SIMON RO

CLASSIC FILM GUIDE

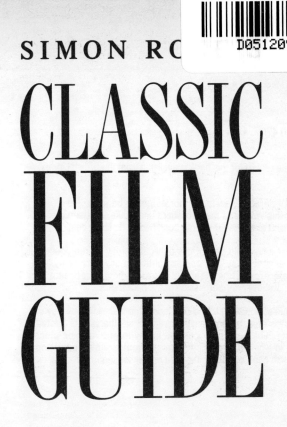

HarperCollins*Publishers*

D0512091

HarperCollins Publishers
PO Box, Glasgow G4 0NB

First published 1995

Reprint 10 9 8 7 6 5 4 3 2 1 0

© Simon Rose, 1995

ISBN 0 00 470734 6

A catalogue record for this book is available from the British Library.

Printed in Great Britain by
HarperCollins Manufacturing, Glasgow

Dedicated to

Carole, Mary, Myrna, Lauren, Cyd, Eleanor,
Jean, Gloria, Rita, Barbara, Marilyn, Peggy, Jessie,
Joan B., Eve and Sandra.

Introduction

*I*t was in my mid-teens that I suddenly developed the peculiar desire to spend large parts of my week in darkness, surrounded by complete strangers, watching highly improbable stories unfolding on the cinema screen which tied up all the loose strands just in time for the words 'The End' to appear. It was so much neater and more exciting than real life and I bought it all, losing myself completely in whatever movie I was watching.

I was lucky to live near The Tyneside Cinema, one of those places that might one day show the three-hour French film, *Celine and Julie Go Boating* and the next *Lucky Lady*, with Liza Minnelli and Burt Reynolds. And when I needed to see the latest film, just across the road was the Odeon where I was so transported by *The Sting* that I set up my own ragtime band.

When, as a student, I came to London, I found true paradise in the form of the Starlight Cinema Club. It showed a double bill of vintage Hollywood movies every night. There were only 40 seats, you could smuggle in wine and peanuts, and it was like having your own preview theatre. Being a student, my vice soon left me out of pocket and I was relegated to the position of projectionist. My only regret about my time there is that I didn't tidy up the projection booth the night that Ingrid Bergman came to see one of her own movies.

It was at The Starlight and the Tyneside Cinema that I developed my taste for 'classic' films. Sadly, not everyone else likes 'old' movies. When a black and white film is shown on television, the duty officers get phone calls from people complaining that they've paid for a colour licence. Part of the fault, I believe, lies with what is written about older movies. There's a too-prevalent attitude that an older film is automatically better than the latest Hollywood blockbuster which is, to my mind, absolutely ridiculous. Some of the films made in 1995 are every bit as good as the 'classics' made in the golden age of cinema when, it should be remembered, the vast majority of films were complete stinkers. Give me a choice of *Raiders of the Lost Ark* or *Battleship Potemkin* and I know which one I'd choose every time.

I wonder when the writers of some tomes on vintage cinema last watched the movies they blather on about. Far too many so-called 'classic' films look antiquated to a modern eye, with clunky dialogue, hammy acting and leaden direction. For this book I have tried to look at these older movies with a fresh eye, as if I was seeing them for the first time. I wanted to judge how they stack up against the latest alternatives available in the video stores.

This guide isn't for film buffs. I recognise that *Die Hard* is one of the greatest thrillers ever made and that *Sleepless in Seattle* or *Shadowlands* can compete with *Brief Encounter* in the tissue-destroying stakes. I'm not going to suggest that you watch a movie because it has an innovative montage sequence or because it was the first time deep-focus photography was used. I am simply interested in knowing whether a film is entertaining or not. So, although the book contains most of the best-known 'classics', I don't like all of them by any means. I have always found *Citizen Kane*, supposedly the greatest movie ever made, dull and no-one is ever likely to change my mind.

The vast majority are films that I have in my own collection. In the late 70s, I

became one of the first people I knew to have a video recorder. Few films existed on video in those days and, with stories abounding of movies being lost for
ever, I had the foolish notion that I might one day be the only person to own a
copy of some great classic. As a result, I taped films avidly as they came up on
TV. You'd be amazed just how much space videos of over a thousand films can
take up.

The word 'classic' in the book's title is interpreted rather loosely. The great
'classics' are here, as well as plenty that are considered to be classics by the
film buffs but don't really deserve the title. But I've also included many of my
favourite films that aren't so well known. I don't suppose *Thunderbirds Are Go*
or the original TV-spinoff film of *Batman* will ever make the Top Ten Films of All
Time lists along with *Double Indemnity* but they are both 'classics' in their own,
modest way. I've also included a selection of movies that are so dreadful, they
are worth looking out for, films like *Double X, Shining Through, Plan 9 From
Outer Space, The Lost Continent, Dinosaurus, The Stud, Mommie Dearest* and
One Million Years B.C.. They are all hugely entertaining in their own inimitable
way. At least one movie, *Grand Prix*, is in only because it gave rise to my
favourite movie anecdote of all time, while *Sanders of the River* became an
essential inclusion for another reason entirely.

By and large, all the films in the book are either available on video or crop up
on TV from time to time. Where a film couldn't be left out, like *A Clockwork
Orange*, I have pointed out how difficult it is to get to see it.

It has been interesting to see what has dated well and what has not.
Humphrey Bogart seems to me to be every bit as fresh on screen as he ever
was, while a once-loved star like George Raft is now virtually unwatchable. Many
60s American movies are now laughably dated, thanks to the silly cinematic
tricks like split screens that were considered so stylish at the time. Many so-
called 'classic' comedies are now frankly embarrassing, with actors doing double-takes as if their lives depended on it, Cary Grant being perhaps the prime
offender among many. To my surprise, many British comedies have held up surprisingly well. Indeed, I was delighted to discover just how enjoyable many
British films still are, and how wide the range of genres and subject matter.

The reviews from the 80s and the early 90s come largely from my *Essential
Film Guide*, although rewatching some of the films I have had to change the rat-
ings, finding myself less or more enthusiastic from a greater critical distance. I
have tried to include all the movies in the more important series. So all the
Bond films are here, even *Casino Royale*, as are the *Star Wars* films, the
Batman movies, the *Indiana Jones* trilogy and so on, but not the interminable
Nightmare on Elm Street or *Friday the 13th* series.

As with *The Essential Film Guide*, I've given not just reviews of the films, but
also a selection of gaffes that film-makers have made, quotes from movies, odd
facts about them and cast lists.

Again, as in *The Essential Guide*, there is a biographical section in the back
of the book. It was far harder to decide who to include and who to leave out.
Problems of space mean that many well known names simply haven't made it.
On the other hand, people like 'Cuddles' Sakall, Eric Blore and Edward Everett
Horton are in because I wanted to include a selection of the great character
actors, who enlivened so many movies with their presence.

Appeal

*T*here must be plenty of wonderful boo-boos, great quotes and mind-boggling bits of trivia that have passed me by. If you want to share some examples of your own for a future edition, then please write to me c/o Rose's Classic Film Guide, PO Box, Glasgow G4 0NB. My thanks to all those who have written in in response to *The Essential Film Guide*.

Thanks

*A*n enormous number of people have helped me along the way, particularly Bill Reiss, my tireless researcher, who has kept me on the straight and narrow and whose incredible breadth of knowledge about movies never ceases to amaze me.

For those who are interested, the database on which the book is based is Helix Express. The information is then output, on a Power Macintosh, to Quark Xpress and automatically formatted. I remain indebted to Mark Pearse and Paul Jackson for initially programming the database and to Stig and Pavla Graham for their continuing assistance. Joe Sudwarts and Steve Caplin also deserve mention for their willingness to field my panicky computer-related phone calls.

I must thank my editor Edwin Moore, for his help, as well as Gail Strachan and Elizabeth McLachlan at Collins for their support and for spotting so many of my own gaffes.

Others who have been generous with their time and brains are Quentin Falk, David Quinlan, James Cameron-Wilson, Hayden Williams, Gill Steene, Herecles, Alan Frank, Dee Pilgrim, David Aldridge, David McGillivray, Mark Kermode, Karen Krizanovich, Antonia Quirke, Bob McCabe, Kevin Brownlow, Bob Monkhouse, Paul Merton, Lois Rathbone, Patrick Walsh, Mike & Sue Bourne, Mitchell Symons, Fiona Moore, Janice Guy, Steve Williams and John Anderson. Lastly, I must also mention, for providing me with liquid sustenance and offering sympathetic ears, Jim, Dawn and Kimberley at the amazing D Lounge and Lucy, Lisa, Polly, Matthew, Martha, Ranu, Julia and Philippa at the Academy.

This book was written on location in London, England, St. Jacut de la Mer, France and New York, USA.

No animal was harmed in the making of this book.

Simon Rose
London, 1995

Contents

The Golden Roses: all-star collection

A

Accidental Hero
Ace in the Hole
Adam's Rib
Adventures of Robin Hood, The
African Queen, The
Aladdin
Alien
Aliens
All About Eve
American Graffiti
Apartment, The
Apollo 13
Arsenic and Old Lace
Asphalt Jungle, The
Assault on Precinct 13

B

Babette's Feast
Back to the Future
Back to the Future, Part III
Bad Day at Black Rock
Ball of Fire
Band Wagon, The
Bank Dick, The
Barefoot in the Park
Barry Lyndon
Beauty and the Beast [1946]
Beauty and the Beast [1991]
Belles of St. Trinians, The
Best Years of Our Lives, The
Big
Big Sleep, The
Blade Runner
Blithe Spirit

Blues Brothers, The
Body Heat
Bonnie and Clyde
Brazil
Breakfast at Tiffany's
Breaking Away
Bride of Frankenstein, The
Brief Encounter
Bronx Tale, A

C

Cabaret
Caine Mutiny, The
Capricorn One
Casablanca
Charade
Charley Varrick
Chien Andalou, Un
Chinatown
Cinema Paradiso
Close Encounters of the Third Kind
Commitments, The
Conversation, The
Cyrano de Bergerac

D

Dances With Wolves
David Copperfield
Days of Heaven
Dead Poets Society
Deliverance
Destry Rides Again
Diaboliques, Les
Die Hard
Diner
Discreet Charm of the Bourgeoisie, The
Dodsworth
Don Juan DeMarco

Double Indemnity
Dr. No
Dr. Strangelove: Or How I Learned to Stop Worrying and Love the Bomb
Duck Soup
Duel
Dumbo

E

Elephant Man, The
Enchanted April
E.T. The Extra-Terrestrial
Eureka

F

Fallen Idol, The
Falling Down
Fanny and Alexander
Field of Dreams
Fish Called Wanda, A
Five Graves to Cairo
Flirting
Fly, The
Footlight Parade
Forbidden Planet
42nd Street
Four Weddings and a Funeral
400 Blows, The
Fried Green Tomatoes at the Whistle Stop Café
From Russia With Love
Funny Bones

G

Gaslight
General, The
Ghost
Ghost and Mrs. Muir, The

Ghostbusters
Gilda
Godfather, The
Gods Must Be Crazy, The
Gold Diggers of 1933
Goldfinger
Gone with the Wind
Goodbye Girl, The
GoodFellas
La Grande Illusion
Grapes of Wrath, The
Great Expectations
Gregory's Girl
Grey Fox, The

H

Hannah and Her Sisters
Happiest Days of Your Life, The
Hard Day's Night, A
Hear My Song
Heiress, The
Hellzapoppin
Henry V
Henry: Portrait of a Serial Killer
High Noon
His Girl Friday
Hope and Glory
Howard's End

I

Indiana Jones and the Last Crusade
Innocents, The
Intolerance
Invasion of the Body Snatchers
It's a Gift
It's a Wonderful Life

J

Jaws
Jean de Florette
Jour de Fête

Judgment at Nuremburg
Jungle Book, The

K

Karate Kid, The
Killers, The
Kind Hearts and Coronets
King of Comedy, The
Kiss of the Spider Woman

L

Last Picture Show, The
Last Seduction, The
Laura
Lavender Hill Mob, The
Lawrence of Arabia
Lethal Weapon 3
Letter, The
Letter from an Unknown Woman
Life and Death of Colonel Blimp, The
Lion King, The
Little Women
Local Hero
Long Good Friday, The
Long Goodbye, The
Lost Horizon
Lost Weekend, The
Love Affair

M

M
Madness of King George, The
Magnificent Ambersons, The
Maltese Falcon, The
Manchurian Candidate, The
Man Escaped, A
Man for All Seasons, A
Manhattan
Manhunter

Manon des Sources
M*A*S*H
Matter of Life and Death, A
Meet Me in St. Louis
Midnight Run
Midnight Sting
Mildred Pierce
Miller's Crossing
Miracle on 34th Street
Misery
Monkey Business
Monsieur Hulot's Holiday
Moonstruck
Movie Movie
Mr. Deeds Goes to Town
Mr. Smith Goes to Washington
Much Ado About Nothing
My Cousin Vinny
My Favorite Year
My Left Foot
My Life as a Dog

N

Name of the Rose, The
Napoleon
Night at the Opera, A
North by Northwest
Notorious

O

Once Upon a Time in America
Once Upon a Time in the West
One Flew Over the Cuckoo's Nest
One Hundred Men and a Girl

P

Paper, The
Partie de Campagne, Une

Passport to Pimlico
Paths of Glory
Patton
Persona
Piano, The
Pinocchio
Postcards from the
  Edge
Pride and Prejudice
Producers, The
Psycho
Pulp Fiction
Pygmalion

R

Raiders of the Lost Ark
Random Harvest
Rear Window
Rebecca
Reservoir Dogs
Rocky
Roger & Me
Room With a View, A
Rules of the Game
Ruthless People

S

Salvador
Scarlet Pimpernel, The
Schindler's List
Scrooge
Seventh Seal, The
Shadowlands
Shadow of a Doubt
Shawshank Redemption,
  The
Shining, The

Shop around the Corner,
  The
Singin' in the Rain
Singles
Sleepless in Seattle
Some Like It Hot
Spartacus
Speed
Splash
Stagecoach
Stalag 17
Star Is Born, A [1954]
Star Trek VI: The
  Undiscovered Country
Star Wars
Sting, The
Strangers on a Train
Strictly Ballroom
Sugarland Express, The
Sullivan's Travels
Sunset Boulevard
Swing Time

T

Terminator, The
That's Entertainment!
Thelma & Louise
Thin Man, The
Third Man, The
39 Steps, The
This is Spinal Tap
Three Days of the
  Condor
Throne of Blood
Tin Drum, The
To Be or Not to Be
Tootsie
Top Hat

Toto the Hero
Trading Places
Trouble in Paradise
Twelve Angry Men
2001: A Space Odyssey

U

Untouchables, The
Usual Suspects, The

V

Vertigo

W

Wages of Fear, The
WarGames
Waterdance, The
Wayne's World
Way Out West
What's Up, Doc?
When Harry Met Sally
White Heat
Wild Bunch, The
Wild Target
Witness
Working Girl
Written on the Wind

Y

Yankee Doodle Dandy
Young Frankenstein

Z

Zulu

Film Music
An introduction, Part 1

Bill Reiss

*T*he importance of a good music soundtrack to the success of a film is still not sufficently appreciated; even silent films in nickelodeons were usually accompanied by a live performer or two. In the Sound era, *Gone With the Wind* is unimaginable without Max Steiner's ripe score, as is *Jaws* without the menacing bass notes of John Williams. The use of Simon & Garfunkel's songs as commentary on the action in *The Graduate* was ground-breaking in its day, as was the use of nostalgic 50s hits for *American Grafitti*.

What follows here is an introduction to some famous film music, for those who wish to find out more. The main criteria for this brief selection, apart from personal taste, was that the music was worth listening to on its own. Many film scores, however right for the movie, don't make for such good listening on their own. All those listed below are available at the time of writing, but deletion of old favourites is often a problem. For further contemporary recommendations, see *The Essential Film Guide* by Simon Rose.

Bernard Herrmann's film scores
Starting off with Orson Welles in the early 40s, through eight assignments for Alfred Hitchcock, and ending with Brian De Palma and Martin Scorsese in the mid-70s, Herrmann is arguably Hollywood's finest ever composer. His skill lay in identifying the key emotions in a film, and underscoring them by using a range of instruments in an innovative way to reflect the character's psychology. Though not strictly a soundtrack collection, it is a useful introduction.

Ennio Morricone's film music 1966-87
Morricone's versatility in identifying the correct register for each project, from violent 60s spaghetti westerns to the nostalgic *Cinema Paradiso*, is extraordinary in its range. This two-disc set is again a good selection for the newcomer to soundtracks. It includes witty classics like *The Good, The Bad and The Ugly*, woodwind melodies for *The Mission* and intriguing tunes for other titles most of us have never heard of.

Once Upon A Time In America
This would be my choice if I had to pick a single Morricone soundtrack. Perfectly matching the film's stylish, elegiac tone, on its own it remains lyrical, rich and haunting.

Schindler's List
John Williams' rousing, full-blown collaborations with George Lucas and Steven Spielberg have been crucial to the success of modern movies like *Star Wars* and *E.T. Schindler's List* was more melancholy and understated, and crucial to the film's subtle and devastating impact.

Cabaret

Everyone should own their favourite musical soundtrack. Here, John Kander's Kurt Weill-inspired music and Fred Ebb's witty barbed lyrics are perfectly delivered by Liza Minnelli as the tragi-comic Sally Bowles and Joel Grey's sinister, all-knowing Master of Ceremonies in the Kit Kat Klub.

Barry Lyndon

Kubrick's fortuitous use of classical music in 1968 for *2001: A Space Odyssey* was groundbreaking, and was followed by *A Clockwork Orange* and *The Shining*. However, *Barry Lyndon* makes for the best listening overall. A range of traditional English and Irish tunes gives way to 18th century pieces by Mozart and Bach, and all bookended by Handel's sombre 'Sarabande' as the Main Title theme.

Blade Runner

Chariots of Fire may have made Vangelis' name, but this recently released soundtrack to Ridley Scott's classic is more impressive, especially played with the bass level turned up high. A dazzling range of music and songs, including some that didn't make it to the final cut, is linked by excerpts of moody dialogue and sound effects from the film.

The Dead Zone

Howard Shore's music for the later Cronenberg films is very fine, but you feel a need to keep all the lights on! Here, Michael Kamen's score for the mellower 1983 *The Dead Zone* is warmer and more wistful, as befits the film's autumnal, melancholy beauty.

The Piano

Michael Nyman hit it big time with this score for the 1993 arthouse smash. It is much more melodic than the rhythmic scores he did for Peter Greenaway, and adds considerable mystery and beauty to Jane Campion's fable set in 19th-century New Zealand.

Film Music
An introduction, Part 2
Stephen Williams of Newsday

*T*he number of notes written to support celluoid images since the Talkie era began would surpass the symphonies churned out by all the real Classical composers. Ennio Morricone, with more than 350 movies to his credit, qualifies as the Mozart of film composers.

I would argue that there are more superior scores than there are superior movies. Populists will rattle off *Gone With the Wind* and *Citizen Kane* and *2001* as common examples of epic movies matched with memorable music. They don't come close to making my Top Ten list. But here are some scores – some familiar, some obscure, some from famous films, most not – that are, to me, classic scores.

Spartacus

King of the 'epic' classics, this Stanley Kubrick colossus capitalised on a remarkable score by Alex North: a lush love theme, a bold, martial main theme, brilliant cues flavoured with extraordinary percussion and overtures so modern they might have been lifted from a Broadway musical.

Hatari
A gem among the dozens of film and television scores fashioned by the late Henry Mancini. This film – produced by Howard Hawks, starring John Wayne, set in Africa's game country – seemed a bit far afield for a guy with Mancini's pop and jazz background. But he pulled it off.

Glory
James Horner's masterpiece (at least until *Apollo 13*) that milks the last tear from every weepy eye in the house. A soaring accompaniment to a sad story about soldiers saddled with sacrifice.

The Man with the Golden Arm
Before jazz music became a film-score cliché in the 60s, Elmer Bernstein pioneered the form with an original, drum-propelled suite that backgrounded Otto Preminger's movie about a junkie who breaks the habit after much aggravation.

The Train
Okay, so it isn't pretty music. But this score by Maurice Jarre is one that works perfectly with the visuals. An example of my rule that a great film score does not have to be great on its own.

The Player and The Shawshank Redemption
For my money, the best of the 90s new composers is Thomas Newman. Minimal amounts of melodic music characterised his work, without the usual histronics and grandiose gestures.

In Harm's Way
Considering the bulk of music Jerry Goldsmith has churned out over the past four decades, it is remarkable how much has survived the test of time. This Preminger picture was released in 1965 and the music remains vibrant and exciting today.

Psycho
Staccato strings set the stage for Hitchcock's classic, if somewhat overwrought, thriller about Norman Bates and his dear old mum. Hitch employed the late Bernard Herrmann, also Martin Scorsese's favourite composer.

The Cowboys and Jaws
Two idioms, Americana and Steven Spielberg, comprise a major chunk of John Williams' repertoire. To me *The Cowboys* and *Jaws* represent his shining moments.

Edwin Moore adds: Mishima
Philip Glass's shimmering score for *Mishima* remains a high point of his work. Highlights include an enchanting pastiche of Western pop music and a lovely waltz at the end.
Also: any score by Erich Korngold. Perhaps the most influential composer of film music ever, his swashbuckling scores are particularly notable. *The Sea Hawk* is regarded as his greatest score ('sublime' – George MacDonald Fraser).

The Guide to The Guide

Ratings
The vast majority of films are included because they are worth watching. However, I consider any 1-star movies to be a complete waste of time. 2-star films may not be outstanding, but with a few reservations, they may still be worth watching. 3-star films provide above-average entertainment value, and 4-star films are those I consider outstanding. However, my tastes are not the same as everybody's, and you will probably need to make allowances for my pet passions and peeves.

Year
Usually this is the year a film was first released theatrically.

Timing
Giving an exact length of movies proves a greater nightmare than it has ever been. Many films exist in several different versions, sometimes because sections have been lost, sometimes because there are directors' cuts, different versions for video or TV, variations in the released films in different countries or, in the case of many silent movies, umpteen different restored versions of films. Don't take any of the timings as gospel, and do remember that the timings given are for movies as shown in the cinema. When played on TV or video, films are run at 25 frames per second, not the usual 24. This means that a film that plays for 100 minutes in the cinema will last only 96 minutes on TV or video. Sometimes TV showings will be speeded up over the credits, or the credits may be dropped altogether.

Colour
I have indicated whether movies are colour or black & white and also used c&b/w for those films which mix the two. I hold no truck with computer-colourised versions of films, considering them the work of the devil. Strike a blow for real movies and boycott them wherever possible.

Director & Screenplay
These may vary from the credits given on the film if other writers and directors have made a significant, but uncredited, contribution to a movie.

Source
I have tried to mention the original plays, books, poems or articles which inspired movies, but have excluded stories written directly for particular movies.

Cast Lists
I have amended many cast lists considerably from the way they appear on films. Where actors who later went on to become well known appear in small bit parts, I have included them on cast lists, and I have sometimes ignored actors who have slipped into obscurity altogether. I would have liked to have listed 30 or so entries for every film, but I would rather that the book be a manageable size.

Oscars
Only the main categories are listed – Best Actor, Best Actress, Best Supporting Actor and Actress, Best Film, Best Director and Best Screenplay.

Blurb
Memorable or amusing tag lines from the film's advertising campaign.

Quote
Noteworthy lines from the movie or quotes about the making of the film.

Showing
A guide to those films that are shown within other films. Nothing stops me enjoying a movie more than trying desperately to recall what one of these is.

OOPS!
A guide to some of those embarrassing slip-ups by film-makers which are so enjoyable to spot. My favourite in the entire canon of movies takes place in the mountain-top café in *North by Northwest*. Frankly, it's worth watching the movie for that alone. After a while, you get the hang of spotting these yourself. Useful things to keep an eye on are clocks, food, dirt, wounds and people in the background who think that they have a chance to become a major movie star by making an ass of themselves.

Psst!
A selection of background information to the making of the film.

Abbott and Costello Meet Frankenstein

★★★ 1948 83min b/w

Director: Charles Barton
Screenplay: Robert Lees, Frederic I. Rinaldo & John Grant
Source: Novel, *Frankenstein* by Mary Shelley

This Universal spoof of the horror films the same studio had such success with in the 30s is the most entertaining of all the Abbott and Costello films. They're railway porters delivering the bodies of Dracula and Frankenstein's monster to a waxworks museum where, to nobody's surprise but their own, they come alive. It's all pretty silly, but there are still plenty of laughs. Known as *Abbott and Costello Meet the Ghosts* in the UK.

Chick Young . . . . .Bud Abbott
Wilbur Grey . . . . .Lou Costello
Lawrence Talbot/Wolf Man . . . . .Lon Chaney Jr.
Dracula . . . . .Bela Lugosi
The Monster . . . . .Glenn Strange
Voice of Invisible Man . . . . .Vincent Price

Blurb More Howls Than You Can Shake A Shiver At ! ! !

Quote 'You don't understand. Every night when the moon is full, I turn into a wolf.' – 'You and fifty million other guys!' • 'I'm a ba-a-ad boy!'

OOPS! Although you aren't supposed to be able to see a vampire's reflection, Dracula is visible in a mirror just as he's about to attack a woman.

Psst! After this success, the comedy duo went on to 'meet' assorted other monsters. The others are watchable, but don't really compare.

Abominable Dr. Phibes

★★★ 1971 93min c.

Director: Robert Fuest
Screenplay: James Whiton & William Goldstein

This incredibly camp, tongue-in-cheek horror pic has the mutilated Price vowing revenge on those he holds responsible for his wife's death. He devises a series of murders taking as their fiendish inspiration the plagues of ancient Egypt. Buoyed by its brilliant art-deco design, it's undoubtedly daft but highly entertaining, as was the sequel *Dr. Phibes Rises Again*.

Dr. Anton Phibes . . . . .Vincent Price
Dr. Vesalius . . . . .Joseph Cotten

Vulnavia . . . . .Virginia North
Dr. Longstreet . . . . .Terry-Thomas
Rabbi . . . . .Hugh Griffith
Goldsmith .Aubrey Woods
Dr. Hargreaves . . . . .Alex Scott
Sergeant .James Grout
Darrow . . . . .John Laurie
Victoria Phibes . . . . .Caroline Munro

Blurb Love Means Never Having To Say You're Ugly.

À Bout de Souffle
SEE: Breathless

Accident

★★ 1967 105min c.

Director: Joseph Losey
Screenplay: Harold Pinter
Source: Novel by Nicholas Mosley

A sour, pre-*Brideshead Revisited* view of lust and betrayal at an Oxford College, after a car accident in a country road. Extremely well acted and unsentimental, it displays the key elements of the Pinter/Losey adaptations which can seem rather irritating these days; enigmatic storylines about the class system, lots ... of irrational ... dialogue ... pauses, and endless gamesplaying between the main characters.

Stephen . . . . .Dirk Bogarde
Charley . . . . .Stanley Baker
Anna . . . . .Jacqueline Sassard
William . . . . .Michael York
Rosalind . . . . .Vivien Merchant
Francesca . . . . .Delphine Seyrig
Provost .Alexander Knox

Psst! Vivian Merchant was married to screenwriter Pinter at the time, who himself appears as Bell.

Accidental Hero

★★★★ 1992 116min c.

Director: Stephen Frears
Screenplay: David Webb Peoples

In this superbly witty satire from the writer of *Unforgiven* and *Blade Runner*, Hoffman is a crooked sleazebag forced by circumstances into rescuing TV reporter Davis from a burning airplane. But when the station offers $1m for the

'Angel of Flight 104' to come forward, it's drifter Garcia who is hailed as the hero. This is cinema entertainment at its finest. It's moving, absorbing and beautifully-acted, keeping us dying to know what's going to happen next. Beginning brilliantly, this movie just gets better as it goes along. With the exception of Davis' squirm-inducing onion-peeling scene, it is quite simply one of the greatest films of the past decade.

Bernie Laplante	Dustin Hoffman
Gale Gayley	Geena Davis
John Bubber	Andy Garcia
Evelyn	Joan Cusack
Chucky (cameraman)	Kevin J. O'Connor
Winston	Maury Chaykin
Wallace	Stephen Tobolowsky
Conklin (reporter)	Christian Clemenson
Chick	Tom Arnold
Station head	Chevy Chase
Bradman (jumper)	Edward Herrmann
TV director	Fisher Stevens

Quote 'It's my story. I did the research.'
• 'Watch my shoes.'

OOPS! The all-important envelope handed to Davis by Garcia when he's on the ledge is never seen again, its existence presumably forgotten by the film-makers.

Psst! The script was written with Hoffman in mind as the lead • Sharon Stone was beaten to the part by Davis, and Kevin Costner lost out to Garcia • So realistic was the crashed plane that pilots coming into land at Los Angeles airport were reporting a disaster to traffic control.

Ace in the Hole

★★★★ 1951 111min b/w

Director: Billy Wilder
Screenplay: Billy Wilder, Lesser Samuels & Walter Newman

A reptilian journalist seizes on a mining accident in a remote community as a chance to make it big, turning the rescue attempt into a circus and even deliberately delaying things for his own ends. Douglas gives a bravura performance in this unsettling Wilder satire that is even more relevant today than it was in the milder 50s. It should be compulsory viewing at journalism school, except that the trainee hacks would probably be rooting for Douglas. Also known as *The Big Carnival*.

Chuck Tatum	Kirk Douglas
Lorraine	Jan Sterling
Herbie Cook	Robert Arthur
Jacob Q. Boot	Porter Hall
Mr. Federber	Frank Cady
Leo Minosa	Richard Benedict
Sheriff	Ray Teal

Quote 'I've met a lot of hard boiled eggs in my time, but you…you're twenty minutes!' • 'I don't go to church. Kneeling bags my nylons.'

Psst! Perhaps it should have been predicted that such an uncomfortable film would have been a box office disaster. The studio changed the title in America to *The Big Carnival* in a vain ploy, presumably, to pretend that it was a circus pic • There were attempts to prevent it being shown abroad in countries friendly to America. It was actually banned in Singapore for the reason that it portrayed a face of American life that 'might be misunderstood' • The film was loosely based on the true-life Floyd Collins cave-in in Kentucky in the 20s.

Across the Pacific

★★★ 1942 97min b/w

Director: John Huston
Screenplay: Richard Macaulay
Source: *Saturday Evening Post* serial, *Aloha Means Goodbye* by Robert Carson

Bogart, as cool as ever, fakes disgrace in order to uncover agents working for the Japanese in World War II. Director Huston is reunited with three of the stars of *The Maltese Falcon* and they work much of the same magic in this entertaining, slightly cheeky, spy yarn.

Rick Leland	Humphrey Bogart
Alberta Marlow	Mary Astor
Dr. Lorenz	Sydney Greenstreet
A.P. Smith	Charles Halton
Joe Totsuiko	Victor Sen Yung
Capt. Morrison	Frank Wilcox
Canadian Major	Lester Matthews
Dan Morton	Monte Blue
Steamship office clerk	Keye Luke

Psst! John Huston was called up for military service towards the end of filming. According to David Niven: 'The word came by phone when he was in the middle of directing Bogie in a scene in which the Japanese enemy had surrounded hero Bogart in a small building. His escape had been carefully rehearsed – who he shot, who he knifed and through which window he would jump, etc. Huston never said a word about the receipt of his 'call-up', he just tripled the number of Japanese around the building, boarded it up with the hero inside and left for Europe. A hastily summoned take-over director found a note on the door: "I'm in the Army – Bogie will know how to get out.'" • There was a shortage of Japanese to play villains during the war as most of them were interred in camps for dangerous aliens. Kam Tong, a Chinese-American who appears in this movie, became so convincing in his portrayal of Japanese that he was recruited into the OSS, later to become the CIA, becoming an undercover agent.

Adam's Rib
★★★★ 1949 101min b/w

Director: George Cukor
Screenplay: Ruth Gordon & Garson Kanin

A happily married pair of lawyers fall out when they find themselves on the opposite sides of a case of attempted murder. This sparkling, sophisticated comedy of the battle of the sexes is occasionally a bit dated by modern standards. But Hepburn and Tracy at their combative, fizzing best more than make up for it.

Adam Bonner	Spencer Tracy
Amanda Bonner	Katharine Hepburn
Doris Attinger	Judy Holliday
Warren Attinger	Tom Ewell
Kip Lurie	David Wayne
Beryl Caighn	Jean Hagen
Judge Reiser	Clarence Kolb

Quote 'I'm old-fashioned. I like two sexes.' • 'What've you got back there? Radar equipment?' • 'Lawyers should never marry other lawyers. This is called inbreeding, from which comes idiot children and more lawyers.' • 'Vive la difference.'

Showing The Mortgage The Merrier.

OOPS! When Hepburn drives them to work near the beginning of the movie, we can see Manhattan projected behind them and also reflected in the gleaming car bonnet. Although it's possibly the way the bonnet curves, it appears to reflect not only the back-projection screen, but also where the screen ends at the sides and the top.

Psst! The inspiration for the film apparently came from the divorce of actor Raymond Massey • Knowing Hepburn's fiery temper, it was suggested that when it came to billing, perhaps ladies ought to come first. Tracy wouldn't play ball: 'This is a movie, not a lifeboat.' • Holliday, making her movie debut,

was desperately nervous about performing with Tracy and Hepburn. Anxiety was exactly what he was after for that first scene, so Cukor did nothing to help her and one take proved all that was needed • Cole Porter wrote the song *Farewell, Amanda* specially for the movie.

The Adventures of Robin Hood
★★★★ 1938 102min c.

Director: Michael Curtiz & William Keighley
Screenplay: Norman Reilly Raine & Seton I. Miller
Source: Novel, *Ivanhoe* by Sir Walter Scott & opera, *Robin Hood* by Reginald De Koven & Harry B. Smith

Accept no substitutes. This is the greatest swashbuckling adventure of them all, with Flynn the dashing Robin and his merry band of character actors taking on the dastardly Rathbone and wooing the lovely De Havilland. Exciting, funny, romantic, beautifully cast and filmed, the whole delicious mix is topped off with rousing music from the great Korngold. This one should be in every video collection.

Sir Robin of Locksley	Errol Flynn
Maid Marian	Olivia De Havilland
Sir Guy of Gisbourne	Basil Rathbone
Prince John	Claude Rains
Will Scarlet	Patric Knowles
Friar Tuck	Eugene Pallette
Little John	Alan Hale
High Sheriff of Nottingham	Melville Cooper
King Richard	Ian Hunter
Bess	Una O'Connor
Much, the miller's son	Herbert Mundin
Bishop of the Black Canons	Montagu Love

Blurb Only The Rainbow Can Duplicate Its Brilliance.

Quote 'You speak treason.' – 'Fluently.'

OOPS! Robin Hood does no more than nibble at a large leg of lamb, but the meat is stripped to the bone in the next shot • When Will Scarlett goes to help Much, a car is visible in the background as he gets off his horse.

Psst! The film was originally conceived as a vehicle for James Cagney but he walked out of Warner Brothers in a contract dispute lasting two years • Way behind schedule and massively over budget, at the time its cost of $1.9m made it Warners' most expensive film • Sherwood Forest was actually a giant park 350 miles northeast of Los Angeles. Fake trees and rocks were brought in to fill it, along with hundreds of bushes and flowers • Flynn did many of his own stunts, including the duelling with Rathbone, who was probably the best swordsman in Hollywood. In one scene, Rathbone was injured by a spear and needed eight stiches in his foot • Flynn professed himself bored with the film later. Others on set were bored with him, for he was frequently late and rarely managed to remember his lines • Flynn still nursed his passion for De Havilland, with whom he made eight movies. However, the base practical jokes that were his way of wooing did not help his cause. In the clinches, he kissed her so passionately that they had to keep retaking the scenes, knowing that they would never get past the censor • The producers offered $150 a time to anyone who would don protection and let the famous archer Howard Hill shoot at them with real arrows • De Havilland's horse later became famous as Roy Rogers' mount Trigger.

The Adventures of Sherlock Holmes
★★★ 1939 85min b/w

Director: Alfred Werker
Screenplay: Edwin Blum & William Drake
Source: Play by William Gillette & the works of Arthur Conan Doyle

Holmes' arch nemesis Moriarty diverts the great detective's attention elsewhere while he plots to steal the Crown Jewels. Lovely characterisation makes up for the rather creaky plot. This was the second of the splendid Rathbone-Bruce pairings after *The Hound of the Baskervilles*. *Pearl of Death* and *The Scarlet Claw* are also worth catching.

Sherlock Holmes	Basil Rathbone
Dr. Watson	Nigel Bruce
Ann Brandon	Ida Lupino
Jerrold Hunter	Alan Marshal
Billy	Terry Kilburn
Prof. Moriarty	George Zucco
Sir Ronald Ramsgate	Henry Stephenson
Insp. Bristol	E.E. Clive

Psst! Holmes is the screen's most-portrayed character, fictional or not, with over 200 movies to his name • After this picture, Fox dropped the idea, thinking nobody would be interested in such fare in wartime. Universal brought the two actors together again in 1942 for another 11 movies, although they were made more cheaply and had contemporary settings involving Nazi villains and the like.

The Adventuress
SEE: I See a Dark Stranger

An Affair to Remember
★★ 1957 114min c.

Director: Leo McCarey
Screenplay: Delmer Daves & Leo McCarey

A couple flirt on board ship and realise it might not just be the bracing sea air that's making their hearts go pitter-patter. To see if it's the real thing, they arrange to meet in six months' time on top of the Empire State Building. But fate throws a stick into the spokes of true love. This wildly melodramatic tear-jerker is regarded by many Americans in the same light the British regard *Brief Encounter*. Sadly, it goes off the boil when it gets on dry land, although those in the right mood may still enjoy it. It's effectively a remake of the more enjoyable 1939 film *Love Affair*, with the same director at the helm.

Nickie Ferrante	Cary Grant
Terry McKay	Deborah Kerr
Kenneth	Richard Denning
Lois Clarke	Neva Patterson
Grandmother	Cathleen Nesbitt
Announcer	Robert Q. Lewis
Courbet	Fortunio Bonanova

Quote 'I ws bored to death. I hadn't seen one attractive woman on this ship since we left, and then I saw you and I was saved.' – 'Tell me, have you been getting results with a line like that?' • 'Do you think it will ever take the place of night baseball?'

Psst! The film is perhaps best known now as the movie Meg Ryan and Rosie O'Donnell get so emotional about in *Sleepless in Seattle* • When a lump on Grant's forehead, a childhood injury, caused problems with the lighting, Grant took a few days off and had it surgically removed • While Kerr is singing 'The Tiny Scout' herself, elsewhere in the film the ubiquitous Marni Nixon dubbed her singing voice.

The African Queen
★★★★ 1951 103min c.

Director: John Huston
Screenplay: James Agee
Source: Novel by C.S. Forester

During World War I, a starchy missionary and a hard-drinking trader are forced to live together on the same boat, enduring a perilous journey down river. One of the great adventure stories of all time, with both leads divine as the couple whose mutual hate turns first into respect and then love. A mite self-indulgent in places perhaps, it's still extremely witty and involving, the action sequences are suitably thrilling and the photography makes the hardships of filming in Africa look well worthwhile. Unfortunately, the stuff filmed on set in London jars because it looks so glaringly obvious.

Charlie Allnut . . . . .Humphrey Bogart
Rose Sayer . . . . .Katharine Hepburn
Rev. Samuel Sayer . . . . .Robert Morley
German captain . . . . .Peter Bull
German 1st officer . . . . .Theodore Bikel
German 2nd officer . . . . .Walter Gotell

Oscars Humphrey Bogart

Quote 'Nature, Mr. Allnut, is what we are put into this world to rise above.' • 'I never dreamed that any mere physical experience could be so stimulating.' • 'I ain't sorry for you no more, you crazy, psalm-singing, skinny old maid.' • "Dear, what is your first name?' • If there's anything in the world I hate it's leeches…filthy little devils!' • 'By the authority vested in me by Kaiser Wilhelm II, I pronounce you man and wife. Proceed with the execution.'

Psst! Bogart won his only Oscar for the film • The project was originally envisaged for Charles Laughton and Elsa Lanchester and then later for Bette Davis and David Niven, with Niven going so far as to brush up his Cockney and grow a beard before being stood down. A later musical version was once suggested, with Lee Marvin and Doris Day the projected leads • Ever the one for doing things the hard way, Huston insisted on filming 1,000 miles up the Congo. It was only the third American film ever to have been made on location in Africa, after *Trader Horn* and *King Solomon's Mines* • Most of the company came down with dysentery. After lambasting Bogart and Huston for their heavy drinking and showing them up by drinking water with her meals, Hepburn realised that it was their abhorrence of water that kept them free of the disease that made her feel she was going to die • Tarantulas, deadly soldier ants, vicious wasps, and crocodiles also posed problems. Hepburn wasn't keen on getting into the water with the crocs. 'Don't worry,' said Huston, 'I'll have my prop men fire a few rounds of ammunition into the water. You'll find the crocodiles get scared by the noise.' 'But what,' queried Hepburn, 'About the deaf ones?' • Bogart, who hated location work, not only grumbled about the discomforts of filming in such conditions but was particularly peeved by the way Hepburn was so exasperatingly cheerful throughout it all • The novel *White Hunter, Black Heart*, made into a movie by Clint Eastwood, was based on those who made *The African Queen*.

After the Thin Man
★★★ 1936 113min b/w

Director: W.S. Van Dyke
Screenplay: Frances Goodrich & Albert Hackett
Source: Story by Dashiell Hammett

Ed and Nora come out of their corners for the second time, trying to solve a rash of murders through their usual alcoholic haze. Although not quite up to the standard of *The Thin Man* itself, it still whizzes along at a fair lick, with wisecracks flying left, right and centre. While Powell and Loy are an absolute dream together, let's not forget the important contribution from the third member of their team, the dog Asta.

Nick Charles . . . . .William Powell
Nora Charles . . . . .Myrna Loy
David Graham . . . . .James Stewart
Selma Landis . . . . .Elissa Landi
Dancer . . . . .Joseph Calleia
Aunt Katherine Forrest . . . . .Jessie Ralph
Robert Landis . . . . .Alan Marshal
Lt. Abrams . . . . .Sam Levene
Casper . . . . .Teddy Hart
Dr. Kammer . . . . .George Zucco
Polly Byrnes . . . . .Penny Singleton
Asta . . . . .Asta

Ai No Corrida
SEE: In the Realm of the Senses

Airplane!
★★★ 1980 88min c.

Director: Jim Abrahams, David Zucker & Jerry Zucker
Screenplay: Jim Abrahams, David Zucker & Jerry Zucker

The team that gave birth to *Kentucky Fried Movie* and, later, *Naked Gun*, here spoof the *Airport* series of disaster movies, with a few digs at *Saturday Night Fever*, *Jaws* and *From*

Here to Eternity thrown in. The jokes and sight gags come thick and fast and it doesn't matter if one doesn't hit home as there'll be another one along a moment later. What little story there is involves a plane whose crew is seriously incapacitated by the in-flight catering. The 1982 sequel isn't quite as good, but still has enough laughs to keep it airborne.

Ted Striker ....Robert Hays
Elaine ....Julie Hagerty
Murdock ....Kareem Abdul-Jabbar
McCroskey ....Lloyd Bridges
Captain Oveur ....Peter Graves
Dr. Rumack ....Leslie Nielsen
Kramer ....Robert Stack

Blurb Thank God It's Only A Motion Picture!

Quote 'Joey, have you ever been in a Turkish prison?' • 'He's alive but unconcious, just like Gerald Ford.' • 'Cream?' – 'No, thank you. I take it black, like my men.'

Psst! After *Kentucky Fried Movie's* success, the trio of Zucker, Abrahams and Zucker wanted to take directorial control. The script was one they had been working on for five years. The film cost $3.5m and grossed $80m around the world • The credits include entries like 'Generally in charge of a lot of things: Mike Finnell' and 'Author of A Tale of Two Cities: Charles Dickens' • The trio who perpetrated the movie appear in cameos, just as their names appear at the beginning. Jim Abrahams is Religious Zealot #6, David Zucker is Ground Crewman #32 and Jerry Zucker is Ground Crewman #1 • The man who thinks he is Ethel Merman is, in fact, Ethel Merman.

Airport

★★★ 1970 137min c.

Director: George Seaton
Screenplay: George Seaton
Source: Novel by Arthur Hailey

The film that started the cycle of disaster movies. It's snowing heavily. The only available runway's blocked. Nobody should be in the air on a night like this, especially when Dean Martin's the pilot. But a bomb's gone off on a plane packed with stereotypical characters and it's gotta land soon. Can anybody be found to act well enough to talk them down to the ground? It's unlikely. In the wake of *Airplane*, it's hard to take it too seriously. Despite some pretty terrible performances from most of those involved, it is surprisingly entertaining. The

sequels were barely good enough to lift off the runway. *Airport 1975* was followed by *Airport '77* and *Airport '79 – The Concorde.*

Mel Bakersfield ....Burt Lancaster
Vernon Demerest ....Dean Martin
Tanya Livingston ....Jean Seberg
Gwen Meighen ....Jacqueline Bisset
Joe Patroni ....George Kennedy
Ada Quonsett ....Helen Hayes
D.O. Guerrero ....Van Heflin
Inez Guerrero ....Maureen Stapleton
Lt. Anson Harris ....Barry Nelson
Harry Standish ....Lloyd Nolan

Oscars Helen Hayes

Quote 'The only thing we've got left in common is the same mattress.' • 'The best film of 1944.' [Critic Judith Crist]

Psst! This was nominated for 10 Academy Awards • Only the 70-year-old Helen Hayes won one which was rather sweet as she enjoyed her role so much she even insisted on doing her wrestling with bomber Van Heflin herself, instead of letting a stand-in do it.

Aladdin

★★★★ 1992 90min c.

Director: John Musker & Ron Clements
Screenplay: John Musker, Ron Clements, Ted Elliott & Terry Rossio

Vastly different to recent Disney cartoons, this is so frenetic and off-the-wall it's more like watching a full-length version of Bugs Bunny or Tex Avery than something like, say, *The Little Mermaid.* Robin Williams was given his head to voice the genie and, of course, improvised wildly. Only then was the animation devised to go with it. Madcap, fast and immensely funny, Aladdin is a delight for the eye and the ear.

Aladdin ....Scott Weinger
Genie ....Robin Williams
Jasmine ....Linda Larkin
Jafar....................Jonathan Freeman
Abu ....Frank Welker
Iago ....Gilbert Gottfried
Sultan ....Douglas Seale

Quote 'Ten thousand years will give you such a crick in the neck.' • 'I'm getting kind of fond of you, kid. Not that I want to pick out curtains or anything.'

Psst! After three years in development and six months of actual production, the first rough screening was a disaster. Studio head Jeffrey Katzenberg told the animators that the story didn't work and that they would have to start all over again • Robin Williams is said to have been given a $7m Picasso painting by way of apology when Disney cheesed him off by making him the focal point of publicity, contrary to their agreement • Look out for the in-joke just before the Genie makes Aladdin a Prince where the crab Sebastian from *The Little Mermaid* appears briefly. There are also other brief references to *The Little Mermaid* and to *Pinocchio* • This is supposedly the first Disney cartoon to show us a belly button, with Jasmine proudly displaying hers throughout • Tim Rice won an Oscar for his songs • The lyrics of *Arabian Nights* were changed after protests from Arabic groups. Instead of the line, 'Where they cut off your ear if they don't like your face. It's barbaric but, hey, it's home' was, 'Where it's flat and immense and the heat is intense, it's barbaric but, hey, it's home.' • On the Internet, rumours were spread that when Aladdin is about to be attacked by Rajah the tiger he says: 'Good teenagers take off their clothes'. In fact, it would appear, he says: 'Good tiger. Take off and go'.

Alfie

★★ 1966 114min c.

Director: Lewis Gilbert
Screenplay: Bill Naughton
Source: Play by Naughton

Cockney Jack-the-Lad Caine beds almost every woman he meets but still has no idea which way happiness lies. The quaintness at seeing the vastly different attitudes of a distant, bygone age still hold some interest although the film becomes rather tough and nasty as it goes on. Unfortunately, Alfie is such a horrible piece of work that we don't really give a shit for the shit as he becomes increasingly pathetic.

Alfie	Michael Caine
Ruby	Shelley Winters
Siddie	Millicent Martin
Gilda	Julia Foster
Annie	Jane Asher
Carla	Shirley Anne Field
Lily	Vivien Merchant
Doctor	Eleanor Bron
Abortionist	Denholm Elliott
Harry	Alfie Bass

Quote 'My understanding of women goes only as far as the pleasures.' • 'So what's the answer? That's what I keep asking meself. What's it all about? Know what I mean?'

Psst! *Alfie* had been a great success on stage in London and in New York • Anthony Newley, Laurence Harvey and Terence Stamp all turned it down before Michael Caine. Each was scared off by the abortion scenes • There were no retakes on the film, not so much because of the professionalism of the actors, but because the filmmakers simply couldn't afford them • It's said that having an actor confide directly to the audience in the form of asides was a novelty, making its first appearance here. This will have come as news to the camel in *Road to Morocco* but certainly it happens more consistently in *Alfie* than before • Shelley Winters says that her moral standards at the time were very different to her character's. 'When I was supposed to be on top of Michael Caine, I had little pillows placed all over his body so we wouldn't touch. He was screaming so much with laughter, we almost didn't get the scene done.' • Although the song 'Alfie' was a hit for Dionne Warwick, it was Cher who sang it in the film.

Algiers

★★★ 1938 95min b/w

Director: John Cromwell
Screenplay: John Howard Lawson & James M. Cain
Source: French novel & film, *Pépé le Moko* by Roger D'Ashelbe

If he had ever said it – which he didn't – then this is the movie in which Charles Boyer would have uttered the much-impersonated phrase, 'Come wiz me to ze Casbah'. Based very closely on a French film, it has Boyer as a jewel thief with an eye for the ladies hiding out in ze Casbah. When Lamarr appears he abandons his principles and falls in love. Although it's the most dreadful tosh, this romantic melodrama is so well handled that it is far more enjoyable than you might expect.

Pépé le Moko	Charles Boyer
Inés	Sigrid Gurie
Gaby	Hedy Lamarr
Slimane	Joseph Calleia
Regis	Gene Lockhart
Grandpére	Alan Hale
Pierrot	Johnny Downs
Aicha	Joan Woodbury
Giroux	Robert Greig
Carlos	Stanley Fields
Max	Charles D. Brown
L'Arbi	Leonid Kinskey

Quote 'I'm sorry, Pepe. He thought you were going to escape.' – 'And so I have, my friend.'

Psst! This was the American debut of Austrian Hedy Lemarr. Boyer was less than impressed by her acting • The world was certainly impressed by her costume. Her white turban, which she designed herself, became all the rage.

Alias Nick Beal

★★★ 1949 93min b/w

Director: John Farrow
Screenplay: Jonathan Latimer
Source: Story by Mindret Lord

One of the best of the cinema's many interpretations of *Faust*, this has an untypically devilish Milland corrupting an honest politician with, naturally, the help of a woman. The intriguing combination of fantasy and *film noir* still makes for a potent mix.

Nick Beal . . . . .Ray Milland
Joseph Foster . . . . .Thomas Mitchell
Donna Allen . . . . .Audrey Totter
Rev. Thomas Garfield . . . . . . .George Macready
Frankie Faulkner . . . . .Fred Clark
Judge Hobson . . . . .Henry O'Neill
Larry Price . . . . .Darryl Hickman

Alice Adams

★ 1935 99min b/w

Director: George Stevens
Screenplay: Dorothy Yost & Mortimer Offner
Source: Novel by Booth Tarkington

If you think Katharine Hepburn is one of the cinema's greatest actresses and incapable of making a clunker, catch her as this obnoxious social climber trying to conceal her modest home and parentage. Although a hit at the time, tastes have changed in a big way in 60 years. Hepburn's acting now seems wildly melodramatic and often cringe-makingly embarrassing. As if that wasn't enough, the ending is not only wildly implausible but comes out of nowhere, as if they couldn't think how else to bring down the final curtain. Shame they didn't do it sooner.

Alice Adams . . . . .Katharine Hepburn
Arthur Russell . . . . .Fred MacMurray
Mr. Adams .Fred Stone
Mildred Palmer . . . . .Evelyn Venable
Walter Adams . . . . .Frank Albertson
Mrs. Adams . . . . .Ann Shoemaker

Mr. Lamb . . . . .Charley Grapewin
Frank Dowling . . . . .Grady Sutton
Mrs. Palmer . . . . .Hedda Hopper
Mr. Palmer . . . . .Jonathan Hale
Maid . . . . .Hattie McDaniel

Psst! Look out for the glorious Hattie McDaniel, best known as Mammy in *Gone With the Wind*, as the maid at the disastrous dinner party • If you're bored, watch out for Fred Stone saying 'Damn' for only the second time in American movie history.

Alice Doesn't Live Here Anymore

★★★ 1974 112min c.

Director: Martin Scorsese
Screenplay: Robert Getchell

A struggling widow and mother working as a waitress is initially unwilling to accept anything more than tips from gentle Kristofferson. Although the pace is leisurely, the performances are smashing and the relationships between the characters are eminently believable. Particularly good is Lutter driving his mum mad. He gives one of the best wise-ass kids' performances in the movies.

Alice Hyatt . . . . .Ellen Burstyn
David .Kris Kristofferson
Donald Hyatt . . . . .Billy "Green" Bush
Tommy Hyatt . . . . .Alfred Lutter
Flo . . . . .Diane Ladd
Audrey . . . . .Jodie Foster
Ben Everhart . . . . .Harvey Keitel
Mel . . . . .Vic Tayback
Vera . . . . .Valerie Curtin
Girl eating ice cream . . . . .Laura Dern

Oscars Ellen Burstyn

Blurb A Picture For Anyone Who Has Ever Dreamed Of A Second Chance.

Showing Coney Island.

Psst! After *Mean Streets*, this was Scorsese's first crack at a mainstream movie • Burstyn was the movie's driving force. It was she who chose Scorsese and she worked on the script as well as helping to choose the cast • Look out for a young Laura Dern, Ladd's daughter, wearing black glasses and scoffing ice-cream in the final scene in the diner • The premise was later turned into the long-running TV sitcom, *Alice*. Only Vic Tayback crossed over from the film to the TV series.

Alien
★★★★ 1979 117min c.

Director: Ridley Scott
Screenplay: Dan O'Bannon

The crew of a distinctly unglamorous spaceship are picked off one by one by a creature that appears to have all the advantages on its side. Bridging the horror and sci-fi genres and with a superbly dark design, this is a truly scary movie packed with its fair share of memorable moments, ,most particularly the famous scene in which Hurt's stomach does the acting. It is also noteworthy for bringing us one of the first instances of the female action hero. The sequel, *Aliens*, was even better.

Dallas . . . . .Tom Skerritt
Ripley . . . . .Sigourney Weaver
Lambert . . . . .Veronica Cartwright
Kane . . . . .John Hurt
Brett . . . . .Harry Dean Stanton
Ash . . . . Ian Holm
Parker . . . . .Yaphet Kotto

Blurb In Space, No One Can Hear You Scream.

Psst! While the film cost $11m, $16m was spent on the ad campaign • A love scene between Weaver and Skeritt was filmed, but not included • In its earliest incarnation, Ripley was a man • Much of the dialogue was ad-libbed • The scene with Hurt's stomach was readied while the other actors were off the set. They weren't told what was going to happen, so their reactions on screen are genuine • It wasn't only the audience who were affected by the scene. In watching the deailies, the director of photography Derek Vanlint, felt so ill, he had to rush from the projection room • The alien was known as 'Big Chap' on set. Inside was Bolaji Badejo, a seven foot two inch tall Masai tribesman • Bountiful entrails and buckets of blood were brought in from a slaughterhouse for the necessary gore. The monster's glossy sheen was KY Jelly while the tendons in its jaw were made from shredded condoms • The model of the spaceship as seen on the outside was only eight feet long.

Alien 3
★ 1992 115min

Director: David Fincher
Screenplay: David Giler, Walter Hill & Larry Ferguson

Shaven-haired Ripley crash-lands on Prison Planet Fury 161 and guess who she's brought with her? The plot and dialogue are largely incomprehensible and the only action comes from interminable chases down dark tunnels as yet another prisoner has his sentence terminated prematurely. The best thing about it is that there definitely won't be an *Alien 4*.

Ripley . . . . .Sigourney Weaver
Dillon .Charles S. Dutton
Clemens .Charles Dance
Golic . . . . .Paul McGann
Andrews . . . . .Brian Glover
Aaron . . . . .Ralph Brown

Quote 'In space no one can hear you yawn.' [Critic Sue Heal]

Psst! The almost complete absence of guns was at the insistence of Weaver, who hadn't liked the excess of weaponry in *Aliens* • Weaver got $5m • Eight scriptwriters and three directors were involved in bringing it to the screen. Fincher's main experience beforehand had been on Madonna videos • The largely British cast referred to the film as 'Skinheads in Space.'

Aliens
★★★★ 1986 137min c.

Director: James Cameron
Screenplay: James Cameron

Ripley wakes after a 57-year nap, only to be told that the planet where she found the alien has been colonised. When contact is lost with the inhabitants, Weaver's sent in with the Marines. Nail-biting, pants-wetting, suspense is complemented by superb action sequences, with Ripley having to mother young Henn as well as save the universe. An outstanding sci-fi actioner.

Ripley .Sigourney Weaver
Newt . . . . .Carrie Henn
Corp. Hicks . . . . .Michael Biehn
Burke . . . . .Paul Reiser
Bishop . . . . .Lance Henriksen
Pte. Hudson . . . . Bill Paxton
Lt. Gorman . . . . .William Hope
Pte. Vasquez . . . . .Jenette Goldstein
Sgt. Apone . . . . .Al Matthews
Pte. Drake . . . . .Mark Rolston

Blurb This Time It's War.

Quote 'Get away from her, you *bitch!*' • 'Game over, man!'

9

OOPS! When the mother alien gets Bishop, the string pulling the stinger through his body is visible.

Psst! The almost complete absence of blood was at the insistence of Weaver, who hadn't liked the excess of gore in the original. She also turned down some planned scenes involving dream sequences flashing back to the incidents in the first film • Goldstein turned up at the audition thinking the movie was about illegal immigrants. Hudson has a line ribbing her about this in the movie • There's an even better Special Edition on video, which has almost 20 minutes not seen in the cinema release.

All About Eve

★★★★ 1950 138min c.

Director: Joseph L. Mankiewicz
Screenplay: Joseph L. Mankiewicz
Source: Story, *The Wisdom of Eve* by Mary Orr

In an untypical moment of weakness a temperamental star befriends a star-struck fan, only to find that she is really a ruthless monster. One of the bitchiest, most caustically witty films ever to hit the screen, brought vividly to life by a cast acting their little cotton socks off. A source of endless joy, with a fascinating early appearance by Monroe as an aspiring actress.

Margo Channing	Bette Davis
Eve Harrington	Anne Baxter
Addison DeWitt	George Sanders
Karen Richards	Celeste Holm
Bill Simpson	Gary Merrill
Lloyd Richards	Hugh Marlowe
Birdie	Thelma Ritter
Miss Casswell	Marilyn Monroe
Max Fabian	Gregory Ratoff

Oscars Best Picture, Best Director, Best Screenplay, George Sanders

Quote 'To those of you who do not read, attend the theatre, or know anything of the world in which you live – it is perhaps necessary to introduce myself.' • 'Bill's 32. He looks 32. He looked it 5 years ago. He'll look it 20 years from now. I hate men.' • 'Fasten your seat belts. We're in for a bumpy night.' • 'Miss Casswell is an actress, a graduate of the Copacabana School of Dramatic Arts.' • 'I am Addison de Witt. I am nobody's fool, least of all yours.'

Psst! The film's 14 Oscar nominations have never been bettered, though it won only six of them • Davis only got the part when Claudette

Colbert put her back out and had to be put in traction. It came at an opportune time, for Warner Brothers, her long-time employers, had dropped her • Fox's boss had wanted Marlene Dietrich to play the lead • Although author Orr claims the original story was based on actress Elisabeth Bergner, others are convinced that Davis based her character on her rival Tallulah Bankhead. Bankhead was less than happy: 'After all the nice things I've said about that hag … When I get hold of her, I'll tear every hair out of her mustache.' • Davis and Merrill, who had never met before filming began, fell in love during the production and married a month and half after filming finished. They divorced 10 years later • Sanders' wife, Zsa Zsa Gabor, did not like her husband spending too much time with Marilyn Monroe and he had to tell her not to get too close to him when Zsa Zsa was around.

All Quiet on the Western Front

★★★ 1930 140min b/w

Director: Lewis Milestone
Screenplay: Del Andrews, Maxwell Anderson, Lewis Milestone & George Abbott
Source: Novel by Erich Maria Remarque

One of the greatest cinematic arguments against war still has enormous power to move today, even if some of the methods used to relate the story appear somewhat archaic now. Told from the German point of view, it follows a group of keen recruits overtaken by the nightmare that was World War I. It's a depressing film, but most definitely a worthwhile experience.

Paul Baumer	Lew Ayres
Katczinsky	Louis Wolheim
Himmelstoss	John Wray
Gerard Duval	Raymond Griffith
Tjaden	Slim Summerville
Muller	Russell Gleason
Kemmerick	Ben Alexander
Mrs. Baumer	Beryl Mercer

Oscars Best Picture, Best Director

Quote 'You'll have to forgive me, comrade.' • 'When it comes to dying for your country, it's better not to die at all.' • 'We live in the trenches out there. We fight. We try not to be killed. But sometimes we are. That's all.'

Psst! Trenches were dug on 20 acres of a ranch in Californian to simulate the battlefields, with 2,000 extras recruited from ex-servicemen. Two miles of pipes were laid to carry the water necessary to make the land water-logged. Real

French and German equipment from the war was imported and the training camp was modelled on genuine German blueprints • The German village was later used by Universal for movies such as *Frankenstein* • The film was originally planned as a silent movie and exists in a longer silent form with music and ZaSu Pitts in place of Beryl Mercer as Mrs. Baumer • Future director Fred Zinnemann, who was to make movies like *High Noon* and *The Day of the Jackal*, appears here as an extra listed as 'Man' on the credits • The film contains the first use of a crane for tracking shots across landscapes • There was pressure from the producers for a happy ending. Fed up of arguing, Milestone once told them: 'I've got your happy ending. We'll let the Germans win the war.' • The film was denounced by Goebbels as anti-German, but the Poles banned it for being pro-German. In France it was prohibited until 1962 • The close-up of Lew Ayres' hand reaching for the butterfly at the end is actually the hand of director Milestone • Although the film has been restored to close to its original 140 minutes, versions still exist ranging right down to just 90 minutes.

All That Jazz

★★ 1979 123min c.

Director: Bob Fosse
Screenplay: Robert Alan Aurthur & Bob Fosse

Frequently compared to Fellini's *8½*, Fosse takes a narcissistic look at what is effectively his own life as a director of musicals. Although some of the song and dance stuff is great, much of it is a rather seedy, self-indulgent wallow.

Joe Gideon . . . . .Roy Scheider
Angelique . . . . .Jessica Lange
Kate Jagger . . . . .Ann Reinking
Audrey Paris . . . . .Leland Palmer
David Newman . . . . .Cliff Gorman
O'Connor Flood . . . . .Ben Vereen
Sandahl . . . . .Sandahl Bergman
Lucas Sergeant . . . . .John Lithgow
Also: C.C.H. Pounder, Wallace Shawn

Quote 'I don't get married again because I can't find anyone I dislike enough to inflict that kind of torture on.' • 'I wonder if Stanley Kubrick has these problems?'

Psst! Richard Dreyfuss was to have played the lead, but he left to make *The Goodbye Girl* so Scheider took over himself • This is probably the first musical number ever performed to open-heart surgery.

All the King's Men

★★★ 1949 109min b/w

Director: Robert Rossen
Screenplay: Robert Rossen
Source: Novel by Robert Penn Warren

A gritty look at the downside of American politics, with Crawford in his best role as a once-honest politician corrupted by power, a character clearly based on the career of the populist Louisiana governor Huey Long. It's gritty stuff, although those who aren't familiar with the workings of the American political system may find their attention wandering occasionally.

Willie Stark . . . . .Broderick Crawford
Anne Stanton . . . . .Joanne Dru
Jack Burden . . . . .John Ireland
Tom Stark . . . . .John Derek
Sadie Burke . . . . .Mercedes McCambridge
Adam Stanton . . . . .John Shepperd
Lucy Stark . . . . .Anne Seymour
Tiny Duffy . . . . .Ralph Dumke

Oscars Best Picture, Broderick Crawford, Mercedes McCambridge

Quote 'Dirt's a funny thing. It rubs off on everybody.'

Psst! The air of authenticity is in large part down to the decision to use hundreds of extras from among the townsfolk of the working-class town, Stockton, in California, where the movie was shot. Some of them were even given lines • John Wayne turned down the part. He thought the novel on which the film was based was disgusting • Long was assassinated in 1935 by a young doctor who believed his sister had been assaulted by the politician.

All the President's Men

★★★ 1976 138min c.

Director: Alan J. Pakula
Screenplay: William Goldman
Source: Book by Carl Bernstein & Bob Woodward

Following the Watergate break-in, two hot-shot journalists dig around and discover a link to the highest office in the land. When the news breaks, the American people are astonished to find that their President is anything other than scrupulously honest. Although often murkily lit and frequently hard to hear, this is nonetheless a fascinating reconstruction of Woodward and

Bernstein's work into uncovering the extraordinary truth about Watergate.

Carl Bernstein	Dustin Hoffman
Bob Woodward	Robert Redford
Harry Rosenfeld	Jack Warden
Howard Simons	Martin Balsam
Deep Throat	Hal Holbrook
Ben Bradlee	Jason Robards
Bookkeeper	Jane Alexander
Debbie Sloan	Meredith Baxter
Dardis	Ned Beatty

Also: Stephen Collins, Polly Holliday, F. Murray Abraham, Lindsay Crouse

Oscars Best Screenplay (adapted), Jason Robards

Blurb The Most Devastating Detective Story Of The Century.

Quote 'Nothing's riding on this except the First Amendment of the Constitution, freedom of the press and maybe the future of the country.'

Psst! Redford was co-producer. It was he who bought the film rights and who had encouraged Bernstein and Woodward to write their book in the first place • Frank Wills, the security guard who uncovered the Watergate break-in, appears playing himself • To make the giant newsroom look as much like the real thing as possible, the filmmakers imported several tons of genuine rubbish from the real-life *Washington Post* newsroom • Bernstein was represented on screen here and in *Heartburn*. He said, 'It's certainly no hardship to be played by Jack Nicholson or Dustin Hoffman. I figure that by now, those guys have gotten about $8-9m to play me. It makes me think that next time, I should play myself.'• Writer William Goldman hated the problems caused by the movie and the interference he faced on the script. He discusses it in his wonderful book, *Adventures in the Screen Trade*.

Amadeus
★★★ 1984 158min c.

Director: Milos Forman
Screenplay: Peter Shaffer
Source: Play by Shaffer

Has-been composer Salieri confesses of his jealousy towards the uncouth but brilliant Mozart and the efforts he went to to keep the upstart languishing in obscurity. Hulce's giggling, ninnyish Mozart is so extraordinarily annoying, we can easily sympathise with Salieri.

Even those who don't go weak at the knees at the music should get swept up in the fascinating story.

Antonio Salieri	F. Murray Abraham
Wolfgang Amadeus Mozart	Tom Hulce
Constanze Mozart	Elizabeth Berridge
Emmanuel Schikaneder	Simon Callow
Leopold Mozart	Roy Dotrice
Katerina Cavalieri	Christine Ebersole
Emperor Joseph II	Jeffrey Jones
Parody Commendatore	Kenny Baker

Oscars Best Picture, F. Murray Abraham, Best Director

Quote 'Why would God choose an obscene child to be his instrument?' • 'There are too many notes.'

Psst! The part of Costanze was Meg Tilly's, but she tore a leg ligament in a soccer game the day before filming began • The two stars identified closely with their roles and formed separate cliques on set, barely speaking to each other • The premiere of *Don Giovanni* was filmed in the Tyl Theatre in Vienna where it had been premiered two hundred years earlier, although it took some persuasion to allow the use of candle-lit chandeliers in the wooden building • Prague, where most of the filming took place, was the only European city with buildings of the right period that had not been damaged in World War II.

The Amazing Dr. Clitterhouse
★★ 1938 87min b/w

Director: Anatole Litvak
Screenplay: John Huston & John Wexley

Robinson is a doctor specialising in the mind of the criminal who, instead of studying more textbooks, joins a gang to find out first hand what happens for himself. Once there, he finds it more difficult to remain detached and gets sucked into the life. Bogart and Robinson are excellent together in this droll but now dated melodrama.

Dr. Clitterhouse	Edward G. Robinson
Jo Keller	Claire Trevor
Rocks Valentine	Humphrey Bogart
Okay	Allen Jenkins
Insp. Lane	Donald Crisp
Nurse Randolph	Gale Page
Judge	Henry O'Neill
Grant	Thurston Hall
Butch	Maxie Rosenbloom

American Gigolo

★ 1980 117min c.

Director: Paul Schrader
Screenplay: Paul Schrader

A highly-paid Beverly Hills gigolo gets falsely accused when one of his clients is murdered. After a great opening, things go downhill from there. Seedy rather than steamy, this is a tacky subject treated in the tackiest way imaginable. The big surprise is not that Gere gets his kit off, but that his career survived his having appeared in this dreadful piffle.

Julian	Richard Gere
Michelle	Lauren Hutton
Sunday	Hector Elizondo
Anne	Nina Van Pallandt
Leon	Bill Duke
Charles Stratton	Brian Davies
Hollywood actor	Macdonald Carey

Blurb Richard Gere Is Neither An Officer Nor A Gentleman [re-release].

Psst! Christopher Reeve is said to have said no to a million dollars when he turned down the lead • Gere was actually a replacement for Travolta, who dropped out at the last minute.

American Graffiti

★★★★ 1973 110min c.

Director: George Lucas
Screenplay: George Lucas, Gloria Katz & Willard Huyck

A group of teenagers cruise around their small town in the early 60s. This influential coming-of-age movie, backed by fabulous music, is witty, entertaining and great, great fun. Based on Lucas' own experiences growing up in Modesto, California, we end up being terribly envious that we weren't there at the same time as him.

Curt Henderson	Richard Dreyfuss
Steve Bolander	Ron Howard
John Milner	Paul LeMat
Terry Fields	Charles Martin Smith
Laurie	Cindy Williams
Debbie	Candy Clark
Falfa	Harrison Ford
Carol	Mackenzie Phillips
Himself	Wolfman Jack
Joe	Bo Hopkins
Peg	Kathleen Quinlan
Blonde in T-Bird	Suzanne Somers

Blurb Where Were You In '62?'

Psst! Universal's executives were unimpressed by the idea of the project and after the premiere threatened not to release it, even though the response from the audience was superb. But when producer Francis Ford Coppola offered to buy the film off them, they changed their minds. The movie, filmed over just 29 days, cost only $750,000 and went on to make over $100m. Its success meant Lucas could make *Star Wars* • The soundtrack of nostalgic pop hits blazed a trail. The rights for the songs used cost 10% of the entire budget • It has been claimed that no other film has launched so many film and TV careers • It inspired the TV sitcom *Happy Days* • Lucas was later criticised, and he agreed with the criticism, for not mentioning at the end what happens to the female characters • Look out for the number plate 'THX 138', virtually the title of Lucas' first feature film, *THX-1138*. It had not been a box office success. The cinema is showing *Dementia 13*, the first movie co-producer Francis Ford Coppola made • Johnny Weissmuller Jr., son of the star of the Tarzan films, appears in a small part • The Universal bigwig who gave the project the green light wanted to change the title to *Another Slow Night in Modesto* for fear that audiences might think it was an Italian movie. Even Coppola tried to get Lucas to change the name, preferring *Rock Around the Block*.

An American in Paris

★★★ 1951 113min c.

Director: Vincente Minnelli
Screenplay: Alan Jay Lerner

A struggling artist in Paris finds love but has to give it up. The aged plot has whiskers so long it risks tripping over them. But you certainly can't complain about the wonderful Gershwin music, including songs like 'I Got Rhythm', 'Swonderful' and 'Embraceable You'. Sadly, Kelly indulges himself with a ballet sequence lasting almost 20 minutes. Some people love these interludes in Kelly films. Others find them tiresome and feel they destroy the mood of what's gone before. I'm with the latter lot.

Jerry Mulligan	Gene Kelly
Lise Bouvier	Leslie Caron
Adam Cook	Oscar Levant
Henri Baurel	Georges Guétary
Milo Roberts	Nina Foch
Mathilde Mattieu	Martha Bamattre

Oscars Best Picture, Best Story and Screenplay

Quote 'Back home everyone said I didn't have any talent. They might be saying the same thing over here, but it sounds better in French.'
• 'With a binding like you've got, people are going to want to know what's in the book.'
• 'That's quite a dress you almost have on.'

OOPS! Artist Kelly takes eight of his pictures to sell and manages to shift two of them. But he still has eight when he gets back home.

Psst! Cyd Charisse was to have been Kelly's partner rather than Caron. But she became pregnant • This was Caron's film debut. She was not particularly fluent in English and was not keen on the dancing, which did not endear her to the impatient and temperamental Kelly, even though he had discovered her • Her gamine haircut was copied around the world • Sadly, the set of the Paris street is built slap bang on top of a mound of debris thrown out from *The Wizard of Oz*.

An American Werewolf in London
★★★ 1981 97min c.

Director: John Landis
Screenplay: John Landis

Two tourists unwisely tramp the Yorkshire moors after dark, only to find themselves in something of a hairy situation. Landis manages the difficult trick of contrasting real scares with belly laughs to disturbing effect. The transformation scenes, carried out in broad daylight, were groundbreaking at the time. In retrospect, however, while some sequences are excellent, it's also showing its age in places.

David Kessler	David Naughton
Alex Price	Jenny Agutter
Jack Goodman	Griffin Dunne
Dr. Hirsch	John Woodvine
Chess player	Brian Glover
Insp. Villiers	Don McKillop
Sgt. McManus	Paul Kember
Gladys	Lila Kaye
Mr. Collins	Frank Oz
Accident victim	John Landis

Blurb From The Director Of *Animal House*...A Different Kind Of Animal.

Quote 'Have you ever talked to a corpse? It's boring.'

OOPS! If the werewolf can only be killed by someone who loves him, how come he is gunned down by the police at the end?

Psst! Landis insisted that the transformations happened on camera, without resorting to trick photography. Rick Baker won the first Academy Award given for makeup • When the wolf runs in front of the car, the man hit and knocked through a plate-glass window by the swerving car is writer-director Landis • The credits include lines like 'Any similarity to persons living, dead or undead, is purely coincidental' and 'Kermit and Frog and Miss Piggy star as themselves.' • The film is dedicated to Charles and Diana • All the songs have 'moon' in their titles • Landis' trademark phrase, 'See You Next Wednesday', crops up as the title of a sex film • Look out for Rik Mayall as one of the hostile drinkers in the *Slaughtered Lamb* pub.

The Americanization of Emily
★★★ 1964 115min b/w

Director: Arthur Hiller
Screenplay: Paddy Chayefsky
Source: Novel by William Bradford Huie

Anyone who only knows Andrews from singing about ribbons and kittens and spoonfuls of sugar is in for a surprise. She's a rather sexy military driver who falls for the cowardly Garner whose boss has plans to turn him into a hero, preferably a dead one. A nicely tart and unusual comedy which shows a very different side of the brass hats at the time of the Normandy invasion.

Lt. Cmdr. Charles Madison	James Garner
Emily Barham	Julie Andrews
Adm. William Jessup	Melvyn Douglas
Lt. Cmdr. 'Bus' Cummings	James Coburn
Mrs. Barham	Joyce Grenfell
Sheila	Liz Fraser
Old sailor	Keenan Wynn
Adm. Thomas Healy	Edward Binns

Psst! Perhaps not too surprisingly, the Pentagon would not cooperate with the filmmakers in any way.

The Amityville Horror
★ 1979 118min c.

Director: Stuart Rosenberg
Screenplay: Sandor Stern
Source: Book by Jay Anson

Visitors drawn to this highly regarded Long Island property are warned that, far from being an exciting and memorable investment, absolutely nothing will disturb their slumber during occupancy. Claims that these supposedly horrific, but actually monumentally tedious events, are based on fact are no doubt as true as the details in any estate agent's blurb. It was followed by three sequels, one in 3-D, which competed with each other to see which could scrape nearest to the bottom of the barrel. It was a dead heat.

George Lutz	James Brolin
Kathy Lutz	Margot Kidder
Father Delaney	Rod Steiger
Father Bolen	Don Stroud
Father Ryan	Murray Hamilton
Father Nuncio	John Larch
Jeff	Michael Sacks
Carolyn	Helen Shaver
Jackie	Amy Wright

Anatomy of a Murder
★★★ 1959 161min b/w

Director: Otto Preminger
Screenplay: Wendell Mayes
Source: Novel by Robert Traver

It is hard for us to imagine just how daring this courtroom drama – with Stewart defending a soldier accused of murder – was at the time. The aspects of the movie that caused such a fuss thentime now seem tame, but although it's very talky, the courtroom stuff is still pretty exciting.

Paul Biegler	James Stewart
Laura Manion	Lee Remick
Lt. Frederick Manion	Ben Gazzara
Parnell McCarthy	Arthur O'Connell
Maida	Eve Arden
Claude Dancer	George C. Scott
Paquette	Murray Hamilton
Mary Pliant	Kathryn Grant

OOPS! Remick is such a great quick-change artiste that she leaves a café wearing a white skirt and emerges onto the street in trousers.

Psst! The movie astonished audiences by talking about condoms, rape and even pink knickers. What was still more astonishing was that James Stewart should be involved • Stewart's father was so offended by his son's part in what he thought a 'dirty' movie that he took out an advertisement in the local paper

advising people not to see it • Lana Turner was replaced by Remick after disagreements with director Preminger. It was said that she slapped him, only for him to slap her back. According to some, the cause of disagreement was his refusal to let her sluttish army-wife character be dressed in designer gowns • The judge at the trial, Joseph N. Welch, was actually a lawyer, later a judge, who had made his name defending members of the Army against Senator McCarthy. Preminger said he always made sure that Welch never had to move and talk at the same time • Burl Ives and Spencer Tracy had both turned down the role before Welch took it.

The Andromeda Strain
★★★ 1970 131min c.

Director: Robert Wise
Screenplay: Nelson Gidding
Source: Novel by Michael Crichton

Scientists race against the clock to find a way to halt a virus from outer space. This early Michael Crichton story suffers from some dreadfully corny acting, irritating split-screen shots and a flat middle section. Despite this, it's still pretty tense and exciting stuff towards the end and has a great set of opening credits.

Dr. Jeremy Stone	Arthur Hill
Dr. Charles Dutton	David Wayne
Dr. Mark Hall	James Olson
Dr. Ruth Leavitt	Kate Reid
Karen Anson	Paula Kelly
Jackson	George Mitchell
Maj. Manchek	Ramon Bieri

Quote 'I never liked red lights. Reminds me of my time in a bordello.'

OOPS! On the third day, the guy squats down and looks at the clock. It says 2.10 as he stands up, but in the cutaway it's 2.25 • In the main control room, the clock on the left which measures minutes and seconds leaps all over the place throughout the movie • During the race to stop the bomb going off, both doors of the airlock are left open at one point • How come the vultures are still alive when everything else dies?

Psst! Although best-known for *Jurassic Park* and *Disclosure*, ex-doctor Crichton's involvement with movies goes back a long way. He went on to direct films like *Westworld* and *Coma*.

And Then There Were None

★★★ 1945 97min b/w

Director: René Clair
Screenplay: Dudley Nichols
Source: Novel *Ten Little Niggers* by Agatha Christie

An excellent small-scale mystery with 10 people invited to an island for reasons they can't fathom. Their enjoyment of the trip is marred slightly when they start being bumped off one by one. An intelligent script and assured direction make it scary, suspenseful and funny, although Christie's original ending is changed.

Judge Quincannon . . . . .Barry Fitzgerald
Dr. Armstrong . . . . .Walter Huston
Philip Lombard . . . . .Louis Hayward
Vera Claythorne . . . . .June Duprez
Blore . . . . .Roland Young
Rogers .Richard Haydn
Gen. Mandrake . . . . .C. Aubrey Smith
Prince Sterloff . . . . .Mischa Auer
Emily Brent . . . . .Judith Anderson

Quote 'Very stupid to kill the only servant in the house. Now we don't even know where to find the marmalade.'

Psst! When first released in the UK, it was under Christie's original title *Ten Little Niggers*.

Angel Street

SEE: **Gaslight**

Angels with Dirty Faces

★★★ 1938 97min b/w

Director: Michael Curtiz
Screenplay: John Wesley & Warren Duff
Source: Story by Rowland Brown

The paths of two childhood friends go in different directions, one becoming a gangster and the other a priest. As adults, the priest is dismayed when the gangster returns to the neighbourhood and is idolised by the local kids. A seminal film of its day, it still works pretty well, although O'Brien fighting to keep the kids from a life of crime is a bit sentimental at times. Still, with Cagney, Bogart and O'Brien all in one picture, who's complaining?

Rocky Sullivan . . . . .James Cagney
Jerry Connelly . . . . .Pat O'Brien
James Frazier . . . . .Humphrey Bogart
Laury Ferguson . . . . .Ann Sheridan
Mac Keefer . . . . .George Bancroft
Also: The Dead End Kids

Quote 'What d'ya hear? What d'ya say?'

Psst! Cagney isn't once seen to reload in any of the gun battles he fights. So many complaints were received from moviegoers that Cagney later made sure he was never seen to fire more than six shots without reloading • Audiences obviously didn't realise just what the actors in the gangster pictures went through. In the 30s, the machine guns in such movies, including this one, fired not blanks but live ammunition. At one point, Cagney refused to stand where he was told for a scene in which bullets landed nearby. It was a sensible decision. A badly-aimed bullet went straight past the spot where his head was supposed to be • Cagney modelled his character on a pimp he had once known back in Manhattan.

Animal Crackers

★★★ 1930 98min b/w

Director: Victor Heerman
Screenplay: Morrie Ryskind
Source: Musical play by Ryskind & George S. Kaufman

Hooray for Captain Spaulding, the African explorer. Groucho, an explorer? Well, believability was never their strong point. This early movie emphasises the zany at the expense of the plot, with the gags flying thick and fast. Fans of the Marx Brothers will love it. Those who don't know their brand of madcap humour ought perhaps to start with *Night at the Opera* or *Duck Soup*.

Capt. Jeffrey Spaulding . . . . .Groucho Marx
The Professor . . . . .Harpo Marx
Signor Emanuel Ravelli . . . . .Chico Marx
Horatio Jamison . . . . .Zeppo Marx
Mrs. Rittenhouse . . . . .Margaret Dumont
Arabella Rittenhouse . . . . .Lillian Roth
Also: Hal Thompson, Louis Sorin, Robert Greig

Quote 'One morning I shot an elephant in my pyjamas. How he got in my pyjamas I'll never know.' • 'You're one of the most beautiful women I've ever seen, and that's not saying much for you.' • 'You go Uruguay and I'll go mine.'

Psst! The Marx Brothers were not the greatest timekeepers in the world, with the card-playing Chico the worst of all. A neighbouring movie had some jail cells that weren't being used, so director Heerman brought in four of them and installed the Brothers there when they weren't needed on set.

Animal House
SEE: National Lampoon's Animal House

Annie Hall
★★★ 1977 93min c.

Director: Woody Allen
Screenplay: Woody Allen & Marshall Brickman

The story of a troubled relationship between a neurotic New York Jewish gag-writer and a flibbertigibbet wannabe singer, with the worst taste in clothes since Abraham Lincoln. Insightful into the problems of dating and living together, it is also extremely funny for much of its length. There are also some more languid stretches, though, and you can't help feeling on occasion that knocking their heads together would achieve rather more than all that jawing. *Manhattan* is far better.

Alvy Singer .Woody Allen
Annie Hall .Diane Keaton
Rob . . . . .Tony Roberts
Allison . . . . .Carol Kane
Tony Lacey . . . . .Paul Simon
Pam . . . . .Shelley Duvall
Mom Hall . . . . .Colleen Dewhurst
Duane Hall . . . . .Christopher Walken
Robin . . . . .Janet Margolin
TV show actress . . . . .Beverly D'Angelo
Alvy's theatre date . . . . .Sigourney Weaver
Party guest . . . . .Jeff Goldblum

Oscars Best Picture, Best Director, Best Screenplay, Diane Keaton

Quote 'Hey! Don't knock masturbation. It's sex with someone I love.' • 'Well, I have to go now Duane, because I'm due back on the planet Earth.' • 'That was the most fun I've ever had without laughing.' • 'A relationship is like a shark. It has to constantly move forward or it dies. And I think what we got on our hands is a dead shark.' • 'California!...I don't want to live in a city where the only cultural advantage is that you can make a right turn on a red light.' • 'Well, lah-dee-dah.' • 'I was thrown out of NYU my freshman year for cheating on my metaphysics final. I looked into the soul of the boy sitting next to me.' • 'That's okay. We can walk to the curb from here.' • 'On alternate days, *Annie Hall*

would appeal to us. Then, we'd get disgusted – who wants to see another love story about New York City? When I saw the rough-cut, I thought it terrible, completely unsalvagable. It rambled and was tangential and just endless.' [Brickman]

Showing The Sorrow and the Pity.

OOPS! Christopher Walken's name is wrongly spelt in the credits.

Psst! Until only three weeks before release, it was called *Anhedonia*, a medical term meaning the inability to experience pleasure. The head of United Artists threatened to throw himself out of a window if the title wasn't changed. In desperation, co-writer Brickman threw out ideas like *Me and My Goy*, *It Had to be Jew* and *A Rollercoster Named Desire* • Come Oscar night and although it won for Best Picture, Best Actress, Best Script and Best Director, Woody wasn't there. Monday night is his night playing clarinet in Michael's Pub in New York and he wasn't going to break his regular habit just to pick up an Oscar or two. He claims to have found out about his success from the following morning's papers • Allen seems almost proud of the fact that no other Oscar-winning film has made so little at the box office, although it is still one of the few movies he's made to turn in a decent profit, taking $36m at the box office worldwide • Allen shot 50 hours of film, and many credit film editor Ralph Rosenblum and Allen's co-writer Brickman with the film's look and feel. Without them, it may have felt more like an hour and a half standing in for Woody's analyst • The film is pretty clearly based on Allen's relationship with Diane Keaton a few years earlier. Hall was her real surname. Allan, however, denies this: 'I was not born underneath a roller coaster on Coney Island, nor was my first wife politically active, nor was my second wife a member of the literary set, nor did Diane leave me for a rock star or to live in California.' • Keep awake and you might spot Jeff Goldblum at the party in LA, Signourney Weaver in her film debut as Allen's date in the cinema queue at the end (you'll need really good eyesight) and Beverly D'Angelo on a TV.

A Nous la Liberté
★★★ 1931 95min b/w

Director: René Clair
Screenplay: René Clair

Master French director Clair brings his extraordinary cinematic flair and showmanship to this tale of an escaped convict who becomes an industrialist. Many of the scenes showing the demoralising and dehumanising effects of mechanisation were nabbed by Chaplin for *Modern Times*. But Chaplin didn't have Clair's eye, and certainly did not have his ear. Although a bit dated now, this operetta-like comedy still zips along, getting its points home without labouring the message or losing the jokes.

Luis . . . . .Raymond Cordy
Emile . . . . .Henri Marchand
Jeanne, the girl . . . . .Rolla France
Paul Imaque . . . . .Paul Olivier

Psst! Although Chaplin was accused of filching ideas from this for *Modern Times*, Clair admitted the character Emile was in any case based on Chaplin's tramp figure • Hungary banned the film as 'dangerous propaganda'.

The Apartment

★★★★ 1960 125min b/w

Director: Billy Wilder
Screenplay: Billy Wilder & I.A.L. Diamond

Lemmon is a slightly pathetic insurance guy climbing the ladder less through his efforts at work than through his willingness to let his apartment be used by his seniors for conducting office affairs. When lift-girl MacLaine is dumped by one of them, Lemmon has to decide whether he's a man or a mouse. This delicious bitter-sweet comedy is a must.

C.C. 'Bud' Baxter . . . . .Jack Lemmon
Fran Kubelik . . . . .Shirley MacLaine
J.D. Sheldrake . . . . .Fred MacMurray
Joe Dobisch . . . . .Ray Walston
Al Kirkeby .David Lewis
Dr. Dreyfuss . . . . .Jack Kruschen
Sylvia . . . . .Joan Shawlee
Miss Olsen . . . . .Edie Adams

Oscars Best Picture, Best Story and Screenplay, Best Director

Quote 'On November 1st, 1959 the population of New York City was 8,042,753. If you laid all these people end to end, figuring an average height of five feet six and a half inches, they would reach from Times Square to the outskirts of Karachi, Pakistan. I know facts like this because I work for an insurance company' • 'When you're in love with a married man, you shouldn't wear mascara.' • 'Some people take and some people get took' • 'That's the way it crumbles, cookie-like.' • 'Did you hear what I said, Miss Kubelik? I absolutely adore you.' – 'Shut up and deal!' [Last line]

Psst! Wilder had promised Lemmon a honey of a part in return for dressing up in drag in *Some Like It Hot*. This was it • Paul Douglas was originally going to play Fred MacMurray's role, but he fell ill and died just two weeks before the production got under way • No-one knew the ending in advance, including the writers. The actors got the pages for the final scene less than half an hour before they were due to film it. They did it in one take • Wilder liked actors to stick to the script and was driven mad by MacLaine's habit of ad-libbing • MacLaine thought she had the Oscar in a bag when Elizabeth Taylor fell ill and had to have an operation. It was widely thought she might die and she received many sympathy votes. But her recovery was swift enough for her to accept the award, with MacLaine commenting ruefully: 'I lost to a tracheotomy.' • MacLaine's nasal spray is actually squirting milk up her nose. Water on its own wouldn't have been as visible on film • The film was turned into a Broadway musical, *Promises, Promises*, in 1968.

Apocalypse Now

★★★ 1979 153min c.

Director: Francis Ford Coppola
Screenplay: John Milius & Francis Ford Coppola

During the Vietnam War, a captain is sent up river into Cambodia to kill a colonel who has gone native in a big way. This extraordinary and unforgettable movie, bizarre and quirky in the extreme, is filled with memorable scenes. However, it isn't a coherent whole and becomes incredibly confusing towards the close. Clearly inspired by Joseph Conrad's novel *Heart of Darkness*, try to catch the documentary made by Coppola's wife Eleanor, *Hearts of Darkness*, which shows the fascinating background to the making of the film.

Col. Kurtz . . . . .Marlon Brando
Lt. Col. Kilgore . . . . .Robert Duvall
Capt. Willard . . . . .Martin Sheen
Chef . . . . .Frederic Forrest
Chief . . . . .Albert Hall
Lance . . . . .Sam Bottoms
Clean . . . . .Laurence Fishburne
Photojournalist . . . . .Dennis Hopper
Colonel .Harrison Ford
General .G.D. Spradlin
Colby (civilian) . . . . .Scott Glenn

Quote 'Terminate with extreme prejudice.'
• 'I love the smell of napalm in the morning. It smells like victory.' • 'Charging a man with murder in this place was like handing out speeding tickets at the Indy 500.' • '*Apocalypse Now* is not *about* Vietnam. It *is* Vietnam. We were in the jungle; there were too many of us; we had access to too much money, too much equipment; and, little by little, we went insane.' [Coppola] • 'I don't see why this amount shouldn't be spent on a morality story, when you can spend it on a giant gorilla, a little fairy tale like *The Wiz* or some jerk who flies up in the sky.' [Coppola]

Psst! One of those movies as fascinating behind the scenes as on screen • A labour of love for Coppola, it was five years in the making. It became something of a joke in Hollywood, picking up the nickname *Apocalypse When?*
• The script had only taken Milius six weeks
• Filming in the Philippines did not go smoothly, to put it mildly. Hurricane Olga wrecked the sets completely, the 24 helicopters lent by Ferdinand Marcos' government kept being commandeered to have a go at rebels and Sheen had a heart attack • They did not lack for luxuries on the set. Some of the Italian members of the crew had their favourite pasta flown in from Italy • Hopper was well under the influence of drugs throughout. He wore the same clothes for the entire two months he was on set and nobody would ride in the same bus as him • Brando turned up late, drunk and heavily overweight. He admitted he hadn't read the script and spent days arguing over motivation and dialogue. Even when he agreed to be filmed, he insisted on remaining in shadow. For long shots, a leaner double was used • Duvall's helicopter attack on the village actually blew up the production's prop and paint shop • The original $12m budget went over $35m, some of which went to grease the palms of Philippine government officials. Coppola had to find several million dollars from his own pocket and is said to have threatened to commit suicide three times before the film was finished. Some of the problems lay at his door. He was such a perfectionist that he would be content if just one shot each day was up to scratch
• In addition to Jack Nicholson, Steve McQueen and Harvey Keitel, Clint Eastwood had been approached to play Sheen's part. When he heard how much the film had cost, he said: 'For that sort of money we could have invaded somewhere.' • Harvey Keitel had Sheen's part originally, but was replaced after two weeks
• When Sheen cuts his hand on the mirror in the hotel room, that's his own blood. He'd gone on a bender for two days at Coppola's instigation to get in the right condition for the part and improvised the scene • Despite his heart attack three-quarters of the way through filming, Sheen was back on set just seven weeks later
• The toughest roles were probably the severed heads in Kurtz's camp. The bodies the heads belonged to were stuck in sweltering heat in underground boxes for 10 hours a day, with only lunch off • The killing of the ox was part of a local native ceremony that Coppola filmed and popped into the movie • Coppola appears in a cameo as the director of the TV news team
• Harrison Ford wears a badge saying 'G. Lucas'. George Lucas of course made *Star Wars* and *American Graffiti*, both starring Ford.

Apollo 13
★★★★ 1995 140min c.

Director: Ron Howard
Screenplay: William Broyles Jr. & Al Reinert
Source: Book, *Lost Moon* by Jim Lovell & Jeffrey Kluger

Just eight months after man first walked on the moon, space travel appeared to have become routine. Then there was an explosion on board Apollo 13 and Mission Control had to figure out a way to get their three astronauts back home in a crippled spacecraft. Despite being a true life story with the outcome well known, this still manages to be an incredibly tense and gripping movie. Thanks to a superb ensemble cast and a lean, surprisingly witty script, every pulse-quick-ening moment is terrifyingly believable. Director Howard has managed what NASA couldn't, awakening our sense of wonder and achieve-ment at man's journey into the unknown.

Jim Lovell . . . . .Tom Hanks
Fred Haise . . . . .Bill Paxton
Jack Swigert . . . . .Kevin Bacon
Ken Mattingly . . . . .Gary Sinise
Gene Kranz . . . . .Ed Harris
Marilyn Lovell . . . . .Kathleen Quinlan
Pete Conrad . . . . .David Andrews
Henry Hurt . . . . .Xander Berkeley
Dr. Chuck . . . . .Christian Clemenson
CAPCOM 1 .Brett Cullen

Blurb 'Houston, We Have A Problem.'

Quote 'I can't deal with cleaning up. Let's sell the house' • 'I could eat the ass out of a dead rhinoceros.' • 'We never lost an American in space. We sure as hell aren't gonna lose one on my watch.' • 'Those people don't put one piece of equipment on my lawn. If they have a problem with that they can take it up with my husband. He'll be home Friday.' • 'It's like trying to drive a toaster through a car wash.'

Psst! Although not mentioned in the movie, the lunar module into which the astronauts had to cram after the command module was damaged was designed to support only two people to survive in for two days. The three Apollo 13 astronauts would have to use it in near freezing conditions for four days if they were to survive to return to earth • Grumman Corporation, which built the lunar module in which the astronauts returned, sent Rockwell a joke bill for towing their damaged command module 300,000 miles • Every shot in the film is original, with nothing taken from previously shot space footage • The actors trained at NASA's Space Camp in Huntsville, Alabama beforehand under the guidance of Jim Lovell and David Scott, the commander of Apollo 15 • The actors playing those in Mission Control enrolled in a Flight Controller School and were even forced to take a crash course in physics • The suits worn by the actor astronauts were genuine, even to the extent of being airtight. Oxygen was pumped in both to cool the actors and to enable them to breathe • The scenes with the astronauts in zero gravity actually were filmed in conditions of weightlessness. Parts of the spacecraft were installed in the KC-135 aircraft in which astronauts train. Although the plane can produce a reduced gravity environment for only 25 seconds at a time, the cast and crew flew a total of three hours 54 minutes while weightless • The real Jim Lovell plays the captain of the ship greeting the returning astronauts • Roger Corman's cameo appearance as a Congressman questioning NASA's funding is something of an in-joke. Corman had given Howard his directing break on a Corman quickie, *Eat My Dust*, back in 1976.

Around the World in 80 Days

★★ 1956 175min c.

Director: Michael Anderson
Screenplay: S.J. Perelman, James Poe & John Farrow
Source: Novel by Jules Verne

A Victorian adventurer bets the old fogeys in the Reform Club that he can get around the world in just 80 days. Although we get to see pretty moving postcards from many parts of the world, the story-telling is terribly flabby and long-winded. Much of the fun now comes from spotting the stars who pop up at regular intervals although the twist in the tail is fun, at least the first time round.

Phileas Fogg	David Niven
Passepartout	Cantinflas
Insp. Fix	Robert Newton
Princess Aouda	Shirley MacLaine
Reform Club member	Robert Morley
Reform Club member	Trevor Howard
Reform Club member	Finlay Currie
Reform Club member	Basil Sydney
M. Casse	Charles Boyer
Stationmaster	Joe E. Brown
Col. Proctor Stamp	John Carradine
Clerk	Charles Coburn
Railway official	Ronald Colman

Also: Melville Cooper, Noël Coward, Reginald Denny, Andy Devine, Marlene Dietrich, Fernandel, John Gielgud, Hermione Gingold, Cedric Hardwicke, Glynis Johns, Buster Keaton, Evelyn Keyes, Beatrice Lillie, Peter Lorre, Edmund Lowe, Victor McLaglen, A.E. Matthews, Mike Mazurki, John Mills, Alan Mowbray, Jack Oakie, George Raft, Gilbert Roland, Cesar Romero, Frank Sinatra, Red Skelton, Harcourt Williams

Oscars Best Picture, Best Screenplay (adapted)

Quote 'An Englishman never jokes about a wager.'

Psst! Producer Mike Todd corralled a raft of famous names to appear briefly in the movie, coining the word 'cameo' to describe their role. It was his hope that audiences would come back a second time to see who they had missed first time around • Gregory Peck got the boot after Todd thought he wasn't taking the film seriously enough • The original director, John Farrow, was dropped after just one day of filming • Ronald Colman's payment came in the form of a new Cadillac • Filming ground to a halt several times while Todd disappeared off to try to chivvy up more cash from somewhere • The use of 140 locations around the world is the greatest for any Hollywood-made movie • Almost 70,000 extras were employed, while a massive 138 actors were actually listed on the cast list. 34 directors filmed in 112 locations in 13 different countries. Where the film established a record, though, was in its use of 8,552 animals, more than any other movie. These comprised: 3,800 Rocky Mountain sheep; 2,448 buffalo; 950 donkeys; 800 horses; 512 monkeys; 17 bulls;

15 elephants; six skunks and four ostriches • Despite the seeming extravagance, the film only cost $6 million. 'I'm ashamed to admit it,' said Todd. 'Take *The Ten Commandments*. That cost $1m a commandment.' • The 'If At First' award should surely go to composer Victor Young, who was nominated on 18 occasions for an Oscar without winning anything. He finally won for this movie, but died before the ceremony • So that audiences didn't watch the clock, Todd ordered theatre managers to remove them from their auditoria • Todd was killed in a plane crash while promoting the movie. Everyone on the plane died. Todd's wife, Elizabeth Taylor, had been suffering from a virus and so had pulled out of the trip. The plane was called *The Lucky Liz* • This remains the only film Todd made.

Arsenic and Old Lace

★★★★ 1944 118min b/w

Director: Frank Capra
Screenplay: Julius J. Epstein & Philip G. Epstein
Source: Play by Joseph Kesselring

Two old ladies take pity on men suffering from loneliness – by poisoning them! Nephew Cary Grant finds out what's going on and nearly breaks his neck doing rapid double-takes. Then the even more psychopathic Massey turns up. Although barely changed from the stage version, this is a delicious farcical black comedy which fairly hums along.

Mortimer Brewster	Cary Grant
Elaine Harper	Priscilla Lane
Jonathan Brewster	Raymond Massey
Dr. Einstein	Peter Lorre
Abby Brewster	Josephine Hull
Martha Brewster	Jean Adair
Officer O'Hara	Jack Carson
Mr. Witherspoon	Edward Everett Horton
Lt. Rooney	James Gleason
'Teddy' Brewster	John Alexander
Rev. Dr. Harper	Grant Mitchell
Officer Brophy	Edward McNamara
Saunders	John Ridgeley
Reporter	Charles Lane

Quote 'One of our gentlemen found time to say 'How delicious!' before he died...' • 'Insanity runs in my family. It practically gallops.' • 'Cha-a-arge.'

Psst! Capra was about to go into the Signal Corps and wanted a quick movie to keep his family while he was away. He got a leave of absence so that he could finish filming

• Although made in 1942, the filmmakers couldn't release it until the smash Broadway run of the play was over. It stayed on the shelf for almost three years as a result • Josephine Hull, John Alexander and Jean Adair had all been in the original play, although Boris Karloff played the Raymond Massey part • Cary Grant's pay of $100,000 went to War Relief • Bob Hope had turned Grant's part down • The original preview flopped, with audiences disgusted that Edward Everett Horton also succumbed to the ladies. It was rapidly changed • The censors wouldn't wear the last line of the play, which had the delighted Grant saying: 'Do you understand? I'm a bastard!' 'I'm the son of a sea cook' isn't quite the same • When Grant is sitting on a tombstone, one of the headstones says 'Archie Leach', his real name.

Arthur

★★★ 1981 97min c.

Director: Steve Gordon
Screenplay: Steve Gordon

A dipsomaniac playboy millionaire falls in love with a girl he sees shoplifting and is threatened with being made penniless by his family. Moore's constant drunkenness now appears a little tacky, but Minnelli is wonderful, as is Gielgud as the wearily sardonic valet. The title of the 1988 sequel, *Arthur 2: On the Rocks*, was only too appropriate.

Arthur Bach	Dudley Moore
Linda Marolla	Liza Minnelli
Hobson	John Gielgud
Martha Bach	Geraldine Fitzgerald
Susan Johnson	Jill Eikenberry
Burt Johnson	Stephen Elliott
Bitterman	Ted Ross
Ralph Marolla	Barney Martin
Stanford Bach	Thomas Barbour
Gloria	Anne De Salvo

Oscars John Gielgud

Blurb I race cars, I play tennis, I fondle women, but I have weekends off and I am my own boss...

Quote 'I wish I had a dime for every dime I have.' • 'I'm going to take a bath.' – 'I'll alert the media.' • 'Are you a hooker? Jesus, I forgot. I just thought I was doing great with you.' • 'Tell me, has there been a death in your family? This is funny stuff.' • 'Isn't this fun? Don't you wish you were me? I know I do.'

The Asphalt Jungle
★★★★ 1950 112min b/w

Director: John Huston
Screenplay: Ben Maddow & John Huston
Source: Novel by W.R. Burnett

This fly-on-the-wall look at the planning and execution of a jewel heist is one of the all-time classic film noirs. Although much copied since, the original remains superb, tense, exciting and packed with masterly acting. The appearance of Marilyn Monroe is an added bonus.

Dix Handley ....Sterling Hayden
Alonzo D. Emmerich ....Louis Calhern
Doll Conovan ....Jean Hagen
Gus Minissi ....James Whitmore
Doc Erwin Riedenschneider ....Sam Jaffe
Police Comm. Hardy ....John McIntire
Cobby ....Marc Lawrence
Angela Phinlay ....Marilyn Monroe

Quote 'Crime is a left-handed form of human endeavour.' • 'That Asphalt Pavement thing is full of nasty, ugly people doing nasty things. I wouldn't walk across the room to see a thing like that.' [Louis B. Meyer, head of MGM, the studio that made it]

Psst! Probably the first film to show a heist from the criminals' point of view, this sparked off a whole new genre • MGM remade the film on three other occasions, as The Badlanders in 1958, as Cairo in 1963 and as Cool Breeze in 1972 • The credits don't even list Marilyn Monroe's name. Small though the part was, she thought it was one of her better performances.

Assault on Precinct 13
★★★★ 1976 91min c.

Director: John Carpenter
Screenplay: John Carpenter

A heavily-armed gang attack an understaffed police station in the process of being run down. This updating of Rio Bravo is tense and incredibly exciting. A masterly piece of film-making and, dare we say it, even better than Hawks' supposed classic.

Ethan Bishop ....Austin Stoker
Leigh ....Laurie Zimmer
Napoleon Wilson ....Darwin Joston
Lawson ....Martin West
Wells ....Tony Burton
Starker ....Charles Cyphers

Julie ....Nancy Loomis
Kathy ....Kim Richards

Quote 'Anyone got a smoke?' • 'Two cops wishing me luck? I'm doomed.'

OOPS! Rather a puzzlingly-titled film, as most of the action happens in Precinct 9 • As a policeman is driving along, a woman pulls up next to him and stares at the camera with understandable curiosity. Even after he has pulled off, she does the same thing again, not just once, but twice more • As two policemen turn into the forecourt of a police station in their car, their caps disappear.

Psst! Carpenter not only wrote and directed the movie but he also edited it and wrote the music • Carpenter acknowledged his source by editing it under the name of John T. Chance, John Wayne's character in Rio Bravo.

Atlantic City
★★★ 1981 104min c.

Director: Louis Malle
Screenplay: John Guare

A seedy, run-down ex-gangster is still hanging on in a seedy, run-down ex-gangster's town. With Susan Sarandon bathing herself with those lemons, can we really blame him? Lancaster is superb here as a guy who has nothing except his past, understandably falling for croupier Sarandon. Sedate and very poignant.

Lou ....Burt Lancaster
Sally ....Susan Sarandon
Grace ....Kate Reid
Chrissie ....Hollis McLaren
Dave ....Robert Joy
Joe ....Michel Piccoli
Waiter ....Wallace Shawn

Quote 'It used to be beautiful, what with the rackets, whoring, guns.' • 'The Atlantic Ocean was something then. Yes, you should have seen the Atlantic Ocean in those days.'

The Awful Truth
★★ 1937 90min b/w

Director: Leo McCarey
Screenplay: Vina Delmar
Source: Play by Arthur Richman

The awful truth is, this isn't anything like as good as everyone seems to think it is. Through a misunderstanding, a happily-married couple begin divorce proceedings. Although considered to be one of the classics of screwball comedy, it now seems pretty tame. Pleasant, but it doesn't raise too many laughs. It was remade in 1953 as a musical, *Let's Do It Again*.

Lucy Warriner . . . . .Irene Dunne
Jerry Warriner . . . . .Cary Grant
Daniel Leeson . . . . .Ralph Bellamy
Armand Duvalle . . . . .Alex D'Arcy
Aunt Patsy . . . . .Cecil Cunningham
Barbara Vance . . . . .Molly Lamont
Toots Binswanger . . . . .Joyce Compton
Mrs. Leeson . . . . .Esther Dale
Mr. Vance . . . . .Robert Warwick
Mrs. Vance . . . . .Mary Forbes
Mr. Smith, the dog .Asta
Also: Claud Allister, Leonard Carey, Byron Foulger, Bess Flowers

Oscars Best Director

Quote 'I guess it was easier for her to change her name than for her whole family to change theirs.' • 'In the spring a young man's fancy lightly turns to what he's been thinking about all winter.' • 'I wouldn't go on living with you if you were dipped in platinum.'

Psst! The film was based on a 1922 hit play which inspired two silent movies • There was no complete script when filming began, McCarey preferring a loose, improvisational style of film-making which often entailed him arriving on set with scraps of paper covered in lines of dialogue • Grant wasn't happy with this method of filming and when his attempt to swap parts with Bellamy failed, he is said to have offered Harry Cohn, head of Columbia, $5,000 to let him leave the movie. McCarey was so annoyed, he offered Cohn another $10,000 to take Grant up on his offer • Mr. Smith is played by Asta from the *Thin Man* films • Playing the part of 'Viola Heath' is Bess Flowers. This grand-looking lady appeared in countless movies but is now known as the Queen of the Hollywood extras. She wasn't often named on the credits but movies where you'll spot her are *Ninotchka*, *Love Affair*, *Double Indemnity*, *All About Eve* and others far, far too numerous to mention.

Babette's Feast
★★★★ 1988 102min c.

Director: Gabriel Axel
Screenplay: Gabriel Axel
Source: Novella by Karen Blixen [Isak Dinesen]

In this Danish film set in the late 19th century Parisian exile Audran, working for two sisters in a primly religious Danish fishing village, wins a fortune in the Paris lottery and uses it to lay on an enormous banquet. A masterly, magical film that has us enraptured as we watch the suspicious villagers try to resist the delights of the 'pagan' feast. Trust me. It's brilliant.

Babette Hersant . . . . .Stéphane Audran
Achille Papin . . . . .Jean-Philippe Lafont
Lorens (young) . . . . .Gudmar Wivesson
Lorens Lowenhielm (old) . . . . .Jarl Kulle

Psst! The original story was by Karen Blixen, portrayed by Streep in *Out of Africa*. It was written as a bet with a friend who told her the best way to get Americans to buy her stuff was to write about food! • In New York, one restaurant did a related promotion. After the film, cinemagoers could sit down to the same amazing banquet as that served up by Audran.

Baby Doll
★★★ 1956 114min b/w

Director: Elia Kazan
Screenplay: Tennessee Williams
Source: Play, *27 Wagonloads of Cotton* by Williams

Seeking revenge, Wallach aims to seduce Malden's child bride. This rather bowdlerised version of Williams' blackly comic play was something of a cinema milestone in its day. Naturally it hardly seems so outrageous now, but the sultry Baker still generates some steam.

Archie . . . . .Karl Malden
Baby Doll . . . . .Carroll Baker
Silva Vacarro . . . . .Eli Wallach
Aunt Rose Comfort . . . . .Mildred Dunnock
Rock . . . . .Lonny Chapman
Also: Rip Torn

Blurb Condemned By Cardinal Spellman.

Quote 'Possibly the dirtiest American picture ever legally exhibited.' [*Time* magazine]

Psst! The Legion of Decency railed against the film, in large part for its portrayal of an unconsummated marriage, and forbade Catholics to see such 'carnal suggestiveness'. The studio could hardly believe its luck at getting such free publicity and stuck the warning on the posters • Diane Cilento had turned down Baker's role. Marilyn Monroe had wanted it, but had been rejected • Baker's baby-doll pyjamas became a fashion craze.

Back to the Future

★★★★ 1985 116min c.

Director: Robert Zemeckis
Screenplay: Bob Gale & Robert Zemeckis

Cracking sci-fi adventure yarn, full of verve, originality, excitement and wacky humour. Inventor Lloyd sends teenager Fox(!) back to the 50s where, to ensure his own existence, he has to bring his parents together, a feat complicated by his mother falling for him. A delight from start to finish.

Marty McFly	Michael J. Fox
Dr. Emmett Brown	Christopher Lloyd
George McFly	Crispin Glover
Lorraine Baines	Lea Thompson
Jennifer Parker	Claudia Wells
Biff Tannen	Thomas F. Wilson
Dave McFly	Marc McClure
Linda McFly	Wendie Jo Sperber
Sam Baines	George DiCenzo
Stella Baines	Frances Lee McCain
Mr. Strickland	James Tolkan

Quote 'Doc, are you telling me that you built a time machine out of a De Lorean?' – 'The way I see it, if you're going to build a time machine into a car, why not do it with some style?'
• 'Ronald Reagan? The actor? Then who's vice-president? Jerry Lewis?' • 'Are you trying to tell me that my mother…has the hots for me?'
• 'Roads? Where we're going we don't need…roads!'

OOPS! How come nobody notices that the money Marty hands over in the café for his coffee is twenty years ahead of its time?
• Watch the mileometer lose a few miles as Marty's trying to escape from the terrorists
• In the same scene, Marty shifts into second gear twice • Doc obviously invented Velcro and didn't tell anybody. It's on his trainers when he's hanging from the clock, several years too early • When Marty returns to the present, the clock in the car showing where he's come from is showing 'November' instead of 'October'.

Psst! Rejected by all the major studios, it was Spielberg who gave the writers their chance • Eric Stoltz was the original lead, but was replaced five weeks into production. Matthew Modine and Ralph Macchio turned the part down • Fox, then a far-from-teenage 24, was working on his TV show *Family Ties* all day. For a month and a half he worked on *BTTF* from six till midnight each day as well • Glover lost his voice through nerves on the first day and had to dub his entire part later • Look out for Billy

Zane as 'Match' and Huey Lewis, who sings 'The Power of Love', in a cameo as the school band judge • The cinema has the same in-joke double-bill as in *Gremlins*.

Back to the Future, Part II

★★ 1989 107min c.

Director: Robert Zemeckis
Screenplay: Bob Gale

The weakest of the series has some stunning effects, with Fox at one point playing three characters at one and the very same time. But the story, involving parallel worlds in which villain Biff can be married to Fox's mum, is overcomplicated while the jokes (*Jaws 19* is playing in the future) aren't so plentiful. The cliff-hanger ending, forcing you to watch the next one, is a bit of a cheek. Shue, however, is delightful as the new Jennifer.

Marty/Marlene McFly	Michael J. Fox
Dr. Emmett Brown	Christopher Lloyd
Lorraine	Lea Thompson
Biff Tannen/Griff	Thomas F. Wilson
Jennifer	Elisabeth Shue
Strickland	James Tolkan
Marvin Berry	Harry Waters Jr.
Terry	Charles Fleischer
George McFly	Jeffrey Weissman
Match	Billy Zane

Quote 'Something's got to be done about your kids, Marty!'

Showing A Fistful of Dollars • Dallas • Taxi • Cheers • Family Ties • Miami Vice.

Psst! Crispin Glover thought he was indispensible as Marty's dad but Universal wouldn't pay the $1m he asked for. Instead they put in some out-takes from the first film and used a double • Judy Ovitz, wife of Mike Ovitz, Hollywood's most powerful agent turned president of Disney, appears as the 'antique store saleswoman', while Elijah Wood, perhaps the best (if not the best-paid) child actor appears in an early role as a 'video game boy' • In the antique shop window is a doll of Roger Rabbit, from another film directed by Zemeckis.

Back to the Future, Part III

★★★★ 1990 118min c.

Director: Robert Zemeckis
Screenplay: Bob Gale

In some ways the best of them all, with Fox nipping back to the 1880s to stop Lloyd being shot. The fun of the original is recreated with the spirit of the Wild West in a rollicking romp that never lets up. Doc gets a love interest, too, in the lovely Steenburgen. Perfect entertainment.

Marty McFly/Seamus McFly . . . . .Michael J. Fox
Dr. Emmett Brown . . . . .Christopher Lloyd
Clara Clayton . . . . .Mary Steenburgen
'Mad Dog' Tannen/Biff . . . . . .Thomas F. Wilson
Maggie McFly/Lorraine . . . . . . .Lea Thompson
Jennifer .Elisabeth Shue
Bartender . . . . .Matt Clark

Blurb They've Saved The Best Trip For Last... But This Time They May Have Gone Too Far.

OOPS! Keep an eye on the shadow of the train near the end of the movie.

Psst! Unusually, because of the work schedules of Fox and director Zemeckis, parts II & III were filmed back-to-back.

The Bad and the Beautiful
★★★ 1952 118min b/w

Director: Vincente Minnelli
Screenplay: Charles Schnee

Although not quite as vicious as *Sunset Boulevard* in its attack on the horrors of Hollywood, Minnelli's Tinseltown satire still has all the fun of a tabloid exposé on dirty doings. A star, a director and a screenwriter all recall in flashback how they were abused years ago by maverick producer Kirk Douglas. Will they help him out now in his hour of need? Much fun can be had trying to match the characters to real-life counterparts. Bitchy and witty, those who love movies will particularly adore it.

Georgia Lorrison . . . . .Lana Turner
Jonathan Shields . . . . .Kirk Douglas
Harry Pebbel . . . . .Walter Pidgeon
James Lee Bartlow . . . . .Dick Powell
Fred Amiel . . . . .Barry Sullivan
Rosemary Bartlow . . . . .Gloria Grahame
Victor 'Gaucho' Ribero . . . . .Gilbert Roland
Henry Whitfield . . . . .Leo G. Carroll

Oscars Gloria Grahame, Best Screenplay

Blurb The Story Of A Blonde Who Wanted To Go Places, And A Brute Who Got Her There...The Hard Way.

Quote 'Jonathan is more than a man. He's an experience, and he's habit-forming. If they could ever bottle him, he'd outsell ginger ale.'

Psst! Douglas' character was thought by some to be based on producer Val Lewton, who made *Cat People*, and by others to be an impression of David O. Selznick, the brains behind *Gone With the Wind*. Selznick considered suing at one point • Ivan Triesault and Leo G. Carroll are supposedly taking off Fritz Lang and Alfred Hitchcock, while Lana Turner supposedly plays Diana Barrymore. Dick Powell's part caricatures F. Scott Fitzgerald • As in the movie, Turner's career started as an extra • Many have noticed the film's multi-flashback structure is similar to that in *Citizen Kane*. John Houseman, the producer, worked on early script drafts of *Kane* with Orson Welles until they had one row too many • The voice of Turner's father, heard reciting Shakespeare on the record, is Louis Calhern.

Bad Day at Black Rock
★★★★ 1955 81min c.

Director: John Sturges
Screenplay: Millard Kaufman
Source: Story, *Bad Time at Hondo* by Howard Breslin

One-armed stranger Tracy gets off the train in a hick Western town on a simple mission. But for some reason his friendliness and politeness is met with extreme hostility from the townsfolk. A simple premise makes for a tense, exciting film as Tracy refuses to be put off and keeps digging until he discovers Black Rock's guilty secret.

John J. Macreedy . . . . .Spencer Tracy
Reno Smith . . . . .Robert Ryan
Liz Wirth .Anne Francis
Tim Horn .Dean Jagger
Doc Velie . . . . .Walter Brennan
Coley Trimble . . . . .Ernest Borgnine
Hector David . . . . .Lee Marvin
Pete Wirth . . . . .John Ericson

Quote 'You look like you need a hand.'
• 'What've you got?' – 'Chili and beans.' – 'Anything else?' – 'Chili without beans.'

Psst! It was originally planned not to have a musical score to heighten the location's bleakness, but this idea was hurriedly changed after the first preview.

Badlands
★★★ 1973 95min c.

Director: Terrence Malick
Screenplay: Terrence Malick

Over twenty years before *Natural Born Killers* a young couple, feeling unappreciated by those around them, go on a killing spree. The debut of writer-director Malick created the sort of stir Tarantino did, but after *Days of Heaven* things went quiet. A compelling look at an inexplicable pair of outcasts which has achieved cult status.

Kit Carruthers	Martin Sheen
Holly	Sissy Spacek
Father	Warren Oates
Cato	Ramon Bieri
Deputy	Alan Vint

Quote 'I wasn't popular at school on account of having no personality and not being pretty.'

Psst! The film was based on a real-life couple, Charles Starkweather and 14-year-old Carol Fugate, who went on a killing spree in 1958, doing away with 10 people, including Fugate's mother, stepfather and half-sister • The film took a week to edit, with Malick taking scripting jobs to raise cash for post-production costs • Although it was not a box office success, it was more popular when it was later re-released.

Bad Timing: A Sensual Obsession
★★★ 1980 123min c.

Director: Nicolas Roeg
Screenplay: Yale Udoff

Two Americans embark on an obsessive affair, and discover that true love is no easier to find in Vienna than it was in *The Third Man* 35 years earlier. Director Roeg and star Russell fell in love while filming and, boy, does it show. Her electric performance overwhelms Art Garfunkel and even veteran scene-stealers Harvey Keitel and Denholm Elliott have trouble keeping up. Stylish and brilliant, but not if you're in therapy.

Dr. Alex Linden	Art Garfunkel
Milena Flaherty	Theresa Russell
Insp. Fredrich Netusil	Harvey Keitel
Stefan Vagnic	Denholm Elliott
Foppish man	Daniel Massey

Quote 'If we don't meet, there's always the possibility it could have been perfect.'

Ball of Fire
★★★★ 1941 111min b/w

Director: Howard Hawks
Screenplay: Charles Brackett & Billy Wilder

Source: Story, *From A to Z* by Thomas Monroe & Billy Wilder.

A streetwise dancer seeks sanctuary with eight unworldly professors researching an encyclopaedia. In return for bed and board, she teaches them about the real world. When naive Cooper is smitten, the other seven Profs offer hilariously inadequate advice on love and dating. Effectively *Snow White and the Seven Dwarfs* in the style of screwball comedy, this is deliciously witty and romantic stuff, with every member of the cast getting their moment of glory. The sort of film that makes you wish real life was more like the movies. Hawks remade the film himself in 1948 as *A Song is Born*.

Prof. Bertram Potts	Gary Cooper
Sugarpuss O'Shea	Barbara Stanwyck
Prof. Gurkakoff	Oscar Homolka
Prof. Jerome	Henry Travers
Prof. Magenbruch	S.Z. "Cuddles" Sakall
Prof. Robinson	Tully Marshall
Prof. Quintana	Leonid Kinskey
Prof. Oddly	Richard Haydn
Prof. Peagram	Aubrey Mather
Garbage man	Allen Jenkins
Joe Lilac	Dana Andrews
Duke Pastrami	Dan Duryea
Miss Bragg	Kathleen Howard
Larsen	Charles Lane
Waiter	Elisha Cook Jr.

Quote 'That is the kind of woman that makes whole civilisations topple' • 'I shall regret the absence of your keen mind. Unfortunately it is inseparable from an extremely disturbing body.' • 'Yes, I love him. I love those hick shirts he wears with the boiled cuffs and the way he always has his vest buttoned wrong. He looks like a giraffe, and I love him. I love him because he's the kind of a guy who gets drunk on a glass of buttermilk and I love the way he blushes right up over his ears. I love him because he doesn't know how to kiss, the jerk. I love him, Joe. That's what I'm trying to tell you.'

Psst! The original story had been co-written by Wilder before he came to America • The original choice for the female lead was Ginger Rogers. She said no, saying that she only wanted to play roles that were ladylike. Producer Sam Goldwyn was irate, famously screaming: 'You tell Ginger Rogers for me that ladies stink up the place!' • Bandleader Gene Krupa is the guy doing the wonderful 'Drum Boogie' on a matchbox in the nightclub• If you think you recognise the voice of the garbage man, perhaps it's because Allen Jenkins was also the voice of Officer Dibble from *Top Cat*

• When Dan Duryea licks the sight of his gun after shooting the place up, it's an in-joke referring to the persistent habit of Gary Gooper in his previous movie, *Sergeant York*.

Bambi

★★★ 1942 70min c.

Director: David Hand
Screenplay: Perce Pearce & Larry Morey
Source: Story by Felix Salten

The ultimate stag movie. When his mother is killed by hunters, a young fawn has to cope on his own, with a little help from his friends of the forest, notably toothsome rabbit Thumper. Very fondly remembered by adults, perhaps undeservedly. Although the moment where mom gets it still brings a lump to the throat and some of the animation is impressive, the winsome songs are truly dreadful while the story is twee and slight. Pales beside some of the recent Disney greats. What's more, it's grossly unfair to skunks, reinforcing harmful stereotypes.

Bambi . . . . Bobby Stewart
Thumper . . . . .Peter Behn
Flower . . . . .Stan Alexander

Quote 'Mother! Mother, where are you mother?' • 'Your mother can't be with you any more.'

Psst! The movie was not a great success financially on first release and took many years to make its money back • Four-year-old Peter Behn auditioned for the part of Thumper but was thought to be dreadful and sent away. When the audition tapes were listened to afterwards, it was clear that he was the one they wanted, but it took some time to find him again • There are only 900 words in the script • A deer carcass was bought so the animators could dissect it and study how it was put together • Two fawns, 'Bambi' and 'Faline' were lent to Disney for the animators to watch. Other relevant animals were also added to the menagerie, among them rabbits, birds, chipmunks and a pair of skunks.

The Band Wagon

★★★★ 1953 112min c.

Director: Vincente Minnelli
Screenplay: Adolph Green & Betty Comden

Quite simply, one of the greatest of movie musicals. In a role close to home, Astaire plays an out-of-favour movie hoofer trying for the big time again in a Broadway show. But with an aloof ballerina, Charisse, as his co-star and arty megalomaniac Buchanan as director, things don't look promising. As in *Singin' in the Rain*, the mix of comedy, backstage drama and music is spot on, with great numbers like 'Triplets' and 'That's Entertainment'. What's more, the 'Girl Hunt Ballet' is cool and mesmerising instead of merely mannered, as when Gene Kelly does it.

Tony Hunter . . . . .Fred Astaire
Gaby Gerard . . . . .Cyd Charisse
Jeffrey Cordova . . . . .Jack Buchanan
Lester Marton . . . . .Oscar Levant
Lily Marton . . . . .Nanette Fabray
Paul Byrd . . . . .James Mitchell
Hal Benton . . . . .Robert Grist
Col. Tripp .Thurston Hall
The Movie Star . . . . .Ava Gardner

Quote 'She was bad. She was dangerous. I wouldn't trust her any further than I could throw her. But she was my kind of woman.' • 'She came at me in sections. More curves than the scenic railway.' • 'We're not quarrelling. We're in complete agreement. We hate each other.'

OOPS! One of the all-time classic gaffes comes just after 'Louisiana Hayride' when the acting troupe are on the train to Baltimore. Out of some carriage windows, it's night-time and cars can be seen with their headlights on. Yet out of other windows, it's bright daylight! • Near the start of the movie, watch the extras walking past Astaire in the amusement arcade as he does his 'Shine On Your Shoes' number. Several come round again and again, with the boy in the checked shirt that Astaire gives his unwanted hot dog to particularly conspicuous as he jumps from place to place • Also in the arcade, you can see the shadow of a Technicolor camera as Astaire jumps on the Electricity for Life machine • Charisse's character's surname, 'Gerard', appears as 'Girard' outside the Alcott Theatre in New York. Inside, the programme gets the theatre's name wrong, calling it the 'Stratton' • The 'Triplets' number first appears as Item six on the programme then, when we see 'Girl Hunt', it's Item two. Rejigging the show on the road? Perhaps.

Psst! Jack Buchanan's role was loosely based on Jose Ferrer who, as a producer in the 50s, had four shows running concurrently on Broadway while acting in a fifth. Astaire's role was modelled fairly closely on his own current situation. The songwriters' parts were based on Adolph Green and Betty Comden themselves, with many scenes taken from incidents in their own lives, such as the early section meeting Astaire at the station • Buchanan got the role after Clifton Webb nixed it, as did Edward G. Robinson and Vincent Price • Oscar Levant had a heart attack just over a month before filming started. His doctors advised him not to exert himself. When Astaire offered to carry him down the long ramp in the 'That's Entertainment' number, Levant threw caution to the winds and did the number as planned • Buchanan was also not happy, having had major dental surgery just before the production • Charisse had to play her scenes with Astaire with her knees bent, so she didn't tower over him too much. It was a problem she frequently had. She did the same in *Singin' in the Rain* with Gene Kelly • Despite its joyous nature on screen, the production was not a happy one with the normally calm Astaire storming off the set at one point in anger at Minnelli's confusing directions.

The Bank Dick
★★★★ 1940 73min b/w

Director: Edward F. Cline
Screenplay: W.C. Fields

One of Fields' greatest. Marginally less haphazardly constructed than some of his other movies, this has him accidentally foiling a bank robbery and unwisely being made a guard there. The wacky gags flow like the water the great man never touched. Although there are some splendidly named characters on the cast list, few of them get much of a look in.

Egbert Sousè	W.C. Fields
Agatha Sousè	Cora Witherspoon
Myrtle Sousè	Una Merkel
Elsie May Sousè	Evelyn Del Rio
Mrs. Hermisillo Brunch	Jessie Ralph
J. Pinkerton Snoopington	Franklin Pangborn
Joe Guelpe	Shemp Howard
Og Oggilby	Grady Sutton
Mackley Q. Greene	Dick Purcell
J. Frothingham Waterbury	Russell Hicks
Drunk	Jack Norton

Quote 'I never smoked a cigarette until I was nine.'

Psst! Fields concealed his identity as writer under the pseudonym Mathatma Kane Jeeves. The name supposedly derives from the hammy old English plays he saw in his youth in which toffs repeatedly said: 'Me hat, Me cane, Jeeves.' • Fields came under pressure from the studio to change the name of the Black Pussy Cat

Café, with its bartender Shemp Howard, one of The Three Stooges. They backed down when he pointed out that a respectable establishment of that name already existed in LA on Santa Monica Boulevard • The inhabitants of the real-life Lompoc protested at the way their town was portrayed on screen, to no avail • If many of the words don't seem to match the lip movements, that's because Fields over-dubbed much of the dialogue after filming. He wasn't very concerned whether it matched up or not.

Barbarella
★★ 1968 98min c.

Director: Roger Vadim
Screenplay: Terry Southern
Source: Comic strip by Jean-Claude Forest

Once an important movie for male adolescents, mainly because of Fonda's striptease under the opening credits. After that, this comic-strip derived tale of a 41st-century astronaut has little to commend it other than some imaginative visuals. What was once erotic, such as O'Shea's sex machine meeting its match in Fonda, is now camp and silly, while the awful rock soundtrack places it firmly in the 1960s rather than the 4060s. A *Highlights of Barbarella* tape would be entertaining but as for the whole thing? I'd rather be plucked from the ground by a blind angel.

Barbarella	Jane Fonda
Pygar	John Philip Law
The Black Queen	Anita Pallenberg
The Concierge	Milo O'Shea
Dildano	David Hemmings
Prof. Ping	Marcel Marceau

Blurb See Barbarella Do Her Thing!

OOPS! When she wants Pygar to shoot the black guard, Barbarella tells him to fire to the right, but he moves the gun to the left.

Psst! Virna Lisi was originally to play Barbarella. But she refused, abandoned her Hollywood career and went home to Italy • Group Duran Duran took their name from a character in the movie • Eight writers worked on the screenplay.

Barefoot in the Park
★★★★ 1967 104min c.

Director: Gene Saks
Screenplay: Neil Simon
Source: Based on play by Simon

A young couple starting married life in a poky flat at the top of their apartment block find that their outlooks on life are diametrically opposed. This classy comedy is one of the most successful screen versions of Neil Simon. It's more than just a collection of good gags. Their relationship and its problems feel real, while there's a lovely subplot involving Natwick, Fonda's mother, and eccentric romeo Boyer.

Paul Bratter	Robert Redford
Corie Bratter	Jane Fonda
Victor Velasco	Charles Boyer
Mrs. Ethel Banks	Mildred Natwick
Harry Pepper, the phone man	Herb Edelman
Aunt Harriet	Mabel Albertson
Restaurant owner	Fritz Feld

Quote 'Next time you're in town, Mr. Bratter, be sure to look me up.' • 'I feel like we've died and gone to heaven... only we had to climb up.'

OOPS! As Fonda and Redford walk in the park, their respective positions switch.

Psst! Redford and Natwick were in the play when it was on Broadway.

Barry Lyndon
★★★★ 1975 184min c.

Director: Stanley Kubrick
Screenplay: Stanley Kubrick
Source: Novel by William Makepeace Thackeray

Slammed on initial release as *Tom Jones* with the projector set to half speed, Thackeray's little-known novel of an Irish lad's attempt to gatecrash European society now looks better than when it baffled audiences 20 years ago. Ryan O'Neal's accent is a bit wobbly, and the pace is certainly slow, but the emotion which Kubrick keeps bottled up in the first half is terrific when it comes pouring out in the second. Visually staggering, it is definitely one of those films that need to be seen in a widescreen version, preferably in the cinema.

Barry Lyndon	Ryan O'Neal
Lady Lyndon	Marisa Berenson
The Chevalier	Patrick Magee
Capt. Potzdorf	Hardy Kruger
Lord Ludd	Steven Berkoff
Nora	Gay Hamilton
Capt. Quin	Leonard Rossiter
Rev. Runt	Murray Melvin
Sir Charles Lyndon	Frank Middlemass
Lord Wendover	André Morell
Barry's mother	Marie Kean
Narrator	Michael Hordern

Quote 'I have taken the ribbon from around my neck, and hidden it somewhere on my person. If you find it, you can have it. You are free to look for it anywhere you will, and I will think very little of you if you do not find it.'

Psst! Kubrick wanted to recreate on screen the look of 18th-century paintings and so set out to film the movie without any artificial lighting at all. Ultra-high speed film was used. The gambling scenes, which were lit only by candlelight, were filmed using this and a specially adapted Zeiss lens which hitherto had only been used by NASA for filming in space.

Basic Instinct
★★ 1992 128min c.

Director: Paul Verhoeven
Screenplay: Joe Eszterhas

Strip out the steamy sex and you're left with a confusing and rather nasty little thriller helped enormously at the box office by the vociferous and useful public protests from concerned homosexuals. Stone's certainly a knockout as the knickerless, bisexual novelist suspected by Douglas of ice-picking her lover to death (how different from the home life of our own dear Barbara Cartland). But the plot is wildly implausible and is, in any case, the identical one Eszterhas uses in most of his films.

Det. Nick Curran	Michael Douglas
Catherine Tramell	Sharon Stone
Gus	George Dzundza
Dr. Beth Garner	Jeanne Tripplehorn
Lt. Walker	Denis Arndt
Roxy	Leilani Sarelle
Andrews	Bruce A. Young
Capt. Talcott	Chelcie Ross
Hazel Dobkins	Dorothy Malone
John Correli	Wayne Knight
Dr. Lamott	Stephen Tobolowsky

Blurb Flesh Seduces. Passion Kills.

Quote 'What are you gonna do? Arrest me for smoking?' • 'It's like ballet. In the rough sex scene between me and Jeanne Tripplehorn it was well rehearsed to the point of boom, up against the wall, kiss, kiss, kiss, boom, her leg comes up, kiss, rip open her blouse etc etc.' [Douglas]

OOPS! In the interrogation room, keep your eye on Stone's cigarette, rather than her legs, and you'll see it vanish and then pop back before disappearing again • When she dresses to go with Douglas to be interrogated, not only her clothes change, but her hairstyle too • The door of Tripplehorn's office spells her first name differently to the record on the computer • Keep an eye on the ketchup bottle top after it lands on the table when Dzunda and Douglas are in the diner.

Psst! Michael Douglas was paid $14m, while scriptwriter Eszterhas got a then record $3m • Sharon Stone got just $300,000 but for *Sliver* she was paid $2.5m plus a percentage of profits • She complained that her thighs were rubbed raw by Douglas' stubble after several hours of filming a love scene • Britain got a stronger version than America, with 43 seconds that were cut in the States. There were unconfirmed stories that some Americans flew across the Pond just to see the meatier cut • Douglas lost 25 pounds to get in shape for the part.

Batman

★★★ 1966 105min c.

Director: Leslie Martinson
Screenplay: Lorenzo Semple Jr.
Source: Characters created by Bob Kane

Holy Crime Wave! Four of the world's campest villains, the Joker, the Riddler, the Penguin and Catwoman combine to steal a dehydration machine that will turn the representatives of the top nations into coloured dust. Can the Caped Crusader and the Boy Wonder stop them in time? Will Batman's heart be broken by Miss Kitka, who's really Catwoman in disguise? Will he get the rubber shark off his leg before he turns back into Bruce Wayne? Biff! Pow! Krunch! Although hardly the epitome of story-telling, this feature-length version of the tongue-in-cheek TV series – complete with Batmobile, Batcopter and Bat Boat – is even better than remembered and makes a splendid contrast to the dark Burton Batmans. Just one question? What do we think of a crime fighter who has to stick labels on absolutely everything, even the Bat Ladder that hangs down from the Batcopter? I mean, anally retentive or what?

Batman/Bruce Wayne . . . . .Adam West
Robin/Dick Grayson . . . . .Burt Ward
Catwoman/Kitka . . . . .Lee Meriwether
The Penguin . . . . .Burgess Meredith
The Joker . . . . .Cesar Romero
The Riddler . . . . .Frank Gorshin
Alfred . . . . .Alan Napier
Commissioner Gordon . . . . .Neil Hamilton
Chief O'Hara . . . . .Stafford Repp

Commodore Schmidlapp . . . . . .Reginald Denny
Aunt Harriet Cooper . . . . .Madge Blake

Quote 'Some days you just can't get rid of a bomb.' • 'They may be drinkers, Robin. But they're still human beings.'

Psst! Originally shot as the pilot episode, this was only released in the cinema when the TV series became such a hit, running eventually to 120 episodes • The movie took just 26 days to make • Interviewed in 1995, Adam West offered several tips for Val Kilmer, taking over in the Batsuit for *Batman Forever*. Among other things, he advised, 'Bad guys are easy to spot. The most heinous ones have bright red hair or wear green Armani suits with question marks all over', 'Large buildings are scary and hard to climb…Have the building turned on its side, as I did', 'Your Batsuit may present problems. Plan bathroom stops carefully. Beware of flushing your cape, as you will strangle', 'Female villains are the most difficult. They're usually quite attractive and may cause strange stirrings in your utility belt. Carry protection.'

Batman

★★ 1989 126min c.

Director: Tim Burton
Screenplay: Sam Hamm & Warren Skaaren
Source: Characters created by Bob Kane

Nice pictures, shame about the story. In a film far removed from the camp TV series, the dark and moody design is everything. The uncharismatic Keaton's an odd choice for the lead and he's over-acted off the screen by Nicholson's Joker. Blurring the boundary between goodie and baddie is one thing, but making the baddie so much more fun unbalances everything. Let's have three cheers, though, for Gough as Alfred.

Batman/Bruce Wayne . . . . .Michael Keaton
Jack Napier/The Joker . . . . .Jack Nicholson
Vicki Vale .Kim Basinger
Alexander .Robert Wuhl
Commissioner Gordon . . . . .Pat Hingle
Harvey Dent . . . . .Billy Dee Williams
Alfred . . . . .Michael Gough
Grissom . . . . .Jack Palance
Alicia . . . . .Jerry Hall
Mayor . . . . .Lee Wallace
Bob the Goon . . . . .Tracey Walter
Eckhardt . . . . .William Hootkins

Quote 'Wait'll they get a load of me.' • 'Have you ever danced with the devil in the pale moonlight?' • 'Can somebody tell me what kind of world we live in where a man dressed up as a *bat* gets all my press?'

OOPS! One give-away sign that the film was made in Britain is the anglicised spelling of 'moisturising' on the foam bath the Joker is peddling • Spelling isn't their strong point. The museum is spelt differently inside and out • In the scene where the hoods are trashing pictures, watch the pink handprints vanish • Although the Batmobile is supposedly driving on its own at one point, if you look carefully you can see a hand on the wheel • When Vicki goes to see Bruce Wayne after hearing about his parents' death, she arrives in a different dress and with her hair redone.

Psst! Nicholson is said to have made more than $50m from the film and its attendant merchandising. That's more than the $40m the film is estimated to have cost • The set was the biggest since *Cleopatra*. One man became wealthy just by supplying the 60 miles of scaffolding • Sean Young was the original Vicki, but had a riding accident just before filming began. The last-minute replacement put an extra $500,000 on the budget • Designer Anton Furst said he wanted Gotham City to look like 'New York without planning permission for 300 years.' • Look out for the artist formerly known as Prince in the Joker's procession • The '12' Certificate was introduced into the UK specifically so that *Batman* could reach its target audience.

Batman Returns

★★★ 1992 127min c.

Director: Tim Burton
Screenplay: Daniel Waters

Armed with even more impressive toys than in *Batman*, the Caped Crusader rides to the rescue of a Gotham City menaced by not one but three villains. Burton's wonderful-looking sequel is crammed with entertaining set-piece action scenes. However, like *Batman*, the plot has more loose ends than Spaghetti Junction. You'd think if they were spending $80m, they could have afforded a script that made sense. Worth seeing for Pfeiffer alone as the whip-wielding leather-clad Catwoman, the stuff dreams – naughty dreams – are made of. A glass of cool milk please, Alfred.

Batman/Bruce Wayne . . . . . . .Michael Keaton
Penguin/Oscar Cobblepot . . . . . .Danny DeVito
Catwoman/Selina Kyle . . . . . . .Michelle Pfeiffer
Max Shreck . . . . .Christopher Walken
Alfred . . . . .Michael Gough
Mayor .Michael Murphy
Ice Princess . . . . .Cristi Conaway
Chip Shreck . . . . .Andrew Bryniarski
Commissioner Gordon . . . . .Pat Hingle
Organ Grinder . . . . .Vincent Schiavelli

Blurb The Bat, The Cat, The Penguin.

Quote 'Life's a bitch. Now so am I.' • 'You're only jealous because I'm a genuine freak and you have to wear a mask.'

OOPS! When Penguin visits his parents' grave, watch for the tombstone that wobbles as he brushes past.

Psst! Pfeiffer studied kick-boxing, yoga, martial arts and weight-lifting. All the tricks with the whip are done by her, though the derrière of her costume was apparently padded • A scene with Catwoman chaining Batman to a bed was cut, as was the idea that she should swallow the bird she puts in her mouth • DeVito ate raw fish to get into the part • Pfeiffer and Keaton revived an old fling during the making of the film • Annette Bening was to have been Catwoman, but became pregnant with Warren's baby. Madonna, Cher and Sean Young particularly coveted the part, with Young apparently turning up in a catsuit on the lot to argue her case • The penguins had their own refrigerated trailer and swimming pool • Pee Wee Herman, disgraced star of Burton's first movie, appears briefly, and almost unrecognisably, as the Penguin's father • Walken's character Max Schreck is named after the actor who played Dracula in the 1921 German film *Nosferatu*.

Batman Forever

★★ 1995 121min c.

Director: Joel Schumacher
Screenplay: Lee Batchler, Janet Scott Batchler & Akiva Goldsman
Source: Characters created by Bob Kane

Same superhero, different jaw. It's all you can see of Batman when he's togged up and this one's not much of an improvement. The film is the manic man Carrey's in the same way that Nicholson stole the first in the series. As the cane-twirling, crazed-cackling, puzzling-posing Riddler, his new device to turn TV into a 3-D experience is sucking the intelligence out of viewers – some might say it's already happened. He teams up with Two-Face to unmask the Caped Crusader. Ex-acrobat O'Donnell pleads to be Batman's sidekick and supposed criminologist Kidman, blonde and busty, tries to get under his cape. It's camp without being witty or in the least bit intelligent. The stunts are so confusingly executed that it is impossible to tell what's happening. A big disappointment. The best thing about the film is once more Michael Gough as the very British butler Alfred. He's the one who keeps pushing the reluctant Batman back into the Batsuit when Batman just wants to give up. So why can't the next in the series be *Batman Retires?* Then we could have Alfred, whose heart *is* in the job, donning the black rubber and heading off into the night to right wrongs.

Batman/Bruce Wayne . . . . .Val Kilmer
Ridler/Edward Nygma . . . . .Jim Carrey
Harvey Two-Face/Harvey Dent . . . .Tommy Lee Jones
Dr. Chase Meridian . . . . .Nicole Kidman
Robin/Dick Grayson . . . . .Chris O'Donnell
Alfred Pennyworth . . . . .Michael Gough
Comm. Gordon . . . . .Pat Hingle
Sugar . . . . .Drew Barrymore
Spice . . . . .Debi Mazar
Fred Stickley . . . . .Ed Begley Jr.

Quote 'Can I persuade you to take a sandwich with you, sir?' • 'It's the car, right? Chicks love the car.' • 'Was that over the top? I never can tell.'

Psst! The film established a new opening weekend record in America, its take of $52.8m exceeding *Jurassic Park* by around $5m, although takings dropped off more quickly afterwards • Robin Williams was originally going to have been The Riddler, but the studio preferred Carrey • Kidman's part was originally offered to Robin Wright, who didn't want it. Kim Basinger wasn't willing to come back, as she hadn't got on with Kilmer on *The Real McCoy* • One of the last black checker taxicabs made, 8S41, appears here painted in black and white. It also appears, in more familiar colours of yellow with black and white checked squares down the side, in over 100 other movies, including *Reversal of Fortune*, *Presumed Innocent* and *Die Hard With a Vengeance*.

Battleship Potemkin
★★ 1925 75min b/w

Director: Sergei Eisenstein
Screenplay: Sergei Eisenstein

A fictionalised account of a mutiny which helped precipitate the Russian Revolution. In 1950 and 1958 this was voted the greatest film of all time by an international panel of film critics, which only goes to show that they ought to get out more. Incredibly influential at the time, particularly because of the montage technique used when Tsarists troops massacre rebels and civilians on the Odessa Steps, it's now pretty boring, inaccurate, agitprop fare. Only the Steps sequence, imitated and parodied many times since, and the rebellion on ship still have much power.

Sailor Vakulincuk . . . . .Alexander Antonov
Commandant Golikov . . . . .Vladimar Barsky
Lt. Giljarovsky . . . . .Grigori Alexandrov

Quote 'We've had enough garbage to eat! A dog wouldn't eat this.'

Psst! Made as part of the 20th anniversary celebrations of the Russian Revolution, the film was only completed on the evening of the premiere and Eisenstein had to ride pillion on a motorbike to get it to the Bolshoi Theatre. In Red Square, the bike broke down and he had to run the rest of the way, just making it in time • The film was banned throughout much of Europe for decades. In Britain, the government was terrified of revolution following the General Strike in 1926 and ensured that no film could be distributed if it so much as mentioned a communist revolution. *Potemkin* premiered in the UK in 1929 at a film society and could occasionally be seen at similar venues, although the authorities frequently interfered. Only in the early 40s, when the Russians were our allies in the war, could copies easily be obtained. The film didn't get a certificate until 1954 and then it was an 'X' • As a result of the film, Eisenstein went to Hollywood. At a meeting with Samuel Goldwyn, one of the more artistic and intelligent of Tinseltown's producers, Eisenstein was told: 'I have seen his film *Potemkin* and admire it very much. What we should like would be for him to do something of the same kind, but rather cheaper, for Ronald Colman.' • Although the massacre on the Odessa Steps is widely considered one of the great atrocities of the Tsarist regime, it only ever took place on celluloid, being invented for the movie.

Beau Geste
★★★ 1939 114min b/w

Director: William Wellman
Screenplay: Robert Carson
Source: Novel by Percival Christopher Wren

Three devoted brothers join the Foreign Legion and have to battle not only Arabs, but also a sadistic Sergeant. Although a little long in the tooth, this old actioner is still stirring stuff, one of those great rainy Sunday afternoon movies. It was remade in 1966 and was parodied by Marty Feldman in 1977 in *The Last Remake of Beau Geste.*

Michael 'Beau' Geste . . . . .Gary Cooper
John Geste .Ray Milland
Digby Geste . . . . .Robert Preston
Sgt. Markoff . . . . .Brian Donlevy
Isobel Rivers . . . . .Susan Hayward
Rasinoff .J. Carrol Naish
Schwartz .Albert Dekker
Hank Miller . . . . .Broderick Crawford
Buddy McMonigal . . . . .Charles Barton
Also: James Stephenson, Heather Thatcher, James Burke, Harold Huber, Donald O'Connor, Harry Woods

Quote 'The love of a man for a woman waxes and wanes like the moon, but the love of brother for brother is steadfast as the stars and endures like the word of the prophet – Arabian proverb.'

Psst! An incredibly young Donald O'Connor plays the young Beau Geste • The sergeant was originally to have been called Lejeune, rather than Markoff, but was changed when the French said that they would otherwise refuse to let the film be screened in France • The pompous Donley was apparently hated by everyone as much off-screen as on it • There had been a silent version in 1926 and it was remade again in 1966 • Gary Cooper had appeared in the 1926 version's sequel, *Beau Sabreaur.* He may be the only actor to appear in a sequel and then the remake of the original • As with the silent film, this was filmed in Buttercup Valley in Arizona where a city of tents for 1,000 people was built, complete with electricity and running water. There was even a cinema.

Beauty and the Beast
★★★★ 1946 90min b/w

Director: Jean Cocteau
Screenplay: Jean Cocteau
Source: Fairy tale by Mme. Leprince de Beaumont

The story's pretty well known now and doesn't get any new twists in this French version. What is remarkable is the sumptuous beauty and

imagination with which it is brought to the screen. Although it won't be to everyone's taste, the visuals are simply staggering, as if a dream or a nightmare by one of the world's greatest painters was brought to life. Cinema has rarely been more magical.

Avenant/The Beast/The Prince . . . .Jean Marais
Beauty . . . . .Josette Day
The Merchant . . . . .Marcel André
Adelaide . . . . .Mila Parely
Felice . . . . .Nane Germon
Ludovic .Michel Auclair

Psst! Despite its beautiful look, the production was dogged by problems, many of them caused by shortages in the immediate aftermath of World War II. Equipment was in short supply and the film stock was sub-standard • Parely was suffering from bruising after the circus horse rolled on top of her and Marais had broken out in a rash of painful boils. Even Cocteau wasn't immune, being plagued by severe eczema on his face • Marais' beast make-up took five hours to put on.

Beauty and the Beast
★★★★ 1991 84min c.

Director: Gary Trousdale & Kirk Wise
Screenplay: Linda Woolverton
Source: Fairy tale by Mme. Leprince de Beaumont

One of the greatest animated films ever. The feminist updating of the story works wonderfully and is mercifully free of the treacly sentiment of so many preceding Disney pics. The supporting characters are splendidly drawn, in both senses of the word. If Belle had any sense, however, she'd have stuck with the Beast, rather than turned him into a Chippendale bimbo of a Prince.

Belle . . . . .Paige O'Hara
Beast . . . . .Robby Benson
Lumiere .Jerry Orbach
Mrs. Potts . . . . .Angela Lansbury
Gaston . . . . .Richard White
Cogsworth/Narrator . . . . . .David Ogden Stiers

Psst! This was the first animated film ever to be nominated for a Best Film Oscar • It was originally planned to be a non-musical cartoon but the plans were changed after *The Little Mermaid* did so well • The best-selling video ever, until the next Disney movie, surpassing *Fantasia's* record in only a few months.

Beetlejuice

★★ 1988 92min c.

Director: Tim Burton
Screenplay: Michael McDowell & Warren Skaaren

Dearly departed couple Davis and Baldwin have difficulty adjusting to the hereafter and to the ghastly new inhabitants of their beloved home. So they call in mad ghoul Keaton to scare them away. Despite the wonderful special effects, Keaton's energetic performance and the interesting look of the picture, it all gets rather tiresome and repetitive.

Adam . . . . .Alec Baldwin
Barbara . . . . .Geena Davis
Betelgeuse . . . . .Michael Keaton
Charles Deetz . . . . .Jeffrey Jones
Delia Deetz . . . . .Catherine O'Hara
Lydia Deetz . . . . .Winona Ryder
Juno . . . . .Sylvia Sidney
Maxie Dean . . . . .Robert Goulet
Otho . . . . .Glenn Shadix
Bernard . . . . .Dick Cavett

Blurb The Name In Laughter From The Hereafter.

OOPS! If you can't see the ghosts in mirrors, how come you can see them reflected in a window?

The Beguiled

★★★ 1971 109min c.

Director: Don Siegel
Screenplay: John B. Sherry & Grimes Grice
Source: Novel by Thomas Cullinan

An interesting, Gothic piece about a wounded Civil War soldier who recuperates in a girls' school. Eastwood, playing one of his few screen villains, is a manipulative cat creating havoc among the sexually frustrated pigeons. The title is appropriate, for this is a rather beguiling movie.

John McBurney . . . . .Clint Eastwood
Martha .Geraldine Page
Edwina . . . . .Elizabeth Hartman
Carol . . . . .Jo Ann Harris
Doris . . . . .Darleen Carr
Amy . . . . .Pamelyn Ferdin
Hallie . . . . .Mae Mercer

Blurb Clint Eastwood Has Never Been In A More Frightening Situation.

Psst! The film was a resounding flop on first release, perhaps because the public wasn't quite yet ready for Clint in such an untypical role.

Being There

★★★ 1979 130min c.

Director: Hal Ashby
Screenplay: Jerzy Kosinski
Source: Novel by Kosinski

A backward gardener, obsessed with watching TV, is thought to be a great sage and rises rapidly up the American ladder of celebrity and success. Sellers is quite wonderful in his last film role but while there are many joys, the storytelling is slack and goes on for far too long.

Chance . . . . .Peter Sellers
Eve Rand . . . . .Shirley MacLaine
Benjamin Rand . . . . .Melvyn Douglas
President 'Bobby' . . . . .Jack Warden
Dr. Robert Allenby . . . . .Richard Dysart
Vladimir Skrapinov . . . . .Richard Basehart
Thomas Franklin . . . . .David Clennon
Louise . . . . .Ruth Attaway

Oscars Melvyn Douglas

Quote 'I like to watch.' • 'You have the gift of being natural. That's a great talent, my boy.'

Psst! Kosinski, who wrote the novel, originally wanted to play the lead role himself, even though Sellers had been pestering him for five or six years to let him portray Chance • Sellers modelled his voice on Stan Laurel's • Some versions of the movie have Peter Sellers' outtakes over the closing credits, which undermine the mood built up over the previous two hours • Chance says he likes to sleep with his head facing North. Sellers in fact insisted in his contracts that wherever he was billeted, the bed should point east-west • MacLaine's masturbation scene needed 17 takes, so nervous was she. It was this scene that caused Laurence Olivier to turn Melvyn Douglas' part down. He thought it 'immoral'.

Belle de Jour

★★★ 1967 100min c.

Director: Luis Buñuel
Screenplay: Luis Buñuel & Jean-Claude Carriere
Source: Novel by Joseph Kessel

A frigid wife takes to working in a brothel during

the afternoons. Although never explicit, thanks largely to Deneuve's smouldering sexuality, it is often infinitely more arousing than many supposedly steamy modern movies. But Buñuel spends so many games with our perceptions of reality and fantasy that it all becomes terribly confusing and frustrating. That may well have been the point, but it's irritating nonetheless.

Séverine Sérizy . . . . .Catherine Deneuve
Pierre Sérizy . . . . .Jean Sorel
Henri Husson . . . . .Michel Piccoli
Mme. Anais . . . . .Genèvieve Page
Marcel . . . . .Pierre Clementi
Hippolyte . . . . .Francisco Rabal
Charlotte . . . . .Françoise Fabian
The Duke . . . . .Georges Marchal

Quote 'You go in. You choose a woman. You spend half an hour with her. You spend the rest of the day depressed.'

La Belle et la Bête

SEE: Beauty and the Beast [1946]

The Belles of St. Trinians

★★★★ 1954 91min b/w

Director: Frank Launder
Screenplay: Frank Launder, Sidney Gilliat & Val Valentine
Source: Inspired by the drawings of Ronald Searle

This glorious comedy about the worst girls' school in England has improved with age, like so much of Launder and Gilliat's work. We can now appreciate just what a fine comic actor Sim was, here playing not only the headmistress but also her bent bookie brother. With a raft of wonderful supporting roles, George Cole as Flash Harry and a bevy of beautiful sixth-formers, this is British movie heaven. While we're at it, doesn't George Cole have absolutely the greatest personal signature tune of all time? It was followed by Blue Murder at St. Trinian's, The Pure Hell of St. Trinian's, The Great St. Trinian's Train Robbery and The Wildcats of St. Trinian's, of which Pure Hell is the best.

Millicent/Clarence Fritton . . . . . . .Alastair Sim
Sgt. Ruby Gates . . . . .Joyce Grenfell
Flash Harry . . . . .George Cole
Miss Drownder . . . . .Hermione Baddeley
Miss Waters . . . . .Betty Ann Davies
Miss Brimmer . . . . .Renée Houston

Miss Wilson . . . . .Beryl Reid
Miss Gale . . . . .Irene Handl
Miss Dawn . . . . .Joan Sims
Manton Bassett . . . . .Richard Wattis
Eric Rowbotton-Smith . . . . .Guy Middleton
Benny Holster . . . . .Sidney James
Sixth-former . . . . .Shirley Eaton

Psst! Look out for Shirley Eaton, the gold-painted girl in Goldfinger, as a sixth-former • Ronald Searle appears as a parent • Classical composer Malcolm Arnold composed the wonderful St. Trinian's school song • The inspiration for the films came from Frank Launder's daughter who brought a book of the cartoons home from school, saying that all the girls were mad on them • Launder, Gilliat and Sim had earlier made The Happiest Days of Your Life, which had many similarities and had been very popular. Despite this, there was little confidence on the part of the studio, right up till the opening night.

Ben-Hur

★★★ 1959 212min c.

Director: William Wyler
Screenplay: Karl Tunberg
Source: Novel by Lew Wallace

This epic tale is once seen, never forgotten, thanks to the grandiosely-staged galley fight and the chariot races. However, it does have some very bald patches which become still more visible if you're watching on the small screen. In an age that pays some actors more than this movie cost, we can but marvel at the days when it was still possible to put such incredible spectacles on celluloid. The original 1925 silent version is also pretty exciting in places.

Judah Ben Hur . . . . .Charlton Heston
Quintus Arrius . . . . .Jack Hawkins
Messala .Stephen Boyd
Esther .Haya Harareet
Sheik Ilderim . . . . .Hugh Griffith
Miriam .Martha Scott
Simonides .Sam Jaffe
Tirzah . . . . .Cathy O'Donnell
Balthasar . . . . .Finlay Currie
Pilate . . . . .Frank Thring
Drusus . . . . .Terence Longden
Sextus .André Morell
Emperor Tiberius . . . . .George Relph
Flavia . . . . .Marina Berti
Doctor . . . . .John Le Mesurier

Oscars Best Picture, Hugh Griffith, Charlton Heston, Best Director

Quote 'Your eyes are full of hate, Forty-One. That's good. Hate keeps a man alive.' • 'Your God, in His eagerness to save you, has also saved the Roman fleet.' • 'One wife? One God, that I can understand. But one wife? That is not civilised. It is not generous.' • 'Loved Ben. Hated Hur.' [Forgotten reviewer]

OOPS! It is said that one of the trumpeters in the chariot scene is wearing a watch, but I can't spot him • Nor have I been able to spot the sports car, apparently a Ferrari, reportedly in the background during the chariot race.

Psst! At the time, the most expensive film ever made, with a cost of almost $15m. The movie nearly sent MGM into bankruptcy, but the film was phenomenally successful, saving the studio for a few more years • It took five years to plan the film, six months to complete filming in Italy and another nine months to edit it all together • Its clutch of 11 Oscars is a record • Marlon Brando, Burt Lancaster and Rock Hudson were all considered for the lead • Charlton Heston was originally going to play Messala and was offered the lead just a few weeks before filming started • Stephen Boyd, who then became Messala, had to wear dark-coloured contact lenses because Heston was the only one permitted by the director to have blue eyes • All the Romans are played by Brits while the Jews are all Americans • The 300 sets which were built covered over 300 acres • The stadium for the chariot race alone occupied 18 acres, making it the largest film set in film history. 1,000 workers took a year to build it, using 40,000 tons of sand brought in from Italy's beaches • The race, which lasts 20 minutes on screen, took three months to film and, at a cost of $1m, was then the most expensive sequence ever seen in the movies. 82 horses were imported from Yugoslavia for it • Stuntman Yakima Canutt, who organised the chariot race, trained Heston and Boyd for weeks in how to drive a chariot. The pair did many of their own stunts and, while Heston was already an experienced handler of horses, Boyd had a far harder time of it, with bloody, blistered hands and severe bruising from the scene where he's dragged underneath his chariot • There have long been rumours that somebody died during the making of the movie but despite a couple of near-misses, nobody did die • Canutt was given a lifetime achievement Oscar, the only stuntman ever to win one • 50,000 extras were employed for the film and 100,000 costumes were used • The

credits include plum acting jobs like 'Leper' and 'Rower #42' • Director Wyler had actually worked in a humbler capacity on the 1925 silent version of the story.

The Best Years of Our Lives
★★★★ 1946 172min b/w

Director: William Wyler
Screenplay: Robert E. Sherwood
Source: Article in *Time* magazine & *Glory For Me* by MacKinlay Kantor

Three veterans of World War II return to their homes and try to readjust to civilian life and the casual attitude so many Americans had to the sacrifices servicemen made on their behalf. This beautifully made film still manages to make us extremely angry, as it was meant to do. The outstanding cast manipulate our emotions expertly, wringing our withers one moment and making us gloriously happy the next. Cinematic story-telling at its very best.

Milly Stephenson	Myrna Loy
Al Stephenson	Fredric March
Fred Derry	Dana Andrews
Peggy Stephenson	Teresa Wright
Marie Derry	Virginia Mayo
Wilma Cameron	Cathy O'Donnell
Butch Engle	Hoagy Carmichael
Homer Parrish	Harold Russell
Hortense Derry	Gladys George

Also: Ray Collins, Minna Gombell, Roman Bohnen, Steve Cochran, Dorothy Adams, Don Beddoe, Charles Halton, Ray Teal, Erskine Sanford

Oscars Best Picture, Fredric March, Harold Russell, Best Screenplay (adapted), Best Director

Quote 'I don't care if it doesn't make a nickel. I just want every man, woman and child in America to see it.' [Producer Sam Goldwyn]

OOPS! March's name is misspelt 'Frederic' on the closing credits.

Psst! Originally an article in *Time* magazine, the writer MacKinlay Kantor was asked to write a short treatment. He came back after three months with a 268 page work, *Glory for Me*, written in free verse. Even when he was given more money to turn it into a screenplay, what was handed in was virtually unusable • Russell was a Canadian war veteran who had lost his hands when a grenade exploded. He became the first of only two non-professionals to win an acting Oscar [the other being Dr. Haing S. Ngor for *The Killing Fields*]. In fact, Russell won two Oscars – the only person to do so for the same performance – because the Academy gave him a special award, only to find him winning Best Supporting Actor as well • To get Russell worked up for his tussle with Ray Teal, Wyler told him that Teal was a closet Fascist and watched the sparks fly • Although Wright plays Loy's daughter, she was actually only 12 years her junior • Wyler made the actors use their own clothes throughout, wanting a lack of glamour.

Betty Blue

★★ 1986 121min c.

Director: Jean-Jacques Beineix
Screenplay: Jean-Jacques Beineix
Source: Book, *37.2° Le Matin* by Philippe Djian.

A frustrated novelist has a wild affair with a nubile teenager before realising that she's going bonkers in a big way. In the interim this pair make the two-backed beast so furiously, you'd think it was on the point of extinction. A typically Gallic tale of mad passion, complete with sombre voice-over and terrific style. But it becomes increasingly tiresome and, when the hero ends up in drag, you know the film has seriously lost its way.

Betty . . . . .Béatrice Dalle
Zorg . . . . .Jean-Hugues Anglade
Lisa . . . . .Consuelo de Haviland

Quote 'I don't walk around naked like that, even at home. I don't like nudity. It's not my style.' [Dalle]

Psst! Dalle was discovered when Beineix saw her picture on a magazine cover. She wasn't a model. The photographer had just snapped her in the street • This is one of those select films where, according to rumour, the actors got carried away and actually made love in front of the camera. The story persists, despite the denials of the stars • There is also a director's cut of 182 minutes.

Beverly Hills Cop

★★★ 1984 105min c.

Director: Martin Brest
Screenplay: Daniel Petrie Jr.

Reasonably funny fish-out-of-water comedy, with Murphy a cop turning up in LA to get revenge

for his mate's murder. Although Murphy is good, there's a nagging feeling that it should all be much funnier and sharper. What's more, it is almost spoiled by the ludicrous ending which has a couple of handguns that never need reloading triumphing over a battery of automatic weapons. The first sequel was dreadful while the third in the series was moderately entertaining.

Axel Foley . . . . .Eddie Murphy
Det. Billy Rosewood . . . . .Judge Reinhold
Sgt. Taggart . . . . .John Ashton
Jenny Summers . . . . .Lisa Eilbacher
Lt. Bogomil . . . . .Ronny Cox
Victor Maitland . . . . .Steven Berkoff
Mickey Tandino . . . . .James Russo
Zack . . . . .Jonathan Banks
Chief Hubbard . . . . .Stephen Elliott
Serge . . . . .Bronson Pinchot
Jeffrey . . . . .Paul Reiser
Banana Man . . . . .Damon Wayans

Quote 'Tell Victor that Ramon…went to the clinic today and I found out that I have…er, herpy simplex ten, and I think Victor should go check himself out with his physician to make sure everything is fine before things start falling off the man.'

Psst! The movie was inspired by a cop stopping studio head Michael Eisner for speeding • This was the film debut of comic Damon Wayans. His first 15 seconds comes as he gives Murphy some bananas • Mickey Rourke and Sylvester Stallone had both been associated with the project when it was still a straight action pic. Stallone backed out just a few weeks before filming was due to start, when writer Petrie wouldn't let him monkey with the script. It didn't stop Nielsen, the then Mrs. Sly, being in the sequel.

Beyond the Valley of the Dolls

★★★ 1970 109min c.

Director: Russ Meyer
Screenplay: Roger Ebert & Russ Meyer

Not a sequel but a spoof of the movie of Jacqueline Susann's blockbuster, with a female rock troupe living life to the full – and beyond – in Hollywood. Although far, far tamer than most of Russ Meyer's extraordinary output, it's still moderately raunchy and delightfully camp with plenty to offend those of delicate sensibilities.

Kelly MacNamara . . . . .Dolly Read
Casey Anderson . . . . .Cynthia Myers
Petronella Danforth . . . . .Marcia McBroom

Ronnie 'Z-Man' Barzell	John La Zar
Lance Rocke	Michael Blodgett
Ashley St. Ives	Edy Williams
Emerson Thorne	Harrison Page
Baxter Wolfe	Charles Napier
Narrator	Russ Meyer

Blurb The World Is Full Of Them, The Super-Octane Girls Who Are Old At Twenty…If They Get To Be Twenty.

Quote 'You will drink the black sperm of my vengeance.' • 'The kind of movie that a maladroit Mack Sennett might have made if he had worked in a sex shop, not a fun factory.' [Alexander Walker]

Psst! Although he may now like to forget it, the script is by Roger Ebert of Siskel & Ebert fame, America's double-team equivalent of Barry Norman. At the time, Ebert called it: 'The first exploitation-horror camp musical.' • Meyer never let his cast know they were acting in a send-up • Edy Williams was Meyer's wife at the time.

Bicycle Thieves
★★★ 1948 90min b/w

Director: Vittorio De Sica
Screenplay: Cesare Zavattini
Source: Novel by Luigi Bartolini

The finest of the films that emerged from the Italian Neo-Realist movement in the mid-40s, which emphasised location shooting and the use of non-professional actors. The story is simplicity itself; a poor man desperately tries to find his stolen bicycle, without which he will lose his job. It's still perceptive, warm and very poignant, although like all realist films the technique does begin to look artificial after a time. Fans of the film should try and catch the hilarious and inventive 1989 spoof by Mauricio Nichetti, *The Icicle Thief*.

Antonio Ricci	Lamberto Maggiorani
Bruno Ricci	Enzo Staiola
Maria Ricci	Lianella Carell
The thief	Vittorio Antonucci
The lady	Elena Altieri

Psst! De Sica had terrible difficulty in finding finance for the film. Desperate though he was, he wasn't so desperate that he would accept producer David O. Selznick's money, for it came with the caveat that Cary Grant would star! • Despite the use of people who weren't actors, the film was not improvised, but was carefully scripted and planned • When he was

in America, De Sica was asked what had happened to the labourer who starred in the film. 'I'm afraid,' he said sadly, 'He has become an actor' • Relations between Italy and America became strained when the Motion Picture Association of America refused to give its approval to the film unless the shot of a boy urinating against a wall was taken out.

Big
★★★★ 1988 105min c.

Director: Penny Marshall
Screenplay: Gary Ross & Anne Spielberg

One of the funniest, most delightful fantasies ever put on film. Hanks is perfect as the boy who wishes that he were grown up – and wakes up 20 years older. Standing out in the adult world by virtue of his innocence (are 12-year-olds *really* that ignorant about sex?), he gets a job at a toy company. The scene with Hanks and boss Loggia dancing out 'Chopsticks' on a giant piano is a classic, while the touching romance between Hanks and the excellent Perkins is perfectly handled.

Josh Baskin	Tom Hanks
Susan	Elizabeth Perkins
Paul	John Heard
Billy	Jared Rushton
MacMillan	Robert Loggia
Young Josh	David Moscow
Scotty Brennen	Jon Lovitz
Mrs. Baskin	Mercedes Ruehl

Quote 'I mean, I like you and I want to spend the night with you.' – 'You mean sleep over?' – 'Well, yeah.' – 'Okay, but I get to be on top.' • 'I'm a kid.' – 'Who isn't?'

Psst! At test screenings, audiences voted that they wanted Perkins and Hanks to live together happily ever after. It's one of the few films in recent years where the studio didn't insist on changing the ending as a result of such comments • The film was originally set to star Harrison Ford, with Spielberg directing.

The Big Blue
★★ 1988 119min c.

Director: Luc Besson
Screenplay: Luc Besson, Robert Garland, Marilyn Goldin, Jacques Mayol & Marc Perrier

Despite some wonderful underwater photography, this French tale of divers develops webbed feet when it's on dry land. Although absolutely magical in places, other parts remind you that magic sometimes means Paul Daniels.

Joanna	.Rosanna Arquette
Jacques Mayol	.Jean-Marc Barr
Enzo Molinari	.Jean Reno
Dr. Laurence	.Paul Shenar
Novelli	.Sergio Castellitto
Duffy	.Griffin Dunne

The Big Carnival
SEE: Ace in the Hole

The Big Chill
★★★ 1983 103min c.

Director: Lawrence Kasdan
Screenplay: Barbara Benedek & Lawrence Kasdan

When a friend kills himself, a group of 60s university students gets back together for a long weekend of talking, rediscovering, bonding, friendship remaking and the odd bit of nookie. Great music and acting but a bit *Thirtysomething* and plotless for some tastes.

Sam	.Tom Berenger
Sarah	.Glenn Close
Michael	.Jeff Goldblum
Nick	.William Hurt
Harold	.Kevin Kline
Meg	.Mary Kay Place
Chloe	.Meg Tilly
Karen	.JoBeth Williams
Alex	.Kevin Costner

OOPS! You can see that Kline is wearing a microphone when his sweatshirt sticks to him.

Psst! Costner was to play Alex, the dead friend, but his 10 minutes of flashback were axed. All we see of him are his hands, torso and legs as the corpse is being dressed • Kasdan is well up with leaders like Coppola in the Nepotism Handicap Stakes, with Jon Kasdan as Harold and Sarah's son, Jacob Kasdan as an autograph seeker and wife Meg as the airline hostess.

The Big Easy
★★★ 1987 108min c.

Director: Jim McBride
Screenplay: Daniel Petrie Jr. & Jack Baran

A series of Mafia murders are investigated by a slightly corrupt New Orleans cop, himself under investigation by Internal Affairs. The whodunnit element is skimmed over pretty fast but the steamy Louisiana atmosphere and even steamier coupling of Quaid and Barkin make this one of the 80's smartest, most attractive thrillers.

Remy McSwain	.Dennis Quaid
Anne Osborne	.Ellen Barkin
Jack Kellom	.Ned Beatty
Andrew De Soto	.John Goodman
McCabe	.Lisa Jane Persky
Ed Dodge	.Ebbe Roe Smith
Bobby McSwain	.Tom O'Brien
Lamar Parmentel	.Charles Ludlam
Mama	.Grace Zabriskie
Chef Paul	.Gailard Sartain

Psst! Jim Garrison, played by Costner in *JFK*, has a cameo as the judge.

The Big Heat
★★★ 1953 90min b/w

Director: Fritz Lang
Screenplay: Sydney Boehm
Source: *Saturday Evening Post* serial by William P. McGivern.

An ex-cop sickened by his wife's murder goes undercover to get the goods on a crime syndicate. The realistic approach to the subject doesn't seem quite as powerful as it once did, but the performances, particularly from vicious Killer Marvin and girlfriend Grahame, still impress. Just over 20 years earlier, audiences had been shocked when Cagney pushed a grapefruit in his girlfriend's face. The memory audiences took away of this movie is of Marvin throwing a pot of scalding coffee in Grahame's face. It still shocks, even now.

Dave Bannion	.Glenn Ford
Debby Marsh	.Gloria Grahame
Katie Bannion	.Jocelyn Brando
Mike Lagana	.Alexander Scourby
Vince Stone	.Lee Marvin
Bertha Duncan	.Jeanette Nolan
Tierney	.Peter Whitney
Lt. Wilkes	.Willis Bouchey
Gus Burke	.Robert Burton
Larry Gordon	.Adam Williams
Cris Alcaide	.George Rose
Atkins	.Dan Seymour
Doris	.Carolyn Jones

Quote 'I've been poor and I've been rich and *believe me*, rich is better.'

Psst! The busting of organised crime was a hot topic in the 50s, with American viewers glued to the extensive TV coverage of the Senate investigations into the subject • Jocelyn Brando is Marlon's sister.

The Big Parade
★★★ 1925 140min b/w

Director: King Vidor
Screenplay: Harry Behn & Laurence Stallings

An idealistic young American enlists in World War I and learns at first hand the reality of the War To End All Wars. Although understandably creaky in places, the battle scenes are still impressive and disturbing, while there is ample humour to offset the horror. The first successful movie to look at World War I, it was also the first to concentrate on the life of the ordinary soldier and the first to show war as anything other than glamorous. Like other so-called 'silent' movies, to do it justice it should really be seen in the cinema with a live orchestra or, at the very least, a musical accompaniment.

Jim Apperson . . . . .John Gilbert
Mélisande .Renée Adorée
Mr. Apperson . . . . .Hobart Bosworth
Mrs. Apperson . . . . .Claire McDowell
Justyn Reed . . . . .Claire Adams
Harry . . . . .Robert Ober

Psst! With its take of $22m, this was the most successful of all silent movies at the box office • ScreenwriterStallings had, like Gilbert in the film, lost a leg in the war • The battle scenes were choreographed to a metronome, so that everything happens to a beat. This is especially noticeable in the scene where the soldiers are walking through the wood being picked off by snipers • Copies exist with running times varying from 115 minutes upwards.

The Big Sleep
★★★★ 1946 114min b/w

Director: Howard Hawks
Screenplay: William Faulkner, Jules Furthman & Leigh Brackett
Source: Novel by Raymond Chandler

One of the greatest of all detective movies, with Bogart's Philip Marlowe coping with smutty photos, murder and blackmail. True, it's sometimes hard to work out exactly what's going on. But there are enormous pleasures to be had from this richly-textured film noir, such as Bogie's seen-it-all gumshoe, the sparks flying between him and Bacall and the wry, witty and often surprisingly sexy dialogue. A classic that well deserves the accolade.

Philip Marlowe . . . . .Humphrey Bogart
Vivian Rutledge . . . . .Lauren Bacall
Eddie Mars . . . . .John Ridgeley
Carmen Sternwood . . . . .Martha Vickers
Joe Brody . . . . .Louis Jean Heydt
Jones . . . . .Elisha Cook Jr.
Bernie Ohis . . . . .Regis Toomey
Proprietess . . . . .Dorothy Malone
Gen. Sternwood . . . . .Charles Waldron
Norris . . . . .Charles D. Brown

Quote 'She tried to sit on my lap while I was standing up.' • 'I don't mind if you don't like my manners. I don't like them myself. They're pretty bad. I grieve over them on long winter evenings.' • 'Speaking of horses…You've got a touch of class, but I don't know how…how far you can go.' – A lot depends on who's in the saddle.' • 'You're not very tall, are you?' – 'I try to be.' • 'Haven't you weaned her yet? She's old enough.'

Psst! Although made in 1944, its release was delayed for two years • Bogart and Bacall, who met making *To Have and Have Now*, had been married for almost a year when *The Big Sleep* came out, although Hawks had tried to persuade protegé Bacall that the relationship could damage her movie career • After seeing how Bacall had gone down in *To Have and Have Not*, she and Bogie filmed some extra scenes to emphasise their screen chemistry • The novel's look at pornography and drug addiction was sharply toned down to pass the censors' scrutiny • Hawks and Bogart argued over how the chauffeur had died. Hawks telegraphed Raymond Chandler to ask him who had actually killed the chauffeur. The writer is said to have replied: 'How should I know?' • Jack Warner found the 70 cent bill for the telegram and rang Hawks personally to ask why the studio's money had been wasted in such a way • Hawks claimed later that 'I never figured out what was going on, but I though that the basic thing had great scenes in it and it was good entertainment. After that got by, I said, "I'm never going to worry about being logical again".'

Billy Liar
★★★ 1963 98min b/w

Director: John Schlesinger
Screenplay: Keith Waterhouse & Willis Hall

Source: Novel & play by Waterhouse and Hall

Walter Mitty transferred from middle-class America to working-class England. Courtenay gives one of his finest performances as the boy whose escape from reality is to create convoluted fantasies that invariably land him in hot water without giving him the freedom he claims to crave. Although sharply observed and trenchantly funny, there's always a nagging feeling that Billy is really a big pain in the arse and that his family and employers are to be pitied.

Billy Fisher	Tom Courtenay
Liz	Julie Christie
Geoffrey Fisher	Wilfred Pickles
Alice Fisher	Mona Washbourne
Florence, grandmother	Ethel Griffies
Duxbury	Finlay Currie
Arthur Crabtree	Rodney Bewes
Barbara	Helen Fraser
Shadrack	Leonard Rossiter

Psst! According to Keith Waterhouse, they had originally planned to call it *Saturday Night at the Roxy* but had to think of something else when Alan Sillitoe published *Saturday Night and Sunday Morning* • A TV series and a musical were also based on *Billy Liar*.

The Birds

★★ 1963 120min c.

Director: Alfred Hitchcock
Screenplay: Evan Hunter
Source: Short story by Daphne du Maurier

A flock of birds congregate in a small West Coast town and begin to attack the human population. This wildly overpraised effort from Hitch has very little point to it, other than showing that birds can be as beastly as things with four legs. The effects used for the birds now look so ropey that relatively few sections are genuinely scary while the characters are so obviously made of cardboard, you can't help wondering why the birds have any problems.

Mitch Brenner	Rod Taylor
Melanie Daniels	Tippi Hedren
Lydia Brenner	Jessica Tandy
Annie Hayworth	Suzanne Pleshette
Cathy Brenner	Veronica Cartwright
Mrs. Bundy	Ethel Griffies
Sebastian Sholes	Charles McGraw
Salesman	Joe Mantell

Blurb The Birds Is Coming!

OOPS! The birds obviously aren't of this world.

When they attack a group of children, even though it's a sunny day, they don't have any shadows.

Psst! Near the opening of the film, Hitch can be seen in front of the pet shop with a pair of white West Highland terriers. They were his own dogs • Some $200,000 was spent on trying to come up with mechanical birds but they never looked genuine enough and Hitch was forced to use real ones that were trained to have a go at people • The scene where Hedren is savaged by the birds took a couple of weeks to complete. Some birds were thrown at her by the crew, while others were fastened to her clothes with thread so they couldn't get away. The scene only took up a minute or so on screen • Melanie Griffith claimed that Hitch had given her a present of a miniature coffin with a doll of her mother, Hedren, inside • Veronica Cartwright was also Lambert in *Alien*, presumably being the person they always call if they want somebody under attack by aggressive animals • Plans to have a final shot of the Golden Gate Bridge covered in birds were abandoned because of the cost • Hitchcock wanted to leave off the card saying 'The End' form the movie's conclusion, to give the impression that the story was still continuing. But this was rejected by the studio.

The Birth of a Nation

★★ 1915 160min c.

Director: D.W. Griffith
Screenplay: D.W. Griffith & Frank E. Woods
Source: Novel & play, *The Clansman* by Thomas Dixon Jr.

This was one of the most successful and innovative films ever on its release, as well as one of the most racist. This epic tale of family strife before, after and during the American Civil War, established D. W. Griffith, rightly or wrongly, as a cinematic genius. But as a film, despite some undoubtedly impressive scenes of spectacle, it's really hard going for anybody but the most dedicated film student.

Benjamin Cameron	Henry B. Walthall
Flora Cameron	Mae Marsh
Elsie Stoneman	Lillian Gish
Margaret Cameron	Miriam Cooper
Ted Stoneman	Robert Harron
Jeff	Wallace Reid
Gen. U.S. Grant	Donald Crisp

Also: Raoul Walsh, Eugene Pallette, Bessie Love, Erich von Stroheim

Psst! This film is possibly the most commercially successful ever, allowing for inflation. It cost $91,000 and made a profit of over $5m • Lilian Gish would go on to achieve the record for the longest acting career of all – 75 years in front of the camera • According to Gish, Griffith used only one take on every scene but one, which took two • In addition to the wonderful Eugene Pallette, look out for director Raoul Walsh and Erich von Stroheim, who's the man who falls off the roof • Tens of thousands of extras were used for the Civil War battle scenes, which took over 100 days to film. When Griffith was asked how he had managed to marshall such spectacular forces, he said: 'I worked out an infallible system. Our soldiers used real bullets' • Despite its subject matter, only one single black person was employed for the movie, white actors blacking up instead • Although Griffith had hoped to use genuine Civil War uniforms, men of 1915 were too large for clothes made 50 years earlier • This was the first film which had a score written for it, Joseph Carl Breil being the composer • It was the first film ever shown in the White House. Woodrow Wilson was President at the time and thought the movie was just wonderful • The membership of the Ku Klux Klan tripled in the months following the movie's release • There were riots against the film in Boston, New York and other cities. The National Association for the Advancement of Colored People persuaded several states to ban it • The film was later prohibited from being shown in American cinemas, although it is available on video and laserdisc. In 1939, a Denver cinema manager was sentenced to 120 days imprisonment and given a $1,400 fine for showing it • In Britain, in 1993, the video was passed with a '15' certificate, although a caption was added to set the fact that the Ku Klux Klan were heroes into historical context. It should be remembered that the attitudes in the film were pretty common at the time, it being only 50 years since the end of the Civil War.

The Birth of the Blues
★★★ 1941 85min c.

Director: Victor Schertzinger
Screenplay: Harry Tugend & Walter de Leon

A delightful, if implausible, concoction about the early days of jazz, with Crosby organising his own jazz band. To be fair, the story isn't terribly impressive, but it has a joyful vitality to it as well as providing us with some great jazz.

Jeff Lambert . . . . .Bing Crosby
Betty Lou Cobb . . . . .Mary Martin
Memphis .Brian Donlevy
Louey . . . . .Eddie "Rochester" Anderson
Pepper .Jack Teagarden
Aunt Phoebe . . . . .Carolyn Lee
Blackie .J. Carrol Naish
Limpy .Warren Hymer

Psst! Mary Martin was the mother of Larry Hagman, *Dallas'* J.R.

Black Narcissus
★★★ 1946 100min c.

Director: Michael Powell & Emeric Pressburger
Screenplay: Michael Powell & Emeric Pressburger
Source: Novel by Rumer Godden

Another gem from those British film industry stalwarts Powell and Pressburger. A group of nuns in the Himalayas are increasingly unsettled not only by the local conditions but also by the dishy Farrar, Her Majesty's man on the spot. Although a mite melodramatic in places, this is a surprisingly erotic movie, which is somewhat unsettling considering it's about nuns. It is also one of the most beautiful films ever made in colour.

Sister Clodagh . . . . .Deborah Kerr
Dilip Rai . . . . .Sabu
Mr. Dean . . . . .David Farrar
Sister Philippa . . . . .Flora Robson
Kanchi .Jean Simmons
General . . . . .Esmond Knight
Sister Ruth . . . . .Kathleen Byron
Sister Briony . . . . .Judith Furse
Sister Honey . . . . .Jenny Laird

Psst! Amazingly the filmmakers never moved outside the Home Counties, with Pinewood and a garden in Horsham, Sussex standing in for the Himalayas • Kerr's flashback of a romance she had before entering the convent was originally cut by the US censors • When Simmons married Stewart Granger, Powell said: When (he) saw Jean eating a squashy fruit with a ring through her nose, he went straight out, proposed to her, and married her. I always said it was the baggy umbrella she carried. It was the final erotic touch.'

Black Sunday
★★★ 1977 143min c.

Director: John Frankenheimer

Screenplay: Ernest Lehman, Kenneth Ross & Ivan Moffat
Source: Novel by Thomas Harris

A group of Middle-Eastern terrorists plot to take over an airship and use it to mow down the crowd watching the Super Bowl in Miami. This tense and nerve-wracking thriller has a surprisingly sophisticated script, but spoils things by being far too long.

Maj. David Kabakov	Robert Shaw
Dahlia Iyad	Marthe Keller
Michael Lander	Bruce Dern
Corley	Fritz Weaver
Moshevsky	Steven Keats
Fasil	Bekim Fehmiu
Muzi	Michael V. Gazzo
Pugh	William Daniels
Col. Riaf	Walter Gotell

Psst! Thomas Harris is also the author of the books about Hannibal Lecter • Director Frankenheimer has a cameo as the TV director in the control room at the Collesium.

Blade Runner
★★★★ 1982 116min c.

Director: Ridley Scott
Screenplay: Hampton Fancher & David Webb Peoples
Source: Short story, *Do Androids Dream of Electric Sheep?* by Philip K. Dick

Ridley Scott's exciting and stylish futuristic thriller is regarded as one of the best and most influential sci-fi pics ever. The original release had an explanatory voiceover and implausible happy ending imposed on it. Everything became confused by the release of the director's cut in 1992. On balance I think I prefer the original, perhaps it's more familiar, but both are brilliant. Ford's job is to 'retire' rogue androids but his dedication to the job in hand wavers when he gets a close look at Sean Young. Disturbingly, the once amazingly futuristic look of the film looks considerably less fantastical over a decade later, as reality moves closer to Scott's bleak vision of city life to come.

Deckard	Harrison Ford
Batty	Rutger Hauer
Rachel	Sean Young
Gaff	Edward James Olmos
Bryant	M. Emmet Walsh
Pris	Daryl Hannah
Leon	Brion James
Zhora	Joanna Cassidy

Quote 'More human than human, is our motto.' • 'You think I'd be working in a place like this if I could afford a real snake?' • 'Wake up. Time to die!'

OOPS! When the snake girl is shot, keep your eye on her hair which changes colour, length and style • When Zhora goes through the glass, it's clearly not her doing the stunt, besides which she's wearing something more solid than the bikini she put on just before • Zhora's wounds appear even before we hear the noise of the bullets.

Psst! Ford's part was at one time a possibility for Dustin Hoffman, while Philip K. Dick, author of the original novel, was keen on Victoria Principal playing Sean Young's part! • Don't get involved in any arguments with friends about the number of escaped replicants. There is no right answer. You will go mad trying to work it out • When the film went over budget, the happy ending (in the original version) used an outtake from the opening of *The Shining* as its backdrop.

Blazing Saddles
★★★ 1974 93min c.

Director: Mel Brooks
Screenplay: Mel Brooks, Norman Steinberg, Andrew Bergman, Richard Pryor & Alan Uger

Mel Brooks' most successful film, about a black sheriff sent to protect a Western town, seemed revolutionary at the time. Now that we have had umpteen imitations, some better than others, it's clear that it doesn't amount to much more than a succession of admittedly brilliant verbal and visual gags in a desperate search for an ending. Best thing by far is Kahn's sexy spoofing of Marlene Dietrich in *Destry Rides Again*.

Bart	Cleavon Little
Jim	Gene Wilder
Taggart	Slim Pickens
Hedley Lemarr	Harvey Korman
Lilly von Shtupp	Madeline Kahn
Gov. Lepetomane/Indian chief	Mel Brooks
Olson Johnson	David Huddleston
Mongo	Alex Karras
Howard Johnson	John Hillerman
Buddy Bizarre	Dom DeLuise
Himself	Count Basie
Rev. Johnson	Liam Dunn

Quote 'Mr. Lamarr, sir, you use your tongue purdier than a twenty dollar whore.' • 'Hold it! The next man makes a move, the nigger gets it.'

43

• 'Excuse me while I whip this out.' • 'Badges? We don't need no stinkin' badges.' • 'Is that a 10-gallon hat, or are you just enjoying the show?'

Psst! It had been planned to cast Richard Pryor, but the studio wouldn't go with him, saying that he wasn't big enough at the box office • Warner Brothers were pushing *Mame*, with Lucille Ball, as part of their 50th anniversary celebrations. To their astonishment, *Mame* attracted few moviegoers but Mel Brooks' movie packed them in • When Lili von Schtupp's playbill appears, listen out for a quick blast on the piano of 'Springtime for Hitler' from Brooks' movie *The Producers* • Brooks appears briefly as the aviator in the queue of bad guys • In Sweden, it was titled *Springtime for the Sheriff* • Until *Dances with Wolves*, this was the highest-grossing Western in movie history.

Blithe Spirit
★★★★ 1945 96min c.

Director: David Lean
Screenplay: Noël Coward, David Lean, Anthony Havelock-Allan & Ronald Neame
Source: Play by Noël Coward.

A novelist is disconcerted, to say the least, when his second marriage is threatened by the arrival on the scene of the exuberant ghost of his first wife. Although the entire cast is on top form, trading Coward's witty repartee back and forth, the movie belongs to the scene-stealing Rutherford as the batty medium Madame Arcati.

Charles Condomine	Rex Harrison
Ruth Condomine	Constance Cummings
Elvira	Kay Hammond
Madame Arcati	Margaret Rutherford
Dr. Bradman	Hugh Wakefield
Mrs. Bradman	Joyce Carey

Blonde Bombshell
SEE: Bombshell

Blood Simple
★★★ 1985 98min c.

Director: Joel Coen
Screenplay: Joel Coen & Ethan Coen

Bloody, complex thriller in which cuckolded Hedaya hires Walsh to kill his wife and her lover. Occasionally implausible, but otherwise terrifi-

cally stylish, exciting and blackly humorous. A dazzlingly original debut by the Coen brothers.

Ray	John Getz
Abby	Frances McDormand
Julian Marty	Dan Hedaya
Private detective	M. Emmet Walsh
Debra	Deborah Neumann
Radio Evangelist	William Preston Robertson

Blurb Dead In The Heart of Texas.

Psst! Astonishingly, the budget was only $1.5m.

Blow-Up
★ 1966 110min c.

Director: Michelangelo Antonioni
Screenplay: Michelangelo Antonioni & Tonino Guerra
Source: Short story by Julio Cortazar

The Emperor's new clothes in cinematic form? A photographer finds something strange in the background when he develops some photos. Is it real or an illusion? Have Boots ballsed up? Can Antonioni develop anything coherent by way of a plot? No he can't and instead of what was once thought chic and exciting, all we have is a bizarrely incomprehensible and pretentious slice of the 60s which has dated badly and now seems so insubstantial that if you breathed on it, it would disappear. Maybe the only reason 60s audiences were so keen was the nudity after all.

Thomas	David Hemmings
Jane	Vanessa Redgrave
Patricia	Sarah Miles
Girl	Jane Birkin
Ron	Peter Bowles
Painter	John Castle

Psst! Redgrave said 'yes' to the part before seeing the script, so much did she want to work with Antonioni • She was exhausted by the end of filming. In addition to the 16-hour days on set, she was acting in a play each evening • This is probably the first instance in which pubic hair was seen in British cinemas, however briefly • Jane Birkin makes her debut here as a girl romping with Hemmings.

The Blue Angel
★★★ 1930 99min b/w

Director: Josef von Sternberg
Screenplay: Robert Liebmann, Carl Zuckmayer & Karl Vollmoeller

Source: Novel, *Professor Unrat* by Heinrich Mann.

A professor falls for a sleazy nightclub singer who toys with him for a while before tossing him back. This German classic now has a touch of arthritis in its joints but there's still a good deal of pathos in the suffering inflicted on Jannings by the bored Dietrich. When she sings, it's all too easy to understand his infatuation.

Prof. Immanuel Rath	Emil Jannings
Lola Frohlich	Marlene Dietrich
Kiepert, the magician	Kurt Gerron
Guste Kiepert	Rosa Valetti
Mazeppa	Hans Albers

Quote 'They call me Lola.' • 'I thought the film was awful and vulgar and I was shocked by the whole thing. Remember, I was a well brought up German girl.' [Dietrich]

Psst! Although this is sometimes referred to as her debut, Dietrich had already made 17 other films. She wasn't very keen on making it and carried on appearing each evening in a play throughout production • It was made in both German and English. As von Sternberg was shooting in sequence, it meant filming one day in German and then doing the same thing the next day in English. The atmosphere on set was miserable. It was very cold and the heating could not be turned on because the unsophisticated sound equipment on what was Germany's first talking picture would pick up the background noise. Bear in mind how chilly it is when you watch the scantily-clad Dietrich • Von Sternberg tore his hair out at Dietrich's inability to sing the word 'moths' in the song *Falling in Love Again*. Her English wasn't too good at that time, and it sounded as if she was singing 'moss around a flame'. After 235 takes over two days, he gave up and ordered one of the musicians to shout 'Bring me a beer' at the crucial moment to drown her out • Despite his annoyance, his working relationship with Dietrich continued for some time, with him acting as her Svengali. Among the many tricks of the trade he thought up for her was the silver makeup line he drew down the centre of her nose, which made it look straighter on film. She used the ploy ever afterwards • Jannings had been one of the big stars of the silent age, winning the first ever Best Actor Oscar. But he didn't survive the talkies and returned to Germany, with this his most notable role. He ended up the head of the company making movies for Goebbels under the Nazis. Two of the other actors in the film, including Gerron, died in the concentration camps.

The Blue Dahlia
★★★ 1946 99min b/w

Director: George Marshall
Screenplay: Raymond Chandler
Source: Based on story by Chandler

A war veteran finds that while he's been away, his wife has been loving and devoted...to lots of guys. When she winds up dead, he's got some explaining to do. Although a pretty competent mystery, it doesn't quite deserve its reputation as a classic film noir. It's quite slackly put together and, hindered by the lacklustre acting, it lacks the verve and vitality of the true greats.

Johnny Morrison	Alan Ladd
Joyce Harwood	Veronica Lake
Buzz Wanchek	William Bendix
Eddie Harwood	Howard da Silva
Helen Morrison	Doris Dowling
Capt. Hendrickson	Tom Powers

Blurb Tamed By A Brunette...Framed By A Blonde...Blamed By The Cops.

Psst! Chandler wasn't too impressed by the lead actress, referring to her as 'Moronica' Lake. Alan Ladd didn't do much for him either: 'Ladd is hard, bitter and occasionally charming, but he is, after all, a small boy's idea of a tough guy.' • It was the only time he wrote an original screenplay, rather than adapting something else.

The Blue Lamp
★★ 1949 84min b/w

Director: Basil Dearden
Screenplay: T.E.B. Clarke

What was once a gritty thriller about the hunt for the killer of a stalwart British bobby now seems a parochial, quaint and tame tale that almost looks like a recruitment film for the boys in blue. More interesting as a social document than for any dramatic value.

P.C. George Dixon	Jack Warner
P.C. Andy Mitchell	Jimmy Hanley
Tom Riley	Dirk Bogarde
Sgt. Roberts	Robert Flemyng
Insp. Cherry	Bernard Lee
P.C. Hughes	Meredith Edwards
Mrs. Dixon	Gladys Henson
Constable Campbell	Bruce Seton
Spud	Patric Doonan
Also: Dora Bryan, Glynis Johns

Psst! The first instance of the word 'bastard' in a British and possibly any English-speaking film • The long-running TV series *Dixon of Dock Green* was spun off from the movie, with Dixon miraculously resurrected.

Blue Velvet
★★ 1986 120min c.

Director: David Lynch
Screenplay: David Lynch

Some find this weird view of small-town America one of the greatest films of the 80s. But for everyone who swears by this movie, there's another who swears at it, finding it a pretentious, violent, meaningless load of tosh. Even by the standards of Lynch's *Twin Peaks* it's bizarre, with MacLachlan doing some amateur sleuthing after the discovery of a severed ear, only to cross paths with beautiful but unstable Rossellini and demented psycho Hopper.

Jeffrey Beaumont . . . . .Kyle MacLachlan
Dorothy Vallens . . . . .Isabella Rossellini
Frank Booth . . . . .Dennis Hopper
Sandy Williams . . . . .Laura Dern
Mrs. Williams . . . . .Hope Lange
Ben . . . . .Dean Stockwell
Paul . . . . .Jack Nance
Raymond .Brad Dourif

Quote 'I don't know if you're a detective or a pervert.' • 'I looked for you in my closet tonight.'

The Blues Brothers
★★★★ 1980 133min c.

Director: John Landis
Screenplay: Dan Aykroyd & John Landis

The world is divided into those who love this movie and those who can't understand why the rest of us go crazy about this tale of Jake and Elwood helping the nuns to raise $5,000 by defying the police and staging a blues concert. Those who are immune to its charms point to the gaping holes in the story, the wild implausibilities, the self indulgence and the wanton destruction of cars along the way. We merely don our shades and pork-pie hats and claim we're on a mission from God. Cab Calloway, Ray Charles, Aretha Franklin, James Brown: what more could anybody want?

Joliet Jake .John Belushi
Elwood . . . . .Dan Aykroyd
Curtis . . . . .Cab Calloway
Rev. Cleophus James . . . . .James Brown
Sister Mary Stigmata . . . . . . .Kathleen Freeman
Burton Mercer . . . . .John Candy
Mystery woman . . . . .Carrie Fisher
Head Nazi . . . . .Henry Gibson
Soul Food Cafe owner . . . . .Aretha Franklin
Ray . . . . .Ray Charles
Also: Charles Napier, Frank Oz, John Landis, Paul Reubens, Twiggy, Steven Spielberg

Quote 'They're not gonna catch us. We're on a mission from God.' • 'Are you boys policemen?' – 'No, ma'am. We're musicians.' • 'It's 106 miles to Chicago, we've got a full tank of gas, half a pack of cigarettes, it's dark and we're wearing sunglasses.' – 'Hit it!'

OOPS! When the police car is overturned in the stadium, the shot from inside the car shows everything outside the wrong way round • Isn't it the same train going past Elwood's apartment window each time?

Psst! Steven Spielberg appears in a cameo towards the end as the Cook County clerk taking their money. Twiggy and Paul Reubens (Pee-wee Herman) also make appearances • Belushi, a heavy drug addict, was unreliable in the extreme and filming was often delayed while he was sought. He would die of his habit two years later • Landis' infamous phrase 'See You Next Wednesday' here appears on a billboard behind which the police are hiding. It was originally a line in *2001* during the phone call back to earth. • 70 names are listed on the credits as being responsible for the stunts • Landis has a fondness for the music of 'The Girl from Ipanema'. Here it's playing in a lift • Like most of Landis' movies, there's a credit for 'Woman on the Cutting Room Floor'.

Body Heat
★★★★ 1981 113min c.

Director: Lawrence Kasdan
Screenplay: Lawrence Kasdan

One of the last great film noirs, with sultry, manipulative Turner taking up with a dim lawyer and convincing him that the world would be a better place without the existence of her husband. It's been done before in many different guises, but rarely with anybody quite as sexy pulling the strings. She passes the test of the great *femme fatale*, in that most red-blooded males would happily act just as stupidly as Hurt if it meant fleeting happiness with her.

```
Ned Racine . . . . . . . . . . . . . . . . . . .William Hurt
Matty Walker  . . . . . . . . . . . . . .Kathleen Turner
Edmund Walker  . . . . . . . . . . . .Richard Crenna
Peter Lowenstein . . . . . . . . . . . . . .Ted Danson
Oscar Grace  . . . . . . . . . . . . . . . . . .J.A. Preston
Teddy Lewis  . . . . . . . . . . . . . . .Mickey Rourke
```

Quote 'You're not too bright, are you? I like that in a man.'

Psst! Of Kathleen Turner's role, Barbara Stanwyck said: 'The only one who could have done it better is me.'

Bombshell

★★★ 1933 95min b/w

Director: Victor Fleming
Screenplay: Jules Furthman & John Lee Mahin
Source: Play by Caroline Francke & Mack Crane

Harlow proves what a fantastic comedienne she could be in this still potent farcical satire of the movie industry, in which she is a film star used and abused by her family and studio. Some of the movie seems extraordinarily topical today, such as her remarkably sudden desire to adopt a baby. It's not exactly *Sunset Boulevard*, but there are more laughs.

```
Lola Burns . . . . . . . . . . . . . . . . . . .Jean Harlow
Space Hanlon . . . . . . . . . . . . . . . . . .Lee Tracy
Pop Burns . . . . . . . . . . . . . . . . . .Frank Morgan
Gifford Middleton . . . . . . . . . . . .Franchot Tone
Brogan. . . . . . . . . . . . . . . . . . . . . . .Pat O'Brien
Miss Mac . . . . . . . . . . . . . . . . . . . . .Una Merkel
Mr. Middleton . . . . . . . . . . .C. Aubrey Smith
Junior Burns . . . . . . . . . . . . . . . . . . .Ted Healy
```

Psst! The film was sadly true to life for Harlow. In real life, her earnings were squandered by her mother. When she died four years later, her estate amounted to only $25,000 • In fact, despite the similarities, it was really modelled more on the life of Clara Bow, the silent screen actress most famous now for having slept regularly with the entire USC Trojans football team, among them a young John Wayne. Frank Morgan's part, however, is too similar to that of Harlow's stepfather, Marino Bello, for it not to have been based on him.

Bonnie and Clyde

★★★★ 1967 111min c.

Director: Arthur Penn
Screenplay: David Newman & Robert Benton

In the midst of the Depression, a pair of outlaws part a series of banks from their cash, caring little who gets in the way of their guns. There's a startling array of cinematic techniques on display here, as the photogenic pair are transformed into modern day Robin Hoods. Although some of the flashiness now irritates and marks it firmly as a product of the 60s, this innovative thriller is still one of the all-time great gangster movies.

```
Clyde Barrow . . . . . . . . . . . . . . .Warren Beatty
Bonnie Parker  . . . . . . . . . . . . . .Faye Dunaway
C.W. Moss . . . . . . . . . . . . . . .Michael J. Pollard
Buck Barrow . . . . . . . . . . . . . .Gene Hackman
Blanche Barrow . . . . . . . . . . . .Estelle Parsons
Eugene Grizzard . . . . . . . . . . . . . . .Gene Wilder
Capt. Frank Hamer . . . . . . . . . . . . .Denver Pyle
Ivan Moss . . . . . . . . . . . . . . . . . . . . . .Dub Taylor
```

Oscars Estelle Parsons

Blurb They're Young...They're In Love...And They Kill People!

Quote 'We rob banks.'

Showing Gold Diggers of 1933.

Psst! While based on real outlaws, it also incorporates a few stories derived from the career of those in John Dillinger's gang • *Time* magazine's reviewer tore into the film and then, the following week, changed his mind and called it one of the most significant films of the decade • This was the first movie to make use of slow-motion violence • The film sparked off a revival of interest in 30s fashions • Hugely influenced by French New Wave filmmaking styles, Jean-Luc Godard and François Truffaut turned down the chance to direct, although they both made creative suggestions. It was Truffaut mentioning the project to Beatty that got him interested in the first place • Tuesday Weld, Natalie Wood and Jane Fonda were among those considered for Bonnie's part. Beatty wanted Leslie Caron, his girlfriend of the moment • This was Gene Wilder's first movie • Although they were no longer in business, the filmmakers used three of the actual banks in Texas that had been robbed by Bonnie and Clyde. Some of the bit parts are played by bystanders who witnessed the real Bonnie and Clyde and provided eye-witness source material for the writers • Dunaway's costumes were heavily copied by the fashion industry. Happiest of all were French beret manufacturers, who saw demand soar from 1,500 a week to 20,000. The other innovative suggestion of the costume designer was that she not wear a bra • Dunaway lost 20 pounds for the part by lugging sandbags around • Bonnie's younger sister sued Warners for more than $1m for the blackening of her sibling's memory. The widow and son of Capt. Hamer also sued for similar reasons • The great music comes courtesy of the wonderfully named blue-grass musicians Flatt and Scruggs, best-known for the theme music to *The Beverly Hillbillies* on TV.

Boom Town

★★★ 1940 117min b/w

Director: Jack Conway
Screenplay: John Lee Mahin
Source: Story by James Edward Grant.

A pair of wildcat oilmen in Texas strike it rich and then fall out over women. If you ever wonder about the value of the great stars, look no further than this movie. Although the story is clearly formulaic and unsurprising, Spencer and Gable put it over with such panache and conviction that it becomes hugely enjoyable hokum.

Big John McMasters . . . . .Clark Gable
Square John Sand . . . . .Spencer Tracy
Betsy Bartlett . . . . .Claudette Colbert
Karen Vanmeer . . . . .Hedy Lamarr
Luther Aldrich . . . . .Frank Morgan
Harry Compton . . . . .Lionel Atwill
Harmony Jones . . . . .Chill Wills

Psst! Joe Yule, playing Ed Murphy, was Mickey Rooney's father • Gable's own father had been an itinerant oil worker.

Born Free

★★ 1966 95min c.

Director: James Hill
Screenplay: Gerald L.C. Copley
Source: Book by Joy Adamson

Husband and wife game wardens raise three lion cubs as if they were their children. Although kids will probably still go gooey-eyed over this true-life tale, there isn't much in it to keep any but the most animal-mad adults enthralled. The sequel, *Living Free*, should never have been released from captivity.

Joy Adamson . . . . .Virginia McKenna
George Adamson . . . . .Bill Travers
Kendall . . . . .Geoffrey Keen
Nuru . . . . .Peter Lukoye
Makkede . . . . .Omar Chambati
Sam . . . . .Bill Godden

Psst! The film was shot entirely on location in East Africa.

Born Yesterday

★★★ 1950 103min b/w

Director: George Cukor
Screenplay: Garson Kanin
Source: Play by Garson Kanin

An uncouth scrap metal tycoon gets a tutor to educate his showgirl mistress, only to discover that a little learning is an extremely dangerous thing. Pleasant without being hilarious, Holliday is a delight. But the film suffers from a serious surfeit of reaction shots, as if we needed cues to be told to be surprised or amused. The 1993 remake with Melanie Griffith and Don Johnson is better than might be expected.

Billie Dawn . . . . .Judy Holliday
Paul Verrall . . . . .William Holden
Harry Brock . . . . .Broderick Crawford
Jim Devery . . . . .Howard St. John
Eddie . . . . .Frank Otto
Norval Hedges . . . . .Larry Oliver

Oscars Judy Holliday

Quote 'You're just not couth!' • 'Will ya do me a favour, Harry? Drop dead!' • 'If you don't act friendly, I don't act friendly, if you know what I mean.' • 'What are you doing?' – 'Well, if you don't know, I must be doing it wrong.' • 'It's a sort of cause. I want everybody to be smart. A world full of ignorant people is too dangerous to live in.'

OOPS! When Crawford hits Holliday, he does it with his right hand. But she clutches her right cheek, when it ought to be the left one that's smarting.

Psst! After a major disagreement with the unpleasant head of Columbia, Harry Cohn, years before over *A Double Life*, Kanin got even by modelling the character of Harry Brock on him in *Born Yesterday* • Although vowing never to work for Cohn again, the offer of $1m for the movie rights to the play were enough to sway Kanin. However, he ghosted the screenplay for no fee, with Albert Mannheimer receiving screen credit • Cohn did all he could to avoid casting 'that fat Jewish broad', even though it was Holliday who was primarily responsible for making it a smash hit on stage. But Rita Hayworth, his main star, went off to marry Aly Khan and after Kanin, wife Ruth Gordon, Hepburn and Tracy conspired to make her so memorable in *Adam's Rib*, Cohn caved in. She lost 15 pounds before filming and went on to win the Oscar, beating Gloria Swanson and Bette Davis • In reality, Holliday had an IQ of 172 • Holliday had only been given the stage role after Jean Arthur had to pull out • Cohn's dislike of Holliday may have had something to do with his chasing round his office, only to have him reach inside her blouse and hand him her falsies, saying, 'I think these are what you're after.' • The censors insisted on obscuring the fact that Brock expected sex in return for keeping Billie in style.

Boudu Saved from Drowning
★★★ 1932 87min b/w

Director: Jean Renoir
Screenplay: Jean Renoir
Source: Play by René Fauchois

This sprightly French black comedy is another delight from the amazing Jean Renoir. A tramp is saved from drowning and given a home. Instead of being grateful, the free spirit instead takes over the lives of his rescuers, thinking nothing of seducing the women in the household. Although it's clearly intended to be a social commentary, that never gets in the way of the rich vein of humour mined by the great Simon. It's French title is *Boudu Sauvé des Eaux*. It was effectively remade, quite creditably, in 1985 as *Down and Out in Beverly Hills* with Richard Dreyfuss, Bette Midler and Nick Nolte.

Boudu . . . . .Michel Simon
Lestingois . . . . .Charles Grandval
Mme Lestingois . . . . .Marcelle Hainia
Anne-Marie . . . . .Severine Lerczinska
The student . . . . .Jean Dasté

The Bowery
★★★ 1933 92min b/w

Director: Raoul Walsh
Screenplay: Howard Estabrook & James Gleason
Source: Novel, *Chuck Connors* by Michael L. Simmons & Bessie Roth Solomon

Rivalry among roustabouts in New York's Bowery district in the Gay 90s, with Beery and Raft the challengers for Wray's affections who start any 'discussion' by putting their dukes up. Although occasionally a little corny, there's plen-

ty of action to keep us occupied, with Walsh ensuring that the screen fairly teams with life.

Chuck Connors . . . . .Wallace Beery
Steve Brodie . . . . .George Raft
Swipes McGurk . . . . .Jackie Cooper
Lucy Calhoun .Fay Wray
Trixie Odbray . . . . .Pert Kelton
Max Herman . . . . .Herman Bing
Slick . . . . .Harold Huber

The Boy Friend
★★★ 1971 135min c.

Director: Ken Russell
Screenplay: Ken Russell
Source: Musical play by Sandy Wilson.

Sandy Wilson's tongue-in-cheek homage to the musicals of the 30s is surprisingly respectfully translated to the screen by Russell. There's a sweet story which even Twiggy can't ruin, delightfully camp humour and some stunningly-staged Busby Berkeley-ish numbers. Among the songs are 'I Could Be Happy' and 'All I Do Is Dream of You'. A veritable knickerbocker glory of a musical.

Polly Browne . . . . .Twiggy
Tony Brockhurst . . . . .Christopher Gable
Max . . . . .Max Adrian
Mme Dubonnet . . . . .Moyra Fraser
De Thrill .Vladek Sheybal
Tommy . . . . .Tommy Tune
Rita . . . . .Glenda Jackson
Hortense . . . . .Barbara Windsor
Percy . . . . .Bryan Pringle

Brazil
★★★★ 1985 142min c.

Director: Terry Gilliam
Screenplay: Terry Gilliam, Tom Stoppard & Charles McKeown

There has never been and there never will be another movie quite like this bizarre, black and bleakly funny fantasy about a Kafkaesque, bureaucratically strangled future world. Pryce is the clerk in Information Retrieval who won't stop dreaming, particularly when he encounters dream-girl Greist. Like a hard-nosed version of Gilliam's Python animations brought to life, Brazil may take more than one viewing to appreciate it fully and still may not make complete sense. Certainly a mite too long but, boy, does it stick in the memory.

Sam Lowry	Jonathan Pryce
Tuttle	Robert De Niro
Ida Lowry	Katherine Helmond
Kurtzmann	Ian Holm
Spoor	Bob Hoskins
Jack Lint	Michael Palin
Warren	Ian Richardson
Helpmann	Peter Vaughan
Jill Layton	Kim Greist
Dr. Jaffe	Jim Broadbent

Also: Charles McKeown, Derrick O'Connor, Bryan Pringle, Nigel Planer, Gorden Kaye

Blurb It's Only A State Of Mind.

Quote 'I generally describe *Brazil* in a pretentious way as a post-Orwellian view of a pre-Orwellian world. That description bores everyone stiff, so they leave me alone.' [Gilliam]

Psst! The studio weren't happy about the film and wanted it cut heavily and given a happy ending. They hung onto the movie while the arguments raged. Eventually Gilliam took an ad in Variety that said: 'Dear Sid Sheinberg. When are you going to release my film?' Only when it won three awards from the LA Film Critics Association was it released • The smoker in the Shangri-La tower who bumps into Pryce is director Gilliam.

Breakfast at Tiffany's
★★★★ 1961 115min c.

Director: Blake Edwards
Screenplay: George Axelrod
Source: Novella by Truman Capote

Capote's novella of the enigmatic Holly Golightly, living off a succession of $50 bills given to her for the powder room by her gentleman friends, is here turned into gloriously sentimental moonshine. Hepburn has the same mesmerising effect on audiences as her character does in the movie, while the dialogue is top notch. The only drawback is the excruciatingly awful appearance of slant-eyed Rooney as her irascible Japanese neighbour. The stereotype is bad enough. The slapstick is worse.

Holly Golightly	Audrey Hepburn
Paul Varjak	George Peppard
2E	Patricia Neal
Doc Golightly	Buddy Ebsen
O.J. Berman	Martin Balsam
Mr. Yunioshi	Mickey Rooney
Tiffany's clerk	John McGiver
Sally Tomato	Alan Reed

Quote 'Cross my heart and kiss my elbow.'
• 'She's a phony, all right, but a *real* phony.

OOPS! Hepburn is bare-legged when she crawls through Peppard's bedroom window. When she's sitting on his bed, she's got black stockings on.

Psst! The studio initially wanted to change the title to *Follow That Blonde*.

Breaking Away
★★★★ 1979 100min c.

Director: Peter Yates
Screenplay: Steve Tesich

A bike-mad boy is so obsessed by his hobby that, to the irritation of his father, he will speak nothing but Italian at home because it's from Italy that the great cyclists come. This refreshing and delightful coming-of-age movie is not only extremely funny, but also contains some exciting sports action.

Dave Stohler	Dennis Christopher
Mike	Dennis Quaid
Cyril	Daniel Stern
Moocher	Jackie Earle Haley
Mrs. Stohler	Barbara Barrie
Mr. Stohler	Paul Dooley
Katherine	Robyn Douglas
Rod	Hart Bochner

Oscars Best Screenplay

OOPS! When Christopher comes off his bike during the race near the conclusion of the movie, his T-shirt gets mucked up. But at the end, his T-shirt is pristine again.

Psst! Many of the residents of Bloomington were roped in as extras • Yates insisted that the only clothes the actors wear should either come from their own homes or be bought locally.

Breathless
★★ 1959 90min b/w

Director: Jean-Luc Godard
Screenplay: Jean-Luc Godard & François Truffaut

Have Gauloise, will travel. A small-time crook who idolises Bogart is wanted for a cop's murder and hides out with his American girlfriend while trying to raise cash. This hugely influential

New Wave homage to the old American B-pictures uses its array of directorial tricks as a magician would use sleight of hand. The flashiness conceals the fact that the plot goes nowhere and what once seemed fresh and exciting now seems gimmicky. However, it is infinitely stylish compared to the 1983 sequel with Richard Gere, which is so devoid of breath it's a stiff.

Michael Poiccard/Laszlo Kovaks ....Jean-Paul Belmondo
Patricia Franchini ....Jean Seberg
Police Inspector ....Daniel Boulanger
Parvulesco ....Jean-Pierre Melville
Informer ....Jean-Luc Godard

Quote 'Killers kill. Squealers squeal.'

Psst! The film has been analysed to death by film critics and students. It was some time after the movie came out that Godard admitted that his striking use of the jump-cut, a radical technique that became much copied, came about simply because he didn't have enough film to shoot the traditional dissolves • No sound was recorded during filming, the whole enterprise more closely resembling a silent movie, with Godard shouting out instructions as they went • Godard appears as the man in sunglasses who fingers Belmondo to the cops.

The Bride of Frankenstein
★★★★ 1935 75min c.

Director: James Whale
Screenplay: John Balderston & William Hurlbut
Source: Novel by Mary Shelley

Sixty years on, still a surprisingly effective example of witty, gothic horror. Dr. Frankenstein is forced to make a friend for the monster he created. But the blind date between the two doesn't go exactly according to plan. A classic worthy of the title. It makes a great double bill with the wonderful Mel Brooks' version, Young Frankenstein.

The Monster ....Boris Karloff
Henry Frankenstein ....Colin Clive
Elizabeth Frankenstein ....Valerie Hobson
Dr. Septimus Pretorius ....Ernest Thesiger
Mary Shelley/The Bride .....Elsa Lanchester
Minnie ....Una O'Connor
Burgomaster ....................E.E. Clive
The hermit ....................O.P. Heggie
Karl ....Dwight Frye
Percy Shelley ....Douglas Walton

Neighbour ....Walter Brennan
Baby ....Billy Barty
Hunter ....John Carradine

Blurb WARNING! The Monster Demands A Mate.

Quote 'Go. You Live. Go. You stay. We belong dead.'

OOPS! When the castle is blowing up, Clive can be seen inside. Yet he's then seen outside embracing Hobson. This is undoubtedly a result of the changed ending.

Psst! Boris Karloff was unhappy that he had dialogue, feeling that having the monster grunt out words weakened its character considerably • Poor Karloff. Having had to endure four hours preparation each day on the original film, the costume and makeup were made still more sophisticated here and needed seven hours to apply and remove. He lost 20 pounds during filming • Elsa Lanchester's makeup as the 'bride' made movement so difficult that she had to be fed through a tube • She modelled her gait on robot Brigitte Helm's in Lang's silent sci-fi film Metropolis • Although originally the movie ended with Dr. Frankenstein dying in the castle, a slightly less downbeat ending was hastily written and substituted in which only those who deserve their comeuppance get it.

The Bridge on the River Kwai
★★★ 1957 161min c.

Director: David Lean
Screenplay: Carl Foreman & Michael Wilson
Source: Novel by Pierre Boulle

Led by an increasingly deranged Colonel who wants to show his Japanese captors just what fine stuff the British are made of, prisoners of war labour under appalling conditions to build a railway bridge in Burma. The memory of this great movie is better than the reality. Once you've seen it once, it seems terribly slow and long-winded in parts with a meandering storyline. Guinness, however, is spellbinding.

Shears ....William Holden
Col. Nicholson ....Alec Guinness
Maj. Warden..................Jack Hawkins
Col. Saito ....Sessue Hayakawa
Maj. Clipton ....James Donald
Lt. Joyce ....Geoffrey Horne
Col. Green ....André Morell
Capt. Reeves ....Peter Williams
Grogan ....Percy Herbert
Maj. Hughes ....John Boxer

Oscars Best Picture, Best Screenplay (adapted), Best Screenplay (adapted), Alec Guinness, Best Director, Best Screenplay (adapted)

Quote 'You and that Colonel Nicholson, you're two of a kind. Crazy with courage. For what? How to die like a gentleman.' • 'You give me powders, pills, baths, injections and enemas…when all I need is love.' • 'Madness! Madness!' [Last line]

OOPS! Alec Guinness' surname is wrongly spelt with only one 'n' on the closing titles • Note the awkward walk of the badly matched stand-in for the final shot in the movie.

Psst! Guinness was billed third on the movie. Charles Laughton had been the first choice for his part, with Humphrey Bogart and Laurence Olivier other ideas • Cary Grant was originally approached for Holden's role. Grant refused because he couldn't stand any more location filming • Guinness originally didn't want to do the movie when he was offered it. The script, he said, was full of silly things like elephant charges while he thought Col. Nicholson a blinkered character: 'Then Sam Spiegel (the producer) took me to dinner. He is a very persuasive character. I started out maintaining that I wouldn't play the role, and by the end of the evening we were discussing what kind of wig I should wear.' • The boss of Columbia, Harry Cohn, was convinced that a film lasting 2 hours 41 minutes which did not have a hero could not possibly succeed financially • Wilson and Foreman were both blacklisted writers, ostracised by the McCarthy Communist witch hunts. So it is Pierre Boulle, author of the novel, whose name appears on the credits. When it won the Best Screenplay Oscar, the statuette was accepted in Boulle's name, everyone ignoring the fact that he could barely speak English, let alone write it. It wasn't until 1985 that the Oscars were handed over – to the mens' widows, both writers having died in the interim • Although the credits claim that the film is from the book of the same name, in fact the book is called ·*The Bridge Over the River Kwai* • The movie was made entirely on location in the Sri Lankan jungle • Guinness claimed to have established a record on set by killing 681 flies on one day • A year in the making, there were some complicated logistics, particularly when it came to making the bridge and then blowing it up. A combination of men and 35 elephants put it together in eight months at a cost of $250,000. But the Hollywood effects people weren't confident of demolishing it at

the same time as a train ran across it. ICI in Ceylon were called in to offer advice. It was one of the most dangerous stunts ever undertaken. The driver had to leap out a quarter of the way across and hare back to safety unseen, just moments before the dynamite went off • The book lad left the bridge standing as a symbol of the futility of war.

Brief Encounter
★★★★ 1945 86min b/w

Director: David Lean
Screenplay: Noël Coward, David Lean, Ronald Neame & Anthony Havelock-Allan
Source: Play, *Still Life* by Noël Coward

This most exquisite of all British love stories goes against all the rules of popular cinema, featuring a far from exciting middle-aged, middle-class, couple – a housewife and a doctor – meeting by chance in a depressing railway station and falling head over heels for each other. But both are married and so it becomes clear that stiff upper lips will be called for. Unbearably poignant, yet not without humour, this is one of those rare films that can be watched again and again.

Laura Johnson	Celia Johnson
Alec Harvey	Trevor Howard
Albert Godby	Stanley Holloway
Myrtle Bagot	Joyce Carey
Fred Jesson	Cyril Raymond
Stephen Lynn	Valentine Dyall
Dolly Messiter	Everley Gregg
Boatman	Jack May
Organist	Irene Handl

Quote 'I believe we would be so different if we lived in a warm climate. We wouldn't be so shy and withdrawn and difficult.'

OOPS! Somehow it seems almost fitting that Celia Johnson shows no sign of being wet after she dashes through a downpour • Keep your eyes skinned and you may spot a signpost showing that the movie was filmed in Lancashire rather than the Home Counties. The accents of the extras are another giveaway.

Psst! Although it's hard to believe, the film was not a box office success at the time, despite winning the top prize at the Cannes Film Festival. After one preview produced hysterical laughter, Lean wanted to set the negative on fire and forget the whole project • Celia Johnson got £1,000 and Trevor Howard just

£500. They received nothing further from the movie's subsequent success and frequent TV showings • Milford Junction was actually Carnforth station in Lancashire on the edge of the Lake District. Chosen because it was far enough from the flight paths of the German bombers that blackouts didn't have to be enforced at night, the station is now in a state of sad delapidation • Filming took place largely at night and in the early hours to avoid the usual train services • The music is Rachmaninoff's Second Piano Concerto • Bizarrely, a Canadian cinema advertised this with the slogan: 'Girls who live dangerously.' • Throughout his career Howard insisted on a clause in his contract allowing him to stay away from work while cricket test matches were being played • Howard recalls that at the premiere, Coward didn't even appear to realise who he was.

Brighton Rock
★★★ 1947 92min b/w

Director: John Boulting
Screenplay: Graham Greene & Terence Rattigan
Source: Novel by Graham Greene

Attenborough has one of his finest screen roles as the nasty young hood who marries the waitress who provided him with an alibi for murder. Unfortunately for her, he's not planning to celebrate too many wedding anniversaries. The film was remarkable in its day for the tough violence it depicted and while that side of it may seem old hat these days, there's still an air of menace while the acting from the leads ensures that the drama still works.

Pinkie Brown . . . . .Richard Attenborough
Ida .Hermione Baddeley
Dallow .William Hartnell
Prewitt . . . . .Harcourt Williams
Cubitt . . . . .Nigel Stock
Rose . . . . .Carol Marsh
Fred Hale (Kolley Kibber) . . . . . . .Alan Wheatley
Spicer . . . . .Wylie Watson

Psst! At the ending, Carol Marsh was supposed to play the record on which she erroneously thinks Pinkie confesses his love. But the censor thought it would be too depressing as planned, so a compromise was struck, with the audience knowing what was on the record but not Marsh. It had to be shot in just one day and hastily tacked on, which is why the lighting looks so odd.

Bringing Up Baby
★★★ 1938 102min c.

Director: Howard Hawks
Screenplay: Dudley Nichols & Hagar Wilde
Source: Story by Hagar Wilde

An introverted zoologist's life is thrown into disarray when he comes into collision with a dizzy socialite and her pet leopard. Once seen as the epitome of screwball comedy, the madcap pace now seems a little too forced. Hepburn's mannered performance has a tendency to get on the nerves, while Grant's repeated double takes have a similar jarring effect. It's still very funny, just not the perfect comic outing it's often claimed to be.

Susan Vance . . . . .Katharine Hepburn
David Huxley . . . . .Cary Grant
Aunt Elizabeth . . . . .May Robson
Major Applegate . . . . .Charles Ruggles
Constable Slokum . . . . .Walter Catlett
Dr. Fritz Lehman . . . . .Fritz Feld
Mr. Gogarty . . . . .Barry Fitzgerald
Also: Jonathan Hale, Asta

Quote 'I'll be with you in a minute, Mr. Peabody.'
• 'I just decided to go gay all of a sudden.'

Psst! Grant's role was apparently first offered to Ronald Colman, Ray Milland and Robert Montgomery • Although the critics liked it, the film flopped at the box office, losing $350,000. Hepburn received much of the blame and it sent her stock still lower, only to be rescued when she took the initiative to rescue her career with *The Philadelphia Story* • Some of the film was improvised, most notably Hepburn's line 'I was born on the side of a hill' when she broke the heel of her shoe • Hepburn later claimed that Grant was afraid of the leopard. She, it seems, was the only one who wasn't. 'I was too dumb to be afraid,' she said • The dog is played by Asta, famous for his part in the *Thin Man* films • The same issue of Colliers magazine, 10 April 1937, in which this short story appeared also contained *Stage to Lordsburg*, which was filmed as *Stagecoach*.

Bring Me the Head of Alfredo Garcia
★★ 1974 112min c.

Director: Sam Peckinpah
Screenplay: Gordon Dawson & Sam Peckinpah

Peckinpah fans love this story of a piano player getting involved in a fight for control of the head of the poor chap who made the mistake of getting a gangster's daughter pregnant. Others, like me, find it not only rather tasteless, confusing and unnecessarily violent but, even more importantly, downright dull.

Bennie	Warren Oates
Quill	Gig Young
Elita	Isela Vega
Sappensly	Robert Webber
Max	Helmut Dantine
Paco	Kris Kristofferson
El Jefe	Emilio Fernandez

Blurb It's Got Guts.

Quote 'Few movies are as tedious. Bring me the head of the studio that released this one.' [Critic Gene Shalit]

Psst! Peckinpah claims this to be the only movie on which he had complete control.

Broadcast News
★★★ 1987 132min c.

Director: James L. Brooks
Screenplay: James L. Brooks

Excellent satire on the world of televison news with Hunter the tough producer who has to choose between Brooks, the unphotogenic reporter who's a good friend, and Hurt, the pretty but oh so dim new anchorman. Not only funny, but frighteningly realistic. Turn off before the daft, tacked-on ending.

Tom Grunick	William Hurt
Jane Craig	Holly Hunter
Aaron Altman	Albert Brooks
Ernie Merriman	Robert Prosky
Jennifer Mack	Lois Chiles
Blair Litton	Joan Cusack
Paul Moore	Peter Hackes
Bobby	Christian Clemenson
Anchorman	Jack Nicholson
Angry messenger	John Cusack

Quote 'If anything happens to me, you tell every woman I've ever gone out with I was talking about her at the end. That way, they'll have to re-evaluate me.'

Psst! Jack Nicholson appears, unbilled, in a cameo as an anchorman while John Cusack, Joan's brother, pops up as the 'angry messenger.' Nicholson left his name off because he didn't want to take attention from the leads • The part was written with Debra Winger in mind, but she became pregnant. Kathleen Turner was also considered. Writer-director Brooks hadn't even heard of Hunter when she read for the part • Hunter noticed when researching the part at CBS that everyone had dirty hands, so she rubbed hers with newspapers at the start of every day's filming.

Broadway Melody of 1940
★★★ 1939 102min b/w

Director: Norman Taurog
Screenplay: Leon Gordon & George Oppenheimer

Although not as well known as some movie musicals, this should be sought out by all fans of the genre. The story of sparring and romancing dancing partners is fairly run of the mill, though nicely handled. What scores is the Cole Porter music and the incredible dancing. In the company of Powell, a far better dancer than Rogers, Astaire seems to strive even harder. Their nine minute routine to 'Begin the Beguine', danced on that wonderful, glossy, black floor, is among the finest ever captured on film.

Johnny Brett	Fred Astaire
Clare Bennett	Eleanor Powell
King Shaw	George Murphy
Bob Casey	Frank Morgan
Bert C. Matthews	Ian Hunter
Amy Blake	Florence Rice
Emmy Lou Lee	Lynne Carver

A Bronx Tale
★★★★ 1993 122min c.

Director: Robert De Niro
Screenplay: Chazz Palminteri
Source: Play by Palminteri

Set in the 60s, when the Bronx was a family neighbourhood with a doo-wop group on every corner, a young boy finds his loyalties are torn between his responsible bus-driver father and the more glamous local Mafia leader. This enthralling coming-of-age story, based on Palminteri's own experiences, so beautifully conjures up the setting and the people who populated it that you can hardly believe they are really actors. A sterling directorial debut for De Niro.

Lorenzo . . . . .Robert De Niro
Sonny . . . . .Chazz Palminteri
Calogero at 17 . . . . .Lillo Brancato Jr.
Calogero at 9 . . . . .Francis Capra
Jane . . . . .Taral Hicks
Rosina . . . . .Kathrine Narducci
Jimmy Whispers . . . . .Clem Caserta
Bobby Bars . . . . .Alfred Sauchelli Jr.
Danny K.O. . . . . .Frank Pietrangolare
Carmine . . . . .Joe Pesci

Psst! Palminteri was getting odd jobs as an actor and so turned his childhood reminiscences into a one-man show which became phenomenally successful. When Hollywood bid for the rights, he refused unless he could both write and star in it, even though they offered $250,000. He was still saying no when they were offering $1m. Then De Niro said he was interested • De Niro, getting into his role as usual, took the New York bus driver's exam. When told that he'd failed for the second time he asked them to check again, only to find that they'd made a mistake and he had passed • The Bronx having changed so much in the interim, it was actually filmed in Queens.

The Browning Version
★★★ 1951 90min b/w

Director: Anthony Asquith
Screenplay: Terence Rattigan
Source: Play by Rattigan

A capable if uninspiring adaptation of Rattigan's play about the public-school teacher approaching retirement, who has to face up to the fact that his younger wife is unfaithful, that his pupils hate him and that he has achieved nothing with his life. The film is still moving, even if the upbeat ending is somewhat implausible.

Andrew Crocker-Harris . . . . .Michael Redgrave
Millie Crocker-Harris . . . . .Jean Kent
Frank Hunter . . . . .Nigel Patrick
Frobisher . . . . .Wilfrid Hyde-White
Fletcher . . . . .Bill Travers
Gilbert . . . . .Ronald Howard
Taplow . . . . .Brian Smith
Carstairs . . . . .Peter Jones
Betty Carstairs . . . . .Sarah Lawson

Bugsy Malone
★★ 1976 93min c.

Director: Alan Parker
Screenplay: Alan Parker

For a while, the idea of playing a spoof of the 20s gangster film as a musical with kids tickles the fancy. Then it becomes tiresome and coy. It needs more subtlety than these youngsters, with the exception of Foster, can provide. Where sex rears its head, it becomes positively disturbing.

Bugsy Malone . . . . .Scott Baio
Tallulah . . . . .Jodie Foster
Blousey . . . . .Florrie Dugger
Fat Sam . . . . .John Cassisi

Psst! Foster's singing voice was dubbed. When she went on to become a star, Parker admitted he wished he hadn't done it.

Build My Gallows High
SEE: **Out of the Past**

Bulldog Drummond
★★ 1929 90min b/w

Director: F. Richard Jones
Screenplay: Sidney Howard
Source: Play, *Sapper* by H.C. McNeil.

An ex-soldier still craving adventure is asked by an American heiress to help free her uncle. Being an early talkie, the action doesn't exactly knock us out but Colman is suitably dashing and debonair. Silly, but fun. Of the numerous sequels the 1934 *Bulldog Drummond Strikes Back* is best, and an improvement on the original.

Drummond . . . . .Ronald Colman
Phyllis Benton . . . . .Joan Bennett
Erma Peterson . . . . .Lilyan Tashman
Carl Peterson . . . . .Montagu Love
Algy Longworth . . . . .Claud Allister

Psst! Ronald Colman's first talkie.

Bull Durham
★★★ 1988 108min c.

Director: Ron Shelton
Screenplay: Ron Shelton

Baseball groupie Sarandon takes one of the local minor-league team each year and coaches him in the finer things in life, believing that good sex produces higher batting averages. Robbins and Costner compete for her affections in this lovely, sassy, often sexy, romantic comedy.

Sarandon's performance is so good, it soars out of the ball park.

Crash Davis	Kevin Costner
Annie Savoy	Susan Sarandon
'Nuke' LaLoosh	Tim Robbins
Skip	Trey Wilson
Larry	Robert Wuhl
Jimmy	William O'Leary
Bobby	David Neidorf
Deke	Danny Gans

Quote 'This is the damnedest season I ever seen. The Durham Bulls can't lose and I can't get laid.' • 'A guy'll listen to anything if he thinks it's foreplay.' • 'It wasn't the first time I went to bed with a guy and woke up with a note.' • 'I believe in the soul, the dawn, the evening, the small of a woman's back, the hanging curve ball, high fibre, good Scotch, long foreplay, show tunes…I believe that Lee Harvey Oswald acted alone, I believe that there ought to be a constitutional amendment outlawing astroturf, I believe in the sweet spot, soft core pornography, chocolate chip cookies…and I believe in long, slow, deep, soft, wet kisses that last three days.'

Psst! There were no takers for this movie from first time writer-director Shelton until Costner picked up the ball and ran with it • Shelton, who later made *White Men Can't Jump*, was in the minor-leagues himself for five years • The scene in the pool hall where Robbins tells Costner he's joining the top league was originally set and filmed in a brothel, then changed a couple of months later.

Bullitt

★★★ 1968 113min c.

Director: Peter Yates
Screenplay: Harry Kleiner & Alan R. Trustman
Source: Novel, *Mute Witness* by Robert L. Pike

More of a chase movie than a detective film, although McQueen is ostensibly supposed to protect a witness in a case against the Mafia. Although McQueen has charisma in abundance, it's only once the staggeringly influential pursuit through San Francisco's streets begins that the excitement gets under way.

Frank Bullitt	Steve McQueen
Walter Chalmers	Robert Vaughn
Cathy	Jacqueline Bisset
Weissberg	Robert Duvall
Capt. Bennett	Simon Oakland

Delgetti	Don Gordon
Baker	Norman Fell

OOPS! The filmmakers must have been short of cars. During the famous chase, the same black and white cars keep appearing, with one green Beetle being particularly persistent • Even better is the guy outside Safeway's signalling which way the cars should head next • The car McQueen is chasing loses three hubcaps at one point and then, when it smashes into the wall, another three come flying off • When McQueen is standing by a table in a restaurant talking to a pair of women, look out for the man behind who wanders into view and is dragged away • Much fun can be had seeing just how many times McQueen changes gear upwards. It seems to be more than 15 times.

Psst! McQueen was initially reluctant to take on the role. 'I'd never expected to play a cop,' he said. 'As a kid, running the streets, I'd been hassled a lot by the police and I'd always figured that they were on one side of the fence with me on the other. I never felt easy around cops.' However, when he agreed, he spent time on patrol with detectives in San Francisco and developed a new-found respect for his old adversaries • McQueen, a keen driver, did his own driving in the movie • Some cinemagoers are said to have become physically sick during the famous chase through Frisco's humpback streets.

Bus Stop

★★ 1956 96min c.

Director: Joshua Logan
Screenplay: George Axelrod
Source: Play by William Inge

A bar singer in the West is wooed by a simple cowboy. Marilyn is the only reason to watch this, with her sexy rendering of 'That Old Black Magic' the highlight of the film. But although it's hard to take our eyes off her, the plot really is Dullsville, USA and we have to face the fact that just because it's got Monroe in doesn't mean it *has* to be brilliant.

Cherie	Marilyn Monroe
Bo	Don Murray
Virgil	Arthur O'Connell
Grace	Betty Field
Vera	Eileen Heckart
Carl	Robert Bray
Elma	Hope Lange

Psst! Monroe had been studying at the Actors' Studio in New York for over a year. When she returned, she was accompanied by Paula Strasberg, the wife of studio head Lee Strasberg. From here on, her acting coaches would be with her on set, a source of irritation to successive directors. It did nothing to help her remember her lines and take after take was ruined by her getting dialogue wrong • Hope Lange had to have her hair darkened when Monroe complained that it was too similar in shade to hers.

Butch Cassidy and The Sundance Kid
★★★ 1969 112min c.

Director: George Roy Hill
Screenplay: William Goldman

This Western based around the story of real-life outlaws was one of the first buddy movies and, with smashing dialogue to back them up, Redford and Newman make a great team. Sadly, the movie now seems too firmly rooted in the 60s. The flashy direction is irritating in the extreme, the music (of which there is, surprisingly, only 12 minutes) is horrendously dated and it's hard to think of a more insipid heroine than Ross. Fun, but flawed. The 1979 'prequel', *Butch and Sundance: The Early Years* is pleasant but uninspiring.

Butch Cassidy	Paul Newman
The Sundance Kid	Robert Redford
Etta Place	Katharine Ross
Percy Garris	Strother Martin
Bike salesman	Henry Jones
Sheriff Bledsoe	Jeff Corey
Agnes	Cloris Leachman
Marshal	Kenneth Mars
Harvey Logan	Ted Cassidy
Card player	Sam Elliott

Oscars Best Story and Screenplay

Blurb Not That It Matters, But Most Of It Is True!

Quote 'Who are those guys?' • 'Well, that ought to do it.' • 'He'll feel a lot better once we've robbed a couple of banks.' • 'I'm not a sore loser or anything, but when we're done, if I'm dead, kill him.' • 'Dammit, why is everything we're good at illegal?' • 'Next time I say let's go some place like Bolivia, let's go some place like Bolivia.' • 'I think we lost 'em. Do you think we lost 'em?' – 'No.' – 'Neither do I.' • 'Good. For a minute there I thought we were in trouble.' [Last line]

OOPS! If your eyes don't mist up during 'Raindrops Keep Fallin' on my Head', keep them on Katharine Ross. She switches from riding on the handlebars to the crossbar and back again as Newman tries out the new-fangled bicycle • Perhaps it isn't the sort of movie where you should count the bullets, but Redford loads both his six-shooters at one point and then lets off well over 15 shots.

Psst! Goldman originally envisaged Newman playing Sundance rather than Butch • Marlon Brando turned down the role of Sundance, with other suggestions including Warren Beatty, Steve McQueen and even Jack Lemmon. McQueen wouldn't countenance it when he discovered that Newman was to get top billing • Director Hill had injured his back and spent most of the shoot being carried around on a stretcher • Logan, the member of The Hole in the Wall Gang that Newman fights, is better known as Lurch in TV's *The Addams Family* • In reality, Butch Cassidy died peacefully in the late 30s in Washington State • The TV series *Alias Smith and Jones* was based on the film. *Alas Smith and Jones* wasn't.

Cabaret
★★★★ 1972 124min c.

Director: Bob Fosse
Screenplay: Jay Presson Allen
Source: Play by Joe Masteroff, play, *I Am a Camera* by John Van Druten & writings of Christopher Isherwood

An Englishman in Berlin in the early 30s gets involved with an American, who's a singer in a trashy nightclub, and a German aristocrat. The rise of Nazism, and all it involved, is beatifully counterpointed with the songs performed at the Kit Kat Klub. Minnelli, in her greatest screen role, is really far too good to be the untalented Sally Bowles but we aren't complaining. Grey is also outstanding as the distinctly discomforting club MC.

Sally Bowles	Liza Minnelli
Brian Roberts	Michael York
Master of Ceremonies	Joel Grey
Maximillian von Heune	Helmut Griem
Fritz Wendel	Fritz Wepper
Natalia Landauer	Marisa Berenson

Oscars Best Director, Joel Grey, Liza Minnelli

Blurb A Divinely Decadent Experience.

Quote 'Willkommen, bienvenue, welcome.'

- 'Leave your troubles outside. Life is disappointing? In here, life is beautiful.'
- 'Screw Maximilian!' – 'I do.' – 'So do I.'

Psst! Minnelli's clothes came from German charity shops that she plundered to find sufficiently tacky clothes. Her hairstyle was modelled on that of Louise Brooks (see *Pandora's Box*) • The Nazi song 'Tomorrow Belongs to Me' was cut from the film when it was shown in Germany, perhaps sensible in the light of the anti-Semitism that Minnelli and other members of the cast and crew encountered there.

La Cage aux Folles
★★★ 1978 91min c.

Director: Edouard Molinaro
Screenplay: Francis Veber, Edouard Molinaro, Marcello Danon & Jean Poiret
Source: Play by Poiret

A young man brought up by his gay father and his partner announces that he is engaged. When his fiancée and her parents want to meet his folks, his father has to act straight. Things rapidly descend into farce. This droll and surprisingly old-fashioned film was a huge international hit which spawned a pair of lacklustre sequels and a stage musical.

Renato	Ugo Tognazzi
Albin/'Zaza'	Michel Serrault
Charrier	Michel Galabru
Simone	Claire Maurier
Laurent	Remi Laurent
Jacob	Benny Luke

The Caine Mutiny
★★★★ 1954 125min c.

Director: Edward Dmytryk
Screenplay: Stanley Roberts
Source: Play & novel by Herman Wouk

A group of naval officers stand out against an obsessive, tyrannical captain and are court-martialled for mutiny. This untypical role for Bogart is also one of his greatest, with the scenes of him giving evidence, ball-bearings in hand, being one of the most memorable moments in the movies. Cracking stuff.

Capt. Philip Francis Queeg	Humphrey Bogart
Lt. Barney Greenwald	Jose Ferrer
Lt. Steven Maryk	Van Johnson
Lt. Tom Keefer	Fred MacMurray
Ensign Willie Keith	Robert Francis
Lt. Cmdr. Challee	E.G. Marshall
May Wynn	May Wynn
Meatball	Lee Marvin

Blurb As Big As The Ocean.

Quote 'You may tell the crew for me there are four ways of doing thigs on baord my ship: the right way, teh wrong way, the Navy way and my way. If they do things my way, we'll get along.'
• 'Ah, but the strawberries! That's where I had them. They laughed and made jokes, but I proved beyond the shadow of a doubt, and with geometric logic, that a duplicate key to the wardroom icebox did exist. And I'd have produced that key if they hadn't pulled the Caine out of action. I know now they were out to protect some fellow officer.'

Psst! The Navy gave its cooperation and lent various ships in return for the caption at the beginning of the movie saying, 'There has never been a mutiny in the United States Navy,' although producer Stanley Kramer denied this, saying he put it in of his own volition • Surprisingly, the film didn't pick up one Oscar • When asked how he prepared for the character, Bogart answered: 'Simple. Everybody knows I'm nuts anyway.' It was a part he had coveted since the novel appeared in 1951 • For some reason May Wynn's character is called May Wynn • Maurice Micklewhite, looking for a good stage name, changed his surname to Caine after seeing this movie advertised. Thus was born Michael Caine.

Camille
★★★ 1937 108min b/w

Director: George Cukor
Screenplay: Frances Marion, James Hilton & Zoe Akins
Source: Novel & play, *La Dame aux Camelias* by Alexander Dumas fils

One of the Garbo's greatest movies, in which she plays the famous doomed courtesan loved by young Taylor but doing the decent thing. It should be risible and daft, but they all take it so seriously that this tragic romance still gives the tear-ducts a good working out.

Marguérite Gautier	Greta Garbo
Armand Duval	Robert Taylor
M. Duval	Lionel Barrymore

Baron de Varville	Henry Daniell
Nichette	Elizabeth Allan
Nanine	Jessie Ralph
Olympe	Lenore Ulric
Prudence	Laura Hope Crews

Also: Rex O'Malley, E.E. Clive

Quote 'I always look well when I'm near death.'
• 'I wouldn't call her a warm personality. Making a film with Greta Garbo does not constitute an introduction.' [Robert Montgomery]

Psst! Irving Thalberg, talented and influential head of production at MGM, died during the making of the film.

The Candidate

★★★ 1972 109min c.

Director: Michael Ritchie
Screenplay: Jeremy Larner

Although coming from a political family, idealistic Redford runs for the Senate, convinced that he can remain a decent chap and keep his principles intact. It al bowls along happily enough but isn't particularly deep or out of the ordinary.

Bill McKay	Robert Redford
Luck	Peter Boyle
Sen. Crocker Jarmon	Don Porter
Howard Klein	Allen Garfield
John J. McKay	Melvyn Douglas
Nancy McKay	Karen Carlson
Rich Jenkin	Quinn Redeker
Paul Corliss	Michael Lerner

Oscars Best Story and Screenplay

Psst! This is said to be the film that persuaded Dan Quayle he should become a politician.

A Canterbury Tale

★★★ 1944 124min b/w

Director: Michael Powell & Emeric Pressburger
Screenplay: Michael Powell & Emeric Pressburger

In a medieval prologue, a hawk turns into a World War II spitfire. A city girl has glue poured in her hair during a wartime blackout. After that, things begin to get strange. A flop on release, and only recently restored to its proper length, A Canterbury Tale is now seen as one of Powell and Pressburger's most beautiful, haunting and eccentric celebrations of British life. There are

no prizes for guessing who the mysterious glue-thrower is, but the evocative music, quirky characters and breathtaking Kentish scenery make this film quite unique.

Thomas Colpepper, J.P.	Eric Portman
Alison Smith	Sheila Sim
Bob Johnson	John Sweet
Peter Gibbs	Dennis Price
Narrator/Soldier/Village idiot	Esmond Knight
Thomas Duckett	Charles Hawtrey
Woodcock	Hay Petrie
Ned Horton	George Merritt
Jim Horton	Edward Rigby
Prudence Honeywood	Freda Jackson
Organist	Eliot Makeham
Sgt. Stuffy	Graham Moffatt

Psst! In America, the film was cut to 95 minutes and had some extra scenes tacked on with Kim Hunter, in an attempt to explain to audiences what was going on. It didn't work, merely destroying the movie's charm.

Cape Fear

★★★ 1962 105min b/w

Director: J. Lee Thompson
Screenplay: James R. Webb
Source: Novel, The Executioners by John D. MacDonald

A psychopathic rapist is released from prison and wages a campaign of intimidation and violence against the man responsible for putting him behind bars. Although slightly melodramatic in places, this thriller still grips and will have you on the edge of your seat towards the close. Mitchum is truly terrifying and the mood is enhanced by Bernard Herrmann's music and keen use of light and shadow. The remake by Scorsese 30 years later was trickier and thus less gripping.

Sam Bowden	Gregory Peck
Max Cady	Robert Mitchum
Peggy Bowden	Polly Bergen
Nancy Bowden	Lori Martin
Mark Dutton	Martin Balsam
Dave Grafton	Jack Kruschen
Charles Sievers	Telly Savalas
Judge	Edward Platt
Officer Brown	Ward Ramsey

Quote 'Didn't remember me right off, did you? Well, I guess I've changed a little. Where I've been, if you don't change, they're real disappointed.' • 'You're strong, Cady. You're going to live a long life. In a cage. That's where you belong and that's where you're going. And this time for life. Bang your head against the walls. Count the years, the months, the hours. Until the day you rot.' [Last line]

Psst! Making the film could have been risky for Mitchum. Filming took place in Georgia where he had been sentenced in the 30s to time on a chain-gang for vagrancy. He had escaped after just six days. Although 30 years had elapsed he was still, technically, a fugitive.

Capricorn One
★★★★ 1978 127min c.

Director: Peter Hyams
Screenplay: Peter Hyams

When the first manned flight to Mars develops a problem, NASA decide to fake it rather than risk losing funds. A journalist gets a whiff of the story while the astronauts become convinced that they're more at risk on land than they would be in space. Although not always plausible, this cracking thriller is choc-a-bloc with great chases, has a lovely sense of humour and maintains a suitably satisfying air of paranoia. The ending is a real corker.

Robert Caulfield . . . . .Elliott Gould
Col. Brubaker . . . . .James Brolin
Mrs. Brubaker . . . . .Brenda Vaccaro
Lt. Peter Willis . . . . .Sam Waterston
Cmdr. John Walker . . . . .O.J. Simpson
Dr. Kelloway . . . . .Hal Holbrook
Albain . . . . .Telly Savalas
Judy Drinkwater . . . . .Karen Black
Hollis Peaker . . . . .David Huddleston

Captain Blood
★★★ 1935 119min b/w

Director: Michael Curtiz
Screenplay: Casey Robinson
Source: Novel by Rafael Sabatini

A young surgeon is forced by circumstances into piracy, buckling his swash and wooing maidens across the Caribbean. Although a little tatty round the edges, Flynn's tongue-in-cheek, devil-may-care demeanour raises this combination of action and romance above the herd.

Dr. Peter Blood . . . . .Errol Flynn
Arabella Bishop . . . . .Olivia De Havilland

Capt. Levasseur . . . . .Basil Rathbone
Col. Bishop . . . . .Lionel Atwill
Hagthorpe . . . . .Guy Kibbee
Lord Willoughby . . . . .Henry Stephenson
Jeremy Pitt . . . . .Ross Alexander
Also: Robert Barrat, J. Carrol Naish, Donald Meek

Psst! The battles were fought in a studio tank with model ships 18 feet long, with clips from two silent movies, *The Sea Hawk* and *Captain Blood*, spliced in • The movie was originally to star Robert Donat, but because of his fragile health, he had to pull out. Leslie Howard wouldn't take the part so Warners gambled heavily on the virtually-unknown Flynn. The film made him a major star • De Havilland and Flynn were to appear together in eight movies • Apparently Curtiz removed the protective tip from Rathbone's blade before the sword fight on the beach. After telling Rathbone to goad Flynn by telling him how much bigger his pay cheques were, the pair set to with a fury and Flynn's face was nicked, giving him a scar • 27 years later Errol Flynn's son, Sean Flynn, starred in *The Son of Captain Blood*.

Captains Courageous
★★★ 1937 116min b/w

Director: Victor Fleming
Screenplay: John Lee Mahin, Marc Connelly & Dale Van Every
Source: Novel by Rudyard Kipling

A spoilt rich kid with the morals of a multinational tycoon falls off a liner and is picked up by a bunch of modest fisherman. Tracy, sporting an uncomfortable Portuguese accent and a hairstyle that looks as if it's borrowed from Harpo Marx, teaches the lad to behave like a human being. It's rather fey at times, but the quality of the acting and the production still shine out.

Harvey Cheyne . . . . .Freddie Bartholomew
Manuel .Spencer Tracy
Capt. Disko Troop . . . . .Lionel Barrymore
Mr. Cheyne . . . . .Melvyn Douglas
Dan . . . . .Mickey Rooney
Uncle Salters . . . . .Charley Grapewin
'Long Jack' . . . . .John Carradine
Old Clement . . . . .Christian Rub
Burns . . . . .Leo G. Carroll

Oscars Spencer Tracy

Quote 'People give presents after someone's been nice to them, don't they? So what's dishonest with giving presents before someone's nice to you?' • 'I used to pray that something would happen to halt production. I was positive I was doing the worst job of my life.' [Spencer Tracy]

Psst! Freddie Bartholomew, who had starred in *David Copperfield*, was billed above both Tracy and Barrymore • Tracy hated the film. He disliked having to adopt an accent, having his hair curled and, most of all, having to sing a couple of sea shanties. He was, however, to win an Oscar and follow it up next year with another one for *Boys Town*, the only back-to-back Best Actor Oscars until Tom Hanks managed it • When Tracy picked his Oscar up, he saw that it was mistakenly inscribed to 'Dick Tracy'. He thought it funny and kept it as it was.

Carnal Knowledge
★★ 1971 96min c.

Director: Mike Nichols
Screenplay: Jules Feiffer

Lecherous rake Nicholson and college buddy Garfunkel spend whatever time they aren't with women talking about women. This endless jawing about relationships has been done so often now, it's all a bit passé, as well as being tame and surprisingly dull. Attitudes have changed so much in the intervening quarter century that even the most chauvinistic are likely to find Nicholson's boorish behaviour cringe-making.

Jonathan	Jack Nicholson
Sandy	Art Garfunkel
Bobbie	Ann-Margret
Susan	Candice Bergen
Louise	Rita Moreno
Cindy	Cynthia O'Neal
Jennifer	Carol Kane

Quote 'It's not as easy getting laid as it used to be. I don't think I fuck more than a dozen new girls a year now.' • 'Women today are better hung than the men.'

Psst! Nicholson and Garfunkel were playing college boys at the ages, respectively, of 34 and 29 • The film was banned in the State of Georgia for being pornographic.

Carousel
★ 1956 128min c.

Director: Henry King
Screenplay: Phoebe Ephron & Henry Ephron

Source: Musical by Rogers & Hammerstein based on play, *Lilliom* by Ferenc Molnar

Despite a couple of good songs, it's hard to see why this tiresome and drab musical has such a high reputation. The tale of a ne'er-do-well carnival barker trying to make amends when he's in heaven is twee and the story never catches light. Stop the carousel, my good man, I want to get off.

Billy Bigelow	Gordon MacRae
Julie	Shirley Jones
Jigger	Cameron Mitchell
Carrie	Barbara Ruick
Starkeeper	Gene Lockhart
Cousin Nettie	Claramae Turner
Mr. Snow	Robert Rounseville

OOPS! I've never managed to spot it, but others say there's a plane visible flying above the harbour at one point • I'm convinced, though, that during 'June is Bustin' Out All Over' a motorboat can be seen in the distance just as the sailors come dancing up the gangplank.

Psst! Frank Sinatra played the lead for just three days' filming. He claimed he walked because Fox were filming two different versions, one in Cinemascope and one in Todd-AO, and he was only being paid for one. Others claim his voice wasn't up to it.

Carrie
★★★ 1976 97min c.

Director: Brian de Palma
Screenplay: Lawrence D. Cohen
Source: Novel by Stephen King

The film for anyone who's ever been humiliated in a school changing room. Put-upon Carrie exacts telekinetic revenge on her convincingly vicious classmates, as well as on her nagging mom at home. Although a little draggy in the middle, the acting is terrific and there's a breath-taking, knock 'em dead finale. *Carrie* put De Palma on the movie map, and the coronory-inducing epilogue still works its magic despite the endless imitations since.

Carrie White	Sissy Spacek
Margaret White	Piper Laurie
Sue Snell	Amy Irving
Tommy Ross	William Katt
Billy Nolan	John Travolta
Chris Hargenson	Nancy Allen
Miss Collins	Betty Buckley
Mrs. Snell	Priscilla Pointer

Quote 'No flinching – that was the hardest part. I had to stand there looking so happy when I knew any minute the bucket was going to fall. For blood they used syrup, the consistency of honey. I couldn't sit down – I'd stick to the chair.' [Spacek]

Psst! Carrie Fisher was the original choice for the lead but wouldn't do the nude scenes. So she swapped with Spacek who was initially cast as Leia in *Star Wars* • Priscilla Pointer and Amy Irving are mother and daughter in real life too • References to *Psycho* abound. It's easy to spot the blood and showers and the snatches of Bernard Herrmann's music but there's also the lethal mother and the name of the school, Bates High • The Royal Shakespeare Company came up with a musical version in 1988 which was a flop both in Britain and on Broadway.

Carry On Cleo
★★ 1964 92min c.

Director: Gerald Thomas
Screenplay: Talbot Rothwell

The usual team spoof Taylor and Burton's disastrous epic on a slightly more modest scale. The budget did not stretch, as is all too obvious, to filming in sunny Egypt. Yet although not always paying strict attention to historical accuracy, everyone seems to be having a lot of fun and there are plenty of decent laughs, even if it isn't particularly inspired.

Cleo . . . . .Amanda Barrie
Mark Anthony . . . . .Sidney James
Julius Caesar . . . . .Kenneth Williams
Calpurnia . . . . .Joan Sims
Hengist Pod . . . . .Kenneth Connor
Horsa . . . . .Jim Dale
Seneca . . . . .Charles Hawtrey
Senna Pod . . . . .Sheila Hancock
The Soothsayer . . . . .Jon Pertwee
Sergeant-Major . . . . .Victor Maddern
Spencius . . . . .Warren Mitchell

Quote 'Infamy! Infamy! They've all got it in for me!' • 'The eunuchs are on strike. They're complaining about loss of assets.' • 'I've seen your bust.' – 'I wish I could say the same.' • 'I have a poisonous asp.' – 'Oh, I wouldn't say that.'

OOPS! The actors cast shadows on the sky, or what passes for the sky in *Carry On* films • At the opening, when the Roman soldiers near the ancient Britons' settlement, look out for the country house in the background.

Psst! Even six years into the series, this entry still only cost £160,000 • Fox, who had made *Cleopatra* the year before, objected to the similarities in the *Carry on Cleo* poster to their own. The future Lord Hailsham defended our lads, but lost the case and the poster had to be changed. The insurance company paid the legal costs and the film benefited from all the extra publicity • Marks and Spencer were also a little miffed at Warren Mitchell playing Spencius, the brother of Marcus, particularly as their familiar shades of green and gold were used. However, they decided not to go to court over the matter.

Carry On Nurse
★★★ 1959 86min b/w

Director: Gerald Thomas
Screenplay: Norman Hudis

The *Carry On* series got into its stride with the second splendid outing. The patients on a hospital ward run on dictatorial principles by the matron can't face waiting for their copies of the Patients Charter and take matters into their own hands. Of the long-running series, which became saucier but also less subtle as it went on, the most worthwhile are *Cleo, Up the Khyber, Cabby, Spying, Henry, Don't Lose Your Head* and *Camping.*

Bernie Bishop . . . . .Kenneth Connor
Oliver Reckitt . . . . .Kenneth Williams
Hinton .Charles Hawtrey
Nurse Dorothy Denton . . . . .Shirley Eaton
Jack Bell .Leslie Phillips
Nurse Stella Dawson . . . . .Joan Sims
Matron .Hattie Jacques
Percy Hickson . . . . .Bill Owen
Ted York . . . . .Terence Longden
Also: Wilfrid Hyde-White, Joan Hickson, Irene Handl, Jill Ireland, Michael Medwin

Quote 'Come come, matron. Surely you've seen a temperature taken like this before.' – 'Yes, colonel. Many times. But never with a daffodil.' • 'What a fuss about such a little thing.'

Psst! The *'Carry On'* series is the longest running in the history of British cinema, beginning with *Carry On Sergeant* in 1958 and ending, temporarily, with *Carry On Emmanuelle* in 1978. The dreadful *Carry On Columbus* was released in 1992 • *Nurse* was a great hit in America where it ran for over two years at one cinema in Los Angeles • Kenneth Williams holds the record for *Carry On* appearances, making 25 films in the series • While Williams and Sid James got around £5,000 a film, the producer and director got £15,000 each and a third each of the profits on every movie. They did very nicely thank you out of the series.

Carry On up the Khyber

★★★ 1968 88min c.

Director: Gerald Thomas
Screenplay: Talbot Rothwell

The *Carry On* team venture to the far-flung reaches of the British Empire, with the kilted Third Foot and Mouth regiment assigned to defend the pink bits of the map against rebellious Afghans. This is many peoples' favourite in the series, perhaps because it has more of a plot than usual. The scene with diners maintaining stiff upper lips in the midst of an attack is one of the highspots in the *Carry On* canon, while the filmmakers make a virtue of their low budget by showing the Khyber Pass itself as a five-bar gate on a barren hillside in North Wales.

Sir Sidney Ruff-Diamond . . . . . . .Sidney James
The Khazi of Kalabar . . . . .Kenneth Williams
Pte. James Widdle . . . . .Charles Hawtrey
Lady Ruff-Diamond . . . . .Joan Sims
Capt. Keene . . . . .Roy Castle
Bunghit Din . . . . .Bernard Bresslaw
Missionary . . . . .Peter Butterworth
Sgt-Major MacNutt . . . . .Terry Scott
Princess Jelhi . . . . .Angela Douglas
The Fakir . . . . .Cardew Robinson

Quote 'Oh dear, I seem to have got a little plastered.'

Casablanca

★★★★ 1942 102min b/w

Director: Michael Curtiz
Screenplay: Julius J. Epstein, Philip G. Epstein & Howard Koch
Source: Play, *Everybody Comes to Rick's* by Murray Burnett & Joan Alison.

If you die and go to movie heaven, then Rick's is where you will surely head. *Casablanca* has got everything – melodrama, thrills, romance, comedy, politics – blended together into a perfect mixture. A tale of a resistance leader, a bar owner and the woman they both love thrown together in wartime North Africa, this is one of those rare films that gets better with every viewing. In large part this is due not only to the leads, but to a splendid supporting cast. Hokum it may be, but whose heart doesn't stop when Rick first catches sight of Ilsa and whose eye is completely dry when the Marseilleise is struck up? Play it, Sam. Again and again and again.

Rick Blaine . . . . .Humphrey Bogart
Ilsa Lund . . . . .Ingrid Bergman
Victor Laszlo . . . . .Paul Henreid
Capt. Louis Renault . . . . .Claude Rains
Maj. Heinrich Strasser . . . . .Conrad Veidt
Senor Ferrari . . . . .Sydney Greenstreet
Ugarte . . . . .Peter Lorre
Carl, headwaiter . . . . .S.Z. "Cuddles" Sakall
Yvonne . . . . .Madeleine LeBeau
Sam .Dooley Wilson
Annina Brandel . . . . .Joy Page
Berger .John Qualen
Sascha . . . . .Leonid Kinskey
Croupier . . . . .Marcel Dalio
Abdul . . . . .Dan Seymour
Jan Brandel . . . . .Helmut Dantine

Oscars Best Picture, Best Director, Best Screenplay (adapted)

Blurb As Big And Timely A Picture As Ever You've Seen! You Can Tell By The Cast It's Important! Gripping! Big!

Quote 'I came to Casablanca for the waters.' – 'The waters? What waters? We're in the desert.' – 'I was misinformed.' • 'I stick my neck out for nobody.' • 'You despite me, don't you.' – 'If I gave you any thought, I probably would.' • 'Play it, Sam. Play 'As Time Goes By'.' • 'That was the day the Germans marched into Paris…I remember every detail. The Germans were gray, you wore blue' • 'We'll always have Paris.' • 'Of all the gin joints in all the towns in all the world, she walks into mine.' • 'You played it for her. You can play it for me…If she can stand it, I can. Play it.' • 'Was that cannon fire, or is it my heart pounding?' • 'If that plane leaves the ground and you're not with him, you'll regret it. Maybe not today and maybe not tomorrow, but soon, and for the rest of your life.' • 'Ilsa, I'm no good at being noble, but it doesn't take much to see that the problems of three little people don't amount to a hill of beans in this crazy world. Someday you'll understand that.' • 'Here's looking at you, kid.' • 'Round up the usual suspects!' • 'Louis, I think this is the beginning of a beautiful friendship.'

OOPS! Although Ilsa remembers wearing a dress when the Germans marched into Paris, it's actually a suit • Notice how quickly Sam and

Rick are dry after being drenched at the Paris railway station • In the flashback to their days in Paris, he's driving a right-hand drive car • Fog? In North Africa? This probably has a lot to do with trying to cover up the fact that the other airplanes in the airport scene are models • 'Cuddles' Sakall's initials have a 'K' instead of a 'Z' in the credits • Although Ugarte mentions General Weygand's name in connection with the Letters of Transit, they're actually signed by General de Gaulle, hardly a name that would have held much sway with Vichy or the Nazis • Bogart's cigarettes and drinks are good things for gaffe-watchers to keep their eyes on.

Psst! More myths have grown up around this than any other film, most of which have never been satisfactorily debunked. Most importantly Ronald Regan was *never* going to play Rick. When the publicity people announced the movie they plucked contract player Reagan's name out of the hat because he needed a bit of press exposure. Nor did George Raft turn the part down as many say, although his rejecting *High Sierra* had given Bogart his big break. In fact, Bogie was the first choice from the moment the script got under way. He was Warner's newest and brightest star, having just signed a $3,500-a-week contract • It isn't true that no-one knew how the film would finish until the end of filming, as Bergman always claimed. Although the film *was* written as they went along, production records show that Bergman filmed for a fortnight *after* the crucial airport scene was in the can. The very last line did elude them until after filming finished. It was dubbed later by Rains over the scene with him and Bogart walking off into the fog • Bogart was given no idea of what was happening when Curtiz ordered him to stand on the balcony of the café and nod. Only later did he find out that it was the cue for the Battle of the Anthems • Although taller than her when they danced, in reality Bogart was five inches shorter than Bergman was, being the same height as Michael J. Fox. He wore wooden blocks strapped to his shoes to make him look taller • According to Bergman, 'Because of the difficulties with the script we'd all been a bit on edge and I'd hardly got to know Humphrey Bogart at all. Oh, I'd kissed him, but I didn't know him. He was polite, naturally, but I always felt there was a distance; he was behind a wall. I was intimidated by him. *The Maltese Falcon* was playing in Hollywood at the time and I used to go there and see it quite often during the shooting of *Casablanca*, because I felt I got to know him a little better through that picture

• Bogart's marriage to the unstable Mayo Methot was on the rocks and she was becoming so violent that Bogie's agents took out life insurance on him for $100,000. Bogart often slept in the studio rather than face going home • Not only does no-one say 'Play it again, Sam', but Dooley Wilson couldn't have played 'As Time Goes By', no matter how he was asked. He was a drummer, not a pianist and was miming to off-camera pianist Elliot Carpenter • The piano was painted pink so that it would look glowingly white on film. It was sold at auction in 1988 for $154,000 • Max Steiner, Warner's top composer, hated the song 'As Time Goes By' and insisted it be taken out. He only backed down when it was pointed out that refilming was impossible as Bergman's hair had been shorn for *For Whom the Bell Tolls*. The song was actually specified in the original play • In this ultimate film about political refugees, the vast majority of the cast, as well as the director, were themselves Nazi refugees • The famous opening sequence was directed by Don Siegel, later to be known for his collaboration with Clint Eastwood on movies like *Dirty Harry* • The censors tampered with dialogue in two of Rains' scenes, wanting the fact that he was selling visas in return for sex played down. Out went the exchange: 'Another visa problem has come up.' – 'Show her up.' • The play on which the film was based, was first performed four years later and revived in 1991, briefly, in London. In it, Ilsa was less of a noble character and was living with another man, not Laszlo, when knocking around with Rick in Paris. It's his discovery of this that sends him to Casablanca. She later agrees to sleep with him to get the exit visa. However, a surprising amount of what is in the film actually comes from the virtually unknown play. 'Here's good luck to you' was improved a little, as was the line, 'Of all the cafés in all the towns in the world, she walks into my café' • Although due for release in June 1943, Allied forces landed at Casablanca in November 1942 and it was rushed out just 18 days later in New York. Its general release in January coincided with the Casablanca Conference between the Allied Powers • Michael Curtiz, whose mangling of English was immortalised in David Niven's *Bring on the Empty Horses* bounded onto the Academy stage on Oscar night and said: 'So many times I have a speech ready but no dice. Always a bridesmaid, never a mother.' • Not long after *Casablanca*, Bogie's new contract made him the highest-paid actor in the world • When the Marx Brothers were making *Night in Casablanca* in 1946, Warner Brothers wrote to them saying that they had the rights to use 'Casablanca' as they had done it first. Groucho retaliated, in an hilarious exchange of letters, by telling Jack Warner that the Marx Brothers were using the word 'Brothers' long before Warner Brothers started up! 'I just don't understand your attitude,' he said. 'Even if you plan on rereleasing your picture, I am sure that the average movie fan could learn in time to distinguish between Ingrid Bergman and Harpo. I don't know whether I could, but I certainly would like to try.' • Co-writer Julius J. Epstein was not as enamoured of the film as many others. He said it was just: 'A routine assignment. Frankly, I can't understand its staying power. If it were made today, line for line, each performance as good, it'd be laughed off the screen. It's such a phoney picture. Not a word of truth in it. It's camp, kitsch. It's just slick shit!'

Casino Royale
★ 1967 131min c.

Director: John Huston, Ken Hughes, Val Guest, Robert Parrish & Joe McGrath
Screenplay: Wolf Mankowitz, John Law & Michael Sayers
Source: Novel by Ian Fleming

The big question about this lamentable send-up of James Bond is: Why? Could anyone possibly have imagined that this mess would be funny? If so, they were woefully mistaken. Even with a raft of famous names, the only interest to be had is in watching the stars going round with eggs on their faces, sunny side up. There's more humour to be had in 10 minutes of a good 'straight' Bond movie than in this whole sorry farrago.

Evelyn Tremble . . . . .Peter Sellers
Vesper Lynd . . . . .Ursula Andress
Sir James Bond . . . . David Niven
Le Chiffre .Orson Welles
Mata Bond . . . . :. . .Joanna Pettet
Jimmy Bond/Dr. Noah . . . . .Woody Allen
Mimi/Lady Fiona McTarry . . . . . . .Deborah Kerr
Ransome . . . . .William Holden
Also: Charles Boyer, John Huston, George Raft, Jean-Paul Belmondo, Jacqueline Bisset, Ronnie Corbett, Kurt Kasznar, Derek Nimmo, Peter O'Toole

OOPS! Although Niven's mansion is destroyed by a mortar shell, there's a shot just afterwards where it's completely undamaged.

Psst! The original novel by an unknown Ian Fleming had sold only 7,000 copies when it was first published • Sellers and Welles hated each other and, although there is a scene with both of them gambling, they were never actually on set together. Instead, each acted to a double and they were spliced together later.

The Cat and the Canary
★★★ 1939 72min b/w

Director: Elliott Nugent
Screenplay: Walter de Leon & Lynn Starling
Source: Play by John Willard

A young woman stands to inherit a fortune, providing she can remain sane in the standard old dark house, packed with revolving bookcases, secret passages and the like, as well as sinister coves like Sondergaard and Zucco. Still, she's got Hope, full of bravado and with a backbone of custard, to protect her. The mixture of comedy and chills still works pretty well and suits Hope's persona down to the ground. There was an earlier silent version in 1927 and it was remade again, with little to recommend it, in 1979. Goddard and Hope were teamed again in 1940 in the similarly enjoyable scare-comedy, The Ghost Breakers.

Wally Campbell . . . . .Bob Hope
Joyce Norman . . . . .Paulette Goddard
Miss Lu . . . . .Gale Sondergaard
Charlie Wilder . . . . .Douglass Montgomery
Fred Blythe . . . . .John Beal
Lawyer Crosby . . . . .George Zucco
Cicily . . . . .Nydia Westman
Aunt Susan . . . . .Elizabeth Patterson
Hendricks, the boatman . . . . .John Wray
Reporter .Charles Lane

Quote 'Don't these big empty houses scare you?' – 'Not me. I was in vaudeville.' • 'I get goose pimples. Even my goose pimples have goose pimples.'

Cat on a Hot Tin Roof
★★★ 1958 108min c.

Director: Richard Brooks
Screenplay: Richard Brooks & James Poe
Source: Play by Tennessee Williams

Overwrought but enjoyable Southern melodrama with the family vultures gathering around the sickbed of wealthy farmer Ives. For his part, he isn't too impressed with any of them. Like most Tennessee Williams brought to the screen, it's heavily bowdlerised. It's also hammy in places and too obviously derived from a play. But there is some electrifying acting from the leads.

Maggie Pollitt	Elizabeth Taylor
Brick Pollitt	Paul Newman
Big Daddy	Burl Ives
Gooper Pollitt	Jack Carson
Big Mama	Judith Anderson
Mae Pollitt	Madeleine Sherwood
Dr. Baugh	Larry Gates
Deacon Davis	Vaughn Taylor

Quote 'You don't know what love means. To you, it's just another four-letter word.' • 'I've not living with you. We occupy the same cage, that's all.'

Psst! The film was considerably toned down from the original play, with any hints of homosexuality in Newman's character erased • Grace Kelly was originally considered for Taylor's part, but Prince Rainier's hand seemed more attractive to her • Taylor kept working, despite hearing of husband Mike Todd's death in a plane crash in the middle of filming • Ives was the only one in the cast who had been in the play on Broadway.

Cat People
★★★ 1942 73min b/w

Director: Jacques Tourneur
Screenplay: DeWitt Bodeen

A Yugoslavian woman won't consummate her marriage for fear that she will turn into a panther and do away with hubbie. This landmark horror film was the first 'monster' movie that left everything to the imagination rather than make-up, and all the more scary it is as a result. Despite daft moments, once it gets going it really does hold the attention, using its limited resources superbly to rack up the tension and keep it there. Sly, subtle and quite sensual. It was followed by the enjoyable *Curse of the Cat People* and by a sexy and under-rated 1982 remake.

Irena Dubrovna	Simone Simon
Oliver Reed	Kent Smith
Dr. Judd	Tom Conway
Alice Moore	Jane Randolph
Commodore	Jack Holt
Carver	Alan Napier
Zoo keeper	Alec Craig

Blurb Kiss Me And I'll Claw You To Death!

Quote 'Moya sestra. Moya sestra.'

Psst! The filmmakers didn't want to show any sign of any physical creature. But the studio insisted on inserting a shot of a black panther at one point, as well as showing some paw-prints leading away from a savaged sheep, making it feel much more like just another monster movie than intended • The New York apartment house set is actually the one built for *The Magnificent Ambersons*. The staircase is quite clearly the same.

Cat Women of the Moon
★★ 1953 64min b/w

Director: Arthur Hilton
Screenplay: Roy Hamilton

One of the funniest bad movies ever, with astronauts travelling to the moon and finding it inhabited by the catsuited Hollywood Cover Girls who plan to steal their ship and take over the earth. Laughably ignorant of even the most basic scientific principles, we are treated to such delights as giant moon spiders dangling from string and a corrugated iron spaceship with the astronauts working in chairs mounted on castors. Ed Wood probably wished he had made it. Originally filmed in 3-D, it did well enough for a sequel, *Missile to the Moon*, to be made. Sadly, it wasn't anything like as funny.

With: Douglas Fowley, Victor Jory, Sonny Tufts, Marie Windsor, The Hollywood Cover Girls

Charade
★★★★ 1963 113min c.

Director: Stanley Donen
Screenplay: Peter Stone
Source: Story, *The Unsuspecting Wife* by Stone and Marc Behm

After her husband is murdered, Hepburn is pestered by three of his shady colleagues who believe she knows where a fortune looted by her husband is. She has help from Matthau and Grant but soon comes to doubt who is friend and who foe. Time has been kind to this classic romantic thriller in the Hitchcock mould which not only has a decent plot, but lashings of black humour, a neat romance and some great action.

Peter Joshua	Cary Grant
Regina Lambert	Audrey Hepburn
Hamilton Bartholomew	Walter Matthau
Tex Penthollow	James Coburn
Herman Scobie	George Kennedy
Leopold Gideon	Ned Glass
Insp. Edouard Grandpierre	Jacques Marin

Quote 'I don't bite, you know…unless it's called for.' • 'Do you know what's wrong with you?' – 'No. What?' – 'Nothing.'

Psst! Cary Grant was originally unwilling to take on the role because of the gap of 25 years between him and Hepburn. He became happier when the writers found a way to make a joke out of it.

The Charge of the Light Brigade

★★★ 1936 115min b/w

Director: Michael Curtiz
Screenplay: Michel Jacoby & Rowland Leigh
Source: Poem by Alfred, Lord Tennyson.

With the exception of the lines of the poem, there's almost nothing historically accurate in this film, which is largely based not in the Crimea but in India. However, taken on its own merits, it's a rousing, swashbuckling, adventure yarn with Flynn getting on the wrong side of an Indian ruler. In addition to some great action sequences there's plenty of time for romance. The more reliable 1968 film of the same name is spoilt by too much 60s tricksiness.

Maj. Geoffrey Vickers	Errol Flynn
Elsa Campbell	Olivia De Havilland
Capt. Perry Vickers	Patric Knowles
Sir Charles Macefield	Henry Stephenson
Sir Benjamin Warrenton	Nigel Bruce
Col. Campbell	Donald Crisp
Capt. Randall	David Niven
Surat Khan	C. Henry Gordon
Count Igor Volonoff	Robert Barrat
Lady Octavia Warrenton	Spring Byington
Sir Humphrey Harcourt	E.E. Clive
Subahdar-Maj. Puran Singh	J. Carrol Naish

OOPS! Almost every time it is seen, the Union Jack is flying upside down. The thin band of white should be on top in the right-hand corner.

Psst! This is the source of one of David Niven's best stories. Director Curtiz had a shaky grasp of English and at one point ordered a hundred riderless horses to be let loose with the command: 'Bring on the empty horses'. When he saw Flynn and Niven laughing, he yelled: 'You and your stinking language! You think I know fuck nothing. Well, let me tell you, I know fuck all.' • After their success together in *Captain Blood*, Flynn fell for De Havilland. His wooing methods, involving pranks like leaving a dead snake in her knickers, did not go down well with the demure De Havilland. Her friend Bette Davis later wrote that Flynn adored her to the end, but that she, almost alone among Hollywood ladies, never capitulated to him • Trip wires were used to get the horses to fall, a fairly standard movie practice in those days. Several horses broke their legs, though, and had to be put down. The Society for the Prevention of Cruelty to Animals protested so vociferously that new rules were brought in to improve animal welfare on films.

Chariots of Fire

★★★ 1981 123min c.

Director: Hugh Hudson
Screenplay: Colin Welland

This story of two dedicated but very different British athletes competing in the 1924 Olympics was wildly overpraised at the time, probably because nobody ever expected the British to make an enjoyable movie again. Now that the fuss has died down, it's clear that it is pleasant, rather than exceptional. However, despite a tendency for the story to meander, there are still several scenes that stir the blood and quicken the pulse. Now it no longer irritates us by pouring incessantly out of every loudspeaker we pass, Vangelis' music helps the mood greatly.

Harold Abrahams	Ben Cross
Eric Liddell	Ian Charleson
Lord Andrew Lindsay	Nigel Havers
Aubrey Montague	Nicholas Farrell
Sam Mussabini	Ian Holm
Master of Trinity	John Gielgud
Master of Caius	Lindsay Anderson
Jennie Liddell	Cheryl Campbell
Sybil Gordon	Alice Krige
Lord Cadogan	Patrick Magee
Lord Birkenhead	Nigel Davenport

Oscars Best Picture, Best Screenplay

Quote 'I believe God made me for a purpose…But He also made me fast. When I run, I feel His pleasure.' • 'The British are coming.' [The sadly over-optimistic Welland picking up his Oscar] • 'A tedious, propagandistic film. How it ever won the Oscar is beyond me...I think the music score swayed the voters...I think if one watches *Chariots of Fire* a second time, one realises there is less there than meets the eye.' [Ian Charleson]

OOPS! The shirts of the American runners bear the American 50-star flag when there were only 48 states • Back then, Canada's flag wasn't the Maple Leaf. They used the Union Jack • During one of his races, Charleson sets off with a note in his hand. It disappears half-way through but is back in his hand at the end • A girl who gets Charleson's autograph at the meeting in East Wemyss, asks him for it again in Edinburgh where she is wearing the same clothes.

Psst! The actors underwent two months of tough training to make them look convincing. By the time filming started, Ben Cross could do 500 push-ups in one session • For his part, Charleson studied the Bible as well as running five miles around Hyde Park each day • The race against the clock in the Great Court of Cambridge's Trinity College never took place. Lord Burghley, a friend of Abrahams and the model for Lord Lindsay, was the one who managed to beat the chimes • Historical inaccuracy wasn't the reason the authorities at Trinity wouldn't let the cameras in. They just didn't want nasty, grubby movie people invading their hallowed portals. So the less stuffy Eton appears instead, director Hudson being an old boy • Liverpool locations substituted for Paris, which was beyond the reach of the modest budget • At the same 1924 Olympics was American swimmer Johnny Weissmuller, later to become *Tarzan*.

Charley Varrick
★★★★ 1973 111min c.

Director: Don Siegel
Screenplay: Dean Riesner & Howard Rodman
Source: Novel, *The Looters* by John Reese.

Matthau is superb in this excellent thriller that looks even better 20 years later, thanks to its ingenious and witty script. He plays a small-time crook who mistakenly steals money from the Mafia and has to use every ounce of his cunning if he is to outwit the hitman they send after him as well as the police. For once in this sort of film, the ending isn't a cop-out.

Charley Varrick . . . . .Walter Matthau
Molly . . . . .Joe Don Baker
Sybil Fort . . . . .Felicia Farr

Harman Sullivan . . . . .Andrew Robinson
Jewell Everett . . . . .Sheree North
Maynard Boyle . . . . .John Vernon
Mr. Garfinkle . . . . .Norman Fell
Honest John . . . . .Benson Fong

Psst! Director Don Siegel appears in a brief cameo as a table tennis player • Siegel said of Matthau: 'One of the funniest men I've ever worked with and didn't understand anything about the movie at all. When i showed him the first cut all he said was, "Well, I got to admit it's a picture, but can anyone tell me what the hell it's all about?"'

Charlie Bubbles
★★ 1968 91min c.

Director: Albert Finney
Screenplay: Shelagh Delaney

A working-class writer strikes it rich but is bored stiff by the good life and just wants to be able to turn the clock back. The romance with secretary Minnelli is touching and one or two scenes, as in the restaurant, are still very funny. By and large, though, it has not improved with age.

Charlie Bubbles . . . . .Albert Finney
Lottie . . . . .Billie Whitelaw
Smokey Pickles . . . . .Colin Blakely
Eliza . . . . .Liza Minnelli
Jack Bubbles . . . . .Timothy Garland
Accountant . . . . .Richard Pearson
Lawyer . . . . .Peter Sallis
Maud .Diana Coupland
Also: Yootha Joyce, Joe Gladwin

Psst! This was Liza Minnelli's screen debut • In America, the Production Code Administration wanted to ban the film for its hint of oral sex. Instead, it was released by a company that wasn't governed by the Code.

Un Chien Andalou
★★★★ 1928 17min b/w

Director: Luis Buñuel
Screenplay: Luis Buñuel & Salvador Dali

There's no point trying to outline the plot in this most famous of avant-garde films. Co-writers Buñuel and Dali rejected any image they could 'explain' at the script stage. Wisely kept as a short, this surreal film remains creepy, bizarre and funny even 60 years later. The eye-slitting opening will still have the most hardened gore-hound gibbering uncontrollably behind the sofa.

The cyclist	.Pierre Batcheff
The woman	.Simone Mareuil

Also: Salvador Dali, Luis Buñuel

Psst! Buñuel appears in the opening sequence. It is him smoking the cigarette and sharpening the razor • Those concerned about the actress' welfare can rest assured that the eye used belonged to a cow • Those concerned about animal welfare had better avoid the film entirely. There is still debate about whether Buñuel killed the donkeys and whether he stole the severed head from a mortuary or not • Some of his critics, including George Orwell, thought that he had a sick mind • Buñuel only directed one other film, *L'Age d'Or*, until 1947.

The China Syndrome
★★★ 1979 122min c.

Director: James Bridges
Screenplay: Mike Gray, T.S. Cook & James Bridges

After a near-major disaster at a nuclear plant is covered up, engineer Lemmon tries desperately to make management realise the danger resulting from cost-saving in its construction. His only ally is TV reporter Fonda. This is one of the better conspiracy thrillers. Although it takes itself a little too seriously at times, it is genuinely chilling. If you want to understand the title, then watch the movie.

Kimberly Wells	.Jane Fonda
Jack Godell	.Jack Lemmon
Richard Adams	.Michael Douglas
Herman De Young	.Scott Brady
Bill Gibson	.James Hampton
Don Jacovich	.Peter Donat
Ted Spindler	.Wilford Brimley

Also: Richard Herd, James Karen

Quote 'I can feel it....'

Psst! Michael Douglas was the movie's producer. He had problems trying to raise the money and found he hadn't enough to pay for Richard Dreyfuss as Adams. His price had soared after the success of *Close Encounters* and *The Goodbye Girl*. So he played the part himself • Although it may have seemed fantastical when they were making it, weeks after the film opened came the accident with the Three Mile Island nuclear reactor, which didn't do the box office any harm at all

• Unusually for a modern mainstream movie, there is no background music at all. A composer did work on a score, but Douglas thought that adding the music made it seem silly.

Chinatown
★★★★ 1974 131min c.

Director: Roman Polanski
Screenplay: Robert Towne

This deliciously tortuous labyrinthine thriller is still quite simply one of the greatest movies of all time. Set in the 30s, Nicholson is the seedy private eye who gets pulled into a quicksand of corruption, murder and incest by *femme fatale* Dunaway. The witty script is so tortuous that it may need more than one viewing before you reckon you've nailed the plot down. But with such a wonderfully atmospheric film, who could complain about having to watch it again? The much-troubled sequel, *The Two Jakes*, was released in 1990. Hated by most critics, it's one of my favourite movies of the past few years.

J.J. Gittes	.Jack Nicholson
Evelyn Mulwray	.Faye Dunaway
Noah Cross	.John Huston
Escobar	.Perry Lopez
Yelburton	.John Hillerman
Hollis Mulwray	.Darrell Zwerling
Ida Sessions	.Diane Ladd
Man with knife	.Roman Polanski

Also: Richard Bakalyan, Roy Jensen, Joe Mantell, James Hong

Oscars Best Screenplay

Quote 'He passed away two weeks ago and he bought the land a week ago. That's unusual.' • 'I don't get tough with anyone, Mr. Gittes. My lawyer does.' • 'She's my sister…and my daughter.' • 'Forget it, Jake. It's Chinatown.'

Psst! Director Polanski appears as the hood who slashes Nicholson's nose • The film was nominated for 11 Oscars, but only won the one for Best Screenplay • Ali MacGraw was going to play Dunaway's part, but her marriage to producer Robert Evans broke up and, when Jane Fonda turned the part down, Dunaway was hired • Dunaway and Polanski did not get on. She found him a tyrant and he found her unnecessarily precious about her role, later saying: 'She was a gigantic pain in the ass. She demonstrated certifiable proof of insanity.' It was a view with which Nicholson agreed, calling her 'certifiable'. • To writer Towne's annoyance,

Polanski rewrote the ending • Nicholson was dreading the scene where he gets washed down the storm drain. He came down so fast his shoes made huge dents in the mesh at the opening. Luckily, only the one take was needed.

Chitty Chitty Bang Bang

★ 1968 144min c.

Director: Ken Hughes
Screenplay: Roald Dahl & Ken Hughes
Source: Novel by Ian Fleming

This vehicle definitely came off the production line late on a Friday. An inventor and two kids in their flying car butt heads with the rules of a kingdom which very sensibly discriminates against children. Although it starts well enough, once the fantasy gets under way it gets steadily more tedious and silly. And, boy, is it long! The special effects, on which the movie hinges, are absolutely pathetic (though I don't remember thinking that when I was a kid). The only high spot is Jeffries singing 'POSH'. Children may still enjoy it, though you may want to farm them out for adoption if they do.

Caractacus Potts	Dick Van Dyke
Truly Scrumptious	Sally Ann Howes
Grandpa Potts	Lionel Jeffries
Baron Bomburst	Gert Frobe
Baroness Bomburst	Anna Quayle
Toymaker	Benny Hill
Lord Scrumptious	James Robertson Justice
Child catcher	Robert Helpmann
Jeremy Coggins	Adrian Hall
Jemima	Heather Ripley
Coggins	Desmond Llewelyn

Also: Victor Maddern, Arthur Mullard, Stanley Unwin, Max Wall, Barbara Windsor

OOPS! Using the freeze-frame on the video, you should see some distinctly modern caravans reflected in the chrome of Chitty's bonnet while Van Dyke takes the kids for a spin, just as they're singing: 'You're sleek as a thoroughbred'.

A Christmas Carol

SEE: Scrooge

Christmas in Connecticut

★★ 1945 101min b/w

Director: Peter Godfrey
Screenplay: Lionel Houser & Adele Comandini

A columnist reknowned for being the efficient housewife has to conjure up a family or face exposure as the result of a publicity stunt arranged by her publisher. Although it has its moments, time hasn't been too kind to this seasonal fare. The humour now seems forced and artificial while the story is so light and insubstantial, it would float away altogether if there was just one breath of fresh air.

Elisabeth Lane	Barbara Stanwyck
Jefferson Jones	Dennis Morgan
Alexander Yardley	Sydney Greenstreet
John Sloan	Reginald Gardiner
Felix Bassenak	S.Z. "Cuddles" Sakall
Dudley Beecham	Robert Shayne
Norah	Una O'Connor
Sinkewicz	Frank Jenks
Mary Lee	Joyce Compton

Christmas in July

★★★ 1940 67min b/w

Director: Preston Sturges
Screenplay: Preston Sturges

Despite his enormous reputation, Sturges' once-great screwball comedies no longer have the bite they did in the past. However, this tale of a chap thinking he's won $25,000 as a result of a practical joke remains a sweet confection. It may be amusing rather than downright hilarious, but the wonderful company of supporting actors that Sturges used time and again keep us glued to the screen.

Jimmy MacDonald	Dick Powell
Betty Casey	Ellen Drew
Dr. Maxford	Raymond Walburn
Schindel	Alexander Carr
Bildocker	William Demarest
Mr. Baxter	Ernest Truex
The announcer	Franklin Pangborn
Mr. Waterbury	Harry Hayden
Mrs. MacDonald	Georgia Caine
Mild gentleman	Arthur Hoyt
Thin sour gentleman	Jimmy Conlin
Mr. Jenkins	Byron Foulger
Cashier	Arthur Stuart Hull
Man at shoeshine stand	Preston Sturges
Large gentleman	Robert Warwick

Quote 'If you can't sleep at night, it isn't the coffee, it's the bunk!'

Cible Emouvante

SEE: Wild Target

Cinema Paradiso
★★★★ 1990 124min c.

Director: Giuseppe Tornatore
Screenplay: Giuseppe Tornatore

A cinema director returning home to Sicily reminisces about his childhood, his obsession with the local cinema and his friendship with gruff projectionist Noiret. This is an utterly delightful, moving and often very funny Italian tribute to the power of the movies. Understandably, this has become one of the favourite films of all those who love the cinema. There is also a director's cut which is half an hour longer and, although more densely layered, it's also rather more downbeat.

Alfredo .Philippe Noiret
Salvatore . . . . .Jacques Perrin
Salvatore as child . . . . .Salvatore Cascio
Salvatore as adolescent . . . . . .Mario Leonardi
Elena . . . . .Agnese Nano
Father Adelfio . . . . .Leopoldo Trieste

Quote 'Life isn't like the movies. Life is harder.

Showing Modern Times • Stagecoach • Dr. Jekyll and Mr. Hyde • And God Created Woman • La Strada.

OOPS! *And God Created Woman* was made in 1957, which makes screening it in a tiny Sicilian cinema in 1954 pretty unlikely.

The Citadel
★★★ 1938 113min c.

Director: King Vidor
Screenplay: Ian Dalrymple, Elizabeth Hill, Frank Wead & Emlyn Williams
Source: Novel by A.J. Cronin

An idealistic doctor gives up his practice in a mining community when the bright lights and easy money of London beckon. Because this is Robert Donat, we just know that events will conspire to open his eyes to his selfishness and folly. Despite the predictability and a feeling that we've seen all this in umpteen TV series, the acting and production values are still good enough to carry us along with it.

Andrew Manson . . . . .Robert Donat
Christine Manson . . . . .Rosalind Russell
Denny . . . . .Ralph Richardson
Dr. Lawford . . . . .Rex Harrison
Owen . . . . .Emlyn Williams
Toppy LeRoy . . . . .Penelope Dudley-Ward

Ben Chenkin . . . . .Francis L. Sullivan
Mrs. Orlando . . . . .Mary Clare
Charles Every . . . . .Cecil Parker
Mrs. Thornton . . . . .Nora Swinburne
Joe Morgan . . . . .Edward Chapman
Lady Raebank . . . . .Athene Seyler
Mr. Boon . . . . .Felix Aylmer

Psst! This was made by MGM's British arm, also responsible for productions like *A Yank at Oxford*. Sadly, it was brought to an end by the onset of war • Cronin was actually a doctor before turning to writing and the book was semi-autobiographical.

Citizen Kane
★★ 1941 119min b/w

Director: Orson Welles
Screenplay: Herman J. Mankiewicz & Orson Welles

It's time for the Emperor to cast off his new clothes. Although widely regarded by critics as the best movie of all time, somebody should point out that this quasi-documentary tale of an increasingly remote newspaper magnate is actually rather tedious. We all know that it was incredibly innovative. Deep focus photography meant you could see foreground and background at one and the same time. We also get to see ceilings for almost the first time in the movies. Big deal. We can see ceilings any time by lying down at home. Despite the fantastic look to *Kane* and all Welles' tricks, the story itself drags along at a snail's pace and has been imitated so many times that it no longer seems in the least bit fresh. It's a cold film about a cold man about whom we care little. As for the resolution, what a load of fuss over a bit of wood. What's more, there's not one good car chase in the whole movie.

Charles Foster Kane . . . . .Orson Welles
Jedediah Leland . . . . .Joseph Cotten
Susan Alexander . . . . .Dorothy Comingore
Mr. Bernstein . . . . .Everett Sloane
Boss J.W. 'Big Jim' Gettys . . . . .Ray Collins
Walter Parks Thatcher . . . . . .George Coulouris
Raymond .Paul Stewart
Mary Kane . . . . .Agnes Moorehead
Kane's father . . . . .Harry Shannon
Emily Norton . . . . .Ruth Warrick
Herbert Carter . . . . .Erskine Sanford
Jerry Thompson . . . . .William Alland
Reporter with pipe . . . . .Alan Ladd

Oscars Best Screenplay

Quote 'Last week, as it must to all men, death came to Charles Foster Kane.' • 'Old age…it's the only disease, Mr. Thompson, that you don't look forward to being cured of.' • 'I run a couple of newspapers. What do you do?' • 'One day back in 1896 I was crossing over to Jersey on the ferry, and as we pulled out there was another ferry pulling in, and on it there was a girl waiting to get off. A white dress she had on. She was carrying a white parasol. I only saw her for one second. She didn't see me at all, but I'll bet a month hasn't gone by since that I haven't thought of that girl.' • 'sure we're speaking, Jedediah. You're fired.' • 'Rosebud…'

OOPS! Because of a shortage of funds, in the scene in the projection room Joseph Cotten can be spotted doubling up as an extra.

Psst! When, aged 25, Welles first walked onto a Hollywood sound stage to start *Kane* he said: 'This is the biggest electric train set any boy ever had.' • Welles reportedly saw *Stagecoach* 40 times to study moviemaking before embarking on the project • Early title ideas were *American* and *John Citizen, USA* • Welles was not one to credit others when he could take credit for himself. Despite his self-publicity, much of the kudos for the script should be placed at the door of Mankiewicz. According to writer Nunnally Johnson: 'Orson looked over the credits for the picture. "Orson Welles, in *Citizen Kane*. Produced by Orson Welles. Directed by Orson Welles. Screenplay by Herman J. Mankiewicz and Orson Welles." And there was something in that list that seemed wrong to Orson.' Johnson claims Welles offered Mankiewicz $10,000 if he would take his name off the film. In the end, Welles had to be forced by the Screenwriters' Guild to credit his co-author • Welles worked his cast hard, with Cotten being forced to stay awake for 24 hours before the scene where he's drunk. 100 takes for a scene wasn't unusual • Comingore was pregnant on the movie and care had to be taken that the camera didn't show her condition • Sadly, the life of Comingore closely mirrored the character of Susan Alexander. Her marriage failed, her husband got custody of the children and she was later arrested for soliciting. Although there was shock in Hollywood when her careworn face appeared in the papers, she died penniless a few years later • Unsurprisingly, newspaper tycoon William Randolph Hearst went to great lengths to prevent the film being made or distributed. MGM's head, Louis B. Mayer, a mate of his, tried to buy up the negative so that it could be burnt. Welles had to threaten to sue RKO before they would release it • Although the critics were generally favourable, many in Hollywood were terrified of upsetting Hearst and, at the Oscar ceremony, the nominations for *Kane* were booed. This may, though, have been in large part industry irritation at Welles' precociousness • Hearst prohibited his newspapers from mentioning Welles' name. But when the Los Angeles Examiner campaigned for cash to help Mexican earthquake victims, the paper offered to print the name of every contribution of $25. Welles sent in his money. After much prevarication, the name was published: 'O. Welles, $25.00.' • Rumour has it that one of the reasons William Randolph Hearst was so incensed by the film was that 'Rosebud' was actually his pet name for mistress Marion Davies' clitoris • A print of *Kane* was sent to Hearst but it was sent back unopened • The reporter with the pipe in the scene where the massive collection of Kane is being packed up is Alan Ladd. His fortunes improved dramatically after he married his agent • The remaining sledge (two having been burned) was bought by Steven Spielberg for $60,000. On hearing this, Orson Welles said: 'Not that he would pay me that to write a script.'

City Lights
★★ 1931 86min b/w

Director: Charles Chaplin
Screenplay: Charles Chaplin

A tramp – actually *the* tramp – falls in love with a blind girl who believes him to be a wealthy man. Although there are some very funny scenes, Chaplin let his sentimental side run away with him here and all but his most adamant fans may find they'll need a sturdy brown bag to hand. Although released four years after talkies began, there's no dialogue. It isn't strictly a silent film, though, as it does have synchronised music and sound effects.

The Little Tramp . . . . .Charles Chaplin
The Blind Girl . . . . .Virginia Cherrill
The Eccentric Millionaire . . . . . . .Harry C. Myers
Prize Fighter . . . . .Hank Mann

Psst! Ever the perfectionist, it took Chaplin a record 342 takes until he was satisfied with the scene where the blind flower girl sells him a flower believing that he's a millionaire • Whereas most films shoot roughly 10 times more film than is needed, Chaplin apparently shot 125 times more than ended up in the movie, one of the most extravagant ratios of all time • Chaplin composed the score himself • Jean Harlow appears as an unbilled extra in the café scene. She then went under the name of Jean Pope.

City Slickers
★★★ 1991 114min c.

Director: Ron Underwood
Screenplay: Lowell Ganz & Babaloo Mandel

Three friends play at cowboys during a cattle drive, watched over by tough guy Palance who deservedly picked up an Oscar for his brilliant, dead-pan performance. This comedy combines an engrossing story with some wonderfully funny lines. A winner, despite a layer of gooey sentiment at the finale. The sequel was watchable, with the only inspired thing about it being the way the film-makers resurrected a dead character.

Mitch Robbins . . . . .Billy Crystal
Phil Berquist . . . . .Daniel Stern
Ed Furillo . . . . .Bruno Kirby
Barbara Robbins . . . . .Patricia Wettig
Bonnie Rayburn . . . . .Helen Slater
Curly . . . . .Jack Palance
Barry Shalowitz . . . . .Josh Mostel
Ira Shalowitz . . . . .David Paymer
Clay Stone . . . . .Noble Willingham

Oscars Jack Palance

Blurb Yesterday They Were Businessmen. Today They're Cowboys. Tomorrow They'll Be Walking Funny.

Quote 'The older you get, the younger your girlfriends get. Pretty soon you'll be dating sperm.' • 'Women need a reason to have sex. Men just need a place.'

OOPS! The flowers on Curly's grave mysteriously vanish • Earlier, as he's riding with Billy Crystal, Curly's cigarette keeps changing length.

Psst! Palance holds the record for the longest gap between an Oscar nomination and getting the statuette. It took 39 years from his first nomination in 1952 to picking up the Oscar and doing one-armed press-ups in front of billions of people • Bonnie is played by Helen Slater, star of the disastrous 1984 film *Supergirl* • Odd, isn't it, how despite all those cows, we never once see a cow-pat? Come to think of it, do we *ever* see a cow-pat in any Western movie? • Known in France as *Life, Love and Cows*.

Cleopatra
★ 1963 243min c.

Director: Joseph L. Mankiewicz
Screenplay: Joseph L. Mankiewicz, Ranald MacDougall & Sidney Buchman
Source: Works of Plutarch, Suetonius, Appian & *The Life and Times of Cleopatra* by C.M. Franzero

If you ever wondered why the big costume epic died out, look no further than this monstrously ineffective four-hour Valentine from Liz Taylor to herself, courtesy of a studio that couldn't control her. Sporting so much cleavage and eyeliner, no self-respecting asp would dare bite her, this Cleo obviously gets her way by boring everyone into submission. Sadly, it isn't bad enough to be funny and anyone curious to see her and Burton smouldering together can get a fix with just a few minutes and do something more useful with their life for the rest of the time. The less well-known 1934 version of the story with Claudette Colbert is exactly the opposite, being shorter and surprisingly sexy in places.

Cleopatra . . . . .Elizabeth Taylor
Mark Antony . . . . .Richard Burton
Julius Caesar . . . . .Rex Harrison
High Priestess . . . . .Pamela Brown
Flavius . . . . .George Cole
Sosigenes . . . . .Hume Cronyn
Also: Cesare Danova, Kenneth Haigh, Andrew Keir, Martin Landau, Roddy McDowall, John Hoyt, Carroll O'Connor, Michael Gwynn, Richard O'Sullivan, Robert Stephens, Francesca Annis

Quote 'I only came to see the asp.' [Addams' Family creator Charles Addams] • 'This picture was conceived in a state of emergency, shot in confusion, and wound up in blind panic.' [Writer-director Joseph L. Mankiewicz] • 'The toughest three pictures I ever made.' [Mankiewicz] • 'Elizabeth Taylor is the first Cleopatra to sail down the Nile to Las Vegas.' [Anonymous critic] • 'I facetiously suggested billing the picture "Elizabeth Taylor in *Heat*" and it took the Fox executives a while to realize that I wasn't really serious.'[Rex Harrison] • 'It will be fun to be the first Jewish Queen of Egypt.' • 'I really don't remember much about *Cleopatra*. There were a lot of other things going on.' [Elizabeth Taylor]

OOPS! When Cleopatra is carried through the gigantic arch in Rome, the tell-tale shadows of scaffolding can clearly be seen on the head of the massive sphinx on which she is riding. If you don't spot this, content yourself with knowing that the arch itself wasn't built until after Cleopatra's death • On a more modest scale, when Cleo is taking a bath, there's a sponge floating in the water that the eagle-eyed have pointed out could be bought for a few pence from any local store.

Psst! At the time, the most expensive film ever made, with a final cost of $44m • Such was the advance publicity, mostly about events behind the camera, that $14m had been taken in advance bookings before it opened • It was the longest mainstream movie ever shown in America until *Gettysburg* in 1993 • Elizabeth Taylor became the first actress to receive over $1m for a movie • Initially the film had been conjured up as a much smaller-scale venture for Joan Collins to star in • Much of the excitement came from prurient interest in the fact that Burton and Taylor, both married to other people, became lovers during the making of the film. Their infatuation led to long and costly delays on the movie, made still worse by Taylor's ill health. Taylor's then-husband Eddie Fisher was reportedly paid $1,500 a day to see that she got to the set on time. Presumably, he didn't receive much of his pay • One day's filming was wiped out when Burton's wife Sybil turned up on set. Taylor cried so much that her eyes were too puffy for shooting the following day • Director Mankiewicz said to one curious reporter: 'The real story is that Richard Burton and I are in love, and Elizabeth Taylor is being used as our cover-up.' • The production started in London but, after nine months filming costing $5m, it relocated to Italy and had to start all over again. Taylor had been ill, the weather had been terrible and director Rouben Mamoulian was replaced by Mankiewicz • 26,000 costumes were used on the movie, with Taylor's wardrobe for the movie establishing a record with a total bill of almost $200,000. Forty out of the 105 costumes designed for Taylor were only used for scenes that were then left on the cutting-room floor. The dress she wears when she enters Rome is covered in 24-carat gold • Taylor moored her own yacht on the barge set and took the opportunity of breaks in filming to get a suntan, popping her costume on over her bikini whenever she was needed for a scene. Her steadily darkening skin caused severe problems and, in the end, they resorted to correcting the colour of the film as the only way of concealing it • Taylor's conversion to Judaism meant it was banned in most Arabian countries, including Egypt • In close-ups, you can sometimes see the scar from Taylor's emergency tracheotomy.

The Clock
★★★ 1945 90min b/w

Director: Vincente Minnelli
Screenplay: Robert Nathan & Joseph Schrank
Source: Story by Paul & Pauline Gallico

A soldier on 48 hours leave in wartime New York meets a girl and they fall in love. This small-scale romantic drama is one of the all-time great charmers, a heart-warming confection that proved just how good an actress Garland could be when she wasn't exercising her pipes.

Alice Mayberry	Judy Garland
Cpl. Joe Allen	Robert Walker
Al Henry	James Gleason
Luncheonette Drunk	Keenan Wynn
Mrs. Al Henry	Lucille Gleason
Bill	Marshall Thompson
Michael Henry	Chester Clute
Cop	Ray Teal

Psst! Garland and director Minnelli would later marry • The man from whom Robert Walker gets a light near the start of the movie is Arthur Freed, the songwriter turned producer who would be responsible for movies like *The Pirate* and *Singin' in the Rain* • Although at the time people swore that the movie was made in New York, it was all studio-based, using a great deal of back-projection. One of the sets was a complete replica of Pennsylvania Station, built to the full size.

A Clockwork Orange
★★ 1971 137min c.

Director: Stanley Kubrick
Screenplay: Stanley Kubrick
Source: Novel by Anthony Burgess

In its day, this was a watershed film in the portrayal of sex and violence, and is still officially unavailable in Britain. Malcolm McDowell is excellent as gang leader Alex who, after his arrest for murder, is subjected to crime-aversion therapy, with disastrous results. Following *Robocop*, it's now hard to see what all the fuss is about. It's visually dazzling, moral and still very topical, although some of the later scenes could use shortening.

Alex	Malcolm McDowell
Mr. Alexander	Patrick Magee
Chief guard	Michael Bates

Mrs. Alexander . . . . .Adrienne Corri
Dim . . . . .Warren Clarke
Stage actor .John Clive
Georgie . . . . .James Marcus
Lodger . . . . .Clive Francis
Cat lady . . . . .Miriam Karlin
Also: Aubrey Morris, Steven Berkoff, David Prowse, John Savident, Margaret Tyzack, Carol Drinkwater

Blurb Being The Adventures Of A Young Man Whose Principal Interests Are Rape, Ultra-Violence And Beethoven.

Quote 'Going out for a bit of the old ultra-violence.' • 'Come and get one in the yarbles, if you have any yarbles, you eunuch jelly thou!'

OOPS! Some of the boo-boos are claimed to be intentional, with Kubrick rearranging dishes on a table and the level of wine in wineglasses to unsettle the viewer.

Psst! The title was based by novelist Anthony Burgess on the cockney saying: 'As queer as a clockwork orange' • The film was released as an 'X' in Britain, without the censors asking for any cuts • After the movie was being blamed as being responsible for several violent attacks, Kubrick withdrew the film from distribution in the UK in the year following release. He claims it will never be shown here again until after his death. In an earlier response to criticism, he had said: 'Sanitised violence in movies has been accepted for years. What seems to upset everybody now is the showing of the consequences of violence.' • To get the effect of Alex trying to kill himself, a camera was thrown off a building. It landed lens downwards on the sixth attempt and, although the lens was broken, the camera itself suffered no damage • The assault on the writer's wife in the film parallels a similar attack on Burgess' wife by wartime American GIs • In a record store there's a copy of the soundtrack for Kubrick's *2001*.

Close Encounters of the Third Kind
★★★★ 1977 135min c.

Director: Steven Spielberg
Screenplay: Steven Spielberg

A group of disparate humans become obsessed by a mountain in Indiana where the authorities are preparing to lay down the red carpet for the first official visit by aliens. This intelligent, moving science fiction classic man-ages to waken our usually dormant sense of wonder and send us out into the dark with tears of joy still fresh on our cheeks.

Roy Neary . . . . .Richard Dreyfuss
Claude Lacombe . . . . .François Truffaut
Ronnie Neary .Teri Garr
Jillian Guiler . . . . .Melinda Dillon
Barry Guiler . . . . .Cary Guffey
Interpreter Laughlin . . . . .Bob Balaban
Robert . . . . .Lance Henriksen
Project leader . . . . .Patrick McNamara
Wild Bill . . . . .Warren Kemmerling
Farmer . . . . .Roberts Blossom
Jean Claude . . . . .Philip Dodds
M.P. . . . . .Carl Weathers
Larry Butler . . . . .Josef Sommer
Robert . . . . .Lance Henriksen

Blurb We Are Not Alone...

OOPS! When Dreyfuss begins building a model of Devil's Tower in his front room, it's pouring down outside. Yet when he looks into the garden, it's nice enough for people to be playing baseball and washing their cars • Among the unexplained phenomena are the number plates of the car taking Dreyfuss and Garr to Devil's Tower. They keep changing.

Psst! Spielberg was annoyed that pressure from the studio resulted in the film being released before he was satisfied. His re-cut Special Edition three years later improves the flabby middle section but spoils our sense of wonder by showing us too much of the aliens at the end • The working title of *Watch the Skies* [see *Gremlins*] is taken from the ending of *The Thing* • Spielberg originally thought of Neary as middle-aged and wanted Jack Nicholson. But commitments prevented him from doing it • The landing pad supposedly inside Devil's Tower was the largest indoor set ever built. It occupied an old airship hanger which was six times the size of the largest of Hollywood's sound stages. Four miles of scaffolding were needed • The aliens were six-year-old girls inside rubber suits, who spoilt several takes by breaking into dance steps.

Coal Miner's Daughter
★★★ 1980 125min c.

Director: Michael Apted
Screenplay: Tom Rickman
Source: Autobiography of Loretta Lynn with George Vecsey

This tale of the stormy life and times of country singer Loretta Lynn ranks not just as one of the greatest musical biographies put on film, but as one of the best biographies on celluloid, full stop. Although Spacek won the Oscar, Jones also shines as her husband, as does D'Angelo playing Patsy Cline.

Loretta . . . . .Sissy Spacek
Doolittle 'Mooney' Lynn . . . . .Tommy Lee Jones
Patsy Cline . . . . .Beverly D'Angelo
Ted Webb . . . . .Levon Helm
Clara Webb . . . . .Phyllis Boyens
Lee Dollarhide . . . . .William Sanderson

Oscars Sissy Spacek

Quote 'I don't want no divorce. I just want the doggone bedroom in the back of the house.'

Psst! Beverly D'Angelo and Sissy Spacek do their own singing. Spacek worked with Lynn's own musicians to perfect her way of singing • Mary Elizabeth Mastrantonio was spotted by director Apted working as a Country and Western singer in a Nashville theme park. He cast her as an extra • As far as Loretta Lynn was concerned, 'The film done us proud.'

The Colditz Story
★★★ 1954 97min b/w

Director: Guy Hamilton
Screenplay: Guy Hamilton & Ivan Foxwell
Source: Book by Pat Reid.

A group of constant escapers in World War II are sent to the supposedly escape-proof Colditz Castle. One of the best of all POW movies. Although it has its gung-ho elements, it isn't afraid to show the tedium of everyday life in captivity, lightening the tougher stuff with a vein of stiff-lipped humour.

Pat Reid . . . . .John Mills
Col. Richmond . . . . .Eric Portman
'Mac' McGill . . . . .Christopher Rhodes
Harry Tyler . . . . .Lionel Jeffries
Jimmy Winslow . . . . .Bryan Forbes
Robin Cartwright . . . . .Ian Carmichael
Richard Gordon . . . . .Richard Wattis
Kommandant . . . . .Frederick Valk

Psst! Although perceived in Britain as a place which could barely hold any British POW, in fact only 14 British officers escaped from Colditz, compared to 37 French and Dutch officers • A British TV series on Colditz ran from 1972 onwards.

Coma
★★★ 1978 113min c.

Director: Michael Crichton
Screenplay: Michael Crichton
Source: Novel by Robin Cook

A doctor suspects that a transplant organisation is trying to improve its turnover by killing those patients with organs it needs. Though sometimes as stiff as some of the victims, this thriller still has the power to chill, cleverly exploiting the paranoia we all feel towards the all-powerful medical profession

Dr. Susan Wheeler . . . . .Genevieve Bujold
Dr. Mark Bellows . . . . .Michael Douglas
Mrs. Emerson . . . . .Elizabeth Ashley
Dr. George A. Harris . . . . .Richard Widmark
Dr. George . . . . .Rip Torn
Nancy Greenly . . . . .Lois Chiles
Sean Murphy . . . . .Tom Selleck
Pathology resident . . . . .Ed Harris

Blurb Someone's Getting Away With Murder.

Psst! Like author Cook, director Crichton is a qualified doctor • Tom Selleck and Ed Harris can be glimpsed in small bit parts.

The Commitments
★★★★ 1991 117min c.

Director: Alan Parker
Screenplay: Dick Clement & Ian La Frenais

Who needs expensive stars when a group of unknowns can light up the screen like this lot? A bunch of Dublin teenagers set up a cracking good soul band that's on the verge of tearing itself apart even at the first gig. Hysterical – albeit salty – dialogue, superlative music and sparkling performances make this a joy from start to finish. Unmissable, and there are a couple of great soundtrack albums to boot.

Jimmy Rabbitte . . . . .Robert Arkins
Deco Cuffe . . . . .Andrew Strong
Steve Clifford . . . . .Michael Aherne
Imelda Quirke . . . . .Angeline Ball
Natalie Murphy . . . . .Maria Doyle
Mickah Wallace . . . . .Dave Finnegan
Bernie McGloughlin . . . . . . .Bronagh Gallagher
Dean Fay . . . . .Félim Gormley
Outspan Foster . . . . .Glen Hansard
Joey "The Lips" Fagan . . . . . . .Johnny Murphy
Mr. Rabbitte . . . . .Colm Meaney

Blurb They Had Absolutely Nothing. But They Were Willing To Risk It All.

Quote 'U2 must be shitting themselves.'
• 'You're working class, right?' – 'We would be if there was any work.' • 'God sent him.' – 'On a Suzuki?'

OOPS! Imelda's caravan holiday in the Isle of Man wouldn't be much to write a postcard home about. Caravans are banned from the island.

Psst! It was Andrew Strong's father who was asked to audition. His son came to the audition as well, and walked away with the lead
• Director Alan Parker appears in a cameo right at the end as 'Eejit Record Producer'. His movies are in abundance on the shelves of the video store • Among the suggestions for the band's title is *The Likely Lads* which was the name of the writers' famous TV sitcom.

The Conversation
★★★★ 1974 113min c.

Director: Francis Ford Coppola
Screenplay: Francis Ford Coppola

Often baffling but nonetheless spellbinding tale about a top surveillance expert who drops his professional guard and questions what the result of his work eavesdropping on a couple will be. His interest, he soon discovers, lands him in hot water. Hackman is outstanding in this splendidly-made exploration of loneliness and paranoia.

Harry Caul	Gene Hackman
Stan	John Cazale
Bernie Moran	Allen Garfield
Mark	Frederic Forrest
Ann	Cindy Williams
Paul	Michael Higgins
Amy	Teri Garr
Martin Stett	Harrison Ford
The director	Robert Duvall

Psst! The film benefitted from being released just after the Watergate break-in. It was coincidental, as Coppola had been working for seven years on the script • Marlon Brando was his first choice for lead, but he turned Coppola down.

Coogan's Bluff
★★★ 1968 93min c.

Director: Don Siegel
Screenplay: Herman Miller, Dean Riesner & Howard Rodman

A deputy from Arizona comes to New York to escort a killer home and gets caught up in a web of red tape. He ends up having to track his man down in the unfamiliar concrete jungle and it isn't long before the country boy is showing those know-it-all city cops a thing or two. Still exciting fare, although its elements have been copied many times since.

Coogan	Clint Eastwood
Sheriff McElroy	Lee J. Cobb
Julie	Susan Clark
Linny Raven	Tisha Sterling
Ringerman	Don Stroud
Mrs. Ringerman	Betty Field
Sheriff McCrea	Tom Tully

Psst! The first in the long line of collaborations between Siegel and Eastwood • Director Siegel appears in a cameo as a man in a lift • The basis for the *McCloud* TV series.

The Cook, the Thief, His Wife and Her Lover
★★ 1989 120min c.

Director: Peter Greenaway
Screenplay: Peter Greenaway

Offal given the nouvelle cuisine treatment – impressive to look at, but rather disgusting. This stylish but repellent allegory on 80s greed owes far more than its director would admit to fine performances from Gambon and Mirren. Although flawed by overwriting and by Greenaway's deep-frozen style, it's still a one-off and the only Greenaway worth the time of day.

Richard, the Cook	Richard Bohringer
Albert, the Thief	Michael Gambon
Georgina, his Wife	Helen Mirren
Michael, her Lover	Alan Howard
Mitchel	Tim Roth
Grace	Liz Smith

Quote 'Try the cock, Albert. It's a delicacy, and you know where it's been.'

Psst! Note for pseuds: The long tracking shots from the restaurant door to the toilet are supposed to represent the passing of food through the body. So now you know!

Cool Hand Luke
★★★ 1967 126min c.

Director: Stuart Rosenberg

Screenplay: Donn Pearce & Frank Pierson
Source: Novel by Pearce

A loner serving time on a chain gang for beating up parking meters locks horns with the authorities and dooms himself. Although there are languid stretches, it's still a pretty powerful movie that also manages to pack in a fair dollop of humour. It was 35 years since Paul Muni had starred in *I am a Fugitive from a Chain Gang*; didn't anybody in authority in America's penal system ever go to the movies?

Lucas 'Luke' Jackson . . . . .Paul Newman
Dragline . . . . .George Kennedy
Society Red . . . . .J.D. Cannon
Koko . . . . .Lou Antonio
Loudmouth Steve . . . . .Robert Drivas
Captain . . . . .Strother Martin
Arletta . . . . .Jo Van Fleet
Carr . . . . .Clifton James
Boss Godfrey . . . . .Morgan Woodward
Babalugats . . . . .Dennis Hopper
Gambler . . . . .Wayne Rogers
Girl washing car . . . . .Joy Harmon
Alibi . . . . .Ralph Waite
Also: Anthony Zerbe, Harry Dean Stanton, Joe Don Baker, Clifton James, Donn Pearce

Oscars George Kennedy

Quote 'What we've got here is a failure to communicate.' • 'Sometimes nothing is a very cool hand.'

Psst! The novel's author, a former safecracker and convict who served in a similar camp, appears as 'Sailor' in the chain gang • Newman spent some time beforehand with leg irons on to see what it was like walking and running in them. He also took guitar lessons • When he cries during the scene where he's playing the guitar, that's not acting. Newman shed tears because he was so annoyed with himself for fluffing a line. The director used the shot for the film • For those taking part in trivia quizzes, it's 50 hard-boiled eggs that Luke claims he can eat.

The Count of Monte Cristo
★★★ 1934 113min b/w

Director: Rowland V. Lee
Screenplay: Philip Dunne, Dan Totheroh & Rowland V. Lee
Source: Novel by Alexandre Dumas

A wrongly-imprisoned man bides his time in the dreadful Chateau d'If, just waiting for his chance to escape and wreak revenge on those who ruined his life. This great swashbuckler is far the best version of the Dumas tale, in large part due to Donat's beautifully-judged performance.

Edmond Dantes . . . . .Robert Donat
Mercedes de Rosas . . . . .Elissa Landi
Raymond de Villefort Jr. . . . . .Louis Calhern
Mondego . . . . .Sidney Blackmer
Danglars . . . . .Raymond Walburn
Abbe Faria .O.P. Heggie
Jacopo . . . . .Luis Alberni
Valentine de Villefort . . . . .Irene Hervey
Capt. Leclerc . . . . .William Farnum
De Villefort Sr. . . . . .Lawrence Grant
Madame de Rosas . . . . .Georgia Caine
Albert de Mondego . . . . .Douglas Walton

Psst! The part was written for Fredric March, but he then dropped out • With filming often going on for 17 hours at a stretch Donat, who was always in delicate health, was on the point of exhaustion by the time he was able to escape back to London.

The Court Jester
★★★ 1956 101min c.

Director: Norman Panama & Melvin Frank
Screenplay: Norman Panama & Melvin Frank

This delightful comedy is the most enjoyable of Kaye's films. He's a revolting peasant who poses as a jester to help overthrow the villainous Rathbone. Along the way, he gets involved in swashbuckling and romance and finds time for some of his great tongue-twisting patter, including the now infamous 'vessel with the pestle' scene.

Hawkins . . . . .Danny Kaye
Maid Jean . . . . .Glynis Johns
Sir Ravenhurst . . . . .Basil Rathbone
Princess Gwendolyn . . . . .Angela Lansbury
King Roderick . . . . .Cecil Parker
Griselda . . . . .Mildred Natwick
Sir Griswold . . . . .Robert Middleton
Sir Locksley . . . . .Michael Pate
Captain of the Guard . . . . .Herbert Rudley
Sir Brockhurst . . . . .Alan Napier
Giacomo . . . . .John Carradine

Quote 'The pellet with the poison's in the flagon with the dragon. The vessel with the pestle has the brew that is true.'

Psst! Kaye was given instructions in fencing by Rathbone. Although Rathbone was acknowledged to be the best swordsman in Hollywood, Kaye took to it like a duck to water and Rathbone, who was admittedly 64, had to be doubled in some long shots • Kaye was forced to wear 'leg falsies' designed to improve the shape of his legs.

Creature from the Black Lagoon
★★ 1954 79min b/w

Director: Jack Arnold
Screenplay: Harry Essex & Arthur Ross

The amphibious Gill Man lurks in the Amazon basin, preying on those daft enough to take a dip. This likeable, archetypal 50s low-budget horror film has influenced umpteen films, with *Jaws* and *Alien* perhaps the most obvious. Try to catch it in 3-D for the full, tacky experience. There were several flaccid sequels, among them *Revenge of the Creature* in 1955 and *The Creature Walks Among Us* in 1956.

David Reed	Richard Carlson
Kay Lawrence	Julia Adams
Mark Williams	Richard Denning
Carl Maia	Antonio Moreno
Lucas	Nestor Paiva
Edwin Thompson	Whit Bissel
Gill Man	Ricou Browning

Blurb Not Since The Beginning Of Time Has The World Beheld Terror Like This.

Psst! It isn't too hard to tell that The Creature is actually a man in a rubber suit. There were two of them. For the underwater scenes, the creature was played by Ricou Browning, a champion swimmer who could hold his breath for up to four minutes under water. The costume kept bobbing to the surface so Browning had to have lead weights added to keep him under the surface. On land, Ben Chapman was the Gill Man • The creature was supposedly modelled on the Oscar statuette.

'Crocodile' Dundee
★★★ 1986 98min c.

Director: Peter Faiman
Screenplay: Paul Hogan & Ken Shadie

Delightful fish-out-of-water comedy has sceptical New York journalist shown around the Oz outback by Hogan, who is then similarly baffled when he returns with her to the Big Apple. Often silly, but frequently beguiling and hilarious, the film is made by Hogan's disarming performance. At long last, a hero we chaps can identify with, a guy who doesn't look as if he's worked out in a gym 26 hours a day.

Mick Dundee	Paul Hogan
Sue Charlton	Linda Kozlowski
Wally Reilly	John Meillon
Richard Mason	Mark Blum
Sam Charlton	Michael Lombard
Nevile Bell	David Gulpilil
Con	Ritchie Singer
Ida	Maggie Blinco
Gus	Reginald Veljohnson

Quote 'That's not a knife. *THAT'S* a knife.'

Psst! An enormous success in Australia, Paramount bought the American rights. Even though they spent more than the original $5.5 million budget on ads, they had only moderate hopes for it. It became one of the biggest-ever sleeper hits • Seven minutes were cut for the American version, with the Aussie slang that couldn't be cut being re-recorded • After considering 200 possible names, they stuck with the original title, adding the quotation marks in case people thought it was a picture about reptiles! • The insurance company wouldn't allow real crocodiles to be used, so the one that gets close is a rubber model on an underwater wire • So eager were Australian investors to put money into the film that, according to Hogan, some $3.5m had to be given back • The video is sadly missing the funny scene where Dundee assumes that someone taking cocaine has a bad cold • The Plaza Hotel in New York received many complaints from guests who couldn't find the bidet that so confused Hogan.

The Crowd
★★ 1928 98min b/w

Director: King Vidor
Screenplay: King Vidor, John V.A. Weaver & Harry Behn

One of the most famous of all silent movies, its less-than-glamorous characters are a lowly clerk and his wife suffering from all the hardships that fate could throw at them. Although it still retains some power, both the directorial innovations and the tale have been copied so many times since (the final scene of *Working Girl*, for instance) that there's no freshness to it.

John	James Murray
Mary	Eleanor Boardman

Bert	Bert Roach
Jane	Estelle Clark
Jim	Daniel G. Tomlinson

Psst! Many of the exteriors were filmed on location in New York with a hidden camera • This was the first American film to show a lavatory • Vidor holds the record for the longest directorial career, lasting from 1913 until 1980 • Murray was so sceptical that Vidor was interested in him that he didn't turn up for his first film test. After his career went into decline, he became an alcoholic and died, forgotten, in the 30s.

The Cruel Sea
★★★ 1953 126min b/w

Director: Charles Frend
Screenplay: Eric Ambler
Source: Novel by Nicholas Monsarrat

Ealing Studios didn't only produce comedies. This was one of their best dramas. It's a gritty look at life on a British warship on convoy duty in World War II, with the sea almost as much an enemy as the Germans. Hawkins gives one of his finest in a long line of stiff-upper-lip performances.

Lt. Cmdr. Ericson	Jack Hawkins
Sub-Lieut. Lockhart	Donald Sinden
Sub-Lieut. Ferraby	John Stratton
Sub-Lieut. Morell	Denholm Elliott
Bennett	Stanley Baker
Julie Hallam	Virginia McKenna
Mrs. Morell	Moira Lister
Tallow	Bruce Seton
Chief Petty Officer Watts	Liam Redmond
Tallow's sister	Megs Jenkins

Also: Meredith Edwards, Glyn Houston, Alec McCowen, Andrew Cruickshank, Sam Kydd

Psst! Leslie Norman, the producer, was Barry Norman's father • The film was actually made in the middle of summer. Making it look like the depths of winter was tricky, with the cast sweating buckets in their heavy Arctic gear • Hawkins was badly seasick during the storm scenes.

The Crying Game
★★ 1992 112min c.

Director: Neil Jordan
Screenplay: Neil Jordan

A bust in Britain but a phenomenal success in America, this confused film is part thriller, part romantic comedy. The middle section, with an IRA man seeking out the girlfriend of a dead squaddie, is touching and delightfully funny, sporting an incredible twist in the tale. The outer sections, involving the IRA, are tedious and pointless. Goodness knows why they'd bring in American Whitaker, only to put a bag over his head most of the time.

Fergus	Stephen Rea
Jude	Miranda Richardson
Jody	Forest Whitaker
Col	Jim Broadbent
Dave	Ralph Brown
Maguire	Adrian Dunbar
Dil	Jaye Davidson

Oscars Best Screenplay

Psst! Costing less than £3m, Jordan was turned down by every studio in Hollywood, yet the film was nominated for six Oscars • British Palace Pictures financed it, but went bust in the middle of filming. The producer is said to have used his ATM machine to get cash to pay the actors • Rea drew on his personal experience for his role as an IRA gunman; his wife was once a member and served eight years in prison for her part in car bombings.

Cyrano de Bergerac
★★★★ 1990 135min c.

Director: Jean-Paul Rappeneau
Screenplay: Jean-Claude Carriere & Jean-Paul Rappeneau
Source: Play by Edmond Rostand

Brilliant French version of the famous Rostand play about the guy with the Pinocchio nose heavily, and forlornly, in love with his cousin Roxane. Depardieu is perfect for the part, Fairbanks-like in the duelling sequences and eminently believable in the more emotional moments. Although it was a clever idea to save money on latex by getting the already nasally-overendowed Depardieu to play the part, it was still, at $20m, France's second most expensive film. The earlier 1950 film with José Ferrer had a wonderful central performance but lacked the imagination and style of this one.

Cyrano de Bergerac	Gérard Depardieu
Roxane	Anne Brochet
Christian de Neuvillette	Vincent Perez
Comte De Guiche	Jacques Weber

The Dam Busters

★★★ 1954 125min b/w

Director: Michael Anderson
Screenplay: R.C. Sherriff
Source: Books by Guy Gibson & Paul Brickhill

Brainy boffin Barnes Wallis devises a bizarre method, using a bouncing bomb, for attacking the dams of the industrial Ruhr region in Germany. But first he has to battle the do-nothing attitude of the bureaucrats. Based on fact, this is an fascinating and stirring account of the extraordinary raid, enlivened by Coates' famous music and only occasionally let down by the odd naff model shot and desperately bad matte explosions.

Wing Cmdr. Guy Gibson	Richard Todd
Dr. Barnes Wallis	Michael Redgrave
Mrs. Wallis	Ursula Jeans
Air Chief Marshal Harris	Basil Sydney
Capt. Joseph 'Mutt' Summers	Patrick Barr
Air Vice-Marshal Cochrane	Ernest Clark
G/Capt. J.N.H. Whitworth	Derek Farr
Official, Nat. Physical Lab.	Raymond Huntley
F/O F.M. Spafford	Nigel Stock
Flt/Sgt. J. Pulford	Robert Shaw
Flt/Lt. Maltby	George Baker
Flt./Lt. Martin	Bill Kerr
Farmer	Laurence Naismith
Gibson's batman	Harold Goodwin

Quote 'What possible argument could I put forward to get you a Wellington?' – 'Well, if you told them that I designed it, do you think that might help?'

OOPS! Even though it's clear that the film opens in March, Redgrave refers to the season as winter when he's talking to Jeans.

Psst! The RAF supplied most of the aircraft at a cost of £130 per hour for each plane. The expense consumed 10% of film's budget • The movie's premiere was 12 years to the day after the original raid • Although many of the original locations were used for those parts of the story based in Britain, Lake Windemere doubled for the Ruhr • The original attack won Guy Gibson the VC. He became Britain's most decorated flyer in World War II and was killed over Holland 18 months after the Dambusters Raid • The raid breached the Moehne and Eder dams and although, using slave labour, the dams were rebuilt within six months, one of the damaged power stations wasn't repaired until 1953 • At 35, Todd was 11 years older than Gibson, who was just 24 during the raid • Gibson's dog

Nigger was dubbed 'Trigger' for the American market • This was Robert Shaw's film debut • Inventor Barnes Wallis was a consultant to the movie. The clips of the bouncing bombs being tested are real, lent to the production by Wallis.

Dances With Wolves

★★★★ 1990 179min c.

Director: Kevin Costner
Screenplay: Michael Blake
Source: Based on novel by Blake

A remarkable directing debut from Costner. Despite its irritating and inaccurate Politically Correct stance, this story of a Civil War hero befriending and then joining the Sioux is a marvel. Proving that epics *can* still work, there's hardly a dull moment in a film which is fascinating, touching, shaming and even pretty funny in places. Despite the Western being such an old genre, the photography also dazzles the eye. Such a pity that Costner also saw fit to bring out a 230-minute ego-puffing 'Special Edition'.

Lt. John J. Dunbar	Kevin Costner
Stands With A Fist	Mary McDonnell
Kicking Bird	Graham Greene
Wind In His Hair	Rodney A. Grant
Ten Bears	Floyd Red Crow Westerman
Black Shawl	Tantoo Cardinal
Timmons	Robert Pastorelli
Lt. Elgin	Charles Rocket

Oscars Best Picture, Best Screenplay (adapted), Best Director

OOPS! The Indians were ahead of us in many areas, one of them obviously being hair-styling. Or is that *not* mousse that Mary McDonnell's wearing? Her hair also changes length when Costner first encounters her • Keep an eye on Timmons, the wagon driver. First he gets egg on his beard, which vanishes then reappears. Then, when he's killed, he still manages a last breath • Isn't that a choke chain around the dead wolf's neck?

Psst! So sure was Hollywood that Costner would come unstuck with this troubled production, which ran 30 days over schedule, that they nicknamed it *Kevin's Gate*, a reference to the disastrous *Heaven's Gate* • Revisionist it may be, but the 90s-style Indians, pacifist and green, certainly aren't historically accurate. According to one scholar: 'The Sioux massacred. They pillaged. They raped. They burned. They carried women and children into captivity. They tortured for entertainment. All this was their long-established custom, carried out, indeed, far more frequently against other Indian tribes than against whites.'

Dangerous Liaisons
★★★ 1988 120min c.

Director: Stephen Frears
Screenplay: Christopher Hampton
Source: Play by Hampton and novel, *Les Liaisons Dangereuses* by Choderlos de Laclos

A visually sumptuous story of two French aristocrats playing sexual games of conquest. Close promises Malkovich a return to her bed if he'll seduce Thurman. He's after the tougher challenge of married Pfeiffer. Although modern accents intrude and it's a little hard to believe in Close as an all-powerful sexual being, Pfeiffer is painfully brilliant as the doomed Madame de Tourvel. Costume drama has rarely been so captivating. The following year Milos Forman's turn on the same story, *Valmont*, was released. It was unfortunate that it was so overshadowed by this movie.

Marquise de Merteuil . . . . .Glenn Close
Vicomte de Valmont . . . . .John Malkovich
Madame de Tourvel . . . . .Michelle Pfeiffer
Madame de Volanges . . . . .Swoosie Kurtz
Chevalier Danceny . . . . .Keanu Reeves
Madame de Rosemonde . . . . .Mildred Natwick
Cecile de Volanges . . . . .Uma Thurman
Azolan .Peter Capaldi

Quote 'To seduce a woman famous for strict morals, religious fervour and the happiness of her marriage, what could possibly be more prestigious?' • 'I think we might begin with one or two Latin terms.' • 'It's beyond my control.'

Psst! Malkovich and Pfeiffer became lovers during filming, although he later returned to his wife • Any thoughts of keeping the original title, *Les Liaisons Dangereuses*, were scuppered when a survey showed only 1 in 50 Americans were willing to see a film with a foreign title • In Malaysia, the film was called *Vipers in Heat*.

Dangerous Moonlight
★★ 1941 98min b/w

Director: Brian Desmond Hurst
Screenplay: Shaun Terence Young, Rodney Ackland & Brian Desmond Hurst

A concert pianist flees from Europe and joins the RAF. This popular wartime tale of courage, romance and amnesia was Utility Issue and not particularly well made or durable. It's probably best remembered today for introducing the immensely successful 'Warsaw Concerto' by Richard Addinsell.

Stefan Radetzky . . . . .Anton Walbrook
Carole Peters . . . . .Sally Gray
Mike Carroll . . . . .Derrick de Marney
Specialist .Cecil Parker
Bill Peters . . . . .Percy Parsons
De Guise . . . . .Kenneth Kent
Shorty .Guy Middleton
British Commander . . . . .John Laurie

The Dark Mirror
★★★ 1946 85min b/w

Director: Robert Siodmak
Screenplay: Nunnally Johnson
Source: Novel by Vladimir Pozner

Enjoyably daft hokum with De Havilland playing identical twins, one of whom is sweetness and light, the other a psychopathic killer. Throw in both of the women falling for the psychologist who has to sort the mess out, fashionable postwar psychology and a split-screen technique which has the twins appearing together and you have a ridiculous but still entertaining thriller.

Terry/Ruth Collins . . . . .Olivia De Havilland
Dr. Scott Elliott . . . . .Lew Ayres
Lt. Stevenson . . . . .Thomas Mitchell
Rusty . . . . .Richard Long
Girard, D.A. . . . . .Charles Evans
Franklin . . . . .Garry Owen
Mrs. O'Brien . . . . .Ida Moore

Blurb One Twin Loves…And One Twin Loves To Kill.

Quote 'I don't mind ordinary music. It's the wonderful stuff that bores me.'

Dark Star
★★★ 1974 83min c.

Director: John Carpenter
Screenplay: John Carpenter & Dan O'Bannon

This cult, low-budget, sci-fi comedy no longer seems the out-and-out scream it once did. But there are still plenty of laughs to be had from a tale involving incredibly bored astronauts, lippy talking computers and an alien that resembles a strawberry on steroids. It remains a pretty good late-night bet.

```
Doolittle . . . . . . . . . . . . . . . . . . . . .Brian Nareille
Talby  . . . . . . . . . . . . . . . . . . . . . . . .Dre Pahich
Boiler  . . . . . . . . . . . . . . . . . . . . . . .Cal Kuniholm
Pinback . . . . . . . . . . . . . . . . . . . . .Dan O'Bannon
Commander Powell . . . . . . . . . . .Joe Saunders
```

Blurb Out In Space With A Spaced-Out Bomb!

OOPS! When bomb number 20 emerges from the bomb bay in the middle of the asteroid storm, someone can be seen on the computer screen sticking their tongue out.

Psst! In addition to directing, co-writing and editing the film, Carpenter also wrote the music, as he did for his subsequent movies
• O'Bannon went on to write *Alien* which is obviously heavily influenced by *Dark Star*
• The astronauts' costumes were made out of vacuum cleaner hosing and styrofoam.

Darling
★★★ 1965 128min c.

Director: John Schlesinger
Screenplay: Frederic Raphael

Many British Swinging Sixties films are now very tiresome and *Darling* is so thoroughly soaked in its era that its fingers and toes have gone wrinkly. Yet this one remains fascinating. Christie is a model who rises up the social ladder only to discover her life is an empty shell. At her loveliest, Christie gives one of her best performances and Schlesinger's cool direction matches Raphael's bitter script.

```
Diana Scott . . . . . . . . . . . . . . . . . .Julie Christie
Robert Gold  . . . . . . . . . . . . . . . . .Dirk Bogarde
Miles Brand  . . . . . . . . . . . . . . .Laurence Harvey
Malcolm . . . . . . . . . . . . . . . . . . . .Roland Curram
Sean Martin . . . . . . . . . . . . . . . . . . . .Alex Scott
Alec Prosser-Jones  . . . . . . . . . . .Basil Henson
Estelle Gold  . . . . . . . . . . . . . . . . .Pauline Yates
```

Oscars Julie Christie, Best Story and Screenplay

Quote 'Your idea of fidelity is not having more than one man in bed at the same time. You're a whore, baby.'

Psst! Christie was paid only $7,500 for the role
• Harvey took no money up front, but opted for what turned out to be a profitable percentage take of the box office • Gregory Peck said no to the part before Bogarde was signed up • The production was so strapped for cash that the only way of finishing it was by selling Christie's contract to David Lean so that he could star her in *Doctor Zhivago*.

Dave
★★★ 1993 110min c.

Director: Ivan Reitman
Screenplay: Gary Ross

Hired as a double to impersonate the President, meek but decent Kline is suddenly thrown into the job for real when the President has a stroke. This charming and highly amusing tale actually improves with each viewing, fairly rare for a comedy.

```
Dave Kovic/Bill Mitchell . . . . . . . . . .Kevin Kline
Ellen Mitchell  . . . . . . . . . . . . .Sigourney Weaver
Bob Alexander . . . . . . . . . . . . . . .Frank Langella
Alan Reed  . . . . . . . . . . . . . . . . . . . .Kevin Dunn
Duane Stevenson . . . . . . . . . . . . . .Ving Rhames
Vice Pres. Nance  . . . . . . . . . . . . .Ben Kingsley
Murray Blum  . . . . . . . . . . . . . . .Charles Grodin
Alice  . . . . . . . . . . . . . . . . . . . . . . . .Faith Prince
Randi . . . . . . . . . . . . . . . . . . . . . . . .Laura Linney
White House tour guide . . . .Bonnie Hunt, Arnold
                                        Schwarzenegger
```

Also: Oliver Stone, Jay Leno

Quote 'Listen! You're very good, but she needs a lot of work.'

OOPS! When Kline turns into the White House in the limo the first time, you can see houses over the road through the back window. But they aren't there in later shots • When Kline and Weaver are out together, they have the shopping in their arms before they've actually bought it, which is a neat trick • There's one mike boom too many at the press conference where Langella resigns.

Psst! Although many of the cameos wheeled in to add verisimilitude will be unfamiliar to British audiences, most should be able to spot Arnie and Oliver Stone, spouting yet another conspiracy theory • Originally, it was to star Warren Beatty, but he dropped out.

David Copperfield
★★★★ 1935 132min b/w

Director: George Cukor
Screenplay: Howard Estabrook & Hugh Walpole
Source: Novel by Charles Dickens

One of the very best screen versions of Dickens. It's a sumptuous production, reasonably honest to the source, and with an all-star cast pulling out all the stops. Fields gives the performance of his career. It was a deserved box office success.

Young David . . . . .Freddie Bartholomew
Adult David . . . . .Frank Lawton
Mr. Micawber . . . . .W.C. Fields
Dan Peggotty . . . . .Lionel Barrymore
Peggotty . . . . .Jessie Ralph
Uriah Heep . . . . .Roland Young
Aunt Betsy . . . . .Edna May Oliver
Mr. Murdstone . . . . .Basil Rathbone
Mrs. Copperfield . . . . .Elizabeth Allan
Dora . . . . .Maureen O'Sullivan
Mr. Dick .Lennox Pawle
Steerforth . . . . .Hugh Williams
Miss Murdstone . . . . .Violet Kemble Cooper
Agnes . . . . .Madge Evans
Mr. Wickfield . . . . .Lewis Stone
Barkis . . . . .Herbert Mundin
Clickett . . . . .Elsa Lanchester
Mrs. Micawber . . . . .Jean Cadell

Blurb Brought To The Screen As Dickens Himself Would Wish It.

Quote 'Young friend, I counsel you. Annual income twenty pounds, annual expenditure nineteen pounds, result…happiness. Annual income twenty pounds, annual expenditure twenty-one pounds, result…misery.'

Psst! Producer David O. Selznick initially wanted to make the film in two halves, each to be seen separately, but he then decided against it • He and director Cukor had to fight Louis B. Mayer to stop him casting Jackie Cooper as the young Copperfield • Fields was initially very reluctant to do Micawber and wanted to relieve his anxiety by including a juggling routine. When he was told that Dickens had not mentioned Micawber juggling, Fields replied: 'He probably forgot.' • Fields was so pickled with whisky that he couldn't remember his lines and cue cards had to be provided • Charles Laughton was originally cast as Micawber, but he departed the film after just a couple of days' shooting, saying that he was obviously wrong for the part • The studio originally cut the film to a more typical length, with Barrymore's role being dropped completely. But after viewing the movie MGM chief Louis B. Mayer restored the majority of the cuts • When Maureen O'Sullivan couldn't cry to order during her deathbed scene, director Cukor pinched her feet painfully out of the camera's view.

Mrs. Gummidge . . . . .Una O'Connor
The Vicar .Hugh Walpole
Donkey man . . . . .Arthur Treacher

Dawn Patrol
★★★ 1938 103min b/w

Director: Edmund Goulding
Screenplay: Seton I. Miller & Dan Totheroh
Source: Story, *The Flight Commander* by John Monk Saunders

This remake of the 1930 Howard Hawks film actually improves on the original. World War I flyers have to face up to the fact that their life expectancy is not much longer than a mayfly's. Playful banter is well mixed with tragedy and pathos, although some of the action scenes now look pretty fake.

Capt. Courtney . . . . .Errol Flynn
Maj. Brand . . . . .Basil Rathbone
Lt. Scott .David Niven
Phipps . . . . .Donald Crisp
Sgt. Watkins . . . . .Melville Cooper
Bott . . . . .Barry Fitzgerald
Von Mueller . . . . .Carl Esmond

Psst! Many of the shots of planes in the air are lifted from the 1930 movie. Even large parts of the script are word for word repetitions of the earlier film.

A Day at the Races
★★★ 1937 109min b/w

Director: Sam Wood
Screenplay: Robert Pirosh, George Seaton & George Oppenheimer

Horse doctor Hackenbush goes to work at a sanatorium under threat of closure, prescribing horse pills to patients and wooing the wealthy Dumont. The usual havoc is wreaked by the brilliant Marx Brothers, but they are let down badly by some dreadful musical numbers, mostly inflicted by Allan Jones. Nevertheless, Groucho trying to get a racing tip out of 'tootsie-fruitsie' Chico remains among their greatest moments.

Dr. Hugo Z. Hackenbush . . . . . . .Groucho Marx
Tony . . . . .Chico Marx
Stuffy . . . . .Harpo Marx
Gil Stewart .Allan Jones
Judy . . . . .Maureen O'Sullivan
Mrs. Upjohn . . . . .Margaret Dumont

Morgan	Douglass Dumbrille
Dr. Steinberg	Sig Rumann
Flo	Esther Muir
Whitmore	Leonard Ceeley

Quote 'Get your ice cream! Tootsie-fruitsie ice cream!' • 'Who are you going to believe, me or your own eyes?' • 'Either this man is dead or my watch has stopped.' • 'Don't point that beard at me. It might go off.' • 'I've never been so insulted in my life!' – 'Well, it's early yet.' • 'Closer. Hold me closer.' – 'If I hold you any closer, I'll be in back of you! • 'One dollar and you'll remember me all your life.' – 'That's the most nauseating proposition I've ever heard.' • 'Marry me, Emily, and I'll never look at any other horse.' [Last line]

Psst! As with some of their other movies, the Marx Brothers took their routines on the road to test them on live audiences first. Only the bits getting the best reponse made it into the movie and spaces were left for the laughter they had received on tour • Irving Thalberg, MGM's production head who had turned the Marxes from a cult into a mainstream success, died during production • As on *A Night at the Opera* The Marx Brothers hated director Wood. He continued to antagonise them with his call for umpteen takes, even though he usually used the first or second • The film was banned in Latvia for being 'worthless' • Dorothy Dandridge, later to star in *Carmen Jones*, appears as one of the child extras • Groucho's character was initially going to be called Dr. Quackenbush, until somebody pointed out just how many real Quackenbush's existed.

Day for Night
★★★ 1973 116min c.

Director: François Truffaut
Screenplay: François Truffaut, Suzanne Schiffman & Jean-Louis Richard

One of the best movies made about the making of movies, with director Truffaut playing a director trying to keep his emotionally fragile cast together long enough to get a Mills and Boon-ish love story in the can. This fascinating and extremely funny look behind the scenes is more enjoyable than many of Truffaut's deeper works.

Julie Baker	Jacqueline Bisset
Alexandre	Jean-Pierre Aumont
Séverine	Valentina Cortese
Alphonse	Jean-Pierre Léaud
Ferrand	François Truffaut
Liliane	Dani

Psst! Truffaut claims everything in the film is based on a real incident in his career • Writer Graham Greene heard Truffaut wanted someone to play an English insurance agent and turned up posing as Henry Graham, a businessman living in Antibes. Truffaut cast him, but became concerned when 'Graham' tried to rewrite his scenes. When Greene confessed, Truffaut thought it a great hoax and insisted on keeping him. He is listed as Henry Graham on the credits • Bisset's part is based on Julie Christie.

The Day of the Jackal
★★★ 1973 142min c.

Director: Fred Zinnemann
Screenplay: Kenneth Ross
Source: Based on the novel by Frederick Forsyth

A professional hitman is hired to assassinate General de Gaulle. Although long, the film's unhurried approach, concentrating on Fox's meticulous preparations, serves to increase the tension. Even though we know the outcome, the last few scenes remain nail-biting stuff.

The Jackal	Edward Fox
Claude Lebel	Michel Lonsdale
Col. Rodin	Eric Porter
Mallinson	Donald Sinden
Insp. Thomas	Tony Britton
The Minister	Alan Badel
Gunsmith	Cyril Cusack
Gen. Colbert	Maurice Denham
Colette	Delphine Seyrig
Berthier	Timothy West
Bernard	Anton Rogers

The Day the Earth Caught Fire
★★★ 1961 99min b/w

Director: Val Guest
Screenplay: Wolf Mankowitz & Val Guest

Nuclear tests have the effect of knocking the earth off its axis and sending it towards the sun. Although obviously dated and marred by unimpressive special effects, it is still pretty suspenseful stuff with a streak of intelligence so often lacking in this sort of movie

Peter Stenning	Edward Judd
Jeannie	Janet Munro
Bill Maguire	Leo McKern
Night editor	Michael Goodliffe
News editor	Bernard Braden

Also: Peter Butterworth, Pamela Green

85

The Day the Earth Stood Still
★★★ 1951 92min b/w

Director: Robert Wise
Screenplay: Edmund H. North
Source: Short story, *Farewell to the Master* by Harry Bates

An alien makes a stopover on Earth, with his giant robot Gort, to warn us to abandon nuclear weapons. Our governments, realising he hasn't got a vote, don't pay too much attention until he gives a demonstration of his powers. Although dated in many respects and with some of the actors looking stiffer than Gort, it is still an interesting little movie, helped enormously by Bernard Herrmann's music. It would be nice to have an American film once in a while in which the word 'democracy' can be mentioned without us having to visit the Lincoln Memorial.

Klaatu ....Michael Rennie
Helen Benson ....Patricia Neal
Tom Stevens ....Hugh Marlowe
Dr. Barnhardt ....Sam Jaffe
Bobby Benson ....Billy Gray
Mrs. Barley ....Frances Bavier

Quote 'Klaatu barada nikto.'

OOPS! The presence of aliens must have unsettled people because while a newsreader claims it's 'a nice spring day', we're later told that it's actually July • Michael Rennie's hospital room is 306. But later he says it was 309.

Psst! Claude Rains and Spencer Tracy were originally thought of for part of the alien Klaatu • The robot Gort was played by J. Lockard Martin in a suit of foam rubber. He was the doorman at the famous Grauman's Chinese Theatre. Although picked for his height, some seven feet seven inches, he couldn't actually lift Patricia Neal unaided • Director Robert Wise was to go on and direct *Star Trek: The Motion Picture* 28 years later.

Days of Heaven
★★★★ 1978 95min c.

Director: Terrence Malick
Screenplay: Terrence Malick

Malick's *other* film after *Badlands* is one of the most exquisitely beautiful of all movies. Three immigrants flee the city hoping to find work in the American Mid-West but find the prospect of getting their hands on farmer Shepard's money even more appealing. Relying heavily on mood and atmosphere, it casts a beguiling spell over the audience and is a treat for the ear as well as the eye.

Bill . . . . .Richard Gere
Abby . . . . .Brooke Adams
The farmer . . . . .Sam Shepard
Linda . . . . .Linda Manz
The farm foreman . . . . .Robert J. Wilke
Linda's friend . . . . .Jackie Shultis
Mill foreman . . . . .Stuart Margolin
Vaudeville leader . . . . .Richard Libertini

Psst! Initially, Malick tried to get John Travolta for Gere's part • Filmed in Alberta in Canada instead of in Texas, Malick took two years to make the movie as he wanted to film scenes in the seasons in which they actually took place.

Dead End
★★ 1937 93min b/w

Director: William Wyler
Screenplay: Lillian Hellman
Source: Play by Sidney Kingsley

A gangster hides out in the New York neighbourhood where he grew up, but doesn't meet with a universal welcome, even from his old mum. Architect McCrea is particularly incensed when he finds him corrupting the impressionable kids on the block. Once a hard-hitting look at the underbelly of New York life, this unrealistic and hammy slice-of-life drama now looks too obviously derived from a stage play.

Dave . . . . .Joel McCrea
Drina . . . . .Sylvia Sidney
'Baby Face' Martin . . . . .Humphrey Bogart
Kay . . . . .Wendy Barrie
Francie . . . . .Claire Trevor
Hank . . . . .Allen Jenkins
Mrs. Martin . . . . .Marjorie Main
Mr. Griswold . . . . .Minor Watson
Doorman . . . . .Ward Bond
Also: James Burke, Elizabeth Risdon, Esther Dale, Charles Halton, The Dead End Kids

Quote 'You dog, you dirty yellow dog, you! You ain't no son of mine!' • 'I killed a guy for looking at me the way you are now.'

Psst! The play on which the movie was based ran for 700 performances on Broadway • Marjorie Main and The Dead End Kids had also starred in the play • The film introduced the Dead End Kids to the screen, who went on to appear in several other movies, most notably

Angels With Dirty Faces • They did not endear themselves to the other actors by comparing them unfavourably to the corresponding actors in the stage play • The film rights were bought by producer Sam Goldwyn for what was then the record sum of $165,000 • Director Wyler wanted to film in New York itself, but Goldwyn insisted on using a set costing $300,000 to construct. He is said to have looked at the squalour of the set and the rubbish strewn over it with some distaste. Querying why it should be so filthy, he was told: 'Because it's supposed to be a slum area, Sam.' 'Well,' said the producer, 'this slum cost a lot of money. It should look better than any ordinary slum' • As so often in his early career, Bogart got the part only when George Raft turned it down • Look for Irving Sindler's name on a delicatessen. He was a props guy who always tried to get his name into movies he worked on in days when credit lists were rather shorter. See also *Intermezzo* and *Wuthering Heights*.

Dead of Night

★★★ 1945 104min b/w

Director: Alberto Cavalcanti, Charles Crichton, Basil Dearden & Robert Hamer
Screenplay: John V. Baines, Angus Macphail & T.E.B. Clarke
Source: Stories by Macphail, Baines, E.F. Benson & H.G. Wells

Widely regarded as the best screen horror anthology, this British classic still has the power to chill. An architect comes face to face with the characters who have been occupying his dreams, each of which reveals the nightmare that has been troubling them. Best of all is the final segment, with Redgrave a ventriloquist who thinks his dummy is taking over. Weakest is the golfing story.

Walter Craig	.Mervyn Johns
Eliot Foley	.Roland Culver
Mrs. Foley	.Mary Merrall
Dr. Van Straaten	.Frederick Valk
Hugh	.Antony Baird
Joyce	.Judy Kelly
Hearse driver/bus conductor	.Miles Malleson
Sally O'Hara	.Sally Ann Howes
Joan	.Googie Withers
Peter	.Ralph Michael
Antique dealer	.Esme Percy
George	.Basil Radford
Larry	.Naunton Wayne
Maxwell Frere	.Michael Redgrave

Dead Poets Society

★★★★ 1989 129min c.

Director: Peter Weir
Screenplay: Tom Schulman

Ignore the carpers and seize the chance to see this brilliant performance from Williams as an unconventional English teacher at a straight-laced 1959 boy's school. His love for poetry inspires them but doesn't always have the desired consequences. Yes, it's sentimental. Yes, the story's a little obvious. But it's one of those rare, life-enhancing films that make you feel so much better about things, even if you can't later explain just why.

John Keating	.Robin Williams
Neil Perry	.Robert Sean Leonard
Todd Anderson	.Ethan Hawke
Knox Overstreet	.Josh Charles
Charlie Dalton	.Gale Hansen
Richard Cameron	.Dylan Kussman
Steven Meeks	.Allelon Ruggiero
Gerard Pitts	.James Waterston
Mr. Perry	.Kurtwood Smith
Mr. Nolan	.Norman Lloyd
Ginny Danburry	.Lara Flynn Boyle

Quote '*Carpe diem*, lads. Seize the day. Make your lives extraordinary.' • 'I was the intellectual equivalent of a ninety-eight pound weakling. I would go to the beach and people would kick copies of Byron in my face.'

Psst! At different stages Alec Baldwin and Liam Neeson were considered for Williams' role. So was Dustin Hoffman, but he wanted to direct the film as well.

Dead Ringers

★★ 1988 115min c.

Director: David Cronenberg
Screenplay: David Cronenberg & Norman Snider
Source: Novel, *Twins* by Bari Wood and Jack Geasland.

Extraordinarily unpleasant – though often fascinating – tale of two gynaecologist brothers. Identical twins, they share everything, even their women, until actress Bujold comes between them. Unfortunately, the amazing cinematic trickery, giving us Irons playing opposite Irons, isn't enough to compensate for the film's lack of heart and its essential macabre nastiness.

Beverly/Elliot Mantle	Jeremy Irons
Claire Niveau	Genevieve Bujold
Cary	Heidi Von Palleske
Danuta	Barbara Gordon
Laura	Shirley Douglas
Anders Wolleck	Stephen Lack

Quote 'The beauty of our business is you don't have to get out to meet beautiful women.'

Psst! Bizarrely, the film is based on a true story, although the brothers were gay rather than heterosexual.

Deadly is the Female
SEE: Gun Crazy

Death Drums along the River
★ 1963 83min c.

Director: Lawrence Huntington
Screenplay: Harry Alan Towers, Nicolas Roeg, Kevin Kavanagh & Lawrence Huntington
Source: Novel, *Sanders of the River* by Edgar Wallace

A police inspector in Africa investigating a murder in a hospital uncovers a diamond smuggling operation. An uninspiring colour remake of a 1935 movie starring Paul Robeson, also known as *Sanders*. There was a sequel in 1964, *Coast of Skeletons*. The only remarkable thing about the movie is that film magazine *Empire* always looks it up in new movie guides to see how comprehensive they are. Jolly good magazine, *Empire*. Always thought so.

Police Insp. Harry Saunders	Richard Todd
Dr. Inge Jung	Marianne Koch
Dr. Weiss	Albert Lieven
Dr. Schneider	Walter Rilla
Nurse Marlene	Vivi Bach
Hamilton	Jeremy Lloyd

Psst! Note Nic Roeg, later to direct movies like *Walkabout* and *Don't Look Now*, as one of the co-writers • Lloyd is better known as the writer and director of *Are You Being Served* • In the 1935 movie, Jomo Kenyata, later to be President of Kenya, appeared as an extra.

Death in Venice
★★ 1971 130min c.

Director: Luchino Visconti

Screenplay: Luchino Visconti & Nicola Badalucco
Source: Novella by Thomas Mann

Deathly in Venice, more like. A composer on the point of cracking up becomes besotted by a beautiful young boy and ignores the approach of the plague. Those who adore the Mahler that floods the soundtrack may be able to stand the turgid pace of this wildly overrated art film. The rest of us will be bored rigid enough to do a perfect impression of an ironing board.

Gustav Von Aschenbach	Dirk Bogarde
Tadzio	Bjorn Andresen
Tadzio's mother	Silvana Mangano
Frau Von Aschenbach	Marisa Berenson
Scapegrace	Luigi Battaglia
Alfred	Mark Burns
Hotel manager	Romolo Valli

Death Takes a Holiday
★★ 1934 79min b/w

Director: Mitchell Leisen
Screenplay: Maxwell Anderson, Gladys Lehman & Walter Ferris
Source: Play by Alberto Casella

Knowing that while curiosity may have killed the cat, it can't do much to him, Death pops down to earth to find out why people don't put him top of their popularity lists. Altlhough an intriguing idea, the film no longer carries much conviction and is positively embarrassing in places. With his monocle, March plays Death like a spectral version of Erich von Stroheim.

Prince Sirki	Fredric March
Grazia	Evelyn Venable
Duke Lambert	Guy Standing
Alda	Katherine Alexander
Rhoda	Gail Patrick
Stephanie	Helen Westley
Princess Maria	Kathleen Howard
Baron Cesarea	Henry Travers

Death Wish
★★ 1974 94min c.

Director: Michael Winner
Screenplay: Wendell Mayes
Source: Novel by Brian Garfield

An easy-going liberal turns into a Rambo-like vigilante when his wife and daughter are raped.

Michael Winner displays his usual light touch with this reasonably well-made movie. Although exciting in parts, it still leaves quite a nasty taste in the mouth. It was followed by four worthless sequels and umpteen imitators.

Paul Kersey ....Charles Bronson
Joanna Kersey ....Hope Lange
Insp. Frank Ochoa ....Vincent Gardenia
Jack Toby....................Steven Keats
Aimes Jainchill ....Stuart Margolin
Sam Kreutzer ....William Redfield
Police Commissioner ....Stephen Elliott
Freak #1 ....Jeff Goldblum
Patrolman Reilly ....Christopher Guest

Blurb Vigilante, City Style...Judge, Jury And Executioner.

Psst! Jeff Goldblum makes his film debut as Freak #1, attacking Bronson's wife and daughter at the opening. At the audition, Winner thrust a chair at him, saying: 'Rape that!' • The film is not available on video in Britain.

The Deer Hunter

★★ 1978 182min c.

Director: Michael Cimino
Screenplay: Deric Washburn

This tale of three steelworking buddies who get caught up in the horrors of war was the first important Vietnam film. It confirmed De Niro as a star, Streep as an actress to watch and Cimino as a director who screamed for attention. Working-class characters are rarely so convincingly shown in Hollywood, and the Vietnam sequences are still terrifying, but the film does seem to go on for ever. Why is it an hour before we get to Vietnam, for goodness sake? *Apocalypse Now*, then considered inferior, now looks better.

Michael ....Robert De Niro
Stan ....John Cazale
Steven ....John Savage
Nick ....Christopher Walken
Linda ....Meryl Streep
John ....George Dzundza
Axel ....Chuck Aspegren

Oscars Best Picture, Best Director, Christopher Walken

Quote 'You have to think about one shot. One shot is what it's all about. The deer has to be taken with one shot. I try to tell people that. They don't listen.'

OOPS! During the deer hunt, De Niro's watch swaps hands, probably because the film was reversed.

Psst! De Niro prepared for the film by living in a steelworking community for a while • Chuck Aspegren actually was a steelworker • De Niro and Savage performed their own stunts, including the jump into the river Kwai from the helicopter • A cable from the helicopter got caught on the strut of a bridge and nearly brought it down. One of the crew had to climb out and free it. The shot was still used in the movie • On location, the production doctor had to carry 27 different types of antidotes to snake bites • Although the Vietcong weren't always terribly nice guys, the Russian Roulette torture was invented for the movie • John Cazale died of bone cancer nine months after the film was completed. His condition was evident at the start of filming and nearly led to the project being cancelled before it began. By the end of filming, he was barely able to say his lines. Streep was his partner at the time.

Delicatessen

★★★ 1992 97min c.

Director: Jean-Pierre Jeunet & Marc Caro
Screenplay: Jean-Pierre Jeunet, Marc Caro & Gilles Adrien

Bizarre and very funny black French comedy about a future world in which meat is hard to come by. Pity the new lodgers in Dreyfus' apartments, for the chap's a butcher as well. Far more enjoyable, and considerably less tasteless, than it sounds, this is one of the most innovative, gag-packed comedies of recent years, cramming cannibalism, farce, love, satire, sex and guerilla warfare into a visually-splendid package.

Louison ....Dominique Pinon
Julie ....Marie-Laure Dougnac
Butcher ....Jean-Claude Dreyfus

Deliverance

★★★★ 1972 109min c.

Director: John Boorman
Screenplay: James Dickey
Source: Novel by Dickey

A quartet of soft-handed businessmen go on a canoeing and hunting trip and rapidly get out of their depth when they are hunted in return by a pair of mountain dwellers. This violent, electrifying film is gripping entertainment. Unlike our heroes, there's barely an ounce of flab on it. And on top of everything else, we get the wonderful 'Duelling Banjos'.

Ed	Jon Voight
Lewis	Burt Reynolds
Bobby	Ned Beatty
Drew	Ronny Cox
Mountain man	Bill McKinney
Toothless man	Herbert "Cowboy" Coward
Sheriff Bullard	James Dickey
Highway patrolman	Ed O'Neill
Ed's son	Charley Boorman

OOPS! Although Voight gets covered with muck when he trips while out trying to kill some food for his friends, when he turns up at camp again he's as spruce as when he set out • Boorman's own son, Charley, has his name spelt 'Charlie' in the credits.

Psst! Unusually, the movie was made in sequence • The stars did their own stunts, despite their dangerous nature • In Britain, the film was passed uncut despite the depiction of male rape • The actors did much of their own stuntwork • The author and screenwriter appears as Sheriff Bullard. He gave Reynolds a copy of *Zen in the Art of Archery* for Reynolds to read as background preparation • Just a few months before the film was released, Reynolds had appeared in the buff in *Cosmopolitan*, the magazine's first celebrity centrefold. A Chicago woman bought 500 copies of the magazine, at a cost of $700, to wallpaper her bedroom. Reynolds said: 'For $700 I would have gone over and seen her myself!' • The hillbilly sodomist had performed in public before, in old-fashioned Wild West shows. When Boorman told him what he had to do, he said: 'Well, that's all right. I done a lot worse than that'.

Demolition Man
★★★ 1993 114min c.

Director: Marco Brambilla
Screenplay: Daniel Waters, Robert Reneau & Peter M. Lenkov

Superb sci-fi actioner, with Sly a renegade cop put into suspended animation for being a mite too enthusiastic about his work. In the next century, when everything is sweetness and light and crime is a thing of the past, a vicious 20th century criminal gets loose. Sly has to be

woken and sent after him. An intriguing story, a fascinating (and depressing) view of the future, wonderful comedy and the glorious Bullock in her first big role make this one a must. It also happens to be a great argument against Political Correctness.

John Spartan	Sylvester Stallone
Simon Phoenix	Wesley Snipes
Lelina Huxley	Sandra Bullock
Dr. Raymond Cocteau	Nigel Hawthorne
Alfredo Garcia	Benjamin Bratt
Chief George Earle	Bob Gunton
Associate Bob	Glenn Shadix
Edgar Friendly	Denis Leary

Quote 'We're police officers. We're not trained to handle this kind of violence.' • 'Excuse me, Rambo. I need to borrow this.' • 'Be well!'

OOPS! When Snipes comes up from the manhole, the blue eye is the wrong one • Stallone swears in Bullock's car at one point and doesn't get fined • When he crashes her police car, it lands upside down but is the right way up in the next shot • Sly claims to be able to fix his shredded T-shirt with a needle and thread, but it doesn't look damaged when he goes to the cryogenic facility.

Psst! Lori Petty was replaced after a few days by Bullock • Scenes involving Stallone meeting his daughter who is now older than him were cut out after test audiences found them too sentimental • Photographic stills of the naked Stallone were stolen from the set and published in *Ciak*, an Italian movie magazine • The original script contained a mention of the fast-food franchise wars. The producers managed to turn this into a $5m tie-in with Taco Bell, although it was changed to Pizza Hut in some territories • Snipes making fun of the Orientals in the museum is presumably an in-joke relating to his previous role in *Rising Sun*.

Desire
★★★ 1936 89min b/w

Director: Frank Borzage
Screenplay: Edwin Justus Meyer, Waldemar Young & Samuel Hoffenstein

Lubitsch works his magic on Dietrich in a sparkling romantic comedy with an American engineer falling for a jewel thief who uses him to get gems across the border. The film's glorious look is the epitome of 30s movie chic. Frothy, but fun.

Madeleine de Beaupre	Marlene Dietrich
Tom Bradley	Gary Cooper
Carlos Margoli	John Halliday
Mr. Gibson	William Frawley
Aristide Duval	Ernest Cossart
Police Official	Akim Tamiroff
Dr. Edouard Pauquet	Alan Mowbray

Psst! Athough films were censored, trailers were free to contain what they wanted until this movie's boasted: 'At last sex has returned to the screen'. After that trailers were as closely scrutinised as the movies they promoted • Dietrich had been seeing John Gilbert, the famous silent star now on the skids. He took it badly when she went out with Cooper while they made *Morocco*. He began drinking again and died of a heart attack the day after Cooper's lead in *Desire* was announced.

Desperately Seeking Susan

★★★ 1985 104min c.

Director: Susan Seidelman
Screenplay: Leora Barish

Once upon a time, there was a pop singer on the verge of fame who starred in a quirky, fast-paced mystery involving mistaken identities that was funny and fresh. Ever since then, she's been desperately seeking Susan Seidelman – or a director as good as her – to make another successful film, failing miserably every time. Well this is the one where Madonna really *does* get it right. She's excellent as the mysterious Susan who so fascinates bored housewife Arquette. A good, fun little movie.

Roberta	Rosanna Arquette
Susan	Madonna
Dez	Aidan Quinn
Gary	Mark Blum
Jim	Robert Joy
Leslie	Laurie Metcalf
Nolan	Will Patton
Larry	Steven Wright
Ray	John Turturro

Showing Rebecca.

Psst! Madonna won her part over 200 other auditioning hopefuls • Arquette was originally the star but, as the film was being made, Madonna's career suddenly took off and her part was rapidly rewritten to give her a more prominent role. Arquette's nose was put considerably out of joint by Madonna and objected to the way her song 'Into the Groove'

was inserted into the movie • Getting the film off the ground took some doing. Producer Midge Sanford said: 'Our standard joke was that if the film ever got made, no-one would be left to see it because everyone had read the screenplay.'

Destry Rides Again

★★★★ 1939 94min b/w

Director: George Marshall
Screenplay: Felix Jackson, Gertrude Purcell & Henry Myers
Source: Novel by Max Brand

This Western spoof is unfettered joy with Stewart the pacifist, milk-drinking new deputy sheriff of Bottleneck who takes on local bad boy Donlevy and his girl Dietrich although he doesn't believe in carrying guns. Even without the splendid humour, this would be a smashing Western, packed as it is with action and splendid characters. With it, it becomes a dream, with one of the highspots Dietrich singing 'See What the Boys in the Backroom Will Have'.

Thomas Jefferson Destry Jr.	James Stewart
Frenchy	Marlene Dietrich
Wash Dinsdale	Charles Winninger
Boris Callahan	Mischa Auer
Kent	Brian Donlevy
Janice Tyndall	Irene Hervey
Lilly Belle Callahan	Una Merkel
Gyp Watson	Allen Jenkins
Bugs Watson	Warren Hymer
Loupgeron	Billy Gilbert
Jack Tyndall	Jack Carson

Quote 'You shoot it out with them and, for some reason, they get to look like heroes. You put 'em behind bars, and they look little and cheap, like they are.'

Psst! Although the censors at the Hays Office allowed Dietrich to stow money in her cleavage, they cut the line: 'There's gold in them thar hills!' • The producer Joe Pasternak wanted to cast against type. Dietrich's career had all but evaporated. After being labelled 'box office poison' like Katharine Hepburn, she fled to Europe. One of the screen's most glamorous stars, she was prepared to risk alienating audiences further by portraying a saloon singer. The studio was far keener on getting Paulette Goddard, but Pasternak prevailed. The film put Dietrich back on top again • Stewart was chosen because he was the most unlikely cowboy the producers could think of. After

Destry, he became a Western regular • Dietrich liked Stewart, but had trouble getting his attention. He seemed keener in reading his *Flash Gordon* comics. One day she had a life-size *Flash Gordon* doll made up and enticed Stewart into her dressing room with the doll there, locking the door • Dietrich wouldn't hear of using a stand-in for the cat-fight with Una Merkel and both actresses emerged badly bruised from filming the scene over five days • Author Max Brand, whose book was adapted here, wrote many other Westerns. He was also the creator of *Doctor Kildare*.

The Devil and Miss Jones
★★ 1941 92min c.

Director: Sam Wood
Screenplay: Norman Krasna

The wealthy owner of a department store poses as a shopworker to nail the troublemaker among his employees. Instead of firebrand radicals, he finds kind intolerable behaviour of the management. Despite its high reputation, this comedy isn't really terribly funny although it remains a sweet little tale, largely thanks to Coburn and Arthur.

Mary Jones . . . . .Jean Arthur
John P. Merrick . . . . .Charles Coburn
Joe O'Brien . . . . .Robert Cummings
Hooper .Edmund Gwenn
Elizabeth Ellis . . . . .Spring Byington
George . . . . .S.Z. "Cuddles" Sakall
Detective . . . . .William Demarest
Allison . . . . .Walter Kingsford
Harrison . . . . .Montagu Love

Les Diaboliques
★★★★ 1954 107min b/w

Director: Henri-Georges Clouzot
Screenplay: Henri-Georges Clouzot & Jerome Geronimi
Source: Novel, *Celle Qui N'etait Pas* by Pierre Boileau and Thomas Narcejac

When the wife and the mistress of an unpleasant headmaster can take it no more, they plot to do away with him. But things don't go according to plan. This classic French thriller may have been imitated many times since, but nothing beats the original. Genuinely surprising and truly scary, it is beautifully acted by the whole

cast. The lack of any incidental music only adds to the tension, which just gets steadily more unbearable. One to watch with the lights out and the chain on.

Nicole Horner . . . . .Simone Signoret
Christina Delasalle . . . . .Vera Clouzot
Michel Delasalle . . . . .Paul Meurisse
Insp. Fichet . . . . .Charles Vanel
M. Raymond . . . . .Michel Serrault
Plantiveau . . . . .Jean Brochard

Psst! Be wary. There are umpteen versions of this, all with different running times.

Dial M For Murder
★★ 1954 105min c.

Director: Alfred Hitchcock
Screenplay: Frederick Knott
Source: Play by Knott

Sub-standard Hitchcock. So little has this adaptation of the successful play about a man plotting to murder his wife been changed for the screen that you can practically see the proscenium arch. It has its moments and remains watchable, but you can't help feeling that making it in 3D was not the brightest of ideas.

Tony Wendice . . . . .Ray Milland
Chief Insp. Hubbard . . . . .John Williams
Margot Wendice . . . . .Grace Kelly
Mark Halliday . . . . .Robert Cummings
Capt. Swan Lesgate . . . . .Anthony Dawson
Sgt. Pearson . . . . .Patrick Allen

Quote 'I was going to pass you off with an indifferent port...'

OOPS! The slo-motion on the video comes in handy when Kelly picks up the scissors to stab Dawson. Very briefly, the scissors can be spotted in his back before she does the deed.

Psst! Hitch can be seen in the reunion photograph which appears about 13 minutes into the movie • Hitch had already begun preparation for *Rear Window* and his heart wasn't in the project, particularly as he was ordered to film it in 3D, necessitating cameras that could barely be moved. Hitch called 3D: 'A nine days wonder, and I am in on the ninth day.' • The telephone being dialled at the opening is actually a giant prop with a big wooden finger. The 3D cameras couldn't cope with closeups • Williams had played the part of the Inspector on stage.

Diamonds Are Forever

★★ 1971 120min c.

Director: Guy Hamilton
Screenplay: Richard Maibaum & Tom Mankiewicz
Source: Novel by Ian Fleming

Bond picks up plenty of interesting labels for his luggage as he visits Amsterdam and Las Vegas on the trail of diamond smugglers. Despite Connery's return, this 007 outing is too flabby, stupidly jokey and camp, and is way from the best in the series.

James Bond	Sean Connery
Tiffany Case	Jill St. John
Victor Blofeld	Charles Gray
Plenty O'Toole	Lana Wood
Willard Whyte	Jimmy Dean
Saxby	Bruce Cabot
Wint	Bruce Glover
Kidd	Putter Smith
'M'	Bernard Lee
Miss Moneypenny	Lois Maxwell
'Q'	Desmond Llewelyn
Felix Leiter	Norman Burton

Quote 'I'll finish dressing.' – 'Oh, please, don't. Not on my account.' • 'Hi, I'm Plenty.' – 'Of course you are.' • 'Good morning, gentlemen. Acme pollution inspection. We're cleaning up the world and thought this was a suitable starting point.'

OOPS! When Bond tips the Mustang onto its side to get through the alley, it's the right wheels that are on the ground. But it comes out the other side on its left wheels • The feather in the logo of Slumber Inc. on the hearse at Los Angeles airport changes direction from one shot to the next • Keep your eyes on the wheels of the moon-buggy that Bond nabs. Not only does it lose one of its wheels but in the next shot the wheel is fixed back on again.

Psst! Desperate to lure Connery back after Lazenby's performance in *On Her Majesty's Secret Service*, he was paid $1.25m up front and given 12.5% of the gross take, making him the highest-paid actor in the world at the time. He donated his fee to the Scottish International Trust • Director Hamilton thought he'd found the perfect Bond when watching a TV talk show and still thought so after meeting him. But the studio decided that stuntman Burt Reynolds was not star material • Among those in mind for Tiffany Case were Faye Dunaway, Raquel Welch and Jane Fonda • Lana Wood, playing Plenty O'Toole, is Natalie Wood's sister • Howard Hughes, the model for Willard Whyte, permitted filming in his casinos in return for a copy of the movie when it was finished • In Hong Kong, the film was entitled *Man as Tough as Iron and Gold and Steel Uncovers the Gang Dealing with Diamonds in Hong Kong.*

Die Hard

★★★★ 1988 131min c.

Director: John McTiernan
Screenplay: Jeb Stuart & Steven E. de Souza
Source: Novel, *Nothing Lasts Forever* by Roderick Thorpe

Terrorists take control of a skyscraper, not realising that supercop Willis is on hand to thwart their plans. Perhaps the best action thriller ever, with an excellent script backing up the rough stuff. The part fits Willis like a glove, while Rickman is superb as the intellectual, Jermyn Street-suited terrorist. One of those rare films that gets better on every viewing, as still further nuances are revealed.

John McClane	Bruce Willis
Hans Gruber	Alan Rickman
Holly Gennaro McClane	Bonnie Bedelia
Karl	Alexander Godunov
Sgt. Al Powell	Reginald Veljohnson
Dwayne T. Robinson	Paul Gleason
Argyle	De'voreaux White
Thornburg	William Atherton
Ellis	Hart Bochner
Takagi	James Shigeta
Big Johnson	Robert Davi
Little Johnson	Grand L. Bush

Quote 'Welcome to the party, pal.' • 'Only John can drive someone that crazy.' • 'Yippee-ki-yea, motherfucker!'

OOPS! When the terrorists fire a missile at the police car, they obviously smash the window. Yet when they fire again, the glass is shattered all over again • Surely the terrorists would find McClane's shoes and socks after he leaves them in plain view in the bathroom? • Holly's surname is spelt both 'Gennero' and 'Gennaro' • The dead guy in the elevator can't quite keep his eyes still when Gruber's there.

Psst! Bruce Willis was not particularly popular when the film was launched, which is why on the posters his face was half obscured by the skyscraper • The building is the 20th Century Fox Tower, HQ of the company that made the pic • When shown on TV, the famous phrase somehow becomes, 'Yippee-ki-yea, Kemosabe', even though the f-word is used in abundance elsewhere • In Germany, the terrorists come from 'Europe' rather than the Fatherland.

Die Hard 2
★★★ 1990 120min c.

Director: Renny Harlin
Screenplay: Steven E. de Souza & Doug Richardson

Yet another Christmas is spoiled for tough cop McClane as he tackles a bunch of right-wing terrorists menacing Washington airport while his wife circles overhead. Fast and exciting and with plenty of wry humour, this sequel would be as good as the original were it not for some wild implausibilities. Not least of them is the idea that a man with a handgun not only never runs out of bullets but is invincible against baddies who play dirty by using automatic weapons.

John McClane . . . . .Bruce Willis
Jolly McClane . . . . .Bonnie Bedelia
Dick Thornberg . . . . .William Atherton
Sgt. Al Powell . . . . .Reginald Veljohnson
Esperanza . . . . .Franco Nero
Col Stuart . . . . .William Sadler
Maj. Grant . . . . .John Amos
Carmine Lorenzo . . . . .Dennis Franz
Leslie Barnes .Art Evans
Trudeau . . . . .Fred Dalton Thompson
Also: Tom Bower, Sheila McCarthy, Don Harvey, Robert Patrick, John Leguizamo, Colm Meaney

Blurb Die Harder • They Say Lightning Never Strikes Twice...They Were Wrong.

Quote 'Just the fax, ma'am. Just the fax.'
• 'How can the same shit happen to the same guy twice?'

OOPS! If the passengers can use the phones on the planes to contact the ground, why don't the pilots use them instead of flying blind?
• Although Willis rings his wife while she's in the air, it would be impossible. Calls only work the other way. • Not long after we're told that Nashville airport is snowed up, flights are told to divert there • Why does a plane with no fuel left burst into flames on crash-landing?
• Samantha Coleman is used through the film but it's 'Copeland' on the credits • According to a pilot friend, all the stuff about the terrorists recalibrating ILS is complete nonsense, as pilots have other ways of checking it.

Psst! The bodycount is said to be 264, possibly the highest in mainstream Hollywood history • The studio laughed when the director suggested filming this winter-set story in his native Scandinavia. An unusually mild American winter meant a frantic search for rapidly-vanishing snow and dry ice bills of $50,000 a day • According to Bedelia, while Willis was paid $7.5m, she actually got less than for the first film • The video is an '18', with scenes not seen in the cinema, where it was cut to get a '15' certificate.

Die Hard With a Vengeance
★★★ 1995 128min c.

Director: John McTiernan
Screenplay: Jonathan Hensleigh

Bomber Irons combines his terror campaign in New York with a series of lethal games involving McClane, against whom he appears to bear a grudge. He has, however, another agenda and with everyone in uniform in the Big Apple looking the other way, it's up to McClane to nail him. A film that starts off with a bang, literally, and never lets up. Although the plot's a trifle contrived and not always completely in touch with reality, Willis and touchy Jackson make a splendid team and there are several very exciting action sequences. The weirdly tonsured and accented Irons can't match Rickman in the villainous European stages and the structure isn't as clever as the original *Die Hard*. But it still outdoes *Die Hard 2*.

John McClane . . . . .Bruce Willis
Simon . . . . .Jeremy Irons
Zeus . . . . .Samuel L. Jackson
Joe Lambert . . . . .Graham Greene
Connie Kowalski . . . . .Colleen Camp
Arthur Cobb . . . . .Larry Bryggman
Ricky Walsh . . . . .Anthony Peck
Targo . . . . .Nick Wyman
Katya . . . . .Sam Phillips

Quote 'You are about to have a very bad day.'

OOPS! Just after the 42nd Street phone call, when the pair commandeer a cab to get them to Wall Street, you can see people watching the filming in the background • Willis gets all muddy after being blown out of the water pipe. But his socks are whiter than white on the boat later • Surely the puzzle with the three and five gallon jugs doesn't work as they do it in the film?

Psst! Despite the sensation at the time of *Die*

Hard 2, just five years earlier, when it was announced that Bruce Willis was going to be paid $7.5m, Willis was paid $15m for *Die Hard 3*. However, by the time the film was released Sylvester Stallone and Jim Carrey had both broken the $20m barrier • This outing was originally going to be set on a cruise ship, until it emerged that *Under Siege* was going to be set at sea • With little love lost between them, Willis had a clause in his contract banning Joel Silver – the action producer of movies like *Die Hard*, *Lethal Weapon* and *Demolition Man* – from the set while he was working • The sandwich board Willis wears in Harlem actually had the indiscriminate message, 'I Hate Every Body' on it. It was thought that local residents might not take kindly to him walking round their neighbourhood with the words 'I Hate Niggers' prominently displayed. The words were changed electronically afterwards • The ending of the film had to be reshot, posing problems as Willis had had his head shaved for his next movie.

Diggstown
SEE: Midnight Sting

Diner
★★★★ 1982 110min c.

Director: Barry Levinson
Screenplay: Barry Levinson

Five young men spend much of their time in the Fells Point Diner trying to get to grips with impending adulthood, continually pressing each other for advice on women. An assured debut from Levinson, it's splendidly evocative and has extraordinarily naturalistic dialogue. Full of memorable moments, particularly the scenes with the popcorn in the cinema and in the strip joint when they decide the music isn't fast enough. Wise, witty and wonderful.

Eddie .Steve Guttenberg
Shrevie . . . . .Daniel Stern
Boogie . . . . .Mickey Rourke
Fenwick . . . . .Kevin Bacon
Billy . . . . .Timothy Daly
Beth . . . . .Ellen Barkin
Modell . . . . .Paul Reiser

Blurb What They Wanted Most Wasn't On The Menu

Quote 'Fenwick. Put the damn sheep down.'

Showing A Summer Place.

Psst! The movie is based on Levinson's own experiences growing up in Baltimore. The original diners, on whom he based the characters, watched much of the film being shot.

Dinner at Eight
★★★ 1933 113min b/w

Director: George Cukor
Screenplay: Frances Marion, Herman J. Mankiewicz & Donald Ogden Stewart
Source: Play by George S. Kaufman & Edna Ferber.

Assorted New Yorkers gather for the dinner party from hell. There is little more to this than witty sparring repartée, with the film barely opened up from the stage play it was based on. However Dressler and Harlow as the women at the opposite ends of life shine out and make the all-star exercise come to life.

Carlotta Vance . . . . .Marie Dressler
Larry Renault . . . . .John Barrymore
Dan Packard . . . . .Wallace Beery
Kitty Packard . . . . .Jean Harlow
Oliver Jordan . . . . .Lionel Barrymore
Max Kane . . . . .Lee Tracy
Dr. Wayne Talbot . . . . .Edmund Lowe
Mr. Oliver Jordan . . . . .Billie Burke
Paula Jordan . . . . .Madge Evans
Joe Stengel . . . . .Jean Hersholt
Also: May Robson, Elizabeth Patterson, Karen Morley, Phillips Holmes, Grant Mitchell, Edwin Maxwell, John Davidson, Edward Woods, Herman Bing

Quote 'If there's one thing I know, it's men. I ought to. It's been my life's work.' • 'I was reading a book the other day. Do you know that the guy said machinery is going to take the place of every profession?' – 'Oh, my dear, that's something you need never worry about.'

Psst! The movie's sets were influential in helping to establish the success of the art deco style in the 30s • Harlow and Beery weren't acting when they sniped at each other. They actually detested each other, with Beery considering her a tramp • Barrymore's drunken has-been is effectively an autobiographical role • Clark Gable was going to have Edmund Lowe's part at one point, but MGM head Louis B. Mayer didn't want Gable to appear in an unsympathetic role • The name of Marie Dressler's dog was changed from Mussolini to Tarzan because of objections from the Italian authorities.

Dinosaurus!
★★ 1960 85min c.

Director: Irvin Yeaworth Jr.
Screenplay: Jean Yeaworth & Dan E. Weisburd

Another of those wonderful so-bad-they're-funny movies, with a caveman and a pair of dreadfully-animated dinosaurs emerging onto a modern desert island. Deliciously silly and incompetent and a source of great laughs.

Bart Thompson . . . . .Ward Ramsey
Chuck . . . . .Paul Lukather
Betty Piper . . . . .Kristina Hanson
Julio . . . . .Alan Roberts
Prehistoric Man . . . . .Gregg Martell

Blurb SEE The Battle Between Primeval Beast And Monster Machine! SEE What Happens When A Prehistoric Man Meets A Modern Girl!

Dirty Dancing
★★ 1987 97min c.

Director: Emile Ardolino
Screenplay: Eleanor Bergstein

Grey, on holiday in the Catskills with her family, falls for the attractions of dancing instructor Swayze. For some reason, her dad isn't too happy. A pleasing but insubstantial soufflé that appeals to young girls but may leave others a little cold. The dancing's good fun, though it's a wonder they don't trip over all those clichés that are lying around the place.

Baby Houseman . . . . .Jennifer Grey
Johnny Castle . . . . .Patrick Swayze
Jake Houseman . . . . .Jerry Orbach
Penny Johnson . . . . .Cynthia Rhodes
Max Kellerman . . . . .Jack Weston
Lisa Houseman . . . . .Jane Brucker
Marjorie Houseman . . . . .Kelly Bishop
Neil Kellerman . . . . .Lonny Price
Tito Suarez . . . . .Charles Honi Coles

Quote 'Have you got sheet music for this stuff?'

OOPS! After the first sex scene together, you can see that Grey's got knickers on as Swayze gets out of bed • When Swayze returns for the final dance number, he takes off his jacket twice • Soon afterwards, he leaps from the stage and gets dirt on his knees. But it vanishes in the next shot.

The Dirty Dozen
★★ 1967 150min c.

Director: Robert Aldrich
Screenplay: Nunnally Johnson & Lukas Heller
Source: Novel by E.M. Nathanson

A bunch of the meanest, nastiest soldiers imprisoned by the US army are recruited to be particularly beastly to the Germans in occupied France. The characters are all cardboard cut-outs, there's some terribly hammy acting and it's a good hour before anything interesting happens. Despite the odd moment of excitement, it's way too long and uncomplicated and isn't helped by the action sequences looking old hat by modern standards.

Maj. Reisman . . . . .Lee Marvin
Gen. Worden . . . . .Ernest Borgnine
Joseph Wladislaw . . . . .Charles Bronson
Robert Jefferson . . . . .Jim Brown
Victor Franko . . . . .John Cassavetes
Col. Everett Dasher-Breed . . . . . . .Robert Ryan
Maj. Max Armbruster . . . . .George Kennedy
Archer Maggott . . . . .Telly Savalas
Vernon Pinkley . . . . .Donald Sutherland
Sgt. Bowren . . . . .Richard Jaeckel
Pedro Jiminez . . . . .Trini Lopez

Quote 'You guys foul up on this one, none of us will ever play the violin again.' • 'Everybody's slipping on soap around here.' • 'Kill every officer in sight.' – 'Ours or theirs?'

OOPS! They aren't supposed to have any dog tags on, but Marvin is wearing his.

Psst! Trini Lopez doesn't last long in the film. He would have survived longer if his agent hadn't tried to get more money for him in the middle of the production • John Wayne was offered Marvin's part and was all set to play it until *The Green Berets* turned up • Jack Palance rejected Savalas' role • The run by Brown at the end, after he's blown the cellars with four extra grenades, was done not by a stuntman but by him. The ex-football star was the only one who could possibly run fast enough to escape the very real explosion.

Dirty Harry
★★★ 1971 102min c.

Director: Don Siegel
Screenplay: Harry Julian Fink, Rita M. Fink & Dean Riesner

Great action from the wonderful Eastwood in his first outing for Callahan, the San Francisco detective who is a law unto himself. Here he gets fed up of the Mayor's pussyfooting around with a psycho who's blackmailing the city and goes after him himself. It was followed by the sequels *Magnum Force, The Enforcer, Sudden Impact* and *The Dead Pool*. None came close to the excitement of the original.

Harry Callahan	Clint Eastwood
Chico	Reni Santoni
Bressler	Harry Guardino
The Mayor	John Vernon
Scorpio	Andrew Robinson
The Chief	John Larch
DiGeorgio	John Mitchum
Mrs. Russell	Mae Mercer

Blurb It's Inspector Callahan Vs. The Psychopath. Dirty Harry's The One With The Badge!

Quote 'When a naked man is chasing a woman through an alley with a butcher knife and a hard-on, I figure he isn't out collecting for the Red Cross.' • 'I know what you're thinking. Did he fire six shots or only five? Well, to tell you the truth, in all this excitement I've kind of lost track myself. But being as this is a 44 Magnum, the most powerful handgun in the world and would blow your head clean off, you've got to ask yourself one question: Do I feel lucky? Well, do ya, punk?' • 'He's basically for good and he's got a morality that's higher than society's morality. He hates bureaucracy and he thinks that the law is often wrong. If that's being called fascistic, as several critics have called it, they're full of it.' [Eastwood]

OOPS! After a shopkeeper wraps up a bottle of wine for a customer, he's hit with it. But although the bottle smashes, there's no liquid inside.

Psst! The role of Callahan was turned down by Paul Newman and John Wayne. Frank Sinatra was due to play him, but a hand injury intervened • The film was based on a real-life psychopath using the name Zodiac who operated in San Francisco in the late 60s. He was never caught and when a copycat killer styling himself The Zebra Killer was around in 1974, graffiti appeared in Frisco saying: 'Dirty Harry, where are you now that we need you?' • A section of the Philippine police force ordered a print of the movie – to use as a training film! • After thwarting the early bank robbery, Eastwood passes a cinema showing his directorial debut, *Play Misty for Me*

• Although that was his only film as director to date, he had to stand in for Siegel in the suicide rescue scene after the director got flu
• Eastwood did most of his own stunts, incluing the jump from the bridge onto the roof of the bus Scorpio hijacks.

Dirty Rotten Scoundrels
★★★ 1988 110min c.

Director: Frank Oz
Screenplay: Dale Launer, Stanley Shapiro & Paul Henning

1964's *Bedtime Story* isn't a patch on this remake, a delicious battle between rival con-men Caine and Martin to see which of them must pack their bags and depart the French Riviera. Despite a mite too much silliness from Martin, the jokes fly thick and fast and are supported by a wonderfully clever, twisting, plot that keeps you guessing. A comic delight.

Freddy Benson	Steve Martin
Lawrence Jamieson	Michael Caine
Janet Colgate	Glenne Headly
Inspector Andre	Anton Rogers
Fanny Eubanks	Barbara Harris
Arthur	Ian McDiarmid
Mrs. Reed	Dana Ivey

Blurb Nice Guys Finish Last. Meet The Winners.

Psst! Originally developed as a musical vehicle for Mick Jagger and David Bowie! • The scene in the film's trailer with Martin pushing the old woman into the water wasn't in the movie, being shot specially for the ad.

The Discreet Charm of the Bourgeoisie
★★★★ 1972 100min c.

Director: Luis Buñuel
Screenplay: Luis Buñuel & Jean-Claude Carriere

A dry martini of a film; intoxicating, sophisticated and lethal, with the middle class the olive Buñuel skewers with his cocktail stick. Six friends keep meeting for dinner, but events always prevent them from enjoying the meal. Buñuel rounds up all his usual suspects here – the state, the church, the importance of dreams – but at this late stage of his Surrealist career, he seems wryly to be conceding that the bourgeoisie are actually indestructable.

Ambassador Acosta	.Fernando Rey
Mme Thevenot	.Delphine Seyrig
Mme Senechal	.Stéphane Audran
Florence	.Bulle Ogier
M. Senechal	.Jean-Pierre Cassel
M. Thevenot	.Paul Frankeur
Home Secretary	.Michel Piccoli

Psst! Buñuel didn't want his actresses to use make-up or have their hair done for some scenes. They usually managed it in secret anyway but, according to Audran: 'Buñuel had a strange contraption like a periscope with which he used to spy on us and catch us out.'
• Buñuel claimed that his favourite characters in the film were the cockroaches.

Diva
★★★ 1981 123min c.

Director: Jean-Jacques Beineix
Screenplay: Jean-Jacques Beineix & Jean Van Hamme
Source: Novel by Delacorta.

An incredibly stylish and exciting French thriller. A mailman obsessed with an American opera singer is pursued both by bootleggers after the only recording of her singing and by gangsters trying to retrieve an incriminating tape. Stunning visuals and a suitably twisting plot make this a transport of delight.

Jules	.Frederic Andrei
Cynthia Hawkins	.Wilhelmenia Wiggins Fernandez
Gorodish	.Richard Bohringer
Alba	.Thuy An Luu
Saporta	.Jacques Fabbri
Le Cure	.Dominique Pinon

Psst! The opera is Alfredo Catalani's *La Wally*, while the other splendid music is by Vladimir Cosma.

Doctor in the House
★★★ 1954 91min c.

Director: Ralph Thomas
Screenplay: Nicholas Phipps
Source: Novel by Richard Gordon

A bunch of incredibly mature-looking medical students show as much interest in drink and debauchery as in their studies. This often hilarious romp shows its age a little but the spirited performances, particularly from the superb

James Robertson Justice, make it well worthwhile. The sequels, of gradually diminishing merit, had the Doctor *At Large, In Love, In Distress, In Clover* and *In Trouble.*

Simon	.Dirk Bogarde
Joy	.Muriel Pavlow
Grimsdyke	.Kenneth More
Benskin	.Donald Sinden
Isobel	.Kay Kendall
Sir Lancelot	.James Robertson Justice
Taffy	.Donald Huston
Stella	.Suzanne Cloutier
Dean	.Geoffrey Keen
Briggs	.George Coulouris

Also: Shirley Eaton, Joan Hickson, Richard Wattis

Quote 'You! What's the bleeding time?'

Psst! In addition to the sequels, the books were also the basis of a long-running TV sitcom.

Doctor Zhivago
★★ 1965 197min c.

Director: David Lean
Screenplay: Robert Bolt
Source: Novel by Boris Pasternak

A doctor and a beautiful girl find that a pesky revolution keeps getting in the way of their love affair. Sharif is woefully out of his depth while the haphazard script seems to have been put together by a Russian welder with a few too many bottles of vodka under his belt. Nonetheless, some of the scenes of spectacle are breathtaking. However, while in the cinema these majestic sequences can just about hold your attention, on the small screen the chances are that few will be able to endure the film into its fourth hour. As for the music, whoever got Maurice Jarre to write it should be marooned between floors in an elevator in which it plays endlessly.

Yuri Zhivago	.Omar Sharif
Lara	.Julie Christie
Tonya	.Geraldine Chaplin
Komarovsky	.Rod Steiger
Pasha	.Tom Courtenay
Yevgraf	.Alec Guinness
Alexander	.Ralph Richardson
Anna	.Siobhan McKenna
The Girl	.Rita Tushingham
Amelia	.Adrienne Corri
Prof. Kurt	.Geoffrey Keen
Petya	.Jack MacGowran

Oscars Best Screenplay (adapted)

Quote 'Although I went all over the world promoting it, I'd never got to see more than the credits before being whisked away. Finally, at Cannes, I was to sit the whole thing through. When I appeared for the first time, I fainted from the shock – and woke up in the ladies' room.' [Geraldine Chaplin']

Psst! It is quite sobering to reflect that, just 10 years earlier, anyone trying to make this film would have been hounded out of Hollywood because of the Communist witch hunts. Writer Robert Bolt was not allowed into America to attend the premiere because he had visited China and had been briefly imprisoned after a CND demonstration • Pasternak had won the Nobel Prize but the Russian authorities refused him permission to collect it • Nicolas Roeg was the original cinematographer but, after arguing with Lean, he was sacked after two months • A giant set was built by 800 workers over two years on a site near Madrid's airport, Spain being a more economical base than Hollywood for such a film • The planned budget of $7.5m was virtually doubled by the time the film was finished • To get the correct look of authenticity, the production moved near to the border between Russia and Finland. The mass retreat was staged in temperatures that went down to 30 degrees below freezing • Sharif had his eyes taped back to make his face look more Russian • His son Tarek plays Zhivago aged seven • Sharif was unimpressed by Christie, particularly after seeing her eating fried-egg sandwiches, which he considered very unfeminine • Marlon Brando was offered Steiger's role, but never replied to Lean's letter • Lean made around $15m from the movie. He gave some of it away to Bolt and members of the crew, as well as to charities and the struggling BAFTA.

Dodsworth

★★★★ 1936 101min b/w

Director: William Wyler
Screenplay: Sidney Howard
Source: Play by Howard adapted from the novel by Sinclair Lewis

When a car tycoon retires, he and his wife take a trip to Europe but their lives begin to go in separate directions. This wholly engrossing melodrama depicting a man forced to readjust his life completely in his later years boasts some fine performances, but none better than from Huston himself.

Sam Dodsworth	Walter Huston
Fran Dodsworth	Ruth Chatterton
Edith Cortright	Mary Astor
Arnold Iselin	Paul Lukas
Maj. Lockert	David Niven
Kurt von Obersdorf	Gregory Gaye
Baroness von Obersdorf	Maria Ouspenskaya
Harry	John Payne
Mme. de Penable	Odette Myrtil
Matey Pearson	Spring Byington
Hazzard	Charles Halton

Also: Grant Mitchell

Quote 'Love has to stop some place short of suicide.'

Psst! Writer Howard told producer Sam Goldwyn that the novel would make an excellent film but Goldwyn turned it down. Howard then wrote a play based on it which was a huge success. Goldwyn bought the rights to that for a substantial $165,000. Howard reminded him he could have bought it for $20,000 earlier. 'I'd rather pay $165,000,' said Goldwyn, 'for a successful play than $20,000 for a novel that I don't know what it's going to be like.' • Although highly regarded, the film was not a commercial success. Goldwyn snapped: 'Don't talk to me about *Dodsworth*. I lost my goddamn shirt. I'm not saying it wasn't a fine picture. It was a *great* picture, but nobody wanted to see it. In *droves* • Huston played the same role in the play on Broadway • David Niven said that director Wyler 'was a Jekyll and Hyde character. Kind, fun and cozy at all other times, he became a fiend the moment his bottom touched down in the director's chair • Only the previous year Astor had starred in one of the most scandalous star divorces of all time. Her husband produced in court a diary in which she recorded intimate details of her affair with playwright George S. Kaufman. Details were leaked to the press and the public lapped up the extracts, full of phrases like, 'It's been years since I felt a man up in public, but I just got carried away' and 'We flew into each other's arms. He was rampant in an instant'. Partly thanks to *Dodsworth*, the scandal didn't seem to harm Astor's career, but her diary was burnt by the court for being pornographic.

Dog Day Afternoon

★★★ 1975 130min c.

Director: Sidney Lumet
Screenplay: Frank Pierson
Source: Magazine article by P.F. Kluge & Thomas Moore

A pair of incompetent robbers hold up a bank to raise the cash to pay for one of their lovers to have a sex change operation. Unfortunately, they don't manage a quick getaway and the thing spirals out of control. A tense script is whacked over by some great acting. Bizarrely enough, it's based on a true story.

Sonny	Al Pacino
Sal	John Cazale
Moretti	Charles Durning
Leon	Chris Sarandon
Mulvaney	Sully Boyar
Sheldon	James Broderick
Jenny	Carol Kane
Murphy	Lance Henriksen

Oscars Best Screenplay

Quote 'I'm a Catholic and I don't want to hurt anybody.'

Psst! During the production, Pacino collapsed from nervous exhaustion and filming came to a halt while he recovered in hospital • John Cazale, who portrays Sal, also played Pacino's weak brother Fredo in the *Godfather* movies • The phone conversation between Pacino and Sarandon in the barbershop was apparently improvised • The character on whom Pacino's part was based was released from prison after serving six years.

La Dolce Vita

★★★ 1960 174min c.

Director: Federico Fellini
Screenplay: Federico Fellini, Tullio Pinelli, Ennio Flaiano & Brunello Rondi

This satire of Rome's high life at the onset of the 1960s has lost some of its power to shock but still holds up surprisingly well against many of Fellini's other pictures, even if he does seem unsure whether he's for or against his chosen targets. There are plenty of splendid moments here, although three hours does seem something of a self-indulgence. If nothing else, it's certainly a fascinating record of a bygone age.

Marcello Rubini	Marcello Mastroianni
Sylvia Rank	Anita Ekberg
Maddalena	Anouk Aimée
Steiner	Alain Cuny
Emma	Yvonne Furneaux
Fanny	Magali Noel
Robert	Lex Barker

Blurb The Most Talked About – The Most Shocked About Film Of Our Years.

Psst! Amazingly, much of the whole movie was shot in a studio, even the scene in the fountain • The movie gave the world the word *paparazzi* to describe the frantic star-popping photographers • Fellini said that he sent out feelers to see if Marilyn Monroe would be interested in being in the film. 'She say no, thank you. Is big star, I am Italian director. She would be divine in the scenes played by Anita Ekberg. But with Marilyn Monroe, whole movie then has to be about the girl in the fountain.'

Don Juan DeMarco

★★★★ 1995 97min c.

Director: Jeremy Leven
Screenplay: Jeremy Leven

A young man believes himself to be the great Latin lover Don Juan and is treated by psychiatrist Brando, who finds his dormant romantic streak being awakened. This luscious deeply romantic comedy sends tingles down the spine. Erotic without being explicit, sensual without being overtly sexual, it put me on such a high I wanted to give flowers to every woman I saw afterwards. The scene with Depp seducing the woman in the hotel restaurant must surely rank with the chess game in *The Thomas Crown Affair* and the food scene in *Tom Jones* as one of the most sensuous examples of foreplay in the movies.

Jack Mickler	Marlon Brando
Don Juan DeMarco	Johnny Depp
Marilyn Mickler	Faye Dunaway
Dona Ana	Geraldine Pailhas
Dr. Paul Showalter	Bob Dishy
Dona Inez	Rachel Ticotin
Dona Julia	Talisa Soto

Quote 'I have made love to over a thousand women. I was twenty-one last Wednesday.'
• 'I hope you went ahead without me.'
• 'It *sings*?' • 'He suffered from a romanticism which was incurable and, what was even worse, highly contagious.' • 'If you can't get laid after seeing this film, you just can't get laid.' [Critic Jan Wahl]

Psst! Brando brought his weight down from 25 stone to 17 stone • Although Brando was not reading off cue-cards as in other recent films, he is said to have had his lines read to him through an earpiece.

Don't Look Now
★★★ 1973 110min c.

Director: Nicolas Roeg
Screenplay: Allan Scott & Chris Bryant
Source: Novel by Daphne du Maurier

This is still one of the few truly scary films, with Sutherland and Christie haunted by the spirit of their dead daughter in a crimson anorak. The atmosphere of England and Venice is brilliantly shot and Roeg's unconventional editing cleverly conveys a sinister world Out There. There are many memorable highlights, though perhaps a few too many aimless wanderings around the canals. Wear red next time you go to a cinema to see this and there won't be a problem with anyone blocking your exit afterwards.

Laura Baxter	Julie Christie
John Baxter	Donald Sutherland
Mystic (Heather)	Hilary Mason
Wendy	Clelia Matania
Bishop Barbarrigo	Massimo Serato
Insp. Longhi	Renato Scarpa
Hotel manager	Leopoldo Trieste
Anthony Babbage	David Tree

Do the Right Thing
★★★ 1989 120min c.

Director: Spike Lee
Screenplay: Spike Lee

Though not a perfect film, this is still a provocative, convincing portrait of American inner-city tensions as frustration boils over into violence. Witty and scorchingly shot, Lee erred only in predicting the uprising taking place in New York rather than Los Angeles.

Sal	Danny Aiello
Da Mayor	Ossie Davis
Mother Sister	Ruby Dee
Vito	Richard Edson
Buggin' Out	Giancarlo Esposito
Mookie	Spike Lee
Radio Raheem	Bill Nunn
Pino	John Turturro
Tina	Rosie Perez

Psst! Robert De Niro was originally signed to play Sal but dropped out • Joie, Lee's real-life sister, plays his sister in the film • The credits have an appeal to audiences to vote. Lee hoped that people would kick out New York's Mayor Koch, perhaps better-known as a guest-star of The Muppets Take Manhattan.

Double Indemnity
★★★★ 1944 107min b/w

Director: Billy Wilder
Screenplay: Billy Wilder & Raymond Chandler
Source: Magazine story by James M. Cain

Like a predatory insect, femme fatale Stanwyck ensnares insurance salesman MacMurray and then persuades him that with hubby out of the way, life would be so much more pleasant. MacMurray doesn't stop to think that some female insects eat their mates when their usefulness is over. This classic film noir never fades. The script sparkles with wit and fire and the photography is superb. But it's the performances that make it such a transport of delight. Stanwyck practically sets the screen on fire while the much underrated Robinson proves what a fine actor he could be when a role let him.

Walter Neff	Fred MacMurray
Phyllis Dietrichson	Barbara Stanwyck
Barton Keyes	Edward G. Robinson
Mr. Dietrichson	Tom Powers
Mr. Jackson	Porter Hall
Lola Dietrichson	Jean Heather
Nino Zachette	Gig Young
Mr. Norton	Richard Gaines
Sam Gorlopis	Fortunio Bonanova
Also: John Philliber, Bess Flowers	

Quote 'I killed Dietrichson. Me, Walter Neff, insurance salesman, 35 years old, unmarried, no visible scars. Until a while ago, that is…'
• 'Yes, I killed him. I killed him for money and for a woman. Well, I didn't get the money and I didn't get the woman. Pretty, isn't it?' • 'There's a speed limit in this state, Mr. Neff, around 45 miles an hour.' – 'How fast was I going, officer?' – 'Around 90.' • 'I wonder if I know what you mean.' – 'I wonder if you wonder.'

OOPS! MacMurray's character is a bachelor but he has on what is presumably his own wedding ring throughout the movie.

Psst! Amazingly, the film did not win one Oscar • The basis of the film was the true Snyder and Gray case of 1927, with a couple doing away with the woman's husband for the insurance money • It is said that 11 actors rejected the part of Neff, among them George Raft and Alan Ladd. MacMurray was for some time unwilling to take on a role so different to his usual clean-cut nice chap • As originally filmed, the ending was to have MacMurray dying in the gas chamber in San Quentin, with Robinson watching. But it was felt too harrowing and the last 20 minutes were dropped. Wilder claims they were among the best scenes he ever made. Legend has it that the footage still exists.

A Double Life

★★★ 1947 103min b/w

Director: George Cukor
Screenplay: Ruth Gordon & Garson Kanin
Source: Play, *Othello* by William Shakespeare.

A theatre actor has increasing trouble distinguishing between reality and the parts he is playing on stage. Although there are probably method actors who would consider it merely sensible preparation, when he plays Othello he develops murderous tendencies towards a woman he thinks is Desdemona. Colman portrays the light and dark side of the one man beautifully but the whole enterprise now comes over as a touch too melodramatic.

Anthony John . . . . .Ronald Colman
Brita . . . . .Signe Hasso
Bill Friend . . . . .Edmond O'Brien
Pat Kroll . . . . .Shelley Winters
Victor Donlan . . . . .Ray Collins
Max Lasker . . . . .Philip Loeb
Al Cooley . . . . .Millard Mitchell
Pete Bonner . . . . .Joe Sawyer
Dr. Stauffer . . . . .Whit Bissell

Psst! The head of Columbia, Harry Cohn, had bought the script years before but had gone back on the deal, neither producing it nor paying for it. Kanin got back at him by making him the model for Harry Brock in *Born Yesterday* • The part was originally planned to go to Laurence Olivier, but other commitments prevented him making the film • Colman said: 'It was the most satisfying role I ever had…It tested my total range and all my resources.' • This is Winters' film debut • John Derek, later better known as Mr. Bo Derek, appears in a bit part early in his acting career.

Double X

★★ 1992 97min c.

Director: Shani S. Grewal
Screenplay: Shani S. Grewal
Source: Short story, *Vengeance* by David Fleming

Candidate for the funniest bad film ever. Gormless Norman Wisdom goes on the run from a criminal organisation led by Hill, hamming

it up with the stagiest limp yet seen on screen. A thriller so atrociously made, it looks like one of those awful generic cinema ads that end with someone saying: 'For really great Chinese food, try Joe's in the High Street.' It's funnier than most of Wisdom's proper comedies. Lovers of all-time turkeys should seek it out.

Edward Ross . . . . .Simon Ward
Michael Cooper . . . . .William Katt
Arthur Clutton . . . . .Norman Wisdom
Iggy Smith .Bernard Hill
Jenny Eskridge . . . . .Gemma Craven

OOPS! Keep an eye on the stuntmen. One of them dies at least twice.

Dracula

★★ 1931 84min b/w

Director: Tod Browning
Screenplay: Garrett Fort
Source: Play by Hamilton Deane & John Balderston & the novel by Bram Stoker

This, the first mainstream horror talkie, is something of a museum piece now. With little of it even mildly scary, it comes across as a largely static rendition of the play on which it was based. So hammily is it acted and so over the top are the mists and sound effects that, in the right mood, you might almost think it a spoof. Worth watching, though, if you're curious to see what it started.

Count Dracula . . . . .Bela Lugosi
Mina Seward . . . . .Helen Chandler
John Harker . . . . .David Manners
Renfield . . . . .Dwight Frye
Dr. Van Helsing . . . . .Edward Van Sloan

Blurb The Strangest Love A Man Has Ever Known!

Quote 'I am Dra-a-a-cula. I bid you welcome.' • 'Listen to them. Children of the night. What music they make.' • 'I never drink…wine.'

OOPS! Dracula mentions that Whitby is 'close to London'. Only, presumably, as the bat flies. To the rest of us it's over 200 miles away.

Psst! Among those considered for the lead were William Powell • Lugosi plays a native of Transylvania. He was himself from Transylvania • Lugosi had already portrayed the Count on Broadway for three years • Although identified with the role for the rest of his life, Lugosi only got $500 for the movie. He died in poverty. Despite all the TV showings of the film, he received nothing more • Towards the end of his life Lugosi, a drug addict, was befriended by Ed Wood, the so-called worst filmmaker of all time and acted in several of his films • The strange stare Lugosi affects is the result of two narrow beams being shone into his eyes, one of which always seems to miss very slightly • This was the first film to use the gimmick of having nurses on duty in the cinemas in case patrons were overcome.

Dracula

★★★ 1958 82min c.

Director: Terence Fisher
Screenplay: Jimmy Sangster
Source: Novel by Bram Stoker

This was the film that revived the horror genre. The best film Hammer ever produced, it cuts back on the fantasy elements of the story – a European aristocrat starts up a blood transfusion service for select young ladies – and emphasises the erotic without sparing the gore. Although it doesn't seem quite as sexy or scary now, it clings close to the original story and has a style of its own, with dapper Lee perfect as the Count. In America, it's known as *The Horror of Dracula*. It was followed by *Dracula, Prince of Darkness* and five other sequels.

Dr. Van Helsing	Peter Cushing
Count Dracula	Christopher Lee
Mina Holmwood	Melissa Stribling
Arthur Holmwood	Michael Gough
Lucy	Carol Marsh
Jonathan Harker	John Van Eyssen
Undertaker	Miles Malleson
Vampire woman	Valerie Gaunt
Dr. Seward	Charles Lloyd Pack
Landlord	George Woodbridge

Blurb Who Will Be His Bride Tonight?

Psst! The film was made for £90,000, of which Lee got just £750.

Dr. Ehrlich's Magic Bullet

★★★ 1940 103min b/w

Director: William Dieterle
Screenplay: John Huston, Heinz Herald & Norman Burnside
Source: Letters & notes owned by the Ehrlich family

In addition to gangster movies, Warner Brothers were also pretty hot on biographies of famous people. Considering the tough censorship rules, they were pretty brave in depicting this life of the man who discovered a cure for venereal disease. It was certainly worthwhile, for Robinson gives a handsome, measured portrayal of a dedicated scientist who overcomes considerable obstacles in his search for the elusive solution.

Dr. Paul Ehrlich	Edward G. Robinson
Mrs. Ehrlich	Ruth Gordon
Dr. Emil von Behring	Otto Kruger
Minister Althoff	Donald Crisp
Franziska Spever	Maria Ouspenskaya
Prof. Hartman	Montagu Love
Dr. Hans Wolfert	Sig Rumann
Mittelmeyer	Donald Meek
Dr. Lentz	Henry O'Neill
Dr. Robert Koch	Albert Basserman
Dr. Morgenroth	Edward Norris
Judge	Harry Davenport
Brockdorf	Louis Calhern
Dr. Kunze	Louis Jean Heydt
Becker	Irving Bacon
Sensenbrenner	Charles Halton
Marianne	Ann E. Todd

Dressed to Kill

★★★ 1980 105min c.

Director: Brian de Palma
Screenplay: Brian de Palma

Unhappy mother Angie Dickinson is picked up by a stranger in a New York art gallery, but someone is lurking in the elevator with a razor. The story makes no sense whatsoever, but you don't particularly care as De Palma's swooning camera takes you from one dazzling set piece to the next. Well acted, witty entertainment for those sadists who find *Psycho* too tame.

Dr. Robert Elliott	Michael Caine
Kate Miller	Angie Dickinson
Liz Blake	Nancy Allen
Peter Miller	Keith Gordon
Det. Marino	Dennis Franz
Dr. Levy	David Margulies
Warren Lockman	Kenny Baker

Psst! All credit to Angie Dickinson for venturing into the shower at 50, even if the body double is a bit obvious • On its release, American feminists picketed cinemas in protest against the film's alleged violent misogyny. The American version was slightly shorter than in European cinemas.

Driving Miss Daisy
★★★ 1989 99min c.

Director: Bruce Beresford
Screenplay: Alfred Uhry
Source: Play by Uhry

Oscar-winning, cosy, soft-centred adaptation of a cosy, soft-centred stage play about the cantankerous and bigoted old Jewish lady who is mellowed by her black chauffeur. The performances are great, but it's all a bit schmaltzy.

Hoke Colburn ....Morgan Freeman
Daisy Werthan ....Jessica Tandy
Boolie Werthan ....Dan Aykroyd
Florine Werthan ....Patti LuPone
Idella ....Esther Rolle

Oscars Best Picture, Jessica Tandy

OOPS! Hoke seems to be taking Miss Daisy for a ride in more senses than one. On the way back from the synagogue, they pass the same house with the same van in front of it twice • When they drive from Georgia into Alabama, the policemen they encounter are wearing Georgia patches.

Psst! The idea of the film was rejected by most of the studios, it needing all of producer Lilli and Richard Zanuck's persuasive power to get Warners to agree to make it, so uncommercial was the concept considered to be. Even then, they had to cut the proposed budget in half. It turned out to be a great success at the box office • At 80, Tandy became the oldest actor to win an Oscar. George Burns had been five months younger than her when he won Best Supporting Actor for *The Sunshine Boys*.

Dr. Jekyll and Mr. Hyde
★★★ 1932 90min b/w

Director: Rouben Mamoulian
Screenplay: Samuel Hoffenstein & Percy Heath
Source: Novel by Robert Louis Stevenson

The best of the many versions of the famous Stevenson story. A chemist finds a cure for baldness which not only produces massive hair growth all over the body, but has the unfortunate side effect of splitting the personality into a light and dark side. March delineates the two well and is genuinely scary as Hyde. Made before the censorship rules really bit, it is also suprisingly racy in places. The 1941 version

with Spencer Tracy really doesn't hit the spot in quite the same way.

Dr. Henry Jekyll/Mr. Hyde ......Fredric March
Ivy Pearson ....Miriam Hopkins
Muriel Carew ....Rose Hobart
Dr. Lanyon ....Holmes Herbert
Brig. Gen. Carew ....Halliwell Hobbes
Poole ....Edgar Norton
Student ....Douglas Walton

Quote 'Good and evil are so close they are chained together in the soul.'

Psst! March's make-up took four hours to apply every day • The first transformation cleverly utilised different, coloured layers of make-up which gave a changed appearance as the colour of the lights shining on them was altered. Later, the makeup became still more involved and utilised stop-motion photography • The sound of director Mamoulian's own heartbeat was among the effects used to accompany March's transformations.

Dr. No
★★★★ 1962 111min c.

Director: Terence Young
Screenplay: Richard Maibaum, Johanna Harwood & Berkely Mather
Source: Novel by Ian Fleming.

The first Bond, and one of the finest. To find out why rockets keep going off course, 007 has to travel to the West Indies. Jamaica? Well, yes it is actually, but they missed that joke. It's quite refreshing to see Bond operating before the toys and self-parody got out of hand. There's still plenty of good action and, of course, the chance to top up the memory banks with that wonderful vision of Andress coming out of the sea.

James Bond ....Sean Connery
Honey ....Ursula Andress
Dr. No ....Joseph Wiseman
Felix Leiter ....Jack Lord
'M' ....Bernard Lee
Miss Moneypenny ....Lois Maxwell
Miss Taro ....Zena Marshall
Sylvia ....Eunice Gayson
Prof. Dent ....Anthony Dawson

Quote 'Bond. James Bond.' • 'Vodka martini, very dry, shaken, not stirred.' • 'Moneypenny, what gives?' – 'Me, given an ounce of encouragement.' • 'I never fail, Mr. Bond.'

OOPS! Bond manages a clever cigarette trick when it jumps from his lips straight into the nearby ashtray.

Psst! *Thunderball* was planned to be the first Bond movie, but it was stalled by legal problems • The production was nearly cancelled when it ran over budget by $100,000, the studio thinking it would never see its money again • Richard Burton, Patrick MacGoohan and Roger Moore were all choices of the producers before Connery's name came to the fore. Fleming had suggested the actor, singer and composer Hoagy Carmichael • Connery got just £6,000. Director Young sent him to his tailor and ordered him to work on his accent before filming started • Ursula Andress set a precedent by posing nude for Playboy, one of the first international film stars to do such a thing. Subsequent Bond girls followed suit • Andress' voice was said to have been dubbed by Nikki van der Zyl • Fleming hoped that neighbour Noel Coward would play Dr. No. Coward replied by telegram: 'Dr. No? No! No! No!' • Some of the scenes were filmed on the Jamaican estates of Noel Coward and Ian Fleming himself • Sadly, a mistranslation of the title into Japanese was spotted before the film was released. Otherwise it would have been called *We Don't Want a Doctor* in Japan • The significance of the painting of the Duke of Wellington in Dr. No's headquarters is that it had been stolen a couple of years earlier and had never been recovered.

Dr. Strangelove: Or How I Learned to Stop Worrying and Love the Bomb

★★★★ 1963 93min b/w

Director: Stanley Kubrick
Screenplay: Stanley Kubrick, Terry Southern & Peter George
Source: Novel, *Red Alert* by Peter George

War may be hell, but it can also be hellishly funny, as the Americans try to stop a renegade general triggering World War III. It's the high spot of Sellers' career as he plays a mad scientist, the American president and an RAF officer who just might be able to stop the ultimate madness. Despite the sadly dated effects of the bomber headed towards its target, it still manages to be both hilarious and chillingly believable.

Dr. Strangelove/Mandrake/Muffley Peter Sellers
Gen. 'Buck' Turgidson . . . . .George C. Scott
Gen. Jack D. Ripper . . . . .Sterling Hayden
Col. 'Bat' Guano . . . . .Keenan Wynn
Maj. T.J. 'King' Kong . . . . .Slim Pickens
Ambassador de Sadesky . . . . .Peter Bull
Lt. Lothar Zogg . . . . .James Earl Jones
Miss Scott . . . . .Tracy Reed

Quote 'Mr. President, I'm not saying we wouldn't get our hair mussed. But I do say no more than ten to twenty million people killed, tops, depending on the breaks.' • 'Gentlemen! You can't fight in here! This is the war room!'

OOPS! At one point when Strangelove is having difficulty controlling his errant arm, Peter Bull can be glimpsed behind him having hysterics.

Psst! According to Kubrick: 'I started work on the screenplay with every intention of making the film a serious treatment…Ideas kept coming to me which I would discard because they were so ludicrous. I kept saying to myself: "I can't do this. People will laugh." But after a month or so I began to realise that all the things I was throwing out were the things which were most truthful.' • A custard-pie fight between the two sides in the War Room was filmed but not used • Some have pointed out that, as Kissinger wasn't yet well known, Strangelove couldn't possibly be based on him. But Kubrick actually made a trip to Harvard to meet Kissinger while preparing for the movie • Sellers was due to play a fourth role, that of Major Kong. But he wasn't keen to do it and so faked an injury to his ankle, letting Pickens take the part • *Fail-Safe* was a similarly-themed, but rather more serious, film on the same subject and released at almost the same time. It's still well worth catching.

Duck Soup

★★★★ 1933 70min b/w

Director: Leo McCarey
Screenplay: Bert Kalmar, Harry Ruby, Arthur Sheekman & Nat Perrin

The purest of all Marx Brothers' films is a masterpiece of zany humour. At the insistence of the wealthy Dumont, Groucho is installed as head of Freedonia and rapidly plunges the country into war. Although the plot's more haphazard than in their later MGM days, the gags flow thick and fast, there's some wonderful comic business and, best of all, that dreadful crooner Allan Jones is nowhere in sight.

Rufus T. Firefly	Groucho Marx
Chicolini	Chico Marx
Brownie	Harpo Marx
Bob Rolland	Zeppo Marx
Mrs. Teasdale	Margaret Dumont
Ambassador Trentino	Louis Calhern
Street vendor	Edgar Kennedy
Vera Marcal	Raquel Torres
Agitator	Leonid Kinskey
Prosecutor	Charles B. Middleton

Quote 'Oh, your Excellency!' – 'You're not so bad yourself.' • 'As chairwoman of the reception committee, I welcome you with open arms.' – 'Is that so? How late do you stay open?' • 'I could dance with you till the cows come home. On second thoughts, I'd rather dance with the cows till you came home.' • 'Why, a four-year-old child could understand this report. Run out and get me a four-year-old child. I can't make head nor tail out of it.' • 'Chicolini here may talk like an idiot and look like an idiot. But don't let that fool you. He really is an idiot.' • 'Will you marry me? Did he leave you any money? Answer the second question first.' • 'Remember, men, we're fighting for this woman's honour, which is probably more than she ever did.'• 'Go! And never darken my towels again.' • 'Take a card. You can keep it. I've got 51 left.'

OOPS! At the opening reception Mrs. Teasdale throws for Firefly, Groucho's grey braided jacket changes to a tailcoat and back again.

Psst! Mussolini was so offended by tinpot dictator Rufus T. Firefly that the film was banned in Italy, to the Marx Brothers' considerable delight. Their movies were already banned in Germany • There were grumblings from the good citizens of a town called Fredonia in the state of New York. Groucho had the answer: they should change the town's name because 'it is hurting our picture' • Amazingly, the film was not a wow at the box office. There weren't even many critics who liked it. As a result, Paramount dropped the Marx Brother's contract • This was Zeppo's last film • Margaret Dumont was actually bald. A prank Harpo never tired of throughout their career was to steal her wig.

Duel

★★★★ 1971 88min c.

Director: Steven Spielberg
Screenplay: Richard Matheson
Source: Story in *Playboy* by Richard Matheson

A driver is terrorised by a large petrol tanker and its unseen occupant and realises that he is engaged in a battle to the death. Although originally made for the small screen, this is one of the tensest, most nerve-wracking of all thrillers, a masterpiece of economical film-making.

David Mann	Dennis Weaver
Mrs. Mann	Jacqueline Scott
Gas station attendant	Tim Herbert
Café owner	Eddie Firestone

OOPS! At the roadside café, Weaver drinks all of a glass of water. But it is full again straight afterwards • Keep an eye out for the camera reflected in the phonebox's glass.

Psst! This was Spielberg's first feature-length film. The short story on which it was based was discovered in *Playboy* by his secretary • Universal were prepared to make it as a feature film only if Gregory Peck would star, but he passed on it • Made as a TV film, it was released in European cinemas two years later and was shown theatrically in the US in 1983 • It was made for the unheard of sum of just $425,000 in 16 days • At the Taormina Film Festival in 1973, four Italian critics walked out in disgust when Spielberg refused to agree it was a Communist portrait of the working class striking back at the oppressive middle class • Versions exist from 73 minutes upwards.

Duel in the Sun

★★★ 1946 138min c.

Director: King Vidor
Screenplay: David O. Selznick & Oliver H.P. Garrett
Source: Novel by Niven Busch

Two brothers fall out over a woman, a common enough plot idea but rarely handled quite like this. This wonderfully bad Western on an epic scale can be hugely entertaining if you're in the right mood, with the inept and sometimes hilarious script emphasising the sex angle every step of the way. Freud would have had a field day, particularly with the gloriously over-the-top and highly bizarre finale.

Pearl Chavez	Jennifer Jones
Jess McCanles	Joseph Cotten
Lewt McCanles	Gregory Peck
Sen. McCanles	Lionel Barrymore
Laura Belle McCanles	Lillian Gish
The Sin Killer	Walter Huston
Scott Chavez	Herbert Marshall
Sam Pierce	Charles Bickford

Helen Langford	Joan Tetzel
Lem Smoot	Harry Carey
Mr. Langford	Otto Kruger
The Lover	Sidney Blackmer
Vashti	Butterfly McQueen

Quote 'Pearl, you're curved in the flesh of temptation. Resistance is going to be a darn sight harder for you than for females protected by the shape of sows.'

Psst! The budget rose to a massive $6m, making it the most expensive movie to date. A then phenomenal $2m was spent on promoting it, with most of the emphasis on its steaminess • The film was nicknamed *Lust in the Dust* • With both Catholic and Protestant spokesmen denouncing it, many towns banned it from being shown or else censored it, even in big cities like Philadelphia. With such wonderful publicity, it was naturally a big success • John Wayne was offered the Peck part, but he had qualms about all the sex involved • Hedy Lamarr and Teresa Wright were up for the Jennifer Jones role, but both became pregnant • Although one of Hollywood's top producers, David O. Selznick's decision to write the script himself was not the wisest decision of his career • Credited director King Vidor stormed out after repeated interference from Selznick, who wanted to have control of every facet of the film. Others, including Josef von Sternberg and Selznick himself, took turns in the director's chair. Selznick was particularly concerned that Jennifer Jones, in whom he took a special interest and who would later be his wife, came across well on film.

Dumbo
★★★★ 1941 64min c.

Director: Ben Sharpsteen
Screenplay: Joe Grant & Dick Huemer
Source: Book by Helen Aberson & Harold Pearl

A small elephant, taunted by everyone about his oversized ears, has a miserable time of it until he discovers they make great wings. A charming story boosted by some great characters, particularly the crows, and some wonderful songs. The 'Pink Elephants on Parade' routine is just one of several treats in store.

Timothy Mouse	Edward Brophy
Mr. Stork	Sterling Holloway
Ringmaster	Herman Bing
Elephant	Verna Felton
Jim Crow	Cliff Edwards

Psst! Disney cast around his staff for anybody with relevant circus experience and uncovered a juggler, a trick rider, a tightrope walker and even a typist who was once a lion-tamer.

Easter Parade
★★★ 1948 103min c.

Director: Charles Walters
Screenplay: Sidney Sheldon, Albert Hackett & Frances Goodrich

Yet another backstage musical, with Astaire picking Garland as his dance partner after being given the heave-ho by Miller. The plot is third-rate but the numbers, by Irving Berlin, are not. In addition to the great finale, highlights are 'Stepping Out With My Baby' and, of course, 'A Couple of Swells', all filmed in that glorious saturated colour that marks it out as an MGM musical.

Hannah Brown	Judy Garland
Don Hewes	Fred Astaire
Jonathan Harrow III	Peter Lawford
Nadine Hale	Ann Miller
François, the headwaiter	Jules Munshin
Mike, the bartender	Clinton Sundberg
Hat model	Lola Albright

Psst! Gene Kelly was to have played the lead, but he cracked his ankle in a softball match two days before filming was due to start. It was his suggestion that Astaire might be coaxed back to the screen. Fred had previously said he had given up the movies and had not been in a movie for two years. But he was keen to work with Garland and so he readily agreed • The film was going to be directed by Vincente Minnelli, but wife Judy Garland's psychiatrist said that the pair, husband and wife, shouldn't work together • Ann Miller, replacing Cyd Charisse – who had broken her leg – wasn't well. She had fallen down some stairs while pregnant and lost her baby. She had to dope herself with pain killers for her bad back throughout • Tiny Liza Minnelli makes her first ever screen appearance here with her mum Judy Garland in the final parade.

East of Eden
★★★ 1955 115min c.

Director: Elia Kazan
Screenplay: Paul Osborn
Source: Novel by John Steinbeck

Two very different brothers compete for their father's affections. It's essentially the Cain and Abel story updated to the early years of the 20th century, somewhat overwrought in places but acted with strong conviction. Dean is excellent as a rebellious teenager in an era 40 years before people knew what teenagers were.

Adam Trask	Raymond Massey
Cal Trask	James Dean
Abra	Julie Harris
Aron Trask	Richard Davalos
Kate	Jo Van Fleet
Sam	Burl Ives
Will	Albert Dekker
Ann	Lois Smith
Joe	Timothy Carey

Oscars Jo Van Fleet

Quote 'I don't have to explain anything to anybody.'

Psst! This was James Dean's film debut
• Learning lines or knowing where he should stand on the set was not something that was a priority with Dean, severely cheesing off the professional Raymond Massey. Their relationship off-screen seems closely to have mirrored the attitudes of their movie characters
• The film was originally planned for Marlon Brando and Montgomery Clift.

Easy Living
★★★ 1937 90min b/w

Director: Mitchell Leisen
Screenplay: Preston Sturges
Source: Story by Vera Caspary.

With two of the greatest talents-to-be in screwball comedy as director and writer, it's not surprising that this is a delightfully funny 90 minutes. When a fur coat lands on Arthur, everyone beats a path to her door, thinking she is the mistress of tycoon Arnold. Arthur is one of those radiant, adorable comediennes whose style doesn't seem to have dated one jot in 60 years.

Mary Smith	Jean Arthur
J.B. Ball	Edward Arnold
John Ball Jr.	Ray Milland
Mr. Louis Louis	Luis Alberni
Mrs. Jennie Ball	Mary Nash
Van Buren	Franklin Pangborn
Wallace Whistling	William Demarest
E.F. Hulgar	Andrew Tombes
Lillian	Esther Dale
Mr. Hyde	William B. Davidson

Mrs. Swerf	Nora Cecil
Butler	Robert Greig
Jeweller	Arthur Hoyt

Easy Rider
★★ 1969 94min c.

Director: Dennis Hopper
Screenplay: Peter Fonda, Dennis Hopper & Terry Southern

In its day, a groundbreaking film, being the first to have drug dealers as heroes. Two bikers encounter various rednecks and dropouts as they head for New Orleans, only to learn that the American Dream is dead. It's interesting to see Hopper in youthful rebel mode, but Jack Nicholson gives the best performance. It's mainly of sociological interest these days.

Wyatt	Peter Fonda
Billy	Dennis Hopper
George Hanson	Jack Nicholson
Karen	Karen Black
Hippie leader	Robert Walker Jr.

Blurb A Man Went Looking For America And Couldn't Find It Anywhere.

Quote 'You know, this used to be a hell of a good country. I can't understand what's wrong with it.' • 'I'm the schmuck who didn't want Jack Nicholson to get the role in Easy Rider' [Dennis Hopper] • 'I hated that movie. I wouldn't work with any of the miscreants in it – never have, never will.' [John Wayne, Hopper's co-star in *The Sons of Katie Elder*] • 'A disaster in the history of film to set beside the loss of Technicolor, the invention of gross participation, the early of Murnau, and the longevity of Richard Attenborough.' [David Thomson]

OOPS! In the desert, Fonda takes off his watch and throws it away. It's obviously a fairly cheap watch, so it isn't too much of a wrench to lose it. But earlier, when he was stashing his cash in the petrol tank, he wore a different, far more expensive timepiece.

Psst! The movie was the inspiration of Fonda, who got the idea in a flash while staying in a Toronto hotel room • Hopper took time off from making *True Grit*, a film that could hardly be more different, to make this • Hopper and Fonda sold the movie to Columbia for $355,000. It ended up taking more than $60m at the box office worldwide • The part of the lawyer was offered to Bruce Dern. When he turned it down, Rip Torn took it but he and

Hopper quarreled. So the associate producer, an unknown part-time actor called Jack Nicholson, stepped in at the last moment • Hopper had been on the point of giving up and becoming a teacher, while Fonda's career was going nowhere until this movie came out • Perhaps not altogether surprisingly, the marijuana being smoked by Hopper, Fonda and Nicholson is said to have been the real stuff • While the New Orleans scenes look as if they're intended to show how somebody who is high might see things, in fact it was an accident which left the film fogged • Many scenes were improvised, particularly those involving locals • The scene in the cemetery with Fonda talking to the statue of the Madonna as if it's his mum affected him badly. His own mother killed herself when he was a kid, following which he tried to shoot himself. He begged Hopper to cut it, but Hopper refused • Although the film received an 'X' certificate in Britain, it was the first movie to show drug taking and not be cut • The bigwig buying the coke at the opening is the record producer Phil Spector • In 1995 German airline Lufthansa arranged a package tour motorcycling through Nevada and California. Rather sadly, as part of the deal, Peter Fonda rode with them.

Edward Scissorhands
★★ 1990 105min c.

Director: Tim Burton
Screenplay: Caroline Thompson

An inventor dies before completing his creation of a boy, leaving him with scissors for hands. Adopted by Avon lady Wiest, he is initially welcomed with open arms by the local community, before hostility to anything alien resurfaces. This imaginative modern fairy tale has some truly weird designs, but it's hard to get involved with the characters. Like Burton's *Batman* films, your view probably depends on whether you love his amazing visual style or whether you prefer a strong story.

Edward Scissorhands	Johnny Depp
Kim Boggs	Winona Ryder
Peg Boggs	Dianne Wiest
Jim	Anthony Michael Hall
Joyce Monroe	Kathy Baker
Bill Boggs	Alan Arkin
Inventor	Vincent Price

Blurb His Story Will Touch You, Even Though He Can't.

Psst! Tom Cruise was offered, but turned down, the lead role.

8 ½
★ 1963 138min b/w

Director: Federico Fellini
Screenplay: Federico Fellini, Ennio Flaiano, Tullio Pinelli & Brunello Rondi

Early Fellini films like *La Strada* and *La Dolce Vita* remain enjoyable. The self-indulgent rot set in with this one. The story of famous Italian film director Mastroianni, with endless problems on the home and work front, mixes reality and fantasy with fiction and autobiography. Most aspiring male directors would give their right eye to have the problems – hit movie, wife Anouk Aimé *and* a mistress – that he has.

Guido Anselmi	Marcello Mastroianni
Claudia	Claudia Cardinale
Luisa Anselmi	Anouk Aimée
Carla	Sandra Milo
Rossella	Rossella Falk
Gloria Morin	Barbara Steele
Actress	Madeleine LeBeau

Psst! The title arises because Fellini had previously directed six films, co-directed another and had made two episodes for anthologies. He considered that counted as having made seven and a half films and so this was his eighth and a half • Fellini was a great fan of improvisation and the actors, many of whom were amateurs, often only got their lines just before a scene was due to be filmed. Marcello Mastroianni was the only one allowed to see the entire script • Because she didn't know her lines, Sandra Milo needed 16 takes of a scene in a restaurant and ended up eating 16 chicken legs.

The Elephant Man
★★★★ 1980 124min b/w

Director: David Lynch
Screenplay: Christopher Devore, Eric Bergren & David Lynch
Source: Books, *The Elephant Man & Other Reminiscences* by Sir Fred Treves & *The Elephant Man, A Study in Human Dignity* by Ashley Montagu.

The Victorian victim of a disease causing massive deformities is exhibited as a sideshow freak before meeting a doctor who treats him as a human being. An immensely moving tale, based on a true story, is handled perfectly, with an intelligent, often witty, script, lovely acting and splendid photography. Not a film you would want to miss.

Dr. Frederick Treves	Anthony Hopkins
John Merrick	John Hurt
Mrs. Kendal	Anne Bancroft
Carr Gomm	John Gielgud
Bytes	Freddie Jones
Mothershead	Wendy Hiller
Night Porter	Michael Elphick
Mrs. Treves	Hannah Gordon
Fox	John Standing
Byte's boy	Dexter Fletcher
Merrick's mother	Phoebe Nicholls

Quote 'I am not an animal!'

Psst! The Elephant Man's head and body were latex foam that originally took seven hours to apply, although it was later cut to just five or six hours. Filming had to take place late in the day and poor John Hurt could eat nothing when in full make-up and had to take sustenance through a straw. So exhausting was the whole thing that he could only work in the full rig every other day • On seeing the film Michael Jackson was said to have immediately set about learning the whereabouts of the real Merrick's body, purchasing the remains and attempting to provide Merrick with a true resting place. However, he denied this story in an interview with Oprah Winfrey in February 1993 • A Canadian version of the story was also released in 1980 but made little impact.

Elmer Gantry

★★★ 1960 146min c.

Director: Richard Brooks
Screenplay: Richard Brooks
Source: Novel by Sinclair Lewis

An unprincipled conman realises that there's money in the God business and joins up with an evangelist outfit. Riches and fame beckon. Although it now lacks much subtlety, it is still rousing and enjoyable, if a little long.

Elmer Gantry	Burt Lancaster
Sister Sharon Falconer	Jean Simmons
Jim Lefferts	Arthur Kennedy
Lulu Bains	Shirley Jones
William L. Morgan	Dean Jagger
Sister Rachel	Patti Page

George Babbitt	Edward Andrews
Rev. Pengilly	John McIntire
Preacher	Rex Ingram
Rev. Garrison	Hugh Marlowe

Oscars Shirley Jones, Burt Lancaster

Quote 'And what is love? Love is the mornin' and the evenin' star.'

Psst! Lancaster spent a day arguing with the Catholic Legion of Decency. It wanted the line 'See you in hell, brother' cut from the end of the film. His arguments were wasted. The line was dropped, but 16 years later he snuck it into *Buffalo Bill and the Indians*. The Protestant Churches didn't raise any significant objections to the movie • Lancaster said he based his character's mannerisms in large part on director John Huston • To get the right look for the evangelists' audiences, director Brooks rounded up many who attended such meetings from among the elderly citizens of Long Beach and transported them to the set. He didn't let on that it was only a movie and many of them participated under the apparent impression that it was all for real.

The Empire Strikes Back

★★ 1980 124min c.

Director: Irvin Kershner
Screenplay: Leigh Brackett & Lawrence Kasdan

The weakest of the three *Star Wars* movies has little of the coherence, fun or wit of the original. While the rebels are in hiding from the Emperor's forces, Luke goes off to learn about life and the meaning of the Universe from Grand Master Yoda, one of the most pretentious and long-winded spiritual teachers encountered on film. If you know how the confrontation between Luke and Darth Vader turns out (doesn't everybody?) there's not that much action to pep things up.

Luke Skywalker	Mark Hamill
Han Solo	Harrison Ford
Princess Leia	Carrie Fisher
Darth Vader	David Prowse
Darth Vader's voice	James Earl Jones
C3PO	Anthony Daniels
Chewbacca	Peter Mayhew
R2-D2	Kenny Baker
Yoda	Frank Oz
Lando Calrissian	Billy Dee Williams
Ben Kenobi	Alec Guinness

Blurb The Adventure Continues...

Quote 'Would it help if I got out and pushed?'
• 'Never tell me the odds.' • 'Try not! Do! Or do not. There is no *try*.'

OOPS! Look carefully when Chewbacca is repairing C3PO and you can catch a glimpse of Anthony Daniels' nose inside.

Psst! The second in the trilogy, although called number five on screen • The $18m budget came out of Lucas' own pocket. Against the advice of all his friends, he put the money up and secured all worldwide rights himself. He made, of course, a fortune • Hamill's scarred face was written in after he had a car accident that noticeably altered the look of his face.

Enchanted April

★★★★ 1991 95min c.

Director: Mike Newell
Screenplay: Peter Barnes
Source: Novel by Elizabeth von Arnim

Slight but delightful little film about a quartet of Edwardian ladies breaking loose and taking an idyllic holiday in an Italian villa. Once you get used to the slowness of pace, the charm and magic wash over you and induce a splendid feeling of well-being. Atmosphere, acting and attention to detail are all top-hole. Financed by the BBC, this got a shamefully limited cinema release here but was a big (by British standards) hit in the States.

Rose Arbuthnot	Miranda Richardson
Mrs. Fisher	Joan Plowright
Mellersh Wilkins	Alfred Molina
Lottie Wilkins	Josie Lawrence
Lady Caroline	Polly Walker
George Briggs	Michael Kitchen
Frederick Arbuthnot	Jim Broadbent

Les Enfants du Paradis

★★★ 1945 195min b/w

Director: Marcel Carné
Screenplay: Jacques Prévert

This 19th-century story of the unrequited love of a mime artist is generally regarded as one of the greatest films of all time. It is certainly beautifully filmed, with the screen generally full of life and vitality and Carné doing a splendid job of recreating theatre life in Paris in the 1830s.

However, sadly, the central story itself is rather dull by comparison with all that is going on around it. Arletty, however, is one of the most watchable actresses to have graced a movie screen.

Garance	Arletty
Baptiste Debureau	Jean-Louis Barrault
Frederick Lemaitre	Pierre Brasseur
Jericho	Pierre Renoir
Lacenaire	Marcel Herrand
Nathalie	Maria Casarès

Psst! Made during the war, it was split into two because the Nazis didn't permit any movie to be longer than 90 minutes • Watching some of the sumptuous scenes, it is hard to believe just what shortages of necessary materials there were • Whole flock-fulls of wool were pulled over the Nazis' eyes by the French film-makers. Although all films were heavily scrutinised by the Germans, they don't appear to have realised that the film is a clear allegory about resisting the occupying forces. Many members of the cast were also resistance members • Probably the most expensive film to have been made in France until then, it was three years in the making, with Carné deliberately delaying progress in the hope that the premiere could be held after the liberation. It was • 25,000 extras were hired for the carnival scenes, many of them circus performers • *Variety's* reviewer called it 'Downright dull' • The title refers to those who sit in 'The Gods', the cheapest, highest seats in the theatre.

The Enforcer

★★★ 1951 87min b/w

Director: Bretaigne Windust & Raoul Walsh
Screenplay: Martin Rackin

A tough District Attorney finds his case against a murderous crime syndicate on the point of collapse when a key witness dies. Bogart is his usual splendid self in this gritty drama which may have lost its edge of topicality but is still exciting stuff. Not to be confused with the third in the *Dirty Harry* series.

Martin Ferguson	Humphrey Bogart
'Big Babe' Lazich	Zero Mostel
Albert Mendoza	Everett Sloane
Joseph Rico	Ted de Corsia
Nina Lombardo	Susan Cabot
Capt. Nelson	Roy Roberts
Sgt. Whitlow	King Donovan
Thomas O'Hara	Don Beddoe

Psst! Reputedly the first film to deal with the subject of organised crime, it was based on testimony about a group called Murder Inc. that emerged in the 40s and which was investigated by The Kefauver Committee in the early 50s • Although not credited, Raoul Walsh was brought in to handle some of the action scenes. There are those who think that he was behind much of the film.

Enter the Dragon
★★ 1973 99min c.

Director: Robert Clouse
Screenplay: Michael Allin

Bruce Lee, the 70s Kung Fu star who hit the big time here, is hired by a government agent to infiltrate the island of a drugs baron. Even 20 years ago, this was a hackneyed plot, so what pleasure there is to be had derives from watching Lee's considerable ability to kick seven bells out of everyone.

Lee ....Bruce Lee
Roper ....John Saxon
Williams ....Jim Kelly
Tania ....Ahna Capri

Psst! The film was released only a few days after Lee's early death, aged just 33 • The production had been a troubled one, with Lee getting cuts from a real broken bottle in one fight scene and being bitten by a cobra – fortunately with its venom removed – in another • Apparently Lee performed one kick so fast the camera wasn't able to record it at the usual 24 frames per second! The kick had to be shot in slow motion instead or it simply couldn't have been believable on screen.

The Entertainer
★★ 1960 96min b/w

Director: Tony Richardson
Screenplay: John Osborne & Nigel Kneale
Source: Play by Osborne

A supremely egotistical comedian on the slope to oblivion is blind to the misery he causes to everyone around him. Although the general air of seediness is well-drawn and Olivier is fascinating to watch in the part he made famous on stage, this is a rather depressing film.

Archie Rice ....Laurence Olivier

Phoebe Rice ....Brenda de Banzie
Jean ....Joan Plowright
Billy ....Roger Livesey
Frank Rice ....Alan Bates
Graham ....Daniel Massey
Tina ....Shirley Anne Field
Mick Rice ....Albert Finney
Mrs. Lapford ....Thora Hird
Soubrette ....Miriam Karlin

Psst! Thirty years before Pacino did the same for the third part of *The Godfather*, Olivier had his teeth filed down to make Rice look sufficiently seedy. On stage, it had only been necessary to blacken one tooth • Although Plowright plays Olivier's daughter, she was to become his wife the following year.

Eraserhead
★★ 1978 90min c.

Director: David Lynch
Screenplay: David Lynch

In between delivering newspapers and installing water systems, David Lynch spent five years making this bizarre film about Henry, who fathers a mutant baby, while trying to ignore a woman living behind the radiator. Lynch's wildly original and disturbing style gets its first major outing here, though it might have worked better as a short rather than a full length feature.

Henry Spencer ....Jack Nance
Mary X ....Charlotte Stewart
Mary's father ....Allan Joseph
Mary's mother ....Jeanne Bates
Girl across the hall ......Judith Anna Roberts
Lady in the radiator ....Laurel Near

OOPS! Henry gets his right foot wet when he steps in a puddle on the way home. But it's his *left* sock that he dries on the radiator.

Psst! One film critic claimed the film had 'one of the most repugnant scenes in film history' • Jennifer Lynch, the director's club-footed daughter, firmly denies that the film is directly autobiographical.

Escape from Alcatraz
★★ 1979 112min c.

Director: Don Siegel
Screenplay: Richard Tuggle
Source: Book by J. Campbell Bruce

A straightforward, occasionally plodding, telling of a break from an escape-proof prison. However, despite a lack of action, Eastwood holds our attention as the taciturn inmate who plans to make it into the record books.

Frank Morris	Clint Eastwood
Warden	Patrick McGoohan
Doc	Roberts Blossom
Clarence Anglin	Jack Thibeau
John Anglin	Fred Ward
English	Paul Benjamin
Charley Butts	Larry Hankin
Inmate	Danny Glover

Psst! Alcatraz was the ultimate American prison, the place where Al Capone was interred. But its escape-proof reputation was destroyed by the real-life break on which this film is based in 1962. It was closed shortly afterwards • Danny Glover can be glimpsed as one of the inmates.

E.T. The Extra-Terrestrial
★★★★ 1982 115min c.

Director: Steven Spielberg
Screenplay: Melissa Mathison

Delightful, timeless family pic guaranteed to bring a lump to the throat and a tear to the eye, even if the effects look a little shaky a decade on. A bunch of kids adopt a wacky little alien and then fight off the adults when he wants to return home. Funny, fascinating and occasionally frightening, this spendidly-directed film (almost all shot from a child's-eye view) deservedly became the most successful of all time, grossing over $700m worldwide. Full marks to Spielberg, too, for never spoiling it by giving us a sequel.

Mary	Dee Wallace
Elliott	Henry Thomas
Keys	Peter Coyote
Michael	Robert MacNaughton
Gertie	Drew Barrymore
Greg	K.C. Martel

Blurb He Is Afraid. He Is Totally Alone. He Is 3 Million Light Years From Home.

Quote 'E.T. Phone home.' • 'I've never driven forward before.' • 'Ouch!' • 'Oh torture. Torture. My pubic hairs went grey.' [Spielberg on directing it]

OOPS! Watch Drew Barrymore's hamburger when she's eating dinner with Mom at the start of the film as it first becomes as good as new and then vanishes • After Elliot has rushed back into the house after seeing E.T., keep an eye on the boy beside him. He's mouthing Elliot's lines with him.

Psst! Both Disney and Universal passed on the film, after tests showed the public wouldn't be interested. The film took more in its opening weekend alone than the $10.5m it cost to make • The drunk scene was done by legless schoolboy Matthew de Merrit, walking on his hands inside the costume • Stardom was too much for Drew Barrymore. She turned to drugs and drink and attempted suicide at 13. At 14 she became the youngest person ever to write an autobiography, recently bouncing back, first as a video star, then moving into main features • The little girl in school who kisses Elliott grew up to be a big girl indeed, *Baywatch's* Erika Eleniak, recently seen in *Under Seige* • Harrison Ford's wife wrote the screenplay and he is said to have played the school principal, though the part was cut out of the film • Sweden wouldn't allow children under 12 to see the movie because it showed parents reprimanding their children • M&M refused permission to use their sweets in the film so E.T. followed a trail of Reese's Pieces instead. Sales promptly doubled • Spielberg designed the face of E.T. by taking a picture of a baby and putting Albert Einstein's eyes and forehead on top • The voice was a combination of a heavy-smoking ex-schoolteacher – overheard in a supermarket – and Debra Winger • Among the exotic plants in the spaceship were some made from polyester blown over inflated condoms. One of them is a triffid • When Spielberg was asked about how they managed the special effects, he said: 'Well, we waited for the sun to get very low, then we told the kids to go fly their bicycles across the sun. We said, "Ride like the wind, ride like the wind." And, wow – they flew right across.'

Eureka
★★★★ 1983 129min c.

Director: Nicolas Roeg
Screenplay: Paul Mayersberg
Source: Book, *Who Killed Sir Harry Oakes* by Marshall Houts.

Dazzlingly powerful story, based on fact, of a gold prospector who strikes it fantastically lucky, only to have those around him close in for the kill 20 years later. Violent, sexy and superbly shot, Hackman and Russell as father and daughter have seldom been better. Disowned by the studio, its reputation is finally beginning to struggle out of the mire.

Jack	Gene Hackman
Tracy	Theresa Russell
Maillot van Horn	Rutger Hauer
Helen	Jane Lapotaire
Perkins	Ed Lauter
Aurelio	Mickey Rourke
Mayakofsky	Joe Pesci

Evergreen
★★★ 1934 90min b/w

Director: Victor Saville
Screenplay: Emlyn Williams & Marjorie Gaffney
Source: Play, *Ever Green* by Benn W. Levy

Matthews, perhaps Britain's greatest musical-comedy star, becomes a big hit when she poses as her own, retired, mother. Although lacking the lustre of Hollywood production values, this is still a sophisticated, sparkling entertainment with Rodgers and Hart music that the big studios must have envied. Although little known now, even in Britain, Matthews has one of the most enchanting of musical screen personalities. Those captivated by her should seek out *Gangway* and *The Good Companions*.

Harriet Green/Harriet Hawkes	Jessie Matthews
Leslie Benn	Sonnie Hale
Maudie	Betty Balfour
Tommy Thompson	Barry Mackay
Marquis of Staines	Ivor MacLaren
George Treadwell	Hartley Power
Lord Shropshire	Patrick Ludlow

Psst! In one of the most regrettable career moves in the history of the movies, Matthews turned down the chance to become Fred Astaire's dancing partner. She ended up as radio's Mrs. Dale in *Mrs. Dale's diary*.

Every Which Way But Loose
★ 1978 114min c.

Director: James Fargo
Screenplay: Jeremy Joe Kronsberg

A no-brain comedy about a lorry driver and the only friend he has with an even lower IQ than himself, an orang-utan called Clyde. Why it should be such an enormous success with the public is one of the great unsolved mysteries of Hollywood but, recognising the teeth of a gift horse when they saw it, a sequel, *Any Which Way You Can*, came out two years later. For all the difference, it might have been scenes from the first movie put together in a different order.

Philo Beddoe	Clint Eastwood
Lynn Halsey-Taylor	Sondra Locke
Orville	Geoffrey Lewis
Echo	Beverly D'Angelo
Tank Murdock	Walter Barnes
Dallas	Bill McKinney
Putnam	Gregory Walcott
Trailer court manager	Hank Worden
Ma	Ruth Gordon
Church's manager	Michael Mann
Church	George P. Wilbur

Quote 'Left turn, Clyde.'

The Evil Dead
★★ 1983 85min c.

Director: Sam Raimi
Screenplay: Sam Raimi

Ultra-low-budget shocker, in which a group of gormless teens are turned into homicidal demons after one of the girls is raped by a tree. After that, sadly, it loses its grip on reality and branches out in all directions. It's energetic stuff and admirable considering the budget, but it's still badly-acted rot. It was followed by a dismal sequel and the miserable *Army of Darkness*.

Ash	Bruce Campbell
Cheryl	Ellen Sandweiss
Linda	Betsy Baker
Scott	Hal Delrich
Shelly	Sarah York

Blurb The Ultimate Experience in Gruelling Terror.

Psst! At 19, Sam Raimi was then Hollywood's youngest-ever director • He made the film for less than £200,000, raising the capital from a group of doctors and lawyers he badgered • Campbell and he were friends from High School. Campbell was appointed the actor because 'he was the ones girls wanted to look at.' • Almost a minute was cut for the cinema release. The video came out when 'video nasties' were in the news and despite the proper certificate, some dealers were prosecuted for carrying it. Even though they were acquitted, a stigma still hung over the video. When, in 1985, it was submitted for a specific video certificate, it was refused one. In 1990, it was finally passed, with another 65 seconds cut. The scene with the tree raping the girl was trimmed, as were six other scenes.

The Exorcist
★ 1973 121min c.

Director: William Friedkin
Screenplay: William Peter Blatty
Source: Novel by Blatty

The biggest horror here is how such a diabolically overlong and tedious film has maintained its reputation. A huge box office hit, and still mysteriously banned on video in Britain, this tale of a demonically-possessed teenage girl has its impressive moments, but unfortunately what seems like hours of nothingness to wade through between them. Still, when leading ladies are meant to turn audiences' heads, it makes a change for one to manage the feat herself. Followed by two dreadful sequels.

Mrs. MacNeil . . . . Ellen Burstyn
Father Merrin . . . . Max Von Sydow
Father Karras . . . . Jason Miller
Regan . . . . Linda Blair
Lt. Kinderman . . . . Lee J. Cobb
Burke . . . . Jack MacGowran
Sharon . . . . Kitty Winn
Voice of demon . . . . . Mercedes McCambridge

Oscars Best Screenplay (adapted)

OOPS! Burstyn throws a cigarette away after just a couple of drags. But then it pops back into her hand again.

Psst! Blatty based his novel on the last official exorcism carried out by the Catholic Church in America in 1949 • His model for Mrs. MacNeil was his neighbour Shirley MacLaine, who was none too happy about it • The $3.5m paid for the rights to the novel was a record for the time • The production was dogged by bad luck, with relatives of Linda Blair and Max von Sydow dying in the first week, a spate of accidents, a fire on set, sprinkler systems going off for no reason and actor Jack MacGowran dying a week after he filmed his death scene in the movie. With filming taking twice as long as it was supposed to, the projected budget of $4m shot up to $10m • The vomit spewed out by Blair is actually a mixture of split pea soup and oatmeal, with a device in her throat to ensure it was projected out with sufficient force. Nonetheless, it was realistic enough to make moviegoers around the world chunder in

sympathy. Many others simply passed out • Mercedes McCambridge, the voice of the demon, swallowed 18 raw eggs to help her produce the horrible noises she makes • The temperature was lowered to 20 degrees below zero so that the actors' breath could be seen • The squealing noise during the exorcism is a recording of pigs on the way to be slaughtered.

Fail-Safe
★★★ 1964 111min b/w

Director: Sidney Lumet
Screenplay: Walter Bernstein
Source: Novel by Eugene Burdick & Harvey Wheeler

Although overshadowed by the better-known *Dr. Strangelove*, this is a tense, gripping thriller about the possible approach of nuclear Armageddon. Fonda, excellent as the President who has to make the most difficult decision of his life, has only one card up his sleeve to prevent catastrophe, but it's one that comes with a very heavy price.

The President . . . . Henry Fonda
Groeteschele . . . . Walter Matthau
Gen. Black . . . . Dan O'Herlihy
Gen. Bogan . . . . Frank Overton
Col. Grady . . . . Edward Binns
Col. Cascio . . . . Fritz Weaver
Britt . . . . Larry Hagman
Mr. Knapp . . . . : . . . . Russell Collins
Also: Sorrell Booke

OOPS! The wrong film clip is used when a pilot is ordered to increase speed by using his afterburners. What we actually see is a plane launching its rockets.

Psst! The US Department of Defense wouldn't cooperate with the movie, so all the pictures of bombers are stock footage of just one plane recycled • Kubrick was furious to discover that Columbia was behind this movie as well as the similarly-themed *Dr. Strangelove*. After he threatened to sue for plagiarism, the studio pushed his film first, causing *Fail Safe* to disappear almost without trace when released seven months later.

The Fallen Idol
★★★★ 1948 94min b/w

Director: Carol Reed

Screenplay: Graham Greene
Source: Short story, *The Basement Room*, by Greene

The son of a London-based ambassador idolises butler Richardson. When his shrewish wife dies, the police not unnaturally assume the butler did it. Desperate to get his only friend off the hook, the boy only manages to get him into even hotter water. While a modest film, it is a nerve-wracking masterpiece of cinematic story-telling.

Baines . . . . .Ralph Richardson
Julie . . . . .Michele Morgan
Felipe . . . . .Bobby Henrey
Mrs. Baines . . . . .Sonia Dresdel
Det. Insp. Crowe . . . . .Denis O'Dea
Det. Lake . . . . .Jack Hawkins
Det. Hart . . . . .Bernard Lee
Det. Davis . . . . .Geoffrey Keen
Also: Walter Fitzgerald, Karel Stepanek, Dandy Nichols

Falling Down
★★★★ 1993 115min c.

Director: Joel Schumacher
Screenplay: Ebbe Roe Smith

Something snaps in Douglas when he's stuck in a traffic jam and he abandons his car and strikes out on foot. As he runs up against the horrors of everyday life, he effectively becomes the first consumer vigilante. But although he sticks up for the rights of the ordinary person, he does so in increasingly violent ways. Despite his appalling behaviour, we understand his frustrations so well that it is extraordinary how far down the road we are prepared to travel with him. Nothing like the bleak film many seemed to expect, it's exciting and darkly humorous.

D-Fens .Michael Douglas
Prendergast . . . . .Robert Duvall
Beth . . . . .Barbara Hershey
Sandra .Rachel Ticotin
Mrs. Prendergast . . . . .Tuesday Weld
Surplus store owner . . . . .Frederic Forrest

Quote 'I'm the bad guy?...How did that happen? I did everything they told me.'

Fanny and Alexander
★★★★ 1983 189min c.

Director: Ingmar Bergman
Screenplay: Ingmar Bergman

Young Alexander's father dies and he and his sister find they have a hard time of it when mom marries a severe pastor. How can the plot do justice to a Bergman film, particularly one as brilliant as this? Autobiographical in nature, it's a collage of echoes from his previous films, with an attractive balance between humour and gloom. Don't be put off by the length or the fact that it's in Swedish.

Helena Ekdahl . . . . .Gunn Wallgren
Prof. Carl Ekdahl . . . . .Boerje Ahlstedt
Lydia Ekdahl . . . . .Christina Schollin
Oscar Ekdahl . . . . .Allan Edwall

Fantasia
★★ 1940 120min c.

Director: Ben Sharpsteen
Screenplay: Various

This project, merging art and popular culture by accompanying assorted pieces of classical music with animated pictures, was dear to Walt's heart. Despite its apparent popularity, it is actually rather dull for much of its inordinate length. Although the dancing hippos are good, as is Mickey's Sorcerer's Apprentice, you'd need to tie me down to get me to sit through the dreadfully twee Pastoral Symphony again. If you want to listen to classical music, let your imagination make the pictures.

Narrator . . . . .Deems Taylor
Conductor . . . . .Leopold Stokowski

Blurb Fantasia Will Amaze-Ya.

OOPS! In the Beethoven's Pastoral Symphony section, a pair of centaurs wander off-screen together and a bush goes with them.

Psst! Disney was so happy with the result that he is said to have said: 'This will *make* Beethoven' • The voice of Mickey was, as when he first appeared in *Steamboat Willie*, Walt himself • It was a financial disaster on first release. Cinemas needed the expensive 'Fantasound' multi-speaker system to do it justice and so only a few cinemas were initially able to show it until it went on general release in 1942. However, it became a constant source of revenue in later years, helped by stories that it took on a whole new light under the influence of drugs • For its 50th birthday, it was released with a re-recorded Dolby stereo soundtrack. Only then was it discovered that for the previous 40 years, the music had been two frames out of synch with the pictures • Disney studios took the Politically Correct advantage of the re-release by erasing a black piccaninny acting as servant to a clearly white centaur • Earlier, at the insistence of the censors at the Hays Office, bra-like flowers had to be painted on lady centaurs in the Pastoral Symphony sequence that had previously been bare-breasted • By claiming that the videos were only going to be available to buy for a limited period in the 90s, it became the best-selling title in Britain to date • A revamped version is due to be released in 1998. Of the original, only Night on Bare Mountain, the Dance of the Hours (dancing hippos), the Nutcracker and the Sorcerer's Apprentice (with Mickey) will survive. Five new sections with classical music will be added. Among them, Beethoven's 5th will have abstract animation while Donald Duck will appear as Noah's assistant in Pomp and Circumstance.

Fantastic Voyage
★★★ 1966 100min c.

Director: Richard Fleischer
Screenplay: Harry Kleiner
Source: Novel by Otto Klement & Jay Lewis Bixby

When a defecting Czech scientist is shot and then develops a blood clot on the brain, a team of medics is miniaturised along with a submarine. The whole lot is then injected into his body, most definitely boldly going where no man has gone before, at least not without the aid of hallucinogenic drugs. Despite the quite ludicrous pretext, this is actually an exciting and entertaining sci-fi thriller, with the crew battling bits of the scientist's body and realising that one of them is a double agent. Considering that it's 30 years old, the effects haven't dated too badly.

Grant . . . . .Stephen Boyd
Cora Peterson . . . . .Raquel Welch
Gen. Carter . . . . .Edmond O'Brien
Dr. Michaels . . . . .Donald Pleasence
Col. Donald Reid . . . . .Arthur O'Connell
Capt. Bill Owens . . . . .William Redfield
Dr. Duval . . . . .Arthur Kennedy
Technician . . . . .James Brolin

Psst! Raquel Welch had actually signed to play Domino in *Thunderball*. But Cubby Broccoli was persuaded to release her to Fox for this film instead.

Farewell, My Lovely
★★★ 1944 95min b/w

Director: Edward Dmytryk
Screenplay: John Paxton
Source: Novel by Raymond Chandler

Hard-boiled private dick Philip Marlowe is hired by a none-too-bright thug to look for his lost girl-friend. Long regarded as one of the classic film noirs, the plot twists and turns like an angry rattlesnake. Unfortunately, it's been imitated so much since that it feels rather passé, as well as being somewhat confusing and talky. It's pretty enjoyable but, for my money, the only true Marlowe is Bogie. Known as *Murder, My Sweet* in the US.

Philip Marlowe . . . . .Dick Powell
Velma/Mrs. Grayle . . . . .Claire Trevor
Ann Grayle . . . . .Anne Shirley
Jules Amthor . . . . .Otto Kruger
Moose Malloy . . . . .Mike Mazurki
Marriott . . . . .Douglas Walton
Mr. Grayle . . . . .Miles Mander
Lt. Randall . . . . .Don Douglas

Quote 'The cops always like to solve murders done with my gun.' • 'It's the sort of place where you have to wear a shirt.' • 'I caught the blackjack right behind my ear. A black pool opened up at my feet. I dived in. It had no bottom.' • '"Okay Marlowe", I said to myself, "You're a tough guy. You've been sapped twice, choked, beaten silly with a gun, shot in the arm until you're as crazy as a couple of waltzing mice. Now let's see you do something really tough…like putting your pants on".' • 'Killing a man with a sap's quiet, but it's no work for a lady.'

Psst! This was real casting against type. At the time Powell, his career going nowhere fast, was known only for his bouncy, innocent roles in Busby Berkeley musicals. Thanks to this movie, he was able to move on to meatier roles • It was Powell's participation that accounted for the change of title to *Murder, My Sweet* in America *after* the film was released. Audiences were staying away, apparently believing that *Farewell, My Lovely* was yet another vacuous musical. When the name changed, business picked up • Although Mazurki was supposed to intimidate Powell with his size, he was actually only a couple of inches taller. In their scenes together, Powell has his shoes off and Mazurki is either standing on a box or Powell is walking in the gutter.

Far from the Madding Crowd
★★ 1967 169min c.

Director: John Schlesinger
Screenplay: Frederic Raphael
Source: Novel by Thomas Hardy

...but not far enough. We're back in Thomas Hardy's Wessex, usually a deathly setting for movies. Christie is the woman who makes the lives of three men miserable. Schlesinger is the director who makes the audience's lives miserable. Only cinematographer Nicolas Roeg's beautiful pictures stave off complete boredom.

Bathsheba Everdene . . . . .Julie Christie
William Boldwood . . . . .Peter Finch
Gabriel Oak .Alan Bates
Sgt. Troy . . . . .Terence Stamp
Liddy . . . . .Fiona Walker
Fanny Robin . . . . .Prunella Ransome
Cainy Ball . . . . .Freddie Jones
Soberness . . . . .Denise Coffey

Fast Times at Ridgemont High
★★★ 1982 92min c.

Director: Amy Heckerling
Screenplay: Cameron Crowe
Source: Book by Crowe

Life and love – mainly the latter – for students in a Californian school. Although there's plenty of smut, as handled by director Amy Heckerling and screenwriter Cameron Crowe it also has wit, compassion and a shrewd eye. An impressive cast of then-unknowns, among them Jennifer Jason Leigh, Forest Whittaker and so on, got their kick-start here.

Jeff Spicoli .Sean Penn
Stacy Hamilton . . . . .Jennifer Jason Leigh
Brad Hamilton . . . . .Judge Reinhold
Mike Damone . . . . .Robert Romanus
Mark 'Rat' Ratner . . . . .Brian Backer
Linda Barrett . . . . .Phoebe Cates
Mr. Hand . . . . .Ray Walston
Mr. Vargas . . . . .Vincent Schiavelli
Lisa . . . . .Amanda Wyss
Charles Jefferson . . . . .Forest Whitaker
Cindy .Kelli Maroney
Stoner Bud .Eric Stoltz
Robber . . . . .James Russo
Brad's bud . . . . .Nicolas Cage
Stoner Bud . . . . .Anthony Edwards

Psst! Nicolas Cage makes his film debut as the student picking up cash by working at the burger joint. It's also the first time on screen for Eric Stoltz and Anthony Edwards • Crowe claims to have infiltrated a college to do the necessary research • To find his character as the doped-up surfer Sean Penn stubbed a cigarette out on his palm.

Fatal Attraction
★★ 1987 119min c.

Director: Adrian Lyne
Screenplay: James Dearden

With his family away, lawyer Douglas has a brief fling with Close. But once he zips his trousers up she becomes somewhat unhinged, threatening him and his family. Despite the quality of the acting, as a thriller it's appallingly unsubtle. Although it probably cut the incidence of infidelity for a while, the over-the-top ending has now been copied by so many other films that it looks plain silly.

Dan Gallagher . . . . .Michael Douglas
Alex Forrest . . . . .Glenn Close
Beth Gallagher . . . . .Anne Archer
Ellen Gallagher . . . . .Ellen Hamilton Latzen
Jimmy . . . . .Stuart Pankin
Hildy . . . . .Ellen Foley
Arthur . . . . .Fred Gwynne

Quote 'I will *not* be ignored.'

OOPS! No wonder Michael Douglas was allegedly treated for sex addiction. When he and Close begin making love at the sink, the clock says 4.45. They're still bonking at 6.15 • Time's a big problem for the family. According to Douglas' watch, when he tucks his daughter in for the night, it's 3.15 • Watch the sheet jump about between shots when Close is in bed chatting to Douglas.

Psst! The film is based on a 45-minute British independent production called *Diversion* • The original ending had Close committing suicide, making sure that Douglas would be blamed for her murder. Test audiences didn't like it, so they reshot the new ending seven months after they'd finished filming. The original version can be seen on the special video edition • The original down-beat ending was retained for Japan • The rumours that writer Dearden based the character of Alex on actress Sean Young appear not to be true.

Father of the Bride

★★★ 1950 93min b/w

Director: Vincente Minnelli
Screenplay: Frances Goodrich & Albert Hackett
Source: Novel by Edward Streeter

Instead of putting it all behind him, father Tracy relives for us the nightmare leading up to his daughter's fraught and expensive wedding. Although it no longer seems terribly funny, it's a pleasant time-waster and makes for a fascinating glimpse of middle-class American life. A sequel, *Father's Little Dividend*, followed in 1951. In 1991, Steven Martin starred in a remake and had his thunder stolen by Martin Short as the wedding organiser.

Stanley T. Banks ....Spencer Tracy
Ellie Banks ....Joan Bennett
Kay Banks ....Elizabeth Taylor
Buckley Dunstan ....Don Taylor
Doris Dunstan ....Billie Burke
Mr. Massoula ....Leo G. Carroll
Herbert Dunstan ....Moroni Olsen
Mr. Tringle ....Melville Cooper
Warner ....Taylor Holmes
Rev. Galsworthy ....Paul Harvey
Joe ....Frank Orth
Tommy Banks ....Russ Tamblyn

Blurb The Bride gets the THRILLS! Father gets the BILLS!

Quote 'Given enough ointment, there's always a fly. Given enough presents, there's bound to be a stinker.' • 'An experience caterer can make you ashamed of your house in 15 minutes.'

Psst! Although it is hard to imagine anyone else in Tracy's part, Jack Benny actually tested for it, MGM production head Dore Schary having promised him a shot at it • The film showed Taylor going down the aisle before she ever did it for real • Russ Tamblyn, billed as 'Rusty', appears as a younger Tommy Banks • A TV series based on the film ran for a year from September 1961 starring Leon Ames.

Ferris Bueller's Day Off

★★ 1986 103min c.

Director: John Hughes
Screenplay: John Hughes

Despite its cult reputation, this is a slightly dis-appointing pic from John Hughes. Broderick skips school to have a riotious day round and about Chicago. The invention and humour sadly run out before the film does but Jones is as good as always as the justifiably suspicious headmaster.

Ferris Bueller ....Matthew Broderick
Cameron Frye ....Alan Ruck
Sloane Peterson ....Mia Sara
Ed Rooney ....Jeffrey Jones
Jeanie Bueller ....Jennifer Grey
Katie Bueller ....Cindy Pickett
Tom Bueller ....Lyman Ward
School secretary ....Edie McClurg
Boy in police station ....Charlie Sheen
Economics student ....Kristy Swanson

Quote 'Cameron's so tight, if you stuck a piece of coal up his ass, in two weeks you'd have a diamond.'

Psst! Keep watching the credits to the end and you'll see a little more of Broderick • This is apparently Dan Quayle's favourite movie • Jack Nicholson said after watching it that it 'made me feel totally irrelevant to anything that any audience could want and made me feel 119 years old…I literally walked out of there thinking my days were numbered in the Hollywood film industry' • Watch out for a cameo from Charlie Sheen in the police station and Kristy Swanson in a tiny part as one of four 'economics students'.

A Few Good Men

★★★ 1992 138min c.

Director: Rob Reiner
Screenplay: Aaron Sorkin
Source: Play by Sorkin

A splendid Hollywood entertainment in the old style. Cruise is the inexperienced, devil-may-care navy lawyer assigned to defend two Marines accused of murdering a colleague. Along the way, he tangles with base commander Nicholson. Despite only having three scenes, Jack dominates the film. Cruise still proves himself a fine actor, while Moore does her best with a sadly under-written part. The film fizzes and crackles throughout, the actors firing off their lines like bullets. Shame about the moment of sentimental Stars-and-Stripes waving at the end, though.

Lt. J.G. Kaffee ....Tom Cruise
Col. Jessep ....Jack Nicholson

Lt. Cdr. Galloway	Demi Moore
Capt. Ross	Kevin Bacon
Lt. Kendrick	Kiefer Sutherland
Lt. Weinberg	Kevin Pollak
Pfc. Downey	James Marshall
Lt. Col. Markinson	J.T. Walsh
Dr. Stone	Christopher Guest
Judge Randoplph	J.A. Preston
Lt. Spradling	Matt Craven
Lance Cpl. Dawson	Wolfgang Bodison

Quote 'Walk softly and carry an armoured tank division, I always say.' • 'So this is what a courtroom looks like.'

Psst! In Cruise's apartment, near the typewriter, is *Misery's Child* by Paul Sheldon, the novel that caused so much grief in Rob Reiner's previous film *Misery* • Cruise got $12.5m, while Nicholson supposedly received $500,000 a day • Michelle Pfeiffer, Penelope Ann Miller, Linda Hamilton and Elizabeth Perkins were among those considered for Moore's role • William Goldman, writer of *Butch Cassidy* and *Marathon Man*, is said to have been paid $300,000 just to give advice to Sorkin who had written the play, but never a film before. Sorkin was so pleased with the end result that he then revised the play to take account of some of the material introduced for the film • Bodison was another first-timer. He had run errands for Reiner on *Misery* and bumped into him a couple of years later just when the director was despairing of ever finding the right person for the part. Within a couple of days, Bodison was rehearsing with the others.

Field of Dreams
★★★★ 1989 106min c.

Director: Phil Alden Robinson
Screenplay: Phil Alden Robinson
Source: Book, *Shoeless Joe* by W.P. Kinsella

A failing farmer hears voices in the cornfield telling him that if he builds a baseball diamond then the late Shoeless Joe Jackson, one of the greatest players of all time, will pop in for a quick knock-up. Don't be put off by the weird-sounding plot. True, it's as corny as Costner's fields, but unless you're wholly immune to whimsy, it is also a magical, heart-warming tale which not only grips totally but is even surprisingly believable. In its own way, a modern *It's a Wonderful Life*.

Ray Kinsella	Kevin Costner
Annie Kinsella	Amy Madigan
Karin Kinsella	Gaby Hoffman
Shoeless Joe Jackson	Ray Liotta
Mark	Timothy Busfield
Terence Mann	James Earl Jones
Dr. 'Moonlight' Graham	Burt Lancaster

Quote 'If you build it, he will come.' • 'Hey, is this heaven?' – 'No, it's Iowa.' • 'Oh my God.' – 'What?' – 'You're from the 60s.'

Showing Harvey.

Psst! It took writer-director Robinson eight years to get the movie made • Filming took place in 1988 during a drought. It cost $200,000 to irrigate the Iowa fields • When filming was over, the farmer kept the diamond in place and it became a massively popular tourist attraction.

First Blood
★★ 1982 93min c.

Director: Ted Kotcheff
Screenplay: Michael Kozoll, William Sackheim & Sylvester Stallone
Source: Novel by David Morrell

A local policeman is beastly to Vietnam vet John Rambo who, understandably, goes on the rampage, topping several of the local police force and torching most of the town. It's difficult to know where credibility and John Rambo part company. Perhaps it's when he jumps a hundred feet onto some rocks with barely a scratch? Or perhaps it's when he survives the mine cave-in? Or an attack by what looks like the bulk of the State's armed forces? Startlingly violent but occasionally exciting, little of it actually makes much sense. It was followed by the moderate *Rambo: First Blood II* and the dreadful *Rambo III*.

Rambo	Sylvester Stallone
Trautman	Richard Crenna
Teasle	Brian Dennehy
Mitch	David Caruso
Galt	Jack Starrett

Psst! Originally Rambo died. But when test audiences gave that the thumbs-down, a new ending was filmed • The name 'Q. Moonblood' on the credits as writer is Stallone himself • Amazingly, Dustin Hoffman was offered the role but turned it down. Dustin Hoffman as Rambo? It would have been interesting to see how a method actor like Hoffman prepared for the part • The first two *Rambo* films were considered by the British press to be a contributory factor in the Hungerford

Massacre, although no evidence was ever produced to link killer Michael Ryan and the films.

A Fish Called Wanda
★★★★ 1988 108min c.

Director: Charles Crichton
Screenplay: John Cleese & Charles Crichton

Uptight, hen-pecked lawyer Cleese gets involved with a gang of crooks including sexy Curtis and her dumb but well-read boyfriend Kline. That it isn't quite as hilarious as you hope for is in part because of the over-obvious attempt to internationalise it. Nonetheless, it's one of the funniest comedies in recent years and, what's more, the familiarity on repeated viewings makes it seem even more fun.

Archie Leach . . . . .John Cleese
Wanda . . . . .Jamie Lee Curtis
Otto . . . . .Kevin Kline
Ken . . . . .Michael Palin
Wendy . . . . .Maria Aitken
George .Tom Georgeson
Mrs. Coady . . . . .Patricia Hayes
Judge . . . . .Geoffrey Palmer

Oscars Kevin Kline

Blurb A Tale Of Murder, Lust, Greed, Revenge, And Seafood.

Quote 'Don't call me stupid.' • 'Let me correct you on a couple of things, okay? Aristotle was not Belgian. The central message of Buddhism is not every man for himself…and the London Underground is not a political movement.' • 'The English contribution to world cuisine… the chip.'

Psst! The original ending had Curtis fleeing alone to South America with the jewels. Test audiences weren't keen on this, so Cleese joined her inside the plane with Kline outside • Director Charles Crighton made some of the greatest Ealing comedies, including The Lavender Hill Mob and The Titfield Thunderbolt • Yet another 'You Can Always Park In The Movies' scene when Cleese dashes out of the Law Courts to his nearby parked car, zooming off in hot pursuit • Cleese's character, Archie Leach, is the real name of Cary Grant • There were objections from many support groups about Palin's stuttering, with one group picketing MGM's studios in Los Angeles. Palin had, in fact, been a bad stutterer himself as a child.

A Fistful of Dollars
★★★ 1964 100min c.

Director: Sergio Leone
Screenplay: Sergio Leone & Duccio Tessari

This was the first successful spaghetti western, shot very cheaply in Spain by an Italian director. A taciturn stranger moseys into town and plays off one feuding family against another. It took Clint Eastwood's squeaky-clean Rawhide image, dragged it through the dust and stamped on it, making him an international film star. Ennio Morricone's score helped enormously. 30 years on, it is still strikingly subversive of the western genre, though technically rough round the edges.

The Man With No Name . . . . .Clint Eastwood
Marisol . . . . .Marianne Koch
Ramon Rojo . . . . .Gian Maria Volonte
John Baxter . . . . .Wolfgang Lukschy
Esteban Rojo . . . . .Sieghardt Rupp
Benito Rojo . . . . .Antonio Prieto

OOPS! Although Clint may claim to be 'The Man With No Name' here, somebody forgot to remove his character's name 'Joe' from the end credits.

Psst! The film is fairly obviously based on Kurosawa's film Yojimbo • With a budget of only $200,000, Leone wanted a leading actor but knew it would have to be somebody who came cheaply. James Coburn wanted too much money but somebody suggested Eastwood, then appearing each week in Rawhide on TV. Eastwood agreed to star in what was then called The Magnificent Stranger for just $15,000 • It was Eastwood who suggested that his character's mystique be increased by giving him no name and junking much of the dialogue that had been written for him.

Five Easy Pieces
★★★ 1970 98min c.

Director: Bob Rafelson
Screenplay: Carole Eastman

It's a strange movie that is best remembered for Jack Nicholson trying to order a piece of toast in a restaurant but this film is something of an oddity. Now an oil-rig worker, it turns out that Nicholson's actually from a good background and once could have made it as a classical pianist. Essentially this is a modest road movie with engrossing performances and a neat script to lift it above the norm.

Robert Eroica Dupea	Jack Nicholson
Rayette Dipesto	Karen Black
Elton	Billy "Green" Bush
Stoney	Fannie Flagg
Catherine Van Ost	Susan Anspach
Partita Dupea	Lois Smith
Carl Dupea	Ralph Waite

Quote 'Now all you have to do is hold the chicken, bring me the toast, give me a check for the chicken salad sandwich, and you haven't broken any rules.'

Psst! Eastman wrote the movie under the name of Adrien Joyce. She claimed the central character was in part her late brother, but also had many elements of Nicholson himself in it.

Five Fingers
★★★ 1952 108min b/w

Director: Joseph L. Mankiewicz
Screenplay: Michael Wilson
Source: Book, *Operation Cicero* by L.C. Moyzisch

An Albanian valet at the British embassy in Ankara is selling secrets to the Nazis. Extraordinarily based on a true story, this is a well-crafted espionage thriller with a nice vein of black humour.

Ulysses Diello/'Cicero'	James Mason
Countess Anna Staviska	Danielle Darrieux
George Travers	Michael Rennie
Sir Frederic	Walter Hampden
L.C. Moyzisch	Oscar Karlweis
Col. von Richter	Herbert Berghof
Morrison	Michael Pate
Steuben	Ivan Triesault

Psst! It is said that Cicero sold the Germans 35 secret papers. Among them was the real date and place of the invasion of Europe, but the Germans were too suspicious to believe it.

Five Graves to Cairo
★★★★ 1943 96min b/w

Director: Billy Wilder
Screenplay: Charles Brackett & Billy Wilder
Source: Play, *Hotel Imperial* by Lajos Biro

This World War II spy drama is a corker, with a British soldier finding himself in grave danger

when the identity of a man he has assumed turns out to be a Nazi agent. The usual witty and clever concoction from Wilder and Brackett is put over with gusto by a great cast, with von Stroheim particularly outstanding as Field Marshal Rommel.

Corp. John Bramble	Franchot Tone
Mouche	Anne Baxter
Field Marshal Rommel	Erich von Stroheim
Farid	Akim Tamiroff
Lt. Schwegler	Peter Van Eyck
British Colonel	Miles Mander
Gen. Sebastiano	Fortunio Bonanova
Maj. von Buelow	Konstantin Shayne

Five Million Years to Earth
SEE: Quatermass and the Pit

Flame over India
SEE: Northwest Frontier

Flesh and the Devil
★★ 1927 110min b/w

Director: Clarence Brown
Screenplay: Benjamin Glazer
Source: Novel, *The Undying Past* by Hermann Sudermann

This silent movie about a *femme fatale* and her effect on the friendship of two men would seem a little risible now were it not for the extraordinary charge obvious in the relationship between Garbo and Gilbert. They became lovers off screen as well as on and this seems so apparent in the film that you almost feel you are intruding on their privacy.

Felicitas von Kletzingk	Greta Garbo
Leo von Sellenthin	John Gilbert
Ulrich von Kletzingk	Lars Hanson
Hertha Prochvitz	Barbara Kent
Uncle Kutowski	William Orlamond

Psst! There have been many instances captured on film of stars falling for each other, but this is one of the most electrifying. Alexander Walker said: 'There are few scenes in American film, silent or talkie, in which two fully clothed people generate so much sexual desire.' • In Britain, the film was cut by 23 minutes because of the 'passionate and unrestrained embraces'.

The Flight of the Phoenix
★★★ 1965 147min c.

Director: Robert Aldrich
Screenplay: Lukas Heller
Source: Novel by Elleston Trevor

A plane in trouble has to put down in the desert where the pilot and passengers despair of ever being rescued. Tempers fray until one of them suggests an ingenious do-or-die solution. Despite the odd longueur, the tension mounts steadily higher in this gripping tale, with some unbearably worrying moments towards the close.

Frank Townes	James Stewart
Lew Moran	Richard Attenborough
Capt. Harris	Peter Finch
Heinrich Dorfmann	Hardy Kruger
Trucker Cobb	Ernest Borgnine
Crow	Ian Bannen
Sgt. Watson	Ronald Fraser
Dr. Renaud	Christian Marquand
Standish	Dan Duryea
Bellamy	George Kennedy

Psst! The stuntman doubling for Stewart, himself no mean pilot, was killed when, after repeated attempts to bring the plane down in the Buttercup Valley location, the plane crashed.

Flirting
★★★★ 1990 100min c.

Director: John Duigan
Screenplay: John Duigan

Bullied but bright boarder Taylor falls for Newton, the only African at the nearby girl's school. This Australian sequel to *The Year My Voice Broke* is an utterly absorbing and charming tale of boarding-school life and love. Sometimes biting, sometimes tender, it is also extremely funny. The performances are excellent, with Kidman particularly good as a snooty head-girl.

Danny Embling	Noah Taylor
Thandiwe Adjewa	Thandie Newton
Nicola Radcliffe	Nicole Kidman
'Gilby' Fryer	Bartholomew Rose
Jock Blair	Felix Nobis

Quote 'They can be pretty desperate, these black women. Look at National Geographic.'

The Fly
★★★★ 1986 96min c.

Director: David Cronenberg
Screenplay: Charles Edward Pogue & David Cronenberg

Director Cronenberg experiments with mixing together two film genres, horror and romantic tragedy, coming up with great results. Loopy scientist (is there any other sort?) Goldblum develops an unhealthy taste for sugar while Davis, worried perhaps about the ozone layer, is just too slow with the fly-spray. The transformations are gross, but terrifically done. A contender for best horror pic of the 80s, it is superior to the 1958 original which has not dated well. As for the 1989 sequel, forget it.

Seth Brundle	Jeff Goldblum
Veronica Quaife	Geena Davis
Stathis Borans	John Getz
Tawny	Joy Boushel
Dr. Cheevers	Les Carlson
Gynaecologist	David Cronenberg

Blurb Be Afraid...Be Very Afraid.

OOPS! At one point, when Goldblum's in the pod, the camera and crew can be seen reflected in the glass.

Psst! Director Cronenberg appears as the gynaecologist. He claims this was at Geena Davis' insistence as she didn't want a stranger fumbling around between her legs.

Footlight Parade
★★★★ 1933 104min b/w

Director: Lloyd Bacon
Screenplay: Manuel Seff & James Seymour

A theatre producer hit by the Depression comes up with an idea for pepping up movie screenings with theatrical spectaculars. If you've only ever seen Cagney in gangster films, then his singing and dancing ability should be a revelation, just as Ruby Keeler is, although for less impressive reasons. Plausibility isn't its strongest suit, but marvel at the great lines topped off at the end by the extraordinary trio of back-to-back Busby Berkeley-staged numbers: the surprisingly risqué 'Honeymoon Hotel', the high kitsch water number 'By a Waterfall' and the wonderfully gritty 'Shanghai Lil'. They don't make films like this any more – they wouldn't dare!

Chester Kent . . . . .James Cagney
Nan Prescott . . . . .Joan Blondell
Bea Thorn . . . . .Ruby Keeler
Scotty Blair . . . . .Dick Powell
Silas Gould . . . . .Guy Kibbee
Harriet Bowers Gould . . . . .Ruth Donnelly
Charlie Bowers . . . . .Hugh Herbert
Francis .Frank McHugh
Vivian Rich . . . . .Claire Dodd
Al Frazer .Arthur Hohl
Also: Herman Bing, John Garfield

Quote 'As long as they've got sidewalks,
you've got a job.'

Psst! Claire Dodd, playing Cagney's ex-wife,
was taller than him, so he had to stand on a box
in their scenes • Dick Powell developed a
problem with his throat and he was replaced by
Stanley Smith. However, Powell then recovered.
The studio decided to junk the footage filmed
with Smith and did it all over again with Powell
• John Garfield can be glimpsed as a bit player,
a sailor, in the 'Shanghai Lil' number.

Forbidden Games
SEE: Les Jeux Interdits

Forbidden Planet
★★★★ 1956 98min c.

Director: Fred M. Wilcox
Screenplay: Cyril Hume

Ignoring the space equivalent of a 'Keep Out'
sign, a spaceship lands on Altair 4 to find out
what happened to colonists sent from earth 20
years earlier. This updating of Shakespeare's
The Tempest is one of the most imaginative
and intelligent of all sci-fi films, although it's fair
to say that the dialogue often sounds daft and
some of the actors are hardly RSC material.
Robby the Robot makes for great comic relief.
All in all, an improvement on Shakespeare's
earthbound original.

Dr. Morbius . . . . .Walter Pidgeon
Altaira Morbius . . . . .Anne Francis
Cmdr. Adams . . . . .Leslie Nielsen
Lt. 'Doc' Ostrow . . . . .Warren Stevens
Lt. Farman .Jack Kelly
Chief Quinn . . . . .Richard Anderson
Cook . . . . .Earl Holliman
Strong . . . . .James Drury

Quote 'It's an old custom. All the really high
civilisations go in for it...It stimulates the whole

system. As a matter of fact, you can't be in tip-
top health without it.' [Kelly to Francis, on
kissing] • 'Guilty! Guilty! My evil self is at that
door – and I have no power to stop it!'

Psst! The first film in which all of the music is
electronic • Robby the Robot was later seen in
other movies and TV series, including the
popular *Lost in Space*.

Foreign Correspondent
★★ 1940 120min b/w

Director: Alfred Hitchcock
Screenplay: Charles Bennett, Joan Harrison,
James Hilton & Robert Benchley

An American foreign correspondent trawling for
stories in wartime Europe gets caught up in the
usual spy nonsense. Despite its high reputation,
this thriller has not worn the years well. There
are still some great set-pieces, like the killing
amongst all the umbrellas in the rain, but it is let
down by some lacklustre acting and the fact
that it all looks so dreadfully fake, particularly
the all-important windmill set. It ends with an
unsubtle message to American audiences that
essentially says: 'If you've enjoyed this motion
picture, then please join our war.'

Johnny Jones . . . . .Joel McCrea
Carol Fisher . . . . .Laraine Day
Stephen Fisher . . . . .Herbert Marshall
Scott Ffolliott . . . . .George Sanders
Van Meer . . . . .Albert Basserman
Stebbins . . . . .Robert Benchley
Rowley . . . . .Edmund Gwenn
Also: Eduardo Ciannelli, Martin Kosleck, Harry
Davenport

Quote 'Hello, America! Hang on to your lights,
they're the only lights left in the world!'

Psst! Gary Cooper was the original choice for
the lead, but he was not interested • Hitch
appears walking past the hotel where McCrea
is staying, reading a newspaper • Geobbels,
the Nazi propoganda minister, was a fan,
calling it 'a first-class production, a
criminological bangup hit, which no doubt will
make a certain impression upon the broad
masses of the people in enemy countries.'
• Humorist Robert Benchley, who brightened
up almost every film he appeared in, wrote
much of his own part • The bombing of London
was remarkably prophetic, as the first attack
happened only five days after that scene was
filmed.

Forrest Gump

★★★ 1994 142min c.

Director: Robert Zemeckis
Screenplay: Eric Roth
Source: Novel by Winston Groom

Dim but gentle Forrest bumbles through life, managing through luck and good fortune to be in the right place so many times that he alters history, becomes a war hero and makes a fortune into the bargain. Although fairly amusing, it's awfully long and disjointed for a piece of romantic whimsy and has a story that could have been told in 90 minutes. The big mystery is why it struck such a chord with so many Americans.

Forrest Gump . . . . .Tom Hanks
Jenny Curran . . . . .Robin Wright
Lt. Dan Taylor . . . . .Gary Sinise
Bubba Blue . . . . .Mykelti Williamson
Mrs. Gump . . . . .Sally Field

Oscars Best Picture, Tom Hanks, Best Screenplay (adapted), Best Director

Quote 'My momma always said, life was like a box of chocolates. You never know what you're gonna get.' • 'Momma says stupid is as stupid does.' • 'Now the good thing about meeting the President of the United States is the food.' • 'I feel as though I'm standing on magic legs in a special effects shot that is too unbelievable to imagine and far too costly to make a reality. The power and the pleasure and the emotion of this moment is a constant…it will never be diminished, nor will my appreciation.' [Hanks' Oscar acceptance speech]

OOPS! When Forrest is told by Wright he's a father, watch the iron go from being upright to flat and back to upright again • One of the clippings in the scrapbook is from USA Today and is dated 1978, although the newspaper didn't exist for another four years.

Psst! This was the third-highest grossing movie of all time, after E.T. and Jurassic Park • It was the first time the Best Actor Oscar was won by the same person two years running since Spencer Tracy got back-to-back statuettes for Captains Courageous in 1937 and Boys Town in 1938 • The project had languished in development hell at Warners for several years before being picked up by Paramount. It still took another six years to get it made • Sinise didn't have to play his part with his legs doubled under him. They were removed from sight electronically.

48 HRS.

★★★ 1982 97min c.

Director: Walter Hill
Screenplay: Roger Spottiswoode, Walter Hill, Larry Gross & Steven E. de Souza

Cop Nolte gets fast-talking con Murphy out of prison for a couple of days to help him track down a killer. Naturally, they hate each other on sight and naturally…well, you know the plot. But it's funny, full of great action and highly entertaining. Murphy, in his film debut, shows what he's capable of when his talents are kept in check. Who can forget the scene in the redneck bar? Followed by the dispiriting Another 48 HRS.

Jack Cates . . . . .Nick Nolte
Reggie Hammond . . . . .Eddie Murphy
Elaine . . . . .Annette O'Toole
Haden . . . . .Frank McRae
Ganz . . . . .James Remar
Luther . . . . .David Patrick Kelly
Billy Bear . . . . .Sonny Landham
Kehoe . . . . .Brion James

Quote 'You'll be sorry you ever met me.' – 'I'm already sorry.' • 'I been in prison for three years. My dick gets hard if the wind blows.' • 'I'm your worst nightmare, a nigger with a badge.'

OOPS! Murphy is handcuffed when he leaves jail. The handcuffs vanish, then reappear again • As they arrive at the redneck bar, look out for the people watching the filming.

42nd Street

★★★★ 1933 89min b/w

Director: Lloyd Bacon
Screenplay: James Seymour & Rian James
Source: Novel by Bradford Ropes

The first of the all-wisecracking, all-singing, all-dancing Warner Bros. backstage musicals is packed with original lines and situations that only later became clichés. Yet it still all seems wonderfully fresh as the boys and girls of the chorus prepare for their big opening night. Among an amazing cast, keep your eye on the surreally-attired Rogers as Anytime Annie and Baxter as the producer desperately trying to hold things together. Audiences were understandably knocked over by choreographer Busby Berkeley's production numbers. Among the songs are 'I'm Young and Healthy', 'Shuffle Off to Buffalo' and 'You're Getting to be a Habit With Me'. Pure joy.

Julian Marsh	Warner Baxter
Peggy Sawyer	Ruby Keeler
Dorothy Brock	Bebe Daniels
Pat Denning	George Brent
Lorraine Fleming	Una Merkel
Abner Dillon	Guy Kibbee
Billy Lawler	Dick Powell
Anytime Annie	Ginger Rogers
MacElroy	Allen Jenkins
Barry	Ned Sparks

Quote 'Do you know that she makes $45 a week and sends her mother a hundred of it?' • 'I don't like his face or any part of him. He looks like a bulgarian bald eagle mourning its firstborn.' • 'She only said "no" once and then she didn't hear the question.' • 'Sawyer, you listen to me and you listen hard. Two hundred people, two hundred jobs, two hundred thousand dollars, five weeks of grind and blood and sweat depend upon you. It's the lives of all these people who've worked with you. You've got to go on, and you've got to give and give and give…Sawyer, you're going out a youngster but you've *got* to come back a star!' • 'Go out there and be so swell you'll make me hate you.'

Psst! The first real movie musical. It was Warners production head, Daryl F. Zanuck, who came up with the idea for an antidote to the Depression in the form of a fantasy musical. Studio head Jack Warner didn't realise it was going to be a musical until it was screened for him. After early dreadful talkie musicals flopped, it is likely that he would have protested and may even have had it stopped • Dance director Busby Berkeley got the taste for choreography as a drill master in World War One. By the time he came to Hollywood, he had worked on over 20 Broadway musicals. This was his first major movie • Berkeley apparently auditioned 5,000 prospective chorus girls, picking out only those he thought the prettiest. They were all put on a strict diet and fitness regime with even their sleeping times being supervised. Berkeley claimed this was the reason not one of them fell prey to the flu epidemic raging through Hollywood in 1932 • Safe though they might have been from influenza, they were not safe from the summonses to the outrageous parties held by Berkeley. According to Betty Grable, who went through the Berkeley mill: 'You'd come out in the early dawn feeling like a piece of meat dogs

has been fighting over all night. If my mother hadn't been with me I'd have killed myself a dozen times over. A lot of girls did. It was soul-destroying but everywhere you turned there were people…telling you stories about how so-and-so made it that way. The message was that either you played their game their way or you got out of town • This was Ruby Keeler's first film. She was married to Al Jolson at the time and it was his pull that got her the part. She and Powell were to go on to make another six musicals together • In the far racier novel on which the film is based, Julian Marsh and Billy Lawler are homosexual lovers • In the 70s, it became a hit Broadway and West End musical.

For Your Eyes Only
★★ 1981 127min c.

Director: John Glen
Screenplay: Richard Maibaum & Michael G. Wilson
Source: Stories, *For Your Eyes Only* & *Risico* by Ian Fleming

There are some great stunts and action sequences as Bond goes haring after the usual MacGuffin, this time a lost device that can launch Britain's Polaris missiles. Although avoiding the daft toys and some of the more ridiculous and unbelievable plot elements of some of the others in the series, nothing of interest happens whenever Bond has got his gun holstered.

James Bond	Roger Moore
Melina	Carole Bouquet
Columbo	Chaim Topol
Bibi	Lynn-Holly Johnson
Kristatos	Julian Glover
Lisi	Cassandra Harris
Brink	Jill Bennett
Locque	Michael Gothard
Miss Moneypenny	Lois Maxwell
'Q'	Desmond Llewelyn
Minister of Defence	Geoffrey Keen
Gen. Gogol	Walter Gotell
Tanner	James Villiers
Claus	Charles Dance

OOPS! It's dark when Moore pokes around in the warehouse in Corfu. But although the guy who sets off the explosion escapes into the night, by the time Moore emerges into the open the sun is shining brightly • If you're interested in seeing what happens *behind* the camera, keep an eye on Moore's sunglasses.

Psst! Tula Cossey, who plays one of the Bond girls listed only as 'Tula', later revealed, to much publicity, that she had been a man until a sex change operation • Bernard Lee, who had played 'M', died before filming began. Instead of replacing him, as a mark of respect the script was altered to say he was away on leave.

The Four Feathers
★★★ 1939 115min c.

Director: Zoltan Korda
Screenplay: R.C. Sherriff, Lajos Biro & Arthur Wimperis
Source: Novel by A.E.W. Mason

One of four brothers is accused of cowardice by his siblings, and his fiancée goes to the most extraordinary lengths to prove that it isn't so. This Boys Own adventure contains some splendid derring-do in the days of the British Empire, with battle scenes that have lost none of their magnificence. But it also contains some painfully dated jingoism and some equally painful acting. Still stirring stuff overall, though.

Harry Faversham . . . . .John Clements
Capt. John Durrance . . . . . . .Ralph Richardson
Gen. Burroughs . . . . .C. Aubrey Smith
Ethne Burroughs . . . . .June Duprez
Gen. Faversham . . . . .Allan Jeayes
Lt. Willoughby . . . . .Jack Allen
Peter Burroughs . . . . .Donald Gray
Khalifa . . . . .John Laurie

Psst! So impressive was the footage shot on location that it was reused in at least four other films. These included the 1955 remake, *Storm Over the Nile* and *East of Sudan*. It says a lot for the quality of the film that it still looked good enough to use 25 years later.

Four Weddings and a Funeral
★★★★ 1994 116min c.

Director: Mike Newell
Screenplay: Richard Curtis

Great modern comedy of friendship, love and English embarrassment. Although all the kudos went to Grant for the central role, the whole cast is wonderful. The episodic structure works beautifully and we really feel we get to know this group of mates by the end. Maybe it doesn't have anything terribly incisive to say. But it's delightful, very funny and endlessly rewatchable. Stick around for the end credits.

Charles . . . . .Hugh Grant
Carrie . . . . .Andie MacDowell
Fiona . . . . .Kristin Scott Thomas
Gareth . . . . .Simon Callow
Tom . . . . .James Fleet
Matthew . . . . .John Hannah
Scarlett . . . . .Charlotte Coleman
David . . . . .David Bower
Hamish . . . . .Corin Redgrave
Father Gerald . . . . .Rowan Atkinson
Henrietta . . . . .Anna Chancellor

Blurb Five Good Reasons To Stay Single • WE'RE SPEECHLESS! Proof The Best Man Doesn't Always Win! [Video ad after losing out at Oscars]

Quote 'The divorce came through a couple of months ago but I'm assured it had absolutely nothing to do with me. Apparently Paula knew that Piers had slept with her younger sister before I mentioned it in the speech. The fact that he'd slept with her mother came as a surprise but I think was incidental to the nightmare of recrimination and violence that became their two-day marriage.' • 'I just wondered if by any chance…um…uh, I mean obviously not because I'm just some git who's only slept with nine people but I just wondered…uh…I really feel…um…er, in short, er, to recap in a slightly clearer version, ah, in the words of David Cassidy in fact, um, while he was still with the Partridge Family… er, I think I love you.' • 'Do you actually know Oscar Wilde?' – 'Not personally, no…though I know someone who could get you his fax number.' • 'Bride or groom?' – 'It should be perfectly obvious I'm neither.'

OOPS! Grant's alarm clock always seems to go off around half an hour after the time it's set for • As soon as Grant goes down the steps in the final sequence, his shirt becomes completely soaked, even though it was barely damp a second before.

Psst! The film cost less than $5m. The production had to fake Scotland as they couldn't afford to travel there and extras had to provide their own wedding outfits • The suits in America weren't happy with the title. Among the 112 suggested were 'Four Weddings, Seven Friends and a Funeral', 'Four Weddings, Nine Bridsmaids and Five Priests' and 'Lots of Weddings, Some Sex and a Cup of Tea.' Eventually, it was going to be called 'The Best Man' until someone pointed out the Henry Fonda film of that name • Kristin Scott Thomas, who lives in France, did her own dubbing for the French version.

The 400 Blows
★★★★ 1959 94min b/w

Director: François Truffaut
Screenplay: François Truffaut

It's hard to see now what was considered so ground-breaking about this autobiographical film about a 13-year-old delinquent in late 50s Paris. However, the fluid camerawork and extensive location shooting where Truffaut grew up brought his first feature and the Nouvelle Vague to the world's attention. Antoine Doinel's story of rebellion against family and school remains poignant, witty and humane, unlike some of Truffaut's later films.

Antoine Doinel . . . . .Jean-Pierre Léaud
Mme. Doinel . . . . .Claire Maurier
M. Doinel .Albert Remy
Rene Bigey . . . . .Patrick Auffay
Woman with dog . . . . .Jeanne Moreau

Psst! This was Truffaut's first film. Until its release, he was known in the film world for being an extremely opinionated critic on Cahiers du Cinema. The film is based on Truffaut's own early life. He too was arrested for truancy and sent for a time to a borstal • The title is a French expression for kicking against authority • Léaud's answers to the woman psychiatrist were actually him responding to Truffaut's questions at the original screen test. Truffaut liked it so much that he wove it into the movie • Look out for Jeanne Moreau appearing briefly walking a dog • Truffaut can be seen in the amusement park on one of the rides • The film is dedicated to André Bazin, a film critic who bailed Truffaut out of jail and took him into his home in the days when he was struggling with his journalistic career back in the early 50s. Sadly, Bazin died on the first day of shooting • This became the first in a series of films Truffaut made mirroring his own life, all starring Léaud. Among them were Love at Twenty, Stolen Kisses, Bed and Board and Love on the Run,

Frankenstein
★★★ 1931 71min b/w

Director: James Whale
Screenplay: Garrett Ford, Francis Edwards Faragoh & John Balderston
Source: Novel by Mary Shelley and play by Peggy Webling

This most famous of all horror films may creak a little in the joints but it's still immensely watchable, if not particularly scary any more. The story of the scientist creating life from dead tissue is always fascinating, of course, but this has the additional benefit of beautiful gothic sets and a great-looking creature that inspires sympathy as well as fear. There were umpteen sequels and remakes, the best being The Bride of Frankenstein and Young Frankenstein.

Henry Frankenstein . . . . .Colin Clive
Elizabeth . . . . .Mae Clarke
The Monster . . . . .Boris Karloff
Victor Moritz . . . . .John Boles
Dr. Waldman . . . . .Edward Van Sloan
Fritz, the dwarf . . . . .Dwight Frye
Baron Frankenstein . . . . .Frederick Kerr
Herr Vogel, the Burgomaster . . .Lionel Belmore

Blurb To Have Seen It Is To Wear A Badge Of Courage!

Quote 'It's alive! It's alive!' • 'Have you never wanted to look beyond the clouds and the stars or to know what causes the trees to bud? And what changes darkness into light? But if you talk like that, people call you crazy.'

OOPS! When Victor, Elizabeth and Dr. Waldman visit Frankenstein's laboratory, the man playing God refers to three spectators. But there are four, as Fritz is there too.

Psst! Bela Lugosi refused the part of the monster because there weren't any lines, only grunts. He did play it later in Frankenstein Meets the Wolf Man. John Carradine was another who turned it down • Bette Davis was the original Elizabeth. But she was given the boot after costume tests • It took four hours for Karloff to be made up as the monster each day, with two hours needed to get it all off again. A brace kept his spine rigid and he wore leg braces to give him that strange gait. A double-quilted suit added to his bulk while the platform boots each weighed 12 pounds. The whole outfit weighed 48 pounds, pretty tough for Karloff as they were filming in the middle of a hot summer. He sweated so much, the monter's head kept melting and needed constant repairs • Karloff needed daily heat-lamp treatment and massage and at one point strained his back carrying Clive. So severe was the effect of the costume that he later needed an operation to repair the damage • So concerened were the filmmakers to keep the look of Frankenstein secret that Karloff was hidden under a sheet when he went from the make-up room to the set • The village had been used in *All Quiet on the Western Front* and the laboratory was reused for the *Flash Gordon* serials • In the original script both Frankenstein and his creation died. But after previews, the studio insisted on a different ending • Horror films were still a rarity then and so the studio added a warning prologue and hired nurses to be on hand in the lobby of many cinemas • Many members of the public truly were terrified. After one preview a man claimed he was going to sue because he couldn't sleep. Another rang the home of the cinema manager every five minutes and told him: 'I can't sleep because of that picture and you aren't going to either.' • The 1987 restoration added several cuts, including the rest of the scene in which Frankenstein drowns the little girl. Many argue that the cut there actually made it more, rather than less, horrific. Also restored was Clive's cry: 'Now I know what it feels like to be God!' which was felt to be too blasphemous in 1931 • Colin Clive was to die of alcoholism just six years later at the age of 37 • For film buffs, the film contains the first 360-degree pan and the first off-camera dialogue where viewers can't see the person speaking.

Freaks

★★ 1932 64min b/w

Director: Tod Browning
Screenplay: Willis Goldbeck, Leon Gordon, Edgar Allan Woolf & Al Boasberg
Source: Short story, Spurs by Ted Robbins

MGM, not a studio associated with the horror genre, came up with such a controversial example here that it was banned in many places. One does feel queasy watching this story of a power struggle between a trapeze artist and the real life 'freaks' in the circus, which begs awkward questions as to what extent the film exploits their condition. Despite its reputation, it's really only the revenge finale that is truly scary.

Cleopatra	Olga Baclanova
Hans	Harry Earles
Phroso	Wallace Ford
Venus	Leila Hyams
Roscoe	Roscoe Ates

Psst! *Freaks* was banned in Britain for 30 years, only finally being passed in 1963 • With audiences and critics shunning the movie in America, it was for many years only possible to see it under the canvas of a travelling circus or in burlesque houses, making it the equivalent of

an exploitation programmer doing the rounds of seedy drive-ins.

The French Connection

★★★ 1971 104min c.

Director: William Friedkin
Screenplay: Ernest Tidyman
Source: Novel by Robin Moore.

A tough, unconventional New York cop obsessively tracks down a drugs shipment. A revelation at the time for blurring the distinctions between the police and the crooks, for its use of locations and for its near-documentary style, it is most memorable for the stunning scenes where Hackman chases a subway train in a car. It's a shame it's so hard to hear what the characters are saying at times, especially as this naturalist sound was then copied by so many other movies. The 1975 sequel, *French Connection II*, was almost as good.

Jimmy 'Popeye' Doyle	Gene Hackman
Alain Charnier	Fernando Rey
Buddy Russo	Roy Scheider
Sal Boca	Tony Lo Bianco
Pierre Nicoli	Marcel Bozzuffi
Devereaux	Frederic De Pasquale

Oscars Best Picture, Best Director, Gene Hackman, Best Screenplay (adapted)

Blurb Doyle Is Bad News…But A Good Cop.

Quote 'Alright, Popeye's here!'

OOPS! During Popeye's stakeout of the Westbury Hotel, you can see the camera attached to the side of the car reflected in the windows.

Psst! The novel and film were based on real narcotics agents Eddie 'Popeye' Egan and Sonny Grosso who solved a major case involving a New York drug syndicate in 1961. As a result, they became celebrities and the most written-about cops in America. However the Police didn't like the way they came across in the film and Egan, who had been a cop for 16 years and made over 8,000 arrests, was sacked just seven hours before he was due to retire. As a result, he didn't qualify for his pension. He received only $240 from the movie • Egan appears in the film as Doyle's boss, Simonson. Hackman spent several weeks with Egan to study police work. Some real-life episodes involving the unconventional Egan appear in the movie • Hackman did the driving in the great chase himself, at speeds of up to 90 miles per hour. It took five weeks to film. Although restricting some of the side routes, the filmmakers weren't able to stop the traffic on the route Hackman takes. Those cars he's dodging are filled with ordinary unsuspecting John Does. Director Friedkin said: 'In New York City, if you drive like that, they don't pay too much attention.'

The French Lieutenant's Woman

★★ 1981 123min c.

Director: Karel Reisz
Screenplay: Harold Pinter
Source: Novel by John Fowles

This adaptation of a complex novel proves rather too obviously just how difficult such translations can be, with a Victorian tale of a young man falling for a woman in disgrace interrupted by a modern story in which two actors play the same parts in a film. The ploy confuses rather than clarifies the issue although the leads look rather handsome, as does Lyme Regis.

Sarah Woodruff/Anna	Meryl Streep
Charles Smithson/Mike	Jeremy Irons
Dr. Grogan	Leo McKern
Mrs. Poulteney	Patience Collier
Sam	Hilton McRae
Mary	Emily Morgan
Mrs. Tranter	Charlotte Mitchell
Ernestina	Lynsey Baxter
Mr. Freeman	Peter Vaughan
Vicar	Colin Jeavons
Mrs. Fairley	Liz Smith

Also: Penelope Wilton, Emily Morgan, David Warner, Richard Griffiths, Edward Duke, Harriet Walter, Doreen Mantle

Psst! Lyme Regis has lived off the reputation of starring in the movie ever since. So pleased were they that their town was going to be the location for a big movie that the place was spruced up before the cameras arrived. But director Reisz was after a more authentic look, so he ordered it to be roughed up again.

Friday the 13th

★ 1980 95min c.

Director: Sean S. Cunningham
Screenplay: Victor Miller

The success of *Halloween* lauched a wave of inferior slice'n'dice movies in the early 80s, of which this was one of the most commercially successful, leading to a zillion sequels – well, alright, seven at the last count. For a time, it *is* fun to watch a group of smug American teenagers being pursued by a gibbering psycho, but tedium sets in well before the end.

Mrs. Voorhees	Betsy Palmer
Alice	Adrienne King
Bill	Harry Crosby
Brenda	Laurie Bartram
Ned	Mark Nelson
Marcie	Jeannine Taylor
Jack	Kevin Bacon

Blurb Fridays Will Never Be The Same Again.

Psst! In Latin America, the series is known as *Tuesday the 13th* • The only surprise here is that the killer isn't Jason, who only takes up the machete from Part 2 onwards.

Fried Green Tomatoes at the Whistle Stop Café

★★★★ 1992 130min c.

Director: Jon Avnet
Screenplay: Fannie Flagg & Carol Sobieski
Source: Novel by Flagg

Bates strikes up a liberating friendship with the elderly Tandy, who regales her with stories of her Southern childhood. Tender, bitter-sweet and often amusing, this is old-fashioned filmmaking at its very best. The photography, story and acting is all top-notch. One of those surprising films people don't expect to enjoy and end up raving about to anyone who will listen.

Evelyn Couch	Kathy Bates
Ninny Threadgoode	Jessica Tandy
Idgie Threadgoode	Mary Stuart Masterson
Ruth	Mary-Louise Parker
Frank	Nick Searcy
Ed Couch	Gailard Sartain
Big George	Stan Shaw
Sipsey	Cicely Tyson
Grady Kilgore	Gary Basaraba
Buddy	Chris O'Donnell
Rev. Scroggins	Richard Riehle
Eva Bates	Grace Zabriskie

Blurb The Secret Is In The Sauce!

Quote 'Face it, lady. We're younger and faster.' – 'Face it, girls. I'm older and I have more insurance.'

OOPS! At the end, Tandy sits on a suitcase. When Bates arrives, it disappears.

Psst! In the scene where Masterson charms the bees, she didn't use a stand-in but insisted on doing it herself.

Friendly Persuasion
★★★ 1956 140min c.

Director: William Wyler
Screenplay: Michael Wilson
Source: Novel by Jessamyn West

As the American civil war impinges on their lives, a pacifist Quaker family find life becomes less simple than they have been used to, especially when one of them joins up. This is a sweet, sentimental and often droll movie which, unfortunately, lasts way too long.

Jess Birdwell . . . . .Gary Cooper
Eliza Birdwell . . . . .Dorothy McGuire
Widow Hudspeth . . . . .Marjorie Main
Josh Birdwell . . . . .Anthony Perkins
Little Jess . . . . .Richard Eyer
Sam Jordan . . . . .Robert Middleton
Prof. Waldo Quigly . . . . .Walter Catlett
Mattie Birdwell . . . . .Phyllis Love
Gard Jordan . . . . .Peter Mark Richman
Elder Purdy . . . . .Richard Hale
Elder .Charles Halton

Quote 'If thee talked as much to the Almighty as thee does to that horse, thee might stand more squarely in the light.'

Psst! Wilson was a blacklisted writer and so he was kept off the credits. Although the script was nominated for an Oscar, his name could not be mentioned in the ceremony • Perkins was going out with Cooper's daughter during the making of the film • Cooper had suggested to West, the author of the novel, that he might not be the right person for the part, telling her: 'My life hasn't been very Quaker-like'.

The Friends of Eddie Coyle
★★★ 1973 102min c.

Director: Peter Yates
Screenplay: Paul Monash
Source: Novel by George V. Higgins

With friends like these... Former crook Eddie Coyle is trying to provide for his family by carrying out his usual dodgy deals, but he's leant on by the police to infiltrate a robbery gang. Mitchum is excellent, as usual, and the dialogue is tough and convincing. It's a shame that Hollywood doesn't make more of these lean, unpretentious thrillers nowadays.

Eddie Coyle . . . . .Robert Mitchum
Dillon . . . . .Peter Boyle
Dave Foley . . . . .Richard Jordan
Jackie Brown . . . . .Steven Keats
Scalise . . . . .Alex Rocco
Waters .Mitchell Ryan
Artie Van . . . . .Joe Santos
Sheila Coyle . . . . .Helena Carroll
The Man's contact man . . . . .James Tolkan
The Beard . . . . .Jack Kehoe

From Here to Eternity
★★ 1953 118min b/w

Director: Fred Zinnemann
Screenplay: Daniel Taradash
Source: Novel by James Jones

Life in an army barracks in Hawaii in the days leading up to the Japanese attack on Pearl Harbor. It's toned down so much from the novel that it seems nothing more than a very tame and predictable war melodrama. If it's soap opera you're after, watch the telly. As for the famous roll in the surf with Kerr and Lancaster, will somebody please shove a hanky in my mouth in case the neighbours complain about the laughter.

Sgt. Milton A. Warden . . . . .Burt Lancaster
Karen Holmes . . . . .Deborah Kerr
Pte. Robert E. Lee Prewitt . . . .Montgomery Clift
Angelo Maggio . . . . .Frank Sinatra
Alma Lorene . . . . .Donna Reed
Sgt. 'Fatso' Judson . . . . .Ernest Borgnine
Capt. Dana Holmes . . . . .Philip Ober
Sgt. Leva . . . . .Mickey Shaughnessy
Cpl. Buckley . . . . .Jack Warden
Mazzioli .Harry Bellaver
Sgt. Maylon Stark . . . . .George Reeves
Baldy Thom . . . . .Claude Akins

Oscars Best Picture, Donna Reed, Frank Sinatra, Best Screenplay, Best Director

Blurb The Boldest Book Of Our Time, Honestly, Fearlessly On The Screen.

Quote 'Only my friends call me "wop".'
• 'Nobody ever lies about being lonely.'
• 'I never knew it could be like this.' • 'I love the Army. A man loves a thing, that doesn't mean it's got to love him back.'

Psst! Unsurprisingly, there were many changes made to the novel, which contained some of the worst language and best sex scenes to date in an openly sold book. Some were concessions to the censorship rules and some to the army's sensibilities. Ober's character gets his comeuppance in the film, but not the novel, while Reed's character was a hooker in the book, but a 'hostess' of a 'conversation club' in the movie • Author Jones thought that 'Columbia Pictures ass-kissed the army' to get permission to film at the real-life Schofield barracks and was furious at the way the book was bowdlerised • The Deborah Kerr part was originally to have been played by Joan Crawford, but she got involved in an argument about her costumes and scarpered • Sinatra's career was in a bad way, with singing temporarily impossible because of a throat problem, and he had to beg to play the part after Eli Wallach dropped out. He did it for just $8,000, but it resuscitated his career. As Wallach never gave a reason for his decision to abandon the role, rumours have persisted that Sinatra asked some of his Italian friends to help Wallach make up his mind • As with so many other directors, Zinnemann had many fights with Columbia's hated boss, Harry Cohn. One of the biggest was over the casting of Clift. Zinnemann had his way, but only after much bad blood had passed under the bridge • Clift learnt to play the bugle for his part but the bugle calls were actually dubbed for the film • Reeves, TV's *Superman*, had a substantial role. But preview audiences yelled out 'Superman' every time he appeared so his part was cut to ribbons. He killed himself six years later, still depressed by his inability to escape from the cape and tights • The film picked up eight Oscars, having been nominated for 13 • Although the US Navy banned the film because it was 'derogatory to a sister service', the army allowed it to be shown at any of its bases around the world.

From Russia With Love
★★★★ 1963 118min c.

Director: Terence Young
Screenplay: Richard Maibaum & Johanna Harwood
Source: Novel by Ian Fleming

007 hares off across Europe to get hold of a Russian decoding machine, the Lektor. The best of all the Bond movies benefits enormous-

ly from witty dialogue, splendid action sequences and a pair of deliciously nasty villains in blonde-haired Robert Shaw and Lotte Lenya's Rosa Klebb, one of the few women Bond *didn't* get into bed.

James Bond	Sean Connery
Tatiana Romanova	Daniela Bianchi
Kerim Bey	Pedro Armendariz
Rosa Klebb	Lotte Lenya
Red Grant	Robert Shaw
'M'	Bernard Lee
Miss Moneypenny	Lois Maxwell
Sylvia	Eunice Gayson
Kronsteen	Vladek Sheybal
Morzeny	Walter Gotell

Quote 'Red wine with fish. Well, that should have told me something.' • 'She's had her kicks.' • 'My whole life has been a crusade for larger families.' – 'So I've heard.'

OOPS! After the fight on the train with Robert Shaw, Bond and the girl escape in a truck filled with flowers. Grenades thrown from a helicopter bring them to a halt, smashing the front right side of the truck, knocking out the lights and necessitating a big paint job. Sheltering in rocks, Bond brings down the chopper. As it hits the ground, his hat vanishes. On the way back to the truck, the all-important Lektor machine which never leaves his side vanishes as well. On the plus side, the truck has been completely repaired, with both the paintwork and the lights in pristine condition.

Psst! Italian Bianchi's voice was dubbed • Pedro Armendariz was critically ill and had to be doubled towards the end of filming by director Young. He commited suicide shortly afterwards • One of the most bizarre examples of film merchandising ever must surely be the Rosa Klebb dolls that had retractable spikes in the shoes • The film ends with the credit: The End. Not quite the end. James Bond will return in the next Ian Fleming thriller.

The Front Page
★★ 1974 105min c.

Director: Billy Wilder
Screenplay: Billy Wilder & I.A.L. Diamond
Source: Play by Ben Hecht and Charles MacArthur

A newspaperman is torn between his fiancée and his manipulative editor. Despite the presence of the great team of Lemmon and

Matthau, one of the funniest of stage plays gets a pretty insipid rendering here, hindered considerably by the dreadful performance of Burnett who looks as if she's never acted before. Although to the average film viewer, this is probably the best known of all the movies derived from the Hect and MacArthur play, there also was a rather better 1931 version with Adolphe Menjou was better and the dreadful 1988 *Switching Channels*. Best of all is the 1940 gender-swap version, *His Girl Friday* which was cinematic magic.

Hildy Johnson	Jack Lemmon
Walter Burns	Walter Matthau
Mollie Malloy	Carol Burnett
Peggy Grant	Susan Sarandon
Sheriff	Vincent Gardenia
Bensinger	David Wayne
Kruger	Allen Garfield
Earl Williams	Austin Pendleton
Murphy	Charles Durning
Schwartz	Herb Edelman
Mayor	Harold Gould

Psst! Carol Burnett was on a plane that showed the movie. She went to the microphone afterwards and, to loud applause, apologised to the passengers for her performance.

The Fugitive
★★★ 1993 127min c.

Director: Andrew Davis
Screenplay: Jeb Stuart & David Twohy
Source: Characters created by Roy Huggins

This feature-film version of the cult 60s TV series has Ford as the man on the run, trying to prove his innocence by finding his wife's murderer before the cops catch up with him. From the incredible train crash onwards, the tension is tightened, notch by notch. Jones is particularly brilliant as the relentless cop who won't let anything deter him from catching Kimble. Sadly, Ford's character is far less interesting, being little more than a cipher.

Dr. Richard Kimble	Harrison Ford
US Marshal Samuel Gerard	Tommy Lee Jones
Helen Kimble	Sela Ward
Cosmo Renfro	Joe Pantoliano
Dr. Charles Nichols	Jeroen Krabbé
Sykes	Andreas Katsulas
Dr. Anne Eastman	Julianne Moore
Biggs	Daniel Roebuck

Oscars Tommy Lee Jones

Quote 'Listen up, ladies and gentlemen. Our fugitive has been on the run for 90 minutes. Average foot speed over uneven ground, barring injury, is four miles an hour. That gives us a radius of six miles. What I want out of each and every one of you is a hard target search of every gas station, residence, warehouse, farmhouse, henhouse, outhouse and doghouse in that area. Checkpoints go up at 15 miles. Your fugitive's name is Dr. Richard Kimble. Go get him.' – 'I didn't kill my wife.' – 'I don't care.'

OOPS! Kimble's hair is almost dry when he collapses on the ground after escaping from the dam.

Psst! This was another film that was originally slated for Alec Baldwin. He had also been replaced by Harrison Ford on *Patriot Games* • Ford claimed never to have seen any of the original TV series • The limp sported by Ford is real. He injured his leg during filming and didn't have it treated until afterwards to add verisimilitude.

Funny Bones
★★★★ 1995 126min c.

Director: Peter Chelsom
Screenplay: Peter Chelsom & Peter Flannery

After the wonderful *Hear My Song*, Chelsom returns to the memories of his Blackpool childhood for a very different movie. Unfunny American comedian Platt, the son of top comic Lewis, turns up at the seaside resort where he was born to plunder local talent. There Platt encounters the staggeringly talented Evans and his father and uncle, the hilarious Parker Brothers, learning a few secrets about his own family's past. Gloriously eccentric and often black humour, astounding music hall acts, bizarre settings, a subplot about stolen happy dust and another about Evans' dark secret, all are combined with a vividly imaginative plot to produce a magical stew. The story telling is rather unconventional, although anyone who has seen *Toto the Hero* may be reminded of that delightful film. I wanted to see this film again the moment it had finished. For those who don't have to be spoofed their movies, *Funny Bones* is a comic masterpiece.

Tommy Fawkes	Oliver Platt
Jack Parker	Lee Evans
Jim Minty	Richard Griffith
Katie Parker	Leslie Caron
George Fawkes	Jerry Lewis

Dolly Hopkins	.Oliver Reed
Stanley Sharkey	.Ian McNeice
Bruno Parker	.Freddie Davies
Thomas Parker	.George Carl
Laura Fawkes	.Ruta Lee
Himself	.Harold Nicholas

Quote 'Why do all the best things in life belong to the past?' • 'Have you lived here all your life?' – 'Not yet.' • 'It's all getting a bit French...I don't like it.'

Funny Face
★★★ 1957 103min c.

Director: Stanley Donan
Screenplay: Leonard Gershe
Source: Unproduced libretto, *Wedding Day* by Gershe

A mature fashion photographer turns a girl he discovers working in a bookshop into a fashion model and falls in love with her. The story's not only dim, but its barbs at fashion and beatniks seem ludicrously dated. However, there is plenty to enjoy, with great Gershwin music, beautiful sets and oodles of charm and sophistication from the two stars.

Jo Stockton	.Audrey Hepburn
Dick Avery	.Fred Astaire
Maggie Prescott	.Kay Thompson
Prof. Emile Flostre	.Michel Auclair
Paul Duval	.Robert Flemyng

Fury
★★★ 1936 94min b/w

Director: Fritz Lang
Screenplay: Bartlett Cormack & Fritz Lang
Source: Story, *Mob Rule* by Norman Krasna

Fritz Lang, having fled Nazi Germany, made a sensational Hollywood debut with this story of an innocent Spencer Tracy being left to burn in a jail by a lynch mob. Although it tails off a little towards the end, *Fury* remains a terrific movie of social injustice and violence, which could teach Oliver Stone more than a thing or two about pace and brevity.

Joe Wilson	.Spencer Tracy
Katherine Grant	.Sylvia Sidney
D.A.	.Walter Abel
Sheriff	.Edward Ellis
Buggs Meyers	.Walter Brennan

Kirby Dawson	.Bruce Cabot
Charlie Wilson	.Frank Albertson
Vickery	.Edwin Maxwell
Defense Attorney	.Jonathan Hale
Mrs. Whipple	.Esther Dale
Ahem	.Christian Rub
Albert's mother	.Nora Cecil
Girl	.Esther Muir
Waiter	.Bert Roach
Judge's wife	.Clara Blandick
Man	.Arthur Hoyt
Objector	.Ward Bond
Pippen	.Clarence Kolb
Peanut vendor	.Eddie Quillan

Psst! This was Lang's first American film • Krasna suggested the idea, based on a real lynching of kidnappers in 1933, over lunch one day with Joseph Mankiewicz. When Mankiewicz was later working at MGM as a producer, he pitched Krasna's idea. Studio head Louis B. Mayer wasn't too keen, MGM being mostly known for its lavish musicals, but he nonetheless agreed to buy it. Mankiewicz was a little surprised to get a phone call from Krasna the next day: 'Listen, could you do me a favour? It's been so long since I told it to you, I've forgotten what I said. Would you put it down for me?' So Mankiewicz dictated a 10-page outline and sent it off to Krasna. Krasna was then nominated for an Oscar for his original screenplay! • MGM was very strict about allowing scripts to be tampered with once they had been approved by the front office. After seeing *Fury* in a preview, Mankiewicz worked himself up into a fury of his own and carpeted director Lang. He accused him of changing the screenplay after it had been agreed. 'How could I change it,' said Lang not unreasonably, 'when I can't even speak English?' Mankiewicz grabbed a script and began reading it. 'Damn you,' he grumbled, 'You're right. But it sounds different on the screen.' • Louis B. Mayer, apparently hopeful that the movie bellyflopping would give him a chance to get rid of the autocratic Lang, was cross at how well-received the film was with the public. He did not extend Lang's contract when it expired and Lang was effectively barred from MGM for 20 years • The film's success was Tracy's first taste of stardom • The original titles of *The Mob* and *Mob Rule* were ruled out of court by the Hays Office • The atmosphere on the set was as mutinous as on many other Lang movies. Lang regularly worked through lunchtime, leading Tracy to organise a walkout one day so the cast and crew could eat. In the scene where the mob attack the jail, Lang threw some of the smoke bombs himself and hit Bruce Cabot on the head. Cabot had to be restrained from beating up Lang. He was told by one of the crew that arrangements were being made 'accidentally' to drop a light on Lang so that the problem would be eradicated. Fortunately for Lang, and movie audiences, it never happened.

Gandhi
★★★ 1982 188min c.

Director: Richard Attenborough
Screenplay: John Briley

One of the best of all movie epics. Kingsley is brilliant as the Indian lawyer who devotes his life to ending the British occupation of India. Although it tapers off a little in the latter stages, the acting, photography and story are all strong enough to make us believe that we are actually witnessing history in the making. If only it wasn't quite so long.

Mahatma Gandhi	Ben Kingsley
Margaret Bourke-White	Candice Bergen
General Dyer	Edward Fox
Lord Irwin	John Gielgud
Judge Broomfield	Trevor Howard
Viceroy	John Mills
Walker	Martin Sheen
Kasturba Gandhi	Rohini Hattangady
Charlie Andrews	Ian Charleson
General Smuts	Athol Fugard
Patel	Saeed Jaffrey
Mirabehn	Geraldine James
Kahn	Amrish Puri
Collins	Richard Griffiths
Kinnoch	Nigel Hawthorne
G.O.C.	Bernard Hepton
Sir George Hodge	Michael Hordern
Nahari	Om Puri
Sir Edward Gait	Richard Vernon
Colin	Daniel Day-Lewis

Oscars Best Picture, Best Director, Best Screenplay, Ben Kingsley

Quote 'You have been guests in our home long enough. Now we would like you to leave.' • 'An eye for an eye only ends up making the whole world blind.'

Psst! The funeral uses 300,000 extras, the most ever used in one scene on film • Although there are only 138 actors on the credits, there are 430 speaking parts • It took Attenborough around 20 years to get the film made. One

studio executive turned him down saying nobody would want to see a movie about 'a little brown man in a loincloth'. • The film won a total of eight Oscars, the most ever for a British film • In preparation for the role, Kingsley turned vegetarian, did Yoga daily, lost 17 pounds and learned how to spin thread • Tom Courtenay, Anthony Hopkins, Peter Finch, Dirk Bogarde and Alec Guinness had all turned the part down • Sheen gave his pay to charity • Long before he was a Mohican, Daniel Day-Lewis can be seen in a bit part roundly abusing Gandhi in the street.

Gangway
★★★ 1937 89min b/w

Director: Sonnie Hale
Screenplay: Lesser Samuels & Sonnie Hale

An assistant film critic who wants to tackle the really big stuff takes a job as a maid and gets caught up with gangsters. Although a bit clumsily made, this great little film is ample proof that we were just as capable as the Americans of making wonderful wise-cracking musicals. Why on earth is Matthews so little known today when she's so funny and such a great dancer and singer? The comedy here is a real eye-opener. Not only are the jokes fired at us as if from a machine-gun, but they're often quite surreal and saucy. How many other 30s musicals can you think of that make sly references to alternative uses for handcuffs?

Pat Wayne	Jessie Matthews
Insp. Bob Deering	Barry Mackay
Carl	Patrick Ludlow
Taggett	Alastair Sim
Nedda Beaumont	Olive Blakeney
Otterman	Noel Madison
Joe	Graham Moffatt

Also: Nat Pendleton

Quote 'Don't be a fool...It's not often a policeman comes into big money. Not without an official enquiry.' • 'Sure three aces beats two aces. But not in the same game.'

Gaslight
★★★★ 1940 88min b/w

Director: Thorold Dickinson
Screenplay: A.R. Rawlinson & Bridget Boland
Source: Play by Patrick Hamilton

Is a new bride having hallucinations, or is her husband trying to unsettle her mind? This superb psychological chiller still delivers the goods even today, suffused as it is with a nicely creepy atmosphere and beautifully understated performances. It was also known in America as *Angel Street*. The MGM remake in 1944 with Charles Boyer and Ingrid Bergman is moderately entertaining, but everyone looks as if they're trying too hard.

Paul Mallen	Anton Walbrook
Bella Mallen	Diana Wynyard
Rough	Frank Pettingell
Nancy	Cathleen Cordell
Ullswater	Robert Newton
Cobb	Jimmy Hanley

Psst! When MGM brought out its own version of *Gaslight*, studio head Louis B. Mayer tried to have the negative and all prints of this one destroyed. He failed, but it was impossible to see the earlier British film for many years.

The General

★★★★ 1926 80min b/w

Director: Buster Keaton & Clyde Bruckman
Screenplay: Al Boasberg & Charles Smith
Source: Book, *The Great Locomotive Chase* by William Pittenger

When a group of Union soldiers hijack a Confederate locomotive, its driver is determined to get it back. This now comes across as Buster Keaton's finest film. Although it may not be as anarchic as some of his films, it is beautifully paced, with an ever more frantic succession of great sight gags.

Johnnie Gray	Buster Keaton
Annabelle Lee	Marion Mack
Capt. Anderson	Glen Cavender
Union Gen. Thatcher	Jim Farley

Psst! The film was based on a true incident, although the episode actually ended with the hijackers being caught and several executed • Keaton had a pair of original locomotives restored for the movie. However, his wish that they be run on wood rather than coal caused a forest fire during production • The scene with the bridge collapsing with the engine on it was, according to Kevin Brownlow, the single most expensive shot in silent film history. Legend has it that the loco is still at the bottom of the ravine but memories are long and, during World War II, it was recovered and shipped out for scrap.

Genevieve

★★★ 1954 86min c.

Director: Henry Cornelius
Screenplay: William Rose

A pair of vintage car enthusiasts turn the return from the London to Brighton rally into a race in which gentlemanly behaviour goes out of the window. Although this comedy is many people's favourite British film, it now looks in places as antiquated as the cars. The four leads are splendid and there are some lovely scenes, particularly with the lovely Kay Kendall playing the trumpet. But it's all too genteel, cosy and charming to do much more than bring a smile to the face.

Alan McKim	John Gregson
Wendy McKim	Dinah Sheridan
Ambrose Claverhouse	Kenneth More
Rosalind Peters	Kay Kendall
Motorcycle policeman	Geoffrey Keen
J.C. Callahan	Reginald Beckwith
Hotel proprietress	Joyce Grenfell
Husband	Michael Medwin
Elderly gentleman	Arthur Wontner

OOPS! Anyone familiar with the geography of London will have a field day near the end of the movie trying to work out where they are. One second they're driving opposite Parliament, the next they're in Lewisham. The confused geography became necessary because the all-important tram lines had just been torn up by Westminster Bridge • As Gregson and Sheridan drive up to the BBC's on-the-spot chappie, the shadows of the crew can be seen at the bottom of the picture • In the pub in Brighton, More is carrying a tray with a pint of beer which magically transforms itself into a half-pint • When Kendall plays the trumpet, the guy who's relinquished the instrument to her manages to shrug to another band member that turns out to be himself.

Psst! Kay Kendall, like John Gregson, was a contract player with Rank and so got only around £100 a week. Even Kenneth More, the big name star, only got £3,000 • Although the action takes place on what is supposed to be a pleasant September weekend, the weather was bitterly cold when they actually filmed in the middle of the winter • Larry Adler is probably best known for having written and played the delightful harmonica music. However, he was blacklisted and Muir Matheson was listed as the composer both on American copies of the movie and when it was nominated for an Oscar

• Although Kendall couldn't actually play the trumpet, she took lessons in faking it from top jazz player Kenny Baker • John Gregson couldn't actually drive and had to take lessons beforehand • Genevieve herself is on display in Queensland's Giltrap Museum • Kendall died of leukaemia aged 32 in 1960.

Gentlemen Prefer Blondes

★★★ 1953 91min c.

Director: Howard Hawks
Screenplay: Charles Lederer
Source: Play by Anita Loos and Joseph Fields

A pair of showgirls are on the hunt for men, but whereas one is after money, the other is looking for love. It's hardly an original plot, but this musical comedy is made for us by the two leads. Marilyn is at her voluptuous best as the calculating gold-digger, while Russell is a delight as the wisecracking romantic. The high-spot is Marilyn singing 'Diamonds are a Girl's Best Friend'. There was an inferior sequel, *Gentlemen Marry Brunettes* in 1955.

Dorothy	Jane Russell
Lorelei Lee	Marilyn Monroe
Sir Francis Beekman	Charles Coburn
Det. Malone	Elliott Reid
Gus Esmond	Tommy Noonan
Henry Spofford III	George "Foghorn" Winslow
Lady Beekman	Norma Varden
Magistrate	Marcel Dalio
Gus Esmond, Sr.	Taylor Holmes
Hotel manager	Steven Geray
Winslow	Harry Carey Jr.
Dancer	George Chakiris

Quote 'I just love finding new places to wear diamonds.' • 'I always say a kiss on the hand might feel very good, but a diamond tiara is forever.' • 'I won't let myself fall in love with a man who won't trust me no matter what I might do.' • 'I like a man who can run faster than I can.'

Psst! Anita Loos' inspiration for Lorelei Lee was a blonde she met in 1924 who later went into movies. She was Mae Clarke, whose most famous movie moment was when Jimmy Cagney shoved a grapefruit into her face • Monroe was on $500 a week against Russell's $200,000 payment • Monroe was irritated that she didn't qualify for a dressing room. 'I said, finally... "Look, after all, I am the blonde and it is *Gentlemen Prefer Blondes!*" Because they always kept saying, "Remember, you're not a star." I said, "Well, whatever I am, I *am* the blonde!"'

The Getaway

★★★ 1972 122min c.

Director: Sam Peckinpah
Screenplay: Walter Hill
Source: Novel by Jim Thompson

McQueen gets out of jail and promptly heads a bank robbery. But there is little honour among thieves and, as the bodies begin piling up, McQueen and wife MacGraw go on the lam. What is essentially another chase movie is transformed into something exciting and out of the ordinary by Peckinpah's kinetic direction. The 1994 remake with Alec Baldwin and Kim Basinger was a scene-by-scene copy and didn't have quite the same fire in its belly.

Doc McCoy	Steve McQueen
Carol McCoy	Ali MacGraw
Jack Benyon	Ben Johnson
Rudy Butler	Al Lettieri
Fran Clinton	Sally Struthers
Cowboy	Slim Pickens
Thief	Richard Bright
Laughlin	Dub Taylor
Frank Jackson	Bo Hopkins

Psst! Steve McQueen and Ali McGraw fell in love on the set and later married.

Get Carter

★★★ 1971 112min c.

Director: Mike Hodges
Screenplay: Mike Hodges
Source: Novel, *Jack's Return Home* by Ted Lewis

A penny-ante crook returns to his Newcastle roots to get to the bottom of his brother's death. Still deliciously seedy, even if the drama seems a little flat. Perhaps not surprisingly given cinema trends in the intervening years, the once tough violence now looks rather fake. Writer Osborne's turn as local Mr. Big is something of a revelation.

Jack Carter	Michael Caine
Eric Paice	Ian Hendry
Anna Fletcher	Britt Ekland
Cyril Kinnear	John Osborne
Peter	Tony Beckley
Con	George Sewell
Keith	Alun Armstrong
Albert Swift	Glynn Edwards
Thorpe	Bernard Hepton
Gerald Fletcher	Terence Rigby

Quote 'I'd almost forgotten what your eyes looked like. Still the same. Pissholes in the snow.'

OOPS! Look out for the camera shadow on the bridge in Newcastle after Caine slaps the whore.

Psst! Probably the first film with a sex scene down the phone line.

Ghost
★★★★ 1990 126min c.

Director: Jerry Zucker
Screenplay: Bruce Joel Rubin

This amazingly popular film deserves every bit of its success. Swayze is the murdered man who refuses to lie down until he's saved the life of girlfriend Moore, communicating with the real world through wacky medium Goldberg. The ads made the film sound a sentimental weepie, but its splendid sense of humour keeps it balanced, making it a great feel-good movie.

Sam Wheat	Patrick Swayze
Molly Jensen	Demi Moore
Oda Mae Brown	Whoopi Goldberg
Carl Bruner	Tony Goldwyn
Willie Lopez	Rick Aviles
Subway Ghost	Vincent Schiavelli

Oscars Whoopi Goldberg

Blurb Believe.

Quote 'Ditto.' • 'All I know is that ever since *Ghost* came out, there's been a high enrolment in pottery classes.' [Demi Moore]

OOPS! For two people who've got themselves all mucky with clay at the potter's wheel, Moore and Swayze are remarkably clean when they get down to the serious nookie straight after • When Willie Lopez is run over, the body jumps from its position in the street to the car bonnet.

Psst! The director, Jerry Zucker, was one of the trio that brought us *Airplane* and *Naked Gun*. His brother David Zucker got his own back by spoofing the potter's wheel sequence in the second *Naked Gun* movie • The studio spent $75,000 on illuminating poster billboards in an eerie blue light to make them look more romantic • At one stage, it was proposed to oust Demi Moore and replace her with Swoozie Kurtz. One reason was that they could then use the ad slogan: 'Swoozie and Swayze are swell together.' • Amy Rochelle body doubled for Moore in the sex scene, most of which was cut.

The Ghost and Mrs. Muir
★★★★ 1947 104min b/w

Director: Joseph L. Mankiewicz
Screenplay: Philip Dunne
Source: Novel by R.A. Dick

When widow Tierney discovers that her dream cottage by the sea is haunted by crusty old seadog Harrison, she refuses to budge. Before long, an unlikely friendship takes root. Even though we've seen it all many times since, this remains an utterly glorious romantic tale which barely puts a foot wrong. The only fly in the ointment is the wooden performance from the suitably-named Natalie Wood.

Lucy	Gene Tierney
Ghost of Capt. Daniel Gregg	Rex Harrison
Miles Fairley	George Sanders
Martha	Edna Best
Anna	Vanessa Brown
Anna (as child)	Natalie Wood
Coombe	Robert Coote
Mrs. Fairley	Anna Lee
Angelica	Isobel Elsom

Quote 'It is easy to understand why the most beautiful poems about England in the spring were written by poets living in Italy at the time.'

Ghostbusters
★★★★ 1984 107min c.

Director: Ivan Reitman
Screenplay: Dan Aykroyd & Harold Ramis

Faced with academic scepticism, a trio of parapsychologists set up their own ghost-busting business just as the spirit world is about to make a concerted attack on the earth. Packed with great gags and amazing effects, this is an infectiously joyous movie with Murray, Weaver and Moranis giving particularly enjoyable performances.

Dr. Peter Venkman	Bill Murray
Dr. Raymond Stantz	Dan Aykroyd
Dr. Egon Spengler	Harold Ramis
Dana Barrett	Sigourney Weaver
Louis Tully	Rick Moranis
Janine Melnitz	Annie Potts
Walter Peck	William Atherton
Winston Zeddmore	Ernie Hudson

Quote 'Back off, man. I'm a scientist.' • 'We came. We saw. We kicked its ass!' • 'He *slimed* me.' • 'This chick is *toast*.' • 'There's something you don't see every day.'

OOPS! One truck has stuff on it *before* the marshmallow man explodes • When the rubble is falling off the building onto the police barricades below, some of it bounces.

Psst! The film was originally intended to star John Belushi with Dan Aykroyd, although this became a little tricky after Belushi's untimely death in 1982. The 'eating and drinking ghost' is their tribute to 'Bluto', Belushi's character in *Animal House* • The story grew out of Aykroyd's own interest in parapsychology • A cinema on a New York street is showing *Cannibal Girls*, one of director Ivan Reitman's first films • The voice of the 'possessed' Weaver as she levitates is that of Reitman, who did many of the other alien voices too • Roberto Goizueta, the head of Coca-Cola, Columbia's parent company, said on coming out of an early screening: 'Gee, we're going to lose our shirts'.

The Ghost Goes West

★★ 1935 85min b/w

Director: René Clair
Screenplay: Robert E. Sherwood & Geoffrey Kerr
Source: Story, *Sir Tristram Goes West* by Eric Keown.

An American millionaire buys a Scottish castle and ships it back home, complete with modern laird and 18th-century ghost. Considering the director and the presence of stars like Donat and Pallette, this should have been a riot. But although there's a pleasing cosiness to it, the humour is rather thin and forced.

Murdoch/Donald Glourie	Robert Donat
Peggy Martin	Jean Parker
Joe Martin	Eugene Pallette
Lady Shepperton	Elsa Lanchester
Ed Bigelow	Ralph Bunker
Sheperdess	Patricia Hilliard
Gladys	Everley Gregg
Gavin	Morton Selten
Cleopatra	Chili Bouchier

Psst! Studio head Alexander Korda meddled consistently in the production, which was French director Clair's first English-langauge film. He reshot scenes of the transatlantic crossing and amended others. Clair was on the point of taking his name off the film, but decided to put up with it and received much kudos when the film became a hit in Britain and America.

Giant

★★★ 1956 201min c.

Director: George Stevens
Screenplay: Fred Guiol & Ivan Moffat
Source: Novel by Edna Ferber

Rancher Hudson marries Taylor and carries her over his Texan threshold while loner Dean still nurses a crush on her. Presumably a keen student of Freud, he drills for oil to take his mind off his obsession. This very typically 50s epic sprawls all over the place and is incredibly long. But it remains watchable, primarily thanks to Taylor and Hudson. Dean is fine until he begins ageing, when he starts looking rather bizarre.

Leslie Benedict	Elizabeth Taylor
Bick Benedict	Rock Hudson
Jett Rink	James Dean
Luz Benedict II	Carroll Baker
Vashti Snythe	Jane Withers
Uncle Bawley	Chill Wills
Luz Benedict	Mercedes McCambridge
Jordan Benedict III	Dennis Hopper
Angel Obregon II	Sal Mineo
Mrs. Horace Lynnton	Judith Evelyn
Sir David Karfrey	Rod Taylor
Bob Dace	Earl Holliman

Quote 'Come on, darling. Why don't you kick off your spurs?'

Psst! Alan Ladd turned down James Dean's role. Sue Carol, his agent and wife said: 'I was used to his being top banana, and we both felt the Jimmy Dean role was a secondary role. It didn't turn out that way.' • It was Dean's last part. By the time the film was released, he was dead, killed just three days after his role in the movie ended in a head-on car crash. Dean was morose on set, depressed at having lost his girlfriend, actress Pier Angeli, to Vic Damone. He apparently predicted his own death to a friend on the set • Before Angeli died of a drug overdose at 39, she claimed she was still in love with him • Feelings on set ran high, with Stevens only too happy to remind Taylor that he had preferred Grace Kelly for the part. He also encouraged bad blood between Dean and Rock Hudson because he felt it would be good for the movie • Some of Dean's lines, as in the 'last supper' monologue, were dubbed by Nick Adams because they were inaudible as Dean had performed them • Filming was held up for a fortnight when Taylor collapsed after being made to work by Stevens the day after Dean died • Not everyone adored Dean. Rock Hudson said: 'I don't mean to speak ill of the dead but he ws a prick – pardon my French. He was selfish and petulant, and believed his own press releases. On the set, he'd upstage an actor and step on his lines.' • The film was banned in Syria because of Taylor's perceived pro-Israeli views • McCambridge's stetson was an old one lent to her by Gary Cooper. It had achieved its well-worn look, he claimed, by being 'pissed on by a lot of horses'.

Gigi
★★★ 1958 119min c.

Director: Vincente Minnelli
Screenplay: Alan Jay Lerner
Source: Play by Anita Loos, from novel by Colette

An enchanting musical, with Caron's family objecting to her marrying rake Jourdan because their tradition is to be mistresses not wives. It oozes charm and sly sauciness from every quarter and looks beautiful throughout. The highlight is probably still the famous Chevalier-Gingold duet 'I Remember It Well'.

Gigi . . . . .Leslie Caron
Honore Lachaille . . . . .Maurice Chevalier
Gaston Lachaille . . . . .Louis Jourdan
Mme. Alvarez . . . . .Hermione Gingold
Liane d'Exelmans . . . . .Eva Gabor
Sandomir . . . . .Jacques Bergerac
Alicia . . . . .Isabel Jeans

Oscars Best Picture, Best Original Story

Quote 'It doesn't matter who gives them as long as you never wear anything second-rate. Wait for the first-class jewels, Gigi. Hold onto your ideals.' • 'The only people who make love all the time are liars.'

Psst! Leslie Caron had played the part in a straight production of the story in the West End. On Broadway, it had been performed by Audrey Hepburn • Caron's singing voice is dubbed by Betty Wand • To the horror of Parisians, Maxim's restaurant closed for three days to allow the movie to film there with a redecorated antique interior • Jacques Bergerac couldn't skate, so he and Eva Gabor were taken round the ice on a small sledge that was out of view of the camera • The production was beset by so many problems that it went way over budget and, after a poor preview, roughly a quarter of it was then reshot • The winner of nine Oscars, Gigi remains third equal in the league table of statuettes won, along with The Last Emperor.

Gilda
★★★★ 1946 110min b/w

Director: Charles Vidor
Screenplay: Marion Parsonnet & Virginia Van Upp
Source: Story by E.A. Ellington

The film that makes grown men go weak and do impressions of quivering jellies. A shifty casino boss hires Ford to do his dirty business, including keeping his gorgeous wife in check. But the pair aren't strangers to each other. The rich dialogue oozes innuendo and double meanings, with a strong gay undertone. Although the sleazy characters don't exactly grab our sympathy, there's one overriding reason for watching and that is Hayworth, giving perhaps the sexiest female performance ever. One of the greatest of film noirs.

Gilda . . . . .Rita Hayworth
Johnny Farrell . . . . .Glenn Ford
Ballin Mundson . . . . .George Macready
Obregon .Joseph Calleia
Uncle Pio .Steven Geray
Casey . . . . .Joe Sawyer
Capt. Delgado . . . . .Gerald Mohr
1st German . . . . .Ludwig Donath
Thomas Langford . . . . .Don Douglas

Blurb There NEVER Was A Woman Like Gilda.

Quote 'Oh, I'm sorry. Johnny is such a hard name to remember and so easy to forget.' • 'Pardon me, but your husband is showing.' • 'If I'd been a ranch, they would've named me the Bar Nothing.' • 'You're a child, Gilda. A beautiful, greedy child. And it amuses me to feed you beautiful things because you eat with such a good appetite.' • 'Statistics show that there are more women living than anything else…except insects.' • 'You wouldn't think that one woman could marry two insane men in a lifetime.''

Psst! The story was originally written specifically for Hayworth, who wanted to get back into movies after a break because her marriage with Orson Welles was on the rocks • Filming began without a finished script. They weren't even sure how things were going to turn out at the end, something of a gamble considering that the film starred Columbia's biggest star. Indeed, pages often turned up only on the day they were due to be performed • Ford was told by Vidor not to pull the blow when he hit Hayworth. She retaliated later, knocking out two of his teeth when she had to hit him • Hayworth's singing voice is dubbed by Anita Ellis, although some film buffs argue that when she sings just a few bars of 'Put the Blame on Mame', accompanying herself on the guitar, it is actually Rita voicing it. Hayworth had, after all, once been a singer with Xavier Cugat and his orchestra • The choreographer's inspiration for Hayworth's movements came from a stripper he had known • Extraordinarily, 'Mame' and another dancer number were only slotted in after most of the rest of the filming had been completed. Some of the great dialogue too was inserted after filming was supposed to have finished to pep up the movie • Hated Columbia boss, Harry Cohn, who regarded his female stars as his personal harem, was furious at the growing friendship of Ford and Hayworth, who briefly became lovers. Cohn bugged her dressing-room to eavesdrop on their conversations. They knew about it and delighted in taunting him with their salacious conversations • With servicemen returning home and women unwilling to revert to their former roles, the film was a big hit, being successfully re-released twice more • The atomic bomb dropped on Bikini Atoll in 1946 was nicknamed 'Gilda' and had Hayworth's picture on it.

The Glenn Miller Story
★★★ 1954 116min b/w

Director: Anthony Mann
Screenplay: Valentine Davies & Oscar Brodney

This look at the tragically-truncated career of bandleader Glenn Miller is a cut or two above most showbiz biographies, helped by the radiant presence of June Allyson. The music, of course, is wonderful and we get Louis Armstrong and Gene Krupa thrown in as a bonus.

Glenn Miller . . . . .James Stewart
Helen Miller . . . . .June Allyson
Don Haynes . . . . .Charles Drake
Si Schribman . . . . .George Tobias
Chummy MacGregor . . . . .Harry Morgan
Mr. Miller .Irving Bacon
Mrs. Miller . . . . .Kathleen Lockhart
Gen. Arnold . . . . .Barton MacLane
Mr. Krantz . . . . .Sig Rumann

Psst! Stewart took trombone lessons from Joe Yukl, so that it would at least look as if he was playing the instrument. However, it soon became clear that he had little or no aptitude for the instrument and Yukl wanted to quit, saying that the noises Stewart was producing

were driving him mad and making him use foul language in front of his wife. Stewart persuaded him to stick with it • The playing heard during the film is dubbed both by Yukl and by Murray MacEachern.

The Go-Between
★★★ 1971 118min c.

Director: Joseph Losey
Screenplay: Harold Pinter
Source: Novel by L.P. Hartley

An old man recalls his memories of being a boy in Edwardian England, when he was asked to act as postman between farmer Bates and engaged Christie. Although a little sedate, it's a rather beguiling and beautiful love story which doesn't always follow the expected course.

Marian Maudsley . . . . .Julie Christie
Ted Burgess .Alan Bates
Leo Colston (younger) . . . . .Dominic Guard
Leo Colston (older) . . . . .Michael Redgrave
Mrs. Maudsley . . . . .Margaret Leighton
Mr. Maudsley . . . . .Michael Gough
Hugh Trimingham . . . . .Edward Fox
Charles . . . . .Roger Lloyd Pack

Quote 'The past is a foreign country. They do things differently there.'

The Godfather
★★★★ 1972 175min c.

Director: Francis Ford Coppola
Screenplay: Francis Ford Coppola & Mario Puzo
Source: Novel by Mario Puzo

The trials and tribulations of running a Family business in the face of cut-throat opposition. This epic Mafia saga is a powerful and entertaining piece of storytelling which was a well-deserved box office smash. An invitation to watch this is an offer you won't be able to refuse, even if understanding Brando can be something of a trial at times. It was followed by *The Godfather Part II* in 1974 and *Part III* in 1990.

Don Vito Corleone . . . . .Marlon Brando
Michael Corleone . . . . .Al Pacino
Sonny Corleone . . . . .James Caan
Clemenza . . . . .Richard Castellano
Tom Hagen . . . . .Robert Duvall
McCluskey . . . . .Sterling Hayden

Kay Adams . . . . .Diane Keaton
Connie Rizzi . . . . .Talia Shire
Jack Woltz .John Marley
Barzini . . . . .Richard Conte
Sollozzo . . . . .Al Lettieri
Tessio . . . . .Abe Vigoda
Fredo Corleone . . . . .John Cazale
Johnny Fontane . . . . .Al Martino
Mama Corleone . . . . .Morgana King

Oscars Best Picture, Marlon Brando, Best Screenplay (adapted)

Quote 'I'm gonna make him an offer he can't refuse.' • 'It's a Sicilian message. It means Luca Brasi sleeps with the fishes.' • 'I had so many complaints about the horse's head. There were 30 or so people killed in the film but everyone said: "You killed a living animal to get the horse's head?" Not I. The horse was killed by the dog food companies to feed your little poodles.' [Coppola]

OOPS! When Pacino shoots police chief Sterling Hayden, Hayden grabs his neck, so that's where we assume the bullet hits. But the blood then comes from his forehead • One scene is set in 1945, but there's the Stars and Stripes waving its 50 stars happily. There should only have been 48 at that time.

Psst! Enthusiasm for a picture about the Mafia wasn't exactly rampant at Paramount. Peter Yates and Arthur Penn were offered the chance to direct it before Coppola • Producer Evans attributed its success to hiring a director with Italian parents: 'I wanted to smell the spaghetti'. • It was Coppola who insisted on Brando for the role. The studio's ideas had included Orson Welles, Edward G. Robinson, Laurence Olivier and even Frank Sinatra • As well as stuffing his mouth, Brando plugged his ears throughout filming, the idea being that he would have to concentrate harder when others were talking • Brando had an appliance made by a dentist to reproduce the effect he had earlier achieved by stuffing his cheeks with cotton wool • As usual, Brando relied on cue cards rather than learning his lines beforehand • Sinatra is reputed to hate the character of singer Johnny Fontaine so much that no-one dare mention the name of the film without him blowing up • After meeting real-life Godfather Anthony Columbo, the film-makers agreed that the words 'Mafia' or 'Cosa Nostra' not be mentioned at any point. However, they are used in the sequel • Columbo ensured that no problems arose on location. The minders were, however, sometimes disparaging about the actors, one comment being: 'They hold their pieces like

flowers'. Columbo was shot and seriously wounded while the film was being made • The baby used in the baptism scene is Sofia Coppola, director Francis Ford Coppola's daughter, who was later to star in the third part of the trilogy • Talia Shire is Coppola's sister • Pacino and Keaton were lovers around the time of the film • The horse's head in the bed is not a prop, but a real head • Lenny Montana, six foot six inches and weighing 23 stone, plays Luca Brasi. He was the world heavyweight wrestling champion, fighting under the names *The Zebra Kid* and *Chief Chicawicki* • Although Brando won the Oscar, he didn't turn up. Instead a woman calling herself Sacheen Little Feather made a speech for him complaining about the treatment of native Americans in the movies. It later turned out she was an actress called Maria Cruz, winner of the 1970 Miss American Vampire contest • Only two years earlier, Brando had asked the Academy if they could supply him with a replacement Oscar, as the one he won for *On the Waterfront* had been stolen • Caan actually broke a couple of Russo's ribs when he had to beat him up on screen • Coppola insisted on directing the film in the style of the period it was set, cutting out modern directorial tricks like zooming or quick-fire cuts • Coppola turned parts 1 & 2 into a TV edition, *The Godfather Saga*, with an extra 15 minutes in it. It was then released on video • The novel sold half a million copies in hardback and over 10m in paperback.

The Godfather, Part II

★★★ 1974 200min c.

Director: Francis Ford Coppola
Screenplay: Francis Ford Coppola & Mario Puzo
Source: Characters from Puzo's novel.

This sequel, with the increasingly remote Pacino having taken over the business, also flashes back to the early days of the Don as an Italian-speaking immigrant in New York. Although many think this one even better than the original, I find the endless flashbacks rob the story of narrative drive and serve to confuse things. But then I like the third in the series better than most do.

Michael Corleone . . . . .Al Pacino
Tom Hagen . . . . .Robert Duvall
Kay Corleone . . . . .Diane Keaton
Vito Corleone . . . . .Robert De Niro
Connie . . . . .Talia Shire

Fredo . . . . .John Cazale
Hyman Roth . . . . .Lee Strasberg
Frank Pentangeli . . . . .Michael V. Gazzo
Sen. Geary . . . . .G.D. Spradlin
Al Neri . . . . .Richard Bright
Young Clemenza . . . . .Bruno Kirby
Mama . . . . .Morgana King
Merle Johnson . . . . .Troy Donahue
Tessio . . . . .Abe Vigoda
FBI Man . . . . .Harry Dean Stanton
Tony Rosato . . . . .Danny Aiello
Senator . . . . .Roger Corman
Sonny Corleone . . . . .James Caan

Oscars Best Picture, Best Screenplay
(adapted), Robert De Niro

Quote 'Keep your friends close, but your
enemies closer.' • 'Fredo, you're nothing to me
now. You're not a brother. I don't want to know
you or what you do. I don't
want to see you at the hotels. I don't want you
near my house. When you see our mother, I
want to know a day in advance so I won't be
there.'

Psst! Although Paramount wanted Marlon
Brando to star in the sequel, apparently he
asked for such an outrageous amount of
money that they couldn't possibly countenance
it • De Niro studied Brando's performance in
the first film assiduously to play his character
as a young man. He became one of only two
actors to win an Oscar for a performance in a
foreign language, the other being Sophia Loren
for *Two Women* • Troy Donahue plays a
character called Merle Johnson. It's his real
name • James Caan and Robert De Niro went
to the same Manhattan high school, Rhodes
High • This was the film debut of Lee
Strasberg, head of the Actor's Studio from
which so many method actors emerged
• Producer Roger Corman has a cameo as
Senator #2. It was he who had given Coppola
his first break as a director with *Dementia 13*.
Ron Howard was to give similar thanks to
Corman on *Apollo 13*.

The Godfather, Part III
★★★ 1990 160min c.

Director: Francis Ford Coppola
Screenplay: Mario Puzo & Francis Ford
Coppola

Michael Corleone tries to buy salvation for his
life of crime but finds that the Vatican is full of
crooks even bigger than him. Despite lacking

the crispness of the brilliant originals and having a plot with a few loose ends, this is a
severely under-rated sequel. As a portrayal of
repentance, salvation and spiritual decay, it
remains very powerful. Had Winona Ryder
played Mary instead of the dreadful Sofia
Coppola it would have been a masterpiece.

Michael Corleone . . . . .Al Pacino
Kay Adams .Diane Keaton
Connie Corleone Rizzi . . . . .Talia Shire
Vincent Mancini . . . . .Andy Garcia
Don Altobello . . . . .Eli Wallach
Joey Zasa . . . . .Joe Mantegna
B.J. Harrison . . . . .George Hamilton
Grace Hamilton . . . . .Bridget Fonda
Mary Corleone . . . . .Sofia Coppola

Quote 'Never hate your enemies. It affects
your judgement.'

OOPS! Popes Paul VI and John Paul I are much
discussed in the film which is odd as they'd
both died by 1979, when the movie is set.

Psst! Al Pacino had his teeth filed down and a
yellow stain applied to make him look more
realistic as an old man. When filming was over,
he had them capped • He is said to have
received $7m for the film. Initially, he asked for
more, only to be told by Coppola that the film
would in that case start with his character's
funeral • His part in the series was originally to
be played by Robert Redford, but he pulled out
• The script was written by Coppola and Puzo
in between gambling sessions in Reno • Sofia
Coppola, the director's daughter, took over
from Winona Ryder at the last minute when
Ryder's doctor warned she was on the verge of
a nervous breakdown • A shooting between
two gangs of teenagers in Long Island on the
opening night wounded four, one of whom died
• One of the two 'women in cafe' is Catherine
Scorsese who often appears in her son's
movies • The video is a director's cut, with an
extra 10 minutes.

The Gods Must Be Crazy
★★★★ 1982 108min c.

Director: Jamie Uys
Screenplay: Jamie Uys

One of the most extraordinary comedies ever,
this Botswanan film has the production values
of an episode of *Daktari* and features actors
who couldn't act their way out of a carrier bag.
Yet it is wonderfully, screamingly, tearfully

funny. A bizarre piece of slapstick about the reaction of a tribe to a Coke bottle falling from an aeroplane, it begins slowly but will soon have you clutching your sides to keep the pain under control. The scene with the Land Rover and the tree is a classic.

Andrew Steyn	Marius Weyers
Kate Thompson	Sandra Prinsloo
Xi	N!xau
Sam Boga	Louw Verwey
Mpudi	Michael Thys
Reverend	Jamie Uys

OOPS! The guns were set to single shot, but they're automatic again when the gunfight starts.

Going My Way

★★★ 1944 126min b/w

Director: Leo McCarey
Screenplay: Frank Butler & Frank Cavett

This tale of a young priest bringing radical ideas to his new New York slum parish is still pretty effective. Even though you try to resist the sentimentality, which is ladled on with a trowel, Crosby and Fitzgerald make a winning combination. There was a pleasant sequel, *The Bells of St. Mary's.*

Father Chuck O'Malley	Bing Crosby
Genevieve Linden	Rise Stevens
Father Fitzgibbon	Barry Fitzgerald
Father Timothy O'Dowd	Frank McHugh
Ted Haines	James Brown
Ted Haines, Sr.	Gene Lockhart
Carol James	Jean Heather
Max Dolan	William Frawley
Mr. Belknap	Porter Hall
Tomaso Bozzani	Fortunio Bonanova

Oscars Best Picture, Best Screenplay (adapted), Bing Crosby, Barry Fitzgerald, Best Director, Best Original Story

Quote 'The joy of giving is indeed a pleasure – especially when you get rid of something you don't want.'

Psst! According to McCarey, who wrote the story on which the film was based, it was inspired by incidents in the life of a real priest • Spencer Tracy and James Cagney both turned down the lead • The was Crosby's first serious dramatic role • The film, and its sequel, delighted the American Catholic Church. Bing Crosby was given a private audience by Pope Pius XII by way of thanks • The studio had been so worried about how the Catholic church would react in advance, that the film's release was held up for six months • Some Latin American countries banned it because it showed a priest in a baseball cap and a sweatshirt • As with many McCarey films, some of the dialogue was improvised as they went along • In the Marianas Islands, when the new film didn't arrive, one group of troops grew to hate *Going My Way*, being shown it on seven successive nights. When a group of Japanese were taken prisoner, they were given the chance of watching the end of the film before being led away. They turned the offer down. Having also watched it before, hidden in the jungle, they hated it just as much • Barry Fitzgerald was nominated both for Best Actor and Best Supporting Actor, both of which he won. The rules were changed afterwards to make sure it didn't happen again • During the Second World War, when metal was diverted to the war effort, Academy Award statuettes were made of plaster instead. Bing had to get a replacement after a practice golf shot decapitated poor Oscar • One of the religiously-minded extras is Gibson Gowland, who starred in Erich von Stroheim's silent classic, *Greed.*

Gold Diggers of 1933

★★★★ 1933 96min b/w

Director: Mervyn LeRoy
Screenplay: Erwin Gelsey, James Seymour, David Boehm & Ben Markson
Source: 1919 Play, *Gold Diggers of Broadway* by Avery Hopwood.

The second Busby Berkeley Warners musical was every bit as good as the first, with wealthy songwriter Powell backing a musical, against the opposition of his family. The snappy dialogue is wonderful, and there are some amazing Berkeley routines, among them 'We're in the Money', 'The Shadow Waltz' and the great Depression number 'Forgotten Man'.

J. Lawrence Bradford	Warren William
Carol King	Joan Blondell
Trixie Lorraine	Aline MacMahon
Polly Parker	Ruby Keeler
Brad/Robert	Dick Powell
Faneuil H. Peabody	Guy Kibbee
Barney Hopkins	Ned Sparks
Fay Fortune	Ginger Rogers
Messenger boy	Sterling Holloway

Clubman . . . . .Ferdinand Gottschalk
Call-Boy . . . . .Busby Berkeley
Gigolo Eddie . . . . .Tammany Young
'Pettin in the Park' baby . . . . .Billy Barty
Society reporter . . . . .Charles Lane

Psst! Although it doesn't show it, this was a somewhat rushed affair, with Warners hastily pushing it into production after the success of *Forty-Second Street* • Even when an earthquake struck during filming, choreographer Busby Berkeley wouldn't let the chorus girls off the set and returned to filming immediately after the damage was put right • Rogers was overheard rehearsing 'We're in the Money' in Pig Latin and it was put into the film • Berkeley himself makes an appearance, as the call-boy in the theatre • Joan Blondell's singing voice was dubbed by Marian Anderson.

Goldfinger

★★★★ 1964 112min c.

Director: Guy Hamilton
Screenplay: Richard Maibaum & Paul Dehn
Source: Novel by Ian Fleming

The third in the Bond series still maintained a high standard, with Bond trying to stop an attack on the gold supply at Fort Knox. It's acked full of memorable moments, with Oddjob and his lethal bowler hat, the gold-painted death of Shirley Eaton and a laser beam that nearly brings tears to Bond's eyes and it's all topped off with a great theme song. What more could any Bond fan want?

James Bond . . . . .Sean Connery
Pussy Galore . . . . .Honor Blackman
Auric Goldfinger . . . . .Gert Frobe
Jill Masterson . . . . .Shirley Eaton
Oddjob .Harold Sakata
'M' . . . . .Bernard Lee
Miss Moneypenny . . . . .Lois Maxwell
'Q' .Desmond Llewelyn
Tilly Masterson . . . . .Tania Mallett
Solo . . . . .Martin Benson
Felix Leiter . . . . .Cec Linder
Smithers . . . . .Richard Vernon

Quote 'Choose your next witticism carefully, Mr. Bond. It may be your last.' • 'You're a woman of many parts, Pussy.' • 'Do you expect me to talk?' – 'No, Mr. Bond. I expect you to die.' • 'He had a pressing engagement.'

OOPS! If it's so hot, why is there a handy electric heater in the bathroom for Bond to

throw in the bath? The flex is rather conveniently but unusually long, too.

Psst! Costing just under $3m, the film made $45m around the world • Fort Knox really is Fort Knox, with the filmmakers granted permission to shoot on location there, at least on the outside. The soldiers overcome by nerve gas were members of the American military • Gert Frobe's part was apparently dubbed by somebody else, with Nikki van der Zyl voicing Shirley Eaton's lines • Honor Blackman handed her P45 to John Steed and left *The Avengers* so she could play Pussy • The producers were well aware how cheeky her character's name was and were fully prepare to have to redub it to Kitty if the censors asked them to • Ian Fleming died a fortnight before *Goldfinger* opened • The producers got wind of an NBC TV show that was then called *Solo* in the pipeline. As this was the name of a character in *Goldfinger*, the producers insisted that it be changed which is why, shortly before *Goldfinger* came out, the new programme emerged under the name of *The Man from Uncle* instead • The Aston Martin DB6 was sold at auction in 1986 for $275,000, the most ever for a movie prop • The Queen Mother declared this the best film she had ever seen.

The Gold Rush

★★★ 1925 82min b/w

Director: Charles Chaplin
Screenplay: Charles Chaplin

Did people ever actually like the sickly sentimentality which was poured into almost every Chaplin movie? It's pretty hard to take these days, but luckily there are several sequences of comic genius in this tale of an impoverished gold prospector. The dance with the bread rolls and the eating of the boots are deservedly considered classics.

Lone prospector . . . . .Charles Chaplin
Georgia .Georgia Hale
Big Jim McKay . . . . .Mack Swain
Black Larsen . . . . .Tom Murray

Psst! As with many of his other silent films, Chaplin didn't have a script when he began. With his own studio at his beck and call, he was content to work it out as they went along. Out of 405 official shooting days, only 170 were taken up with actual filming • Scenes like the opening, with all the prospectors, were shot on location in the Californian Rockies. Chaplin hired 2,500 vagrants for a day, although they had to provide their own costumes • Chaplin was a man who would do much for his art, but even he wouldn't go as far as eating real leather boots. They were made of liquorice • In 1942, he reissued the film, 10 minutes shorter, with a musical soundtrack and a rather irritating voice-over by him. The silent version is far better.

Gone with the Wind

★★★★ 1939 220min c.

Director: Victor Fleming, George Cukor & Sam Wood
Screenplay: Sidney Howard & Others
Source: Novel by Margaret Mitchell

The ultimate soap opera is a one-off the like of which we shall never see again. Leigh was surely the right choice for feisty, selfish Scarlett O'Hara, around whom this tale of love and betrayal at the time of the American Civil War revolves. With the possible exception of the miscast Leslie Howard, every single actor does their bit. Despite its running time, there are surprisingly few flat patches and the tedium is soon dispelled when the compelling story sweeps us along again.

Rhett Butler .Clark Gable
Scarlett O'Hara . . . . .Vivien Leigh
Ashley Wilkes . . . . .Leslie Howard
Melanie Hamilton . . . . .Olivia De Havilland
Gerald O'Hara . . . . .Thomas Mitchell
Ellen O'Hara . . . . .Barbara O'Neil
Mammy . . . . .Hattie McDaniel
Prissy . . . . .Butterfly McQueen
Aunt 'Pittypat' Hamilton . . . . .Laura Hope Crews
Jonas Wilkerson . . . . .Victor Jory
Suellen O'Hara . . . . .Evelyn Keyes
Carreen O'Hara . . . . .Ann Rutherford
Stuart Tarleton . . . . .George Reeves
Dr. Meade . . . . .Harry Davenport
Mrs. Merriwether . . . . .Jane Darwell
Belle Watling . . . . .Ona Munson
Tom, a Yankee captain . . . . .Ward Bond
Frank Kennedy . . . . .Carroll Nye
Yankee deserter . . . . .Paul Hurst
Emmy Slattery . . . . .Isabel Jewell
Uncle Peter . . . . . .Eddie "Rochester" Anderson

Oscars Best Picture, Best Screenplay, Vivien Leigh, Hattie McDaniel

Quote 'Fiddle-dee-dee! War! War! War! This war talk's spoiling all the fun at every party this Spring.' • 'He looks as if he knows what I look like without my shimmy.' • 'You should be

kissed, and often, and by someone who knows how.' • 'Frankly, my dear, I don't *give* a damn!' • 'As God is my witness, they're not going to lick me! I'm going to live through this and, when it's all over, I'll never be hungry again. No, nor any of my folks, if I have to lie, steal, cheat or kill. As God is my witness, I'll never be hungry again!' • 'I don't know nothin' 'bout birthin' babies, Miss Scarlett!' • 'I'll go home and I'll think of some way to get him back. After all, tomorrow is another day!' [Last line]

OOPS! A movie ahead of its time, especially when we see an electric street lamp in Atlanta as Scarlett runs to get Dr. Meade! • Someone who timed Melanie's pregnancy by the dates of the Civil War battles referred to, worked out that she was pregnant for 21 months! • The credits get the parts played by George Reeves and Fred Crane mixed up • When Scarlett and Melanie are tending to a wounded soldier, their shadows don't match what they're doing • Just before Bonnie's death, Scarlett puts her cup on the table but it is not there in the next shot.

Psst! At the time, the most expensive film ever made, costing $4,250,000 • It won eight Oscars and was the highest-grossing movie of all time until *The Sound of Music* in 1964. If inflation is taken into account, it's still Number One • Based on Margaret Mitchell's 1,037-page bestseller, written out of boredom when she was resting after breaking an ankle, it was initially suggested to Irving Thalberg at MGM. He is reputed to have said to studio head Louis B. Mayer: 'Forget it, Louis, no Civil War picture ever made a nickel' • Mitchell's only casting suggestion was for her favourite star to play Rhett. It was Groucho Marx! • Although Gable was the only serious choice for Rhett, a nationwide talent competition was launched to find Scarlett, providing excellent advance publicity. Every actress in Hollywood was desperate for the role, among them Joan Crawford, Bette Davis, Claudette Colbert, Talullah Bankhead, Katharine Hepburn and Carole Lombard. Almost 2,000 women were considered over two years. Hopefuls even had themselves delivered to producer Selznick in packages, the most notable being the naked girl who appeared from a box on Christmas Day in 1937 in the midst of the Selznick family celebrations • Some unscrupulous souls took advantage of 'Scarlett Fever' and visited small towns, posing as talent scouts for Selznick. Although most probably went undetected, two were jailed for statutory rape in Flagstaff, Arizona while five more were arrested in Alabama and then released when the embarrassed girls wouldn't testify. Several hundred turned up at Selznick's office with letters from bogus talent scouts offering screen tests. Most were too shame-faced to return home and many ended up on the streets • Some genuine talent scouts were working for Selznick. Only one was considered impressive enough to be tested was Edith Marriner, whose name was changed to Susan Hayward when she began acting • Legend has it that it was only when the first scenes, the burning of Atlanta, were under way that Selznick's brother turned up with Leigh and said: 'I'd like you to meet your Scarlett O'Hara'. However, it is clear from Selznick's copious memos that he had been considering her for the part for many months. What's more she was screen-tested along with Jean Arthur, Joan Bennett and Paulette Goddard, who had been the frontrunner • The Selznick brothers invited all the actresses who had wanted the part to a big party. It was an icy failure • While Gable got $120,000 for 71 days' work, Leigh received only $25,000 for 125 days' work and had to settle for fourth billing • There were 1,250,000 items on the props list for the movie • Leigh, who was punctilious about hygiene, refused to do any more love scenes with Gable until he did something about his breath. He wore dentures and they apparently produced a foul stench • Gable got two days off filming for his honeymoon with new bride Carole Lombard • Filming began with George Cukor at the helm but Gable was said to be unhappy with the 'woman's director' and he was replaced with Victor Fleming, who was taken off *The Wizard of Oz*. When he had a nervous breakdown, Sam Wood took over his duties for a time • Fleming turned down a share of the profits, telling Selznick, 'Don't be a damn fool, David. This picture is going to be one of the biggest white elephants of all time.' • The burning of Atlanta used old unwanted sets for the fire, among them the Great Gate from *King Kong* • This was the first movie to have an intermission • The musical score by Max Steiner was the longest ever written and was finished just over a week before the premiere • Although the Mayor of Atlanta asked the audience at the premiere to applaud the 'Negro members of the cast', none of them were at the event as the cinema was for whites only • It had taken protests from the National Association for the Advancement of Colored People to get the word 'nigger' removed from the script • Hattie McDaniel was the first black actor to win an Oscar. It would be 24 years before it happened again, with Sidney Poitier picking up Best Actor for *Lilies of the*

Field • The only white member of the cast to be absent was Leslie Howard, who had returned to Britain to enlist in the RAF. Howard thought himself miscast and wouldn't learn the lines beforehand, distracted perhaps by working on *Intermezzo* at the same time • Although barred from the premiere, Butterfly McQueen, who played Prissy, was the guest of honour when the film's 50th anniversary was celebrated • The white horse that Thomas Mitchell rides was later to achieve stardom itself as Silver of *Lone Ranger* fame. It is one of only three animals to have its print on the famous pavement outside Grauman's Chinese Theatre • Despite all the fuss, the word 'damn' had appeared in movies before. Nonetheless, Selznick had to pay a fine of $5,000 for using it. He considered that preferable to changing it to, 'Frankly, I don't care' as the censors wanted. It would be another 12 years before the word turned up again in a movie • Taking a leaf out of *GWTW*'s book, Cecil B. De Mille told the papers he was launching a nationwide search for a cigar-store Indian for *Union Pacific* • The film wasn't shown in Russia until 1989.

The Goodbye Girl
★★★★ 1977 110min c.

Director: Herbert Ross
Screenplay: Neil Simon

One of the loveliest of all romantic comedies. Mason is sublime as the divorced dancer and mother who discovers that her departing louse of a lover has rented out their apartment to an actor. The relationship between her and the newcomer is turbulent, particularly given her hatred of actors, but their burgeoning affection for each other is sensitively and believably handled. With a winning combination of humour and sentiment, it stands up well to repeated viewing.

Elliot Garfield . . . . .Richard Dreyfuss
Paula McFadden . . . . .Marsha Mason
Lucy McFadden . . . . .Quinn Cummings
Mark Morgenweiss . . . . .Paul Benedict
Donna Douglas . . . . .Barbara Rhoades
Mrs. Crosby . . . . .Theresa Merritt
Ronnie . . . . .Michael Shawn
Oliver Fry . . . . .Nicol Williamson

Oscars Richard Dreyfuss

Quote 'Oh God, please let me get hit by a rich man in a Rolls Royce.' • 'Listen, I can't stand you. But you got a ten-year-old in there I'm nuts about.' • 'What is it about you that makes a man with a 147 I.Q. feel like a dribbling idiot?' – 'I don't know. But whatever it is, I thank God for it.'

Psst! This was to be Robert De Niro's next role after *Taxi Driver*. But after two weeks, filming was stopped. Neil Simon said that he 'doesn't play joy very well'. The director was changed and the part rewritten for Dreyfuss, who won an Oscar. At 29, he was the youngest-ever winner of the Best Actor statuette • When De Niro was involved, it was called *Bogart Slept Here*.

Goodbye, Mr. Chips
★★★ 1939 114min b/w

Director: Sam Wood
Screenplay: R.C. Sherriff, Claudine West & Eric Maschwitz
Source: Novella by James Hilton

A stuffy, unliked schoolteacher finds love in middle age. Although terribly slow getting under way, once the delightful Garson appears it becomes one of the most glorious and charming love stories of the era. Sadly, Garson's not around for nearly enough of the film and things are a mite creaky elsewhere, particularly the now risible passing-of-the-years inserts about telephones, the Boers, the death of Queen Victoria and the like. Give the 1969 musical remake with Peter O'Toole a wide berth.

Charles Chipping	Robert Donat
Katherine Ellis	Greer Garson
John/Peter Colley	Terry Kilburn
Peter Colley as young man	John Mills
Staefel	Paul Henreid
Flora	Judith Furse
Dr. Wetherby	Lyn Harding
Charteris	Milton Rosmer
Mrs. Wickett	Louise Hampton
Raiston	Austin Trevor

Oscars Robert Donat

Quote 'I thought I heard you saying it was a pity I never had...any children, eh? But you're wrong...I have...thousands of them... thousands of them...and all boys.'

OOPS! Director Wood paid no attention to Henreid when he pointed out that the name of the Austrian Railway company would have been different in the last years of the 19th century. Wood thought hardly anyone would notice, but trainspotters don't go off-duty when they're in the cinema and there were hundreds of letters pointing the error out.

Psst! Not yet fully anglicised, Paul Henreid is

listed on the credits as Paul von Hernreid • It was Henreid's English-language debut, as well as Garson's first film. She had been spotted by MGM head Louis B. Mayer in a play in London's West End • Donat's part was originally going to go to Charles Laughton • The movie was made at 400-year-old Repton School, from which came the schoolboy extras.

The Good Companions
★★★ 1933 113min b/w

Director: Victor Saville
Screenplay: W.P. Lipscomb, Angus Macphail & Ian Dalrymple
Source: Novel by J.B. Priestley

Edmund Gwenn gives up his dull existence and runs away to a life on the road as the odd-job man with the Dinky Doos pierrot outfit. This delightful screen adaptation of Priestley's backstage novel is one of the best British films of the 30s. With the glorious Jessie Matthews enchanting us and greats like Max Miller popping in, it's an absolute joy, even if it comes as something of a shock to see John Gielgud as a young romantic lead.

Susie Dean	Jessie Matthews
Jess Oakroyd	Edmund Gwenn
Inigo Jolifant	John Gielgud
Miss Trant	Mary Glynne
Joe Brundit	Dennis Hoey
Sam Oglethorpe	Frank Pettingell
Milbrau	Max Miller

Also: Finlay Currie, Jack Hawkins, George Zucco

GoodFellas
★★★★ 1990 146min c.

Director: Martin Scorsese
Screenplay: Nicholas Pileggi & Martin Scorsese
Source: Book, *Wiseguy* by Nicholas Pileggi

A dazzlingly brilliant depiction of the allure and often sad reality of life within the Mafia, centring around the criminal career of Liotta. Although violent, direction, script, photography and performances are all out of the top drawer. One expects great things of Pesci and De Niro, but Liotta and Bracco, as the mistreated wife turned-on by the violence, are also both superb.

James Conway	Robert De Niro
Henry Hill	Ray Liotta
Tommy DeVito	Joe Pesci

Karen Hill . . . . .Lorraine Bracco
Paul Cicero . . . . .Paul Sorvino
Frenchy . . . . .Mike Starr
Billy Batts . . . . .Frank Vincent
Morris Kessler . . . . .Chuck Low
Tommy's mother . . . . Catherine Scorsese

Oscars Joe Pesci

Quote 'As far back as I can remember, I've always wanted to be a gangster. To me, being a gangster was better than being President of the United States. You were treated like a film star.' • 'Funny, how?' • 'Saturday night was for wives, but Friday at the Copa was for girlfriends.'

Showing The Jazz Singer.

OOPS! As the caption 'Idlewild Airport, 1963' comes up near the beginning of the film, two jumbos fly past. They didn't exist for another five years • When Bracco drives off after believing De Niro is about to top her, watch the fake number plate of the brown estate car in front fall off as she passes it. Apparently, New York plates have changed colour since the 60s.

Psst! Based on the real-life story of gangster Henry Hill, now in the Witness Protection Plan. Hill's response to the film was: 'That's really the way it was. It's all true.' • According to the Entertainment Research Group, the F-word appears 246 times, beating the previous record-holder Scarface. Together with assorted S-words, '-words and others, there's an obscenity on average every thirty seconds, probably the current record • Although often seen briefly in his films, Scorsese's mother has a proper part this time as Pesci's screen mom, while Charles Scorsese is Vinnie • Look out for Samuel L. Jackson in a small role as 'Stacks Edwards'.

The Good, The Bad and The Ugly
★★★ 1967 161min c.

Director: Sergio Leone
Screenplay: Luciano Vincenzoni & Sergio Leone

An ironic title, as director Leone has to put one of the above labels over each of his three main characters to distinguish them for the audience. This third and most ambitious of the Dollars trilogy is really a prequel, with Clint's cool almost overshadowed by Wallach's endearing hamming. Impressive, though perhaps rather too long.

Joe . . . . .Clint Eastwood
Tuco . . . . .Eli Wallach
Setenza .Lee Van Cleef

Quote 'In this world there's two kinds of people, my friend – those with loaded guns and those who dig. You dig.'

The Graduate
★★★ 1967 105min c.

Director: Mike Nichols
Screenplay: Calder Willingham & Buck Henry
Source: Novel by Charles Webb.

His college days over, a young graduate tries to resist the universal pressures to decide what he should do with his life. He is seduced by his parents' best friend, while falling in love with her daughter. This mould-breaking comedy hasn't dated as badly as the 60s fashions, but it's still looking a little old hat with an air of the sitcom about it. Nonetheless, Hoffman has never been funnier while Bancroft is so electrifyingly sexy that it is impossible to understand why Ben would choose the insipid Elaine over her.

Mrs. Robinson . . . . .Anne Bancroft
Ben Braddock . . . . .Dustin Hoffman
Elaine Robinson . . . . .Katharine Ross
Mr. Braddock . . . . .William Daniels
Mr. Robinson . . . . .Murray Hamilton
Mrs. Braddock . . . . .Elizabeth Wilson
Mr. McCleery . . . . .Norman Fell
Mrs. Singleman . . . . .Alice Ghostley
Room clerk . . . . .Buck Henry
Miss de Witt . . . . .Marion Lorne
Also: Richard Dreyfuss, Mike Farrell

Oscars Best Director

Blurb This is Benjamin. He's A Little Worried About His Future!

Quote 'I just want to say one word to you, just one word…Plastics!' • 'Mrs. Robinson! You're trying to seduce me, aren't you?' • 'Do you find me undesirable?' – 'Oh no, Mrs. Robinson. I think…I think yoiu're the most attractive of all my parents' friends. I mean that.' • 'The whole character is one moment out of my life, me at 21 years old in a drugstore trying to ask for prophylactics, sweating, and walking out as soon as the druggist's wife started to wait on me.' [Hoffman]

Psst! The original novel was autobiographical, with Webb including real episodes from his life such as his hiding in the swimming pool • Although a lot of it is old hat now, director

Nichols introduced many new camera techniques that had been used in commercials but not in commercial cinema • Another innovation was to use popular songs on the soundtrack that were not related to what was happening on screen. Simon and Garfunkel's 'The Sound of Silence' had been at the top of the charts in 1966. 'Mrs. Robinson' went to Number One in 1968 • Robert Redford was the first choice for the lead. He rejected it on the sensible grounds that he thought no-one would believe he found it difficult to get to meet girls. Charles Grodin seemed about to get it at one point, but he was rejected as being a 'difficult' actor, something of an irony in view of Hoffman's later reputation • Doris Day was asked to play Mrs. Robinson but was not willing to damage her image. Jeanne Moreau had already turned it down, while Patricia Neal was still suffering the after-effects of a stroke • Gene Hackman began playing the part of Mr. Robinson but was replaced with Hamilton by Nichols • Bancroft was actually 36 when the film was made, only 11 years older than her screen daughter, while Hoffman was 30 • After filming was over, Hoffman went back onto the dole, not expecting the film to be the success it was • Look out for Richard Dreyfuss in his film debut as a student in the Berkeley rooming house • Writer Buck Henry appears as the hotel clerk • Nichols later said that he expected Ben and Elaine to turn out exactly like their parents.

La Grande Illusion
★★★★ 1937 117min b/w

Director: Jean Renoir
Screenplay: Jean Renoir & Charles Spaak

The masterpiece from a man who made several. This story of prisoners of war in a supposedly escape-proof prison was a most timely anti-war film, even though it clearly proved futile. Elegiac and beautifully told, it still has much of interest to say about class, nationality and patriotism.

Lt. Marechal .Jean Gabin
Capt. de Boeldieu . . . . .Pierre Fresnay
Capt. von Rauffenstein . . . . .Erich von Stroheim
Rosenthal . . . . .Marcel Dalio
Elsa . . . . .Dita Parlo
Cartier, the actor . . . . .Julien Carette
The engineer . . . . .Gaston Modot
The teacher .Jean Dasté

Quote 'A golf course is to play golf, a tennis court is to play tennis, and a prison camp is to

escape from.' • 'Frontiers are an invention of man. Nature doesn't give a hoot.'

Psst! Renoir based the story on the wartime experiences of a friend of his who was shot down and escaped several times • Veteran director Von Stroheim brought many of his own touches to his character, adding the neck brace and corset to make him even stiffer • The film was banned in Germany by Nazi proaganda chief Josef Goebbels. He also persuaded the Italians to ban it, which made it rather embarrassing when it won the 'Best Artistic Ensemble' award at the 1937 Venice Film Festival • It was being shown when German troops marched into Vienna in 1938. Soldiers confiscated the film in the middle of the performance. It's not known if the punters got their money back • The occupying German forces were thought to have destroyed all the copies of the movie. However, one turned up at the end of the war in, of all places, the Germans' own archives. When it was re-released, it was attacked in some quarters for being anti-semitic and pro-German.

Grand Hotel
★★ 1932 115min b/w

Director: Edmund Goulding
Screenplay: William Drake
Source: Novel, *Menschen im Hotel* by Vicki Baum

The first all-star movie is now as famous for one line uttered by Garbo as anything else. Set in a luxury hotel, it's really several different stories. Although decidedly dated in direction and act-ing (particularly from Garbo), there's still some pleasure to be had from watching these stars from the Golden Age of Hollywood. It was remade, badly, as *Weekend at the Waldorf* in 1945.

Grusinskaya . . . . .Greta Garbo
Baron Felix von Gaigern . . . . . .John Barrymore
Flaemmchen . . . . .Joan Crawford
Preysing .Wallace Beery
Otto Kringelein . . . . .Lionel Barrymore
Dr. Otternschlag . . . . .Lewis Stone
Seng . . . . .Jean Hersholt
Meierheim . . . . .Robert McWade
Pimenov . . . . .Ferdinand Gottschalk
Suzette . . . . .Rafaela Ottiano
Gerstenkorn . . . . .Tully Marshall
Honeymooner . . . . .Mary Carlisle

Oscars Best Picture

Quote 'I vant to be alone.' • 'Did you ever see a stenographer with a decent fur coat?' – 'I have indeed.' – 'One she had bought herself?' • 'The Grand Hotel. Always the same. People come, people go…nothing ever happens.' [Last line] • 'We had no scenes together. Alas. For her, and her alone, I could have been a lesbian.' [Joan Crawford on Garbo]

Psst! With the Depression biting terribly, it was MGM's production head, Irving Thalberg, who came up with the idea of a film brimming with stars • This was one of those rare films made in the same sequence that it appeared on screen • Garbo had hoped she could play opposite her former lover John Gilbert, but Thalberg wouldn't agree • Crawford had hoped to play opposite her, but Garbo filmed her scenes on a separate sound stage • The upstaging was said to be rampant throughout production, with the Barrymores having enormous fun in trying to outdo each other • The film was marketed cleverly by having a Hollywood premiere, but holding the film back from the public for months until the 'must see' factor was at its highest. In London, moviegoers camped out on the pavement overnight outside the Palace Theatre so they could be the first to see it • Author Baum took a job as a parlourmaid in a Berlin hotel for six weeks to gather material for her novel.

Grand Prix
★ 1966 179min c.

Director: John Frankenheimer
Screenplay: Robert Alan Aurthur

Seemingly endless shots of racing cars are interspersed with dull dramas about the drivers' personal lives. These guys obviously risk their lives on the track just so they can avoid having to converse with their tedious competitors. Full of split-screen 60s trickery, even the most astonishing of shots are now bettered every time there's a real Grand Prix. Only die-hard motor-racing fans would be interested.

Pete Aron	James Garner
Louise Frederickson	Eva Marie Saint
Jean-Pierre Sarti	Yves Montand
Izo Yamura	Toshiro Mifune
Scott Stoddard	Brian Bedford
Pat	Jessica Walter
Lisa	Francoise Hardy
Agostini Manetta	Adolfo Celi

Psst! Frankenheimer, while filming at Brands

Hatch, could not persuade the British extras to display satisfactory looks of horror at a disaster that was supposed to be happening on the track. So, just before a refreshment break was due, he arranged for the tea trolley to be blown up! He got the horrified reactions he was after. In fact, he later said, he got enough for a dozen movies.

The Grapes of Wrath
★★★★ 1940 129min b/w

Director: John Ford
Screenplay: Nunnally Johnson
Source: Novel by John Steinbeck

A family of poor farmers, under pressure from big business interests that want machines to cultivate the land, abandon their dust-bowl farm and head off to California in search of a better life. But they aren't the only ones. Not just one of the finest social dramas but one of the most heart-rending films of all time.

Tom Joad	Henry Fonda
Ma Joad	Jane Darwell
Casey	John Carradine
Grampa Joad	Charley Grapewin
Rosaharn	Dorris Bowden
Pa Joad	Russell Simpson
Muley	John Qualen
Connie	Eddie Quillan
Al	O.Z. Whitehead
Grandma Joad	Zeffie Tilbury
Guardian	Grant Mitchell
Winfield	Darryl Hickman
Policeman	Ward Bond
Tim	Frank Faylen
Accountant	Joe Sawyer
Conductor	Charles B. Middleton

Oscars Jane Darwell, Best Director

Quote 'Ma, there comes a time when a man gets mad.' • 'I jus' trying to get on without shovin' anybody, that's all.' • 'We keep a-comin'. We're the people that live. They can't wipe us out. They can't lick us. We'll go on forever, Paw…cause…we're the people.' [Last line]

OOPS! Sloppy editing means that Tom Joad's brother Noah disappears with no explanation from the movie.

Psst! It was extraordinary that the film ever got made, particularly as so little of the story was changed. The novel had been banned and burnt across the States. In addition, the Hollywood studios were in the middle of a war against attempts to unionise its workers • Before proceeding with the production, Fox head Darryl Zanuck had teams of investigators head for the migrant camps to see if the book told the truth about the situation. If anything, came back the reports, the novel was too optimistic • Security on the set was high in case there were attempts to disrupt filming, with armed guards posted who had to gather up all the scripts each evening. To stop gossip on the lot, the film was called *Highway 66* during production • Ford tried to keep the film as fresh as possible by getting as many scenes as he could in the can the first time • The first three rows at the premiere were occupied by the directors of Chase National Bank and their wives. As bankers to the production company, the bank will have profited from the film, even though it was also one of those which controlled the land companies that pushed tens of thousands of people like the Joads off their land • Although initially welcomed in Russia because of its depiction of the downside of capitalism, it was then banned after Russians marvelled that the poorest of Americans could still afford a car • Beulah Bondi had thought she'd been offered the part of Ma Joad and went to visit five camps dressed as an Okie to get into the role. Then she found Jane Darwell was cast instead • The ending of the film was dropped in parts of Europe, the film concluding with the departure of Tom from the government camp • Author Steinbeck seemed happy with the result: 'A lean, stringy, dark-faced piece of electricity walked out on the screen and he had me. I believed my own story again.'

Grease

★★★ 1978 110min c.

Director: Randal Kleiser
Screenplay: Bronte Woodard & Allan Carr
Source: Musical by Jim Jacobs and Warren Casey

There's nothing particularly spectacular about this 'teen' musical, and it isn't a patch on the stage version. But the enjoyable songs, including 'You're the One That I Want' and 'Summer Nights', are put over with enthusiasm. Despite the filmmakers' worst intentions, it is still supremely innocent. Now that Travolta's had his comeback, why can't Tarantino write something for Olivia Newton-John? As for *Grease 2*, the least said, the better.

Danny Zuko . . . . .John Travolta
Sandy . . . . .Olivia Newton-John
Rizzo . . . . .Stockard Channing
Kenickie . . . . .Jeff Conaway
Frenchy .Didi Conn
Marty .Dinah Manoff
Jan . . . . .Jamie Donnelly
Putzie . . . . .Kelly Ward
Principal . . . . .Eve Arden
Teen Angel . . . . .Frankie Avalon
Coach Calhoun . . . . .Sid Caesar
Vi . . . . .Joan Blondell
Also: Alice Ghostley, Michael Biehn

Quote 'If you can't be an athlete, be an athletic supporter.'

OOPS! Just after waitress Joan Blondell listens sympathetically to a student grumbling about beauty school, she tries to switch off the lights as she goes into the kitchen. She misses the switch completely but the lights still go off • When Travolta and Newton-John meet in the malt shop, look for the reflection of the boom mike on the jukebox • During the song 'Greased Lightning', Travolta flings his jacket onto the shelf. Look in vain for it after that, because, like magic, it vanishes • Atlhough Travolta plays a guy called Danny Zuko, at the drive-in cinema the name 'John' is clearly visible on his car • After 'Summer Nights', keep an eye out for the modern motorway packed with cars which can be seen in the background.

Psst! Although the play had already been running on Broadway for seven years before the film was released, it began life in a tiny Chicago experimental theatre. It wound up notching up 3,388 performances on Broadway • While the movie cost $4m, the promotion budget was $5m • With a box office take of almost $100m in North America alone, it was the most successful musical ever • Travolta only completed filming *Saturday Night Fever* 10 days before *Grease* began production • The producers encouraged a party-like atmosphere on set. The doors of the sound stage were left open so that the entire Paramount lot could hear the music. The director of the movie next door complained about the noise. In the middle of making *Goin' South*, Jack Nicholson told them either to keep the volume down or else give him a role in the movie • It was called *Brillantina/Brilliantine* in Spain, *Gummina* in France, *Brilliantino* in Italy and *Vaselina* in Venezuela • The film has some of the oldest of all screen high-school kids, with Travolta 24, Newton-John 30 and Channing 34 • Susan Dey and Henry Winkler turned down the lead roles.

The Great Escape
★★★ 1963 169min c.

Director: John Sturges
Screenplay: James Clavell & W.R. Burnett
Source: Book by Paul Brickhill

This exciting Prisoner of War movie is more a part of Easter to many in Britain than the story of the crucifixion. A great blend of action, humour and pathos is put across by a superb international cast. Sadly, it is self-indulgently overlong and it is rather worrying that every last one of the British prisoners gets killed while the Americans mostly survive.

'Cooler King' Hilts . . . . Steve McQueen
'The Scrounger' Hendley . . . . . . James Garner
'Bix X' Bartlett . . . . Richard Attenborough
Senior Officer Ramsey . . . . James Donald
Danny Velinski . . . . Charles Bronson
'The Forger' Blythe . . . . Donald Pleasence
'The Manufacturer' Sedgwick . . .James Coburn
Ashley-Pitt . . . . David McCallum
MacDonald . . . . Gordon Jackson
Willie . . . . John Leyton
Cavendish . . . . Nigel Stock

Quote 'Good luck!' – 'Thank you.'

OOPS! Drag your attention away from Steve McQueen and his motorbike looking for a way through to the Swiss border and you'll see a man trying his best to get out of the shot. By falling over, he becomes twice as obvious.

Psst! Although some liberties were taken with the story, it was based on a true-life mass breakout from Stalag Luft III at Sagan, western Poland, in the middle of the war. 76 members of the RAF got through a tunnel that had taken a year to build. 73 were caught. Of them, 47 were shot. Only three reached Britain, a Dutchman and two Norwegians • Pleasence had been a POW during World War II for 12 months after being shot down over France. Four of the German actors had been prisoners of war in the US • Bronson, who gets claustrophia digging a tunnel, had been a miner in Pennsylvania, paid $1 for every ton he dug • Bronson was later to take David McCallum's wife Jill Ireland away from him • Despite McQueen's obsession with motorbikes – he raced professionally – most of the stunt work on his bike was not done by him. However, he did play the German with the motorbike and sidecar chasing his own character • Although it has what now looks like an all-star cast, few of the actors were well-known internationally when they made the film.

Great Expectations
★★★★ 1946 118min b/w

Director: David Lean
Screenplay: Ronald Neame, David Lean, Kay Walsh, Anthony Havelock-Allan & Cecil McGivern
Source: Novel by Charles Dickens

This screen adaptation of Dickens' novel about the young lad who is rewarded in later life for helping an escaped convict, cannot be faulted. From the glorious atmospheric opening in the graveyard, we know we are in capable hands. Not only does it look beautiful throughout, but this great ensemble cast put it across so well you can't help but feel that Dickens would have been delighted.

Pip Pirrip . . . . John Mills
Estella . . . . Valerie Hobson
Joe Gargery . . . . Bernard Miles
Jaggers . . . . .Francis L. Sullivan
Miss Havisham . . . . .Martita Hunt
Abel Magwitch . . . . .Finlay Currie
Herbert Pocket . . . . .Alec Guinness
Pip, as child . . . . .Anthony Wager
Estella, as child . . . . Jean Simmons
Wemmick . . . . .Ivor Barnard
Also: Freda Jackson, Hay Petrie, O.B. Clarence, Torin Thatcher

Psst! When produced by the BBC on TV in 1989 Jean Simmons, here young Estella, played Miss Haversham.

The Great Train Robbery
★ 1903 11min b/w

Director: Edwin S. Porter
Screenplay: Edwin S. Porter

A group of outlaws rob a train and...er, that's it. This was the first movie ever to tell a proper story following on from another. It scared the blue blazes out of the audiences at the time, particularly when one of the baddies points his gun at the audience and fires it. But it's really only of interest now to film students. It is shown to good effect in *The Grey Fox*.

With: Bronco Billy Anderson, George Barnes, A.C. Abadie, Marie Murray

Psst! Despite its running time of 11 minutes, this was then one of the longest films made and was innovative in that it introduced both the pan and the close-up • At the time, the nickelodeon had to compete with theatre, magic lantern shows, music hall and the like. This film was the first sign that cinema could provide a serious threat to its competitors. Audiences would demand to be shown the movie again and again, many hoping that it would turn out differently the following time • Bronco Bill Anderson made 400 Westerns before retiring in 1920 • Tom London, a train driver, played that role in the movie. He went on to act in over 2,000 other movies until 1959, more than any other performer in movie history.

Greed

★★ 1925 120min b/w

Director: Erich von Stroheim
Screenplay: Erich von Stroheim
Source: Novel, McTeague by Frank Norris

A man is driven to madness by the greed of his wife. This is thought by many to be one of, if not *the* greatest of all silent films, even in its truncated version. However, although one or two scenes still retain some power, unless you are prepared to make significant allowances for the style of acting or the melodramatic way of telling a story over 70 years ago, you're unlikely to get much out of it.

McTeague . . . . .Gibson Gowland
Trina . . . . .ZaSu Pitts
Marcus Schouler . . . . .Jean Hersholt
'Popper' Sieppe . . . . .Chester Conklin
Maria Miranda Macapa . . . . .Dale Fuller

Psst! At the premiere, the was said to have lasted seven hours. Perhaps not surprisingly, the studio took it out of Stroheim's hands and cut it down savagely to under three hours • Stroheim went out on location to film, not something that was done much at the time. However, he insisted in filming in the locations in the book, which meant they had to visit Death Valley. It is not supposed to be possible to survive there in midsummer temperatures of 142 degrees, let alone make a movi. But this lot did ite • When Pitts rushes into the street after finding the body, the reactions of passers-by are genuine. Von Stroheim had gone out on location with a hidden camera • At one time the film was called *McTeague*. The four or so missing hours aren't believed to survive. It is though that someone unaware of the alternative name disposed of the other reels so that the silver could be reclaimed.

Green for Danger

★★★ 1946 91min c.

Director: Sidney Gilliat
Screenplay: Sidney Gilliat & Claud Gurney
Source: Novel by Christianna Brand

A medical whodunnit is given a new twist by being set in a hospital under constant threat of bombardment from doodlebugs in wartime. Although this tongue-in-cheek mystery has acquired a glowing reputation over the years, it's jolly without being exceptional. What makes it worthwhile is not so much the story as Sim's role as an unconventional police inspector.

Insp. Cockrill . . . . .Alastair Sim
Nurse Freddi Linley . . . . .Sally Gray
Dr. Barnes . . . . .Trevor Howard
Nurse Sanson . . . . .Rosamund John
Nurse Woods . . . . .Megs Jenkins
Dr. Eden . . . . .Leo Genn
Joseph Higgins, postman . . . . . .Moore Marriott
Dr. White . . . . .Ronald Adam
Sister Bates . . . . .Judy Campbell
Det. Sgt. Henricks . . . . . . .George Woodbridge

Psst! Although no operations were actually seen, the British censor wanted to ban the movie in case any wounded soldiers thought that their nurses might try to murder them. Gilliat pointed out that it was in the novel, not the film, that the action took place in a *military* hospital. According to him: 'a splendid lunch at the best black market restaurant in Soho restored amity and *amour propre* and he finally passed the picture with only one cut.' • Judy Campbell, playing Sister Bates, is the mother of Jane Birkin.

The Green Man

★★★ 1956 80min c.

Director: Robert Day & Basil Dearden
Screenplay: Sidney Gilliat & Frank Launder
Source: Play, *Meet a Body* by Launder and Gilliat

A clockmaker who does a little assassination work on the side is hired to kill a politician. He takes up residence in the sleepy hotel where it is to happen. Sim is as wonderfully batty as always. The film is also packed with the cream of British comic acting talent and, while the story may not be as hilarious as it might have been, the cast make it all extremely enjoyable.

Hawkins	Alastair Sim
William Blake	George Cole
Boughtflower	Terry-Thomas
Ann Vincent	Jill Adams
Sir Gregory Upshott	Raymond Huntley
Marigold	Avril Angers
McKecknie	John Chandos
Lily	Dora Bryan
Gen. Niva	Peter Bull
Radio salesman	Arthur Lowe
Radio salesman	Willoughby Goddard

Psst! Sim was originally going to direct but he backed out after disagreements over casting. It ended up with Basil Dearden directing much of it • The head of British Lion told Launder and Gilliat he didn't like the film. He hated it so much that he told them that if they'd agree not to be paid until later, they could have most of the profits. They said 'yes' and found it one of the most profitable deals they ever did • Look out for Arthur Lowe as a radio salesman.

Gregory's Girl
★★★★ 1980 91min c.

Director: Bill Forsyth
Screenplay: Bill Forsyth

A lanky lad gets a pash for the only girl on the school football team. One of the greatest depictions of the appalling suffering of the teenage boy as he develops a yen for girls, this is a delicious romantic comedy packed full of smashing witty dialogue and weird and eccentric characters. A treat to be savoured again and again.

Gregory	John Gordon Sinclair
Dorothy	Dee Hepburn
Phil Menzies	Jake D'Arcy
Susan	Clare Grogan
Andy	Robert Buchanan
Steve	William Greenlees
Head	Chic Murray
Eric	Alan Love
Alec	Alex Norton

Quote 'It doesn't look nice. If women were meant to play football, they'd have their tits somewhere else.' • 'That's good. You've stopped kissing me like I was your auntie.'

Psst! Bill Forsyth tried without success for two years to get the British Film Institute Production Board to back the film. Then he made *That Sinking Feeling*, backed by a small film-making cooperative. It was a hit at the Edinburgh and London film festivals and it then took him just

three months to raise the necessary £210,000 • The voices were dubbed for the American market, where it was felt that the original Scottish brogue wouldn't be understood.

Gremlins
★★★ 1984 111min c.

Director: Joe Dante
Screenplay: Chris Columbus

Billy's Christmas present is an eminently merchandisable cuddly creature bought from Creatures-R-Us in Chinatown. For a townful of instant little monsters, just add water. There are some great gags and some occasionally OTT violence. Film buffs could spend a year trying to find all the in-jokes.

Billy	Zach Gilligan
Rand Peltzer	Hoyt Axton
Kate	Phoebe Cates
Lynn	Frances Lee McCain
Mrs. Deagle	Polly Holliday
Sheriff	Scott Brady
Hanson	Glynn Turman
Pete	Corey Feldman
Futterman	Dick Miller
Grandfather	Keye Luke
Gerald	Judge Reinhold

Blurb Cute. Clever. Mischievous. Intelligent. Dangerous.

Quote 'Keep him out of the light…don't get him wet. And never, never feed him after midnight.' • 'Gremlins are not good. You can't trust them. You don't want one for a pet. You don't want your daughter to marry one.' [Director Joe Dante]

Showing It's a Wonderful Life • Snow White and the Seven Dwarfs.

OOPS! After Billy drops Gizmo into the bin, you can catch a glimpse of another Gizmo by his feet. [Not spottable on the video] • They were careless spraying the 'snow' because some of it has stuck to the underside of the branches.

Psst! Columbus thought up the pic after dreaming dream that mice were nibbling his • The cinema is advertising *A Boy's Life* and *Watch the Skies*, the working titles for producer Spielberg's films *E.T.* and *Close Encounters* respectively• There are cameos from the likes of Bugs Bunny animator Chuck Jones and Spielberg. Some say George Lucas is spottable riding a bicycle at the inventor's convention.

The Grey Fox
★★★★ 1983 92min c.

Director: Phillip Borsos
Screenplay: John Hunter

Stagecoach holdup man Farnsworth is released from prison after 33 years to find the world much changed. Unwilling to give up his line of business, he turns his attention towards locomotives. This superb, quirky, true-life Western is a little-known delight, with the laid-back performance of the mature Fransworth a particular joy.

Bill Miner	Richard Farnsworth
Kate Flynn	Jackie Burroughs
Shorty	Wayne Robson
Jack Budd	Ken Pogue
Fernie	Timothy Webber
Det. Seavey	Gary Reineke

Showing The Great Train Robbery.

Groundhog Day
★★★ 1993 103min c.

Director: Harold Ramis
Screenplay: Danny Rubin & Harold Ramis

Obnoxious weatherman Murray, reluctantly covering a small town festival, wakes up to discover that he is cursed to live through the same day again...and again and again. From this slender idea is spun a comedy of great delight and charm, as Murray's character explores first the impish fun that's to be had from knowing what everyone will do and then the misery of being unable to break out of a recurring nightmare.

Phil	Bill Murray
Rita	Andie MacDowell
Larry	Chris Elliott
Ned	Stephen Tobolowsky
Buster	Brian Doyle-Murray
Nancy	Marita Geraghty
Mrs. Lancaster	Angela Paton
Gus	Rick Ducommun
Neurologist	Harold Ramis

Blurb He's Having The Worst Day Of His Life... Over, And Over...

OOPS! The groundhog at the steering wheel? Honestly! • There's a prominent boom mike when the old guy collapses and Murray takes him into hospital.

Psst! All that snow in the final scene is real. Just as they were about to spend a fortune on the artificial stuff, the area was struck by the biggest blizzard of the year, just as happens in the film • Buster, the guy saved from choking by Bill Murray, is Murray's elder brother • Writer-director Harold Ramis appears in a cameo as the neurologist • There really *is* a Punxsutawney and they really *do* have a Groundhog Day.

Guess Who's Coming to Dinner?
★★ 1967 108min c.

Director: Stanley Kramer
Screenplay: William Rose

A middle-class white family are thrown into turmoil when their daughter announces she plans to marry a black scientist. It's a sign of how far we have come that this tame movie could ever have seemed daring. There's little insight or intelligence in the script and Poitier is such a *nice* potential son-in-law that it's hard to imagine the Draytons having any qualms. Those who want to remember Tracy and Hepburn in their heyday may find this a saddening experience.

Matt Drayton	Spencer Tracy
Christina Drayton	Katharine Hepburn
John Wade Prentice	Sidney Poitier
Joey Drayton	Katharine Houghton
Monsignor Ryan	Cecil Kellaway
Mrs. Prentice	Beah Richards
Mr. Prentice	Roy Glenn
Tillie	Isabel Sanford

Oscars Katharine Hepburn, Best Story and Screenplay

Quote 'You're two wonderful people who happened to fall in love and happen to have a pigmentation problem.' • 'Well, Tillie, when the hell are we going to get some dinner?' [Tracy's last line in the movies]

Psst! This was Hepburn and Tracy's ninth film together • Spencer Tracy was ill and hadn't worked for four years when director-producer Kramer suggested reuniting them. Hepburn also hadn't been seen for years because she'd been nursing Tracy. No insurance company would agree to insure the production because of Tracy's condition, so director Kramer and the pair paid for much of it themselves • Filming proved difficult with Tracy only able to work for short periods at a time • He died just 12 days after the film was in the can • Although they were both nominated for Oscars, Hepburn

learnt on the phone while filming *The Lion in Winter* that only she had won. 'Oh well,' she said, 'I'm sure mine is for the two of us.'
• Houghton, playing Hepburn's daughter, is actually her niece • There were demonstrations against the film in the South. At the time of its release, mixed marriages were still illegal in over a dozen American states. It was only eight years since a couple in Virginia were sent to prison for a year for their mixed-race marriage. Their conviction was overturned on appeal only a few months before the movie came out.

Gun Crazy

★★★ 1949 86min b/w

Director: Joseph H. Lewis
Screenplay: MacKinlay Kantor & Dalton Trumbo

A sharp-shooter who wouldn't hurt a fly falls under the influence of a *femme fatale*. Although put together on a very low budget and with acting slightly under par, this neat little film noir in the Bonnie and Clyde tradition has understandably acquired a cult following, not least among modern directors like Martin Scorsese. It's fast, exciting, fascinatingly filmed and surprisingly steamy. Great stuff. Also known as *Deadly is the Female*.

Annie Laurie Starr	Peggy Cummins
Bart Tare	John Dall
Packett	Berry Kroeger
Judge Willoughby	Morris Carnovsky
Ruby Tare	Anabel Shaw
Clyde Boston	Harry Lewis
Bart Tare (younger)	Russ Tamblyn

Blurb Thrill Crazy...Kill Crazy...

Psst! Although the credits list the co-writer as Millard Kaufman, it was a front for blacklisted Trumbo, who also wrote *Spartacus* and *Roman Holiday* • Peggy Cummins is probably the first *femme fatale* born in Prestatyn, North Wales.

Gunfight at the OK Corral

★★ 1957 122min c.

Director: John Sturges
Screenplay: Leon Uris
Source: Magazine article, *The Killer* by George Scullin

One of the most-often filmed of all Western stories gets the big-budget treatment. It's perfectly competent but doesn't really have any fire in its belly and is now almost as well known for its Dmitri Tiomkin music and the irritatingly catchy Frankie Laine theme tune.

Wyatt Earp	Burt Lancaster
Doc Holliday	Kirk Douglas
Laura Denbow	Rhonda Fleming
Kate Fisher	Jo Van Fleet
Johnny Ringo	John Ireland
Cotton Wilson	Frank Faylen
Ed Bailey	Lee Van Cleef
Bat Masterson	Kenneth Tobey
Morgan Earp	DeForest Kelley
Charles Bassett	Earl Holliman
Billy Clanton	Dennis Hopper
Ike Clanton	Lyle Bettger
Shanghai Pierce	Ted de Corsia
John P. Clum	Whit Bissell

Quote 'Why don't you buy yourself a new halo? The one you're wearing's too tight.'

Psst! The real gunfight lasted just 30 seconds or so against the five minutes it takes in the movie • 'You know what we've got to do with Wyatt and Doc,' said Lancaster to Douglas? 'We're in love with each other and we don't know how to express ourselves that way – so we just kind of look at each other and grunt and don't say very much.'

The Gunfighter

★★★ 1950 84min b/w

Director: Henry King
Screenplay: William Bowers, William Sellers & Andre De Toth

Peck is a gunslinger who wants to put his reputation behind him and be reunited with the son he left behind years ago. But the brothers of a man shot in a fair fight are out for revenge and time may be running out. This is a tense, well-drawn portrait of man desperate to shrug off the past but knowing how slim is the chance that it will happen. Not only was it made before *High Noon*, but with hindsight it stands up almost as well.

Jimmy Ringo	Gregory Peck
Peggy Walsh	Helen Westcott
Marshall Mark Strett	Millard Mitchell
Molly	Jean Parker
Mrs. O'Brien	Mae Marsh
Mac	Karl Malden
Hunt Bromley	Skip Homeier
Mrs. Pennyfeather	Verna Felton
Mrs. Devlin	Ellen Corby
Eddie	Richard Jaeckel

Blurb His Only Friend Was His Gun. His Only Refuge, A Woman's Heart.

Quote 'Here I am, 35, and I ain't even got a good watch.'

Psst! The moustache which Peck grew didn't go down to well with the top brass at 20th Century Fox. It was felt that it might reduce his appeal at the box office but when the head of the company realised how much it would cost to reshoot the movie with a hairless Peck, he let it stay.

Gunga Din

★★ 1939 117min b/w

Director: George Stevens
Screenplay: Joel Sayre, Fred Guiol, Ben Hecht & Charles MacArthur
Source: Poem by Rudyard Kipling

Long regarded as one of the great action adventures, this tale of three soldiers battling Thugs to get at their gold now seems terribly dated and draggy. Grant's cockney accent grates badly, the action sequences no longer thrill, the humour is terribly forced and even the least Politically Correct of us is likely to squirm at the patronising depiction of the savage natives.

Cutter	Cary Grant
MacChesney	Victor McLaglen
Ballantine	Douglas Fairbanks Jr.
Gunga Din	Sam Jaffe
Guru	Eduardo Ciannelli
Emmy Stebbins	Joan Fontaine
Col. Weed	Montagu Love
Higginbotham	Robert Coote
Chota	Abner Biberman
Maj. Mitchell	Lumsden Hare
Mr. Stebbins	Cecil Kellaway

Quote 'Take him to the tower and teach him the error of false pride.' • 'You're looking very regimental, Din.' • 'See them down there, coiling and wiggling, sticking their pretty tongues out.' • 'Mad? Mad? Hannibal was mad. Caesar was mad. And Napoleon was surely the maddest of the lot!'

OOPS! When the Thugs threaten to throw McLaglen into the snake pit, you can see the strings making the snakes bob up and down • It's said that one of the non-English-speaking natives screams 'Watch out' in the middle of a battle scene.

Psst! Costing nearly $2m, this was the most expensive film ever made by RKO, which had been in bankruptcy for six years • Although it didn't make its money back at the time, the profits started rolling in when it was reissued several times • In the 50s, it was cut to run at just 94 minutes • William Faulkner worked, uncredited, on the script. The script hadn't been completed when filming started, and some scenes were improvised • Grant persuaded Douglas Fairbanks Jr. to switch parts before they began filming. That way Grant could play a character with his real first name • The film was made in the Sierras, where filming was often held up by a succession of serious dust storms • It was banned in India for fairly obvious reasons. The *Bombay Chronicle* reviewed it nonetheless: 'The scenarists… seem to have heard of Pathas, of Kali, of idols and priests and temples, of elephants, of loin-cloth and of upright British soldiers…they have put them all together in a most amazing jumble. It is all like producing a film of Hollywood life and showing glamour girls riding on the back of Alaskan bears and cigar-chewing producers going about with feathers stuck in their hair like the Red Indians!' • After Kipling's widow claimed that people were laughing at the depiction on screen of the author, he was removed from the movie.

The Guns of Navarone

★★★ 1961 157min c.

Director: J. Lee Thompson
Screenplay: Carl Foreman
Source: Novel by Alistair MacLean

This wartime yarn of a group of Allied comman-does setting out on a near-impossible mission to spike two gigantic German naval guns is not always terribly plausible. It's also a great shame that screenwriter Foreman bores us so with us pompous thoughts about the nature of war. But, although it's too long, the action sequences really are pretty exciting. The sequel, *Force 10 From Navarone*, appeared 17 years later.

Capt. Mallory	Gregory Peck
Corp. Miller	David Niven
C.P.O. Borwn	Stanley Baker
Andrea Stavros	Anthony Quinn
Maj. Franklin	Anthony Quayle
Spyros Pappadimos	James Darren
Maria Pappadimos	Irene Papas
Squadron Ldr. Barnsby	Richard Harris

Jensen	James Robertson Justice
Anna	Gia Scala
Cohn	Bryan Forbes
Baker	Allan Cuthbertson
Grogan	Percy Herbert
Weaver	Michael Trubshawe

Psst! Over 1,000 Greek soldiers were brought in to impersonate the Germans • The cliffs used in the film could only be reached by a two-hour journey by donkey, with all the available animals in a 30-mile radius being collared by the filmmakers • David Niven nearly died after an accident in the tank at Shepperton Studios. He cut his lip and got septicemia, putting him in hospital for a month. He came back to the set but, after finishing his scenes, he had a relapse that put him out of commission for another couple of months • Although the water scenes were filmed in the safety of the studio tank, spare a thought for what the actors are going through. The water was practically freezing cold and copious quantities of spirits were imbibed in an attempt to keep themselves warm.

Hail the Conquering Hero
★★★ 1944 101min b/w

Director: Preston Sturges
Screenplay: Preston Sturges

Rejected by the army on medical grounds, through a misunderstanding Bracken is welcomed back to his home town as a war hero. Although it must have been brave to take pot-shots at the adulation of the military in the middle of the War, this comedy's enormous reputation no longer seems justified. Sturges always used wonderful character actors in his movies and the cast are great fun to watch but, as a satire it doesn't really wash any more.

Woodrow Truesmith	Eddie Bracken
Libby	Ella Raines
Mayor Noble	Raymond Walburn
Sergeant	William Demarest
Forrest Noble	Bill Edwards
Mrs. Truesmith	Georgia Caine
Political boss	Alan Bridge
Committee chairman	Franklin Pangborn
Western Union man	Chester Conklin

Also: Freddie Steele, Elizabeth Patterson, Jimmy Conlin, Torben Meyer, Jack Norton

Quote 'Well that's the war for you – always hard on women. Either they take your men away and never send them back at all or they send them back unexpectedly just to embarrass you.' • 'Opportunity's only got one hair on its head and you got to grab it while it's going by.' • 'If it wasn't for graft you'd get a very low type of people in politics.'

Psst! Sturges was nominated for a Best Screenplay Oscar both for this and for The Miracle of Morgan's Creek in the same year. Neither won • The studio wasn't happy about using the same actors as is Sturges' other films, but the writer-director battled hard to keep them, saying that by contributing to those movies' success, they had a moral right to continue to work with him. However, the relationship with Paramount became sufficiently sour for this to be the last film Sturges made there.

Halloween
★★★ 1978 93min c.

Director: John Carpenter
Screenplay: John Carpenter & Debra Hill

A Psycho rip-off which itself has spawned umpteen rip-offs. The story, what little there is, concerns newcomer Jamie Lee Curtis and her babysitting chums being terrorised by an escapee from a lunatic asylum whose security, presumably, is handled by Group 4. It's very stylish, with scares leaping right out of the frame, and there's surprisingly little blood. Carpenter and his co-screenwriter Hill succeed primarily because they make you care about the teens being chased. As a result, this is a modern horror classic. Of the four sequels, Halloween III is the only one that is watchable.

Dr. Loomis	Donald Pleasence
Laurie	Jamie Lee Curtis
Annie	Nancy Loomis
Lynda	P.J. Soles
Brackett	Charles Cyphers
Lindsay	Kyle Richards
Tommy	Brian Andrews
Graveyard keeper	Arthur Malet
Dr. Winn	Robert Phalen
Michael Myers (older)	Nick Castle

Showing Forbidden Planet • The Thing [1951].

OOPS! A good example of a movie where the weather during filming must have been 'changeable', judging by the number of times the ground alternates between being dry and wet.

Psst! Made for under $500,000, it grossed over $50m • This was Jamie Lee Curtis' film debut • The horror mask is actually a Captain Kirk mask with William Shatner's features obliterated by spraying it white and altering the hair • Pleasence's Dr.Loomis is a nod to Sam Loomis, Janet Leigh's boyfriend in *Psycho*. It's no coincidence that Leigh's daughter is the star of *Halloween* • For what it's worth, the now wildly overused movie cliché of the killer who keeps coming back from the dead probably started here.

Hamlet
★★ 1948 153min b/w

Director: Laurence Olivier
Screenplay: Alan Dent
Source: Play by William Shakespeare

Not a patch on Olivier's earlier *Henry V*. With the silly blonde wig on, it's hard to take Olivier seriously and you keep thinking it's about to turn into *Carry On Up The Castle*. It's all too arty and pretentious. Too much Old Vic and not enough Queen Vic.

Hamlet	Laurence Olivier
Queen Gertrude	Eileen Herlie
King Claudius	Basil Sydney
Ophelia	Jean Simmons
Polonius	Felix Aylmer
Gravedigger	Stanley Holloway
Francisco	John Laurie
Bernardo	Esmond Knight
Hatio	Norman Wooland
Laertes	Terence Morgan
Osric	Peter Cushing
Marcellus	Anthony Quayle
First player	Harcourt Williams
Player King	Patrick Troughton
Voice of Hamlet's Ghost	John Gielgud

Oscars Best Picture, Laurence Olivier

Psst! Olivier's wife Vivien Leigh was upset not to have been chosen to play Ophelia. During filming, she became convinced that he was having an affair with Jean Simmons • Neither Simmons nor Holloway had ever acted in a Shakespeare play before • Although playing his mother, Herlie was actually 13 years younger than Olivier • Anthony Quayle made his screen debut here • The then-unknown actor off-screen who shouts the word 'Lights! is Christopher Lee • At the Oscars, Olivier became the only person to win the Best Actor Oscar for a film directed by themselves.

Hammett
★★★ 1982 97min c.

Director: Wim Wenders
Screenplay: Ross Thomas & Dennis O'Flaherty
Source: Book by Joe Gores

Before turning his hand to writing detective novels like *The Maltese Falcon*, Dashiel Hammett was a detective himself. This clever movie, a homage to the classic detective movies, imagines that Hammett got involved in a mystery that provided the inspiration for his later stories. Although the plot in the film itself is a little confusing, the atmosphere and mood is wonderfully redolent of the great 30s private eye films. A must for those who wished they still made them like that.

Hammett	Frederic Forrest
Jimmy Ryan	Peter Boyle
Kit Conger/Sue Alabama	Marilu Henner
English Eddie Hagedorn	Roy Kinnear
Eli, the taxi driver	Elisha Cook Jr.
Lt. O'Mara	R.G. Armstrong
Det. Bradford	Richard Bradford

Also: Lydia Lei, David Patrick Kelly, Michael Chow, Sylvia Sidney, Royal Dano, Sam Fuller

Psst! It is often rumoured that executive producer Francis Ford Coppola directed, or re-directed, much of the movie himself • It had been in pre-production for five years and began filming in 1980. That version was then abandoned, and Sylvia Miles and Brian Keith were told their services were no longer required. Filming on this version began the following year.

Hands across the Table
★★★ 1935 81min b/w

Director: Mitchell Leisen
Screenplay: Norman Krasna, Vincent Lawrence & Herbert Fields

A gold-digging manicurist thinks she has the choice of two wealthy man, but one isn't quite as well off as he seems. With Lombard, cinema's greatest comedienne, on top form this is a delightful, bewitching comedy with more heart than most.

Regi Allen	Carole Lombard
Theodore Drew III	Fred MacMurray
Allen Macklyn	Ralph Bellamy
Vivian Snowden	Astrid Allwyn

Laura	Ruth Donnelly
Nona	Marie Prévost
Natty	William Demarest

Hannah and Her Sisters
★★★★ 1986 107min c.

Director: Woody Allen
Screenplay: Woody Allen

Astoundingly brilliant Allen film about three sisters and the intertwining stories of the characters involved with them. Shot through with wit, intelligence and little of Woody's tiresome, guilt-ridden angst, this is a perfect ensemble movie with excellent performances from everyone, but particularly Caine, never better than as Farrow's husband who falls for sister Hershey. Endlessly rewatchable.

Micky	Woody Allen
Elliot	Michael Caine
Hannah	Mia Farrow
April	Carrie Fisher
Lee	Barbara Hershey
Hannah's Father	Lloyd Nolan
Hannah's Mother	Maureen O'Sullivan
Dusty	Daniel Stern
Frederick	Max Von Sydow
Holly	Dianne Wiest
The Architect	Sam Waterston
Mickey's Friend	Tony Roberts
Himself	Bobby Short
Gail	Julie Kavner
Ed Smythe	J.T. Walsh
Writer	John Turturro

Oscars Michael Caine, Dianne Wiest

Quote 'How the hell do I know why there were Nazis? I don't know how the can opener works.'

Showing Duck Soup.

Psst! A large part of the movie was filmed in Farrow's apartment, which presumably made it pretty easy to get to work in the morning • According to Caine, Farrow would disappear off to the kitchen to make food for the children, several of whom appeared in the film, taking off her apron and going into the other room when needed for filming. Caine said it was tricky enough doing love scenes with Farrow when Woody was there but that, even worse, on one occasion her former husband André Previn, also turned up • An old man who arrived on the set trying to sell watches was, says Caine, Woody's father • O'Sullivan plays Farrow's mother, which she is in real life • This was

veteran actor Lloyd Nolan's last role. He died before the film came out • The doctor giving Allen the bad news on his sperm count is Benno C. Schmidt, Jr., President of Yale • Although probably alone in his opjnion, Woody was not happy with the ending, which he found too upbeat, feeling that life never worked out as neatly for people as that.

The Happiest Days of Your Life
★★★★ 1950 81min b/w

Director: Frank Launder
Screenplay: Frank Launder & John Dighton
Source: Play by Dighton

The men from the Ministry slip up and billet a girl's school on an all boys' establishment. With the two heads at...er...loggerheads, the scene is set for a superb, very British, farce. Seeing those two great comic talents, Rutherford and Sim, together is a joy no matter how many times it is repeated.

Wetherby Pond	Alastair Sim
Miss Whitchurch	Margaret Rutherford
Miss Gossage	Joyce Grenfell
Rainbow	Edward Rigby
Victor Hyde-Brown	Guy Middleton
Arnold Billings	Richard Wattis
Miss Jezzard	Muriel Aked
Richard Tassell	John Bentley
Miss Harper	Bernadette O'Farrell
Anthony Ramsden	Arthur Howard
Dr. Collet	Laurence Naismith
Mrs. Hampstead	Gladys Henson

Psst! The play ran for 605 performances in the West End. Rutherford was in it, but not Sim.

A Hard Day's Night
★★★★ 1964 85min b/w

Director: Richard Lester
Screenplay: Alun Owen

This farce purports to show us a day and a half in the company of a popular musical singing group of the 60s, with life complicated by the rascally grandfather of one of the band members. This innovative farce, utilising lots of techniques popular in the commercials world, would have bene funny whoever starred in it. As it features The Beatles just after they had made it, it is not only hilarious, but absolutely riveting. The music, it hardly needs to be said, is out of this world. The numbers, accompanied by much teenage screaming, include 'Can't Buy Me Love' and, of course, 'A Hard Day's Night'.

John	John Lennon
Paul	Paul McCartney
George	George Harrison
Ringo	Ringo Starr
Grandfather	Wilfrid Brambell
Norm	Norman Rossington
Shake	John Junkin
TV director	Victor Spinetti
Police Inspector	Deryck Guyler
Millie	Anna Quayle
Shirt advertising man	Kenneth Haigh
Man on train	Richard Vernon
Magician	Derek Nimmo
Dancer at disco	Jeremy Lloyd
Dancer	Lionel Blair
Floor manager	Robin Ray

Quote 'He's a *clean* old man.' • 'The *Citizen Kane* of jukebox movies.' [Critic Andrew Sarris]

OOPS! As the Beatles race onto the train at the opening, their clothes change from what they came onto the set with to what they were supposed to be wearing. The continuity girl was in the loo at the time.

Psst! Filmed in just six and a half weeks, the budget was only £180,000, with United Artists more interested in the soundtrack album than they were in the movie • With Beatlemania at its height, most of the filming outside had to be got in the can in the first or second take before a mob of fans appeared • Much of the filming was done by Lester himself using a hand-held Ariflex camera • Although it has the feel of an ad-libbed movie, it was only the press conference that was improvised. Elsewhere, Lester would simply say what the next line was and film the respective Beatle saying it until he was happy enough to move on • The title came from John's description of Ringo's weird way with English. One all-night recording session was, according to him, 'a hard day's night'. The producer liked the title and asked Paul to write a song to go with it. It was ready the following morning, the lyrics having been written on a book of matches. Like 'Can't Buy Me Love', it got to number one • George Harrison met future wife Patti Boyd during the movie. When John, Paul and George are in the dining car, she is the blonde one of the two schoolgirls the lads give the glad eye to • Lester also directed the Beatles in *Help!* in 1965 and said he preferred that.

Harold and Maude
★★★ 1971 90min c.

Director: Hal Ashby
Screenplay: Colin Higgins

One of those cult comedies that has to be seen to be believed. A death-obsessed youngster only manages to attract his mother's attention once he begins a love affair with a 79-year-old woman he meets at a funeral. Needless to say, mom isn't wildly happy. This exceptionally weird and wonderful movie is about as black as black humour can go and still be funny. It's a tightrope that is great fun to walk.

Maude	Ruth Gordon
Harold	Bud Cort
Mrs. Chasen	Vivian Pickles
Glaucus, the sculptor	Cyril Cusack
Uncle Victor	Charles Tyner
Sunshine Dore	Ellen Gere
Priest	Eric Christmas

Quote 'I go to funerals.' • 'You sure have a way with people.' – 'Well, they're my species.'

Psst! The script started life as a 20-minute student thesis by Higgins • Although the film flopped when it first came out, it became a cult in places with large student populations.

Harvey
★★★ 1950 104min b/w

Director: Henry Koster
Screenplay: Mary Chase & Oscar Brodney
Source: Play by Mary Chase

In this sweet comic fantasy, Stewart is something of a lush who claims to be accompanied everywhere by an invisible six-foot-high white rabbit who is something of a bar-room philosopher. Not everyone loves Harvey as much as he does, though and the doors of the lunatic asylum beckon. It isn't as funny as seeing Stewart playing the part on stage and lacks sparkle. However, you'll chuckle the whole way through and the chances are you'll have a big, stupid smile on your face for ages afterwards.

Elwood P. Dowd	James Stewart
Veta Louise Simmons	Josephine Hull
Myrtle Mae	Victoria Horne
Miss Kelly	Peggy Dow
Dr. Chumley	Cecil Kellaway
Dr. Sanderson	Charles Drake
Wilson	Jesse White

Judge Gaffney	.William Lynn
Taxi driver	.Wallace Ford
Harvey	.Himself

Oscars Josephine Hull

Quote 'I started to walk down the street when I heard a voice saying: "Good evening, Mr. Dowd." I turned and there was this big white rabbit leaning against a lamppost. Well, I thought nothing of it, because when you've lived in a town as long as I've lived in this one, you get used to the fact that everybody knows your name.' • 'I've wrestled with reality for 35 years and I'm happy, Doctor. I finally won out over it.' • 'Harvey has overcome not only time and space, but any objections.' • 'Myrtle Mae, you have a lot to learn, and I hope you never learn it.'

Psst! The movie rights of the play were the first to be sold for over a million dollars • Josephine Hull had played the part on Broadway.

Has Anybody Seen My Gal?
★★★ 1952 89min c.

Director: Douglas Sirk
Screenplay: Joseph Hoffman

A crusty millionaire contemplates leaving his money to the family he nearly had, but wants to see what they're like first. Pretending to be poor as a church mouse, he arranges to stay with them. Although never hilarious, this 20s-set comedy has charm in abundance. Coburn is as great as always, turning the enterprise into a lovely, happy experience.

Samuel Fulton	.Charles Coburn
Millicent	.Piper Laurie
Dan	.Rock Hudson
Roberta	.Gigi Perreau
Harriet Blaisdell	.Lynn Bari
Howard	.William Reynolds
Charles Blaisdell	.Larry Gates
Carl Pennock	.Skip Homeier
Judge Wilkins	.Paul Harvey
Alvarez	.Fritz Feld
Youth	.James Dean

Psst! Look sharp and you'll see James Dean as a 'youth'.

Hear My Song
★★★★ 1992 103min c.

Director: Peter Chelsom
Screenplay: Peter Chelsom & Adrian Dunbar

One of the most unashamedly joyful films of the past decade. Unscrupulous night-club owner Dunbar risks losing his love unless he can persuade a reclusive Irish singer to warble for him. As his girlfriend is the delectable Fitzgerald, his extraordinary efforts are understandable. With a similar feel to films like *Gregory's Girl*, this tale is heart-warming, hysterically funny and huggingly romantic. A delight from start to finish, there are two scenes – the bill-posting dance and the cow with the chain – that would surely be in anybody's *Desert Island Filmclips* list.

Josef Locke	.Ned Beatty
Micky O'Neill	.Adrian Dunbar
Cathleen Doyle	.Shirley Anne Field
Nancy Doyle	.Tara Fitzgerald
Mr X	.William Hootkins
Benny Rose	.Harold Berens
Jim Abbott	.David McCallum

Quote 'I was born in peacetime. I haven't seen what you've seen. I haven't been where you've been.'

Psst! The story is based in part on the life of popular post-war singer Josef Locke, who fled England to avoid charges of tax evasion • The video contains some scenes not seen in the cinema.

Heaven Can Wait
★★★ 1943 112min c.

Director: Ernst Lubitsch
Screenplay: Samson Raphaelson
Source: Play, *Birthdays* by Ladislaus Bus-Fekete

A rake believes that he has led a life of sin, and confesses all to the devil. But his application for membership of Club Hell is turned down. Although it doesn't hit the funnybone as hard as it once did, Lubitsch gives it a flair, gloss and charm all of its own, while Ameche has never been better as he recalls his life back in the 1890s.

Henry van Cleve	.Don Ameche
Martha van Cleve	.Gene Tierney
Hugo van Cleve	.Charles Coburn
Mrs. Strabel	.Marjorie Main
His Excellency	.Laird Cregar
Bertha van Cleve	.Spring Byington
Albert van Cleve	.Allyn Joslyn
E.F. Strabel	.Eugene Pallette
Mademoiselle	.Signe Hasso
Randolph van Cleve	.Louis Calhern
James	.Aubrey Mather
Jasper	.Clarence Muse

Flogdell .Leonard Carey
Mrs. Craig . . . . .Florence Bates

Psst! Although Warren Beatty called his 1978 film *Heaven Can Wait*, it was really a remake not of this but *Here Comes Mr. Jordan*.

Heaven's Gate
★★★ 1980 219min c.

Director: Michael Cimino
Screenplay: Michael Cimino

One of the most self-indulgent wastes of money in the history of Hollywood or one of the greatest Westerns ever made? It depends on who you talk to. The butchered, studio-released film about the Johnson County Wars of 1892, with cattle barons setting out to massacre small farmers, is incredibly confusing and is largely a waste of time. The full version is far better, makes a great deal more sense and is in places mind-bogglingly wonderful, breathtaking in its scope and with some superb set-pieces. But the movie has flaws like a cat has fleas. It's incredibly long, suffers from some dreadful dialogue and gets pretty pretentious and worthy in places. Nonetheless, this a breathtaking two-hour cinematic experience packed into a four hours.

Marshal James Averill . . . . . . .Kris Kristofferson
Nathan D. Champion . . . . . .Christopher Walken
Billy Irvine . . . . .John Hurt
Frank Canton . . . . .Sam Waterston
Ella Watson . . . . .Isabelle Huppert
John H. Bridges . . . . .Jeff Bridges
The Reverend Doctor . . . . .Joseph Cotten
Mr. Eggleston . . . . .Brad Dourif
Trapper . . . . .Geoffrey Lewis
Also: Mickey Rourke, Willem Dafoe, Elizabeth McGovern, Tom Noonan

Blurb The Most Talked About Film Of The Decade!

OOPS! Although set over a century ago, eagle-eyed viewers spotted a GPO manhole cover in what is supposed to be Massachusetts.

Psst! 220 hours of film were shot for this $50m epic that was budgeted at only a little over $10m • It took Cimino 10 years before he got permission to make it, with the success of *The Deer Hunter* being enough to get the green light • The proper version runs at 219 minutes but a few days after it was savaged in by critics it was withdrawn and cut down to 149 minutes • Cimino appears almost to have a death wish

as a director. Fields were stained to look better on camera, a contemporary steam train was brought hundreds of miles to the set, genuine firearms were bought, the smallest extras had incredibly lavish costumes, while some had lessons in how to skate, shoot and ride • This was Willem Dafoe's film debut. Although he acted prominently in several scenes, his part was cut so much that, in the shorter version, he is effectively no more than an extra • Cimino's contract said that his name had to be as big as the title of the film. The studio was as good as its word. However, while his name is amazingly prominent on the film, they managed to put it in such a thin type on the posters that it is almost unreadable • The book *Final Cut* tells the fascinating story behind the making of the film.

The Heiress
★★★★ 1949 115min b/w

Director: William Wyler
Screenplay: Ruth Goetz & Augustus Goetz
Source: Play by the Goetz's and novel, *Washington Square* by Henry James

In the mid-19th century, a plain but wealthy woman oppressed by her dominant, unkind father, finally receives attentions from a young man who may possibly be a fortune hunter. This is a wholly engrossing drama with beautiful photography complemented by great performances from the leads, particularly De Havilland, for whom this is probably the best part in her career.

Catherine Sloper . . . . .Olivia De Havilland
Morris Townsend . . . . .Montgomery Clift
Dr. Austin Sloper . . . . .Ralph Richardson
Lavinia Penniman . . . . .Miriam Hopkins
Maria . . . . .Vanessa Brown
Marian Almond . . . . .Mona Freeman
Jefferson Almond . . . . .Ray Collins
Mrs. Montgomery . . . . .Selena Royle

Oscars Olivia De Havilland

Quote 'Yes, I can be very cruel. I have been taught by masters.'

Psst! Although Basil Rathbone and Wendy Hiller had played the leads on Broadway, the studio thought they were not big enough names to attract people to the movie • De Havilland later called Richardson a 'wicked, selfish man' for his blatant scene-stealing. She was not terribly taken with Clift, either, who she felt never thought of anyone but himself when he was acting.

Hellzapoppin

★★★★ 1941 84min b/w

Director: H.C. Potter
Screenplay: Nat Perrin & Warren Wilson
Source: Play by Nat Perrin

If it's zany comedy you're after, feast yourself on this transfer of Olson and Johnson's stage show which manages to make even the Marx Brothers look sedate. Forget what little plot there is and marvel at the quickest succession of wacky gags you're ever likely to see. They don't all work, but a surprising number are still hilarious, despite the fact that the formula's been copied umpteen times since. Even though the songs are defused by great visual stuff, they're still a little tiresome, but then you can't have everything. One of a kind. Oh, and if you see Mrs. Jones, someone's got a message for her.

Ole	Ole Olson
Chic	Chic Johnson
Betty	Martha Raye
Quimby	Hugh Herbert
Jeff Hunter	Robert Paige
Kitty Rand	Jane Frazee
Pepi	Mischa Auer
Woody Tyler	Lewis Howard
Mr. Rand	Clarence Kolb
Mrs. Rand	Nella Walker
Selby	Elisha Cook Jr.
Director	Richard Lane
Louis	Shemp Howard
Messenger	Frank Darien
Orchestra leader	Gus Schilling
Lena	Katherine Johnson
Cellist	Sig Arno

Quote 'MRS. JONES! MRS JONES!' • 'You can't hurt me. I always wear a bullet-proof vest around the studio.'

Psst! The stage version of *Hellzapoppin* ran for 1,404 performances from September 1938. There was little demarcation between stage and auditorium, with as much happening off-stage as on.

Henry V

★★★★ 1944 137min c.

Director: Laurence Olivier
Screenplay: Laurence Olivier & Alan Dent
Source: Play by William Shakespeare

At a time when the British desperately needed a boost to morale, old Will Shakespeare was wheeled in to the rescue. This best of all screen versions of his plays cleverly starts as a filmed piece of theatre, gradually becomes more realistic, and then comes round full circle to end as a stage play again. Olivier gives one of his greatest performances. Even in peacetime, it can get the patriotic blood racing. At the time, it must have been an amazing tonic to embattled Britons. The 1989 version with and by Kenneth Branagh plays down the patriotism and can't match this masterpiece. But it is still an excellent movie.

King Henry V	Laurence Olivier
Ancient Pistol	Robert Newton
Chorus	Leslie Banks
Princess Katherine	Renée Asherson
Fluellen	Esmond Knight
Contable of France	Leo Genn
Archbishop of Canterbury	Felix Aylmer
Mountjoy	Ralph Truman
King Charles VI of France	Harcourt Williams
Sir John Falstaff	George Robey

Also: Ernest Thesiger, Max Adrian, Valentine Dyall, John Laurie, George Cole

Psst! Olivier was given leave from his duties with the Fleet Air Arm • He only agreed to direct the movie when William Wyler, Terence Young and Carol Reed turned the project down • Olivier's wife Vivien Leigh couldn't get permission from Selznick to come to England to play Queen Katherine. Asherson was chosen in large part because she was a similar size to Leigh and the costumes had already been made • Costumes were tricky to make in wartime, so the designers were delighted when research showed that Henry's troops didn't wear shoes, but instead wrapped their feet in coarse cloth. The chain mail was actually knitted twine that was then sprayed with aluminium paint. The tiaras were made out of papier-maché and the weapons were wood painted to look like metal. • Despite wartime economies, the £300,000 budget still wasn't enough, the eventual cost being almost £500,000 • Filmed in neutral Ireland, the production used the only Technicolor camera in the British Isles • Many of the extras were local farmers and soldiers from Enniskerry in Ireland where it was filmed • Olivier's lip was split when a horse hit the camera, scarring him for life • Olivier had to revoice the phrase 'Norman bastards' for the Americans, making it 'Norman dastards' instead • Keep your eyes skinned for a teenage George Cole as 'The Boy'.

Henry: Portrait of a Serial Killer

★★★★ 1990 83min c.

Director: John McNaughton
Screenplay: John McNaughton & Richard Fire

Quietly spoken Henry introduces a new friend to his hobby, bumping people off. An immensely chilling, understated and creepily-acted portrayal of a modern nightmare. Black humour and blacker psychology are skilfully employed, even in the mutilated corpse of the slashed-up video version. Be warned, it is a *really* disturbing film.

Henry .Michael Rooker
Otis . . . . .Tom Towles
Becky . . . . .Tracy Arnold

Showing Becket.

Psst! The video had almost 50 seconds cut, mostly from the scene where Henry and Otis are playing their home video of the family being killed • Although made in 1986, the film only received a certificate and full release in 1990.

Here Comes Mr. Jordan

★★ 1941 93min b/w

Director: Alexander Hall
Screenplay: Sidney Buchman & Seton I. Miller
Source: Play, *Heaven Can Wait* by Harry Segall

A boxer is taken to heaven 40 years too early and, unsurprisingly, creates a stink about it. But plans to bring him back are complicated when it's discovered his body was cremated. Some clever plot ideas are frittered away by a cast all at sea, even the normally dependable Horton. Montgomery is dire, Keyes is infuriatingly wet and only Rains and boxing manager Gleason can save us from nodding off. Although important in its day and well-regarded for sparking off innumerable heavenly comedies, you'd do better watching one of those that has stood the test of time, such as *A Matter of Life and Death*.

Joe Pendleton . . . . .Robert Montgomery
Bette Logan . . . . .Evelyn Keyes
Mr. Jordan . . . . .Claude Rains
Julia Franswroth . . . . .Rita Johnson
Messenger #7013 . . . . .Edward Everett Horton
Max Corkle . . . . .James Gleason
Tony Abbott . . . . .John Emery
Insp. Williams . . . . .Donald MacBride
Sisk . . . . .Halliwell Hobbes
Also: Lloyd Bridges

Oscars Best Screenplay (adapted), Best Original Story

Psst! There was a dull sequel, *Down to Earth*, while the story was uninspiringly remade with a football background in 1978 starring Warren Beatty • Keep your eyes open and you may spot a very young Lloyd Bridges.

High Noon

★★★★ 1952 85min b/w

Director: Fred Zinnemann
Screenplay: Carl Foreman
Source: Story, *The Tin Star* by John W. Cunningham

There is little that's particularly fresh in the story of Gary Cooper standing alone to defend Hadleyville from four gunmen. What has kept this film a classic is Zinnemann's brisk pace (one of those rare films set in 'real time') and the elimination of a lot of tiresome background characterisation. Grace Kelly had yet to be thawed out by Hitchcock, but the cast is otherwise excellent, and the theme tune and rhythmic editing help immeasurably.

Will Kane .Gary Cooper
Amy Kane .Grace Kelly
Jonas Henderson . . . . .Thomas Mitchell
Harvey Pell . . . . .Lloyd Bridges
Helen Ramirez . . . . .Katy Jurado
Percy Mettrick . . . . .Otto Kruger
Martin Howe . . . . .Lon Chaney Jr.
William Fuller . . . . .Harry Morgan
Cooper . . . . .Harry Shannon
Jack Colby . . . . .Lee Van Cleef

Oscars Gary Cooper

Blurb When These Hands Stand Straight Up...The Excitement Starts.

Quote 'It's no good. I've got to go back. They're making me run. I've never run from anyone before.' • 'You're asking me to wait an hour to find out if I'm going to be a wife or a widow.'

OOPS! There are children alongside their parents in church. Then they vanish, leaving only adults there, before popping back again • The town's newspaper changes from the *Clarion* to the *Chronicle* throughout the film • There's a crane shot at the end that goes from Cooper to the empty streets and goes just that little bit too far, so that part of Los Angeles and its modern telegraph poles can be glimpsed in the background • Watch the ground as Cooper throws away his star at the end. There's another half-buried in the dust behind his feet. Was this from an earlier take, or a legacy of the last marshall in town?

Psst! One of the few mainstream movies to be filmed in 'real time', a nightmare for the continuity girl who had to make sure that the clocks were always properly set. It doesn't work completely. The film's running time of 85 minutes actually covers 90 minutes • Cooper was not the first choice for the role, Charlton Heston and Marlon Brando being leading contenders, but the lettuce tycoon who financed the movie was a fan of Cooper's and threatened to withdraw if his man didn't get the part • After years at the top of the box office tree, Cooper's movies had been doing poorly of late. He agreed to do *High Noon* for a fifth of his usual price, $60,000, together with a share of the profits. The film put him back in favour with the public. He made the Top Ten list for 15 years of his career. It was once considered impressive that he earned over $10m throughout his career. Now, some actors get double that for just one movie, even before the profits come in • Cooper had only recently had a hernia operation and he later discovered that he had had a bleeding duodenal ulcer during filming which explained why he was in agony for much of the time • When at the first screening producer Stanley Kramer realised that the movie was too slow in places, he inserted lots of closeups of Cooper's tired face as well as repeated shots of clocks counting the minutes to noon • After the first preview fell flat, Kramer asked composer Dmitri Tiomkin to come up with a song. 'Do Not Forsake Me, Oh My Darling' won an Oscar • Writer Carl Foreman was blacklisted as a Communist after he was brought before the House Un-American Activities Committee during filming. He refused to name names or discuss his political affiliations and was forced to continue his career in Britain, where he wrote *Bridge on the River Kwai* and *The Guns of Navarone* • Foreman knew he would be compelled to testify when he wrote *High Noon* and many read the film – particularly the throwing away of the marshall's badge – as a condemnation of the McCarthy era and the way in which the Hollywood community rolled over for McCarthy • John Wayne, a rabid anti-Communist, was so disgusted with the film, particularly the scene with the badge, that he agreed to do *Rio Bravo* as a counterblast • In the story on which the film is based, the sheriff dies • Kane was originally called 'Doane' but Katy Jurado couldn't pronounce it • Lee Van Cleef appears as one of the bad guys with a harmonica.

High Sierra
★★★ 1941 100min b/w

Director: Raoul Walsh
Screenplay: John Huston & W.R. Burnett
Source: Novel by Burnett

A gangster plans one last job to see him into a comfortable retirement, but things don't go according to plan. The by-the-numbers story lets it down a little but Bogie and Lupino, as a gangster's moll, are so watchable we don't really care. The dog's pretty good, too. The story was used again in *Colorado Territory* in 1949, again with Walsh at the helm, and again in 1955 as *I Died a Thousand Times*.

Roy 'Mad Dog' Earle	Humphrey Bogart
Marie Garson	Ida Lupino
Babe Kozak	Alan Curtis
Red Hattery	Arthur Kennedy
Velma	Joan Leslie
Doc Banton	Henry Hull
Jake Kranmer	Barton MacLane
Pa	Henry Travers
Ma	Elizabeth Risdon
Louis Mendoza	Cornel Wilde
Mrs. Baughman	Minna Gombell
Mr. Baughman	Paul Harvey
Big Mac	Donald MacBride

Blurb He Killed...And There On The Crest Of Sierra's Highest Crag...He Must Be Killed!

Quote 'Of all the fourteen-caret saps, starting out on a caper with a woman and a dog.' • 'Sometimes I feel like I don't know what it's about any more.' • 'He's free! He's free!'

Psst! Humphrey Bogart was made up to look like gangster John Dillinger • This was yet another film turned down by George Raft, helping Bogie to climb one more rung up the ladder to fame. Edward G. Robinson, James Cagney and John Garfield also refused it • As always, Bogart complained vociferously about having to film on location • He was second on the billing to Lupino.

High Society
★★★ 1956 107min c.

Director: Charles Walters
Screenplay: John Patrick
Source: Play, *The Philadelphia Story* by Philip Barry

It's fashionable to say this musical remake of *The Philadelphia Story* isn't a patch on the original. But while time has been unkind to the 1940 movie, it hasn't done much harm to this version. The leads all seem to be enjoying themselves with the witty dialogue and their joy comes across, while the Cole Porter songs, all but one written specially for the film, still sparkle brightly.

C.K. Dexter-Haven	Bing Crosby
Tracy Lord	Grace Kelly
Mike Connor	Frank Sinatra
Liz Imbrie	Celeste Holm
George Kittredge	John Lund
Uncle Willie	Louis Calhern
Seth Lord	Sidney Blackmer
Himself	Louis Armstrong

Psst! This was Grace Kelly's last movie before becoming Princess Grace of Monaco. She got engaged a month before production began and married a month after it wrapped, even though her MGM contract still had four years to run • Crosby and Kelly, not quite the virginal type she usually portrayed, had an affair a few years earlier • The film was banned in Monaco, but whether it was because Prince Rainier didn't want his people to see the new Princess on screen or whether it was because he had heard the rumours about Crosby and Kelly, we shall never know • 'True Love' sold over a million copies. According to Crosby, "They didn't want her to sing on the record; they thought it should have a better voice. Of course, I was determined to have Grace on a record that I thought had a chance to be a gold one, and we had quite a squabble about it. She didn't care whether she sang on it or not.' It became Crosby's 20th gold disc, while Kelly's one and only gold disc was hung in the palace at Monte Carlo • This is said to be the first movie in which a black person comes to the front door of a house.

His Girl Friday

★★★★ 1940 92min b/w

Director: Howard Hawks
Screenplay: Charles Lederer
Source: Play, *The Front Page* by Ben Hecht and Charles MacArthur.

Many think this the greatest comedy ever made. Certainly unlike any other film, it is well-nigh impossible to find anyone who has a bad word to say about it. It's a remake of *The Front Page*, with the lead journalist role switched from male to female and made the ex-wife of the manipulative editor. Sex enters the equation and adds a great new dimension to an already jam-packed

play. Played at an extraordinarily frenetic speed, packed with good lines and a nice line in black gallows humour, this screwball comedy knocks all its competitors for six, including Hawks' own *Bringing Up Baby*. Irresistible, madcap fun.

Walter Burns	Cary Grant
Hildy Johnson	Rosalind Russell
Bruce Baldwin	Ralph Bellamy
Sheriff Hartwell	Gene Lockhart
Mollie Malloy	Helen Mack
Murphy	Porter Hall
Roy Bensinger	Ernest Truex
Endicott	Cliff Edwards
Mayor	Clarence Kolb
McCue	Roscoe Karns
Wilson	Frank Jenks
Sanders	Regis Toomey
Diamond Louie	Abner Biberman
Duffy	Frank Orth
Earl Williams	John Qualen
Silas F. Pinkus	Billy Gilbert

Quote 'Will you take your hands off me? What are you playing – osteopath?' • 'I'm more or less particular about whom my wife marries.' • 'He's got a lot of charm.' – 'Well he comes by it naturally. His grandfather was a snake.' • 'Listen, the last man who said that to me was Archie Leach, just a week before he cut his throat.' [Grant, mentioning his own real name]

Psst! The first film to use realistic-sounding overlapping dialogue effectively, although many think it was the later *Citizen Kane* that broke that mould • Someone timed the speed of the actors' delivery at around 240 words a minute, whereas the usual speed in movies at that time was 110! • Jean Arthur, Carole Lombard, Katharine Hepburn, Claudette Colbert, Irene Dunne and Ginger Rogers all turned down Russell's part • Grant, trying to describe Russell's beau, says that he looks like 'that film actor, Ralph Bellamy'. He is played by Bellamy.

The History of Mr. Polly

★★ 1949 94min b/w

Director: Anthony Pelissier
Screenplay: Anthony Pelissier
Source: Novel by H.G. Wells

A Victorian draper's assistant grows to hate his shop and his shrewish wife and cuts loose. Although the production has some charm, Polly's irritating way with words jars and the story-telling is too slight and clumsy. Something of a museum piece.

Alfred Polly . . . . .John Mills
Cristabel . . . . .Sally Ann Howes
Plump woman . . . . .Megs Jenkins
Uncle Jim .Finlay Currie
Miriam . . . . .Betty Ann Davies
Mr. Johnson . . . . .Edward Chapman
Mrs. Larkins . . . . .Gladys Henson
Little Polly . . . . .Juliet Mills
Old gentleman . . . . .Miles Malleson
Uncle Pentstemon . . . . .Moore Marriott
Lady on roof . . . . .Edie Martin
Mrs. Johnson . . . . .Dandy Nichols
Also: Irene Handl, Doris Hare, Wylie Watson

Hobson's Choice

★★★ 1953 107min b/w

Director: David Lean
Screenplay: David Lean, Norman Spencer & Wynyard Browne
Source: Play by Harold Brighouse

One of the three daughters of a domineering bootmaker turns the table on him with the help of her meek husband. This funny and touching version of a famous play is still extremely enjoyable, in large part thanks to Laughton's masterly performance as the bully brought low.

Henry Horatio Hobson . . . . . .Charles Laughton
Willis Mossop .John Mills
Maggie Hobson . . . . .Brenda de Banzie
Alice Hobson . . . . .Daphne Anderson
Vicky Hobson . . . . .Prunella Scales
Albert Prosser . . . . .Richard Wattis
Mrs. Hepworth . . . . .Helen Haye
Freddy Beenstock . . . . .Derek Blomfield
Jim Heeler . . . . .Joseph Tomelty

Psst! Robert Donat was to have been Mossop but, as so often, his delicate health let him down, and Mills was rushed into his shoes • If you wonder where you've seen 'Vicky' before, it's probably quite a few years later as Sybil Fawlty in *Fawlty Towers*.

Holiday

★★★ 1938 93min b/w

Director: George Cukor
Screenplay: Donald Ogden Stewart

Free-spirited Grant acts like a breath of fresh air to a conformist society family. With Grant and Hepburn sparring so well with each other and a script that sparkles while still managing to bite

a few well-chosen targets firmly in the rump, this romantic comedy is a transport of delight.

Linda Seton . . . . .Katharine Hepburn
Johnny Case .Cary Grant
Ned Seton . . . . .Lew Ayres
Julia Seton . . . . .Doris Nolan
Prof. Nick Potter . . . . . .Edward Everett Horton
Laura Cram . . . . .Binnie Barnes
Edward Seton . . . . .Henry Kolker
Susan Potter . . . . .Jean Dixon
Seton Cram . . . . .Henry Daniell
Banker . . . . .Charles Trowbridge
Also: Ruth Donnelly, Bess Flowers

Quote 'When I find myself in a position like this, I ask myself what would General Motors do? And then I do the opposite!'

Psst! Edward Everett Horton had played the same part in a 1930 version • When the play was on Broadway 10 years before, Hepburn had been understudy to the lead. In two years, she never had to go on once • Harry Cohn, the head of Columbia, wanted Irene Dunne for the lead, but Cukor said it had to be Hepburn. She had been labelled 'box office poison' and the studio tried to turn this to advantage by publicising the film with the catchline, "Is it true what they say about Hepburn?'

Home Alone

★★ 1990 103min c.

Director: Chris Columbus
Screenplay: John Hughes

A family leave smug, smart-alec, eight-year-old Culkin behind when they go on holiday to Paris, then try to pretend it's all a mistake rather than something they've been planning all year. Then burglars Pesci and Stern try to break in to the family home. Despite being one of the most popular films ever, relatively little happens until the fun-filled final quarter of an hour. Although kids love to see one of their own making fools of a couple of adults, it's violent and nothing like as inventive as might be expected. There are those who find that a little Mac goes an awfully long way. The sequel is pretty much a reprise of this, with the violence even more exaggerated.

Kevin McCallister . . . . .Macaulay Culkin
Harry . . . . .Joe Pesci
Marv . . . . .Daniel Stern
Peter McCallister . . . . .John Heard
Kate McCallister . . . . .Catherine O'Hara
Marley . . . . .Roberts Blossom
Uncle Frank . . . . .Gerry Bamman

Gus Polinski . . . . .John Candy
Fuller . . . . .Kieran Culkin

Showing It's a Wonderful Life [in French].

OOPS! When Mum flies home, she arrives on a different type of plane than the one she left Paris on • Watch Pesci forget which hand he's burnt on the hot doorknob. Its image on his palm is also upside down.

Psst! Hughes was inspired to write the script after he lost one of his own children briefly in a department store • Culkins' goldfish died on the night of the end-of-filming party.

Hope and Glory
★★★★ 1987 113min c.

Director: John Boorman
Screenplay: John Boorman

A spellbinding evocation of family life in wartime suburban Britain, as seen through the eyes of a nine-year-old. Despite the privations and upheavals caused by the Blitz, for the young-sters it's a wildly exciting time. Often funny, occasionally sad, but always with the ring of truth, there has never been a better portrayal of life on the home front.

Bill Rohan . . . . .Sebastian Rice-Edwards
Sue Rohan . . . . .Geraldine Muir
Grace Rohan . . . . .Sarah Miles
Clive Rohan . . . . .David Hayman
Dawn Rohan . . . . .Sammi Davis
Mac .Derrick O'Connor
Molly . . . . .Susan Wooldridge
Cpl. Bruce Carey . . . . .Jean-Marc Barr
Grandfather George . . . . .Ian Bannen

Quote 'Thank you, Adolf.' [When school is bombed] • 'All my life nothing ever quite matched the perfect joy of that moment. My school lay in ruins; the river beckoned with a promise of stolen days.' [Last line]

Psst! The voice narrating at the beginning is that of writer-director Boorman • His son Charley Boorman, star of The Emerald Forest plays the downed Luftwaffe pilot.

Hopscotch
★★★ 1980 104min c.

Director: Ronald Neame
Screenplay: Brian Garfield & Bryan Forbes
Source: Novel by Brian Garfield

A thoroughly entertaining spy yarn, with Matthau the former CIA agent who decides to get his own back on the Agency for doing the dirty on him. Teaming up with Jackson, he has to stay out of the CIA's clutches while writing a book that will blow the lid on the spy business. Cleverly plotted, with umpteen neat twists, Matthau's taunting of his former bosses has the same irrepressible fun about it that his earlier Charley Varrick had.

Miles Kendig . . . . .Walter Matthau
Isobel von Schmidt . . . . .Glenda Jackson
G.P. Myerson . . . . .Ned Beatty
Mikhail Yaskov . . . . .Herbert Lom
Joe Cutter . . . . .Sam Waterston
Westlake . . . . .George Baker

Horror of Dracula
SEE: Dracula [1958]

Horse Feathers
★★★ 1932 69min b/w

Director: Norman Z. McLeod
Screenplay: Bert Kalmar, Harry Ruby & S.J. Perelman

Groucho is the new President of Huxley College, determined that by fair means or foul – prefer-ably foul – the football team will win its match against rivals Darwin. The usual madcap humour seems even faster-paced than usual with several memorable scenes, best of which is the scene trying to discover the password at the speakeasy.

Prof. Quincey Adams Wagstaff . .Groucho Marx
Pinky . . . . .Harpo Marx
Barovelli . . . . .Chico Marx
Frank Wagstaff . . . . .Zeppo Marx
Connie Bailey . . . . .Thelma Todd
Jennings .David Landau
McCarthy . . . . .Nat Pendleton
Prof. Hornsbogle . . . . .Robert Greig
Peggy Carrington . . . . .Florine McKinney
Mullens . . . . .Guinn "Big Boy" Williams

Quote 'I'd horsewhip you if I had a horse.' • 'I married your mother because I wanted children. Imagine my disappointment when you arrived.' • 'Barovelli, you've got the brain of a four-year-old boy and I bet he was glad to get rid of it.' • 'There's a man outside with a big black moustache.' – 'Tell him I've got one.' • 'Why don't you bore a hole in yourself and let the sap run out?' • 'You're a disgrace to our family name of Wagstaff, if such a thing is possible.'

Psst! Thelma Todd, nicknamed 'Hot Toddy' in her social circle, had also been in *Monkey Business* with the Marx Brothers. She died in 1935, aged 30, discovered in her garage with her car engine on. There was some speculation that, far from being suicide, it was a Mob-related murder with her gangster boyfriend reckoned to be the most likely suspect.

The Hound of the Baskervilles
★★★ 1939 80min b/w

Director: Sidney Lanfield
Screenplay: Ernest Pascal
Source: Story by Arthur Conan Doyle

This was the first of the Rathbone-Bruce outings as the famous detective and his sidekick. It and *The Adventures of Sherlock Holmes* were the only ones set in the right period. Dripping with great Victorian atmosphere, much of it courtesy of umpteen fogs, this is the one about Holmes trying to nail a supernatural mutt that's been the bane for generations of a family living on Dartmoor.

Sherlock Holmes . . . . .Basil Rathbone
Dr. Watson . . . . .Nigel Bruce
Sir Henry Baskerville . . . . .Richard Greene
Beryl Stapleton . . . . .Wendy Barrie
Dr. James Mortimer . . . . .Lionel Atwill
Barryman . . . . .John Carradine
Jennifer Mortimer . . . . .Beryl Mercer
John Stapleton . . . . .Morton Lowry
Sir Hugo Baskerville . . . . .Ralph Forbes
Cabby . . . . .E.E. Clive

Quote 'Quick, Watson. The needle.'

Psst! Rathbone would go on to make 16 films in which he was Sherlock Holmes, as well as playing the character in 200 radio plays.

How Green Was My Valley
★★★ 1941 118min b/w

Director: John Ford
Screenplay: Philip Dunne
Source: Novel by Richard Llewellyn

The trials and tribulations of a Welsh mining community at the turn of the century. This is Wales, Hollywood style and is made still more unsettling by the fact that everyone has Irish accents. But if it's all pretty unbelievable, it's an effective tear-jerker nonetheless. A great Sunday afternoon movie.

Mr. Gruffydd . . . . .Walter Pidgeon
Angharad . . . . .Maureen O'Hara
Mr. Morgan . . . . .Donald Crisp
Bronwyn . . . . .Anna Lee
Huw Morgan . . . . .Roddy McDowall
Ianto Morgan . . . . .John Loder
Mrs. Morgan . . . . .Sara Allgood
Cyfartha . . . . .Barry Fitzgerald
Ivor . . . . .Patric Knowles
Mr. Jonas . . . . .Morton Lowry
Parry . . . . .Arthur Shields
Cienwen . . . . .Ann E. Todd
Also: Frederic Worlock, Richard Fraser, Rhys Williams

Oscars Best Picture, Donald Crisp, Best Director

Psst! With the war in progress, it was not possible to film in Wales, so an entire village with a coal mine was built in the San Fernando Valley. It took 150 workers six months to complete the set, covering 80 acres • It came in for a great deal of stick in Wales itself, in part due to what they felt was the fake look to the film, but more importantly for glossing over a period that some recalled as being considerably less rosy than depicted in the movie.

Howard's End
★★★★ 1992 140min c.

Director: James Ivory
Screenplay: Ruth Prawer Jhabvala
Source: Novel by E.M. Forster

At last, a Forster adaptation that not only has pretty frocks, meadows and steam-trains, but a cracking good story too. Independently-minded Thompson is cheated out of the eponymous house by widower Hopkins, only to end up marrying him. A superb ensemble cast carry off this tale of class and family conflict brilliantly, showing up the horrors and hypocrisy of Edwardian society. A superlative entertainment.

Henry Wilcox . . . . .Anthony Hopkins
Ruth Wilcox . . . . .Vanessa Redgrave
Helen Schlegel . . . . .Helena Bonham Carter
Margaret Schlegel . . . . .Emma Thompson
Charles Wilcox . . . . .James Wilby
Leonard Blast . . . . .Samuel West
Evie Wilcox . . . . .Jemma Redgrave
Jacky Bast . . . . .Nicola Duffett

Aunt Juley . . . . .Prunella Scales
Lecturer .Simon Callow

Oscars Best Screenplay (adapted), Emma Thompson

OOPS! Jacky Bast has a vaccination scar on her upper arm.

Hud
★★★ 1963 112min b/w

Director: Martin Ritt
Screenplay: Irving Ravetch & Harriet Frank
Source: Novel, *Horseman, Pass By* by Larry McMurtry

A lazy, high-living rancher's son disagrees with his traditional father about the future of the business. The film broke new ground, including many words never before heard in a mainstream movie, while the attempted rape caused outrage in some quarters. Newman's anti-hero is pretty unpleasant throughout but he plays it so well that the movie remains compelling viewing.

Hud Bannon . . . . .Paul Newman
Alma Brown . . . . .Patricia Neal
Homer Bannon . . . . .Melvyn Douglas
Lon Bannon . . . . .Brandon de Wilde
Hermy . . . . .John Ashley
Burris . . . . .Whit Bissell
Jesse . . . . .Crahan Denton

Oscars Melvyn Douglas, Patricia Neal

Quote 'The only question I ever ask any woman is: "What time is your husband coming home?"' • 'I've done my time with one cold-blooded bastard. I'm not looking for another.' • 'There's so much *crap* in this world. You're going to wallow in it sooner or later, like it or not!' • 'You look pretty good without your shirt on, you know. The sight of that through the kitchen window made me put down my dishtowel more than once.'

Psst! Newman prepared for the part by spending time on a cattle ranch in Texas and had already developed some pretty impressive calluses by the time filming began.

Hue and Cry
★★★ 1946 82min b/w

Director: Charles Crichton
Screenplay: T.E.B. Clarke

Although not well known, this was the first of the Ealing comedies. A group of lads enlist the help of the man who writes the detective stories in their favourite comic to trap a gang of crooks. Exciting and droll kids' fare that won't bore adults, it is also fascinating for the extraordinary look it gives us of bomb-damaged London as it emerged from war.

Felix H. Wilkinson . . . . .Alastair Sim
Nightingale . . . . .Jack Warner
Joe Kirby .Harry Fowler
Rhona . . . . .Valerie White
Mr. Kirby . . . . .Frederick Piper

The Hunchback of Notre Dame
★★★ 1939 115min b/w

Director: William Dieterle
Screenplay: Sonya Levien & Bruno Frank
Source: Novel by Victor Hugo

The best version of Victor Hugo's novel set in medieval Paris. The archdeacon has gypsy girl Esmeralda kidnapped by bellringer Quasimodo, a dead ringer 'before' picture in a Clearasil ad. Charles Laughton is in fine, if much-parodied, form as the mis-shapen Quasimodo and the set designs still look impressive. It's pretty obvious that much of it is intended to be an allegory on the Nazi threat in Europe, although some of the dialogue now has the ring of *Monty Python* about it. There have been plenty of other versions, the best known being the 1923 Lon Chaney outing and the 1956 film with Anthony Quinn and Gina Lollobrigida.

The Hunchback . . . . .Charles Laughton
Frollo . . . . .Cedric Hardwicke
Clopin . . . . .Thomas Mitchell
Esmeralda . . . . .Maureen O'Hara
Gringoire . . . . .Edmond O'Brien
Proebus . . . . .Alan Marshal
Claude . . . . .Walter Hampden
Louis XI . . . . .Harry Davenport
Procurator . . . . .George Zucco
Mme. De Lys . . . . .Katherine Alexander
Also: Fritz Leiber, George Tobias

Quote 'Do you recollect that letter we had from …er…what'shisname... Chris... Christopher Columbus?' • 'Ouch! You're hurting me. I should have made you my chief torturer' • 'Sanctuary! Sanctuary!' • 'Why was I not made of stone like thee.' [Last line]

Psst! Getting Laughton made up took five and a half hours, a record for the time. Considering how ugly he always considered himself, perhaps it's no wonder he was able to put so much into the role. He certainly relished not having to wear corsets or lose weight beforehand, as he had with other parts • In the earlier 1923 version, Lon Chaney had to endure a costume that weighed 34 pounds against the six Laughton had to cope with • In the flogging scene, Laughton was actually whipped, with the scene needing over a dozen takes! • The scene where Quasimodo rings the bells took place on the day that Britain declared war on Germany. When the scene finished, Laughton didn't stop pealing the bells, but just kept ringing them and ringing them • In this one extraordinary year, generally regarded as moviedom's *annus miraculus*, Thomas Mitchell appeared in this, *Only Angels Have Wings*, *Stagecoach*, *Gone With the Wind* and *Mr. Smith Goes to Washington* • This was the American film debut of O'Hara.

The Hustler
★★★ 1961 135min b/w

Director: Robert Rossen
Screenplay: Sidney Carroll & Robert Rossen
Source: Novel by Walter Tevis

Never has the smoke-filled pool room in all its seediness been captured so well as in this beautifully filmed movie, marked out by a trio of superlative performances from Newman, Laurie and Scott. A little overlong perhaps, but well worth while. So is the sequel, *The Color of Money*, which appeared 25 years later and starred Newman again, as well as Tom Cruise.

'Fast' Eddie Felson . . . . .Paul Newman
Minnesota Fats . . . . .Jackie Gleason
Bert Gordon . . . . .George C. Scott
Sarah Packard . . . . .Piper Laurie
Charlie Burns . . . . .Myron McCormick
James Findlay . . . . .Murray Hamilton
Big John . . . . .Michael Constantine
Bartender . . . . .Jake LaMotta
Bartender . . . . .Vincent Gardenia

Quote 'Eddie, you're a born loser.' • 'Fat man, you shoot a great game of pool.'

Psst! The initial ideas for the title were *Sing of Angels* and *Stroke of Luck* • This was the film that turned Newman from just another pretty-boy actor into a star • Newman was coached in pool technique by the great Willie Mosconi, whose hands stood in for Newman's in the close-ups • George C. Scott asked for his

nomination for an Oscar to be withdrawn because he thought the Oscars were 'bull'. The Academy refused to do so • Jack La Motta, the subject of *Raging Bull*, appears as a bartender.

I Am a Fugitive from a Chain Gang
★★★ 1932 93min b/w

Director: Mervyn LeRoy
Screenplay: Sheridan Gibney & Brown Holmes
Source: Autobiography, *I am a Fugitive from a Georgia Chain Gang* by Robert E. Burns.

Searing drama about an innocent man unjustly imprisoned and made to work under inhuman conditions on a chain gang. This powerful tale of an individual being turned into a criminal by the justice system is probably Muni's greatest film. The treatment meted out to him makes you well with pity and anger, particularly when you know that it is largely a true story. Unfortunately, despite Muni's brilliance, parts of the movie look distinctly artificial now.

James Allen .Paul Muni
Maria Woods . . . . .Glenda Farrell
Helen . . . . .Helen Vinson
Peter . . . . .Preston Foster
Barney Sykes . . . . .Allen Jenkins
Bomber Wells . . . . .Edward Ellis
Judge .Berton Churchill
Nordine . . . . .John Wray
Warden .David Landau
Second Warden . . . . .Edward McNamara
Ramsey . . . . .Robert McWade
wJudge .Berton Churchill
Red . . . . .James Bell
D.A. . . . . .Douglass Dumbrille
Fuller . . . . .Robert Warwick
Train conductor . . . . .Charles B. Middleton

Quote 'How do you live?' – 'I steal.' [Last line]

Psst! The film was based on the story of Robert Elliot Burns, who was sentenced to serve 10 years hard labour on a chain gang in 1920 after stealing $5.29 for food and who escaped two years later. Although the film-makers were careful not to mention that the events took place in Georgia, the state still banned the film and even tried to sue for libel. The film was considered so shocking that reforms were made in many states afterwards. Georgia, however, kept trying to recapture Burns and threatened director LeRoy and anybody connected with the movie with retribution if they

ever visited crossed the Georgia state line
• Still a fugitive, Burns worked on the movie under an assumed name. Since gaining his freedom he had become a magazine editor. He was arrested in New Jersey but after the public rallied to his defence, three different governors refused to send him to Georgia. In 1945, his sentence was commuted and he died in 1955.
• Muni always believed in throwing himself into his parts and, although the heat was intense during the quarrying scene, he refused to let a double stand in for him • The movie was originally intended for Jimmy Cagney, but he was on suspension as a result of one of his periodic fights with the studio • The final fade-out, probably the first in movies, was accidental. The lights had failed at an earlier rehearsal and director LeRoy decided he liked the effect of the screen becoming black.

if...

★★★ 1968 111min c&b/w

Director: Lindsay Anderson
Screenplay: David Sherwin

Unhappy pupils at an English public school mount a violent rebellion against their oppressors. Although so surrealistic that at times you have little idea what's going on, it is still very funny and its pointed barbs haven't developed much rust in the intervening years. One of those movies that everyone should watch at least once. Travis appeared in two sequels, the interesting *O Lucky Man!* and the near-unwatchable *Britannia Hospital*.

Mick Travis	Malcolm McDowell
Johnny	David Wood
Wallace	Richard Warwick
The Girl	Christine Noonan
Bobby Philips	Rupert Webster
Rowntree	Robert Swann
Headmaster	Peter Jeffrey
Matron	Mona Washbourne
Mr. Kemp, Housemaster	Arthur Lowe
Chaplain	Geoffrey Chater
History master	Graham Crowden
Classics master	Charles Lloyd Pack
Keating	Robin Askwith

Quote 'Education in Britain is a nubile Cinderella, sparsely clad and often interfered with.'

Psst! Anderson filmed at his old *alma mater*, Cheltenham College. It is thought that the school wasn't entirely aware of the nature of

the movie when they granted permission
• There was much discussion among film buffs about the significance of the switch from colour to black and white, with many theories being advanced. It was some time before Anderson admitted that they had simply run out of money and could only afford black and white film!

I Know Where I'm Going!

★★★ 1945 91min b/w

Director: Michael Powell & Emeric Pressburger
Screenplay: Michael Powell & Emeric Pressburger

The amazing team of Powell and Pressburger chalk up another winner. A woman travels to Scotland, determined to marry an elderly millionaire solely for his money. But she meets a naval officer and love tries to bar her way. Although the story is slight, the film has considerable wit and charm, as well as an ethereal atmosphere all of its own which casts a powerful spell.

Joan Webster	Wendy Hiller
Torquil MacNeil	Roger Livesey
Ruairidh Mor	Finlay Currie
Catriona Potts	Pamela Brown
John Campbell	John Laurie
Mr. Robinson	Valentine Dyall
Cheril	Petula Clark
Mr. Webster	George Carney
Hunter	Walter Hudd
Postmistress	Jean Cadell
Mrs. Robinson	Catherine Lacey
RAF Sergeant	Graham Moffatt

I'm All Right Jack

★★★ 1959 104min c.

Director: John Boulting
Screenplay: Frank Harvey & John Boulting
Source: Novel, *Private Life* by Alan Hackney

Carmichael, the usual innocent, starts work at his uncle's factory and manages to upset the delicate balance between capital and labour, precipitating massive industrial unrest. Surprisingly, this satire on trade unionism hasn't dated too badly, even though the attitudes expressed by management and workers now appear to belong to another planet. Maybe the delight that there are some things which have changed for the better increases our pleasure. While a whole raft of great British comic talent strut their stuff, this is really Sellers' film as the blinkered trade union leader Fred Kite.

Stanley Windrush . . . . .Ian Carmichael
Fred Kite .Peter Sellers
Maj. Hitchcock . . . . .Terry-Thomas
Sidney de Vere Cox . . . . .Richard Attenborough
Bertram Tracepurcel . . . . .Dennis Price
Aunt Dolly . . . . .Margaret Rutherford
Mrs. Kite .Irene Handl
Cynthia Kite . . . . .Liz Fraser
Windrush Sr. . . . . .Miles Malleson
Mr. Mohammed . . . . .Marne Maitland
Waters . . . . .John Le Mesurier
Magistrate . . . . .Raymond Huntley
Knowles . . . . .Victor Maddern
Dai . . . . .Kenneth Griffith
Also: Sam Kydd, Malcolm Muggeridge

Quote 'We've got men here who can break into a muck sweat merely by standing still.'

I Married a Witch
★★ 1942 82min b/w

Director: René Clair
Screenplay: Robert Pirosh & Marc Connelly
Source: Novel, *The Passionate Witch* by Thorne Smith and Norman Matson

A woman burned as a witch and her cherub-like father return to haunt the descendent of the Puritan who condemned them 250 years earlier. As he's now about to get married and stand for state governorship, their presence is less than convenient. Despite Lake's undoubted sexiness and the presence of that great supporting actor Robert Benchley, the humour now seems rather forced and slow. It's a cheerful enough movie, but not the inspired comedy many seem to think it is.

Wallace Wooley . . . . .Fredric March
Jennifer . . . . .Veronica Lake
Dr. Dudley White . . . . .Robert Benchley
Estelle Masterson . . . . .Susan Hayward
Daniel .Cecil Kellaway
Margaret . . . . .Elizabeth Patterson
J.B. Masterson . . . . .Robert Warwick
Tabitha Wooley . . . . .Eily Malyon
Town Crier . . . . .Robert Greig
Harriet . . . . .Nora Cecil
Allen . . . . .Emory Parnell
Also: Aldrich Bowker, Emma Dunn, Al Bridge, Chester Conklin, Arthur Stuart Hull

Blurb She Knows All About Love Potions...And Lovely Motions.

Psst! This was the inspiration for the TV sitcom *Bewitched* • Comic author Thorne Smith, one of the great humorists of the 20s and 30s, also wrote the books on which the *Topper* films were based.

The Immortal Battalion
SEE: **The Way Ahead**

I'm No Angel
★★★ 1933 87min b/w

Director: Wesley Ruggles
Screenplay: Mae West

A circus performer tames men just as easily as she tames lions. The larger-than-life West is at her most outrageous here in the days before the censors took most of the fun out of her movies. The double entendres fly thick and fast from one of cinema's true one-offs.

Tira . . . . .Mae West
Jack Clayton . . . . .Cary Grant
Benny Pinkowitz . . . . .Gregory Ratoff
Bill Barton . . . . .Edward Arnold
Slick Wiley . . . . .Ralf Harolde
Kirk Lawrence . . . . .Kent Taylor
Alicia Hatton . . . . .Gertrude Michael
Harry . . . . .Nat Pendleton
Flea Madigan, the barker . . . . .Russell Hopton
Thelma . . . . .Dorothy Peterson
Ernest Brown, the chump . .William B. Davidson
Rajah . . . . .Nigel de Brulier

Quote 'It's not the men in my life, but the life in my men that counts.' • 'Beulah, peel me a grape.' • 'When I'm good, I'm very good, but when I'm bad, I'm better.' • 'I'm a one-man woman. One man at a time.'

Psst! This film and her previous movie *She Done Him Wrong* are credited with helping to rescue studio Paramount from impending bankruptcy • Although Grant claimed to have learnt more about comedy working with West than anyone else, he also said she was the most difficult person he ever acted with. "I thought she was brilliant with that one character she portrayed, but she was an absolute fake as a person. She wore so much make-up and all that figure and those tall high heels. You couldn't find Mae West in there. I'm not attracted to artificiality. Mae wore more of it than anyone I've ever seen in my life.' • An RAF life jacket was named after West in World War II, making her the only fillm star to make it into the dictionary.

The Importance of Being Earnest
★★★ 1952 95min c.

Director: Anthony Asquith
Screenplay: Anthony Asquith
Source: Play by Oscar Wilde

No attempt has been made to pretend this is anything other than a filmed version of a play. But what a play! Wilde's wittiest work is in extremely capable hands here, with a stunning cast putting it over with considerable aplomb. Best of all, of course, is Edith Evans. Just two words of hers, 'A Handbag?', are among the most famous in the entire movie canon. See her and weep…with laughter.

Mr. Jack Worthing	Michael Redgrave
Mr. Algernon Moncrieff	Michael Denison
Lady Bracknell	Edith Evans
Miss Prism	Margaret Rutherford
Miss Gwendolen Fairfax	Joan Greenwood
Miss Cecily Cardew	Dorothy Tutin
The Rev. Dr. Chasuble	Miles Malleson
Seton	Richard Wattis
Lane	Walter Hudd
Merriman	Aubrey Mather

In a Lonely Place
★★★ 1950 93min b/w

Director: Nicholas Ray
Screenplay: Andrew Solt
Source: Novel by Dorothy B. Hughes

Cynical screenwriter Bogart, prone to violent outbursts, is accused of murdering a hat-check girl last seen leaving his apartment. This doesn't unsettle him so much that he can't start up a romance with the great Grahame, who provides his alibi. This wonderful moody film noir with a Hollywood background toys with us as we try to decide whether Bogie is guilty. The subtext is clearly about the hunt for Communists in the film industry at the time.

Dixon Stelle	Humphrey Bogart
Laurel Gray	Gloria Grahame
Brub Nicolai	Frank Lovejoy
Capt. Lochner	Carl Benton Reid
Mel Lippman	Art Smith
Sylvia Nicolai	Jeff Donnell
Mildred Atkinson	Martha Stewart
Charlie Waterman	Robert Warwick
Lloyd Barnes	Morris Ankrum

Quote 'Thank you, but I always go home with the man who brought me.' • 'I was born when she kissed me. I died when she left me. I lived a few weeks while she loved me.'

Psst! Some think that the plot of the film is closely related to director Ray's own life. He was married to Grahame but they divorced shortly afterwards. She raised eyebrows when, in 1961, she married Ray's son, Tony, by another marriage. She already had a son with Nicholas Ray called Timothy. So Tony was not only Timothy's stepbrother but also his stepfather • Ray said that Ginger Rogers was the first choice for the lead.

The Incredible Shrinking Man
★★★ 1957 81min b/w

Director: Jack Arnold
Screenplay: Richard Matheson
Source: Novel by Matheson

What would 50s sci-fi film-makers have done without those pesky atomic scientists? This time, a cloud of atomic vapour causes a guy to shrink. When it becomes clear that the shrinking isn't going to stop, he reflects on the nature of man and the universe as well as fighting off seemingly giant animals and insects. Although a little silly in places, it has a more thoughtful and intelligent script than you'd expect from this sort of film.

Scott Carey	Grant Williams
Louise Carey	Randy Stuart
Clarice	April Kent
Charlie Carey	Paul Langton
Dr. Thomas Silver	Raymond Bailey
Midget	Billy Curtis

Blurb So Incredible You'll Talk About It For Years To Come.

Quote 'That's silly, honey. People just don't get smaller.' • 'All this vast majesty of creation, it had to mean something. And then I meant something, too. Yes, smaller than the smallest, I meant something too. To God there is no zero. I still exist.' [Last line]

Psst! To simulate the giant raindrops, giant water-filled condoms were used. Director Arnold said he remembered from his childhood 'that they made dandy bombs when you fill them with water. I used to drop them on top of people from windows. And I remembered that they used to hold a tear-shaped form on their way down.' • The studio accountants wanted to know why they were suddenly presented with a bill for 14,400 condoms. They received the answer that they had been needed for the post-production party!

Indiana Jones and the Last Crusade

★★★★ 1989 127min c.

Director: Steven Spielberg
Screenplay: Jeffrey Boam

An excellent third outing for Indiana Jones, this time teamed up with dad Connery in a search for the Holy Grail. Although full of implausibilities (didn't anyone use passports in the 30s?) it's rollicking good fun, packed with great action sequences, villainous Nazis, great locations and wonderful bantering dialogue between Dad and Junior.

Indiana Jones	Harrison Ford
Prof. Henry Jones	Sean Connery
Marcus Brody	Denholm Elliott
Dr. Elsa Schneider	Alison Doody
Sallah	John Rhys-Davies
Walter Donovan	Julian Glover
Young Indy	River Phoenix
Vogel	Michael Byrne
Kazim	Kevork Malikyan
Grail Knight	Robert Eddison
Fedora	Richard Young
Sultan	Alexei Sayle

Blurb He's Back, And This Time He's Brought His Dad • You'll Have The Time Of Your Life Keeping Up With The Jones's

Quote 'Nazis! I hate these guys.' • 'Does anyone here speak English, or even ancient Greek?'

OOPS! Where to start? After Dad and Junior escape from the castle, the signpost they stop at has directions to different places on each side • When Hitler signs his autograph for Indy, the world's most notorious left-hander does so with his right hand and, what's more, writes 'Adolph' instead of 'Adolf' • The Jones boys would have had difficulty riding in the *Hindenberg* in 1938. It blew up the year before • Indy would have trouble with his transatlantic flight east. He made the journey a year before the service began • In the airport lounge, a couple of passengers are reading a newspaper dated 1918 • After the speedboat has been sliced up, watch the wheel of Indy's boat switch suddenly from right to left • In the library in the old church, the all-important letter 'X' is clearly

white when seen from the staircase but it's a much fainter green when they're back downstairs again • Despite the lettering on screen reading 'The Republic of Hatay', the ruler is immediately afterwards referred to as 'Your Royal Highness' • The tank going over the cliff is clearly a fake as there's no hole visible when the turret comes off.

Psst! Although Connery is playing Ford's father, he is actually only 12 years older • The script originally had the relationship between Dad and Junior all lovey-dovey, with Dad a fount of much Yoda-like wisdom. It was toughened up at Connery's insistence • Phoenix, here playing the young Indy, had starred with Ford three years earlier in *The Mosquito Coast* • Lt. Col. Hugh Dickens, the CO of the 9th/12th Royal Lancers appears as a Nazi officer • 3,000 rats were bred specially for the catacombs scene.

Indiana Jones and the Temple of Doom

★★ 1984 117min c.

Director: Steven Spielberg
Screenplay: Willard Huyck & Gloria Katz

This prequel to *Raiders* is gruesome and unsubtle, undermined by a weak story involving Eastern religious fanatics. The endless succession of action set-pieces are suprisingly unconvincing, even the expensively-staged underground railway escape.

Indiana Jones	Harrison Ford
Willie Scott	Kate Capshaw
Short Round	Ke Huy Quan
Mola Ram	Amrish Puri
Chattar Lal	Roshan Seth
Weber	Dan Aykroyd

Psst! The Club Obi-Wan, home to the opening sequence, is a *Star Wars* in-joke • Keep an eye out early on for Dan Aykroyd in a cameo as 'Weber', leading Indy and the others to the plane. The cameo was a quid pro quo for Spielberg's appearance in *The Blues Brothers*. Spielberg himself appears as a background tourist in the airport scene • Although the PG-13 rating was introduced for this film, The American National Coalition of Television Violence thought it should have been an X, logging 14 killings and 39 attempted murders by Indy and over a hundred other incidents of killing, maiming and torture. A sacrifice involving a heart being ripped out was cut by the UK censor • The rope suspension bridge could only be shown from one side, or the Grand Coulee Dam would have been visible.

Indiscreet

★★ 1958 100min c.

Director: Stanley Donan
Screenplay: Norman Krasna
Source: Play, *Kind Sir* by Krasna

American man-about-town Grant falls for famous actress Bergman but escapes commitment by pretending to be married. There's real chemistry on screen between the two stars but although it's sweet, the film moves far too slowly to get terribly excited.

Philip Adams	Cary Grant
Anna Kalman	Ingrid Bergman
Alfred Munson	Cecil Parker
Margaret Munson	Phyllis Calvert
Carl Banks	David Kossoff
Doris Banks	Megs Jenkins
Mr. Finleigh	Oliver Johnston
Oscar	Michael Anthony
Leading man	Richard Vernon

Quote 'How dare he make love to me and not be a married man!' • 'There is no sincerity like a woman telling a lie.'

OOPS! She says they are going to the Players' Club on their first date but the mat as they enter says 'Garrick Club' • Their stroll to Cleopatra's Needle, the Mall and Hyde Park Corner demonstrates a rather cavalier attitude towards London geography.

The Innocents

★★★★ 1961 99min c.

Director: Jack Clayton
Screenplay: William Archibald & Truman Capote
Source: Novel, *The Turn of the Screw* by Henry James

A Victorian governess is troubled that the apparent innocence of the children in her charge conceals something sinister. Then she starts seeing ghosts. This stunningly effective chiller takes hold of your guts early on and twists them tighter and tighter until you can barely stand it. If you get a chance to see it, cancel any other engagements, take the phone off the hook and put the chain on the door.

Miss Giddens	Deborah Kerr
Peter Quint	Peter Wyngarde
The Uncle	Michael Redgrave
Mrs. Grose	Megs Jenkins
Miles	Martin Stephens
Flora	Pamela Franklin

The Inn of the Sixth Happiness

★★ 1958 158min c.

Director: Mark Robson
Screenplay: Isobel Lennart
Source: Book, *The Small Woman* by Alan Burgess

An English missionary in China before World War II leads a group of children on a hazardous journey to safety. Almost as saccharine at times as *The Sound of Music*, its similar theme will probably appeal most to lovers of that movie. Others may decide to cancel their subscriptions to the NSPCC.

Gladys Aylward	Ingrid Bergman
Capt. Lin Nan	Curt Jurgens
Mandarin	Robert Donat
Mrs. Lawson	Athene Seyler
Sir Francis Jamison	Ronald Squire
Also: Richard Wattis	

Quote 'Once in her life, every woman should have that said to her. I thank you for being the one who said it to me.'

Psst! Based on a true story about missionary Gladys Aylward, it was filmed in North Wales • This was Robert Donat's final screen performance. He spent much of the time using oxygen tanks to help his laboured breathing. His last line on screen was: 'We shall not see each other again, I think.' • Audrey Hepburn turned down the lead role.

Intermezzo

★★★ 1939 70min b/w

Director: Gregory Ratoff
Screenplay: George O'Neil

A young pianist falls in love with a famous pianist. But he is married and she worries if taking him away from his family is the right thing to do. Bergman and Howard are just right for this sort of romantic tosh, managing to elevate it into a superior, albeit extremely sentimental, love story. It's a shame that it's so short. It was originally called *Intermezzo: A Love Story*.

Holger Brandt	Leslie Howard
Anita Hoffman	Ingrid Bergman
Margit Brandt	Edna Best
Charles Moler	Cecil Kellaway
Thomas Sternborg	John Halliday
Greta Sternborg	Ann E. Todd

Psst! This was Ingrid Bergman's first American film. She had been in a Swedish production of the same tale in 1937. Producer David O. Selznick told Ratoff to copy the first film scene for scene • One of producer Selznick's infamous memos said, 'I note Bergman is 69 and a half inches tall. Is it possible she is actually this high, and do you think we will have to use stepladders with Leslie Howard?' • Director Ratoff replaced William Wyler who Selznick thought was dragging his feet • Howard's violin playing was dubbed by Toscha Seidel. When we see Howard playing the violin there are, in fact, two players on either side of him, one bowing the instrument and the other the fingering • Props master Irving Sindler compensated for the lack of a credit on the movie by putting the name 'Sindler & Son' on a bakery sign. See also *Wuthering Heights* and *Dead End*.

In the Heat of the Night
★★★ 1967 109min c.

Director: Norman Jewison
Screenplay: Stirling Silliphant
Source: Novel by John Ball

A Southern sheriff is astounded to find a black detective sent along to help him solve a murder case. As the two work together, however, they develop a mutual respect and affection. Steiger and Poitier are both splendid, with Steiger particularly believeable as the man having to reconsider lifelong beliefs. Unfortunately, there isn't much to the movie apart from these two. Poitier would later go on to play the same role in *They Call Me* Mister *Tibbs* and *The Organization*.

Virgil Tibbs	Sidney Poitier
Bill Gillespie	Rod Steiger
Deputy Sam Wood	Warren Oates
Delores Purdy	Quentin Dean
Purdy	James Patterson
Webb Schubert	William Schallert
Mrs. Leslie Colbert	Lee Grant
Eric Endicott	Larry Gates

Mama Baleba	Beah Richards
Harvey Oberst	Scott Wilson
Packy Harrison	Matt Clark
Ralph Henshaw	Anthony James

Oscars Best Picture, Best Screenplay (adapted), Rod Steiger

Quote 'They call me *Mr.* Tibbs.'

Psst! Steiger stayed in character even when the cameras weren't rolling and was never without gum in his mouth • When director Jewison said he wasn't tubby enough, Steiger was only too delighted to pig himself on desserts. 'I gladly sacrificed myself to art. If I had only two pieces of pecan pie, they went mad. So I gorged myself.'

In the Line of Fire
★★★ 1993 128min c.

Director: Wolfgang Petersen
Screenplay: Jeff Maguire

An ageing secret agent who hasn't forgiven himself for not preventing JFK being topped is toyed with by a former CIA hitman with a grudge against the President. Malkovich makes a truly memorable villain and there's plenty of excitement here, even if it's not always terribly plausible. The major drawback is that Clint doesn't do much in the line of detective work, instead being led all the way by the manipulative Malkovich.

Frank Horrigan	Clint Eastwood
Mitch Leary	John Malkovich
Lilly Raines	Rene Russo
Al D'Andrea	Dylan McDermott
Bill Watts	Gary Cole
Harry Sargent	Fred Dalton Thompson
Sam Campagna	John Mahoney

Quote 'If she looks back, that means she's interested. Come on, now. Give me a little look. A little glance back. Give me that smug look and be on your way.'

OOPS! Even though we've established that Frank's no longer too hot in the running stakes, when they all hare off to the park, guess who gets there first?

Psst! New digital techology was used to replace President Clinton in footage of one of his campaign rallies with the actor who played the President in the movie. It also came in handy for giving Eastwood the first ever movie digital haircut.

In the Name of the Father

★★★ 1993 132min c.

Director: Jim Sheridan
Screenplay: Terry George & Jim Sheridan

Based on real life, this purports to tell the story of Gerry Conlon, who went to London looking for free love and found himself looking through iron bars for 15 years, convicted of the 1974 Guildford pub bombing. Despite some pretty wild distortions of the facts, as a piece of storytelling about a gross miscarriage of justice it's hard to fault, with Day-Lewis and Postlethwaite superb as the son and father who only come close to understanding each other when they share the same cell. Gripping stuff, which makes something like *JFK* look tame indeed.

Gerry Conlon	Daniel Day-Lewis
Giuseppe Conlon	Pete Postlethwaite
Gareth Peirce	Emma Thompson
Paul Hill	John Lynch
Robert Dixon	Corin Redgrave
Carole Richardson	Beatie Edney

Showing The Godfather.

OOPS! There's a very visible boom mike as they go to have their first meal in Park Royal prison.

Psst! Among the artistic liberties taken are putting Conlon and his father in the same cell, which never happened, showing Conlon was robbing the prostitute's flat at the time of the bombing, when in fact several days separated the two and having solicitor Thompson addressing the court • Day-Lewis insisted on being kept awake in a cell for two days to get in the right condition for one scene.

In the Realm of the Senses

★★ 1976 105min c.

Director: Nagisa Oshima
Screenplay: Nagisa Oshima

After careful scrutiny, Oshima's very controversial and explicit film probably *is* a serious examination of sexual obsession in repressive 1930s Japan. Not that such high artistic intent continues to attract most audiences to a film still banned on British video. Nevertheless, 'Based On A True Story' is for once a recommendation and the main actors go at it with rare conviction. Adventurous couples may wish to stock up on boiled eggs beforehand, but please don't attempt the finale in your own home.

Sada	Tatsuya Fuji
Kichi-zo	Eiko Matsuda
Toku	Aoi Nakajima
Geisha Matsuko	Maika Seri

Psst! The true-life story of a couple's affair in 1936 ended with the wife, an early Lorena Bobbitt, arrested for murder with the missing item from her husband's body 'concealed about her person' • In Japan, Oshima was charged with obscenity, not for the movie, but for the book of the movie • The American censors confiscated the film before it was due to be shown at the New York Film Festival in 1976 • In Britain, it was shown at the London Film Festival in December 1976 where it won the Critics' Circle prize. The BBFC recommended that it only be shown in clubs, not cinemas. Even so, one scene with Sada grabbing the penis of a small boy was cut because of the risk that it might fall foul of the Protection of Children Act. The film was submitted to the BBFC only in 1989. Chief censor James Ferman wanted to pass the film without any cuts at all. By playing with the image so that what happened with the boy could be inferred but not seen, he got round it and, in March 1991, it got an 18 certificate. However, a video release is not thought to be likely.

Intolerance

★★★★ 1916 175min b/w

Director: D.W. Griffith
Screenplay: D.W. Griffith

Few epics come bigger than this. Four narratives – the fall of Babylon, the Massacre of St Bartholomew, the life of Christ and a modern-day execution – are interwoven to contrast intolerance across the ages. The sentiments are sometimes Victorian, but on a big screen with music it is amazing how well this film, called by some the most important movie ever made, still works.

The Woman Who Rocks the Cradle	Lillian Gish
The Boy	Robert Harron
The Dear One	Mae Marsh
Girl from the Mountains	Constance Talmadge
The Bride of Cana	Bessie Love
Prosper Latour	Eugene Pallette
Pharisee (and others)	Erich von Stroheim

Quote 'The only film fugue' [Terry Ramsaye] • 'The greatest commercial anticlimax in film history.' [Gene Fowler]

OOPS! In one of the big crowd scenes – with the Persians attacking Babylon – one of director Griffith's assistants is said to be visible in a jacket and tie.

Psst! Although film buffs point out many firsts for the film, such as the giant crane used for the Babylon sequence, just as important was Griffith's invention to make Princess Beloved's eyes more exciting: false eyelashes • The reconstruction of ancient Babylon was extraordinary and has never been equalled for Hollywood excess. Spread out over several hundred acres, the sets stood 300 feet high and one scene alone used 5,000 extras • So many flames were shooting up when they filmed the night battle sequence that the local fire brigade turned out • Griffith hired some prostitutes to appear naked at the orgiastic Belshazar's Feast. When the movie was re-released in 1942, New Yorks' censors insisted on them being struck out • Because of this scene, which Griffith didn't want cut out, the film was not submitted to the BBFC in Britain. As a result, the film had a limited release here • *Intolerance* was not a success with audiences. After initial interest, takings fell off, its final plea for tolerance and peace being out of tune with a nation gearing up for war.

Invasion of the Body Snatchers

★★★★ 1956 80min b/w

Director: Don Siegel
Screenplay: Daniel Mainwaring
Source: Novel, *The Body Snatchers* by Jack Finney

A doctor discovers aliens are doing away with his fellow townspeople and replacing them with inhuman replicas. Despite its low budget, this is one of the all-time great paranoia movies, chilling in its concept and terrifyingly plausible in its execution. A 76-minute version, without the daft, tacked-on prologue and epilogue, is better than the original release. If you can't see that, just try to ignore the first and last bits. The 1978 remake was competent, but not quite so chilling. A third version by Abel Ferrara, again quite watchable, came out on video only in the UK.

Dr. Miles Bennel . . . . .Kevin McCarthy
Becky Driscoll . . . . .Dana Wynter
Dr. Dan Kauffman . . . . .Larry Gates
Jack . . . . .King Donovan
Theodora . . . . .Carolyn Jones

Wilma Lentz . . . . .Virginia Christine
Nick Grivett . . . . .Ralph Dumke
Uncle Ira . . . . .Tom Fadden
Psychiatrist . . . . .Whit Bissell
Gas man . . . . .Sam Peckinpah

Blurb …There Was Nothing To Hold On To – Except Each Other.

Quote 'Desire, ambition, faith. Without them, life is so simple.' • 'While you're asleep, they'll absorb your mind, your memories, and you'll be reborn into an untroubled world.' • 'You're next!'

Psst! The working title was *Sleep No More* • The studio bosses were so frightened when they saw the film that they insisted on explanatory bookends being tacked on at the start and end of the film, just in case people though it was all for real • Although it was ignored by the critics, it became a big hit with the public. For a while, the word 'pod' became one of the most popular in the language • Sam Peckinpah appears as a meter reader. He was down on his luck, so Siegel gave the role to him out of friendship. Siegel himself appears in the 1978 remake as a taxi driver while Kevin McCarthy also had a bit part.

The Invisible Man

★★★ 1933 71min b/w

Director: James Whale
Screenplay: R.C. Sherriff & Philip Wylie
Source: Novel by H.G. Wells

A scientist finds a way to make himself invisible but he gets progressively loopier as well, until he becomes a dangerous menace. Some of the performances now seem a little melodramatic but, amazingly, most of the special effects look fine even today while the joky tone makes it all good fun. There were umpteen sequels and imitators, among them *The Invisible Man Returns*, *The Invisible Woman*, *Abbott and Costello Meet the Invisible Man*, as well as the more recent *Memoirs of an Invisible Man*.

Jack Griffin . . . . .Claude Rains
Flora Cranley . . . . .Gloria Stuart
Dr. Kemp . . . . .William Harrigan
Dr. Cranley . . . . .Henry Travers
Mrs. Hall . . . . .Una O'Connor
Chief of Detectives . . . . .Dudley Digges
Mr. Hall . . . . .Forrester Harvey
Jaffers . . . . .E.E. Clive
Also: Holmes Herbert, Walter Brennan, John Carradine, Dwight Frye

Quote 'We'll start with a reign of terror, a few murders here and there. Murders of great men, murders of little men. Just to show we make no distinction.'

OOPS! Rains, completely invisible, escapes from the burning barn and dashes across the snow. The reason he's invisible is that he is totally naked. Yet in one of the greatest of all cinema gaffes, he leaves, not footprints for the police to follow in the snow, but *shoeprints*! • Would a British police station really have the words 'Police Department' on the door?

Psst! This was Claude Rains' cinema debut, although moviegoers didn't get to see much of him • Boris Karloff was the original choice for the lead, but he didn't want to play a part where he couldn't largely be seen.

In Which We Serve

★★★ 1942 114min b/w

Director: Noël Coward & David Lean
Screenplay: Noël Coward
Source: Experiences of Lord Louis Mountbatten

The captain and survivors of a warship sunk by a torpedo reflect on their ship's glorious life. A patriotic flagwaver of inestimable value in the middle of the war, it still carries enormous emotional power even now. Although the differences of class now look extraordinarily dated, this tribute to the stiff upper lip is likely to bring a tear to even the most cynical eye.

Capt Kinross	Noël Coward
O/S 'Shorty' Blake	John Mills
CPO Walter Hardy	Bernard Miles
Alix Kinross	Celia Johnson
Mrs. Hardy	Joyce Carey
Freda Lewis	Kay Walsh
'Flags'	Michael Wilding
Maureen Fenwick	Penelope Dudley-Ward
Mrs. Blake	Kathleen Harrison
'Torps'	Philip Friend
'Number One'	Derek Elphinstone
Mr. Blake	George Carney
Joey Mackridge	Geoffrey Hibbert
Edgecombe	Frederick Piper
Col. Lumsden	Walter Fitzgerald
Bobby Kinross	Daniel Massey
Young stoker	Richard Attenborough
Engineer Commander	Ballard Berkeley
Pilot	Hubert Gregg
Doctor	James Donald

Psst! Coward based the film on the experiences of Lord Louis Mountbatten whose ship, HMS Kelly, was sunk. Although he denied that Mountbatten was the inspiration, it was his naval cap that Coward wore in the film • At one point, the film was nearly cancelled because it was thought it might be detrimental to morale • A full-size replica of the destroyer was built in the studio, the largest set ever made in Britain at the time. It could tilt to either side by 15 degrees and many of the actors became seasick while working on it • Coward was scriptwriter, director, star, producer and even composed the music • He got back at Lord Beaverbrook, the press baron against whom he had a long-standing grudge, by showing a copy of *The Daily Express* with its banner headline, 'No War This Year', floating in the sea just after war was declared • While Coward was performing the Dunkirk speech, the Royal Family was actually on set watching the filming • When Mills was shot at and wounded in the water, the gunfire effect came from a row of condoms below the water that were burst by compressed air. Mills believed himself the only actor ever to have been 'shot in the arm by a French letter' • The film saw the debuts of Richard Attenborough as 'young stoker', Daniel Massey, and Celia Johnson • Juliet Mills appears as an infant • If Ballard Berkeley looks familiar, it's probably because he was also the Major in *Fawlty Towers*.

The Ipcress File

★★★ 1965 105min c.

Director: Sidney J. Furie
Screenplay: Bill Canaway & James Doran
Source: Novel by Len Deighton.

Caine plays down-market spy Harry Palmer to perfection in this who-can-you-trust espionage yarn. The story's still pretty good although the twist at the end obviously only surprises the first time. The direction, however, is firmly rooted in the 60s and is as old hat as flares and kipper ties. Caine played Harry Palmer again in the dull sequels, *Funeral in Berlin* and *Billion Dollar Brain*.

Harry Palmer	Michael Caine
Dalby	Nigel Green
Maj. Ross	Guy Doleman
Jean	Sue Lloyd
Jock Carswell	Gordon Jackson
Radcliffe	Aubrey Richards
Bluejay	Frank Gatliff

Psst! Christopher Plummer was first choice for the lead, but he preferred to make *The Sound of Music* • Len Deighton didn't name his hero in the novels on which this and the sequels are based • As filming was about to start, the director called the actors around him, put his script on the ground, and set it alight. 'That's what I think of it,' he said to the astonished actors. The amazed Caine was then approached by Furie, wanting to know if he could borrow a script so that he could see what was in the first scene.

I See a Dark Stranger

★★★ 1945 112min b/w

Director: Frank Launder
Screenplay: Frank Launder, Sidney Gilliat & Wolfgang Wilhelm

A young Irishwoman who hates the British believes she is working for the IRA. In fact, it is the Germans who are giving her her orders. One of our chaps is on her tail, but isn't so sure that he wants to catch her. It seems an extraordinary subject for a comedy-thriller so soon after the war ended, but it comes off beautifully thanks, in large part, to the contribution of Launder and Gilliat, responsible for movies such as *The Lady Vanishes* and *The Belles of St. Trinians*. Tophole stuff. Known as *The Adventuress* in America.

Bridie Quitty	Deborah Kerr
Lt. David Bayne	Trevor Howard
Miller	Raymond Huntley
Timothy	Liam Redmond
Hawkins	Michael Howard
Intelligence Officer	David Tomlinson
Straw hat man	Norman Shelley
O'Callaghan	Brefni O'Rourke
Capt. Goodhusband	Garry Marsh
Lt. Spanswick	Tom Macaulay
Walter	George Woodbridge
Old lady in train	Katie Johnson
Policeman	Torin Thatcher
Hotel manageress	Joan Hickson
American girl	Brenda Bruce

Psst! The film was originally supposed to feature Charters and Caldicott, the cricket-obsessed characters who starred in other movies like *The Lady Vanishes*. But when they insisted on their parts being made larger their services were dispensed with and a new pair of buffoons, Goodhusband and Spanswick, were conjured up.

The Italian Job

★★★ 1969 100min c.

Director: Peter Collinson
Screenplay: Troy Kennedy Martin

This fondly remembered caper movie has Caine planning to nab gold bullion in Turin during a massive traffic jam that he's engineered. It's terribly slow and oh-so-Sixties to begin with, with Caine giving the impression he's auditioning for an episode of the TV puppet show *Thunderbirds*. Despite the irritations, the heist itself is still extremely enjoyable and well worth hanging around for.

Charlie Crocker	Michael Caine
Mr. Bridger	Noël Coward
Computer expert	Benny Hill
Altabani	Raf Vallone
Freddie	Tony Beckley
Beckerman	Rossano Brazzi
Lorna	Maggie Blye
Miss Peach	Irene Handl
Governor	John Le Mesurier
Birkinshaw	Fred Emney
Garage manager	John Clive
Yellow	Robert Powell
Vicar	David Kelly
Shirtmaker	Simon Dee

Quote 'Just remember this. In this country, they drive on the wrong side of the road.'

OOPS! The mini changes colour as it tumbles down the mountain • Surely there's some confusion over money? When the police chief comes to the computer centre he says $3m is at stake. But elsewhere, Caine and the others have said it's $4m.

Psst! Paramount originally suggested Robert Redford for the lead • Look out for Robert Powell as 'Yellow' and Simon Dee as a shirtmaker.

It Always Rains on Sunday

★★ 1947 92min b/w

Director: Robert Hamer
Screenplay: Robert Hamer, Henry Cornelius & Angus Macphail
Source: Novel by Arthur La Bern

An escaped convict makes his way to tne East End and the house of his old girlfriend, who's now married. If it had Jean Gabin or Humphrey

Bogart in it, the film might have dated better. Although considered shocking and exciting at the time, this Ealing production is not only now drab and depressing, but rather unrealistic too.

Rose Sandigate	Googie Withers
Sgt. Fothergill	Jack Warner
Tommy Swann	John McCallum
George Sandigate	Edward Chapman
Whitey Williams	Jimmy Hanley
Lou Hyams	John Slater
Vi Sandigate	Susan Shaw
Morry Hyams	Sydney Tafler
Dicey Perkins	Alfie Bass
Mrs. Spry	Hermione Baddeley
Ted Edwards	Nigel Stock

It Happened One Night

★★★ 1934 105min c.

Director: Frank Capra
Screenplay: Robert Riskin
Source: Short story, *Night Bus* by Samuel Hopkins Adams

A runaway heiress is dogged by a troublesome reporter eager to write her story. Two people who so obviously detest each other are always certain to fall in love in the movies, but the inevitability is part of the great pleasure to be had in this splendidly unsentimental Capra comedy (his first success) which only occasionally drags its heels.

Peter Warne	Clark Gable
Ellie Andrews	Claudette Colbert
Alexander Andrews	Walter Connolly
Oscar Shapeley	Roscoe Karns
Danker	Alan Hale
Bus driver	Ward Bond
King Westley	Jameson Thomas
Zeke	Arthur Hoyt
Station attendant	Irving Bacon
Drunken boy	Henry Wadsworth
Mrs. Meriwether	Bess Flowers

Oscars Best Picture, Best Director, Claudette Colbert, Clark Gable, Best Screenplay (adapted)

Blurb Together For The First Time!

Quote 'Shapeley's the name and that's the way I like 'em.' • 'I proved, once and for all, that the limb is mightier than the thumb' – 'Why didn't you take off *all* your clothes? You could have stopped forty cars.' • 'Behold the walls of Jericho! Maybe not as thick as the ones that Joshua blew down with his trumpet, but a lot safer. You see, I have no trumpet.' • 'I just had

the unpleasant sensation of hearing you referred to as my husband.'

OOPS! Notice the clock in the cabin when Gable leaves Colbert in the morning. He leaves for New York, where he writes a piece before driving back. The clock still says 2.30.

Psst! The first movie to win Oscars in the five main categories, a triumph matched since only by *One Flew Over the Cuckoo's Nest* and *Silence of the Lambs* •MGM turned down the story because boss Louis B. Mayer didn't think enough respect was shown to a captain of industry in the person of Ellie Andrews' father • Gable was given the part as punishment for asking for a pay rise from MGM who lent him to 'Poverty Row' studio Columbia. He had just spent nine weeks in hospital having his appendix and tonsils removed • Myrna Loy, Margaret Sullavan, Miriam Hopkins and Constance Bennett all turned down the part. Colbert didn't want it either. Under contract to Paramount, she claimed she only had a four-week gap before a holiday and asked for double her usual salary. To her surprise, Columbia gave her the requested $40,000 and made the film at breakneck speed • Gable enjoyed himself on set, making Colbert jump once by hiding a hammer in his trousers before a close clinch. He broke up laughing so often, there were worries that the film wouldn't be made within its tight schedule • Colbert disliked Capra's laisser-faire style of directing and was difficult for much of the production. Initially, she would not do the famous hitch-hiking scene, refusing to show her leg to the camera. Only when Capra hired a chorus girl to double for her legs did she agree • In the 'Walls of Jericho' scene, Colbert again refused to undress. Capra instead had her drape her clothes on the dividing blanket which turned out to be far sexier • The scene was revolutionary at the time because Gable was seen to wear no vest. Sales of vests plummeted, prompting complaints to the studios from manufacturers • Bus companies reported an increase in trade, particularly from unattached women, presumably hoping to be picked up by the likes of Clark Gable. The newly introduced concept of motels also got a boost from the film • Cartoon character Bugs Bunny was apparently inspired by the way Gable eats a carrot in the movie • When Colbert finished filming, she told friends: 'I've just finished the worst picture of the year.' • On the day of the Oscar ceremony, she was not even going to attend and had to be dragged away from the train taking her East in order to get there in time to collect the statuette.

It's a Gift

★★★★ 1934 73min b/w

Director: Norman Z. McLeod
Screenplay: Jack Cunningham & W.C. Fields
Source: Play, *The Comic Supplement* by J.P. McEvoy

A put-upon shopowner heads West with his horrendous family to the orange grove he's bought sight unseen. More a succession of gags and routines than a coherent story, it showcases Fields at his absolute best. For fans, it's a nonstop delight.

Harold Bissonette . . . . .W.C. Fields
Mildred Bissonette . . . . .Jean Rouverol
Baby Dunk .Baby LeRoy
Amelia Bissonette . . . . .Kathleen Howard
Norman Bissonette . . . . .Tommy Bupp
Everett Ricks . . . . .Tammany Young

Quote 'I'll be sober tomorrow, but you'll be crazy the rest of your life.' • 'Shades of Bacchus.'

Psst! Fields co-wrote the film under the pseudonym of Charles Bogle • Not one of the greatest of children lovers, Fields spiked Baby LeRoy's milk with gin. When he had to be led from the set, Fields shouted after him: 'The kid's no trouper!'

It's a Mad Mad Mad Mad World

★ 1963 154min c.

Director: Stanley Kramer
Screenplay: William Rose & Tania Rose

It's a Sad Sad Sad Sad World when this sort of over-the-top, underwhelming marathon knocks the public for six at the box office, as this movie did at the time. A dying motorist tells his rescuers about the whereabouts of $350,000 and they all drop everything and hare off after it. At half the length, this frenetic, madcap, all-star comedy might have been moderately amusing. As it is, it just goes on and on and on and on, so that the smile freezes on your face. Individual moments still shine out, but nobody should be made to sit through it all except as a punishment …and then only for something *very* naughty.

Capt. C.G. Culpepper . . . . .Spencer Tracy
J. Russell Finch . . . . .Milton Berle
Melville Crump . . . . .Sid Caesar
Benjy Benjamin . . . . .Buddy Hackett
Mrs. Marcus . . . . .Ethel Merman
Ding Bell . . . . .Mickey Rooney
Sylvester Marcus . . . . .Dick Shawn
Otto Meyer .Phil Silvers
J. Algernon Hawthorne . . . . .Terry-Thomas
Lennie Pike . . . . .Jonathan Winters
Monica Crump . . . . .Edie Adams
First cab driver . . .Eddie "Rochester" Anderson
Tyler Fitzgerald . . . . .Jim Backus
Union official . . . . .Joe E. Brown
Chief Aloysius . . . . .William Demarest
Sheriff . . . . .Andy Devine
Second cab driver . . . . .Peter Falk
Detective .Norman Fell
Deputy Sheriff . . . . .Stan Freberg
Fire Chief . . . . .Sterling Holloway
Dinckler . . . . .Edward Everett Horton
Jimmy the Crook . . . . .Buster Keaton
Airport manager . . . . .Charles Lane
Sarge . . . . .Mike Mazurki
Switchboard operator . . . . .ZaSu Pitts
Tower Control . . . . .Carl Reiner
Smiler Grogan . . . . .Jimmy Durante
Mad driver .Jerry Lewis
Man on road . . . . .Jack Benny

Quote 'The whole bloody place [America] is the most unspeakable matriarchy in the whole history of civilization…And this positively infantile preoccupation with bosoms. I'll wager you anything you like if American women stopped wearing brassieres, your whole national economy would collapse overnight.'

Psst! Spencer Tracy was very ill during production, this being his penultimate movie. A double, wearing a Tracy mask, stood in for him in any scene where it could be got away with • Word has it that a new, even longer, director's cut is currently in preparation. The mind boggles, particularly as rumour has it that the original version was five-and-a-half hours long before being drastically reduced.

It's a Wonderful Life

★★★★ 1946 129min b/w

Director: Frank Capra
Screenplay: Frances Goodrich, Albert Hackett & Frank Capra
Source: Story, *The Greatest Gift* by Philip Van Doren Stern

An all-round nice guy finds himself so beset by troubles that he toys with the idea of killing himself, only to have an angel appear to show him what life in Bedford Falls would be like without him. Once the slightly twee opening with the angels nattering in heaven is out of the way, we can luxuriate in one of the loveliest, kindliest, happiest and most emotional films ever made. Although occasionally a little stilted and rather jumpily edited, there are few movies that can coax the tears out every time on cue like this one. By the end, you're so glad to be alive, you just want to go round and hug everyone you meet. Beware, nice people, of the appalling colourised version.

George Bailey	James Stewart
Mary Hatch	Donna Reed
Mr. Potter	Lionel Barrymore
Clarence Oddbody	Henry Travers
Uncle Billy	Thomas Mitchell
Mrs. Bailey	Beulah Bondi
Ernie	Frank Faylen
Bert	Ward Bond
Violet Bick	Gloria Grahame
Mr. Gower	H.B. Warner
Harry Bailey	Todd Karns
Mr. Bailey	Samuel S. Hinds
Sam Wainwright	Frank Albertson
Cousin Millie	Mary Treen
Nick	Sheldon Leonard
Potter's rent collector	Charles Lane
Carter, Bank Examiner	Charles Halton
Tollhouse keeper	Tom Fadden
Miss Davis	Ellen Corby
Cousin Eustace	Charles Williams
Owner of house	J. Farrell MacDonald
Mr. Potter's secretary	Almira Sessions

Quote 'What is it you want, Mary? What do you want? You want the moon?' • 'Aw, youth is wasted on the wrong people.' • 'Get me back. I don't care what happens to me. Get me back to my wife and kids. Help me, Clarence. Please! Please! I wanna live again. I wanna live again. I wanna live again. Please, God, let me live again!' • '*It's a Wonderful Life* is such a *pure* movie. It wasn't taken from a novel or play. It was developed from one little paragraph. Simple story, no message, no violence, no mob scenes. When the movies have a story like this they do it better than any medium there is.' [James Stewart]

OOPS! Watch the wreath Stewart is carrying when he comes into the newspaper office. He throws it away but then it reappears on his arm • I refuse to watch colourised versions of movies, but I'm told that even though everybody of the period had black and white cameras, the technicians coloured the family photographs in the Bailey house along with everything else.

Psst! Probably the only movie to be based on a Christmas Card! Van Doren Stern sent the story out to his friends one year on his cards and got such a good response that it was published • RKO bought the rights for Cary Grant but when Capra came on board, Stewart was his first choice • Both men had been in the services and had had no offers of work during the months since they had left. Stewart remained grateful to Capra for the job that got him back into movies for the rest of his life • Writers Hackett and Goodrich remembered working with Capra as 'The only unpleasant experience we've ever had.' • Look out for the raven on Thomas Mitchell's desk, a feature of almost all Capra's films • Amazingly, the film was a flop at the box office at the time, losing over half a million dollars. Only later, when TV picked it up as a seasonal offering, did it gain in popularity. Sadly, Capra did not benefit as its copyright had elapsed and not been renewed • Nominated for five Oscars, it didn't win one • The film was colourised, even though Capra fought hard to prevent it happening.

I Was a Male War Bride

★★★ 1949 105min b/w

Director: Howard Hawks
Screenplay: Charles Lederer, Leonard Spiegelgass & Hagar Wilde
Source: Novel by Henri Rochard

A WAC falls in love with a French officer but comes up against a bureaucratic nightmare when she tries returning with him to America. Although not all the farce works it remains gently amusing throughout, never going over the top. The relationship between Sheridan and Grant is rather sweet, even if Grant is the unlikeliest Frenchman you could imagine. Known as *You Can't Sleep Here* when released in the U.K.

Capt. Henri Rochard	Cary Grant
Lt. Catherine Gates	Ann Sheridan
Capt. Jack Rumsey	William Neff
WAC	Marion Marshall
WAC	Randy Stuart
Seaman	Ken Tobey

Quote 'I just went gay, all of a sudden.'

OOPS! Just after they have to get off the river because of the weir and are heading across country on the motorbike, we can see a giant barge heading the way they've been told they can't go.

Psst! The film is based on a true story written by the male war bride in question, Henri Rochard, played here by Grant • Grant performed all his own stunts.

Jabberwocky
★★★ 1977 100min c.

Director: Terry Gilliam
Screenplay: Charles Alverson & Terry Gilliam

The traditional tale of the knight and the dragon ...except that the prince is rather more lowly than a prince, it's full of base, lewd and lavatorial humour and is directed by Python member Gilliam. As he's proved since, Gilliam has a wonderful visual sense and this must be one of the best portrayals of medieval filth and degredation yet put on film. This scatalogical comedy has worn better than the similarly-themed but sillier *Monty Python and the Holy Grail*.

Dennis Cooper	Michael Palin
King Bruno	Max Wall
Princess	Deborah Fallender
Chamberlain	John Le Mesurier
Griselda Fishfinger	Annette Badland
Mr. Fishfinger	Warren Mitchell
Squire	Harry H. Corbett
Other squire	Rodney Bewes
Landlord	Bernard Bresslaw
First Herald	John Bird
First merchant	Peter Cellier
Fanatics leader	Graham Crowden
Man with rock	Terry Gilliam
Armourer	Brian Glover
Second Herald	Neil Innes
Poacher	Terry Jones
Sister Jessica	Gorden Kaye
Second gate guard	Bryan Pringle
Red Herring Knight	David Prowse
Prince	Simon Williams

Quote 'Rats on a stick!' Rats on a stick!'

Jagged Edge
★★★ 1985 108min c.

Director: Richard Marquand
Screenplay: Joe Eszterhas

The age-old story of the lawyer falling for the accused murderer. Here it's Close getting steamed up over Bridges, suspected of having topped his wife for her money in a pretty grisly manner. Slickly produced and with some great performances from the leads, it just about moves fast enough to stop you thinking about the silliness of the plot, which has more holes than a string vest. If you're under 30 you may need to get some old-timer to explain to you what a typewriter was. The countless attempts to imitate this movie since, including those by writer Eszterhas himself, only make you realise how well-crafted it is.

Jack Forrester	Jeff Bridges
Teddy Barnes	Glenn Close
Thomas Krasny	Peter Coyote
Sam Ransom	Robert Loggia
Judge Carrigan	John Dehner
Julie Jensen	Karen Austin

OOPS! Keep an eye on Close's suit in court as it changes from grey on the way in to dark blue and then to brown. Her blouse changes from white to brown as well.

Psst! There are those who maintain that this set the pattern for all Joe Eszterhas' scripts, making him the highest-paid scriptwriter ever. An entertaining parlour game is to spot the similarities in the plotlines of this, *Music Box*, *Sliver* and *Basic Instinct* • Much of the opening of the film has been lost when shown on TV in the past.

Jailhouse Rock
★★★ 1957 96min b/w

Director: Richard Thorpe
Screenplay: Guy Trosper

This movie, Elvis' third, set the pattern for all the rest, with a daft story involving the King being imprisoned for manslaughter then making it in the music business when he gets out. Most of his other movies were far more anodyne than this. For many fans, this is the true Elvis, still a rockabilly, still dangerous, still electric, still exciting. Best number is the title song.

Vince Everett	Elvis Presley
Peggy Van Alden	Judy Tyler
Hunk Houghton	Mickey Shaughnessy
Mr. Shores	Vaughn Taylor
Sherry Wilson	Jennifer Holden
Teddy Talbot	Dean Jones

OOPS! Elvis' prison number changes from 6239 to 6240.

Psst! When Presley made his first movie, *Love Me Tender*, he was blond. After a tour of duty with the Army, he returned to the screen for this film with black hair • Jailhouse Rock sold two million in just two weeks • After Presley's appearance on TV had rocked the young generation and shocked the rest, Presley's manager, Col. Parker, decided that the small screen would only lead to a quick burn-out of Elvis fever. Far better, he reasoned, to make the public pay to see him at the movies. They stuck to that policy through 10 years and roughly 30 films • Jailhouse Rock was re-released just after Elvis was discharged from the army • Judy Tyler was killed in a car crash shortly after making the movie.

Jane Eyre
★★ 1943 96min b/w

Director: Robert Stevenson
Screenplay: Aldous Huxley, Robert Stevenson & John Houseman
Source: Novel by Charlotte Brontë

This is the best of all the screen versions of Charlotte Brontë's tale of the governess falling for her gloomy employer. There had already been four before it and another was to follow in 1970. But despite this it's hardly scintillating stuff. It's terribly sluggish, Fontaine is insipid and Welles appears to have something else on his mind.

Jane Eyre	Joan Fontaine
Edward Rochester	Orson Welles
Adéle	Margaret O'Brien
Jane (as child)	Peggy Ann Garner
St. John Rivers	John Sutton
Bessie	Sara Allgood
Brockelhurst	Henry Daniell
Mrs. Reed	Agnes Moorehead
Helen Burns	Elizabeth Taylor
Col. Dent	Aubrey Mather
Lady Ingram	Barbara Everest
Blanche Ingram	Hillary Brooke
Leah	Mae Marsh

Blurb A Love Story Every Woman Would Die A Thousand Deaths To Live!

Psst! Keep your eyes open for Elizabeth Taylor as the girl dying of neglect.

Jason and the Argonauts
★★ 1963 104min c.

Director: Don Chaffey
Screenplay: Jan Read & Beverley Cross

This film is best enjoyed at about the age of 11, and then it can be fondly recalled for the rest of your life without your recollection actually being spoilt by watching it again. Jason and Co. set out in the Argo, doing battle with an impressive range of Ray Harryhausen monsters in order to obtain a golden sheepskin. Tacky, fast-moving fun, helped immeasurably by Bernard Herrmann's score.

Jason	Todd Armstrong
Hera	Honor Blackman
Phalerus	Andrew Faulds
Medea	Nancy Kovack
Acastus	Gary Raymond
Argus	Laurence Naismith
Hercules	Nigel Green
Phineas	Patrick Troughton

OOPS! Look for an out-of-place zipper sported by one of the dancing priestesses.

Psst! This is probably Ray Harryhausen's finest work. His was a painstaking job, with the creatures being animated through the stop-motion process which means taking a picture, moving the monster imperceptibly, and then taking the next.

Jaws
★★★★ 1975 124min c.

Director: Steven Spielberg
Screenplay: Peter Benchley & Carl Gottlieb
Source: Novel by Benchley

Okay, okay. So the shark looks just a little rubbery 20 years on. But with that one caveat, this tale of a Great White treating holiday time at a New England resort as an eat-all-you-can buffet is still rivetting stuff. That's due, in the main, to beautifully assured direction from a 27-year-old Spielberg and a trio of splendid performances from Scheider, Shaw and Dreyfuss. Scheider hung around for the limp sequel, but sensibly opted out of the further two dreadful Jaws films.

Martin Brody	Roy Scheider
Capt. Quint	Robert Shaw
Matt Hooper	Richard Dreyfuss
Ellen Brody	Lorraine Gary
Mayor Vaughan	Murray Hamilton
Meadows	Carl Gottlieb
Deputy Hendricks	Jeffrey C. Kramer
Chrissie Watkins	Susan Backlinie
Cassidy	Jonathan Filley
Interviewer	Peter Benchley

Blurb She Was The First.

Quote 'This was no boating accident.' • 'Here's to swimmin' with bow-legged women.' • 'You're gonna need a bigger boat.' • 'A shark, he's got lifeless eyes, black eyes, like a doll's eyes. When he comes at you he doesn't seem to be living until he bites you and those black eyes roll over white, and then, oh, then you hear that terrible high-pitch screaming.' • 'One of the better films I have seen.' [Fidel Castro]

OOPS! Although Amity is partying for the 4th of July holiday weekend, there are no leaves on the trees for some scenes • At the end of the film, the fishing boat *Orca* has a visible serial number painted on the bow. In *Jaws 2*, when divers inspect the wreck, there's no serial number. Instead, there's a shiny nameplate • Maybe its my maths that are up the spout, but when Scheider tells the mayor that two people have died, surely it should be three as they've just found Ben Gardner's body?

Psst! The budget soared from $2.5m to $8m, largely because of problems relating to filming in water. This caused apoplexy among Universal executives. Twenty years later, the cost of the same studio's *Waterworld* would approach $200m • The opening shark attack was simulated by having five guys pulling on ropes attached to the girl in the water. They were so enthusiastic, they broke two of her ribs • It took just 78 days for *Jaws* to beat all previous box office records, including those set by *Gone with the Wind*, *The Sound of Music* and *The Godfather*. It was beaten in turn by *Star Wars* • Three hydraulically-controlled sharks were made at a cost of $150,000 each. They were extremely temperamental and were nicknamed 'Bruce' • The main Bruce now lives in Alice Cooper's Hollywood swimming pool • The scene in which the shark sinks the *Orca* happened for real but was not planned. Fortunately, the film was recovered by divers and immediately sluiced down and developed • Lee Marvin was the first choice for Quint, but he turned the role down because, 'I'm interested in catching fish, not acting with them.' • The actors who did star weren't terribly enthusiastic. Richard Dreyfuss thought it would be 'the turkey of the year' and Robert Shaw thought the plot was 'a piece of shit' • The American release was deliberately delayed until the beginning of the summer beach season. Unsurprisingly, there was a wave of shark sightings and relatively few people ventured into the water that year • This was the first big merchandised movie, with *Jaws* T-shirts, bikinis, socks, beach towels, lunch boxes, tote bags, blow-up toys, posters and plastic fins to create jollity on the beaches • In France, it was known as *The Teeth of the Sea* • Author Robert Benchley appears as a reporter • Three sequels vied with each other in their ghastliness.

The Jazz Singer

★ **1927 89min b/w**

Director: Alan Crosland
Screenplay: Alfred A. Cohn
Source: Play by Samson Raphaelson

Those kids, they're always the same. Dad wants them to do one thing, they want to do another. Instead of being content to wow them with his singing in the synagogue, cantor's son Eddie goes into showbiz. But then he always was a mammy's boy. The first feature film that had someone talking in it created a sensation. Unsurprisingly, it now holds very little interest to anybody other than film students, although numbers like 'My Mammy' and 'Toot, Toot, Tootsie Goodbye' aren't too bad. Remade twice, in 1953 and 1980. Both versions were dreadful and didn't even have novelty value.

Jakie Rabinowitz/Jack Robin	Al Jolson
May McAvoy	Mary Dale
Cantor Rabinowitz	Warner Oland
Sara Rabinowitz	Eugenie Besserer
Moisa Yudelson	Otto Lederer
Buster Billings	William Demarest
The agent	Roscoe Karns
Chorus girl	Myrna Loy

Quote 'Wait a minute, wait a minute. You ain't heard nothin' yet!' • 'I had a simple, corny, well-felt little melodrama, and they made an ill-felt, silly, maudlin, badly timed thing of it.' [Playwright Raphaelson]

Psst! The star of the play on Broadway was George Jessel. He was announced for the role in the film but only a week after getting to Hollywood, Jolson – then the biggest star in Vaudeville – was given the part • In large part the film was a silent with some musical interludes synchronously recorded. However, Jolson broke into unrehearsed speech before a couple of his numbers, ad-libbing. It was this that caused the furore, even though there are only 354 words in the film. The director wanted to cut these unscripted bits out, but Darryl F. Zanuck, Warner's production head, insisted on keeping them in and adding some more. Boss Jack Warner told him to cut out these 'talking tricks', believing the studio could be ruined if people thought them ridiculous • It wasn't the first talking picture. Edison had experimented with them back in 1889 and *Don Juan* in 1926 was the first film with synchronised musical accompaniment • If you look quickly, you may spot Myrna Loy as a chorus girl.

Jean de Florette
★★★★ 1987 122min c.

Director: Claude Berri
Screenplay: Claude Berri & Gérard Brach
Source: Novel by Marcel Pagnol

Magical, wholly captivating French story of hunchback Depardieu and his family trying to scratch a living on their new land, unaware that neighbour Montand and his half-witted nephew have blocked up their spring. A winner in every department, but particularly strong on photography and acting, this is one of those rare films that sticks in the memory long after you've seen it. It was made back-to-back with the equally brilliant sequel, *Manon des Sources*.

Cesar Soubeyran . . . . Yves Montand
Jean de Florette . . . . Gérard Depardieu
Ugolin . . . . Daniel Auteuil
Aimee . . . . Elisabeth Depardieu
Manon . . . . Ernestine Mazurowna
Pique-Bouffigue . . . . Marcel Champel

Les Jeux Interdits
★★★ 1952 84min b/w

Director: René Clément
Screenplay: Jean Aurenche, Pierre Bost & René Clément
Source: Novel, *Les Jeux Inconnus* by François Boyer

In the midst of the Fall of France in World War II, an orphaned girl and the son of the family who take her in try to come to terms with death by making their own pet cemetery. It doesn't go down too well with the adults when it's discovered. The message elements of the film, mostly to do with war, aren't terribly subtle. But as a portrait of childhood it is still utterly charming, thanks in no small part to the incredibly naturalistic performances by the young leads.

Michael Dollé . . . . George Poujouly
Paulette . . . . Brigitte Fossey
M. Dollé . . . . Lucien Hubert
Mme. Dollé . . . . Suzanne Courtal

Georges Dollé . . . . Jacques Marin
Berthe Dollé . . . . Laurence Badie
Francis Gouard . . . . Amedée

Jezebel
★★★ 1938 104min b/w

Director: William Wyler
Screenplay: Clements Ripley, Abem Finkel & John Huston
Source: Play by Owen Davis Sr.

The pre-Civil War South, a spirited, wilful heroine, a mismanaged love affair...no, it's not *Gone With the Wind* but it's still pretty jolly hokum. Davis may never have been better on screen, even persuading us at one of the more dramatic moments that she is wearing a red dress, a neat trick for a black and white movie.

Julie Morrison . . . . Bette Davis
Preston Dillard . . . . Henry Fonda
Buck Cantrell . . . . George Brent
Amy Bradford Dillard . . . . Margaret Lindsay
Aunt Belle Massey . . . . Fay Bainter
Ted Dillard . . . . Richard Cromwell
Dr. Livingstone . . . . Donald Crisp
Gen. Theopholus Bogardus . . . . . . Henry O'Neill
Mrs. Kendrick . . . . Spring Byington
Jean LeCour . . . . John Litel
Dick Allen . . . . Gordon Oliver
Gros Bat . . . . Eddie "Rochester" Anderson
Molly Allen . . . . Janet Shaw
Huger . . . . Irving Pichel
Drunk . . . . Jack Norton

Oscars Fay Bainter, Bette Davis

Quote 'I like my convictions undiluted, same as I do my bourbon.'

Psst! When Bette Davis lost out in the fight to play Scarlett in *Gone With the Wind*, this was offered to her instead. Although she didn't rate it particularly highly, it won her her second Oscar • Miriam Hopkins had played the part on Broadway and was disappointed not to get the lead in the film version as well • Davis and director Wyler began a year-long affair during filming • So similar to *GWTW* was it that Selznick alleged Warners were indulging in unfair trade practices. There was a race to be first into the cinemas which *Jezebel* won by nine months • Fonda was made to do so many retakes by Wyler that Hal B. Wallis, the head of production, suspected Wyler of resenting Fonda because they had both been married to Margaret Sullavan: 'Possibly Wyler likes to see these big numbers on the slate, and maybe we could arrange to have them start with number six on each take, then it wouldn't take so long to get up to nine or ten.' There was an attempt to replace him but, although she often fought him on set, Davis insisted that she would walk if he was sacked • Fonda had an arrangement to leave the production so that he could be with his wife for the birth of their first child, which would be Jane. As the film was behind schedule, Davis had to perform many of her close-ups without Fonda opposite her.

JFK
★★ 1991 190min c.

Director: Oliver Stone
Screenplay: Oliver Stone & Zachary Sklar
Source: Books, *Trial of the Assassins* by Jim Garrison & *Crossfire: The Plot that Killed Kennedy* by Jim Mars

Can you remember where you were when *JFK* came out? Stone lays the blame for Kennedy's assassination squarely with the industrial-military complex, the FBI, the CIA, Cuban dissidents, the Cuban Government, Lee Harvey Oswald, Jack Ruby, Uncle Tom Cobbley and indeed almost anyone else who'd ever heard of the man. An undoubted filmic *tour-de-force* with some splendid acting, its overlong blend of fact and fiction muddies the waters for anyone hoping to understand events. Vietnam isn't forgotten, of course, Stone's slant here being that it wouldn't have happened if JFK hadn't been blown away.

Jim Garrison . . . . .Kevin Costner
Liz Garrison . . . . .Sissy Spacek
David Ferrie .Joe Pesci
Clay Shaw . . . . .Tommy Lee Jones
Lee Harvey Oswald . . . . .Gary Oldman
Lou Ivon . . . . .Jay O. Saunders
Bill Broussard . . . . .Michael Rooker
Susie Cox . . . . .Laurie Metcalf
Al Oser . . . . .Gary Grubbs
Dean Andrews . . . . .John Candy
Jack Martin . . . . .Jack Lemmon
Sen. Russell Long . . . . .Walter Matthau
Guy Bannister .Ed Asner
Colonel 'X' . . . . .Donald Sutherland
Willie O'Keefe . . . . .Kevin Bacon
Jack Ruby . . . . .Brian Doyle-Murray

OOPS! When Garrison and his colleagues meet in his house there's a Christmas tree. Yet a meeting with Clay Shaw the following Sunday turns out to be during Easter!

Psst! Earl Warren of the Commission of the same name is played by the real-life Jim Garrison • The books in Garrison's study are exactly the same as those in the real Garrison's room, with the exception of the designer substituting a set of Lincoln's speeches for the set of Shakespeare that was usually kept on the desk • There is a director's cut on video with an extra 17 minutes of footage not seen in the cinema release.

Johnny Belinda
★★★ 1948 102min b/w

Director: Jean Negulesco
Screenplay: Irmgard Von Cube & Allen Vincent
Source: Play by Elmer Harris

A deaf-mute girl is befriended by a doctor who brings her out of her shell. But when she becomes pregnant after being raped, the locals assume the doctor is responsible. Rape, deafness, not a word uttered...what else could it mean but an Oscar for Wyman? Yes, it's a real tearjerker, but a handsomely produced and well-acted one.

Belinda McDonald . . . . .Jane Wyman
Dr. Robert Richardson . . . . .Lew Ayres
Black McDonald . . . . .Charles Bickford
Aggie McDonald . . . . .Agnes Moorehead
Locky McCormick . . . . .Stephen McNally
Stella McGuire . . . . .Jan Sterling
Mrs. Poggety . . . . .Rosalind Ivan
Pacquet .Dan Seymour
Mrs. Lutz .Mabel Paige
Mrs. McKee . . . . .Ida Moore
Defence attorney . . . . .Alan Napier
Ben . . . . .Monte Blue

Oscars Jane Wyman

Quote 'I accept this award gratefully for keeping my mouth shut for once. I think I'll do it again.' [Wyman picking up her Oscar]

Psst! Wyman – then Mrs. Ronald Reagan – is one of three actors who have an Oscar without saying a word, the others being John Mills for *Ryan's Daughter* and Marlee Matlin for *Children of a Lesser God*. Holly Hunter for *The Piano* doesn't really count as she was allowed some inner vocalising • Wyman studied the behaviour of the deaf intensely for six months for her role, learning signing and lip-reading. On set, she played the part with her ears blocked so that she would respond in the same way as someone who was actually deaf. This had its drawbacks, though. As she couldn't read lips, she had trouble telling when the other actors were giving her the cues for her lines. A system of signs and signals had to be invented for communicating with her on set.

Johnny in the Clouds
SEE: The Way to the Stars

The Jolson Story
★★ 1946 128min c.

Director: Alfred E. Green
Screenplay: Stephen Longstreet

Parks acts and sings up a storm in this bright and breezy musical biopic of Al Jolson. The film displays a blatant disregard for the truth, glossing over the fact that Jolson was one of the biggest egomaniacs in a profession not reknowned for modesty. But as a piece of entertainment it still has its moments, even if the blackface minstrel stuff now appears bizarre in the extreme. A sequel, *Jolson Sings Again*, followed in 1949.

Al Jolson . . . . .Larry Parks
Julie Benson . . . . .Evelyn Keyes
Steve Martin . . . . .William Demarest
Tom Baron . . . . .Bill Goodwin
Cantor Yoelson . . . . .Ludwig Donath
Mrs. Yoelson . . . . .Tamara Shayne
Lew Dockstader . . . . .John Alexander
Jolson (as boy) . . . . .Scotty Beckett
Ann (as girl) . . . . .Ann E. Todd
Oscar Hammerstein . . . . .Edwin Maxwell
Voice of Jolson . . . . .Al Jolson

Quote 'Broadway. What a street! You know something, baby? It belongs to me. You know something else? If you want, I'll give it to you.'

OOPS! As Jolson goes on his first American tour, watch the scenery flash by the ubiquitous train taking him between venues. Isn't that the same shed and telegraph pole we saw earlier?

Psst! Although in his 60s, Jolson – never the most modest of men – desperately wanted to play himself. He did get to dub Parks' singing voice and benefitted from a surge in his popularity when the film was released. He was also on a percentage of the film's profit and got an extra $25,000 for re-recording all the songs • He can also be seen in blackface in longshots in 'Swanee' • Jolson's third wife, gauche hoofer Ruby Keeler, refused to cooperate with the

making of the film, so her character's name was changed to Julie Benson.

Jour de Fête
★★★★ 1949 70min b/w

Director: Jacques Tati
Screenplay: Jacques Tati & Henri Marquet

A small village postman sees a film about the American postal system and decides to adopt a few of their more modern methods. Tati is one of the screen's greatest clowns, adept at physical comedy like no-one since silent days. He turns this often hilarious French comedy into a work of genius which also happens to be a charming portrait of French post-war village life.

Francois, the postman . . . . .Jacques Tati
Roger, a showman . . . . .Guy Decomble
Marcel, a showman . . . . .Paul Frankeur
Roger's wife . . . . .Santa Relli

Psst! It was still a novelty to make a film completely on location in 1949. Sainte-Sévère-sur-Indre was the town in which the soldier Tati sheltered for three months after the French surrendered in 1939 • The film was actually filmed in colour, but the processing went wrong. Fortunately, a black-and-white copy was also made • Tati couldn't find a distributor for the film until he arranged a preview in Paris which was a great success • The film critic of *Le Canard Enchainé*, France's equivalent of *Private Eye*, challenged anyone to a duel who preferred this to *M. Hulot's Holiday* • The film almost disappeared late in the 50s. Some think that Tati withdrew it out of respect to de Gaulle after he became President, knowing how everyone thought the two incredibly alike • Tati is said to have been a major influence on the editing techniques later used so famously by Francois Truffaut and Jean-Luc Godard.

Journey to the Center of the Earth
★★★ 1959 132min c.

Director: Henry Levin
Screenplay: Charles Brackett & Walter Reisch
Source: Novel by Jules Verne

A professor and his party nip into a extinct Icelandic volcano on the first step of their trip to the earth's core, working on the assumption that what occasionally goes up might go right down too. The film begins in the most ludicrous manner and simply gets more ridiculous as it goes on. But Mason brings his usual gravitas to his part and the script is surprisingly witty. All in all, it's still a highly entertaining romp.

Prof. Oliver Lindenbrook	James Mason
Alec McEwen	Pat Boone
Carla	Arlene Dahl
Jenny	Diane Baker
Count Saknussemm	Thayer David
Dean	Alan Napier
Hans	Peter Ronson

Judgment at Nuremberg

★★★★ 1961 190min c.

Director: Stanley Kramer
Screenplay: Abby Mann

An electrifying account of the tail-end of the Nuremberg trials. Tracy is a judge on the slide in the States sent to Germany to preside over the trial of his peers, the judges who were in office while the Nazis were in power. Although a trifle stagy and long, it's still a gripping movie. Oddly, having a cast composed of big star names actually works in the movie's favour.

Judge Dan Haywood	Spencer Tracy
Ernst Janning	Burt Lancaster
Col. Tad Lawson	Richard Widmark
Mme. Bertholt	Marlene Dietrich
Hans Rolfe	Maximilian Schell
Irene Hoffman	Judy Garland
Rudoph Petersen	Montgomery Clift
Sen. Burkette	Edward Binns
Werner Lammpe	Torben Meyer
Capt. Byers	William Shatner
Judge Kenneth Morris	Kenneth MacKenna
Gen. Merrin	Alan Baxter
Judge Curtiss Ives	Ray Teal

Oscars Best Screenplay (adapted), Maximilian Schell

Blurb The Things You'll See And The Things You'll Feel Are The Things That Will Be Part Of You As Long As You Live.

Quote 'This, then, is what we stand for: truth, justice and the value of a single human being.'

Psst! Laurence Olivier turned down the part that went to Burt Lancaster • Originally a TV drama, the words 'gas ovens' had to be bleeped out during the broadcast. The segment's sponsor was the American Gas Association! • The courtroom was built as an exact replica of the one in Nuremberg

• Montgomery Clift was in a sorry state, both physically and mentally, when he made the movie and had to be led gently through his part by Spencer Tracy.

The Jungle Book

★★★★ 1967 78min c.

Director: Wolfgang Reitherman
Screenplay: Larry Clemmons, Ralph Wright, Ken Anderson & Vance Gerry
Source: Book, *The Jungle Book* by Rudyard Kipling

The funniest, most enjoyable and endlessly rewatchable of all Disney cartoons. It may not have too much to do with Kipling but the characters are voiced so well that the animals all have the spirit of life about them. Who can resist Baloo the Bear and numbers like 'The Bare Necessities' and 'I Wanna Be Like You'? Only the feeble ending lets it down. The 1942 Korda live-action film is now embarrassingly bad but the 1994 Disney live-action tale, *Rudyard Kipling's The Jungle Book*, is a rousing family adventure.

Baloo, the Bear	Phil Harris
Bagheera, the Panther	Sebastian Cabot
Shere Kahn, the Tiger	George Sanders
Kaa, the Snake	Sterling Holloway
King Louie of the Apes	Louis Prima

Quote Man! That's what I call a swinging party!'

Psst! This was the last animated film to be supervised by Walt Disney, who died eight months before the film was released • Singer and bandleader Phil Harris had gone into semi-retirement and turned the part of Baloo down at first, thinking the script and songs were banal. He eventually agreed, only on condition that he could improvise. The film and soundtrack were so popular that he thought the first royalty cheque he was sent must be a mistake • Sterling Holloway also provided the voice for Pooh in Disney's *Winnie the Pooh* cartoons • This is the best-selling video in the UK, with over five million sold, raking in more money than *Jurassic Park* took at the box office.

Jurassic Park

★★★ 1993 126min c.

Director: Steven Spielberg
Screenplay: Michael Crichton & David Koepp
Source: Novel by Crichton

When are movie scientists going to wake up to the fact that whenever they tamper with nature, things go wrong? Bonkers boffin Attenborough sets up a theme park with DNA-cloned dinosaurs instead of dodgems and the creatures demonstrate all too clearly the answer to that age-old question: 'Are dinosaurs vegetarians or carnivores?' The re-creation of the dinosaurs is stunning, particularly in the sequences with the T-Rex and the velociraptors. However, the effects are everything. Dern and Attenborough give worse performances than the dinosaurs and the story is completely at sea, with loose ends left lying all over the place, a fault that becomes more glaringly obvious on subsequent viewings.

Dr. Alan Grant	Sam Neill
Ellie Sattler	Laura Dern
Ian Malcolm	Jeff Goldblum
John Hammond	Richard Attenborough
Robert Muldoon	Bob Peck
Donald Gennaro	Martin Ferrero
Dr. Wu	B.D. Wong
Tim	Joseph Mazzello
Lex	Ariana Richards
Arnold	Samuel L. Jackson
Dennis Nedry	Wayne Knight

Blurb An Adventure 65 Million Years In The Making.

Quote 'God creates dinosaurs. God destroys dinosaurs. God creates man. Man destroys God. Man creates dinosaurs...' – 'Dinosaurs eat man. Woman inherits the earth.' • 'If The Pirates of the Caribbean breaks down, the pirates don't eat the tourists.' • 'Hammond, after careful consideration, I've decided not to endorse your park.'

OOPS! When Nedry steals the embryos, the spelling of 'stegosaurus' is instead 'stegasaurus' • Jackson appears to be mouthing Attenborough's lines when he's asking them to find Nedry.

Psst! Originally it was going to be directed by Martin Scorsese. Spielberg was intially attached to the remake of *Cape Fear* until, in 1990, they swapped movies • The film took $50m on its opening weekend in America, establishing a record unbeaten until *Batman Forever*. It went on to become the most successful film of all time, taking over $900m around the world • Filming on the Hawaiian island of Kauai was badly hit by Hurrican Iniki • A year's work by technicians to create a baby triceratops that one of the children rides was wiped out when Spielberg cut the scene,

believing it would destroy the movie's pacing
• The secret ingredients to re-create the sound of the dinosaurs were elephants, elephant seals, geese and horses slowed down
• Coincidentally, Dern's mother Diane Ladd starred in a low-budget rip-off released around the same time called *Carnosaur* • Spielberg banned his own four children, of ages up to eight, from seeing the film when it came out, as he thought it would be too scary for them.

The Karate Kid
★★★★ 1984 126min c.

Director: John G. Avildsen
Screenplay: Robert Mark Kamen

Forget the sneers. This is a brilliant movie about an underdog winning out, in the *Rocky* vein (they have the same director) but about karate. When Macchio moves with his mum to California, he's picked on by some bullies who are martial arts experts. Luckily, the janitor of his block knows a bit about chop-socky himself. Undoubtedly manipulative, if you just go with the flow you'll have a hugely entertaining time.

Daniel	Ralph Macchio
Miyagi	Pat Morita
Ali	Elisabeth Shue
Kreese	Martin Kove
Lucille	Randee Heller
Johnny	William Zabka

Quote 'Wax on. Wax off.' • 'Man who catch fly with chopstick, accomplish anything.'

Psst! In reality, Pat Morita knows nothing about karate. 'It mystifies me. All that stuff about breaking bricks. Why don't they just pick up the brick and him 'em over the head with it?'

Kentucky Fried Movie
★★★ 1977 90min c&b/w

Director: John Landis
Screenplay: David Zucker, Jerry Zucker & Jim Abrahams

Although directed by Landis, this unconnected series of sketches were actually written by the team that went on to make *Airplane* and the *Naked Gun* movies. That should give you a pretty good idea what to expect although, as they hadn't long left college, it's rather ruder than their later movies. Not all of it works, but those bits that do, like the newsreader and his colleagues watching the couple making out on the living-room sofa, are absolutely hilarious.

Cleopatra . . . . .Evan C. Kim
Schwartz . . . . .Saul Kahan
Housewife . . . . .Marcy Goldman
Paul . . . . .Joe Medalis
Lo . . . . .Evan C. Kim
The Architect . . . . .George Lazenby
Himself . . . . .Henry Gibson
Himself . . . . .Bill Bixby
The Clumsy Waiter . . . . . . .Donald Sutherland

Psst! Zucker, Abrahams and Zucker abandoned their jobs in favour of their sketch show, *Kentucky Fried Theater*. They spent $35,000 videoing it to take to the Hollywood studios, which led to this movie • At a cost of just $700,000, the film grossed $20m • Look out for Landis' trademark phrase: 'See you next Wednesday'. It appears here as the title of the 'Feel-a-Rama' movie • Landis' earlier film, *Schlock*, appears as a poster in the cinema in the same section.

Kes

★★★ 1969 112min c.

Director: Ken Loach
Screenplay: Barry Hines, Ken Loach & Tony Garnett
Source: Novel, *A Kestrel for a Knave* by Hines

A Yorkshire lad who has a miserable existence finds a baby kestrel, rears it and bonds with it. Although ultimately downbeat, as it probably had to be, there are moments where this picture soars like the bird itself, lifting the heart and spirit and making it fly. Like a lot of Loach's other films, it's also funny where you least expect it to be.

Billy Casper . . . . .David Bradley
Jud . . . . .Freddie Fletcher
Mrs. Casper . . . . .Lynne Perrie
Mr. Farthing . . . . .Colin Welland
Mr. Sugden . . . . .Brian Glover

Key Largo

★★★ 1948 101min b/w

Director: John Huston
Screenplay: Richard Brooks & John Huston
Source: Play by Maxwell Anderson

An ex-serviceman turns up at a hotel in the Florida Keys and finds hot and cold running gangsters controlling the place. With a storm approaching and the numbers augmented by a pair of escaped convict Indians, the scene is set for a slightly stagy but still enjoyably tense thriller. Bogie and Robinson give it all they've got, though you will need to turn a deaf ear to a bit of post-war philosophising

Frank McCloud . . . . .Humphrey Bogart
Johnny Rocco . . . . .Edward G. Robinson
Nora Temple . . . . .Lauren Bacall
James Temple . . . . .Lionel Barrymore
Gaye Dawn . . . . .Claire Trevor
Curley .Thomas Gomez
Ziggy . . . . .Marc Lawrence
Angel . . . . .Dan Seymour
Sheriff Ben Wade . . . . .Monte Blue

Oscars Claire Trevor

Blurb A Storm Of Fear And Fury In The Sizzling Florida Keys.

Quote 'One Rocco more or less isn't worth dying for.' • 'If your head says one thing and your whole life says another, your head always loses.' • 'You don't like it, do you, Rocco? The storm. Show it your gun, why don't you? If it doesn't stop, shoot it.'

Psst! The original play was set against the background of the Spanish Civil War. Robinson's part was originally not a gangster, but an unpleasant gambler • As the arthritic Barrymore defends President Roosevelt, bear in mind that he actually loathed the man and all that he had stood for • Trevor didn't want to have to sing 'Moanin' Low' and Huston kept postponing it. Although she didn't think she had done it particularly well, Huston was happy with it and she went on to win the Oscar.

The Killers

★★★★ 1946 105min b/w

Director: Robert Siodmak
Screenplay: Anthony Veiller
Source: Story by Ernest Hemingway

A gangster stoically awaits the two men he knows have been sent to kill him. As an insurance investigator digs around, we learn through flashback the events leading to his death. This superbly plotted film noir hooks us from the off and never lets us go. It was remade, competently but rather more violently, in 1964.

Swede Lunn . . . . .Burt Lancaster
Jim Riordan . . . . .Edmond O'Brien
Kitty Collins . . . . .Ava Gardner
Big Jim Colfax . . . . .Albert Dekker
Lt. Sam Lubinsky . . . . .Sam Levene
Lilly Lubinsky . . . . .Virginia Christine
Jake . . . . .John Miljan
Max . . . . .William Conrad
Kenyon . . . . .Donald MacBride
Blinky . . . . .Jeff Corey

Quote 'I'm poison – to myself and everybody
around me!'

Psst! John Huston worked on the script,
although he was not credited • Elements of the
music by Miklos Rosza became famous when
they were used by the TV series *Dragnet* • This
was Lancaster's first movie, aged 32 • Ronald
Reagan played his last film role in the remake,
the one and only time he was a villain on
screen.

Kind Hearts and Coronets
★★★★ 1949 105min b/w

Director: Robert Hamer
Screenplay: Robert Hamer & John Dighton
Source: Novel, Israel Rank by Roy Horniman

Hating those disdainful relatives that stand
between him and the dukedom he considers
rightfully his, a young man increases his chance
of inheritance by doing away with those nearer
the title. In this splendid black comedy,
Guinness outdoes himself playing eight of the
D'Ascoynes, Price is suitably cold-blooded and
Greenwood is incredibly sexy. The wonderfully
witty and literate script keeps the film fresh no
matter how many times you watch it. Not just
one of the best of British comedies, but one of
the best films this country has ever produced.

Louis Mazzini . . . . .Dennis Price
Edith D'Ascoyne . . . . .Valerie Hobson
Sibella .Joan Greenwood
The Duke/ The Banker/
The Parson/ The General/
The Admiral/ Young Ascoyne
D'Ascoyne/ Young Henry/
Lady Agatha . . . . .Alec Guinness
Mama . . . . .Audrey Fildes
Hangman . . . . .Miles Malleson
Prison Governor . . . . .Clive Morton
Lionel . . . . .John Penrose
Lord High Steward . . . . .Hugh Griffith
Reporter .Arthur Lowe
Crown Counsel . . . . .Cecil Ramage

Quote 'It is so difficult to make a neat job of
killing people with whom one is not on friendly
terms.' • 'I was sorry about the girl, of course,
but took heart in the certainty that she had in
the course of the weekend already suffered a
fate popularly supposed to be worse than
death.' • 'Revenge is the dish which people of
taste prefer to eat cold.'

Psst! It was originally intended that Alec
Guinness would play just four members of the
D'Ascoyne family. Playing eight posed him
some problems. 'I had to ask myself from time
to time: "Which one am I now?" It would have
been quite disastrous to have faced the camera
in the make-up of the suffragette and spoken
like the admiral.' • For the scene with the
balloon, a Belgian balloonist was brought in.
Things didn't go according to plan, however,
and the chap couldn't bring the balloon down to
earth again for 50 miles • The ending was
originally much vaguer and thus more
satisfying. Then came word from the
Americans that the censors would not allow the
movie to be released as it stood. Crime could
not be seen to pay, so the final scene had to be
tacked on.

The King and I
★★★ 1956 133min c.

Director: Walter Lang
Screenplay: Ernest Lehman
Source: Musical by Rodgers and Hammerstein
from Book, *Anna and the King of Siam* by
Margaret Landon

An English governess locks horns with the autocratic King of Siam, with the inevitable
conclusion. Well, this *is* the movies. This hand-
somely-mounted production of the stage
musical retains its spirit of fun and is blessed by
some superb musical numbers, among them
'Getting to Know You' and 'Hello, Young Lovers'.
The same story had been filmed 10 years earlier in *Anne and the King of Siam*, an enjoyable
non-musical version with Irene Dunne and Rex
Harrison.

Anna Leonowens . . . . .Deborah Kerr
The King . . . . .Yul Brynner
Tuptim . . . . .Rita Moreno
Kralahome . . . . .Martin Benson
Lady Thiang . . . . .Terry Saunders
Louis Leonowens . . . . .Rex Thompson
British Ambassador . . . . .Alan Mowbray

Oscars Yul Brynner

Quote 'Et cetera. Et cetera. Et cetera.'

OOPS! While Brynner is singing 'It's a Puzzlement' his earring suddenly vanishes, then reappears. Just in case you missed it the first time, it does it several times and even swaps ears.

Psst! Brynner played the role for years on stage. When he died in 1985, it was estimated that he had performed the part about 4,000 times • Brynner had hair in an earlier film but shaved it to play the part of the King of Siam on Broadway. He kept it that way for the rest of his life • When he picked up his Oscar, he said he was the only person who had won the statuette who was as bald as Oscar was • Originally, Brynner had wanted to direct Marlon Brando in the movie version, but Brando said no and so Brynner agreed to star instead. Although not the director in name, his insistence on how it should be done – and several walk-outs – meant that he might as well have been • Although it is often said that Kerr's voice was dubbed by Marni Nixon, Kerr had taken singing lessons in preparation for the film. It is certainly Nixon singing on 'Hello Young Lovers' but it may only have been for the higher notes that she stood in for Kerr elsewhere. Nixon was also responsible for Audrey Hepburn's singing voice in *My Fair Lady* and for Natalie Wood's in *West Side Story*.

King Kong

★★★ 1933 100min b/w

Director: Merian C. Cooper & Ernest B. Schoedsack
Screenplay: James Creelman & Ruth Rose
Source: Story by Edgar Wallace.

A giant ape is brought back by an expedition to New York to be exhibited but it escapes and creates havoc. Like so many movies in which enormous effort was expended on the effects, the story isn't always strong enough to carry the strain. The effects themselves have held up surprisingly well considering how innovative they then were and there are many delights along the way, not least the less-than-subtle sexual subtext of this Beauty and the Beast tale. *The Son of Kong*, a disappointing sequel, followed immediately afterwards. It was, however, considerably better than the dreadful 1976 version with Jessica Lange.

Ann Darrow . . . . .Fay Wray
Carl Denham . . . . .Robert Armstrong
John Driscoll . . . . .Bruce Cabot
Capt. Englehorn . . . . .Frank Reicher
Charles Weston . . . . .Sam Hardy
Native chief . . . . .Noble Johnson
2nd mate Briggs . . . . .James Flavin
Socrates . . . . .Paul Porcasi

Blurb The Eighth Wonder Of The World.

Quote 'Wa saba ani mako. O tar vey, Rama Kong.' • 'Oh, no, it wasn't the airplanes. It was beauty killed the beast.' [Last line] • 'The tallest, darkest leading man in Hollywood.' [Wray on her co-star]

OOPS! As Fay Wray emerges from the water, her dress slips just enough to be momentarily revealing. Keep an eye on her after discussing food with the cook, Charley, though. Either she's cold or she's hot, if you get the drift • In New York, we hear that there were 12 deaths. But if you count them as they happen, you won't be able to get past 10 • If the natives wanted to keep King Kong safely penned in, why did they build a door in the wall big enough for him to get through?

Psst! Another of those movies that saved the studio, this time RKO, from financial disaster in the depths of the Great Depression • King Kong is mainly an 18-inch model, filmed by taking a frame of film, moving the model's limbs and eyes imperceptibly, then filming another frame, and so on. It took an hour to produce each second of screen time. For some shots, as where Wray is in Kong's paw, large models were built. There have been claims that some shots are of a man in a gorilla suit, but although possible these have never been substantiated • Because filming was so drawn out, Fay Wray starred in two other movies, *Doctor X* and *The Most Dangerous Game* at the same time • Both Ginger Rogers and Jean Harlow were considered for Fay Wray's part • Edgar Wallace was commissioned to pen the screenplay, but died soon afterwards • When the film was released again in 1938, RKO cut bits from some of the more sensational scenes to get them past the censors. Sadly, it is this version that is most often shown on TV although restored editions now exist • One scene that had made preview audiences scream or flee had people being eaten by giant insects and snakes after falling in a chasm. It was cut by the film-makers before release. This is the only one of the scenes cut over the years that has never been traced • Although the native language was pure gibberish, invented for the movie, the film couldn't get past the censors until an English translation was provided for them to peruse • Cooper and Schoedsack appear at the end as the Flight Commander and his observer delivering the death blow to Kong. They thought it was only fitting that they killed their own creation • Those who have taken their slide-rules to the film reckon that while Kong is 18 feet tall on the island, in New York he has grown to 24 feet • Hitler said this was his favourite movie.

The King of Comedy
★★★★ 1983 108min c.

Director: Martin Scorsese
Screenplay: Paul D. Zimmerman

This superb black comedy from Scorsese was a failure on release, but its reputation has deservedly grown since. De Niro is the stage-door johnny Rupert Pupkin who believes he can be a great comic like his hero Jerry Langford. When Langford brushes him off, Pupkin and his friends take more drastic action. A frighteningly realistic satire on the world of entertainment, it is extremely funny, providing you like your comedy black, with no milk or sugar. Surprisingly, Lewis turns out to be rather a fine actor.

Rupert Pupkin . . . . .Robert De Niro
Jerry Langford . . . . .Jerry Lewis
Rita . . . . .Diahnne Abbott
Masha . . . . .Sandra Bernhard
Also: Ed Herlihy, Liza Minnelli, Victor Borge, Tony Randall, Martin Scorsese

Quote 'Look, I figure it this way: better to be king for a night than schmuck for a lifetime.'

OOPS! When De Niro is in the restaurant with Abbott, watch how his glass keeps emptying and then refilling • There's a wonderful moment when De Niro and Abbott are arguing on the street, with a member of the public in a white shirt quite openly staring at the camera.

Psst! The credits thank the late Dan Johnson, Scorsese's former cook • As usual Scorsese's mother Catherine plays her part, here as the off-screen voice of Pupkin's mother. His both appears in a bar • There are cameos from Scorsese as the director of the TV show, as well as Liza Minnelli, Victor Borge and Tony Randall • Scorsese wanted Johnny Carson for the Lewis part, but he wouldn't do it • If you look carefully at the start of the film, you'll see Mary Elizabeth Mastrantonio in the crowd. This was her first film part, but it was almost completely cut out of the final version.

Kings Row
★★★ 1942 127min b/w

Director: Sam Wood
Screenplay: Casey Robinson
Source: Novel by Henry Bellamann

It's best known for containing Ronald Reagan's best movie role and one of the most famous of all movie lines. But this look through the stuff swept under the carpet of a small American town in the early years of the century is still a very superior and enjoyable soap.

Randy Monoghan . . . . .Ann Sheridan
Parris Mitchell . . . . .Robert Cummings
Drake McHugh . . . . .Ronald Reagan
Dr. Alexander Tower . . . . .Claude Rains
Cassandra Tower . . . . .Betty Field
Dr. Henry Gordon . . . . .Charles Coburn
Harriet Gordon . . . . .Judith Anderson
Mme. Von Eln . . . . .Maria Ouspenskaya
Louise Gordon . . . . .Nancy Coleman
Col. Skeffington . . . . .Harry Davenport
Elise Sandor . . . . .Karen Verne
Sam Winters . . . . .Minor Watson
Randy (as child) . . . . .Ann E. Todd

Blurb The Town They Talk Of In Whispers.

Quote 'KING'S ROW...A GOOD TOWN TO LIVE IN.' • 'Where's the rest of me?'

Psst! The film was made the year before, but although based on a best-selling novel the studio delayed its release because they felt it was so depressing • Even so, elements of the novel were softened or cut for the film, such as the odd death from cancer and a mercy killing. Joseph Breen, who was chief censor, thought it 'a very questionable undertaking'. • Bette Davis and Olivia De Havilland both wanted to play the part that went to Betty Field. Ida Lupino turned it down, refusing to play yet another neurotic • Reagan talked of little but politics during production. Robert Cummings apparently said to him at one point: 'Ronnie, you ought to run for President.' – 'President of What?' – 'Of the United States.' – 'Bob,' came the plaintive response, 'Don't you like my acting either?'

Kipps
★★ 1941 110min b/w

Director: Carol Reed
Screenplay: Sidney Gilliat
Source: Novel by H.G. Wells

A draper's assistant inherits a fortune but doesn't find it terribly easy fitting into high society. Despite the solid reputation of the director and writer, this is an uninspiring, almost plodding, rendition of Wells' tale. It was remade as the musical *Half a Sixpence* in 1967 which had some good musical numbers but even more problems with the story.

Arthur Kipps . . . . .Michael Redgrave
Helen Walshingham . . . . .Diana Wynyard
Harry Chitterlow . . . . .Arthur Riscoe
Ann Pornick . . . . .Phyllis Calvert
Chester Coote . . . . .Max Adrian
Mrs. Walshingham . . . . .Helen Haye
Ronnie Walshingham . . . . .Michael Wilding
Shalford . . . . .Lloyd Pearson
Buggins . . . . .Edward Rigby
Miss Mergle . . . . .Hermione Baddeley
Flo Bates . . . . .Betty Ann Davies
Old Kipps . . . . .Frank Pettingell
Also: Beatrice Varley, George Carney, Irene Browne, Philip Frost, Diana Calderwood, Kathleen Harrison, Felix Aylmer

Psst! A prologue from H.G. Wells himself was filmed, but it was cut from the movie because of his peculiar high voice.

Kiss Me Deadly
★★★ 1955 105min b/w

Director: Robert Aldrich
Screenplay: A.I. Bezzerides
Source: Novel by Mickey Spillane

Truly bizarre, apocalyptic film noir with thuggish Mike Hammer brutally trying to track down a suitcase containing the Great Whatsit. Hammer is one of the least sympathetic heroes in the history of film. Everything about this extraordinary movie is strange and fascinating, from the back-to-front credits to the obscure camera angles. Check out Hammer's reel-to-reel ansaphone in the wall too.

Mike Hammer . . . . .Ralph Meeker
Dr. Soberin . . . . .Albert Dekker
Carl Evello . . . . .Paul Stewart
Gabrielle/Lily Carver . . . . .Gaby Rodgers
Velda .Maxine Cooper
Christina . . . . .Cloris Leachman
Pat . . . . .Wesley Addy
Eddie Eager . . . . .Juano Hernandez
Nick . . . . .Nick Dennis
Friday . . . . .Marian Carr
Sugar . . . . .Jack Lambert

Charlie Max .Jack Elam
Carmen Trivago . . . . .Fortunio Bonanova
Truck driver . . . . .Strother Martin

Blurb I Don't Care What You Do To Me, Mike – Just Do It Fast.

Quote 'If we don't make that bus stop... remember me' • 'You're one of those self-indulgent males who thinks about nothing but his clothes, his car, himself. Bet you do push-ups every morning just to keep your belly hard.'

OOPS! Time accelerates when Hammer buys some popcorn in the street. The clock in the background shows him about to get the popcorn at 2.10 but it's 10 minutes later when he moves on up the street.

Psst! Tarantino buffs have noted that the glowing suitcase which Travolta opens in *Pulp Fiction* is a nod to this film's finale.

Kiss Me Kate
★★★ 1953 109min c.

Director: George Sidney
Screenplay: Dorothy Kingsley
Source: Play by Cole Porter, Sam Spewack, Bella Spewack from *The Taming of the Shrew* by Shakespeare

The actors in a musical production of *The Taming of the Shrew* quarrel as much off stage as on. Although generally a spirited and enjoyable musical, it isn't half as funny as it thinks it is. What's more, we also have to endure 'Wunderbar', surely one of the worst songs in any musical? Still, much can be forgiven for the joys of Wynn and Whitmore in 'Brush Up Your Shakespeare' and the great tap dancing of Miller.

Lilli Vanessi/Katherine . . . . . . .Kathryn Grayson
Fred Graham/Petruchio . . . . .Howard Keel
Lois Lane/Bianca . . . . .Ann Miller
Lippy . . . . .Keenan Wynn
Gremio . . . . .Bobby Van
Bill Calhoun/Lucentio . . . . .Tommy Rall
Slug .James Whitmore
Hortensio .Bob Fosse

Psst! The film was made in 3-D but was almost never shown that way as the craze had virtually died out by the time it was released. It explains why things keep being flung towards the camera • Bob Fosse appears in the number 'From This Moment On'.

Kiss of Death

★★ 1947 98min b/w

Director: Henry Hathaway
Screenplay: Ben Hecht & Charles Lederer

When a gangster turns informer, a vicious killer is sent to silence him. Once considered *the* word in tough, gritty, crime dramas, it hasn't stood the test of time!. Mature not only looks like a statue but acts like one, while Widmark's unhinged psychopath now seems well over the top. His pushing an old lady in a wheelchair down the stairs is still shocking, though.

Nick Bianco	Victor Mature
D'Angelo	Brian Donlevy
Nettie	Coleen Gray
Tommy Udo	Richard Widmark
Sgt. William Cullen	Karl Malden
Earl Howser	Taylor Holmes
Ma Rizzo	Mildred Dunnock
Max Schulte	Millard Mitchell
Judge	Robert Keith

Quote 'You know what I do with squealers? I let 'em have it in the belly so they can roll around for a long time thinking it over.'

Psst! Director Hathaway insisted upon shooting the entire film in New York. Although this film wasn't the first to do so, it was so effective that it became almost obligatory for future crime movies set in the Big Apple to be shot there • This was the screen debut of Widmark.

Kiss of the Spider Woman

★★★★ 1985 119min c&b/w

Director: Hector Babenco
Screenplay: Leonard Schrader
Source: Novel by Manuel Puig

A flamboyant gay shares a South American prison cell with a radical activist and reminisces about old Hollywood movies. But the relationship between the two is not what it appears. This is one of those rare films which tackles a host of tricky issues and emerges with flying colours. Funny, scary, original and thought-provoking, it has a brilliant performance from Hurt. One of the great movies of the 80s.

Molina	William Hurt
Valentin	Raul Julia
Leni Lamaison/Marta	Sonia Braga
Warden	Jose Lewgoy

Oscars William Hurt

Quote 'It's just a romance. But it's *so* beautiful.'

Psst! Hurt's part was originally to have been played by Burt Lancaster, but he had to withdraw for a heart operation • Julia lost 30 pounds, reckoning that 'there are no fat revolutionaries' • The actors worked for expenses only, deferring their salaries against box office receipts • At one point, Hurt's beach house was broken into by thieves high on drugs. They held him hostage with a gun at his head, teasing him for half an hour before escaping • Hurt is said to detest California so much that he has to have his ticket to New York about his person at all times, even when filming, when it may be hidden in swimming trunks or, as in this case, in the rags he wears in the prison cell.

Klute

★★★ 1971 114min c.

Director: Alan J. Pakula
Screenplay: Andy Lewis & Dave Lewis

A private eye trying to find a scientist who has disappeared gets involved with a hooker. Although the thriller aspects aren't always terribly convincing, as a character study it stands out, with Fonda giving one of her best and most believable performances as the call-girl who dare not let her professional front drop.

Bree Daniels	Jane Fonda
John Klute	Donald Sutherland
Peter Cable	Charles Cioffi
Frank Ligourin	Roy Scheider
Arlyn Page	Dorothy Tristan
Trina	Rita Gam
Goldfarb's secretary	Jean Stapleton
Sugarman	Richard B. Shull

Oscars Jane Fonda

Quote 'Men have paid $200 for me and here you are, turning down a freebie. You could get a perfectly good dishwasher for that.'

Psst! Fonda spend a month studying the life of high-class hookers • Not all those in the crew respected Fonda's outspoken views on Vietnam and they hung out an American flag on set.

The Knack...and How to Get It

★★★ 1965 84min b/w

Director: Richard Lester
Screenplay: Charles Wood
Source: Based on the play by Ann Jellicoe

Lester's attempt to duplicate the success of *A Hard Day's Night* with a look at swinging 60s London hasn't worn the years quite as happily. But there's still much to enjoy in this tale of meek Crawford pleading with Brooks to explain his success with women. The gags come thick and fast and the camera never stops long enough for us to catch our breath.

Nancy Jones . . . . .Rita Tushingham
Tolen . . . . .Ray Brooks
Colin .Michael Crawford
Tom . . . . .Donal Donnelly
Angry father . . . . .John Bluthal
Picture owner . . . . .Peter Copley
Tom's landlady . . . . .Dandy Nichols
Water skier . . . . .Charlotte Rampling

Psst! Jacqueline Bisset can be seen briefly, while Charlotte Rampling appears quickly as a water-skier.

Kramer vs. Kramer

★★★ 1979 105min c.

Director: Robert Benton
Screenplay: Robert Benton
Source: Novel by Avery Corman

A mother ups sticks to 'find herself', leaving dad to endure a crash course in single parenting. If you like nothing more than snuggling into the sofa with a box of tissues than this emotionally draining tug of war melodrama, as mom returns to claim her child, will be for you. There are those, however, who can't stand this sort of thing, particularly as Streep is so extraordinarily mannered in this film.

Ted Kramer . . . . .Dustin Hoffman
Joanna Kramer . . . . .Meryl Streep
Margaret Phelps . . . . .Jane Alexander
Billy Kramer . . . . .Justin Henry
John Shaunessy . . . . .Howard Duff
Jim O'Connor . . . . .George Coe
Phyllis Bernard . . . . .JoBeth Williams
Gressen . . . . .Bill Moor

Oscars Best Picture, Best Director, Best Screenplay (adapted), Dustin Hoffman, Meryl Streep

Blurb There Are Three Sides To This Love Story.

Quote 'I'd like to know what law is it that says that a woman is a better parent simly by virtue of her sex.' • 'I'd like to thank my mother and father for not practising birth control.' [Hoffman collecting his Oscar]

Psst! Originally François Truffaut was to direct, until writer Benton demanded to have a crack • Streep rewrote most of her own dialgoue and it's said that she and Hoffman clashed often during filming • 6-year-old Justin Henry became the youngest actor to be nominated for an Oscar • Hoffman divorced from his own wife, Anne Bryne, around this time.

The Lady Eve

★★★ 1941 97min b/w

Director: Preston Sturges
Screenplay: Preston Sturges
Source: Play, *The Faithful Heart* by Monckton Hoffe

A shapely confidence trickster gets a shy millionaire in her sights but finds herself falling for him. Although once considered the epitome of sophisticated romantic comedy, the mechanics of the plot are far too visible and Fonda is so wooden he could pass for a cigar-store Indian. There's no denying, though, the comic ability or the amazing force of Stanwyck's sexual attraction when she turns the heat on. If only the film didn't have such an implausible ending. It was remade badly as *The Birds and the Bees* in 1956.

Jean Harrington . . . . .Barbara Stanwyck
Charles Pike . . . . .Henry Fonda
'Colonel' Harry Harrington . . . . .Charles Coburn
Mr. Pike . . . . .Eugene Pallette
Mugsy . . . . .William Demarest
Sir Alfred McGlennan Keith . . . . .Eric Blore
Gerald .Melville Cooper
Martha . . . . .Martha O'Driscoll
Mrs. Pike . . . . .Janet Beecher
Burrows . . . . .Robert Greig
Pike's chef . . . . .Luis Alberni
Steward .Jimmy Conlin
Steward . . . . .Al Bridge
Lawyer . . . . .Arthur Hoyt

Quote 'See anything you like?' • 'Hopsie, you don't know very much about girls. The best ones aren't as good as you probably think and the bad ones aren't as bad...not nearly as bad.' • 'Would you care to come in and see Emma?' – 'That's a new one, isn't it?' • 'They say a moonlit deck is a woman's business office.'

Psst! Famous costume designer Edith Head even made a diamond necklace for Emma, the snake: 'The only problem was that it was the hibernating season for snakes and Emma just wanted to sleep, so she proceeded to shed her skin in the middle of production...We finally had to let her do scenes without the necklace, one of my few costuming failures.'

The Lady from Shanghai
★★★ 1948 87min b/w

Director: Orson Welles
Screenplay: Orson Welles
Source: Novel, *If I Die Before I Wake* by Sherwood King

A seaman gets dragged into a murder plot by a *femme fatale*. This beautiful film noir is incredibly confusing the first time round. Don't worry, though. It's equally inexplicable on further viewings. But it remains one of the most visually dazzling thrillers ever, particularly in the final much-copied Hall of Mirrors sequence, and it's all cloaked in an effective air of mystery.

Elsa Bannister . . . . .Rita Hayworth
Michael O'Hara . . . . .Orson Welles
Arthur Bannister . . . . .Everett Sloane
Grisby . . . . .Glenn Anders
Sidney Broome . . . . .Ted de Corsia
Judge .Erskine Sanford
Goldie . . . . .Gus Schilling
Cab driver . . . . .Harry Shannon

Quote 'When I start out to make a fool of myself, there's very little can stop me.' • 'The only way to stay out of trouble is to grow old, so I guess I'll concentrate on that. Maybe I'll live so long that I'll forget her. Maybe I'll die trying.' [Last line]

Psst! Desperately needing cash for a play, Welles tried borrowing money from Columbia head Harry Cohn. He offered to direct a movie for him and mentioned he knew of a great thriller. When Cohn wanted to know what it was, Welles happened to spot someone nearby reading *If I Die Before I Wake*, so he precised its plot. He got his loan in return for making the movie, with the title changed to *The Lady from Shanghai*. Who knows why? There's nobody from Shanghai in the film • There was shock among the Columbia bigwigs when they saw that Hayworth's gorgeous red hair had been transformed into in a blonde bob. Columbia head Harry Cohn said: 'The six people who saw what Orson Welles did to Rita wanted to kill him, but they had to get behind me in line.' Welles' marriage to Hayworth was in trouble, and some have speculated that he may have tried to destroy her screen image out of personal animosity • As so often, Welles lost control of the film at the editing stage. He was furious at the way the studio mucked around with it, believing they had destroyed it. He also claimed that the music chosen was less suitable for a thriller and more sensible for a Disney cartoon • Welles borrowed his friend Errol Flynn's yacht, Zaca, for the sea scenes. Although unseen, it is Flynn sailing the boat.

The Ladykillers
★★ 1955 97min c.

Director: Alexander Mackendrick
Screenplay: William Rose

A gang of crooks planning a robbery are hindered by their seemingly potty landlady. Many people consider this one of the best of all comedies, which just goes to show how varied tastes can be. For a black comedy to work, there ought to be not just a dark plot but also some element of humour. But the script makes little concession in this direction. Instead, in a desperate attempt to inject some laughs, we get Guinness with a set of silly teeth and the others overacting like mad. Thanks largely to Johnson as the landlady, it's quite watchable. But funny it ain't.

Prof. Marcus . . . . .Alec Guinness
Mrs. Louisa Alexandra Wilberforce . . . . . . .Katie
Johnson
Maj. Courteney . . . . .Cecil Parker
Harry Robinson . . . . .Peter Sellers
Louis Harvey . . . . .Herbert Lom
One-Round Lawson . . . . .Danny Green
Police Superintendent . . . . .Jack Warner
Barrow Boy . . . . .Frankie Howerd
Cab Driver . . . . .Kenneth Connor
Lettice . . . . .Edie Martin
Police Sergeant . . . . .Philip Stainton

The Lady Vanishes
★★★ 1938 97min b/w

Director: Alfred Hitchcock
Screenplay: Sidney Gilliat & Frank Launder
Source: Novel, *The Wheel Spins* by Ethel Lina White

Long considered one of the greatest of all thrillers of all time, this tale of a young woman prying into the mysterious disappearance of an old lady on a train now looks distinctly cheesy round the edges. Although Charters and Caldicott as the cricket-mad buffers are wonderful and the young leads are fine, some of the rest of the actors look as if they belong to the School of Coarse Acting and it is also impossible to overlook Hitch's usual dreadful back-projection work and the cheapo models. Although the script is witty, unless you can believe in what is happening on screen, you can't really be expected to be biting your nails in fear. It's all jolly good English fun. It just isn't terribly thrilling any more. The least said about the 1979 version with Cybill Shepherd and Elliott Gould the better.

Iris Henderson	Margaret Lockwood
Gilbert Redman	Michael Redgrave
Dr. Hartz	Paul Lukas
Miss Froy	Dame May Whitty
Caldicott	Naunton Wayne
Charters	Basil Radford
Eric Todhunter	Cecil Parker
'Mrs' Todhunter	Linden Travers
Baroness	Mary Clare
Hotel manager	Emile Boreo
Blanche	Googie Withers

Quote 'Never climb a fence if you can sit on it. An old Foreign Office proverb.' • 'I've been everywhere and done everything. I've eaten caviar at Cannes, sausage rolls at the dogs. I've played baccarat at Biarritz and darts with the rural dean. What is there left for me but marriage?'

OOPS! Look carefully at the window when Whitty writes the name 'Froy' on it. In between shots it moves and looks nothing like the first version.

Psst! The original title was *Lost Lady* but an American company had already registered that title • Hitchcock was apparently the second choice for director after the American Roy William Neill, who had directed *Dr. Syn* • Michael Redgrave was also starring each night in a play in the West End and regarded this as a job for hire, having little respect at the time for movies • Hitch appears towards the end of the film at Victoria Station smoking a cigarette • The film was so popular in America that it paved the way for Hitchcock's move there. After *Jamaica Inn*, he made only two more movies in Britain, *Frenzy* and *Stage Fright* • The second unit went off to film in Yugoslavia, but they were ordered out of the country because the script contained a shot of Nazis goose-stepping • Charters and Caldicott were originally called Charters and Spanswick. The pair appeared in other movies like *Night Train to Munich* as well as a radio series. Then they continued under the different names of

Spenser and Woolcot. Spanswick wasn't lost. Named after Gilliat's gardener, he resurfaced in *I See a Dark Stranger* when Wayne and Radford proved difficult.

The Last Detail
★★★ 1973 104min c.

Director: Hal Ashby
Screenplay: Robert Towne
Source: Novel by Darryl Ponicsan

Two sailors are picked to escort a young prisoner to the place where he'll serve his eight year sentence for stealing $40. They determine to make it a trip he won't forget. Nicholson is superb in this gritty, often funny, but ultimately downbeat drama. The language in the script is still quite salty.

Buddusky	Jack Nicholson
Mulhall	Otis Young
Meadows	Randy Quaid
Master-at-Arms	Clifton James
Young prostitute	Carol Kane
Marine Duty Office	Michael Moriarty
Nancy	Nancy Allen
Kathleen	Kathleen Miller
Donna	Luana Anders
Nicheren Shoshu disciple	Gilda Radner

Quote 'It isn't exactly a recruiting film.' [Nicholson]

Psst! The Navy would not cooperate with the film-makers because of the salty language and the sailors' less than exemplary behaviour • Gilda Radnercan be spotted in a bit part in the church.

Last Holiday
★★★ 1950 88min b/w

Director: Henry Cass
Screenplay: J.B. Priestley

When a man is told that he has not got long to live, he determines that his last days will go with a swing. Along the way, he improves the lives of those he meets. Thanks to Guinness, this droll and occasionally tearful comedy-drama lingers fondly in the memory long afterwards.

George Bird	Alec Guinness
Sheila Rockingham	Beatrice Campbell
Mrs. Poole	Kay Walsh
Insp. Wilton	Bernard Lee

Chalfont ....Wilfrid Hyde-White
Joe Clarence ....Sidney James
Sir Trevor Lampington ....Ernest Thesiger
Gambini ....Grégoire Aslan
Lady Oswington ....Muriel George
Daisy Clarence ....Jean Colin
Miss Fox ....Esma Cannon
Also: Brian Worth, Arthur Howard, David McCallum

Psst! Look out for David McCallum, with *The Man from Uncle* still in the future, as the 'blind fiddler'.

The Last Picture Show
★★★★ 1971 118min b/w

Director: Peter Bogdanovich
Screenplay: Larry McMurtry & Peter Bogdanovich
Source: Novel by McMurtry.

A beautiful slice-of-life look centring on the lives of assorted youngsters in a fading Midwestern American town. Although ultimately rather bleak, it is a beautifully observed piece of nostalgia. Some grumble that Bogdanovich's style is terribly derivative but, at a time when directors were cramming any old gimmick into their movies in a desperate attempt to liven things up, it now comes as a relief to see something from that period that isn't so showy. It was followed, 19 years later, by the dismal sequel *Texasville*.

Sonny Crawford ....Timothy Bottoms
Duane Jackson ....Jeff Bridges
Jacy Farrow ....Cybill Shepherd
Sam the Lion ....Ben Johnson
Ruth Popper ....Cloris Leachman
Lois Farrow ....Ellen Burstyn
Genevieve ....Eileen Brennan
Abilene ....Clu Gulager
Lester Marlow ....Randy Quaid
Teacher ....John Hillerman
Chester ....Noble Willingham
Charlene Duggs ....Sharon Taggart
Bill ....Sam Bottoms

Oscars Ben Johnson, Cloris Leachman

Showing Father of the Bride • Red River.

Psst! When Ben Johnson originally refused to do the film, Bogdanovich told him that he would win an Oscar if he did it. Leachman claims he said the same to her, claiming that anyone playing her part would win one • John Hillerman became best known for his continuing role in TV's *Magnum* with Tom Selleck.

The Last Seduction
★★★★ 1994 109min c.

Director: John Dahl
Screenplay: Steve Barancik

Who says they don't make *femme fatales* like they used to? Scheming, sexy Fiorentino is one of the best ever. First she runs off with the cash that hubbie stole from the guys whose first and last names end in vowels. Then she hides out with dumb Berg, wrapping him round her little finger and treating him as nothing more than a sex object. Completely amoral, she is totally irresistible in this clever little thriller that twists and turns so many times we have to cling on for dear life. Absolutely, unequivocally superb.

Bridget Gregory ....Linda Fiorentino
Mike Swale ....Peter Berg
Clay Gregory ....Bill Pullman
Frank Griffith ..................J.T. Walsh
Harlan ....Bill Nunn
Bob Trotter ....Herb Mitchell

Quote 'Anybody checked you for a heartbeat lately?' • 'How about going on an actual date sometime?' • 'Maybe it's my quaint small town morals, but I don't do murder.' – 'You would if you loved me.'

Psst! Although generally reckoned to have given one of the best performances of the year, Fiorentino was disqualified for being nominated from an Oscar nomination because the movie had premiered on a TV channel.

Last Tango in Paris
★ 1973 129min c.

Director: Bernardo Bertolucci
Screenplay: Bernardo Bertolucci & Franco Arcalli

How things can change in 20 years. Banned, censored and much debated, this doom-laden account of an American widower's anonymous affair with a young woman was a major scandal in the early 70s. Now no amount of Parisian scenery, Brando's mumbling or Schneider's buttered butt will convince that this is anything but a tedious, self-indulgent bore.

Paul ....Marlon Brando
Jeanne ....Maria Schneider
Tom ....Jean-Pierre Léaud
Concierge ....Darling Legitimus
TV script girl ....Catherine Sola
TV cameraman ....Mauro Marchetti

Quote 'I don't think Bertolucci knew what *Last Tango in Paris* was about. And *I* didn't know what it was about. He went around telling everybody it was about his prick.' [Brando]
• 'When I read *Last Tango in Paris*, I didn't see anything that worried me. I was 20. I didn't want to be a star, much less a scandalous actress – simply to be in cinema. Later, I realised I'd been completely manipulated by Bertolucci and Brando...People were insulting me in the street. In restaurants, waiters would bring me butter with a funny smile.' [Schneider]

Psst! In Britain, just ten seconds were cut out by the censors. They were restored in 1977
• The film was prosecuted in Italy under the obscenity laws. The director argued that it was not an erotic film but a film about eroticism
• Apparently Hollywood offered Bertolucci the chance to make *Last Tango in Paris 2*. 'I reminded them Brando had died at the end, but they said he'd gone to hospital and recovered.'
• Bertolucci had approached several actresses for the lead, among them Catherine Deneuve. Brando hadn't been his first choice either, but Jean-Louis Trintignant turned it down
• Schneider's frizzy hair sparked off a resurgence in perming, which had all but died out • Brando improvised the scene where he tells Schneider about his childhood. It was filmed in just one take and Bertolucci claims that it reveals more about the real Brando than almost anything else he has done in the movies
• The appearance of Truffaut's star, Jean-Pierre Léaud, as a New Wave director is an in-joke, though not many split their sides.

Laura

★★★★ 1944 88min b/w

Director: Otto Preminger
Screenplay: Jay Dratler, Samuel Hoffenstein & Betty Reinhardt
Source: Novel by Vera Caspary

'Tis Pity She's a Corpse. A detective finds himself falling in love with the young woman whose murder he is investigating. Obsession has never been as mesmerising as in this ever-so-stylish and witty film noir. It's easy to understand Andrews' feelings towards the enigmatic Tierney. But the best thing is undoubtedly the egotistical, rude and narcissistic Webb who can't cope with having to love someone else. With scenes like his typing in the bath, he's one of the most memorable characters in the movies.

Laura Hunt	Gene Tierney
Mark McPherson	Dana Andrews
Waldo Lydecker	Clifton Webb
Shelby Carpenter	Vincent Price
Anne Treadwell	Judith Anderson
Bessie Clary	Dorothy Adams
McAvity	James Flavin
Corey	Grant Mitchell
Louise	Kathleen Howard
Bullitt	Clyde Fillmore

Quote 'I shall never forget the weekend Laura died. A silver sun burned through the sky like a huge magnifying glass. It was the hottest Sunday in my recollection. I felt as if I were the only human being left in New York.' • 'It's lavish, but I call it home.' • 'Haven't you heard of science's newest triumph – the doorbell?'
• 'In my case, self-absorption is completely justified. I have never discovered any other subject quite so worthy of my attention.'
• 'I don't use a pen. I write with a goose quill dipped in venom.'

Psst! Originally this was planned to be a B-picture. Although Preminger had developed the project, studio head Darryl Zanuck wouldn't let him direct it, only produce it. Rouben Mamoulian was hired as director but then, after the start of filming, he was fired. Preminger, whom Zanuck hired reluctantly because he couldn't find anybody else, started all over again, even junking the costumes and a picture of Laura that had been painted by Mamoulian's wife • Hedy Lamarr and Jennifer Jones turned down the lead • Waldo Lydecker is modelled in large part on critic Alexander Woolcott, the famous member of the Algonquin Round Table who was also the inspiration for *The Man Who Came to Dinner* • Although Clifton Webb had made a few silent films, this was his first sound movie • Preminger wanted to use Duke Ellington's 'Sophisticated Lady' as the theme. When composer David Raksin objected one Friday, Preminger gave him till Monday to come up with something better. He wrote 'Laura' immediately after opening an unexpected letter from his wife, saying that she was leaving him. After the movie was a smash, Johnny Mercer was asked to write some lyrics. The record went to the top of the charts
• Zanuck didn't like the ending and reassembled the cast to shoot another. Fortunately, Walter Winchell saw the revised version and said he didn't understand the conclusion. So the original was restored
• Irritatingly, three minutes of dialogue were cut after the film was released. The full version should be 88, not 85 minutes.

The Lavender Hill Mob

★★★★ 1951 82min b/w

Director: Charles Crichton
Screenplay: T.E.B. Clarke

Along with *Kind Hearts and Coronets* and *Passport to Pimlico*, this is one of the best things Ealing Studios ever produced. A meek clerk dreams up a way to rob his employers – The Bank of England. Even without the delicious humour, this would be an enjoyable heist movie. But thanks to the wonderful tongue-in-cheek script and stand-out performances from Guinness and Holloway, the film is an absolute joy from the beginning until the very final moments. What a shame, though, that it was decreed that crime couldn't be seen to pay.

Henry Holland . . . . .Alec Guinness
Pendlebury . . . . .Stanley Holloway
Lackery .Sidney James
Shorty . . . . .Alfie Bass
Mrs. Chalk . . . . .Marjorie Fielding
Miss Evesham . . . . .Edie Martin
Farrow . . . . .John Gregson
Godwin . . . . .Gibb McLaughlin
Chiquita . . . . .Audrey Hepburn
Turner .Ronald Adam
Station Sergeant . . . . .Clive Morton
Clayton .Sydney Tafler
Senora Gallardo . . . . .Marie Burke
British Ambassador . . . . . . .Michael Trubshawe
Also: James Fox, Peter Bull

Oscars Best Story and Screenplay

Quote 'I like the bullion office. It holds all I ever wished for.'

OOPS! During the car chase the Lavender Hill Mob jump from west London to east of St. Paul's in the twinkling of an eye.

Psst! When writer 'Tibby' Clarke was stumped for a way for Guinness to rob the Bank of England, he approached the Bank itself to see if they could help. His appointments form read: 'Information required on means of stealing gold bullion'. Amazingly, the Bank set up a committee to work out how somebody could gain access to their vaults.● Keep your eyes peeled for the 22-year-old Audrey Hepburn as Chiquita in the first scene • James Fox has a small role as Gregory, although he is on the credits as William Fox • The film was banned in Czechoslovakia and Hungary. It was also prohibited to be shown in Northern Rhodesia, apparently on the orders of the British Government, which felt it might undermine respect for the law there.

Lawrence of Arabia

★★★★ 1962 216min c.

Director: David Lean
Screenplay: Robert Bolt
Source: Autobiography, *The Seven Pillars of Wisdom* by T.E. Lawrence

This epic tale of British war hero Lawrence leading the Arabs against the Turks in World War I is one of the greatest spectacles the cinema has produced. Although the photography and the use of the wide screen is breathtaking, as is the score by Maurice Jarre, much of its success is down to just one man, O'Toole. He gets across the determination and near madness of the man, about whom the script really tells us far too little. It's a shame the second half is less memorable than the first but this is less of a problem in the restored version. See it on the small screen and you really are missing out on something special.

T.E. Lawrence . . . . .Peter O'Toole
Sherif Ali . . . . .Omar Sharif
Prince Feisal . . . . .Alec Guinness
Auda Abu Tayi . . . . .Anthony Quinn
Gen. Allenby . . . . .Jack Hawkins
Jackson Bentley . . . . •Arthur Kennedy
The Bey . . . . .Jose Ferrer
Col. Harry Brighton . . . . .Anthony Quayle
Dryden . . . . .Claude Rains
Gen. Murray . . . . .Donald Wolfit
Farraj . . . . .Michel Ray

Oscars Best Picture, Best Director

Quote 'He was a poet, a scholar and a mighty warrior. He was also the most shameless exhibitionist since Barnum and Bailey.' • 'Of course it hurts. The trick is not *showing* that it hurts.' • 'Of course I'm the man for the job. What is the job, by the way?' • 'A man who tells lies merely hides the truth, but a man who tells half-lies has forgotten where he put it.' • 'I should not have recognised my brother.' [Prof. Arnold Lawrence]

Psst! Director Lean and producer Spiegel had previously collaborated on *The Bridge on the River Kwai*. They briefly considered a film about Gandhi before settling on Lawrence • Although Lawrence's brother approved of the early draft of the script, he publicly attacked the final version and would not let the movie use the title of Lawrence's memoirs, *The Seven Pillars of Wisdom* • Lawrence's biographer Stanley Weintraub said: 'Its Lawrence bears much the same relation to Colonel Thomas Edward Lawrence that Elizabeth Taylor's Cleopatra does to that famous lady.' • Marlon Brando and Albert Finney were among those considered for the lead. Finney was offered it, but turned it down. Producer Sam Spiegel said of O'Toole: 'You make a star, you make a monster.' • When approached about *Lawrence*, O'Toole, who had only made a minor Disney movie, *Kidnapped*, is reputed to have asked if it was a speaking part • O'Toole had his nose and squint straightened before joining the production • There was not one speaking role for a woman in the entire movie • Jack Hawkins' part was dubbed • The film took two years to make, a year of that on location in the desert. The budget rose from an initial estimate of $2.5m to a final $13m • The famous shot of Snarif approaching through the desert was actually carried out by a stand-in, until the moment for him to dismount • Lean was not one to cosset his actors. They filmed for a year in 120-degree heat in the desert. The scene with O'Toole looking into the sandstorm with his eyes open took 19 takes and caused the actor great pain • O'Toole insisted on doing his own stunts. As the whole movie couldn't be insured, if he was seriously hurt the film would have had to be shelved. It's likely most modern stars *would* consider themselves seriously hurt by what O'Toole suffered. He was bitten by a camel at one point, losing the use of two of his fingers for a while. This was in addition to assorted pulled ligaments, strains, severe sunburn and a cracked skull and concussion. He lost two stone during filming but, as he later said, there were compensations: 'How many young men get to live with Bedouins for a year?' • Filming the motorbike scene, O'Toole's bike was actually mounted on a trailer. The towing bar came loose at one point and the trailer careered away. For a moment, it looked as if history could have bene repeated, but O'Toole was not seriously hurt • O'Toole learnt to ride a camel for the film, only becoming comfortable when he put a layer of foam rubber under the saddle blanket. It was an innovation that was then copied by Bedouin tribesman working on the movie • While Alec Guinness had a swank caravan to keep him comfortable, O'Toole was apparently given nothing more luxurious than a deckchair to relax in • The only way Spiegel could get Lean to finish the movie was by arranging for it to be shown at the Royal Command Film Performance • It won seven Oscars • When O'Toole returned to the UK, he downed as much alcohol as he could and was done for drunk driving, losing his licence for a year • He couldn't face watching the film for another 20 years although, when he did finally see it, he professed himself pleased. Noel

Coward told him: 'If you had been any prettier, it would have been *Florence of Arabia* • In 1989, Lean oversaw a newly-minted restored version. 20 minutes had been cut between the premiere and the first general release and another 15 minutes was dropped when it was re-released in 1970. The cast had to redub some of their dialogue for the new version. O'Toole's voice had changed in the intervening 26 years, so it was electronically altered to sound younger.

The League of Gentlemen
★★★ 1960 116min b/w

Director: Basil Dearden
Screenplay: Bryan Forbes
Source: Novel by John Boland

An officer reacts angrily to being kicked out of the army by organising what he hopes will be the perfect robbery, using military methods and blackmailed colleagues to execute the plan. While the Americans would turn this into a dark, moody film noir, here it's treated with a substantial sense of humour. It's a jolly good show from all concerned but suffers, as did other crime caper films of the time, from an ending that leaves the audience feeling it has been robbed.

Hyde	Jack Hawkins
Race	Nigel Patrick
Mycroft	Roger Livesey
Lexy	Richard Attenborough
Porthill	Bryan Forbes
Stevens	Kieron Moore
Rupert Rutland-Smith	Terence Alexander
Bunny Warren	Robert Coote
Weaver	Norman Bird
Peggy	Melissa Stribling
Elizabeth	Nanette Newman
Molly Weaver	Doris Hare
CSM	David Lodge
Wylie	Patrick Wymark
Capt. Saunders	Gerald Harper
Grogan	Brian Murray
Ballet dancer	Oliver Reed

Psst! Bryan Forbes wrote the script as well as acting in the film • Oliver Reed can be glimpsed briefly as a ballet dancer!

The Leopard
★★★ 1963 205min c.

Director: Luchino Visconti
Screenplay: Luchino Visconti & Others

Source: Novel, *Il Gattopardo* by Giuseppe Tomasi de Lampedusa

Burt Lancaster may not be everyone's first choice to play a 19th-century Sicilian aristocrat in a costume adaptation of a Lampedusa novel. But it was his participation which presumably persuaded 20th Century Fox to hand over millions of dollars to Marxist aristocrat Visconti to recreate the era sumptuously and with his customary style. Now restored, after the studio had wrecked both the colour and the running time, it is still looking impressive, if not quite top drawer.

Don Fabrizio	Burt Lancaster
Tancredi	Alain Delon
Angelica Sedara	Claudia Cardinale
Don Calogero Sedara	Paolo Stoppa
Maria Stella	Rina Morelli
Father Pirrone	Romolo Valli
Don Ciccio Tumeo	Serge Reggiani

Quote 'I sometimes think Burt the most perfectly mysterious man I ever met in my life.' [Visconti]

Psst! Visconti originally wanted the Russian actor Nicolai Cherkassov to play the lead, then tried for Laurence Olivier or Marlon Brando. With none of them free Fox, who were handling the film internationally, provided him with a short list that included Anthony Quinn, Spencer Tracy and Burt Lancaster. Choosing what he felt was the lesser of the evils presented to him, Visconti opted for Lancaster. But he wasn't happy: 'Argh! Lancaster – he's a cowboy, no?' However, they found they worked together so well they got together again in 1974 for *The Conversation Piece* • The amazing ball scene, considered one of the most spectacular sequences ever made, took 36 days of filming to complete.

Let George Do It
★★ 1940 82min b/w

Director: Marcel Varnel
Screenplay: John Dighton, Austin Melford, Angus MacPahil & Basil Dearden

This wartime comedy, with the gormless Formby mistakenly travelling to Norway and getting involved in a spy caper, is generally considered to be his best film. Not everyone takes to the grinning chappie with his ukelele in his hand. Those who do will be able to overlook the weak little plot, almost identical to all his

other films, and enjoy the musical numbers. The rest will probably want to overlook the entire movie.

George	George Formby
Mary	Phyllis Calvert
Mendez	Garry Marsh
Slim	Romney Brent
Nelson	Bernard Lee
Ivy	Coral Browne
U-boat commander	Torin Thatcher

Lethal Weapon
★★★ 1987 110min c.

Director: Richard Donner
Screenplay: Shane Black

A cracking thriller with Gibson the Vietnam vet cop so unhinged by his wife's death that he doesn't care what happens, just so long as he brings down a few baddies. Glover, the more mature family man, has reservations about being teamed with someone so suicidal. The first in the series very much puts the top-notch action before the wisecracks.

Martin Riggs	Mel Gibson
Roger Murtaugh	Danny Glover
Joshua	Gary Busey
The General	Mitchell Ryan
Michael Hunsaker	Tom Atkins
Trish Murtaugh	Darlene Love
Rianne Murtaugh	Traci Wolfe
Amanda Hunsaker	Jackie Swanson
Nick Murtaugh	Damon Hines
Carrie Murtaugh	Ebonie Smith
Psychologist	Mary Ellen Trainor

Quote 'You ever meet anybody you didn't kill?' • 'I'm too old for this.' [Last line]

Showing A Christmas Carol.

OOPS! Watch carefully as Riggs and the jumper leap from the ledge. The fake handcuffs come apart as the slow-motion begins, so they have to hold hands to make it look right • The gear lever of the car Murtagh is driving is clearly in 'Park' at one point.

Psst! A cinema claims to be showing 'The Lost Boys – This Year's Hit'. It was one of the studio's forthcoming films • Isn't Mel just a touch boyish to have been a Vietnam vet? • In 1994, a 14-year-old boy quoted the line from the Russian roulette scene, 'This is what I do each day to see if I am going to have a good day or a bad day,' before shooting himself in the head in front of a classmate while watching TV at home. He died in hospital.

Lethal Weapon 2

★★ 1989 111min c.

Director: Richard Donner
Screenplay: Jeffrey Boam

Although it's still got its exciting moments, this is the weakest of the bunch, let down by a tiresomely illogical script about South African drug runners. Although the gags aren't bad and Pesci's great fun, you keep asking yourself questions. How can Riggs run after a BMW and nearly catch it? How come when he sets off on foot after those with transport have departed, he still arrives before them? How come automatic weapons are so popular with villains if they aren't a patch on Riggs' and Murtagh's revolvers?

Martin Riggs	Mel Gibson
Roger Murtaugh	Danny Glover
Leo Getz	Joe Pesci
Arjen Rudd	Joss Ackland
Pieter Vorstedt	Derrick O'Connor
Rika Van Den Haas	Patsy Kensit

Quote 'We're back. We're bad. He's black. I'm mad.' • 'What you doin' Saturday?'

Psst! Probably the first movie in which a villain's head is removed with a surfboard • A '15' in the cinema, the video is a slightly longer '18' • On TV, much amusement can be had from watching Mel's lips as he says, 'You fold up your tents and get your friends out of my country'.

Lethal Weapon 3

★★★★ 1992 118min c.

Director: Richard Donner
Screenplay: Jeffrey Boam & Robert Mark Kamen

Murtagh's just a few days away from retirement when he and Riggs discover weapons confiscated by the Police turning up on the streets. The addition of tough woman cop Russo to the team is a bonus. When she and Riggs compare scars incurred in the line of duty, it turns into one of the cleverest foreplay scenes in the movies. With a clearer plot than usual, this is simply one of the greatest, funniest action pics of all time.

Martin Riggs	Mel Gibson
Roger Murtaugh	Danny Glover
Leo Getz	Joe Pesci
Lorna Cole	Rene Russo
Jack Travis	Stuart Wilson
Captain Murphy	Steve Kahan

Quote 'Nobody's dead.' – 'Hey, the night's young.'

OOPS! Note the speed with which the bloodstains disappear after the killing in the police interrogation room • Mel's boots change to shoes during the chase in the underground tunnel, then back again.

Psst! Keep watching the credits to the end to hear more of our heroes • After taking $100m in America, the stars were each presented with a new Range Rover • Instead of Rene Russo, John Goodman was originally intended as the new addition to the team • Among the uncredited writers working on the script was Carrie Fisher • Our heroes pass a cinema showing *Radio Flyer*, another movie directed by Donner.

The Letter

★★★★ 1940 95min c.

Director: William Wyler
Screenplay: Howard Koch
Source: Story by W. Somerset Maugham

Set in the world of the Malaysian rubber plantations, a woman kills a man, claiming it is self-defence. Then a letter turns up proving that they were lovers. Considering how so many of Davis' other films now come across as overmelodramatic, it is suprising that this one has worn its years so well. On the page, the script might now seem ridiculous but all concerned bring it off with great panache.

Leslie Crosbie	Bette Davis
Robert Crosbie	Herbert Marshall
Howard Joyce	James Stephenson
Mrs. Hammond	Gale Sondergaard
Dorothy Joyce	Frieda Inescourt
John Withers	Bruce Lester
Prescott	Cecil Kellaway
Ong Chi Seng	Victor Sen Yung
Fred	Leonard Mudie

Quote 'Yes, I killed him. And I'm glad, I tell you. Glad! Glad! Glad!' • 'Juries can sometimes be very stupid and it's just as well not to worry them with more evidence than they can conveniently deal with.'

Psst! It was filmed in 1929 as well. In that movie Marshall played the lover • The censors imposed a rather more moralistic ending than Maugham had in his original story.

Letter from an Unknown Woman

★★★★ 1948 89min b/w

Director: Max Ophuls
Screenplay: Howard Koch
Source: Novel, *Brief Einer Unbekannten* by Stefan Zweig

A woman falls in love with a concert pianist who is something of a ladies' man. While she is constant in love, he is not quite as steadfast. When you reflect on the film afterwards, you wonder why you should be taken in by such a ridiculous story. But when it's running, it's wonderfully weepy stuff, beautifully filmed, and will have you straining to see the screen through the tears.

Lisa Berndle	Joan Fontaine
Stefan Brand	Louis Jourdan
Frau Berndle	Mady Christians
Johann Stauffer	Marcel Journet
John	Art Smith
Marie	Carol Yorke
Herr Kastner	Howard Freeman
Porter	Erskine Sanford
Carriage driver	Torben Meyer

A Letter to Three Wives

★★★ 1949 103min b/w

Director: Joseph L. Mankiewicz
Screenplay: Joseph L. Mankiewicz
Source: Novel, *A Letter to Five Wives* by John Klempner

Three women who believe themselves happily married go through torment when they each receive a letter from a friend saying that she has run off with one of their husbands. In turn they review their relationships. Mankiewicz penned a crisp, witty script that was laid into with relish by the cast, best of whom are the two Douglases, Darnell and the ever priceless Ritter.

Deborah Bishop	Jeanne Crain
Lora May Hollingsway	Linda Darnell
Rita Phipps	Ann Southern
George Phipps	Kirk Douglas
Porter Hollingsway	Paul Douglas
Babe	Barbara Lawrence

Brad Bishop	Jeffrey Lynn
Mrs. Finney	Connie Gilchrist
Mrs. Manleigh	Florence Bates
Sadie	Thelma Ritter
Mr. Manleigh	Hobart Cavanaugh
Addie Ross	Celeste Holm

Oscars Best Director, Best Screenplay

Blurb A Peek Into The Other Woman's Male.

Quote 'Do you know what I like about your programme? Even when I'm running the vacuum, I can understand it.' • 'I don't understand this conversation at all. How drunk am I?'

Libeled Lady

★★ 1936 98min b/w

Director: Jack Conway
Screenplay: Maurine Watkins, Howard Emmett Rogers & George Oppenheimer

When the wealthy Loy sues Tracy's newspaper, he delays his wedding to Harlow for the umpteenth time and orders ladies' man Powell to romance Loy so that he will have a hold over her. As in every other comedy since time immemorial, love gets in the way. Once considered one of the best of the screwball comedies, the plot now seems as limp as a stick of yesterday's celery. The all-star cast makes it watchable but it's hardly one of the greats. Remade as *Easy to Wed* in 1946.

Bill Chandler	William Powell
Connie Allenbury	Myrna Loy
Gladys Benton	Jean Harlow
Warren Haggerty	Spencer Tracy
James B. Allenbury	Walter Connolly
Hollis Bane	Charley Grapewin
Mrs. Burns-Norvell	Cora Witherspoon
Evans	E.E. Clive
Graham	Charles Trowbridge
Maid	Hattie McDaniel

Psst! Powell and Harlow were lovers off-screen, despite the fact that Powell was 20 years her senior. It was said that they planned to marry, plans marred by her untimely death.

Licence to Kill

★★★ 1989 133min c.

Director: John Glen
Screenplay: Michael G. Wilson & Richard Maibaum

Dalton shook and stirred a few Bond fans with this first film written specially for him. Adding a touch – just a touch – of realism to the character, he disobeys orders and goes after drug baron Davi. Lowell makes a wonderfully sassy heroine. Although the plot's as ropey as ever, the stunts are great.

James Bond	.Timothy Dalton
Pam Bouvier	.Carey Lowell
Franz Sanchez	.Robert Davi
Lupe Lamora	.Talisa Soto
Milton Krest	.Anthony Zerbe
Sharkey	.Frank McRae
Killifer	.Everett McGill
Prof. Joe Butcher	.Wayne Newton
'Q'	.Desmond Llewelyn
Felix Leiter	.David Hedison
'M'	.Robert Brown
Miss Moneypenny	.Caroline Bliss

Quote 'He disagreed with something that ate him.'

Psst! Although there's an unusual warning against the health dangers of tobacco at the end of the film, the film-makers accepted $350,000 from Philip Morris for the scene in which 007 lights up a *Larks* cigarette
• Originally the film had the book's title, *Licence Revoked*, until a survey found only one in five Americans knew what 'revoked' meant. Presumably, that didn't include the film-makers for, as Bond's licence *is* revoked in the film, the new title is nonsensical.

The Life and Death of Colonel Blimp

★★★★ 1943 163min c.

Director: Michael Powell & Emeric Pressburger
Screenplay: Michael Powell & Emeric Pressburger
Source: Cartoons by David Low

A stuffy British military man reflects on his life and loves from the Boer War to World War II. An extraordinary film, as with so many Powell-Pressburger collaborations, but particularly so as it was made in wartime. Not only is the central character not the stuff of which heroes are made, but we also get a sympathetic German soldier, a friend no less, thrown in. Although the story meanders a little, just as it would if such an old buffer told it, it is witty and wistful and Livesey gives a commanding lead. Some of the medals should go to Kerr who plays three different women in his life.

Clive Candy	.Roger Livesey
Edith/Barbara/Johnny	.Deborah Kerr
Theo Kretschmar-Schuldorff	.Anton Walbrook
Col. Betteridge	.Roland Culver
Spud Wilson	.James McKechnie
Von Ritter	.Albert Lieven
Embassy Counsellor	.Arthur Wontner
President of Council	.A.E. Matthews
Hoppy	.David Hutcheson
Frau von Kalteneck	.Ursula Jeans
Murdoch	.John Laurie
Maj. Davis	.Harry Welchman
Von Schonborn	.Valentine Dyall
Von Reumann	.Carl Jaffe
Van Zill	.Reginald Tate

Psst! The lead was originally intended for Laurence Olivier • The central character was based on a series of cartoons in the Evening Standard which led to crusty military men being nicknamed 'Colonel Blimp'. The cartoons were far harsher than the character in the movie
• Winston Churchill hated the film. He tried to stop it being made and then, against the advice of the Ministry of Information, he prohibited its export, undoubtedly illegally, because it was 'detrimental to the morale of the Army'. Only when it proved such a big hit on the Home Front was the ban finally lifted, although the film was cut for distribution to the Allied nations
• Although the third collaboration between Powell and Pressburger, this was the first 'Archers' production, opening with their logo of an archery target • A vastly inferior American version just 93 minutes long exists. Another cut verson, with the narrative 'straightened out' is used on some videos over here.

Life of Brian

SEE: Monty Python's Life of Brian

The Life of Emile Zola

★★★ 1937 123min b/w

Director: William Dieterle
Screenplay: Norman Reilly Raine, Heinz Herald & Geza Herczeg

J'accuse! Ostracised and outrageous novelist Emile Zola gains a reputation as one of France's top scribblers. He uses his power to fight on behalf of Jewish officer Alfred Dreyfus, framed and sent to Devil's Island. Paul Muni here gives the best of all his biographical roles. The story of the case that split France keeps closer to the true facts than we might expect and is utterly fascinating, as well as providing good drama.

Emile Zola	.Paul Muni
Capt. Alfred Dreyfus	Joseph Schildkraut
Lucie Dreyfus	.Gale Sondergaard
Alexandre Zola	.Gloria Holden
Maitre Labori	.Donald Crisp
Nana	.Erin O'Brien-Moore
Charpentier	.John Litel
Col. Picquart	.Henry O'Neill
Maj. Dort	.Louis Calhern
Chief of Staff	.Harry Davenport
Maj. Walsin Esterhazy	.Robert Barrat
Paul Cezanne	.Vladimir Sokoloff
Pierre Dreyfus	.Dickie Moore
Albert	.Frank Darien
M. Richards	.Lumsden Hare
Commander of Paris	.Holmes Herbert
Col. Sandherr	.Walter Kingsford
Cavaignac	.Montagu Love
Georges Clemenceau	.Grant Mitchell
Capt. Guignet	.Moroni Olsen
M. Perreux	.Frank Reicher
Maj. Henry	.Robert Warwick

Oscars Best Picture, Best Screenplay, Joseph Schildkraut

Psst! For a time, biographies of famous men were all the rage. It's hard to credit now, but pics about Pasteur, Schubert, Juarez, Schubert and the like wowed them at the box office around the world • Lubitsch was shown the script but couldn't find the right actor and so passed it to Warner Brothers who had Muni under contract • Despite being in large part about anti-Semitism, the word 'Jew' is never mentioned.

Life with Father

★★ 1947 118min c.

Director: Michael Curtiz
Screenplay: Donald Ogden Stewart
Source: Play by Howard Lindsay & Russel Crouse and book by Clarence Day Jr.

Rambling reminiscences of Victorian life in a family dominated by a father of fixed opinions on women and religion. A series of episodes rather than a straight narrative, the film has to get by on the charm of Powell and Dunne and our interest in their little brood. While the period detail is interesting, this isn't quite another *Meet Me in St. Louis*.

Clarence Day	.William Powell
Vinnie Day	.Irene Dunne
Mary	.Elizabeth Taylor
Rev. Dr. Lloyd	.Edmund Gwenn
Cora	.ZaSu Pitts
John	.Martin Milner
Clarence	.Jimmy Lydon
Margaret	.Emma Dunn
Dr. Humphries	.Moroni Olsen
Mrs. Whitehead	.Elizabeth Risdon

Quote 'Why did God make so many dumb fools and Democrats?'

Psst! The play ran on Broadway for an extraordinary 3,224 performances lasting eight years • In the book and the play, the last line is: 'I'm going to be baptised, damn it!' The censors wouldn't wear the blasphemy • Fredric March had lobbied for the role and took *The Best Years of Our Lives* as a consolation prize • Mary Pickford and Bette Davis were among those coveting the role that went to Irene Dunne • The real Mrs. Clarence day was Technical Adviser on the film • *Life With Father* became an early sitcom, playing from 1953 to 1955 with Leon Ames in the title role.

The Lion in Winter

★★ 1968 134min c.

Director: Anthony Harvey
Screenplay: James Goldman
Source: Play by Goldman

Many families squabble at Christmas. Henry II's brood are no different, with the king summoning his kin together and letting them go at it hammer and tongs. Its witty, literate script is just the sort of thing actors love to get their teeth into and O'Toole and Hepburn gnaw their parts down to the bone. It is rather stagy, though, and all the talk gets a bit tiresome after a while.

King Henry II	.Peter O'Toole
Eleanor of Aquitaine	.Katharine Hepburn
Richard the Lion-Hearted	.Anthony Hopkins
Prince Geoffrey	.John Castle
Prince John	.Nigel Terry
King Philip II	.Timothy Dalton
Princess Alais	.Jane Merrow
William Marshall	.Nigel Stock
Bishop of Durham	.O.Z. Whitehead
Strolling player	.Kenneth Griffith

Oscars Best Screenplay (adapted), Katharine Hepburn

212

Quote 'How dear of you to let me out of jail.' – 'It's only for the holidays.' • 'In a world where carpenters get resurrected, anything is possible.' • 'Well, what family doesn't have its ups and downs?' • 'Give me a little peace.' – 'A little? Why so modest? How about eternal peace?' • 'In a world where carpenters get resurrected, anything is possible.' • 'I could listen to you lie for hours.'

Psst! This was Hopkins' film debut. He broke several bones when he fell off his horse • Hepburn won her third Oscar for this role, making her the first actress to do so. She went on to win one more. It was her first film since longtime lover Spencer Tracy died.

The Lion King
★★★★ 1994 87min c.

Director: Roger Allers & Rob Minkoff
Screenplay: Irene Mecchi, Jonathan Roberts & Linda Woolverton

Despite the dreadful songs, this is one of the best of the recent Disney cartoons. With echoes of *Robin Hood* and nods to the like of Leni Riefenstahl, the evil lion Scar (the best thing Irons has ever done) plots to overthrow his brother and usurp his throne as King of the Beasts. Only Prince Simba can stand in his way. Less of a romp than *Aladdin*, it brilliantly conjures up the majesty of Africa, throwing in a stampede to outdo the one in *Jurassic Park*. At times, it's almost *too* realistic and a little scary for very young ones. A thing of beauty and a joy to behold.

Zazu	Rowan Atkinson
Simba	Matthew Broderick
Shenzi	Whoopi Goldberg
Rafiki	Robert Guillaume
Scar	Jeremy Irons
Mufasa	James Earl Jones
Nala	Moira Kelly

Quote 'Slimy...yet satisfying.' • 'Kid, what's eating you?' – 'Nothing. He's at the top of the food chain.'

Psst! For the first time in an animated Disney movie, there were no human characters. It was also the first Disney movie not based on a published story or a fairy tale • The video became the most popular consumer product in American history, selling even more than Michael Jackson's *Thriller* album.

Little Big Man
★★★ 1970 147min c.

Director: Arthur Penn
Screenplay: Calder Willingham
Source: Novel by Thomas Berger

This is one of the oddest Westerns ever, with Hoffman a sort of half-White, half-Indian *Forrest Gump*. As a reminiscing 121-year-old, he claims to have been present at umpteen historical events, including the massacre at the Little Big Horn, bouncing between one side and the other. An extraordinary movie, which is sometimes tragic, sometimes comic but always fascinating.

Jack Crabb	Dustin Hoffman
Mrs. Pendrake	Faye Dunaway
Allardyce T. Merriweather	Martin Balsam
Gen. George A. Custer	Richard Mulligan
Old Lodge Skins	Chief Dan George
Wild Bill Hickock	Jeff Corey
Historian	William Hickey
Lieutenant	Jesse Vint
Major	Alan Oppenheimer
Rev. Silas Pendrake	Thayer David
Jack Crabb (as adolescent)	Alan Howard
Shotgun guard	M. Emmet Walsh

Quote 'My heart soars like a hawk.' • 'Does she smile when you mount her?'

Psst! Hoffman's make-up as the 121-year-old, comprising a 14-piece mask, took five hours to complete • He was the only non-authentic Indian among the cast • Hoffman claimed that the key to his character was that 'he hadn't had a decent bowel movement in 46 years.' • No other actor has played a character with such a large age span during a movie • The massacre in Oklahoma by Custer was filmed in Calgary with wind-chill taking the temperature to 60 degrees below freezing. In some of the worst conditions endured by the cast and crew of any movie, the cameras kept freezing and filming had to be stopped repeatedly while they were thawed out.

Little Caesar
★★ 1931 80min b/w

Director: Mervyn LeRoy
Screenplay: Francis Edwards Faragoh & Robert E. Lee
Source: Novel by W.R. Burnett

Edward G. Robinson launched the Gat Pack with this thinly-veiled biography of Al Capone, starting out as a small-time crook and killer who builds a criminal empire. Although Robinson is suitably menacing and well worth watching, the film itself is now incredibly dated.

'Rico' Bandello	Edward G. Robinson
Joe Massara	Douglas Fairbanks Jr.
Olga Strassof	Glenda Farrell
Tony Passa	William Collier Jr.
Diamond Pete Montana	Ralph Ince
Otero	George E. Stone
Sgt. Flaherty	Thomas Jackson
Sam Vettori	Stanley Fields
The Big Boy	Sidney Blackmer
Ma Magdalena	Lucille La Verne

Quote 'You want me, you're going to have to come and get me.' • 'Mother of Mercy…Is this the end of Rico?' [Last line]

Psst! Although 37-year-old Robinson had been acting on stage and screen for 17 years, he had had little success until this film. Sadly for him, he was typecast for the rest of his life • He had originally been slated for playing Otero, but he persuaded director LeRoy to let him play the lead • Clark Gable was among those screen tested. Jack Warner thought him too ugly • Robinson did not like guns. Every time he fired one, his eyes blinked involuntarily. They had to tape his eyelids up so that his eyes didn't close whenever his piece went off. The taping made him look even more menacing • The church steps on which Robinson takes his last breath are the same ones James Cagney would die on in *The Roaring Twenties*.

The Little Foxes
★★★ 1941 115min b/w

Director: William Wyler
Screenplay: Lillian Hellman, Arthur Kober, Dorothy Parker & Alan Campbell
Source: Play by Hellman

This tale of an avaricious family in the South in the days after the Civil War is a splendid potboiler, with vivid performances putting over the lines that had already done sterling service in the theatre. Director Wyler's gentle handling, along with the lovely cinematography, makes it much more than just a filmed play.

Regina Giddens	Bette Davis
Horace Giddens	Herbert Marshall
Alexandra Giddens	Teresa Wright
David Hewitt	Richard Carlson
Leo Hubbard	Dan Duryea
Birdie Hubbard	Patricia Collinge
Ben Hubbard	Charles Dingle
Oscar Hubbard	Carl Benton Reid
William Marshall	Russell Hicks
Sam Manders	Lucien Littlefield
Lucy Hewitt	Virginia Brissac

Quote 'Cynicism is an unpleasant way of telling the truth.'

Psst! Talullah Bankhead had played Davis' role on Broadway and relations between Davis and the director were not helped by Wyler's constant cry: 'We'll have to get Bankhead'. The two had furious fights and, although they had workedg together on *Jezebel* and *The Letter*, they were not to collaborate again.

The Little Mermaid
★★★ 1989 82min c.

Director: John Musker & Ron Clements
Screenplay: John Musker & Ron Clements

Disney was almost back on top form with this Hans Christian Andersen story about the mermaid who wants to be human. The animation's great, the characters are fun and the songs are pretty good. Perhaps it's all a little unmemorable compared to the great features of Disney's past, but let us give thanks for the absence of icky sentimentality.

Louis	Rene Auberjonois
Eric	Christopher Daniel Barnes
Ariel	Jodi Benson
Ursula	Pat Carroll

Quote 'Look what the catfish dragged in.'

Psst! As if Disney hadn't had enough problems with *Three Men and a Baby* over the alleged ghost, they were then inundated with calls this time from people who thought that an erect penis had been surreptitiously drawn into the design of the towers on the video box.

Little Women
★★★★ 1933 115min b/w

Director: George Cukor
Screenplay: Sarah Y. Mason & Victor Heerman
Source: Novel by Louisa May Alcott

A splendidly big, vibrant adaptation of the

famous novel handled expertly by Cukor, who acquired a reputation as a 'woman's director'. Although it doesn't shy away from the sentimental stuff, there are plenty of laughs as well. Utterly charming and easily the best of all the screen versions of the book, best known of which are those of 1949 and 1994.

Jo	Katharine Hepburn
Amy	Joan Bennett
Prof. Fritz Bhaer	Paul Lukas
Aunt March	Edna May Oliver
Beth	Jean Parker
Mr. Laurence	Henry Stephenson
Laurie	Douglass Montgomery
Marmee	Spring Byington
Meg	Frances Dee
Brooke	John Lodge
Mr. March	Samuel S. Hinds
Mr. Davis	Olin Howlin

Psst! Hepburn arranged picnics and afternoon each day for the cast and crew to encourage the atmosphere of it being one big family • Joan Bennett's pregnancy was relatively easy to hide initially. However, a three-week strike by technicians meant some hurried alterations in her costumes when filming started again.

Live and Let Die
★★ 1973 121min c.

Director: Guy Hamilton
Screenplay: Tom Mankiewicz
Source: Novel by Ian Fleming

Moore, on his first outing as 007, is as stiff as a board while the plot, conversely, is as limp as can be. The story, involving drugs and voodoo, is weak but the funeral scene and the massive boat chase are still worthwhile. James' increasingly exasperated Sheriff provides welcome comic relief.

James Bond	Roger Moore
Dr. Kananga	Yaphet Kotto
Solitaire	Jane Seymour
Sheriff Pepper	Clifton James
Baron Samedi	Geoffrey Holder
Felix Leiter	David Hedison
'M'	Bernard Lee
Miss Moneypenny	Lois Maxwell
Tee Hee	Julius Harris

OOPS! Pay attention during Bond's fight on the train with Tee Hee and you'll notice that, depending on which window you look out of, the train is going in different directions!

Psst! Connery turned down $5.5m to play Bond again • Known as *The Dead Slave* in Japan • Hedison was to repeat his role as Leiter in *Licence to Kill*, the only actor who has played the character twice.

The Lives of a Bengal Lancer
★★★ 1935 109min b/w

Director: Henry Hathaway
Screenplay: Waldemar Young, John Balderston, Achmed Abdullah, Grover Jones & William Slavens McNutt
Source: Novel by Maj. Francis Yeats-Brown

Stirring heroics in the days of the British Empire, as the 41st Bengal Lancers quell the unruly natives. The action scenes are still exciting, the buddy stuff is enjoyable and there's plenty of wit to keep the whole enterprise bubbling along. It also contains one of the most famous and often imitated lines in all of moviedom.

Lt. Alan McGregor	Gary Cooper
Lt. John Forsythe	Franchot Tone
Lt. Donald Stone	Richard Cromwell
Col. Stone	Guy Standing
Maj. Hamilton	C. Aubrey Smith
Hamzulia Khan	Monte Blue
Tania Volkanskaya	Kathleen Burke
Lt. Barrett	Colin Tapley
Mohammed Khan	Douglass Dumbrille
Emir	Akim Tamiroff
Also: Lumsden Hare, J. Carrol Naish	

Quote 'We have ways of making men talk.'

The Living Daylights
★★★ 1987 130min c.

Director: John Glen
Screenplay: Richard Maibaum & Michael G. Wilson
Source: Story by Ian Fleming

At 40, Dalton takes his bow as James Bond. Although he isn't as quick with the wisecracks as earlier incarnations of 007, there's plenty of great action, a delicious damsel in distress and some wonderful scenery. What more do you want from a Bond film?

James Bond	Timothy Dalton
Kara Milovy	Maryam d'Abo
Gen. Georgi Koskov	Jeroen Krabbé

Brad Whitaker ....Joe Don Baker
Gen. Leonid Pushkin ....John Rhys-Davies
Kamran Shah....................Art Malik
'Q' ....Desmond Llewelyn
'M' ....Robert Brown
Minister of Defence ....Geoffrey Keen
Miss Moneypenny ....Caroline Bliss

OOPS! At the end, when they can't land the plane because it is too hilly, they eject the jeep. But we then see the jeep driving along a perfectly flat road where you could land a plane with no difficulty at all.

Psst! Pierce Brosnan was apparently set to step into Roger Moore's shoes but was then called back to TV for another series of *Remington Steele*. He would have to wait until *Goldeneye* in 1995 before getting his chance at playing 007 • Known as *The Breeze of Death* in Germany • Ex-Royal girlfriend Katie Rabett appears in a small part as 'Liz' • This was the debut of Caroline Bliss as Miss Moneypenny, replacing the glorious Lois Maxwell.

Local Hero
★★★★ 1983 111min c.

Director: Bill Forsyth
Screenplay: Bill Forsyth

Utterly delightful, magical comedy from the director of *Gregory's Girl*. Riegert's the oil executive sent to Scotland to buy an entire fishing village so his company can build a refinery. But playing politics with guys in suits hasn't quite prepared him for the canniness of the villagers' negotiating tactics. Just as Riegert succumbs to the charms of the landscape, so you'll succumb to the charms of this warm-hearted film, peopled with wonderfully eccentric characters.

Happer ....Burt Lancaster
Mac ....Peter Riegert
Ben ....Fulton Mackay
Urquhart ....Denis Lawson
Moritz ....Norman Chancer
Oldsen ....Peter Capaldi
Geddes ....Rikki Fulton
Watt ....Alex Norton
Marina ....Jenny Seagrove
Stella ....Jennifer Black
Ricky ....John Gordon Sinclair

Quote 'I wonder what the poor people are doing tonight?'

Psst! Apparently this was the main influence behind the TV series *Northern Exposure*.

Lolita
★★★ 1962 152min b/w

Director: Stanley Kubrick
Screenplay: Vladimir Nabokov
Source: Novel by Nabokov

A middle-aged professor leches after an underage girl, and marries her mother just so that he can be near her. Nabokov's novel, which gave us the word 'nymphet', has been turned into a surprisingly good movie. Although it is long, there are many bright and funny moments, as well as some touching scenes. It's also, despite its age, uncomfortably titillating.

Humbert Humbert ....James Mason
Charlotte Haze ....Shelley Winters
Lolita Haze ....Sue Lyon
Clare Quilty ....Peter Sellers
Vivian Darkbloom ....Marianne Stone
Jean Farlow ....Diane Decker
Nurse Lore ....Lois Maxwell

Blurb However Did They Make A Film Of *Lolita*?

Psst! Despite the controversy over the movie, it cheated by making Nabokov's 'nymphet' 14 years old rather than 12, which weakened considerably the central idea of sexual attraction to a child. However, the change was made at the insistence of the BBFC who had been shown the script • For a while, it was thought that Errol Flynn might star. The public would probably have loved the idea. His predilection for young girls was well known and he had recently announced his engagement to a 17-year-old. Although some say he pulled out when his fiancée couldn't star with him, he was also extremely ill with an assortment of diseases like T.B., hepatitis, malaria and gonorrhea, and he died of a heart attack shortly afterwards. Noël Coward was another possibility who was considered, as was Cary Grant. Both men turned it down • The producers initially wanted to cast Hayley Mills for the lead. But she was under contract to Disney and neither they nor her father, John Mills, were keen on the idea • The character Vivian Darkbloom is an anagram of Vladimir Nabokov • In 1973, Sue Lyon married Gary Adamson, a prisoner in Colorado State Penitentiary, who was serving a long sentence for murder and armed robbery • Winters claimed that, as morality was so different then, she had to be given drugs to calm her down when she was doing a scene in bed with James Mason.

Lonely Are the Brave
★★★ 1962 107min b/w

Director: David Miller
Screenplay: Dalton Trumbo
Source: Novel, *The Brave Cowboy* by Edward Abbey

Lovely, elegiac Western with Douglas a cowboy out of tune with the modern world who takes on the forces of law enforcement and all their technological gadgetry. Thanks to Douglas and Matthau as the sheriff whose heart is not in the chase, this wistful tip of the hat to a bygone era sticks in the memory long afterwards.

Jack Burns	.Kirk Douglas
Sheriff Johnson	.Walter Matthau
Jerri Bondi	.Gena Rowlands
Paul Bondi	.Michael Kane
Hinton, the truck driver	.Carroll O'Connor
Guitierrez	.George Kennedy
Harry	.William Schallert
'One Arm'	.Bill Bixby

Quote 'Believe you me, if it didn't take men to make babies I wouldn't have anything to do with any of you!'

Psst! This was the last project that Douglas initiated and brought to the screen himself. The studio showed little interest and, despite wonderful reviews, the film was shown for just one week in most places before being pulled. Over the years, its reputation has grown enormously but too late for Douglas, who tried for 10 years to film *One Flew Over the Cuckoo's Nest* without success. It was his son Michael who managed to get it made.

The Long Good Friday
★★★★ 1980 105min c.

Director: John Mackenzie
Screenplay: Barrie Keefe

Although you can't help feeling at times that he's about to go into an impersonation of Jimmy Cagney, Hoskins is superb in this gripping British gangster movie. He's a terrifying hoodlum who bites off considerably more than he can chew when he goes after the people attacking his organisation and receives splendid support from Mirren. The script could perhaps have been a little more lucid but it still looks fresh and chills the blood.

Harold	.Bob Hoskins
Victoria	.Helen Mirren

Charlie	.Eddie Constantine
Parky	.Dave King
Harris	.Bryan Marshall
Gus	.George Coulouris
1st Irishman	.Pierce Brosnan
Erroll	.Paul Barber
Priest	.Alan Devlin
Kid	.Dexter Fletcher
Colin	.Paul Freeman

Quote 'Colin never hurt a fly. Well, only when it was necessary.' • 'There's a lot of dignity in that, going out like a raspberry ripple.' • 'What I'm looking for is someone who can contribute to what England has given the world: culture, sophistication, genius – a little more than a hot dog, you know what I mean?'

Psst! It was originally made for television. Lew Grade was all set to chop out all the blood and bad language but George Harrison's Handmade Films rescued it and aimed it at the cinema • Keep an eye out for *Eastender* Gillian Taylforth as 'Sherry'.

The Long Goodbye
★★★★ 1973 112min c.

Director: Robert Altman
Screenplay: Leigh Brackett
Source: Novel by Raymond Chandler

Although Chandler purists froth at the mouth at the merest mention of it, Altman's homage-cum-spoof of the private eye movies is great fun. Forget whether it trashes Marlowe's good name or not and sit back and enjoy Gould subvert the genre as a shambling, bumbling tec investigating the murder of a friend's wife.

Philip Marlowe	.Elliott Gould
Eileen Wade	.Nina Van Pallandt
Roger Wade	.Sterling Hayden
Marty Augustine	.Mark Rydell
Dr. Verringer	.Henry Gibson
Harry	.David Arkin
Morgan	.Warren Berlinger
Hood	.Arnold Schwarzenegger
Also: Rutanya Alda, David Carradine	

Blurb Nothing Says Goodbye Like A Bullet.

Quote 'Robert Altman's *The Long Goodbye* was a Raymond Chandler thriller. I don't remember a thing about making it as I was smashed at the time.' [Sterling Hayden]

Psst! The writer, Brackett, was co-author of *The Big Sleep* • Arnold Schwarzenegger in the days when he was billed as Arnold Strong, appears briefly as a hood, while David Carradine has a bit part.

The Lost Continent

★★ 1968 98min c.

Director: Michael Carreras
Screenplay: Michael Nash
Source: Novel, *Uncharted Seas* by Dennis Wheatley

A lost classic in the Hilariously Overimaginative stakes, based on a Dennis Wheatley novel. A boat becomes stranded mid-ocean among carnivorous seaweed. If you think this is a little unlikely, wait until they discover an entire Spanish colony living there too! Considering the slavish attention the fashion industry paid to movies in the 60s, it's a little odd that the inflatable, walking-on-water shoes never caught on in Carnaby Street.

Lansen ....Eric Porter
Eva ....Hildegarde Neff
Unity ....Suzanna Leigh
Tyler ....Tony Beckley
Webster ....Nigel Stock
Pat ....Jimmy Hanley
Sparks ......Donald Sumpter, James Cossins,
Victor Maddern

Lost Horizon

★★★★ 1937 131min b/w

Director: Frank Capra
Screenplay: Robert Riskin
Source: Novel by James Hilton

Four refugees from war in China are taken against their will to a beautiful, remote, Tibetan valley where peace reigns and people live well past a ripe old age. Despite the odd turgid bit of fortune-cookie philosophy, this utopian romantic fantasy is still one of the most delightful bits of Hollywood moonshine. Who wouldn't join with Colman in his search to find Shangri-La again ? If you can put up with the missing sections, the full version is the one to watch. Avoid the dreadful 1972 musical remake if you value your lunch.

Robert Conway ....Ronald Colman
Sondra ....Jane Wyatt
Alexander P. Lovett ....Edward Everett Horton
Chang ........................H.B. Warner

High Lama ....Sam Jaffe
Henry Barnard ....Thomas Mitchell
George Conway ....John Howard
Maria ....Margo
Gloria Stone ....Isabel Jewell
Lord Gainsford ....Hugh Buckler

Quote 'Every man carried in his heart a Shangri-La.' • 'If I had my life to live over again, I would do everything the exact same way, with the possible exception of seeing the movie remake of *Lost Horizon*. [Woody Allen]

OOPS! When he's wandering, lost, in the blizzard, Colman rolls down a mountain where nobody's ever been before. Nobody, that is, except for whoever left the footprints just in front of the camera • If that ledge with the precipitous drop is the only entrance, can someone please explain how they got the grand piano in? • When you see Colman collapsing when he gets to the remote Tibetan village, his hair and beard in close-up are much tidier and shorter than in the long shot, which is actually taken from a German film.

Psst! Author Hilton claimed to have written the novel in six weeks • At the time, the set of Shangri-La was the largest Hollywood had seen • The movie's $2.5m cost was half of Columbia's total annual budget • The first preview went dreadfully. People were laughing and Capra overheard someone saying: 'The people who made that picture should be shot'. After agonising over what had gone wrong, he simply dropped the first two reels altogether, taking its time down to 118minutes. It was released in that form and proved immensely popular, although it still lost money to begin with. However, it was re-released many times over the years, with the running time cut further to 109 minutes. There is now an almost complete version, although six minutes exist only in dialogue and stills are used on screen while they are playing • They began filming with no High Lama and still didn't have one after 75 days of the production. A.E. Anson was hired, but died before he got to the set. Another, Henry B. Walthall, died before he could be tested. Finally they settled on someone younger, the 38-year-old Sam Jaffe • Among other methods experimented with by the make-up people to get Jaffe's skin looking old enough, they plaed around cigarette paper, oatmeal and fish skins. In the end, they took a cast of his face and built that up • Capra insisted that the cold should not look phony. In order to get the actors' breath to show, they had to film where it was at least 20 degrees below zero. They used a cold-storage warehouse that had its own artificial snow machines which would blow ground-up ice blocks over the frozen swordfish stored there. They filmed there for six weeks while it was 90 degrees outside • The long shots of the mountains were taken from a couple of German feature films of the early 30s.

The Lost Patrol
★★★ 1934 74min b/w

Director: John Ford
Screenplay: Dudley Nichols
Source: Novel, *Patrol* by Philip MacDonald.

Although slightly stiff in places, this drama about a lost group of British soldiers being picked off one by one by an unseen force is still enjoyable and has a fine, doom-laden atmosphere. Itself a remake of a 1929 British silent, its core idea has been copied time and time again, both on earth and in space.

The Sergeant	Victor McLaglen
Sanders	Boris Karloff
Morelli	Wallace Ford
Brown	Reginald Denny
Quincannon	J.M. Kerrigan
Hale	Billy Bevan
Cook	Alan Hale
Bell	Brandon Hurst

The Lost Weekend
★★★★ 1945 101min b/w

Director: Billy Wilder
Screenplay: Charles Brackett & Billy Wilder
Source: Novel by Charles R. Jackson

Although the subject has been covered umpteen times since, this first serious look at the world of the alcoholic still carries a tremendous punch. Milland gives his greatest, and most untypical, performance as the writer who uses booze to clear his writer's block, getting sucked down and down. A disturbing movie which is as literate and compelling as most of Wilder and Brackett's stuff.

Don Birnam	Ray Milland
Helen St. James	Jane Wyman
Nick Birnam	Phillip Terry
Nat, the bartender	Howard da Silva
Gloria	Doris Dowling
Bim	Frank Faylen

Oscars Best Picture, Best Screenplay (adapted), Ray Milland, Best Director

Blurb The Picture That Dares To Bare A Man's Soul.

Quote 'What I'm trying to say is, I'm not a drinker – I'm a drunk.' • 'One's too many and a hundred's not enough.' • 'Ray Milland did not deserve an oscar, but *The Lost Weekend* was the first picture to tackle alcoholism. Tremendous impact. In the same role, W.C. Fields would have won.' [John Huston]

Psst! The film very nearly wasn't released at all, with Paramount's top brass utterly horrified at what Billy Wilder had done. Lobbyists for the drinks industry offered $5m to destroy the negative while temperance groups attacked it because they thought it would actually encourage drinking. The studio held up its release for a year until Wilder persuaded them to go for a limited showing in New York alone. After the critics lauded it, it was released across the country and was very successful • The first preview had had library music added to it instead of Miklos Rozsa's fine score and the audience took the film as a comedy and laughed their way through it. When the proper music was added, audience reactions were completely different • Much of the realism came from shooting on location in New York with concealed cameras • The film differed from the novel in having a rather more hopeful ending and in not revealing that the reason for the character's drinking was the repressed homosexuality • Wilder hadn't wanted Ray Milland for the lead, preferring José Ferrer, but he was overruled by the studio • For years afterwards Milland was the target of jokes about drink wherever he went • As he leaves a bar, a woman's arm is seen handing him his hat. It is Loretta Young's • Lillian Fontaine, the mother of both Joan Fontaine and Olivia De Havilland, plays Mrs. St. James.

Love Affair
★★★★ 1939 87min b/w

Director: Leo McCarey
Screenplay: Delmer Daves & Donald Ogden Stewart

One of the all-time great romantic movies, with a couple testing the strength of their shipboard attraction by arranging to meet six months hence on top of the Empire State Building.

Unfortunately, fate plays a cruel trick on them. Although it's heavily sentimental, in the early stages in particular it is also very funny and touching. It was remade, less successfully, by the same director, as *An Affair to Remember* in 1957 and once more by Warren Beatty starring him and Annette Bening in 1994.

Terry McKay	Irene Dunne
Michel Marnet	Charles Boyer
Grandmother Janou	Maria Ouspenskaya
Kenneth Bradley	Lee Bowman
Lois Clarke	Astrid Allwyn
Maurice Cobert	Maurice Moscovitch
Boy on ship	Scotty Beckett
Woman on deck (in couple)	Bess Flowers
Autograph seeker	Joan Leslie

Quote 'My mother told me never to enter any man's room in months ending in R.'

Psst! One of those movies that succeeded despite apparently being written as it went along.

The Love Bug
★★★ 1969 107min c.

Director: Robert Stevenson
Screenplay: Bill Walsh & Don da Gradi

A car with a mind of its own helps its racing driver owner in love and on the track while managing to foil the villains as well. It doesn't seem any less daft now than in did then but it's fun family fare with enough slapstick and stunts to keep everyone occupied. Herbie, a surprisingly sweet character when you consider that he's a car, was popular enough to spawn three sequels, all of which needed more fine tuning before being allowed out on the road.

Jim	Dean Jones
Carole	Michele Lee
Thorndyke	David Tomlinson
Tennessee Steinmetz	Buddy Hackett
Havershaw	Joe Flynn
Mr. Wu	Benson Fong
Detective	Joe E. Ross
Carhop	Iris Adrian

Quote 'There's nothing essentially wrong with the car. It's just that it wants to go one way, and I'd like to go another.'

OOPS! When Herbie goes for a drive in San Francisco he passes several other Volkswagens, blue, red then white. The same cars are there, in the same places, the second

time • The mineshaft that Herbie is diverted to during the race is rectangular on the way in, but round when seen through the back window.

Psst! A large number of identical 'Herbies' were rigged up by the special effects department. There was one souped-up for racing scenes, another that could appear to be driving on its own, a pair of front and half VWs that would both operate independently, one that would run on three wheels and another on just two. There was even one that could appear drunk and another afraid.

Lover Come Back
★★★ 1961 107min c.

Director: Delbert Mann
Screenplay: Paul Henning & Stanley Shapiro

Advertising executive Day aims to wrest a big ad account from Hudson, who epitomises everything she hates in a man. It's not too hard to work out what's going to happen. But after some early stuff that now seems terribly sexist, it exudes considerable charm, helped by Randall's great comic support. It's also fascinating for its glimpse at a far more innocent era.

Jerry Webster	Rock Hudson
Carol Templeton	Doris Day
Peter Ramsey	Tony Randall
Rebel Davis	Edie Adams
J. Paxton Miller	Jack Oakie
Dr. Linus Tyler	Jack Kruschen
Hadley	Joe Flynn
Brackett	Howard St. John
Fred	Jack Albertson
Modges	Ward Ramsey

Love Me or Leave Me
★★★ 1955 122min c.

Director: Charles Vidor
Screenplay: Daniel Fuchs & Isobel Lennart
Source: Story by Daniel Fuchs.

If you've only ever seen Doris Day in soft, fluffy comedies then try to catch her in this moderately true-life story of 20s torch singer Ruth Etting. Her successful career was entirely down to the help she got from a less-than-charming gangster who didn't take kindly to her displaying any sort of independence or falling for any other men. The strain of it all tells heavily on her. Both Day and Cagney are outstanding in this sad, touching tale of love and despair. There's also some great music', with Day making the hairs on the back of the neck rise with 'Ten Cents a Dance'.

Ruth Etting	Doris Day
Martin 'The Gimp' Snyder	James Cagney
Johnny Alderman	Cameron Mitchell
Bernard V. Loomis	Robert Keith
Frobisher	Tom Tully
Georgie	Harry Bellaver
Paul Hunter	Richard Gaines
Fred Taylor	Peter Leeds

Oscars Best Original Story

Psst! Ava Gardner preferred to be suspended by MGM than play the lead role.

Love Me Tonight
★★★ 1932 104min b/w

Director: Rouben Mamoulian
Screenplay: Samuel Hoffenstein, Waldemar Young & George Marion Jr.
Source: Play, *Tailor in the Chateau* by Leopold Marchant & Paul Armont

A delightful romantic comedy musical about a love affair between a tailor and a princess. Jeanette MacDonald is surprisingly adept at comedy, it's innovatively filmed and full of great Rodgers and Hart songs. The story may just be a bit of fluff, but what particularly marks the film out is the continuous stream of splendidly cheeky repartee and double entendres that are still enjoyable today. There has surely never been a nymphomaniac quite as appealing or outrageous as Loy. If you want to know what was missing from films once the censorship under The Hays Code began to bite, watch this gorgeous concoction and weep for what might have been.

Maurice Courtelin	Maurice Chevalier
Princess Jeanette	Jeanette MacDonald
Viscount Gilbert de Varese	Charles Ruggles
Count de Savignac	Charles Butterworth
Countess Vantine	Myrna Loy
The Duke	C. Aubrey Smith
First aunt	Elizabeth Patterson
Second aunt	Ethel Griffies
Major Domo	Robert Greig
Emile	Bert Roach
Laundress	Cecil Cunningham
Valet	Edgar Norton

Quote 'Could you go for a doctor?' – 'Oh yes! Send him in.'

Psst! Chevalier had learnt to speak English while held in a German prisoner of war camp in the World War I.

Love Story
★ 1970 100min c.

Director: Arthur Hiller
Screenplay: Erich Segal

This saccharine, maudlin tale of doomed love from the opposite sides of the track just goes to show that you'll never go broke underestimating the taste of the cinema-going public. Trite, clichéd, grossly sentimental and with two of the least charismatic leads we've ever seen, you'll need some tissues handy...not for your eyes but for wiping up after you've been violently sick. The sequel, *Oliver's Story*, starred O'Neal, this time with Candice Bergen, and is even worse.

Jenny Cavilleri	Ali MacGraw
Oliver Barrett IV	Ryan O'Neal
Oliver Barret III	Ray Milland
John Marley	Phil Cavilleri
Mrs. Oliver Barrett III	Katharine Balfour
Dean Thompson	Russell Nype
Hank	Tommy Lee Jones
Dr. Shapely	Sydney Walker

Quote 'What can you say about a twenty-five-year-old girl who died? That she was beautiful and brilliant? That she loved Mozart and Bach, the Beatles, and me?' [Opening line] • 'Love means never having to say you're sorry.' [Last line]

Psst! Although Paramount's production chief Robert Evans had been warned that such old-fashioned romanticism couldn't possibly work in the 70s, the film was an enormous success and introduced a new, remarkably irritating, saying into the language • Robert Redford, Beau Bridges and Michael York turned down the lead role, while even Ryan O'Neal was initially reluctant to take it • He learnt to ice-skate while Mac Graw took harpsichord lessons • This is the first time Ray Milland appeared in a movie without his hairpiece • Segal wrote the 'novelisation' of the film at the same time as the script for the movie. It was the first such book of the movie and sold 418,000 in hardback and over four million in paperback in the first editions alone • The mansion was the same one that appears in *North by Northwest* • For the sake of the movie, Evans looked the other way when O'Neal and wife MacGraw got together for some unscheduled love scenes off camera • One of the scenes in the film was considered so risible by everyone who saw it that they substituted a long shot of the window, only letting us hear the dialogue, 'You were under the mistaken impression that I wanted to make love to you.' • Producer Robert Evans believes 'there were more pregnancies over *Love Story* than any film ever made. It was an aphrodisiac. Was it corny? Sure.' • Film buffs now love to talk of 'Ali McGraw's disease'. It's defined as a mysterious wasting disease unknown to medical science which makes the sufferer look more beautiful as death approaches. Other examples can be seen in *Beaches* and *Terms of Endearment*.

M
★★★★ 1931 118min b/w

Director: Fritz Lang
Screenplay: Fritz Lang, Thea von Harbou, Paul Falkenberg, Adolf Jansen & Karl Vash
Source: Article by Egon Jacobson

Berlin is gripped with terror because of a wave of killings of small girls. When the police get nowhere, the city's criminals decide to catch the killer themselves. This dark chase movie was Lang's first time working with sound, yet he uses it extremely effectively. Incredibly atmospheric, with a pathetic protagonist with whom we can almost sympathise, many of the images stick indelibly in the mind. Still a deeply disturbing and gripping film.

Franz Becker ....Peter Lorre
Insp. Karl Lohmann ....Otto Wernicke
Schraenker ....Gustav Gründgens
Bauetnfaenger ....Theo Lingen

Quote 'I can't help myself! I haven't any control over this evil thing that's inside me…the fire, the voices, the torment…I want to escape…but it's impossible.'

Psst! The film was based on a real case history of a psychopathic paedophile in Düsseldorf • It was originally titled *Murderers Among Us*. But Lang was threatened by members of the Nazi party who got to hear of the title and assumed the movie was going to be about them. They backed off when Lang explained what the movie was about. Despite being half-Jewish, Lang was held in high esteem by the Nazis. When Goebbels asked him if he would head up the Nazi film unit, Lang decided it was time to leave Germany and departed that evening

• Lorre was acting on stage each night after filming finished • The whistling was dubbed by Lang himself.

Mad Max
★★ 1979 93min c.

Director: George Miller
Screenplay: George Miller & James McCausland

In a desolate and bleak future, an ex-cop goes on a revenge binge when his family are killed. Although what's been achieved on such a low budget is amazing, if you imagine horses instead of cars it's really little more than another Western. Some of the car chases and smash-ups are exciting but as for story or characterisation, forget it. The first sequel was better.

Max Rockatansky ....Mel Gibson
Jessie ....Joanne Samuel
The Toecutter ....Hugh Keays-Byrne
Jim Goose ....Steve Bisley
Johnny the boy ....Tim Burns
Fifi Macaffee ....Roger Ward

Psst! Miller had lost three friends in car crashes and, as a medical student, saw umpteen horrendous motor injuries passing through the casualty department • Made on an incredibly low budget, Miller edited much of the movie in his bedroom • The American distributors weren't sure what to make of the film and ruined it by dubbing American dialogue over the Aussie voices.

Mad Max 2
★★★ 1981 94min c.

Director: George Miller
Screenplay: Terry Hayes, Dean Semler & George Miller

Max is still out there, getting drawn into helping a commune with a supply of precious petrol survive an attack by a bunch of grotesque weirdoes with very few manners. Some stunning car chases and rather more of a plot to get our teeth into make this superior to the first in the series and most definitely superior to the next, *Mad Max Beyond Thunderdome*, which was only so-so.

Max Rodeatansky ....Mel Gibson
Gyro Captain ....Bruce Spence

Wez	Vernon Welles
Feral Kid	Emily Minty
Warrior Woman	Virginia Hey
Big Rebecca	Moira Claux

Psst! With the Americans finally cottoning on, the film took over $100m worldwide • I haven't counted, but it is reckoned that there are fewer than 50 lines of dialogue.

The Madness of King George
★★★★ 1994 107min c.

Director: Nicholas Hytner
Screenplay: Alan Bennett
Source: Play, *The Madness of George III* by Bennett

This Bennett-scripted account of King Farmer George's first bout of madness is spellbinding, right from the sumptuous opening where the King is being readied for the opening of the Parliament. It has everything: tragedy, high comedy, love, madness, political intrigue, bizarre medical practices, all rendered in Bennett's inimitable style. While Hawthorne is brilliant, even Rupert Everett rises to the occasion and gives the best performance of his career as the bored Prince of Wales. One of the best historical movies ever.

George III	Nigel Hawthorne
Queen Charlotte	Helen Mirren
Dr. Willis	Ian Holm
Prince of Wales	Rupert Everett
Greville	Rupert Graves
Thurlow	John Wood
Lady Pembroke	Amanda Donohoe

Blurb His Majesty Was All Powerful And All Knowing. But He Wasn't Quite All There.

Quote 'Good evening, Mr. King.' – 'Good evening, Mrs. King.'

OOPS! Surely we can hear but not see trumpets during the performance of 'The Water Music' that Hawthorne wrecks! • The statue outside St. Paul's Cathedral at the end is not, as many thought, that of Queen Victoria. In fact, it's Queen Anne and so, sadly, isn't a boo-boo at all.

Psst! Although the play was called *The Madness of George III*, the title was changed for the movie in case American audiences thought that this was a sequel to two movies that they had never heard of.

The Magnificent Ambersons
★★★★ 1942 88min b/w

Director: Orson Welles
Screenplay: Orson Welles
Source: Novel by Booth Tarkington

For those who don't agree with all the fuss made about *Citizen Kane*, *this* is Orson Welles' great masterpiece. Despite being hacked to ribbons by the studio, there's plenty to marvel at in this tale of a wealthy family at the turn of the century refusing to bow in the face of progress. Whereas Welles showed off mercilessly with *Kane*, he exhibits much more control when playing with his 'train set' this time. A marvel to both the eye and the ear, he makes what is actually a slight story into a wholly absorbing, fascinating glimpse into a bygone era.

Eugene Morgan	Joseph Cotten
Isabel Amberson Minafer	Dolores Costello
Lucy Morgan	Anne Baxter
George Amberson Minafer	Tim Holt
Fanny Amberson	Agnes Moorehead
Jack Amberson	Ray Collins
Benson	Erskine Sanford
Maj. Amberson	Richard Bennett
Narrator	Orson Welles

Quote 'At twenty-one or twenty-two, so many things appear solid, permanent and terrible, which forty sees as nothing but disappearing miasma. Forty can't tell twenty about this. Twenty can find out only by getting to be forty.' • 'Life and money, both behave like loose quicksilver in a nest of cracks. When they're gone, you can't tell what the devil you did with them.' • 'They let the studio janitor cut *The Magnificent Ambersons* in my absence.'

Psst! The original release was taken out of Welles' hands and butchered by the studio. He had already lost 17 minutes from its 148 minitess, but when Welles was in Brazil working on another project the top brass at RKO changed. The new regime had the film cut further to 88 minutes and got somebody to write a happier ending which was filmed by Freddie Fleck. Welles considered that the changes had wiped out the heart of the film, saying that it looked 'as though somebody had run a lawnmower through the celluloid.' Worst of all, the missing 50 minutes was destroyed, without Welles' knowledge, so that the film can never be restored • It was released as the lesser portion of a double bill with *The Mexican Spitfire Sees a Ghost* starring Lupe Velez. Despite this, it took $1.5m and picked uo four

Oscar nominations • Unusually, the credits at the end are all spoken and end with: 'I wrote and directed the picture • The long crane shot through three rooms was made possible by putting the walls on invisible chains that were raised noiselessly as the camera moved • The ice warehouse that had been used for filming *Lost Horizon* was utilised for the snow scenes. It was later to be used again memorably for *The Thing*. In the cold, filming was constantly disrupted by the lighting bulbs exploding • Rather than have an inviolable script, Welles went through rehearsals with his cast, then let them improvise. The need for take after take apparently drove Agnes Moorehead in particular to distraction • Richard Bennett, playing Maj. Amberson, was the father of actresses Constance, Joan and Barbara Bennett • Welles had originally planned to follow *Citizen Kane* with a version of *The Pickwick Papers*, with W.C. Fields as Pickwick • The mansion house set can be spotted in many other RKO films such as *Cat People*.

The Magnificent Seven

★★★ 1960 138min c.

Director: John Sturges
Screenplay: William Roberts
Source: Film, *The Seven Samurai* by Akira Kirosawa

A Mexican village fed up of constant attacks from bandits hire a group of gunmen to defend them. But they can only afford to hire seven, making the odds a little uneven. The action sequences are still suitably magnificent. The movie is only let down by a tendency for too much talk to intrude in between the shooting. Still, unlike the Japanese original, at least you don't have to read your way through it. Three vastly inferior sequels followed, *The Return of the Seven, The Guns of the Magnificent Seven* and *The Magnificent Seven Ride*.

Chris . . . . .Yul Brynner
Vin . . . . .Steve McQueen
Chico . . . . .Horst Buchholz
O'Reilly . . . . .Charles Bronson
Lee . . . . .Robert Vaughn
Harry Luck . . . . .Brad Dexter
Britt . . . . .James Coburn
Calvera . . . . .Eli Wallach
Old man . . . . .Vladimir Sokoloff

Quote 'Never rode shotgun on a hearse before.'

Psst! The film was based on the Japanese *The Seven Samurai*. Its director, Kurosawa, intended it to be a Japanese Western and came up with the idea of substituting wandering Samurai for cowboys. As soon as he saw it, Sturges wanted to remake it as a Western • After seeing this film, Kurosawa presented director Sturges with a sword as a token of his esteem • With the exception of Brynner, the others in the Seven were virtual or relative unknowns at the time. The film was good to all their careers bar Brad Dexter, who almost vanished without trace • McQueen was working on a TV series, *Dead or Alive*. After being refused permission to be in the movie, he had a car crash in which he claimed to get whiplash. Free of his TV commitments for a while, he appeared to have no problems with his neck during filming • There was considerable on-set rivalry between Brynner and McQueen, with each trying to outdo each other on screen. As the latter had grown up on a farm, he was far better able to handle guns and horses than Brynner, who had no experience of them. Brynner claimed that McQueen was always trying to draw attention away from him by playing with his hat and other scene-stealing tricks • This was the first major Western to be shot in Mexico. Sturges hired real bandits to advise on the movie. They took to Wallach in a big way. He was escorted everywhere by a 30-man escort who taught him to ride and shoot • Buchholz's character was changed to a Mexican when the government refused permission to shoot there if only the baddies were Mexican • When the film-makers dammed the river to get extra water for the horses to splash through as they crossed, the local villagers did not need to hire any gunmen to fight their quarrel for them. They turned up on set armed with machetes and ordered the dam to be torn down • The film was the first to be opened in as many cinemas as possible, rather than building up from a small start.

The Major and the Minor

★★★ 1942 100min b/w

Director: Billy Wilder
Screenplay: Charles Brackett & Billy Wilder
Source: Play, *Connie Goes Home* by Edward Childs Carpenter and story, *Sunny Goes Home* by Fannie Kilbourne

Rogers disguises herself as a 12-year-old to get her train fare for half price and ends up having to maintain the pretense at a military academy. She has a startling effect on the boys, and the men, with whom she comes into contact. This surprisingly risqué comedy still has much to commend it, with Rogers proving a suitably attractive Lolita and the likes of Benchley and Lynn among the supporting cast putting the witty Brackett and Wilder script over with vigour. It was remade as *You're Never Too Young*.

Susan Applegate	Ginger Rogers
Maj. Kirby	Ray Milland
Pamela Hill	Rita Johnson
Mr. Osborne	Robert Benchley
Lucy Hill	Diana Lynn
Col. Hill	Edward Fielding
Cadet Osbourne	Frankie Thomas
Cadet Korner	Charles Smith

Blurb Is She A Kid Or Is She Kidding?

Quote 'Why don't you get out of that wet coat and into a dry martini?'

Psst! This was Billy Wilder's directorial debut • Lela Rogers, Ginger's mother and – so it is said – the bane of Fred Astaire's professional life, appears near the end as her screen mom.

The Maltese Falcon

★★★★ 1941 100min b/w

Director: John Huston
Screenplay: John Huston
Source: Novel by Dashiell Hammett

While investigating the death of his partner, cynical private eye Sam Spade is drawn into the search for a priceless statue of a black bird. Nobody was ever better as the hard-bitten detective than Bogie, though he's helped by an outstanding supporting cast including *femme fatale* Astor, sneaky Lorre and avuncular, dangerous Greenstreet. Most detective stories don't bear repeated viewing once you know who's done it. This is one of those rarities that improves with age and repeated visits. Watch the 1931 version, also known as *Dangerous Female*, which uses much of the same dialogue and realise just how bad the same yarn with the wrong actors and director can be.

Sam Spade	Humphrey Bogart
Brigid O'Shaughnessy	Mary Astor
Iva Archer	Gladys George
Joel Cairo	Peter Lorre
Kasper Gutman	Sydney Greenstreet
Wilmer Cook	Elisha Cook Jr.
Det. Lt. Dundy	Barton MacLane
Effie Perine	Lee Patrick
Det. Tom Polhaus	Ward Bond
Miles Archer	Jerome Cowan
Capt. Jacobi	Walter Huston

Blurb He's As Fast On The Draw As He Is In The Drawing Room.

Quote 'In 1539 the Knights Templar of Malta paid tribute to Charles V of Spain by sending him a Golden Falcon encrusted with rarest jewels…But pirates seized the galley carrying this priceless token.' [Opening crawl] • 'We didn't exactly believe your story, Miss O'Shaughnessy. We believed your 200 dollars. You paid us more than if you'd been telling the truth, and enough more to make it all right.' • 'When you're slapped, you'll take it and like it.' • 'By *gad*, sir! You *are* a character, that you are. There's never any telling what you'll say or do next, except that it's bound to be something astonishing.' • 'Well, sir, here's to plain speaking and clear understanding.' • 'Don't be too sure I'm as crooked as I'm supposed to be.' • 'What is it?' – 'The stuff that dreams are made of.' [Last line] • '*The Maltese Falcon* was produced three times before I did it, but never with very much success, so I decided on a radical procedure: to follow the book rather than depart from it. This was practically an unheard-of thing to do with any picture taken from a novel and marks the beginning of a great epoch in picture making.' [John Huston] • 'The actors were all in their places – looking at me expectantly. I'd no idea what was required. Finally, my assistant, the splendid Jack Sullivan, whispered: "Say action!" I did so and *The Maltese Falcon* was underway.' [John Huston]

OOPS! Bogie is on a chair talking to Astor at one point when he suddenly jumps and is sitting beside her on the sofa • Keep your eye on Peter Lorre's bow tie when Bogie slaps him about. One moment it's got polka dots on, the next stripes.

Psst! The film had been made twice before, first in 1931 and then in 1936, the second version being called *Satan Met a Lady* • This was John Huston's first film as director and he planned it meticulously in advance with storyboards, filming largely in sequence • It was adapted by getting a secretary to copy the novel in script format, keeping the dialogue intact. Some say that's as Huston wanted it, others that he planned to change things but that Jack Warner saw the script at that stage and approved it before Huston had a chance to make further changes • When the previews revealed that audiences found the plot a little confusing, some extra scenes were filmed, which necessitated Bogart being brought back from *All Through the Night* • Huston took out from the script Spade's ordering Brigid to strip to prove that she hadn't stolen a $1,000 bill. It was in the first movie version but he knew he'd never get away with it in the prevailing climate. The censors also insisted on further changes, ordering Huston to make the fact that Spade had been having an affair with his partner's widow less explicit, to make it less obvious that Cairo was homosexual, and to remove the hints that Spade and O'Shaughnessy spent a night together. One thing slipped through unnoticed. Bogart calls Cook a 'gunsel', which was hobo slang for a homosexual side-kick. The 1931 movie had been far saucier, with the Spade character bedding or having bedded practically every woman in sight • According to Astor, one day's shooting scheduled was completed in less than ten minutes, so the cast and crew were able to spend the day around the pool. A great deal of socialising among the principals went on, usually at the Lakeside Country Club. Filming still finished two days ahead of schedule • Astor signals when character is lying by appearing to be out of breath • George Raft was offered the part of Spade but he didn't think the picture 'important' enough and he wasn't prepared to take a chance with a novice director. As with *Dead End* and *High Sierra*, Raft's loss was Bogart's gain, leading to the actor's return from two months' suspension • At 62, this was the first film for Greenstreet who, after starting out as a tea planter, had spent his life on stage • Walter Huston, director John's father, makes a cameo appearance as the seaman who brings Spade the falcon and then drops down dead. He complained that having to do twenty takes had left him black and blue. At Huston's instigation, Astor rang Walter the following day pretending to be a secretary and telling him that the scene would have to be done over again. Walter's answer was pure Anglo-Saxon • At one time, it was planned to call the film *The Gent from Frisco* • This is one of those movies which you think *must* have won at least one Oscar. But it didn't get any • Greenstreet, Bogart, Astor and Huston all got together again soon afterwards for *Across the Pacific* • Both Lee Patrick and Elisha Cook Jr. appeared in a 1975 parody of the movie, *The Black Bird*.

The Man Who Fell to Earth
★★★ 1976 140min c.

Director: Nicolas Roeg
Screenplay: Paul Mayersberg
Source: Novel by Walter Tevis

ET for adults. An alien landing on Earth in search of water becomes fabulously rich but all he really wants is to Go Home. With its prescient vision of the power of multi-media conglomerates, this film looks better with every passing year. America has seldom seemed more breathtaking, the witty ideas keep bubbling away, and Roeg even gets a convincing performance out of Bowie. The loud, cross-cutting sex scenes have dated, though.

Thomas Jerome Newton . . . . .David Bowie
Nathan Bryce .Rip Torn
Mary-Lou . . . . .Candy Clark
Oliver Farnsworth . . . . .Buck Henry
Peters . . . . .Bernie Casey
Prof. Canutti . . . . .Jackson D. Kane

Psst! Originally released at 140minutes, it was then cut down in America until assorted versions were around from 117minutes up to 125minutes. It was restored to its full length in the 80s, but the other versions are probably still knocking around.

A Man and a Woman
★★★ 1966 102min c&b/w

Director: Claude Lelouch
Screenplay: Claude Lelouch & Pierre Uytterhoeven

This famous romantic French movie about a racing driver and a widow falling in love ought not to work at all. It's full of intrusive 60s cinematic trickery and the plot barely exists. Yet it still retains its winning charm. There's a real spark between the couple, with Aimée rarely more radiant than here. Instead of being irritating, the music, which almost never lets up, keeps the mood bubbling along nicely. It's still a great movie to watch while cuddling up on the sofa. It was followed by a sequel 20 years later and was virtually remade by Lelouch in 1977 under the title *Another Man, Another Chance*. Also known as *Un Homme et une Femme*.

Anne Gauthier . . . . .Anouk Aimée
Jean-Louis Duroc . . . . . . .Jean-Louis Trintignant
Pierre Gauthier . . . . .Pierre Barouh
Valerie Duroc . . . . .Valerie Lagrange

Oscars Best Story and Screenplay

Quote 'I think he's upset. We didn't order enough.' – 'Shall we cheer him up? Waiter! Do you have any rooms?' • 'I wonder why, when things are far-fetched, we say it's like the movies. Have you ever thought why people don't take films seriously?'

The Manchurian Candidate
★★★★ 1962 126min c.

Director: John Frankenheimer
Screenplay: George Axelrod
Source: Novel by Richard Condon

A war hero returns form the Korean War having been programmed by his captors to be an assassin. This nerve-tingling conspiracy thriller, brilliantly written, manages to fit in many satirical sideswipes along the way. Claustrophic and gripping, it features the performance of a lifetime from Angela Lansbury as the ultimate Mother from Hell. Compelling and truly frightening.

Bennett Marco . . . . .Frank Sinatra
Raymond Shaw . . . . .Laurence Harvey
Rosie . . . . .Janet Leigh
Raymond's mother . . . . Angela Lansbury
Sen.John Iselin . . . . .James Gregory
Chunjin . . . . .Henry Silva
Jocie Jordan . . . . .Leslie Parrish
Sen. Thomas Jordan . . . . .John McGiver
Yen Lo . . . . .Knigh Dhiegh
Corp. Melvin . . . . .James Edwards
Sec. of Defence . . . . .Barry Kelley
Medical officer . . . . .Whit Bissell

Quote 'His brain has not only been washed, as they say. It has been dry cleaned.'

Psst! The film was planned as an independent production after the major studios had shown no interest. When Sinatra said he wanted to star, United Artists picked it up. But it was still shot cheaply in just 39 days • The film was reported to be one of President John F. Kennedy's favourite movies. His assassination took place just over a year after its release • Several years after the Kennedy shooting the film was withdrawn from circulation, apparently because some considered that it might have sown the seeds of the idea to do away with JFK. It was only in 1988 that it was re-released • Bizarrely, Frankenheimer, who was a friend of Robert Kennedy, drove him to the hotel where he was killed later that evening • Although

playing Harvey's mother, Lansbury was only three years older than him, 37 to his 34
• Sinatra broke a finger during the fight with Henry Silva.

A Man Escaped
★★★★ 1957 102min b/w

Director: Robert Bresson
Screenplay: Robert Bresson
Source: Articles by André Devigny

A captured member of the resistance is sentenced to be executed, but he is determined to escape before it can be carried out. This incredibly tense French film is one of the greatest movies made about a prison break. Not only is it beautifully crafted, an example of the cinematic art at its finest, but the story is absolutely gripping. It puts almost all other prison movies to shame. It'll take some time for your nails to grow back afterwards.

Lt. Fontaine . . . . .François Leterrier
François Jost . . . . .Charles Le Clainche
Blanchet . . . . .Maurice Beerblock
De Leiris the Pastor . . . . .Roland Monod
Orsini .Jacques Ertaud
Hebrard . . . . .Jean-Paul Delhumeau

Psst! The story is based on the true experiences of André Devigny. He was technical adviser on the film and the cell depicted in the movie is the one in which he was imprisoned • As with other films by Bresson, the cast is made up not of professional actors, but amateurs. Leterrier was a graduate of philosophy who was a lieutenant in the army.

A Man for All Seasons
★★★★ 1966 120min c.

Director: Fred Zinnemann
Screenplay: Robert Bolt
Source: Play by Bolt

Despite being given umpteen opportunities to change his mind, Sir Thomas More refuses to condone King Henry VIII's split with Rome or his divorce. An already superb play is actually improved for the screen. The wise and witty script is complemented by outstanding acting, unobtrusive direction and some gorgeous cinematography. One of the best period films ever made and endlessly rewatchable.

Sir Thomas More	Paul Scofield
Alice More	Wendy Hiller
Thomas Cromwell	Leo McKern
King Henry VIII	Robert Shaw
Cardinal Wolsey	Orson Welles
Margaret More	Susannah York
Duke of Norfolk	Nigel Davenport
Richard Rich	John Hurt
William Roper	Corin Redgrave
Matthew	Colin Blakely
Anne Boleyn	Vanessa Redgrave

Oscars Best Picture, Best Screenplay (adapted), Paul Scofield, Best Director

Quote 'Some men think the Earth is round. Others think it flat. It is a matter capable of question. But if it is flat, will the King's word make it round. And if it is round, will the King's word flatten it?' • 'I die His Majesty's good servant, but God's first.'

Psst! This was Scofield's first starring role on screen. He had played the part on stage • Charlton Heston desperately wanted the lead. He got to play it later on stage in the West End and in a 1988 TV version of the play • Orson Welles' Cardinal Wolsey uses a real quill pen and sheepskin parchment. Wolsey's seal was duplicated to ensure authenticity. Even the axe used for the execution was of the right period • Never one to make life easy for himself, Welles used eyedrops to make his eyes appear bloodshot • Vanessa Redgrave, Corin Redgrave's sister, appears as Anne Boleyn in an uncredited cameo • Some American critics read the film as an anti-Vietnam piece.

Manhattan
★★★★ 1979 96min c.

Director: Woody Allen
Screenplay: Woody Allen & Marshall Brickman

One of Allen's true masterpieces, this story of a middle-aged comedy writer in love with a teenager now has added resonances from its creator's own life. It walks a difficult tightrope with great confidence, managing to mix its intelligent observations with wit and a great deal of tenderness in a way that Allen hasn't quite managed in any other film. The Gershwin score is divine, the icing on a perfect cake.

Isaac Davis	Woody Allen
Mary Wilke	Diane Keaton
Yale	Michael Murphy
Tracy	Mariel Hemingway
Jill	Meryl Streep

Emily	Anne Byrne
Connie	Karen Ludwig
Jeremiah	Wallace Shawn
TV actor	Karen Allen
Shakespearean actor	Mark Linn-Baker

Quote 'He adored new York City. He idolised it out of all proportion.' • 'My wife left me for another woman.' • 'There must be something wrong with me because I've never had a relationship with a woman that's lasted longer than the one between Hitler and Eva Braun.' • 'If my film makes one more person feel miserable, I'll feel I've done my job.' [Allen]

OOPS! Woody says he is 42 while Tracy is just 17. But in the café later, he agrees with her that when she is 36 and at the height of her sexual power, he will be 63. Poor maths from the Woodman; he'll only be 61.

Psst! When asked why he had filmed it in black and white, Allen replied: 'Because that's how I remember it when I was small.' • Mariel Hemingway is the granddaughter of novelist Ernest Hemingway.

Manhunter
★★★★ 1986 118min c.

Director: Michael Mann
Screenplay: Michael Mann
Source: Novel, *Red Dragon* by Thomas Harris

This is the Hannibal Lecter film you should not miss, a chilling thriller that gets a good grip early on and refuses to let go until the credits have finished. Petersen is the FBI man who catches serial killers by putting himself in the murderers' minds. Here, he risks his sanity by consulting Lecter, the man he put behind bars. It makes *Silence of the Lambs* look like *Blue Peter*.

Will Graham	William Petersen
Molly Graham	Kim Greist
Reba	Joan Allen
Dr. Lecter	Brian Cox
Jack Crawford	Dennis Farina
Freddie	Stephen Lang
Francis	Tom Noonan
Mrs. Sherman	Patricia Charbonneau

OOPS! When Petersen is talking to his son in the supermarket about evil, the packets of cereal on the shelves behind him suddenly turn into tinned fruit • In the book, Hannibal's name is *Lecter*. Here it's mis-spelt *Lecktor* both on the end credits and when a pile of newspapers is being cut open.

Psst! Although based on the Thomas Harris book *Red Dragon*, producer Dino de Laurentiis had just made the flop *Year of the Dragon* and didn't want to chance fate by using the word 'Dragon' again.

The Man in the White Suit

★★★ 1951 84min b/w

Director: Alexander Mackendrick
Screenplay: Roger Macdougall, John Dighton & Alexander Mackendrick

When a research scientist invents a material that never wears out or needs cleaning, labour and management combine against the threat to both their interests. Guinness is excellent as the bewildered boffin and Greenwood very sensual as his reluctant nemesis. Unlike the fabric, this satire has faded a little. But although it seems not to know where to go with its central idea, it is still jolly and eminently watchable. The noise made by Guinness' equipment is one of the most memorable sound effects in the movies.

Sidney Stratton . . . . .Alec Guinness
Daphne Birnley . . . . .Joan Greenwood
Alan Birnley . . . . .Cecil Parker
Michael Corland . . . . .Michael Gough
Sir John Kirlaw . . . . .Ernest Thesiger
Cranford . . . . .Howard Marion-Crawford
Bertha . . . . .Vida Hope
Also: Duncan Lamont, Patric Doonan, Miles Malleson, George Benson, Edie Martin

Manon des Sources

★★★★ 1987 114min c.

Director: Claude Berri
Screenplay: Claude Berri & Gérard Brach
Source: Novel *L'Eau des collines* by Marcel Pagnol, in turn based on Pagnol's 1953 film.

This sequel to *Jean de Florette* has Depardieu's daughter Beart, now a beautiful shepherdess, discovering the truth behind her father's death and plotting revenge. If at all possible, this is better than the earlier film, becoming almost heart-rendingly unbearable when Montand realises the true enormity of his crime. Also known as *Manon of the Spring*.

Cesar Soubeyran . . . . .Yves Montand
Ugolin . . . . .Daniel Auteuil
Manon . . . . .Emmanuelle Beart
Bernard Olivier . . . . .Hoppolyte Girardot
Aimee . . . . .Elisabeth Depardieu

The Man Who Came to Dinner

★★★ 1941 112min b/w

Director: William Keighley
Screenplay: Julius J. Epstein & Philip G. Epstein
Source: Play by George Kaufman & Moss Hart

A viciously uncharitable radio commentator becomes the Guest From Hell after injuring himself on a patch of ice on a family's doorstep. He meddles in the lives of all around him, treating their home as Liberty Hall, and his brain moves into overdrive when he realises that love may lose him his efficient secretary. Although the topical references are now largely lost, the play is sufficiently funny and is performed with enough vigour and vim to more than compensate. A delightful comedic gem.

Maggie Cutler . . . . .Bette Davis
Lorraine Sheldon . . . . .Ann Sheridan
Sheridan Whiteside . . . . .Monty Woolley
Bert Jefferson . . . . .Richard Travis
Banjo . . . . .Jimmy Durante
Beverly Carlton . . . . .Reginald Gardiner
Mrs. Ernest Stanley . . . . .Billie Burke
June Stanley . . . . .Elisabeth Fraser
Ernest Stanley . . . . .Grant Mitchell
Dr. Bradley . . . . .George Barbier
Nurse . . . . .Mary Wickes

Quote 'I guess you are sort of attractive in a corn-fed sort of way. You can find youself a poor girl falling for you if…well, if you threw in a set of dishes.' • 'Go in and read the life of Florence Nightingale and learn how unfitted you are for your chosen profession.' • 'I am not only walking out on this case, Mr Whiteside, I am leaving the nursing profession…after one month with you, Mr Whiteside, I am going to work in a munitions factory. From now on, anything I can do to help exterminate the human race will fill me with the greatest of pleasure.' • ';My great-aunt Jennifer ate a whole box of candy every day of her life. She lived to be 102, and when she had been dead three days, she looked better than you do now.' • 'And now will you all leave quietly, or must I ask Miss Cutler to pass among you with a baseball bad.' • 'I can feel the hot blood pounding through your varicose veins.' • 'You have the touch of a love-starved cobra.' • 'If you ever come to New York, try and find me.'

Psst! The original hit play was based on the wits of the Algonquin Round Table, with Alexander Woollcott the basis of Whiteside, Harpo Marx as Banjo and more occasional visitor Noël Coward as Beverly Carlton

• Although John Barrymore was hired for the main part, he had to be replaced because he couldn't remember his lines. Robert Benchley and Charles Laughton tested for the role and it nearly went to Orson Welles, but RKO dug their heels in and would not lend him to Warners
• Mary Wickes, who plays the Nurse, is best known now for her role in the *Sister Act* films.

The Man Who Could Work Miracles

★★★ 1936 82min b/w

Director: Lothar Mendes
Screenplay: Lajos Biro
Source: Story by H.G. Wells

Playful gods decide to give a meek clerk unlimited powers. Young is just right as the mouse who wakes up to find himself the King of the Jungle and whose newfound abilities go straight to his head. Although a trifle faded, it's still appealing, with some interesting ideas behind it.

George Fotheringay ....Roland Young
Col. Winstanley ....Ralph Richardson
Ada Price ....Joan Gardner
Mr. Maydig ....Ernest Thesiger
Maj. Grigsby ....Edward Chapman
Maggie Hooper ....Sophie Stewart
Mr. Banfylele ....Lawrence Hanray
Also: George Zucco, George Sanders, Torin Thatcher

Psst! Wells caused considerable friction on set with his constant interference. Frank Wells, his eldest son who worked for Korda's London Films, was deputed to keep his father as far away from the film-makers as possible.

The Man Who Would Be King

★★★ 1975 129min c.

Director: John Huston
Screenplay: John Huston & Gladys Hill
Source: Short story by Rudyard Kipling

Two of Her Majesty's less noble officers head off into Afghanistan with the intention of getting their hands on riches beyond the dreams even of their considerable avarice. Although rather plodding in its early stages, it becomes a fascinating action yarn once the pair cross the mountains, even if Connery and Caine often come across like a comedy double act, a sort of Imperial Morecambe and Wise.

Daniel Dravot ....Sean Connery
Peachy Carnehan ....Michael Caine
Rudyard Kipling ....Christopher Plummer
Billy Fish ....Saeed Jaffrey
District Commissioner ....Jack May
Roxanne ....Shakira Caine
Kafu-Selim ....Karroum Ben Bouih
Ootah ....Doghmi Larbi

Quote 'Not Gods. Englishmen. The next best thing.' • 'Peachy, I'm heartily ashamed for getting you killed instead of going home rich like you deserve to, on account of me being so bleedin' high and bloody mighty. Can you forgive me?' – 'That I can and that I do, Danny.' • 'The typhoid is particularly unpleasant because you go dizzy and can't stand up. But apart from that, it was a big laugh.' [Michael Caine]

Psst! Huston had been fascinated by the story since he read it as a bedridden teenager. His plans to film it with Humphrey Bogart and Clark Gable went by the board when Bogie died and he wasn't able to raise the cash to make it with Richard Burton and Peter O'Toole. He then rewrote it envisaging Paul Newman and Robert Redford in the leads but Newman said he thought it would be best if a pair of Britons were cast • Roxanne, the tribal princess, is played by Mrs. Caine. She was not an actress and, when she found herself unable to portray fear, Huston taught her to raise her eyes so that just the whites were showing • The movie was made in Morocco and substantial funds had to be handed over to corrupt officials to prevent filming being shut down on various flimsy pretexts • Berber tribesmen were coralled in as extras but their womenfolk could not be photographed and so the necessary ladies were obtained from brothels in Marrakesh • The three ancient tribesmen that played the High Priests had never seen a movie before. When they saw themselves on the rushes, they were delighted, believing that their spirits had been preserved and that they would never die • There were money problems with the studio and both Caine and Connery had to sue Allied Artists to get the cash due to them.

The Man with the Golden Arm

★★ 1956 119min b/w

Director: Otto Preminger
Screenplay: Walter Newman & Lewis Meltzer
Source: Novel by Nelson Algren

This once-shocking story of a poker player trying to shake off his heroin addiction may have been ground-breaking in its day, but it looks rather pallid and obvious now. Sinatra does play the lead, going through the hell of cold turkey, pretty well though.

```
Frankie Machine . .,. . . . . . . . . . . .Frank Sinatra
Molly . . . . . . . . . . . . . . . . . . . . . . . .Kim Novak
Zosch Machine  . . . . . . . . . . . . .Eleanor Parker
Sparrow . . . . . . . . . . . . . . . . . . . .Arnold Stang
Louie . . . . . . . . . . . . . . . . . . .Darren McGavin
Schwiefka . . . . . . . . . . . . . . . .Robert Strauss
Drunky . . . . . . . . . . . . . . . . . . . . . .John Conte
Vi . . . . . . . . . . . . . . . . . . . . . . . .Doro Merande
Markette . . . . . . . . . . . . . . . . .George E. Stone
Williams . . . . . . . . . . . . . . . .George Matthews
Dominowski  . . . . . . . . . . . . . .Leonid Kinskey
```

Psst! Marlon Brando was also up for the lead, but Sinatra agreed to do it without seeing a complete script and was signed, to Brando's apparent fury • The film was an important step in doing away with Hollywood's self-censorship. It broke new ground in showing someone addicted to heroin. Preminger knew full well that drug addiction was on the list of forbidden topics for movies. He expected that the rules would be altered for his movie. When they weren't, United Artists released it without the MPAA seal which had hitherto been all-important. A year later, the first changes in the Code since 1930 were made, allowing the depiction within limits of drugs, prostitution, kidnapping and abortion • Novak was paid just $100 a week, her regular salary. But the film-makers had to pay Columbia, the studio from which they'd hired her, $100,000 for her services.

The Man with the Golden Gun

★ 1974 125min c.

Director: Guy Hamilton
Screenplay: Richard Maibaum & Tom Mankiewicz
Source: Novel by Ian Fleming

One of the worst of all the Bonds, as 007 goes head-to-head with the assassin Scaramanga. The plot and the gadgets are tiresome and implausible, the humour is crass, Ekland and Adams don't cut the mustard, and having the sheriff from *Live and Let Die* turn up smacks of desperation. Also, silly double entendres like 'Something just came up' and 'She's just coming, sir' are hardly worthy of a Carry On film. And while we're at it, since when did James Bond resort to twisting a woman's arm to get information?

```
James Bond . . . . . . . . . . . . . . . . . .Roger Moore
Scaramanga  . . . . . . . . . . . . . .Christopher Lee
Mary Goodnight  . . . . . . . . . . . . . . .Britt Ekland
Andrea  . . . . . . . . . . . . . . . . . . . .Maud Adams
Nick Nack  . . . . . . . . . . . . . . .Hervé Villechaize
J.W. Pepper . . . . . . . . . . . . . . . .Clifton James
'M'  . . . . . . . . . . . . . . . . . . . . . . . .Bernard Lee
Miss Moneypenny . . . . . . . . . . . . .Lois Maxwell
'Q'  . . . . . . . . . . . . . . . . . . . .Desmond Llewelyn
```

Quote 'I like a girl in a bikini...no concealed weapons.'

OOPS! Keep an eye on the dressing table in the Beirut club when the fight breaks out. When it gets knocked, the camera crew are visible momentarily in the reflection.

Psst! Lee was the cousin of Bond author Fleming. Before Connery was cast as the first Bond, Lee had been one of Fleming's suggestions for an actor to play 007.

Marathon Man

★★★ 1976 125min c.

Director: John Schlesinger
Screenplay: William Goldman
Source: Novel by Goldman

A prospective marathon runner unwittingly finds himself on the receiving end of some unwanted dental treatment from an ex-Nazi trying to find a hoard of jewels stolen from concentration camp victims. Incredibly tense and packed with great action sequences, parts of the film are deeply disturbing and hard to scrub from the memory afterwards.

```
Babe Levy . . . . . . . . . . . . . . . . .Dustin Hoffman
Szell . . . . . . . . . . . . . . . . . . . . .Laurence Olivier
Doc Levy . . . . . . . . . . . . . . . . . .Roy Scheider
Janeway  . . . . . . . . . . . . . . . .William Devane
Else  . . . . . . . . . . . . . . . . . . . . . .Marthe Keller
Prof. Biesenthal . . . . . . . . . . . . . . .Fritz Weaver
Carl . . . . . . . . . . . . . . . . . . . . . . .Richard Bright
Erhard . . . . . . . . . . . . . . . . . . . .Marc Lawrence
LeClerk . . . . . . . . . . . . . . . . . . . .Jacques Marin
```

Quote 'Is it safe?'

Psst! The film resulted in one of the most famous of all movie anecdotes. Told in many different forms, it is said that Hoffman needed to look as if he had been awake for three days on the trot. Ever the method actor, he actually stayed awake for that time so that he was sufficiently disorientated on the set. After the scene was filmed, Olivier said to him: 'Why don't you try acting next time, Dustin. It's so much easier.' Other versions of the story say it happened after Hoffman ran round the block so that he would appear out of breath.

The Mark of Zorro

★★★ 1940 93min b/w

Director: Rouben Mamoulian
Screenplay: John Taintor Foote, Garrett Fort & Bess Meredyth
Source: Novel, *The Curse of Capistrano* by Johnston McCulley

When a young man returns to California in pre-movie days, he finds a vicious tyrant has taken over. Donning the briefest of masks, which renders him totally unrecognisable even to his nearest and dearest, he rushes around the place despatching baddies and leaving grafitti wherever he goes in the form of the letter 'Z'. Rathbone is particularly good as the villain of the piece in this exuberant old-fashioned adventure yarn which has plenty of good sword fights and which Fox intended as their riposte to Warner's *Robin Hood*. Not quite as good, but fun nonetheless.

Don Diego Vega/Zorro . . . . .Tyrone Power
Lolita Quintero . . . . .Linda Darnell
Capt. Esteban Pasquale . . . . . .Basil Rathbone
Inez Quintero . . . . .Gale Sondergaard
Fra Felipe . . . . .Eugene Pallette
Don Luis Quintero . . . . . . .J. Edward Bromberg
Don Alejandro Vega . . . . .Montagu Love
Isabella Vega . . . . .Janet Beecher
Rodrigo .Robert Lowery

Quote 'Most men have objects they play with. Churchmen have their beads. I toy with a sword.'

Psst! Rathbone, acknowledged to be the best swordsman in Hollywood, claimed that: 'Power was the most agile man with a sword I've ever faced before a camera. Tyrone could have fenced Errol Flynn into a cocked hat.'

Marty

★★★ 1955 91min b/w

Director: Delbert Mann
Screenplay: Paddy Chayefsky
Source: TV play by Chayefsky

Unprepossessing butcher Borgnine finally meets a girl who doesn't run a mile when he says 'hello'. Thanks to its honest portrayal of the dating scene, using actors who looked like real people instead of movie stars pretending to be real people, it was an immense success. It's now lost much of its power and seems little more than sweet. It's worth it, though, for Borgnine's finest hour and a half.

Marty .Ernest Borgnine
Clara . . . . .Betsy Blair
Mrs. Pilletti . . . . .Esther Minciotti
Angie . . . . .Joe Mantell
Virginia . . . . .Karen Steel
Thomas . . . . .Jerry Paris
Ralph . . . . .Frank Sutton
Catherine . . . . .Augusta Ciolli

Oscars Best Picture, Ernest Borgnine, Best Screenplay, Best Director

Quote 'What do you feel like doing tonight' – 'I don't know, Ange. What do *you* feel like doing?' • 'I've been looking for a girl every Saturday night of my life. I'm 34 years old. I'm just tired of looking, that's all.' • 'Dogs like us, we ain't such dogs as we think we are.'

Psst! This was the first TV drama to be turned into a motion picture. The TV version starred Rod Steiger as a Jewish, rather than Italian, butcher • Studio chiefs were so unenthusiastic about the film that they came close to cancelling the project. Its success led to a succession of low-key, small-scale dramatic movies, many based on TV plays • When they were working together on *Bad Day at Black Rock*, Borgnine asked Spencer Tracy whether he should make the film. Tracy reckoned it would do nothing and that he should reject it. Both men were nominated for Oscars and, as Borgnine passed Tracy to pick his statuette up, Tracy said: 'You never listen, do you?' • Betsy Blair was Gene Kelly's wife • This was the first film since the end of World War II to be shown in the Soviet Union, where it proved to be immensely successful.

Mary Poppins

★★★ 1964 140min c.

Director: Robert Stevenson
Screenplay: Bill Walsh & Don DaGradi
Source: Mary Poppins books by P.L. Travers

Travers' tale of the nanny with magical powers is Disneyfied almost beyond recognition. Kids are less likely than discriminating adults to scream with anguish at Dick van Dyke's mangling of a Cockney accent or to quail at Julie Andrews' incessant cheerfulness. They might realise that the special effects are pretty feeble by modern standards and that the second half of a long movie flags. But they'll undoubtedly enjoy it nonetheless. Altogether now, 'Supercalifragilisticexpialidocious.'

Mary Poppins	Julie Andrews
Bert/Old Dawes	Dick Van Dyke
Mr. Banks	David Tomlinson
Mrs. Banks	Glynis Johns
Ellen	Hermione Baddeley
Katie Nanna	Elsa Lanchester
Jane Banks	Karen Dotrice
Michael Banks	Matthew Garber
Uncle Albert	Ed Wynn
Bird Woman	Jane Darwell
Constable Jones	Arthur Treacher
Adm. Boom	Reginald Owen

Oscars Julie Andrews

Quote 'I shall stay until the wind changes.'

OOPS! Watch Mary's gloves as she's reading a letter change from white to black and back to white again.

Psst! Andrews was surprised and disappointed not to transfer her stage role of Eliza in *My Fair Lady* to the screen. She wasn't considered a big enough star, however, and so she made this instead. It was her first film and she won an Oscar for it, depriving Audrey Hepburn of the statuette • Picking up her Oscar, she said: 'You Americans are famous for your hospitality, but this is ridiculous' • For those curious about the origins of 'supercalifragilisticexpialidocious', it was apparently a word the songwriters Richard and Robert Sherman heard at a summer camp before the war.

M*A*S*H
★★★★ 1970 116min c.

Director: Robert Altman
Screenplay: Ring Lardner Jr.
Source: Novel by Richard Hooker

Two doctors at a Mobile Army Surgical Hospital in the Korean War try to make life for themselves as comfortable as possible while irritating the hell out of anyone behaving in a vaguely military manner. This freewheeling, anarchic comedy is still incredibly fresh and funny, hitting most of its targets exactly where it hurts. There are moments, though, when it plays almost like an adult *Porky's*.

Hawkeye Pierce	Donald Sutherland
Trapper John McIntyre	Elliott Gould
Duke Forrest	Tom Skerritt
Maj. Hotlips Houlihan	Sally Kellerman
Maj. Frank Burns	Robert Duvall
Lt. Hot Dish	Jo Ann Pflug
Dago Red	Rene Auberjonois
Col. Henry Blake	Roger Bowen
Radar O'Reilly	Gary Burghoff
Me Lay	Michael Murphy
Sgt.-Maj. Vollmer	David Arkin
Spearchucker	Fred Williamson
Painless Pole	John Schuck

Oscars Best Screenplay (adapted)

Quote 'Frank, were you on this religious kick at home or did you crack up over here?' • 'I wonder how a degenerated person like that could have reached a position of responsibility in the Army Medical Corps.' – 'He was drafted.' • 'This isn't a hospital. It's an insane asylum!'

OOPS! Early on, there's an operating room scene where all we see are the surgeons' feet. Although Elliott Gould hasn't yet arrived at the outfit, you can clearly hear his voice.

Psst! Fourteen potential directors were either unavailable or turned the film down before Altman got the chance to make his first comedy. One of the top brass of 20th Century Fox later admitted that if he'd seen Altman's earlier film, *That Cold Day in the Park*, he would never have been allowed to direct this one • Altman had to fight the top brass long and hard to keep all the blood and gore in • At the preview for the foreign press, there was a mass walkout at the sight of all the blood • The film, which was released during the Vietnam War, was immensely popular, but was banned from Army and Air Force bases. The Navy, however, which got off scot-free in the movie, was happy to show it • Encouraging input and improvisation, Altman made the cast and crew live under canvas on the Fox lot, where they behaved rather like the characters in the movie. Many of the scenes that were supposedly rehearsals were the ones printed • Angie Dickinson was originally offered the part of Hotlips Houlihan, but she wasn't keen to go on location and turned it down. The part originally contained just nine lines. More were made up as they went along • Kellerman was terribly shy of doing her nude scene in the shower, so Altman got all the cast to stand behind the camera with no clothes on. When the canvas vanished, Kellerman's look of surprise was exactly what the director had wanted • Gould and Sutherland hated Altman's methods and tried to have him sacked • The book was written by an ex-Army doctor. It was rejected by 17 publishers before finally finding a home • The films that are ridiculed over the tannoy are all Fox movies • This movie was later turned into a TV comedy series that ran for 11 years. The Korean War itself had lasted only three years! Gary Burghoff was the only member of the cast to make the transfer to TV • Altman got no benefit from this, as he'd taken his fee up front. But his son, who had written the lyrics to the theme music, did very nicely thank you out of the royalties each week • The film marked the rehabilitation of Ring Lardner Jr., who had been imprisoned for 10 months as a Member of the Hollywood Ten who stood out against HUAC and then ostracised for 15 years. He got an Oscar to put on the mantlepiece along with the one he won for *Woman of the Year* in 1942 • This is probably the only movie to have the end credits read out over a PA system.

The Mask

★★★ 1994 101min c.

Director: Charles Russell
Screenplay: Mike Werb

A meek bank clerk finds a mask which turns him into a hip, wisecracking, babe-chasing super-hero. Although irritating as in his Jerry Lewis-like persona as Ipkiss, once Carrey gets the mask on he virtually becomes a Tex Avery cartoon, with his eyes popping out on stalks and his jaw hitting the floor when he sees gang-ster's babe Diaz. The combination of Carrey's schtick and the most amazing effects we've seen for ages click, turning the film into a funny, eye-boggling experience. The dog's pretty good too.

Stanley Ipkiss/The Mask . . . . .Jim Carrey
Tina Carlyle . . . . .Cameron Diaz
Lt. Mitch Kellaway . . . . .Peter Riegert
Dorian Tyrel . . . . .Peter Greene
Peggy Brandt . . . . .Amy Yasbeck
Charlie Schumacher . . . . .Richard Jeni
Niko .Orestes Matacena
Mrs. Peeman . . . . .Nancy Fish

Blurb From Zero To Hero.

Quote 'That girl will tear your heart out, put it in a blender and hit "frappe".' • 'Most of the men in this town think monogamy is some kind of wood.'

The Mask of Dimitrios

★★★ 1944 95min b/w

Director: Jean Negulesco
Screenplay: Frank Gruber
Source: Novel, *A Coffin for Dimitrios* by Eric Ambler

This is a wonderfully atmospheric film noir, with Lorre as a novelist turning over the stone of a criminal's past and finding all sorts of nasty things crawling around there. Not only is the script a corker which keeps you hooked throughout, but the whole enterprise is carried by a great team of character actors, without a star in sight.

Mr. Peters . . . . .Sydney Greenstreet
Cornelius Latimer Leyden . . . . .Peter Lorre
Dimitrios .Zachary Scott
Irana Preveza . . . . .Faye Emerson
Grodek . . . . .Victor Francen
Bulic . . . . .Steven Geray
Mme. Chevez . . . . .Florence Bates
Marukakis . . . . .Eduardo Ciannelli
Col. Haki . . . . .Kurt Katch
Abdul . . . . .Monte Blue

Quote 'Ingenuity is never a substitute for intelligence.'

Psst! The film is partly based on fact, the central villain being a thinly disguised version of munitions tycoon Basil Zaharoff.

The Masque of the Red Death

★★ 1964 86min c.

Director: Roger Corman
Screenplay: Charles Beaumont & R. Wright Campbell
Source: Novels, *The Masque of the Red Death* & *Hop-Frog, or the Eight Chained Orang-Outangs* by Edgar Allan Poe

While the plague rages outside, a Satanist and his cronies hold a ball. Death turns up, but can't find his invitation card for a while. Although con-sidered Roger Corman's best stab at Poe, this film is wildly overrated, presumably because it looks vaguely like something Ingmar Bergman might have made if he'd gone into this field instead of, say, Carry On movies. It's all rather amateurish and about as scary as an early episode of Dr. Who.

Prince Prospero . . . . .Vincent Price
Juliana . . . . .Hazel Court

Francesca	Jane Asher
Alfredo	Patrick Magee
Ludovico	Nigel Green
Man in Red	John Westbrook
Senora Escobar	Gaye Brown
Gino	David Weston

A Matter of Life and Death
★★★★ 1946 104min c&b/w

Director: Michael Powell & Emeric Pressburger
Screenplay: Michael Powell & Emeric Pressburger

A pilot bales out from a burning plane and survives, but imagines that he is ordered to report for his wings in Heaven. He's reluctant to obey, having fallen in love with a girl he's never seen. Although occasionally a little over the top in the scenes with Massey at the end, this utterly delightful fantasy is packed full of great ideas, such as the staircase that leads up to Heaven. The romance between Niven and Hunter is so believable that you feel almost as much pain at the impending parting as they do. A pinnacle of British film-making from the great team of Powell and Pressburger and one of my Top Ten of all time. Known in the US as *Stairway to Heaven*.

Peter Carter	David Niven
June	Kim Hunter
Dr. Reeves	Roger Livesey
Bob Trubshawe	Robert Coote
Conductor 71	Marius Goring
Abraham Farlan	Raymond Massey
Judge/Surgeon	Abraham Sofaer
English pilot	Richard Attenborough
American pilot	Bonar Colleano
Angel	Kathleen Byron
Chief Recorder	Joan Maude

Quote 'One is starved for Technicolor up there.'

OOPS! When Niven is discarding his stuff on the beach, the sand is very damp. In the long shot just after he takes his boot off, it's perfectly dry.

Psst! The film was initiated by The Ministry of Information with the aim of promoting goodwill between America and Britain • It was the film shown at the first Royal Command Film Performance • Of the title change in America, Michael Powell said: 'It was only the United States that had to be protected from the realities of life and death.'

McCabe and Mrs. Miller
★★★ 1971 120min c.

Director: Robert Altman
Screenplay: Robert Altman & Brian McKay
Source: Novel, *McCabe* by Edmund Naughton

Altman debunks the Western. Gambler Beatty sets up a brothel which, with Christie's help, becomes a thriving business, only to attract attention from some unpleasant types. It offers an intriguingly different slant on the West and looks divine, although the songs by Leonard Cohen seem ridiculously out of period.

John McCabe	Warren Beatty
Constance Miller	Julie Christie
Sheehan	Rene Auberjonois
Smalley	John Shuck
Bart Coyle	Bert Remsen
Cowboy	Keith Carradine
Lawyer	William Devane
Ida Coyle	Shelley Duvall
Sears	Michael Murphy

Psst! Altman had to fight the studio, as so often, to get his choice of Beatty for the lead over their preference of George C. Scott
• Christie and Beatty were lovers at the time
• There was the usual element of improvisation, as in any Altman film. This was most successful in the cake-eating scene in the brothel, which was filmed after the cast had been happily downing vodka for hours.

The McKenzie Break
★★★ 1970 108min c.

Director: Lamont Johnson
Screenplay: William Norton
Source: Novel, *The Bowmanville Break* by Sidney Shelley

A refreshing variation on the familiar POW story, with German soldiers trying to escape from a Scottish camp in World War II. There's a great standoff rivalry between intelligence agent Brian Keith and U-Boat captain Helmut Griem, with the film bolstered by a witty, twisty script and lots of wild scenery. A tight, unpretentious genre piece. More like this, please.

Capt. Jack Connor	Brian Keith
Capitan Willi Schluetter	Helmut Griem
Maj. Perry	Ian Hendry
Gen. Kerr	Jack Watson
Sgt. Maj. Cox	Patrick O'Connell

Lt. Nauchl	.Horst Janson
Lt. Schmidt	Tom Kempinski

Mean Streets
★★★ 1973 110min c.

Director: Martin Scorsese
Screenplay: Martin Scorsese & Mardik Martin

The film that made director Martin Scorsese's reputation, portraying the struggle between Redemption and Damnation on New York's streets. Harvey Keitel stars as the divided loner torn between the Church and the Mob, though ironically it was Robert de Niro who went on to be the star. It was groundbreaking in its use of colour, camera and rock music, although it's not the most coherent of Scorsese's films.

Charlie	.Harvey Keitel
Johnny Boy	.Robert De Niro
Tony	.David Proval
Teresa	Amy Robinson
Michael	Richard Romanus
Giovanni	Cesare Danova
Mario	.Victor Argo
Assassin	Robert Carradine
Drunk	David Carradine
Joey Catucci	George Memmoli
Car gunman	.Martin Scorsese
Neighbour on staircase . . .	Catherine Scorsese

Showing The Searchers.

Psst! With the exception of a few exteriors it was filmed, not in New York where it is set, but in Los Angeles • Scorsese, who was film editor on several movies of 70s rock concerts, envisaged the movie not just in terms of pictures, but of pictures and music simultaneously • Roger Corman, for whom he had been working, had slightly different ideas about the film, reckoning that it would make a good, quickly-shot, black exploitation movie • At the preview screening at Warner Brothers, sandwiches were served in the middle of the movie. So little attention was being paid to the film that the waiter simply stood in front of the projector and yelled out: 'Who's got the tuna on rye?' • Scorsese appears in a cameo as an assassin

Meet Me in St. Louis
★★★★ 1944 113min c.

Director: Vincente Minnelli
Screenplay: Irving Brecher & Fred Finklehoffe
Source: Stories by Sally Benson

A big, happy family in turn-of-the-century St. Louis go through misery when a move to New York is threatened. Although the script is little more than a series of incidents strung together, it is visually sumptuous, bright and lively and packed with great songs from Garland at the peak of her career like 'Have Yourself a Merry Little Christmas', 'The Trolley Song' and the smashing title number.

Esther Smith	.Judy Garland
'Tootie' Smith	Margaret O'Brien
Mrs. Anne Smith	.Mary Astor
Rose Smith	Lucille Bremer
Lulille Ballard	June Lockhart
John Truett	.Tom Drake
Katie	Marjorie Main
Grandpa	Harry Davenport
Mr. Alonzo Smith	Leon Ames
Agnes Smith	.Joan Carroll
Col. Darly	.Hugh Marlowe
Mr. Neely	.Chill Wills

Quote 'Personally, I wouldn't marry a man who proposed to me over an invention.'

OOPS! Keep your ears peeled for one of the all-time best boo-boo's during 'The Trolley Song'. At one point, you can clearly hear someone call out, 'Hi, Judy'. Presumably the visitor didn't realise that they were actually recording. But they were, and that was the take they used • During the slightly twee dance, 'If You Like-a-Me' by Garland and O'Brien, O'Brien's slippers change colour from pink to blue.

Psst! According to producer Arthur Freed, it was the hardest film he ever had to sell to the MGM top brass. 'Finally we had a meeting and (Louis B.) Mayer said: "Arthur's record has been so good, either he'll learn a lesson or we'll learn a lesson. So go make the picture." And it was the biggest-grossing picture they had for five years.' • Initially, Garland had refused to make the film, not wanting to play any more teenage parts now that she was 21. But she was threatened with suspension by Mayer and her early antagonism on set towards director Minnelli gradually evaporated so that, by the time filming finished, they were going steady. They married the following year • For once, the seven-year-old O'Brien was unable to cry when needed. So Minnelli told her that her dog had died horribly and, as he went into gorier and gorier details about how it had died, he got the tears he was after. He said later: 'I went home feeling like a monster. I marvel tht Margaret didn't turn out to be one too. That sort of preparation struck me as most unhealthy.' • O'Brien was later to perfect the art of crying.

She is reputed once to have asked a director: 'When I cry, do you want the tears to run all the way down or should I stop half way?' • When songwriter Ralph Blane was researching the period, he saw a picture of a trolley bus, with a caption: 'Clang, Clang, Here Comes the Trolley'. He said to his partner Hugh Martin, 'Clang, Clang, Clang Went the Trolley' and, so they claim, the song was finished in 10 minutes • Garland sang 'Buzz, Buzz, Buzz' by mistake in the song instead of 'Bump, Bump, Bump' but they kept the take and she had to sing it wrongly every time she performed it in future • Producer Arthur Freed, who in his song-writing days wrote the numbers used in 'Singin' in the Rain', dubbed Ames' singing voice in 'You and I'.

The Men
★★★ 1950 85min b/w

Director: Fred Zinnemann
Screenplay: Carl Foreman

A World War II veteran is left paralysed by a sniper's bullet and initially refuses either to cooperate with the doctors or nurses, or to see his loyal girlfriend. This is one of Brando's best performances, though he's helped by a clever and often witty script which avoids too much sentimentality. The little-known 1991 movie *Waterdance* covered the same ground but is more inspired and enjoyable.

Ken Wilozek	Marlon Brando
Ellen	Teresa Wright
Dr. Brock	Everett Sloane
Norm	Jack Webb
Leo	Richard Erdman
Angel	Arthur Jurado
Ellen's father	Howard St. John
Man at bar	Ray Teal
Nurse Robbins	Virginia Farmer
Ellen's mother	Dorothy Tree

Psst! This was Brando's first movie role. Two years earlier he had been given a screen test but nobody had shown any interest • Ever the method actor, he insisted before filming on spending time living with some paraplegics in an army hospital • Brando was drinking with them in a bar when they were disturbed by a woman from the Salvation Army. 'Oh Lord,' she cried, when she saw them in their wheelchairs, 'Grant that these men may be able to walk again!' Perspiration breaking out on his brow, Brando struggled to his feet and shuffled over to her. Her astonishment caused great delight among Brando's new friends.

Merrily We Live
★★★ 1938 90min b/w

Director: Norman Z. McLeod
Screenplay: Eddie Moran & Jack Jevne

A wealthy family finds their new chauffeur more than a match for their extraordinary ways. It's really an inferior version of *My Man Godfrey*. But while the plot's a little insipid, the wacky family is still very funny and the jokes are fast and zany. To think there was a time when Hollywood could make screwball comedies like this at the drop of a hat.

Jerry Kilbourne	Constance Bennett
Wade Rawlins	Brian Aherne
Mrs. Emily Kilbourne	Billie Burke
Grosvenor	Alan Mowbray
Cook	Patsy Kelly
Minerva Harlan	Ann Dvorak
Marion Kilbourne	Bonita Granville
Senator's wife	Marjorie Rambeau
Mr. Kilbourne	Clarence Kolb

Metropolis
★★ 1926 120min b/w

Director: Fritz Lang
Screenplay: Thea von Harbou
Source: Novel by von Harbou

In a futuristic society the workers are encouraged to revolt by a robot. Although undoubtedly incredibly influential in the sci-fi and horror fields and with many startling images, the actual storyline is bogged down in treacle. Anyone with an interest in the history of film will want to catch it but others may find it heavy going.

Maria	Brigitte Helm
John Fredersen	Alfred Abel
Freder	Gustav Frölich
Rotwang	Rudolf Klein-Rogge

Psst! It took almost a year and a half to make, had a cast of 36,000 and bankrupted the giant German Ufa studios • There are umpteen versions, including the most complete at 139 minutes, a BBC print from the 70s with an electronic music soundtrack and an 83-minute 1984 tinted version with music by Giorgio Moroder • Von Harbou was Lang's wife and it seems amazing they ever collaborated. While he hated the Nazis and fled Germany to get away from them, she became one of the top screenwriters in the Third Reich.

Midnight
★★★ 1939 94min c.

Director: Mitchell Leisen
Screenplay: Charles Brackett & Billy Wilder
Source: Story by Edwin Justus Mayer & Franz Shulz

Colbert is a hoofer posing as a countess, chased around Paris by lovestruck cabbie Ameche. Despite flashes of brilliance, sadly this is another highly-regarded comedy which has paled with the passing of time. Although it remains rather sweet, the humour is too clumsy and unsubtle for it still to be called a classic.

Eve Peabody	.Claudette Colbert
Tibor Czerny	.Don Ameche
Georges Flammarion	.John Barrymore
Jacques Picot	.Francis Lederer
Helen Flammarion	.Mary Astor
Simone	.Elaine Barrie
Stephanie	.Hedda Hopper
Marcel	.Rex O'Malley
Judge	.Monty Woolley

Quote 'Oh, I think it's a dream on you. You know, it does something to your face. It…it gives you a chin.' • 'The moment I saw you, I had an idea you had an idea.'

Psst! Mary Astor was heavily pregnant during the production and considerable efforts had to be made to conceal her condition with roomy costumes or by making her act from behind substantial pieces of furniture • Astor had been given her start in the business by Barrymore after her parents encouraged her to take 'acting lessons' with him at the age of 15 despite his ferocious reputation as a rake. Astor later said her parents knew exactly what the sessions involved but the 40-year-old Barrymore, unlike so many others in the business, was honourable enough to give her a leading role opposite him in *Beau Brummel*, a film that turned her into a star overnight.

Midnight Cowboy
★★★ 1969 113min c.

Director: John Schlesinger
Screenplay: Waldo Salt
Source: Novel by James Leo Herlihy

Cowboy Voight, a Mensa reject, turns up in the Big Apple expecting to rake it in as a stud for wealthy women. Instead, he meets up with a diseased con man who becomes his agent.

This seamy look at the underbelly of New York life is still powerful meat but it all seems rather less subtle or startling than it once did.

Enrico 'Ratso' Rizzo	.Dustin Hoffman
Joe Buck	.Jon Voight
Cass	.Sylvia Miles
Shirley	.Brenda Vaccaro
Mr. O'Daniel	.John McGiver
Towny	.Barnard Hughes
Sally Buck	.Ruth White
Annie	.Jennifer Salt
Woodsy Niles	.Gil Rankin
Also: M. Emmet Walsh, Bob Balaban

Oscars Best Picture, Best Screenplay (adapted), Best Director

Quote 'Frankly, you're beginning to smell. And for a stud in New York, that's a handicap.'
• 'Well, I'll tell you the truth now. I ain't a real cowboy. But I am one helluva stud.'

Psst! After *The Graduate*'s success, Hoffman's friends and agent advised him not to make this picture, claiming that he might never act again • This was the only X-rated film to have won the Best Picture Oscar, although the rating was later downgraded after some judicious minor editing. There were plans at one point to have a homosexual love scene between the two.

Midnight Express
★★★ 1978 121min c.

Director: Alan Parker
Screenplay: Oliver Stone
Source: Book by Billy Hayes & William Hoffer

An American student caught smuggling drugs gets thrown into a Turkish prison that isn't rated terribly highly in the Michelin Guide. Stone's script goes wildly over the top as usual, twisting the facts of the true story on which the movie is based, and coming close at times to giving us the male equivalent of the top-shelf female prison movie. It's well made, though, and the acting of the leads is first-rate.

Billy Hayes	.Brad Davis
Jimmy Booth	.Randy Quaid
Tex	.Bo Hopkins
Max	.John Hurt
Susan	.Irene Miracle
Mr. Hayes	.Mike Kellin
Hamidou	.Paul Smith
Erich	.Norbert Weisser
Stanley Daniels	.Michael Ensign

Oscars Best Screenplay (adapted)

Blurb For Billy, Dying Would Have Been The Easy Way Out.

Quote 'One of the ugliest sado-masochistic trips, with heavy homosexual overtones, that our thoroughly nasty movie age has yet produced.' [Richard Schickel, *Time* magazine]

OOPS! Almost at fade-out, Brad Davis is being dragged along by a guard. He is screaming out, 'No! No! No!' and his cries are beautifully captured by the sound man we can see running along with the boom mike.

Psst! The Turkish government objected to the movie which apparently exaggerated some of the incidents in the book.

Midnight Run
★★★★ 1988 126min c.

Director: Martin Brest
Screenplay: George Gallo

This tense and exciting thriller is also hilariously funny as a comedy. De Niro's the bounty hunter hired to bring in accountant Grodin who's stolen $15m from the mob. But the mob, the FBI and a rival bounty hunter are also after Grodin. The two stars really strike sparks off each other in what is a near-perfect action flick.

Jack Walsh . . . . .Robert De Niro
Jonathan Mardukas . . . . .Charles Grodin
Alonzo Mosely . . . . .Yaphet Kotto
Marvin Dorfler . . . . .John Ashton
Jimmy Serrano . . . . .Dennis Farina
Eddie Moscone . . . . .Joe Pantoliano

Psst! The studio had wanted Robin Williams for Grodin's part and Williams was willing, but Brest preferred Grodin • Dustin Hoffman turned down the film so that he would not miss his chance to be in the delayed *Rain Man* • In order to persuade Charles Grodin to throw himself into the freezing white-water rapids, the director did the jump himself first • Grodin has scars from the handcuffs he had to wear for much of the movie • The video is missing a scene with De Niro picking a door lock, for fear it might be used as an instruction manual.

Midnight Sting
★★★★ 1992 98min c.

Director: Michael Ritchie
Screenplay: Steven McKay

Source: Novel, *The Diggstown Ringers* by Leonard Wise

Despite the really cheeky title change on this side of the pond from *Diggstown*, this excellent caper-cum-con movie *is* reminiscent of *The Sting*. On getting out of jail, Woods wants to scam sleazebag Dern, the bigwig in boxing-obsessed Diggstown, and bets that his man can beat 10 of theirs in just one day. Often hilariously funny, this brilliant film has such great twists in the plot that by the end you'll be whooping and hollering in the one-and-nines.

Gabriel Caine . . . . .James Woods
'Honey' Roy Palmer . . . . .Louis Gossett Jr.
John Gillon .Bruce Dern
Fitz . . . . .Oliver Platt
Emily Forrester . . . . .Heather Graham
Wolf Forrester . . . . .Randall "Tex" Cobb

Blurb This Much Fun Can Get You Killed.

Psst! Called *Diggstown* in the States, the film opened to ecstatic reviews. But after $14m spent on a bizarre marketing campaign, it grossed only $3.5m in two weeks.

A Midsummer Night's Dream
★★ 1935 132min b/w

Director: Max Reinhardt & William Dieterle
Source: Play by William Shakespeare

Not quite a *Midsummer Night's Nightmare*. It seems bizarre that a Shakespeare adaptation could possibly look dated, but that's what's happened here. Despite a wonderful lustrous look to everything, some of these actors reciting the Bard's blank verse have the worried look of a rabbit caught in a car's headlights. Rooney is irritating in the extreme and it's really only James Cagney who seems truly at home.

Bottom . . . . .James Cagney
Lysander . . . . .Dick Powell
Flute . . . . .Joe E. Brown
Helena . . . . .Jean Muir
Snout . . . . .Hugh Herbert
Hermia . . . . .Olivia De Havilland
Theseus . . . . .Ian Hunter
Quince .Frank McHugh
Oberon . . . . .Victor Jory
Demetrius . . . . .Ross Alexander
Puck . . . . .Mickey Rooney
Titania, Queen of the Fairies . . . . .Anita Louise
Hippolyta, Queen of the Amazons . . . . . .Verree Teasdale
Ninus Tomb . . . . .Arthur Treacher

Also: Billy Barty, Grant Mitchell, Victor Jory, Hobart Cavanaugh, Kenneth Anger

Blurb Three Centuries In The Making.

Psst! Reinhardt was one of the pre-eminent theatre directors in Europe but he had little experience with film, as early tests all too clearly proved. So Dieterle was brought in to stave off disaster • This was De Havilland's film debut. She had been an understudy on Reinhardt's production of the play at the Hollywood Bowl the year before. On opening night she'd had to go on in place of the actress who played Hermia and she'd kept the part • Cagney hadn't wanted to be in the film. His performance is now considered one of the best he ever gave • Kenneth Anger, who wrote the two *Hollywood Babylon* books, is the child prince riding the unicorn • Mickey Rooney was hampered by a broken leg from a tobogganing accident and was wheeled round on a hidden tricycle most of the time • Perhaps not too surprisingly, Dick Powell later said that he didn't understand what he was saying • The gigantic forest designed by Anton Grot used up two sound stages but was too dark to film. Hal Mohr came in, took the tops off the trees, resprayed the forest and put sequins everywhere to give it that extraordinary sparkle • A record 2,971 cinemas cancelled their order for the film when they realised what it was they were expected to show their customers. Cancellations usually ran at about the 30 to 50 mark. Not surprisingly, the movie was a box office flop.

Mildred Pierce
★★★★ 1945 111min b/w

Director: Michael Curtiz
Screenplay: Ranald MacDougall
Source: Novel by James M. Cain

One of the all-time great soapers, with over-emoting Crawford perfect as the woman who lavishes everything on spoilt daughter Blyth, only to find that gratitude isn't one of the words in the little minx's vocabulary. Dark, with deliciously sharp dialogue and deft direction.

Mildred Pierce . . . . .Joan Crawford
Wally Fay . . . . .Jack Carson
Monte Beragon . . . . .Zachary Scott
Ida . . . . .Eve Arden
Veda . . . . .Ann Blyth
Bert Pierce . . . . .Bruce Bennett
Mr. Chris .George Tobias
Maggie Binderhof . . . . .Lee Patrick
Also: Moroni Olsen, Butterfly McQueen

Oscars Joan Crawford

Blurb Don't Tell What Mildred Pierce Did!
• The Kind Of Woman Most Men Want...And Shouldn't Have.

Quote 'Personally, Veda's convinced me that alligators have the right idea. They eat their young.' • 'Oh, men! I never yet met one of them who didn't have the instincts of a heel. Sometimes I wish I could get along without them.' • 'I love you, mother, really I do. But let's not be sticky about it.'

Psst! The part was turned down by Bette Davis and Ann Sheridan. Crawford, who had moved to Warners from MGM and whose career was on the slide, fought to stop it going to Barbara Stanwyck. The success of the film put her back on top • The script was being completed as production went on, with actors receiving pages only a day or two before they were to be filmed • Curtiz found working with Crawford so frustrating that at one point he ripped the shoulder pads out of her dress.

Miller's Crossing
★★★★ 1990 115min c.

Director: Joel Coen
Screenplay: Ethan Coen & Joel Coen

Stylish, moody, wonderfully atmospheric 30s gangster picture from the extraordinary Coen Brothers. Byrne's the bright mobster who opts for the transfer from Finney's side to Polito's lot. Or does he? Little is what it seems in this complex, witty and hypnotically mesmerising cinematic *tour-de-force*. Superb performances and tough, if slightly cartoonish, action make this one of the greatest gangster movies ever.

Tom Reagan . . . . .Gabriel Byrne
Verna . . . . .Marcia Gay Harden
Bernie Bernbaum . . . . .John Turturro
Johnny Caspar . . . . .Jon Polito
Eddie Dane . . . . .J.E. Freeman
Leo . . . . .Albert Finney
Mink . . . . .Steve Buscemi

Quote 'What's the rumpus?'

OOPS! In the scene where Finney decks Byrne, his drink first changes colour then vanishes completely.

Psst! The film's distributors were so worried that British audiences might not understand the slang (despite years of exposure to American films) that, at some cinemas, they gave out sheets translating it into English • Even after her superb performance in such a critically-acclaimed movie, Marcia Gay Harden was forced back to waitressing for a full year afterwards! This despite the fact that she's also a skilled dancer, juggler, trapeze artist and tightrope walker • Joel Coen's wife, Frances McDormand, who starred in *Blood Simple* cameos as the mayor's secretary. Horror director Sam Raimi appears briefly as 'snickering gunman' in the police shootout. The Coens and he had co-written Raimi's film *Crime Wave* and would later work together on *The Hudsucker Proxy* • In addition to writing, producing and directing their films, the Coens also edit them, using the pseudonym of Roderick Jaynes. Jaynes has been quoted on occasion complaining about the difficulties of working with the Coens!

Le Million
★★★ 1931 85min b/w

Director: René Clair
Screenplay: René Clair
Source: Musical play by Georges Berr & M. Guillemaud

A delightful comic fantasy musical about a search for a winning lottery ticket. Clair's French films tend to resemble nobody else's, although much in them was imitated afterwards by others, among them Lubitsch and the Marx Brothers. Despite coming so soon after the invention of sound, this is lively, witty and quite remarkable in its use of visuals and sound. It has dated a little, but it's well worth sticking with.

Beatrice	Annabella
Michel	René Lefèvre
'Father Tulipe' Crochard	Paul Olivier
Prosper	Louis Allibert
Vanda	Vanda Greville
Taxi driver	Raymond Cordy

Ministry of Fear
★★★ 1944 85min b/w

Director: Fritz Lang
Screenplay: Seton I. Miller
Source: Novel by Graham Greene

A man released from a mental institution gets caught up in a twisted, ingenious spy thriller involving nasty Nazis. A scintillating and terrifying film noir, largely thanks to the deft direction

from Lang, who manages to make the most innocuous of objects seem menacing.

Stephen Neale	Ray Milland
Carla Hilfe	Marjorie Reynolds
Willi Hilfe	Carl Esmond
Cost/Travers	Dan Duryea
Mrs. Bellane	Hillary Brooke
Dr. Forrester	Alan Napier
Mr. Rennit	Erskine Sanford

The Miracle of Morgan's Creek
★★★ 1944 99min b/w

Director: Preston Sturges
Screenplay: Preston Sturges

Pregnant by an unknown soldier, a girl picks out a meek bank clerk to marry rather than face the disgrace of single parenthood. But as this is a Preston Sturges film, nothing is that simple. Unbelievably daring for its day and long considered the ultimate in screwball comedy, like other Sturges films the years haven't been kind. It's still rather sweet, thanks largely to the wonderful array of actors, but most of the taboos that it aims at have long since been shattered

Trudy Kockenlocker	Betty Hutton
Norval Jones	Eddie Bracken
Emmy Kockenlocker	Diana Lynn
Officer Kockenlocker	William Demarest
Gov. McGinty	Brian Donlevy
The Boss	Akim Tamiroff
Justice of the Peace	Porter Hall
Mr. Johnson	Alan Bridge
Justice's wife	Almira Sessions
Mayor	Jimmy Conlin
Mr. Tuerck	Emory Parnell
Sally	Esther Howard
Sheriff	J. Farrell MacDonald
McGinty's secretary	Byron Foulger
McGinty's secretary	Arthur Loft
Doctor	Torben Meyer

Quote 'I practice the law. I'm not only willing, but anxious, to sue anyone anytime for anything, but they got to be real people with names and corpuses and meat on their bones. I can't work with spooks.' • 'If you don't mind my mentioning it, father, I think you have a mind like a swamp.' • 'Some kind of fun lasts longer than others, if you get what I mean.'

Psst! When the film was attacked by some people who believed that the birth of sextuplets meant that Hutton had slept with six different

men, Sturges said: 'Education, though compulsory, seems to be spreading slowly.'
• One scene that he had to drop had a minister warning his female congregation to 'beware of confusing patriotism with promiscuity.'

Miracle on 34th Street
★★★★ 1947 96min b/w

Director: George Seaton
Screenplay: George Seaton
Source: Story by Valentine Davies

The ultimate Christmas movie. Although O'Hara's too practical a career woman to believe in Santa, she employs Santa-lookalike Kris Kringle in her department store. But things get complicated when he claims to be the *real* Father Christmas. Although it is a little sluggish in places, it's a terribly sweet and charming confection with several scenes that are pure movie magic. Is there *anybody* who can watch the final courtroom scene without the tears flowing? Beware the appalling colourised version.

Doris Walker . . . . .Maureen O'Hara
Fred Gailey . . . . .John Payne
Kris Kringle . . . . .Edmund Gwenn
Susan Walker . . . . .Natalie Wood
Judge Harper . . . . .Gene Lockhart
Mr. Sawyer . . . . .Porter Hall
Charles Halloran . . . . .William Frawley
Thomas Mars . . . . .Jerome Cowan
Mother . . . . .Thelma Ritter
Postal employee . . . . .Jack Albertson

Oscars Best Original Story, Edmund Gwenn, Best Screenplay (adapted)

Quote 'Faith is believing in things when common sense tells you not to.' • 'Now wait a minute, Susie. Just because every child can't get its wish, that doesn't mean there isn't a Santa Claus.' • KRIS KRINGLE KRAZY? KOURT KASE KOMING; 'KALAMITY,' KRIES KIDS [Paper headline]

OOPS! As Gwenn and Payne are walking together, the shadow of the camera is quite clearly visible.

Psst! Not surprisingly, Macy's cooperated wholeheartedly with the film, shot around the Christmas of 1946. The studio didn't think much of it and, instead of waiting until the next Noel, they released it in June • After hearing the outline of the idea, Darryl F. Zanuck, head of 20th Century Fox, had said: 'Who the hell is going to care about an old man who thinks he's

Santa Claus?' • Despite its unseasonal release in summer, the film was a great success. It seemed to bring about spirit of goodwill in the unlikeliest places. Macy's big rival, Gimbel's, ran an full-age ad in the *New York Times* not only praising the film, but patting Macy's on the back for being involved. Perhaps they were taken by the idea in the movie of a store benefiting by recommending the competition • This was the debut of the wonderful Thelma Ritter • The original title for the film, used during production, was *It's Only Human* • The 1994 remake was far better than it was given credit for, though it still pales beside the original.

The Miracle Worker
★★★ 1962 106min b/w

Director: Arthur Penn
Screenplay: William Gibson
Source: Play by Gibson based on the book, *The Story of My Life* by Helen Keller

Tough, no-holds-barred, depiction of the true life story of blind and deaf Helen Keller. Bancroft is the teacher who wants to help her communicate with the world around her, using methods that seem rather harsh by modern standards. With two excellent performances, this is an incredibly moving story that never seems to exploit its subject matter. You'll probably cry so much you'll think a dam behind your eyes has just burst.

Annie Sullivan . . . . .Anne Bancroft
Helen Keller . . . . .Patty Duke
Capt. Keller . . . . .Victor Jory
Kate Keller . . . . .Inga Swenson
James Keller . . . . .Andrew Prine
Aunt Ev . . . . .Kathleen Comegys
Viney . . . . .Beah Richards

Oscars Anne Bancroft, Patty Duke

Psst! The novel became a TV play, then a Broadway production which Penn directed, with the same two actors in the lead roles • Until Tatum O'Neal won for *Paper Moon*, 16-year-old Duke was the youngest person to win a Best Supporting Actress Oscar • According to Duke's memoirs, the film was doubly troubling for her as, during the period the movie was being made, she was the victim of sexual abuse from her guardian and personal manager • Bancroft, whose participation director Penn had had to fight for against a reluctant studio, worked herself into the ground and was admitted to hospital when she finished filming, suffering from pneumonia • Watch Bancroft's lips as she slips in the stream. She loudly declaimed 'Shit', but there were no microphones being used at the time • In the days before Steadicams, the camera operators were often pushed in wheelchairs to give the camera mobility • It was remade as a TV movie in 1979 with Duke playing Sullivan instead of Keller.

Les Miserables
★★★ 1935 108min b/w

Director: Richard Boleslawski
Screenplay: W.P. Lipscomb
Source: Novel by Victor Hugo

Sentenced to 10 years' hard labour for stealing a loaf of bread, March escapes and becomes a model citizen devoting his life to helping the less fortunate. But he is pursued relentlessly by the cold-blooded police chief who is determined that the letter of the law be upheld. Pretty solid and dependable version of the Hugo classic.

Jean Valjean . . . . .Fredric March
Javert . . . . .Charles Laughton
Bishop Bienvenu . . . . .Cedric Hardwicke
Big Cosette . . . . .Rochelle Hudson
Eponine . . . . .Frances Drake
Marius . . . . .John Beal
Mme. Magloire . . . . .Jessie Ralph
Fantine . . . . .Florence Eldridge
Thenardier . . . . .Ferdinand Gottschalk
Genflou . . . . .Leonid Kinskey
Enjolras . . . . .John Carradine
Mlle. Baptiseme . . . . .Mary Forbes
Prison governor . . . . .Robert Greig

Psst! Although largely faithful to the novel, this does have a less downbeat, more Hollywood finale than Hugo penned • This is one of the most-filmed of all novels, with other versions in 1909, '13, '17, '23, '29, '34, '46, '52 (twice), '56 and '78. It also became a phenomenally successful stage musical • Look out for John Carradine in a bit part as one of the students.

Misery
★★★★ 1990 107min c.

Director: Rob Reiner
Screenplay: William Goldman
Source: Novel by Stephen King

Terrifically tense thriller. Novelist Caan crashes in a blizzard and is rescued by his 'greatest fan',

the mentally unstable Bates. When she discovers his plans for her favourite character, she persuades him to stay and do a little rewriting. And she can be *very* persuasive. Edge-of-the seat stuff. You'll have your hand in your mouth, not your popcorn carton, begging them to switch away from that bedroom so you can breathe again for a while.

Paul Sheldon . . . . .James Caan
Annie Wilkes . . . . .Kathy Bates
Buster . . . . .Richard Farnsworth
Virginia . . . . .Frances Sternhagen
Marcia Sindell . . . . .Lauren Bacall
Park ranger .J.T. Walsh

Oscars Kathy Bates

Blurb Paul Sheldon Used To Write For A Living...Now He's Writing To Stay Alive.

Quote 'I'm your number one fan.'

OOPS! Bates' car mysteriously reappears outside the house after she has driven it away • The correcting fluid wasn't there when Bates first brought the typewriter in • The Post-It notes on the sheriff's board keep changing position • The curtain is still alight after Caan's put it out.

Psst! Originally, Warren Beatty and Bette Midler were to be the stars • A copy of *When Harry Met Sally*, also directed by Reiner, is on display in the video store • Reiner has a cameo as a helicopter pilot.

The Misfits
★★ 1961 124min b/w

Director: John Huston
Screenplay: Arthur Miller

It's a terrible thing to say of Gable and Monroe's last film, but this look at the sad twilight days of the cowboy and the involvement of one of them with an ex-stripper really doesn't cut the mustard. Although there are moments when it comes alive, for the large part it's horribly talky and the talk is pretentious and often pointless. A big disappointment.

Gay Langland . . . . .Clark Gable
Roslyn Taber . . . . .Marilyn Monroe
Perce Howland . . . . .Montgomery Clift
Guido . . . . .Eli Wallach
Isabelle Steers . . . . .Thelma Ritter
Old man in bar . . . . .James Barton
Church lady . . . . .Estelle Winwood
Raymond Taber . . . . .Kevin McCarthy

Quote 'A man who's too afraid to die's too afraid to live.' • 'How do you find your way back in the dark?' – 'Just head for that big star straight on. The highway's under it and it'll take us right home.' [Monroe's and Gable's last movie lines] • 'John Huston treats me like an idiot – "Honey, this" and "Honey, that".' [Monroe] • 'I'm not just a dumb blonde this time, I'm a crazy dumb blonde. And to think, *Arthur* did this to me. He was supposed to be writing this for me. He could've written *anything* and he came up with *this*.'

Psst! Monroe was at her most difficult on the film, with drugs causing violent mood swings. She had considerable difficulty remembering lines and was usually either late on set or didn't turn up at all • Gable, who had dieted from 16-and-a-half to 14 stones for the part, did some of his own stunts, often out of boredom while waiting for Monroe to make an appearance. One of these involved being dragged by a rope at 30 miles per hour behind a truck. On the last day Gable had to work, he said: 'Christ, I'm glad this picture's finished. She [Monroe] damn near gave me a heart attack. I've never been happier when a film ended.' He had a heart attack the next day and died 11 days later, before the film was finished. His fifth wife gave birth to his only child, a boy, several months later • Although Gable was kind on set to Monroe, despite his frustration with her, he hated Wallach, referring to him as 'boiled ham' • Monroe was herself kind to Montgomery Clift, whose insecurities were so bad that she probably felt emotionally rock-solid in comparison • Her marriage to writer Arthur Miller was on the rocks and when he *was* on set, she openly abused and taunted him, to the embarrassment of everyone • Studio executives weren't happy with the way the film was turning out. But although Huston and Miller agreed to refilm some scenes, Gable turned the idea down • One shot that was dropped from the final cut was in the bedroom scene and showed Monroe's bare breast.

Mister Roberts

★★ 1955 123min c.

Director: John Ford & Mervyn LeRoy
Screenplay: Joshua Logan & Frank S. Nugent
Source: Novel by Thomas Heggen & play by Logan & Heggen

The hit comedy about a World War II supply ship captained by a martinet who makes his crew's life miserable hasn't translated too well to the screen. There are some bright patches, mostly provided by Lemmon, but elsewhere time drags almost as heavily for the audience as for Mister Roberts himself, desperate to get away from the ship and into the heat of battle. There was a waterlogged sequel in 1964, *Ensign Pulver*.

Mister Roberts	Henry Fonda
Captain	James Cagney
Doc	William Powell
Ensign Pulver	Jack Lemmon
Lt. Ann Girard	Betsy Palmer
C.P.O. Dowdy	Ward Bond
Mannion	Phil Carey
Reber	Nick Adams
Dolan	Ken Curtis
Stefanowski	Harry Carey Jr.

Oscars Jack Lemmon

Quote 'Captain, it is I, Ensign Pulver and I just threw your stinking palm tree overboard. Now, what's all this crud about no movie tonight?' [Last line]

Psst! Ford refused to direct unless Fonda, who had created the part on Broadway, was in it. But Fonda did not like the levity being introduced into the movie and the two of them, despite being old friends, argued furiously. They even exchanged punches on one occasion, with Ford ending their friendship by flooring Fonda. Ford then feigned illness and was replaced by LeRoy • This was Jack Lemmon's screen debut. He had actually been an ensign on the *USS Lake Champlain* during World War II • As on other films (see *The Pink Panther*) the soap bubbles used for the laundry scenes turned out to be less than kind to hands and other parts of the body. Both Lemmon and his double developed severe rashes.

Modern Times

★★ 1936 87min b/w

Director: Charles Chaplin
Screenplay: Charles Chaplin

Only Chaplin would have the chutzpah to bring out what is essentially a silent film nine years after the talkies had changed the movies forever. Although some consider this satire on the mechanised age a classic, any but the greatest Chaplin fans will surely now find it grossly sentimental and unfunny for long stretches. Most of the best comedy sequences are retreads of Chaplin's earlier two-reelers and even the great scene on the production line is a lift.

Tramp	Charles Chaplin
A Gamin	Paulette Goddard
Cafe owner	Henry Bergman
Mechanic	Chester Conklin
Big Bill	Stanley "Tiny" Sanford
Gamin's sister	Gloria De Haven

Psst! Chaplin's voice was heard on screen for the first time singing in the nonsense song. Chaplin wrote all the music • This was the last appearance of Chaplin's tramp • The film took three years to make • Goddard was Chaplin's third wife at the time. Until this, she'd only appeared in Hal Roach comedy shorts and was a platinum blonde. Chaplin remodelled her as a dark-haired beauty and taught her how to act and to speak. She arrived on the set wearing an expensive dress, only to have Chaplin say: 'That isn't it, baby.' He threw a bucket of water over her, 'and that's how I got my hairstyle in *Modern Times*. It broke my heart and I cried and cried and cried. And he said: "Cry, dammit, cry! Camera! Goddammit, get down on your knees and look up at me!" And the tears were running and it was the best shot I ever had!' • The extraordinarily close similarities to René Clair's film *A Nous La Liberté* didn't escape that movie's producers. They started a suit for plagiarism but dropped it when Clair himself said that he was flattered • The film was banned in Nazi Germany and Mussolini's Italy.

Mommie Dearest
★★ 1981 129min c.

Director: Frank Perry
Screenplay: Frank Yablans, Frank Perry, Tracy Hotchner & Robert Getchell
Source: Book by Christina Crawford

As we now know from her adopted daughter's book, Joan Crawford was not the mother any of us would have chosen for ourselves. While her life story is fascinating, this movie is compelling for other reasons. It is so badly scripted, acted and directed that it is very largely screamingly funny. It has now understandably become one of the favourite camp classics.

Joan Crawford	Faye Dunaway
Christina Crawford	Diana Scarwid
Greg Savitt	Steve Forrest
Louis B. Mayer	Howard da Silva
Carol Ann	Rutanya Alda
Barbara Bennett	Jocelyn Brando

Quote 'Yes, Mommie Dearest.' – 'When I told you to call me that, I wanted you to mean it.'

• 'Helga, I'm not mad at you. I'm mad at the dirt.' • 'NO WIRE HANGERS!' • 'I'd rather you go bald to school than looking like a tramp!' • 'Don't fuck with me, fellas. I've fought bigger sharks than you.' • 'Faye Dunaway says she is being haunted by mother's ghost. After her performance in *Mommie Dearest*, I can understand why.' [Christina Crawford]

Psst! Before she died, Crawford had been quoted as saying: 'Of all the actresses, to me, only Faye Dunaway has the talent and class and the courage it takes to make a real star' • Initially, Anne Bancroft was signed for the role • For some reason, the film avoids mentioning Crawford's early screen roles in stag movies.

Mona Lisa
★★★ 1986 104min c.

Director: Neil Jordan
Screenplay: David Leland & Neil Jordan

When Hoskins emerges from seven years inside, crime boss Caine gives him a job chauffeuring hooker Tyson. Gradually he is drawn into her search for a lost friend, discovering that much has changed in the underworld since he's been away. The air of menace hanging over this powerful human drama gets steadily heavier until it is brought to a head by the superbly menacing Caine.

George	Bob Hoskins
Simone	Cathy Tyson
Mortwell	Michael Caine
Thomas	Robbie Coltrane
Anderson	Clarke Peters
Cathy	Kate Hardie

Monkey Business
★★★★ 1931 77min b/w

Director: Norman Z. McLeod
Screenplay: S.J. Perelman, Will B. Johnstone & Arthur Sheekman

The Marx Brothers on top form as staggeringly unobtrusive stowaways on a luxury liner. There's no Margaret Dumont, but Thelma Todd is a great *femme fatale*, a role she'd repeat in *Horse Feathers*. This is the one in which the four brothers impersonate Maurice Chevalier.

Groucho	Groucho Marx
Harpo	Harpo Marx

Chico	.Chico Marx
Zeppo	.Zeppo Marx
Lucille	.Thelma Todd
Tom Helton	.Rockliffe Fellowes
Mary Helton	.Ruth Hall

Quote 'How about you and I pasing out on the veranda. Or would you rather pass out here?' • 'Look at me: I worked my way up from nothing to a state of extreme poverty.' • 'Do you suppose I could buy back my introduction to you?' • 'Mrs. Briggs, I've known and respected your husband Alky for years and what's good enough for him is good enough for me.' • 'I want to register a complaint. Do you know who sneaked into my room at three o'clock this morning?' – 'Who?' – 'Nobody, and that's my complaint.' • 'You're awfully shy for a lawyer.' – 'You bet I'm shy. I'm a shyster lawyer.'

OOPS! Their father, Sam 'Frenchie' Marx, had always wanted to be in a movie, so he appears as an extra in a white hat among the passengers on the ship getting ready to sail. So enthusiastic was he that, wearing the same hat, he also appears on the dock, waving goodbye to those on the ship!

Psst! This was the first Marx Brothers film written specifically for the screen • The film was banned in Ireland, the censors fearing it might create anarchy among the populace • Winston Churchill asked for the film to be run for him in 1941 in the middle of the London blitz to keep his spirits up.

Monsieur Hulot's Holiday
★★★★ 1953 85min b/w

Director: Jacques Tati
Screenplay: Jacques Tati & Henri Marquet

On his first appearance here, Tati's gangly, clumsy M. Hulot became one of the greatest comic characters of all time. Universally adored because of the limited dialogue, this rambling French account of Hulot's holiday in a Brittany seaside resort is full of wonderful sight gags. It's true they aren't all hilarious, but the characters are so well drawn that even when we aren't roaring with laughter we are beguiled by the film's utter charm. A joy to be savoured again and again, particularly as it becomes even more enjoyable when you know what's coming next. Also known as Les Vacances de Monsieur Hulot.

M. Hulot	.Jacques Tati
Martine	.Nathalie Pascaud

Fred	.Louis Perrault
The Aunt	.Michelle Rolla
The Englishwoman	.Valentine Camax

Psst! The script received an Oscar nomination • Many of the supporting cast weren't actors, but tourists and inhabitants of the Brittany seaside town where the exterior scenes were filmed • Much of the dubbing of the voices into English was done by Christopher Lee.

Monty Python's Life of Brian
★★ 1979 93min c.

Director: Terry Jones
Screenplay: John Cleese, Terry Gilliam, Michael Palin, Eric Idle, Graham Chapman & Terry Jones

A man living at the same time as Christ is mistaken throughout his life for the Messiah. Because of the ridiculous uproar from religious groups about the film's supposed blasphemy, we all desperately wanted to like the movie at the time. In fact, although sporadically funny, it's really little more than a succession of sketches, not all of which strike the funny bone with a resounding twang. It opens well and closes brilliantly, with the striking scene accompanying the song 'Always Look on the Bright Side of Life'. Also known as plain Life of Brian.

Brian/Biggus Dickus, etc.	.Graham Chapman
Reg, etc.	.John Cleese
Jailer/Prophet, etc.	.Terry Gilliam
Mr. Cheeky/ Stan Called Loretta, etc.	.Eric Idle
Virgin Mandy/Brian's mother, etc.	.Terry Jones
Pontius Pilate, etc.	.Michael Palin
Jesus the Christ	.Kenneth Colley
Mrs. Big Nose, etc.	.Gwen Taylor
Roman soldier Stig, etc.	.Charles McKeown
Mrs. Gregory/Elsie	.Carol Cleveland
Also:	George Harrison, Neil Innes, Chris Langham, Spike Milligan

Quote 'Blessed are the cheesemakers.'

OOPS! There's a boom mike at the top of the screen when Brian's mother is buying rocks for the stoning.

Psst! Several local authorities banned the film in Britain • Mary Whitehouse decided against prosecuting it under the law of blasphemy after taking legal advice • George Harrison appears in a cameo as Mr. Papadopolous, the owner of The Mount • Watch to the end to see the credit: 'If you have enjoyed this film, why not go and see "La Noxie"?'

The Moon and Sixpence
★★★ 1942 89min c&b/w

Director: Albert Lewin
Screenplay: Albert Lewin
Source: Novel by W. Somerset Maugham

A splendid adaptation of Maugham's story of the stockbroker who abandons family and career to devote his life to painting, moving to Tahiti. Clearly based in large part on Gaugain's life, Sanders gives of his best, particularly during the artist's caddish period. There was nobody to touch Sanders when it came to playing a cad.

Charles Strickland	George Sanders
Geoffrey Wolfe	Herbert Marshall
Dirk Stroeve	Steven Geray
Blanche Stroeve	Doris Dudley
Capt. Nichols	Eric Blore
Tiara Johnson	Florence Bates
Rose Waterford	Heather Thatcher
Dr. Coutras	Albert Basserman
Mrs. Strickland	Molly Lamont
Ata	Elena Verdugo
Maitland	Robert Greig

Moonraker
★ 1979 126min c.

Director: Lewis Gilbert
Screenplay: Christopher Wood
Source: Novel by Ian Fleming

Bond goes chasing after missing space shuttles and encounters the usual mad megalomaniac. This one plans to populate the earth with a new race of supermen. This outing for 007 is not just bad, but dire. Even Moore's energetic eyebrows can't raise much interest in this pathetic plot which makes Bond seem weightless even before he gets into space. Although a fortune was spent on the effects, even some of these look rather ropey.

James Bond	Roger Moore
Holly Goodhead	Lois Chiles
Hugo Drax	Michel Lonsdale
Jaws	Richard Kiel
Corinne Dufour	Corinne Clery
'M'	Bernard Lee
Frederick Gray	Geoffrey Keen
'Q'	Desmond Llewelyn
Miss Moneypenny	Lois Maxwell
Consumptive Italian	Alfie Bass
Gen. Gogol	Walter Gotell
Cavendish	Arthur Howard
US Shuttle Captain	Brian Keith

Psst! The film is said to have cost as much as the first eight in the series combined • The part of Drax was originally offered to James Mason • Lois Chiles had turned down the part of Anya in *The Spy Who Loved Me* and got this part when she happened to sit next to director Gilbert on a plane trip • The code for the electronic lock in Drax's laboratory is the same as in *Close Encounters*.

Moonstruck
★★★★ 1987 102min c.

Director: Norman Jewison
Screenplay: John Patrick Shanley

An utter charmer of a movie about an Italian-American family in Brooklyn and, in particular, the nearly-Fortysomething widow Cher. She falls for Cage, the estranged brother of her fiancé Aiello. Wit and wisdom shine out from this beautifully written and acted tale of love and family as the characters, so we're to believe, are driven by the influence of the moon.

Loretta	Cher
Ronny Cammareri	Nicolas Cage
Cosmo Castorini	Vincent Gardenia
Rose Castorini	Olympia Dukakis
Mr. Johnny Cammareri	Danny Aiello
Rita Cappomaggi	Julie Bovasso
Perry	John Mahoney
Raymond Cappomaggi	Louis Guss
Old man	Feodor Chaliapin

Oscars Cher, Olympia Dukakis

Quote 'God took a rib from Adam and made Eve. Now maybe men chase women to get the rib back.' • 'No matter where you go or what you do, you're gonna die.' [Rose to errant husband Cosmo]

Psst! The script was originally about a Jewish family but was changed at the studio's insistence • It was written with Sally Field in mind.

Morocco
★★★ 1930 90min b/w

Director: Josef von Sternberg
Screenplay: Jules Furthman
Source: Novel, *Amy Jolly* by Benno Vigny

A cabaret singer who attracts men like light attracts moths is torn between a wealthy suitor and the man she truly loves. The plot is corny and dated, as are many of the performances. But it still has a lovely exotic air about it and is campily enjoyable.

Tom Brown . . . . .Gary Cooper
Amy Jolly . . . . .Marlene Dietrich
M. Le Bessiere . . . . .Adolphe Menjou
Adjutant Caesar . . . . .Ullrich Haupt
Anna Dolores . . . . .Juliette Compton
Cpl. Barney Latoche . . . . . . .Francis McDonald
Mme. Caesar . . . . .Eve Southern

Psst! This was Dietrich's first film in Hollywood. Although she made *The Blue Angel* earlier, its release was held back until after *Morocco* came out • Cooper hated director Sternberg speaking German on set and favouring Dietrich on camera. Nonetheless, he still had an affair with her • With the nightclub scene Marlene Dietrich became the first leading actress to kiss another woman in a mainstream movie.

The Most Dangerous Game
★★ 1932 63min b/w

Director: Ernest B. Schoedsack & Irving Pichel
Screenplay: James Creelman

When ships are marooned on rocks around a mysterious island, the survivors are initially welcomed by its hunting-mad occupant. Then they discover that they are to be his next prey. Copied umpteen times since, this no longer seems as frightening as it must have done on first release. But the chase is still quite exciting and the whole film remains watchable, if slightly dated.

Bob Rainsford . . . . .Joel McCrea
Eve Trowbridge . . . . .Fay Wray
Count Zaroff . . . . .Leslie Banks
Martin Trowbridge . . . . .Robert Armstrong
Tartar servant . . . . .Noble Johnson

Quote 'First the hunt. Then the revels.' • 'My life has been one glorious hunt. It would be impossible for me to tell you how many animals I have killed.'

Psst! The film was made at around the same time as *King Kong*. It used some of the same jungle sets, as well as actress Fay Wray, who sometimes had to dash between the two films on the same day to shoot scenes for each • A scene involving the stuffed and mounted heads of victims was cut before release.

The Mouse that Roared
★★ 1959 83min c.

Director: Jack Arnold
Screenplay: Roger Macdougall & Stanley Mann
Source: Novel, *The Wrath of the Grapes* by Leonard Wibberley

A tiny European nation decides that the best way of getting funds into the state coffers is to lose a war with America. This is one of those films that seems funnier in recollection than when you're actually watching it. Despite the clever idea behind it, the script isn't really sufficiently witty or inspired, although it's a pleasant enough way to pass the time. The sequel about them going into space, *The Mouse on the Moon*, was just plain daft.

Tully Bascombe/Gloriana/
Prime Minister . . . . .Peter Sellers
Helen . . . . .Jean Seberg
Prof. Kokintz . . . . .David Kossoff
Willy . . . . .William Hartnell
Benter . . . . .Leo McKern
BBC Annnouncer . . . . .Colin Gordon

Quote 'Whereas other countries rarely forgive anything, the Americans forgive everything. There isn't a more profitable undertaking for any country than to declare war on the United States and to be defeated.' • 'I warn you, madam. I know the Geneva Convention by heart.' – 'Oh, how nice. You must recite it to me some evening. I play the harpsichord.'

Movie Crazy
★★★ 1932 82min b/w

Director: Clyde Bruckman
Screenplay: Harold Lloyd & Others

Although he is now remembered as a silent comedian, Harold Lloyd actually made quite a few talkies. This one is the best of them, with the bespectacled one heading for Hollywood to become a film actor. It's not only pretty funny, with some great sight gags, but is also a fascinating look behind the scenes of early filmmaking.

Harold Hall . . . . .Harold Lloyd
Mary Sears . . . . .Constance Cummings
Vance, a gentleman heavy . . .Kenneth Thomson
The Director . . . . .Sidney Jarvis
Bill, the Assistant Director . . . .Eddie Fetherston

Movie Movie

★★★★ 1978 106min c&b/w

Director: Stanley Donen
Screenplay: Larry Gelbart & Sheldon Keller

Two movies for the price of one. There have been many movie pastiches, but none as lovingly or brilliantly rendered as this. It's like an old movie-house double bill, with boxing movie *Dynamite Hands* followed by *Baxter's Beauties of 1933*. All the old clichés are there, in spades, in this hilarious tribute to the 'them' in the phrase: 'They don't make them like that any more'. Those who love old movies will adore it.

Gloves Molloy/Spats Baxter	George C. Scott
Betsy McGuirse/Isobel Stuart	Trish Van Devere
Peanuts Miller/Jinks Murphy	Red Buttons
Trixie Lane	Barbara Harris
Vince Marlow/Pop	Eli Wallach
Dr. Blaine/Dr. Bowers	Art Carney
Johnny Danko/Dick Cummings	Barry Bostwick
Joey Popchik	Harry Hamlin
Troubles Moran	Ann Reinking
Mama Popchik/Mrs. Updike	Jocelyn Brando

Quote 'That's show business. One moment you're in the wings, the next you're wearing them.' • 'Awful awful.' [Variety]

Mr. Blandings Builds His Dream House

★★ 1948 94min b/w

Director: H.C. Potter
Screenplay: Norman Panama & Melvin Frank
Source: Novel by Eric Hodgins

A family plan to move out of crowded Manhattan into their ideal home in the country. This comedy is charmingly played by its leads, who are always good value. But it's been done umpteen times since and the targets of the humour now all seem pretty obvious. Blandings by name, bland by nature. It was effectively remade in 1986 as *The Money Pit*.

Jim Blandings	Cary Grant
Muriel Blandings	Myrna Loy
Bill Cole	Melvyn Douglas
Simms	Reginald Denny
Joan Blandings	Sharyn Moffett
Betsy Blandings	Connie Marshall
Gussie	Louise Beavers
Smith	Ian Wolfe
Tesander	Harry Shannon

John Retch	Jason Robards
Mary	Lurene Tuttle

Quote 'You've been taken to the cleaners and you don't even know your pants are off.' • 'I refuse to endanger the health of my children in a house with less than three bathrooms.' • 'If you ain't eating Wham, you ain't eating ham!'

Mr. Deeds Goes to Town

★★★★ 1936 115min b/w

Director: Frank Capra
Screenplay: Robert Riskin
Source: Story, *Opera Hat* by Clarence Budington Kelland

A small-town hick inherits a vast fortune and is targeted by a newspaper that wants to dig up some dirt on him, especially when he starts giving his money away. Capra can be terribly irritating, especially when it comes to the politics in his movies, which here are incredibly naive and simplistic. The production also looks rather threadbare, while the pace is too slow. And yet Cooper and Arthur are both wonderfully endearing and the final courtroom scene is so beautifully, heart-twistingly, life-enhancingly brilliant that you fall for it every time.

Longfellow Deeds	Gary Cooper
Babe Bennett	Jean Arthur
MacWade	George Bancroft
Cornelius Cobb	Lionel Stander
John Cedar	Douglass Dumbrille
Walter	Raymond Walburn
Morrow	Walter Catlett
Judge Walker	H.B. Warner
Bodyguard	Warren Hymer
Mabel Dawson	Ruth Donnelly
Mrs. Meredith	Emma Dunn
Budington	Arthur Hoyt
Farmer	John Wray
Mr. Semple	Jameson Thomas
Mrs. Semple	Mayo Methot
Hallor	Charles Lane
Frank	Irving Bacon
Tailor	Franklin Pangborn
Cabby	Billy Bevan

Oscars Best Director

Quote 'Why, everybody in Mandrake Falls is pixilated – except us.' • 'The most enjoyable film I ever made. I liked Mr. Deeds. Heck of a good fellow. Wish I could meet him somewhere.' [Cooper]

Psst! Capra's insistence that the lead be played

by Cooper led to filming being held up for six months, at a cost of $100,000 • Although Arthur had acted in movies before, they were pretty minor and she is said to have shaken with nerves before each scene.

Mrs. Doubtfire
★★★ 1993 125min c.

Director: Chris Columbus
Screenplay: Randi Mayem Singer & Leslie Dixon
Source: Novel, *Alias Madame Doubtfire* by Anne Fine.

Divorced father Williams goes TV and gets a job as a nanny, the only way he can think of to get to see his children. Williams is often incredibly funny, particularly in a couple of farcical scenes. Unfortunately, the film drags on for too long and becomes over-sentimental. At the end, it almost becomes a self-help lecture for the children of divorced parents.

Daniel Hillard/Mrs. Doubtfire	Robin Williams
Miranda Hillard	Sally Field
Stu	Pierce Brosnan
Frank	Harvey Fierstein
Gloria	Polly Holliday
Lydia Hillard	Lisa Jakub
Chris Hillard	Matthew Lawrence
Natalie Hillard	Mara Wilson
Mr. Lundy	Robert Prosky

Blurb She's A Blessing In Disguise.

Quote 'Winston's idea of foreplay was, "Effie, brace yourself".'

OOPS! Prosky arranges dinner for Friday. The next scene, *before* the dinner, is Williams with his kids. Yet we've been told that access day is Saturday.

Psst! Given a '12' certificate in Britain, there were loud protests from parents whose children were turned away. A small cut was made and, four months after being released, it was reclassified a 'PG'.

Mrs. Miniver
★★ 1942 134min b/w

Director: William Wyler
Screenplay: Arthur Wimperis, George Froeschel, James Hilton & Claudine West
Source: Novel by Jan Struther

A wartime British village family make jam, hold fetes and generally behave in such a way that the Germans will despair of ever destroying their spirit, stop bombing and wave the white flag. There'll always be an England, but England Hollywood style looks as if it's drawn from a collection of biscuit tin lids. Although it's all a bit twee now, it was a very important movie in its day, doing much to cement American resolve that they had done the right thing in entering the war. It was followed by the rather dour *The Miniver Story* in 1950.

Kay Miniver	Greer Garson
Clem Miniver	Walter Pidgeon
Carol Beldon	Teresa Wright
Lady Beldon	Dame May Whitty
Mr. Ballard	Henry Travers
Foley	Reginald Owen
German agent's voice	Miles Mander
Vin Miniver	Richard Ney
Vicar	Henry Wilcoxon
German flyer	Helmut Dantine
Pilot	Peter Lawford
Horace	Rhys Williams
Dentist	Ian Wolfe
Fred	John Abbott
Conductor	Billy Bevan

Oscars Best Picture, Best Screenplay (adapted), Greer Garson, Teresa Wright, Best Director

Quote 'This is the people's war. It is our war. We are the fighters. Fight it, then. Fight it with all that is in us. And may God defend the right.' • 'Looking at *Mrs. Miniver* on videotape and looking at *Mrs. Miniver* on 35mm good black and white film is the difference between observation and inspiration.' [Steven Spielberg]

Psst! Churchill, who wasn't always cinema's greatest friend [see *The Life and Death of Colonel Blimp*], claimed that this film would be more useful to the war effort than six divisions. The Queen Mother said: 'It was such a morale booster for us when we most needed it. We had no idea that we were quite so brave.' • The closing speech of the film was printed on propaganda leaflets which were dropped over Europe • Goebbels, Germany's minister of propaganda, said it was 'an exemplary propaganda film for the German industry to copy' • Garson didn't want to make the film. Although only 34, she was worried that having a 27-year-old son [Ney] in the film would make her look old. She later married Ney, although the wedding was delayed until the movie had run its course. Norma Shearer turned the part down for the same reason • Garson holds the record for giving the longest-ever Oscar acceptance speech. Despite reports that it went on for up to an hour, it was actually five and a half minutes long. It merely seemed much longer to those who were there. One attendee said: 'Her acceptance speech was longer than her part.'

Mr. Smith Goes to Washington
★★★★ 1939 125min b/w

Director: Frank Capra
Screenplay: Sidney Buchman
Source: Story, *The Gentleman from Montana* by Lewis R. Foster

An idealistic boy scout leader becomes a Senator but finds that in Washington playing corrupt political games takes precedence over doing good. Luckily, this is Frank Capra's world, one in which the little people *can* make a difference. It's rather corny in places – particularly in its heart-on-the-sleeve patriotism – as well as being too long. But it still packs a hell of a punch at times and brings tears to the eyes on more than one occasion. Stewart is, well, Stewart but let's not forget the cynical and utterly delightful Arthur.

Saunders . . . . .Jean Arthur
Jefferson Smith . . . . .James Stewart
Sen. Joseph Paine . . . . .Claude Rains
Jim Taylor . . . . .Edward Arnold
Gov. Hubert Hopper . . . . .Guy Kibbee
Diz Moore . . . . .Thomas Mitchell
Chick McGann . . . . .Eugene Pallette
Ma Smith .Beulah Bondi
Sen. Fuller .H.B. Warner
Pres. of Senate . . . . .Harry Carey
Susan Paine . . . . .Astrid Allwyn
Emma Hopper . . . . .Ruth Donnelly
Sen. Monroe . . . . .Porter Hall
Nosey . . . . .Charles Lane
Sweeney . . . . .Jack Carson
Bill Griffith . . . . .William Demarest
Sen. MacPherson . . . . .Grant Mitchell
Sen. Barnes . . . . .Pierre Watkin
Hopper's secretary . . . . .Byron Foulger
Reporter . . . . .Dub Taylor

Oscars Best Original Story

Quote 'Dad always used to say the only causes worth fighting for were the lost causes.' • 'I wouldn't give you two cents for all your fancy rules if, behind them, they didn't have a little bit of plain, ordinary, everyday kindness and a little looking out for the other fellow, too.'

OOPS! Kibbee tells Arnold, Rains and Pallette that Smith knows Lincoln and Washington by heart. Yet a minute later Rains says a guy who quotes Lincoln and Jefferson would be a great patsy • Maybe one shouldn't bring it up but how, during the filibuster, does Smith answer the calls of nature if he can't leave the Chamber?

Psst! The film created a storm, with America's politicians up in arms against it. The Majority Leader said, 'It was a source of disgust and hilarity to every member of Congress who saw it.' Some congressmen tried to get it withdrawn from release • Joseph P. Kennedy, then ambassador to Britain, thought it shouldn't be shown in Europe because it would undermine the morale of America's allies and be seen as propaganda for the Axis powers: 'I feel that to show this film in foreign countries will do inestimable harm to American prestige all over the world.' • The famous American broadcaster of the 30s and 40s, H.V. Kaltenborn, appears as himself.

Much Ado About Nothing
★★★★ 1993 110min c.

Director: Kenneth Branagh
Screenplay: William Shakespeare & Kenneth Branagh
Source: Play by William Shakespeare.

This splendid Shakespeare adaptation is both hilarious and moving and, what's more, extremely accessible to modern audiences, be they Bard groupies or not. Maybe the plot's a bit creaky, but it *is* a few hundred years old. Forget the mix of American and British accents and revel in Ken and Emma's superb comic performances. Only the all-at-sea Reeves and Branagh's over-fussy direction let down this otherwise superb comedy.

Benedick . . . . .Kenneth Branagh
Dogberry . . . . .Michael Keaton
Claudio . . . . .Robert Sean Leonard
Don John . . . . .Keanu Reeves
Beatrice . . . . .Emma Thompson
Don Pedro . . . . .Denzel Washington
Leonato . . . . .Richard Briers
Hero . . . . .Kate Beckinsale
Antonio .Brian Blessed
Verges . . . . .Ben Elton
Ursula . . . . .Phyllida Law
Margaret . . . . .Imelda Staunton

OOPS! During the crying scene in the chapel, Thompson's make-up is in disarray from the tears one moment, then perfect again the next.

Murder on the Orient Express

★ **1974 127min c.**

Director: Sidney Lumet
Screenplay: Paul Dehn
Source: Novel by Agatha Christie

An all-star cast murder a story by the queen of crime fiction. Poirot tries to find the culprit. Is it director Lumet, with his heavy hand on the tiller? Is it writer Dehn who has the actors talk the most atrocious tosh? Is it the overabundance of stars? Or is it the over-acting Finneyf? Someone pull the communication cord. I want to get off.

Insp. Hercule Poirot	Albert Finney
Mrs. Hubbard	Lauren Bacall
Bianchi	Martin Balsam
Greta Ohlsson	Ingrid Bergman
Countess Andrenyi	Jacqueline Bisset
Col. Arbuthnot	Sean Connery
Beddoes	John Gielgud
Princess Dragomiroff	Wendy Hiller
Hector McQueen	Anthony Perkins
Ratchett	Richard Widmark
Mary Debenham	Vanessa Redgrave
Count Andrenyi	Michael York
Pierre Michel	Jean-Pierre Cassel
Hildegarde Schmidt	Rachel Roberts
Dr. Constantine	George Coulouris
Hardman	Colin Blakely
Foscarelli	Denis Quilley

Oscars Ingrid Bergman

Psst! This was Bacall's first movie part in eight years. She apparently couldn't resist starring with husband Humphrey Bogart's most famous co-star, Ingrid Bergman • Bergman was also acting on stage every night at the same time.

Murder, Inc.
SEE: The Enforcer

Murder, My Sweet
SEE: Farewell My Lovely

The Music Man

★★★ **1962 151min c.**

Director: Morton da Costa
Screenplay: Marion Hargrove
Source: Musical by Meredith Willson & Franklyn Lacey

In the early years of the century, a con-man persuades a town to start up a band, his intention being to run off with the funds. Preston is outstanding in this musical's central role with which he had wowed audiences on Broadway. It's bright, lively and funny, has a superior period look to it and contains some corkers in the way of songs, such as '76 Trombones'.

Harold Hill	Robert Preston
Marian Paroo	Shirley Jones
Marcellus Washburn	Buddy Hackett
Eulalie Shinn	Hermione Gingold
Mayor Shinn	Paul Ford
Mrs. Paroo	Pert Kelton
Winthrop Paroo	Ron Howard
Mrs. Squires	Mary Wickes
Oscar Jackson	Rance Howard
Constable Locke	Charles Lane

Psst! Ron Howard, here but a nipper, went on to star in *Happy Days* before becoming a successful director of movies like *Splash* and *Parenthood*.

Mutiny on the Bounty

★★★ **1935 135min b/w**

Director: Frank Lloyd
Screenplay: Talbot Jennings, Carey Wilson & Jules Furthman
Source: Novels, *Mutiny on the Bounty* & *Men Against the Sea* by Charles Nordhoof & James Norman Hall

By and large this most famous version of the true(ish) tale of 18th-century sailors mutinying against their martinet captain moves along with a fair wind behind it. But there's no denying that it gets becalmed in some stretches. The acting is great, though, with Laughton splendidly over the top in one of the most imitated of all movie roles. Credit must also go to Gable who gives the role far more depth than we might expect. It was remade in 1962, and again as *The Bounty* in 1984.

Capt. William Bligh	Charles Laughton
1st Officer Fletcher Christian	Clark Gable
Robert Byam	Franchot Tone
Smith	Herbert Mundin
Ellison	Eddie Quillan
Bacchus	Dudley Digges
Burkitt	Donald Crisp
Sir Joseph Banks	Henry Stephenson
Chief's daughter	Movita
Capt. Nelson	Francis Lister

Also: Spring Byington, Jane Wyman

Oscars Best Picture

Quote 'Mr. Christian. Come here!' • 'We'll be men again if we hang for it!' • 'I'll take my chances against the law. You'll take yours against the sea.'

OOPS! In using the word 'sabotage', Charles Laughton is a couple of centuries too early. It didn't come into use until the 20th century.

Psst! As with the previous year's *It Happened One Night*, Gable was extremely reluctant to take the part. He didn't want to have to shave off his moustache and kicked against the idea of wearing wigs and silly trousers • The production was beset with difficulties. Not only were there arguments among the cast, particularly between Gable and Laughton, but the humidity on location ruined some footage and valuable equiment • Laughton researched his part thoroughly, even going so far as to have uniforms run up for him by the firm that had outfitted Bligh and which was still in existence, insisting that they be exact copies of the original • The ships were also copies of the original pair, the *HMS Bounty* and *HMS Pandora*. During the exterior filming, they were sailed to Tahiti and back again • Movita Castaneda, who plays the chief's daughter who has the romance with Christian, was later married to Marlon Brando who was Christian in the 1962 remake • This was the only instance when three actors from the same film, Gable, Laughton and Tone, were nominated for Best Actor Oscars • Wallace Beery and Robert Montgomery had been the original choices for Laughton and Tone's part • Both James Cagney and David Niven apparently appear in the movie as unbilled extras, although I've yet to spot Cagney. It was Niven's first appearance before the cameras.

My Beautiful Laundrette
★★★ 1985 97min c.

Director: Stephen Frears
Screenplay: Hanif Kureishi

A young Pakistani entrepreneur runs an advanced laundrette with the help of an ex-skinhead. Social, racial and class tensions in South London don't help business. Despite a couple of weak performances and, perhaps, the raising of too many unresolved issues, this remains an original, unpredictable and thought-provoking drama which cleverly tapped into the mood of mid-80s Britain.

Johnny	Daniel Day-Lewis
Nasser	Saeed Jaffrey
Pap	Roshan Seth
Omar	Gordon Warnecke
Rachel	Shirley Anne Field
Tania	Rita Wolf

Quote 'Take my advice, there's money in muck.'

My Brilliant Career
★★★ 1979 100min c.

Director: Gillian Armstrong
Screenplay: Eleanor Witcombe
Source: Novel by Miles Franklin.

A 19th-century Australian farmer's daughter refuses to remain in the place that society has allotted her and determines to have a career of her own. Although less impressive and rather more sluggish than it seemed at the time, this apparently true tale of an early feminist is still buoyed up by Davis' outstanding performance in the lead.

Sybylla Melvyn	Judy Davis
Harry Beecham	Sam Neill
Aunt Helen	Wendy Hughes
Frank Hawdon	Robert Grubb
Mr. McSwat	Max Cullen
Aunt Gussie	Patricia Kennedy
Grandma Bassier	Aileen Britton
Uncle Julius	Peter Whitford
Mother	Julia Blake

My Cousin Vinny
★★★★ 1992 119min c.

Director: Jonathan Lynn
Screenplay: Dale Launer

Uproariously funny tale of incompetent Brooklyn lawyer Pesci turning up in Wahzoo, Alabama in leather jacket and cowboy boots to defend a young cousin and his friend on a murder rap. Not only has Pesci never won a case; he's never even fought one before. As if that wasn't bad enough, he has to contend with the by-the-book hostility of the judge, the wonderful Fred Gwynne. Although the film's a mite draggy in a couple of places, Pesci's brilliant in his first leading role. Despite this, he's almost acted off the screen by Tomei as his fiery, gum-chewing, wisecracking girlfriend, giving one of the most electrifying comedy performances in years.

Vinny	.Joe Pesci
Bill Gambini	.Ralph Macchio
Mona Lisa Vito	.Marisa Tomei
Stan Rothenstein	.Mitchell Whitfield
Judge Haller	.Fred Gwynne
Jim Trotter	.Lane Smith
John Gibbons	.Austin Pendleton

Oscars Marisa Tomei

Quote 'Oh yeah. You blend.' • 'Sure, I've heard of grits. I've just never actually seen a grit before.' • 'Your Honour, may I have permission to treat Miss Vito as a hostile witness?' – 'You think I'm hostile now, wait till you see me tonight.'

OOPS! The tapes used to pull Pesci's skin upwards on his face and make him look younger can occasionally be spotted.

Psst! If it's bugging you where you've seen the judge before, it's probably from his long-running TV role as Hermann Munster.

My Darling Clementine
★★★ 1946 97min b/w

Director: John Ford
Screenplay: Samuel G. Engel & Winston Miller
Source: Novel, *Wyatt Earp, Frontier Marshall* by Stuart N. Lake

This is the Wild West as it almost certainly never was, with a languid Wyatt Earp and Doc Holliday taking on the Clantons. One of the most beautiful Westerns ever filmed, with the most gorgeous skies full of luminous clouds. You could practically take any shot and frame it for your wall. On the other hand, while it has a nice, brooding atmosphere about it, it does tend to drag its feet in places. It's much more of a mood piece than the action-packed movie you might expect.

Wyatt Earp	.Henry Fonda
Chihuahua	.Linda Darnell
Doc Holliday	.Victor Mature
Old Man Clanton	.Walter Brennan
Clementine	.Cathy Downs
Earp	.Tim Holt
Morgan Earp	.Ward Bond
Granville Thorndyke	.Alan Mowbray
Billy Clanton	.John Ireland
Mayor	.Roy Roberts
Kate Nelson	.Jane Darwell
Ike Clanton	.Grant Withers

Blurb She Was Everything The West Was – Young, Fiery, Exciting.

Quote 'Mac, you ever been in love?' – 'No. I've been a bartender all ma life.' • 'Ma'am, I sure like that name, Clementine.' [Last line]

Psst! One of umpteen films about Wyatt Earp, among them *Gunfight at the OK Corral, House of the Gun, Tombstone* and *Wyatt Earp* • Ford had actually met Earp who would come and visit his cowboy friends when Ford was working as an assistant prop boy in the early days of silent movies: 'I used to give him a chair and a cup of coffee, and he told me about the fight at the O.K. Corral. So...we did it exactly the way it had been. They didn't just walk up the street and start banging away at each other; it was a clever military manoeuvre.' • It was shot in Ford's favourite location, Monument Valley, even though the scenery bore no resemblance to that around Tombstone.

My Fair Lady
★★★ 1964 170min c.

Director: George Cukor
Screenplay: Alan Jay Lerner
Source: Musical play by Lerner & Loewe based on the play, *Pygmalion* by George Bernard Shaw

Hepburn is so elegant, however hard she tries, that it's hard to believe in her transformation from flower girl to society lady in this musical version of *Pygmalion*. But, although slow in places, it looks lovely and the rest of the cast have a high time with Shaw's dialogue and the great Lerner and Loewe songs, including 'Get Me to the Church on Time' and 'I've Grown Accustomed to Her Face'.

Prof. Henry Higgins	.Rex Harrison
Eliza Doolittle	.Audrey Hepburn
Alfred P. Doolittle	.Stanley Holloway
Col. Hugh Pickering	.Wilfrid Hyde-White
Mrs. Higgins	.Gladys Cooper
Freddy Eynsford-Hill	.Jeremy Brett
Zoltan Karpathy	.Theodore Bikel
Mrs. Eynsford Hill	.Isobel Elsom
Mrs. Burke	.Mona Washbourne
Prince Gregor	.Henry Daniell
Ambassador	.Alan Napier

Oscars Best Picture, Best Director, Rex Harrison

Quote 'The rain in Spain stays mainly in the plain.' • 'Eliza, where the devil are my slippers?'

Psst! The rights to the musical cost $5.5m, with the production itself costing another $17m. Unfortunately for Warner Bros., despite the movie's popularity at the box office, it didn't manage to recoup its costs • The Broadway musical ran for six years, notching up 2,717 performances • Julie Andrews had played the role on stage with Rex Harrison opposite her, but it was felt they needed a bigger name for the movie • Hepburn's singing was dubbed by the ubiquitous Marnie Nixon, even though Hepburn had gone to considerable trouble preparing for the role. Because her performance was thus considered 'synthetic', she was disqualified from the Oscar nominations. In the newly restored version, Hepburn can be heard to have quite a pleasing singing voice • The film won eight Oscars, including all the other major categories • Cary Grant and Rock Hudson both turned down the part of Higgins, with Grant saying he'd only pay money to see the film if Harrison played it. Harrison had played the part for three years on stage and, because he wasn't asked to be in the movie, he went off to his place in Spain for a holiday. Director Cukor rang him there to ask if he would come to California for a screen test. Harrison refused, saying he'd play the role happily but wouldn't test for it. Later he sent some nude pictures of himself fooling around on the beach to Cukor saying: 'If you want a photographic test, this is it'. He got the part immediately • There was an attempt to get Jimmy Cagney to play Eliza's dad, but he couldn't be budged from retirement on his farm, even for the million dollars that was being offered • To make Hepburn's hair sufficiently bedraggled Cukor ordered it to be coated in vaseline and Fuller's earth. Hepburn agreed, but compensated by spraying herself liberally with Givenchy perfume 'to keep up my morale'.

My Favorite Wife
★★★ 1940 88min b/w

Director: Garson Kanin
Screenplay: Sam Spewack & Bella Spewack

After spending seven years shipwrecked on a desert island, Dunne returns to find that husband Grant has got over her sufficiently to get married again. She determines to end his days as an accidental bigamist. It's more enjoyable than the pair's earlier teaming for *The Awful Truth*. Although never stitch-creatingly funny, it's pleasant and amusing throughout.

Nick Arden ....Cary Grant
Ellen Arden ....Irene Dunne
Stephen Burkett ....Randolph Scott

Bianca ....Gail Patrick
Ma ....Ann Shoemaker
Hotel clerk ....Donald MacBride
Judge ....Granville Bates
Tim ....Scotty Beckett

Quote 'Oh, by the way, how was my funeral?'

My Favorite Year
★★★★ 1982 92min c.

Director: Richard Benjamin
Screenplay: Norman Steinberg & Dennis Palumbo

...and My Favourite Film. Well, one of them. Linn-Baker's the young writer on a 50s TV show given the unwanted task of looking after swash-buckling film star O'Toole, a renowned lush, womaniser and hell-raiser. The film delights on all levels. Not only is it an astonishingly funny, fast-paced comedy with some incredible lines, a few thrills and a little romance thrown in, but it also gives us a remarkable view of the early days of live television. Ninety-two minutes of pure, cinematic joy.

Alan Swann ....Peter O'Toole
Benjy Stone ....Mark Linn-Baker
K.C. Downing ....Jessica Harper
King Kaiser ....Joseph Bologna
Sy Benson ....Bill Macy
Belle Carroca ....Lainie Kazan
Alice Miller ....Anne DeSalvo
Uncle Morty ....Lou Jacobi
Alfie Bumbacelli ....Tony Di Benedetto
Myron Fein ....George Wyner
Karl Rojeck ....Cameron Mitchell

Quote 'Jews know two things in this world: suffering, and where to get really great Chinese food.' • 'Live? I can't go on live! I'm a movie star, not an actor!' • 'This is for ladies only!' [Woman in lavatory] – 'So is this, madam. But every now and again I have to run some water through it.'

Psst! Made by Mel Brooks' company, the basis for the story was the occasion when Brooks, a writer on Sid Caesar's TV show, had to look after guest Errol Flynn • As well as Brooks, the programme *The Show of Shows* had writers like Woody Allen, Larry Gelbart (creator of TV's *M*A*S*H*) and writer-performer Carl Reiner, later a top director and father of director Rob • Writer Palumbo later became a psychotherapist dealing specifically with the problems of actors, writers and directors and offering 'supportive therapy'.

My Left Foot
★★★★ 1989 98min c.

Director: Jim Sheridan
Screenplay: Shane Connaughton & Jim Sheridan
Source: Book by Christy Brown

The remarkable story of Christy Brown, the best-selling writer who suffered from cerebral palsy from birth and was able to control his left foot and nothing else. While the idea might sound depressing, this turns out to be a remarkably joyous and witty film, superbly acted by the entire cast. It has its sentimental moments, to be sure, but the overall experience is wonderfully uplifting.

Christy Brown . . . . .Daniel Day-Lewis
Mrs. Brown . . . . .Brenda Fricker
Mr. Brown . . . . .Ray McAnally
Mary . . . . .Ruth McCabe
Dr. Eileen Cole . . . . .Fiona Shaw
Lord Castlewelland . . . . .Cyril Cusack
Peter . . . . .Adrian Dunbar

Oscars Daniel Day-Lewis, Brenda Fricker

Psst! Although it only cost £1m to make, writer Connaughton told everyone in Hollywood that it had cost £5m, fearing they wouldn't take him seriously if they knew the truth • Brown was one of 13 surviving children out of a total of 22 born.

My Life as a Dog
★★★★ 1984 101min c.

Director: Lasse Hallström
Screenplay: Lasse Hallström, Reidar Jönsson, Brasse Brännstrom & Per Berglund
Source: Novel by Jonsson.

Just when you think you've had enough coming-of-age movies, one comes along that knocks the others into a cocked hat. In this delightful little Swedish film, a mischievous 12-year-old is sent to the country for the summer when his mother falls ill. Full of oddball humour, the impish Glanzelius convinces as a real human being having to grow up all too quickly. Made in 1984 but not released in Britain or America until 1987.

Ingemar . . . . .Anton Glanzelius
Uncle Gunnar . . . . .Tomas von Bromssen
Mother . . . . .Anki Liden
Saga .Malinda Kinnaman

Psst! Unusually for a foreign film it received two Oscar nominations in the main – rather than foreign – categories, for director and screenplay.

My Man Godfrey
★★★ 1936 90min b/w

Director: Gregory La Cava
Screenplay: Morrie Ryskind, Eric Hatch & Gregory La Cava
Source: Short story, *1101 Park Avenue*, by Eric Hatch.

One of the greatest of the screwball comedies still delights today, with the glorious Lombard a deliciously scatty society gal besotted with new butler Powell, a 'forgotten man' picked up in a Park Avenue scavenger hunt. This Depression satire labours the disdain of the wealthy for the poor to an almost embarrassing extent at times. But the acting is wonderful, with the bullfrog-voiced Pallette – the father driven to distraction by the madnesses of his family – turning in one of the greatest comic performances in the movies. Insipidly remade in 1957 with David Niven and June Allyson, it also inspired the fun *Merrily We Live* in 1938.

Godfrey Parke . . . . .William Powell
Irene Bullock . . . . .Carole Lombard
Angelica Bullock . . . . .Alice Brady
Alexander Bullock . . . . .Eugene Pallette
Cornelia Bullock . . . . .Gail Patrick
Tommy Gray . . . . .Alan Mowbray
Molly, the maid . . . . .Jean Dixon
Carlo . . . . .Mischa Auer
M.C. . . . . .Franklin Pangborn
Van Rumple . . . . .Grady Sutton
Girl at party . . . . .Jane Wyman

Quote 'What this family needs is discipline. I've been a pretty patient man. But when people start riding horses up the front steps and parking them in the library, that's going a little bit too far.' • 'I've just been going over last month's bills and I find that you people have confused me with the Treasury Department.' • 'Stand still, Godfrey. It'll all be over in a minute.'

Psst! Powell and Lombard were married from 1931 to 1933, when they went through what was said to have been one of the most amicable divorces in Hollywood • Lombard's career had been going nowhere before Powell insisted she be hired. Afterwards, she became the highest-paid actress in the movies • At the time of the film, Lombard was living with Clark Gable. Alice Brady, playing her mother, had had a fling with Gable several years earlier but claimed to remember little about it when Lombard asked for some pointers • The actors were often only given their dialogue on the morning they had to say their lines • Jane Wyman can be spotted briefly in her film debut in the party scene.

The Mystery of the Wax Museum

★★★ 1933 73min c.

Director: Michael Curtiz
Screenplay: Don Mullaly & Carl Erickson
Source: Play by Charles Belden

Like so many of the 30s horror films, this tale of a fire-damaged sculptor resurrecting his destroyed waxworks museum with real bodies, is no longer particularly scary. But it has much to admire, including its abundant humour, its great visuals and one of the all-time great crazies in Atwill.

Ivan Igor . . . . .Lionel Atwill
Charlotte Duncan . . . . .Fay Wray
Florence Dempsey . . . . .Glenda Farrell
Jim . . . . .Frank McHugh
Ralph Burton . . . . .Allen Vincent
Harold Winton . . . . .Gavin Gordon
Dr. Rasmussen . . . . .Holmes Herbert

Quote ' I offer you immortality, my child. Think of it! In a thousand years you shall be as lovely as you are now!

Psst! The film, remade in 1953 as the 3-D *House of Wax*, was lost for many years. Then a print turned up in the 60s.

The Naked City

★★★ 1948 96min b/w

Director: Jules Dassin
Screenplay: Albert Maltz & Malvin Wald

Two detectives try to track down a killer in the city that wears no clothes but displays no shame. This first docudrama was incredibly influential in its storytelling method and use of real locations. Although that no longer strikes us as being in the least out of the ordinary, the investigation is pretty good entertainment in itself.

Lt. Dan Muldoon . . . . .Barry Fitzgerald
Frank Niles . . . . .Howard Duff
Ruth Morrison . . . . .Dorothy Hart
Jimmy Halloran . . . . .Don Taylor
Capt. Donohue . . . . .Frank Conroy
Willie Garzah . . . . .Ted de Corsia

Quote 'There are eight million stories in the naked city. This has been one of them.'

Psst! This was the first Hollywood movie with an urban setting that was filmed on location in its entirety. The film-makers utilised over 100 locations in New York. Most of the scenes outside were shot from inside a parked van with tinted windows and a one-way mirror. The interiors were also real, with no sets being used at all • According to Dassin 'the very heart of the film was cut out' at the editing stage. 'I could have wept,' he said • There was a TV series of the same title that ran for five years from 1958.

The Naked Gun: From the Films of Police Squad!

★★★ 1988 85min c.

Director: David Zucker
Screenplay: Jim Abrahams, David Zucker, Jerry Zucker & Pat Proft

Yet another triumph from the team that brought the world *Airplane* and *Kentucky Fried Movie*. Former straight actor Nielsen is incompetent cop Frank Drebin, out to foil an assassination attempt on the Queen during a visit to LA. Pratfalls, slapsticks, gags old and even older, jostle for position in this zany, fast-paced comedy. The jokes come so thick and fast, it's almost impossible to catch them all the first time through. The two sequels were much of a muchness, with plenty to enjoy but proving rather less inventive than the original.

Frank Drebin . . . . .Leslie Nielsen
Jane Spence . . . . .Priscilla Presley
Vincent Ludwig . . . . .Ricardo Montalban
Ed Hocken . . . . .George Kennedy
Nordberg . . . . .O.J. Simpson
Mrs. Nordberg . . . . .Susan Beaubian
Mayor . . . . .Nancy Marchand

Quote 'Same old story. Boy finds girl. Boy loses girl. Girl finds boy. Boy forgets girl. Boy remembers girl. Girl dies in a tragic blimp accident over the Orange Bowl on New Year's Day.' • 'It's a topsy-turvey world, Jane. And maybe the problems of two people don't amount to a hill of beans. But this is our hill and these are our beans.' • 'You don't know real heat until you've spent several hours inside a giant condom.' [Priscilla Presley]

Psst! Keep an eye on the closing credits, as you should in all ZAZ films. They include the line: 'In Case Of Tornado…Southwest Corner Of Basement' as well as credits for 'Man and Woman deleted from fireworks scene', 'Mr. Weiss's Divorce Attorney' and an explanation of just what it is that grips do • The film is based on, and many of the jokes are taken from, a sadly discontinued TV series in the same vein called *Police Squad*. Only six episodes were ever made • Sexologist Dr. Joyce Brothers appears as a baseball commentator.

The Name of the Rose
★★★★ 1986 131min c.

Director: Jean-Jacques Annaud
Screenplay: Andrew Birkin, Gérard Brach, Howard Franklin & Alain Godard
Source: Novel by Umberto Eco

Take what might be a conventional detective yarn, set it in a 14th-century Italian abbey where the power of life and death lies with the Inquisition, make the private eye a less-than-reverential English monk, and you have one of the most remarkable films of recent years. Connery is superb as William of Baskerville, who becomes the bloodhound of the Baskervilles if you like, accompanied by his novice Slater as they try to prove that a series of murders are not the work of the Devil. This gripping and fascinating film oozes atmosphere so thick you can practically eat it. Once seen, never forgotten.

William of Baskerville	Sean Connery
Bernardo Gui	F. Murray Abraham
Adso of Melk	Christian Slater
Severinus	Elya Baskin
Jorge de Burgos	Feodor Chaliapin
Ubertino de Casale	William Hickey
The Abbot	Michel Lonsdale
Salvatore	Ron Perlman

Psst! After looking at over 300 monasteries around Europe, filming eventually took place at Klöster Eberbach near Frankfurt, where time has stood still since the 12th century. The outside was built on a hill near Rome, the largest exterior set Europe has seen since the making of *Cleopatra*.

Napoleon
★★★★ 1927 313min c&b/w

Director: Abel Gancé
Screenplay: Abel Gancé

This epic telling of the early part of Napoleon's career is one of the great masterpieces of the silent era. It's packed with memorable scenes which use the visual medium in ways that have never been equalled, although it's hardly an unbiased portrait of the man and is extremely long. There is only one way to watch this film – in a cinema with a live orchestra playing Carl Davis' music. If you ever get the opportunity to beg, steal or borrow a ticket, then do so. At one stage Gancé has arranged it so that we have contiguous images on three screens simultaneously, side by side. To be part of an audience rising to its feet and cheering wildly as the screens colour red, white and blue is one of the most exciting cinematic experiences I have ever had. As for watching it on TV, unless you're an avid film scholar, you can't possibly appreciate the majesty of it.

Napoléon	Albert Dieudonné
Joséphine de Beauharnais	Gina Manés
Tristan Fleuri	Nicolas Koline
Napoléon (as boy)	Wladimir Roudenko
Rouget de Lisle	Harry Krimer
Violine	Annabella
Marat	Antonin Artaud
Danton	Alexandre Koubitzky
Saint-Just	Abel Gancé
Maximilien Robespierre	Edmond Van Daele
Gen. Hoche	Pierre Batcheff

Psst! Gance originally planned six full length films covering the life of Napoleon. When he returned from filming in Corsica, the original backer had died and the finances for the movie fell apart. He scraped enough together to finish the first film, ending with Napoleon's invasion of Italy • The premiere at the Paris Opera in April 1927 was a huge success. The score on that occasion was by Arthur Honegger and the film ran to 210 minutes. A six-hour version was shown later that year • With the advent of sound, interest in the film waned. It received a limited release in Europe and America and the available versions became shorter and shorter over the years • In 1934 Gancé, ever the innovator, showed his film with an early version of stereophonic sound • It came to be thought by film historians that the film had been a failure. Only when the restored version was released in 1981 could everyone see that a masterpiece had been re-discovered. Film historian Kevin Brownlow spent 30 years piecing what could be found of the film back together again. Its current length of 313 minutes is accompanied in the UK by Carl Davis' score and in the States by the music of Carmine Coppola.

Narrow Margin

★★★ 1952 71min b/w

Director: Richard Fleischer
Screenplay: Earl Fenton

A cop taking a mobster's widow to give evidence by train has to fight off determined attempts to stop her getting there, or indeed anywhere. Regarded by some as one of the greatest B-movies ever, it's got some wonderful visuals and clever camerawork. Unfortunately, B-movies tend to have B-movie actors in them and it's their inadequacies which stop the film, which has more twists than the track, from becoming truly nail-biting stuff. It's still pretty good, though.

Walter Brown	.Charles McGraw
Mrs. Neil	.Marie Windsor
Ann Singlair	.Jacqueline White
Tommy Sinclair	.Gordon Gebert
Mrs. Troll	.Queenie Leonard
Kemp	.David Clarke

Quote 'What are you going to do? Shoot something for breakfast?' • 'Nobody loves a fat man, except his grocer and his tailor.'

Nashville

★★ 1975 159min c.

Director: Robert Altman
Screenplay: Joan Tewkesbury

Satirist Robert Altman's contribution to the American Bicentennial celebrations and, unsurprisingly, it's a caustic one. All his usual traits are on display: overlapping sound, a multitude of interconnected characters, and stars appearing as themselves. To some a masterpiece, to others – especially those resistant to Country and Western music – something of an ordeal.

Norman Chauffeur	.David Arkin
Lady Pearl	.Barbara Baxley
Delbert Reese	.Ned Beatty
Connie White	.Karen Black
Barbara Jean	.Ronee Blakley
Tom Frank	.Keith Carradine
Opal	.Geraldine Chaplin
Wade	.Robert DoQui
L.A. Joan	.Shelley Duvall
Haven Hamilton	.Henry Gibson
PFC Glenn Kelly	.Scott Glenn
Tricycle man	.Jeff Goldblum
John Triplette	.Michael Murphy
Linnea Reese	.Lily Tomlin
Mr. Green	.Keenan Wynn

Also: Barbara Harris, Bert Remsen, Gwen Welles, Elliott Gould, Julie Christie

Psst! The actors in the film wrote many of their own songs, with Carradine winning an Oscar for his lyrical 'I'm Easy' • Everything was recorded live, with no post-dubbing as is normal on a movie • Much of the dialogue was improvised and the whole film was made in less than 45 days for just $2m.

National Lampoon's Animal House

★★★ 1978 109min c.

Director: John Landis
Screenplay: Harold Ramis, Douglas Kenney & Chris Miller

As with movies such as *The Blues Brothers* and *Kentucky Fried Movie*, this comedy about a college dean waging war on the worst frat house on campus has acquired a massive cult status and is one of those films you either love or hate. If you like gross, puerile, base, raucous, vulgar comedy then it could be right up your street, hitting the funny bone again and again until the sadly lacklustre finale. It also has some great music. If you're not certain it's your sort of thing, perhaps you'd do best staying well clear.

John 'Bluto Blutarsky	.John Belushi
Eric 'Otter' Stratton	.Tim Matheson
Donald 'Boon' Schoenstein	.Peter Riegert
Dean Wormer	.John Vernon
Dave Jennings	.Donald Sutherland
Larry 'Pinto' Kroger	.Tom Hulce
Mayor Carmine De Pasto	.Cesare Danova
Marion Wormer	.Verna Bloom
Gregg Marmalard	.James Daughton
Kent 'Flounder' Dorfman	.Stephen Furst
Daniel 'D-Day' Simpson	.Bruce McGill
Chip Diller	.Kevin Bacon

Also: Karen Allen, James Widdoes

Quote 'I'm a zit. Get it?' • 'Toga! Toga! Toga! • 'Food fight!' • 'Greg, honey. Is it supposed to be this soft?'

OOPS! The girl Matheson is fooling with in the car has no bra when she jumps out of the car. But she's got one on when she gets back in again • The 'T' in the word 'SATAN' that Sutherland writes on the blackboard leaps from one side of the crack to the other.

Psst! Allegedly based on the screenwriters' own college experiences, the movie grossed over $80m, making it the most successful comedy to date • Chevy Chase turned down Matheson's role • The production had some difficulty finding a campus to film on. Fifty turned them down before they were finally welcomed at the University of Oregon • The movie was made in only 30 days • The character Babs becomes a tour guide at Universal Studios and the credits [as well as for other John Landis films] include an ad saying: 'Ask for Babs'. Until recently, Universal was said to offer free entry or a discount to anybody who did.

National Velvet

★★★ 1944 125min b/w

Director: Clarence Brown
Screenplay: Theodore Reeves & Helen Deutsch
Source: Novel by Enid Bagnold

When young Taylor wins a racehorse, she gets Rooney to help her train the nag to run in the Grand National. Once we've seen the flying pigs, nothing that happens afterwards can surprise us. Despite the gross implausibilities, it's an extremely enjoyable family movie, as much fun now as when it was released. The sequel, *International Velvet*, didn't trot onto the screen until 1978, 32 years later, but should have been sent straight to the knacker's yard.

Mi Taylor	Mickey Rooney
Mr. Brown	Donald Crisp
Velvet Brown	Elizabeth Taylor
Mrs. Brown	Anne Revere
Edwina Brown	Angela Lansbury
Farmer Ede	Reginald Owen
Miss Sims	Norma Varden
Donald Brown	Jackie "Butch" Jenkins
Malvolia Brown	Juanita Quigley
Ted	Terry Kilburn
Tim	Alec Craig
Mr. Hallam	Arthur Shields

Mr. Greenford	Dennis Hoey
Entry official	Aubrey Mather
Steward	Frederic Worlock
Man with umbrella	Arthur Treacher
Constable	Billy Bevan

Oscars Anne Revere

Psst! Taylor was only chosen for the role after Shirley Temple, Margaret Sullavan and even Katharine Hepburn had turned it down. As she tells it: 'I was 12 at the time, very short and the producer told me I was absolutely right for the part other than my height. I said: "Well, I'll grow." And he patted me on the head: "That's very sweet…Just don't set your heart on it." But I *did*…and in three months, I grew three inches. I did everything. I hung from doors, ate steak for breakfast, lunch and dinner, rode four hours a day. I guess I was in that period where children just shoot up. But I thought I'd willed myself into it.' • Taylor did most of her own riding, other than the really tricky jumps.

Network

★ 1976 120min c.

Director: Sidney Lumet
Screenplay: Paddy Chayefsky

A newsreader announces his forthcoming suicide on air and finds himself transformed into a guru for the nation. Where did this film's high reputation come from? Have things really changed so much? With its haphazard plotting and heavy-handed and ultimately ridiculous satire, it comes across as pretentious and even tedious in the later stages, a cinematic equivalent of a strident bad fringe play. Only the extraordinary scene with everyone yelling with rage from their windows still has any real power.

Diana Christensen	Faye Dunaway
Max Schumacher	William Holden
Howard Beale	Peter Finch
Frank Hackett	Robert Duvall
Arthur Jensen	Ned Beatty
Nelson Chaney	Wesley Addy
Louise	Beatrice Straight
Bill Herron	Darryl Hickman

Oscars Best Screenplay, Faye Dunaway, Peter Finch, Beatrice Straight

Quote 'I want all of you to get up out of your chairs. I want you to get up right now and go to the window, open it and stick your head out and yell: "I'm mad as hell and I'm not going to take this any more!"' • 'This was the story of Howard Beale, the first known instance of a man who was killed because he had lousy ratings.' [Last line]

Psst! Finch died just two months before the Academy Awards ceremony and is the only actor to have had an Oscar awarded posthumously • Glenn Ford, Henry Fonda and George C. Scott all turned down the role of Howard Beale • Finch was originally thought of for Holden's part and Holden for Beale, but they were then switched.

Never Say Never Again

★★ 1983 134min c.

Director: Irvin Kershner
Screenplay: Lorenzo Semple Jr.
Source: Novel, *Thunderball* by Ian Fleming

Although it's great to see Connery back as Bond after an absence of 12 years, it's something of a pity that the film should really just be *Thunderball* bunged under the grill and warmed up again under a different name. Despite the stunts, the girls and the wisecracks, it's just a little bit too thin to be completely satisfying.

James Bond	Sean Connery
Largo	Klaus Maria Brandauer
Blofeld	Max Von Sydow
Fatima	Barbara Carrera
Domino	Kim Basinger
Leiter	Bernie Casey
Q/Algy	Alec McCowen
'M'	Edward Fox
Miss Moneypenny	Pamela Salem
Small-Fawcett	Rowan Atkinson

Quote 'Do you lose as gracefully as you win?' – 'I wouldn't know. I've never lost.' • 'Mr. Bond, I need a urine sample. If you could fill this beaker for me.' – 'From here?' • 'My Scots accent was stronger in this new Bond film than in the others. I suppose you get more relaxed the nearer you get to the grave.' [Connery]

OOPS! When he goes spying on the yacht, Bond has no mask when he gets into the water. But he has when he comes out again.

Psst! The title is a dig at Connery, suggested by his wife, because he had said after *Diamonds are Forever* that he would 'never again' do another Bond film. Presumably the $5m, the most ever paid to a British star at the time, helped cushion the blow. Originally, it was to be called *Warhead* • Connery's hairpiece

cost $52,000, and was said to be most expensive ever made for a film star • At one time, Orson Welles was slated for Blofeld, with Trevor Howard asked to play 'M' • The film was a direct rival to *Octopussy*, a competition which it lost.

A New Leaf

★★★ 1970 102min c.

Director: Elaine May
Screenplay: Elaine May
Source: Story, *The Green Heart* by Jack Ritchie

An impecunious playboy plans to marry and then kill a woman who is as wealthy as she is dowdy. This fine, beautifully written comedy is one of those films with a charm that steals over you and which becomes still more enjoyable on repeated viewings.

Henry Graham	Walter Matthau
Henrietta Lowell	Elaine May
Andrew McPherson	Jack Weston
Harold	George Rose
Beckett	William Redfield
Uncle Harry	James Coco
Sharon Hart	Renee Taylor

Psst! May disowned the film after it was taken out of her hands and re-edited.

Niagara

★★★ 1953 89min c.

Director: Henry Hathaway
Screenplay: Charles Brackett, Walter Reisch & Richard Breen

A tight little black number, with Monroe visiting Niagara Falls with older hubbie Cotton, where she plans to do away with him. Although it's a little irritating that the area of natural beauty that the camera lingers on is more often MM than NF, this is still an absorbing – if rather silly – suspense movie along Hitchcockian lines.

Rose Loomis	Marilyn Monroe
George Loomis	Joseph Cotten
Polly Cutler	Jean Peters
Ray Cutler	Max Showalter
Insp. Starkey	Denis O'Dea
Patrick	Richard Allan
Mr. Kettering	Don Wilson
Mrs. Kettering	Lurene Tuttle
Mr. Qua	Russell Collins

Doctor . . . . .Lester Matthews
Sam . . . . .Sean McClory
Taxi driver . . . . .Harry Carey Jr.

Quote 'I'm meeting somebody, just anybody handy as long as he's a man.'

Psst! Director Hathaway thought the film would have been better if James Mason had played it as he wanted. But apparently Mason's daughter told her father that she had seen him die in too many films • Peters married reclusive millionaire Howard Hughes. One of the stipulations of the marriage was that she give up movies.

Night of the Living Dead
★★★ 1968 96min b/w

Director: George A. Romero
Screenplay: John A. Russo

Like *Psycho*, a groundbreaking 60s horror movie in which the dead rise up and devour the living. Shot incredibly cheaply in black and white, Romero's sly script subverts the rules of horror films, with a black hero, the besieged group bickering rather than pulling together, the romantic leading couple not surviving, etc. Although very rough round the edges, it still delivers the chills. Endlessly sequelised, ripped-off and imitated, by *Assault on Precinct 13* among others. The sequels, which were even gorier than the original, were *Dawn of the Dead* and *Day of the Dead*, while there was a no-more-than-competent colour remake in 1990 under the same title.

Barbara . . . . .Judith O'Dea
Ben . . . . .Duane Jones
Johnny .Russell Streiner
Harry Cooper . . . . .Karl Hardman
Tom . . . . .Keith Wayne

Psst! The film was made for less than $150,000 which was rustled up by Romero with his cap in his hands. Filming had to be fitted in with everyone's other commitments and so went in fits and starts • Among suggested titles were *The Flesheaters* and *Night of Anubis*, while the working title was *The Monster Flick* • Columbia turned it down because it was in black and white, while American International Pictures apparently weren't impressed that there was no central romance • When it was released, despite the title it often turned up at childrens' matinées, presumably scarring the unprepared little tots

for life. When it found its natural slot on the late-night and campus circuit, it became one of the most successful independent films ever • Despite its reputation, the original investors lost money initially and Romero lost control of the movie's rights, which became public domain. Only in 1988, when it was remade in order to get the rights back, did the profits flow in • The movie was black and white only because colour stock was beyond their budget • If you're still looking at the screen when the zombies begin snacking, console yourself with the thought that it isn't really people they're eating but lamb entrails picked up at the local slaughterhouse • Film freak Romero worked as a grip on *North by Northwest* while still at college.

A Night at the Opera
★★★★ 1935 96min b/w

Director: Sam Wood
Screenplay: George S. Kaufman & Morrie Ryskind

The Marx Brothers wreak their usual havoc on the world of opera. Despite the dreadful songs from Jones and the twee love interest, it contains some of their greatest moments and is a more coherent movie than their earlier films. The hilarious stateroom scene on the boat is here, as is the business with The Party of the First Part and the backstage destruction of *Il Trovatore*. Bliss.

Otis B. Driftwood . . . . .Groucho Marx
Fiorello . . . . .Chico Marx
Tomasso .Harpo Marx
Rosa Castaldi . . . . .Kitty Carlisle
Ricardo Baroni . . . . .Allan Jones
Herman Gottlieb . . . . .Sig Rumann
Mrs. Claypool . . . . .Margaret Dumont
Rodolfo Lassparri . . . . .Walter Woolf King
Captain .Edward Keane
Steward .Gino Corrado
Engineer's assitant/Peasant . . . . .Billy Gilbert
Stage manager . . . . .Jonathan Hale

Quote 'That's…that's in every contract. That's…that's what they call a sanity clause.' – 'Ha, ha, ha. You can't fool me. There ain't no Sanity Clause.' • 'Are you sure you have everything, Otis?' – 'I've never had any complaints yet.' • 'Is my aunt Minnie in here?' – 'Well you can come in and prowl around if you want to. If she isn't in here, you could probably find someone just as good.' • 'Let joy be unconfined. Let there be dancing in the streets, drinking in the saloons and necking in the park.'

Psst! This was the Marx Brothers' first movie at MGM after being sacked by Paramount. It only came about, so legend has it, because Chico got in a card game with MGM production chief Irving Thalberg • Thalberg made them go out on the road, testing the gags and routines they planned to use on real audiences until they were sure they were right. It seemed to work. The movie was their biggest hit. Sadly for the Marxes, Thalberg died during the making of their next movie, *Day at the Races* • On both this film and *A Day at the Races*, the out of favour Buster Keaton worked thinking up business for Harpo • The Marx Brothers quarrelled with director Wood, who they considered had no sense of humour and they did their utmost to force him to resign. They also hated his habit of doing umpteen retakes but still using the first or second take • Although an ordeal to those who want the funny stuff to begin again, the song 'Alone' became a big hit. It's sung by Allan Jones, Jack Jones' dad • This was the Marx Brothers' first movie without Zeppo • Mike Nichols, director of films like *The Graduate* once said to Groucho: 'I've seen *A Night at the Opera* 17 times.' – 'Really?' – 'Yes. I just couldn't get over that love story between Allan Jones and Kitty Carlisle.'

A Nightmare on Elm Street
★★★ 1984 91min c.

Director: Wes Craven
Screenplay: Wes Craven

A group of teens find they are being attacked in their dreams. Only young Nancy can save them, assuming she can stay awake. An ingenious new concept for a horror movie (then), with Freddy Krueger a genuinely sinister figure. The dream/reality trick is cunningly exploited, but the surprise ending fooled nobody. It was followed by umpteen, inferior, sequels and then rose from the dead again with the interesting *Wes Craven's New Nightmare*.

Freddy Krueger ....Robert Englund
Lt. Thompson ....John Saxon
Nancy Thompson ....Heather Langenkamp
Tina Grey ....Amanda Wyss
Rod Lane ....Nick Corri
Marge Thompson ....Ronee Blakley
Glen Lantz ....Johnny Depp
Dr. King ....Charles Fleischer

Blurb Sleep Kills.

Quote 'God! I look 20 years old.'

Showing The Evil Dead.

OOPS! A close shot of a wristwatch shows an arm with a long sleeve. But the character is actually wearing a short-sleeved nightdress • When Nancy walks past a tree, it appears to contain the tickets that she is given in the next scene.

Psst! This was Johnny Depp's screen debut • Craven says he named Kruger after a boy who bullied him in his schooldays.

The Night of the Hunter
★★ 1955 93min b/w

Director: Charles Laughton
Screenplay: James Agee
Source: Novel by Davis Grubb

Psychopathic preacher Mitchum terrorises a widow and her two children to get his hands on hubby's stolen loot. Film buffs claim this, Laughton's only outing as director, is a masterpiece. True, Mitchum is genuinely scary and there are a few extraordinary and beautifully-composed scenes. But it's all terribly melodramatic, the boy can't act and the dreadful sets are so deliberately obvious that the film keeps losing its grip on reality. One for the buffs only.

Preacher Harry Powell ....Robert Mitchum
Willa Harper ....Shelley Winters
Rachel.......................Lillian Gish
Icey Spoon ....Evelyn Varden
Ben Harper ....Peter Graves
Birdie ....James Gleason
John ....Billy Chaplin
Pearl ....Sally Jane Bruce

Quote 'Lord, you sure knew what you was doing when you put me in this very cell at this very time. A man with $10,000 hid somewhere, and a widder in the make.' • 'Would you like me to tell you the little story of right hand, left hand? The story of good and evil? H.A.T.E. It was with this left hand that old brother Cain struck the blow that laid his brother low. L.O.V.E. You see these fingers, dear hearts? These fingers has veins that run straight to the soul of man. The right hand, friends, the hand of love.' • 'A significant role for me? Seems to be – now! Charles called me up: "I've a book here about a thoroughly unredeemable shit." And I said: "Present!" [Mitchum]

Psst! Although Agee is listed as the writer, he apparently wrote a screenplay that was four times the size of the novel. Laughton helped trim and adapt it until he was satisfied it was a decent adaptation of the novel • Mitchum was making *Not as a Stranger* simultaneously and had to do much of his filming late at night or on Sundays • The frightening scene where the children spot Mitchum on horseback from the hay loft where they are hiding was actually a shot of a midget on a pony to make the perspective more interesting • The studio didn't know what to make of the film and sent it out on a double bill with a B-movie western. Most often screened at childrens' matinees, it may well be responsible for traumatising a generation of cinemagoers • The film was banned in Memphis.

A Night to Remember
★★★ 1958 123min b/w

Director: Roy Ward Baker
Screenplay: Eric Ambler
Source: Book by Walter Lord

The story of the sinking of the Titanic, a cocktail with umpteen British character actors telling the story straight up with a chunk of ice on the side. Although an expensive British movie at the time, on which much care and attention was lavished, the special effects now sadly look pretty naff. Nonetheless, it's still a pretty exciting tale.

Herbert Lightoller . . . . .Kenneth More
Mr. Clarke . . . . .Ronald Allen
Mrs. Lucas . . . . .Honor Blackman
Peuchen . . . . .Robert Ayres
Capt. Rostron . . . . .Anthony Bushell
Bride . . . . .David McCallum
Phillips . . . . .Kenneth Griffith
Thomas Andrews . . . . .Michael Goodliffe
Chairman . . . . .Frank Lawton
Cottam . . . . .Alec McCowen
Capt. Smith . . . . .Laurence Naismith

Psst! The line 'Still here, Miss Evans?' refers to one of the two women in first class who didn't survive the sinking.

Night Train to Munich
★★ 1940 93min b/w

Director: Carol Reed
Screenplay: Frank Launder & Sidney Gilliat

Source: Novel, *Report on a Fugitive* by Gordon Wellesley.

British spy Harrison spirits a Czech inventor away from the Nazis. This attempt by Launder & Gilliat to replicate the success of their earlier film *The Lady Vanishes* was very popular at the time. Now, though, it s too old-fashioned and silly to get up a head of steam and is hampered by some dreadful models. On the other hand, cricket-obsessed Charters and Caldicott are as delightful as ever.

Anna Bomasch . . . . .Margaret Lockwood
Gus Bennett . . . . .Rex Harrison
Karl Marsen . . . . .Paul Henreid
Charters . . . . .Basil Radford
Caldicott . . . . .Naunton Wayne
Dr. Fredericks . . . . .Felix Aylmer
Dryden . . . . .Wyndham Goldie
Roberts . . . . .Roland Culver
Schwab . . . . .Eliot Makeham
Kampenfeldt . . . . .Raymond Huntley
Also: Kenneth Kent, Austin Trevor, Irene Handl

Quote 'You know, if a woman ever loved you like you love yourself, it'd be one of the romances of history.' • 'The nation is behind the Fuehrer.' – 'Yes, but how far behind?'

OOPS! At the cable car station, Harrison gets off a hundred or more shots from a revolver, making it perhaps one of the least realistic shoot-outs in the movies.

Psst! The original story on which the film was based was set in a mythical state called Ironia. After the outbreak of war, however, the film-makers were allowed to identify it clearly as Nazi Germany • Look out for a glimpse of Irene Handl 'Heil Hitler'-ing as people get off the train • Paul Henreid is on the credits as Paul von Hernreid.

Nikita
★★ 1990 116min c.

Director: Luc Besson
Screenplay: Luc Besson

After being involved in a violent robbery, punky junkie Parillaud is turned into a Government hit-person. Initially very exciting, the movie ultimately goes nowhere, uncertain if it's an art film or a shoot-'em-up. The mini-skirted Parillaud is tremendous, but you might as well look at the wonderful poster for a couple of hours. Also known as *La Femme Nikita*. Remade in Hollywood as *Assassin*.

Nikita	Anne Parillaud
Marco	Jean-Hugues Anglade
Bob	Tcheky Karyo
Amande	Jeanne Moreau

9 ½ Weeks

★★ 1986 116min c.

Director: Adrian Lyne
Screenplay: Patricia Louisianna Knop, Zalman King & Sarah Kernochan
Source: Novel by Elizabeth McNeil

It only seems that long. Even in the more explicit European version, this examination of an obsessive relationship between Basinger and Rourke is tiresome stuff. For once 'all mouth and no trousers' is a perfectly apt description. Style is everything, with the hi-fi equipment getting more attention from the camera than Basinger. Some of the much-touted sex scenes raise nothing more than a snigger. Surprisingly, perhaps, the film appears to be more popular with women than men.

John	Mickey Rourke
Elizabeth	Kim Basinger
Molly	Margaret Whitton
Harvey	David Margulies
Thea	Christine Baranski
Sue	Karen Young

Quote 'I became an actress in my own eyes...I was electrically disturbed after it was over; marbles were rolling off the table.' [Basinger] • 'I had the impression we were going to break new territory; certain paranoias and fantasies, certain delicate, subtle things that go on between two people that I wanted to delve into and capture. But that wouldn't sell as many tickets as me humping Kim Basinger on a coffee table.' [Rourke]

OOPS! After Rourke buys her a scarf in the market, it vanishes from her shoulders as they walk, as does the shopping bag.

Psst! Basinger and Rourke didn't get on. He didn't think she was sexy enough for the part and she thought necking him was like kissing an ashtray • Cut by the American distributor for being too steamy, it was far more popular abroad, where it was complete • Worthing Council wouldn't let the film be shown until the councillors had a private screening to check if it was decent. In its place was offered *Body Lust, Best Bit of Crumpet in Denmark* • The credits include a 'physical fitness consultant'.

9 to 5

★★ 1980 110min c.

Director: Colin Higgins
Screenplay: Colin Higgins & Patricia Resnick

Three female office workers hatch a plot to get their own back on their nasty, chauvinistic male boss. Although this comedy was immensely successful at the box office, one gets the impression that the writers only clocked in at 12 and left at three. Little of any interest is done with the premise and it only very occasionally raises more than a titter. Rather more Tipp-Ex would not have come amiss.

Judy Bernly	Jane Fonda
Violet Newstead	Lily Tomlin
Doralee Rhodes	Dolly Parton
Franklin Hart, Jr.	Dabney Coleman
Tinsworthy	Sterling Hayden
Roz	Elizabeth Wilson

OOPS! Tomlin is stopped by a cop on a motorbike because her rear lights are faulty. When she drives away afterwards, they are both working fine.

Psst! The film was made by Jane Fonda's production company • This was Dolly Parton's first screen role.

Ninotchka

★★★ 1939 110min b/w

Director: Ernst Lubitsch
Screenplay: Charles Brackett, Billy Wilder & Walter Reisch
Source: Original screen story by Melchior Lengyel

It's hard to understand why everyone goes into such raptures about this tale of the hard line Communist falling for the Parisian playboy. What is supposedly the peak of sophisticated romantic comedy doesn't half look clunky these days, in large part because Garbo is such an abysmal comedienne. When, as the ad puts it, Garbo laughs, it looks as though she's read how to do it from a book. Still, Douglas is charming, Rumann and Bressart are as funny as ever and there are some neat lines. In 1957 it became the musical *Silk Stockings*.

Comrade Ninotchka	Greta Garbo
Count Leon Dolga	Melvyn Douglas
Grand Duchess Swana	Ina Claire
Michael Ironoff	Sig Rumann

Buljanoff	Felix Bressart
Kopalski	Alexander Granach
Commissar Razinin	Bela Lugosi
Count Alexis Rakonin	Gregory Gaye

Blurb Garbo Laughs!

Quote 'This picture takes place in Paris in those wonderful days when a siren was a brunette and not an alarm – and if a Frenchman turned out the light it was not on account of an air raid!' [Prologue] • 'There is an old Turkish proverb that says: If something smells bad, why put your nose in it?' – 'And there is an old Russian saying: The cat who has cream on his whiskers had better find good excuses.' • 'Ninotchka, it's midnight. One half of Paris is making love to the other half.' • 'Never did I dream I could feel this toward a sergeant.' • 'Ninotchka, you like me just a little bit?' – 'Your general appearance is not distasteful.' – 'Thank you.' – 'The whites of your eyes are clear. Your cornea is excellent.' • 'Must you flirt?' – 'I don't have to, but I find it natural.' – 'Suppress it.' • 'That was restful…Again.'

Psst! This was Garbo's penultimate film. Her next, *Two-Faced Woman*, was so poorly received that she gave up acting and became a recluse • Garbo became good friends with co-star Ina Claire who had married the late silent star John Gilbert, with whom Garbo had had a much publicised affair.

Nobody's Fool
★★★ 1994 110min c.

Director: Robert Benton
Screenplay: Robert Benton
Source: Novel by Richard Russo

Newman plays Sully, a charmer but one of nature's losers, who has managed to bumble along avoiding any responsibility, but has little now to show for his life. Only ex-teacher Tandy still has any faith left in him. Then his son and grandson appear out of the blue and he is given one final chance to redeem himself. This delightful film is so gentle and beguiling that it is half way through before you realise how completely and utterly hooked you are. In addition to Paul Newman's superlative performance, boss Willis and Griffith, with whom he constantly flirts, prove themselves here to be far better actors than they are usually given credit for. This is one of those feel-good movies that sweeps you off your feet and gives you a great big hug.

Sully	Paul Newman
Miss Beryl	Jessica Tandy
Carl Roebuck	Bruce Willis
Toby Roebuck	Melanie Griffith
Peter	Dylan Walsh
Rub Squeers	Pruitt Taylor Vince
Wirf	Gene Saks
Clive Peoples Jr.	Josef Sommer
Officer Raymer	Philip Seymour Hoffman
Judge Flatt	Philip Bosco

Psst! It feels rather spooky when Jessica Tandy, seen here on screen for the very last time, says: 'I've got a feeling God's creeping in on me. I think this is the year he lowers the boom.' • The same title was confusingly used for a romantic comedy in 1986 starring Rosanna Arquette. Although studios can register film titles with The Motion Picture Association of America, Island Pictures, who made the movie, wasn't an MPAA member.

North by Northwest
★★★★ 1959 136min c.

Director: Alfred Hitchcock
Screenplay: Ernest Lehman

The ultimate comedy-thriller. Ad-man Grant finds his life in danger when he is mistaken for a spy. This delicious blend of thrills, humour, mystery and great chases is full of memorable scenes, including the crop-dusting plane and the climax on Mount Rushmore. Although there's one desperately bad fake wood, at least Hitch doesn't inflict any of his lousy back-projection work on us to destroy the mood. Pretty damn perfect.

Roger Thornhill	Cary Grant
Eve Kendall	Eva Marie Saint
Phillip Vandamm	James Mason
The Professor	Leo G. Carroll
Leonard	Martin Landau
Clara Thornhill	Jessie Royce Landis
Lester Townsend	Philip Ober
Valerian	Adam Williams
Handsome woman	Josephine Hutchinson
Victor Larrabee	Edward Platt

Quote 'You gentlemen aren't really trying to kill my son, are you?' • 'That's funny. That plane's dusting crops where there ain't no crops.' • 'This matter is best disposed of from a great height. Over water.' • 'That wasn't very sporting, using real bullets.'

OOPS! My very favourite movie boo-boo happens in the mountainside café where Saint pretends to shoot Grant. The gun must have made a lot of noise in previous takes because, just as she draws the gun, a little lad who isn't even looking in their direction puts his fingers in his ears • As Thornhill is bundled into his car by Mason's heavies, one goes the wrong way so that his head vanishes behind the painting of the background • Look out of the train window during the earlier scene when the pair first meet on the train. As they chat, they pass many interesting sights such as some woods and a timber-yard, and a timber-yard and some woods and some familiar woods and the same timber-yard again. All this, while on the table the wilting flowers keep reviving miraculously • A car with its rear wheel over a cliff wouldn't be able to drive away, as happens here • Grant muffs a line, saying 'our friend who's *assembling* the General Assembly' as he looks at a photo, instead of 'addressing'.

Psst! Hitch was actually hired to direct a version of Hammond Innes' novel, *The Wreck of the Mary Deare*. He and writer Lehman soon discovered it was too difficult to adapt and worked together on conjuring up an original spy thriller • It was originally intended for James Stewart • According to Hitchcock: 'Our original title was *The Man in Lincoln's Nose*. Couldn't use it, though. They also wouldn't let us shoot people on Mount Rushmore. Can't deface a national monument. And it's a pity, too, because I had a wonderful shot in mind of Cary Grant hiding in Lincoln's nose and having a sneezing fit.' • The faces had to be re-created in the studio for close-up work • Hitchcock intentionally wouldn't let the cast know the whole plot. He wanted them to seem bewildered and uncertain about what was going to happen • The United Nations refused permission for Hitchcock to film in their building. The shot of Grant entering it was taken with a hidden camera • Although Landis plays Grant's mother, he was actually 10 months older than her • Fans of the film should try to watch the 1995 Johnny Depp movie *Arizona Dream* for the great re-creation of the crop-dusting scene.

Northwest Frontier

★★★ 1959 129min c.

Director: J. Lee-Thompson
Screenplay: Robin Estridge

Great Boy's Own action-adventure with English officer More and governess Bacall trying to get a young Indian prince away to safety on a rickety train, with dangers besetting them on all sides. Counting the clichés as they fly past is half the fun. Also known as *Flame over India*.

Capt. Scott	Kenneth More
Catherine Wyatt	Lauren Bacall
Van Leyden	Herbert Lom
Bridie	Wilfrid Hyde-White
Lady Windham	Ursula Jeans
Gupta	I.S. Johar

Nothing Sacred

★★ 1937 75min c.

Director: William Wellman
Screenplay: Ben Hecht
Source: Story, *Letter to the Editor* by James H. Street.

A young woman, believed to be dying of a rare disease, is built up into a national celebrity by a sleazy journalist. Problems arise when she doesn't die on cue. Once seen as a razor-sharp satire on the press and the public's obsession with disease-of-the-week true-life stories, this comedy now looks rather cosy and safe, even though it stars the glorious Lombard. In spite of its incredibly high reputation, it no longer seems anything out of the ordinary. The plot was used for a 1953 stage musical called *Hazel Flagg* which was then turned into the 1954 film *Living It Up* with Jerry Lewis and Dean Martin.

Hazel Flagg	Carole Lombard
Wally Cook	Fredric March
Oliver Stone	Walter Connolly
Dr. Enoch Downer	Charles Winninger
Dr. Emile Egglehoffer	Sig Rumann
M.C.	Frank Fay
Max Levinsky	Maxie Rosenbloom
Drugstore lady	Margaret Hamilton
Dr. Vunch	Monty Woolley
Fireman	John Qualen
Baggage man	Olin Howlin
Mrs. Walker	Hattie McDaniel
Dowager 'Katinka'	Jinx Falkenberg

Quote 'I'll tell you briefly what I think of newspapermen. The hand of God, reaching down into the mire, couldn't elevate one of them to the depths of degradation.'

Psst! Hecht drew on his experiences as a reporter in Chicago, writing the film on a train from New York to Los Angeles specifically for Carole Lombard • Lombard did not get on with March. Ever one for practical jokes, she decided to end his unwanted attentions once and for all. She invited him to her dressing room one evening and led him on, only for him to discover that she was wearing a rubber dildo • For film buffs, this was the first film to contain colour back-projection.

Notorious
★★★★ 1946 101min b/w

Director: Alfred Hitchcock
Screenplay: Ben Hecht

This sensational wartime spy-thriller-cum-love-story is one of Hitchcock's finest movies. American Government agent Grant puts Bergman in immense danger by getting her to marry dangerous Nazi agent Rains. It's tense, exciting, romantic and surprisingly sexy with one of the greatest of all screen kisses and a subtext you could practically drown in.

Devlin	Cary Grant
Alicia Huberman	Ingrid Bergman
Alexander Sebastian	Claude Rains
Paul Prescott	Louis Calhern
Mme. Sebastian	Leopoldine Konstantin
Dr. Anderson	Reinhold Schünzel
Walter Beardsley	Moroni Olsen
Eric Mathis	Ivan Triesault
Mr. Hopkins	Wally Brown

Blurb The Longest Kiss In History.

Quote 'We are protected by the enormity of your stupidity.' • 'Alex, will you come in, please? I wish to talk to you.' [Last line]

Psst! Hitch can be spotted roughly an hour into the film, drinking champagne at the party in Rains' mansion • Clifton Webb was Hitchcock's first choice for the role that went to Claude Rains • At the time, the Production Code allowed kisses to last only three seconds. Hitch got round this by getting Grant and Bergman to keep breaking off to do other things like talk, nibble earlobes and so on. It comes across as one long stupendous snog without at any time breaking the rule • Hitch claimed that he was watched by the FBI because the plot involved uranium ore. When the film was being prepared, the atomic bomb had not yet been exploded and The Manhattan Project was the most secret operation in America. Hitch and the writers claimed to have chosen the subject of uranium as their MacGuffin by chance. Others say it was only included *after* the bomb exploded at Hiroshima. • Film buffs go into

raptures about the amazing crane shot that swoops down from the top of the stairs to the key nestling in Bergman's hand.

No Way Out
★★★ 1987 114min c.

Director: Roger Donaldson
Screenplay: Robert Garland
Source: Novel, *The Big Clock* by Kenneth Fearing

This tense and racy thriller has Pentagon naval officer Costner sharing lover Young with Secretary of Defence Hackman. When Hackman kills her in a fit of jealousy, Costner is put in charge of the investigation. Like all good thrillers, the tension is steadily racked up notch by notch. Although not always entirely plausible, Young is excellent compensation, and never sexier than here. Others hated the ending. I think it's great.

Tom Farrell	Kevin Costner
David Brice	Gene Hackman
Susan Atwell	Sean Young
Scott Pritchard	Will Patton
Senator Duvall	Howard Duff
Sam Hesselman	George Dzundza

Psst! The project was in 'turnaround', indicating nobody wanted to make it, when Costner came across it and championed its cause • The movie is a remake, although not a very close one, of the 1948 *The Big Clock*, starring Charles Laughton • Apparently limousine hire companies saw a noticeable pick-up in business after the famous back-seat sex scene in the film! • Young hates doing love scenes and downed four beers before feeling able to cope with it.

Now, Voyager
★★★ 1942 118min b/w

Director: Irving Rapper
Screenplay: Casey Robinson
Source: Novel by Olive Higgins Prouty

An unhappy, mother-dominated spinster is turned into a chic socialite by three months of psychiatry and embarks on her first brief, but inevitably doomed, love affair in Rio. It's utter tosh and it's also utterly irresistible. Davis is at her over-emoting best and if you don't cry buckets on cue to Max Steiner's music then you've a stronger constitution than me. The film does, of course, contain the most famous cigarette-lighting scene in the movies.

Charlotte Vale	.Bette Davis
Jerry Durrance	.Paul Henreid
Dr. Jaquity	.Claude Rains
Mrs. Vale	.Gladys Cooper
June Vale	.Bonita Granville
Elliott Livingston	.John Loder
Lisa Vale	.Ilka Chase
Deb McIntyre	.Lee Patrick
Leslie Trotter	.Charles Drake
Mr. Thompson	.Franklin Pangborn
Frank McIntryre	.James Rennie
Tina	.Janis Wilson
Donna Pickford	.Mary Wickes

Quote 'No one ever called me darling before.'
• 'Oh, Jerry, don't let's ask for the moon. We have the stars!' [Last line]

Psst! The lead was originally intended for Irene Dunne, but Davis fought tooth and nail to get it • She rewrote many of her scenes, restoring much of the dialogue from the original novel • After the famous cigarette-lighting scene, Paul Henreid claimed not be able to go anywhere without women beseeching him to 'light me' • Gossip columnist Louella Parsons thought she'd got an amazing exclusive when she wrote in her column that 'one of the World's greatest living psychoanalysts, Sigmund Freud', was going to act as technical adviser on the film.

La Nuit Américaine
SEE: Day for Night

The Nun's Story
★★★ 1959 149min c.

Director: Fred Zinnemann
Screenplay: Robert Anderson
Source: Book by Kathryn C. Hulme

A nun's dedication to her vocation is tested by war and love in the Belgian Congo at the outbreak of World War II. Based on a true story, this absorbing and worthwhile tale is a good deal less sentimental and pious than you might expect.

Gabrielle Van Der Mal/Sister Luke	.Audrey Hepburn
Dr. Fortunati	.Peter Finch
Mother Emmanual	.Edith Evans
Mother Mathilde	.Peggy Ashcroft
Dr. Van Der Mal	.Dean Jagger
Sister Margharita	.Mildred Dunnock
Sister William	.Patricia Collinge
Mother Christophe	.Beatrice Straight
Archangel	.Colleen Dewhurst
Mother Marcella	.Ruth White
Sister Eleanor	.Rosalie Crutchley
Dr. Goovaerts	.Lionel Jeffries

Psst! The scenes with the nuns going through assorted rituals were carried out by members of Rome's Royal Opera Ballet • Unusually, there was no music over the end titles. There was argument among the top brass over whether it should be upbeat or downbeat, while Zinnemann didn't want music to say what the film didn't. He won and got the silence he sought • Although nominated for six Oscars, it didn't win one.

Octopussy
★★★ 1983 130min c.

Director: John Glen
Screenplay: George Macdonald Fraser, Richard Maibaum & Michael G. Wilson

The plot's ludicrous, all about a Russian general trying to start World War III by himself, but who cares? This is still a pretty droll, action-packed outing for Bond, culminating in one of those wonderful disarming-the-device races in which the clock gets slower and slower as zero approaches, much like the train indicators on the London Underground.

James Bond	.Roger Moore
Octopussy	.Maud Adams
Kamal	.Louis Jourdan
Magda	.Kristina Wayborn
Gobinda	.Kabir Bedi
Orlov	.Steven Berkoff
'Q'	.Desmond Llewelyn
'M'	.Robert Brown
Gogol	.Walter Gotell
Minister of Defence	.Geoffrey Keen
Moneypenny	.Lois Maxwell

Psst! The film was in competition with the rival *Never Say Never Again* starring Connery • Tennis star Vijay Amritraj appears as himself • Maud Adams, here a villain, was the love interest nine years earlier in *The Man With the Golden Gun*, where she was killed. She is the only actress to appear in more than one Bond film, with the exception of Lois Maxwell and Caroline Bliss, of course, who play Moneypenny.

The Odd Couple
★★★ 1968 105min c.

Director: Gene Saks
Screenplay: Neil Simon
Source: Play by Simon

Although Simon's play still looks stage-bound on screen, it's just as funny as in the theatre. A pair of veterans from wrecked marriages set up home together and bicker like man and wife. Full of delicious one-liners, it's one of the best of the screen teamings of Matthau and Lemon.

Felix Ungar ....Jack Lemmon
Oscar Madison ....Walter Matthau
Vinnie ....John Fielder
Murray ....Herb Edelman
Roy ....David Sheiner
Speed ....Larry Haines
Cecily ....Monica Evans
Gwendolyn ....Carole Shelley
Waitress ....Iris Adrian

Quote 'I got brown sandwiches and green sandwiches. Which one do you want?' – 'What's the green?' – 'It's either very new cheese or very old meat.' • 'It took me three hours to figure out 'F.U.' was Felix Ungar. It's not your fault, Felix; it's a rotten combination, that's all.' • 'He wears a seat belt in a drive-in movie.' • 'He's the only man in the world with clenched hair.' • 'Don't point that finger at me unless you intend to use it.' • 'Let's spend one night talking to someone with higher voices than us.' • 'Every actor looks all his life for a part that will combine his talents with his personality. *The Odd Couple* was mine. The plutonium I needed. It all started happening after that.' [Walter Matthau]

Psst! While Matthau reprised his stage role, Lemmon's part had been played on Broadway by Art Carney • Matthau and Lemmon had earlier appeared together in *The Fortune Cookie* • The premise was turned into a long-running TV sitcom, then in the early 80s it had an outing as a sitcom with two black actors. Neil Simon even turned it into a stage vehicle for two women, *Oliver and Florence*, which starred Sally Struthers and Rita Moreno.

Odd Man Out
★★★ 1947 115min c.

Director: Carol Reed
Screenplay: F.L. Green & R.C. Sherriff
Source: Novel by Green

An escaped IRA man is wounded and seeks help from a succession of Belfast citizens, some well-meaning and some less so. It is almost impossible to take your eyes off Mason in this beautifully-photographed, at times almost ethereal, chase movie.

Johnny McQueen ....James Mason
Lukey.......................Robert Newton
Kathleen ....Kathleen Ryan
Dennis ....Robert Beatty
Shell .......................F.J. McCormick
Pat ....Cyril Cusack
Rosie ....Fay Compton
Fencie ....William Hartnell
Nolan ....Dan O'Herlihy
Cabby ....Joseph Tomelty

An Officer and a Gentleman
★★ 1982 124min c.

Director: Taylor Hackford
Screenplay: Douglas Day Stewart

An officer, maybe. But a *gentleman*? Gere's the lad from the slums who wants to be a pilot. But first he has to endure training under bully Gossett. Mild consolation comes from local girl Winger. The plot's as old as the Hollywood sign and there's something rather disquieting about Winger's only means of escape being on Gere's coat-tails. Still, there are compensations, not least of them Gossett and his wonderful performance as the martinet.

Zack Mayo ....Richard Gere
Paula Pokrifki ....Debra Winger
Sgt. Emil Foley ....Louis Gossett Jr.
Sid Worley ....David Keith
Lynette Pomeroy ....Lisa Blount
Byron Mayo ....Robert Loggia
Casey ....Lisa Eilbacher
Emiliano Serra ....Tony Plana
Topper Daniels ....David Caruso
Esther Pokrifki ....Grace Zabriskie
Voice of Altitude
Chamber instructor ....Ed Begley Jr.

Oscars Louis Gossett Jr.

Blurb It'll Lift You Up Where You Belong.

Quote 'So there I am, on top of him, with tears coming out of my eyes and people thinking it's because I'm so moved, when actually I'm really crying because I'm so unhappy' [Winger]

Psst! The studio had little faith in the movie and spent very little promoting it. Word of mouth made it into a hit • The smouldering looks between Gere and Winger are not the result of off-screen attraction. They are said to have loathed each other [see above] • Richard Gere's role was apparently written with John Denver in mind • Gossett's part was written with a white actor in mind • Writer Stewart had been through the school himself, and survived • 'On the sand [says the script] Lynette's fingers work at the gold buttons on Sid's tunic while Sid's fingers grope for the zipper that would unlock all the mysteries…' • The production had to use a deserted base when the Navy, upset by the sexual explicitness of the film, would not offer any help.

Oh, Mr. Porter!

★★★ 1937 84min b/w

Director: Marcel Varnel
Screenplay: Marriott Edgar, Val Guest & J.O.C. Orton
Source: Story by Frank Launder

A new stationmaster arrives at Buggleskelly, on the border of the Irish Free State and Northern Ireland, and gets involved with ghosts and gun-runners. Although as creaky as the windmill's sails in places, Hay, old man Marriott and chubby youth Moffatt were never better teamed together than here. If there was ever a British version of the zany humour epitomised by The Marx Brothers, it was this trio. Warm yourself at the brazier. It's full of delightful comic chestnuts.

William Porter	Will Hay
Jeremiah Harbottle	Moore Marriott
Albert	Graham Moffatt
Grogan	Dennis Wyndham
Postman	Dave O'Toole
Charles Trimbletow	Sebastian Smith
Mrs. Trimbletow	Agnes Lauchlan
An old Victorian Engine	Gladstone

Quote 'He haunts the hill, He haunts the mill, And the land that lies between.' – 'Is he a house agent?' • 'Next train's gone.' • 'You're wasting your time.' – 'Well, what are you doing?' – 'Just watching you wasting your time.'

Oh! What a Lovely War

★★ 1969 144min c.

Director: Richard Attenborough
Screenplay: Len Deighton

Source: Joan Littlewood's stage production of Charles Chilton's radio play, *The Long, Long Trail*

A patchy attempt to transfer Joan Littlewood's successful stage musical about the senseless futility of war to the screen. There are scenes that work, but on the whole it tries far too hard and lacks subtlety.

Sir Edward Grey	Ralph Richardson
Lady Grey	Meriel Forbes
Count Berchtold	John Gielgud
Kaiser Wilhelm II	Kenneth More
Field Marshal Sir John French	Laurence Olivier
Gen. Sir Henry Wilson	Michael Redgrave
Field Marshal Sir Douglas Haig	John Mills
Sylvia Pankhurst	Vanessa Redgrave
Eleanor	Susannah York
Music hall star	Maggie Smith
Emperor Franz Josef	Jack Hawkins
President Poincare	Ian Holm
Gen. Von Moltke	John Clements
Czar Nicholas II	Paul Daneman
Also: Dirk Bogarde, Phyllis Calvert, Joe Melia, Corin Redgrave, Juliet Mills, Jane Seymour	

Psst! This was Attenborough's directorial debut • Author Len Deighton, who with the producer had bought the film rights to the property, had his name taken off the film because of differences of opinion with Attenborough.

Oklahoma!

★★ 1955 145min c.

Director: Fred Zinnemann
Screenplay: Sonya Levien & William Ludwig
Source: Musical by Rodgers & Hammerstein from play by Lynn Riggs

Although this rendering of the famous Rodgers and Hammerstein musical is pretty uninspiring, the great songs still come across well, among them 'Oh, What a Beautiful Morning' and 'The Surrey with the Fringe on Top'.

Curly	Gordon MacRae
Ado Annie	Gloria Grahame
Will Parker	Gene Nelson
Aunt Eller	Charlotte Greenwood
Laurey	Shirley Jones
Jud Fry	Rod Steiger
Ali Hakim	Eddie Albert
Carnes	James Whitmore
Gertie	Barbara Lawrence
Skidmore	Jay C. Flippen
Dream Curly	James Mitchell

Quote 'I wanted to marry her when I saw the moonlight shining on the barrel of her father's shotgun.'

Psst! The movie was actually filmed in Arizona where the weather was supposed to be better than Oklahoma. In fact it rained for much of the shoot and a flash flood swept away a car containing the footage of a whole week's work.

The Old Dark House

★★★ 1932 71min b/w

Director: James Whale
Screenplay: Benn W. Levy & R.C. Sherriff
Source: Novel, *Benighted* by J.B. Priestley

A group of travellers wonder if they were wise to seek shelter in a gothic monstrosity inhabited by an extremely weird family who obviously don't get many visitors. More comedy than horror to modern tastes, much of it is pretty silly. But the sheer eccentricity of it all is still very appealing.

Morgan	Boris Karloff
Roger Penderell	Melvyn Douglas
Sir William Porterhouse	Charles Laughton
Horace Femm	Ernest Thesiger
Philip Waverton	Raymond Massey
Margaret Waverton	Gloria Stuart
Gladys DuCane	Lillian Bond
Rebecca Femm	Eva Moore
Sir Roderick Femm	Elspeth Dudgeon

Quote 'No beds! They can't have beds.' • 'Have a potato.'

Psst! Although billed as John Dudgeons, Sir Roderick Femm is actually played by Elspeth Dudgeons.

Oliver Twist

★★★ 1948 116min b/w

Director: David Lean
Screenplay: David Lean & Stanley Haynes
Source: Novel by Charles Dickens

This wonderfully dark and atmospheric version of Dickens' classic tale of the orphan falling in with a gang of young thieves looks as if Dore's nightmarish pictures of Victorian London have been brought to life. Sadly, it is impossible to overlook Guinness' stereotypical Fagin. While his portrayal may be true to the novel, it does serve to unbalance the film.

Bill Sikes	Robert Newton
Fagin	Alec Guinness
Nancy	Kay Walsh
Mr. Bumble	Francis L. Sullivan
Mr. Brownlow	Henry Stephenson
Oliver Twist	John Howard Davies
The Artful Dodger	Anthony Newley
Mrs. Cornley	Mary Clare
Oliver's mother	Josephine Stuart

Also: Henry Edwards, Ralph Truman, Diana Dors

Psst! Young Oliver is John Howard Davies who left acting to become one of the BBC's top comedy producers, making series like *Monty Python* and *Fawlty Towers* • The filming schedule actually broke the regulations governing child labour, but the authorities turned a blind eye • There is said to be one scene for which Guinness was unavailable, in which David Lean stood in for him • Protests from Jewish groups in America about Guinness' portrayal of Fagin delayed the release of the film for three years and resulted in seven minutes being cut out. It only became possible to see it in its full version in 1970 • In West Berlin in 1949, there were violent demonstrations when the film opened • In China, it was retitled *Lost Child in Foggy City*.

Oliver!

★★★ 1968 153min c.

Director: Carol Reed
Screenplay: Vernon Harris
Source: Play by Lionel Bart from the novel by Charles Dickens.

A splendidly exuberant musical version of Dickens' novel, every bit as enjoyable as on the stage. There are a few dull stretches but plenty of wonderfully staged songs to compensate, among them 'Consider Yourself', 'Food Glorious Food' and 'Who Will Buy This Wonderful Morning?'

Fagin	Ron Moody
Bill Sikes	Oliver Reed
Nancy	Shani Wallis
Mr. Bumble	Harry Secombe
Oliver	Mark Lester
The Artful Dodger	Jack Wild
Magistrate	Hugh Griffith
Mr. Brownlow	Joseph O'Conor
Widow Corney	Peggy Mount
Mr. Sowerberry	Leonard Rossiter
Mrs. Sowerberry	Hylda Baker
Noah Claypole	Kenneth Cranham

Mrs. Bedwin . . . . .Megs Jenkins
Chairman .Fred Emney

Oscars Best Picture, Best Director

Quote 'Please, sir. I want some more.'

Psst! Director Carol Reed was Oliver Reed's uncle • Moody had played the part of Fagin on stage • Reed originally wanted Shirley Bassey to play Nancy but Columbia refused to countenance a black actress in the part, reluctant to lose the bookings in the Southern states that would undoubtedly result • It won six Oscars.

The Omega Man

★★★ 1971 98min c.

Director: Boris Sagal
Screenplay: John William Corrington & Joyce M. Corrington
Source: Novel, *I am Legend* by Richard Matheson

A truly memorable and scary sci-fi thriller, with Heston apparently the last normal human being alive after germ warfare has wiped most of mankind out. There are, however, considerable numbers of zombie-like disease carriers for him to battle. Although not the best-made of movies, this one is likely to stay in the memory long afterwards.

Neville . . . . .Charlton Heston
Matthias .Anthony Zerbe
Lisa . . . . .Rosalind Cash
Dutch . . . . .Paul Koslo
Zachary . . . . .Lincoln Kilpatrick
Tommy . . . . .Brian Tochi
Family member . . . . .John Dierkes

The Omen

★★ 1976 111min c.

Director: Richard Donner
Screenplay: David Seltzer

The American Ambassador to London, Gregory Peck, swaps his stillborn child with that delivered to a dead mother, but rashly ignores the 666 on the lad's forehead. He's subsequently soon having to dial 999 to cope with the endless diabolically-inspired deaths of anyone who comes close to the little imp. Even the Common Market gets blamed at one point! This is a silly, stylish *Exorcist* rip-off, with Billie Whitelaw splen-

did as the original Nanny From Hell. It gave birth to three revolting offspring.

Robert Thorn . . . . .Gregory Peck
Katherine Thorn . . . . .Lee Remick
Mrs. Baylock . . . . .Billie Whitelaw
Jennings .David Warner
Damien .Harvey Stevens
Bugenhagen . . . . .Leo McKern
Father Brennan . . . . .Patrick Troughton
Father Spiletto . . . . .Martin Benson

Blurb Good Morning. You Are One Day Closer To The End Of The World.

Psst! According to the director, some parents shaved their childrens' heads after seeing the film, looking for a '666' birthmark • Charlton Heston was the original choice for Peck's part • Probably the first film to have a character decapitated by a sheet of glass falling off the back of a lorry.

Once Upon a Time in America

★★★★ 1984 228min c.

Director: Sergio Leone
Screenplay: Sergio Leone, Leo Benvenuti, Piero De Bernardi, Enrico Medioli, Franco Arcalli & Franco Ferrini
Source: Novel, *The Hoods* by Harry Grey (David Aaronson)

The story of a group of Jewish gangsters, known as the Kosher Nostra, in 20s and 30s New York. Leone's best film is a corrective to the sentimentality of *The Godfather*. Brutal, ambitious, even affectionate, it's shot through with Hollywood-fed fantasies of the American Dream and its betrayal by Prohibition's institutionalisation of crime. Although the plot isn't always plausible, the mood and action is terrific, as is the acting. Avoid any of the truncated versions of the film that are around.

Noodles .Robert De Niro
Max . . . . .James Woods
Deborah . . . . .Elizabeth McGovern
Jimmy O'Donnell . . . . .Treat Williams
Carol . . . . .Tuesday Weld
Joe . . . . .Burt Young
Frankie . . . . .Joe Pesci
Police Chief Aiello . . . . .Danny Aiello
Cockeye . . . . .William Forsythe
Young Deborah . . . . .Jennifer Connelly

Quote 'Age cannot wither me, Noodles.'

Once Upon a Time in the West

★★★★ 1969 165min c.

Director: Sergio Leone
Screenplay: Sergio Leone & Sergio Donati

Despite the absence of Clint, this is Leone's best spaghetti western. Combining echoes of many famous others with an unfathomable plot about water rights, the film benefits from location shooting in John Ford's sacred Monument Valley, flamboyant camerawork and tough performances, including Cardinale. Morricone's wildly overblown score helps immeasurably. One to be seen in widescreen if at all possible.

Frank	Henry Fonda
Jill McBain	Claudia Cardinale
Cheyenne	Jason Robards
'Harmonica'	Charles Bronson
Morton	Gabriele Ferzetti
Sheriff	Keenan Wynn
Stony	Woody Strode
Knuckles	Jack Elam
Barman	Lionel Stander
Brett McBain	Frank Wolff

Blurb There Were Three Men In Her Life. One To Take Her...One To Love Her...And One To Kill Her.

Quote 'He's whittling on a piece of wood. I got a feeling when he stops whittling, something's gonna happen.' • 'How can you trust a man who wears both a belt and suspenders? Man can't even trust his own pants'

Psst! When originally released in America, it was in a much shorter version so that more screenings could be fitted into each day. It was released again, in its full version, in 1984 • The opening credits last for 10 minutes, making it the joint record-holder with *Superman* for the lengthiest, although that film splits them whereas Leone's has them all in one chunk during the opening 14-minute scene.

One Flew Over the Cuckoo's Nest

★★★★ 1975 133min c.

Director: Milos Forman
Screenplay: Lawrence Hauben & Bo Goldman
Source: Novel by Ken Kesey & play by Dale Wasserman

A prisoner thinks life will be cushier if he fakes madness. But although he tries to brighten up life at the mental institution he is transferred to, he meets implacable opposition from the sadistic head nurse. This deeply black comedy about rebellion and the power of the human spirit is a breath-taking experience, one of those rare films that seems to hit all the right buttons, making for electrifying entertainment throughout.

Randle P. McMurphy	Jack Nicholson
Nurse Ratched	Louise Fletcher
Harding	William Redfield
Chief Bromden	Will Sampson
Billy Bibbit	Brad Dourif
Ellis	Michael Berryman
Taber	Christopher Lloyd
Martini	Danny DeVito
Col. Matterson	Peter Brocco
Turkle	Scatman Crothers
Cheswick	Sydney Lassick
Rose	Louisa Moritz
Dr. John Spivey	Dean R. Brooks
Patient	Vincent Schiavelli

Oscars Best Picture, Louise Fletcher, Best Director, Best Screenplay (adapted), Jack Nicholson

Quote 'I bet in one week I can put a bug so far up her ass, she don't know whether to shit or wind her wristwatch.' • 'Medication time.' • 'They was giving me 10,000 watts a day, you know, and I'm hot to trot. The next woman takes me on is going to light up like a pinball machine and pay off in silver dollars.'

Psst! Kirk Douglas, who had initiated many of his films, was very successful in the stage version of the play in the 60s. But his attempts to get the movie off the ground over more than a decade failed. By the mid 70s, he was too old to play the lead role. But son Michael managed to get it made • The film marked the screen debut of Christopher Lloyd • Among those who turned down the part of Nurse Ratched were Angela Lansbury, Ellen Burstyn, Geraldine Page and Anne Bancroft • James Caan turned down Nicholson's part, as did Gene Hackman, Burt Reynolds and Marlon Brando • Dean R. Brooks, playing Dr. John Spivey, was the superintendent of the Oregon State Hospital where the movie was made. 40 other similar institutions had turned the film-makers down • Some of the extras are hospital patients. Other extras were recruited through an ad in the local paper that said: 'Do you have a face that scares timberwolves?' • It is said by some sources that Nicholson disappeared for two months before filming started. When the crew arrived at the hospital to begin setting ther equipment up, they found he had admitted himself as a voluntary patient. True or not, it certainly is the case that Forman and writer Hauben stayed at the hospital while they put the finishing touches to the script • This was the first film since It Happened One Night to win all five top Oscars. The Silence of the Lambs is the only other movie to manage it • When Fletcher picked up her Oscar, she signed as she gave her speech. Her parents were deaf and she wanted to show them her 'special gratitude.' • Kesey only received $5,000 for the film rights and sued the producers, unsuccessfully, for a share of the profits • Christopher Lloyd and Danny de Vito were to star together 10 years later in the TV sitcom Taxi.

One Million Years B.C.

★★ 1966 100min c.

Director: Don Chaffey
Screenplay: Michael Carreras

With little regard to pre-history, dinosaurs battle it out with a bunch of cavemen in skins or, in the case of the shapely Raquel Welch, in a fur bikini. This is another of those dreadfully bad films that deserves to be revered for its unintentional entertainment value. Camp and extremely silly. The dialogue, largely consisting of grunts, is wonderful.

Loana . . . . .Raquel Welch
Tumak .John Richardson
Sakana . . . . .Percy Herbert
Akhoba .Robert Brown
Nupondi . . . . .Martine Beswick

Blurb Travel Back Through Time And Space To The Edge Of Man's Beginnings…Discover A Savage World Whose Only Law Was Lust!

OOPS! This lot got their priorities right. Even before the invention of the wheel, they'd invented false eyelashes.

Psst! This was the most profitable movie Hammer ever made.

One Hundred and One Dalmations

★★★ 1961 79min c.

Director: Wolfgang Reitherman & Hamilton Luske
Screenplay: Clyde Geronimi & Bill Peet
Source: Book by Dodie Smith

Keen to get herself a new fur coat, Cruella de Vil (surely the model for Patsy in Absolutely Fabulous?) rounds up dalmation puppies for their pelts. Can the parents of 15 of the pups rescue them before it's too late? The interesting stylised animation looks as if Raoul Dufy decided to paint London rather than Paris. The story is sweet, but a little spotty and, sadly, there are only two songs.

Pongo . . . . .Rod Taylor
Anita . . . . .Lisa Davis
Perdita . . . . .Cate Bauer
Cruella De Vil . . . . .Betty Lou Gerson
Horace . . . . .Frederic Worlock
Nani/Goose/Cow . . . . .Martha Wentworth

Quote 'The humans have tried everything. Now it's up to us dogs.' • 'I've got the knob for this job.'

Showing Thunderbolt.

OOPS! Near the end, the lorry is supposed to be going to London, but it turns right at the sign which says London is straight on.

Psst! There are exactly 6,469,952 spots in the movie on the back of 101 Dalmations dogs and puppies. A spot check would reveal that Pongo has 72, Perdita 68 and each pup an even 32. With 113,760 frames of film to colour, the spots and other colour effects required 800 gallons of a special paint that weighed nearly five tons and would have been enough to have coating the outsides of 135 homes. Disney's publicists estimated that 1,218,750 pencils were 'consumed' by artists during the course of making the film.

One Hundred Men and a Girl

★★★★ 1937 84min b/w

Director: Henry Koster
Screenplay: Bruce Manning, Charles Kenyon & Hans Kraly

Not quite as racy as it sounds. Durbin sets out to persuade the great Stokowski to conduct an orchestra of unemployed musicians, including her dad. Yes, it's a little bit silly and maybe a trifle twee in places. But Durbin has the loveliest voice and the sweetest temperament of all the young singing stars and it's a tough heart that can resist such beautifully handled schmaltz.

Patricia Cardwell . . . . .Deanna Durbin
Himself . . . . .Leopold Stokowski
John Cardwell . . . . .Adolphe Menjou
Mrs. Frost .Alice Brady

John R. Frost . . . . .Eugene Pallette
Michael Borodoff . . . . .Mischa Auer
Garage owner . . . . .Billy Gilbert
Mrs. Tyler . . . . .Alma Kruger
Taxi driver . . . . .Frank Jenks
Marshall, the doorman . . . . .Jack Smart
Bitters . . . . .Jed Prouty
Russell . . . . .Jameson Thomas
Brandsetter . . . . .Christian Rub
Theatre patron . . . . .Mary Forbes
Pianist . . . . .Leonid Kinskey

Psst! Although Durbin first appeared on film in a short for MGM with Judy Garland, they kept Judy and dropped her. MGM's loss was Universal's gain for *Three Smart Girls* and this one did so well that it saved the studio from impending bankruptcy.

On Golden Pond
★★ 1981 109min c.

Director: Mark Rydell
Screenplay: Ernest Thompson
Source: Play by Thompson

On Golden Syrup. Treacly, sentimental tale of a professor going through late-life crisis, supported by a loyal wife and sparring with his daughter. It's beautifully filmed and well acted. Whether you'd actually rush anywhere to go and see it is another matter.

Ethel Thayer . . . . .Katharine Hepburn
Norman Thayer, Jr. . . . . .Henry Fonda
Chelsea Thayer Wayne . . . . .Jane Fonda
Billy Ray . . . . .Doug McKeon
Bill Ray . . . . .Dabney Coleman
Sumner Todd . . . . .Christopher Rydell

Oscars Henry Fonda, Katharine Hepburn, Best Screenplay (adapted)

Quote 'You wanna dance? Or would you rather just suck face?'

Psst! Jane Fonda's company took out an option on the play specifically intending it to be a film for her father, with whom she had never acted • Hepburn had not only not worked with Fonda before, but had never even met him. On the first day of filming, she gave him a hat that had been given to Spencer Tracy by John Ford. He wears it in the film • Henry Fonda was too ill to attend the Oscar ceremonies but later said: 'I thank God every morning that I lived long enough to play that role' • Jane accepted his statuette on his behalf. He died five months later.

On Her Majesty's Secret Service
★★ 1969 140min c.

Director: Peter Hunt
Screenplay: Richard Maibaum
Source: Novel by Ian Fleming

Neither Her Majesty nor we are particularly well-served by this one, and mercifully only, outing as 007 for George Lazenby, a former model (presumably the plastic sort that you put together with glue). It's a pity, because both the stunts and the action sequences are fantastic in this race to find Blofeld before he sterilises the world. Without an even half-way decent Bond, though, the film has no heart. This is the one in which Bond gets married. If it seems long, that's because it's the longest in the series.

James Bond . . . . .George Lazenby
Tracy Draco . . . . .Diana Rigg
Ernst Stavro Blofeld . . . . .Telly Savalas
Irma Bunt . . . . .Ilse Steppat
Marc Ange Draco . . . . .Gabriele Ferzetti
Sir Hilary Bray . . . . .George Baker
'M' . . . . .Bernard Lee
Miss Moneypenny . . . . .Lois Maxwell
'Q' . . . . .Desmond Llewelyn

Quote 'This never happened to the other fellow.' • 'Some fellow named Lazenby filled the role – the way concrete fills a hole.' [*Time*]

Psst! George Lazenby had never acted before. But when Sean Connery refused to star, the producers thought this Australian car salesman turned model would fit the bill just as well • Brigitte Bardot and Catherine Deneuve were among those considered for Diana Rigg's part. Rigg is reputed not to have got on with Lazenby.

Only Angels Have Wings
★★ 1939 121min b/w

Director: Howard Hawks
Screenplay: Howard Hawks & Jules Furthman

A group of hard-bitten pilots flying dangerous missions in the Andes are sent all a twitter by a pair of even tougher women. This is another movie that fails to live up to its high reputation. For a film that's supposedly about flying, there's surprisingly little action and an awful lot of talk, not all of it terribly scintillating. It's always interesting seeing these stars, but they've all made far better movies than this.

Geoff Carter	Cary Grant
Bonnie Lee	Jean Arthur
Bat McPherson	Richard Barthelmess
Judith McPherson	Rita Hayworth
Kid Dabb	Thomas Mitchell
Dutchman	Sig Rumann
Gent Shelton	John Carroll
Sparks	Victor Kilian
Les Peters	Allyn Joslyn
Joe Souther	Noah Beery Jr.

Blurb Romance As Glorious As The Towering Andes.

Quote 'The only thing I can tell you about him, he's a good guy for gals to stay away from.' • 'Look, I hardly know the man.' – 'Sure, but you'll get over it.' • 'Got a match?'

Psst! Until this movie, Richard Barthelmess had made little since his days as one of the top silent movie stars. Although this film was important to his career if he was to survive in movies, much of his part seems to have been cut out. He never made another significant film after it.

Only Two Can Play
★★★ 1962 106min b/w

Director: Sidney Gilliat
Screenplay: Bryan Forbes
Source: Novel, *That Uncertain Feeling* by Kingsley Amis

A married Welsh librarian dallies in the adultery section and stamps the ticket of one of what passes for the upper set in that part of the world. Peter Sellers is splendid in this witty and earthy comedy which has moments of sheer brilliance.

John Lewis	Peter Sellers
Liz	Mai Zetterling
Jean	Virginia Maskell
Gareth Probert	Richard Attenborough
Ievan Jenkins	Kenneth Griffith
Nyman	Graham Stark
Slater	John Le Mesurier
Vernon	Raymond Huntley

Psst! The always gloomy Sellers believed that the film was going to be a failure and begged British Lion to buy out his profit share. They did, and he lost out considerably when the film became a big hit.

On The Town
★★★ 1949 98min c.

Director: Gene Kelly & Stanley Donen
Screenplay: Adolph Green & Betty Comden
Source: Musical play by Comden, Green & Bernstein, from the ballet *Fancy Free* by Jerome Robbins

The adventures of three sailors on one day's shore leave in New York. The novelty of a musical filmed on location has worn off and, although the three romances are very sweet and Ann Miller is a tap-dancing goddess, the songs really aren't too hot. As for the ballet that Kelly always throws in to his films – wake me up when it's over. Musical fans love the film for its sheer vitality. For others, it doesn't work half as well as the later Donen-Kelly collaboration, *Singin' in the Rain*.

Gabey	Gene Kelly
Chip	Frank Sinatra
Brunhilde Esterhazy	Betty Garrett
Claire Huddesen	Ann Miller
Ozzie	Jules Munshin
Ivy Smith	Vera-Ellen
Mme. Dilyovska	Florence Bates
Lucy Shmeeler	Alice Pearce

OOPS! At the end of 'Wonderful Town' it's hard to miss all the people watching the filming from above.

Psst! This was the first musical that actually went out on location to film. Kelly and Donen wanted to film all of it on the streets of New York. MGM chief Louis B. Mayer wasn't too keen on the project and wanted it to stay in Hollywood. A compromise gave Kelly just one week to get as much in the can as possible. Most of the scenes were filmed using a hidden camera • When they first saw the script, the censors found 'It's a helluva town' an unacceptable lyric in 'New York, New York' • Throughout, Sinatra wore padded buttocks, much against his own wishes.

On the Waterfront
★★★ 1954 108min b/w

Director: Elia Kazan
Screenplay: Budd Schulberg
Source: Pulitzer Prize-winning articles by Malcolm Johnson

A still-impressive story of Union skullduggery in

New York, with Marlon Brando standing up to the bully boys in between caring for his pigeons and wooing Eva Marie Saint. Once famed for its location realism, Elia Kazan's direction now looks rather arty. But the acting is still very impressive, and not only from The Great Mumbler himself. The underlying message about the need to be an informant remains controversial.

Terry Malloy	Marlon Brando
Edie Doyle	Eva Marie Saint
Father Barry	Karl Malden
Johnny Friendly	Lee J. Cobb
Charley Malloy	Rod Steiger
'Kayo' Dugan	Pat Henning
Glover	Leif Erickson
Big Mac	James Westerfield

Also: John Hamilton, Tony Galento, Martin Balsam, Fred Gwynne, Pat Hingle, Nehemiah Persoff

Oscars Best Picture, Marlon Brando, Best Director, Best Story and Screenplay

Quote 'The only arithmetic he ever got was hearing the referee count up to ten.' • 'You want to hear my philosophy of life? Do it to him before he does it to you.' • 'I don't like the country. Crickets make me nervous.' • 'I could've had class. I could've been a contender. I could've been somebody, instead of a bum, which is what I am.'

Psst! The film won eight Oscars • Director Kazan admitted that the film was a penance for turning informer himself and testifying before the House Un-American Activities Committee. Because of his testimony, Arthur Miller refused to pen the screenplay and Kazan had to turn to Schulberg, who had also testified • This was the film debut of Saint, Gwynne, Hingle and Balsam. Grace Kelly had originally been offered Saint's part but she wanted to do *Rear Window* instead • The film was extremely controversial at the time, with the phrase 'Go to hell' shocking audiences. The depiction of the unions in a negative manner was another first. The mob still ran the docks in New Jersey where the movie was filmed and the police provided protection for the production in case there was trouble • Marlon Brando got the role when Montgomery Clift and Frank Sinatra wouldn't do it • Frank Sinatra obviously thought that he had been offered the role because he sued producer Sam Spiegel for breach of contract • During the famous taxi scene, Rod Steiger stayed around on the set so that Brando would have someone to play off during his 'contender' speech. However, when it was time for Steiger to perform his part of the scene, he was faced not by Brando, who had already gone home, but by an assistant director. Steiger never forgave Brando • Although Steiger plays Brando's elder brother, he is actually a year younger • The Hays Office insisted that the ending be changed. As originally written, Brando was to have been killed by the bent union officials. Crime could still not be seen to win at this stage, so it had to be altered.

Operation Petticoat

★★★ 1959 124min c.

Director: Blake Edwards
Screenplay: Stanley Shapiro & Maurice Richlin

A damaged American wartime sub tries to get back home but the book is thrown out of the porthole when it picks up a party of nurses, refugees and livestock. A rather sweet, often very funny and fondly-remembered comedy, with Grant at his exasperated best.

Adm. Matt Sherman	Cary Grant
Lt. Nick Holden	Tony Curtis
Lt. Dolores Crandall	Joan O'Brien
Lt. Barbara Duran	Dina Merrill
Molumphrey	Gene Evans
Sam Tostin	Arthur O'Connell
Stovall	Dick Sargent
Dooley	Frankie Darro
Maj. Edna Hayward	Virginia Gregg
Cap. J.B. Henderson	Robert F. Simon
Lt. Claire Reid	Madlyn Rhue
Lt. Ruth Colfax	Marion Ross

OOPS! As if the colour of the submarine isn't embarrassing enough, as he comes ashore Curtis' boy calls Cary 'Mr. Grant'.

Psst! Amazingly, the film is based largely on true incidents. An American submarine operating in the Pacific, *Sea Dragon*, lost her paint in an explosion and went round with the red primer exposed. Other events, like the kerfuffle over the toilet paper, the evacuation of nurses and the birth on ship were all true, although they happened on vessels other than the *Sea Dragon*. Even the torpedoing of a *bus* of Japanese sailors really happened, with the USS *Bowfin* firing the chance shot • There was also a TV series along the same lines • Marion Ross was later better known as Mrs. Cunningham in TV's *Happy Days* • A TV movie of the same title in 1977 had Curtis' daughter Jamie Lee Curtis in it as a nurse.

Ordinary People

★★ 1980 124min c.

Director: Robert Redford
Screenplay: Alvin Sargent
Source: Novel by Judith Guest

Ordinary people, ordinary film. An off-the-peg middle-class family go to pieces after the elder son dies. Interesting though the attempt was, Tyler Moore was *not* the right choice for mom. This wildly overpraised directorial debut from Redford is as dry and superficial as his other movies. They're all glossy enough but there's usually nothing underneath the pretty surface.

Calvin	Donald Sutherland
Beth	Mary Tyler Moore
Berger	Judd Hirsch
Conrad	Timothy Hutton
Swim coach	M. Emmet Walsh
Jeannine	Elizabeth McGovern

Also: Dinah Manoff, Fredric Lehne, James B. Sikking, Meg Mundy, Adam Baldwin

Oscars Best Picture, Timothy Hutton, Best Director, Best Screenplay (adapted)

Quote 'A little advice about feeling, kiddo. Don't expect it always to tickle.'

Psst! The first choice for Beth was Ann-Margret • Mary Tyler Moore separated from her husband, to whom she'd been married for 17 years, during the production • This was Hutton's debut.

Our Hospitality

★★ 1923 70min b/w

Director: Buster Keaton & Jack Blystone
Screenplay: Clyde Bruckman, Jean Havez & Joseph Mitchell

Set in the mid-19th century, Buster returns to the South to collect his inheritance and falls in love with a girl from a family on less than friendly terms with his. Although there are some nice gags, yet another train and a great stunt at a waterfall, this now looks sweet and charming rather than hilariously funny. As with other silents, it is best appreciated in a cinema with an accompanying orchestra.

Willie McKay	Buster Keaton
Virginia Canfield	Natalie Talmadge
Lem Doolittle	Joe Keaton
Willie (as baby)	Buster Keaton Jr.
Aunt Mary	Kitty Bradbury
Joseph Canfield	Joe Roberts

Psst! Keaton and Talmadge married after the movie • Keaton didn't use a double for the extraordinary scene at the waterfall near the end.

The Outlaw Josey Wales

★★★ 1976 135min c.

Director: Clint Eastwood
Screenplay: Philip Kaufman & Sonia Chernus
Source: Novel, *Gone to Texas* by Forrest Carter

Turning outlaw and rebel after the death of his family, former farmer Eastwood vows revenge. Although a little too languid, this extended chase movie is often exciting, albeit quite violent in places. The sequel, *The Return of Josey Wales* didn't even have Eastwood in, and was dreadful.

Josey Wales	Clint Eastwood
Lone Watie	Chief Dan George
Laura Lee	Sondra Locke
Terrill	Bill McKinney
Fletcher	John Vernon
Grandma Sarah	Paula Trueman
Little Moonlight	Geraldine Keams
Jamie	Sam Bottoms
Chief	Will Sampson

Quote 'I guess we all died a little in that damn war.' • 'Dyin' ain't no way of livin'.' • 'The buzzards got to eat, same as the worms.' • 'I myself never surrendered. But they got my horse and *it* surrendered.'

Out of Africa

★★★ 1985 161min c.

Director: Sydney Pollack
Screenplay: Kurt Luedtke
Source: Writings by Isak Dinesen (Karen Blixen), Judith Thurman and Errol Trzefinski

'I haard a faaarm in Aaafreekar.' Overlong and slight of plot, this story of writer Karen Blixen tiring of boorish husband Brandauer and falling for dashing hunter Redford is still exquisitely shot and acted. A little imagination is needed to believe that Redford is English, but perhaps it's better than him trying an accent and getting it wrong.

Karen	Meryl Streep
Denys	Robert Redford
Bror	Klaus Maria Brandauer
Berkeley	Michael Kitchen
Farah	Malick Bowens
Kamanto	Joseph Thiaka
Felicity	Suzanna Hamilton
Lady Belfield	Rachel Kempson
Delamere	Michael Gough
Lord Belfield	Graham Crowden
Sir Joseph	Leslie Phillips

Oscars Best Picture, Best Director

Quote 'You should have asked permission.' – 'I did. She said yes.' • 'The earth was made round so we would not see too far down the road.' • 'When the Gods want to punish you, they answer your prayers.' • 'Robert Redford's the very best kisser I ever met.' [Streep]

OOPS! If you're getting just the teensiest bit bored, try counting the fluctuating number of oranges when they're having a picnic • When Redford returns from a hunting trip and is about to make love, his tie comes off three times.

Psst! The film-makers had to cope with restrictions making it illegal to touch or interfere with any wild animal. Five trained lions were imported from California, as there were none in Africa. An eagle and three dogs were brought in as well • In the overall view of the coffee plantation flowering, the blooms are actually dollops of shaving foam • At one time Orson Welles, David Lean and Nicolas Roeg had all considered making a film about Blixen.

Out of the Past
★★★ 1947 97min b/w

Director: Jacques Tourneur
Screenplay: Daniel Mainwaring
Source: Novel, *Build My Gallows High* by Geoffrey Homes (Mainwaring)

For the first three-quarters, this rivals *Double Indemnity* as the great film noir. Mitchum, in voice-over, recounts how he was hired by Douglas to trace icy *femme fatale* Greer, only to become ensnared in an ever-tightening trap. There's lots of smart dialogue and it's atmospherically shot by Tourneur. So it's a real pity the plot gets rather garbled in the last reel which means it just misses being a true classic.

Jeff Bailey	Robert Mitchum
Kathie Moffett	Jane Greer

Whit Sterling	Kirk Douglas
Meta Carson	Rhonda Fleming
Jim	Richard Webb
Fisher	Steve Brodie
The Kid	Dickie Moore
Sheriff Douglas	Frank Wilcox

Blurb You're No Good And Neither Am I. We Deserve Each Other.

Quote 'Maybe love is like luck – you have to go all the way to find it.' • 'Don't you believe me?' – 'Baby, I don't care.'

Psst! Until just before release, the title was *Build My Gallows High*, by which name it was still known in early prints in the UK • Before Robert Mitchum got the part, Humphrey Bogart, Dick Powell and John Garfield turned it down • Jane Greer also appeared in the bad 1984 remake *Against All Odds*, playing the mother of her original character.

The Overlanders
★★★ 1946 91min b/w

Director: Harry Watt
Screenplay: Harry Watt

A team of cattle drovers take their herd on an epic trek to keep them out of the hands of the Japanese in World War II. This interesting Australian Western, made by Ealing Studios, is fascinating and beautifully filmed.

Don McAlpine	Chips Rafferty
Bill Parons	John Heyward
Mary Parsons	Daphne Campbell
Mrs. Parsons	Jean Blue

Psst! The story is based on fact.

The Ox-Bow Incident
★★★ 1943 75min b/w

Director: William Wellman
Screenplay: Lamar Trotti
Source: Novel by Walter Van Tilburg Clark

Henry Fonda witnesses the attempted lynching of three men he believes are innocent. It was hardly a subject likely to be a big hit during wartime and so it proved. The stylised studio settings used for scenes like the big confrontation actually help keep the atmosphere tense and claustrophic as the defendants' rights are debated, although the preachy aftermath is a mistake.

Gil Carter	Henry Fonda
Martin	Dana Andrews
Rose Mapen	Mary Beth Hughes
Juan Martines	Anthony Quinn
Mexican	William Eythe
Art Croft	Harry Morgan
Ma Grier	Jane Darwell
Davies	Harry Davenport
Maj. Tetley	Frank Conroy
Farnley	Marc Lawrence
Darby	Victor Kilian
Monty	Paul Hurst
Mrs. Swanson	Almira Sessions
Mrs. Larch	Margaret Hamilton

Psst! Clint Eastwood claims this is his favourite Western • The film is based on a true story of events in Nevada back in 1885 • Wellman bought the rights to the book himself and spent some time trying to find a studio that would make it before he and Fonda finally persuaded Darryl Zanuck at Fox to go with it, even though Zanuck was convinced – rightly – that it wouldn't make money. However, they got the go-ahead only on condition that in return they agreed to make other films for the studio • Wellman claimed that the project was originally pitched to him by a writer as a Mae West vehicle!

The Paleface

★★★ 1948 91min c.

Director: Norman Z. McLeod
Screenplay: Edmund Hartman & Frank Tashlin

Hope, a dentist who is incompetent and a coward to boot, is picked out by Russell's Calamity Jane, on a secret mission, as giving her the cover she needs – and boy does she need a lot of cover! There are some good jokes as well as the Oscar-winning song 'Buttons and Bows'. The sequel, *Son of Paleface*, is better still.

'Painless' Peter Potter	Bob Hope
Calamity Jane	Jane Russell
Terris	Robert Armstrong
Pepper	Iris Adrian
Toby Preston	Robert Watson
Jasper Martin	Jack Searle
Indian scout	Joseph Vitale

Quote 'What do you want? A happy ending?' [Last line]

OOPS! This is one of those movies where it is all too apparent that the star isn't doing his own stunts. Use the video to slow the action down when 'Painless' Potter is slugged by a patient. A stuntman who is quite clearly nothing like Hope

goes over the counter where Hope is hiding, ready to jump up.

Psst! The version of *Buttons and Bows* that soared up the chart was sung, not by Hope, but by Dinah Shore.

The Palm Beach Story

★★★ 1942 90min b/w

Director: Preston Sturges
Screenplay: Preston Sturges

When an architect can't get anyone to back his airport scheme, his wife sets off to find a new wealthy husband who will plough money into it. Despite Sturges' usual witty lines, fast pace and screwball plot, the story is pretty insubstantial and is damned near spoilt by the daft, wildly implausible ending. This comes out of nowhere and, as it has had no set-up whatsoever, is incredibly irritating.

Gerry Jeffers	Claudette Colbert
Tom Jeffers	Joel McCrea
J.D. Hackensacker III	Rudy Vallee
Princess Centimillia	Mary Astor
Toto	Sig Arno
Mr. Hinch	Robert Warwick
Mr. Osmond	Arthur Stuart Hull
Dr. Cluck	Torben Meyer
Mr. Asweld	Jimmy Conlin
The Wienie King	Robert Dudley
Manager	Franklin Pangborn
Ale & Quail Club	William Demarest
Ale & Quail Club	Jack Norton
Ale & Quail Club	Robert Greig
Ale & Quail Club	Chester Conklin
Pullman conductor	Arthur Hoyt
Conductor	Al Bridge

Quote 'I've never bought things for a girl before – I mean in any such quantity.' – 'You've been denying yourself, monsieur, one of the basic pleasures in life.' • 'Chivalry is not only dead, it's decomposed.' • 'That's one of the tragedies of this life, that the men most in need of a beating up are always enormous.' • 'You have no idea what a long-legged gal can do without doing anything.' • 'I grow on people – like moss.'

Pandora's Box

★★ 1928 110min b/w

Director: G.W. Pabst
Screenplay: G.W. Pabst & Laszlo Wajda

Source: Plays, *Erdgeist & Pandora's Box* by Franz Wedekind

A German silent version of the Lulu tale with Brooks mesmerising as the nymphomaniac who leaves emotional wrecks, male and female, in her wake. As a piece of storytelling, it's pretty stilted, despite managing to drag Jack the Ripper in. But Brooks is another matter, coming across even now as one of most mysterious, sexy and alluring women ever to appear on screen. Eat your heart out Marlene Dietrich.

Lulu	Louise Brooks
Dr. Peter Schön	Fritz Kortner
Alwa Schön	Francis Lederer
Schigolch	Carl Goetz
Jack the Ripper	Gustav Diessl
Stage director	Sig Arno

Psst! The original running time was 131 minutes. In 1929, the version released in America was only 85 minutes, with a third of the movie cut out. In Britain, the scene with Lulu and the lesbian countess at Lulu's wedding, the first example of a lesbian character in the movies, was cut. The restored 1983 version is 110 minutes • An American, Brooks was under contract to Paramount and was released to make this film in Germany because Pabst considered the alternative, Marlene Dietrich, 'too old and too obvious'. Brooks' attempts to return to Hollywood were unsuccessful and, after a spell as a dancer and a sales assistant, she turned to writing about movies, penning the splendid *Lulu in Hollywood*.

The Paper
★★★★ 1994 110min c.

Director: Ron Howard
Screenplay: David Koepp & Stephen Koepp

A day in the life of a New York tabloid. The sort of fast, furious, funny all-star movie Hollywood did brilliantly in the 40s and as good as any of them. From the second the great opening credits start we are hooked by a film that packs enough excitement, action, melodrama and laughs for five other movies. Highly recommended.

Henry Hackett	Michael Keaton
Bernie White	Robert Duvall
Alicia Clark	Glenn Close
Martha Hackett	Marisa Tomei
McDougal	Randy Quaid
Graham Keighley	Jason Robards
Marion Sandusky	Jason Alexander
Paul Bladden	Spalding Gray
Susan	Catherine O'Hara

Blurb Never Let The Truth Get In The Way Of A Good Story.

Quote 'Stop the presses!' • 'The Sun: It Shines For All.'

OOPS! Just after the fight scenes, Keaton's cuts and bruises vanish • Although pregnant Tomei has a cellular phone, isn't it a little too convenient for the plot that neither Keaton, Quaid nor Close has one?

Paper Moon
★★★ 1973 102min b/w

Director: Peter Bogdanovich
Screenplay: Alvin Sargent
Source: Novel, *Addie Pray* by Joe David Brown

In the 30s a conman is lumbered with an ex-girl-friend's daughter but, after early animosity, they find they make a great team for parting suckers from their money. Despite the backlash against this comedy, it remains delightful fun with a lovely period feel and splendid authentic music on the soundtrack.

Moses Pray	Ryan O'Neal
Addie Loggins	Tatum O'Neal
Trixie Delight	Madeline Kahn
Sheriff/Jess Hardin	John Hillerman
Imogene	P.J. Johnson
Miss Ollie	Jessie Lee Fulton
Mr. Robertson	Noble Willingham

Oscars Tatum O'Neal

Psst! The original plan was for John Huston to direct Paul Newman and his daughter. When that didn't work out, Ryan O'Neal and his daughter were approached • This was Tatum O'Neal's acting debut. She was then 10 and is still the youngest actor to have received a regular Oscar, although Shirley Temple got a special Oscar before her sixth birthday • Bogdanovich hated the experience of working with Tatum O'Neal, believing her to be no actress. 'I had to feed her her lines one at a time. I couldn't believe it when she won the Oscar.' • Look out for Randy Quaid in a bit part.

The Parallax View
★★ 1974 102min c.

Director: Alan J. Pakula

Screenplay: David Giler & Lorenzo Semple Jr.
Source: Novel by Loren Singer

A reporter investigates the mysterious deaths of those who witness an assassination. A well-conjured air of conspiracy and some nice locations are not enough on their own to make a great thriller, as this massively over-rated effort shows. Wildly implausible and incredibly confusing, it raises far more questions in the viewer's mind than it answers. In the end it's considerably less than the sum of its parts.

Joe Frady	Warren Beatty
Lee Carter	Paula Prentiss
Austin Tucker	William Daniels
Rintels	Hume Cronyn
Jack	Walter McGinn
Sheriff L.D.	Kelly Thordsen
Art	Bill McKinney
Schwartzkopf	Anthony Zerbe
Turner	Kenneth Mars

Quote 'A martini is like a woman's breasts. One ain't enough and three is too many.'

Parenthood
★★★ 1989 124min c.

Director: Ron Howard
Screenplay: Lowell Ganz & Babaloo Mandel

A massive starry cast give us four generations of a large family practising just about every method of parenting yet devised, from Dr. Spock to Mr. Spock. Although occasionally sentimental, the film is warm-hearted and funny enough to carry it off. A really pleasing couple of hours, with the scene where Steenburgen tries to 'relax' husband Martin a particular delight. One of the few 'family' films aimed at the adults, rather than the kids.

Gil	Steve Martin
Karen	Mary Steenburgen
Helen	Dianne Wiest
Frank	Jason Robards
Nathan	Rick Moranis
Larry	Tom Hulce
Julie	Martha Plimpton
Tod	Keanu Reeves
Susan	Harley Jane Kozak

Blurb It Could Happen To You.

Quote 'No, no, no. I'm too young. You know, grandmothers are old. They bake and they sew and they tell you stories about the Depression. I was at Woodstock, for Chrissake. I peed in a field! • 'Would you like to see me make strange animals with balloons?' • 'I give 'em six months. Four if she cooks.'

Psst! Rance Howard, Ron's dad, regularly crops up in his movies. Here he's the 'dean at college'.

Une Partie de Campagne
★★★★ 1936 40min b/w

Director: Jean Renoir
Screenplay: Jean Renoir
Source: Short story by Guy de Maupassant

In the aftermath of a Sunday picnic, the men fish while some of the women indulge in fishing of another kind. This delightful French movie from the great Jean Renoir merits its frequent comparison to a French impressionist painting brought to life. Vibrant, witty and joyful, it establishes a beautiful happy mood and keeps it afloat throughout its sadly truncated length.

Henriette	Sylvie Bataille
Mme. Dufour	Jeanne Marken
Henri	Georges Darnoux
Rudolphe	Jacques Brunius
Papa Poulain, innkeeper	Jean Renoir

Psst! The film was never completed, although it was only planned to be an hour long. It was not released until 1946.

A Passage to India
★★★ 1984 163min c.

Director: David Lean
Screenplay: David Lean
Source: Novel by E.M. Forster & play by Santha Rami Rau.

Despite its unnecessary length, there's much to admire in this E.M. Forster tale of the clash of cultures revolving around early friendship and then recriminations between British woman Davis and Indian doctor Banerjee. Acting, photography, atmosphere and period are all top-hole. But it's still way too long.

Adela Quested	Judy Davis
Dr. Aziz	Victor Banerjee
Mrs. Moore	Peggy Ashcroft
Richard Fielding	James Fox
Godbole	Alec Guinness
Ronny Heaslop	Nigel Havers

Turton	Richard Wilson
Mahmoud Ali	Art Malik
Hamidullah	Saeed Jaffrey
Maj. Callendar	Clive Swift
Amritrao	Roshan Seth

Oscars Peggy Ashcroft

Psst! This was David Lean's first film for 14 years. It was also his last • Lean's wife appears briefly as James Fox's wife.

Passport to Pimlico
★★★★ 1949 84min b/w

Director: Henry Cornelius
Screenplay: T.E.B. Clarke

An area of London discovers it doesn't belong to Britain at all, but to Burgundy. So it sets up its own government – without the rationing restrictions everyone else was suffering from. Although a slight tale, this is a delightful evocation of post-war London, attempting to recapture that spirit of togetherness that was already evaporating just four years after the war. Packed full of great British comic actors and with some lovely tongue-in-cheek comedy, it is a delight to be savoured over and over again.

Arthur Pemberton	Stanley Holloway
Edie Randall	Hermione Baddeley
Prof. Hatton-Jones	Margaret Rutherford
Straker	Naunton Wayne
Gregg	Basil Radford
Bashford	Michael Hordern
Duke of Burgundy	Paul Dupuis
Mr. Wix	Raymond Huntley
Molly	Jane Hylton
Connie Pemberton	Betty Warren
Shirley Pemberton	Barbara Murray
Fred Cowan	Sydney Tafler
Garland	Frederick Piper
Bert Fitch	Charles Hawtrey
Inspector	Michael Hordern
Sapper	Sam Kydd

Quote 'You never know when you're well off until you aren't.' • 'It is just because we are English that we are sticking to our right to be Burgundians.'

Pat and Mike
★★★ 1952 95min b/w

Director: George Cukor
Screenplay: Garson Kanin & Ruth Gordon

A rather shifty sports promoter latches onto an all-round athlete and takes her under his wing. As in all the other Hepburn-Tracy pairings, after initial animosity they begin to find each other's company less repulsive. The plot's no great shakes but the relationship between the two is as delightful as it ever was on screen.

Mike Conovan	Spencer Tracy
Pat Pemberton	Katharine Hepburn
Davie Hucko	Aldo Ray
Collier Weld	William Ching
Charles Barry	Jim Backus
Hank Tasling	Charles Bronson
Police Captain	Chuck Connors
Spec Cauley	George Matthews

Quote 'You see her face? A real honest face. Only disgusting thing about her.' • 'Not much meat on her, but what there is is cherce.' • 'Well, I don't know if I can lick you or you can lick me. But I'll tell you one thing I do know…together we can lick them all.'

Psst! The film includes many sports stars of the day such as Babe Didrickson Zaharias, golfers Betty Hicks and Helen Dettweiler and tennis players Pancho Gonzales and Don Budge • Look out for Charles Bronson in an early role, credited as Charles Buchinski.

Paths of Glory
★★★★ 1957 86min b/w

Director: Stanley Kubrick
Screenplay: Stanley Kubrick, Calder Willingham & Jim Thompson
Source: Novel by Humphrey Cobb

In the middle of World War I, three randomly-chosen French soldiers are made scapegoats for the military incompetence of the generals and court-martialled. This anti-war movie is still incredibly powerful, with its numbing indictment of the commanders and vivid and horrifying portrait of life on the battlefield.

Col. Dax	Kirk Douglas
Cpl. Paris	Ralph Meeker
Gen. Broulard	Adolphe Menjou
Gen. Mireau	George Macready
Lt. Roget	Wayne Morris
Maj. Saint-Auban	Richard Anderson
Pte. Ferol	Timothy Carey
The German girl	Susanne Christian
Pte. Arnoud	Joseph Turkel
Priest	Emile Meyer

Psst! It was Douglas who bought the rights to the novel, based on a true story, and who hired the almost unknown director Kubrick • The film was made entirely in Germany with 800 German policemen playing the French troops • Kubrick insisted on 56 takes of the execution scene, an early example of the meticulousness he was going to display throughout his career • The film was a failure on release • It was ruled out of court a time by the American armed forces from its bases in Europe and banned altogether in France until 1975 • The young German woman at end of film, Susanne Christian, became Kubrick's third wife.

Patton
★★★★ 1970 170min c.

Director: Franklin J. Schaffner
Screenplay: Francis Ford Coppola & Edmund H. North
Source: Books, *Patton: Ordeal and Triumph* by Ladislas Farago & *A Soldier's Story* by Gen. Omar N. Bradley

The story of one of the most unorthodox of Allied generals in World War II, 'Old Blood And Guts' Patton. Scott is totally believable as the man who made our own Field Marshall Montgomery look modest. As Patton, he is completely convinced of his merits as a commander and prone to flying wildly off the handle. Complemented by some amazing battle scenes, this is one of the great war movies and one of the great movie biographies to boot.

Gen. George S. Patton Jr.	George C. Scott
Gen. Omar N. Bradley	Karl Malden
Maj. Gen. Walter Bedell Smith	Edward Binns
Maj. Gen. Lucian K. Truscott	John Doucette
Field Marshal Montgomery	Michael Bates
Field Marshal Erwin Rommel	Karl Michael Vogler
Capt. Chester B. Hansen	Stephen Young
Brig. Gen. Hobart Carver	Michael Strong
Lt. Col. Henry Davenport	Frank Latimore
Capt. Richard N. Jenson	Morgan Paull
Col. John Welkin	Peter Barkworth

Oscars Best Picture, Best Story and Screenplay, Best Director, George C. Scott

Quote 'I want you to remember that no bastard ever won a war by dying for his country. He won it by making the other poor dumb bastard die for his country.' • 'Rommel, you beautiful bastard. I read your book.' • 'There's only one proper way for a professional soldier to die. That's from the last bullet of the last battle of the last war.' • 'Compared to war, all other forms of human endeavour shrink to insignificance.' [George S. Patton] • 'I was much better playing Shylock in a Central Park performance.' [Scott]

Psst! Lee Marvin was offered the role but turned it down, as did Rod Steiger and Robert Mitchum. Burt Lancaster and John Wayne were among those who wanted to play it • George C. Scott had his nose straightened, shaved his head, wore false teeth, a plate, a fake nose and even a mole to get into the part. He did not, however, imitate Patton's voice, which was high and rather weedy • General Bradley allowed himself to be portrayed by Karl Malden and served as an adviser on the movie, insisting on getting 10% of the film's profits • Scott didn't attend the ceremony to pick his Oscar up, having earlier called the whole business 'bull'. He was the first actor to turn the statuette down • This was Richard Nixon's favourite movie. Unusually, both militarists and pacifists seemed to think the movie took their point of view.

Peeping Tom
★★★ 1959 109min c.

Director: Michael Powell
Screenplay: Leo Marks

At first sight, this is a slowish and rather implausible horror movie about a shy man with a lethal movie camera. On reflection, though, it is more clearly an extremely creepy meditation on filming and voyeurism which benefits from the cool underplaying, with Karl Boehm rivalling Anthony Perkins in *Psycho* in that department. The wave of revulsion from British critics at the time virtually finished Powell's career, despite his amazing past contribution to British cinema, mostly in the company of Emeric Pressburger. Martin Scorsese, who arranged for the film's 1979 re-release, is almost solely responsible for re-establishing it as a classic that has been much imitated, from *Manhunter* to *Raising Cain*.

Mark Lewis	Carl Boehm
Vivian	Moira Shearer
Helen Stephens	Anna Massey
Mrs. Stephens	Maxine Audley
Arthur Baden	Esmond Knight
Don Jarvis	Michael Goodliffe
Diane Ashley	Shirley Anne Field
Insp. Gregg	Jack Watson
Sgt. Miller	Nigel Davenport
Milly	Pamela Green
Dr. Rosen	Martin Miller
Dora	Brenda Bruce

Elderly gentleman . . . . .Miles Malleson
Mark's father . . . . .Michael Powell

Blurb WARNING! Don't See *Peeping Tom*
Unless You Are Prepared To See The
Screaming Shock And Raw Terror In The Faces
Of Those Marked For Death!

Quote 'All this filming isn't healthy.' • 'The only
really satisfactory way to dispose of *Peeping
Tom* would be to shovel it up and flush it swifly
down the nearest sewer.' [The Tribune]

Psst! The film was banned in Reading • In the
midst of all the fuss, the movie was cut to
ribbons by distributors and only seen again in
its proper form in the 80s. Even then, many still
criticised it as viciously as on its first release
• Powell never recovered from the knockout
blows he was given over *Peeping Tom*. He died
in 1990 • Powell appears as Mark's dad, while
his son Columba is the persecuted boy • Moira
Shearer had earlier starred in Powell's movies
The Red Shoes and *The Tales of Hoffman* •
Pamela Green appears as a victim. She was a
doyenne of the early British sex film industry,
appearing in movies like *The Window Dresser*
and *Naked as Nature Intended*.

Performance

★★ 1970 105min c.

Director: Nicolas Roeg & Donald Cammell
Screenplay: Donald Cammell

Definitely the death knell for Swinging London.
Cammell and Roeg's flamboyant directorial
debut starts off as a gangster flick with lashings
of psychedelic sex and violence, and evolves
into a philosophical debate on art, gender and
identity. Very sixties, very weird, and very much
an acquired taste.

Chas Devlin . . . . .James Fox
Turner . . . . .Mick Jagger
Pherber . . . . .Anita Pallenberg
Lucy . . . . .Michèle Breton
Moody . . . . .John Bindon
The lawyer . . . . .Allan Cuthbertson
Joey Maddocks . . . . .Anthony Valentine
Tony Farrell . . . . .Ken Colley

Blurb Vice. And Versa.

Quote 'Halfway through shooting, they'd
already started to hate it. Do you recall the
scene in the bath with Mick, Anita and Michele?
Someone from Hollywood complained the bath
water was too dirty. I mean…!' [Nicolas Roeg]

Psst! When the top brass at Warners saw the
film, they insisted on 15 minutes being taken
out. They thought the film was 'decadent' and
its release was held back for two years in the
States • After his terrifying portrayal of a
cockney thug, star James Fox dropped out of
mainstream acting to become an evangelist in
Leeds. He returned to the big screen in 1978.

Persona

★★★★ 1966 81min b/w

Director: Ingmar Bergman
Screenplay: Ingmar Bergman

Not all Bergman's films stand the test of time,
but this one most certainly does. Liv Ullman
falls silent on stage and she is cared for by Bibi
Andersson on a remote island. A terrifying psychological battle takes place between the
women as their identities merge. Icily shot, and
brilliantly acted, blatant rip-offs like *Single White
Female* don't come close.

Nurse Alma . . . . .Bibi Andersson
Elisabeth Vogler . . . . .Liv Ullmann
Dr. Lakaren . . . . .Margareta Krook
Mr. Vogler . . . . .Gunnar Björnstrand

The Petrified Forest

★★ 1936 83min b/w

Director: Archie Mayo
Screenplay: Charles Kenyon & Delmer Daves
Source: Play by Robert E. Sherwood

Petrified is right. Far too little was changed
from the hit play about the gangster holding a
group hostage in a roadside restaurant.
Although the role of the doomed idealistic writer
fits Howard like a glove and some of the acting
is fine, the dialogue is nauseatingly pretentious
and the whole set-bound enterprise is itself like
some fossilised dinosaur.

Alan Squier . . . . .Leslie Howard
Gabrielle Maple . . . . .Bette Davis
Duke Mantee . . . . .Humphrey Bogart
Mrs. Chisholm . . . . .Genevieve Tobin
Boze Hertzlinger . . . . .Dick Foran
Jackie . . . . .Joe Sawyer
Jason Maple . . . . .Porter Hall
Gramp . . . . .Charley Grapewin

Quote 'Living, I'm worth nothing to her. But
dead, I can buy her the tallest cathedrals,

golden vineyards and dancing in the streets. One well-directed bullet will accomplish all that.'

Psst! Jack Warner had wanted Edward G. Robinson to star. Howard, who had starred in the play with Bogart, told Warner that unless Bogart was in the movie, he would pull out. Bogart remained grateful for the rest of his life to Howard, even naming his daughter Leslie after him • The character of Mantee was heavily modelled on Jack Dillinger, America's Public Enemy Number One and Bogart studied newsreel footage of the gangster so that he could mimic his mannerisms.

The Phantom Tollbooth

★★★ 1969 90min c.

Director: Chuck Jones
Screenplay: Chuck Jones & Sam Rosen
Source: Book by Norton Juster

One of the most delightful of all childrens' films requires a bit more work from the young ones' little grey cells than usual. A boy takes his car into a cartoon land where two rival societies, one worshipping letters and the other numbers, fight it out. Milo has to battle through the Doldrums and restore the captured Rhyme and Reason to their rightful place. Full of clever ideas and some moderately enjoyable tunes.

Milo . . . . .Butch Patrick
Also: Mel Blanc, Hans Conried, Candy Candido

Philadelphia

★★ 1993 122min c.

Director: Jonathan Demme
Screenplay: Ron Nyswaner

In typical American manner, the first mainstream Hollywood AIDS movie tries to boil the whole issue of the disease and discrimination against those who have it to a standard court case. Despite the subject matter, it all seems terribly pat and over-melodramatic. Goodness knows why Hanks got the Oscar. Perhaps all those Californina voters were impressed by his dieting ability? Washington is far more impressive as the homophobic lawyer who has to rethink his deeply-held prejudices.

Andrew Beckett . . . . .Tom Hanks
Joe Miller . . . . .Denzel Washington
Charles Wheeler . . . . .Jason Robards

Belinda Conine . . . . .Mary Steenburgen
Miguel Alvarez . . . . .Antonio Banderas
Bob Seidman .Ron Vawter
Walter Kenton . . . . .Robert Ridgely
Judge Garnett . . . . .Charles Napier
Sarah Beckett . . . . .Joanne Woodward

Oscars Tom Hanks

Quote 'I don't want to go to bed with anybody who's stronger than me or who has more hair on their chest than me.' • 'These people make me sick, but a law's been broken.'

OOPS! After Hanks describes the opera, the music stops without him turning it off.

The Philadelphia Story

★★★ 1940 112min b/w

Director: George Cukor
Screenplay: Donald Ogden Stewart
Source: Play by Philip Barry

Grant tries to sabotage former wife Hepburn's society wedding but Stewart, the reporter he brings in, finds his earlier objections to the idle rich evaporate when he's exposed to Hepburn. Although regarded as one of the greatest comedies of all time, to modern tastes it seems rather slow and talky. It's still all very pleasant, but only occasionally is it actually very funny. It was remade as the musical *High Society.*

C.K. Dexter Haven . . . . .Cary Grant
Tracy Lord . . . . .Katharine Hepburn
Macaulay Connor . . . . .James Stewart
Elizabeth Imbrie . . . . .Ruth Hussey
George Kittredge . . . . .John Howard
Uncle Willie . . . . .Roland Young
Margaret Lord . . . . .Mary Nash
Dinah Lord . . . . .Virginia Weidler
Sidney Kidd . . . . .Henry Daniell
Seth Lord .John Halliday

Oscars James Stewart, Best Screenplay (adapted)

Blurb Uncle Leo's Bedtime Story For You Older Tots. The Things They Do Among The Playful Rich – Oh Boy!

Quote 'You're slipping, Red. I used to be frightened of that look – the withering glance of the goddess.' • 'My, she was ya.' • 'Put me in your pocket, Mike.' • 'No mean Machiavelli is smiling, cynical Sidney Kidd. The world is his oyster, with an 'R' in every month.' • 'Oh, this is one of those days that the pages of history teach us are best spent lying in bed.' • 'You were extremely attractive. But you were a little worse, or better, for wine…and there are rules about that.'

Psst! Only a couple of years earlier, Hepburn was considered 'box office poison'. She persuaded Barry to write *The Philadelphia Story* for her and made it a great success on stage with Van Heflin as Connor and Joseph Cotten as Dexter Haven • Hepburn was fairly close in attitude and upbringing to her character. She was from a prominent New England family and educated at Bryn Mawr • Shrewdly, in addition to her investment in the play, she also bought the film rights. MGM were forced not only to pay her $250,000 for them but also had to give her casting and directorial control • Grant accepted only if he got top billing. He donated his near-record fee of $137,000 to the British War Relief Fund • The film was a big hit, putting Hepburn back on top of the Hollywood heap and breaking records at Radio City Music Hall • When Stewart rang his father to tell him about winning the Oscar, he was told to send it home so his dad could place it in the window of his hardware store. It remained there for 20 years.

The Piano
★★★★ 1993 120min c.

Director: Jane Campion
Screenplay: Jane Campion

In the 19th century, a deaf woman who's a dab hand with the ivories is sent to New Zealand with her daughter to marry a farmer. When he leaves her beloved piano on the beach, she becomes increasingly obstreperous and begins an affair with uncultivated Keitel. This shatteringly powerful film is incredibly erotic without being explicit. Hunter's outstanding performance is enhanced by sumptuous visuals and Michael Nyman's extraordinary score. A cinematic experience quite unlike any other although, having said that, there were a small – misguided – minority who hated it as much as the rest of us loved it.

Ada McGrath . . . . .Holly Hunter
George Baines . . . . .Harvey Keitel
Stewart . . . . .Sam Neill
Fiona McGrath . . . . .Anna Paquin
Aunt Morag . . . . .Kerry Walker
Nessie . . . . .Genevieve Lemon

Oscars Best Screenplay, Holly Hunter, Anna Paquin

Quote 'Something to be said for silence.'

Psst! According to Anna Paquin, her parents didn't allow her to see the entire film • The Maori actors described themselves as 'The Blackground' and throughout the movie are apparently passing disparaging remarks to each other about the production and the stars.

Picnic at Hanging Rock
★★★ 1975 110min c.

Director: Peter Weir
Screenplay: Cliff Green
Source: Novel by Joan Lindsay

If beauty and mood are what you look for in a film, look no further, for this atmospheric tale of three schoolgirls who go missing on an outing in 1900 has both in spades. Although based on a true story, it is a puzzle that has never been solved and no real answer is supplied here. But the landscapes are breathtaking and there is an air of fear and repressed sexuality to this movie that some find enchanting. Others, however, think it a load of pretentious, arty twaddle.

Mrs. Appleyard . . . . .Rachel Roberts
Michael Fitzhubert . . . . .Dominic Guard
Dianne De Poitiers . . . . .Helen Morse
Minnie . . . . .Jacki Weaver
Miss Greta McGraw . . . . .Vivean Gray
Dora Lumley . . . . .Kirsty Child

The Picture of Dorian Gray
★★★ 1945 110min c&b/w

Director: Albert Lewin
Screenplay: Albert Lewin
Source: Novel by Oscar Wilde

A splendid telling of Wilde's story about the beautiful young man who trades his soul for eternal youth. Instead of him ageing, it's his portrait that does, becoming ever more grotesque as he is led further down the path of decadence and depravity. Hatfield's impassive face, intentional or not, makes the story seem all the more effective while Lansbury is outstanding as the woman Dorian jilts.

Lord Henry Wotton . . . . .George Sanders
Dorian Gray . . . . .Hurd Hatfield
Gladys Hallward . . . . .Donna Reed
Sybil Vane . . . . .Angela Lansbury
David Stone . . . . .Peter Lawford
Basil Hallward . . . . .Lowell Gilmore

James Vane	Richard Fraser
Lord George Farmoor	Reginald Owen
Adrian Singleton	Morton Lowry
Sir Robert Bentley	Miles Mander
Lady Agatha	Mary Forbes
Sir Thomas	Robert Greig
Malvolio Jones	Billy Bevan
Narrator	Cedric Hardwicke

Quote 'I apologise for the intelligence of my remarks, Sir Thomas. I had forgotten that you were a Member of Parliament.' • 'If I could get back my youth, I'd do anything in the world… except get up early, take exercise or be respectable.' • 'When a man says he has exhausted life, you may be sure life has exhausted him.' • 'A good influence is the worst influence of all.'

Psst! The pictures of Dorian Gray were painted by Ivan and Malvin Albright. They went to lunatic asylums and centres for alcoholics to study the faces of those who had lived debauched lives • For the last portrait, which appears in Technicolor (in some prints at least), fresh chicken blood was used to get the bright red shade they were after • Angela Lansbury's mother, Moyna MacGill, appears as the Duchess • The narrator is Cedric Hardwicke.

The Pink Panther
★★★ 1963 113min c.

Director: Blake Edwards
Screenplay: Blake Edwards & Maurice Richlin

A bumbling French police inspector finds catching a famous jewel thief difficult. The fact that his wife is the chap's lover may have something to do with it. Although Clouseau was supposed to be a supporting character, he fairly takes over the picture. In fact, it is rather dull when he isn't on. Sellers proves himself a wonderful comic clown and did even better in the sequel, *A Shot in the Dark*. After that the series became more erratic, with *The Return of the Pink Panther*, *The Pink Panther Strikes Again* and *The Revenge of the Pink Panther*. *The Trail of the Pink Panther* and *The Curse of the Pink Panther* used outtakes after Sellers' death while *Son of the Pink Panther* starred Roberto Benigni. In 1968, Alan Arkin played the role in *Inspector Clouseau*.

Sir Charles Lytton	David Niven
Insp. Jacques Clouseau	Peter Sellers
George Lytton	Robert Wagner
Simone Clouseau	Capucine
Princess Dala	Claudia Cardinale
Angela Danning	Brenda de Banzie
Greek 'cousin'	Fran Jeffries
Defence attorney	John Le Mesurier
The novelist	Michael Trubshawe
Tucker	Colin Gordon
Saloud	James Lanphier

Quote 'When you've seen one Stradivarius, you've seen them all.' • 'If I were my father, I'd have you tortured.' – 'If you were your father, I doubt very much if I would have kissed you.'

OOPS! When Niven is seducing Cardinale on the tigerskin rug, her cigarette swaps hands then vanishes.

Psst! Clouseau was originally conjured up with Peter Ustinov in mind but he pulled out shortly before filming. Ava Gardner was at one point also slated to star • Sellers is said to have based his character on the image of Captain Webb, the first person to swim the channel back in 1875, as seen on the box of a brand of matches • Capucine and Wagner received bad burns from the industrial foam used when they are in the bath together. Wagner was also temporarily blinded by it and ordered to spend four weeks in a dark room. The producer was all set to junk him from the movie but faced a mutiny from Edwards, Niven and Sellers • The success of the Pink Panther character, seen in the opening credits, was such that he got his own cartoon series • For Sellers' first date with young Swedish actress Britt Ekland, he took her to a screening of *The Pink Panther* • The *Pink Panther* was actually the diamond around which the plot revolves, having nothing to do with Inspector Clouseau • Film critic Leslie Halliwell said once of Blake Edwards: 'A man of many talents, all of them minor.'

Pinocchio
★★★★ 1940 88min c.

Director: Ben Sharpsteen & Hamilton Luske
Screenplay: Ted Sears, Otto Englander, Webb Smith & Others
Source: Story by Carlo Collodi

One of the greatest of Disney's feature-length cartoons. Technically superb, it's also a classic piece of storytelling as the wooden puppet dreams of being a real boy, only to find that being flesh and bone isn't such a doddle as he expected. Jiminy Cricket's a great sidekick, but all the rest of the characters are great fun too, as are songs like 'An Actor's Life For Me'.

Pinocchio	.Dick Jones
Jiminy Cricket	.Cliff Edwards
Geppetto	.Christian Rub
J. Worthington Foulfellow	.Walter Catlett
The Blue Fairy	.Evelyn Venable
Lampwick	.Frankie Darro
Gideon	.Mel Blanc

Quote 'Always let your conscience be your guide.'

OOPS! During the pool game, the yellow number one ball changes to a red number three ball.

Psst! For the opening, 11 midgets were hired to dress in Pinocchio outfits and frolic above the cinema's entrance. Unfortunately, the food passed up to them at lunchtime also included a quantity of booze. By mid-afternoon a crowd had gathered, not to see the movie, but to gaze at 11 naked midgets playing dice and belching at the spectators. Police armed with ladders mounted a raid and carried them away in pillowcases • Is it only me that thinks it spookily prescient that in the earlier *Snow White* Sneezy yells out 'Jiminy Crickets!' when the dwarfs think there's a monster in their house? • After six months of work, Disney told the animators that Pinocchio's character was without warmth and made them start all over again • Gideon the Cat was silent except for one hiccough. It was voiced by Mel Blanc, the man who made Bugs Bunny, Sylvester and Elmer Fudd what they are today • Jiminy Cricket is voiced by Cliff Edwards, known to many as Ukulele Ike, one of the most popular Vaudeville entertainers of his day • The multiplane camera, used in *Snow White*, was refined further here, giving viewers the impression of moving through a three-dimensional image • Disney varied the original story a little. In the book, the puppet listens to the cricket which tells him it wants to be his conscience. He listens...and then he stamps on him with his foot and goes on his merry way.

The Pirate
★★ 1948 102min c.

Director: Vincente Minnelli
Screenplay: Albert Hackett & Frances Goodrich
Source: Play by S.N. Behrman

Although it has the colour, sweep and spectacle of the usual MGM musical, far too little attention was paid to the silly script about a street performer, Kelly, who pretends to be an infamous pirate to woo Garland, only to discover that her fiancé Slezak is the real pirate. There are some reasonably good songs and some nice dancing, but it's not one of the greats.

Manuela	.Judy Garland
Serafin	.Gene Kelly
Don Pedro Vargas	.Walter Slezak
Aunt Inez	.Gladys Cooper
The Advocate	.Reginald Owen
The Viceroy	.George Zucco

Also: The Nicholas Brothers

Psst! MGM originally bought the rights to the play intending it to be a straight farce with William Powell, Charles Laughton and Myrna Loy • Garland's impending nervous breakdown and massive attacks of paranoia delayed proceedings considerably. As soon as filming finished, she checked into a sanatorium for a rest • The appearance in the 'Be a Clown' number of the Nicholas Brothers, among the greatest tap dancers of all time, was cut out of the film when it played in some Southern states.

Planes, Trains and Automobiles
★★★ 1987 93min c.

Director: John Hughes
Screenplay: John Hughes

This fun comedy has yuppie Martin trying desperately to get home to his family for a snowy Thanksgiving, but finding himself lumbered with overbearing slob of a shower-curtain ring salesman Candy every step of the way. The gags don't always sit well with the more sentimental aspects of the tale, but there's plenty to enjoy, with both stars giving excellent performances.

Neal Page	.Steve Martin
Del Griffith	.John Candy
Susan Page	.Laila Robbins
State Trooper	.Michael McKean
Taxi Racer	.Kevin Bacon
Owen	.Dylan Baker

Showing She's Having a Baby [another Hughes film].

Psst! As no transport business would co-operate in having themselves sent up, the film-makers had to build an airport terminal, create a fictitious car-hire firm and rent 20 miles of train track on which they could run their train • The film was called *Better To Be Alone Than In Bad Company* in Spain.

Planet of the Apes

★★★ 1968 112min c.

Director: Franklin J. Schaffner
Screenplay: Michael Wilson & Rod Serling
Source: Novel, *Monkey Planet* by Pierre Boulle

The crew of a crashed spaceship find themselves on a planet where apes are the cultured masters and humans are the subservient savages picking fleas off themselves. There isn't much in this famous sci-fi film that is terribly surprising, except for wonderfully haunting ending. But it's all highly enjoyable and is open to some pretty weird, deep and unlikely analysis. The first two sequels, *Beneath the Planet of the Apes* and *Escape from the Planet of the Apes*, weren't bad but the other two, *Conquest of the Planet of the Apes* and *Battle for the Planet of the Apes*, are missing the link to the earlier quality.

George Taylor . . . . .Charlton Heston
Cornelius . . . . .Roddy McDowall
Zira . . . . .Kim Hunter
Dr. Zaius . . . . .Maurice Evans
President of Assembly . . . . . .James Whitmore
Honorious . . . . .James Daly
Nova . . . . .Linda Harrison
Landon . . . . .Robert Gunner
Lucius . . . . .Lou Wagner

Quote 'Get your stinking paws off me, you damn dirty ape.' • 'He was a model for all of us, a gorilla to remember.'

Psst! Instead of using masks, the actors had to endure their faces being made up as apes. Although it is their ability to show facial expressions that makes them so realistic, it meant five hours in make-up each day for the actors. The make-up won an Oscar and took up a staggering 20% of the budget • Edward G. Robinson was to play Dr. Zaius but he had an adverse reaction to the make-up and had to bow out • The underground New York sets were originally built for *Hello Dolly* • There were three different competing endings. The one Heston came up with is the one used in the film.

Plan 9 from Outer Space

★★ 1959 79min b/w

Director: Edward D. Wood
Screenplay: Edward D. Wood

Edward D. Wood Jr. is to movies what William McGonagall is to poetry, Florence Foster Jenkins is to singing and Eddie the Eagle is to ski-jumping. Commonly believed to be the most inept filmmaker of all time, this is his most famous movie. A group of improbable aliens plan to use zombies they have raised from the dead to take over the world. A cast who can't act (one of whom was dead!), a director who can't write or direct, cardboard sets that fall apart, unrelated stock footage, wobbling tombstones, the same furniture appearing in several locations, all this is joy unconfined to the fans of those movies that are so bad they're good. Most watchable of Woods' other films is undoubtedly the incredibly bizarre transvestite movie *Glen or Glenda*.

Jeff Trent . . . . .Gregory Walcott
Paula Trent . . . . .Mona McKinnon
Lt. Harper . . . . .Duke Moore
Col. Tom Edwards . . . . .Tom Keene
The Ghoul Woman . . . . .Vampira
The Ghoul Man . . . . .Bela Lugosi
Police Insp. Clay . . . . .Tor Johnson
Himself . . . . .Criswell
Gen. Roberts . . . . .Lyle Talbot
Eros . . . . .Dudley Manlove
The Ruler . . . . .John 'Bunny' Breckinridge

Quote 'Greetings, my friends. We are all interested in the future, for that is where you and I are going to spend the rest of our lives. Future events, such as these, will affect you in the future!' • 'Visits? That would indicate visitors?' • 'This is the most fantastic story I've ever heard.' – 'And every word of it's true, too.' – 'That's the fantastic part of it.' • 'My friends, you have seen this incident based on sworn testimony. Can you prove that it didn't happen? Perhaps, on your way home, someone will tap you in the dark and you will never know it, for they will be from outer space!' • 'Aim for the stars, and if at the end of your life you've only reached Mars, remember one thing. Stars flicker in and flash out...Mars is a planet.'

OOPS! The entire film.

Psst! The film professes to be the 'sworn testimony of miserable souls who survived the ordeal of grave-robbers from outer space!' • It was originally to be called *Grave Robbers from Outer Space* and this title is referred to in the film • Wood's friend Bela Lugosi died before the production and was buried in his *Dracula* cape. But that didn't stop Wood. He used a couple of minutes he had shot of Lugosi and put that in, getting his own wife's chiropractor to impersonate the dead actor elsewhere. Although he holds a cape up in front of his face, it's hard to disguise the fact that he's far taller and of a completely different build • The flying saucers are said by some to be plates although Wood claimed that they were car hubcaps dangled from fishing rods • Ed Wood was one of the fastest film-makers in Hollywood, shooting up to 30 scenes a day. Undaunted by having a colour-blind cameraman and having to use stock footage and film thrown out by other movies, he managed to make 35 movies, all costing less than $15,000 • Serving as a Marine in World War II, life-long transvestite Ed Wood wore pink panties and a bra under his service uniform. Although afraid of what would happen if he were wounded and treated, he served with great bravery, being one of the few to survive the terrible battle of Tarawa in the Pacific. He was awarded several medals.

Platoon

★★★ 1986 120min c.

Director: Oliver Stone
Screenplay: Oliver Stone

It's Vietnam. It's war. It's hell. Stone's version is more hellish than most with Sheen the volunteer – like Stone himself – who finds that his new platoon is divided between those who follow the more compassionate Dafoe and those who go for Berenger's brutal approach. In its portrayal of life as a soldier on the ground in 'Nam, this semi-autobiographical film is realistic, fascinating and harrowing. Whether you'd want to watch it twice is another matter.

Sgt. Barnes . . . . Tom Berenger
Sgt. Elias . . . . .Willem Dafoe
Chris . . . . Charlie Sheen
Big Harold . . . . .Forest Whitaker
Rhah . . . . .Francesco Quinn
Sgt. O'Neill . . . . .John C. McGinley
Sal . . . . .Richard Edison
Bunny . . . . .Kevin Dillon
Junior .Reggie Johnson
King . . . . Keith David
Lerner . . . . .Johnny Depp

Oscars Best Picture, Best Director

Quote 'O'Neill, take a break. You don't have to be a prick every day of your life, you know.'
• 'We did not fight the enemy. We fought ourselves. And the enemy was in us.'

Psst! Stone spent over ten years trying to get the film made, which he said he wrote inspired by acid and Jim Morrison • Little was expected of the film. But it grossed well over $100m, despite costing only $6m, and was probably the biggest word-of-mouth hit since *Easy Rider*

• Stone appears briefly near the close as an officer in the command bunker that's blown up by the suicide runner • The cast underwent a gruelling fortnight's training in the Philippine jungles before filming, led by an ex-Marine Captain. Stone then started filming immediately to capture their discomfort on camera • Military equipment came from the Philippine government, but the US Defence Department wouldn't cooperate in any other way on the movie • Johnny Depp's helmet has *Sherilyn* on it. At the time, he was engaged to Sherilyn Fenn • Listen out for the real Adrian Cronauer, the Williams character in *Good Morning, Vietnam* calling out his famous catchphrase • Mickey Rooney felt the film was so disturbing women should be banned from seeing it.

The Player

★★★ 1992 124min c.

Director: Robert Altman
Screenplay: Michael Tolkin
Source: Novel by Tolkin

This wickedly delicious satire on Hollywood tells us more about the industry than any documentary ever could. A pressured studio executive over-reacts in a big way to a series of threatening postcards. It's almost impossible to concentrate on the slender thriller plot because of the countless stars who pop in and out of the picture for a few seconds at a time. Full of delicious in-jokes, it doesn't hold up too well to a second viewing, but is a must at least once.

Griffin Mill . . . . .Tim Robbins
June Gudmundsdottir . . . . .Greta Scacchi
Walter Stuckel . . . . .Fred Ward
Det. Avery . . . . .Whoopi Goldberg
Larry Levy . . . . .Peter Gallagher
Joel Levison . . . . .Brion James
Bonnie Sherow . . . . .Cynthia Stevenson
David Kahane . . . . .Vincent D'Onofrio
Andy Civella . . . . .Dean Stockwell
Tom Oakley . . . . .Richard E. Grant
Dick Mellen . . . . .Sydney Pollack
Det. DeLongpre . . . . .Lyle Lovett
Also: Steve Allen, Richard Anderson, Rene Auberjonois, Harry Belafonte, Shari Belafonte, Karen Black, Michael Bowen, Gary Busey, Robert Carradine, Charles Champlin, Cher, James Coburn, Cathy Lee Crosby, John Cusack, Brad Davis, Paul Dooley, Thereza Ellis, Peter Falk, Felicia Farr, Kasia Figura, Louise Fletcher, Dennis Franz, Teri Garr, Leeza Gibbons, Scott Glenn, Jeff Goldblum, Elliott Gould, Joel Grey, David Alan

Grier, Buck Henry, Anjelica Huston, Kathy Ireland, Steve James, Maxine John-James, Sally Kellerman, Sally Kirkland, Jack Lemmon, Marlee Matlin, Andie MacDowell, Malcolm McDowell, Jayne Meadows, Martin Mull, Jennifer Nash, Nick Nolte, Alexandra Powers, Bert Remsen, Guy Remsen, Patricia Resnick, Burt Reynolds, Jack Riley, Julia Roberts, Mimi Rogers, Annie Ross, Alan Rudolph, Jill St. John, Susan Sarandon, Adam Simon, Rod Steiger, Joan Tewkesbury, Brian Tochi, Lily Tomlin, Robert Wagner, Ray Walston, Bruce Willis, Marvin Young

Quote 'It's *Out of Africa* meets *Pretty Woman*.'
• 'Rumours are always true. You know that.'
• 'This is a red wine glass. Can I have my water in a water glass?' • 'Traffic was a bitch.'

Showing The Bicycle Thieves.

Psst! Sixty-five stars agreed to take part for next to nothing. If they'd been paid their usual rate, the wages bill would have come to over $100m • For film buffs, the opening scene is a continuous tracking shot lasting seven minutes. Among the dialogue is a discussion of other famous tracking shots in the movies • The lead was nearly played by Chevy Chase until he was talked out of it, Patrick Swayze's part was left on the cutting-room floor and Warren Beatty was apparently furious that, because he didn't return Altman's calls, he wasn't in it • Screenwriter Michael Tolkin is the right-hand one of the pair of writers who land a deal with Mill.

Play it Again, Sam
★★★ 1972 86min c.

Director: Herbert Ross
Screenplay: Woody Allen
Source: Play by Allen

A nerdy film fanatic, obsessed with *Casablanca*, gets advice on wooing women from the ghost of Humphrey Bogart. Largely because of the dreadfully unfunny slapstick elements, this isn't quite as wonderful as memory would have it. Although film buffs adore it (it makes an excellent double bill with *Casablanca*), the smashing central idea isn't dealt with as inventively as it would have been if Allen had directed it himself.

Allan Felix . . . . .Woody Allen
Linda Christie . . . . .Diane Keaton
Dick Christie . . . . .Tony Roberts
Humphrey Bogart . . . . .Jerry Lacy
Nancy Felix . . . . .Susan Anspach
Sharon . . . . .Jennifer Salt
Julie . . . . .Joy Bang

Jennifer . . . . .Viva
Tough #1 . . . . .Michael Greene
Tough #2 .Ted Markland

Quote 'I never met a dame who didn't understand a slap in the mouth or a slug from a 45.'

Showing Casablanca.

Psst! The principal four actors appeared in Allen's popular play which ran for 453 performances • Jerry Lacy went on star as Bogie in umpteen commercials.

Play 'Misty' for Me
★★★ 1971 102min c.

Director: Clint Eastwood
Screenplay: Jo Heims & Dean Riesner

A late-night D.J. has a fling with a fan which turns into a nightmare as it emerges that she is not only completely screwy, but also extremely dangerous. This is a generally assured directorial debut from Eastwood. Despite some awkwardness in the love scenes and the dripping wet performance from Mills, it is still a neat little thriller which pulls all the right strings while also exploring the subjects of loneliness and sexual obsession. A great late-night movie.

Dave Garland . . . . .Clint Eastwood
Evelyn Draper . . . . .Jessica Walter
Tobie Williams . . . . .Donna Mills
Sgt. McCallum . . . . .John Larch
Madge Brenner . . . . .Irene Hervey
Dr. Frank Dewan . . . . .Jack Ging
Murphy, the bartender . . . . .Don Siegel

Blurb The Scream You Hear May Be Your Own.

Quote 'For lonely lovers on a cool, cool night.'

Psst! Look out for Don Siegel, Eastwood's mate and regular director, as the bartender.

Plaza Suite
★★★ 1971 114min c.

Director: Arthur Hiller
Screenplay: Neil Simon
Source: Play by Simon

Three stories in the life of a suite at New York's Plaza Hotel, with Walter Matthau playing a different character in each. Despite the slightly contrived and stagy premise, the laughs come thick and fast, helped by Simon's witty script and the ever enjoyable Matthau.

Nash/Kiplinger/Hubley	Walter Matthau
Karen Nash	Maureen Stapleton
Miss McCormack	Louise Sorel
Muriel Tate	Barbara Harris
Norma Hubley	Lee Grant
Mimsey	Jenny Sullivan
Borden Eisler	Tom Carey

Quote 'Why do you always start the most serious discussions in our life when I'm halfway out the door?'

Pocahontas

★★★ 1995 87min c.

Director: Mike Gabriel & Eric Goldberg
Screenplay: Carl Binder, Susannah Grant & Philip LaZebnick

Although the tale is unknown outside America, this Disney feature-length cartoon is a true-ish story of an Indian princess who befriends one of the early English settlers. The settlers, commanded by the evil Governor, plunder the land in search of gold while the Indians are all committed environmentalists. Mercifully, the PC message is treated with restraint, the romance between civilised man and supposed savage is sweet and the songs are a vast improvement on those in *The Lion King*, with Mel Gibson's singing far better than might be expected. Best of all though, are the hilarious animal friends of Pocahontas, a racoon and a hummingbird, quite the funniest and most delightful creatures Disney have given us for years.

Pocahontas	Irene Bedard
John Smith	Mel Gibson
Gov. Ratcliffe/Wiggins	David Ogden Stiers
Chief Powhatan	Russell Means
Thomas	Christian Bale
Grandmother Willow	Linda Hunt
Ben	Billy Connolly

OOPS! The Union Jack, as shown in the opening scene, didn't appear in that form until 1801.

Psst! The film was first shown at a free open-air screening in New York's Central Park attended by 100,000, chosen by lottery from applicants from every one of America's 50 states • The four giant screens were eight storeys high, each backed by 45 sea containers stacked on top of one other • Pocahontas' singing voice was provided by Judy Kuhn. Mel Gibson did his own singing • Although based on a true story, Disney didn't always stick to the facts. The real Pocahontas – who would have been topless like all the other women – was just 11 when she met John Smith. Whatever their relationship, she married another settler, John Rolfe, seven years later. Lady Rebecca Rolfe, as she was called after her baptism, sailed with her husband and son to England. There, they were presented at court and became the toast of society although Disney omits to mention her habit of doing cartwheels while wearing no underwear. She fell ill with smallpox as they were returning to America and is buried in Gravesend.

Point Blank

★★ 1967 92min c.

Director: John Boorman
Screenplay: Alexander Jacobs, David Newhouse & Rafe Newhouse
Source: Novel, *The Hunter* by Donald E. Westlake

A crook double-crossed by his wife and shot and left for dead by his partner plans revenge. Although some people love it, this still-violent thriller is all terribly flashy, with its undeniable style insufficient compensation for the fact that the plot is incredibly obscure and confusing.

Walker	Lee Marvin
Chris	Angie Dickinson
Yost	Keenan Wynn
Brewster	Carroll O'Connor
Frederick Carter	Lloyd Bochner
Stegman	Michael Strong
Mal Reese	John Vernon
Lynn	Sharon Acker
Hired gun	James B. Sikking
Citizen	Kathleen Freeman

Psst! Boorman insisted that the film have WASP gangsters, rather than the usual stereotypical Italians.

Poltergeist

★★ 1982 114min c.

Director: Tobe Hooper
Screenplay: Steven Spielberg, Michael Grais & Mark Victor

To this day, Steven Spielberg's level of input is hotly debated, and probably accounts for the very mixed tones to the movie. To make a horror film without a single death is an achievement of sorts, and the special effects are beyond reproach. We could do without the mystical babble from the munchkin psychic, however. It was followed by two pathetic sequels.

Steve Freeling	Craig T. Nelson
Diane Freeling	JoBeth Williams
Dr. Lesh	Beatrice Straight
Dana Freeling	Dominique Dunne
Robbie Freeling	Oliver Robins
Carol Anne	Heather O'Rourke

Blurb It Knows What Scares You!

Quote 'They're he-e-e-ere!'

Showing A Guy Named Joe.

Porky's
★ **1982 98min c.**

Director: Bob Clark
Screenplay: Bob Clark

A depressingly influential 50s-era student 'comedy' with 80s smut. Its sophistication never rises above the level of leering through peepholes in female shower rooms. Badly paced and shoddily made, its great success and the two sequels (*Porky's II* and *Porky's Revenge*) it spawned are dishearteningly depressing to all those with an IQ in treble or even double figures.

Pee Wee	Dan Monahan
Billy	Mark Herrier
Tommy	Wyatt Knight
Mickey	Roger Wilson
Honeywell	Kim Cattrall
Brian Schwartz	Scott Colomby

Quote 'You're too stupid to even be a good bigot.'

Port of Shadows
SEE: Quai des Brumes

The Poseidon Adventure
★★ **1972 117min c.**

Director: Ronald Neame
Screenplay: Stirling Silliphant & Wendell Mayes
Source: Novel by Paul Gallico

When a luxury liner turns turtle in a tidal wave, those actors whose agents couldn't get them any better work try to get to the bottom of the ship, which is now the top. The script is dreadful, the characters risible stereotypes and the clichés pour in faster than the water. But for all that, it's all so ridiculous that it's actually rather enjoyable. Not so the 1979 sequel, *Beyond the Poseiden Adventure*.

Rev. Frank Scott	Gene Hackman
Mike Rogo	Ernest Borgnine
James Martin	Red Buttons
Belle Rosen	Shelley Winters
Manny Rosen	Jack Albertson
Acres	Roddy McDowall
The Captain	Leslie Nielsen
The Chaplain	Arthur O'Connell
Linda Rogo	Stella Stevens
Nonnie Parry	Carol Lynley

Blurb They Were In Hell, Upside Down!

Quote 'In the water, I'm a very skinny lady.'

Psst! Author Gallico got the original idea back in 1937 when he was on the Queen Mary and it was nearly capsized in a storm • The ship used on the movie is the Queen Mary, although it was permanently moored as a maritime museum in Long Beach • The film cost $5m and grossed over 20 times that amount. Its success spawned a series of 'disaster' movies, the 70s most popular genre • In Hong Kong, it was called *The Story of a Ship Called God of the Sea Meeting Danger*.

Postcards from the Edge
★★★★ **1990 104min c.**

Director: Mike Nichols
Screenplay: Carrie Fisher
Source: Novel by Fisher

An excellent, consistently amusing, satire about the wacky world of Hollywood. It is told from the viewpoint of Streep, drug-taking actress daughter of showbiz mom MacLaine, always trying to upstage her daughter. Mercifully unsentimental, it's funny and sharp and an excellent glimpse of Tinseltown at work. Even Streep's a joy in this.

Suzanne Vale	Meryl Streep
Doris Mann	Shirley MacLaine
Jack Falkner	Dennis Quaid
Lowell	Gene Hackman
Dr. Frankenthal	Richard Dreyfuss
Joe Pierce	Rob Reiner
Grandma	Mary Wickes
Grandpa	Conrad Bain
Evelyn Ames	Annette Bening
Simon Asquith	Simon Callow

Blurb Having A Wonderful Time, Wish I Were Here.

Quote 'I don't mind *getting* old. What I mind is *looking* old.'

Psst! Although not strictly autobiographical, Carrie Fisher's novel, on which this is based, bears some close resemblances to her relationship with her own showbiz mother, Debbie Reynolds • Rob Reiner, director of *When Harry Met Sally*, appears as Joe Pierce.

The Postman Always Rings Twice

★★★ 1946 113min b/w

Director: Tay Garnett
Screenplay: Harry Ruskin & Niven Busch
Source: Novel by James M. Cain

Tramp Turner falls for Garfield and together they murder her husband. Even although the censors toned down the novel considerably, the sparks really fly between these two. Unfortunately, the movie is let down by a story strongly reminiscent of *Double Indemnity*, without being half as good. The 1981 remake with Jack Nicholson and Jessica Lange is rather unfocussed and lifeless. Although it is far more explicit, the original is actually much steamier.

Cora Smith .Lana Turner
Frank Chambers . . . . .John Garfield
Nick Smith . . . . .Cecil Kellaway
Arthur Keats . . . . .Hume Cronyn
Kyle Sackett . . . . .Leon Ames
Madge Gorland . . . . .Audrey Totter
Ezra Liam Kennedy . . . . .Alan Reed
Doctor .Charles Williams

Blurb Their Love Was A Flame That Destroyed!

Quote 'You've been trying to make a tramp out of me ever since you've known me.' • 'There'll be kisses, kisses with life and not death.' • 'I don't especially like the way I look sometimes, but I never met a man since I was 14 that didn't want to give me an argument about it.'

Psst! The film nearly starred Cameron Mitchell because Garfield was in the Army. But Garfield had a weak heart and was discharged in time for him to make the movie • Novelist Cain was so impressed with Turner's performance that he gave her a first edition of the novel inscribed: 'For my dear Lana, thank you for giving a performance that was even finer than I expected.' • For her part, Turner gave the director a fur-lined jockstrap at the end of filming.

Potemkin

SEE: Battleship Potemkin

Pretty Baby

★★ 1978 109min c.

Director: Louis Malle
Screenplay: Polly Platt
Source: Book, *Storyville, New Orleans: Being an Authentic Account of the Notorious Redlight District* by Al Rose

In the red-light district of New Orleans, a 12-year-old girl's virginity is auctioned off in a brothel. Despite the salacious subject matter of the movie, Malle's first American movie is so slow-paced, it would be overtaken by a doped snail. It all looks very beautiful, but that's not enough.

E.J. Bellocq . . . . .Keith Carradine
Hattie .Susan Sarandon
Violet Marr . . . . .Brooke Shields
Mme. Nell Livingston . . . . .Frances Faye
Professor . . . . .Antonio Fargas
Highpockets . . . . .Gerrit Graham
Mama Mosebery . . . . .Mae Mercer
Frieda . . . . .Diana Scarwid
Josephine . . . . .Barbara Steele

Psst! In Britain, the Protection of Children Act had recently come in and a scene where the naked Brooke Shields had her legs slightly apart was optically retouched.

Pretty Poison

★★★ 1968 89min c.

Director: Noel Black
Screenplay: Lorenzo Semple Jr.
Source: Novel, *She Let Him Continue* by Stephen Geller

Kooky arsonist Perkins links up with sexy teenager Weld, only to discover there are people around with even weirder ideas than him. This is a great thriller, splendidly tense. While Perkins gives his usual batty young man role, Weld proves truly chilling as a manipulative psychotic.

Dennis Pitt . . . . .Anthony Perkins
Sue Ann Stepanek . . . . .Tuesday Weld
Mrs. Stepanek . . . . .Beverly Garland
Azenauer . . . . .John Randolph
Bud Munsch . . . . .Dick O'Neill
Mrs. Bronson . . . . .Clarice Blackburn
Pete . . . . .Joseph Bova
Detective . . . . .Don Fellows

Psst! Weld possessed an outstanding ability to turn down movies that became very successful. Among those she said 'No' to were *Bob and Carol and Ted and Alice*, Polanski's *Macbeth*, *Lolita* and *True Grit*.

Pretty Woman
★★★ 1990 120min c.

Director: Garry Marshall
Screenplay: J.F. Lawton

Morally dubious but otherwise highly entertaining modern fairy tale. Roberts is the street hooker lucky enough to proposition tycoon Gere just when he needs a companion for the week. No prizes for guessing what happens next, but it is handled in such a manipulatively enjoyable manner that the predictability's part of the fun. Roberts is so divine in the part, it's hard to imagine anybody else bringing it off as well. All credit to Elizondo, too, for his delightful portrayal of the hotel manager. If only more films these days had such decent supporting roles.

Edward Lewis . . . . .Richard Gere
Vivian Ward . . . . .Julia Roberts
James Morse . . . . .Ralph Bellamy
Philip Stuckey . . . . .Jason Alexander
Kit De Luca . . . . .Laura San Giacomo
Hotel manager . . . . .Hector Elizondo
David Morse . . . . .Alex Hyde-White
Elizabeth Stuckey . . . . .Amy Yasbeck

Quote 'Close your mouth, dear.' • 'Listen, I appreciate this whole seduction scene you've got going, but let me give you a tip. I'm a sure thing, okay?' • 'Pick one. I got red, I got green, I got yellow. I'm out of purple.'

Showing Charade.

OOPS! A delight for those spotting boo-boos. Gere's tie pops back on after Roberts first removes it • At breakfast the next morning, her croissant changes to a pancake • A man watching Gere play the piano vanishes • Gere's shoes and socks are on again in the park just after she's taken them off • At the polo match, we see sticking plaster on her toes. It's gone when she's back at the hotel • In one of the first shots at the polo match, as the camera pulls back ahead of the horses, you can see the tracks of what is, presumably, the camera car on the grass • At the posh restaurant, the dessert dishes in front of Gere and Bellamy vanish then reappear • In some versions, as the usher seats them at the opera, he appears to call Vivian 'Miss Roberts'.

Psst! The opening dressing scene isn't Roberts at all, but body double Shelley Michelle. She got just $750 a day, about the same amount Vivian charges in the film. Model Donna Scoggins stood in for Roberts on the famous poster, with the star's face superimposed on her body. Some claim the man on the poster isn't Gere either. Unlike in the film, his hair on the poster isn't grey, but brown • Until late on, the film was to be called *Three Thousand*, Vivian's fee for the week. The real-life hotel room costs more than that each night • Before being given the Disney treatment, the script was darker [she was a cocaine addict, among other things] and it ended with her walking out on him • The beautiful music that Gere is making at the piano, prior to making beautiful music on top of it with Roberts, is a little thing of his own.

Pride and Prejudice
★★★★ 1940 117min b/w

Director: Robert Z. Leonard
Screenplay: Aldous Huxley & Jane Murfin
Source: Play by Helen Jerome & the novel by Jane Austen

This film is an outstanding example of MGM at its sumptuous, elegant best. It may lack some of the nuances of Jane Austen's novel of the husband-hunting sisters, one of whom is blind to the catch right under her nose. But the acting is spot on, there's some nice humour and the whole thing has a charm and sophistication that is not always present in period Hollywood drama.

Mr. Darcy . . . . .Laurence Olivier
Elizabeth Bennet . . . . .Greer Garson
Mr. Bennet . . . . .Edmund Gwenn
Mrs. Bennet . . . . .Mary Boland
Lady Catherine de Bourgh . . . .Edna May Oliver
Jane Bennet . . . . .Maureen O'Sullivan
Mr. Collins . . . . .Melville Cooper
Mary Bennet . . . . .Marsha Hunt
Lydia Bennet . . . . .Ann Rutherford
Kitty Bennet . . . . .Heather Angel
Mrs. Collins . . . . .Karen Morley
Mrs. Bingley . . . . .Frieda Inescourt
Mr. Bingley . . . . .Bruce Lester
Sir William Lucas . . . . .E.E. Clive

Blurb Girls! Take A Lesson From These Husband Hunters.

OOPS! Listen out for a snatch of Mendelssohn, a mite too early.

The Prime of Miss Jean Brodie
★★★ 1969 116min c.

Director: Ronald Neame
Screenplay: Jay Presson Allen
Source: Play adaptation of the novel by Muriel Spark

There is little that is inspiring about the actual making of this film version of the famous play. However, Maggie Smith is mesmerising in the role that she made her own, as the teacher who not only encourages the best of her pupils, but who also tries to control their lives.

Jean Brodie . . . . .Maggie Smith
Teddy Lloyd . . . . .Robert Stephens
Sandy . . . . .Pamela Franklin
Gordon Lowther . . . . .Gordon Jackson
Miss MacKay . . . . .Celia Johnson
Jenny .Diane Grayson
Mary McGregor . . . . .Jane Carr
Miss Alison Kerr . . . . .Molly Weir

Oscars Maggie Smith

Blurb Out Of One Jean Brodie Would Come A Whole Generation Of Jean Brodies... Experimenting With Sex, Society And Everything Else.

Quote 'I am in the business of putting old heads on young shoulders, and all my pupils are the crème de la crème. Give me a girl at an impressionable age and she is mine for life.' • 'I won't have to do with girls who roll up the sleeves of their blouses. We are civilised beings.'

Psst! Smith was then married to Stephens • Although Smith had enormous success with the part on stage, the film role was first offered to Julie Andrews.

The Prisoner of Zenda
★★★ 1937 101min b/w

Director: John Cromwell
Screenplay: John Balderston, Wills Root & Donald Ogden Stewart
Source: Novel by Anthony Hope & the play by Edward Rose

A handsome rendition of the tale of the English tourist in Ruritania who gets roped in to impersonate his distant cousin, the King, something that wasn't mentioned in the holiday brochure. There's some great swashbuckling and a raft of

great actors doing their stuff in this time-old story. It's a little too stiff, though, to rank in the same class as The Adventures of Robin Hood. The yarn was filmed earlier, in 1913, 1915 and 1922 and was made again in 1952 (with the same music) as well as in 1979, starring Peter Seller, which was the worst of them all.

Rudolph Rassendyll/Rudolf V . . .Ronald Colman
Princess Flavia . . . . .Madeleine Carroll
Rupert of Hentzau . . . . . .Douglas Fairbanks Jr.
Antoinette de Mauban . . . . .Mary Astor
Col. Zapt . . . . .C. Aubrey Smith
Black Michael . . . . .Raymond Massey
Capt. Fritz von Tarlenheim . . . . . . .David Niven
Johann . . . . .Byron Foulger
Detchard . . . . .Montagu Love

Quote 'If I see your eyes, I might forget to be a king.'

Private Benjamin
★★ 1980 109min c.

Director: Howard Zieff
Screenplay: Nancy Meyers, Charles Shyer & Harvey Miller

A widowed Jewish-American Princess joins the Army, only to find that it isn't the holiday camp she was expecting. A great concept is only occasionally brought to life. For the most part, it is frittered away with feeble jokes, uninteresting situations and a tiresome romance.

Judy Benjamin . . . . .Goldie Hawn
Capt. Doreen Lewis . . . . .Eileen Brennan
Henri Tremont . . . . .Armand Assante
Col. Clay Thornbush . . . . .Robert Webber
Teddy Benjamin . . . . .Sam Wanamaker
Harriet Benjamin . . . . .Barbara Barrie
Pte. Mary Lou Glass . . . . .Mary Kay Place
Sgt. Jim Ballard . . . . .Harry Dean Stanton
Yale Goodman . . . . .Albert Brooks

Quote 'Excuse me, sir. Is green the only colour these come in?

Psst! It was later turned into a TV series.

A Private Function
★★★ 1985 94min c.

Director: Malcolm Mowbray
Screenplay: Alan Bennett

In ration-bound 1947 Britain, snobby Smith persuades timid chiropodist hubby Palin to steal a pig being fattened up by the town's top brass for the impending royal nuptials. Bennett's first feature-film script brings home the bacon in a big way. Wonderfully observed, with his usual incredible ear for eccentric dialogue, it is also hugely funny.

Gilbert Chilvers	Michael Palin
Joyce Chilvers	Maggie Smith
Betty the Pig	Himself
Dr. Swaby	Denholm Elliott
Allardyce	Richard Griffiths
Sutcliff	Tony Haygarth
Wormold	Bill Paterson
Mother	Liz Smith
Mrs. Allardyce	Alison Steadman
Insp. Noble	Jim Carter
Nuttal	Pete Postlethwaite

Psst! Probably the first movie in which a pig gets third billing.

The Private Life of Henry VIII
★★★ 1933 97min b/w

Director: Alexander Korda
Screenplay: Lajos Biro & Arthur Wimperis

Laughton has the time of his life as the boisterous King whose divorce settlements tended to be on the severe side. Although it shows the odd sign of its splendid old age, the movie is still great fun, being gloriously irreverent and packed with an abundance of bawdy humour.

Henry VIII	Charles Laughton
Thomas Culpepper	Robert Donat
Catherine Howard	Binnie Barnes
Anne of Cleves	Elsa Lanchester
Anne Boleyn	Merle Oberon
Jane Seymour	Wendy Barrie
Catherine Parr	Everley Gregg
Wriothesley	Miles Mander

Oscars Charles Laughton

Quote 'Am I a King or a breeding bull?' • 'The things I do for England.'

Psst! Some stories say that Alexander Korda, searching for a film for Laughton and his wife Lanchester, was inspired by seeing a statue of bluff King Harry. Others say that soon after arriving in Britain he heard a cabbie singing 'I'm 'Enery the Eighth' and thought the song was about the monarch • Although it doesn't look it, the film only cost £60,000 and was made in just five weeks. The largely cardboard sets held

out until the end of filming and the movie made back 10 times its budget • Many of the cast and crew had agreed to defer their full payment until after the movie was made • Laughton spent a great deal of time boning up for his role by devouring everything he could find on Henry VIII. He even took wrestling lessons • Laughton's Oscar was the first for a British movie • Merle Oberon later married Korda • The film was such a success in America as well as in Europe that a succession of period films were put into production. In Kansas City, one cinema owner told a Hollywood rep that his audiences wouldn't put up with any more pictures 'in which men wrote with feathers'.

Prizzi's Honor
★★ 1985 129min c.

Director: John Huston
Screenplay: Richard Condon & Janet Roach
Source: Novel by Condon

Wildly overrated Huston-directed black comedy. Nicholson's the dim mob hitman who falls for Turner only to discover she's in the same line of business. A potentially hilarious idea is taken at the pace of a funeral procession and has about as many laughs. The characters and the acting are splendid but, black though it is, it simply isn't very funny.

Charley Partanna	Jack Nicholson
Irene Walker	Kathleen Turner
Eduardo Prizzi	Robert Loggia
Angelo 'Pop' Partanna	John Randolph
Don Corrado Prizzi	William Hickey
Dominic Prizzi	Lee Richardson
Filargi 'Finlay'	Michael Lombard
Maerose Prizzi	Anjelica Huston

Oscars Anjelica Huston

Quote 'Come on, Charley. You wanna do it? Let's do it, right here on the Oriental.' • 'Do I ice her or marry her?

Psst! When Anjelica Huston won her Best Supporting Oscar, the Hustons became the first family with three generations to win the coveted statuettes, with father John and grandfather Walter preceding her for directing and acting in *Treasure of the Sierra Madre* • Huston and Nicholson were a long-standing couple when the film was made • Nicholson gained 30 pounds for the part • William Hickey's other claim to fame is playing the drunk in the bar in *The Producers*.

The Producers

★★★★ 1968 88min c.

Director: Mel Brooks
Screenplay: Mel Brooks

An ageing theatrical producer with a cardboard belt realises that if a production flops he can keep all the money raised. With a pro-Hitler musical written by a Nazi and starring an amnesiac hippy, how can he go wrong? This hilarious monument to bad taste has now been recognised as one of great comedy classics. Get any two devotees together in a room and they'll invariably act out their favourite scenes. You should be warned that there could be many. Sadly, on the tenth or eleventh viewing, one or two stretches flag a little.

Max Bialystock	Zero Mostel
Leo Bloom	Gene Wilder
Frank Liebkind	Kenneth Mars
Lorenzo St. Du Bois	Dick Shawn
Ulla	Lee Meredith
'Hold me, touch me'	Estelle Winwood
Roger De Bris	Christopher Hewett
Carmen Giya	Andreas Voutsinas
Drunk	William Hickey
Eva Braun	Renee Taylor

Oscars Best Story and Screenplay

Quote 'He who hesitates is poor.' • 'You miserable, cowardly, wretched little caterpillar! Don't you ever want to become a butterfly?' • 'A week? Are you kidding? This play has got to close on page four.' • 'Let me tell you this, and you are hearing this straight from the horse, Hitler was better looking than Churchill, he was a better dresser than Churchill, he had more hair, he told funnier jokes and he could dance the pants off of Churchill.' • 'That's exactly why we want to produce this play: to show the world the true Hitler, the Hitler you loved, the Hitler you knew, the Hitler with a song in his heart.' • 'He who hesitates is poor.' • 'Flaunt it, baby! Flaunt it!' • 'I want... everything...I've ever seen...in the movies.' • 'He's perhaps the worst director that ever lived. He's the only director whose plays close on the first day of rehearsal.' • 'You are the audience. I am the author. I outrank you.' • 'How could this happen? I was so careful. I picked the wrong play, the wrong director, the wrong cast. Where did I go right?' • 'Have you lost your mind? How can you kill the actors? Actors are not animals. They're human beings.' – 'They are? Have you ever eaten with one?' • 'We find the defendants incredibly guilty.'

Psst! The original title was *Springtime for Hitler* but producer Joe Levine forced Brooks to change it • Kenneth Mars' part was written by Brooks with the intention that he play it himself. He then decided against it and was considering a request from a young, unknown actor called Dustin Hoffman to play the part when Hoffman chose to make *The Graduate* instead • Despite winning the Oscar for the Best Screenplay, the film was a flop on first release and only emerged from obscurity after the success of *Blazing Saddles* • The rows between Brooks and Mostel have gone down in Hollywood lore as being among the most furious in the industry's history • The voice in 'Springtime for Hitler' saying 'Don't be stupid, be a smarty, Come and join the Nazi Party' is that of Brooks • William Hickey's other claim to fame is playing Don Corrado Prizzi in *Prizzi's Honor*.

Psycho

★★★★ 1960 109min b/w

Director: Alfred Hitchcock
Screenplay: Joseph Stefano
Source: Novel by Robert Bloch

A woman on the run stops at the Bates Motel, where the main provision is a hot and cold running maniac with a mother fixation. Filmed cheaply and looking as if it was destined for the TV, this pulse-quickening, stomach-churning thriller is still an excellent remedy for narcolepsy. Oddly, it actually gets more frightening on future viewings, even though Hitch's jet-black humour is also then more apparent. The first sequel, *Psycho II* didn't appear until 23 years later. It wasn't much good but *Psycho III* in 1986 and a TV movie in 1990 that was a pilot for a proposed series appeared to be using psychological warfare on suffering audiences.

Norman Bates	Anthony Perkins
Marion Crane	Janet Leigh
Lila Crane	Vera Miles
Sam Loomis	John Gavin
Milton Arbogast	Martin Balsam
Sheriff Chambers	John McIntire
Dr. Richmond	Simon Oakland
Tom Cassidy	Frank Albertson
Caroline	Patricia Hitchcock
Mrs. Chambers	Lurene Tuttle

Blurb Don't Give Away The Ending...It's The Only One We Have.

Quote 'Mother...what's the phrase?...isn't quite herself today.' • 'We all go a little mad sometimes.' • 'A boy's best friend is his mother' • 'There are plenty of motels in the area. You should have…I mean, just to be safe.'

OOPS! When Leigh is packing to leave town, the camera crew's shadow can be seen on the bed • At the end of the shower scene Leigh visibly swallows • The calendar is all to pot in the motel. The film opens on Friday, 11th December and ought, if you follow it through, to finish on the 20th. But the date shown in the motel office is the 17th.

Psst! The story was based on the real-life tale of the necrophiliac killer Ed Gein from Wisconsin, whose less than charming behaviour was also the inspiration for *The Texas Chainsaw Massacre* and *Silence of the Lambs* • *Psycho* didn't win one Oscar • Hitch teased the press by announcing that Helen Hayes and Judith Anderson were being considered for the role of the mother. It appealed to Hitch's sense of humour that none of them would ever get a chance to play the part • It was savaged by critics on both sides of the Atlantic when it opened but became one of the most profitable films ever, with $14m taken at the box office in the first year against a cost of just $780,000. Hitch had been refused a bigger budget because the studio thought it would be a failure • Hitch used the crew from his TV series and at one point considered changing *Psycho* from a movie to just another TV episode • Although Hitchcock had never made a horror movie before, this one established the slasher genre • One of his reasons for making the movie was his curiosity in seeing what happened if you killed off the star early in the film • Among the actresses considered for Leigh's part were Lana Turner, Shirley Jones, Piper Laurie and Eva Marie Saint • Hitch insisted that everyone involved in the production keep every detail of it absolutely secret • Hitchcock can be seen standing outside Leigh's office in a cowboy hat • One of the most famous sequences in movies, the shower scene, lasts only 45 seconds. It involved 78 shots and took seven days to get in the can. The blood is actually chocolate sauce • The latest view is that Saul Bass *didn't* direct it. He produced the storyboards for the scene, but Hitch was actually in the chair at the time • It's claimed that just as the scene started, Hitch arranged for the water to turn ice-cold, getting a satisfying reaction from Leigh • Leigh wore three strategically-placed pieces of fur when being filmed in the shower. A stand-in, Margo Epper, was used for the nude scenes. Stars very rarely did their own nude scenes in

those days • Three of the panel of five censors claimed that they had seen a nipple in the shower scene and demanded Hitch take out the nudity. Hitch took the film away and sent it back the following day unchanged. This time the three who had complained before were satisfied, but the other two now claimed they saw a glimpse of nipple • The British censors cut the number of knife strokes from 17 to just three • The sound of the knife going into flesh is actually that of a blade penetrating a watermelon. Fruit and vegetables play a considerable part in the sound technician's armoury • It isn't Perkins that can be glimpsed through the shower curtain. He was preparing for a play in New York at the time. Some say that for the close-ups, it was Hitch who held the knife • Many opticians pointed out that Leigh's eyes should be dilated after the shower scene rather than pinpoints, which were caused by the strong lighting. They advised using belladonna in eyedrops in future, which the Master did, although why he bothered with such detail and didn't fix the appalling back-projection in his films is beyond me • To test how frightening 'mother' was, Hitch put her in Leigh's dressing room and waited to see how loudly Leigh screamed when she returned • In the opening love scene, John Gavin was proving too nervous for Hitchcock's taste. He took Leigh aside and suggested that if she was able to get Gavin a little worked up the scene would play better. The prurient Hitch was delighted when Leigh's fingers worked the necessary magic and was convinced that Gavin's more fevered performance came from playing the scene with an erection. Gavin became American Ambassador to Mexico in 1980 • Hitchcock was fairly obsessed with lavatories. This movie is supposed to contain the first shot of a toilet flushing in American movies, a moment considered more distasteful by many than anything happening in the shower • Hitch made it a condition of cinemas booking the film that nobody be admitted after it had begun. The posters read: 'No one…BUT NO ONE…will be admitted to the theatre after the start of each performance of *PSYCHO*.'. One cinema owner complaining about his furious patrons made to stand out in the rain was told by Hitch: 'Buy them umbrellas' • It is said that after buying the rights to the novel anonymously, Hitchcock then bought up as many copies of the book as he could so that nobody would be around who knew the ending • If you ever get a chance to see the trailer narrated by Hitch, do so: it's wonderful • A man wrote to Hitch saying that since seeing the film, his wife was scared of bathing or showering. What did Hitch suggest? 'Sir,' replied Hitch, 'Have you ever considered sending your wife to the dry cleaner?'

The Public Enemy

★★★ 1931 84min b/w

Director: William Wellman
Screenplay: Kubec Glasmon, John Bright & Harvey Thew
Source: Story, *Beer and Blood* by John Bright

A pair of kids from the gutter become gangsters before ending up back where they started from. *Little Caesar* and this really kicked off the gangster genre and appalled and appealed to audiences in equal measure. However, like its contemporary starring Edward G. Robinson, while there's much to appreciate, particularly in Cagney's acting, it hasn't worn the years too happily. Dated, but still with flashes of fire and, of course, the famous grapefruit scene.

Tom Powers	James Cagney
Gwen Allen	Jean Harlow
Matt Doyle	Edward Woods
Marnie	Joan Blondell
Ma Powers	Beryl Mercer
Mike Powers	Donald Cook
Kitty	Mae Clarke
Nails Nathan	Leslie Fenton

Quote 'I wish you was a wishing well, so I could tie a bucket to you and sink you.'

OOPS! Although Louise Brooks, best known for her role in *Pandora's Box*, is listed on the credits as 'Bess', she doesn't appear in the final movie.

Psst! Considering Cagney's later career, it seems extraordinary that until two days before filming started he was going to play the good guy. He and Edward Woods then swapped parts. At the time, Cagney was known for being a song and dance man. Some say Woods asked for a less violent part, others that it was the director's idea after seeing early rushes • Louise Brooks was originally slated to play Clarke's role. Although she is listed on the credits as 'Bess', no such character appears in the movie • The film was made for just $150,000 in only 26 days. Warner's head of production, Darryl Zanuck claimed 'the gangster picture's dead' but Wellman said he'd make 'the toughest, the most violent, most realistic picture you ever did see.' • Cagney's character is supposedly based on Chicago

gangster Charles Dion 'Deanie' O'Bannion • The scene where Cagney pushes a grapefruit into Mae Clarke's face was cut by the censors in Britain • Several versions of how it came about exist. Cagney and Clarke claimed that the pair were horsing around for the crew during the rehearsal and the camera just happened to be turning. Others say Wellman told Cagney what to do in private and that it came as a complete surprise to Clarke • For years afterwards, Cagney suffered from being offered umpteen grapefruits whenever he ate out • *The New York Times* referred to 'Sensational and sometimes sensationally incoherent murders' which ended in 'general slaughter'. There are in fact only eight deaths in the film, each of which takes place off camera • Excluding silents, this holds the record for being the least-edited feature film. Only 360 feet out of 8,760 feet of film shot didn't make it into the final cut.

Pulp Fiction

★★★★ 1994 153min c.

Director: Quentin Tarantino
Screenplay: Quentin Tarantino

Although it's overlong and plays a few too many tricks with cinema conventions, this more than amply demonstrates that *Reservoir Dogs* was no flash in the pan. Packed with Tarantino's witty, fizzing dialogue, it cleverly weaves together three stories set deep within the gore found inside the underbelly of American society. Although Jackson and Travolta were lauded for their roles, let's not forget how wonderful Willis is as the boxer told to throw a fight. Hugely entertaining, but be warned that it is pretty violent in places.

Vincent Vega	John Travolta
Jules	Samuel L. Jackson
Mia	Uma Thurman
The Wolf	Harvey Keitel
Pumpkin	Tim Roth
Honey Bunny	Amanda Plummer
Fabienne	Maria De Madeiros
Marsellus Wallace	Ving Rhames
Lance	Eric Stoltz
Jody	Rosanna Arquette
Koons	Christopher Walken
Butch	Bruce Willis

Oscars Best Screenplay

Quote 'Come on. Let's get in character.'

Showing The Losers.

OOPS! Before the first shooting, Travolta tells Jackson he doesn't know what a TV pilot is because he never watches the box. Yet later he talks in detail about the show *Cops* • Bullet holes appear in the wall behind Jackson before the shots that are supposed to make them are actually fired • During Walken's speech about the watch it shows a different time than the 12 o'clock displayed in the close-up • Although Thurman turns off the alarm when she and Travolta return to her place, surely there's an outside door at the back that is ajar?

Psst! It was hoped that Travolta would be at the Japanese opening. But he wanted to fly his own jet over and, when nobody volunteered to pay the $100,000 fuel cost, he refused to go, even first class • Although Willis gets $15m for *Die Hard* movies, he worked for minimum wages on this, getting just $1,400. In Cannes, he threw the dinner to celebrate the movie winning the Palme D'Or and probably ended up $100,000 poorer after making the film • The support fight for Willis' bout is 'Vossler vs. Martinez', these being the names of two of Tarantino's buddies from the video store days • The credits include one guy listed as 'Long Hair Yuppie Scum' • The film started a run on stocks of Chanel Rouge Noir nail varnish, as used by Uma Thurman in the movie • In Britain, the published film script became the first ever to top The Times best seller lists, with over 80,000 copies sold.

Pygmalion

★★★★ 1938 96min b/w

Director: Anthony Asquith & Leslie Howard
Screenplay: George Bernard Shaw, W.P. Lipscomb, Cecil Lewis & Ian Dalrymple
Source: Play by George Bernard Shaw

Although many now think of this as *My Fair Lady* without the music, this is pretty close to the original form of Shaw's original play of the phonetics professor embarking on a bet to turn a flower girl into a society lady. Witty, sophisticated entertainment with sparkling performances all round.

Prof. Henry Higgins	Leslie Howard
Eliza Doolittle	Wendy Hiller
Alfred Doolittle	Wilfrid Lawson
Mrs. Higgins	Marie Lohr
Col. Pickering	Scott Sunderland
Mrs. Pearce	Jean Cadell
Freddy Eynsford-Hill	David Tree
Mrs. Eynsford-Hill	Everley Gregg
Count Aristid Karpathy	Esme Percy
Hairdresser	Anthony Quayle

Oscars Best Screenplay

Quote 'Yes, you squashed cabbage leaf, you disgrace to the noble architecture of these columns, you incarnate insult to the English language, I can pass you off as the Queen of Sheba.' • 'Where the devil are my slippers, Eliza? • 'I'm a good girl, I am.'

Psst! Although the film sticks fairly well to Shaw's play, some of the heavier philosophising was cut, while Shaw added the scene at the Ambassador's Ball • Features the first instance in a British movie of the words 'bloody' and also 'damn', before Rhett got to say it in *Gone With the Wind*.

Q Planes

★★★ 1939 82min b/w

Director: Tim Whelan
Screenplay: Ian Dalrymple, Brock Williams, Jack Whittingham & Arthur Wimperis

Eccentric spymaster Richardson enlists pilot Olivier's help to discover why new experimental planes keep disappearing. While hardly terribly plausible, it's all rollicking fun, with wonderfully fast, furious and funny banter worthy of the *Thin Man* films. Full marks, too, for the great running gag of Richardson always missing his dates with Daphne.

Maj. Hammond	Ralph Richardson
Tony McVane	Laurence Olivier
Amy	Valerie Hobson
Jenkins	George Curzon
Barrett	George Merritt
Blenkinsop	Gus McNaughton
MacKenzie	David Tree
Stage door keeper	Hay Petrie

Quote 'Less enthusiasm, please. This is Britain.'

OOPS! At the end, as Daphne gets up from the piano to meet Richardson, it keeps playing.

Psst! The film was based on a newspaper article spotted by studio head Alexander Korda • Korda's company, London Films, was responsible for some of the best movies ever made in Britain. The shot of Big Ben with which all their films begin is, at the very least, an indication that what will follow will display a fair degree of quality, verve and imagination.

Quadrophenia
★★★ 1979 120min c.

Director: Franc Roddam
Screenplay: Dave Humphries, Martin Stellman & Franc Roddam

This is a surprisingly good British youth movie, set in 60s Brighton. About the clash between Mods and Rockers, it is based on Pete Townshend's Who album of the same name. What could have been another self-pitying yoof tragedy is given directorial energy and convincing performances, though some of the anachronisms cause unintentional hilarity. Leave your parka or leather jacket in the wardrobe if you want to avoid trouble.

Jimmy	Phil Daniels
Dave	Mark Wingett
Chalky	Philip Davis
Steph	Leslie Ash
Pete	Garry Cooper
Monkey	Toyah Wilcox
The Ace Face	Sting
Jimmy's father	Michael Elphick
Mr. Fulford	Benjamin Whitrow
Danny	Daniel Peacock
Agency man	Jeremy Child
Projectionist	Timothy Spall
Tailor	Olivier Pierre
Mr. Cale	Hugh Lloyd

OOPS! The number plates are from completely the wrong era.

Psst! This was Sting's acting debut.

Quai des Brumes
★★★ 1938 90min b/w

Director: Marcel Carné
Screenplay: Jacques Prévert
Source: Novel by Pierre Mac Orlan

A deserter searching for a way to flee France holes up in Le Havre and falls for a young girl. This is a wonderfully atmospheric, moody, fatalistic melodrama with a great brooding performance from Gabin, France's Bogart. There's so much studio-created fog around, it's a wonder the actors aren't continually coughing their guts out. To be fair, despite the fog's disguise, the sets are rather obvious but the whole affair is as French as Gitanes.

Jean	Jean Gabin
Nelly	Michele Morgan
Zabel	Michel Simon
Lucien	Pierre Brasseur

Psst! The film was originally going to be made in Germany, but Nazi propaganda head Gobbels thought a story about a deserter decadent • The French minister of war forbade the word 'deserter' from being used • The film was banned during the German occupation of France • In the original novel, Nelly is a prostitute who kills her pimp.

Quatermass and the Pit
★★★ 1967 97min c.

Director: Roy Ward Baker
Screenplay: Nigel Kneale

Work on the London underground uncovers a strange object. It seems to contain a mysterious and deadly power and scientists race against the clock to understand and contain it. This third in the *Quatermass* series was the best of the bunch. Although occasionally betraying its modest budget, this is one of the most imaginative and gripping of all sci-fi films, full of interesting ideas and with a real sockeroo finale. As a youngster, I found it terrifying. The first two films in the series were 1955's *The Quatermass Experiment*, known in America as *The Creeping Unknown*, and the 1957 *Quatermass II*, known in the States as *Enemy from Space*. Both are worth catching. The later *Quatermass Conclusion* was made for TV and received a short theatrical release in 1979.

Dr. Roney	James Donald
Quatermass	Andrew Keir
Barbara Judd	Barbara Shelley
Col. Breen	Julian Glover
Sladden	Duncan Lamont
Capt. Potter	Bryan Marshall
Howell	Peter Copley
Journalist	Sheila Steafel

Psst! The Quatermass films were based on a TV series.

Queen Christina
★★ 1933 97min b/w

Director: Rouben Mamoulian
Screenplay: Salka Viertel, H.M. Harwood & S.N. Behrman

Back in the 17th century, the Queen of Sweden

gets tired of life at court and pops out for a spot of incognito slumming. After donning men's clothes, she falls for Don Antonio, the Spanish ambassador. In other hands, this would seem like Mills and Boonish drivel. But Garbo is at her luminescent best and the scenes between her and Gilbert are almost as electrically charged as in *Flesh and the Devil*. It's tosh, and an acquired taste, but Garbo fans will love it.

Queen Christina	Greta Garbo
Don Antonio De la Prada	John Gilbert
Magnus	Ian Keith
Chancellor Oxenstierna	Lewis Stone
Aage	C. Aubrey Smith
Prince Charles	Reginald Owen
Ebba	Elizabeth Young
General	Gustav von Seyffertitz
Innkeeper	Akim Tamiroff

Quote 'I have been memorising this room. In the future, in my memory, I shall live a great deal in this room.' • 'I shall die a bachelor.'

OOPS! Audiences were so entranced by that final shot of Garbo in the prow of the ship that they usually didn't notice that the wind mussing her hair in such an appealing manner came from a different direction than the one filling the sails.

Psst! Garbo had taken a break from filming for 18 months and was living in Sweden when a friend gave her a couple of books about Queen Christina • After Garbo rejected Franchot Tone and Leslie Howard, Laurence Olivier was hired for the male lead. But during rehearsals Garbo changed her mind and had him booted off the production in favour of her former lover and co-star John Gilbert. Her contract gave her the right to choose everyone involved in the film • Until the last moment Louis B. Mayer, the head of MGM, tried everything in his power to get someone other than Gilbert. It is widely thought that it was Mayer who had torpedoed the former silent star by claiming that his voice was too thin and weedy for the talkies • Knowing of the real Queen Christina's bisexuality, the censors kept a close eye on the script • There was a Swedish historial adviser on the movie but his constant protests about the almost complete lack of historical accuracy were to no avail • The final scene is probably the most famous image of Garbo, as she stands in the prow of the ship, the wind blowing her hair. According to Mamoulian, he said to her: 'I want your face to be a blank sheet of paper. I want the writing to be done by every member of the audience.' • The film did poorly in America, although it was popular in Europe.

Quest for Love
★★★ 1971 90min c.

Director: Ralph Thomas
Screenplay: Terence Feely
Source: Story, *Random Quest* by John Wyndham

Blown into a parallel dimension, a physicist loves a woman who snuffs it. Back on familiar territory, he races to find the same woman and save her. Although its production values would disgrace an episode of *Crossroads*, the intriguing sci-fi plot keeps it all bubbling along merrily.

Colin	Tom Bell
Ottille	Joan Collins
Tom Lewis	Denholm Elliott
Sir Henry Larnstein	Laurence Naismith
Jennifer	Lyn Ashley
Geraldine Lambert	Juliet Harmer
Also: Simon Ward	

The Quiet Man
★★★ 1952 129min c.

Director: John Ford
Screenplay: Frank S. Nugent
Source: Story by Maurice Walsh

An American boxer returns to his roots in Ireland and makes it his mission to tame a local bigwig and his beautiful but tempestuous sister. Although it's an Ireland that only exists in the imaginations of second- or third-generation Americans, it's all very beautiful and lusciously filmed. If you can ignore the shamrock-waving, it's got some great action, a nice line in self-deprecating humour and an enjoyable romance between two very charismatic stars. A four-leafed clover of a movie.

Sean Thornton	John Wayne
Mary Kate Danaher	Maureen O'Hara
Michaeleen Flynn	Barry Fitzgerald
'Red' Will Danaher	Victor McLaglen
Father Lonergan	Ward Bond
Mrs. Tillane	Mildred Natwick
Dan Tobin	Francis Ford
Rev. Cyril Playfair	Arthur Shields
Mrs. Playfair	Eileen Crowe
Woman at station	May Craig
Forbes	Charles Fitzsimmons

Oscars Best Director

Quote 'No patty fingers, if you please.' • 'He'll regret it to his dying day…if he ever lives that long.'

OOPS! For his fight with McLaglen, Wayne doesn't wear his toupée. He doesn't need to because he's wearing a hat. But the hat gets knocked off and we see that the Duke is becoming folically-challenged.

Psst! This was something of an incestuous project. Fitzgerald and Shields were brothers, while O'Hara was FitzSimmons' sister. Ford got his brother Francis to play the chap with the white beard, although they were barely on speaking terms. Wayne didn't miss out on getting work for the family, either. Four of his children, two of each sex, had small roles in the movie • The big fight between Wayne and McLaglen is said to be the longest in any movie and took four days to film.

Raging Bull

★★★ 1980 128min c.

Director: Martin Scorsese
Screenplay: Paul Schrader & Mardik Martin
Source: Book by Jake La Motta with Joseph Carter & Peter Savage

In this downbeat biog of selfish, self-destructive boxer Jake La Motta, De Niro gives an amazing portrayal of a man whose animal side lurks just below the surface, ever ready to erupt. No punches are pulled in the often repellent boxing scenes. Although technically brilliant and voted by many critics their favourite 80s movie, De Niro plays so unsympathetic a character that the experience is not just bleak and uncomfortable, but also rather nasty.

Jake La Motta . . . . .Robert De Niro
Vicki . . . . .Cathy Moriarty
Joey . . . . .Joe Pesci
Salvy . . . . .Frank Vincent
Tommy . . . . .Nicholas Colasanto
Lenore . . . . .Theresa Saldana

Oscars Robert De Niro

Quote 'Can you prove that you're 21? Prove it to me.' • 'C'mon. You're my brother. Be friends, ya fuckin' bum. Give me a break. C'mon, kiss me. Give me a kiss. C'mon.'

Showing Of Mice and Men.

Psst! Throwing himself into the role as always, De Niro trained with La Motta for six months, putting on 50 pounds to play the boxer in his later years. It took him years to regain his former weight. La Motta claimed that if De Niro ever tired of acting, he would acquit himself

well in the boxing ring as a middleweight. The actor had broken the caps on La Motta's teeth, given him more than one black eye and damaged his chin. La Motta billed the film company the $4,000 his dental bills came to • The camera flashes were accompanied by the sound effects of gunshots. The noises for the punches were made by squashing tomatoes and melons • De Niro accidentally broke a couple of Pesci's ribs in a sparring bout. The scene, where Pesci can be heard to groan, is in the movie • Moriarty, a model, had never acted before. She was discovered by Pesci, who thought she looked identical to La Motta's wife • Pesci himself was running a restaurant when Scorsese persuaded him to do the movie • Scorsese appears in a cameo, asking De Niro to go on stage.

Raiders of the Lost Ark

★★★★ 1981 115min c.

Director: Steven Spielberg
Screenplay: Lawrence Kasdan

An unorthodox archaeologist races the Nazis to get hold of the legendary Ark of the Covenant. Spielberg gave us a great new hero in this wonderful Boy's Own adventure yarn which combines thrills, comedy, fantasy, damsels in distress, religion, nasty Nazis and even a spot of romance. Hold on tight! It starts at full throttle and never lets up. There were two sequels, *Indiana Jones and the Temple of Doom* and *Indiana Jones and the Last Crusade*.

Indiana Jones . . . . .Harrison Ford
Marion Ravenwood . . . . .Karen Allen
Belloq . . . . .Paul Freeman
Toht . . . . .Ronald Lacey
Sallah . . . . .John Rhys-Davies
Marcus Brody . . . . .Denholm Elliott
Satipo . . . . .Alfred Molina
Dietrich . . . . .Wolf Kahler

Quote 'Well, Jones, at least you haven't forgotten how to show a lady a good time.' • 'Snakes! Why did it have to be snakes?' • 'There've been a lot of heroes on television who are champagne heroes. Indiana Jones is not a champagne hero. He's a cheap wine hero.' [Spielberg] • 'I think *Raiders of the Lost Ark* was probably the most fun I've had on a film.' [Harrison Ford]

OOPS! Although Thailand is clearly visible on the map showing the plane's progress, the country was still called Siam then • When Indy is facing the cobra, light briefly glints off the glass we aren't supposed to know is there • Keep an eye on Allen's medallion that leaps from neck to hand in a trice • When the truck explodes, a pole can be seen underneath that pushes it over • If the staff is indeed five feet tall, that doesn't say much for Indy's height because it is far taller than him, even after it's inserted into the hole in the map room.

Psst! The original choice for Indiana Jones was a then unknown Tom Selleck. But his option was taken up on a pilot he'd done for *Magnum*. He couldn't get out of it, even though Spielberg held up the film for five weeks. A TV actor's strike then meant that *Raiders* actually finished before *Magnum* even started • The name 'Indiana Jones' was that of producer George Lucas's dog • Of the 12,000 snakes used in the film, around 2,000 went missing • The day before they were due to start filming, someone found out that the antidote for cobra bites was out of date. More was hurriedly flown in from Paris • Karen Allen was so frightened when filming the scene with the snakes that she wasn't able to scream. Spielberg apparently dropped a snake onto her from above and she suddenly found her voice • The great moment when Indy shoots the sword-wielding baddie was not planned. There was supposed to be a long fight between them. But many of those on the production, including Ford, were ill with diarrhea and his change to the scene meant they could move to a more comfortable location • The submarine pens were the genuine item, former U-boat hideouts in France • When Indy is rescued by the bi-plane in the opening sequence, its number is OB-3PO and as the Ark is taken by the Nazis, keep your eye out for the sneaky appearance of R2D2 and C3PO from *Star Wars* among the hieroglyphics on the wall • The throaty noise of the truck on which Indy is fighting includes the sounds of lions roaring • Ford did the scenes with him being dragged by the truck himself. Asked if it was dangerous, he said: 'No. If it really was dangerous, they would have filmed more of the movie first.'

The Railway Children
★★★ 1970 108min c.

Director: Lionel Jeffries
Screenplay: Lionel Jeffries
Source: Novel by E. Nesbit

Three Edwardian children, living near a railway

line, scheme to get their father released from prison. Although rough round the edges and with less-than-brilliant acting from the younger kids, it still manages to wring the withers every time, with the deeply Freudian final reunion on the train platform the main catalyst for the tears. Charming family fare.

Mother . . . . .Dinah Sheridan
Perks, the porter . . . . .Bernard Cribbins
Old Gentleman . . . . .William Mervyn
Father .Iain Cuthbertson
Bobbie . . . . .Jenny Agutter
Phyllis . . . . .Sally Thomsett
Peter . . . . .Gary Warren

Rain Man
★★★ 1988 133min c.

Director: Barry Levinson
Screenplay: Ronald Bass & Barry Morrow

How rare to find an 'issue' movie that is so immensely enjoyable. Cruise is the self-centred hotshot, furious to discover that his father's money has been left to an unknown autistic brother. Cruise nabs him from the asylum in the hope he can con him out of the money but, as they drive, both their characters begin to change. Tacky though it might sound, the film is not only a moving insight into the world of the *idiot savant*, but also an incredibly funny buddy movie. Hoffman naturally relishes his part, but Cruise, with no autistic acting props to fall back on, is less showy but every bit as impressive.

Raymond Babbitt . . . . .Dustin Hoffman
Charles Babbitt . . . . .Tom Cruise
Susanna .Valeria Golino
Dr. Bruner . . . . .Gerald R. Molen
John Mooney . . . . .Jack Murdock
Vern . . . . .Michael D. Roberts
Lanny .Ralph Seymour
Iris . . . . .Lucinda Jenney
Sally Dibbs . . . . .Bonnie Hunt

Oscars Best Picture, Dustin Hoffman, Best Director

Quote 'K-Mart sucks!'

Psst! Warners turned *Rain Man* down because of its similarity to another film they had on their books called *Forrest Gump*. After *Rain Man's* success, they junked *Gump* and Paramount took it up • In the restaurant, the last two names memorised by Hoffman are Marsha and William Gottsegen, his real in-laws • Hoffman received a total of around $20m • He was originally offered the Cruise part but preferred to be Raymond. He was the one who suggested that the disability be switched from simple retardation to autism • Every airline in the world bar one cut the scene where Raymond's afraid to fly. Only Qantas showed it, as Raymond quoted statistics that it was the only airline never to have had a fatal crash. Quantas had every reason to be grateful. Ticket sales rose after the film came out • This is said to be Princess Diana's favourite film • Among the directors associated with the project before Levinson were Martin Brest, Steven Spielberg and Sydney Pollack, who quarrelled with Hoffman as he had done on *Tootsie* • Spielberg turned down $5m to direct it. Levinson said later that among the Spielberg ideas he jettisoned were some wacky chase scenes • Levinson appears in a cameo as the psychiatrist near the end of the movie.

Rancho Notorious

★★★ 1952 89min c.

Director: Fritz Lang
Screenplay: Daniel Taradash
Source: Story, *Gunsight Whitman* by Sylvia Richards

A man out to avenge his fiancée's death infiltrates a ranch run by a one-time barroom singer. Despite the familiar sounding plot, this is a splendidly quirky Western, peopled by extraordinary characters and with an unusual visual style. Dietrich is particularly good, and not only when she's singing. Offbeat and very enjoyable, with the 'Chuck-a-luck' song an unforgettable movie moment.

Altar Keane	Marlene Dietrich
Vern Haskell	Arthur Kennedy
Frenchy Fairmont	Mel Ferrer
Beth Forbes	Gloria Henry
Baldy Gunder	William Frawley
Geary	Jack Elam
Kinch	Lloyd Gough
Harbin	Francis McDonald
Wilson	George Reeves
Comanche Paul	Dan Seymour

Psst! Lang and Dietrich fought furiously on set and ended up not talking to each other. One of Dietrich's problems was that she didn't look as good on film as she had when cinematographer Hal Mohr had filmed her for *Destry Rides Again* 13 years earlier. She asked Mohr why that should be so and received the tactful reply that,

regrettably, he was 13 years older • Lloyd Gough, who plays Kinch, had his name taken off the credits by RKO studio head Howard Hughes when he was blacklisted after refusing to testify to the House Un-American Activities Committee.

Random Harvest

★★★★ 1942 126min b/w

Director: Mervyn LeRoy
Screenplay: Claudine West, George Froeschel & Arthur Wimperis
Source: Novel by James Hilton

Ronald Colman is a shell-shocked ex-soldier with amnesia who suddenly recalls his previous life but forgets about his more recent wife and child. It's a pretty ludicrous plot and, with other actors in the leads, we'd no doubt be reaching for the 'off' button but Colman and Garson make it all extremely moving and supremely enjoyable.

Charles Rainier	Ronald Colman
Paula	Greer Garson
Dr. Jonathan Benet	Philip Dorn
Kitty	Susan Peters
Dr. Sims	Henry Travers
'Biffer'	Reginald Owen
Mrs. Deventer	Margaret Wycherly
Harrison	Bramwell Fletcher
Sam	Rhys Williams

Quote 'I would like to recommend this film to those who can stay interested in Ronald Colman's amnesia for two hours and who could with pleasure eat a bowl of Yardley's shaving soap for breakfast.' [Critic James Agee]

Reach for the Sky

★★ 1956 135min b/w

Director: Lewis Gilbert
Screenplay: Lewis Gilbert
Source: Book, *The Story of Douglas Bader* by Paul Brickhill

Despite the loss of his legs, a flyer joins the RAF and becomes a thorn in the Germans' side after he is captured. One of the most extraordinary tales of wartime heroism is told in a rather plodding manner. But, thanks to More's great performance in the central role, it is never really dull.

Douglas Bader	Kenneth More
Thelma Bader	Muriel Pavlow
Johnny Sanderson	Lyndon Brook
Stan Turner	Lee Patterson
Mr. Joyce	Alexander Knox
Nurse Brace	Dorothy Alison
Robert Desoutter	Sydney Tafler

Rear Window

★★★★ 1954 112min c.

Director: Alfred Hitchcock
Screenplay: John Michael Hayes
Source: Story, *It Had to Be Murder* by Cornell Woolrich

A photographer with his leg in plaster spends his time gazing out of the window and comes to suspect one of his neighbours of murder. This is one of Hitch's best, a great suspense movie made all the more gripping by the claustrophobia of the single set. Even as we watch it, we feel uncomfortable that we are slipping so easily into the role of voyeur. Among the added bonuses to this great film are the wisecracking Thelma Ritter, Grace Kelly at her sexiest best and the great soundtrack. Listen out for appropriate songs like 'Lisa' and 'To See You Is To Love You'.

L.B. 'Jeff' Jeffries	James Stewart
Lisa Fremont	Grace Kelly
Det. Thomas J. Doyle	Wendell Corey
Stella	Thelma Ritter
Lars Thorwald	Raymond Burr
Miss Lonelyhearts	Judith Evelyn

Quote 'We've become a race of Peeping Toms. What people ought to do is get outside their own house and look in for a change.' • 'Preview of coming attractions.' • 'Sure, he's a snooper, but aren't we all?' [Hitchcock]

OOPS! While Kelly and Stewart are arguing, Stewart's cast leaps from the left leg to the right for an instant. Much as one might like to think of such a monumental gaffe not being noticed at the time, it's more likely the shot was reversed at the editing stage.

Psst! Hitchcock appears roughly an hour into the movie, winding the clock in the songwriter's flat • This is one of the five 'lost Hitchcocks'. Along with *Rope*, *The Man Who Knew Too Much* (1956), *Vertigo* and *The Trouble with Harry*, the rights were bought back by Hitch as a legacy for his daughter. They were unseen for around 30 years, only being re-released in the mid-80s.

Rebecca

★★★★ 1940 130min b/w

Director: Alfred Hitchcock
Screenplay: Robert E. Sherwood & Joan Harrison
Source: Novel by Daphne du Maurier

After a whirlwind romance, a young bride is nearly driven mad by constant reminders of her husband's first wife. Despite, or perhaps because of, the wettest heroine in all Hitch's films, this is a sublime, Gothic melodrama, a mystery that simply oozes with atmosphere and menace. A slab of cinematic perfection from its wonderful opening shot to the final moments, only dragging its heels in the overlong legal wrangles. The real standout is the deliciously menacing housekeeper, Judith Anderson.

Maxim de Winter	Laurence Olivier
Mrs. de Winter	Joan Fontaine
Jack Favell	George Sanders
Mrs. Danvers	Judith Anderson
Maj. Giles Lacy	Nigel Bruce
Col. Julyan	C. Aubrey Smith
Frank Crawley	Reginald Denny
Beatrice Lacy	Gladys Cooper
Mrs. Van Hopper	Florence Bates
Coroner	Melville Cooper
Dr. Baker	Leo G. Carroll
Chalcroft	Forrester Harvey
Tabbs	Lumsden Hare

Oscars Best Picture

Quote 'Last night I dreamt I went to Manderley again.'[Opening line] • 'Most girls would give their eyes for a chance to see Monte.' – 'Woudn't that rather defeat the purpose.' • 'I wish there could have been an invention that bottled up a memory, like perfume, and it never faded, never got stale. Then whenever I wanted to, I could uncork the bottle and live the memory all over again.' • 'I'm asking you to marry me, you little fool.'

Psst! This was Hitchcock's first Hollywood film • War between Britain and Germany was declared just as filming started • Hitch doesn't appear in the film, although some stills taken on set show him standing outside a phone box with Sanders inside • Among those mentioned in connection with the lead were Olivia De Havilland, Anne Baxter, Loretta Young and Margaret Sullavan. Vivien Leigh, Olivier's lover, was also considered, but producer Selznick didn't want to risk having them on screen together while they were still married to other people • The 22-year-old Fontaine was far from a star at the time and both Hitch and Olivier advised against using her • Olivier was second choice for the part after Ronald Colman had turned it down • Hitch got the performance he wanted from Fontaine by keeping her unsettled on set, telling her that he was the only one who thought she could act at all. Olivier, still smarting from not being able to co-star with Leigh, apparently whispered obscenities into Fontaine's ear in the love scenes. Hitch did nothing to stop him as he adored the expression on the timid and naive Fontaine's face • As in the novel, Fontaine's character has no first name • The ending is changed from the book, where Rebecca's death is a murder. In the film, it is an accident • This is the only one of Hitchcock's films that won an Oscar for Best Picture.

Rebel Without a Cause

★★ 1955 111min c.

Director: Nicholas Ray
Screenplay: Stewart Stern
Source: Story, *The Blind Run* by Dr. Robert M. Lindner

If you adore James Dean then you won't hear a word against this movie. But for the rest of us it now seems a rather turgid look at angry, inarticulate teenagers rebelling against the fact that they've got nothing to rebel against. If Dean hadn't died, this probably wouldn't be remembered as anything other than the exploitation pic about misunderstood youth that was originally planned.

Jim	James Dean
Judy	Natalie Wood
Jim's father	Jim Backus
Jim's mother	Ann Doran
Plato	Sal Mineo
Goon	Dennis Hopper
Buzz	Corey Allen
Judy's father	William Hopper
Judy's mother	Rochelle Hudson
Moose	Nick Adams
Psychiatrist	Edward Platt
Jim's Grandmother	Virginia Brissac

Blurb Teenage Terror Torn From Today's Headlines.

Quote 'I saw you and I said, "Boy, this is going to be one terrific day, so you better live it up 'cause tomorrow you'll be nothing," see, and I almost was.'

Psst! The original title was *Blind Run* • The casting suggested by Warner Brothers was Tab Hunter and Jayne Mansfield. It was director Ray who insisted on Wood and Dean • Ray studied police cases involving teenagers by the score as research, going with the screenwriter to interview police and judges and spending time with a gang of youths • If Jim Backus' voice sounds familiar, that may be because he voiced the *Mr. Magoo* cartoons. As a tribute, Dean imitates *Mr. Magoo* in the movie • In the knife fight between Dean and Allen, they used real flick-knives, with chainmail under their tops to protect them. Despite it, Dean was slightly cut • The scene was axed by the censors in Britain • Dean psyched himself up for the scene where he smashes the desk by getting drunk and working himself up into a fury. The scene was done in one take, but Dean broke two bones in his hand • The three young stars all met with premature deaths. Mineo was murdered in 1976, Wood died in a boating accident in 1981 and Dean was killed later in 1955 speeding in his car. He was already dead when both *Rebel* and *Giant* were released. Former girlfriend Pier Angeli, the recent split with whom had depressed Dean so much, died of a drug overdose aged 39. Nick Adams also died of an overdose in 1968 • The mansion is the one used in *Sunset Boulevard* • Director Ray is the solitary person walking up to the planetarium at the end of the movie.

Red Dust

★★ 1932 83min b/w

Director: Victor Fleming
Screenplay: John Lee Mahin
Source: Play by Wilson Collison

Jean Harlow is on top steamy form in a steamy Indochina plantation, distracting Clark Gable from his rubber extraction and the attentions of Mary Astor. The pre-Production Code dialogue is surprisingly racy as well as witty, and the leads manage pretty well to conceal the fact that the plot isn't as hot as the weather. It was remade as *Congo Maisie* in 1940 and in 1954 as *Mogambo*, with Clark Gable starring again.

Dennis Carson	Clark Gable
Vantine	Jean Harlow
Gary Willis	Gene Raymond
Barbara Willis	Mary Astor
Guidon	Donald Crisp
McQuarg	Tully Marshall
Limey	Forrester Harvey

Quote 'I've been looking at her kind ever since my voice changed.' • 'This place certainly reeks of hospitality and good cheer, or maybe it's this cheese.'

Psst! Jean Harlow's second husband Paul Bern, a leading producer at MGM, killed himself while the movie was being made. A year later she married Harold Rosson, the cinematographer on *Red Dust*.

Red River

★★★ 1948 133min b/w

Director: Howard Hawks
Screenplay: Borden Chase & Charles Schnee
Source: Novel, *The Chisholm Trail* by Chase

This epic Western about the battle for authority on a cattle drive is virtually *Mutiny on the Chisholm Trail*, with Wayne as Captain Bligh and Clift as Mr. Christian. Beautifully filmed and acted, it has a tendency to meander like those Western rivers in places but is generally utterly absorbing.

Tom Dunson . . . . .John Wayne
Matthew Garth . . . . .Montgomery Clift
Tess Millay . . . . .Joanne Dru
Groot Nadine . . . . .Walter Brennan
Fen . . . . .Coleen Gray
Cherry Valance . . . . .John Ireland
Buster McGee . . . . .Noah Beery Jr.
Mr. Millville . . . . .Harry Carey
Dan Latimer . . . . .Harry Carey Jr.
Quo . . . . .Chief Yowlachie
Simms .Hank Worden
A Quitter . . . . .Tom Tyler
Naylor .Glenn Strange
Dance-hall girl . . . . .Shelley Winters

Quote 'Fill a man full of lead and stick him in the ground and then read on him. Why, when you killed a man, why try to bring the Lord in as a partner on the job?' • 'You shoulda let 'em kill me 'cause I'm gonna kill you. I'll catch up with you. I don't know when, but I'll catch up . Every time you turn around, expect to see me. Because one time you'll turn around and I'll be there. And I'll kill you, Matt.' • 'There's quitters to be buried.'

Psst! Hawks was hoping to get Gary Cooper for the lead and Cary Grant for the part that was eventually played by John Ireland • Ireland, who got on badly with Hawks and had his part cut to ribbons as a result, married Dru after filming finished • This was Montgomery Clift's

second film • Much against Brennan's better judgement, Hawks persuaded him to play the part with his false teeth out. After this, it was hard to get him to keep them in • More than 5,000 head of cattle were used, costing $10 per head per day. Some of them had to have their faces painted • The cattle stampede involved thousands of head of cattle being scared by wranglers off camera into running towards the stuntmen, who could then appear to be trampled underneath. Although the film in the 15 cameras recording the scene over 10 days were under-cranked, so that the animals would appear to be running faster when it was played back at normal speed, seven of the stuntmen were still injured • Howard Hughes believed that the fight between Wayne and Clift was stolen from his 1943 movie *The Outlaw* and sued Hawks, although he later dropped the matter after Wayne intervened • John Ford said to Hawks about Wayne: 'I never knew the big son of a bitch could act.' • Look out for Shelley Winters in the dance hall.

The Red Shoes

★★ 1948 133min c.

Director: Michael Powell & Emeric Pressburger
Screenplay: Michael Powell & Emeric Pressburger
Source: Fairy tale by Hans Christian Anderson

Ballet lovers adore this tragic Powell and Pressburger tale of a ballerina unable to choose between ballet and love. Although, as in most P&P movies, it makes wonderful use of colour and contains some great ballet sequences, the story itself is unworthy of the talent behind it being, frankly, downright dull. Although it is undoubtedly the best movie there has been on ballet, there haven't been that many.

Boris Lermontov . . . . .Anton Walbrook
Victoria Page . . . . .Moira Shearer
Julian Craster . . . . .Marius Goring
Grischa Ljubov . . . . .Leonide Massine
Ivan Boleslawsky . . . . .Robert Helpmann
Sergei Ratov . . . . .Albert Basserman
Livingstone Montague . . . . .Esmond Knight

OOPS! As the students run up the steps of the Royal Opera House to get to the gods, the wall shakes.

Psst! Ten years earlier, the script had been commissioned by Alexander Korda for his wife Merle Oberon to star in, the plan being to bring in a double for the dancing sequences. But

Powell and Pressburger bought the script back off him • Shearer was a ballerina with Sadler's Wells at the time • The movie was the top box office earner in America in 1948, beating *Red River*, *The Paleface*, *The Three Musketeers* and *Johnny Belinda*.

La Règle du Jeu
SEE: Rules of the Game

The Remarkable Mr. Kipps
SEE: Kipps

Rembrandt
★★★ 1936 84min c.

Director: Alexander Korda
Screenplay: Lajos Biro, June Head & Carl Zuckmayer

A staggeringly beautiful look at the latter half of the life of the great artist. With relatively little in the way of story, this is much more of a mood piece. While Laughton is splendid as the great man, the biggest applause must go to Alexander Korda's brother Vincent who designed such amazing sets that you believe you are looking at the living versions of Rembrandt's paintings.

Rembrandt van Rijn . . . . .Charles Laughton
Geertje Dirx . . . . .Gertrude Lawrence
Hendrickje Stoffels . . . . .Elsa Lanchester
Fabrizius . . . . .Edward Chapman
Banning Cocq . . . . .Walter Hudd
Beggar Saul . . . . .Roger Livesey
Ludwig . . . . .Raymond Huntley
Baron Leivens . . . . .Marius Goring
Gavaert Flink . . . . .John Clements

Psst! Unlike Alexander Korda's earlier biopic, *The Private Life of Henry VIII*, the public stayed away from this one • Korda, himself an art collector, offered free admission to anyone who could prove that they owned a genuine Rembrandt.

Repo Man
★★ 1984 92min c.

Director: Alex Cox
Screenplay: Alex Cox

Another of those independent movies whose reputation far exceeds what we get. Estevez gets involved in the car repossession business with Stanton. There's a man with something malevolent glowing in his car boot, the odd car chase and some sort of government conspiracy. Whenever Cox – that irritating man who used to put our backs up before *Moviedrome* films – runs out of ideas, he throws a new genre in. The sort of disjointed film that gives 'cult' a bad name.

Bud . . . . .Harry Dean Stanton
Otto .Emilio Estevez
Miller . . . . .Tracey Walter
Leila . . . . .Olivia Barash
Lite . . . . .Sy Richardson

Psst! The film is distinctive for having credits that scroll down instead of upwards, a nod to the 1955 *Kiss Me Deadly* • The characters are mainly named after beers • After the producers failed to get any product placement money, they simply labelled everything generically, with names like 'Food', 'Beer', etc.

Repulsion
★★★ 1965 105min b/w

Director: Roman Polanski
Screenplay: Roman Polanski & Gérard Brach

Roman Polanski's first English-language film (and it sometimes shows on the soundtrack) is still a very vivid journey into a deranged mind. Catherine Deneuve is left alone in a Kensington flat, has horrific hallucinations and gives her few visitors a really hard time. It's not easy viewing, but it shows that not all of 60s London was swinging.

Carol . . . . .Catherine Deneuve
Michael .Ian Hendry
Colin .John Fraser
Landlord . . . . .Patrick Wymark
Helen . . . . .Yvonne Furneaux
Miss Balch . . . . .Renée Houston
Bridget . . . . .Helen Fraser
Mme. Denise . . . . .Valerie Taylor
John . . . . .James Villiers
Spoons player . . . . .Roman Polanski

Psst! The gore was made by mixing Nescafé with cochineal and firing it out of a bicycle pump • Polanski appears in a cameo as a spoons player • Polanski is proud of the fact that he is the first film-maker to have included the sound of a woman's orgasm in a British movie.

Deneuve hears it through the wall. He believes he got away with it because the film was considered to be artistic • The scene was particularly poignant to Deneuve because Polanski had insisted that, in order to play her part properly, she must have been celibate for some time. He arranged her accomodation in London and ensured that it was impossible for anyone of the opposite sex to be left alone with her.

Reservoir Dogs
★★★★ 1992 105min c.

Director: Quentin Tarantino
Screenplay: Quentin Tarantino

Startlingly good debut by writer-director Tarantino, depicting in real time the aftermath of a bungled jewel robbery. Be warned that one scene is horrifically violent. But the acting and dialogue fairly fizz with wit and energy. If only film-makers didn't forget how to make tight little thrillers like this once they're given big bucks to spend.

Mr. White	Harvey Keitel
Mr. Orange	Tim Roth
Nice Guy Eddie	Chris Penn
Mr. Pink	Steve Buscemi
Joe Cabot	Lawrence Tierney
Mr. Blonde	Michael Madsen
Mr. Brown	Quentin Tarantino
Mr. Blue	Eddie Bunker

Blurb Let's Get To Work.

Quote 'Somebody's shoved a red-hot poker up our ass and I want to know whose name is on the handle.'

Psst! Tarantino was working as a video-store manager when he wrote the script. To add to his credibility, he claimed to have acted in Jean-Luc Godard's *King Lear*, on the pretty safe assumption that no-one in Hollywood would actually have seen it • Although prepared to shoot it in black and white with his mates as the actors, a script got to Harvey Keitel, who loved it so much he helped Tarantino raise money • Eddie Bunker, playing Mr. Blue, was at 17 the youngest prisoner in San Quentin, serving several sentences over the years for forgery and armed robbery before turning to writing and acting • Madsen's role as the psycho was so convincing that his sister Virginia was subsequently able to ward off unwanted advances by simply mentioning who her

brother was • James Woods was several times offered a part, but his agent never mentioned it to him as the money was less than he would usually receive. When Woods later met Tarantino and heard about it, he changed his agent. It is thought he was offered Roth's part • Roth had a hard time with his dialogue teacher. At his suggestion, it is her he gets to shoot in the movie • There has been much discussion among film buffs, particularly those who wear anoraks, about who could possibly have shot Nice Guy Eddie. Like the issue of the replicants in *Blade Runner*, there is no answer to this conundrum. Should anyone try to get you into conversation on the subject, you should make your excuses and leave immediately • This wasn't the first crime movie where the principals used colours for names, as those who remember the wonderful *The Taking of Pelham, One, Two, Three* will recall • I have my own theory about the inspiration of the opening scene. A café, guys in suits talking, 'Time for work, boys', off to do a robbery. Pretty conclusive, eh? The movie: *Nuns on the Run*. I rest my case.

Return of the Jedi
★★★ 1983 133min c.

Director: Richard Marquand
Screenplay: Lawrence Kasdan & George Lucas

A near-clone of *Star Wars*, this third in the series has some great effects, Vader building an unbeatable new Death Star (ha!), Luke going off to play with daddy and Leia getting some unwanted sexual harrassment. But it also has Yoda and the Ewoks and some pretty icky sentimental stuff along the way. That's not to say it's not great entertainment. It's just not quite as good as the first.

Luke Skywalker	Mark Hamill
Han Solo	Harrison Ford
Princess Leia	Carrie Fisher
Lando Calrissian	Billy Dee Williams
Yoda	Frank Oz
C-3PO	Anthony Daniels
Chewbacca	Peter Mayhew
Anakin Skywalker	Sebastian Shaw
Emperor	Ian McDiarmid
Darth Vader	David Prowse
Darth Vader's voice	James Earl Jones
Ben Obi-Wan Kenobi	Alec Guinness
R2-D2	Kenny Baker

Quote 'I'm glad I did it. I'm glad I did all three of them. But I'm glad I don't have to do any more.' [Harrison Ford]

OOPS! During one of the battle scenes, it looks as if a shoe is passing the Falcon's window in space. Members of the special effects team have claimed since that they snuck in a sneaker, as it were • When Jabba the Hutt drops the dancer into the pit, she loses her top.

Psst! Even after some of the posters were printed, it was still called *Revenge of the Jedi*, possibly to mislead merchandising pirates. Then they changed the title, deciding that noble Jedi didn't go in for revenge. Those few posters which were printed are now worth quite a few bob • Mark Hamill was once the voice of *Flipper* and of Jeannie in the *I Dream of Jeannie* cartoon TV series • In theory this is the third of the middle of the middle of three trilogies, with *Star Wars* said to be number four. George Lucas is now working on the next three *Star Wars* films, with the first expected in 1998 • There are those who reckon they can spot bits of the San Francisco skyline in the uncompleted Death Star.

Reversal of Fortune
★★★ 1990 111min c.

Director: Barbet Schroeder
Screenplay: Nicholas Kazan
Source: Book by Alan Dershowitz

The comatose Sunny von Bulow reflects on her insulin overdose and the case for murder brought against her husband. This brilliantly original approach to the stuff of TV docudramas, pits European decadence against American naivety. A devastating exposé of the seductions and corruptions of the ultra-rich, with the show stolen by Irons as the charming, enigmatic Claus.

Sunny Von Bulow . . . . .Glenn Close
Claus Von Bulow . . . . .Jeremy Irons
Alan Dershowitz . . . . .Ron Silver
Sarah . . . . .Annabella Sciorra
Maria . . . . .Uta Hagen
David Marriott . . . . .Fisher Stevens
Peter Macintosh . . . . .Jack Gilpin
Andrea Reynolds . . . . .Christine Baranski

Oscars Jeremy Irons

Showing The Crimson Pirate.

OOPS! The first time we see Irons in the courtroom, there's a boom mike visible.

Rififi
★★★ 1955 117min b/w

Director: Jules Dassin
Screenplay: Jules Dassin, René Wheeler & Auguste le Breton
Source: Novel by le Breton

This French classic is the granddaddy of all heist movies. You would think that after 40 years, the jewel robbery itself would seem passé, especially as it has been imitated so many times. Not a bit of it. It lasts almost half an hour, is carried out in complete silence and is still incredibly tense. Perhaps the rest of the movie doesn't seem quite so vivid and exciting now but it still stands head and shoulders over most of its rivals.

Tony le Stephanois . . . . .Jean Servais
Jo le Suedois . . . . .Carl Mohner
Mario . . . . .Robert Manuel
Mado .Marie Sabouret
Cesar . . . . .Jules Dassin
Viviane .Magali Noel

Quote 'I sometimes ask myself whether so much of the film is silent because of my own lack of French.' [Dassin]

Psst! Writer-director Dassin, who appears as Cesar under the name of Perlo Vita, was an American who chose go to France after being blacklisted as a suspected Communist • The title is French vernacular for 'trouble'.

The Right Stuff
★★★ 1983 193min c.

Director: Philip Kaufman
Screenplay: Philip Kaufman
Source: Book by Tom Wolfe

Long but often exhilarating account of the early days of America's space programme, largely centred around the story of test pilot Chuck Yeager. Based on the book by Tom Wolfe, it's nothing like the straightforward documentary you would expect, but has some sharp and funny satire mixed in with the exciting aerial footage. Despite its length, *The Right Stuff* is just that.

Chuck Yeager . . . . .Sam Shepard
Glennis Yeager . . . . .Barbara Hershey
Alan Shepard . . . . .Scott Glenn
John Glenn . . . . .Ed Harris
Gordon Cooper . . . . .Dennis Quaid

314

Gus Grissom	Fred Ward
Pancho Barnes	Kim Stanley
Betty Grissom	Veronica Cartwright

Also: Pamela Reed, Scott Paulin, Charles Frank, Lance Henriksen, Donald Moffat, Peggy Davis, Jeff Goldblum

Quote 'Our Germans are better than their Germans.' • 'Hey, Ridley. You got any Beemans?' • 'I wanted to play Gordon Cooper in *the Right Stuff* a year before they even thought about the movie. I mean, *he fell asleep on the launch pad!* [Dennis Quaid]

Psst! Brigadier General Chuck Yeager, played in the film by Sam Shepard, has a small part as Fred, the barman • A stuntman was killed filming the scene where an ejecting pilot doesn't pull his rip-cord in time • The space suit material was left over from some silver costumes that had been made for Cher! • The original NASA mould was used to construct a Mercury rocket for the movie.

Rio Bravo
★★ 1959 141min c.

Director: Howard Hawks
Screenplay: Jules Furthman & Leigh Brackett
Source: Story by Barbara Hawks McCampbell

Intended by Wayne and Hawks to counteract the isolated pessimism of *High Noon*, this is for some one of the great westerns of all time. A sheriff rounds up a motley crew to defend a jail from siege, and while they wait they sort out their individual problems. Unfortunately, the likeable Angie Dickinson can't hack it as a Hawksian heroine, the obligatory singalongs with Ricky Nelson and Dean Martin become very tiresome, and the whole thing ambles on for far too long. Hawks obviously didn't think so, as his later films *El Dorado* and *Rio Lobo* are both pretty similar to this. However, John Carpenter's *Assault on Precinct 13* is much better than all of them.

John T. Chance	John Wayne
Dude	Dean Martin
Colorado Ryan	Ricky Nelson
Feathers	Angie Dickinson
Stumpy	Walter Brennan
Pat Wheeler	Ward Bond
Nathan Burdette	John Russell
Carlos	Pedro Gonzalez-Gonzalez
Joe Burdette	Claude Akins
Matt Harris	Bob Steele
Harold	Harry Carey Jr.

Quote '"Sorry" don't get it done, Dude.' • 'Well, if I'm gonna get shot at, I might as well get paid for it. How do I get a badge?'

Psst! Hawks had, like John Wayne, detested *High Noon*: 'I didn't think a good sheriff was going to go running around town like a chicken with his head off asking for help, and finally his Quaker wife had to save him.' • It was Howard Hawks' daughter, Barbara Hawks McCampbell, who came up with the basic story • Most scenes had to be filmed in one take where possible because the set was invaded by a plague of grasshoppers. They were attracted by the lights and so Hawks tried to get each shot in the camera before too many of the insects arrived and fried themselves.

Riot in Cell Block 11
★★★ 1954 80min c.

Director: Don Siegel
Screenplay: Richard Collins

Despite its small budget, this realistic drama of prisoners seizing hostages among the guards and barricading themselves in, still packs a pretty good punch. In addition to the powerful drama, it makes a reasonably good job of its plea for penal reform.

Dunn	Neville Brand
The Warden	Emile Meyer
Haskell	Frank Faylen
Carnie	Leo Gordon
The Colonel	Robert Osterloh
Reporter	Don Keefer
Snader	Whit Bissell
Ambrose	Robert Burton
Delmar	Roy Glenn
Russell	Jonathan Hale
Reporter	William Schallert

Risky Business
★★ 1983 98min c.

Director: Paul Brickman
Screenplay: Paul Brickman

Every parent's nightmare brought to life. As soon as young puppy Cruise's folks go away, he starts dallying with delightful hooker De Mornay, only to find things going seriously wrong when she pushes him into a money-making scheme. There are some things Yellow Pages *can't* put right before your parents get home. Despite the film's high reputation, it's only slightly better than the average 'first time' teen-sex comedy. It's interesting to see two stars just starting out, but it's a crime it took De Mornay almost another 10 years to make it after this. Worth checking out that famous subway ride, though.

Joel Goodsen	Tom Cruise
Lana	Rebecca De Mornay
Guido	Joe Pantoliano
Rutherford	Richard Masur
Barry	Bronson Pinchot
Miles	Curtis Armstrong
Joel's Father	Nicholas Pryor
Joel's Mother	Janet Carroll

OOPS! Keep your eye on the van taking away the furniture from the house and watch the furniture vanish.

Psst! The film originally ended with Cruise losing De Mornay and failing to get into college. But when only 38% of a test audience said they 'would recommend' the movie to friends, the studio hurriedly filmed two extra minutes. This time 70% said they 'would recommend' the film • Cruise dieted to lose a stone in a month for the movie, then gave up on exercise to put on 'a little layer of baby fat.' • He also did Ray-Ban something of a favour. Their Wayfarers, designed in the early 50s, were shifting only 18,000 a year until *Risky Business*. The following year 360,000 were sold. It's now up to four million a year. *Top Gun* had the same effect with another Ray-Ban model. The company now pays to put its glasses in a couple of hundred movies and TV shows each year.

Road to Morocco
★★★ 1942 83min b/w

Director: David Butler
Screenplay: Frank Butler & Don Hartman

This third in the *Road* series is the best of all. The surprising thing is how the movies, starring the cowardly and lecherous Hope, and the untrustworthy and more successfully lecherous Crosby, have worn so well. The quick-fire humour in these films still seems surprisingly zany, with plenty of asides to the camera, in-jokes and even, in this one, a talking camel. Among the others in the series, *Rio* and the exceptionally zany *Utopia* are the best, with *Hong Kong*, *Bali*, *Singapore* and *Zanzibar* completing the set.

Jeff Peters	Bing Crosby
Oliver 'Turkey' Jackson	Bob Hope
Princess Shalmar	Dorothy Lamour
Sheikh Kasim	Anthony Quinn
Mihirmah	Dona Drake
Hyder Khan	Vladimir Sokoloff
Oso Bucco	Andrew Tombes
Hand maiden	Yvonne De Carlo

Quote 'It's the old, old story. Boy meets girl, Romeo and Juliet, Minneapolis and St. Paul.'
• 'This is the screwiest picture I was ever in.' [The camel]

Psst! The original choice for the role was George Burns and Gracie Allen. They turned it down and Fred MacMurray and Jack Oakie were then considered before Hope and Crosby were approached. Bob and Bing had already been paired on stage and had appeared on each other's radio shows. They were conveniently both under contract to Paramount • Both stars had teams of gag writers working for them and the script tended only to be a rough guide to what Bing or Bob might say. The movie's writers, Butler and Hartman, were prone to shout out 'Bingo' whenever they heard one of the lines they'd penned • Yvonne de Carlo, later to star in the TV sitcom *The Munsters*, can be seen as a hand maiden • The *Road* movies made over $50m in total, the greatest for any film series until James Bond came along.

The Road Warrior
SEE: **Mad Max 2**

The Roaring Twenties
★★★ 1939 104min b/w

Director: Raoul Walsh & Anatole Litvak
Screenplay: Jerry Wald, Richard Macaulay & Robert Rossen
Source: Story by Mark Hellinger

A World War I veteran gets involved in bootlegging. But one of his wartime buddies doesn't prove too trustworthy. Although there are a few tiresome patches, this has probably worn better than any of the other 30s gangster pics, thanks in large part to Walsh's lightning direction and the playing of Cagney as the decent gangster and Bogart as the villain with no redeeming features at all.

Eddie Bartlett	James Cagney
George Hally	Humphrey Bogart

Jean Sherman	.Priscilla Lane
Lloyd Hart	.Jeffrey Lynn
Panama Smith	.Gladys George
Danny Green	.Frank McHugh
Nick Brown	.Paul Kelly
Mrs. Sherman	.Elizabeth Risdon
Sgt. Pete Jones	.Joe Sawyer
Lefty	.Abner Biberman
Drunk	.Jack Norton

Quote 'What was his business?' – 'He used to be a big shot.' [Last line]

OOPS! As Bogart talks to Cagney at one point, the brush he's using is in his right hand, but it jumps to his left hand in the next shot.

Psst! This film's original title was *The World Moves On* • James Cagney's character is based on the New York gangster Larry Fay, who was the driving force behind the career of singer Texas Guinan. *The Great Gatsby* was also based on Fay • After almost a decade of playing gangsters, Cagney didn't play another one until *White Heat*, 10 years later • The church steps in the last scene were the same as those used in *Little Caesar* • In Russia, the movie was known as *The Fate of a Soldier in America*.

Robin Hood: Prince of Thieves
★★★ 1991 143min c.

Director: Kevin Reynolds
Screenplay: Pen Densham & John Watson

Deservedly the more successful of the two 1991 Robin Hoods. Although it starts sluggishly, once the film-makers forget about Political Correctness, it all becomes rollicking good fun, full of spectacle and great gags. Costner makes a likeable Hood, although his West Coast of Nottingham accent takes some getting used to. While Costner is the outlaw, it's Rickman who steals the picture as the hysterically funny, yet never less than evil, Sheriff of Nottingham.

Robin of Locksley	.Kevin Costner
Azeem	.Morgan Freeman
Sheriff of Nottingham	.Alan Rickman
Marian	.Mary Elizabeth Mastrantonio
Will Scarlett	.Christian Slater
King Richard	.Sean Connery
Mortianna	.Geraldine McEwan
Friar Tuck	.Michael McShane
Lord Locksley	.Brian Blessed

Quote 'Cancel the kitchen scraps for lepers and orphans. No more merciful beheadings. And call off Christmas.' • 'You! My room. 10.30 tonight…You! 10.45. And bring a friend.'

OOPS! Some say the use of gunpowder and a telescope wouldn't have been possible in the 12th century. My old history professor claims it's feasible a Moor might have known about these, if a little unlikely • However, printing definitely wasn't invented for another 200 years, so where do the 'Wanted' posters come from? • The Sheriff's codpiece is well ahead of its time, as is his use of '10.30' to make assignations. Clocks didn't exist then • Even in the 12th century, Hadrian's Wall wasn't anywhere near Nottingham, yet they're on it just before they arrive.

Psst! That isn't Costner's bottom in the bathing scene. A body double was used, not apparently because Costner was shy, but because the water was so cold! • Sean Connery was paid an estimated $250,000 to $500,000 for his cameo turn, not a bad return for one day's work and one minute's screen time. He donated his fee to charity • Several scenes with Rickman were cut when it seemed he was in danger of running away with the movie. Amongst the bits lost is the revelation that the Sheriff is the witch's son • The video has 30 further seconds gone, particularly noticeable when the Sheriff is trying to consummate his 'marriage'. The chopping off of a prisoner's hand is also cut, as is the hanging of the boy, while priceless dialogue like 'I've never seen the breasts of a noblewoman' and 'Bugger me' have gone • Look out for Jack Wild, star of the film musical *Oliver* as Much, one of Robin's men.

Robocop
★★★ 1987 103min c.

Director: Paul Verhoeven
Screenplay: Edward Neumeier & Michael Miner

Weller's the cop in ultra-violent future Detroit killed in the line of duty. Soon he's back as a rebuilt super-cyborg, the perfect policeman. Then his human memory returns and he realises that company OCP isn't such a philanthropic employer after all. Great action-sci-fi that's more stylish, violent and grittier than most of its ilk, yet still has plenty of wit to dispense. Such a shame that the effects used to animate the robot ED209 have dated so quickly.

Murphy/RoboCop ....Peter Weller
Lewis ....Nancy Allen
Jones ....Ronny Cox
Clarence Boddiker ....Kurtwood Smith
Morton ....Miguel Ferrer
Sgt. Reed ....Robert DoQui
The Old Man ....Dan O'Herlihy

Blurb Part Man. Part Machine. All Cop. The Future Of Law Enforcement.

Quote 'I'd buy that for a dollar!' • 'Your move, creep!'

Psst! The TV anchorwoman who says 'You give us three minutes and we'll give you the world' is Leeza Gibbons, the reporter for the popular American TV show *Entertainment Tonight*. As well as the sequel, she pops up in *Maxie*, *Soapdish* and *The Player* • According to the credits: 'This motion picture is protected under the laws of the United States and other countries and its unauthorized duplication, distribution or exhibition may result in civil liability and criminal prosecution by enforcement droids.' • 36 seconds of violence were cut from the cinema release while a further four seconds, showing how to break into a car, disappeared from the video.

Rock around the Clock
★★ 1956 77min b/w

Director: Fred F. Sears
Screenplay: Robert E. Kent & James B. Gordon

The joint is jumping, cat. The film that brought rock'n'roll to the world is now something of a museum piece, with slang that seems hilarious today. Forget the plot about D.J. Alan Freed discovering the bequiffed one, Bill Haley, and his Comets and revel in the music from them, the Platters and others.

With: Bill Haley and the Comets, The Platters, Tony Martinez and His Band, Frankie Bell and His Bellboys, Alan Freed

Psst! Amazingly, the film produced riotous behavour in cinemas in several countries. In Britain, over a thousand Teddy Boys went on the rampage after seeing it. The movie was subject to local bans in some places in the UK • The producer must have been delighted. It was actually his intention from the start to replicate in the cinema the outrageous behaviour displayed by audiences at some rock concerts.

Rocky
★★★★ 1976 119min c.

Director: John G. Avildsen
Screenplay: Sylvester Stallone

Although the plot could belong to any one of a hundred boxing movies, this tale of the underdog boxer getting a shot at the big one sweeps you up and carries you along with it until you're punching the air as the big boys are punching each other. With a charming accompanying love story and a fair helping of sentiment, this is an incredibly uplifting film, the sort of movie that makes you think an individual really can do anything, if only they put their mind to it. Although Rocky took his punches, he wouldn't lie down. There were four sequels, of which Rocky III was the only one of any interest.

Rocky Balboa ....Sylvester Stallone
Adrian ....Talia Shire
Mickey....................Burgess Meredith
Paulie ....Burt Young
Apollo Creed ....Carl Weathers
Miles Jergens ....Thayer David
Tom Gazzo ....Joe Spinell
Timekeeper ....Frank Stallone
Apollo's trainer ....Tony Burton

Oscars Best Picture, Best Director

Quote 'Apollo Creed meets The Italian Stallion. Sounds like a damn monster movie.'

Psst! The story behind the film is one of the nicest true Hollywood fairy tales of all. The acting career of one-time beautician, girl's gym instructor and lion cage cleaner Stallone was going nowhere. He had had 32 script reject when he wrote this one in three-and-a-half days. Even though he was down to his last $100 and his wife was pregnant, he turned down $75,000 for it because he wanted to star in it himself. He was still holding out at $265,000 when they finally agreed to let him have the part. The film grossed $55m and won the Best Picture Oscar • Stallone was nominated both for Best Actor Oscar and for the best script. Only Charles Chaplin and Orson Welles had managed the same feat • The studio initially wanted to cast James Caan or Burt Reynolds in the lead • The fight scenes were filmed by three cameras, one of which was a hand-held Steadicam. It was the first time it had been used in a movie although it didn't really make its presence felt until *The Shining* • Rocky's dog was Stallone's own, a bull mastiff called Butkus • Stallone's father Frank plays a timekeeper while brother Frank Jr. is a street singer • The story was inspired by Stallone watching the fight between part-time New Jersey boxer Chuck Wepner and Muhammad Ali. Although not expected to last long after the opening bell, the fight went 15 rounds.

The Rocky Horror Picture Show

★★ 1975 100min c.

Director: Jim Sharman
Screenplay: Jim Sharman & Richard O'Brien
Source: Stage musical by O'Brien

A conventional, strait-laced couple seek help in the traditional old dark house. But this one's full of rather kinky, cross-dressing Transylvanian wackos and weirdos. Brilliant though it is on stage, the movie is rather tame and anaemic, stuck together with glue and Sellotape rather than being welded into a coherent whole. Best to see it live or go to a late night screening where everyone else will dress up and shout out the dialogue.

Dr. Frank N. Further . . . . .Tim Curry
Janet Weiss . . . . .Susan Sarandon
Brad Majors . . . . .Barry Bostwick
Riff Raff . . . . .Richard O'Brien
Magenta .Patricia Quinn
Columbia .Nell Campbell
Dr. Everett Scott . . . . .Jonathan Adams
Rocky . . . . .Peter Hinwood
Eddie . . . . .Meat Loaf
Criminologist . . . . .Charles Gray
Transylvanian . . . . .Christopher Biggins
Transylvanian . . . . .Gaye Brown
Transylvanian . . . . .Koo Stark

Quote 'It thrills me that one day my grandchildren may see their grandmother in her little half-slip and bra – seducing a monster.' [Sarandon]

OOPS! Although we're told the events unfolding take place one November evening, on the car radio Nixon is announcing his resignation, something that happened in August. What a shame, when the film otherwise has such a firm grip on reality • There's a trail of blood leading into the freezer, but Meat Loaf doesn't get the pick until he's inside the freezer • Adams is carried out of the castle by Sarandon and Bostwick. But somehow the wheelchair is outside too to be crushed in the next scene.

Psst! After terrible reviews and initially poor business, the film was about to be written off

as a tax loss, when cinema owners reported that the same people were coming back for performance after performance. As the cult spread, so more prints were minted and the film became a popular bill for midnight screenings and student-patronised cinemas • Although cinemas don't mind audiences turning up in stockings and suspenders, many now have a ban on people bringing in the rice that is part of the ritual, to throw during the wedding scene • Meat Loaf has a cameo as the ill-fated Eddie, while Koo Stark and Christopher Biggins are in there as well.

Roger & Me

★★★★ 1989 91min c.

Director: Michael Moore
Screenplay: Michael Moore

If you see only one documentary in your life, make it this one. Moore's film is about the deadly effect on Flint, Michigan, of the closure of General Motors' plant there. Moore decides to track down GM's boss Roger Smith and ask him a few pertinent questions. The indifference to the personal tragedies by company officials is shocking, but what could have been so dull turns out instead to be lively and frequently hysterically funny. Much of the pleasure comes from knowing that this documentary was so startlingly successful that it will take GM years to recover from the public relations disaster.

With: The citizens of Flint, Michigan

Quote 'I was having a hard time finding my business card because I don't have any business cards. So I gave Mr. Slaughter my discount pass to Chucky Cheese.'

Psst! The one town in America where you couldn't see *Roger & Me* was Flint, Michigan. The cinema had closed down! • Moore sold his home and most of his possessions to finance the film. He ran bingo games in Flint to raise cash and even collected empty drinks bottles for the refundable deposits! His phone was disconnected for non-payment shortly after completion.

Romancing the Stone

★★★ 1984 105min c.

Director: Robert Zemeckis
Screenplay: Diane Thomas

319

Shy romantic novelist Turner travels to Colombia when her sister's in trouble, falling into big doo-doo herself and finding only the reluctant Douglas to help her. A splendid tongue-in-cheek old-fashioned adventure, with lots of gags, plenty of top-notch action and superb hate-each-other chemistry between the two stars. DeVito also scores as a slimy villain. The next year's sequel, *Jewel of the Nile*, wasn't a patch on this.

Jack Colton	Michael Douglas
Joan Wilder	Kathleen Turner
Ralph	Danny DeVito
Ira	Zack Norman
Juan	Alfonso Arau
Zolo	Manuel Ojeda

OOPS! Although Douglas gives Turner a pretty necklace, what she takes in the next shot is completely different and looks rather crummy • Douglas must be putting on weight. As he swings on a rope into a rockface, it moves.

Roman Holiday

★★★ 1953 119min b/w

Director: William Wyler
Screenplay: Ian McLellan Hunter, John Dighton & Dalton Trumbo

A cossetted princess on a visit to Rome cuts loose and goes on the town, falling in love with the American journalist who thinks he's got the scoop of his career. It's a pity that Wyler got quite so excited by being able to film in Rome, for there's rather too much of the city and too little of the stars. However, Hepburn is at her most delightful and the romance is deftly handled, making the movie still seem one of the great charmers even today.

Joe Bradley	Gregory Peck
Princess Anne	Audrey Hepburn
Irving Radovich	Eddie Albert
Mr. Hennessy	Hartley Power
Ambassador	Harcourt Williams
Countess Vereberg	Margaret Rawlings
Gen. Provno	Tullio Carminati
Hennessy's secretary	Laura Solari

Oscars Audrey Hepburn, Best Original Story

Quote 'Will you help me get undressed, please?' • 'This is very unusual. I've never been alone with a man before – even with my dress on. With my dress off, it's *most* unusual.'

Psst! The film was nominated for 10 Oscars and won three • The real author of the film is believed to have been the blacklisted writer Dalton Trumbo, but his name didn't appear on the credits. Hunter fronted for him, passing the money to Trumbo. When the story won the Oscar, Hunter collected it and kept it in his attic • Wyler wanted desperately to film on location but it was then still relatively rare to pop across to Europe for a movie. He was told by the studio that he could only make the film in colour if he stayed in Hollywood. He opted for pasta and black and white • Filming was held up at the outset when the Italian authorities cut up rough about the way that Italians were treated as jokes in the movie • Hepburn is amazingly popular in Japan where this was the most popular video ever, selling 370,000. It was then beaten by *Fantasia*, which sold over a million.

La Ronde

★★★ 1950 97min b/w

Director: Max Ophuls
Screenplay: Jacques Natanson & Max Ophuls
Source: Play, *Reigen* by Arthur Schnitzler

Although nothing like as salacious as it must have seemed at the time, this French comedy is still a charming, witty and surprisingly erotic rendition of the famous play. The plot, essentially, is that A bonks B, who bonks C, who bonks D and so and so on until we get back to A again, showing us the circuitry of love.

Destiny, Master of Ceremonies	Anton Walbrook
Leocadie, a prostitute	Simone Signoret
Marie, a chambermaid	Simone Simon
Robert, a poet	Jean-Louis Barrault
Franz, a soldier	Serge Reggiani
Albert, a young man	Daniel Gélin

Psst! The film was considered so immoral by the New York State censorship board that it wasn't possible to see it in America for four years after it was first released.

Room at the Top

★★★ 1958 117min b/w

Director: Jack Clayton
Screenplay: Neil Paterson
Source: Novel by John Braine

A single-minded young man determines to fight his way up from his working-class roots by whatever means he can. The sexual side of this kitchen-sink drama, which so scandalised and excited audiences at the time, now naturally seems rather tame. But ambitious characters like Lampton haven't died out and so that side of the film still holds the attention, as does the wonderful Signoret as the older woman sacrificed to Lampton's ladder-climbing. The 1965 sequel, *Life at the Top*, wasn't a patch on this, nor was the 1975 *Man at the Top*.

Joe Lampton	Laurence Harvey
Alice Aisgill	Simone Signoret
Susan Brown	Heather Sears
Mr. Brown	Donald Wolfit
Mrs. Brown	Ambrosine Phillpotts
Charles Soames	Donald Huston
Mr. Hoylake	Raymond Huntley
Jack Wales	John Westbrook
George Aisgill	Allan Cuthbertson
Elspeth	Hermione Baddeley
June Samson	Mary Peach
Aunt	Beatrice Varley
Mayoress	Everley Gregg
Joan	Wendy Craig
Gertrude	Miriam Karlin
Cyril	Ian Hendry
Meg	Prunella Scales

Oscars Simone Signoret

Quote 'The first British film in which a man and a woman went to bed without one of them having one foot on the floor.' [Harvey]

Psst! There can't be many British films set in Bradford and banned in Australia for their sexual explicitness. This one managed it and was attacked by the Catholic Legion of Decency in the USA, as well as by some moralists in Britain • Although married, Harvey had an affair during filming, and briefly afterwards, with the more mature Baddeley • For the scene in which he gets thrown into the canal, Harvey didn't use a double. Although it was filmed in the early hours of the morning, the police were called by several worried locals, unaware that a film was being made.

A Room With a View
★★★★ 1986 115min c.

Director: James Ivory
Screenplay: Ruth Prawer Jhabvala
Source: Novel by E.M. Forster

The Merchant-Ivory team and E.M. Forster were made for each other. Set in Italy in 1907, everyone is scandalised when young Bonham Carter gets a kiss from Sands and bags are packed. This beautifully photographed and acted comedy of manners may be predictable, but it's also utterly delightful. There are times when it seems a pity that practically the only decent British films are costume dramas, but at least we do do them awfully, awfully well.

Charlotte Bartlett	Maggie Smith
Lucy Honeychurch	Helena Bonham Carter
Mr. Emerson	Denholm Elliott
George Emerson	Julian Sands
Cecil Vyse	Daniel Day-Lewis
Reverend Beebe	Simon Callow
Miss Lavish	Judi Dench
Freddy Honeychurch	Rupert Graves

Rope
★★★ 1948 80min c.

Director: Alfred Hitchcock
Screenplay: Arthur Laurents & Hume Cronyn
Source: Play, *Rope's End* by Patrick Hamilton

Two college students murder a friend and then hold a cocktail party around the chest where they've stashed the corpse. Although very tastless in 1948, this artificial jet-black comedy looks very modern in the era of Tarantino, with the audience's initial fascination for the killers being morally confronted by an increasingly suspicious James Stewart. Cedric Hardwicke movingly portrays the bewildered father of the murdered student and Joan Chandler is sparky as a rare brunette Hitchockian leading lady.

Rupert Cadell	James Stewart
Shaw Brandon	John Dall
Philip	Farley Granger
Janet Walker	Joan Chandler
Mr. Kentley	Cedric Hardwicke
Mrs. Atwater	Constance Collier
Mrs. Wilson, governess	Edith Evanson
Kenneth Lawrence	Douglas Dick

Quote 'Nobody commits murder just for the experience of committing it. Nobody except us.' • 'Who's the cat and who's the mouse?' • 'I undertook *Rope* as a stunt.' [Hitchcock]

OOPS! Can anyone spot whether there's actually a bedroom in this flat?

Psst! Hitchcock appears in the skyline ad for Reduco in a before and after silhouette • Hitchcock had tried to get Cary Grant for Stewart's part, but he was not free • Hitch wanted the film to look as if it was made in one continuous take. In fact, because of the limited length of film reels, about every 10 minutes there's a cut, noticable by somebody's back or some other dark object filling the screen • The walls to the set were built on rollers so they could be moved away to give the roving camera freedom • The film was out of circulation for years as one of the 'Lost Hitchcocks'. See *Rear Window* • The characters played by Dall and Granger are based on the infamous exploits of wealthy Chicago teenagers Richard Leopold and Nathan Loeb who killed 14-year-old Bobbie Franks in 1924 purely for academic interest • Even though the homosexual aspect to the two main characters was barely hinted at in the film, it was still banned in Chicago, as well as in other towns like Seattle and Memphis.

Rosemary's Baby
★★★ 1968 136min c.

Director: Roman Polanski
Screenplay: Roman Polanski
Source: Novel by Ira Levin

One wonders if Mia Farrow's fondness for adopting other people's children had anything to do with her role here. She sets up home in a stylish Manhattan apartment, but dreams she may be carrying the devil's child. For some reason, the neighbours don't seem to take her fears seriously. Polanski winds up the atmosphere and paranoia in his usual, cunning way as the awful truth emerges. Not a movie to recommend to pregnant mums.

Rosemary Woodhouse ....Mia Farrow
Guy Woodhouse ....John Cassavetes
Minnie Castevet ....Ruth Gordon
Roman Castevet ....Sidney Blackmer
Hutch ....Maurice Evans
Dr. Sapirstein ....Ralph Bellamy
Laura-Louise ....Patsy Kelly
Mr. Nicklas ....Elisha Cook Jr.
Dr. Hill ....Charles Grodin

Oscars Ruth Gordon

Blurb Pray For Rosemary's Baby.

Quote 'Oh, Andy...Andy or Jennie...I'm sorry, my little darling. Forgive me.'

Psst! Jane Fonda was the first choice for Farrow's part • Both Warren Beatty and Robert Redford coveted the lead and Polanski came to wish he hadn't chosen Cassavetes, with whom he disagreed violently throughout filming • The film was produced by William Castle, who was best known for a series of low-budget exploitation movies such as *The Tingler* and the gimmicks he used to promote them. See *Shampoo* • Farrow's husband Frank Sinatra had wanted her to star against him in *The Detective* and hadn't wanted her to make *Rosemary's Baby*. She was actually on set working when Sinatra had her divorce papers delivered • This was Charles Grodin's film debut • The voice of 'Donald Baumgart' is actually Tony Curtis • In Britain, a few seconds were cut from the satanic rape scene • It was only a year after this movie came out, with its theme of people having designs on a young pregnant wife, that Polanski's own pregnant wife, actress Sharon Tate, was murdered by the Manson cult.

Roxanne
★★★ 1987 107min c.

Director: Fred Schepisi
Screenplay: Steve Martin
Source: Play, *Cyrano de Bergerac* by Edmond Rostand

Martin is the big-nosed, big-hearted chief of an incompetent crew of firemen. In this modern version of *Cyrano de Bergerac*, he helps Rossovich woo astronomer Hannah, despite loving her himself. Martin wrote this brilliant romantic comedy, the most satisfying of all his films. It's only a pity about the odd bit of misguided slapstick.

C.D. Bales ....Steve Martin
Roxanne ....Daryl Hannah
Chris ....Rick Rossovich
Dixie ....Shelley Duvall
Chuck ....John Kapelos
Mayor Deebs ....Fred Willard
Dean ....Max Alexander
Andy ....Michael J. Pollard
Jerry ....Damon Wayans

Quote 'My dream, and I hope you don't find this too crazy, is that I would like the people of this community to feel that if, God forbid, there were a fire, calling the Fire Department would actually be a wise thing to do.' • 'Laugh and the world laughs with you. Sneeze and it's "Goodbye Seattle".'

OOPS! After telling 19 nose jokes in the restaurant, Martin asks the diners how many he's done and is told that it's 14. Telling another six, he brings the total to 25. But the challenge was only to tell 20.

Psst! Hannah's penchant for insisting that she always have a career to go with her looks [Interior designer in *Wall Street*, documentary maker for the Smithsonian Institute in *Memoirs of an Invisible Man*, etc.] doesn't disappoint here.

Ruggles of Red Gap

★★ 1935 90min b/w

Director: Leo McCarey
Screenplay: Walter de Leon, Harlan Thompson & Humphrey Pearson
Source: Play & novel by Harry Leon Wilson

Taste in comedy has changed enormously. How else can we explain why this story of the English butler lost in a poker game to a Western rancher seems so stupendously unfunny now? Although some critics still claim it as a classic comedy, it's only really worth watching to see how Laughton handles one of his few comedy roles. It was remade as *Fancy Pants* starring Bob Hope, which now seems the better of the two.

Marmaduke Ruggles	Charles Laughton
Effie Fooud	Mary Boland
Egbert Floud	Charles Ruggles
Mrs. Judson	ZaSu Pitts
Hon. George Van Bassingwell	Roland Young
Nell Kenner	Leila Hyams
Ma Pettingill	Maude Eburne
Charles Belknap-Jackson	Lucien Littlefield
Jeff Tuttle	James Burke
Barfly	Jack Norton

Rules of the Game

★★★★ 1939 110min b/w

Director: Jean Renoir
Screenplay: Jean Renoir & Carl Koch

This sublime French classic examines the aristocracy, class and love over a weekend hunting party at a country estate. One of a kind, it manages with extraordinary success to mix pathos, farce, black comedy and romance into one spellbinding whole. Beautifully filmed and acted, it may not have been a success when released, but is now generally acknowledged, deservedly so, as one of the true classics of cinema. Also known as *La Règle du Jeu*.

Marquis de la Chesnaye	Marcel Dalio
Christine de la Chesnaye	Nora Gregor
André Jurieu	Roland Toutain
Octave	Jean Renoir
Geneviève de Marrast	Mila Parely
Lisette	Paulette Dubost
Schumacher	Gaston Modot
The General	Pierre Magnier

Psst! The film was booed at its premiere in Paris in 1939. A near riot ensued and some people tried burning down the cinema • Although cuts were made in the scenes that caused most objections, it closed after three weeks • It was banned by the French government, then the Vichy authorities and then by the occupying German government • The original negative was destroyed in 1942 in an air raid. Only in 1959 was it restored from different prints to its original length • In the days before animals were given more consideration than humans on film sets, the rabbit-hunting sequence was shot so many times over two months than the local rabbit population was decimated.

Ruthless People

★★★★ 1986 94min c.

Director: Jim Abrahams, David Zucker & Jerry Zucker
Screenplay: Dale Launer

One of the very best comedies of the 80s. Reinhold and Slater kidnap the awful Midler and hold her to ransom. But her still more obnoxious hubbie DeVito had been planning to murder her anyway and has no wish to see her back. Although from the *Airplane* guys, it's more realistic than their other films, with a fiendishly clever plot. But it's still hysterically, manically, blackly and deliciously funny.

Sam Stone	Danny DeVito
Barbara Stone	Bette Midler
Ken Kessler	Judge Reinhold
Sandy Kessler	Helen Slater
Carol	Anita Morris
Earl	Bill Pullman
Police Commissioner	William G. Schilling

Quote 'I'm being marked down? I've been kidnapped by K-Mart!' • 'Let's face it, she's not Mother Teresa. Gandhi would have strangled her.'

OOPS! There's a very obvious boom mike when Morris and Pullman put the video into the machine in the store.

Psst! At one point, writer Launer was told that Madonna was to play Bette Midler's part.

However, even although the plot hinges on it, Madonna was not willing to be seen as a fat person.

Sabrina
★★★ 1954 113min b/w

Director: Billy Wilder
Screenplay: Samuel Taylor & Ernest Lehman
Source: Novel, *Sabrina Fair* by Taylor

It wasn't often that Humphrey Bogart got involved in sophisticated romantic comedies, but he gave it a pretty good thwack here. Of two wealthy brothers, Bogie is the shy, business-like one and Holden the playboy who spurns chauffeur's daughter Hepburn until she arrives back from Paris transformed into a stunning beauty. To stop him wooing her, Bogie pretends he fancies her himself. Although the plot is pretty insubstantial, the script is delightfully witty and Bogart and Hepburn made a charming pair. Remade with Harrison Ford in 1995.

Linus Larrabee . . . . .Humphrey Bogart
Sabrina Fairchild . . . . .Audrey Hepburn
David Larrabee . . . . .William Holden
Thomas Fairchild . . . . .John Williams
Oliver Larrabee . . . . .Walter Hampden
Elizabeth Tyson . . . . .Martha Hyer
Gretchen Van Horn . . . . .Joan Vohs
Baron . . . . .Marcel Dalio
The Professor . . . . .Marcel Hillaire
Maude Larrabee . . . . .Nella Walker
Margaret, the cook . . . . .Marjorie Bennett
Mr. Tyson . . . . .Francis X. Bushman

Quote 'An egg…is a living thing. It has a heart. So when we crack it we must not torment it. We must be merciful and execute it quickly, like with a guillotine.'

Psst! Humphrey Bogart's part was originally offered to Cary Grant • Bogie never seemed happy with it. He argued constantly with Billy Wilder over what was funny, thought William Holden an overripe juvenile but admitted that Audrey Hepburn was 'awright…if you don't mind a dozen takes.' He really wanted to co-star with his wife Lauren Bacall • At one point, the production had to be shut down for a while after a disgruntled Bogart simply walked off the set • Mr. Tyson is played by Francis X. Bushman, the star of silent pictures, whose best-known role was as Messala in *Ben Hur* and who was once known as the most handsome man in the world.

Safety Last
★★★ 1923 70min b/w

Director: Sam Taylor & Fred Newmeyer
Screenplay: Harold Lloyd, Sam Taylor, Tim Whelan & Hal Roach

Although it takes its time getting going, this becomes one of the funniest and most thrilling of all silent films when it culminates in the famous climb up the side of a skyscraper, with Lloyd beset by accidents from all sides. Despite its age, it still has the power to make you catch your breath, while the common man Lloyd's personality has worn far better than Chaplin's over-the-top sentimentality.

The clerk . . . . .Harold Lloyd
The girl . . . . .Mildred Davis
The pal . . . . .Bill Strothers
The law . . . . .Noah Young

Psst! Although Lloyd always maintained that he carried out all his stunts himself, there were elements of cheating involved here. It appears that Lloyd was inspired to make the movie by Bill Strothers, a steeplejack he saw a year earlier making a 14-storey climb, after which he cycled round the top ledge and shinned along a flagpole before standing on his head. Lloyd hired Strothers, planning to use him as a double. Although Lloyd claimed that Strothers broke his leg and so couldn't be used as a double, it is now thought that it is Strothers we see in the long shots. He also plays 'The pal' • After Lloyd's death in 1971 another stunt man, Harvey Parry, claimed that he had also worked on the climb • When Lloyd is seen clinging to the disintegrating clock, there's actually a platform a few feet below him. Advantage was taken of perspective to persuade viewers that the building was in fact on the opposite side of the street, with a big drop below it • Despite all this, Lloyd was actually a very accomplished stuntman, even though he had lost a thumb and forefinger when an explosives effect went wrong. He wore prosthetic fingers and a flesh-coloured glove to disguise the injury.

Salvador
★★★★ 1986 123min c.

Director: Oliver Stone
Screenplay: Richard Boyle & Oliver Stone

Seedy journalist Woods tricks his D.J. friend

Belushi into travelling down to El Salvador for some easy drinks, drugs and women. Instead, they are thrown into the horrors of the Salvadorean revolution. After a scrappy start, Oliver Stone's best movie brilliantly combines a personal and political story with terrifying scenes of a country falling apart. This is also James Woods' finest role yet, energising the true narrative with wit, compassion and his hyper-kinetic drive.

Richard Boyle	James Woods
Dr. Rock	James Belushi
Ambassador Kelly	Michael Murphy
Maria	Elpidia Carrillo
John Cassady	John Savage
Major Max	Tony Plana
Jack Morgan	Colby Chester
Cathy Moore	Cynthia Gibb

Quote 'If God gave me this woman, then there must be a God.'

Psst! A one-time extreme right-winger, it was while making *Salvador* that Stone did a volte-face, emerging as Hollywood's most aggressive liberal.

Same Time, Next Year
★★★ 1978 119min c.

Director: Robert Mulligan
Screenplay: Bernard Slade
Source: Play by Slade

A couple who have an affair at a hotel then go on to meet for an annual adulterous weekend every year for the next 25 years. Although not opened up at all from the stage play, this romantic comedy is still great fun, with Bernard Slade pointing up some of the more ridiculous fads and fancies that Americans were prey to over the course of a generation. The leads, Burstyn and Alda, are absolutely perfect, while the dialogue is as good as the best of Neil Simon.

Doris	Ellen Burstyn
George	Alan Alda

Quote 'He runs four miles a day and has a body like Mark Spitz. Unfortunately, he still has a face like Ernest Borgnine.'

Sanders
SEE: **Death Drums along the River**

San Francisco
★★★ 1936 115min b/w

Director: W.S. Van Dyke
Screenplay: Anita Loos
Source: Story by Robert E. Hopkins

When Gable makes love, the earth *really* moves. He's owner of the Pardise Club, a gambler and an atheist, trying to make out with religious nut MacDonald. She's torn between him and her career, until the Big One happens and it's the buildings and streets that get torn. Even before the still-stupendous special effects take their 20-minute bow, this is superior entertainment, marred only by MacDonald's irritating goody-goodiness and a sickly religious finale. Who says disaster movies only began in the 70s?

Blackie Norton	Clark Gable
Mary Blake	Jeanette MacDonald
Father Mullin	Spencer Tracy
Jack Burley	Jack Holt
Maisie Burley	Jessie Ralph
Matt	Ted Healy
Bailiff	Edgar Kennedy
Professor	Al Shean
Trixie	Shirley Ross
'Babe'	Harold Huber

Psst! Gable was keen to work with Tracy, whom he considered the finest actor in movies, but was less enamoured with the idea of 'America's Sweetheart', Jeanette MacDonald. He only agreed to play the role after hearing she had given up her salary to help pay for him. On set, though, he sent her into tears by studiously avoiding her • Watch for the look of suprise on MacDonald's face when she and Gable first kiss. Apparently Gable had overdosed on garlic beforehand, not the only instance of one of his co-stars being staggered by his breath [see *Gone With the Wind*] • Director Van Dyke found work for many silent movie actors on the film who were now having a hard time of it in the Depression. Rumour has it that D.W. Griffith, the silent movie director, helmed one scene, but no-one seems to know which.

Saturday Night and Sunday Morning
★★★ 1960 89min b/w

Director: Karel Reisz
Screenplay: Alan Sillitoe
Source: Novel by Sillitoe

Effectively *Saturday Night Fever* with the kitchen sink taking the place of disco and, even better, no Bee-Gees. A factory worker is keen to keep his independence and sows his wild oats before eventually buckling down to the same drab life as his mates. Finney is remarkably good in his first lead role. Although obviously not as shocking now, its acerbic and witty script was extremely frank about sex for the time and the film proved another watershed for British movies

```
Arthur Seaton . . . . . . . . . . . . . . . .Albert Finney
Doreen Gretton . . . . . . . . . . .Shirley Anne Field
Brenda . . . . . . . . . . . . . . . . . . . .Rachel Roberts
Aunt Ada . . . . . . . . . . . . . . . . . . . . .Hylda Baker
Bert . . . . . . . . . . . . . . . . . .Norman Rossington
Jack . . . . . . . . . . . . . . . . . . . . . .Bryan Pringle
Robboe . . . . . . . . . . . . . . . . . .Robert Cawdron
Mrs. Bull . . . . . . . . . . . . . . . . . . . . .Edna Morris
Loudmouth . . . . . . . . . . . . . . . . .Colin Blakely
```

Quote 'Don't let the bastards grind you down.'
• 'I was the first man to be seen sleeping with another man's wife in an English film.' [Finney]

Psst! Diana Dors turned down the role of the older, married woman, giving Rachel Roberts one of her greatest parts • After the producers refused to cut out two of the love scenes, Warwickshire Council banned the film. David Kingsley of British Lion said: 'We are not prepared to agree that a film of outstanding importance and merit should be re-edited by the Mrs. Grundys of the Warwickshire County Council. It is fortunate for the world that Warwickshire's greatest and often bawdy son, William Shakespeare, was not subject in his day to the restrictions of prim and petty officialdom.'

Saturday Night Fever
★★ 1977 119min c.

Director: John Badham
Screenplay: Norman Wexler
Source: Magazine article, *Tribal Rites of the New Saturday Night* by Nik Cohn

This look at 70s working-class youths boogieing on down in their ridiculous flared clothes is unintentionally but gloriously funny. However, it becomes impossible to ignore the gratuitously nasty behaviour of Travolata and his chums towards women, with the gang-rape scene in particular leaving an extremely unpleasant taste in the mouth. In retrospect, apart from the one dance, it's hard to see why it was so popular, especially as Gorney must be one of the least

charismatic leads in the history of movies. She can't even dance particularly well. The 1983 sequel, *Staying Alive*, should have been put out of its misery before release.

```
Tony Manero . . . . . . . . . . . . . . . .John Travolta
Stephanie . . . . . . . . . . . . . .Karen Lynn Gorney
Bobby C. . . . . . . . . . . . . . . . . . . . .Barry Miller
Joey . . . . . . . . . . . . . . . . . . . . . . . .Joseph Cali
Double J. . . . . . . . . . . . . . . . . . . . .Paul Pape
Annette . . . . . . . . . . . . . . . . . .Donna Pescow
Flo . . . . . . . . . . . . . . . . . . . . . . .Julie Bovasso
```

Quote 'Will you just watch the hair? You know, I work on my hair a long time and you hit it.'
• 'You guys have the Moses effect. You arrive and the crowd parts like the Red Sea.'

Psst! Travolta learnt disco dancing over a five-month period specially for the film • The soundtrack album sold 35 million copies
• There are two versions, the later, tamer one being around 10 minutes shorter • Travolta's long-time lover Cynthia Hyland, who was 40 to his 22, died of cancer in his arms during filming
• The famous white suit was sold at auction in June 1995 for $145,000. The seller was film critic Gene Siskel, who had bought it along with the black shirt for just $2,000 in 1979.

Scaramouche
★★★ 1952 115min c.

Director: George Sidney
Screenplay: Ronald Miller & George Froeschel
Source: Novel by Rafael Sabatini

Granger poses as an actor in Revolutionary France as he prepares to exact revenge for his brother's death. The romantic interest is a little sickly but swashbuckling has rarely been as beautifully staged and exciting as here. With dollops of splendid humour, it's all great fun in the Robin Hood vein. Stick with it for the last great gag about Napoleon.

```
Andre Moreau . . . . . . . . . . . . . .Stewart Granger
Lenore . . . . . . . . . . . . . . . . . . . .Eleanor Parker
Aline de Gavrillac . . . . . . . . . . . . . . .Janet Leigh
Noel, Marquis de Maynes . . . . . . . . .Mel Ferrer
Chevalier de Chabrillaine . . . . . .Henry Wilcoxon
George de Valmorin . . . . . . . . . . . .Lewis Stone
Marie Antoinette . . . . . . . . . . . . . . . .Nina Foch
Gaston Binet . . . . . . . . . . . . . . . .Robert Coote
Philippe de Valmorin . . . . . . .Richard Anderson
President . . . . . . . . . . . . . .Douglass Dumbrille
```
Also: John Dehner, John Litel, Elizabeth Risdon, Ursula Andress

Quote 'I once said to Spencer Tracy, who was a great friend, "I wish I'd made just one film like *Inherit the Wind*." And you know what he said? "Jim, I'd love to have done *Scaramouche*.' [Stewart Granger]

OOPS! Surely at one point they're riding furiously on what is clearly a modern golf course?

Psst! The climactic swordfight is reputed to be the longest ever put on film, lasting six-and-a-half minutes • Look out for Ursula Andress.

Scarface

★★★ 1932 99min b/w

Director: Howard Hawks
Screenplay: Ben Hecht, Seton I. Miller, John Lee Mahin, W.R. Burnett & Fred Pasley
Source: Novel by Armitage Traill

The third of the original trilogy of Gat Pack movies, along with *Little Caesar* and *Public Enemy*. This is a thinly-veiled portrait of Al Capone, with the gangster portrayed as an out-and-out murderer who hasn't even got society to blame for his behaviour. His only Achilles' heel is his near incestuous relationship with his sister. Still surprisingly vivid and exciting, particularly when compared with the 1983 remake.

Tony Camonte . . . . .Paul Muni
Cesca Camonte . . . . .Ann Dvorak
Guino Rinaldo . . . . .George Raft
Gaffney . . . . .Boris Karloff
Poppy . . . . .Karen Morey
Angelo .Vince Barnett
Johnny Lovo . . . . .Osgood Perkins
Insp. Guarino . . . . .C. Henry Gordon
Chief of Detectives . . . . .Edwin Maxwell
Editor . . . . .Tully Marshall

Psst! Although it appeared after *Little Caesar* and *Public Enemy*, it was actually made earlier, but was held back for over a year because of difficulties with the censors • After word of it got out that the film was really about Al Capone, writer Hecht was visited at his hotel room by two of Capone's henchmen. With his knowledge of Chicago gangster life from his days as a reporter, he managed to persuade them that it was about another gangster altogether and that it was only called *Scarface* so that the public would be keener to see it • Capone enjoyed the film so much he bought himself a print of it • Although both Hawks and Hecht claim credit for the idea, the pair were agreed that part of the inspiration came from the story of the Borgia family • This was the most violent movie ever seen in its day, with 28 deaths and many more off-camera • So ferociously did producer Howard Hughes and director Hawks squabble that the picture was nearly cancelled. Hughes later kept the film out of distribution and it was only after his death in 1979 that it could be seen again.

Scarface

★★ 1983 170min c.

Director: Brian DePalma
Screenplay: Oliver Stone
Source: 1932 film by Ben Hecht.

A Cuban refugee arrives in Miami and sets about taking, rather than making, his fortune. This remake of the 30s Hawks gangster classic looks better than when it opened, thanks to De Palma's stylised direction, Pacino's energy and a smart pair of early appearances by Pfeiffer and Mastrantonio. It's very violent and the chainsaw sequence still chills, even in the…er…cut version. But it's way too long and offers nothing new.

Tony Montana . . . . .Al Pacino
Manny Ray . . . . .Steven Bauer
Elvira . . . . .Michelle Pfeiffer
Gina . . . . .Mary Elizabeth Mastrantonio
Frank Lopez . . . . .Robert Loggia
Omar . . . . .F. Murray Abraham
Alejandro Sosa . . . . .Paul Shenar

Quote 'The only thing that gives orders in this world is balls.'

Psst! Until the arrival of *Goodfellas*, this film held the record for the most uses of the F-word, notching up 206 of them.

The Scarlet Pimpernel

★★★★ 1934 93min b/w

Director: Harold Young
Screenplay: Robert E. Sherwood, Sam Berman, Arthur Wimperis & Lajos Biro
Source: Novel by Baroness Orczy

An effete aristocrat is really the Scarlet Pimpernel, the daring rescuer of French aristocrats from the reign of revolutionary terror. This rousing costume drama, superbly acted by all, but particularly by Howard and the villainous

Massey, is still a rattling good yarn even now. The 1938 *Return of the Scarlet Pimpernel* had little to commend it but the David Niven remake in 1950 is good fun, even thought it was originally a musical that then had the musical numbers taken out. Howard also starred in *Pimpernel Smith*, a similarly-themed movie with Nazis standing in for the French revolutionaries.

Sir Percy Blakeney . . . . .Leslie Howard
Lady Blakeney . . . . .Merle Oberon
Chauvelin . . . . .Raymond Massey
The Prince of Wales . . . . .Nigel Bruce
Priest . . . . .Bramwell Fletcher
Sir Andrew Ffoulkes . . . . .Anthony Bushell
Suzanne de Tournay . . . . .Joan Gardner
Armand St. Just . . . . .Walter Rilla
Also: Mabel Terry-Lewis, O.B. Clarence, Melville Cooper

Quote 'They seek him here, they seek him there, Those Frenchies seek him everywhere. Is he in Heaven? Is he in hell? That damned elusive Pimpernel.'

Psst! Original director Roland V. Brown was fired on his first day at work after arguing with studio head Alexander Korda • Although it seems the epitome of British film-making, the hero was of Hungarian descent, as was one of the scriptwriters, the author of the original novel and the head of the studio. The heroine was Anglo-Indian, while two of the other writers were American • Howard and Oberon became lovers while filming, causing her to break off her engagement to Joseph Schenk, the head of United Artists. She was later to marry Korda.

Schindler's List
★★★★ 1993 195min c&b/w

Director: Steven Spielberg
Screenplay: Steven Zaillian
Source: Novel by Thomas Keneally

Based on a true story, a Nazi industrialist protects his workers from The Final Solution. Although long, the time passes staggeringly quickly. The use of hand-held cameras gives the film a documentary flavour and the story is grippingly and convincingly told. Fiennes is a particular standout as one of the most complex, vicious and almost pitiable villains in movie history. The film is moving, heart-rending and life-affirming. Although the Holocaust is not trivialised, the movie is less depressing than might be expected both because this is one tale that has a happy ending and because it is shot

through with wry humour. What's more, it improves on further viewings. The only miscalculation is Neeson's final speech and the colour coda, which almost takes us into *Sound of Music*-style schmaltz. That apart, this is simply one of the most remarkable movies ever made.

Oskar Schindler . . . . .Liam Neeson
Itzhak Stern . . . . .Ben Kingsley
Amon Goeth . . . . .Ralph Fiennes
Emilie Schindler . . . . .Caroline Goodall
Poldek Pfefferberg . . . . .Jonathan Sagalle
Helen Hirsch . . . . .Embeth Davidtz

Oscars Best Picture, Best Director, Best Screenplay (adapted)

Blurb Whoever Saves One Life Saves The World Entire.

Quote 'What if I got here five minutes later? Then where would I be?' • 'Good-bye, Jews!' • 'I realise you're not a person in the strictest sense of the word.' • 'If this factory ever produces a shell that can actually be fired, I'll be very unhappy.'

Psst! As if Spielberg's achievement wasn't great enough, after filming *Schindler* during the day in Poland, by night he was editing *Jurassic Park* using a satellite link • Spielberg had to fight long and hard to persuade Universal to allow him to make it in black and white, the industry view being that colour films will always make more money • Spielberg was refused permission to film inside Auschwitz, even though other films had done so before. The Auschwitz set was built *beside* the real location and the train seen is actually moving *out* of Auschwitz rather than into it • Fiennes added weight for his part by drinking substantial quantities of Guinness • John Williams' score is surely one of the 10 best soundtracks of all time.

School for Scoundrels
★★★ 1960 94min b/w

Director: Robert Hamer
Screenplay: Patricia Mayes & Hal E. Chester
Source: *Lifemanship* books by Stephen Potter.

Ever feel that the cads and bounders of life always get the better of you ? Bested in love by Terry-Thomas and saddled with a dinosaur of the road by rapacious car salesmen Price and Jones, nice chap Carmichael enrols in the College of Lifemanship. There he learns the secrets of coming out on top and turns the table on his tormentors. Although episodic, it's got plenty of laughs and its dated quaintness actually seems a plus.

Henry Palfrey . . . . .Ian Carmichael
Raymond Delauney . . . . .Terry-Thomas
Stephen Potter . . . . .Alastair Sim
April Smith . . . . .Janette Scott
Dunstan Dorchester . . . . .Dennis Price
Dudley Dorchester . . . . .Peter Jones
Gloatbridge . . . . .Edward Chapman
Head waiter . . . . .John Le Mesurier
Mrs. Stringer . . . . .Irene Handl
First instructress . . . . .Hattie Jacques
Instructor . . . . .Hugh Paddick

OOPS! In the bonnet of Terry-Thomas' car, you can see not only the reflection of the sky but also where the fake sky ends!

Scrooge
★★★★ 1951 86min b/w

Director: Brian Desmond
Screenplay: Noel Langley
Source: Novel, *A Christmas Carol* by Charles Dickens

There have been umpteen versions of Dickens' classic Christmas fable but this is the best. After seeing the goggle-eyed Sim as the famous miser, you'll imagine him every time you think of Ebenezer Scrooge in the future. Known as *A Christmas Carol* in the US. Among the other versions are the 1970 musical *Scrooge* with Albert Finney and *Scrooged*, the 1988 Bill Murray version, playing it for laughs and not getting them.

Scrooge . . . . .Alastair Sim
Mrs. Dilber . . . . .Kathleen Harrison
Bob Cratchit . . . . .Mervyn Johns
Mrs. Cratchit . . . . .Hermione Baddeley
Jacob Marley . . . . .Michael Hordern
Mr. Jorkins . . . . .Jack Warner
Scrooge (younger) . . . . .George Cole
Old Joe .Miles Malleson
Fan . . . . .Carol Marsh
Fred . . . . .Brian Worth
Undertaker . . . . .Ernest Thesiger
Mrs. Fezziwig . . . . .Hattie Jacques
Laundress . . . . .Louise Hampton
Snedrig . . . . .Eliot Makeham
First businessman . . . . .Peter Bull
Also: Patrick Macnee, Michael Dolan, Eleanor Summerfield, Noel Howlett, Richard Pearson

OOPS! Keep an eye on a mirror behind Sim and you'll spot the camera crew.

The Sea Hawk
★★★ 1940 126min b/w

Director: Michael Curtiz
Screenplay: Howard Koch & Seton I. Miller

Once more Errol Flynn buckles on the swash that was never far from his side, this time as an English captain who believes war with Spain is in the offing. With Queen Elizabeth's encouragement, he raises funds by plundering Spain and its ships. The plot is pretty familiar, but it's all carried out with a good deal of panache, with Rains relishing his role as the baddie. There's a strong, but not terribly subtle, allegory about the war in Europe as well. The score by Erich Wolfgang Korngold is one of the most famous from the classic era.

Capt. Geoffrey Thorpe . . . . .Errol Flynn
Donna Maria . . . . .Brenda Marshall
Don Jose .Claude Rains
Sir John Burleson . . . . .Donald Crisp
Queen Elizabeth . . . . .Flora Robson
Carl Pitt . . . . .Alan Hale
Lord Wolfingham . . . . .Henry Daniell
Miss Latham . . . . .Una O'Connor
Abbott . . . . .James Stephenson
Capt. Lopez . . . . .Gilbert Roland
Oliver Scott . . . . .Julien Mitchell
King Philip II . . . . .Montagu Love

Blurb If You Miss It, You Will Owe Yourself An Apology.

Quote 'They say that Elizabeth surrounds herself with beauty in the hope that it may be contagious.'

Psst! Sets from *The Private Lives of Elizabeth and Essex* and *Juarez* were used, along with action sequences from *Captain Blood*. In the studio's tank were two full-size ships which could be rocked with hydraulic jacks, causing some of the actors to suffer from seasickness • Henry Daniell was so bad at fencing that he had to be doubled and can rarely be seen even holding a sword • The English version came complete with a stirring backs-to-the-wall morale-building speech from Queen Elizabeth I herself.

Sea of Love
★★★ 1989 113min c.

Director: Harold Becker
Screenplay: Richard Price

Cracking thriller with cop Pacino investigating the murders of lonely hearts advertisers by placing an ad himself. Although it seems barking, he's soon bonkin' Barkin, the lead suspect. Is she the killer or not? The plot's not the greatest ever, but what really grabs is the raw sensuality, the wonderful characterisation and dialogue and the fantastic observation of the singles scene. If only more erotic thrillers aped this rather than *Basic Instinct*, what a wonderful world it would be.

Frank Keller	Al Pacino
Helen Cruger	Ellen Barkin
Sherman Touhy	John Goodman
Terry	Michael Rooker
Frank Sr.	William Hickey
Gruber	Richard Jenkins

OOPS! Look carefully when Pacino is getting dressed after making love with Barkin the first time and, as he puts on his briefs, you can see that he's already wearing a pair.

Psst! There's another, longer, version around that also has Lorraine Bracco in it as Pacino's ex-wife • The original script had a far more ambiguous ending with the person who's the killer in the released film committing suicide, leaving us unsure who's the guilty one.

The Searchers

★★★ 1956 119min c.

Director: John Ford
Screenplay: Frank S. Nugent
Source: Novel by Alan LeMay

The Western that film buffs go into raptures over. Wayne is the bigoted ex-Confederate who searches for seven years for the daughter of his brother and sister-in-law who was taken prisoner by the Indians who murdered her parents. While it's true that it's extremely beautiful and that Wayne gives an untypically deep performance, if you aren't reading deep, deep meaning into it all the time, it can also be somewhat tedious in places. I keep rewatching it, but if there's more to this than meets the eye, it escapes me.

Ethan Edwards	John Wayne
Martin Pawley	Jeffrey Hunter
Laurie Jorgensen	Vera Miles
Capt. Rev. Sam Clayton	Ward Bond
Debbie Edwards	Natalie Wood
Lars Jorgensen	John Qualen
Brad Jorgensen	Harry Carey Jr.

Emilio Figueroa	Antonio Moreno
Mrs. Jorgensen	Olive Carey
Chief Scar	Henry Brandon
Charlie McCorry	Ken Curtis
Mose Harper	Hank Worden

Quote 'That'll be the day.' • 'Let's go home, Debbie.'

OOPS! Wayne gives his niece a medal he won fighting for the Confederate side. Smarter alecs than me have pointed out that the Confederates didn't mint any medals.

Psst! John Wayne was so taken with his character in this film, which he considered his best, that he named his third son John Ethan • The part of Debbie as a child was played by Natalie Wood's younger sister, Lana. She was later admirably to flesh out the role of Plenty O'Toole in *Diamonds Are Forever*.

The Sea Wolf

★★★ 1941 90min b/w

Director: Michael Curtiz
Screenplay: Robert Rossen
Source: Novel by Jack London

Knox and Lupino are the survivors of a shipwreck, picked up by a ship on which the clock seems to have been turned back two centuries or more. Most of the sailors have been pressganged and Lupino and Knox find that, instead of being taken to shore, they too are pressed into service. Although there's rather too much pseudo-philosophical talk, Robinson plays the megalomaniac monster of a captain as if he was born to the role.

'Wolf' Larsen	Edward G. Robinson
Ruth Webster	Ida Lupino
George Leach	John Garfield
Humphrey Van Weyden	Alexander Knox
Dr. Louis Prescott	Gene Lockhart
Cooky	Barry Fitzgerald
Johnson	Stanley Ridges
Harrison	Howard da Silva
Smoke	Frank Lackteen
Young sailor	David Bruce
Agent	Ralf Harolde

Psst! The premiere was a disaster. Good though the idea of having it on board the SS *America* might have been, a storm blew up and many of those present found themselves with better things to do than watch a movie which itself had its fair share of stormy weather at sea.

The Secret Life of Walter Mitty

★★★ 1947 105min c.

Director: Norman Z. McLeod
Screenplay: Ken Englund & Everett Freeman
Source: Story by James Thurber

Although many do this comedy down, Kaye is at his hilarious best as the hen-pecked man who continually loses himself in daydreams where he invariably commits conspicuous acts of bravery. There are moments during the fantasy sequences where Kaye's immodesty is somewhat cringe-making, but generally it's good-natured knockabout fun.

Walter Mitty	Danny Kaye
Rosalind van Hoorn	Virginia Mayo
Dr. Hugo Hollingshead	Boris Karloff
Mrs. Mitty	Fay Bainter
Gertrude Griswold	Ann Rutherford
Bruce Pierce	Thurston Hall
Mrs. Griswold	Florence Bates
RAF Colonel	Reginald Denny
Peter van Hoorn	Konstantin Shayne
Tubby Wadsworth	Gordon Jones
Anatole	Fritz Feld

Quote 'Your small minds are muscle-bound with suspicion. That's because the only exercise you ever get is jumping to conclusions.' • 'Pocketa, pocketa, pocketa…'

Psst! Humorist James Thurber is reputed to have offered producer Samuel Goldwyn $10,000 *not* to film his famous short story.

Sergeant York

★★ 1941 134min b/w

Director: Howard Hawks
Screenplay: Abem Finkel, Harry Chandlee, Howard Koch & John Huston
Source: War Diary of Sgt. York and book *Sgt York & His People* by Sam K. Cowan and *Sergeant York* by Tom Skeyhill

In World War I, a pacifist backwoods farmer – an ace with his gun – reluctantly goes to France to take part in a war he thinks is wrong. Despite his reservations, he becomes America's biggest war hero. This true story is told in far too leisurely a manner but is held together by the calm, measured performance of Cooper.

Alvin C. York	Gary Cooper
Pastor Rosier Pile	Walter Brennan
Gracie Williams	Joan Leslie

'Pusher' Ross	George Tobias
Maj. Buxton	Stanley Ridges
Mother York	Margaret Wycherly
Ike Botkin	Ward Bond
Buck Lipscomb	Noah Beery Jr.
Rosie York	June Lockhart
George York	Dickie Moore
Zeke	Clem Bevans
Lem	Howard da Silva
Cordell Hull	Charles Trowbridge
Bert Thomas	David Bruce
German major	Carl Esmond
Sgt. Early	Joe Sawyer

Oscars Gary Cooper

Quote 'This is where we change cars, Alvin. The end of the line.'

Psst! The film is based on the true story of one of America's most decorated heroes who, on one day in 1918, killed 25 German solders and took another132 hostage single-handedly • It took producer Jesse Lasky many years to convince the unassuming York that his story should be filmed. York eventually capitulated, provided that the profits went to charity and that Gary Cooper play him on screen. Cooper was reluctant, so Lasky faked a telegram, purporting to come from York, asking him to take the part • June Lockhart would go on to become better-known as the mother in TV's *Lost in Space*.

The Servant

★★ 1964 115min b/w

Director: Joseph Losey
Screenplay: Harold Pinter
Source: Novel by Robin Maugham

A creepy servant and his sister undermine and come to dominate a wealthy toff. Although often tedious, pretentious and depressing drivel, Bogarde and Fox are both very good. It's also something of a surprise seeing Wendy Craig in a sexy role. If it ever had anything of importance to say about class, it says it extremely slowly.

Hugo Barrett	Dirk Bogarde
Tony	James Fox
Vera	Sarah Miles
Susan	Wendy Craig
Lady Mounset	Catherine Lacey
Lord Mounset	Richard Vernon
Bishop	Patrick Magee
Society woman	Ann Firbank

Curate . . . . .Alun Owen
Society man . . . . .Harold Pinter

Psst! Losey, who had fled to Britain because of his alleged Communist sympathies, came across the novel in 1956 and suggested it to Bogarde. They had trouble getting it off the ground until the climate of censorship had relaxed a little and still only managed to get a budget of £140,000. In fact, the production came in under budget and cleaned up at the box office.

Seven Days in May
★★★ 1964 120min b/w

Director: John Frankenheimer
Screenplay: Rod Serling
Source: Novel by Fletcher Knebel & Charles Waldo Bailey II

The aide to an American general discovers a plot by the military to stage a coup d'état and overthrow what they see as a pacifist President. An intelligent, gripping and all too believable thriller which moves along at a rapid lick.

Gen. James M. Scott . . . . .Burt Lancaster
Col. Martin 'Jiggs' Casey . . . . . . .Kirk Douglas
President Jordan Lyman . . . . .Fredric March
Eleanor Holbrook . . . . .Ava Gardner
Sen. Raymond Clark . . . . .Edmond O'Brien
Paul Girard . . . . .Martin Balsam
Christopher Todd . . . . .George Macready
Sen. Prentice . . . . .Whit Bissell
Adm. Barnswell . . . . .John Houseman
Also: Hugh Marlowe, Bart Burns, Victor Buono

Psst! Perhaps understandably, the film-makers did not bother approaching the military to ask if they would cooperate with the movie. However, the Kennedy administration did offer considerable assistance. President Kennedy disappeared off to his place in Hyannisport so that the production could shoot for a week outside the White House.

Seven Days to Noon
★★★ 1950 94min c.

Director: John Boulting
Screenplay: Frank Harvey, Roy Boulting, Paul Dehn & James Bernard

An atomic scientist holds the government to ransom when he threatens to blow up London.

Although much of the philosophising is now old hat, the thriller aspects still work well thanks to the Boulting Brothers' decision to keep it a modest, almost austere, movie instead of pulling out all the stops.

Prof. Willingdon . . . . .Barry Jones
Goldie . . . . .Olive Sloan
Superintendent Folland . . . . .André Morell
Ann Willingdon . . . . .Sheila Manahan
Stephen Lane . . . . .Hugh Cross
Mrs. Peckett . . . . .Joan Hickson
The Prime Minister . . . . .Ronald Adam
Also: Joss Ackland

Oscars Best Original Story

The Seven Samurai
★★★ 1954 208min b/w

Director: Akira Kurosawa
Screenplay: Shinobu Hashimoto, Hideo Oguni & Akira Kurosawa

In 16th century Japan a village suffering from repeated attacks hires an ageing samurai and six of his buddies to help defend them. This atmsopheric movie has some fantastically-staged battle scenes and is considered by many one of the great masterpieces of the cinema. But critics are always more enthusiastic about a film where they have to read the dialogue at the bottom of the screen. After three hours of this, you do begin to wish that you were watching *The Magnificent Seven* instead. It's exciting enough to be well worth watching once, even for those who don't care too much for subtitles. But if given the choice of one or the other to pop into the video machine for an entertaining evening, I know which one I'd choose. There are umpteen different versions knocking around, with lengths varying from 141minutes right up to the full 208 minutes.

Kambei . . . . .Takashi Shimura
Kikuchiyo . . . . .Toshiro Mifune
Gorobei .Yoshio Inaba

Psst! The most expensive film ever made in Japan at the time. Funding difficulties during production and problems in finding enough horses, meant that filming took over a year • Writer-director Kurosawa was a great fan of Westerns and dreamed up the idea of using wandering Samurai knights instead of gunfighters so that he could make an Eastern Western • This was the inspiration for *The Magnificent Seven.*

The Seventh Seal

★★★★ 1957 95min b/w

Director: Ingmar Bergman
Screenplay: Ingmar Bergman
Source: Radio & stage play, *Trämaining* by Bergman

Ingmar Bergman has a lot to answer for. *Love and Death, Last Action Hero* and *Bill and Ted's Bogus Journey* are just a few of the spoofs of the memorable imagery in *The Seventh Seal*, in which a crusader plays chess with Death. Its enduring popularity with film-makers seeking inspiration testifies to its lasting visual power. This is the film that really got Bergman noticed on the world stage and is still a very effective evocation of the medieval world, plagues and all.

Antonius Block	Max Von Sydow
Jöns	Gunnar Björnstrand
Death	Bengt Ekerot
Jof	Nils Poppe
Mia	Bibi Andersson

Psst! The famous image of the Dance of Death underneath the dark cloud was not the result of detailed preparation. Most of the cast and crew had knocked off for the day when Bergman noticed the cloud, thought it too good to miss, and decided to try for the shot. The few people left on the set and a couple of tourists were roped in and quickly dressed up in costume. Ignoring sound, the camera was turned on and, with just 10 minutes' rehearsal, the scene shot before the cloud could disappear.

The Seventh Veil

★★★ 1945 94min b/w

Director: Compton Bennett
Screenplay: Muriel Box & Sydney Box

A pianist with a fear of losing her hands seeks psychiatic help and recalls the influence on her life of her cruel guardian. Psychiatry was all the rage in movies in the 40s. The advice from the head-shrinker here seems rather peculiar, but what could audiences expect for their two bob? The performers put this romantic tripe over as if they believe in it, with Mason making a wonderfully hissable villain and it's hard not to get swept along by it all.

Nicholas	James Mason
Francesca Cunningham	Ann Todd
Dr. Larsen	Herbert Lom

Maxwell Leyden	Albert Lieven
Peter Gay	Hugh McDermott
Susan Brook	Yvonne Owen
Dr. Kendal	David Horne

Oscars Best Screenplay

Psst! The film-makers were undecided how to end the movie and asked audiences at special previews which man Todd should end up with, going with their decision.

The Seven Year Itch

★★ 1955 105min c.

Director: Billy Wilder
Screenplay: Billy Wilder & George Axelrod
Source: Play by Axelrod

When his wife and children get away from sultry New York for the summer, a publisher married for seven years begins to fantasise about having an affair with the gorgeous girl in the apartment above. Sadly, the play was sanitised for the screen and although there are some splendid moments here, with Monroe looking at her most appealing throughout, they never really gel. For a comedy, there are surprisingly few good laughs and, after a time, Ewell's daydreams and incessant chattering simply becomes tedious.

The girl	Marilyn Monroe
Richard Sherman	Tom Ewell
Helen Sherman	Evelyn Keyes
Tom McKenzie	Sonny Tufts
Krukulik	Robert Strauss
Dr. Brubaker	Oscar Homolka
Plumber	Victor Moore
Miss Morris	Marguerite Chapman
Mr. Brady	Donald MacBride
Miss Finch	Carolyn Jones

Quote 'My fan is caught in the door.'

Psst! Billy Wilder wanted Walter Matthau to star, but he was over-ruled by the head of Fox, Darryl Zanuck • Monroe's marriage to baseball player Joe DiMaggio was already in trouble when the movie started. But DiMaggio was present on the night when the scene with the air from the subway grating blowing up her skirt was filmed in front of the Trans-Lux Theatre in New York. The crowd of several thousand roared their appreciation every time MM's dress blew up and pictures of it appeared throughout the world. Divorce proceedings began soon afterwards • Carolyn Jones, who appears as Miss Fitch, was later to achieve fame as Morticia in *The Addams Family*.

sex, lies, and videotape
★★★ 1989 100min c.

Director: Steven Soderbergh
Screenplay: Steven Soderbergh

This remarkable debut from writer-director Soderbergh has Spader as the old college friend visiting the repressed MacDowell while hubby Gallagher is cheating with her sister Giacomo. Spader's a teensy bit weird, getting his kicks from taping women talking intimately about sex, a pastime that has dramatic consequences. More talk than action, this is a timely reminder that the sexiest films don't have to feature much of the act at all. Intelligent and witty, it's a beautifully-constructed film that draws you deeper and deeper into these peoples' lives.

Graham Dalton . . . . .James Spader
Ann Millaney . . . . .Andie MacDowell
John Millaney . . . . .Peter Gallagher
Cynthia Bishop . . . . .Laura San Giacomo
Therapist . . . . .Ron Vawter

Quote 'It's all downhill from here' [The all-too-prescient Soderbergh on winning the Palme D'Or at Cannes]

OOPS! Watch for the vanishing necklace as MacDowell tackles Gallagher on whether he's having an affair or not.

Psst! During Cannes the Rob Lowe video scandal broke, with the actor's tape of sex with young girls becoming the most popular pirate tape in America. The publicity also helped Soderbergh's movie.

Shadowlands
★★★★ 1993 130min c.

Director: Richard Attenborough
Screenplay: William Nicholson
Source: Play by Nicholson

The best British love story since *Brief Encounter*. Confirmed academic bachelor C.S. Lewis, he of the Narnia books, finds love late in life in the person of fiery American poet Winger. Although Attenborough, amazingly for him, never lets it become too sentimental, the tears will still flow so freely that the dye in your socks will run. It's also surprisingly funny in places. One of those rare films you want to go more slowly so that it won't come to an end.

Jack Lewis . . . . .Anthony Hopkins
Joy Gresham . . . . .Debra Winger

Warnie Lewis . . . . .Edward Hardwicke
"Harry" Harrington . . . . .Michael Denison
Christopher Riley . . . . .John Wood
Dr. Craig . . . . .Peter Firth
Douglas Gresham . . . . .Joseph Mazzello

Quote 'The pain now is part of the happiness then. That is the deal.' • 'One can always be friendlier to people who can't stay long.'

Shadow of a Doubt
★★★★ 1943 108min b/w

Director: Alfred Hitchcock
Screenplay: Thornton Wilder, Alma Reville & Sally Benson
Source: Story by Gordon McDonnell

After murdering the latest in a long line of widows for her money, Cotten hides out with his sister and her family. Wright dotes on her uncle until she meets a detective who is on his trail. Although this thriller is relatively low-key, being set in a sleepy small town, the Master still racks the suspense up to near unbearable levels, helped enormously by Cotten's wonderful portrayal of an intelligent monster.

Uncle Charlie . . . . .Joseph Cotten
Young Charlie . . . . .Teresa Wright
Jack Graham . . . . .Macdonald Carey
Emma Newton . . . . .Patricia Collinge
Joseph Newton . . . . .Henry Travers
Herbie Hawkins . . . . .Hume Cronyn
Fred Saunders . . . . .Wallace Ford
Ann Newton . . . . .Edna May Wonacott
Station master . . . . .Irving Bacon
Pullman porter . . . . .Clarence Muse

Quote 'You see them in the hotels, the best hotels, every day by the thousands, drinking the money, eating the money, losing the money at bridge, playing all day and all night, smelling of money. Horrible, faded, fat, greedy women.'

OOPS! Without doubt, there's a shadow of the camera on Teresa Wright's back as she is doing research in the library.

Psst! Hitch appears early in the film as a passenger on the train that Cotten gets on. He's playing cards and has the full suit of spades in his hand • He claims that this was his favourite movie • The story was based on Earle Leonard Nelson, whose killing spree in the 30s, earned him the nickname 'The Merry Widow Murderer' • Wilder had not written a screenplay before and adopted a rather leisurely attitude to the work. He still hadn't finished when he enlisted in the Army, so Hitchcock got on the train with him on his way to basic training in Florida while Wilder finished. Legend has it that he finished the final page as the train was pulling in • Carey was a heavy drinker and, at one point, he shook so much from a hangover that Hitchcock called for a bottle of bourbon.

Shaft

★★ 1971 100min c.

Director: Gordon Parks
Screenplay: John D.F. Black & Ernest Tidyman
Source: Novel by Tidyman

A hip black private eye, something of a stud, is hired to find a Harlem gangster's kidnapped daughter. Although notable for being the first 'blaxploitation' film, it now looks a fairly routine programmer with dashes of violence and sex thrown in to stop us realising how dull the story is. It was followed by *Shaft's Big Score* and *Shaft in Africa*.

John Shaft	Richard Roundtree
Bumpy Jonas	Moses Gunn
Lt. Vic Androzzy	Charles Cioffi
Ben Buford	Christopher St. John
Ellie Moore	Gwenn Mitchell
Charlie	Victor Arnold

Psst! There was a TV series, which was rather tamer than the movies.

Shampoo

★ 1975 109min c.

Director: Hal Ashby
Screenplay: Robert Towne & Warren Beatty

A fashionable Beverly Hills hairdresser devotes his attention to more than just the heads of his women clients. This shampoo hasn't been tested for irritancy on humans and it results in a dull, unmanageable mess with split ends all over the place. Few films have dated quite as badly . What was once supposedly a sexy West Coast satire now simply won't wash, being lacklustre, seedy and incredibly tiresome. Fisher's great debut is about the only thing worth sticking around for.

George Roundy	Warren Beatty
Jackie Shawn	Julie Christie
Jill	Goldie Hawn
Felicia	Lee Grant

Lester Carr	Jack Warden
Lorna Carr	Carrie Fisher
Johnny Pope	Tony Bill
Senator	Brad Dexter
Norman	Jay Robinson
Producer	William Castle

Oscars Lee Grant

Quote 'Want me to do your hair?' • 'I've got the heads.'

Psst! Beatty produced and co-wrote the film, working for six years to bring it to the screen • This was Carrie Fisher's film debut, although mom Debbie Reynolds was said to be livid that she had done it • The producer is played by producer-director William Castle, known less for his B-movies than for the gimmicks he used to promote them, such as free insurance policies, having nurses on hand in case of heart attacks, rigging seats to tingle with electricity, and so on. The movie *Matinee* in 1993 was based on him.

Shane

★★ 1953 118min c.

Director: George Stevens
Screenplay: A.B. Guthrie Jr.
Source: Novel by Jack Schaefer

No one denies *Shane* is a staggeringly beautiful film, exquisitely composed and lit. But its reputation far exceeds what's actually on offer. The plot, concerning Alan Ladd's arrival to sort out villainous black-clad Jack Pallance, offers no great surprises and the attempts of George Stevens to inflate it to the level of myth are irritating. This sort of thing is best left to veterans like John Ford.

Shane	Alan Ladd
Marion Starrett	Jean Arthur
Joe Starrett	Van Heflin
Wilson	Jack Palance
Joey Starrett	Brandon de Wilde
Chris	Ben Johnson
Lewis	Edgar Buchanan
Torrey	Elisha Cook Jr.
Ryker	Emile Meyer

Quote 'Prove it!' • 'A gun is a tool, no better, no worse, than any other tool, an axe, a shovel, or anything. A gun is as good or as bad as the man using it.' • 'A man's gotta do what a man's gotta do.' • 'Pa's got things for you to do. And mother wants you. I know she does...Shane!... SHANE. COME BACK!...Thank you.' [Last line]

OOPS! Elisha Cook Jr. is more animated dead than alive, judging by the way his body moves around • It's supposed to be possible to see the glare reflecting from a car window in the distance early on in the movie. Others say you can see a bus towards the end of the film. I've yet to spot either.

Psst! This was Jean Arthur's last film • Jack Palance was actually scared of horses and it often took many takes to get him to mount or dismount a horse with any conviction • Despite cinematographer Loyal Griggs' best efforts, Paramount was so taken with the new widescreen process that it lopped the top and the bottom of his carefully composed scenes and released it in an inappropriate wide version.

Shanghai Express

★★★ 1932 80min b/w

Director: Josef von Sternberg
Screenplay: Jules Furthman

A woman gone bad in a big way meets up with an old flame on a train and, when they are captured by bandits, does the selfless thing. Although dialogue and direction are sometimes stilted, it's all so wonderfully camp that it becomes compulsive, with Dietrich at her vampish, noble best.

Shanghai Lily	Marlene Dietrich
Capt. Donald Harvey	Clive Brook
Henry Chang	Warner Oland
Hui Fei	Anna May Wong
Sam Salt	Eugene Pallette
Rev. Carmichael	Lawrence Grant
Mrs. Haggerty	Louise Closser Hale

Quote 'It took more than one man to change my name to Shanghai Lily.' • 'The white woman stays with me.'

The Shawshank Redemption

★★★★ 1994 142min c.

Director: Frank Darabont
Screenplay: Frank Darabont
Source: Novella by Stephen King

If you thought you'd seen enough prison movies, think again. Robbins is the meek banker convicted of murdering his wife who gets sent to hellhole of a prison, Shawshank. There he is befriended by lifer Freeman, who

shows him how to survive the harsh regime. Conditions improve when the governor discovers how useful Robbins' financial knowledge can be, but is he becoming *too* useful? In an intelligent, moving and often witty film, both leads give masterly, compelling performances. That is why we not only feel their suffering but also why we want to punch the air with delight at their eventual 'Redemption'. A mite too long perhaps, but nonetheless a wonderful, moving experience.

Andy Dufresne	Tim Robbins
Ellis Boy "Red" Redding	Morgan Freeman
Warden Samuel Norton	Bob Gunton
Heywood	William Sadler
Capt. Byron Hadley	Clancy Brown
Tommy Williams	Gil Bellows
Brooks Hatlen	James Whitmore

OOPS! Twist-off tops for beer bottles didn't exist in 1949. The prisoners working on the roof would have needed bottle openers.

Psst! Freeman's role was originally written for a red-haired Irishman, which explains his otherwise baffling surname.

She Done Him Wrong

★★★ 1933 66min b/w

Director: Lowell Sherman
Screenplay: Mae West, Harvey Thew & John Bright
Source: Play, *Diamond Lil* by West

A saloon keeper fond of baubles finds, to her surprise, that she is falling for a member of the Salvation Army. Then she discovers there is rather more to him than meets the eye, although not quite in the way she was hoping for. Mae West in her undiluted form is still something. Even though some of the more salacious aspects of her stage play – like the white slave traffic racket – were toned down, this is still a very funny and extremely cheeky movie with Mae singing, in her inimitable way, 'A Guy What Takes His Time'.

Lady Lou	Mae West
Capt. Cummings	Cary Grant
Chick Clark	Owen Moore
Serge Stanieff	Gilbert Roland
Gus Jordan	Noah Beery
Dan Flynn	David Landau
Russian Rita	Rafaela Ottiano
Ragtime Kelly	Fuzzy Knight
Sally	Rochelle Hudson

Quote 'Is that a gun in your pocket or are you just glad to see me?' • 'One of the finest women who ever walked the streets.' • 'When women go wrong, men go right after them.' • 'Why don't you come up sometime 'n' see me. I'm home every evening.' • 'You know, it takes two to get one in trouble.' • 'I wasn't always rich. No, there was a time I didn't know where my next husband was coming from.'

Psst! The film was completed in only 18 days • Along with West's *I'm No Angel*, it helped rescue Paramount from bankruptcy • West is said to have spotted Grant wandering around the Paramount lot • The film was cut by eight minutes by Paramount before release. Another six minutes were lopped off by the censors in Britain. It was banned in Austria.

Shining Through
★★ 1992 132min c.

Director: David Seltzer
Screenplay: David Seltzer & Laurie Frank
Source: Novel by Susan Isaac

One of the funniest bad movies ever. Despite superb production values, the script is so silly and the dialogue so priceless that audiences were shrieking with laughter. Secretary Griffith convinces Douglas she can be a spy by baking him apple strüdel and is sent into Nazi Germany as a nanny-cum-secret agent. There she takes her charges – children of a top Nazi – to look for the hiding place of her Jewish relatives, photographs some documents with the important bits conveniently circled in red and makes her escape in a full-length ballgown. Douglas meanwhile pops in and out of Germany as if it were his club, despite speaking not a word of the lingo. All this is framed by a hilarious BBC documentary with Griffith in terrible old-age make-up yet talking in the same little-girl voice. Hugely entertaining, for *all* the wrong reasons.

Ed Leland . . . . .Michael Douglas
Linda Voss . . . . .Melanie Griffith
Franze-Otto Dietrich . . . . .Liam Neeson
Margrete . . . . .Joely Richardson
Sunflower . . . . .John Gielgud

Quote 'I knew it was on a Friday that Ed and I said goodbye because the next day was Saturday.' • 'Mein Gott, you've got guts.' • 'There would be no symphonies for me and Ed.' • 'By late October of '41 London was reeling under a hailstorm of German bombs called The Blitz and life in America was energised with the knowledge of what was inevitable.'

Showing The Mortal Storm.

OOPS! When she escapes, she's dressed in a white ballgown and runs from Potsdam to Berlin, no mean feat as it's 15 miles.

Psst! Griffith raised a few eyebrows when she was quoted as saying that, until she worked on the film, 'I didn't know that six million Jews were killed. That's a lot of people.'

The Shining
★★★★ 1980 120min c.

Director: Stanley Kubrick
Screenplay: Stanley Kubrick & Diane Johnson
Source: Novel by Stephen King

On release, Kubrick's adaptation of Stephen King's ghost novel was dismissed as a commercial cop-out. In fact, this story of the Overlook Hotel taking over the soul of blocked writer Nicholson became one of the great 80s horror movies, breaking all the rules by keeping the lights on, having classical music playing, and so on. The first film extensively to use the Steadicam for prowling round the hotel corridors, *The Shining* is atmospheric, creepy and a sly allegory on modern America.

Jack Torrance . . . . .Jack Nicholson
Wendy Torrance . . . . .Shelley Duvall
Danny Torrance . . . . .Danny Lloyd
Halloran . . . . .Scatman Crothers
Ullman . . . . .Barry Nelson
Grady, the waiter . . . . .Philip Stone

Quote 'He-e-e-e-re's Johnnie!' • 'Wendy. Darling. Light of my life. I don't want to hurt you. I want to bash your fucking brains out.'

Showing The Class of 44.

OOPS! During the shot showing the family approaching the hotel, the camera helicopter's shadow is visible • When Nicholson hacks at the bathroom door with the axe, he only chops through one panel. But we then see the door with *both* panels hacked out.

Psst! Stanley Kubrick insisted on filming one scene with Shelley Duvall 127 times, supposedly a record for a scene with dialogue [see *City Lights*] • The American version of the film is 142 minutes. Kubrick cut it to 120 minutes for the British release • Kubrick is said to have rung author Stephen King in the early hours of the morning to ask him questions like: 'Do you believe in God?' • The colour scheme in the hall was carefully chosen to resemble dried blood • Some out-takes from early on in the film were used for the original ending of *Blade Runner*.

The Shop around the Corner
★★★★ 1940 97min b/w

Director: Ernst Lubitsch
Screenplay: Samson Raphaelson
Source: Play, *Parfumerie* by Nikolaus Laszlo

Two battling employees of a Budapest perfume shop find an outlet for their romantic spirit in their correspondence with pen pals. Guess who the pen pals turn out to be? Although a little sluggish in places now and clearly based on a play, Lubitsch turns the charm on full blast and the characters are all so delightful that it's impossible not to get caught up in it.

Alfred Kralik	James Stewart
Klara Novak	Margaret Sullavan
Hugo Matuschek	Frank Morgan
Ferencz Vadas	Joseph Schildkraut
Flora	Sara Haden
Pirovitch	Felix Bressart
Pepi Katona	William Tracy
Detective	Charles Halton
Doctor	Edwin Maxwell
Rudy	Charles Smith

Psst! Remade as the musical *In the Good Old Summertime* • The play on which the film was based was also the basis for the award-winning stage musical, *She Loves Me*.

A Shot in the Dark
★★★ 1964 101min c.

Director: Blake Edwards
Screenplay: Blake Edwards & William Peter Blatty
Source: Play, *L'Idiote* by Marcel Achard & *A Shot in the Dark* by Harry Kurnitz

The best of all the *Pink Panther* films, with bumbling, incompetent, accident-prone Inspector Clouseau convinced that chambermaid Sommer is far too pretty to be guilty of murder. Gag follows gag in a relentless machine-gun-like assault. Not all of it hits the funny bone, but what does is hilarious enough to make up for the rest.

Insp. Clouseau	Peter Sellers
Maria Gambrelli	Elke Sommer
Benjamin Ballon	George Sanders
Insp. Charles Dreyfus	Herbert Lom
Dominique Ballon	Tracy Reed
Kato	Burt Kwouk
Hercule Lajoy	Graham Stark
François	Andre Maranne

Quote 'I suspect everyone, and I suspect no one.'

Psst! After filming *The Pink Panther*, Edwards was due to direct this adaptation of a French farce. He agreed only if he could make it a vehicle for Sellers as Clouseau. Filming was actually finished even before *The Pink Panther* was released • Writer Blatty later found fame writing *The Exorcist*.

Show People
★★★ 1928 82min b/w

Director: King Vidor
Screenplay: Agnes Christine Johnson, Laurence Stallings & Wanda Tuchock

It's the old tale of the girl who comes to Hollywood to be an actress but made in the days when the story couldn't be anything but fresh. Seeing this silent movie in a cinema with an orchestra playing Carl Davis' accompanying music was a real eye-opener. Not only is it an extremely funny and fascinating look at the world of early movies, but Marion Davies turns out to be one of the greatest of screen comediennes. We all know of her as the untalented model for the mistress in *Citizen Kane*. After seeing this, it is a crying shame that William Randolph Hearst insisted on her tackling dramatic roles that were completely wrong for her.

Peggy Pepper	Marion Davies
Billy Boone	William Haines
Oldfish Pepper	Dell Henderson
Andre Telefair	Paul Ralli

Also: Charles Chaplin, King Vidor, Douglas Fairbanks, John Gilbert, Elinor Glyn, Mae Murray, Louella Parsons, Lew Cody

The Silence of the Lambs
★★★ 1991 119min c.

Director: Jonathan Demme
Screenplay: Ted Tally
Source: Novel by Thomas Harris

A great but overrated chiller with FBI trainee Foster deputed to seek help from 'Hannibal the Cannibal' Hopkins in tracking down a serial killer. The scenes with the brilliant but dangerous Hopkins burrowing into Foster's mind are compulsive and deeply disturbing. But when Hopkins disappears half-way through, the pic turns into a daft and implausible thriller. If you want to be *really* frightened, try the other Hannibal movie, *Manhunter*, whose events take place before those in this movie.

Clarice Starling	Jodie Foster
Dr. Hannibal Lecter	Anthony Hopkins
Jack Crawford	Scott Glenn
Jame Gumb	Ted Levine
Dr. Frederick Chilton	Anthony Heald
Catherine Martin	Brooke Smith
Senator Ruth Martin	Diane Baker

Oscars Best Picture, Best Director, Jodie Foster, Anthony Hopkins, Best Screenplay (adapted)

Quote 'A census taker once tried to test me. I ate his liver with some fava beans and a nice Chianti.' • 'Goodbye Clarice…I do wish we could chat longer, but I'm having an old friend for dinner.'

OOPS! Clarice improves herself in many ways but even she couldn't have changed her eye colour from the dark brown sported by the young Clarice, to blue, as the adult Clarice has • If you want to distract yourself, look out for the boom mike in a couple of shots.

Psst! This was only the third film to win the top five Oscars, after *It Happened One Night* and *One Flew Over the Cuckoo's Nest* • As a sick joke, they opened it in America on Valentine's Day • Look out for horror director Roger Corman as FBI director Burke and singer Chris Isaak as leader of the SWAT team • The magazine Hopkins reads in his temporary cell is *Bon Appetit!* • The death's head at the centre of the moth on the ads is actually made up of six naked women • When the film came to Britain, Hopkins apparently delighted in waiting for the first scream, then turning round and smiling devilishly at the person behind him • He claimed to have based his character on a combination of Katharine Hepburn, Truman Capote and HAL, the computer in *2001* • This was to have been Gene Hackman's first film as director but, although he also planned to play Lecter, he pulled out, deciding it was too violent • Michelle Pfeiffer was offered the part of Clarice at one point • Among those working on the film was a 'Moth Wrangler/Stylist'.

Silent Running
★★★ 1971 89min c.

Director: Douglas Trumbull
Screenplay: Deric Washburn, Michael Cimino & Steven Bocho

In the future, Earth no longer supports plant life, the only vegetation being in several space stations in outer space. When the project is closed down, Bruce Dern decides to take matters into his own hands. This early ecological sci-fi pic is gently paced but has considerable charm and poses some interesting ideas. Comic relief is provided by Dern's little mechanical friends, Huey, Louie and Dewey.

Freeman Lowell	Bruce Dern
Wolf	Cliff Potts
Barker	Ron Rifkin
Keenan	Jesse Vint

OOPS! Dern's injured leg changes sides.

Psst! This was the first film as director for Trumbull, who had created the special effects for *2001*.

Silk Stockings
★★★ 1957 117min c.

Director: Rouben Mamoulian
Screenplay: Leonard Gershe & Leonard Spigelgass
Source: Musical play by George S. Kaufman, Leueen McGrath & Abe Burrows based on the film, *Ninotchka*

This musical remake of *Ninotchka*, the tale of a coldly efficient Russian commissar warmed by Paris and love, doesn't have as witty a script as its predecessor. But it has great style, Cole Porter songs and some lovely dancing from Astaire and Charisse. It also has Peter Lorre in a comedy role!

Steve Canfield	Fred Astaire
Ninotchka	Cyd Charisse
Brankov	Peter Lorre
Peggy Dainton	Janis Paige
Bibinski	Jules Munshin
Commissar Vassili Markovitch	George Tobias
Ivanov	Joseph Buloff
Russian Embassy official	Ivan Triesault

Quote 'Where is the little comrade's room?'

OOPS! When Fred takes Cyd onto her hotel room balcony, the typewriter she's been using and the adjacent vase of flowers vanish into thin air • In one number, Charisse's skirt switches to culottes and back again several times.

Psst! Carol Richards provided Cyd Charisse's singing voice.

Silver Streak

★★★ 1976 113min c.

Director: Arthur Hiller
Screenplay: Colin Higgins

A publisher on a cross-country train journey witnesses a murder and is soon in danger himself. Critics hate this blend of thrills, romance and humour for being so derivative of Hitchcock, but I confess to being bowled over the first time I saw it. Although not quite as funny on repeated viewings, some of the scenes with Wilder and Pryor are pure comic gold. It seems a little odd that Pryor arrives so late in the film, though.

George Caldwell	Gene Wilder
Hilly Burns	Jill Clayburgh
Grover Muldoon	Richard Pryor
Roger Devereau	Patrick McGoohan
Sweet	Ned Beatty
Goldtooth	Richard Kiel
Sheriff Chauncey	Clifton James
Mr. Whiney	Ray Walston
Ralston	Scatman Crothers

Quote 'In 10 minutes you're going to have 200 tons of locomotive smashing its way through Central Station on its way to Marshall Field!' • 'I don't know about you, but next time I'm going to take the bus.'

OOPS! As the train moves out of the station, with McGoohan burning the letters, look out of the window. Clearly visible in the reflection of the windows of the station is the camera crew on the handcar who filmed the pictures being used as the back projection.

Psst! Kiel's villain would go on to play virtually the same role in *The Spy Who Loved Me* the following year.

Since You Went Away

★★ 1944 172min b/w

Director: John Cromwell
Screenplay: David O. Selznick
Source: Book, *Together* by Margaret Buell Wilder

Life on the American home front in World War II, centring on Colbert and her two daughters. This US-set equivalent of *Mrs Miniver* is very much a film of its time, aimed at and about those who stayed at home while the men were away fighting. It will just about suffice for one of those rainy Sunday afternoons on the sofa, but it is rather dated, long and episodic. With lapses into outright xenophobia, the patriotic flag-waving all seems a bit much, especially as it's such an ostentatious flag compared to the elegance and simplicity of our own dear Union Jack. You'll probably need to keep the tissues handy.

Anne Hilton	Claudette Colbert
Jane Hilton	Jennifer Jones
Lt. Tony Willet	Joseph Cotten
Bridget Hilton	Shirley Temple
Cpl. William G. Smollett II	Robert Walker
Col. Smollett	Monty Woolley
Emily Hawkins	Agnes Moorehead
Fidelia	Hattie McDaniel
Danny Williams	Craig Stevens
Lt. Solomon	Keenan Wynn
Clergyman	Lionel Barrymore

Also: Guy Madison, Rhonda Fleming, John Derek, Dorothy Dandridge, Albert Basserman, Alla Nazimova

Quote 'When I finishes with my work, I wants my solitude and I wants my privitation.'

Psst! The book on which the film is based was originally a newspaper column consisting of letters written by a columnist to her husband in the forces overseas • Jones and Walker were actually married in real life • Rhonda Fleming and Dorothy Dandridge appear in bit parts.

Sing As We Go

★★ 1934 80min b/w

Director: Basil Dean
Screenplay: J.B. Priestley & Gordon Wellesley

Unemployed millworker Gracie gets on her bike and picks up assorted jobs in Blackpool. When did the habit of workers cheering themselves up with a good singsong die out? Looking at how it boosts morale here, companies ought to consider introducing it into the work day. Our Gracie is as exuberant as always in her best picture but while it's socially and historically interesting, the movie itself now needs a zimmer frame.

Gracie Platt	Gracie Fields
Hugh Phillips	John Loder
Phyllis Logan	Dorothy Hyson

Policeman	Stanley Holloway
Murgatroyd Platt	Frank Pettingell
Sir William Upton	Lawrence Grossmith

Singin' in the Rain
★★★★ 1952 103min c.

Director: Gene Kelly & Stanley Donan
Screenplay: Adolph Green & Betty Comden
Source: Songs by Arthur Freed

The greatest musical ever made, a boisterous, fizzing firecracker of a film. Although it only came about as a way to string some of MGM's songs together (all written by producer Arthur Freed), this tale of the early days of talking pictures is pure cinematic magic. The story, of a young actress forced to dub the voice of an obnoxious silent star, is often extremely funny. The acting is splendid, with Kelly and O'Connor making a great buddy team while Gene and Debbie strike great sparks off each other. Some of the musical numbers are simply out of this world, particularly 'Moses Supposes', 'Make 'Em Laugh', 'Good Morning' and, of course, the title song. Even Kelly's balletic interlude, 'Broadway Ballet', doesn't jar as much as in his other films. The sort of movie you want to watch all over again as soon as you've seen it.

Don Lockwood	Gene Kelly
Cosmo Brown	Donald O'Connor
Kathy Selden	Debbie Reynolds
Lina Lamont	Jean Hagen
R.F. Simpson	Millard Mitchell
Dancer	Cyd Charisse
Zelda Zanders	Rita Moreno
Roscoe Dexter	Douglas Fowley
Dora Bailey	Madge Blake
Rod	King Donovan
Phoebe Dinsmore	Kathleen Freeman
Diction coach	Robert Watson

Quote 'Dignity, always dignity.' • 'Simpson, I once gave you a cigar. Can I have it back?' • 'People? I ain't people. I'm a... 'a shimmering, glowing star in the cinema firmament.' It says so, right there.' • 'If we bring a little joy into your humdrum lives, it makes us feel our work ain't been in vain fer nothin'.'

OOPS! As Millard Mitchell gets up after the unsuccessful screening of the early sound film, the edge screen that is supposed to be behind him cuts off his shoulder.

Psst! The film received only two Oscar nominations and didn't win one. It was overshadowed by *An American in Paris*, also starring Kelly, which won the Best Picture Oscar that year • The silent movie sequences and costumes were all based on real examples • We see Reynolds dubbing Hagen's atrocious voice for her new talking picture. But Reynolds' own voice wasn't felt to be sufficiently resonant, so it is actually Hagen that we are hearing. Hagen even sings 'Would You' rather than Reynolds • Reynolds, the ex-Miss Burbank, received just $300 a week against Gene Kelly's $2,500 a week salary. To get to work, she took the bus, having to change twice • Before this film, Reynolds' dancing and singing experience was almost zero while Kelly and O'Connor had been performing since they could walk. In addition to his own taps, Kelly also dubbed those for Reynolds • Angry that Reynolds had been foisted on him, Kelly pushed her hard. During 'Good Mornin'', she burst blood vessels in her feet and was ordered to rest for three days. She was back after just one • Kelly lost his temper, as he was often prone to do, during the number 'You Were Meant for Me', where the two of them were alone on a sound stage. As Kelly played around the ladder on which Reynolds stood, he got the chewing gum she'd left on it stuck in his hair! She claims never to have chewed gum again • Producer and ex-songwriter Arthur Freed wrote the 'Make 'Em Laugh' number overnight for O'Connor. Nobody saw fit to tell Freed that it was a rip-off of Cole Porter's song, 'Be a Clown', that was used in *The Pirate* which Freed had produced. O'Connor needed three days' rest after the incredibly energetic routine. But the negative was damaged and so he had to do it again, needing another three days off • The staging of the 'Singin' in the Rain' number was Kelly's idea. He asked for holes to be dug in the ground so that the water would collect in puddles. According to writers Betty Comden and Adolph Green: 'We knew from the start there was a scene where there was rain, and the leading man was singin' in it. What we hadn't written into the script was: "Here Gene Kelly does perhaps the outstanding solo number of his career".' • The rain that Kelly so memorably dances in was adulterated with milk to show up better on film. The sequence was actually filmed by day. The street set was covered with a tarpaulin to make it dark. But it was very hot under the tarpaulin and Kelly, who had a bad cold and had to wear a thick wool suit, was soaked to the skin and scared he would develop pneumonia. Yet throughout the day and a half it took to get it in the can, he looked as if he hadn't a care in the world. Now that's acting • When the scene was rehearsed one day at five o'clock, the water changed from a torrent to a dribble. It was, the panicky technicians soon discovered, the time that local residents tended to turn on their water spinklers • According to Francois Truffaut, Hitchcock once claimed that his favourite scene in any movie is where, at the end of 'Good Morning', the sofa goes backwards and Reynolds quickly has to pull her skirt down • One of the most infamous of all backstage quotations was uttered before the scarf sequence in the Broadway Ballet was filmed. There were problems with Charisse's costume, which was apparently not covering all of her pubic hair. Finally, the costume designer Walter Plunkett was satisfied, and happily and innocently shouted out: 'We've got Cyd Charisse's crotch licked' • The car driven by Reynolds was the same one that had been used by Mickey Rooney in the Andy Hardy films.

Singles
★★★★ 1992 99min c.

Director: Cameron Crowe
Screenplay: Cameron Crowe

A wonderfully funny romantic comedy, following the wiggly course of love, true or otherwise, for half a dozen Twentysomethings in Seattle. Spot-on in its examination of dating rituals, particularly the use of the telephone, this film from former rock journalist Crowe is a true original. The pull-back ending, showing an ever-widening circle of people having exactly the same hassles in their lives, is particularly memorable.

Janet Livermore . . . . .Bridget Fonda
Steve Dunne . . . . .Campbell Scott
Linda Powell . . . . .Kyra Sedgwick
Debbie Hunt . . . . .Sheila Kelley
David Bailey .Jim True
Cliff Poncier . . . . .Matt Dillon
Dr. Jamison . . . . .Bill Pullman
Also: James Le Gros, Devon Raymond, Camilo Gallardo, Ally Walker, Eric Stoltz, Jeremy Piven, Tom Skerritt

Blurb Love Is A Game. Easy To Start. Hard To Finish.

Psst! Look out for *Batman* director Tim Burton in a brief cameo as the chap picking up 20 bucks to direct Debbie's dating video • Adam Ant is Sedgwick's date on the roller coaster • Keep watching after the credits of the video version for some outtakes.

Sitting Pretty
★★★ 1948 84min b/w

Director: Walter Lang
Screenplay: F. Hugh Herbert
Source: Novel, *Belvedere* by Gwen Davenport

A desperate couple hire a prissy, self-confessed genius to look after their over-boisterous brood. Sweeping in like a male Mary Poppins, Mr. Belvedere soon imposes order. But he is not all he seems. Webb is oustanding in this still highly amusing comedy. It's easy to see why two sequels were made, *Mr. Belvedere Goes to College* and *Mr. Belvedere Rings the Bell*, but they had little of the first film's wit or inspiration.

Harry King . . . . .Robert Young
Tacey King . . . . .Maureen O'Hara
Lynn Belvedere . . . . .Clifton Webb
Mr. Appleton . . . . .Richard Haydn
Edna Philby . . . . .Louise Allbritton
Peggy . . . . .Randy Stuart
Hammond . . . . .Ed Begley
Larry . . . . .Larry Olsen

Quote 'May I ask what your profession is?' – 'Certainly. I am a genius.' • 'Your husband has a great deal to be modest about.' • 'Don't ever again, so long as you live, dare to call me uncle. By no stretch of the imagination could I possibly be a relative of yours.'

Sleeper
★★★ 1973 88min c.

Director: Woody Allen
Screenplay: Woody Allen & Marshall Brickman

A nebbish in hospital for an operation on an ulcer wakes up 200 hundred years later and winds up plotting to overthrow a totalitarian government. Woody Allen proves himself adept at slapstick, although he doesn't stint on the verbal gags. Although some contemporary 70s humour has dated and there are a few dull stretches, this remains an extremely funny sci-fi parody from Woody's pre-navel gazing days.

Miles Monroe . . . . .Woody Allen
Luna Schlosser . . . . .Diane Keaton
Erno Windt .John Beck
Dr. Melik . . . . .Mary Gregory
Dr. Tyron .Don Keefer
Dr. Agon .Don McLiam
Dr. Orva . . . . .Bartlett Robinson

Quote 'I can't believe this. My doctor said I'd be up and on my feet in five days. He was off by 199 years.' • 'It's hard to believe that you haven't had sex for 200 years.' – '204 if you count my marriage.'

Psst! The costumes for this movie were designed by Joel Schumacher, who later became a director of films like *Batman Forever* and *Falling Down* • The voice of the nasty computer is Douglas Rain, who was 'HAL' in *2001* and *2010*.

Sleepless in Seattle
★★★★ 1993 104min c.

Director: Nora Ephron
Screenplay: Nora Ephron, David S. Ward & Jeff Arch

One of the most unashamedly romantic films of recent years, with journalist Ryan getting the idea into her head that although she's never met him, widower Hanks may be the only man in the world for her. Her ally, Hanks' son, does his best to bring the two together. Grab a few tissues, tuck your feet up and prepare for a witty, tearful treat.

Sam Baldwin	Tom Hanks
Annie Reed	Meg Ryan
Walter	Bill Pullman
Jonah Baldwin	Ross Malinger
Becky	Rosie O'Donnell
Jessica	Gaby Hoffman
Greg	Victor Garber
Suzy	Rita Wilson
Maggie Baldwin	Carey Lowell
Jay	Rob Reiner
Victoria	Barbara Garrick
Claire	Dana Ivey

Quote 'Things are a little different now. First, you have to be friends. You have to like each other. Then, you neck. This could go on for years. Then you have tests, and then you get to do it with a condom. The good news is, you split the check.'

Showing An Affair to Remember.

OOPS! How come Annie doesn't recognise Sam when she has already seen his picture at her office?

Psst! In America, people paid projectionists to flash up proposals of marriage, feeling that if their intended wasn't in the right mood then, they never would be.

Sleuth
★★★ 1972 138min c.

Director: Joseph L. Mankiewicz
Screenplay: Anthony Shaffer
Source: Play by Shaffer

A crime writer with a taste for mechanical toys suggests a plot for an insurance scam to his wife's lover. But the stakes are higher than he lets on. This wonderfully labyrinthine thriller is a *tour de force* for the two leads, who seem to be having as much fun as the audience. There can't be many plays or films which switch direction as often as this. Good clean macabre fun which is enjoyable even on repeated viewings when you know what's going to happen.

Andrew Wyke	Laurence Olivier
Milo Tindle	Michael Caine
Insp. Doppler	Alec Cawthorne
Marguerite	Margo Channing
Det. Sgt. Tarrant	John Matthews
PC Higgs	Teddy Martin

Quote 'This, as they say, is where the plot thickens.' • 'I understand you want to marry my wife.'

Psst! After a successful West End run, the play ran for 1,222 performances on Broadway • Albert Finney was first choice for Milo • Margo Channing is, of course, an in-joke, a homage to *All About Eve* • The portrait on Olivier's wall of his wife was posed for by Joanne Woodward.

Slither
★★★ 1973 97min c.

Director: Howard Zieff
Screenplay: W.D. Richter

This off-the-wall comedy involves a hoard of stolen cash, gangsters and a pair of incredibly sinister-looking Recreational Vehicles. Probably the only conspiracy road movie ever, it's sometimes a little too confusing for its own good. But it harbours a deliciously tongue-in-cheek sense of humour and those vans are an amazingly effective way of keeping the mood tense.

Dick Kanipsia	James Caan
Barry Fenaka	Peter Boyle
Kitty Kopetzky	Sally Kellerman
Mary Fenaka	Louise Lasser
Vincent J. Palmer	Allen Garfield
Harry Moss	Richard B. Shull
Man with ice cream	Alex Rocco

The Small Back Room

★★★ 1949 106min b/w

Director: Michael Powell & Emeric Pressburger
Screenplay: Michael Powell & Emeric Pressburger
Source: Novel by Nigel Balchin

An offbeat wartime drama with bomb expert Farrar fighting red tape, a new type of German bomb and his own desire for a few stiff ones. Occasionally nerve-wracking and with the usual raft of interesting characters we expect from Powell and Pressburger, there's also an extraordinary surreal section where Farrar fights the demon drink.

Sammy Rice	David Farrar
Susan	Kathleen Byron
R.B. Waring	Jack Hawkins
Capt. Stewart	Michael Gough
Minister	Robert Morley
Col. Holland	Leslie Banks
Corp. Taylor	Cyril Cusack
Landlord	Sidney James
Bandaged soldier	Bryan Forbes

Smokey and the Bandit

★ 1977 96min c.

Director: Hal Needham
Screenplay: James Lee Barrett, Charles Shyer & Alan Mandel

A modern-day bootlegger is chased around the American Midwest by an irate sheriff, grinning all the time to camera just to show us how funny it's all supposed to be. Consisting of little more than a series of chases tied together, this extraordinarily popular movie has been compared to the *Road Runner* cartoons. Sadly, it doesn't have *Road Runner's* depth of characterisation or subtlety of humour. To be fair, some of the stunts are okay. The fact that there were two even more appaling sequels is just too depressing for words, although even Burt Reynolds had the sense to miss out on the last one.

Bandit	Burt Reynolds
Sheriff Buford T. Justice	Jackie Gleason
Carrie	Sally Field
Cledus	Jerry Reed
Junior	Mike Henry
Little Enos	Paul Williams
Big Enos	Pat McCormick
Trucker	Hank Worden

OOPS! Either Sheriff Gleason has umpteen cars or an incredibly quick body shop because dents appear and disappear in quick order throughout.

Psst! Field and Reynolds were then an item.

Snow White and the Seven Dwarfs

★★★ 1937 83min c.

Director: Various
Screenplay: Various
Source: Fairy tale by the Brothers Grimm

A beautiful princess fleeing her evil step-mother bunks down with seven besotted but extraordinarily well-behaved little diamond miners and ends up being rescued by the usual wimpish prince on a white horse. The lashings of sentiment in the first ever feature-length cartoon are now a little hard to take in places. However, there's ample compensation in the charming animation, the dwarfs' humour, the timeless songs and the truly scary Queen.

Snow White	Adriana Caselotti
Prince Charming	Harry Stockwell
The Queen	Lucille La Verne
Sneezy	Billy Gilbert

Blurb The Show Sensation of the Generation!

Quote 'Mirror, mirror, on the wall, who is the fairest of them all?' • 'The only film that made money in 1937… And it would have made more money if they woulda let *me* play Snow White.' [Mae West]

Psst! So certain was Hollywood that the public wouldn't sit still for a feature cartoon that the project was dubbed 'Disney's folly'. Louis B. Mayer, head of MGM, said: 'Who'd pay to see a drawing of a fairy princess when they can watch Joan Crawford's boobs for the same price?' • Among the names rejected for the dwarfs were Weepy, Dirty, Shirty, Woeful, Sniffy, Puffy, Lazy, Deafy, Wheezy, Shorty, Gloomy, Snoopy and Awful who 'steals and drinks and is very dirty'. In case you get involved in one of those infuriating 'Name the seven dwarfs' discussions, the names finally chosen were Sneezy, Sleepy, Grumpy, Happy, Bashful, Dopey and Doc • With costs escalating, Disney had to borrow heavily. If the film had flopped, the studio would have collapsed • Disney threw a celebratory weekend party for its employees when the film was completed. Letting off three years of steam, it quickly degenerated into a drunken orgy remarkable even by Hollywood's wild standards, forcing Disney into a cover-up operation to protect the studio's reputation • In Britain, there was a censorship storm, with the flight of Snow White through the forest considered so frightening that nobody under the age of 16 could see it unless accompanied by an adult • Several scenes were cut at the planning stage, such as the Huntsman being led away to be tortured and Snow White's mother dying in childbirth. They decided against including the original ending of the aptly-named Brothers Grimm, with Snow White forcing her stepmother to dance at her wedding in red-hot shoes until she drops down dead! • This was the first screen musical to generate its own soundtrack album • When Disney received a special award for the movie, Shirley Temple handed over a regular Oscar, together with seven little ones.

Some Like It Hot

★★★★ 1959 120min b/w

Director: Billy Wilder
Screenplay: Billy Wilder & I.A.L. Diamond
Source: Screenplay, *Fanfares of Love*, by Robert Thoeren & M. Logan

Two musicians witness the Valentine's Day Massacre and hide out in drag with an all girl jazz band. As one of them is the insufferably gorgeous Marilyn Monroe, life in womens' clothing proves something of a strain for this randy pair. A splendid re-creation of the Jazz Age, the Roaring in these Twenties is of laughter, for this is as nearly perfect as a comedy can be. The script is lively, witty and imaginative, the action moves at a smart lick and the performances from Lemmon, Curtis and particularly Monroe, are out of this world. Has Monroe ever been sexier or more delightfully naive? Has there ever been a funnier Cary Grant impression? The movie is full of memorable moments, the best of which is probably when Curtis is pretending that Monroe's attempts to seduce him are having no effect at all.

Sugar Kane . . . . .Marilyn Monroe
Joe/Josephine . . . . .Tony Curtis
Jerry/Daphne . . . . .Jack Lemmon
Osgood E. Fielding III . . . . .Joe E. Brown
Spats Columbo . . . . .George Raft
Mulligan . . . . .Pat O'Brien
Little Bonaparte . . . . .Nehemiah Persoff

Sweet Sue . . . . .Joan Shawlee
Toothpick Charlie . . . . .George E. Stone
Spat's henchman . . . . .Mike Mazurki
Sig Poliakoff .Billy Gray

Quote 'Well, that's it for tonight, folks. This is Sweet Sue, saying good night, reminding all you daddies out there that every girl in my band is a virtuoso – and I intend to keep it that way.' • 'Look how she moves. It's just like Jello on springs. I tell you, it's a whole different sex.' • 'I always get the fuzzy end of the lollipop.' • 'All they have to do is play eight bars of 'Come to Me, My Melancholy Baby', and my spine turns to custard. I get goose pimply all over and I come to 'em.' • 'I think you're on the right track.' – 'I must be. Your glasses are beginning to steam up.' • 'You don't understand, Osgood. I'm a man!' – 'Well, nobody's perfect.' [Last line] • 'She has breasts like granite and a brain like Swiss cheese, full of holes. Extracting a performance from her is like pulling teeth…Would I direct a third film with her? I am too old and too rich to go through this again.' [Wilder]

Psst! In the early stages, the film was planned to star Danny Kaye and Bob Hope. Then Lemmon was signed, only to be sacked when it looked as if the audience-pulling Frank Sinatra would sign up. When Monroe agreed to star, however, Sinatra was not needed and Lemmon was back in. Monroe's signing meant Mitzi Gaynor was booted out • Monroe apparently agreed to do the film without even reading the script. She had been away from movies for two years and needed the money. When she read it, she was horrified that she was being asked to play a blonde so dumb she couldn't tell her two girlfriends were really men in drag. In an effort to avoid doing it, she pointed out that her contract insisted that all her movies should be in colour. Finally, she went on an eating spree in the hope she would become too fat to play Sugar • However wonderful she looks on screen, Monroe was, as so often, a nightmare to work with. 'Kissing Marilyn was like kissing Hitler,' said the less than enamoured Curtis. Marilyn apparently responded: 'He only said that because I wore prettier dresses than he did.' Curtis was not alone, however, in his view that, 'Marilyn was as mad as a hatter. She had a woman's body but the mind of a four-year-old. If she hadn't had that sexy look and 38-inch bust she'd have been locked up for sure.' • One of her lines in Daphne and Josphine's room, 'Where's the Bourbon?', had to be shot 59 times because she fluffed the words. The line was written in one of the drawers she opens, but when she couldn't remember which drawer it was, it was pasted in all of them. The line, 'It's me. Sugar' took 47 takes, even though the lines were written on a blackboard from take 30 onwards • In addition to constantly fumbling her lines, Monroe was extremely unpunctual and sometimes didn't turn up at all. So unpopular was she on set that she wasn't invited to the end of shooting party. However, in her defence, she had not long before suffered a miscarriage and it transpired later that she became pregnant again during filming with a baby she would lose soon afterwards • George Raft was apparently delighted by her tardiness. He had only been hired for a week but stayed on for all four months as a result of Marilyn's antics and all at a time when he was strapped for cash. His casino in Havana had recently been shut down by Castro without compensation • Raft asks one of the younger gangsters, 'Where did you pick up that cheap trick?' when he sees him flipping a coin. Raft himself had made the gesture famous in *Scarface* back in 1932. The chap he's talking to is Edward G. Robinson Jr., following in dad's footsteps • In one scene, Raft had to kick a toothpick out of Toothpick Charlie's mouth. Raft fretted that he would kick actor George E. Stone by mistake. To show him how easy it was, director Wilder tried it himself and kicked Stone so hard he was hospitalised • Ex-Broadway dancer Raft taught Lemmon and Joe E. Brown how to tango for their scene together • Wilder hired a female impersonator to teach Curtis and Lemmon the tricks of the trade. To prove that they had mastered it they were told they had to use the ladies' lavatory without being discovered • Curtis claims to have based his Josephine on Grace Kelly • The ending of the movie had to be changed because Monroe was not around. One of the famous last lines in movie history was only thought up the night before it was filmed • Was Curtis' millionaire character based on Alexander Korda? The king of pre-war British movies used a very similar seduction technique, claiming to his latest conquest-to-be that the most beautiful women in the world had tried and failed to cure his impotence. Almost inevitably, the challenge would be accepted and a 'miracle' would occur.

Something Wild
★★★ 1986 113min c.

Director: Jonathan Demme
Screenplay: E. Max Frye

Meek pencil-pusher Daniels is virtually kidnapped by the anarchic, totally OTT, Griffith and dragged along on a wild trip that involves that famous handcuff scene and attending her high school reunion. The film switches abruptly from farce to something darker when violent ex Liotta turns up. Constantly confounding your expectations of where it's going, possibly because it doesn't know itself, this is still a highly entertaining and blackly amusing film. Griffith is just wonderful.

Charles Driggs	Jeff Daniels
Audrey Hankel	Melanie Griffith
Ray Sinclair	Ray Liotta
Irene	Margaret Colin
The Country Squire	Tracey Walter
Peaches	Dana Preu
Larry Dillman	Jack Gilpin
Also: John Sayles, John Waters

Psst! There are cameos from directors John Sayles and John Waters as, respectively, the motorcycle cop and used-car guy.

Sommersby
★★★ 1993 112min c.

Director: Jon Amiel
Screenplay: Nicholas Meyer & Sarah Kernochan
Source: Film, *The Return of Martin Guerre* by Daniel Vigne & Carriere.

After seven years away fighting in the Civil War, Southern gentlewoman Foster's husband returns home a much changed man. The question is, is he the same man? Jodie Foster and Richard Gere are both superb in this fascinating period love story, which is old-fashioned filmmaking at its finest with a story that keeps you guessing right up to the final minute. How rare to find a film that really is about love, rather than lust. Without being too explicit, this pair's passion practically burns a hole in the screen. A shame that Gere's character has to be quite such a 90s liberal, but you can't have everything.

Jack Sommersby	Richard Gere
Laurel Sommersby	Jodie Foster
Judge Isaacs	James Earl Jones
Orin Meecham	Bill Pullman
Lawyer Dawson	Maury Chaykin
Buck	Lanny Flaherty
Travis	Wendell Wellman
Little Rob	Bretty Kelley
Dick Mead	R. Lee Ermey

Psst! The cow is called Clarice, presumably a reference to Foster's part in *Silence of the Lambs* • Some apparently hot love scenes filmed between Gere and Foster never made it to the screen. According to Gere, they took a heavy toll: 'If the day is filled with explicit sex scenes I seldom feel like even more sex at night.'

The Song of Bernadette
★★ 1943 156min c.

Director: Henry King
Screenplay: George Seaton
Source: Novel by Franz Werfel

Nuns and Hollywood are a deadly mixture and should never be allowed to come into contact with each other. Sadly, they couldn't resist telling – at staggering length – the story of the nun whose visions led to the discovery of the waters of Lourdes, which can allegedly cure any physical ailment. Perhaps all future Hollywood executives should be dunked there to cure them of greenlighting movies with wimples in them.

Bernadette Soubirous . . . . Jennifer Jones
Peyramale, Dean of Lourdes . . Charles Bickford
Antoine Nicolau . . . . William Eythe
Prosecutor Dutour . . . . Vincent Price
Dr. Dozous . . . . Lee J. Cobb
Sister Marie Theresa Vauzous . . Gladys Cooper
Louise Soubirous . . . . Anne Revere
François Soubirous . . . . Roman Bohnen
Croisine Bouhouhorts . . . . Edith Barrett
Louis Napoleon III . . . . Fortunio Bonanova
Napoleon . . . . Jerome Cowan
Callet, the Policeman . . . . Marcel Dalio
Virgin Mary . . . . Linda Darnell
Jacomet . . . . Charles Dingle
Monk . . . . Fritz Leiber
Woman . . . . Mae Marsh
Lacade . . . . Aubrey Mather
Adolar . . . . Dickie Moore
Psychiatrist . . . . Alan Napier
Chaplain . . . . Moroni Olsen
Louis Bouriette . . . . Sig Rumann
Doctor . . . . Edward Van Sloan

Oscars Jennifer Jones

Quote 'For those who believe in God, no explanation is necessary. For those who do not believe in God, no explanation is possible.' [Opening caption]

Psst! Jennifer Jones was groomed by producer David O. Selznick for stardom. This was her first major film role. She was married at the time of the film to Robert Walker but divorced him a couple of years later and married Selznick in 1949 • Sex siren Linda Darnell appeared, unbilled, as the Virgin Mary in what, considering her colourful private and professional life, was surely the single most inappropriate casting decision in Hollywood history. According to one version of the story, so sensitive was the issue of the Virgin Mary considered to be that nobody wanted to cast the part without the approval of studio head Darryl F. Zanuck. He was abroad serving in the army and was so annoyed at being bothered with such inconsequentialities that he replied with the most facetious suggestion he could think of. Back in Hollywood, his message was treated seriously! The fully-embroidered story has Darnell initially giving such a sexy portrayal of the role that it had rapidly to be reshot with the camera distinctly out of focus.

Sons of the Desert
★★★ 1934 68min b/w

Director: William A. Seiter
Screenplay: Frank Craven & Byron Mogan

One of the best of Stan and Ollie's feature films (the best being *Way Out West*). The lads tell their wives they're off to Honolulu but it's all just a ruse so that they can attend their mason-like convention. Anyone who thinks they stand a chance of getting away with that can't have watched any Laurel and Hardy before. The hilarious hi-jinks are capped by the song 'Honolulu Baby'.

Stan . . . . Stan Laurel
Oliver . . . . Oliver Hardy
Charley . . . . Charley Chase
Mrs. Betty Laurel . . . . Dorothy Christy
Mrs. Lottie Chase Hardy . . . . Mae Busch
Dr. Horace Meddick . . . . Lucien Littlefield
Extra . . . . Hal Roach

Quote 'If I have to go to Honolulu alone, he's going with me.' • 'Well, here's another nice mess you've gotten me into.' • 'To catch a Hardy, they've got to get up very early in the morning.' – 'What time?'

Psst! The international fan club of Laurel and Hardy call themselves after this film's title • Mae Busch had been a star in the silent era • Robert Cummings can be glimpsed briefly in a bit part.

Sophie's Choice
★★ 1982 151min c.

Director: Alan J. Pakula
Screenplay: Alan J. Pakula
Source: Novel by William Stryon

A Polish woman's disintegration in postwar New York is revealed to have been caused by her suffering in a concentration camp. The revelation of the awful choice Sophie has to make is devastatingly chilling. But the incredible time it takes for us to discover what it is and the irritating mannerisms of Meryl in Polish mode make the whole film's handling of its subject matter exploitative and distasteful. Does anybody know what Streep's real voice sounds like?

Sophie	Meryl Streep
Nathan	Kevin Kline
Stingo	Peter MacNicol
Narrator	Josef Sommer
Yetta	Rita Karin
Larry	Stephen D. Newman
Morris Fink	Josh Mostel

Oscars Meryl Streep

Psst! William Stryon, the novel's author, said he always visualised Ursula Andress in the lead and Pakula originally wanted Liv Ullmann • Streep lost 25 pounds [and shaved her head] for the Auschwitz scenes and gained 10 pounds for those in New York. She also learnt to speak Polish and German • This was Kline's film debut.

Sorry, Wrong Number
★★★ 1948 89min b/w

Director: Anatole Litvak
Screenplay: Lucille Fletcher
Source: Radio drama by Fletcher

A hypochondriac woman, confined to bed, gets a crossed line and hears two men planning a murder. She tries frantically to raise help before it's too late. Although there are several serious plot implausibilities which have to be glossed over, this remains a good, suspenseful film noir.

Leona Stevenson	Barbara Stanwyck
Henry Stevenson	Burt Lancaster
Sally Lord Dodge	Ann Richards
Dr. Alexander	Wendell Corey
Waldo Evans	Harold Vermilyea
James Cotterill	Ed Begley
Fred Lord	Leif Erickson
Morano	William Conrad

Psst! This was originally a short radio play in which the lead was played by Agnes Moorehead. If was felt a bigger star was needed to play the part on screen • Rather than use costume jewellery, a local firm lent a small fortune in gems for the movie. This meant that whenever she was in character, Stanwyck was followed by an armed guard.

The Sound of Music
★★ 1965 174min c.

Director: Robert Wise
Screenplay: Ernest Lehman
Source: Musical play by Rogers & Hammerstein

What is it about nuns and Hollywood? Andrews is the naughty novice who becomes governess to an uptight widower and his flock of pre-Osmond singing angels. Then those beastly Germans spoil things and everyone has to flee. If you feel like fleeing yourself, you aren't the only one. Barmen claim to be inundated by *Sound of Music* refugees whenever it comes on the telly. If 'Edelweiss', 'Do Re Mi' and 'Climb Every Mountain' are for you, and you can ignore the dreadful direction and acting, then fine. It certainly isn't among My Favourite Things.

Maria	Julie Andrews
Capt. Von Trapp	Christopher Plummer
The Baroness	Eleanor Parker
Max Detweiler	Richard Haydn
Mother Abbess	Peggy Wood
Sister Sophia	Marni Nixon
Frau Schmidt	Norma Varden
Sister Margaretta	Anna Lee

Oscars Best Picture

Quote 'There's nothing more irresistible to a man than a woman who's in love with him.'
• '*The Sound of Mucus*' [Plummer] • 'Working with her is like being hit over the head with a Valentine card.' [Plummer about Andrews]
• 'The most evil film to ever come out of Hollywood.' [Alfred Hitchcock] • 'Calorie counters, diabetics and grown-ups from 8 to 80 had best beware.' [Critic Judith Crist]

OOPS! In the market, take your eyes off Andrews and the kids and look instead for the crate marked: 'Jaffa Oranges – Product of Israel.' Israel didn't come about until 1948. Although very visible in the cinema, sadly on TV or video this blunder may not be apparent though it is in some photos of the film
• Geography wasn't the film-makers' strong point. The way the Von Trapps flee across the

mountains is not towards Switzerland, but is actually the route to Germany and the Nazis! In any case, the Von Trapps got out through Italy, not Switzerland.

Psst! The film was so successful, taking $160m around the world, that it knocked *Gone With the Wind* off its perch as the most successful movie of all time. It cost $8m with another $12m spent on prints and promotion • The weather during filming was appaling, being cold with heavy rainstorms. Ox carts had to be used in the mountains because jeeps couldn't manage the quagmires that the tracks had turned into. Julie Andrews sang music-hall songs to the cast and crew to cheer everyone up while they waited for the weather to clear • Many would agree with the Korean distributors who decided the film was too long. They cut it, by losing all the songs! • In Germany, everything to do with the Nazis had to be cut out, leaving the film only two-thirds of its original length • Top movie critic Pauline Kael was fired from McCall's Magazine for writing: 'Will probably be the single most repressive influence on artistic freedom in movies for the next few years.' • The real Baroness Von Trapp, the character played by Andrews, appears in the movie as an extra • Marni Nixon, who dubbed stars for films like *My Fair Lady*, *The King and I* and *West Side Story*, appears in the flesh for the one and only time as Sister Sophia • She also dubbed Peggy Wood's singing, despite the fact that Wood had been an opera singer • Christopher Plummer refused to have his singing dubbed until his efforts were played back to him. Appaled at how he sounded, he promptly agreed to let Bill Lee voice his songs • Mary Martin, Larry Hagman's mother, played the part of Maria on Broadway • Mia Farrow was turned down for the role of one of the Von Trapp children. She was one of 300 child actors who auditioned • Despite the pickup in bar takings, some people go out of their way to watch the film whenever they can. Mrs. Myra Franklin of Cardiff is listed by the *Guinness Book of Records* as having seen it some 940 times, more than anyone else has seen any film in the cinema.

South Pacific
★★ 1958 171min c.

Director: Joshua Logan
Screenplay: Paul Osborn
Source: Musical by Rodgers & Hammerstein from book, *Tales of the South Pacific* by James A. Michener

Great songs. Shame about the movie. The story, of love and warfare on an island in the South Pacific in World War II, is incredibly slackly handled, is filled with irritating coloured hues and seems to go on forever. Even the presence of Rodgers and Hammerstein greats like 'Some Enchanted Evening' and 'There is Nothing Like a Dame' aren't enough to compensate. You'd be better off listening to the soundtrack while flicking through a handful of holiday brochures.

Emile de Becque	Rossano Brazzi
Nellie Forbush	Mitzi Gaynor
Lt. Joe Cable	John Kerr
Luther Billis	Ray Walston
Bloody Mary	Juanita Hall
Liat	France Nuyen
Pilot	Doug McClure

Also: Joan Fontaine

Psst! The director had wanted Elizabeth Taylor for Mitzi Gaynor's role, but the nervous Liz flunked an audition in front of Rodgers and Hammerstein • Although Hall had played the role in London, her voice was still dubbed by Muriel Smith. Brazzi was dubbed by Giorgio Tozzi and Bill Lee's tonsils substitute for Kerr's. Of the leads, only Gaynor got to hear her own pipes in the movie • Joan Fontaine appears in an unbilled cameo • Unusually for a musical, it was filmed on location in Hawaii • 20,000 Marines and sailors were lent by the American Government for the show at Thanksgiving, while the battle scenes were genuine Marine war games • Richard Rodgers is said to have taken only five minutes to write 'Bali Hi'.

Spartacus
★★★★ 1960 196min c.

Director: Stanley Kubrick
Screenplay: Dalton Trumbo
Source: Novel by Howard Fast

Long it may be, but this tale of the slaves led by he of the chiselled dimple, revolting against the Roman Empire, still has awesome power to move and entertain. Get the dreadful American narrator's history lesson out of the way, ignore the odd bit of coarse acting and prepare to be chilled by the callousness of the Romans, moved by the desire of the gladiators to rule their own destiny and thrilled by some of the greatest battle scenes ever put on celluloid. A winner.

Spartacus	Kirk Douglas
Marcus Crassus	Laurence Olivier
Gracchus	Charles Laughton

Varinia	Jean Simmons
Antoninus	Tony Curtis
Batiatus	Peter Ustinov
Julius Caesar	John Gavin
Helena	Nina Foch
Tigranes	Herbert Lom
Crixus	John Ireland
Marcellus	Charles McGraw
Claudia	Joanna Barnes
Draba	Woody Strode
David	Harold J. Stone
Caius	John Hoyt

Oscars Peter Ustinov

Quote 'I'm Spartacus!' • 'My taste includes both snails and oysters.' • 'Corpulence makes a man reasonable, pleasant and phlegmatic. Have you noticed that the nastiest of talents are invariably thin?'

OOPS! As Kirk Douglas arrives at the gladiator school, you can clearly see a vaccination scar on his arm • Many people claim to have seen extras wearing wristwatches and a truck in the background during a battle scene. I've yet to catch either.

Psst! Director Anthony Mann was fired after a week and Douglas, whose project it was, signed up Kubrick. The two, however, fought furiously throughout much of the production after Kubrick wanted to change the screenplay • The original screenplay was by Dalton Trumbo. This was the first time his name had appeared publicly on a film since he was imprisoned for 10 months for refusing to testify before HUAC and then blacklisted • There was plenty of bad blood on set. Douglas told each star that theirs was the most important role, doctoring the script he sent to each to prove it. But when the cast compared their scripts, there was uproar, particularly as Laughton and Olivier were far from the best of mates • Ingrid Bergman was among those who turned down Jean Simmons' part • 8,500 extras were involved in the final battle scenes. They were Spanish soldiers who were trained in the fighting tactics of the Romans • Several scenes were attacked by the Catholic Legion of Decency and were dropped • When the restored version was being prepared, the soundtrack was missing for the bathing scene – cut from the original release after objections from the censors – where Olivier probes Curtis about his sexual preferences. Although Curtis could dub his part again, Anthony Mann had to be brought in to impersonate Olivier. Listen carefully, and you can just tell it's him • Although Presidents often have movies

screened for them in the White House, President Kennedy apparently played hookey and nipped out to his local fleapit, incognito, to see this • The sound of the excited crowd watching the fighting gladiators is actually a recording of the crowd at an American football game • Although the film was popular with the public, it still failed to make its substantial cost of $12m back at the box office.

Speed
★★★★ 1994 115min c.

Director: Jan De Bont
Screenplay: Graham Yost

One of the best action-thrillers for years, with psycho Hopper wiring a bus to explode if it goes slower than 50 mph. There are plenty of implausibilities: a member of the bomb squad with no radio or cellphone, for instance, and the idea of a bus in the LA rush hour even getting to 50, let alone staying above it. The last action sequence is also somewhat risible. But the rest is such a humdinger that we can forgive its drawbacks easily. Our hearts pop into our mouths in the opening scene and don't emerge again till the closing credits. Who'd have thought Reeves could ever cut it as an action hero? And let's not forget the wonderful Bullock, surely the best young actress in movies today?

Jack Traven	Keanu Reeves
Howard Payne	Dennis Hopper
Annie	Sandra Bullock
Lt. McMahon	Joe Morton
Harry	Jeff Daniels
Stephens	Alan Ruck
Jaguar owner	Glenn Plummer
Norwood	Richard Lineback

Quote 'Anything else that'll keep this lift from falling?' – 'Yeah, the basement.' • 'Interactive TV, Jack. Wave to the future.' • 'Poor people are crazy, Jack. I'm eccentric.' • 'I have to warn you. I've heard relationships based on intense experiences never work.' – 'Okay, we'll have to base it on sex, then.' – 'Whatever you say, ma'am.'

OOPS! Although Reeves shoots Daniels in the left leg, he limps on the right • When the first bus explodes, Reeves is trying to get his car door unlocked. When he rushes back to the car, he opens the door without unlocking it • When the bomb-rigged bus does its incredibly sharp turn, a device is visible underneath it helping the right wheels lift off the ground

• While the credits say McMahon is a captain, he's referred to as a lieutenant throughout the movie • As Reeves and Bullock emerge so spectacularly onto the street at the movie's conclusion, notice all the bystanders gawping at the filming.

Psst! Like *Forrest Gump*, this was a film that wasn't wanted. Paramount put it in turnaround and Fox were roundly ridiculed for picking it up. But with a new studio head, they wanted stuff they could make quickly and surprised themselves as well as everybody else when they came up trumps • Originally the script was much darker and the villain was the Jeff Daniels' character. But this was felt to be too bleak, so Hopper's character was invented.

Spellbound
★★★ 1945 111min b/w

Director: Alfred Hitchcock
Screenplay: Ben Hecht & Angus Macphail
Source: Novel, *The House of Dr. Edwardes* by Francis Beeding [Hilary St. George Saunders, John Palmer]

Dr. Bergman becomes suspicious of Peck, the new head of a mental hospital. There was an outbreak of mental instability in the mid-40s, with a rash of Hollywood directors suffering from a compulsion to make movies about psychiatry. Despite the bogus medical stuff, which pretty much says that love can cure amnesia, Hitch gives us enough of his inimitable touch to keep us happy. Let's be honest, if the man had filmed the phone book, we'd be jumping at every name, terrified that it concealed a murderer.

Dr. Constance Peterson . . . . . . .Ingrid Bergman
John 'J.B.' Ballantine . . . . .Gregory Peck
Dr. Murchison . . . . .Leo G. Carroll
Mary Carmichael . . . . .Rhonda Fleming
Dr. Fleurot . . . . .John Emery
Matron . . . . .Jean Acker
Dr. Alex Brulov . . . . .Michael Checkhov
Garmes .Norman Lloyd
Harry . . . . .Donald Curtis

Quote 'As my old friend Zannebaum used to say, "Women make the best psychoanalysts till they fall in love. After that, they make the best patients".'

OOPS! You try turning your wrist 180 degrees while holding something like, say, a gun. I say it isn't possible. Perhaps that's why it looks so odd.

Psst! Hitch can be seen around 40 minutes into the film, coming out of the hotel lift carrying a violin • Dr. Alex Brulov is played by Michael Chekhov, the nephew of Russian playwright Anton Chekhov • The two-frame splash of red which ought to be in the film near the end [not all prints have it] is the shortest use of colour in a black and white movie. The momentary flash of colour as the gun fired at *them* had audiences of the time jumping and then returning to see the movie again to catch it all over. Perhaps that's why the film was Hitch's most successful in the 40s • The surrealist dream sequences were designed by Salvador Dali, who provided five paintings and over 100 sketches. Although only lasting two minutes in the film, much of their original length of 22 minutes was actually shot, although not a planned scene in which Bergman was covered with ants. It was William Cameron Menzies who directed them, though, as Hitchcock had left for London. Producer David O. Selznick hated the Dali sequences and was behind cutting them right down. Menzies asked for his name to be taken off the credits.

The Spiral Staircase
★★★ 1946 83min b/w

Director: Robert Siodmak
Screenplay: Mel Dinelli
Source: Novel, *Some Must Watch* by Ethel Lina White

A killer is attacking handicapped girls in 19th-century New England and mute Dorothy Mc Guire is worried that she is next. Every trick in the horror director's book has been thrown in, with billowing curtains, creaking doors and the like. Amazingly, the excellent acting and Siodmak's expressionist direction ensure that it still works on a modern audience. Ignore the dreadful 1975 British remake.

Helen Capel . . . . .Dorothy McGuire
Prof. Warren . . . . .George Brent
Mrs. Warren . . . . .Ethel Barrymore
Dr. Parry .Kent Smith
Blanche . . . . .Rhonda Fleming
Steve Warren . . . . .Gordon Oliver
Mrs. Oates . . . . .Elsa Lanchester
Nurse Barker . . . . .Sara Allgood
Mr. Oates . . . . .Rhys Williams

Psst! Apart from being moved from a present-day setting in the book, the central character also changed from being crippled to a mute.

The producers thought if she couldn't talk, it would make audiences still more worried for her.

Splash

★★★★ 1984 110min c.

Director: Ron Howard
Screenplay: Lowell Ganz, Babaloo Mandel & Bruce Jay Friedman

This superb comic fantasy has Hannah as the mermaid emerging onto dry land and Hanks as the gawky young man who falls for her, unaware that there's something fishy about her story. Their sweet romance is complicated by the interest shown in Hannah by the usual sinister scientist types. Perfect casting, a witty and inventive script and reasonably brisk direction make this a wholly delightful, if a trifle whimsical, movie.

Allen Bauer	Tom Hanks
Madison	Daryl Hannah
Walter Kornbluth	Eugene Levy
Freddie Bauer	John Candy
Mrs. Simler	Dody Goodman
Dr. Ross	Richard B. Shull

Blurb She Was The Woman Of Allen's Dreams. She Had Large Dark Eyes, A Beautiful Smile And A Great Pair Of Fins.

Quote 'All my life I've been waiting for someone, and when I find her she's a fish.'

OOPS! Keep an eye out for the boom mike which appears on several occasions.

Psst! This was the first Disney movie to feature bare breasts. Some Disney employees held a prayer meeting to protest about it. The studio originally tried out devices to cover up Hannah's nipples, until somebody pointed out that, without them, the audiences were even *more* likely to stare at her breasts • The posters emphasise Hannah's legs, rather than her tail because, according to a marketing man at the studio 'the target audience of young men just didn't believe you could screw a fish.' • Hanks claims he got the part after almost everybody else turned it down. Those who were asked include Michael Keaton, Chevy Chase, Dudley Moore, Bill Murray and John Travolta • Ron Howard's dad Rance here plays 'McCullough', while the writers Ganz and Mandel (who later wrote *City Slickers* and *League of Their Own*) can be seen as 'Stan' and 'Rudy' • Keep watching after the credits to see where Hanks and Hannah end up.

The Spy Who Came in from the Cold

★★★ 1965 112min b/w

Director: Martin Ritt
Screenplay: Paul Dehn & Guy Trosper
Source: Novel by John Le Carré

For his final mission, a British spy has to pretend to be a double agent in East Germany. But not all the danger comes from the Communist side. Despite the gritty realistic plot, or perhaps because of it, the film wasn't popular at the time. But this is the perfect antidote to the lunacy of Bond and now that the more complex Le Carré's have done so well on TV, it's time to give this another go. Although it's bleak, Burton has rarely been better.

Alec Leamas	Richard Burton
Nan Perry	Claire Bloom
Fiedler	Oskar Werner
Hans-Dieter Mundt	Peter Van Eyck
East German Defence Attorney	George Voskovec
Peters	Sam Wanamaker
Smiley	Rupert Davies
Control	Cyril Cusack
Ashe	Michael Hordern
Carlton	Robert Hardy
Patmore	Bernard Lee
Holten	Walter Gotell
Old judge	Esmond Knight
Mr. Zanfrello	Warren Mitchell

The Spy Who Loved Me

★★ 1977 125min c.

Director: Lewis Gilbert
Screenplay: Christopher Wood & Richard Maibaum
Source: Novel by Ian Fleming

There's no respite for Bond from the succession of nutters who want to dominate the world. Stromberg is next off the block, with his aim to wipe man from the face of the Earth while he and his mates live at the bottom of the sea. Although some of the stunts are great, and Kiel's metal-toothed villain provides some interest, Moore and the script both appear to need the kiss of life desperately.

James Bond	Roger Moore
Maj. Anya Amasova	Barbara Bach
Karl Stromberg	Curt Jurgens

Jaws	Richard Kiel
Naomi	Caroline Munro
Gen. Gogol	Walter Gotell
Minister of Defence	Geoffrey Keen
'M'	Bernard Lee
Moneypenny	Lois Maxwell
'Q'	Desmond Llewelyn
Capt. Carter	Shane Rimmer
Commander Talbot	Bryan Marshall
Capt. Benson	George Baker
Sergei	Michael Billington
Capt. of Liparus	Sydney Tafler
Adm. Hargeaves	Robert Brown

Quote 'He just dropped in for a quick bite.'

Psst! The incredible opening ski chase culminating in the leap off the cliff, followed by the opening of the Union Jack parachute, caused wild applause in cinemas. It took 10 days and $30,000 to get the stuntman to get it on film • Demand for white Lotus Esprit's became so strong, the waiting list grew to three years. The standard model was, sadly, not amphibious.

Stagecoach
★★★★ 1939 96min b/w

Director: John Ford
Screenplay: Dudley Nichols
Source: Short story, *Stage to Lordsburg* by Ernest Haycox

The one Western everybody seems to like. In essence, it's just a group of seven people with assorted problems who are crammed into a tiny room. What makes this gabfest different from countless similar movies is that the 'room' is on its way through Indian territory while the savages are on the warpath. Sure enough, the Indians attack and the scene is set for some exciting action. It could so easily have been another B-Western doomed to obscurity, but the mix gelled and what came out the other end was a classic that has endured and will continue to enchant moviegoers. The 1966 remake with Ann-Margret and Bing Crosby didn't quicken anybody's pulse.

Dallas	Claire Trevor
The Ringo Kid	John Wayne
Dr. Josiah Boone	Thomas Mitchell
Hatfield	John Carradine
Buck Rickabaugh	Andy Devine
Sheriff Curly Wilcox	George Bancroft
Mr. Samuel Peacock	Donald Meek
Lucy Mallory	Louise Platt

Lt. Blanchard	Tim Holt
Henry Gatewood	Berton Churchill
Chris	Chris Martin
Hank Plummer	Tom Tyler

Oscars Thomas Mitchell

Quote 'Somewhere, sometime, there may be the right bullet or the wrong bottle waiting for Josiah Boone. Why worry when or where?'

OOPS! There are several instances in the film of modern tyre tracks appearing where only stagecoach wheels are supposed to have gone • When the stage is crossing the river, you can see the shadow of the camera reels on the back of the driver.

Psst! Although he is now thought of primarily for Westerns, this was Ford's first film in the genre for 13 years. He bought the story from *Colliers* magazine for $2,500 but had trouble finding anyone who would let him make it as Westerns were out of fashion • The same issue of *Colliers* also contained the story *Bringing Up Baby* • When Ford found some cash he invited his old friend Wayne to take the part of Johnny Ringo. Ford had earlier given the ex-USC football star a few bit parts. Since then he had been appearing only in B-Westerns. There was considerable opposition to Wayne being offered the part • When Ford had trouble getting the performance he wanted out of Wayne in a scene with Claire Trevor, he simply said: 'Just raise your eyebrows and wrinkle your forehead'. Wayne later claimed that he used the technique over and over again in his movies • Ford almost never attended rushes. He 'cut in the camera', only filming scenes as he intended them to appear, instead of from countless angles as other directors did. There was thus little opportunity for an editor to change Ford's vision of the movie • The stunts were performed by the amazing Yakima Canutt, who also appears as the cavalry scout. Despite the amazing stunts he performed over the years, Canutt lived to be 90 • The method of getting horses to fall on cue in those days was to pull wires attached to their legs. It often resulted in animals having to be put down and has long since been abandoned • There were no special camera cars in those days and cameras had to be mounted on ordinary cars which were driven after the stage. To keep up with it usually involved driving at over 40 mph • The film popularised the use of the amazing Monument Valley as a location. Some say that it was the idea of the Navaho Indians there who desperately needed cash. Ford claimed that he had seen it years earlier and was ever since planning on filming there again. It had been on the stagecoach trail in the 1880s, and the trails still existed. No other place in the main United States is further from a railway line • One of the original Concord stagecoaches that had travelled the route was used for location work • Chief John Big Tree who appeared in this and other Westerns was the model for the 'Indian Head' nickel • Ford insisted on paying the Navajo extras the same as everyone else, against the opposition of the front office. Ford was afterwards made an honorary chief by the Navajo • Although *Citizen Kane* is commonly thought to be the first major movie to show ceilings, in fact there are several here • The movie also contains the first ever shot of a train going over the camera • Ford had music played on set while rehearsals were under way, as had happened in the silent days. It was generally accordian music from Danny Borzage, who was the brother of the director Frank • Tom Tyler, who plays Hank Plummer, was the world heavyweight weightlifting champion for 14 years. He appeared in other films such as *Gone with the Wind* and *She Wore a Yellow Ribbon* • The original prints of *Stagecoach* all disappeared over the years and the current prints of the film were struck from John Wayne's own copy in 1970 • Literary buffs claim that the original source of the story is *Boule de Suif* or *Ball of Lard*, the first story Guy de Maupassant published. The coach in it is racing through the suburbs of Paris during the Franco-Prussian war, with the Prussians the bad guys.

Stage Door
★★★ 1937 93min b/w

Director: Gregory La Cava
Screenplay: Morrie Ryskind & Anthony Veiller
Source: Play by Edna Ferber & George S. Kaufman

A group of aspiring actresses yoked to the same boarding house keep their chins up and the wisecracks coming as they wait for work that may never come. A deliciously catty script is put across with vim and vigour by some of the best young actresses around at the time.

Terry Randall . . . . .Katharine Hepburn
Jean Maitland . . . . .Ginger Rogers
Anthony Powell . . . . .Adolphe Menjou
Linda Shaw . . . . .Gail Patrick
Catherine Luther . . . . .Constance Collier
Judy Canfield . . . . .Lucille Ball

Eve . . . . .Eve Arden
Annie . . . . .Ann Miller
Henry Sims . . . . .Samuel S. Hinds
Harcourt . . . . .Franklin Pangborn
Kaye Hamilton . . . . .Andrea Leeds
Richard Carmichael . . . . .Pierre Watkin
Milbank . . . . .Jack Carson
Actor in play . . . . .Ralph Forbes
Butcher .Grady Sutton

Quote 'The calla lilies are in bloom again.' • 'It'd be a terrific innovation if you could get your mind to stretch a little further than the next wisecrack' • 'Hold on! Gangrene just set in.' • 'When I get back to my room you're the only thing I want to find missing.'

Psst! Although based on a stage play, director La Cava wanted to make it as realistic as possible and had a team of people monitoring the lifestyle, behaviour and conversation of struggling bit players. Some of the dialogue overheard made it into the picture • La Cava hated the fact that movie actors often wore clothes that their characters wouldn't have been able to afford and insisted that the actors used their own clothes • While the film was about starving actresses, the alley cat featured in the movie received a salary of $150 per week. It had cost just 25 cents • Ann Miller had faked her birth certificate to prove that she was old enough to be in the film. But she was only 17 and thus under-age • The actresses did not all get on together, with La Cava, frequently drunk, encouraging dissension on set as he thought it was good for the film. Feeling that Miller was too tall for her, Rogers took to wearing top hats and high heels • When Rogers couldn't cry to La Cava's satisfaction, he told her that her house had burnt down. It was an old trick, but it worked • Hepburn's often repeated line about 'the calla lilies' were from her 1933 Broadway play, *The Lake*, which had been a flop.

Stairway to Heaven
SEE: A Matter of Life and Death

Stalag 17
★★★★ 1953 120min b/w

Director: Billy Wilder
Screenplay: Billy Wilder & Edwin Blum
Source: Play by Donald Bevan & Edmund Trzcinski

Perhaps the greatest of all POW films, this is not the standard one-dimensional, stiff-upper-lip tale of prisoners making a home from home behind the barbed wire. It's a rather black comedy, with the prisoners suspecting that loner Holden is the fink who rats on them to the Germans. Although the guards play their parts as silly goons who look as if they are already auditioning for *Hogan's Heroes*, on the whole this is a far more realistic view of POW life than usual, funny, gritty and sometimes nasty. Highly recommended.

Sefton	.William Holden
Lt. Dunbar	.Don Taylor
Oberst Von Scherbach	.Otto Preminger
'Animal' Stosh	.Robert Strauss
Harry	.Harvey Lembeck
Hoffy	.Richard Erdman
Price	.Peter Graves
Duke	.Neville Brand
Schultz	.Sig Rumann

Oscars William Holden

Quote 'Just one more word. If I ever run into any of you bums on the street corner, just let's pretend we never met before.'

Psst! Charlton Heston was originally going to play William Holden's role • Although Otto Preminger may seem a stereotypical tyrant, he was pretty much playing himself, as those who worked in his movies would have confirmed
• The long-running TV sitcom, *Hogan's Heroes*, was inspired by the film.

A Star Is Born

★★★ 1937 111min c.

Director: William Wellman
Screenplay: Dorothy Parker, Alan Campbell & Robert Carson
Source: Story by Wellman & Carson based on the film, *What Price Hollywood?*

A starlet on her way up marries a once-great star on his way down and soon has to hold onto him for grim life to prevent him plummeting to his doom. Thanks, presumably, to the venomous wit of Algonquin Round Table member Dorothy Parker and her husband and collaborator Campbell, this gives the best warts-and-all backstage view of Hollywood and the film-making process of all three versions. Some prefer it to the 1954 version, but wonderful though Gaynor and March are, they can't quite match up to Garland and Mason.

Esther Blodgett/Vicki Lester	.Janet Gaynor
Norman Maine	.Fredric March
Oliver Niles	.Adolphe Menjou
Lettie	.May Robson
Danny McGuire	.Andy Devine
Libby	.Lionel Stander
Billy Moon	.Franklin Pangborn
Pop Randall	.Edgar Kennedy
Casey Burke	.Owen Moore
Anita Regis	.Elizabeth Jenns
Theodore Smythe	.J.C. Nugent
Aunt Mattie	.Clara Blandick
Miss Phillips	.Peggy Wood
Ward	.Arthur Hoyt
Posture coach	.Guinn "Big Boy" Williams

Oscars Best Original Story

Quote 'He has a heart of gold – only harder.'
• 'First drink of water he's had in 20 years, and then he had to get it by accident. How do you wire congratulations to the Pacific Ocean?'
• 'Hello, everybody. This is Mrs. Norman Maine.' [Last line]

Psst! The film was a remake of the 1932 movie *What Price Hollywood?* • The story was apparently based on the lives of silent actor John Bowers and his wife Marguerite de la Motte • Lana Turner received her first professional payment, $25, as an extra in this movie. Carole Landis was another of the extras, also in her first part.

A Star Is Born

★★★★ 1954 154min c.

Director: George Cukor
Screenplay: Moss Hart
Source: Screenplay by Parker, Campbell & Carson from story by Wellman & Carson, based on the film, *What Price Hollywood?*

A starlet on her way up marries a once-great star on his way down and soon has to hold onto him for grim life to prevent him plummeting to his doom. This version is far more emotional than the 1937 version and while the musical numbers may not add much to the story, they are among the best numbers Garland ever performs on film. Her acting is top notch, too, as is Mason's, who is superb as the man suffering from the swings of fame while his wife is happily playing on the roundabouts.

Esther Blodgett/Vicki Lester	.Judy Garland
Norman Maine	.James Mason
Matt Libby	.Jack Carson

Oliver Niles	Charles Bickford
Danny McGuire	Tommy Noonan
Lola Lavery	Lucy Marlow
Susan Ettinger	Amanda Blake
Graves	Irving Bacon
Glenn William	James Brown

Quote 'If you'll be kind enough to glance betwen my shoulder blades...you'll find a knife buried to the hilt. On its handle are your initials.' • 'Hello, everybody. This is Mrs. Norman Maine.' • 'The biggest robbery since Brink's.' [Groucho Marx to Garland when Grace Kelly won the Oscar for *The Country Girl*]

Psst! Originally the film ran to a full three hours. But after the premiere it was cut savagely to 154 minutes. There is a splendid restored version available which runs 170 minutes although, as with movies like *Lost Horizon*, there are some stills for scenes where only the dialogue remains. Sadly, director Cukor died the night before he was due to see it • The film didn't win one Oscar • Cary Grant, Humphrey Bogart and Marlon Brando were among the names discussed before James Mason was signed • George Cukor also directed the 1932 movie, *What Price Hollywood*, on which the three *Stars Are Born* were based • Although the man who asks Garland to sing 'Melancholy Baby' is an extra, the voice is Humphrey Bogart's • For the 1976 version, Barbra Streisand initially approached Elvis Presley for the role of Norman Maine.

Stargate
★★★ 1994 120min c.

Director: Roland Emmerich
Screenplay: Dean Devlin & Roland Emmerich

Archaeologist Spader solves the secret behind a gateway to the stars. Soldier Russell and a bunch of grunts accompany him on a trip to a desert planet ruled by all-powerful androgynous Egyptian deity Davidson and encounter a few problems getting their return tickets validated. Although it is riddled with plot inconsistences, this epic sci-fi adventure is one of the few movies of recent years to get our sense of wonder and imagination flowing. Its soundtrack by David Arnold, a cross between *Star Wars* and *Lawrence of Arabia*, is also highly recommended.

Col. Jack O'Neil	Kurt Russell
Dr. Daniel Jackson	James Spader
Ra	Jaye Davidson

Catherine	Viveca Lindfors
Skaara	Alexis Cruz
Sha'uri	Mili Avital

Quote 'I guess the word dweeb doesn't mean anything to you guys?'

Psst! Kurt Russell picked up $7m for his role • Davidson was going to be bare-chested but when he appeared for filming sporting nipple-rings, the producers hurriedly had a breast-plate made for him • The product placement for the 5th Avenue chocolate bar on a world a million light-years from earth must surely rank as one of the most blatant yet.

Star Trek: The Motion Picture
★★ 1979 132min c.

Director: Robert Wise
Screenplay: Harold Livingston & Gene Roddenberry
Source: Star Trek TV story by Alan Dean Foster

The Enterprise's crew is brought back together to help stop the earth being destroyed. Although the special effects are fine, the story itself is as wrinkly and ancient as many of the actors and hardly a fitting tribute to the original TV series. Trekkers won't care, of course. It was followed by five sequels, the even numbers being the best, and then by the disappointing *Star Trek: Generations*.

Adm. James T. Kirk	William Shatner
Mr. Spock	Leonard Nimoy
Dr. Leonard 'Bones' McCoy	DeForest Kelley
Cmdr. Willard Decker	Stephen Collins
Montgomery 'Scotty' Scott	James Doohan
Sulu	George Takei
Chekov	Walter Koenig
Uhura	Nichelle Nichols
Ilia	Persis Khambatta
Dr. Christine Chapel	Majel Barrett

OOPS! Although Vulcan appears to have two moons, Treckers with good memories have pointed out that in the TV series, Spock claims Vulcan has no moon.

Psst! Although the TV series had ended 10 years earlier, the popularity of the constant reruns ensured that the movie was a box office success • There's a longer and less disjointed 143-minute version on video • I can't face watching it again to check, but others say that when Spock sees the weird images, after his line 'Who or what are we dealing with?', you can see Miss Piggy and Darth Vader.

Star Trek IV – The Voyage Home

★★★ 1986 119min c.

Director: Leonard Nimoy
Screenplay: Harve Bennett, Steve Meerson, Peter Krikes & Nicholas Meyer
Source: TV series created by Gene Roddenberry.

Our gallant lads (ha!) have to fetch a pair of future-extinct whales from 20th-century Earth if 23rd-century Earth isn't to be wiped out. Played largely for the fish-out-of-water laughs, and getting them, this is an immensely entertaining outing for the Enterprise and all who sail in her, even if the TV-standard acting's a mite embarrassing in places. Spock wears his pyjamas and dressing gown throughout.

Kirk	William Shatner
Spock	Leonard Nimoy
McCoy	DeForest Kelley
Scotty	James Doohan
Sulu	George Takei
Chekov	Walter Koenig
Uhura	Nichelle Nichols
Amanda	Jane Wyatt
Gillian	Catherine Hicks

Quote 'Don't tell me. You're from outer space.' – 'No, I'm from Iowa. I only work in outer space.'

Psst! V.J. Armitraj is the captain of the *Yorktown* who gives the distress message.

Star Trek VI: The Undiscovered Country

★★★★ 1991 109min c.

Director: Nicholas Meyer
Screenplay: Nicholas Meyer & Denny Martin Flinn

The crew of the Enterprise boldly push their zimmer frames where no man has pushed them before. Despite looking as if they should be travelling on senior citizen passes, this is the best of the bunch, with Kirk framed by the Klingons and deported to a prison planet. A rattling good yarn is enlivened by plenty of thrills, lots of cod Shakespearian references and some delightful dead-pan humour. It closes, however, with the corniest of end credits, as they all literally sign off.

Captain James T. Kirk	William Shatner
Spock	Leonard Nimoy
Dr. McCoy	DeForest Kelley
Scotty	James Doohan
Chekov	Walter Koenig
Uhuru	Nichelle Nichols
Captain Sulu	George Takei
Lt. Valeris	Kim Cattrall
Chancellor Gorkon	David Warner

Also: Christopher Plummer, Mark Lenard, Brock Peters, Kurtwood Smith, Christian Slater

Quote 'You've not discovered Shakespeare until you've read him in the original Klingon.'
• 'Once again, we have saved civilisation as we know it.'

OOPS! Under attack, Sulu drops a cup which shatters. Obviously there's some incredible cleaning system available in the future, because the bits disappear incredibly quickly
• Surely Romulan ale was blue in Star Trek II? These bally breweries; always tinkering with the formula.

Psst! When Shatner saw the rushes, he was upset at how big his bottom looked in a scene where he walks away from the camera across a bridge. He insisted on the whole scene being airbrushed to improve on what nature had given him • Klingon is now a living language which can be studied at several American universities. There are even two competing Klingon Bibles in preparation • The film is dedicated to Gene Roddenberry, creator of the TV series, who died just before the film opened • Christian Slater appears in a doorway of the *Excelsior* receiving orders from Sulu, a cameo so short he doesn't even have time to whip his shirt off. His mum, a devoted Trekker, was casting director and wanted nothing more than for her boy to appear in a Star Trek pic • The video has a couple of minutes not seen in the cinema.

Star Wars

★★★★ 1977 121min c.

Director: George Lucas
Screenplay: George Lucas

Rebels loyal to a beautiful princess take on the evil Empire, with the help of a knight trained by a wise old man. Although transferred into outer space, this is an old, old story and that's probably the reason for its amazing success. Too many films, especially in the sci-fi genre, bombard us with special effects and pay no attention to the ancient art of story-telling. Not

Star Wars. It's the believable fight between good and evil that ensures we can watch it again and again, not the expensive FX. In fact, amazing though they were at the time, some of these now look a little dated. And although others delight at the jokey robots, on the umpteenth viewing their banter becomes rather irritating, while the naffness of some of the acting becomes more obvious. These are only minor drawbacks, though, to a cracking adventure yarn which works up to a terrifically exciting finale. Strictly speaking, the fourth of nine parts, it was followed by *The Empire Strikes Back* and *Return of the Jedi.*

Luke Skywalker . . . . .Mark Hamill
Han Solo .Harrison Ford
Princess Leia Organa . . . . .Carrie Fisher
Ben Obi-Wan Kenobi . . . . .Alec Guinness
Grand Moff Tarkin . . . . .Peter Cushing
C3PO . . . . .Anthony Daniels
R2-D2 . . . . .Kenny Baker
Lord Darth Vader . . . . .David Prowse
Darth Vader's voice . . . . .James Earl Jones
Chewbacca . . . . .Peter Mayhew
Chief Jawa . . . . .Jack Purvis
Gen. Taggi . . . . .Don Henderson
Red Two .Denis Lawson

Quote 'A long time ago in a galaxy far, far away...' • 'May the Force be with you!' • 'Acting in *Star Wars*, I felt like a raisin in a gigantic fruit salad.' [Mark Hamill] • 'I don't know what my part is about. Take my name, Obi-Wan Kenobi. I haven't a clue what it's meant to mean.' [Alec Guinness]

OOPS! As the stormtroopers break into the control room, one bangs his head • Near the movie's conclusion, the actors must have been getting tired because, as Fisher greets Hamill on his return from the battle, he calls her 'Carrie' • Know-alls have pointed out that a parsec is a unit of time, not distance and that you can't hear explosions in space • There's a pair of metal dice hanging in the Millenium Falcon's cockpit early on, but they've vanished later.

Psst! At one point, George Lucas toyed with the idea of remaking the *Flash Gordon* serials, but the rights proved prohibitively expensive. His ideas for his own movie were turned down by United Artists and Universal and finally picked up by Fox • He said that: 'The title *Star Wars* was an insurance policy. We calculated that there are something like $8m worth of science fiction freaks in the USA and they will go to see absolutely anything with a title like *Star Wars.*' • It made back not only its budget, but also the costs of advertising and

promotion, within just two months and became the most successful film ever, knocking *Jaws* from the pole position, and sparking a massive merchandising bonanza. It was beaten in turn by *E.T.* • The amazing effects, then seen as revolutionary in the film business, were the work of the now-famous Industrial Light and Magic, a company Lucas set up with some of the money he had made from *American Grafiti* • The Death Star is the most expensive model ever, costing $100,000. It is said to have had 250,000 portholes • The FX boys studied dogfights from *The Bridges at Toko-Ri* and *The Battle of Britain* as inspiration for their own • Lucas struck a deal where he got less up front, but had 40% of the movie's profits, as well as the merchandising rights. He became very, very, very, very rich • Alec Guinness struck a lucrative deal, too, getting 2.25% of profits. He threatened to quit at one point, though, when the script was revised to kill him off in the middle of the movie • The John Williams soundtrack became the highest-selling original soundtrack ever, with over three million copies shifted • On set, both cast and crew were fairly unhappy. Without any concept of the special effects that would be added later, the script seemed a complete mess and little of it made sense. Harrison Ford told Lucas: 'You can type this shit, George, but you can't say it.' • At the insistence of George Lucas, Carrie Fisher had to have her breasts taped to her chest. Lucas ordered, she said, 'No jiggling in the Empire.' Fisher claimed she toyed with the idea of setting up a lottery to see who could rip the tape off at the end of each day's filming • Sissy Spacek was the original choice as Leia, but when Carrie Fisher wouldn't do the nude scenes in *Carrie* they swopped roles • The swing with Hamill across the chasm in the Death Star terrified Fisher. They were actually 30 feet up and weren't allowed to use doubles. Fortunately, they got it right on the first take • Hamill's character was called Luke Starkiller until the very start of filming • Despite his role in Lucas' *American Graffiti*, Ford had found acting work hard to come by and had returned to working as a carpenter when Lucas offered him the part of Han Solo. Christopher Walken and Nick Nolte were among those he thought about for the part before Ford • James Earl Jones asked not to be credited, feeling he hadn't done enough work to justify it. Rumour has it that David Prowse had not been told that his voice would be dubbed • The cost of the closing credits is said to be more than the entire cost of *Airplane* and *Friday the Thirteenth* combined • Most of the crowd watching the medals being awarded at the end are said to be cardboard cutouts. Some of the starfighters in the rebels' hideout were also cardboard • The Directors' Guild of America told Lucas he had to put some credits at the beginning of the movie. Lucas refused, paid the fine they levied, and then quit the Guild • Look out for the reference to cell number 'THX-1138', the title of George Lucas' first feature film • R2-D2 is a movie in-joke, being the film editor's term for 'Reel 2, Dialogue 2' • In the early desert filming in Tunisia, R2-D2's controls didn't work and Kenny Baker, who was just three feet eight inches and baking inside the metal shell, had to be dragged along by a rope. Anthony Daniels, inside C3PO, was naked apart from a layer of vaseline. The heavy weight of the arms of his costume rested on his thumbs, in which he had no feeling for weeks afterwards • Old pro Peter Cushing is said to have reverted to wearing carpet slippers whenever he knew his feet would be out of shot • It was never originally planned to be anything more than a one-off, except perhaps in Lucas' imagination. After the first release's success, a new caption was inserted at the opening saying: 'EPISODE IV – A NEW HOPE'.

Steelyard Blues
★★★ 1973 92min c.

Director: Alan Myerson
Screenplay: David S. Ward

A convict and a bunch of his extremely odd anarchist pals trying to resurrect an old aero-plane clash with the authorities. One of the great anti-establishment movies, this offbeat comedy-drama enjoyed cult status for a while but seems to have disappeared from view now. Shame. It's weird, but very entertaining.

Iris Caine . . . . .Jane Fonda
Jesse Veldini . . . . .Donald Sutherland
Eagle Throneberry . . . . .Peter Boyle
Duval Jacks . . . . .Garry Goodrow
Frank Veldini . . . . .Howard Hesseman
The Kid . . . . .John Savage
Police Captain . . . . .Morgan Upton

Stella Dallas
★★★ 1937 105min b/w

Director: King Vidor
Screenplay: Sarah Y. Mason & Victor Heerman
Source: Novel by Olive Higgins Prouty

One of the ultimate tear-jerkers with Stanwyck acting fit to bust as the brassy woman who comes to realise that she is standing in the way of her daughter getting on in life. It's all utter tosh, of course, but if the actors knew that they manage to keep their contempt well hidden. Their conviction carries the picture along. It aims to wring the withers and it does so magnif-icently.

Stella Martin Dallas . . . . . . .Barbara Stanwyck
Stephen Dallas . . . . .John Boles
Laurel Dallas . . . . .Anne Shirley
Helen Morrison . . . . .Barbara O'Neil
Ed Munn . . . . .Alan Hale
Mrs. Martin . . . . .Marjorie Main
Richard Grosvenor III . . . . .Tim Holt
Margaret Phillibrown . . . . .Ann Shoemaker
Mrs. Grosvenor . . . . .Nella Walker

Quote 'All right, folks. You've seen enough. Move along, please. Come on, clear the sidewalk.' [Last line]

The Stepford Wives
★★★ 1975 115min c.

Director: Bryan Forbes
Screenplay: William Goldman
Source: Novel by Ira Levin

The female half of a couple new to a Connecticut town is puzzled by the cheerful and subservient demeanour of the other wives. Then she begins to suspect there's a sinister reason for it. Get over the slow opening and this is an enjoyable little sci-fi thriller, albeit with more than a nod to Invasion of the Body Snatchers. Sadly, both Ross and Newman are so miscast that we have trouble telling which versions are robots and which are human.

Joanna Eberhart . . . . .Katharine Ross
Bobby . . . . .Paula Prentiss
Walter Eberhart . . . . .Peter Masterson
Carol . . . . .Nanette Newman
Dale Coba . . . . .Patrick O'Neal
Charmaine . . . . .Tina Louise
Dr. Fancher . . . . .Carol Rossen
Ike Mazzard, artist . . . . .William Prince
Mrs. Cornell . . . . .Judith Baldwin
Claude Axhelm . . . . .George Coe
Raymond Chandler . . . . .Robert Fields
Mr. Cornell . . . . .Michael Higgins
Ted Van Sant . . . . .Josef Sommer
Welcome Wagon lady . . . . .Paula Trueman
Mr. Atkinson . . . . .Remak Ramsay
Kim Eberhart . . . . .Mary Stuart Masterson

Psst! Newman is director Forbes' wife • Seven-year-old Mary Stuart Masterson appears in a bit part as Kim Eberhart, playing the daughter of her real dad. Her first line in the movies is: 'Daddy, I just saw a man carrying a naked lady.'

The Sting
★★★★ 1973 129min c.

Director: George Roy Hill
Screenplay: David S. Ward

A pair of confidence tricksters go for the big one, avenging a friend's death by setting up a Chicago gangster. Re-teaming the actors who had made *Butch Cassidy and the Sundance Kid* with the same director, this film hit it big at the box office. It has a wonderful 30s atmosphere, thanks in large part to Marvin Hamlisch's revival of Scott Joplin's music. There's also a humdinger of a plot, clever in its construction and immensely enjoyable in its execution. Although its reputation isn't as high as *Butch Cassidy*, *The Sting* is much the better movie. The sequel, *The Sting II*, in 1983, is utterly dreadful.

Henry Gondorff . . . . .Paul Newman
Johnny Hooker . . . . .Robert Redford
Doyle Lonnegan . . . . .Robert Shaw
Lt. William Snyder . . . . .Charles Durning
J.J. Singleton . . . . .Ray Walston
Billie . . . . .Eileen Brennan
Kid Twist . . . . .Harold Gould
Eddie Niles . . . . .John Heffernan
FBI Agent Polk . . . . .Dana Elcar
'Erie Kid' .Jack Kehoe
Luther Coleman . . . . .Robert Earl Jones
Crystal .Sally Kirkland

Oscars Best Picture, Best Director, Best Story and Screenplay

Blurb All It Takes Is A Little Confidence.

Quote 'He's not as tough as he thinks.' – 'Neither are we.' • 'You're not gonna stick around for your share?' – 'Nah. I'd only blow it.' [Last line]

Psst! It won seven Oscars • The film was the first in over 25 years to begin with the Universal logo of the glass globe which had been the studio's hallmark in the 40s • Although Scott Joplin's music now seems irretrievably linked with the movie, it isn't of the right period. Rather than the 30s, ragtime was all the rage around the turn of the century, a generation earlier.

Stormy Weather
★★★ 1943 77min b/w

Director: Andrew L. Stone
Screenplay: Frederick Jackson & Ted Koehler

There's almost no story here, just an excuse to showcase some of the greatest black entertainers of the day in a movie that was actually aimed as much at white audiences. The great Bill 'Bojangles' Robinson is joined by Lena Horne, Fats Waller ('Ain't Misbehavin'), The Nicholas Brothers, Cab Calloway and many more. Sheer heaven to those who love the music.

Selina Rogers . . . . .Lena Horne
Corky . . . . .Bill Robinson
Ada . . . . .Ada Brown
Gabe . . . . .Dooley Wilson
Himself .Cab Calloway
Himself . . . . .Fats Waller
Themselves . . . . .The Nicholas Brothers

Psst! Although they play husband and wife, Horne was just 26 to Robinson's 65.

The Stranger
★★★ 1946 95min b/w

Director: Orson Welles
Screenplay: Anthony Veiller
Source: Story by Victor Trivas & Decla Dunning

In the months after World War II, Robinson is on the trail of one of the most infamous Nazis who organised the Holocaust. His suspicions fall on Welles, a professor in a small Connecticut town. Although understated, this thriller still delivers tension in spades, culminating in a cracking climax in a clock tower. Welles' villain is one of the best, most believable and most chilling Nazis seen in the cinema.

Wilson . . . . .Edward G. Robinson
Prof. Charles Rankin . . . . .Orson Welles
Mary Longstreet . . . . .Loretta Young
Judge Longstreet . . . . .Philip Merivale
Noah Longstreet . . . . .Richard Long
Dr. Jeff Lawrence . . . . .Byron Keith
Konrad Meinike . . . . .Konstantin Shayne
Sara . . . . .Martha Wentworth

Psst! Welles hoped to get Agnes Moorehead to play the part that went to Robinson, but he was overruled by the producer • The clock tower was, at the time, the tallest set built in Hollywood since *Intolerance*, D.W. Griffith's extraordinary silent epic.

Strangers on a Train
★★★★ 1951 101min b/w

Director: Alfred Hitchcock
Screenplay: Raymond Chandler & Czenzi Ormonde
Source: Novel by Patricia Highsmith.

It is suggested to Granger, a tennis player tied down by an unhappy marriage, that the perfect killing would be if two complete strangers swapped murders. When Granger's wife is killed, it becomes clear this was no academic discussion and psychotic Walker demands that Granger fulfil his side of the bargain. Despite some insipid casting among the leads, this is one of Hitchcock's true nail-biting master-pieces, with the nightmare situation into which Granger is thrown gripping us as it approaches its thrilling climax. The film contains one of Hitch's most memorable scenes, the tennis match where everyone in the crowd is following the ball except Walker. The splendid 1987 com-edy *Throw Momma from the Train* was a homage to this film.

Guy Haines . . . . .Farley Granger
Anne Morton . . . . .Ruth Roman
Bruno Anthony . . . . .Robert Walker
Senator Morton . . . . .Leo G. Carroll
Barbara Morton . . . . .Patricia Hitchcock
Miriam . . . . .Laura Elliot
Mrs. Anthony . . . . .Marion Lorne
Mr. Anthony . . . . .Jonathan Hale
Capt. Turley . . . . .Howard St. John
Prof. Collins . . . . .John Brown

Quote 'You're a naughty boy, Bruno.' • 'Some people are better off dead...like your wife and my father, for instance.' • 'I may be old-fashioned, but I thought murder was against the law.'

Psst! Hitch can be seen early in the film trying to get on the train with a double bass as Granger gets off • He had wanted William Holden for the part that went to Farley Granger • Although Raymond Chandler and Hitchcock didn't find working together a comfortable experience, the finished film is still largely Chandler's work in outline although, according to Chandler: 'Hitchcock succeeded in removing almost every trace of my writing from it.' • Chandler handed the script in to Warner Brothers one morning at 8.30. Half an hour later, his agent received a telegram saying that Chandler had been taken off the payroll, thus saving the studio half a day's wages • The scene with the man crawling under the out-of-control roundabout was done for real. Hitchcock later said it was the most dangerous stunt on any of his films • Barbara Morton is played by Hitch's own daughter, who was also Janet Leigh's co-worker in *Psycho*. Not even she was free from Hitch's penchant for cruel jokes. He left her at the top of the Ferris Wheel at night when it was pitch black, ignoring her hysterial cries • Robert Walker died the year the movie was released from the effects of drugs prescribed to calm him down.

The Strawberry Blonde
★★★ 1941 97min c.

Director: Raoul Walsh
Screenplay: Julius J. Epstein & Philip G. Epstein

In turn-of-the-century New York a dentist still besotted with one woman wonders if he did the right thing by marrying another. This delightfully charming and often witty romantic drama has Cagney on top form, showing that there was so much more to this versatile actor than just play-ing gangsters.

Biff Grimes . . . . .James Cagney
Amy Lind . . . . .Olivia De Havilland
Virginia Brush . . . . .Rita Hayworth
Old Man Grimes . . . . .Alan Hale
Hugo Barnstead . . . . .Jack Carson
Nicholas Pappalas . . . . .George Tobias
Mrs. Mulcahey . . . . .Una O'Connor
Harold . . . . .George Reeves

Quote 'When I want to kiss my wife, I'll kiss her anytime, anyplace, anywhere. That's the kind of hairpin I am.' [Last line]

Psst! Stick with the credits for the sing-along.

Straw Dogs
★ 1971 118min c.

Director: Sam Peckinpah
Screenplay: David Z. Goodman
Source: Novel, *The Siege of Trencher's Farm* by Gordon M. Williams

The Cornish Tourist Board's least favourite film. Mild mathematician Dustin Hoffman sets up home in Cornwall with Susan George but fails to take into account the effect that her standing by windows with her kit off will have on the locals. The gothic all-stops out final siege has some force – any takers for putting your head in a mantrap? – but it's generally risible, unpleasant nonsense whose reputation has only grown because it is so difficult to see in Britain.

David Sumner	Dustin Hoffman
Amy Sumner	Susan George
Henry	David Warner
Tom Hedden	Peter Vaughan
Maj. Scott	T.P. McKenna
Rev. Hood	Colin Welland
Charlie Venner	Del Henney
Scutt	Ken Hutchison
Cawsey	Jim Norton
Janice	Sally Thomsett
John Niles	Peter Arne

Blurb The Knock At The Door Meant The Birth Of One Man And The Death Of Seven Others!

Psst! There is much debate over whether the cuts in the film ordered by the British censors in the rape sequence actually made the scene look worse, giving the impression of buggery. The film is banned on video because the scene can be taken out of context • The film inspired some copycat crimes, such as the sexual asault and killing of a female patient in a psychiatric hospital. It had been shown to patients there in the previous month, apparently as part of the patients' rehabilitation • What the film doesn't find time to explain is the title. To help jog memories, it derives from the Chinese philospher Lao Tzu: 'Heaven and Earth are ruthless, and treat the myriad of creatures as straw dogs.'

A Streetcar Named Desire

★★★ 1951 122min b/w

Director: Elia Kazan
Screenplay: Tennessee Williams
Source: Play by Williams

Blanche Du Bois visits her sister Stella in New Orleans, but gets entangled with her brutish brother-in-law Stanley. If one is tempted to dismiss Method acting as a load of mumbo-jumbo, a film like *Streetcar* shows just how effective it can be in the right project. Brando was seldom better than as the passionate, inarticulate Kawalski in Tennessee William's electric play, fascinatingly contrasted with the theatrical technique of Vivien Leigh. Still compelling viewing.

Blanche DuBois	Vivien Leigh
Stanley Kowalski	Marlon Brando
Stella Kowalski	Kim Hunter
Mitch	Karl Malden
Steve Hubbell	Rudy Bond
Pablo Gonzales	Nick Dennis
Eunice Hubbell	Peg Hillias
Collector	Wright King

Oscars Kim Hunter, Vivien Leigh, Karl Malden

Quote 'I don't want realism…I want magic.' • 'He's like an animal. He has an animal's habits. There's even something subhuman about him. Thousands of years have passed him right by and there he is. Stanley Kowalski, survivor of the Stone Age, bearing the raw meat home from the kill in the jungle!' • 'I have always depended on the kindness of strangers.' • 'I can't stand a naked night bulb any more than I can stand a rude remark or a vulgar action.'

Psst! Brando had first come to the public's attention as a 23-year-old playing the part on Broadway for two years • Director Kazan brought with him almost everyone from the stage production, with the exception of Jessica Tandy as Blanche. The studio felt that she was not a big enough star to carry the role on film • Olivia De Havilland was approached for the lead, but she did not feel that a lady should behave that way, even if it was acting • Leigh had been playing the part in the London production where she was directed by husband Laurence Olivier • Leigh, who was becoming steadily more unbalanced, hated Brando's slobbish behaviour on set which, as a Method actor, mirrored his character's behaviour. He enjoyed her revulsion and played up to it whenever he could. She is said to have spent much of her time locked in her dressing room ironing her gloves. Leigh suffered from manic depression and in later life became confused between her own personality and that of Blanche DuBois • The play was bowdlerised to get past the tighter cinema censors, with references to Blanche's first husband's homosexuality taken out and her own nymphomania made less prominent. Nonetheless, by the standards of what had gone before on screen, it was still considered quite shocking • The Catholic Legion of Decency was going to ban Catholics from seeing the movie, so the studio agreed to make certain changes that they asked for, cutting out three minutes from the movie. Kazan said: 'I want to put myself on record that I may be sore as hell about what the hell is done to please the Legion, and if I'm sore as hell, nothing in this wide world will keep me silent. To quote an old Jewish proverb, if someone spits in my face, I will not say it's raining.' • Jack Palance is responsible for Brando's broken nose, which he has never had reset. Palance was Brando's understudy during the Broadway run of the play and accidentally hit Brando while they were mucking around backstage • A director's cut has recently become available on video, with some of the censored scenes restored.

Strictly Ballroom
★★★★ 1992 94min c.

Director: Baz Luhrmann
Screenplay: Baz Luhrmann & Craig Pearce

The ideal pick-you-up picture. Mercurio wants to break with convention and perform his own steps in the forthcoming dancing championships but no-one will partner him except ugly duckling Morice. The time-honoured storyline of youth rebelling against authority conceals one of the freshest, funniest and happiest films to hit the cinema in years. A joy from start to finish.

Scott Hastings	Paul Mercurio
Fran	Tara Morice
Barry Fife	Bill Hunter
Doug Hastings	Barry Otto
Shirley Hastings	Pat Thompson
Liz Holt	Gia Carides
Les Kendall	Peter Whitford

Psst! The film was originally a $50 student theatrical production that grew like Topsy. Nicknamed *Dirty Dancing Down Under*, it swept Australia like wildfire. There were even ballroom dancers performing at half-time in the national rugby championships • It received a 15-minute standing ovation when it was shown at Cannes. It didn't do too well when released in France, though, where its title was changed to *Ballroom Dancing*.

The Stud
★ 1978 90min c.

Director: Quentin Masters
Screenplay: Jackie Collins
Source: Novel by Collins

Joan Collins' bid to regain star status paid off in this highly successful adaptation of her sister's book, which led to her playing Alexis in TV's *Dynasty*. The film is hilariously awful, including a wonderfully tacky 70's disco scene, Oliver Tobias in jacket lapels you could land a plane on and rumpy-pumpy in a lift.

Mrs. Fontaine Khaled	Joan Collins
Tony Blake	Oliver Tobias
Vanessa	Sue Lloyd
Leonard	Mark Burns
Sammy	Doug Fisher
Ben Khaled	Walter Gotell

The Sugarland Express
★★★★ 1974 109min c.

Director: Steven Spielberg
Screenplay: Hal Barwood & Matthew Robbins

Refusing to give up her baby for adoption, Hawn springs hubbie Atherton from prison and they go on the lam, chased by most of the law enforcement officers of Texas. Based on a true story, Spielberg demonstrates his usual skill behind the camera, giving us a tense and exciting little movie. Considering how things turn out, though, it seems a little unfair that it should have such a jolly tone at the outset.

Lou Jean Poplin	Goldie Hawn
Capt. Tanner	Ben Johnson
Officer Maxwell Slide	Michael Sacks
Clovis Poplin	William Atherton
Officer Mashburn	Gregory Walcott
Jessup	Steve Kanaly
Mrs. Looby	Louise Latham
Baby Langston	Harrison Zanuck
Mrs. Nocker	Jessie Lee Fulton

Psst! This was Spielberg's first film for the cinema, his previous movie *Duel* being made for TV.

Sullivan's Travels
★★★★ 1941 91min b/w

Director: Preston Sturges
Screenplay: Preston Sturges

When he tires of making mindless comedies like *Ants in Your Pants of 1939* and *So Long, Sarong*, a Hollywood director determines to make a meaningful social drama. He sets off with just 10 cents in his pocket to see what poverty is like first hand, but ends up in a brutal prison camp, where he realises that the ability to make others laugh and forget their surroundings is one of the greatest talents a man can have. A witty and wise script manages its own move into the field of social drama adeptly and contains not just laughs, but action, pathos and romance. Unlike most of Sturges' other comedies, which haven't worn too well, this remains one of the greatest ever. Any comic actor or film-maker who starts getting an urge to do *Hamlet* should be forced to watch this film.

John L. Sullivan	Joel McCrea
The girl	Veronica Lake
LeBrand	Robert Warwick
Jones	William Demarest
Casalais	Franklin Pangborn
Hadrian	Porter Hall
Valdelle	Byron Foulger
Butler	Robert Greig
Valet	Eric Blore

Also: Margaret Hayes, Jimmy Conlin, Torben Meyer, Al Bridge

Quote 'You know, the nice thing about buying food for a man is that you don't have to laugh at his jokes.' • 'There's a lot to be said for making people laugh. Did you know that's all some people have? It isn't much…but it's better than nothing in this cockeyed caravan.' [Last line]

Psst! The studio didn't want Veronica Lake in the lead, preferring actresses like Lucille Ball, Ruby Keeler or Claire Trevor.

Sunday, Bloody Sunday
★★★ 1971 110min c.

Director: John Schlesinger
Screenplay: Penelope Gilliatt

The central idea of Finch and Jackson discovering that they have a lover, Head, in common is no longer the daring concept it was at the time. But although Head is an exceptionally weak link in this chain, this remains an absorbing and intelligent, if rather too talkative, melodrama.

Alex Greville	Glenda Jackson
Dr. Daniel Hirsh	Peter Finch
Bob Elkin	Murray Head
Mrs. Greville	Peggy Ashcroft
Mr. Greville	Maurice Denham
George Harding	Tony Britton
Answering service lady	Bessie Love
Alva Hodson	Vivan Pickles
Bill Hodson	Frank Windsor
Daniel's father	Harold Goldblatt
Prof. Johns	Thomas Baptiste
Middle-aged patient	Richard Pearson
Vandal	Daniel Day-Lewis

Psst! Ian Bannen was the original Dr. Hirsh but he fell ill just before filming began and Peter Finch was offered the part. It meant he had to fly straightaway to London from his house in

Rome, and Finch almost turned the part down because he disliked flying so much • He had to wear his own clothes because he didn't fit the clothes run up for Bannen and there was no time to make more • Vanessa Regrave was the original choice for Glenda Jackson's role, but she went off to make *The Devils* instead • Daniel Day-Lewis has a bit part as a vandal • Bessie Love, a silent film star in movies like *Intolerance*, had settled in London and had a small role as the woman at the answering service.

The Sundowners
★★★ 1960 133min c.

Director: Fred Zinnemann
Screenplay: Isobel Lennart
Source: Novel by Jon Cleary

Westerns didn't have to be set in America. This top-notch tale is set in Western Australia in the 20s, with Mitchum and Kerr the sheep-herding couple who hope to be able to settle down before too long. Great scenery, masterly acting and some fine action makes this a splendidly memorable experience.

Ida Carmody	Deborah Kerr
Paddy Carmody	Robert Mitchum
Venneker	Peter Ustinov
Mrs. Firth	Glynis Johns
Jean Halstead	Dina Merrill
Quinlan	Chips Rafferty
Sean	Michael Anderson Jr.
Herb Johnson	Wylie Watson
Bluey	John Meillon
Ocker	Ronald Fraser
Jack Patchogue	Mervyn Johns

Sunset Boulevard
★★★★ 1950 110min b/w

Director: Billy Wilder
Screenplay: Billy Wilder, Charles Brackett & D.M. Marshman Jr.

A scriptwriter with no cash or prospects goes to work on a futile project for a former silent movie star with extreme delusions of fame and grandeur. But eventually he wakes up to the fact that he is virtually being held a prisoner by the woman and her menacing butler. Although it pleases as straight storytelling, this is a multi-layered film, with elements of melodrama, satire, gothic horror and black humour woven in. It is also one of the most interesting and insightful peeps behind the curtain of Hollywood, rendered still more fascinating by the use of many of the true stars of the silent era. Although all of the acting is of a high calibre, Swanson should be singled out. In her comeback role, she gives a masterly performance. A masterpiece that creates that magic tingle in the spine every time you watch it.

Joe Gillis	William Holden
Norma Desmond	Gloria Swanson
Max von Mayerling	Erich von Stroheim
Betty Schaefer	Nancy Olson
Sheldrake	Fred Clark
Morino	Lloyd Gough
Artie Green	Jack Webb
Himself	Cecil B. DeMille
Herself	Hedda Hopper
Himself	Buster Keaton
Himself	H.B. Warner
Herself	Anna Q. Nilsson

Oscars Best Story and Screenplay

Blurb A Hollywood Story.

Quote 'We didn't need dialogue. We had *faces* then.' • 'You're Norma Desmond. Used to be in silent pictures. Used to be big.' – 'I *am* big. It's the pictures that got small.' • 'Audiences don't know somebody sits down and writes a picture. they think the actors make it up as they go along.' • 'Alright, Mr. De Mille. I'm ready for my close-up.' [Last line] • 'I had to sit on Gloria Swanson's bed with one foot firmly on the floor – and my overcoat on! Hell, I was living off her in the film. Everybody in the audience knew I was a kept man so why did they have to be so modest?' [Holden]

Showing Queen Kelly.

Psst! The nature of the film was kept a secret from the studio, being hidden behind the title of *A Can of Beans*. Wilder and Brackett never let anyone see a full script, fearing that if word got out the industry would pressure Paramount to drop the project. It was the last time they worked together • When Louis B. Mayer, the head of MGM, saw the film he called Wilder a 'bastard' and said: 'You have disgraced the industry that made you and fed you! You should be tarred and feathered and run out of Hollywood!' • Early previews were disastrous. The film originally opened with corpses in the Los Angeles Morgue sitting up and discussing how they had died. This was cut and the opening of the film delayed by six months while the opening and closing scenes were changed.

Wilder said that the original scenes were among the best he had ever filmed • When the film opened at the Radio City Music Hall, the queue stretched for three blocks • Wilder and Brackett discussed the possibility of using many of the silent movie stars who were still around, among them Mae Murray and Mary Pickford. Pola Negri and Mae West turned the lead down. 52-year-old Swanson was unhappy at having to test for the part, but eventually agreed • Despite the plaudits for her performance, she still had a gap of 18 years between making *Nero's Mistress* in 1956 and making her second comeback in *Airport 75* in 1974 • Although much of Swanson's real silent movie career is woven into the film, she was a very different character to the actress depicted here. As she said: 'It's amazing to find so many people who I thought really know me could have thought that *Sunset* was autobiographical. I've got nobody floating in my swimming pool.' • She had one of the briefest of all Hollywood marriages. Her union with Wallace Beery lasted just three weeks • Montgomery Clift was due to play the male lead, but backed out just two weeks before filming. It was thought he was unhappy about the similarities between his character and his own relationship with the heiress Libby Holman, 30 years his senior. Fred MacMurray had turned the part down as being 'morally repugnant'. Gene Kelly was also approached, but wasn't free • When the cinematographer queried the camera set-up for the scene where Swanson attempts suicide, Wilder told him: 'Johnny, it's the usual slashed-wrist shot.' • Later, Wilder ordered him to: 'Keep it out of focus. I want to win the foreign picture award.' • Wilder was treading on dangerous ground working with egos the size of Stroheim's and Swanson's but apparently both were extremely courteous and helpful. Stroheim let Wilder use clips from *Queen Kelly*, his unreleased movie starring Swanson • Von Stroheim couldn't drive, so when he appeared as Swanson's chauffeur, the car was actually being towed while he merely steered • When he asked Cecil B. De Mille to play himself in the scenes that were filmed on the set of *Samson and Delilah*, De Mille's current film, Wilder said: 'We made an agreement; he wouldn't tell me how to direct *Sunset Boulevard* and I wouldn't tell him how to direct *Samson and Delilah*.' • The mansion in the movie belonged to the Getty family and wasn't at 10086 Sunset but 3810 Wilshire Boulevard. The film-makers built a swimming pool there in return for the use of the place. It was also used for *Rebel Without a Cause* and was demolished in 1957.

The Sunshine Boys
★★★ 1975 111min c.

Director: Herbert Ross
Screenplay: Neil Simon
Source: Play by Simon

Two old-time vaudeville comedians, fondly remembered by those with very long memories, are asked to get together one more time for a TV show. But they actually hated each other and are no happier in one other's company decades later. Containing as many funny lines as Simon's scripts normally do, this one is given more depth than usual by the performances of the two stars, who add considerable pathos to the film. Aspiring comedy writers will also learn that words with a 'K' in them are intrinsically funny.

Willy Clark . . . . .Walter Matthau
Al Lewis . . . . .George Burns
Ben Clark . . . . .Richard Benjamin
Nurse in sketch . . . . .Lee Meredith
Doris . . . . .Carol Arthur
Nurse .Rosetta Le Noire
Mechanic . . . . .F. Murray Abraham
Commercial director . . . . . .Howard Hesseman
TV floor manager . . . . .Ron Rifkin
Man at audition . . . . .Fritz Feld

Oscars George Burns

Quote 'As an actor, no one could touch him. As a human being, no one wanted to touch him.' • 'I can't tell the difference between our act and us any more.' • 'The finger! You're starting with the finger again!'

Psst! The play was inspired by real-life vaudeville team Smith and Dale who came together to re-create one of their sketches on the Ed Sullivan show • It was originally intended for Burns and Jack Benny, but Benny died in 1974. Matthau, who replaced him, had to be aged considerably with make-up • This was Burns' first starring role since *Honolulu* in 1939. It relaunched his screen career at the age of 81. He was the oldest actor ever to win an Oscar, until Jessica Tandy picked up hers for *Driving Miss Daisy*.

Superman
★★★ 1978 143min c.

Director: Richard Donner
Screenplay: Mario Puzo, David Newman, Leslie Newman & Robert Benton
Source: Comic strip created by Jerry Siegel & Joe Shuster

The man from Krypton comes to earth as a baby, grows up with superhuman powers and saves the earth from the evil Lex Luthor. There's plenty to enjoy here, particularly the tongue-in-cheek humour and the delightful romance with Lois Lane. But it's far too long, the early stuff on Krypton is dull, the flying effects now look naff and the saving of Lois Lane is staggeringly unbelievable. Still good fun, although its sequel was even more enjoyable.

Superman/Clark Kent . . . . . .Christopher Reeve
Lex Luthor . . . . .Gene Hackman
Lois Lane . . . . .Margot Kidder
Jor-El . . . . .Marlon Brando
Otis . . . . .Ned Beatty
Eve Teschmacher . . . . .Valerie Perrine
Perry White . . . . .Jackie Cooper
Pa Kent . . . . .Glenn Ford
1st elder . . . . .Trevor Howard
Gen. Zod .Terence Stamp
Vond-Ah . . . . .Maria Schell
Lara . . . .Susannah York, Harry Andrews, Sarah Douglas, Jack O'Halloran, Marc McClure, Larry Hagman, Lise Hilboldt, John Ratzenberger

Blurb You'll Believe a Man Can Fly.

Quote 'Easy, miss. I've got you.' – 'You've got me? Who's got you?' • 'I'm here to fight for truth, justice and the American way.' • 'I never drink when I fly.' • 'The greatest screen actor in the history of cinema, perhaps, and he's running round with white hair and a Krypton suit. Just something wrong about that.' [James Woods]

OOPS! As pedants have pointed out, why does the Man of Steel have fillings? • Why, too, does Superman's dad Jor-El, played by Brando, have what looks like a Rolex on his wrist as he pops Supe into the capsule.

Psst! The film was in planning for five years. It sparked one of the most publicised hunts for a movie lead for years. Among those considered were Burt Reynolds, Kris Kristofferson, Sylvester Stallone, Clint Eastwood, James Caan, Steve McQueen, Paul Newman, Robert Redford and even Ryan O'Neal. Nick Nolte apparently said, when approached: 'I'll do it if I can play him as a schizophrenic.' • Reeve, best known until then for his role in TV soaps, was announced to have got the part just a month before production was due to start. He was ordered to start a course of physical fitness to build up his rather scrawny body. His instructor was David Prowse, who played Darth Vader in *Star Wars*. Reeve put on 30 pounds and increased his chest measurement two inches in 10 weeks. Unfortunately, he kept working out and the shots of him flying at the end of the movie showed him much bulkier than at the start, so reshoots had to be done • Although special effects played their part in making us think that a man could fly, the flying scenes were tough stuff for Reeve. He was fastened by the waist and had to keep his arms and legs fully outstretched and stiff while the cameras were turning, developing massive bruises and callouses • A midget wearing a latex mask of Reeve's face was said to have been used as a double for some of the long shots • Steven Spielberg was to direct the movie at one time, but proved too expensive • At the time, its $44m cost made it the most expensive film ever made • Brando was reportedly paid $3.7m for 12 days work, almost $300,000 a day. His performance lasted less than 10 minutes on screen. That still didn't stop him suing the producers for a share of the box office. Billy Wilder said: 'Mr. Marlon Brando got, for an aggregate of 20 minutes on the screen in *Superman* and *Apocalypse Now*, more money than Clark Gable got for 20 years at MGM • The producers had hoped to get Joan Crawford to play Clark Kent's mother but her death soon after their approach ruled it out • The film holds the joint record for the longest credits in a movie with *Once Upon a Time in the West*. There are 10 minutes of them • One scene had to be reshot when someone spotted that the contents of Reeves' lunchbox had switched sides • Noel Neill, who was Lois Lane in the TV series and Kirk Alyn, who played Superman in two serials, have small roles as Lois Lane's parents, although they are visible only in the extended version shown by some TV stations.

Superman II
★★★ 1980 127min c.

Director: Richard Lester
Screenplay: Mario Puzo, David Newman & Leslie Newman
Source: Comic strip created by Jerry Siegel & Joe Shuster

Three renegades from Supe's old home planet, Krypton, come to earth and behave with considerable impropriety. This is one of those rare instances where a sequel is actually an improvement on the original. With plenty of great action scenes, this outing isn't ashamed to be funny and is not as po-faced as the original. It's still too long, but you can't have everything. It was followed by the less exciting *Superman III* and the dire *Superman IV: The Quest for Peace*.

Superman/Clark Kent	Christopher Reeve
Lex Luthor	Gene Hackman
Otis	Ned Beatty
Perry White	Jackie Cooper
Lois Lane	Margot Kidder
Ursa	Sarah Douglas
Non	Jack O'Halloran
Gen. Zod	Terence Stamp
Eve Teschmacher	Valerie Perrine

Also: Susannah York, Clifton James, E.G. Marshall, Marc McClure, Richard Griffiths, John Ratzenberger, Shane Rimmer, Antony Sher

Quote 'From the look of them, I'll bet $10 they're from Los Angeles.'

Psst! Some scenes were filmed in 1977 when the first in the series was made. The plan then was to film two *Superman* films back to back • The film was released in America six months after it appeared in other parts of the world • Hackman was billed above Reeve • Anthony Sher appears in a bit part as a bellboy.

Support Your Local Sheriff
★★★ 1968 93min c.

Director: Burt Kennedy
Screenplay: William Bowers

This delightful Western spoof is made by the irresistible performance of cheeky and charming Garner as the sheriff who uses his brains rather than brawn to tame a wild town. Brennan's appearance in what amounts to a parody of practically half of his earlier movie roles is a big bonus. Although it wasn't strictly speaking a sequel, there was an equally amusing follow-up two years later, *Support your Local Gunfighter*.

Jason McCullough	James Garner
Prudy Perkins	Joan Hackett
Pa Danby	Walter Brennan
Mayor Olly Perkins	Harry Morgan
Jake	Jack Elam
Joe Danby	Bruce Dern
Preacher Henry Jackson	Henry Jones
Tom Danby	Gene Evans

Suspicion
★★ 1941 99min b/w

Director: Alfred Hitchcock
Screenplay: Samson Raphaelson, Joan Harrison & Alma Reville
Source: Novel, *Before the Fact* by Frances Iles

A woman escapes from the shelf on which she's been left by marrying a playboy. But she comes to believe that he is a murderer and she will be his next victim. Despite a brace of fine actors, this never takes flight in the best Hitchcock manner. And if ever a movie was spoilt by changing a book's plot, this was it. The ending Hitch filmed is an immense bellyflop, making a nonsense of the paranoia generated before. Sadly, he never filmed the book's real ending so there is no chance of somebody announcing that they've discovered it in a vault somewhere.

Johnnie Aysgarth . . . . .Cary Grant
Lina McLaidlaw . . . . .Joan Fontaine
Gen. McLaidlaw . . . . .Cedric Hardwicke
Beaky Thwaite . . . . .Nigel Bruce
Mrs. McLaidlaw . . . . .Dame May Whitty
Mrs. Newsham . . . . .Isabel Jeans
Ethel . . . . .Heather Angel
Capt. Melbeck . . . . .Leo G. Carroll

Oscars Joan Fontaine

Quote 'Hello, monkey face!'

Psst! Hitch appears 45 minutes in, posting a letter • Terrified that the public would recoil from the idea of Cary Grant as a killer, the studio and Hitchcock changed the ending in the novel • During the famous milk sequence, Hitch achieved the glow in the glass by putting a light inside it • Fontaine won the Oscar for Best Actress. Her sister, Olivia De Havilland, was one of the other nominees. The two did not get on and Fontaine winning only fanned the flames of their enmity • Grant got on no better with Fontaine, thinking that her 'bitchy behaviour' made it all too likely that a husband would want to murder her.

Sweet Smell of Success
★★★ 1957 96min b/w

Director: Alexander Mackendrick
Screenplay: Clifford Odets & Ernest Lehman
Source: Short story, *Tell Me About It Tomorrow* by Lehman

Malevolent newspaper columnist Lancaster and slimy PR man Curtis scheme to break up Lancaster's daughter's romance with a musician. There is little to like in the main characters in this gripping tale of media manipulation and the abuse of power, neither displaying any redeeming features whatsoever. Perhaps that's why the public hated it so. But it is grippingly made with two stunning performances from Lancaster and Curtis.

J.J. Hunsecker . . . . .Burt Lancaster
Sidney Falco . . . . .Tony Curtis
Susan Hunsecker . . . . .Susan Harrison
Steve Dallas . . . . .Marty Milner
Frank D'Angelo . . . . .Sam Levene
Rita . . . . .Barbara Nichols
Sally . . . . .Jeff Donnell
Robard . . . . .Joseph Leon
Mary . . . . .Edith Atwater
Harry Kello .Emile Meyer
Herbie Temple . . . . .Joe Frisco
Mrs. Bartha . . . . .Lurene Tuttle

Quote 'From now on, the best of everything is good enough for me.' • 'I'd hate to take a bite out of you. You're a cookie full of arsenic.'
• 'You're walking around blind, Frank, without a cane.' • 'Match me, Sidney.'

Psst! Lancaster starred with Curtis in *Trapeze* and suggested him for this part • British director Mackendrick had made *Whisky Galore* and *The Ladykillers* • There were similarities between Lancaster and columnist Walter Winchell who had also tried, without success, to keep his sister out of the papers • Lancaster's own production company made the film. 'It was,' he said, 'the greatest failure our company ever made. We lost a fortune on it but it has become a critics' darling over the years.'

Swing Time
★★★★ 1936 103min b/w

Director: George Stevens
Screenplay: Howard Lindsay & Allan Scott
Source: Story by Erwin Gelsey

After missing his own wedding, gambler and dancer Astaire sets off to prove to his prospective father-in-law that he can hold a job. But in New York, he falls for dance instructor Rogers. It's a toss-up whether this or *Top Hat* is the best Astaire-Rogers musical. There are many things wrong with this one. Stevens isn't adept at handling comedy – the scene with everyone laughing at the end is a serious miscalculation and the business with the trouser turn-ups is a blatant reworking of a gag in *Top Hat*. But the musical numbers, including 'A Fine Romance', 'Never Gonna Dance' and 'Pick Yourself Up', are out of this world. There's even a surprisingly inoffensive blackface number, in Astaire's homage to the great Bill 'Bojangles' Robinson.

John 'Lucky' Garnett . . . . .Fred Astaire
Penny Carrol . . . . .Ginger Rogers
'Pop' Cardetti . . . . .Victor Moore

Mabel Anderson ....Helen Broderick
Gordon ....Eric Blore
Margaret Watson ....Betty Furness
Ricardo Romero ....George Metaxa
Al Simpson ....Pierre Watkin

OOPS! It's impossible to concentrate during *A Fine Romance* once you notice Fred put a lit pipe into his pocket.

Psst! The amazing series of turns in 'Never Gonna Dance' took 40 takes to get right. In the middle of shooting they discovered that Rogers' feet were bleeding but, like the old trouper she was, she kept going until the shot was in the can • Look at Victor Moore's lips when he's swearing at the cop. Even though a car horn drowns him out, it's clear his words are rather inappropriate for a romantic comedy • Helen Broderick was the mother of Broderick Crawford • Possibly the only movie in which somebody in top hat and tails jumps onto a freight car • The director's father, Landers Stevens, plays Astaire's fiancée's father • When Rogers appears with her hair covered in shampoo, it's actually whipped cream. It was the actress' own suggestion after egg whites and soap hadn't achieved the right look.

Take the Money and Run
★★★ 1969 85min c.

Director: Woody Allen
Screenplay: Woody Allen & Mickey Rose

Woody Allen's first outing as a director is a pseudo-documentary look at the life of an incompetent criminal. Essentially little more than a collection of sketches and gags loosely strung together, not all of it works. However, there are still plenty of good gags as well as a few moments of absolute unrestrained hilarity.

Virgil Starkwell ....Woody Allen
Louise ....Janet Margolin
Fritz ....Marcel Hillaire
Miss Blaire ....Jacquelyn Hyde
Jake ....Lonny Chapman
Al ....Jan Merlin
Also: Mark Gordon, Louise Lasser

Quote 'I used to make obscene phone calls to her, collect, and she used to accept the charges all the time.' • 'The psychiatrist asked me if I thought sex was dirty and I said: "It is if you're doing it right".' • 'You know, he never made the ten most wanted list. It's very unfair voting. It's who you know.' • 'He told me he was a gynecologist. He couldn't speak any foreign

languages. Who was he kidding?' • 'Nobody wears a beige suit to a bank robbery.'

Psst! Originally Allen hoped Jerry Lewis would direct the movie • The prison sequences were shot at San Quentin, and the guards told Allen: 'If you're held hostage, we'll do everything we can to get you out short of opening the gates.'

The Taking of Pelham One Two Three
★★★ 1974 104min c.

Director: Joseph Sargent
Screenplay: Peter Stone
Source: Novel by John Godey

A New York subway train is hijacked and the city authorities given just an hour to produce $1m in cash before the first hostage is killed. This is an incredibly exciting thriller with a cracking plot. Kidnapper Shaw and negotiator Matthau are perfect for their roles as sparring partners. The only drawback is, as in other movies of the period, that the naturalistic recording of dialogue sometimes makes it hard to hear what is being said.

Lt. Garber ....Walter Matthau
Blue ....Robert Shaw
Green ....Martin Balsam
Grey ....Hector Elizondo
Brown ....Earl Hindman
Denny Doyle ....James Broderick
Correll ....Dick O'Neill
The Mayor ....Lee Wallace
Lt. Rico Patrone ....Jerry Stiller
Police Commissioner ....Rudy Bond
Borough Commander ......Kenneth McMillan

Psst! Walter Matthau claimed: 'There was no part for me except the black Transit Authority patrolman – who was about 32. I said, "Well, I'm a little older than 32, but I think there's a lot of black in my background – although I'm not sure." So they gave me the part.' • The use by criminals of colours as codenames was copied by Tarantino for *Reservoir Dogs* • Posters advertising the film in US underground stations were withdrawn after travellers complained.

A Tale of Two Cities
★★★ 1935 121min b/w

Director: Jack Conway
Screenplay: W.P. Lipscomb & S.N. Behrman
Source: Novel by Charles Dickens

At the time of the French Revolution, a British lawyer in love with a woman who has married another man finds a way to help her when her husband is condemned to death. This is the best of the many versions of Dickens' famous tale, sumptuously brought to the screen with Colman making a perfect Carlton. It looks a little fake in places, but still numbs the emotions in its famous final scene. In addition to four silent versions, it was remade in a competent 1958 version with Dirk Bogarde.

Sydney Carton	Ronald Colman
Lucie Manette	Elizabeth Allan
Miss Pross	Edna May Oliver
Marquis St. Evremonde	Basil Rathbone
Mme. Defarge	Blanche Yurka
Striver	Reginald Owen
Dr. Manette	Henry B. Walthall
Charles Darnay	Donald Woods
Barsad	Walter Catlett
Gaspard	Fritz Leiber
Gabelle	H.B. Warner
Jerry Cruncher	Billy Bevan
Seamstress	Isabel Jewell
Woodcutter	Tully Marshall
Mrs. Cruncher	Eily Malyon
Judge in Old Bailey	E.E. Clive

Quote 'With what I get from these peasants, I can hardly afford to pay my perfume bills.' • 'Hunger is an indulgence with these peasants as gout is with us.' • 'It is a far, far better thing I do than I have ever done. It is a far, far better rest I go to than I have ever known.'

OOPS! Although there's a 'despatch from Reuter's' in a newspaper report, Mr. Reuter himself wasn't born until 1816.

Psst! Ronald Colman was not keen to take on the role to begin with and it took much cajoling both to get him to accept and then to get him to shave off his moustache • Blanche Yurka, of Czech extraction, was the 67th actress to test for the part of the evil Madame Defarge. Then it turned out that she did not know how to knit and had to be taught • The sequence with the Bastille being stormed involved 17,000 extras.

The Talk of the Town
★★★ 1942 118min b/w

Director: George Stevens
Screenplay: Irwin Shaw & Sidney Buchman
Source: Story by Sidney Harmon, adapted by Dale Van Every

Suspected murderer Grant is sheltered by Arthur. But a top lawyer who is a stickler for the letter of the law is also staying there. It soon becomes clear that both have designs on their landlady. Although a trifle worthy in places, this comedy with lashings of romance and drama still works, thanks to the talents of the three leading actors. With hindsight, Arthur emerges as the most durable of all the comedy actresses from Hollywood's golden period.

Leopold Dilg	Cary Grant
Nora Shelley	Jean Arthur
Michael Lightcap	Ronald Colman
Regina Bush	Glenda Farrell
Sam Yates	Edgar Buchanan
Andrew Holmes	Charles Dingle
Mrs. Shelley	Emma Dunn
Tilney	Rex Ingram
Jan Pulaski	Leonid Kinskey
Clyde Bracken	Tom Tyler
Forrester	Lloyd Bridges
Chief of Police	Don Beddoe

Psst! Two endings were shot, with Arthur ending up with both Grant and Colman. Preview audiences voted for which they preferred and the winner was the one used.

Tarzan and His Mate
★★★ 1934 105min b/w

Director: Jack Conway & Cedric Gibbons
Screenplay: Leon Gordon & Howard Emmett Rogers
Source: Characters created by Edgar Rice Burroughs

The second in the MGM Weissmuller *Tarzan* series after *Tarzan, the Ape Man* two years earlier is generally held to be the best Tarzan film of all. After being kidnapped and then falling in love with Tarzan in the first film, the scantily-clad Jane now lives in unmarried bliss with the jungle man and his incredibly tame family of animals. Her former boyfriend turns up with some nefarious cronies, plotting to plunder the elephants' graveyard. The daftness of the plot and the animals' behaviour only adds to the enjoyment of this good-natured jungle romp. Weissmuller and O'Sullivan made six *Tarzan* films, and he did another five on his own. There were numerous other *Tarzans* in films going back to 1918. The best of the rest is 1984's *Greystoke*, notably for being the only time an animal has been an Oscar nominee. The worst is almost certainly the 1981 *Tarzan, the Ape Man* with Bo Derek.

Tarzan . . . . .Johnny Weissmuller
Jane Parker . . . . .Maureen O'Sullivan
Harry Holt . . . . .Neil Hamilton
Martin Arlington . . . . .Paul Cavanagh
Beamish . . . . .Forrester Harvey
Pierce . . . . .William Stack
Van Ness . . . . .Desmond Roberts
M. Gironde . . . . .Paul Porcasi

Quote 'Cheetah, that bastard, bit me whenever
he could. The apes were all homosexuals,
eager to wrap their paws around Johnny
Weissmuller's thighs. They were jealous of me
and I loathed them.' [Maureen O'Sullivan]

Psst! Weissmuller won five Olympic medals in
1924 and 28 and broke over 60 world records.
Legend has it he actually went to MGM to visit
his friend Clark Gable, but that the only way in
was by joining the queue of actors auditioning
for the part of Tarzan • Despite being so
closely identified with the role, Weissmuller only
got the part at the last minute when American
footballer Herman Brix, who had been chosen,
injured his shoulder • When Weissmuller signed
up for the Tarzan films, he was under contract
to the company BVD to model their swimming
costumes and underwear. The only way BVD
would allow MGM to take on Weissmuller was if
they agreed to have stars like Marie Dressler,
Greta Garbo, Joan Crawford and Jean Harlow
model their swimwear. MGM was so desperate
that they agreed • The famous line, 'Me Tarzan,
You Jane' existed only in the public's
imagination. What Weissmuller actually said
was just: 'Tarzan…Jane.' • MGM had problems
with the Hays Office over a scene in which Jane
swam naked, with a double standing in for
O'Sullivan, Mia Farrow's mum. Although
ordering her to be covered up, the censors
then discovered that versions, some with her
topless and some with her nude, had also gone
into circulation. After their further objections,
the scene was cut altogether. The master copy
discovered in the 80s is the nude version • As
censorship became tougher, so Jane's
costume became less skimpy in future movies
• This is probably the only example of an
American Olympic swimming champ playing an
English Lord • Weissmuller was doubled for the
vine-swinging sequences by acrobat Alfredo
Codona of The Flying Codonas. The same clips
were used again and again in other *Tarzan* films
• MGM's zoo had Indian, not African elephants,
because they are easier to train. So larger ears
and tusks were made for them, and others
brought in from circuses, to wear • O'Sullivan
complained later that she was 'never more

consistently sick and miserable in my life'. She
had a constant cold from so much time spent in
cold water and was regularly bitten by monkeys.

A Taste of Honey
★★★ 1962 100min b/w

Director: Tony Richardson
Screenplay: Shelagh Delaney & Tony
Richardson
Source: Play by Delaney

As most Kitchen Sink movies feature Angry
Young Men, the quieter heroine here makes a
pleasant change. The 'controversial' aspects of
Shelagh Delaney's play, such as miscegenation
and homosexuality, are now the stuff of any day-
time soap opera. But here they are portrayed
with honesty and a close attention to detail on
northern locations.

Jo . . . . .Rita Tushingham
Peter .Robert Stephens
Helen . . . . .Dora Bryan
Geoffrey .Murray Melvin
Jimmy . . . . .Paul Danquah
Bert . . . . .David Boliver
Doris . . . . .Moira Kaye

Quote 'I'm not just talented. I'm geniused.'
• 'Geoffrey, you're just like a big sister to me.'

Psst! Although an American producer was keen
to make the film, he wanted to junk the idea of
Jo having Jimmy's baby. Otherwise, the whole
of the Southern United States wouldn't take the
movie. Richardson and Osborne decided to
make it independently instead • The film-
makers opted for realism by going on location
to Salford and Manchester. The interiors were
shot in a pad in Chelsea, perhaps the first
movie to use such a locale for real
• Tushingham was almost completely
inexperienced but she saw the job advertised
and decided to audition on the spur of the
moment. The film's success turned her into one
of the faces of the 60s.

Taxi Driver
★★★ 1976 113min c.

Director: Martin Scorsese
Screenplay: Paul Schrader

An inarticulate Vietnam veteran, now a taxi driver, is dehumanised and brutalised by the crime

and sordid behaviour he sees around him. When he comes across a young prostitute, he vows to rescue her from her predicament. De Niro's edgy, surprisingly sympathetic, performance is electrifying and the depiction of the underbelly of New York life sordid and realistic. This is a bleak, uncompromising, mind-blowing film. On repeated viewings, however, the realistic violence becomes still more worrying, while the ridiculous and unbelievable sub-plot about De Niro and Shepherd serves to undermine the film's plausibility.

Travis Bickle	Robert De Niro
Betsy	Cybill Shepherd
Iris Steensman	Jodie Foster
Wizard	Peter Boyle
Sport	Harvey Keitel
Tom	Albert Brooks
Charles Palantine	Leonard Harris
Man in taxi	Martin Scorsese
Personnel officer	Joe Spinell
Concession girl	Diahnne Abbott

Blurb On Every Street In Every City, There's A Nobody Who Dreams Of Being A Somebody.

Quote 'All the animals come out at night: whores, scum, pussies, buggers, queens, fairies, dopers, junkies. Sick. Venal. Some day a real rain will come and wash this scum off the streets.' • 'Are you talkin' to me?' Well, I'm the only one here. Who the fuck do you think you're talking to?' • 'I spent four hours with a shrink to prove I was normal enough to play a hooker.' [Jodie Foster] • 'Bickle is somewhere between Charles Manson and Saint Paul.' [Scorsese]

Psst! The producers couldn't find a major studio to back the movie unless Jeff Bridges played the part of Bickle. But when writer Schrader saw *Mean Streets*, he knew he'd found the right director. His addition to the team persuaded Columbia to back the movie • The 'You talkin' to me?' scene was ad-libbed by De Niro • With his usual dedication, De Niro lost two-and-a-half stone and worked as a taxi driver to prepare for his role. A passenger is reputed to have recognised him and said: 'You're the actor, aren't you? Guess it's hard to find steady work.' • For his preparation, Keitel hung around with real-life pimps • Jodie Foster not only had to be checked out by a psychiatrist before filming but was accompanied everywhere by a social worker during production • Her sister Connie doubled for her in the more risqué scenes, most of which were cut anyway • Composer Bernard Herrmann, reknowned for his work on Hitchcock's movies, died the day afer finishing

his score for *Taxi Driver*. He is said to have refused the commission until he was shown the scene where Bickle pours Schnapps on his cereal • In addition to his cameo in the back of Bickle's cab as a furious passenger playing with his gun while he looks up at the window where his wife is cheating on him, director Scorsese can be glimpsed behind Shepherd as De Niro walks into the campaign headquarters in slo-mo • De Niro's wife of the time, Diahnne Abbott, has a bit part on the concession stand in the porn cinema • John Hinckley watched the movie 15 times and somehow imagined that in order to rescue Jodie Foster he had to shoot Ronald Reagan. De Niro felt in no way responsible. 'There are always people who jump with a towel from the roof because they think they *are* Superman.'

10

★★ 1979 122min c.

Director: Blake Edwards
Screenplay: Blake Edwards

A songwriter suffering from mid-life crisis is knocked out when he meets Derek, who rates 11 on his babe-o-meter. But his all-too-sensible aversion to Ravel's *Bolero* causes him problems. There are a few funny scenes, but they don't adequately compensate for the tedium elsewhere. And while Derek is certainly statuesque, unfortunately she not only looks as if she is made out of stone, but acts like it too.

George	Dudley Moore
Sam	Julie Andrews
Jenny	Bo Derek
Hugh	Robert Webber
Mary Lewis	Dee Wallace
David	Sam Jones
Bartender	Brian Dennehy
The Reverend	Max Showalter

Blurb Just When He Thought It Was Safe To Go Back In The Water.

Quote 'I wouldn't mind losing like a man if you weren't so damned determined to win like one.' • 'Actually, I'm opposed to bartenders making value judgements while on duty.' • 'I'm very big in elevators.' • 'Whenever Mrs. Kissell breaks wind, we beat the dog.' • 'I could tell I got the part immediately because Blake Edwards took his sunglasses off.' [Bo Derek]

Psst! George Segal was originally intended to play Moore's part and actually began filming before quitting.

10 Rillington Place
★★ 1971 111min c.

Director: Richard Fleischer
Screenplay: Clive Exton
Source: Book by Ludovic Kennedy

This tale of murderer John Christie would be unbelievable if we didn't know it was true. Hurt is Evans, the man who was hanged for murdering his wife and child, killings actually carried out by Christie, who didn't stop there. The filmmakers bend over too far backwards to avoid sensationalising events and, although the facts are absorbing, as a piece of storytelling it suffers from being too long and low-key.

John Reginald Christie	. . .Richard Attenborough
Beryl Evans	. . . . .Judy Geeson
Timothy John Evans	. . . . .John Hurt
Mrs. Ethel Christie	. . . . .Pat Heywood
Alice	. . . . .Isobel Black
Judge Lewis	. . . . .André Morell
Christmas Humphreys	. . . . . .Geoffrey Chater
Malcolm Harris	. . . . .Robert Hardy
Furniture dealer	. . . . .Sam Kydd

Psst! The movie was filmed in the building next door to Christie's house.

The Terminator
★★★★ 1984 108min c.

Director: James Cameron
Screenplay: Gale Anne Hurd & James Cameron

Highly influential sci-fi thriller with Arnie in pre-superstar days as an evil cyborg, sent back from the future to stop a potential rebel leader being born to a bewildered Linda Hamilton. One of those rare films in which splendid action sequences are complemented by an intelligent and witty script. It holds up brilliantly no matter how many times you watch it, even if some of the stop-motion special effects now look a mite ropey.

Terminator	. . . . .Arnold Schwarzenegger
Kyle Reese	. . . . .Michael Biehn
Sarah Connor	. . . . .Linda Hamilton
Traxler	. . . . .Paul Winfield
Vukovich	. . . . .Lance Henriksen
Matt	. . . . .Rick Rossovich
Ginger	. . . . .Bess Motta
Silberman	. . . . .Earl Boen
Pawn shop clerk	. . . . .Dick Miller
Punk leader	. . . . .Bill Paxton

Quote 'I'll be back.' • 'Come with me if you want to live.'

OOPS! Arnie finds three addresses for Sarah Connor in the phone book. The first house he pays a housecall on is numbered 14239, which wasn't one of them • Although the phone is knocked off the hook in Hamilton's apartment, it rings later • When Arnie makes his famous return to the police station, there's the dazzle of headlights. But the car that crashes into the station doesn't have its lights on • The cops say that Hamilton's mother will not at the cabin for an hour. Yet Sarah thinks she's talking to her on the phone, even though it's Arnie. Surely the mother has to be there so that the cyborg can impersonate her voice?

Psst! Harlan Ellison successfully sued, claiming the plot came from an *Outer Limits* TV episode he wrote • O.J. Simpson was considered for the terminator's role, but the film-makers worried that audiences wouldn't take him seriously • Henrikson and Schwarzenegger originally had each other's roles. After reading the script, Arnie asked to swop over.

Terminator 2: Judgment Day
★★★ 1991 136min c.

Director: James Cameron
Screenplay: James Cameron & William Wisher

Now that he's a superstar Arnie has to be the good guy, even though he looks exactly like the baddie in the first film. He's sent back in time to save the future leader of the rebels fighting the machines. The script isn't as clever or witty as the original, but the effects are out of this world. You can tell Arnie's a goodie because he only shoots people in the leg, not anywhere it'll hurt!

Terminator T-800	. . . . .Arnold Schwarzenegger
Sarah Connor	. . . . .Linda Hamilton
John Connor	. . . . .Edward Furlong
Terminator T-1000	. . . . .Robert Patrick
Dr. Silberman	. . . . .Earl Boen
Miles Dyson	. . . . .Joe Morton
Tarissa Dyson	. . . . .S. Epatha Merkerson
Tim	. . . . .Danny Cooksey

Blurb It's Nothing Personal.

Quote 'On August 29th, 1997…anybody not wearing two million sunblock is gonna have a real bad day.' • 'Hasta la vista, baby.' • 'Who sent you?' – 'You did, 35 years from now.'

OOPS! As the truck dives off the bridge, the glass in the cab shatters. Yet it's back for the evil Terminator to smash soon after • When Arnie and Furlong are on the motorbike and he causes the lorry to crash by shooting its tyre, they're going through the left hand side of the small tunnel. Then they disappear. Then they're there again • As the evil Terminator flies the helicopter, he reloads his gun using both hands. So whose is the other hand we see now flying the chopper? • When Linda Hamilton runs through the hospital barefoot, the noise is of someone wearing shoes • If we're quibbling, the boy should actually only be six or seven to fit in with the first film.

Psst! The most expensive film ever made – until *Waterworld* – with a cost reckoned to be of the order of $100m, with the studio spending another $20m on publicity • Schwarzenegger is said to have been given a Gulfstream G-III jet as part of his $15m fee • You could argue that his rate of pay was lower than on the first *Terminator*. Then he was eventually paid $6m for the 133 words he uttered, $45,000 a word. In the sequel he had 474 words, which works out at just $31,500 a word.

Terms of Endearment

★★★ 1983 132min c.

Director: James L. Brooks
Screenplay: James L. Brooks
Source: Novel by Larry McMurtry

This highly emotional Oscar-winner is TV soap opera played at Gale Force Ten, yet is still worth watching for the acting. MacLaine's the overbearing mother who drives daughter Winger into an unsuitable marriage while being wooed by wisecracking ex-astronaut Nicholson. Kleenex sales must have soared when it came out.

Aurora Greenway . . . . .Shirley MacLaine
Emma Greenway Horton . . . . . . .Debra Winger
Garrett Breedlove . . . . .Jack Nicholson
Flap Horton . . . . .Jeff Daniels
Vernon Dahlart . . . . .Danny DeVito
Sam Burns . . . . .John Lithgow

Oscars Best Picture, Best Director, Shirley MacLaine, Jack Nicholson

Blurb Come To Laugh, Come To Cry, Come To Care, Come To Terms.

Quote 'I like the lights *on*.' — 'Then go home and turn them on.' • 'It sure would be nice to have a mother that somebody liked.'

Psst! It took writer-director Brooks four years to find a studio that would back the project

• Winger went to some lengths to get into her part, wearing a fake pregnancy prosthetic for three months, even in bed, although she's only seen pregnant very briefly in the film. She also insisted MacLaine call her by her character's name when they spoke • Winger and MacLaine did not see eye to eye and, to the delight of the public, carried their quarrels over into the media after finishing the film • Collecting her Oscar, MacLaine said: 'I really deserve this'.

The Texas Chainsaw Massacre

★ 1974 83min c.

Director: Tobe Hooper
Screenplay: Kim Henkel & Tobe Hooper

The only point in this film's favour is that, desite the lurid title, it is actually quite restrained when it comes to pouring out the tomato ketchup. A couple of well-staged shocks apart, this tale of Leatherface and his family keeping the deep freeze stocked with prime cuts of over-inquisitive visitors is draggy and misses the black comic tone Tobe Hooper is obviously striving for.

Sally . . . . .Marilyn Burns
Leatherface . . . . .Gunnar Hansen
Hitchhiker . . . . .Edwin Neal
Jerry . . . . .Allen Danziger
Franklin . . . . .Paul A. Partain
Kirk . . . . .William Vail
Narrator . . . . .John Larroquette

Blurb Who Will Survive And What Will Be Left Of Them?

Psst! Like *Psycho*, the film is based on the real-life Wisconsin killer Ed Gein • The BBFC refused to pass the film and it was left to the GLC to grant it a London-only 'X' certificate so it could be shown. Mysteriously, it is still banned on video in Britain • The actress chased through undergrowth by Leatherface actually cut herself on the branches quite badly, so much of the blood on her body and clothes is actually hers.

That's Entertainment!

★★★★ 1974 137min c&b/w

Director: Jack Haley Jr.
Screenplay: Jack Haley Jr.

Musical fans will adore this collection of clips from the golden age of musicals, all garnered from the archives of MGM and presented by great stars such as Astaire, Kelly, Stewart and

Taylor. They aren't all brilliant, but as everyone's favourite tends to be different, there should be something among the 100 musicals represented for everyone. *That's Entertainment, Part 2*, released in 1976 was a little less scintillating, but still a treasure trove with clips from drama and comedy as well as musicals. In 1994 *That's Entertainment! III* included some rarely-seen outtakes and is a must for musical fans. *That's Dancing* is pretty ropey, but still includes some wonderful dancing scenes.

With: Fred Astaire, Bing Crosby, Gene Kelly, Peter Lawford, Liza Minnelli, Donald O'Connor, Debbie Reynolds, Mickey Rooney, Frank Sinatra, James Stewart, Elizabeth Taylor

Psst! The producer, Jack Haley Jr., reckoned that the cost of staging the musical numbers would be around $250m, even before the actors' pay was taken into account.

Thelma & Louise
★★★★ 1991 130min c.

Director: Ridley Scott
Screenplay: Callie Khouri

Waitress Sarandon gets meek housewife Davis away from her sexist husband for the weekend. But things go wrong when a rape attempt forces them to go on the run. Although widely acclaimed as a feminist film, this is really just another buddy road movie (with a relatively well-worn tread on the script) where the genders have been switched. However, the two women are so good in their gutsy, often very funny roles, and the photography is so stylish that we get carried along for the ride. A hugely enjoyable movie, whichever sex you are.

Thelma Dickinson . . . . .Geena Davis
Louise Sawyer . . . . .Susan Sarandon
Hal . . . . .Harvey Keitel
Jimmy . . . . .Michael Madsen
Darryl . . . . .Christopher McDonald
Max . . . . .Stephen Tobolowsky
J.D. . . . . .Brad Pitt

Oscars Best Screenplay

Blurb Someone Said Get A Life...So They Did.

Quote 'He's got a cute butt. Not like Darryl. You could park a car in the shadow of his ass.' • 'I always believe that, done properly, armed robbery doesn't have to be a totally unpleasant experience.' • 'Take all the cash out of that drawer and put it in a paper bag. You're gonna have an amazing story to tell all your friends. If

not, you'll have a tag on your toe. You decide.' • 'How do you like your vacation so far?'

OOPS! In the C&W bar, Sarandon's marguerita is in one of those magical movie glasses where the drink level keeps bobbing around.

Psst! Incredible though it may seem, the originally planned ending had the two landing their car safely at the bottom of the Grand Canyon and driving off free as birds. For some reason someone thought this a little implausible. Despite the actual ending, in the wake of the film's success one executive still suggested to Sarandon the possibility of a sequel.

Them!
★★★ 1954 94min b/w

Director: Gordon Douglas
Screenplay: Ted Sherdeman

Don't you just hate it when meddlesome scientists upset the balance of nature yet again? Here, their desert nuclear tests spawn a race of monster...well, you'll have to watch to see what 'Them' are. Suffice it to say that it's one of the best of the batch of 50s monster sci-fi movies and, as we don't see much of 'Them', there isn't too much time spent laughing at dated effects.

Sgt. Ben Peterson . . . . .James Whitmore
Dr. Harold Medford . . . . .Edmund Gwenn
Dr. Patricia Medford . . . . .Joan Weldon
Robert Graham . . . . .James Arness
Brig. Gen. O'Brien . . . . .Onslow Stevens
Maj. Kibbee . . . . .Sean McClory
Crotty . . . . .Fess Parker
Sergeant . . . . .Leonard Nimoy

Blurb Don't Tell Anyone What *Them* Are.

Psst! Two giant 'Thems' were built, one just the front section and the other a 12-foot model of the whole creature. They were operated by pulleys and levers operated by the technicians • James Arness would soon be better known as Marshall Matt Dillon in the TV series *Gunsmoke* • If you're quick, you can spot a young Leonard Nimoy as a sergeant at a teletype machine.

They Live by Night
★ 1949 95min b/w

Director: Nicholas Ray
Screenplay: Charles Schnee
Source: Novel, *Thieves Like Us* by Edward Anderson

Nicholas Ray's high reputation remains a mystery, as this first film shows. Two criminal lovers on the run can make a great story, as is shown in the contemporaneous *Gun Crazy*, made on a tiny budget. However, any film which aspires to tragedy with the opening caption, 'This boy and girl were never properly introduced to the world we live in', is destined to sink into whingeing self-pity. Nor does Farley Granger, who could suggest evil in Hitchcock films, convince here as a criminal.

Keechie	Cathy O'Donnell
Bowie	Farley Granger
Chicamaw	Howard da Silva
T-Dub	Jay C. Flippen
Mattie	Helen Craig
Mobley	Will Wright
Hawkins	Ian Wolfe
Lambert	Byron Foulger
Policeman	Ralph Dunn
Doctor	Erskine Sanford

Psst! As the crooks are chased by the Police, there's a camera shot from a helicopter. Although copter shots are wildly over-used in movies now, this was revolutionary at the time.

They Shoot Horses, Don't They?

★★★ 1969 129min c.

Director: Sydney Pollack
Screenplay: James Poe & Robert E. Thompson
Source: Novel by Horace McCoy

A harrowing look at a dance marathon in the Depression years, with couples moving around the dance floor till they drop. Even if they don't win the cash prize, they want to keep going just for the three square meals a day. Overseeing it all is the sleazy, sadistic Young. You are likely to boil over with anger at the injustice of it all. A depressing experience, but one everybody ought to try once.

Gloria Beatty	Jane Fonda
Robert Syverton	Michael Sarrazin
Alice	Susannah York
Rocky	Gig Young
Sailor	Red Buttons
Ruby	Bonnie Bedelia
James	Bruce Dern
Rollo	Michael Conrad
Joel	Robert Fields
Turkey	Al Lewis

Oscars Gig Young

Quote ' Yowsah! Yowsah! Yowsah! Here they are again, these wonderful, wonderful kids, still struggling, still hoping as the clock of fate ticks away. The dance of destiny continues. The marathon goes on and on and on. How long can they last? Let's hear it. C'mon, let's hear it. Let's hear it.' • 'There can only be one winner, folks, but isn't that the American way?'

Psst! Some of the shots of the dancers were taken by a cameraman on roller skates • In order to make the cast appear sufficiently tired, director Pollack made them run around the set several times at the start of each day's filming • The film rights of the 1935 novel were first purchased by Charles Chaplin • Fonda wanted the part to put her sex kitten persona behind her • Al Lewis is best known for for his role in the TV sitcom *The Munsters* • Director Mervyn LeRoy, who had made movies like *Little Caesar* and *Gold Diggers of 1933* has a tiny cameo as a member of the audience introduced by Gig Young • Young, who won the Oscar, had until this been known mostly for frothy comedies. Less than 10 years later he was to kill his fifth wife and then shoot himself • This was the first Hollywood movie ever shown on Russian TV.

The Thief of Bagdad

★★★ 1940 102min c.

Director: Michael Powell, Ludwig Berger, Tim Whelan, Zoltan Korda, William Cameron Menzies & Alexander Korda
Screenplay: Lajos Biro & Miles Malleson

This Arabian Nights adventure, involving a light-fingered street rat trying to thwart the plans of the evil Jaffar with the help of a genie, was once considered the epitome of screen fantasy. Unfortunately, the world of special effects has moved on so far that some of it, such as the flying horse, now creaks terribly. Also on the debit side, the songs are pretty dreadful and there's too much talk and too little action. However, it still tickles the imagination enough to keep kids interested and adults will marvel at the glorious early use of Technicolor. The plot was plundered heavily for the Disney version of *Aladdin*.

Jaffar	Conrad Veidt
Abu	Sabu
Princess	June Duprez
Ahmad	John Justin
Djinni	Rex Ingram
Sultan	Miles Malleson
Old King	Morton Selten

Halima . . . . .Mary Morris
Astrologer .Hay Petrie

Quote 'I'm Abu the Thief, son of Abu the Thief, grandson of Abu the Thief, most unfortunate of ten sons with a hunger that yearns day and night.' • 'There are but three things that men respect: the lash that descends, the yoke that breaks, and the sword that slays. By the power and terror of these; you may conquer the earth.'

Psst! The film was begun in Britain but, because of the war, it had to be completed in America • With six directors ultimately involved, it was extraordinary that it got finished at all • The sets were designed by William Cameron Menzies. When the courtyard of Bagdad didn't look right, the whole one and a half acres was cemented over, painted black and then polished so that it would have a sufficient lustre to reflect the surrounding buildings.

The Thin Man

★★★★ 1934 93min c.

Director: W.S. Van Dyke
Screenplay: Frances Goodrich & Albert Hackett
Source: Novel by Dashiell Hammett

Let's face it: the detective story is rather tedious, with wooden direction and some dreadfully melodramatic acting from the supports. But the two stars turn it into movie magic. As played by Powell and Loy, the hard-drinking, wisecracking, affectionate Nick and Nora still rank as one of the most scintillating husband and wife combos ever seen on screen. There were five sequels, the best of them After the Thin Man.

Nick Charles . . . . .William Powell
Nora Charles . . . . .Myrna Loy
Dorothy Wynant . . . . .Maureen O'Sullivan
Lt. John Guild . . . . .Nat Pendleton
Mimi Wynant . . . . .Minna Gombell
MacCauley . . . . .Porter Hall
Tommy . . . . .Henry Wadsworth
Gilbert Wynant . . . . .William Henry
Chris Jorgenson . . . . .Cesar Romero
Nunheim . . . . .Harold Huber
Joe Morelli . . . . .Edward Brophy
Clyde Wynant . . . . .Edward Ellis
Asta . . . . .Asta

Quote 'I haven't time. I'm much too busy seeing that you don't lose any of the money I married you for.' • 'The important thing is the rhythm. Always have rhythm in your shaking. Now a Manhattan you shake to foxtrot time, a Bronx to two-step time, a dry martini you always shake

to waltz time.' • 'The next person who says Merry Christmas to me, I'll kill him.' • 'I think it's a dirty trick to bring me all the way to New York just to make a widow of me.' – 'You wouldn't be a widow long.' – 'You bet I wouldn't. Not with your money.'

Psst! MGM wasn't keen on the project, reckoning that the detective movie had had its day. Even when Van Dyke managed to convince Louis B. Mayer to make it, the MGM boss didn't want Powell and Loy because they were serious actors and wouldn't be able to handle comedy • Mayer was so parsimonious with the budget, effectively relegating it to B-movie status, that it had to be made with almost no retakes in just 16 days • Many of its more wonderful touches, such as Nora's first entrance, were improvised as they went along • So popular were Loy and Powell on screen together that they were teamed for a total of 13 films • The Thin Man isn't Nick Charles, but Clyde Wynant, the murder victim • Asta was so popular that he started off a craze for wirehaired terriers. He appeared, not only in other Thin Man films, but also in Bringing Up Baby and The Awful Truth.

The Thing

★★ 1951 87min b/w

Director: Christian Nyby
Screenplay: Charles Lederer
Source: Story, Who Goes There by J.W. Campbell Jr.

Scientists at the North Pole make the mistake of thawing out an unfriendly alien whose spaceship has crashed into the permafrost. Copied so many times since that it no longer looks fresh, there are still a few thrills to be had. Very sensibly, the 'Thing' is rarely glimpsed clearly. Without silly gimmicks, the audience's imagination is free to run riot. Also known as The Thing From Another World. Remade, with some panache, by John Carpenter in 1982.

Capt. Pat Henry . . . . .Kenneth Tobey
Nikki Nicholson . . . . .Margaret Sheridan
Dr. Carrington . . . . .Robert Cornthwaite
'The Thing' . . . . .James Arness
Corp. Barnes . . . . .William Self
Bob . . . . .Dewey Martin
Scotty . . . . .Douglas Spencer

Quote 'An intellectual carrot! The mind boggles!' • 'I bring you warning, to every one of you listening to the sound of my voice. Tell the world, tell this to everyone wherever they are: Watch the skies, everywhere, keep looking. Keep watching the skies.' [Last line]

Psst! This is apparently the first film to feature a creature from outer space • Although many seem to believe that producer Howard Hawks must have directed much of the movie, those actors who were in the film claim he was barely even seen on the set • Arness, who plays 'The Thing' would later become better known as Marshall Dillon on TV's *Gunsmoke* • The same Los Angeles warehouse used to simulate below-zero conditions in *Lost Horizon* and *The Magnificent Ambersons* was utilised here • The American Air Force would not cooperate with the film-makers because they felt that it would be tantamount to admitting that UFOs existed.

Things to Come
★★ 1936 100min b/w

Director: William Cameron Menzies
Screenplay: H.G. Wells & Lajos Biro
Source: Book, *The Shape of Things to Come* by H.G. Wells

Wells' view of the future was amazingly pre-scient, with forecasts of a forthcoming war with blanket bombing and rocket travel to the moon. The futuristic sets still look stupendous, Arthur Bliss' music is considered one of the great scores and the scenes of wartime devastation are chillingly accurate. But the screenplay Wells constructed from his novel was probably stilted and stagy even at the time. The story's human side is lamentable, a perfect example of what happens when a genius is allowed to run riot in a field he later confessed he knew little about.

John/Oswald Cabal . . . . .Raymond Massey
Pippa/Raymond Passworthy .Edward Chapman
The Boss . . . . .Ralph Richardson
Roxana/Rowena . . . . .Margaretta Scott
Theotocopulos . . . . .Cedric Hardwicke
Dr. Harding . . . . .Maurice Braddell
Mrs. Cabal . . . . .Sophie Stewart
Mary Gordon .Ann Todd
Richard Gordon . . . . .Derrick de Marney
Airman .John Clements

Quote 'If we don't end war, war will end us.' • 'I don't suppose any man has ever understood any woman since the beginning of things.'

Psst! Seventy-year-old Wells penned the screenplay from his novel. He found it harder than he expected and even his fourth attempt after two years of work had to be considerably

reworked • Wells became fascinated with the mechanics of filming and constantly interfered, not just with the story but with the actors, design and music as well. Wells brought Arthur Bliss in before filming started, so that the score could be integrated with the film. The recording of it became the first movie soundtrack to be sold to the public and it remains one of Bliss' best known works • The film itself, which cost an amazing $1.5m, was not a hit with the public, although it recouped its money through re-releases • Although some see similarities in the vision of the future with *Metropolis*, Wells thought Lang's view of the future 'hopelessly silly…you may take it that whatever Lang did in *Metropolis* is the exact opposite of what is wanted here.' • The scenes of Everytown in ruins were used by the Air Ministry and Winston Churchill to argue how effective heavy bombing could be, while Neville Chamberlain used the same scenes as proof of the danger we were in from the Luftwaffe and of the need for peace • As with so many other films, such as *Duck Soup*, Mussolini took offence at Richardson's portrayal of a dictator and the film was banned in Italy • Several different versions exist. The original ran for 130 minutes, but most of those now available vary from 90 to 113 minutes.

The Third Man
★★★★ 1949 104min b/w

Director: Carol Reed
Screenplay: Graham Greene

A perfect movie? As near as they come. Writer Cotten searches for an old friend in devastated postwar Vienna, not realising what sort of man he'd turned into. A cracking yarn made flesh by outstanding acting, a fantastic sense of time and place, pacy direction and superlative pho-tography. Maybe a touch less of the evocative zither music wouldn't have hurt. One of those rare films that can be watched again and again.

Holly Martins . . . . .Joseph Cotten
Harry Lime .Orson Welles
Anna Schmidt .Alida Valli
Maj. Calloway . . . . .Trevor Howard
Sgt. Paine .Bernard Lee
Crabbin . . . . .Wilfrid Hyde-White
'Baron' Kurtz . . . . .Ernst Deutsch
British policeman . . . . .Geoffrey Keen
Porter .Paul Hoerbiger

Quote 'In Italy for 30 years under the Borgias, they had warfare, terror, murder and bloodshed. But they produced Michelangelo,

Leonardo da Vinci and the Renaissance. In Switzerland, they had brotherly love and they had 500 years of democracy and peace. And what did they produce? The cuckoo clock!'
• 'What can I do, old man? I'm dead, aren't I?'
• 'Honest, sensible, sober, harmless Holly Martins. Holly …what a silly name.'

OOPS! Lime has amazingly clean shoes for someone who commutes through the sewers.

Psst! After making *The Fallen Idol*, director Reed and writer Greene wanted to work together again but were stumped for an idea. Then Greene found an envelope on which, years before, he had written: 'I had paid my last farewell to Harry a week ago, when his coffin was lowered into the frozen February ground, so it was with incredulity that I saw him pass by, without a sign of recognition, among the host of strangers in the Strand.' Greene worked it up as a novel and then turned that into the screenplay • If the narration is by Cotten then you're watching the shorter 93-minute American version. Director Reed narrated the longer British version • Cary Grant was the original casting idea for the Joseph Cotten part • Trevor Howard claimed to have discovered zither player Anton Karas playing outside a restaurant in Vienna • The music was immensely popular but isn't playable on the zither as it sounds. Karas used early multi-tracking techniques to play alongside himself • Many think that Welles came up with much of his own dialogue but, with the exception of writing the speech about cuckoo clocks, in fact he largely stuck to the script as written. He did, however, come up with directorial suggestions for the scenes in which he appeared • Welles initially asked for a double to be used for the sewer scenes because of his asthma but then couldn't bear remaining on the sidelines • The first choice for Harry Lime had been Noel Coward • Welles took the part to raise money for his film of *Othello*. He later regretted taking cash straight up front rather than going for a share of the profits. Nonetheless it remained his favourite film, despite the zither music being played at him wherever he went • Against objections from others, including Greene, it was Reed who insisted on keeping the downbeat ending • Filming in occupied Vienna wasn't always easy. With just five weeks there, the crew was divided into two, one working during the day and one at night. Reed had to be around all the time, and survived the shoot with just a couple of brief naps each day • Trevor Howard went on a bender one evening, forgetting that he was still in his colonel's

uniform. He was picked up by the Military Police who wanted to charge him with impersonating an officer • American co-producer David O. Selznick tried to persuade Reed to change the title to *Night in Vienna*. He had also wanted Noël Coward to play Harry Lime.

The 39 Steps
★★★★ 1935 85min b/w

Director: Alfred Hitchcock
Screenplay: Charles Bennett & Alma Reville
Source: Novel by John Buchan

A Canadian on holiday in London is pitched into a search for enemy spies, even while he is being hunted by the authorities as a murderer. Hitchcock excelled himself with this thriller. Although some of the sets now look a bit ropey, it remains a great chase movie with lashings of comic touches, wonderful thrills, deft dialogue and the still sexy predicament of Donat and the reluctant Carroll handcuffed together. It was remade in 1959 and 1978. Neither can hold a candle to this masterpiece.

Richard Hannay	Robert Donat
Pamela	Madeleine Carroll
Miss Smith	Lucie Mannheim
Prof. Jordan	Godfrey Tearle
Crofter's wife	Peggy Ashcroft
Crofter	John Laurie
Mrs. Jordan	Helen Haye
Mr. Memory	Wylie Watson
Sheriff Watson	Frank Cellier
Commercial traveller	Gus McNaughton
Commercial traveller	Jerry Verno

Quote 'There are twenty million women in this island and I've got to be chained to you.'
• 'Thank you, sir. thank you. I'm glad it's off my mind at last.' [Last line]

Psst! Hitch can be glimpsed five or six minutes from the opening, dropping litter as Donat and Mannheim flee from the music hall • One of Hitchcock's cruellest gags was played on this set, with the great man handcuffing Donat and Carroll together before they properly knew each other. He claimed it was preparatory to rehearsing a scene, but he then disappeared with the key and could not be found. The two unfortunate actors had to spend most of the day locked together. Hitch's main interest, he later confessed, was in seeing how they coped with calls of nature! • Three score of Hertfordshire sheep were used in the studio for the scene where the car is held up. They ate bits of the set and assorted props before their moment of stardom was over • When Robert Donat and Peggy Ashcroft couldn't stop corpsing for a scene together, the annoyed Hitchcock punched a studio light, smashing it. It stopped the laughter stone dead.

This Gun for Hire
★★★ 1942 80min b/w

Director: Frank Tuttle
Screenplay: Albert Maltz & W.R. Burnett
Source: Novel, *A Gun for Sale* by Graham Greene

This great film noir mixes glamorous Veronica Lake with cold assassin Alan Ladd and a tale involving fifth columnists, a staple plot element in many thrillers of the time. Although downbeat, there's plenty of suspense and Ladd is amazingly creepy in the part. Although there wasn't a romance between the two, the public liked the pairing so much that they made three more movies together, *The Glass Key*, the fine *Blue Dahlia* and *Saigon*. This one was remade as *Short Cut to Hell*, with James Cagney directing.

Philip Raven .Alan Ladd
Ellen Graham . . . . .Veronica Lake
Michael Crane . . . . .Robert Preston
Willard Gates . . . . .Laird Cregar
Alvin Brewster . . . . .Tully Marshall
Sluky .Mikhail Rasumny
Tommy .Marc Lawrence
Steve Finnerty . . . . .Harry Shannon
Show girl . . . . .Yvonne De Carlo

Psst! As in the novel, the film was originally centred around the Lake and Preston characters. But as filming began, they realised how good Ladd was and the script was rejigged to make him the co-star • Ladd was never one of the world's greatest actors and became as well-known for the trench coat that he wore as for his acting ability • Lake was one of the few co-stars the five-foot four-inch star didn't have to disguise his height against. She was three inches shorter than him • Lake had no dancing or singing experience prior to the movie and took lessons from a professional magician for the magic act. She wasn't best pleased when director Tuttle made her do it 64 times and then used the fourth take. It didn't help that she was bitten twice by the monkey • Although the novel was set in 1936, it was updated to wartime and the location switched to California • As the production ended, Ladd was struck by a serious bout of pneumonia

which looked for a time as if it might prove fatal • Yvonne de Carlo, later to star in the TV sitcom *The Munsters*, made her film debut here in a tiny part as a show girl • This film was one of the main sources of clips used in the Steve Martin film *Dead Men Don't Wear Plaid*.

This Happy Breed
★★ 1944 110min c.

Director: David Lean
Screenplay: David Lean, Ronald Neame & Anthony Havelock-Allan
Source: Play by Noël Coward

This episodic tale of a working-class family between the wars, taken from his play, gives little impression that Coward had ever met anyone from the working classes, let alone known them well enough to write about them. Despite the odd decent performance which manages to wrench out an involuntary tear or two, its main interest now is to see the jingoistic flag-waving and the way in which domestic life has changed in the intervening period.

Frank Gibbons . . . . .Robert Newton
Ethel Gibbons . . . . .Celia Johnson
Billy Mitchell . . . . .John Mills
Queenie Gibbons . . . . .Kay Walsh
Bob Mitchell . . . . .Stanley Holloway
Mrs. Flint .Amy Veness
Aunt Sylvia . . . . .Alison Leggatt
Reg . . . . .John Blythe
Narrator . . . . .Laurence Olivier

Psst! A scene with an 11-year-old girl in the bath was cut by the censors in Britain because 'the girl can be seen from the waist up' • It wasn't until 1947, three years after the UK release, that the film was seen in America • Lean had co-directed *In Which We Serve* with Coward and the collaboration continued with Lean filming this, *Blithe Spirit* and *Brief Encounter* • Kay Walsh was Mrs. Lean at the time.

This is Spinal Tap
★★★★ 1984 82min c.

Director: Rob Reiner
Screenplay: Christopher Guest, Michael McKean, Harry Shearer & Rob Reiner

A beautifully observed and often hilarious satire on the rock scene, following a declining heavy-metal band as they make a steadily less successful tour of America, filmed by a 'rocku-mentary' team. It is amazing how well these guys ape the real thing, the only problem being that they are so bad, they would surely be more successful. Catch those great speakers with the knobs going all the way to eleven.

David St. Hubbins . . . . .Michael McKean
Nigel Tufnel . . . . .Christopher Guest
Derek Smalls . . . . .Harry Shearer
Mick Shrimpton . . . . .R.J. Parnell
Marti DiBerti . . . . .Rob Reiner
Tommy Pischedda . . . . .Bruno Kirby
Also: Billy Crystal, Anjelica Huston, Patrick Macnee, Dana Carvey

Quote 'He died in a bizarre gardening accident.' • 'You should have seen the cover they *wanted* to do. It wasn't a glove, believe me.' • 'There is such a fine line between genius and stupidity.' • 'These go to 11.'

Psst! Many of the scenes were improvised on the basic script • There are cameos from Anjelica Huston, Patrick Macnee and Billy Crystal, with Reiner himself playing the director of the documentary • In the film the band decide to seek their fortune in Japan because the 'Smell the Glove' album was doing so well there. Oddly enough, in Japan the spoof *Spinal Tap* album became a big hit • The band are all musicians in their own right and play on the albums and on tour to plug them • Guest, the lead guitarist and husband of Jamie-Lee Curtis, is in line to inherit the title of Baron and a seat in the House of Lords.

This Man Is News
★★★ 1938 77min b/w

Director: David MacDonald
Screenplay: Allan Mackinnon, Roger Macdougall & Basil Dearden

Perhaps the nearest the British film industry came to replicating the witty banter and excite-ment of the *Thin Man* films. Barnes is the reporter on the trail of jewel thieves, Hobson his wisecrack-spitting wife and Sim the delightfully irascible editor. On the debit side, it's a bit hammy, Barnes is on the dull side and there are some terribly unconvincing fights. But who cares? The banter is glorious, there's a lisping villain with white mice crawling all over him and a memorable evening a *deux* with the two stars knocking off three bottles of champagne from massive brandy glasses. The British film indus-try needed more heroes like this.

Simon Drake . . . . .Barry K. Barnes
Pat Drake . . . . .Valerie Hobson
Macgregor .Alastair Sim
Insp. Hollis . . . . .Edward Lexy
Sgt. Bright . . . . .Garry Marsh
Johnny Clayton . . . . .John Warwick
Ken Marquis . . . . .Kenneth Buckley
'Harelip' Murphy . . . . .Philip Leaver

OOPS! When the Police appear for the shootout in the newspaper offices, they shout out 'Drake' and call for him to drop the gun. But it isn't Drake they're talking to. It's Clayton.

This Sporting Life
★★★ 1963 134min b/w

Director: Lindsay Anderson
Screenplay: David Storey
Source: Novel by Storey

A self-destructive miner leaves the pit behind and becomes a professional rugby player. Although it's hard to sympathise with Harris' character, this remains a gritty, disturbing drama. Among the fine performances, most memorable are Roberts, as the widow Harris pursues, and Hartnell as the homosexual scout who first discovered Harris. Watching the dis-passionate way the rugby players are treated by the owners of the club is a little like watching the Romans overseeing the gladiators in *Spartacus*. Tough meat, but still well worth get-ting your teeth into.

Frank Machin . . . . .Richard Harris
Mrs. Hammond . . . . .Rachel Roberts
Weaver . . . . .Alan Badel
Johnson . . . . .William Hartnell
Maurice Braithwaite . . . . .Colin Blakely
Mrs. Weaver . . . . .Vanda Godsell
Slomer . . . . .Arthur Lowe
Judith . . . . .Anne Cunningham
Len Miller . . . . .Jack Watson
Jeff . . . . .George Sewell
Phillips . . . . .Leonard Rossiter
Dentist . . . . .Frank Windsor

The Thomas Crown Affair
★★ 1968 102min c.

Director: Norman Jewison
Screenplay: Alan R. Trustman

A bored millionaire plots what he thinks will be the perfect robbery but he reckons without a beautiful ace insurance investigator. The movie is still remembered fondly for its theme music, 'The Windmills of Your Mind', and for the chess game which serves as foreplay, still one of the sexiest scenes in the movies. Unfortunately, like so many 60s movies, this is filled with silly directorial tricks that make it almost too irritating to watch at times. It's the filmic equivalent of the lava lamp. What seemed chic and clever at the time is rather tacky and embarrassing now.

Thomas Crown	Steve McQueen
Vicky Anderson	Faye Dunaway
Eddy Malone	Paul Burke
Erwin Weaver	Jack Weston
Carl	Yaphet Kotto
Sandy	Biff McGuire
Abe	Addison Powell

OOPS! The first bank robbery is supposed to net over $2.5m. But a secretary later announces how it breaks down – 16,240 $20 bills, 19,871 $10 bills, 34,645 $5 bills and 129,000 $1 bills. That's only $825,735.

Psst! This supposedly features the longest-ever screen kiss – McQueen and Dunaway suck face for just five seconds short of a minute.

Three Days of the Condor
★★★★ 1975 117min c.

Director: Sydney Pollack
Screenplay: Lorenzo Semple Jr. & David Rayfiel
Source: Novel, *The Six Days of the Condor* by James Grady

A researcher for a rather literary branch of the CIA pops out for coffee and returns to find the entire office slaughtered. Expecting that whoever did it will want to kill him too, he goes on the run. But he doesn't know who he can trust among his former employers. This is one of the all-time great conspiracy thrillers, thanks to a witty, literate and eminently believable script. Redford is splendid as the bookworm who turns, having to learn the wrinkles of being an agent in the field in incredibly quick order.

Joe Turner	Robert Redford
Kathy Hale	Faye Dunaway
Higgins	Cliff Robertson
Joubert	Max Von Sydow
Mr. Wabash	John Houseman
Atwood	Addison Powell
Sam Barber	Walter McGinn
Fowler	Michael Miller

The Three Faces of Eve
★★ 1957 91min b/w

Director: Nunnally Johnson
Screenplay: Nunnally Johnson
Source: Book by Corbett H. Thigpen M.D. & Hervey M. Cleckley M.D.

A psychiatrist discovers that a woman he is treating has three different personalities. The Academy for Motion Picture Arts and Sciences loves actors portraying people with mental illness at one and the same time. As Woodward was playing three people with mental illness, it's no wonder they gave her an Oscar. She does give a creditable performance, to be fair, and the film's moderately entertaining if rather simplistic. It doesn't really ring true, though, making us wonder about the real details of the true-life case on which the film is based.

Eve	Joanne Woodward
Dr. Luther	Lee J. Cobb
Ralph White	David Wayne
Mrs. Black	Nancy Kulp
Dr. Day	Edwin Jerome
Narrator	Alistair Cooke
Mr. Black	Douglas Spencer

Oscars Joanne Woodward

Quote 'Life's a city of straying streets and death's the marketplace where each one meets. Just that. Someday it'll happen.'

Three Men and a Baby
★★ 1987 102min c.

Director: Leonard Nimoy
Screenplay: James Orr & Jim Cruickshank
Source: Film, *Trois Hommes et un Couffin*

Immensely popular remake of a French comedy about three bachelors who have a baby foist upon them. The plot, thinner than Danson's hair, is wholly unrealistic. These chaps endure sleepless nights, nappy changings, feeding, bathtime, urinations and yet, despite their wealth, never contemplate paid help? Come on! The jokes are pathetic, the sentiment is slapped on with a trowel and the daft drugs subplot is a miscalculation. The baby's pretty sweet, though.

Peter	Tom Selleck
Michael	Steve Guttenberg
Jack	Ted Danson
Sylvia	Nancy Travis
Rebecca	Margaret Colin

Detective Melkowitz	.Philip Bosco
Jack's mother	.Celeste Holm
Vince	.Paul Guilfoyle

Blurb They Changed Her Diapers. She Changed Their Lives.

Quote 'The man is one giant gland.' • 'I'll give you a thousand dollars if you'll do it.' • 'I'm an actor. I can do a father.'

Psst! Watch closely as Celeste Holm, Danson's mum, picks up the baby and moves out of the room. In the background, you can see the outline of what looks like a little boy peering through the window. The Disney switchboard was swamped for months as people claimed to have seen a ghost. Rumours said it was a boy who had died in the house where filming took place. The studio claims it's a cutout of Danson in a fez and that, in any case, the scene was shot on a Toronto soundstage where no-one has ever died. Have a look for yourself • In the interests of in-depth research Guttenberg, Selleck and Danson apparently spent as much time as they could investigating the singles scene in Toronto!

The Three Musketeers

★★★ 1948 125min c.

Director: George Sidney
Screenplay: Robert Ardrey
Source: Novel by Alexandre Dumas

Richelieu and the Lady de Winter plot to overthrow the king, but the Three Musketeers aim to stop them. Let's hope their skill with the sword is better than their maths, as there are actually four of them. This is the best of all the versions of the Dumas tale, full of wit and vigour and with splendid acrobatic, even sometimes balletic, swash-buckling.

Lady de Winter	.Lana Turner
D'Artagnan	.Gene Kelly
Constance Bonacieux	.June Allyson
Athos	.Van Heflin
Queen Anne	.Angela Lansbury
King Louis XIII	.Frank Morgan
Richelieu	.Vincent Price
Planchet	.Keenan Wynn
Duke of Buckingham	.John Sutton
Porthos	.Gig Young
Aramis	.Robert Coote
Tréville	.Reginald Owen

Psst! Lana Turner initially refused the role and was put on suspension by MGM, only returning

when they agreed to pad out her part
• Apparently she wore trousers and comfortable shoes underneath all the period finery
• Kelly took two months of intensive lessons in swordsmanship before the movie and insisted on doing all his own fighting and stunts • Some of the duelling sequences were filmed in public parks in Pasadena, and Kelly hoped that enough would be going on in the foreground for audiences not to notice • Have you ever wondered why Richelieu isn't a cardinal here? The Catholic Legion of Decency had objected to the part and, rather than lose the role entirely, this was the studio's compromise solution • Kelly later tried to persuade MGM to let him make a musical version of Cyrano de Bergerac, but without success.

The Three Musketeers

★★ 1973 107min c.

Director: Richard Lester
Screenplay: George Macdonald Fraser
Source: Novel by Alexandre Dumas

Richard Lester's tongue-in-cheek version of the Dumas tale is as much concerned with unbuttoning bodices as with buckling swashes. I'm embarrassed that I once thought this was funny. The slapstick's terribly contrived and unamusing, with Milligan going way, way over the top. Richard Briers appears to have dubbed the King's voice, but even the real English actors give the impression of being badly dubbed. On top of everything else, Michel Legrand's music is more suitable for a lift than a movie. A film of its day. And its day has long gone.

Athos	.Oliver Reed
D'Artagnan	.Michael York
Aramis	.Richard Chamberlain
Porthos	.Frank Finlay
Constance	.Raquel Welch
Rochefort	.Christopher Lee
Queen Anne	.Geraldine Chaplin
Cardinal Richelieu	.Charlton Heston
Duke of Buckingham	.Simon Ward
Milady	.Faye Dunaway
Louis XIII	.Jean-Pierre Cassel
Planchet	.Roy Kinnear
M. Bonaciux	.Spike Milligan

OOPS! After the studs are returned to the Queen, Dunaway tells Heston that D'Artagnan gained entrance to the hotel. 'Palace', surely?

Psst! Although the cast were paid for making one film, the producer shot enough for another without mentioning it to them. When the sequel, *The Four Musketeers*, came out in 1975, the actors got together to sue for further payment. Although the courts awarded them more cash, it still probably cost the producers less than if they'd been paid the correct amount for both movies.

Throne of Blood

★★★★ 1957 109min b/w

Director: Akira Kurosawa
Screenplay: Hideo Oguni, Shinobu Hashimoto, Ryuzo Kikushima & Akira Kurosawa
Source: Play, *Macbeth* by William Shakespeare

It is ironic that the best screen version of *Macbeth* is actually set in feudal Japan without a line of Shakespeare in it. When Toshiro Mifune meets a sinister witch in the forest – Chieko Naniwa and a heap of skulls more than making up for Shakespeare's three weird sisters – he plans to slaughter his way to power with the support of his sinister wife. With intense Noh theatre performances from all concerned, in the finale, when the forest starts to move as prophesied, you'll be under the seat. An incredibly beautiful film.

Taketoki Washizu . . . . .Toshiro Mifune
Asaji . . . . .Isuzu Yamada
Noriyasu Odagura . . . . .Takashi Shimura
Yoshaki Miki . . . . .Minoru Chiaki

Thunderball

★★ 1965 132min c.

Director: Terence Young
Screenplay: Richard Maibaum & John Hopkins
Source: Novel by Ian Fleming

SPECTRE get hold of a NATO bomber and its nuclear bombs and threaten to blow up Miami. Considering Bond's impeccable taste, you'd have thought he would have let them get on with it. Instead of concentrating on getting a half-way decent script, the producers seemed happy to lavish money on the special effects instead. It was a regrettable trend that continued with subsequent films. Although some of the stunts, many of them underwater, are well staged, this outing is not among the best. It was remade 18 years later as Connery's Bond comeback movie, *Never Say Never Again*.

James Bond . . . . .Sean Connery
Domino Derval . . . . .Claudine Auger
Emilio Largo . . . . .Adolfo Celi
Fiona Volpe . . . . .Luciana Paluzzi
Felix Leiter . . . . .Rik Van Nutter
Paula Caplan . . . . .Martine Beswick
'M' . . . . .Bernard Lee
Miss Moneypenny . . . . .Lois Maxwell
'Q' . . . . .Desmond Llewelyn
Foreign Secretary . . . . .Roland Culver
Count Lippe . . . . .Guy Doleman
Varga . . . . .Philip Locke

Quote 'Try to be a little less than your usual frivolous self, 007.' • 'Well, he got a point.' • 'You don't think I enjoyed what we did this evening, do you? What I did tonight was for Queen and country.'

OOPS! Keep your eye on Leiter when he and Bond prepare to dive from the helicopter. One moment he's wearing trousers, the next he's got shorts on.

Psst! This was the most commercially-successful of the entire Bond series • Adolpho Celli spoke with such a strong Italian accent that the villain had to be dubbed by Robert Rietti, saviour of many a weak verbal performance • Claudine Auger, a one-time Miss France, was also dubbed • Raquel Welch was due to play Domino, but Fox wanted her for *Fantastic Voyage* and persuaded producer Cubby Broccoli to let her go. Julie Christie and Faye Dunaway were two others who were considered for the role • Stuntman Bill Cumming got $450 extra to jump into the shark-infested pool.

Thunderbirds Are Go

★★ 1966 90min c.

Director: David Lane
Screenplay: Gerry Anderson & Sylvia Anderson

Manned space mission Zero-X gets into trouble and the call goes out for International Rescue. Before you know it, Thunderbirds are go. This feature length version is probably only going to be appreciated by fans of the TV puppet series. For us, there are some wonderful incidental pleasures along the way such as Gerry and the Pacemakers' appearance as puppets in a space bar and the erotic fantasies of one of the Tracy boys about Lady Penelope. Well, who hasn't been there?

With: Scott Tracy, Virgil Tracy, Alan Tracy, John Tracy, Gordon Tracy, Mr. Jeff Tracy, Brains, Lady Penelope, Parker, Tin Tin

Psst! The Zero-X also appeared in the very first episode of the Sylvia and Gerry Anderson TV puppet series, *Captain Scarlet.*

Tight Little Island
SEE: **Whisky Galore**

Time After Time
★★★ 1979 112min c.

Director: Nicholas Meyer
Screenplay: Nicholas Meyer

H.G. Wells discovers that a mate of his is Jack the Ripper. Sadly, Jack escapes to the present day in the time machine that Wells has built and the author feels honour bound to chase after him. Although a mite too violent for its tongue-in-cheek plot, this is nonetheless a highly inventive and witty time-travel movie, with Jack the Ripper Warner finding himself far more at ease in our disturbed era than Wells. There's even a charming romance thrown in.

H.G. Wells	Malcolm McDowell
Dr. John Stevenson	David Warner
Amy Robbins	Mary Steenburgen
Lt. Mitchell	Charles Cioffi
Assistant	Kent Williams
Shirley	Patti D'Arbanville
Adams	Joseph Maher
Boy at museum	Corey Feldman
Dorent	Shelley Hack
Sergeant	Michael Evans

Time Bandits
★★★ 1981 113min c.

Director: Terry Gilliam
Screenplay: Terry Gilliam & Michael Palin

An unhappy schoolboy is dragged off on adventures through time by six dwarfs who have stolen a map from the Supreme Being showing where the holes in time are. While they see it as a means of plundering different ages, the forces of darkness are after the map for another reason entirely. This is the most imaginative and satisfying movie to come from the Python stable, being a mind-boggling blend of myth and legend, humour, fantasy and dark drama.

Robin Hood	John Cleese
King Agamemnon	Sean Connery
Pansy	Shelley Duvall
Mrs. Ogre	Katherine Helmond
Napoleon	Ian Holm
Vincent	Michael Palin
Supreme Being	Ralph Richardson
Ogre	Peter Vaughan
Evil Genius	David Warner
Randall	David Rappaport

OOPS! The supposedly bottomless chasm has a rather obvious floor not far beneath the ropes on which the bandits are swinging.

The Tin Drum
★★★★ 1979 142min c.

Director: Volker Schlondorff
Screenplay: Jean-Claude Carriere, Franz Seitz & Volker Schlondorff
Source: Novel by Günter Grass

Not many German films from the 70s hold up well, but this one's dark humour and bizarre imagery have kept it fascinating. In Nazi Germany, three-year-old Oskar resolves never to grow up and stunts his growth by leaping down the cellar steps. Things get even more surreal when his sex life takes off, and people start dying by eating. The tiny, 12-year-old David Bennent is hauntingly brilliant in the lead role.

Oskar Matzerath	David Bennent
Alfred Matzerath	Mario Adorf
Agnes Matzerath	Angela Winkler
Jan Bronski	Daniel Olbrychski
Maria Matzerath	Katharina Thalbach
Lina Greff	Andrea Ferreol

Quote 'Once there was a credulous people who believed in Santa Claus, but Santa Claus turned out to be the gas man.'

Psst! Schlondorff did not want to use a dwarf to portray the boy. He was introduced to the son of an actor with whom he had worked, who had a son of 12 whose facial characteristics had aged far more rapidly than the rest of the body • Schlondorff had originally intended that he would follow the story of the boy in later life, but Bennett's arrested development made this impossible • In Britain, because of the Child Protection Act, a scene with the 12-year-old boy snuggling up to the naked groin of his nurse was cut out.

Tin Pan Alley

★★★ 1940 94min b/w

Director: Walter Lang
Screenplay: Robert Ellis & Helen Logan

The plot of this film, for what it's worth, is about a songwriting duo and their relationship with a pair of singing sisters around the time of World War I. Don't be put off by the fact that the story isn't up to much, for this is still a splendidly boisterous musical, full of wonderfully witty banter and great tunes. Plausibility isn't it's strongest point, judging by the way the lads keep trying to find words for the tune that became 'K-K-K-Katie'.

Katie Blane	Alice Faye
Lily Blane	Betty Grable
Harry Calhoun	Jack Oakie
Skeets Harrigan	John Payne
Sgt. Casey	Allen Jenkins
Nora Bayes	Esther Ralston
Themselves	The Nicholas Brothers
Joe Codd	Elisha Cook Jr.

Psst! The 'Sheik of Araby' number had to be toned down after the Hays Office complained that too much flesh was on show.

The Titfield Thunderbolt

★★★ 1952 84min c.

Director: Charles Crichton
Screenplay: T.E.B. Clarke

A village reacts to the closure of its branch line by setting up their own railway service. But before it can be approved by the authorities, they have to contend with foul play from the local bus company. Both the plot and the characterisations in this Ealing comedy are a little below par. Nonetheless, it remains a fascinating and gently humorous portrait of a lost way of life. England as it appears here probably never existed except in our imaginations, but that doesn't lessen our nostalgic fondness for it.

Valentine	Stanley Holloway
Weech	George Relph
Blakeworth	Naunton Wayne
Gordon	John Gregson
Bishop	Godfrey Tearle
Joan	Gabrielle Brune
Dan	Hugh Griffith
Hawkins	Sidney James
Crump	Jack McGowran

Emily	Edie Martin
Coggett	Reginald Beckwith
Ruddock	Michael Trubshawe

To Be or Not to Be

★★★★ 1942 99min b/w

Director: Ernst Lubitsch
Screenplay: Edwin Justus Mayer

Released in the middle of World War II, this daring black comedy still has a dangerous edge to it. A group of Jewish actors in occupied Poland get involved in trying to stop a spy contacting the Nazis. Drama, romance, pathos, humour, satire and wartime propaganda combine to produce the perfect Lubitsch movie, sadly misunderstood during the war, but gaining in reputation with every year. What a loss the early death of Lombard was to Hollywood comedy. And what a pleasant surprise Benny's rounded performance is too. Remade, with none of the style or panache of the original, by Mel Brooks in 1983 and worth watching only for *Sweet Georgia Brown* performed in Polish.

Maria Tura	Carole Lombard
Joseph Tura	Jack Benny
Lt. Stanislav Sobinski	Robert Stack
Greenberg	Felix Bressart
Rawtich	Lionel Atwill
Prof. Siletsky	Stanley Ridges
Col. Ehrhardt	Sig Rumann
Bronski	Tom Dugan
Dubosh	Charles Halton
Anna	Maude Eburne
Wilhelm Kunze	Peter Caldwell

Quote 'What he did to Shakespeare, we are now doing to Poland!' • 'So, they call me Concentration Camp Erhardt?'

OOPS! When Stack jumps out of the plane, we see a shot of him by day, even though it's supposedly night • When Lombard puts the all-important letter in the typewriter, she puts it in the wrong way round, so that the signature would be on the back, not the side she is typing on.

Psst! Brilliant comedienne Lombard, the wife of Clark Gable, was killed in a plane crash just before the film was released, while on her way to raise funds for the war effort on Jack Benny's radio show. She never got to see the film, but had claimed it was the most enjoyable movie of her career • A line with her saying, 'What can happen in a plane?' was cut from the film after her death • Miriam Hopkins had been down to play Lombard's role but she had pulled out early on after she rowed with Benny • America was still neutral when filming started, the attack on Pearl Harbor happening towards the end of filming • Even though Lubitsch himself was a refugee from the Nazis, there was a ludicrous but widespread feeling at the time that the movie was somehow mocking the Poles.

To Catch a Thief
★★★ 1955 103min c.

Director: Alfred Hitchcock
Screenplay: John Michael Hayes
Source: Novel by David Dodge

This bit of fluff, about a jewel thief on the Riviera trying to find out who's copying his style, is hardly classic Hitch. Anyone who hasn't solved the mystery in the first quarter of an hour should go and stand in the corner. But, thanks to the painfully beautiful Kelly, the double entendres littering the script seem more sophisticated than they deserve and the movie still comes across as stylish, sensual and entertaining.

John Robie . . . . .Cary Grant
Frances Stevens . . . . .Grace Kelly
Mrs. Stevens . . . . .Jessie Royce Landis
H.H. Hughson . . . . .John Williams
Bertani . . . . .Charles Vanel
Danielle . . . . .Brigitte Auber

Quote 'Do you want a leg or a breast?' • 'I have a feeling that tonight you're going to see one of the Riviera's most fascinating sights...I was talking about the fireworks.'

Psst! Hitchcock appears 10 minutes in, sitting next to Grant on a bus • Set in Monaco, it wasn't long before Kelly would marry Prince Rainier of Monaco. They met during filming and he tried, unsuccessfully, to stop the film being released • The road where Kelly and Grant are chased by the police is the same one on which she died 27 years later in a car crash • Hitchcock hated eggs, possibly because his father was a poulterer. 'I regard eggs as loathsome and, to me,' he said, 'the most repulsive smell in the world is that which reeks up from a hard-boiled eggs.' He often put them in his films, finding the piercing of a yolk in *Shadow of a Doubt*, for instance 'much more effective than oozing blood'. Here he has Jesse Royce Landis stub out a cigarette in a yolk.

To Have and Have Not
★★★ 1944 100min b/w

Director: Howard Hawks
Screenplay: Jules Furthman & William Faulkner
Source: Novel by Ernest Hemingway

Bogart grudgingly allows his boat, *Queen Conch*, to be chartered by the French resistance. He also finds time to fall in love with Bacall. Although the story's a hand-me-down version of *Casablanca*, there's fun to be had from rummy Walter Brennan and piano player Hoagy Carmichael. But it's the relationship between Bogie and Bacall that makes the movie live. They were falling for each other in real life and it's all up there on the screen, as sultry and hot as its Martinique setting.

Harry Morgan . . . . .Humphrey Bogart
Eddie . . . . .Walter Brennan
Marie Browning . . . . .Lauren Bacall
Helene De Bursac . . . . .Dolores Moran
Cricket . . . . .Hoagy Carmichael
Lt. Coyo . . . . .Sheldon Leonard
Capt. Renard . . . . .Dan Seymour
Gerard ('Frenchie') . . . . .Marcel Dalio

Quote 'You don't have to say anything and you don't have to do anything. Not a thing. Oh, maybe just whistle. You know how to whistle, don't you, Steve? Just put your lips together and blow.' • 'It's even better when you help.' • 'Was you ever bit by a dead bee?' •'I'm hard to get, Steve. All you have to do is ask me.'

Psst! On a fishing trip Hawks boasted to Hemingway that he could make a film even out of his worst book. Hemingway said this was it, although Hawks pretty much threw out everything other than the title • The book was set in Cuba but the American government didn't want to upset the authorities there and threatened to withhold an export licence. As a result, the setting was switched to French Martinique • Filming progressed in sequence as the story unfolds, although the revised script pages were sometimes only a day or two old when they were filmed • Lauren Bacall was an unknown 19-year-old model called Betty Bacall at the time and was spotted on the cover of *Vogue* by director Hawks' wife • Bacall's sexy way of looking up from her lowered head only came about because she was so nervous she had to keep her head down to stop it shaking • Steve and Slim were the nicknames director Hawks and his wife had for each other. Mrs. Hawks took Bacall out of town to a remote spot where she made her scream until her voice became hoarse and husky like her own • Bacall's singing voice was to have been dubbed by a very young Andy Williams. However, Williams himself claims that a combination of different takes of Bacall herself singing were spliced together and used instead of him • Bogart and Bacall fell in love while making the film. Even though Bogie had married for the third time before Bacall finished High School, they got spliced the following year, and lived happily together for 12 years until his death from cancer in 1957 • Bogart gave Bacall a gold whistle. When she tried attracting his attention with it, several dogs rushed at her – it was a dog whistle. When he died, she placed it in his urn. It was inscribed: 'If you want anything, just whistle.' • This was singer-composer Hoagy Carmichael's screen debut.

To Kill a Mockingbird

★★ 1962 129min b/w

Director: Robert Mulligan
Screenplay: Horton Foote
Source: Novel by Harper Lee

In a the deep South in the 30s, lawyer Peck defends a black man accused of rape. Although a little too pat and predictable at times, this is still an affectionate nostalgic look at old-time small-town America with dollops of social conscience thrown in.

Atticus Finch	Gregory Peck
Jean Louise 'Scout' Finch	Mary Badham
Jem Finch	Phillip Alford
Dill Harris	John Megna
Sheriff Heck Tate	Frank Overton
Miss Maudie Atkinson	Rosemary Murphy
Boo Radley	Robert Duvall
Mrs. Dubose	Ruth White
Tom Robinson	Brock Peters
Mr. Raley	Richard Hale
Stephanie Crawford	Alice Ghostley

Oscars Best Screenplay (adapted), Gregory Peck

Psst! The book, based on author Harper Lee's childhood memories, was originally brought to Universal's attention by Rock Hudson, but the studio didn't want to make it with him. Only later, when Peck seemed interested, was the project revived • Peck went to Alabama to meet Lee's real father. He died before the film was finished. Lee was so pleased with Peck's

performance that she gave him her father's old pocket watch • This was Robert Duvall's film debut. He named all his dogs Boo Radley afterwards in gratitude.

Tom Jones

★★ 1963 129min c.

Director: Tony Richardson
Screenplay: John Osborne
Source: Novel by Henry Fielding

The amorous adventures of an 18th-century foundling. This period comedy pulled them in at the box office, with many attracted by the bawdy humour. This is now practically all the film has to recommend it. For like so many films of the time, the cinematic tricks with which it is filled now seem irksome rather than clever. We get silent movie slapstick, titles on the screen, undercranking to give quick-motion chases, all this in period costume. The most famous scene, with Redman and Finney using food as foreplay, is still extremely sensual. Whether it's worth sitting through the rest of a tiresomely long museum piece is a matter of personal choice.

Tom Jones	Albert Finney
Sophie Western	Susannah York
Squire Western	Hugh Griffith
Miss Western	Edith Evans
Lady Bellaston	Joan Greenwood
Molly Seagrim	Diane Cilento
Mrs. Waters	Joyce Redman
Lord Fellamar	David Tomlinson
Blifil	David Warner
Thwackum	Peter Bull
Patridge	Jack McGowran
Fitzpatrick	George A. Cooper
Susan	Lynn Redgrave
Honour	Patsy Rowlands
Black George	Wilfrid Lawson
Mrs. Seagrim	Freda Jackson
Lt. Northerton	Julian Glover
Bridget Allworthy	Rachel Kempson

Oscars Best Picture, Best Screenplay (adapted), Best Director

Quote 'Tom Jones. Of whom the opinion of all was that he was born to be hanged.' • 'Tom had always thought that any woman was better than none, while Molly never felt that one man was quite as good as two.' • 'Edith Evans asked me, "I don't look seventy, do I? Now be honest." I replied, "No love, you don't. Not any more".' [Richardson]

Psst! When first released, the film couldn't get a booking from a major cinema chain. Then it broke box office records at the London Pavilion and became a hit across Britain as well as internationally • Henry Fielding's novel became a best-seller 200 years after first being published • Keep an eye on the extras in the execution scene. Director Richardson asked those who had them to take out their dentures to add a bit of authenticity • This was the screen debut of David Warner and Lynn Redgrave, sister of director Richardson's wife Vanessa • The film was re-released in a restored version in 1989, with Richardson re-editing it and losing another seven minutes which he said he would have done if he'd been smarter 25 years previously.

Tootsie

★★★★ 1982 116min c.

Director: Sydney Pollack
Screenplay: Larry Gelbart & Murray Schisgal

Unemployable actor Hoffman puts on a frock and high heels and promptly lands a leading role in a soap. This is a constantly entertaining and frequently hilarious movie which also reveals many truths about the behaviour of the sexes towards each other. A witty script is complemented by a raft of excellent performances from leads and supports alike.

Michael Dorsey/Dorothy . . . . . .Dustin Hoffman
Julie . . . . .Jessica Lange
Sandy . . . . .Teri Garr
Ron . . . . .Dabney Coleman
Les . . . .,. . . .Charles Durning
Jeff . . . . .Bill Murray
George Fields . . . . .Sydney Pollack
John Van Horn . . . . .George Gaynes
April . . . . .Geena Davis

Oscars Jessica Lange

Quote 'I'd like to make her a little more attractive. How far can you pull back?' – 'How do you feel about Cleveland?' • 'Don't you find being a woman in the 80s complicated?' – 'Extremely!' • 'The only reason you're still living is because I never kissed you.' • 'If I met Dorothy – me as a woman – at a party, I'd turn her down.' [Hoffman]

OOPS! When Garr comes to see Hoffman, his purse is on the table as she knocks. Then it disappears.

Psst! Being a Method actor, Hoffman insisted on testing out his character in real life. Not content with a visit to his daughter's school, where he wasn't recognised, he propositioned actor José Ferrer in a lift, offering him a blow job. Ferrer politely declined • Asked if he would do a sequel, Hoffman said it was a possibility only if he could push the character still further, perhaps by giving birth • The make-up gave Hoffman terrible acne and a constant watch had to be kept on set for signs of stubble • Director Pollack appears as Hoffman's agent. He and Hoffman often had furious rows during filming, similar in nature to the one they have in the movie • With eight writers involved in the troubled gestation of the project, the Writer's Guild had to arbitrate the fight over who was to be credited. Barry Levinson was one of those who lost out • When the script was originally bought, the producer thought it would be a great role for George Hamilton • It was then called *Would I Lie To You?* Hoffman suggested the new title. Tootsie was a nickname he had as a child • This was Geena Davis' first film • Estelle Getty, Sophia from *The Golden Girls*, has a bit part as 'middle-aged woman'.

Top Gun

★★ 1986 110min c.

Director: Tony Scott
Screenplay: Jim Cash & Jack Epps Jr.

To help him remember his characterisation, maverick pilot Cruise is called Maverick. He's got a problem with authority, is a whizz in a plane, has a guilt trip over his father and is irresistible to his teacher. Fortunately, she's a woman. Although it's fantastic while in the air, albeit a little confusing at times, it's rather more leaden on the ground. McGillis is perhaps not the most convincing flying instructor in the history of the movies.

Maverick . . . . .Tom Cruise
Charlie . . . . .Kelly McGillis
Ice . . . . .Val Kilmer
Goose . . . . .Anthony Edwards
Viper . . . . .Tom Skerritt
Jester .Michael Ironside
Cougar .John Stockwell
Wolfman . . . . .Barry Tubb
Slider . . . . .Rick Rossovich
Merlin . . . . .Tim Robbins
Also: Clarence Gilyard, Whip Hubley, James Tolkan, Meg Ryan

Quote 'I feel the need...the need for speed!'

OOPS! Cruise miraculously changes planes in mid-air in the concluding battle. Just watch the number on his tail • Robbins at one point says 'we're running low on gas'. He's sitting in the back seat when he says it but manages to tap the fuel gauge in the front seat.

Psst! Director Tony Scott wasn't hired on the basis of his previous film, *The Hunger*, which was thought rather too arty in Hollywood. What swung it was a commercial he had made that involved both a jet and a car • The inspiration for the film was a 1983 magazine article entitled *Top Guns* • In preparation for the film Cruise attended classes at the Miramar Naval Air Station and flew with Navy pilots. He also drank with them and was sick over Anthony Edwards' BMW! • Cruise couldn't have been a pilot, even if he'd wanted to be. They insist that their chaps be at least five feet ten inches, an inch higher than Cruise • Although the Navy gave the film-makers an amazing degree of cooperation, they also gave them a bill for over $1m. When the film came out, levels of recruitment soared • Sales of Ray-Ban Aviators, sported by Cruise in the movie, also soared [see *Risky Business*] • Initial tests screenings weren't good enough, so six months after filming ended the actors had to return for some additional scenes, including some extra steam between Cruise and McGillis. Unfortunately, she no longer had blonde hair and had had it cut for another film, so had to wear a cap in one scene in a lift • Admiral T.J. Cassidy plays himself • For a hilarious explanation of the homosexual subtext of *Top Gun*, see Quentin Tarantino's cameo at the part in the 1994 movie *Sleep With Me*.

Top Hat
★★★★ 1935 101min b/w

Director: Mark Sandrich
Screenplay: Dwight Taylor & Allan Scott
Source: Musical, *The Gay Divorcee* by Dwight Taylor & Cole Porter, adapted from the play, *The Girl Who Dared* by Alexander Farago & Aladar Laszlo

When dancer Astaire falls for Rogers, she believes he's actually her friend's husband and isn't too keen on his wooing her. Not only is the slightly feeble plot second-hand, but it was taken from one of their own films, *The Gay Divorcee*, which had only come out the previous year and had much the same cast. The last quarter of an hour of the film also comes across as rather rushed and contrived. But Astaire and Rogers have an almost magical relationship here and the film contains some very funny scenes. The sets are art deco splendour at its best, even if there isn't one room that has a carpet. Best of all is the Irving Berlin music, including numbers like 'Isn't This a Lovely Day?', 'Top Hat, White Tie and Tails' and 'Cheek to Cheek'.

Jerry Travers	Fred Astaire
Dale Tremont	Ginger Rogers
Horace Hardwick	Edward Everett Horton
Madge Hardwick	Helen Broderick
Alberto Beddini	Erik Rhodes
Bates, the butler	Eric Blore
Flower shop clerk	Lucille Ball
Flower salesman	Leonard Mudie
Hotel manager	Edgar Norton
Hotel manager	Gino Corrado

Quote 'If I'd have forgotten myself with that girl, I'd remember it.' • 'Oh, I'm sorry. I didn't realise I was disturbing you. You see, every once in a while I suddenly find myself dancing.' – 'I suppose it's some kind of affliction.' • 'Sic transit gloria mundi, sir.' • 'Beddini has the motto: "For the woman the kiss, for the man the sword".'

OOPS! As they are crossing the bridge in London with Astaire taking the place of the cabby, they appear to be driving on the right at one point.

Psst! This was the fourth screen teaming for Astaire and Rogers and the first time a screenplay had been written directly for them • Although all their movies featured them in a romance, there were never any real clinches. According to Rogers' autobiography, this was because Fred Astaire's wife didn't wanting him kissing any other women • The feather dress that Rogers wears in 'Cheek to Cheek' was a major source of irritation to Astaire as the feathers not only tickled him, but kept coming off and floating around. Astaire blew his top, precipitating one of the few real crises in their relationship in which Rogers' strident mother played a large part. The designer spent all night sewing each feather into position and they managed to get through the dance the following day without too many coming adrift. From then on, Astaire insisted on vetting his partners' costumes beforehand • Lucille Ball can be spotted as the clerk in the flower shop, still playing bit parts in her 18th film. RKO later fired her because they thought she was never going to make it as an actress. She ended up buying the entire studio 23 years after making *Top Hat* • Rhodes' stereotypical Italian so offended Mussolini that this film was banned in Italy, as *The Gay Divorcee* was before it • Rhodes' line, 'For the women the kiss, for the men the sword' was orginally written as, 'For the men the sword, for the women the whip,' but, perhaps not surprisingly, the Hays Office weren't having it • Writer Allan Scott later said: 'If Ginger was having trouble with a scene, she always said, "There's something radically wrong with this scene." It took us a couple of pictures to realize that when Ginger said this, it meant that she was not prepared and doubtless had been on the town the night before.'

Topper
★★★ 1937 98min b/w

Director: Norman Z. McLeod
Screenplay: Jack Jevne, Eric Hatch & Eddie Moran
Source: Novel, *The Jovial Ghosts* by Thorne Smith

A high-living couple wrap their car round a tree and are disconcerted to find themselves ghosts. With time on their hands and possessing the same playful spirits as when they were alive, they devote themselves to shaking up their stuffy banker friend Topper. That this rather bowdlerised version of Smith's saucy comic novel is so amusing is largely thanks to the bewildered Young. The two sequels, *Topper Takes a Trip* and *Topper Returns* lacked Grant and weren't quite up to the standard of the first.

Marion Kerby . . . . .Constance Bennett
George Kerby . . . . .Cary Grant
Cosmo Topper . . . . .Roland Young
Henrietta Topper . . . . .Billie Burke
Wilkins . . . . .Alan Mowbray
Casey .Eugene Pallette
Elevator boy . . . . .Arthur Lake
Mrs. Stuyvesant . . . . .Hedda Hopper
Policeman . . . . .J. Farrell MacDonald

Psst! The original casting idea of producer Hal Roach, best known for short comedies starring the likes of Laurel & Hardy, was for W.C. Fields and Jean Harlow to co-star but Fields wasn't available and Harlow died a month before filming was due to start • A TV series was based on the *Topper* films • The house was later used often for the *Batman* TV series.

Total Recall
★★★ 1990 109min c.

Director: Paul Verhoeven
Screenplay: Ronald Shusett, Dan O'Bannon & Gary Goldman
Source: Short story, *We Can Remember It For You Wholesale* by Philip K. Dick

In the future, Arnie's a mere construction worker who dreams of being a secret agent travelling to Mars on a mission. Then he remembers that he *is* a secret agent and this confuses him considerably. A constantly intriguing and often amusing sci-fi actioner is needlessly violent and nothing like as clever as the Philip K. Dick short story on which it's based. But the effects are astounding and the action's highly entertaining.

Doug Quaid . . . . .Arnold Schwarzenegger
Melina . . . . .Rachel Ticotin
Lori . . . . .Sharon Stone
Cohaagen .Ronny Cox
Richter . . . . .Michael Ironside
George/Juato . . . . .Marshall Bell

Blurb They Stole His Mind, Now He Wants It Back.

Quote 'Consider that a divorce.'

OOPS! Although Arnie shoots the psychiatrist who has tried to convince him that he's just having a very vivid dream, we can see the chap again later prior to the reprogramming treatment.

Psst! It took writer Shusett 15 years to get the film made. At one time Matthew Broderick was the projected star • One watchdog group counted 110 acts of violence an hour and 35 slayings, 18 of them by Arnie.

Toto the Hero
★★★★ 1991 90min c.

Director: Jaco van Dormael
Screenplay: Jaco van Dormael

A film so unique it's difficult to explain why it's so wonderful. In old age Bouquet still blames his wealthy next-door neighbour for stealing his life after a mix-up in the maternity ward, and vows revenge. This Belgian film is movie storytelling at its very best, with flashbacks to youth and middle-age fleshing out the compelling yarn. Extraordinarily witty and inventive, and utterly spell-binding, it's hard to believe that this is Jaco van Dormael's first film, or that he was once a circus clown! Be warned, the song *Boum* is one of the catchiest ever used in a movie.

```
Thomas van Hasebroeck . . . . .Michael Bouquet
Thomas (as young man) . . . . . . . .Jo De Backer
Thomas (as child) . . . . . . . . . . . .Thomas Godet
Evelyne . . . . . . . . . . . . . . . . . . . . . .Gisela Uhlen
Evelyn (as young woman) . . . . . .Mireille Perrier
Alice . . . . . . . . . . . . . . . . . . . . . .Sandrine Blancke
Alfred . . . . . . . . . . . . . . . . . . . . . . .Peter Böhlke
```

A Touch of Class
★★ 1973 105min c.

Director: Melvin Frank
Screenplay: Melvin Frank & Jack Rose

Married American Segal begins an affair with divorcée Jackson, but life has a whole toolbox of spanners ready to throw in the works. Some of this near-farcical romantic comedy still works well, with the odd very funny moment. Sadly, Jackson looks rather uncomfortable attempting to play comedy; it's like someone trying to become an artist by using a painting-by-numbers picture.

```
Steve Blackburn . . . . . . . . . . . . .George Segal
Vicki Allessio . . . . . . . . . . . . . . .Glenda Jackson
Walter Menkes . . . . . . . . . . . . . . .Paul Sorvino
Gloria Blackburn . . . . . . . . . . . . .Hildegard Neil
Wendell Thompson . . . . . . . . . . . . . .Cec Linder
Patty Menkes . . . . . . . . . . . . . . . . . .K. Callan
Night hotel manager . . . . . . . .Nadim Sawalha
Dr. Alvarez . . . . . . . . . . . . . . .David De Keyser
```

Oscars Glenda Jackson

Quote '"Very nice" is hardly the phrase to describe two bodies locked in heavenly transport. "Very nice" is when you get a get well card from your butcher.'

Touch of Evil
★★★ 1958 108min b/w

Director: Orson Welles
Screenplay: Orson Welles
Source: Novel, *Badge of Evil* by Whit Masterson

Narcotics agent Heston, on honeymoon in a Mexican border town, gets involved in a murder case, tangling with corrupt local police chief Welles. The extraordinary three-minute opening crane shot is said by many to be the greatest single shot ever captured on celluloid. Although the rest of the film can't possibly live up to it, it does have a wonderful sleazy atmosphere, some extraordinary characters and it looks fabulous. Sadly, the mystery plot needed rather more work and comes across as confusing, even on repeated viewings.

```
Ramon Miguel 'Mike' Vargas . . .Charlton Heston
Susan Vargas . . . . . . . . . . . . . . . . . .Janet Leigh
Hank Quinlan . . . . . . . . . . . . . . . .Orson Welles
Peter Menzies . . . . . . . . . . . . . . .Joseph Calleia
'Uncle Joe' Grandi . . . . . . . . . . . .Akim Tamiroff
Tanya . . . . . . . . . . . . . . . . . . . .Marlene Dietrich
Adair . . . . . . . . . . . . . . . . . . . . . . . . .Ray Collins
Motel clerk . . . . . . . . . . . . . . . .Dennis Weaver
Coroner . . . . . . . . . . . . . . . . . . . .Joseph Cotten
Also: Mercedes McCambridge, Zsa Zsa Gabor
```

Psst! Welles was initially hired just as an actor. But Heston suggested to the studio that Welles direct it: 'It genuinely seemed to strike them as a radical suggestion, as though I'd asked to have my mother direct the picture.' • Welles roped in mates like Dietrich and Cotten for small parts • Leigh made the film despite breaking her left arm shortly before filming. Her cast had to be disguised and occasionally removed • The opening sequence is one of the most famous in movie history, with one long tracking shot showing several different scenes as it covers an extraordinary three blocks • As ever with Welles' movies, once production finished he lost control. The studio recut the film and some additional scenes directed by Harry Keller were added • Different versions exist varying from 95 to 115 minutes. The original Welles cut is believed to be the rediscovered 108-minute version.

The Towering Inferno
★★★ 1974 165min c.

Director: John Guillermin & Irwin Allen
Screenplay: Stirling Silliphant
Source: Novels, *The Tower* by Richard Martin Stern & *The Glass Inferno* by Thomas N. Scortia & Frank M. Robinson

The world's tallest building catches fire on opening night, while there's a party up top attended by a group of actors willing to do pretty near anything to resuscitate their ailing careers. Although critics sneer at this most famous of disaster movies, it's pretty exciting stuff with the effects wearing their age pretty well. It isn't perfect by any means. It's too long and some of the characters are so wet they could put the fire out on their own. But there's no better film in the disaster genre.

Michael O'Hallorhan . . . . .Steve McQueen
Doug Roberts . . . . .Paul Newman
James Duncan . . . . .William Holden
Susan Franklin . . . . .Faye Dunaway
Harlee Claiborne . . . . .Fred Astaire
Roger Simmons . . . . .Richard Chamberlain
Patty Simmons . . . . .Susan Blakely
Lisolette Mueller . . . . .Jennifer Jones
Dan Bigelow . . . . .Robert Wagner
Jernigan .O.J. Simpson
Sen. Gary Parker . . . . .Robert Vaughn
Also: Felton Perry, Gregory Sierra, Don Gordon, Susan Flannery, Dabney Coleman

Quote 'When are you architects going to learn?' • 'Hell, we all know who the real star of this movie is – that damned fire.' [Paul Newman]

Psst! After *The Poseiden Adventure* did so well, 20th Century Fox looked for another similar project. They wanted to buy the book, *The Tower*, but Warner Brothers got there first. Although they snapped up a similar novel, *The Glass Inferno*, they realised it would be commercial suicide for two studios to bring out such similar films. So, uniquely, the two studios worked together on one giant disaster movie • McQueen and Newman were both on $1m salary up front and 7.5% of the box office take, which meant they ultimately received $12m each • McQueen, who had originally had Newman's part and then asked to switch, complained that Newman had 12 more lines of dialogue than him and the script had to be rejigged • After arguments about billing, McQueen's name eventually came first in the movie's credits but on the poster, while his name appears to the left of Newman's, Newman's name is slightly higher • McQueen ended up earning $12m from the film • Holden tore Dunaway off a strip about her habitual lateness on set, usually a result of her being inordinantly fussy about make-up or her hair • Real fire crews were on the set most of the time in case things got out of hand. Amazingly, not one person was injured in the entire production • For the scene where a million gallons of water poured onto the set and the tethered stars, 12 cameras were used. As the water tore the set to bits, there was no opportunity for any retakes • A few months after the film came out, a fire broke out at the World Trade Centre in New York, raging through six floors before being brought under control.

Trading Places
★★★★ 1983 116min c.

Director: John Landis
Screenplay: Timothy Harris & Herschel Weingrod

Near-perfect comedy about a couple of crusty old buffers switching the life of pompous, wealthy commodity trader Aykroyd with that of sassy beggar Murphy for the sake of a bet. Murphy's never been better and there's excellent support from Curtis and Elliott. A total delight which is eminently re-watchable.

Louis Winthorpe III . . . . .Dan Aykroyd
Billy Ray Valentine . . . . .Eddie Murphy
Coleman . . . . .Denholm Elliott
Randolph Duke . . . . .Ralph Bellamy
Mortimer Duke . . . . .Don Ameche
Ophelia . . . . .Jamie Lee Curtis
Also: Kristin Holby, Robert Earl Jones, Paul Gleason, Frank Oz, Bo Diddley, James Belushi, Philip Bosco

Quote 'When I was growing up and we wanted a Jacuzzi, we had to fart in the tub.'

Psst! For years John Landis put the words 'See you next Wednesday' in every film. Here it's on a poster in Curtis' room • When Eddie Murphy discovered that Ralph Bellamy had made 99 films and Don Ameche 49, he said, 'That means between the three of us, we've made 150 movies!'

The Train
★★★ 1965 140min b/w

Director: John Frankenheimer
Screenplay: Franklin Coen, Frank Davis & Walter Bernstein
Source: Novel, *Le Front de l'Art* by Rose Valland

As the Germans begin their retreat in the summer of 1944, German colonel Scofield is ordered to grab a pile of famous paintings and hare back to the Fatherland with them. The French resistance, art lovers to a man, move into action. A mite long, perhaps, but overall an extremely exciting action movie backed by some sterling acting work all round.

Labiche . . . . .Burt Lancaster
Col. von Waldheim . . . . .Paul Scofield
Christine . . . . .Jeanne Moreau
Papa Boule . . . . .Michel Simon

Miss Villard . . . . .Suzanne Flon
Herren .Wolfgang Preiss
Didont . . . . .Albert Remy
Jacques .Jacques Marin

Psst! The film was originally directed by Arthur Penn [*Bonnie & Clyde*] but he had some early run-ins with the producer and was sent packing. Frankenheimer, who directed Lancaster's previous movie, *Seven Days in May*, was called in • Filming took place entirely on location in France and used no model shots.

Treasure Island

★★★ 1950 96min c.

Director: Byron Haskin
Screenplay: Lawrence E. Watkin
Source: Novel by Robert Louis Stevenson

Ar, Jim me lad. Shiver me timbers. Yo ho ho and a dead man's chest and all that guff. This be the one, the only, true version of Stevenson's tale of pirates and treasure. Don't you be acceptin' no imitations now, lad. That chap Newton, a mighty fine actor he be. Not only be he larger than life itself, but he gave work to countless others down the years impersonating him. No-one else gets a look in, not even the parrot. But rollicking fun nonetheless.

Jim Hawkins . . . . .Bobby Driscoll
Long John Silver . . . . .Robert Newton
Capt. Smollett . . . . .Basil Sydney
Squire Trelawney . . . . .Walter Fitzgerald
Dr. Livesey .Denis O'Dea
Capt. Bones . . . . .Finlay Currie
George Merry . . . . .Ralph Truman
Pew . . . . .John Laurie
Also: Patrick Troughton, Geoffrey Keen, John Gregson

Psst! This was Disney's first live-action feature film • Unusually for a Disney movie, when the studio came to re-release the film in the 70s, the censors took objection to some of the violence and wanted to give it a 'PG' rating. In more innocent days, this would have been anathema to the Disney studios, so they cut the film to make it acceptable to all • Bobby Driscoll was the first flesh-and-blood actor to be given a long-term contract by Disney but, when his career petered out in his teens, he turned to drugs. He died, aged 31, in an abandoned building in New York and was buried in a pauper's grave. It was only the following year, thanks to fingerprinting, that it was it discovered who he was.

The Treasure of the Sierra Madre

★★★ 1948 126min b/w

Director: John Huston
Screenplay: John Huston
Source: Novel by Berwick Traven Torsvan (B. Traven)

A trio of gold prospectors are transformed from decent human beings into jackals by greed and machismo. It could have been preachy and dull, but is saved largely by Bogart who gives one of his best ever performances as the easy-going bum who changes gradually into a monster. Considering how much time they spent out on location, you think they could have done a little better with the sets, though.

Fred C. Dobbs . . . . .Humphrey Bogart
Howard . . . . .Walter Huston
Curtin . . . . .Tim Holt
Cody . . . . .Bruce Bennett
McCormick . . . . .Barton MacLane
'Gold Hat' . . . . .Alfonso Bedoya
'White Suit' .John Huston

Oscars Best Director, Walter Huston, Best Screenplay

Quote 'I know what gold does to men's souls.' • 'Badges? We ain't got no badges! We don't need no badges! I don't have to show you any stinkin' badges!' • 'Nobody ever put anything over on Fred C. Dobbs.' • 'I caught this guy stealing our water. Next time you try that, I'll let it out of you through little round holes.' • 'You gotta get up early in the morning to outsmart Fred C. Dobbs.'

Psst! Director Huston appears near the opening as the white-hatted American tourist that Bogie keeps pestering for cash. The close-ups were actually directed by Bogart, who bugged Huston by insisting on endless retakes • This is the only time that father and son won Oscars for the same movie • When Anjelica Huston won one for *Prizzi's Honor*, the Hustons became the first family in which three generations won Oscars • When Walter Huston turned up for the first day's filming, he had his teeth out, the toothless look serving him so well on *Red River*, Bogart ripped off his toupée saying: 'I'll be damned if I'm going to let that old bum upstage me.' Sadly, the studio pointed out that his contract specified that he had to keep it on • The 'stinkin' badges' line appears in several other movies, most notably *Blazing Saddles* • Huston asked the secretive novelist,

B. Traven, if he could come and chat to him in Mexico. But Traven sent a representative instead, H. Croves, who Huston hired as a technical adviser. Croves was camera shy and elusive about Traven. When they left the location and returned to the studio, Huston found an old photo of Traven. 'Recognise him?' he asked Bogart. 'Sure,' said Bogie. 'That's old Croves. I'd know him anywhere.'

A Tree Grows in Brooklyn

★★★ 1945 128min b/w

Director: Elia Kazan
Screenplay: Tess Slesinger & Frank Davis
Source: Novel by Betty Smith

The trials and tribulations of a poor Irish family in New York at the turn of the century. This splendidly observed film is one of the best, most accomplished, tear-jerkers Hollywood ever produced, a great, big, sentimental, one-eyed teddy bear of a movie.

Katie .Dorothy McGuire
Aunt Sissy . . . . .Joan Blondell
Johnny Nolan . . . . .James Dunn
McShane .Lloyd Nolan
Francie Nolan . . . . .Peggy Ann Garner
Neeley Nolan . . . . .Ted Donaldson
McGarrity . . . . .James Gleason
Miss McDonough . . . . .Ruth Nelson
Steve Edwards . . . . .John Alexander
Also: Charles Halton

Oscars James Dunn

Psst! Dunn was pretty much playing himself, being well-known for having ruined his own acting career through drink. He swore off the booze during filming, although this apparently didn't include his days off.

Tremors

★★★ 1990 95min c.

Director: Ron Underwood
Screenplay: Brent Maddock & S.S. Wilson

Giant earthworms are burrowing through the desert and snacking on unwary campers. Witty, fast and highly enjoyable, this delivers the thrills while at the same time parodying the monster genre. Note, too, the ingenious way in which the Politically Correct 90s heroine still manages to get separated from her jeans.

Valentine McKee . . . . .Kevin Bacon
Earl Basset .Fred Ward
Rhonda LeBeck . . . . .Finn Carter
Burt Gummer . . . . .Michael Gross
Heather Gummer . . . . .Reba McEntire
Melvin Plug . . . . .Bobby Jacoby

Psst! The credits include a 'dirt' wrangler and a 'sage' wrangler.

Trouble in Paradise

★★★★ 1932 83min b/w

Director: Ernst Lubitsch
Screenplay: Grover Jones & Samson Raphaelson
Source: Play, *The Honest Finder* by Laszlo Aladar

A pair of jewel thieves, Miriam Hopkins and Herbert Marshall, fall out when Marshall begins falling for their latest mark, Kay Francis. This Lubitsch masterpiece remains one of the funniest, most stylish and most sophisticated of all romantic comedies, full of delightful visual and verbal nuggets. Set in Venice, the stylish art deco sets are simply stunning. From the famous opening scene with the singing gondolier, the smile never leaves our face throughout. As the movie predated the Hays Code, it is also surprisingly saucy, particularly in one memorable scene between Hopkins and Marshall, when they use the competing theft of trinkets as foreplay.

Lily Vautier . . . . .Miriam Hopkins
Gaston Monescu . . . . .Herbert Marshall
Mariette Colet . . . . .Kay Francis
The Major . . . . .Charles Ruggles
Francois Filiba . . . . .Edward Everett Horton
Adolph Giron . . . . .C. Aubrey Smith
Jacques, the butler . . . . .Robert Greig
Radical . . . . .Leonid Kinskey
Annoyed opera fan . . . . .Luis Alberni
Mme. Bouchet . . . . .Nella Walker

The Trouble With Harry

★ 1955 99min c.

Director: Alfred Hitchcock
Screenplay: John Michael Hayes
Source: Novel by Jack Trevor Story

Various characters in a small Vermont town believe that they've killed Harry, whose corpse just won't lie down. If you didn't know this rather tedious, slow-paced farce, was directed by Hitchcock, you'd probably give it a miss completely, despite the wonderful cast. Some people, desperate to find an undiscovered great among the Master's misunderstood works, now claim it is a comic classic. Piffle. The public didn't ignore it because it was tasteless, as is sometimes claimed, but because while Hitch knew all there was to know about skeletons, he wasn't too hot at finding the funny bone if there wasn't any menace involved.

Capt. Albert Wiles	Edmund Gwenn
Sam Marlowe	John Forsythe
Miss Gravely	Mildred Natwick
Jennifer Rogers	Shirley MacLaine
Mrs. Wiggs	Mildred Dunnock
Arnie Rogers	Jerry Mathers
Calvin Wiggs	Royal Dano

Quote 'What seems to be the trouble, Captain?' • 'He looked exactly the same when he was alive, only he was vertical.'

Psst! Hitch appears 20 minutes in, walking past the car of a man who is examining the pictures • This was MacLaine's film debut. She had been an understudy on *The Pyjama Game*, and had to go on on the very night that producer Hal B. Wallis was in the audience. He signed her and lent her out to Hitchcock for this film • It was also the debut of composer Bernard Herrman on a Hitchcock movie. Their collaboration lasted eight years • This was one of the 'Lost Hitchcocks' [see *Rear Window*].

True Grit
★★★ 1969 128min c.

Director: Henry Hathaway
Screenplay: Marguerite Roberts
Source: Novel by Charles Portis

A girl wanting revenge for the death of her father pins her hopes on a one-eyed, paunchy, drunk marshal. Although it drags a little at times, this is still an enjoyably boisterous Western with Wayne on fine form taking the mickey out of himself. The sequel, the 1975 *Rooster Cogburn* with Katharine Hepburn, had little to recommend it.

'Rooster' Cogburn	John Wayne
La Boeuf	Glen Campbell
Mattie Ross	Kim Darby
Emmett Quincy	Jeremy Slate
Ned Pepper	Robert Duvall
Moon	Dennis Hopper

Col. G. Stonehill	Strother Martin
Tom Chaney	Jeff Corey

Oscars John Wayne

Quote 'Fill your hands, you son of a bitch!' • 'Come and see a fat old man sometime.'

Psst! Wayne claimed that his scene reminiscing with Kim Darby was the best he ever did • Wayne's hat-band had once belonged to Gary Cooper • Mia Farrow was set to co-star but changed her mind when she heard stories that working with director Hathaway could be an unhappy experience. She said later it was the biggest mistake she ever made. Tuesday Weld was another who turned down the part, but she seemed to specialise in turning down good roles • This was singer Glen Campbell's screen debut.

True Lies
★★★ 1994 141min c.

Director: James Cameron
Screenplay: James Cameron
Source: Film, *La Totale!*

The nearest thing we've had to a good James Bond movie for years. Arnie's the secret agent who always saves the world in time to get home for tea with the wife and kids, who have no idea what he does for a living. In addition to some outstanding action sequences, we get superb comic support from Tom Arnold, Curtis at her sexiest for years and Arnie doing everything but ask for a martini, shaken not stirred. Yes, it's too long, sagging badly in the middle, it's misogynistic and wildly implausible. But then, so were the James Bond films. Action fans will love it.

Harry	Arnold Schwarzenegger
Helen	Jamie Lee Curtis
Gib	Tom Arnold
Simon	Bill Paxton
Juno	Tia Carrere
Aziz	Art Malik
Dana	Eliza Dushku
Spencer Trilby	Charlton Heston

Blurb When He Said I Do, He Didn't Say What He Did.

Quote 'Have you ever killed anyone?' – 'Yeah. But they were all *bad*.'

OOPS! After Arnie makes a surprise visit to his wife at work, there's a little old lady standing behind the van watching them.

Psst! Keep your eyes open for Charlton Heston sporting an eye patch • The film-makers hired three Marine Harrier Jump Jets from the US Navy, together with pilots. They cost over $100,000 in all, working out at $2,400 an hour.

Tunes of Glory

★★★ 1960 106min c.

Director: Ronald Neame
Screenplay: James Kennaway
Source: Novel by Kennaway

The nose of the experienced commander of a peacetime Scottish regiment, Guinness, is put out by the arrival of his replacement Mills, a by-the-book pen-and-paper soldier. Heads are lowered and battle commences. There isn't too much by the way of plot, but it's enough to sit back and marvel at the two splendid central performances.

Lt. Col. Jock Sinclair	Alec Guinness
Lt. Col. Basil Barrow	John Mills
Morag Sinclair	Susannah York
Maj. Charlie Scott	Dennis Price
Mary	Kay Walsh
Pipe Maj. MacLean	Duncan Macrae
Cpl. Piper Ian Fraser	John Fraser
Capt. Eric Simpson	Allan Cuthbertson
Capt. Jimmy Cairns	Gordon Jackson
Maj. Hugo MacMillan	Gerald Harper
Lt. David MacKinnon	Peter McEnery

Twelve Angry Men

★★★★ 1957 95min b/w

Director: Sidney Lumet
Screenplay: Reginald Rose
Source: Television play by Rose

One jury member holds out against the other eleven, who are initially convinced that a boy is guilty of killing his father. Although imitated so many times since that it no longer looks fresh, this is still a mesmerising movie. The performances from a group who were then largely unknown are wonderful, while filming it in that one, stiflingly hot room gives the movie a suitably claustrophic feel.

Juror #8	Henry Fonda
Juror #3	Lee J. Cobb
Juror #4	E.G. Marshall
Juror #10	Ed Begley
Juror #7	Jack Warden
Juror #1	Martin Balsam
Juror #2	John Fielder
Juror #5	Jack Klugman
Juror #11	George Voskovec
Juror #12	Robert Webber
Juror #6	Edward Binns
Juror #9	Joseph Sweeney
Judge	Rudy Bond
Court clerk	Bill Nelson

Quote 'Pardon me, but don't you ever sweat?'

Psst! The movie didn't win a single Oscar • As with several other landmark 50s movies, this initially began as a TV play and marked Sidney Lumet's directorial debut for the cinema • Lumet insisted on two weeks of rehearsals. Filming itself, in a real New York jury room, took just 20 days • The film was not a commercial success in America, but it did do well overseas. Lumet had deferred his pay and never actually received any money for his work • Henry Fonda produced the film and, after its poor reception, said he would never do so again • Jack Warden had been a boxer in his younger days, fighting under the name of Johnny Costello.

Twentieth Century

★★ 1934 91min b/w

Director: Howard Hawks
Screenplay: Ben Hecht & Charles MacArthur
Source: Play, *Napoleon of Broadway* by Charles Bruce Milholland.

Barrymore, a melodramatic Broadway producer on the slide, collars Lombard, the girl he turned into a star, on a train trip and tries to persuade her to star in his latest show. Although this was once considered the height of witty sophisticated comedy, with lines sharp enough you could cut yourself on them, it has dated badly. The humour no longer looks fresh and Barrymore's hammy acting style is well over-ripe.

Oscar Jaffe	John Barrymore
Lily Garland	Carole Lombard
Owen O'Malley	Roscoe Karns
Oliver Webb	Walter Connolly
George Smith	Ralph Forbes
Max Jacobs	Charles Lane
Matthew J. Clark	Etienne Girardot
Mr. McConigle	Edgar Kennedy

Quote 'Chicago! What a town! They should never have taken it away from the Indians.'
• 'I could cut my throat.' – 'If you did, greasepaint would run out of it.' • 'He won't kill himself. It'd please too many people.'

Psst! John Barrymore asked Hawks if he thought he'd be any good in the film. 'It's the story of the greatest ham in the world,' said Hawks. 'And God knows you fit that.' – 'I'll do the picture,' said Barrymore.

20,000 Leagues under the Sea

★★★ 1954 127min c.

Director: Richard Fleischer
Screenplay: Earl Felton
Source: Novel by Jules Verne

In the mid-19th century, a mysterious sea creature is attacking and sinking ships and a battleship is sent to destroy it. The monster turns out to be a submarine, captained by the crazed Mason. This is one of the greatest of all so-called 'family' films. Based on Verne's prescient novel, it manages the difficult trick of appealing to adults and children at the same time. The highlight is the fight with the giant squid.

Ned Land	Kirk Douglas
Capt. Nemo	James Mason
Prof. Aronnax	Paul Lukas
Conseil	Peter Lorre
First Mate	Robert J. Wilke
Capt. Farragut	Ted de Corsia
John Howard	Carleton Young

OOPS! When Prof. Aronnax books a trip with the Great Western Steam Packet Company, San Francisco Harbour, crammed with ships, can be seen through the window. But on the outside, instead of the ships' reflections in the window, there are some trees, a billboard and a man fiddling with a lamp.

Psst! Mason fought long and hard before accepting second billing to Douglas • When the fight with the giant squid was first filmed, the wires moving the tentacles around were far too obvious. So the director ordered that it be shot at night and that a storm be created in the tank so that audiences would be too distracted to spot the wires • Director Fleischer is the son of Max Fleischer, the cartoonist who created *Betty Boop*.

2001: A Space Odyssey

★★★★ 1968 141min c.

Director: Stanley Kubrick
Screenplay: Stanley Kubrick & Arthur C. Clarke
Source: Short story, *The Sentinel* by Clarke.

A spaceship is sent off to Jupiter in search of the recipient of a signal sent from a black monolith on the moon, but the computer and crew don't see eye to eye. This visually arresting spectacle was generally held to be deeply profound, probably because it's impossible to understand what's going on for much of the time. Nonetheless, it fills us with wonder at the majesty of the universe and man's insignificance within it. Considering that it was made before anyone had even walked on the moon, it is remarkable how realistic the space sequences still look. If you've never seen it before, you really ought to wait until you can watch it on the big screen. Followed by a so-so sequel, *2010*, in 1984.

David Bowman	Keir Dullea
Frank Poole	Gary Lockwood
Dr. Heywood Floyd	William Sylvester
Moonwatcher	Daniel Richter
Smyslov	Leonard Rossiter
Voice of Hal 9000	Douglas Rain
Elena	Margaret Tyzack
Mission controller	Frank Miller
Halvorsen	Robert Beatty

Blurb The Ultimate Trip.

Quote 'I'm sorry, Dave. I'm afraid I can't do that.' • 'It can only be attributed to human error.' • 'I know everything hasn't been quite right with me, but I can assure you now, very confidentially, that it's going to be all right again.' • 'Stop, Dave. I'm afraid. I'm afraid, Dave. Dave, my mind is going. I can feel it. I can feel it.'

OOPS! The rotating space station changes direction three times • Although the astronauts are hibernating, their respective positions keep changing • Scientists have pointed out that distant stars shouldn't appear to move slowly relative to the Discovery • There are occasional lapses in the illusion of zero gravity, as when Dr. Floyd's food being sucked from a container drops back instead of remaining where it is • When Dave comes back to the Discovery and enters HAL's logic centre, his left glove comes loose from what is supposedly an airtight space suit.

Psst! Arthur C. Clarke's short story came first. Stanley Kubrick planned a movie around it, then called *Journey Beyond the Stars*, that was almost a documentary. Then he adapted his vision as the project developed. The novel came after the screenplay, and offers rather more explanation of what's going on than the film does • There is no dialogue at all for the first 22 minutes • Originally 160 minutes long, Kubrick then cut it to its current length • Transpose HAL by one letter and you get IBM. Clarke and Kubrick claimed this was a coincidence. Kubrick said his original idea was to have a woman voice the computer, which was to be called Athena. When he changed his mind, the name came about from a combination of buzz-words 'heuristic' and 'algorithmic' • Martin Balsam originally voiced HAL but was replaced by Rain after Kubrick found him 'too emotional' • Kubrick put some classical music onto early edited footage to show composer Alex North the sort of thing he was after. But the director wasn't happy with North's score and, with no time left to commission another composer, he had to stick with the classical music. It proved immensely popular and is the only time that Richard Strauss has made the top 40, thanks to his catchy little number *Also Sprach Zarathustra* • It's said that some people watched the film while stoned, timing it so that they were most out of it during the psychedelic sequences near the end • The Dawn of Man sequence used only two real baby chimpanzees. The rest were people in suits. Among those rejected as being the wrong shape was apparently aspirant ape Ronnie Corbett • Perhaps what has dated most is the idea that a person can fit comfortably inside a computer's memory bank • Keir Dullea is probably best remembered now for Noel Coward's cutting comment on him: 'Keir Dullea and gone tomorrow.'

Two Way Stretch
★★★ 1960 87min b/w

Director: Robert Day
Screenplay: John Warren & Len Heath

Sellers and his mates reckon that they have the perfect alibi when they plan a robbery; they are in prison! But suspicious warder Jeffries has his eye on them. Although hardly the height of sophisticated comedy, this remains a pretty amusing romp put over by a wonderful array of great British comic actors.

Dodger Lane	Peter Sellers
'Rev' Basil Fowler/Soapy	Wilfrid Hyde-White
Jelly Knight	David Lodge
Lennie Price	Bernard Cribbins
Cmdr. Horatio Bennet	Maurice Denham
Sidney Crout	Lionel Jeffries
Mrs. Price	Irene Handl
Ethel	Liz Fraser
Miss Pringle	Beryl Reid
Warder Jenkins	George Woodbridge
Col. Arkwright	Thorley Walters
Tailor	Warren Mitchell
Fred	Arthur Mullard

Under the Clock
SEE: The Clock

Unforgiven
★★★ 1992 131min c.

Director: Clint Eastwood
Screenplay: David Webb Peoples

A group of prostitutes offer a reward for the murder of the man who cut one of them up. Hog-farmer Eastwood saddles up one more time and sets off to do what a man's got to do. This Eastwood-directed Western is good, but nothing like as brilliant or unconventional as the critics maintained. There are several over-indulgent scenes of Clint riding through fields of swirling corn, while its supposed message preaching against violence is not particularly clear. But Hackman's superb as the psychotic sheriff and Harris and Rubinek are delightful as the Royalist killer and his biographer sidekick.

Bill Munny	Clint Eastwood
Little Bill Daggett	Gene Hackman
Ned Logan	Morgan Freeman
English Bob	Richard Harris
The 'Schofield Kid'	Jaimz Woolvett
W.W.Beauchamp	Saul Rubinek
Strawberry Alice	Frances Fisher

Oscars Best Picture, Best Director, Gene Hackman

Quote 'I ain't like that any more, kid.' • 'Hell, I even thought I was dead, till I found out it was just that I was in Nebraska.' • 'It's a hell of a thing killing a man. You take away all he's got and all he's ever gonna have.' • 'I've killed women and children. Killed just about everything that walks or crawls at one time or another. And I'm here to kill you, Little Bill, for what you done to Ned.' • 'I guess he had it coming.' – 'We all got it coming, kid.'

OOPS! Although English Bob shoots at pheasants from the train, they weren't introduced into America until 1882, the year after the film is set.

Psst! The film is dedicated to 'Sergio and Don', Sergio Leone and Don Siegel respectively • The script had been written around 20 years earlier. Along the way Gene Hackman was one of those who had rejected the lead role • Frances Fisher, playing 'Strawberry Alice', was Eastwood's partner at the time • Despite his association with Westerns, Eastwood is allergic to horses and has to take medication when he's around them.

The Uninvited

★★★ 1944 98min b/w

Director: Lewis Allen
Screenplay: Dodie Smith
Source: Novel, *Uneasy Freehold* by Dorothy Macardle

A couple buy one of those photogenic houses on the tops of cliffs that ghosts love so much, presumably for the sea air. Sure enough, as soon as they move in, strange things begin happening. Rather than sue the surveyor, they want to find out the story behind the spectres. One of the few serious ghost stories ever filmed, this remains pretty scary in places because so much is left to the audience's imagination.

Roderick Fitzgerald . . . . .Ray Milland
Pamela Fitgerald . . . . .Ruth Hussey
Cmdr. Bench . . . . .Donald Crisp
Stella Meredith . . . . .Gail Russell
Miss Holloway . . . . .Cornelia Otis Skinner
Miss Hird . . . . .Dorothy Stickney
Lizzie Flynn . . . . .Barbara Everest
Dr. Scott . . . . .Alan Napier

Blurb A Love Haunted By Nameless Evil Which Fought To Live In Their Hearts.

Quote 'Who ever heard of a poisonous cat?'

The Untouchables

★★★★ 1987 119min c.

Director: Brian de Palma
Screenplay: David Mamet

In the midst of Prohibition in Chicago, Treasury agent Eliot Ness decides to get tough with Al Capone, helped by gnarled cop Connery and a group of incorruptable colleagues. Although a little slow to start and rather confusing in the shoot-out scene with the horses, this is a taut, exciting gangster picture taken to a higher level by some excellent acting and occasionally inspired direction. Never mind that Ness really had nothing to do with convicting Capone. Just sit back and enjoy.

Eliot Ness . . . . .Kevin Costner
Jim Malone . . . . .Sean Connery
Oscar Wallace . . . . .Charles Martin Smith
George Stone . . . . .Andy Garcia
Al Capone . . . . .Robert De Niro
Mike .Richard Bradford
Payne . . . . .Jack Kehoe

Oscars Sean Connery

Quote 'You just fulfilled the first rule of law enforcement: Make sure when your shift is over you go home alive. Here endeth the lesson.' • 'He's in the car.' • 'They say they're going to repeal Prohibition. What will you do then?' – 'I think I'll have a drink.' [Last line]

OOPS! In a warehouse raid, the crates have Canada's maple leaf symbol on them, 30 years before it was first used • The amazing station steps sequence only lasts three minutes (even in slow motion), yet the clock shows that 10 minutes passes • The camera can be seen in the reflection from a window in Connery's flat when the guy with the knife gets in.

Psst! The final shootout on the station steps, arguably the film's finest scene [albeit a ripoff of Eisenstein's *Battleship Potemkin*] was improvised by De Palma in a matter of hours when he was told that there was no money for the period train he wanted. The money, $200,000, had gone to pay off Bob Hoskins when Robert De Niro became available to play Al Capone • De Niro shoved plugs up his nose and added 25 pounds in weight in Italy where he gorged himself on pasta and puddings. He also wore silk underwear bought from the firm that had supplied Capone.

The Usual Suspects

★★★★ 1995 106min c.

Director: Bryan Singer
Screenplay: Christopher McQuarrie

There are few greater cinematic pleasures than a complicated crime yarn which is beautifully arranged and executed. This is one of those rare movies, reminding us of greats of the genre like *Chinatown* and *The Big Sleep*. It flashes between a police investigation into a massacre on a moored ship and the incident itself, with cop Palminteri convinced that Byrne is the mastermind while survivor Spacey maintains it's the work of a mysterous, feared gangster. The plot twists and turns like an angry serpent, with writer McQuarrie playing with us as someone might tease a kitten with a ball of string, keeping the solution out of our reach even though it always seems tantalisingly close. This is one of those rare thrillers that reveals further layers on repeated viewings. A truly tasty movie.

McManus . . . . .Stephen Baldwin
Keaton . . . . .Gabriel Byrne
Dave Kujan . . . . .Chazz Palminteri
Hockey . . . . .Kevin Pollak
Kobayashi . . . . .Pete Postlethwaite
Verbal .Kevin Spacey
Edie Finneran . . . . .Suzy Amis
Jack Baer . . . . .Giancarlo Esposito
Fenster . . . . .Benicio Del Toro
Jeff Rabin .Dan Hedaya

Quote 'The greatest trick the devil ever pulled was persuading the world he didn't exist.'

Psst! Writer McQuarrie was a private detective in New Jersey for four years.

Vertigo
★★★★ 1958 128min c.

Director: Alfred Hitchcock
Screenplay: Alec Coppel & Samuel Taylor
Source: Novel, *D'Entre les Morts* by Pierre Boileau & Thomas Narcejac

Hitchcock, often seen only as the Master of Suspense, baffled contemporary audiences with this slow, operatic love story of agoraphobic James Stewart falling for his client's blonde wife. The normally secretive director for once bares his soul, and the film's re-release in 1983 revealed a haunting, despairing portrait of romantic obsession which improves on each viewing. Stewart was seldom better and for once Kim Novak's artificiality is just right. Occasionally absurd, frequently brilliant, it is now seen as one of Hitchcock's finest, most imitated films.

John 'Scottie' Ferguson . . . . . . .James Stewart
Madeleine/Judy . . . . .Kim Novak

Midge . . . . .Barbara Bel Geddes
Gavin Elster . . . . .Tom Helmore
Coroner . . . . .Henry Jones
Doctor .Raymond Bailey
Manageress . . . . .Ellen Corby
Pop Leibel . . . . .Konstantin Shayne
Older Mistaken Identity . . . . .Lee Patrick

Blurb A Tall Story About A Pushover.

OOPS! James Stewart is able to leap across a gap from one building to another at roof-top level. But when he is suspended from the gutter, the distance has widened to that of a normal city street!

Psst! When French writers Pierre Boileau and Thomas Narcejac heard that Alfred Hitchcock was interested in acquiring the rights to their book on which *Les Diaboliques* was based, they decided to write another novel specifically to interest him. The book, *From Among the Dead* in English, became *Vertigo*. Hitch only found out several years later that far from him cleverly spotting a good property, it had his name on it from the start • Hitch appears 10 minutes in walking past the shipyard • Hitchcock invented the famous combination of zooming the lens in while moving the camera backwards to create the sensation of vertigo to the audience. The view down the mission stairwell cost $19,000 to achieve for just a couple of seconds of screen time • Hitchcock had hoped to use Vera Miles again, after enjoying working with her in *The Wrong Man*. But she became pregnant, to his vociferous dismay • James Stewart recalled that Kim Novak was terribly serious throughout filming. 'She came up to Hitchcock and said, "About the next scene. I'd like to go over it with you because I'm not sure of the reason for the motivation that I have in dealing with the problem that I have." And Hitchcock just looked at her and said, "Kim, it's only a movie!"' • This is one of the 'lost Hitchcocks' [see *Rear Window*].

Victim
★★ 1961 100min b/w

Director: Basil Dearden
Screenplay: Janet Green & John McCormick

An eminent lawyer, a bisexual, realises after an ex-lover hangs himself that the man was being blackmailed. He then sets out to bring the blackmailers to justice, despite the risks to himself. This was an important film of its day, and considered extremely daring for its tackling issues of homosexuality in a straightforward manner. But without this novelty to add extra spice, the thriller aspects aren't really terribly exciting.

Melville Farr	Dirk Bogarde
Laura Farr	Sylvia Syms
Calloway	Dennis Price
Lord Fullbrook	Anthony Nicholls
Paul Mandrake	Peter Copley
Harold Doe	Norman Bird
Jack Barrett	Peter McEnery
Henry	Charles Lloyd Pack
Phip	Nigel Stock
Frank	Alan Howard

Psst! This was the first British movie to use the word 'homosexual' and to deal with the subject openly. It was given an 'X' certificate after a few small cuts were insisted upon by the censor • The movie was said to have played a part in the shift in attitudes that let to a partial decriminalisation of homosexuality in Britain in 1967 • In America it was not permitted the Seal of the Motion Picture Association of America and had to be released without it.

Victor/Victoria

★★ 1982 133min c.

Director: Blake Edwards
Screenplay: Blake Edwards
Source: 1933 film, *Victor Und Viktoria*

Aided by camp Preston, broke singer Andrews becomes a success when she pretends to be a man pretending to be a woman. This is one of those movies whose reputation is way too high. It does have some hilarious scenes, as when playboy Garner tries to prove what a man he is by ordering milk in a rough bar, and those involving waiter Stark. But there are also long, dull patches and Julie Andrews is far too squeaky-clean to convince. Without the central conceit working, the film never really catches wing.

Victor/Victoria	Julie Andrews
King	James Garner
Toddy	Robert Preston
Norma	Lesley Ann Warren
Squashy	Alex Karras
Cassell	John Rhys-Davies
Waiter	Graham Stark
Also: Peter Arne, Michael Robbins, Norman Chancer, Maria Charles

Quote 'Oh, it's nothing serious. A few nights flat on his back under a specialist and he'll be as good as new.' • 'There's nothing more inconvenient than an old queen with a head cold.'

OOPS! Although the word 'gay' is used throughout to refer to homosexuality, it hadn't acquired that meaning in the 30s.

A View to a Kill

★ 1985 131min c.

Director: John Glen
Screenplay: Richard Maibaum & Michael G. Wilson

A View to Retirement, Moore like. Roger Moore said goodbye to Bond with something of a whimper in this overlong and rather tired tale which sees baddie Walken planning to wipe out California's Silicon Valley. There's far too much boring talk and not enough action, and there's also something rather distasteful about seeing the ageing Moore in bed with girls young enough to be his daughter. The only plus point is the great airship scene above the Golden Gate Bridge.

James Bond	Roger Moore
Max Zorin	Christopher Walken
Stacey Sutton	Tanya Roberts
May Day	Grace Jones
Tibbett	Patrick Macnee
Scarpine	Patrick Bauchau
Pola Ivanova	Fiona Fullerton
Jenny Flex	Alison Doody
'Q'	Desmond Llewelyn
'M'	Robert Brown
Miss Moneypenny	Lois Maxwell
Also: Walter Gotell, Geoffrey Keen, Dolph Lundgren

Psst! The film was known in Hong Kong as *The Indestructible Iron Man Fights Against the Electronic Gang* • Filming was delayed when the '007' soundstage at Pinewood Studios burnt down. It was rebuilt in less than four months • On every picture, Roger Moore insisted on being given an unlimited supply of Montecristo havanas. The bill on one Bond film came to over £3,000 • Look out for Dolph Lundgren in a bit part as a KGB goon. He was then the boyfriend of singer Grace Jones boyfriend • As well as being Moore's last Bond, it was also the Lois Maxwell's last outing as Moneypenny.

Village of the Damned

★★★ 1960 78min b/w

Director: Wolf Rilla
Screenplay: Wolf Rilla, Stirling Silliphant &
George Barclay
Source: Novel, *The Midwich Cuckoos* by John
Wyndham

After a sleeping sickness hits an English village,
a dozen of the women find they're pregnant.
The children they produce are identical, blonde
with staring eyes, and have a phenomenal intelligence. It soon becomes clear, however, that
these menacing kids have more on their mind
than MENSA membership. Although it doesn't
match the book's creepiness, a nicely eerie
atmosphere is maintained throughout. The film
did well enough to inspire a sequel, *Children of
the Damned*, which had little to commend it.

Gordon Zellaby . . . . .George Sanders
Anthea Zellaby . . . . .Barbara Shelley
David Zellaby . . . . .Martin Stephens
Maj. Alan Bernard . . . . .Michael Gwynn
Dr. Willers . . . . .Laurence Naismith
Mrs. Harrington . . . . .Jenny Laird
Janet Pawle . . . . .Charlotte Mitchell
Sir Edgar Hargraves . . . . .Richard Vernon
Vicar .Bernard Archard
Mrs. Plumpton . . . . .Susan Richards
P.C. Gobbey . . . . .Peter Vaughan

The Wages of Fear

★★★★ 1953 140min c.

Director: Henri-Georges Clouzot
Screenplay: Henri-Georges Clouzot
Source: Novel by Georges Arnaud.

When an oil well catches fire in Central America,
a group of drivers are chosen to take a highly
volatile cargo of nitroglycerine 300 miles
through murderous terrain. Even a trip right the
way round the M25 pales in comparison to the
problems these guys have. You have nothing to
fear but fear itself, and this French film oozes it
out of every pore. Although it starts slow starting,
it then just gets scarier and scarier. There isn't
a sofa built that's big enough to hide behind.

Mario . . . . .Yves Montand
Jo . . . . .Charles Vanel
Linda . . . . .Vera Clouzot
Bimba .Peter Van Eyck
Louigi . . . . .Folco Lulli
Bill O'Brien . . . . .William Tubbs

Psst! The American release was cut drastically,
losing a fifth of its length.

Wait until Dark

★★★ 1967 108min c.

Director: Terence Young
Screenplay: Robert Carrington & Jane Howard
Carrington
Source: Play by Frederick Knott

Hepburn, coming to terms with being blinded in
an accident, is virtually imprisoned in her apartment by crooks who want the drugs stashed in
a doll. This Hitchcockian thriller is real nails-bit-
ten-down-to-the-stub stuff. Arkin makes an
amazingly menacing villain while Hepburn is
magnificent as the vulnerable woman who isn't
quite the easy target they had bargained for.

Susy Hendrix . . . . .Audrey Hepburn
Harry Roat Jr. . . . . .Alan Arkin
Mike Talman . . . . .Richard Crenna
Sam Hendrix . . . . .Efrem Zimbalist Jr.
Carlino . . . . .Jack Weston
Lisa . . . . .Samantha Jones

Psst! Hepburn closely researched her role. She
wore shades on her eyes for long periods and
learnt how to function without sight, as did the
director • A box office success, some cinema
managers turned the house lights off
completely for the latter stages of the film in
order to heighten the tension.

Walkabout

★★★ 1971 100min c.

Director: Nicolas Roeg
Screenplay: Edward Bond
Source: Novel by James Vance Marshall

A brother and sister have to fend for themselves in the Outback when their father
commits suicide. They are befriended by an
aborigine, and a bond develops between him
and the girl. With Roeg's fine visual powers
turned up full, this is a lyrical, mystical and
haunting film that is most definitely a one-off.

Girl . . . . .Jenny Agutter
Brother . . . . .Lucien John
Aborigine . . . . .David Gulpilil
Father . . . . .John Meillon

Psst! This was Roeg's first solo outing as a
director. The project had to be shelved for a

time because of a lack of funds, so in the interim he co-directed *Performance*.

Wall Street
★★★ 1987 124min c.

Director: Oliver Stone
Screenplay: Stanley Weiser & Oliver Stone

This tale of an Ivan Boesky-like corporate raider is now almost as fascinating as a picture of a bygone era as it is a rattling good yarn. Sheen is excellent as the young broker so eager to get in with Douglas that he'll do almost anything. But it's Douglas' compelling performance as the lord of all he surveys that makes the picture so riveting even if, as so often with Stone, things are rather too black and white to be wholly convincing.

Gordon Gekko	Michael Douglas
Bud Fox	Charlie Sheen
Carl Fox	Martin Sheen
Darien Taylor	Daryl Hannah
Sir Larry Wildman	Terence Stamp
Kate Gekko	Sean Young
Realtor	Sylvia Miles
Roger Barnes	James Spader
Marvin	John C. McGinley
Lou Mannheim	Hal Holbrook

Oscars Michael Douglas

Quote 'If you need a friend, get a dog.'
• 'Greed…is good. Greed is right. Greed works'
• 'Lunch is for wimps!'

Psst! The movie was originally called *Greed* • It is dedicated to Louis, Oliver's stockbroker father • Stone appears very briefly during a split-screen Wall Street sequence • Martin and Charlie Sheen are, of course, father and son • Young was fired during filming, only finding out when she discovered Hannah on set delivering one of her lines. The story that when she was tackled leaving the studio with a costume on she simply stripped off all her clothes is, it appears, another of those legends with little basis in fact.

WarGames
★★★★ 1983 113min c.

Director: John Badham
Screenplay: Lawrence Lasker & Walter F. Parkes

Computer whiz-kid Broderick hacks into a computer and starts playing a game called Thermonuclear War, only to discover that the game's for real. An invigoratingly entertaining and nail-biting thriller, with plenty of laughs, a little romance and just the teeniest bit of preaching. Surprisingly re-watchable, too.

David Lightman	Matthew Broderick
Jennifer	Ally Sheedy
McKittrick	Dabney Coleman
Falken	John Wood
General Berringer	Barry Corbin
Pat Healy	Juanin Clay
Cabot	Kent Williams
Watson	Dennis Lipscomb

Quote 'Goddamn it. I'd piss on a spark plug if I thought it would do any good!' • 'A strange game. The only winning move is not to play. How about a nice game of chess?'

Psst! Originally a 'message' film, when market research showed how little the public wanted a film about nuclear war, director Martin Brest [*Beverly Hills Cop*] was fired, the film was pepped up and the original ending, which had the Biggest Bang of all, was junked • MGM head honcho Freddie Fields was dissuaded from including one more shot showing Broderick and Sheedy walking into the sunset • Broderick practised for two months beforehand on arcade games machines which the studio bought for him • This is the movie Costner left *after* filming had begun in order to be in *The Big Chill*, only to have his part in that film dropped almost entirely • This is said to be one of Ronald Reagan's favourite films.

The War of the Worlds
★★★ 1953 85min c.

Director: Byron Haskin
Screenplay: Barre Lyndon
Source: Novel by H.G. Wells

The Martians invade earth, take one look at the world's leaders, decide that they don't want to be taken to them, and start shooting the place up. The action from Wells' original book is updated from the 19th to 20th century although, sadly, the acting and the dialogue are not. The locale is also changed to California where, judging by the movies, 99% of all extraterrestrial encounters take place. You really only want to watch this for the special effects, which still look surprisingly good. It's filmed in a very artificial looking colour which helps the mood considerably.

Dr. Clayton Forrester	.Gene Barry
Sylvia Van Buren	.Ann Robinson
Gen. Mann	.Les Tremayne
Dr. Pryor	.Robert Cornthwaite
Pastor Matthew Collins	.Lewis Martin
Salvatore	.Jack Kruschen
Cop	.Henry Brandon
Buck Monahan	.Ralph Dumke
Narrator	.Cedric Hardwicke
Blonde	.Carolyn Jones

OOPS! Look out for the wires holding up the Martian spacecraft which are visible from time to time.

Psst! The screenplay was as heavily inspired by Orson Welles' infamous radio broadcast in 1938 as by H.G. Wells' novel • Paramount sent a film crew to shoot an atomic bomb test in Nevada. But the flash and mushroom cloud they filmed were thought not to be spectacular enough, so the special effects department was set to work to produce something more exciting! • At one time both Sergei Eisenstein and Cecil B. DeMille had hoped to make a movie version of Wells' story.

The Waterdance
★★★★ 1992 107min c.

Director: Neal Jimenez & Michael Steinberg
Screenplay: Neal Jimenez

Don't be put off by the subject matter. Far from being depressing, this story of a group of para- plegics in a hospital ward coming to terms with their lot is a life-enhancing, often downright hilarious, tale of the triumph of the human spirit. We are caught up from the word go as Stoltz tries to cope with his fragile and now uncon- summated relationship with married Hunt. A superlative piece of storytelling, with excellent performances from everyone but particularly Forsythe as the racist biker and Snipes as the lippy erstwhile ladies' man.

Joel	.Eric Stoltz
Anna	.Helen Hunt
Bloss	.William Forsythe
Ray	.Wesley Snipes
Rosa	.Elizabeth Pena

Psst! The story is based on the personal experiences of writer Jimenez, wheelchair- bound after a similar accident.

Waterloo Bridge
★★★ 1940 103min b/w

Director: Mervyn LeRoy
Screenplay: S.N. Behrman, Hans Rameau & George Froeschel
Source: Play by Robert E. Sherwood

In World War I, a ballerina and a soldier fall in love. But he's sent off to the front before they can marry and, believing him killed in action, she turns to prostitution. Then he comes back. This depressing wartime weepie, although heavily sanitised from the original play, is still moving thanks to Leigh's emotive performance.

Myra Lester	.Vivien Leigh
Capt. Roy Cronin	.Robert Taylor
Lady Margaret Cronin	.Lucille Watson
Kitty	.Virginia Field
Mme. Olga Kirowa	.Maria Ouspenskaya
Elsa	.Steffi Duna
Policeman	.Leo G. Carroll

Psst! Leigh, in the middle of a divorce, had hoped the lead role would go to her lover, Laurence Olivier.

The Way Ahead
★★★ 1944 115min b/w

Director: Carol Reed
Screenplay: Eric Ambler & Peter Ustinov

A platoon of Army recruits in World War II are moulded into a fighting unit and go off to war. Bearing in mind that this was intended as a wartime morale-booster, it is amazing how well it has worn the years. A film full of spirit and not a little humour still comes across as one of the finest movies about a group of fighting men. Also known as *The Immortal Battalion.*

Lt. Jim Perry	.David Niven
Brewer	.Stanley Holloway
Davenport	.Raymond Huntley
Sgt. Fletcher	.William Hartnell
Lloyd	.James Donald
Luke	.John Laurie
Beck	.Leslie Dwyer
Parsons	.Hugh Burden
Stainer	.Jimmy Hanley
Marjorie Gillingham	.Renée Asherson
Also:	Trevor Howard, Leo Genn, Penelope Dudley-Ward, Reginald Tate, Peter Ustinov

Psst! Based on an idea by Lt. Col. David Niven, it was originally intended as a training film but, perhaps not surprisingly considering the talent involved, became rather more than that • It was still being used as an official training film until the early 60s • Niven's batman was an enlisted man called Peter Ustinov • The caption at the end reads: 'The Beginning'.

Wayne's World
★★★★ 1992 95min c.

Director: Penelope Spheeris
Screenplay: Mike Myers, Bonnie Turner & Terry Turner

A pair of dweebish teenagers running a public-access cable show from their mum's basement get a shot at the big-time. This comedy, full of references to 60s TV shows and heavy metal is infantile, silly, pointless and thus hysterically funny to those who love childish humour. On top of that, the babes are great, with Carrere particularly babelicious. Deep philosophy question, NOT! Which came first? Wayne and Garth or Bill and Ted? Who knows? Who cares? Love 'em all. For those of mature years, this should be essential viewing for its perceptive insights into youth culture. The sequel is also surprisingly good.

Wayne Campbell . . . . .Mike Myers
Garth Algar . . . . .Dana Carvey
Benjamin Oliver . . . . .Rob Lowe
Cassandra . . . . .Tia Carrere
Noah Vanderhoff . . . . .Brian Doyle-Murray
Stacy .Lara Flynn Boyle
Russell . . . . .Kurt Fuller
Mrs. Vanderhoff . . . . .Colleen Camp

Blurb You'll Laugh. You'll Cry. You'll Hurl.

Quote 'Party on.' • 'Excellent.' • 'NOT!' • 'Schwing!' • 'And monkeys might fly out my butt.' • 'That is a babe! She makes me feel kinda funny, like when we used to climb the rope in gym class.' • 'If she were a President, she'd be Baberaham Lincoln.'

OOPS! Rob Lowe is playing 'Benjamin Oliver' according to the credits, but he introduces himself as 'Benjamin King' • Wayne actually plays the white guitar he covets before he buys it.

Psst! There are plenty of cameos. Alice Cooper's easy to spot, that's Meat Loaf as a bouncer, Ione Skye as Lowe's suspiciously underage-looking girlfriend and Donna Dixon [Dan Aykroyd's wife] as Garth's dream girl

• Robert Patrick from *Terminator 2* appears in a cameo similarly dressed as a policeman • Keep watching right through the credits for Wayne and Garth's sign-off • Known in Taiwan as *The Rambunctious and Clever Ones* • The bit where Wayne tries out the first few notes of 'Stairway to Heaven' had to be changed for all overseas versions and any American versions other than in the cinemas. The rights for those markets couldn't be obtained and so a special riff was written.

Way Out West
★★★★ 1937 65min b/w

Director: James W. Horne
Screenplay: Charles Rogers, James Parrott & Felix Adler

In their finest feature film, Laurel and Hardy are sent West to deliver the deeds to a gold mine. Not unnaturally, there are a few hiccoughs in their mission. The film, in which their relationship seems terribly natural and touching, contains some of their best routines as well as the great song 'The Trail of the Lonesome Pine'. Best of all, though, is their hilarious little dance, 'Commencin' Dancing' on the steps of the saloon. Tear-weeping, side-splitting joy.

Stanley . . . . .Stan Laurel
Ollie . . . . .Oliver Hardy
Lola Marcel . . . . .Sharon Lynne
Mickey Finn . . . . .James Finlayson
Mary Roberts . . . . .Rosina Lawrence
Sheriff . . . . .Stanley Fields

Quote 'Now that you've got the mine, I'll bet you'll be a swell gold-digger.'

Psst! Laurel and Hardy were having personal problems at the time and both separated from their wives during filming • The boys' rendition of 'The Trail of the Lonesome Pine' got to number two in the British charts in 1975.

The Way to the Stars
★★★ 1945 109min b/w

Director: Anthony Asquith
Screenplay: Terence Rattigan & Anatole de Grunwald
Source: Poem by John Pudney.

Far too few films set in wartime focused on the home front. This provided a different angle by concentrating on the war as it was seen from the viewpoint of a hotel close by an airfield. There are many story threads, the most important involving romance and the attitude of British airmen to the arrival of the Johnny-come-lately Americans. While people may sneer at the stiff upper lips on show, this is still a very tender and moving film, with a good eye and ear and plenty of humour to keep it afloat. Also known as *Johnny in the Clouds*.

David Archdale	Michael Redgrave
Peter Penrose	John Mills
Toddy Todd	Rosamund John
Johnny Hollis	Douglass Montgomery
Mr. Palmer	Stanley Holloway
Iris Winterton	Renée Asherson
Tiny Williams	Basil Radford
Rev. Charles Moss	Felix Aylmer
Squadron Ldr. Carter	Trevor Howard
Miss Winterton	Joyce Carey
Joe Friselli	Bonar Colleano
Singer	Jean Simmons
Prune Parsons	David Tomlinson

Psst! Rosamund John's line: 'Get the hell out of here' had to be dubbed: 'Get the heck out of here' for the sensitive Americans • Bill Owen, later to find fame as Compo in *Last of the Summer Wine* made his film debut here.

The Way We Were
★★ 1973 118min c.

Director: Sydney Pollack
Screenplay: Arthur Laurents
Source: Novel by Laurents

Jewish political activist Streisand falls in love with Waspish Redford. Although there are those who love this and weep buckets at it, to me it's always seemed one of the least likely and least believable of all movie romances and isn't helped by the fact that the music is now so familiar. While we're at it, isn't the scene where she fondles the drunk and naked Redford date rape?

Katie Morosky	Barbra Streisand
Hubbell Gardiner	Robert Redford
J.J.	Bradford Dillman
George Bissinger	Patrick O'Neal
Paula Reisner	Viveca Lindfors
Carol Ann	Lois Chiles
Brooks Carpenter	Murray Hamilton
Bill Verso	Herb Edelman
Frankie McVeigh	James Woods

Pony Dunbar	Sally Kirkland
Guest	Dan Seymour

Quote 'May I ask you a personal question? Do you smile all the time?'

OOPS! I'm sorry, but if somebody has just thrown up, wouldn't their breath be just a teensy bit revolting? Despite her oversized olefactory equipment, Streisand doesn't even notice.

Psst! It took director Sydney Pollack eight months to persuade Robert Redford to take the part. He was keen at the time on changing his public persona and thought the film would merely reinforce his pretty-face image • The atmosphere on set was so bad, it was described by one crew member as 'doing overtime at Dachau.' • After taking us through American politics from the 30s to the 50s, the film suddenly becomes vague just as McCarthy hoves into sight. Although shot, this section was apparently chopped out just before the film was released • Keep your eye out for a young James Wood as Streisand's politically sympathetic colleague in the early days, as well as a glimpse of composer Marvin Hamlisch at the Hollywood screening.

Went the Day Well?
★★★ 1942 92min b/w

Director: Alberto Cavalcanti
Screenplay: John Dighton, Angus Macphail & Diana Morgan
Source: Story by Graham Greene

A group of German paratroopers lands in an English village and takes it over with the aid of the turncoat local squire. However, they reckon without the pluck and courage of John Bull. The interesting idea, wondering how the average British citizen would behave if we suffered the fate of much of Europe, is deftly handled and makes for an absorbing movie.

Oliver Wilsford	Leslie Banks
Ortler	Basil Sydney
Tom Sturry	Frank Lawton
Peggy	Elizabeth Allan
Nora Ashton	Valerie Taylor
Sims	Mervyn Johns
Poacher	Edward Rigby
Mrs. Fraser	Marie Lohr
Land Girl	Thora Hird
Daisy	Patricia Hayes
George Truscott	Harry Fowler

Western Union

★★★ 1941 93min c.

Director: Fritz Lang
Screenplay: Robert Carson
Source: Story by Zane Grey

A Fritz Lang film in Technicolor takes a bit of getting used to, but the fine cinematography is just one strength of this intriguing western. Randolph Scott becomes involved with the building of the telegraph line, but his outlaw past catches up with him. A crisp, beautiful and witty Western, it has a moving theme about the price of taming the wilderness.

Vance Shaw	Randolph Scott
Richard Blake	Robert Young
Edward Creighton	Dean Jagger
Sue Creighton	Virginia Gilmore
Doc Murdoch	John Carradine
Herman	Slim Summerville
Homer	Chill Wills
Jack Slade	Barton MacLane
Governor	Russell Hicks
Charlie	Victor Kilian

Psst! When the film-makers needed to stampede the cattle, they were inspired by someone's memory of the effect Stuka dive-bombers had on troops. A handful of aircraft were ordered up and dived on the cattle to get them moving.

West Side Story

★★ 1961 155min c.

Director: Robert Wise & Jerome Robbins
Screenplay: Ernest Lehman
Source: Play by Arthur Laurents inspired by the play *Romeo and Juliet* by Shakespeare

Some consider this version of Romeo and Juliet, transferred to the world of New York gangs, the Jets and the Sharks, one of the greatest of all screen musicals. Some of the musical numbers, which include songs like 'America', and 'I Feel Pretty' are energetically staged. But the performances of some of the actors, particularly Beymer and Wood, are so dreadful that the mood is destroyed almost every time they open their mouths. Although it must have seemed a great idea to film it on location, it really does detract from the enterprise. You either love it or hate it. Me, I head for the door whenever a musical number is coming to a close.

Maria	Natalie Wood
Tony	Richard Beymer
Riff	Russ Tamblyn
Anita	Rita Moreno
Bernardo	George Chakiris
Social worker	John Astin
Doc	Ned Glass
Lt. Shrank	Simon Oakland

Oscars Best Picture, George Chakiris, Rita Moreno, Best Director

Psst! The film holds second place in the Oscar league table, winning for 10 of its 11 nominations, with only *Ben-Hur* doing better • Robbins was the director of the Broadway version of the musical. But he was something of a perfectionist and, after running badly behind schedule, he was removed to make way for Wise, who was already doing the non-musical scenes. Both directors were credited, though, and it was the first time co-directors had won Oscars • The members of the rival gangs were encouraged to needle each other and play practical jokes off set to keep the mood going between them • In Britain, the president of the BBFC wanted to ban the picture altogether because of the gang violence • Natalie Wood was dubbed by Marni Nixon, Richard Beymer by Jim Bryant and Rita Moreno by Betty Wand • Wood wasn't much of a dancer, so the choreography had to disguise the fact that she was given simple steps by making a lot happen around her and keeping the camera otherwise occupied • For some time, the producers toyed with the idea of getting Elvis Presley to star in the film, much to Robbins' horror • This was John Astin's film debut. He is best known for being Gomez in TV's *The Addams Family*.

Westworld

★★★ 1973 89min c.

Director: Michael Crichton
Screenplay: Michael Crichton

A vacation resort offers people the chance to live in one of several fantasy worlds. Benjamin dons a stetson to play at being a cowboy. But things go wrong when one of the robots, looking remarkably like Yul Brynner, blows a fuse and begins blowing punters away for real. Although betraying its low budget at times, this early Michael Crichton movie still has plenty going for it. Like all good sci-fi, it is imaginative while the action sequences are well staged and pretty exciting. It was followed by *Futureworld* three years later, which wasn't bad as sequels go.

Gunslinger	Yul Brynner
Peter Martin	Richard Benjamin
John Blane	James Brolin
Medieval Knight	Norman Bartold
Banker	Dick Van Patten
Chief supervisor	Alan Oppenheimer
Medieval Queen	Victoria Shaw
Miss Carrie	Majel Barrett

Whatever Happened to Baby Jane?

★★ 1962 132min b/w

Director: Robert Aldrich
Screenplay: Lukas Heller
Source: Novel by Henry Farrell

Two sisters, former well-known actresses who live in a crumbling mansion, display little in the way of sisterly love. An already bad relationship gets considerably worse when one learns the other intends putting her in a home. If it is fascinating to watch stars who were actually an item doing love scenes on the screen, then it ought to be utterly compelling watching these two act out their real-life animosity. But although many find this slice of hammy over-the-top black comedy both funny and thrilling, it's actually rather sad to watch two once-great talents resorting to making a bad horror pic. There's a feeling that you're gazing in on a cheap freak show and matters aren't helped by a running time that's more heavily padded than Crawford's shoulders.

Jane Hudson	Bette Davis
Blanche Hudson	Joan Crawford
Edwin Flagg	Victor Buono
Mrs. Bates	Anna Lee
Della Flagg	Marjorie Bennett
Elvira Stitt	Maidie Norman

Blurb Sister, Sister, Oh So Fair, Why Is There Blood All Over Your Hair?

Quote 'The best time I ever had with Joan Crawford was when I pushed her down the stairs.' [Davis] • 'Bette and I work differently, Bette screams and I knit. While she screamed, I knitted a scarf that stretched clear to Malibu!' [Crawford] • 'I wouldn't give you one dime for those two washed-up bitches' [Jack Warner]

Showing Sadie McKee • Parachute Jumper • Ex-Lady.

Psst! It was Crawford who bought the movie rights to the novel and offered the part to Davis. She had always admired her and regretted that they had never worked together before • Davis got a higher salary but Crawford was on points • The pair did everything they could to upset each other. Davis is said accidentally to have kicked Crawford in the head during one scene. Crawford got her own back when Davis had to drag her at one point. She put weights under her clothes, causing Davis to put her back out • The neighbour, Liza, was played by Davis' 14-year-old daughter, B.D. Merrill. Crawford needled Davis by remarking on the girl's lack of acting talent and, like Crawford's daughter, Merrill was later to pen an acerbic book about her mother • When Davis donated her scrapbooks to Boston University in 1985, every picture of Joan Crawford had its teeth blacked out.

What's Up, Doc?

★★★★ 1972 94min c.

Director: Peter Bogdanovich
Screenplay: Buck Henry, David Newman & Robert Benton

Kooky, unembarrassable Streisand latches onto mild-mannered musicologist O'Neal and throws his life into disarray just as he's pitching for a big grant to study the music inherent in rocks. Bogdanovich's frenetic homage to the screwball comedy makes me roar with laughter no matter how many times I see it. Mars and Kahn provide beautiful comic support, while the scene with the banner in the street is one any of the top silent comedians would have been proud of. One of the all-time great comedies.

Judy Maxwell	Barbra Streisand
Howard Bannister	Ryan O'Neal
Eunice Burns	Madeline Kahn
Hugh Simon	Kenneth Mars
Frederick Larrabee	Austin Pendleton
Harry	Sorrell Booke
Fritz	Stefan Gierasch
Mrs. Van Hoskins	Mabel Albertson
Mr. Smith	Michael Murphy
Bailiff	Graham Jarvis
Judge Maxwell	Liam Dunn
Hotel manager	John Hillerman
Arresting officer	M. Emmet Walsh
Prof. Hosquith	Randy Quaid

Quote 'Once upon a time, there was a plaid overnight case.' • 'Must you stand quite so close?' – 'I'm very nearsighted.' • 'What are you doing? This is a one-way street!' – 'I'm only going one way.' • 'Love means never having to say you're sorry.' – 'That's the dumbest thing I ever heard!'

OOPS! Streisand is in a different outfit on the piano from the one she wore at the dinner and yet another one when she leaves the hotel. Yet we know that the bag containing her clothes is not the one she is carrying • When they come off the transporter, the Beetle they're in has only three tin cans hanging off the bumper. In the next shot, there are loads of them.

Psst! O'Neal and Streisand had signed up to make a movie called *A Glimpse of Tiger*. When that was abandoned, Bogdanovich had the writers come up with a new script for the stars • Bogdanovich shot footage of the rehearsals and showed it to Howard Hawks, director of *Bringing Up Baby*, the screwball comedy that was the model for this film. Hawks said that, like Hepburn, Streisand was trying to be funny and it wasn't' working. "Tell them to just read the lines. They've got to play off each other and get the laughs from their attitudes."

When Harry Met Sally
★★★★ 1989 95min c.

Director: Rob Reiner
Screenplay: Nora Ephron

Hilarious examination of the age-old question: Can men and women be friends as well as lovers? Extraordinarily witty and wise, everything about this movie is spot on. The actors are perfect for their roles, the direction keeps it rolling smoothly and the mix between humour, sentiment and plot is just right. Unlike so many other comedies, it also works well on repeated viewings.

Harry Burns . . . . .Billy Crystal
Sally Albright . . . . .Meg Ryan
Marie . . . . .Carrie Fisher
Jess . . . . .Bruno Kirby
Joe . . . . .Steven Ford
Alice .Lisa Jane Persky

Blurb Can Two Friends Sleep Together And Still Love Each Other In The Morning?

Quote 'I'll have what she's having.' • 'You made a woman *miaow*?' • 'It's not the same for men. Charlie Chaplin had babies when he was 73.' – 'Yeh, but he was too old to pick them up.' • 'I love that you get cold when it's 71 degrees out.

I love that it takes you an hour and a half to order a sandwich. I love that you get a little crinkle above your nose when you're looking at me like I'm nuts. I love that after I spend a day with you I can still smell your perfume on my clothes. And I love that you are the last person I want to talk to before I go to sleep at night.'

Showing Casablanca.

OOPS! On the car trip, after Harry has opened the window, it alternates between open and closed.

Psst! At the end of the justly-famous restaurant episode, Meg Ryan was presented with a salami by the crew • The famous reaction line to Ryan's performance is said by Estelle Reiner, the director's mother • Crystal can be seen reading Stephen King's *Misery* at one point. It would be director Reiner's next project. The film was going to be called *It Had To Be You*, but another film in development already had that name. Another rejected name was *Boy Meets Girl* • For the New Year's Eve scene, 200 bulbs in the Empire State Building were changed to a seasonal red and green for three days. It appears in the background for only 20 seconds.

Where Eagles Dare
★★★ 1969 155min c.

Director: Brian G. Hutton
Screenplay: Alistair MacLean
Source: Novel by MacLean

Hi-jinks in wartime Bavaria, with a group of paratroops dropping into Nazi territory to rescue an American general. You have to put your brain on hold to watch this, so many are its implausibilities. But despite the fact that it should have been at least half an hour shorter, there is plenty of stirring action to be enjoyed.

Maj. John Smith . . . . .Richard Burton
Lt. Morris Schaffer . . . . .Clint Eastwood
Mary Ellison . . . . .Mary Ure
Col. Turner . . . . .Patrick Wymark
Vice Adm. Rolland . . . . .Michael Hordern
Christiansen . . . . .Donald Houston
Berkeley . . . . .Peter Barkworth
Cartwright Jones . . . . .Robert Beatty
Kramer .Anton Diffring
Heidi . . . . .Ingrid Pitt

Psst! Eastwood's character is said to kill more people in this film than in any of his other movies.

Whisky Galore
★★★ 1948 82min c.

Director: Alexander Mackendrick
Screenplay: Compton Mackenzie & Angus Macphail
Source: Novel by Compton Mackenzie

When a ship full of whisky is wrecked off a small island in the Hebrides during the Second World War, the islanders decide that there are better homes for it than the hands of the Customs and Excise. Although delightful throughout, this Ealing comedy doesn't quite have the wit or inventiveness to put in the very top class. But just because it resembles 10-year-old whisky rather than the 25-year-old stuff is no reason to say 'no' to it. The 1957 sequel, *Mad Little Island*, was closer to a naff supermarket blend.

Capt. Paul Waggett	Basil Radford
Peggy Macroon	Joan Greenwood
Mrs. Campbell	Jean Cadell
Dr. McLaren	James Robertson Justice
George Campbell	Gordon Jackson
Joseph Macroon	Wylie Watson
Sammy MacCodrum	John Gregson
The Biffer	Morland Graham
Angus MacCormac	Duncan Macrae
Mrs. Waggett	Catherine Lacey
Sgt. Odd	Bruce Seaton

Psst! This was Mackendrick's first film as director. He had been employed by Sir Michael Balcon as a storyboard artist and writer and, although Balcon let him sit in the director's chair, he kept his pay at £35 a week, only half what the cameraman was getting • The weather in the Hebrides was dreadful and communication with the mainland was often impossible. The film went over budget and was subject to long delays and, on one occasion, Mackendrick rang his fiancée and told her he was going to kill himself • Balcon was so unhappy with the result that he would not release it. Charles Crichton, who had directed *The Lavender Hill Mob*, thought it showed promise and he re-edited it into releasable shape even though he received no pay or credit • The American title of *Tight Little Island* was necessitated by the refusal of the Hays Office to allow any mention of alcohol in a film title • The novel's author, Sir Compton Mackenzie, appears as Captain Buncher • The novel was inspired by a true story, when the *SS Politican* sank off the coast of Scotland. Fourteen bottles, supposedly the last left, came up for auction in 1993 and fetched £12,000.

Whistle Down the Wind
★★★ 1961 99min c.

Director: Bryan Forbes
Screenplay: Keith Waterhouse & Willis Hall
Source: Novel by Mary Hayley Bell

Three children on a farm in Lancashire find a bearded man sheltering in their barn and assume that he is Jesus Christ. In fact he's a dangerous criminal on the run. Mawkish and twee though it may sound in summary, this allegory is still a very touching tale of childhood innocence and trust which doesn't eschew the use of humour.

Kathy Bostock	Hayley Mills
Mr. Bostock	Bernard Lee
The Man	Alan Bates
Eddie	Norman Bird
Auntie Dorothy	Elsie Wagstaffe
Charles Bostock	Alan Barnes
Nan Bostock	Diane Holgate

Psst! The novel was written by Hayley Mill's mother who was also, of course, Mrs. John Mills.

White Christmas
★★ 1954 120min c.

Director: Michael Curtiz
Screenplay: Norman Krasna, Norman Panama & Melvin Frank

Two song-and-dance men decide to help raise money for a skiing resort in trouble that's run by an old mate from the army. To a large extent, an inferior remake of *Holiday Inn* from 12 years earlier, the good tunes by Irving Berlin aren't enough to lift this perennial season favourite above the herd.

Bob Wallace	Bing Crosby
Phil Davis	Danny Kaye
Betty	Rosemary Clooney
Judy	Vera-Ellen
Gen. Waverly	Dean Jagger
Emma	Mary Wickes
Also: Grady Sutton, Sig Rumann	

Psst! Fred Astaire was approached for Kaye's part but he wasn't interested. Donald O'Connor was going to take it, but he put his back out so it went to Kaye • Neither Kaye nor Crosby were keen to think of themselves as Number Two, so the production was riven by almost interminable arguments • The song 'White

Christmas' was first used in *Holiday Inn*. Irving Berlin presented the Oscar for best song that year and opened the envelope to find that the winner was himself! It only happened one other time, to Walt Disney • 'White Christmas' is the best-selling record ever, with well over 30m bought • This was the first film made in the new widescreen VistaVision process, which produces rich, high-quality colour images.

White Heat

★★★★ 1949 114min b/w

Director: Raoul Walsh
Screenplay: Ivan Goff & Ben Roberts
Source: Story by Virginia Kellogg

A policeman infiltrates the gang of a psychotic mother-fixated mobster. This is still one of the all-time great gangster movies, thanks partly to a script packed with action and sharp dialogue but still more to the great performance from Jimmy Cagney. Not quite as shocking as when it first came out, but still pretty exciting, it's topped by one of the most famous moments in the history of movies, with Cagney shouting out to his dead mother from the top of an oil refinery. Unmissable.

Cody Jarrett . . . . .James Cagney
Vic Pardo/Hank Fallon . . . . . . .Edmond O'Brien
Verna Jarrett . . . . .Virginia Mayo
Ma Jarrett . . . . .Margaret Wycherly
Big Ed Somers . . . . .Steve Cochran
Phillip Evans . . . . .John Archer
Cotton Valetti . . . . .Wally Cassell
The Trader . . . . .Fred Clark
Roy Parker . . . . .Paul Guilfoyle

Quote 'Made it, Ma! Top of the world!' [Last line]

Psst! The inspiration for Cagney's character was the real-life gangster Arthur 'Doc' Barker, with Wycherley playing the 'Ma' Barker role • Cagney improvised the scene where he gets on his mother's lap. He and Walsh were surprised when the censors allowed it through.

White Palace

★★★ 1990 105min

Director: Luis Mandoki
Screenplay: Ted Tally & Alvin Sargent

Young yuppie Spader is feeling low until he's picked up by sexy older Sarandon. Can their relationship survive the difference in their social and ethnic backgrounds? Although a little unbelievable in places, the superb performances from the leads sweep us along in this often sexy love story with a difference.

Nora Baker . . . . .Susan Sarandon
Max Baron . . . . .James Spader
Neil . . . . .Jason Alexander
Rosemary .Kathy Bates
Judy . . . . .Eileen Brennan
Sol Horowitz .Steven Hill

Blurb The Story Of A Younger Man And A Bolder Woman.

Quote 'We get naked and touch each other and you get inside me and you can't tell me how much *rent* you pay?

OOPS! Although the electricity is off, the little light in the fridge still comes on when the door is opened.

Psst! Sarandon added 20 pounds for the part.

Who Framed Roger Rabbit?

★★★ 1988 103min c.

Director: Robert Zemeckis
Screenplay: Jeffrey Price & Peter S. Seaman
Source: Novel, *Who Censored Roger Rabbit?* by Gary K. Wolf

...or *Who Rogered Jessica Rabbit*, as some wags had it. In 40s Los Angeles, cartoon characters exist alongside humans. When Roger is accused of murder, he turns to private eye Hoskins for help. Despite the presence of the sexiest cartoon character ever in Jessica Rabbit, it's mainly worth watching to admire the technical achievement, rather than the lacklustre story. You never really get involved in what's going on, although Hoskins does his best when you consider that he was acting against thin air for much of the time.

Eddie Valiant . . . . .Bob Hoskins
Judge Doom . . . . .Christopher Lloyd
Dolores . . . . .Joanna Cassidy
Marvin Acme . . . . .Stubby Kaye
R. K. Maroon . . . . .Alan Tilvern
Raoul, the director . . . . .Joel Silver
Roger .Charles Fleischer
Jessica (speaking) . . . . .Kathleen Turner
Jessica (singing) . . . . .Amy Irving
Baby Herman . . . . .Lou Hirsch
Daffy Duck . . . . .Mel Blanc
Singing Sword . . . . .Frank Sinatra

Quote 'I'm not bad. I'm just drawn that way.'
• 'My problem is that I got a fifty-year lust and a three-year-old dinkie.' • 'I love you more than any woman's ever loved a rabbit.'

Psst! At the time, the most expensive film ever made, with a cost of $70m • The book's title was *Who Censored Roger Rabbit?*, appropriately perhaps as a momentary flash of her boobs by Betty Boop was excised by the studio from the video version. However, slow down the moment early on when Baby Herman storms off the set and through a woman's legs and you'll see something the studio probably wishes had been cut out • On the laserdisc, as Jessica is thrown out of the taxi she's riding in with Hoskins, her dress rides up and, as *Variety* tastefully put it: 'You can see right down Broadway.' • Felix and Popeye refused to appear, claiming that the $5,000 on offer wasn't enough • To help Hoskins, Fleischer wore a rabbit costume for the four months he did Roger's voice. For much of the time, Hoskins was acting on his own. He claimed for a time afterwards to be suffering from cartoon hallucinations • 743 people were credited on the film, a record • In Golders Green, a storm changed the title at one cinema to *Who Framed Roger Rabbi?* • The exterior of the Acme factory is actually London Transport's Shepherd's Bush bus depot • The director of the film at the beginning is Joel Silver, producer of some of the best action pictures of the past decade.

The Whole Town's Talking

★★★ 1935 95min b/w

Director: John Ford
Screenplay: Jo Swerling & Robert Riskin
Source: Novel by W.R. Burnett

A meek shop clerk is the spitting image of a gangster who has just been released from prison. After discovering the resemblance, the mobster uses it for his own ends, kidnapping the poor sap's aunt and the girl he loves to ensure his cooperation. Edward G. Robinson proved he had a gift for comedy, albeit of the black kind, in this superb movie which is all the more fascinating for being so untypical both of its leading star and its director.

Arthur Jones/Killer Mannion	Edward G. Robinson
'Bill' Clark	Jean Arthur
Det. Sgt. Boyle	Arthur Hohl
Healy	Wallace Ford

D.A. Spencer	A.S. Byron
Hoyt	Donald Meek
J.G. Carpenter	Paul Harvey
'Slugs' Martin	Edward Brophy
Seaver	Etienne Girardot
Det. Sgt. Pat Howe	James Donlan
Warden	J. Farrell MacDonald

Who's Afraid of Virginia Woolf?

★★★ 1966 129min b/w

Director: Mike Nichols
Screenplay: Ernest Lehman
Source: Play by Edward Albee

The barometer in Burton and Taylor's living room reads stormy and the pressure is falling. This far from cosy campus couple invite Seagal and Dennis back for a nightcap and, as the sparks fly, the language becomes stronger than the drink. Although the four-letter words won't make chins drop as they once did, this pitch-black comedy still has plenty of bite left in it. You could hardly call it an uplifting experience, but you can't deny that you've witnessed some pretty amazing acting...always assuming Burton and Taylor *were* actually acting.

Martha	Elizabeth Taylor
George	Richard Burton
Nick	George Segal
Honey	Sandy Dennis

Oscars Sandy Dennis, Elizabeth Taylor

Blurb You Are Cordially Invited To George And Martha's For An Evening Of Fun And Games.

Quote 'Martha, will you show her where we keep the...er...euphemism?' • 'I swear, if you existed I'd divorce you.' • 'Musical beds is the faculty sport around here.'

Psst! The play was so full of vitriol and bad language that it had even managed the difficult feat of shocking seasoned New York theatregoers. It was assumed by everyone that it would be diluted considerably for the screen. But after initially being denied the Seal of the Production Code, Jack Warner threw his weight behind the film and persuaded them to pass it, even arguing for the inclusion of words like 'bastard' and 'bitch'. It was, however, the first film to get the new American rating of R, meaning that nobody under 18 could see it without a parent or guardian • Lehman so loved the play that he could hardly bear to change any of it. Legend has it that his contribution was just 27 words, four of which were: 'Screenplay by Ernest Lehman'. When Albee read it, his reponse was: '27 words, all bad.' • Albee's choice for the leads had been James Mason and Bette Davis • Robert Redford and Jack Lemmon were among the actors who had turned down the movie • Out of a total budget of $5m, $1m went to each of the Burtons • Part of the movie's success was undoubtedly due to the public's fascination with the details of the Burtons' private life, which was known to be every bit as tempestuous as that depicted on screen • Sandy Dennis was pregnant during filming but lost the baby afterwards • This was Mike Nichols' directorial debut.

The Wicked Lady

★ 1945 104min b/w

Director: Leslie Arliss
Screenplay: Leslie Arliss
Source: Novel, *The Life and Death of the Wicked Lady Skelton* by Magdalen King-Hall

A lady of noble birth slums it, becoming a high-wayman in the company of the nasty Mason. This costume drama was the most successful of the Gainsborough films but is so badly made, falling down in almost all departments, that it holds little interest now. A remake by Michael Winner in 1983 was, despite displaying rather more female flesh, even less enticing.

Barbara . . . . .Margaret Lockwood
Capt. Jerry Jackson . . . . .James Mason
Caroline . . . . .Patricia Roc
Sir Ralph Skelton . . . . .Griffith Jones
Kit Locksby . . . . .Michael Rennie
Hogarth . . . . .Felix Aylmer
Doxy . . . . .Jean Kent
Agatha Trimble . . . . .Martita Hunt

Psst! Many scenes had to be reshot for the American market because Margaret Lockwood was displaying a slight cleavage which would not have got past the censors • In Britain, despite the implication of sex outside marriage, no cuts were called for.

The Wicker Man

★★★ 1973 87min c.

Director: Robin Hardy
Screenplay: Anthony Shaffer

A strange cult has taken to worshipping a little-known but wonderful early 70s movie. Their influence appears to be growing and almost everyone who comes into contact with the film succumbs. A God-fearing policeman visits a remote Scottish island to investigate the reported disappearance of a young girl. He is dismayed to find the islanders follow a pagan religion which places a heavy emphasis on sex and nudity. He comes to believe that the girl is going to be sacrificed. Sadly, the film is poorly directed, with production values no higher than the drama output of a badly-equipped local TV station. There is also some pretty dreadful music, a throwback to the hippyish 60s, to contend with. But the film overcomes these drawbacks and establishes a truly eerie atmosphere. It is compulsive viewing, building up strongly to a memorable and harrowing final scene. Genuinely unsettling, this is the sort of film whose images stay with you long afterwards.

Sgt. Neil Howie . . . . .Edward Woodward
Lord Summerisle . . . . .Christopher Lee
Willow MacGregor . . . . .Britt Ekland
Miss Rose . . . . .Diane Cilento
Librarian . . . . .Ingrid Pitt
Alder MacGregor . . . . .Lindsay Kemp
Harbourmaster . . . . .Russell Waters
Old Gardener/Gravedigger . . . . .Aubrey Morris

Psst! With an unsuccessful marketing campaign the film, which was butchered by the distributors to just 87 minutes, disappeared from view on its initial release and only came to be sought out after Christopher Lee said that he gives his best performance of his career here • The original version of 103 minutes has now been restored in America. Sadly, most prints in Britain, including the latest video release, are in the truncated form, which misses the events of entire night • Singer Rod Stewart is said to have tried to obtain the negative of the film, so that he could destroy the nude performance of his girlfriend of the time, Britt Ekland.

The Wild Bunch

★★★★ 1969 144min c.

Director: Sam Peckinpah
Screenplay: Walon Green & Sam Peckinpah

After a failed armed robbery, a group of old-fashioned outlaws arrange one more do-or-die job so that they can retire. This film, set against the background of the Mexican Revolution, aroused enormous controversy over the extent of the violence, which pushed the already bulging envelope out still further. It is easy to agree with Peckinpah that, unlike some of his other films, the movie is about violence rather than being violent for violence's sake. Those scenes will give few viewers pause for thought now and the film remains an elegiac sunset Western with some great action scenes. The atmosphere and detail is so rich that it is hard at times to remember that you are watching a movie rather than real life.

Pike Bishop	William Holden
Dutch Engstrom	Ernest Borgnine
Deke Thornton	Robert Ryan
Sykes	Edmond O'Brien
Lyle Gorch	Warren Oates
Hector Gorch	Ben Johnson
Angel	Jaime Sanchez
Coffer	Strother Martin
T.C.	L.Q. Jones
Menacing man	Albert Dekker
Kid outlaw	Bo Hopkins
Wainscoat	Dub Taylor

Quote 'It ain't like it used to be, but it'll do.'

OOPS! A sniper shoots O'Brien in the right thigh, and he limps off out of the film for a while. When he comes back just before the closing credits, the filthy bandage is on his *left* thigh.

Psst! After the film was shown to reviewers in the United States it was cut heavily by the studio while Sam Peckinpah was away on holiday. Although the previews had been positive, it appears the studio wanted a shorter film so that it could make more at the box office. Sadly, the sections cut out meant that the film was less intelligible • The longer version has been restored and is now easy to get hold of. Peckinpah has also added another 10 minutes to a new director's cut which adds little to the movie but is worth watching because sound and vision have both been greatly improved. Quite why the blood looks like paint in the director's cut remains a mystery • When the director's cut was shown to the censors in 1992, they threatened to give it an NC-17 certificate, the kiss of death in American cinemas, even though it had only been an R in 1969 and no scenes of violence had been added. The battle over its certificate lasted until late 1994 before it was allowed to keep the R rating • It is said that more blank ammunition was fired during the making of

film than live ammunition was used in the entire Mexican Revolution of 1914 • 12,000 Red Harvester ants and 12 grey scorpions were imported to the Mexican location from Hollywood • Alfonso Arau, one of Mapache's lieutenants, later became a director of films such as *Like Water for Chocolate* and *A Walk in the Clouds*. At the time of writing, he is preparing a sequel to *The Wild Bunch* called *The Greaser*.

The Wild One
★★ 1953 79min b/w

Director: Laslo Benedek
Screenplay: John Paxton
Source: Magazine story, *The Cyclists' Raid* by Frank Rooney

A group of motorcyclists led by leather-jacketed Brando ride into a small town and find that the local residents aren't exactly laying out the red carpet. Not only the first biker pic, but also – two years ahead of *Rebel Without a Cause* – the first movie which explored the subject of alienated youth. It looks a little dated and tame now, but while the narrative doesn't really go anywhere, it is hard to take your eyes off the early Brando.

Johnny	Marlon Brando
Kathie	Mary Murphy
Harry Bleeker	Robert Keith
Chino	Lee Marvin
Sheriff Singer	Jay C. Flippen
Mildred	Peggy Maley
Frank Bleeker	Ray Teal

Quote 'What are you rebelling against?' – What have you got?'

Psst! Although its is usually womens' fashions that are inspired by the movies, it was Brando's look here that started the wearing of zipped leather jackets • The film was based on a true incident in 1947 when the small Californian town of Hollister was taken over for the 4th of July holiday weekend by a gang of 4,000 bikers who trashed the place • To Brando's disgust, much of the gritty dialogue, which was what had made him want to do the film in the first place, was taken out before filming began • He prepared for his role by mixing with bike gangs and drove his own motorbike in the movie • In Britain, the censors thought the film encouraged antisocial behaviour by young people and the movie was banned until 1968.

Wild Target
★★★★ 1993 87min c.

Director: Pierre Salvadori
Screenplay: Pierre Salvadori

When an anally-retentive French assassin takes on an apprentice, he finds his well-ordered life is thrown upside down. With Rochefort's inimitable comic performance complementing an out-standingly witty script, this is an incredibly funny and inventive black comedy. It probably won't be too long before Hollywood gets round to a remake of this amazing French film. How could they possibly improve on such brilliance? The French title is *Cible Émouvante*.

Victor Meynard	Jean Rochefort
Renée Dandrieux	Marie Trintignant
Antoine	Guillaume Depardieu
Mme. Meynard	Patachou

Quote 'How heavy are you?'

Psst! No prizes for guessing who Guillaume Depardieu's father is.

Winchester '73
★★★ 1950 92min b/w

Director: Anthony Mann
Screenplay: Robert L. Richards & Borden Chase
Source: Story by Stuart N. Lake

Stewart has a rifle that he won in a shooting contest stolen from him. Rather than claim on the insurance and risk losing his no-claims bonus, he goes after the thief, pursuing him with a relentless, obsessive determination. Seen by some as the first 'psychological' Western, even if you don't want to look too far beneath the surface it still comes across as one of the classic manhunt movies. Great stuff.

Lin McAdam	James Stewart
Lola Manners	Shelley Winters
Waco Johnnie Dean	Dan Duryea
Dutch Henry Brown	Stephen McNally
Johnny 'High Spade' Williams	Millard Mitchell
Steve Miller	Charles Drake
Joe Lamont	John McIntire
Wyatt Earp	Will Geer
Sgt. Wilkes	Jay C. Flippen
Young Bull	Rock Hudson
Jack Riker	John Alexander
Latigo Means	Abner Biberman
Wesley	Steve Brodie
Doan	Tony Curtis

Psst! This was the film that revived the Western genre in the 50s and was the first collaboration between Stewart and Mann • Among the bit players are Rock Hudson, who plays an Indian, and Tony Curtis, who plays a soldier.

The Winslow Boy
★★★ 1948 117min b/w

Director: Anthony Asquith
Screenplay: Terence Rattigan & Anatole de Grunwald
Source: Play by Rattigan

In pre-World War I days, a naval cadet is accused of stealing a postal order. Now he'd be sent for a period of adjustment in Barbados. But in harsher days, he was expelled. Father Hardwicke rifles his savings to hire Donat, the top lawyer in the country, to clear his son's name. Based on a true-life case, a splendid cast turn this into a fascinating and stirring court-room drama.

Sir Robert Morton	Robert Donat
Catherine Winslow	Margaret Leighton
Arthur Winslow	Cedric Hardwicke
Attorney General	Francis L. Sullivan
John Watherstone	Frank Lawton
Dickie Winslow	Jack Watling
Esmond Curry	Basil Radford
Violet	Kathleen Harrison
Ronnie Winslow	Neil North
Grace Winslow	Marie Lohr
First Lord	Walter Fitzgerald
Also:	Wilfrid Hyde-White, Ernest Thesiger

Winter Kills
★★★ 1979 97min c.

Director: William Richert
Screenplay: William Richert
Source: Novel by Richard Condon

The ultimate conspiracy theory about the Kennedy assassination, and a parody of all con-spiracy thrillers. The younger son of shot president Kegan hears a deathbed confession from a gunman and, as he investigates the claims, people die mysteriously. The film's unpolished feel was due to an 11th hour funding withdrawal – another conspiracy perhaps? – but the film takes satirical potshots at every American sacred cow. The stellar cast is to die for. Half the length of *JFK*, this is just as plausi-ble and twice the fun.

Nick Kegan	Jeff Bridges
Pa Kegan	John Huston
John Ceruti	Anthony Perkins
Z.K. Dawson	Sterling Hayden
Joe Diamond	Eli Wallach
Emma Kegan	Dorothy Malone
Frank Mayo	Tomas Milian
Keifitz	Richard Boone
Lola Comante	Elizabeth Taylor
Yvette Malone	Belinda Bauer
Gameboy Baker	Ralph Meeker

Psst! Richert had never directed before, but he managed to get John Huston, Anthony Perkins, Jeff Bridges and Elizabeth Taylor to commit to the movie in writing so that he could raise funds • Just a week before filming was due to be completed, the studio shut the movie down without explanation. Richert continued off his own bat but the film was never distributed properly • He re-edited the film in 1983 and put back the original ending which had been changed, since when its reputation has kept rising • The efficent PA Rosemary is played by Gladys Hill, for many years John Huston's assistant and co-scriptwriter.

Witness

★★★★ 1985 112min c.

Director: Peter Weir
Screenplay: Earl W. Wallace & William Kelley

A young boy witnesses a killing and, when cop Ford realises his boss is involved, they take refuge in the lad's Amish community. How refreshing to come across a completely new background for a thriller. Weir spins a superb, steadily tension-tightening yarn as he contrasts the violent outside world with the peaceful Amish and brings Ford together with McGillis in an obviously doomed romance. Excellent, eminently rewatchable, stuff.

John Book	Harrison Ford
Rachel	Kelly McGillis
Schaeffer	Josef Sommer
Samuel	Lukas Haas
Eli Lapp	Jan Rubes
Daniel Hochleitner	Alexander Godunov
McFee	Danny Glover

Quote 'You never had your hands on a teat before?' – 'Not one this big.' • 'You be careful out among them English.'

OOPS! As Godunov goes into the room at the wake to commiserate with McGillis, there's a very prominent mike boom • The train leaving the station appears to be a different one from that which pulled in. This is most obvious just after Godunov is showing off by standing on the wagon • Odd, isn't it, how the Amish come at the double when the bell rings but don't notice the earlier gunfire?

Psst! Having Ford work at the carpentry bench is an in-joke. Before making it as an actor, he was a carpenter by trade and it's still his hobby • The Amish community wanted nothing to do with the film. Their religion forbids them either to be photographed or to watch movies. McGillis did live briefly with an Amish family to study the life and the accent, but she was turfed out when they discovered why she was there.

Witness for the Prosecution

★★★ 1957 114min c.

Director: Billy Wilder
Screenplay: Billy Wilder & Harry Kurnitz
Source: Novel and play by Agatha Christie

A QC who is supposed to have given up on medical grounds can't resist getting involved on the defence side in a murder case where, there being no butler, everything clearly points to the accused having done it. There can't be many Agatha Christie adaptations where one of the cast plays the accordian and sings, but why have Dietrich and not show off her legs? Not all the performances are up to scratch, but the plot is one of Christie's best and Wilder makes the courtroom stuff fairly whizz along.

Leonard Vole	Tyrone Power
Christine Vole	Marlene Dietrich
Sir Wilfrid Robarts	Charles Laughton
Miss Plimsoll	Elsa Lanchester
Brogan-Moore	John Williams
Mayhew	Henry Daniell
Carter	Ian Wolfe
Janet MacKenzie	Una O'Connor
Mr. Meyers	Torin Thatcher
Judge	Francis Compton

Quote 'If I'd known how much you talked, I'd never have come out of my coma.'

Psst! Dietrich was taught in the felicities of the Cockney twang by Laughton • This was Tyrone Power's last movie • The courtroom of the Old Bailey was meticulously reconstructed using the plans of the original • Agatha Christie said this was the first decent movie that had been made from one of her stories.

The Wizard of Oz

★★★ 1939 101min c&b/w

Director: Victor Fleming
Screenplay: Noel Langley, Florence Ryerson &
Edgar Allan Woolf
Source: Book by Frank L. Baum

An unhappy girl runs away to the fantasy world
of Oz and searches for happiness at the end of
the Yellow Brick Road. Surely the fondness so
many feel for this musical has more to do with
nostalgia for a simpler age than anything else?
Some of the minor songs are exceptionally dull
while the storyline and humour will seem banal
in the extreme to all but the youngest children.
Still, there are some neat performances and the
good songs, like 'Somewhere Over the
Rainbow' and 'We're Off to See the Wizard' really are humdingers. Bearing in mind how hard it
is to find people who don't think this is one of
the greatest films ever made, perhaps those of
us who aren't friends of Dorothy ought to form
an Enemies of Dorothy support group?

Dorothy . . . . .Judy Garland
Prof. Marvel/Wizard . . . . .Frank Morgan
Hunk/Scarecrow . . . . .Ray Bolger
Zeke/Cowardly Lion . . . . .Bert Lahr
Hickory/The Tin Man . . . . .Jack Haley
Glinda . . . . .Billie Burke
Miss Gulch/Wicked Witch . . .Margaret Hamilton
Uncle Henry . . . . .Charley Grapewin
Auntie Em . . . . .Clara Blandick

Quote 'Toto, I've a feeling we're not in Kansas
anymore.' • 'I'll get you, my pretty, and your little
dog too!' • 'Hearts will never be practical until
they can be made unbreakable.' • 'Surrender
Dorothy or die.' • 'Pay no attention to that man
behind the curtain. The…er…great Oz has
spoken!' • 'Toto, we're home! Home! And this is
my room…and you're all here! And I'm not
going to leave here ever, ever again…because
I love you all and, oh, Aunt Em…there's *no*
place like home. [Last line]

OOPS! There are umpteen boo-boo's to pick
from. Among the most obvious is Auntie Em's
lack of mathmatical ability when she's counting
the chickens with Dorothy early on • After
Hamilton exits for the first time, one of the
female Munchkin shouts 'Judy' instead of
'Dorothy' as she runs to her • Dorothy's hair is a
source of continual fascination, switching as it
does between resting on her shoulders,
reaching down to her waist and points in
between • During the tornado, although
Dorothy's bed is thrown all over the place, the

bottles on the table remain immobile • Brainy
the Scarecrow may be when it all ends happily
ever after. But that doesn't make him right
when he claims: 'The sum of the square roots
of any two sides of an isosceles triangle is
equal to the square root of the remaining side.'
It only works for right-angled triangles • When
Dorothy chases the Tin Man, she drops the oil
can. But it reappears in her basket later • When
they're singing 'We're Off to See the Wizard',
someone can be glimpsed in the background
dodging about, presumably one of the crew.

Psst! Both Shirley Temple and Deanna Durbin
were considered for the part before Garland.
Fox refused to lend Temple to MGM after the
prearranged swap with Clark Gable and Jean
Harlow fell through when Harlow died • Garland
was ordered by the studio to fast every other
day so that the 16-year-old would pass for 11.
She was also heavily corseted so that her
increasingly prominent breasts wouldn't be
visible • *Over the Rainbow* was added to the
film very late on and, after previews, was
ordered by the men in suits to be taken out
again. Associate producer Arthur Freed said:
'The song stays – or I go! It's as simple as that.'
He stayed, the song stayed, and it won the
Oscar for Best Song • Although the movie was
very popular, children's tickets were much
cheaper than for adults and the film took 20
years for it to make back its costs, through
becoming a favourite on TV. To be fair, MGM
had always thought of it as a prestige film
anyway, rather than one which would wow them
in Wyoming • In New York on the day of opening
15,000 people were queueing to see it by eight
in the morning • Director Richard Thorpe was
replaced by Victor Fleming after two weeks,
with King Vidor coming in for the last week to
do the black and white sequences. Fleming had
been called to *Gone With the Wind* to replace
George Cukor • Garland got paid just $500 a
week. About the only featured player who got
less was Terry, the Cairn Terrier playing Toto.
He was on $125 a week • Initially Garland was
told to play the part in a blonde wig and heavy,
doll-like make-up • Frank Morgan was drunk
much of the time, keeping the libations coming
from a briefcase in which he kept hidden the
ingredients of a good martini • The part of the
wizard was offered to W.C. Fields, but he
turned it down when they wouldn't pay him
enough • Buddy Ebsen was originally to have
played the Scarecrow and Ray Bolger the Tin
Man. Bolger persuaded Ebsen to change parts,
but Ebsen's lungs became inflamed from the
metallic paint and he had to spend six weeks in

an iron lung, suffering breathing difficulties for the rest of his life. His voice can still be heard in 'Off to See the Wizard'. The make-up process was changed, but Haley, his replacement, was not told what had happened to Ebsen until after filming finished. Ebsen is now best known for playing Jed Clampett in the TV sitcom *The Beverly Hillbillies* • Haley's son, Jack Haley Jr., married Liza Minnelli, Judy Garland's daughter, in 1974. They divorced four years later • The film-makers had planned painting the horse that takes our heroes to the Emerald City. But animal groups found out and protested. So the horses used had to be covered with coloured gelatine. Unfortunately, the animals loved the stuff and kept licking it off • Margaret Hamilton got badly burnt by a special effect which went wrong as she was supposed to vanish. She was hospitalised for a month and, considering that she was completely engulfed in flame, she was lucky it wasn't worse. The take that went wrong is the one that's used in the movie. When she returned to work, she refused to do any scenes in which fire was involved. Her stand-in, Betty Danko, did the broomstick ride for her. There was an explosion and Danko was burnt and hospitalised, with her legs scarred • Bert Lahr grumbled that after the film: 'I was typecast as a lion-and there aren't all that many parts for lions.' The suit he wears is made out of real lion skin • Garland remembered Bolger, Lahr and Haley unkindly, finding them unfriendly and prone to stealing scenes, although they later remembered things differently • In addition, she had to contend with being groped and propositioned by the midgets playing the Munchkins • When the Munchkins sing out 'Ding, dong, the Witch is dead' after the Wicked Witch of the East is killed, some of them improvised. In rushes, it was discovered that they had used the word 'bitch' instead of 'witch' and the proper words had to be over-dubbed • The tornado was created by swirling, not a lady's stocking as some have said, but a 35-foot muslin wind sock in front of the camera • One of the four identical pairs of ruby slippers was sold in 1988 for $165,000. In 1970, a pair had gone for $15,000 • Of all the bizarre facts about the movie, two stand out. Professor Marvel's coat was discovered in a second-hand store. After wearing it for some time, Frank Morgan found a label saying 'L. Frank Baum' inside. Suspecting a prank, they contacted the tailor and Baum's widow. Both confirmed the coat had indeed belonged to the author of *The Wizard of Oz* • Persistent rumours that a man committed suicide on the set and that his body can be seen on the left as Dorothy, The Tin Man

and the Scarecrow walk down the Yellow Brick Road after meeting the Wicked Witch are untrue. The object is actually an exotic bird • The restored print has the Kansas scenes in sepia, rather than the more familiar black and white most of us are used to • On the day Judy Garland died, June 23rd 1969, there was a tornado in Kansas • The movie wasn't seen in East Germany until 1989, 50 years after its release • The 46 years it took for the sequel, *Return to Oz*, to turn up in 1985 is a record.

The Woman in the Window
★★★ 1944 99min b/w

Director: Fritz Lang
Screenplay: Nunnally Johnson
Source: Novel, *Once Off Guard* by J.H. Wallis

Married professor Robinson makes the mistake of having a chat with gorgeous Bennett. Before he knows it he's up to his neck in a nasty murder case. What makes it worse, his friend Massey is investigating the crime. This tasty little film noir has Robinson excelling in a role a little out of the ordinary for him. Bennett is suitably alluring as the woman innocently responsible for it all. Opinion is divided over whether the ending is a cop-out or a sweet little coda.

Prof. Richard Wanley	Edward G. Robinson
Alice Reed	Joan Bennett
District Attorney	Raymond Massey
Heidt	Dan Duryea
Dr. Barkstone	Edmond Breon
Police Inspector	Thomas Jackson
Mazard	Arthur Loft
Mrs. Wanley	Dorothy Peterson

Woman of the Year
★★★ 1942 112min b/w

Director: George Stevens
Screenplay: Ring Lardner Jr. & Michael Kanin

Sports writer Tracy and famous columnist Hepburn wage war on each other through their newspaper writing but they get on far better in person. However, their relationship is not on the firmest of ground. She knows nothing of sport and even less of domestic science while he thinks a woman's place should be in the home. It's hardly PC, but the script is generally witty and lively. It might not be their best film together, but there's a magic between them you won't find in many other movie pairings.

Sam Craig	Spencer Tracy
Tess Harding	Katharine Hepburn
Ellen Whitcomb	Fay Bainter
Clayton	Reginald Owen
Pinkie Peters	William Bendix
William Harding	Minor Watson
Phil Whittaker	Roscoe Karns
Gerald	Dan Tobin
Flo Peters	Gladys Blake
Ellis	William Tannen
Matron at refugee home	Sara Haden
Reporter	Jimmy Conlin
Reporter	Ray Teal

Oscars Best Screenplay

Quote 'You know, it's too bad I'm not covering this dinner of yours tonight, because I've got an angle that would really be sensational. The outstanding woman of the year isn't a woman at all.'

Psst! This was the first teaming of Hepburn and Tracy, a partnership that would last for 25 years and end just before Tracy's death with *Guess Who's Coming to Dinner* • When the movie started, Hepburn was dating director Stephens. But the end, she had switched to Tracy. Although the pair became lovers and remained so until Tracy died, the Hollywood gossip columnists never mentioned it once • The film was based partly on the life of famous American columnist Dorothy Thompson • The film was Hepburn's idea and she picked up not only an extraordinarily attractive salary, but also the choice of director and co-star. She wouldn't consider anybody else but Tracy • At their first meeting Hepburn, five feet seven inches plus her four-inch heels, towered over her future co-star and lover. 'I'm afraid I'm a little tall for you, Mr. Tracy,' she is alleged to have said. Producer Joseph Mankiewicz told her, 'Don't worry, he'll cut you down to size.' • Hepburn hated the scene where she has to play at being a housewife and show Tracy she can cook, but it stayed in despite her protestations.

The Women

★★★ 1939 132min c&b/w

Director: George Cukor
Screenplay: Anita Loos & Jane Murfin
Source: Play by Clare Boothe Luce

An all-women cast have considerable fun with Clare Booth Luce's witty and caustic play. Although the women seem to be interested in little other than how they, their friends and their enemies are getting on with men – their own and others' – the catty dialogue is a dream. The opening credits, with each actress paired with an animal, are pretty famous on their own.

Mary Haines	Norma Shearer
Crystal Allen	Joan Crawford
Sylvia Fowler	Rosalind Russell
Countess de Lave	Mary Boland
Miriam Aarons	Paulette Goddard
Peggy Day	Joan Fontaine
Mrs. Moorhead	Lucile Watson
Edith Potter	Phyllis Povah
Little Mary	Virginia Weidler
Miss Watts	Ruth Hussey
Mrs. Wagstaff	Margaret Dumont
Lucy	Marjorie Main
Ingrid	Esther Dale
Dolly de Peyster	Hedda Hopper

Also: Mary Beth Hughes, Butterfly McQueen

Blurb 135 Women With Men On Their Minds!

Quote 'L'amour, l'amour. Toujours l'amour!' • 'She's got those eyes that run up and down men like a searchlight.' • 'You know, the first man that can think up a good explanation how he can be in love with his wife *and* another woman is going to win that prize they're always giving out in Sweden.' • 'Don't you believe in marriage?' – 'Sure I do - for women. But it's the sons of Adam that they gotta marry.' • 'I hate to tell you, dear, but your skin makes the Rocky Mountains look like chiffon velvet.' • 'Say, can you beat him? He almost stood me up for his wife!' • 'There's a name for you ladies, but it isn't used in high society – outside of a kennel.'

Psst! With three stars whose egos matched their box office status, billing precedence wasn't the only source of squabbling. Even the order in which Crawford, Russell and Shearer were called to the set created difficulties. Director Cukor had to call them over the tannoy so they could arrive together. When this went wrong on one tempestuous occasion, they had to switch to getting messengers to knock simultaneously on the three stars' doors • Although it had been a hit Broadway play which ran to 666 performances, Povah and Main were the only members of the cast who had also played in it on stage • In addition to the all-woman cast, the books in the library scene were by women writers, all the art objects were by women and even the animals, apparently, were female only • F. Scott Fitzgerald worked, uncredited, on the screenplay • Cukor disliked the idea of the Technicolor fashion show but was overruled by the front office.

Women in Love
★★ 1969 130min c.

Director: Ken Russell
Screenplay: Larry Kramer
Source: Novel by D.H. Lawrence

A group of actors talk about sex and love a great deal, take their 20s clothes off, run through cornfields, wrestle naked and make love. It's based on D.H. Lawrence, so it must be art. But it's made by Ken Russell, so it must irritate the life out of us. Although as pretty as a shampoo commercial in places, it's also pretentious, confusing and occasionally unintentionally funny. It was followed in 1989 by a prequel, *The Rainbow*, in which Jackson plays the mother of her character in this film.

Rupert Birkin .Alan Bates
Gerald Crich . . . . .Oliver Reed
Gudrun Brangwen . . . . .Glenda Jackson
Ursula Brangwen . . . . .Jennie Linden
Hermione Roddice . . . . .Eleanor Bron
Thomas Crich . . . . .Alan Webb
Tom Brangwen . . . . .Michael Gough
Loerke .Vladek Sheybal
Minister . . . . .James Laurenson

Oscars Glenda Jackson

Quote 'How are your thighs? Are they strong? Because I want to drown in hot, physical, naked flesh.' • 'They should take all the pretentious dialogue off the soundtrack and call it *Women in Heat*. [Critic Rex Reed]

Psst! This was the first film openly to show full frontal male nudity. According to some sources, Oliver Reed felt slightly concerned at the relative attributes of Alan Bates and himself and, er, revived the memory of J. Arthur Rank before the famous scene. It's certainly true that the pair got horrendously drunk the night before to calm their nerves • The censors insisted on blurring the scene slightly • Russell later said that he should have turned the whole thing into a musical and claimed that 'it wasn't far off in some ways.'

Working Girl
★★★★ 1988 113min c.

Director: Mike Nichols
Screenplay: Kevin Wade

Griffith is superb as the ambitious secretary who discovers that new boss Weaver has been passing off her ideas as her own. Taking advantage of Weaver's absence, she latches onto banker Ford as her key to doing the deal herself. It's pointless carping that the business machinations aren't realistic. Just sit back and enjoy one of the funniest, sharpest and liveliest fairy tales of the decade. And, while we're at it, three cheers for Cusack for her wonderful supporting performance.

Tess McGill . . . . .Melanie Griffith
Jack Trainer . . . . .Harrison Ford
Katharine Parker . . . . .Sigourney Weaver
Cyn . . . . .Joan Cusack
Mick Dugan . . . . .Alec Baldwin
Oren Trask . . . . .Philip Bosco
Ginny . . . . .Nora Dunn
Lutz . . . . .Oliver Platt
Also: James Lally, Kevin Spacey, Robert Easton, Olympia Dukakis, Ricki Lake

Quote 'I've a head for business and a bod for sin.' • 'Sometimes I sing and dance around my house in my underwear. Doesn't make me Madonna. Never will.' • 'Can I get you anything? Coffee? Tea? Me?' • 'Never burn bridges. Today's junior prick, tomorrow's senior partner.'

OOPS! The electronic tickertape in stockbrokers' offices is derived directly from the New York Stock Exchange and can't be tapped into in the way that Griffith does in the movie.

Psst! When Weaver returns to New York with her leg in plaster, she is carrying a giant stuffed gorilla. Her previous film had been *Gorillas in the Mist*, released in the States just three months earlier • Ricki Lake appears in a bit part as a bridesmaid.

Written on the Wind
★★★★ 1956 99min c.

Director: Douglas Sirk
Screenplay: George Zuckerman
Source: Novel by Robert Wilder

The best of Douglas Sirk's glossy melodramas, anticipating the tacky glamour of *Dallas* by 20 years and with a deliciously subversive undercurrent the TV soaps never aspired to. Rich kid Robert Stack has marriage problems with Lauren Bacall, while nymphomaniac kid sister Dorothy Malone vents her frustrated passion for Rock Hudson by picking up men on the wrong side of town. Dazzling decor, lurid Technicolor and blatant phallic imagery make for compelling kitsch.

Mitch Wayne	Rock Hudson
Lucy Moore Hadley	Lauren Bacall
Kyle Hadley	Robert Stack
Marylee Hadley	Dorothy Malone
Jasper Hadley	Robert Keith
Biff Miley	Grant Williams
Dan Willis	Robert J. Wilke
Dr. Paul Cochrane	Edward Platt
Hoak Wayne	Harry Shannon
Roy Carter	John Larch
Sam	Roy Glenn
Bertha	Maidie Norman
Reporter	William Schallert

Oscars Dorothy Malone

OOPS! Watch for the shadow when the camera observing the party moves through the open window.

Wuthering Heights

★★★ 1939 103min b/w

Director: William Wyler
Screenplay: Ben Hecht & Charles MacArthur
Source: Novel by Emile Brontë.

The most famous version of Brontë's novel only actually tackles the first half of it. Although it's a little hard now not to find the shouts of 'Cathy' – 'Heathcliff' on the moors amusing, the story of the Yorkshire lass marrying one chap but still fancying her rugged childhood gypsy friend is still a winner. Oberon doesn't seem quite right for the part, but Olivier is fine and it all looks splendid. There are assorted other versions, including Luis Bunuel's in 1954, a creditable British attempt in 1970 and a rather laughable 1992 version.

Cathy Linton	Merle Oberon
Heathcliff	Laurence Olivier
Edgar Linton	David Niven
Ellen Dean	Flora Robson
Dr. Kenneth	Donald Crisp
Hindley Earnshaw	Hugh Williams
Isabella Linton	Geraldine Fitzgerald
Joseph	Leo G. Carroll
Lockwood	Miles Mander
Mr. Earnshaw	Cecil Kellaway

Quote 'What do they know of Heaven and Hell, Cathy, who know nothing of life?' • 'Take me to the window. Let me look at the moors with you once more, my darling.'

OOPS! As she is on her way to meet Heathcliff on the Moors, Cathy's outfit changes completely.

Psst! Olivier was unknown to American audiences of the day until the film made him a star there • Initially Olivier agreed to make the film only if his lover and future wife Vivien Leigh was his co-star. But Oberon had already been signed. Leigh was offered Geraldine Fitzgerald's part but turned it down. In the end, Olivier accepted anyway. Wyler said he was astounded when Leigh said no to the lesser role: 'I told Vivien she was totally unknown in America and that she wouldn't get anything better than Isabella for her first Hollywood part.' • On set, Olivier was brutally unkind to Oberon and refused to talk to her away from the cameras • Studio boss Sam Goldwyn switched the period from the Regency period to the Georgian era, primarily because the womens' costumes would be prettier • Writers Hecht and MacArthur were invited by critic Alexander Woollcott to work on the screenplay in the quiet of his island estate. He was a great fan of the novel, so the pair left fake pages lying around which filled in Heathcliff's progress when away in America, when he became a gunfighter taking on Indians and the like. When Woollcott found the pages, he went ballistic, screaming: 'You vandals! You have raped Emily Brontë!' MacArthur taunted him: 'She's been waiting for it for years.' • Wyler resisted Goldwyn's pleas to make it all a little bit more glamorous. When Goldwyn told him he wanted the final scene to show the two lovers united in heaven, Wyler categorically refused. The scene was shot without him, using doubles • $100,000 was spent transforming the Conejo Hills 50 miles from Hollywood into the Yorkshire Moors. 14,000 tumbleweeds gathered by schoolkids for a cent each were scattered around. Sprinkled with purple sawdust, they resembled heather on film. 1,000 heather plants brought in for more detailed work had to be fumigated and sterilised before being allowed across the state line • Although everyone down to the tea boy now gets a mention on credits, it wasn't always the case. Props guy Irving Sindler used to sneak his name in somehow, here on a gravestone reading: 'I. Sindler. A Good Man' [see also *Dead End* and *Intermezzo*].

Yankee Doodle Dandy

★★★★ 1942 126min b/w

Director: Michael Curtiz
Screenplay: Robert Buckner & Edmund Joseph
Source: Story by Robert Buckner

James Cagney stars as George M. Cohan, one of America's most famous song-and-dance artists. Not only is it not an accurate portrayal of Cohan's life (which biopic is?) but the drama is rather run-of-the-mill and extraordinarily jingoistic. However, the musical numbers are among the greatest ever put on film. Anyone who only know Cagney for his tough guy roles will be astounded by his energy, vitality and skill as a tapdancer and singer. It's amazing to see that, 10 years after becoming typecast as a gangster, he can still get his feet to perform complex tap steps like wings as if he were falling off a log. Mr. Cagney, the critics thank you, the moviegoing public thanks you, and I thank you.

George M. Cohan	James Cagney
Mary	Joan Leslie
Jerry Cohan	Walter Huston
Sam Harris	Richard Whorf
Fay Templeton	Irene Manning
Dietz	George Tobias
Nellie Cohan	Rosemary DeCamp
Josie Cohan	Jeanne Cagney
Schwab	S.Z. "Cuddles" Sakall
Erlanger	George Barbier

Also: Walter Catlett, Eddie Foy Jr.

Oscars James Cagney

Quote 'Ladies and gentlemen, my mother thanks you, my father thanks you, my sister thanks you, and I thank you.'

OOPS! The newspaper photograph of the sinking of the Lusitania shows a ship with two funnels, rather than the correct four • Among the labels on Cagney's luggage is one showing Trafalgar Square's Nelson's Column and reading 'Nelson Square Hotel'.

Psst! This was Cagney's favourite film, winning him his only Oscar. Initially, however, he turned the role down, as did Fred Astaire. It took much persuasion, involving the intervention of Cohan himself, to get Cagney to do it • Cagney had a staircase from the movie put up in his own home in Martha's Vineyard • Filming began the day after the Japanese attacked Pearl Harbor. The New York premiere raised $6m for the war effort, with the top seat costing $25,000 • $100,000 of the budget went to Cohan, who was convalescing from a serious operation. After seeing the film at a private screening, he said: 'My God, what an act to follow.' • Cagney had auditioned for Cohan when much younger, but Cohan had done the 'Don't call us, we'll call you' routine. He also once fired Clark Gable from one of his plays • Cagney played Cohan

again, in a cameo role in *The Seven Little Foys* in 1955. Although not a good film, Cagney's tabletop tap dance with Bob Hope is among the most wonderful musical moments in the movies. He accepted no payment for the film, because Foy had been so kind to him early in his career • Cohan had written 500 songs, 41 musicals and plays and produced over 100 others • Rosemary DeCamp is actually 14 years younger than Cagney, whose mother she plays here • Cagney's sister Jeanne is here his screen sister • This was the first film to be subjected to the hideous practice of computer colourisation. Strike a blow for pure movies. Boycott it!

Yellow Submarine
★★★ 1968 85min c.

Director: George Dunning
Screenplay: Lee Minoff, Al Brodax, Erich Segal & Jack Mendelsohn

All you need is love? Would that it were true. Still, this smashing animated movie will go some way towards making us forget real life for a while. A delightfully silly story about the Blue Meanies attacking Pepperland and sucking the colour out of people is complimented by some good jokes, bright and vivacious animation and songs like 'Lucy in the Sky with Diamonds', 'Eleanor Rigby' and, of course, the title number. The Fab Four appear at the end too.

John	John Clive
Paul	Geoffrey Hughes
George	Peter Batten
Ringo/Chief Blue Meanie	Paul Angelis
Lord Mayor/Nowhere Man/Max	Dick Emery
Old Fred	Lance Percival

Also: Paul McCartney, John Lennon, Ringo Starr, George Harrison

Psst! This was the first British animated film for 14 years • Contrary to some advance expectations, despite the references to drugs the movie still received a 'U' certificate in Britain.

You Can't Take It with You
★★ 1938 127min b/w

Director: Frank Capra
Screenplay: Robert Riskin
Source: Play by George S. Kaufman & Moss Hart

A decidedly eccentric family who have dropped out of the rat race pursue an anarchic way of life in their homely little mansion. But conflict with the real world arises when daughter Arthur falls in love with Stewart, son of the rapscallion banker who wants to tear their place down. The play on which this is based now seems quite old hat, but the film is made still worse by Frank Capra imposing his simplistic politics on top of it. It is this aspect of Capra's films which have dated his movies more than anything else. Frankly, this cock-eyed lambasting of capitalism just doesn't wash any more. The family's oddities don't seem as funny as they did, and the whole bunch of them seem more like sanctimonious parasites than the liberating free spirits we are supposed to think them. There are still some witty lines and nothing with Jean Arthur in can be all bad. But a classic it's not.

Alice Sycamore	Jean Arthur
Martin Vanderhof	Lionel Barrymore
Tony Kirby	James Stewart
Anthony P. Kirby	Edward Arnold
Kolenkhov	Mischa Auer
Essie Carmichael	Ann Miller
Penny Sycamore	Spring Byington
Paul Sycamore	Samuel S. Hinds
Poppins	Donald Meek
Ramsey	H.B. Warner
De Pinna	Halliwell Hobbes
Ed Carmichael	Dub Taylor
Mrs. Anthony Kirby	Mary Forbes
Donald	Eddie "Rochester" Anderson
Judge	Harry Davenport
Henderson	Charles Lane
Kirby's assistant	Byron Foulger
Kirby's secretary	Ian Wolfe
Henry	Irving Bacon
Jailer	James Flavin
Detective	Ward Bond
Detective	James Burke
Diner	Robert Greig

Oscars Best Picture, Best Director

Psst! The screen rights to the play cost a record $200,000 • During filming, Lionel Barrymore was suffering badly from the serious arthritis which would eventually cripple him. Director Capra got round it by having him wear a cast on his leg and pretend he'd broken it while sliding down a banister • Many directors, like Hitchcock, have little trademark signatures they like to pop into their movies. For Capra, beginning with this film, it was a raven.

Young and Innocent
★★★ 1937 80min b/w

Director: Alfred Hitchcock
Screenplay: Charles Bennett & Alma Reville
Source: Novel, *A Shilling for Candles* by Josephine Tey

The daughter of a policeman helps a murder suspect she believes is innocent. Although hardly terribly deep and bearing many similarities to *The 39 Steps*, this Hitchcock thriller has great charm. True, it looks rather dated, with some dreadful train models and slightly hammy acting. But the jolly story still sweeps you along. Sixty years later, the extraordinary crane shot in the hotel ballroom, as the camera moves towards the murderer with the twitching eyes, is still amazingly effective, as is the tense kids' tea party.

Erica Burgoyne	Nova Pilbeam
Robert Tisdall	Derrick de Marney
Col. Burgoyne	Percy Marmont
Old Will	Edward Rigby
Aunt Margaret	Mary Clare
Uncle Basil	Basil Radford
Insp. Kent	John Longden
Guy	George Curzon
Lorry driver	Jerry Verno

Psst! Hitch appears standing outside the courtroom with a camera as de Marney makes his escape.

Young Frankenstein
★★★★ 1974 108min b/w

Director: Mel Brooks
Screenplay: Gene Wilder & Mel Brooks
Source: Characters from the novel *Frankenstein* by Mary Wollstonecraft Shelley

The grandson of the infamous Baron Frankenstein, a doctor who pronounces the name *Fronk*-en-steen, inherits the family estate along with its attendant hunchback and assorted weirdoes. When he finds granddad's notes, he just has to have another go. This wonderful spoof of the horror genre by Mel Brooks works beautifully, thanks to a far stronger storyline than we usually get from him. That's not say that there aren't great gags. There are loads of them, along with superb set designs and the monster himself giving us a rendition of 'Puttin' on the Ritz' that would make Fred Astaire weep.

Dr. Frederick Frankenstein	Gene Wilder
Monster	Peter Boyle
Igor	Marty Feldman
Elizabeth	Madeline Kahn
Frau Blucher	Cloris Leachman
Inga	Teri Garr
Insp. Kemp	Kenneth Mars
Blind hermit	Gene Hackman
Herr Falkstein	Richard Haydn
Mr. Hilltop	Liam Dunn
Village elder	Arthur Malet
Insp. Kemp's aide	Richard Roth

Quote 'Pardon me, boy. Is this the Transylvania station?' – 'Ya, ya. Track 29. Can I give you a shine?' • 'Elevate me.' • 'Oh, you men are all alike! Seven or eight quick ones and you're off with the boys, to boast and brag.' • 'From what was once an inarticulate mass of lifeless tissues, may I now present a cultured, sophisticated man about town.'

Psst! The castle in which they filmed *Young Frankenstein* was the same as that used in the 1910 version of *Frankenstein* • The laboratory set was the one used in the 1931 *Frankenstein*, which had been lying around in storage in a garage for decades • There was a real Baron Franckenstein on the film, appearing under his screen name of Clement St. George • Mel Brooks' only acting contribution was to voice the cat that screams off-screen when it is hit by a dart. His face appears as one of the gargoyles on the castle • According to him, Cloris Leachman ate her facial wart when it 'fell in her tuna salad and was swallowed in a glob of mayonnaise'.

The Young in Heart
★★★ 1938 91min b/w

Director: Richard Wallace
Screenplay: Paul Osborn & Charles Bennett
Source: Novel, *The Gay Banditti* by I.A.R. Wylie

A family of confidence tricksters target Dupree as their next mark. But the charming old lady has an extraordinary influence on them. This delightful comedy has no real satirical bite or black underbelly. It's just out and out fun, sweet and very funny, with a few dollops of acceptable sentiment thrown into the mix.

George-Anne Carleton	Janet Gaynor
Richard Carleton	Douglas Fairbanks Jr.
Leslie	Paulette Goddard
'Sahib' Carleton	Roland Young

'Marmy' Carleton	Billie Burke
Duncan MacCrae	Richard Carlson
Miss Ellen Fortune	Minnie Dupree
Mrs. Jennings	Lucille Watson
Det. Chief	Walter Kingsford
Mr. Hutchins	Lawrence Grant
Mr. Anstruther	Henry Stephenson
Kennel proprietor	Bill Bevan

Young Mr. Lincoln
★★★ 1939 100min b/w

Director: John Ford
Screenplay: Lamar Trotti

Fonda is splendid, noble if not downright saintly, as the tyro lawyer who stops a lynching and then proves himself in the courtroom defending a murder case. Can anyone really have been as decent as this? If only the Confederacy had been able to watch this enjoyable bit of Hollywood moonshine, they'd never have dared start the Civil War.

Abraham Lincoln	Henry Fonda
Abigail Clay	Alice Brady
Mary Todd	Marjorie Weaver
Hannah Clay	Arleen Whelan
Efe Turner	Eddie Collins
Ann Rutledge	Pauline Moore
Matt Clay	Richard Cromwell
John Felder	Donald Meek
Adam Clay	Eddie Quillan
Judge Bell	Spencer Charters
John Palmer Cass	Ward Bond
Stephan A. Douglas	Milburn Stone
Juror	Robert Lowery
Frank Ford	Francis Ford
Woman	Virginia Brissac
Hawthorne	Charles Halton
Adam (as boy)	Dick Jones

Psst! Ford was under contant pressure from Darryl F. Zanuck, the executive producer, to give the film a faster pace. Knowing how the studio system worked, Ford had no wish for an editor to change his vision of the film. So, as with other movies of his, he edited in the camera, filming only what he knew he wanted to use and actually destroying everything else so that it couldn't be cut in a different way while he was working on another project • The rain into which Fonda walks at the end was not prearranged, but just happened along when they were filming and Ford decided to take advantage of it.

You Only Live Once
★★★ 1937 86min b/w

Director: Fritz Lang
Screenplay: Gene Towne & Graham Baker

Trying to go straight, Fonda is accused of murder and snaps, fighting back against the system and going on the run with wife Sidney. Based to some extent on Bonnie and Clyde, this is a gripping, but also rather depressing, melodrama. As intended, it makes the blood boil against the injustice meted out to the couple and is very much a film of its Depression Era time. Its expressionist style, though, harks forward to the onset of film noir.

Joan Graham	Sylvia Sidney
Eddie Taylor	Henry Fonda
Stephen Whitney	Barton MacLane
Bonnie Graham	Jean Dixon
Father Dolan	William Gargan
Muggsy	Warren Hymer
Ethan	Charles "Chic" Sale
Hester	Margaret Hamilton
Rogers	Guinn "Big Boy" Williams
Dr. Hill	Jerome Cowan
Warden	John Wray
D.A.	Jonathan Hale
Guard	Ward Bond
Gas station attendant	Jack Carson

Psst! Lang worked his cast and crew extremely hard, often forcing them to go without sleep to get the effect of exhaustion that he wanted. They frequently had to work until three in the morning. It was, according to cameraman Leon Shamroy, a 'tortured nightmare'.

You Only Live Twice
★★★ 1967 117min c.

Director: Lewis Gilbert
Screenplay: Roald Dahl
Source: Novel by Ian Fleming

With Russia and America all ready to blow the whistle to start The Big One over rockets they keep losing, Bond hops from bed to bed until he gets to Blofeld's hideout in a volcano in Japan. Another of those Bond films where the effects and action take precedence over the quality of the script. But it's still got enough going on to keep fans of the series pretty happy.

James Bond	Sean Connery
Aki	Akiko Wakabayashi
Tiger Tanaka	Tetsuro Tamba
Kissy Suzuki	Mie Hama
Helga Brandt	Karin Dor
Ernst Stavro Blofeld	Donald Pleasence
'M'	Bernard Lee
Miss Moneypenny	Lois Maxwell
'Q'	Desmond Llewelyn
Henderson	Charles Gray
Spectre #3	Burt Kwouk

Psst! There were many Bond-related bits of merchandise over the year. Shortly before this movie, Colgate-Palmolive brought out a range of products for men. Among them was 007 aftershave. On the bottle it said: 'Gives Any Man the Licence to Kill…Women'. In smaller letters, it read: 'Dangerous? Sure, but what a way to go!'

You're Telling Me
★★★ 1934 67min c.

Director: Erle C. Kenton
Screenplay: Paul M. Jones & Walter de Leon
Source: Novel by David Benedictius

Fans of the bulbous-nosed comedian will have a Fields day with this superb comedy which is sadly neglected compared to others such as *The Bank Dick*. Here he is an inventor who has come up with a tyre that can't be punctured. Naturally there are obstacles between him and success, mostly of his own making. As usual Fields cribs from his earlier shorts, this time roping in his wonderful and rightly famous golf routine.

Sam Bisbee	W.C. Fields
Pauline Bisbee	Joan Marsh
Bob Murchison	Larry 'Buster' Crabbe
H.R.H. Princess Lescaboura	Adrienne Ames
Mrs. Bessie Bisbee	Louise Carter
Mrs. Murchison	Kathleen Howard

Quote 'It's a funny old world – a man's lucky if he can get out of it alive.'

Psst! Crabbe was best known for his part as Flash Gordon in the long-running film serial.

You Were Never Lovelier
★★★ 1942 97min b/w

Director: William A. Seiter
Screenplay: Michael Fessier, Ernest Pagano & Delmer Daves

Fred Astaire had been paired with Rita Hayworth before in *You'll Never Get Rich*. Enjoyable though it was, they were even better together here. Rita's father is desperate to marry her off but she's having none of it. So he hires Fred, an impecunious dancer, to pretend to be her secret admirer. Although the plot is as thin as Astaire's hair, the Jerome Kern music is great and the leads rarely did look lovelier.

Robert Davis	Fred Astaire
Maria Acuna	Rita Hayworth
Edwardo	Adolphe Menjou
Cecy Acuna	Leslie Brooks
Lita Acuna	Adele Mara
Mrs. Maria Castro	Isobel Elsom
Fernando	Gus Schilling
Grandmother Acuna	Kathleen Howard
Tony	Larry Parks

Psst! Nan Wynn dubbed Hayworth's singing voice • Xavier Cugat appears with his orchestra. Hayworth was once a singer with the band.

Zulu

★★★★ 1964 135min c.

Director: Cy Endfield
Screenplay: John Prebble & Cy Endfield

A handful of British soldiers are attacked by an overwhelming force of Zulu warriors at Rorke's Drift in 1879. Every part is splendidly characterised in a clever and often witty script and the tension is racked higher and higher as they await the attack. With some of the most horrifyingly realistic battle scenes on celluloid, this is one of the greatest of all war films and, what's more, one that is remarkably true to the facts. As with the Battle of the Bands in *Casablanca*, the rival Zulu chanting and Redcoats singing *Men of Harlech* brings a pretty solid lump to the throat. If you're watching a good copy, the deeply-saturated colours will amaze you. The 1979 prequel, *Zulu Dawn*, is pretty good too.

Lt. John Chard	Stanley Baker
Rev. Otto Witt	Jack Hawkins
Margareta Witt	Ulla Jacobsson
Pte. Henry Hook	James Booth
Lt. Gonville Bromhead	Michael Caine
Colour Sgt. Bourne	Nigel Green
Pte. Owen	Ivor Emmanual
Sgt. Maxfield	Paul Daneman
Cpl. Allen	Glynn Edwards
Surgeon Reynolds	Patrick Magee
Cetewayo	Chief Buthelezi
Narrator	Richard Burton

OOPS! The film company paid the extras with watches and some of the Zulu warriors show their gratitude by sporting them during the movie.

Psst! The film-makers had trouble getting the Zulu extras to understand what they had to do while they were filming in Natal. When it became clear that they had never seen a film before Stanley Baker, also the film's producer, had some old Gene Autry Westerns flown in • When he had trouble finding finance, Baker sank much of his own money into the movie • The 11 Victoria Crosses handed out to those who fought at Rorke's Drift is a record for one engagement • Chief Buthelesi appears as his own ancestor Cetewayo, who led the Zulus • This was Michael Caine's first major film part. He was so sick from nerves after watching the rushes that he never watched them for this or any other movie again • Although Caine has been sneered at for his accent, he spent time with the Scots Guards in the officers' mess beforehand trying to get it right • Jack Hawkins was so annoyed by the way his missionary character came across as a buffoon that he stormed out of the premiere, calling the film a 'fiasco'.

Filmographies

Almost 200 actors and directors are covered in this section. Most are very well known but I have also included a range of character actors who do so much to add to our enjoyment of movies but who can also often set off that frustrating 'Who is that?' game that does so much to spoil our concentration. Although I would have liked to have included far more actors and directors, there simply isn't enough space. Even so, I have been forced to restrict the films listed against each actor to a selection of their better-remembered and most easily-available films.

Those films for which there is an entry in the main body of the guide are in bold type, while the others are in plain type.

Abbreviations: (a) Actor; (b) Indicates an actor's role is just a small bit-part; (c) Indicates an actor only played a cameo in the film; (d) Director; (s) Screenplay; (v) Indicates that just the actor's voice is used in the film.

Woody Allen (b. 1935)

***Real name:* Allen Stewart Konigsberg**

WRITER-DIRECTOR & ACTOR. The one-time gag writer and stand-up comic is an actor-director people either love or hate. Even his fans are split into two; those who love the funny films and those who love the serious ones. Of late, Allen's movies have begun emphasising the comic rather than tortured side of his psyche, thank goodness. After years of what was, by normal standards, a pretty bizarre relationship with Mia Farrow, there was then an acrimonious split after he took up with their adopted daughter. He has an amazing record for putting future stars in bit parts. Sylvester Stallone, Sigourney Weaver and Sharon Stone all appeared in brief, wordless parts in Allen movies.

Quote: 'I've never made a film that could remotely be considered a masterpiece. Not even remotely.' • 'Love is the answer, but while you are waiting for the answer, sex raises some pretty good questions.' • 'Sex between two people is beautiful – if you can get between the right two people.' • 'A face that convinces you that God is a cartoonist.' [Jack Kroll]

Films: What's New, Pussycat? •• (65; a&s only), What's Up, Tiger Lily? •• (66; s only), **Casino Royale • (67; a only), Take the Money and Run ••• (69; also a&s),** Bananas •••• (71; also a&s), Everything You Always Wanted To Know About Sex (But Were Afraid To Ask) ••• (72; also a&s), **Play it Again, Sam ••• (72; a&s only), Sleeper ••• (73; also a&s),** Love and Death ••• (75; also a&s), The Front •••• (76; a only), **Annie Hall ••• (77; also a&s),** Interiors • (78; also s), **Manhattan •••• (79; also a&s),** Stardust Memories • (80; also a&s), A

Midsummer Night's Sex Comedy ••• (82; also a&s), Zelig •• (83; also a&s), Broadway Danny Rose ••• (84; also a&s), The Purple Rose of Cairo •• (85; also s), **Hannah and Her Sisters •••• (86; also a&s),** Radio Days ••• (87; also a&s), September • (87; also s), Another Woman • (88; also s), Crimes and Misdemeanors •• (89; also a&s), New York Stories •• (89; also a&s), Alice ••• (90; also s), Scenes from a Mall •• (91; a only), Shadows and Fog ••• (92; also a&s), Husbands and Wives ••• (92; also a&s), Manhattan Murder Mystery ••• (93; also a&s), Bullets Over Broadway •• (94; also s)

Robert Altman (b. 1925)

DIRECTOR. A one-time bomber pilot and dog-tattoo machine inventor, Altman specialises in anti-Hollywood, iconoclastic, satirical movies with large casts and several interweaving plots. He has a devoted following but his films are wildly uneven. Occasionally he hits the button, however, and the fireworks fly.

Quote: 'Nobody has ever made a good movie. Someday, someone will make half a good one.' • 'It's very hard to find anyone with any decency in the business. They all hide behind the corporate structure. They're like landlords who kick people out of tenement buildings. There's no compassion, and there's certainly no interest in the arts.'

Films: M*A*S*H •••• (70), Brewster McCloud ••• (70), **McCabe and Mrs. Miller ••• (71; also s), The Long Goodbye •••• (73),** Thieves Like Us ••• (74), **Nashville •• (75),** A Wedding •• (78), Health •• (79), Popeye • (80), Come Back to the Five and Dime, Jimmy Dean, Jimmy Dean ••• (82), Streamers •• (83), Secret Honor •• (84), Fool for Love •• (85), Aria • (87), Beyond Therapy • (87; also s), Vincent and Theo ••• (90), **The Player** ••• **(92)**, Short Cuts ••• (93; also s), Pret-a-Porter • (94; also s)

Jean Arthur (1905-91)

Real name: Gladys Georgianna Greene

One of the screen's most natural and radiant comediennes, Arthur was a favourite actress of Frank Capra. Her style of zany playfulness has survived the years well, making many of her movies pure joy to watch. Despite her natural persona on screen, she is said to have suffered from the worst nerves in Hollywood, often being violently sick before having to film.

Quote: 'The fact that I did not marry George Bernard Shaw is the only real disappointment I've had.' • 'She has the sexiest voice in the history of the talkies.' [Derek Owen] • 'Everyone who went to the movies *liked* her, and that's unusual. Every movie star is disliked by some people – Gable, Crawford, Dietrich certainly, even Garbo, Ronald Colman – but everyone liked Jean Arthur.' [John Cromwell] • 'That poor girl suffered for her art. In front of the camera, she was bubbling and radiant, but when it wasn't running, she was in torment.' [Cary Grant] • 'Jean Arthur was an enigmatic figure because she doesn't do very well in crowds, and she doesn't do very well with people, and she doesn't do very well with life, but she does very well as an actress.' [Frank Capra]

Films: **The Whole Town's Talking** ••• **(35),** Diamond Jim ••• (35), If You Could Only Cook •• (35), **Mr. Deeds Goes to Town** •••• **(36),** The Plainsman • (36), The Ex-Mrs. Bradford •• (36), **Easy Living** ••• **(37),** History Is Made at Night ••• (37), **You Can't Take It with You** •• **(38),** Only Angels Have Wings •• (39), **Mr. Smith Goes to Washington** •••• **(39),** Too Many Husbands ••• (40), **The Devil and Miss Jones** •• **(41),** The Talk of the Town ••• **(42),** The More the Merrier ••• (43), Foreign Affair ••• (48), **Shane** •• **(53)**

Fred Astaire (1899-87)

Real name: Frederick Austerlitz

The evaluation on his first screen test said:

'Can't sing. Can't act. Slightly balding.' The last was certainly true, but he proved time and again that the first two were way off beam. Performing professionally from the age of seven, Fred and his sister Adele were a popular dance team for many years. He turned to the movies when she married an English lord. It wasn't long before he was teamed through a series of movies with Ginger Rogers. Oddly, they had gone out together a few times in New York years earlier but nothing had come of it, apart from the story that Astaire was no great shakes as a ballroom dancer. One of cinema's perfectionists, he rehearsed endlessly the routines that look so effortless on screen. Despite people's belief that he only made movies with Rogers, he was wonderful with other partners like Cyd Charisse, Rita Hayworth and Eleanor Powell and also proved himself in several straight dramatic roles. His legs were insured for a million dollars.

Quote: 'I just put my feet in the air and move them around.' • 'I'm just a hoofer with a spare set of tails.' • 'I have no desire to prove anything by it. I have never used it as an outlet or as a means of expressing myself. I just dance.' • 'The difference is that there have been a lot of imitators of Gene Kelly, but no one has been able to imitate Fred Astaire. I wish I did know what it was with Astaire. If I knew I'd add it to my own bag of tricks.' [Gene Kelly] • 'He can give the audience pleasure just by walking across the floor.' [Gene Kelly] • 'I know a doctor in Los Angeles who's a better dancer than Fred Astaire ever was. There are many men who never danced professionally who are superb ballroom dancers. Fred was never much better than an average dancer at parties. He always felt a little awkward at parties when we danced together. I'm not taking anything away from him, though. He's a great dancer. He was able to do what so many professional dancers cannot do – be perfect in front of a camera time after time after time.' [Ginger Rogers]

Films: Flying Down to Rio •• (33), Dancing Lady •• (33), The Gay Divorcee ••• (34), **Top Hat** •••• **(35),** Roberta ••• (35), **Swing Time** •••• **(36),** Follow the Fleet ••• (36), Shall We Dance ••• (36), A Damsel in Distress •• (37), Carefree ••• (38), **Broadway Melody of 1940** ••• **(39),** The Story of Vernon & Irene Castle •• (39), You'll Never Get Rich ••• (41), **You Were Never Lovelier** ••• **(42),** Holiday Inn •• (42), The Sky's the Limit •• (43), Ziegfeld Follies •• (46), Blue Skies •• (46), **Easter Parade** •••

(48), The Barkleys of Broadway •• (49), Royal Wedding •• (51), **The Band Wagon •••• (53)**, Daddy Long Legs •• (55), **Funny Face ••• (57)**, **Silk Stockings ••• (57)**, On the Beach ••• (59), Finian's Rainbow •• (68), **That's Entertainment! •••• (74)**, **The Towering Inferno ••• (74)**, That's Entertainment, Part 2 ••• (76)

Mary Astor (1906-87)

Real name: Lucille Vasconcellos Langehanke

After achieving stardom overnight with her role opposite John Barrymore in *Beau Brummel* (see *Midnight*), the strikingly handsome Astor made the transition to sound films, excelling particularly in the part of the *femme fatale* or the sophisticated seen-it-all woman. Her flamboyant private life (see *Dodsworth*) did little to harm her career. She won an Oscar for *The Great Lie*.

Quote: 'I was never totally involved in movies. I was making my father's dream come true.' • 'We were the hope peddlers; we pushed it in all sorts of brightly coloured capsules: Love Conquers All, Crime Doesn't Pay, Honesty is the Best Policy, Hard Work Reaps Rewards, The Rich Are Unhappy – The Poor Are Happy, Good Triumphs Over Evil. These silver linings to all clouds were the stuff of dreams, and human beings like to dream.'

Films: Red Dust •• (32), The Kennel Murder Case ••• (33), Upperworld ••• (34), **Dodsworth •••• (36)**, **The Prisoner of Zenda ••• (37)**, **Midnight ••• (39)**, **The Maltese Falcon •••• (41)**, The Great Lie (41), **The Palm Beach Story ••• (42)**, **Across the Pacific ••• (42)**, **Meet Me in St. Louis •••• (44)**, Little Women •• (49), Hush Hush Sweet Charlotte •• (65)

Richard Attenborough (b. 1923)

DIRECTOR & ACTOR. A talented character actor frequently seen as a killer or a coward, Attenborough graduated to become a producer and director of personally-felt liberal, historical epics. Much ridiculed for his tear-stained performances at awards ceremonies, many of his films have a tendency to tug a little too severely at the heart-strings. However, the lovely British love story *Shadowlands* shows he is capable of greatness. Attenborough is a tireless champion of the British film industry, which

would be in an even sorrier state were it not for his efforts. He won an Oscar for directing *Gandhi*.

Quote: 'It is my honest belief that it is much more edifying and aesthetically pleasing to have a beautiful painting to look at than a healthy bank balance.' • 'By far the finest, most decent human being I've ever met in the picture business.' [William Goldman]

Films: In Which We Serve ••• (b)(42; a only), A Matter of Life and Death •••• **(46; a only)**, **Brighton Rock ••• (47; a only)**, The Magic Box • (c)(51; a only), Private's Progress •• (56; a only), **I'm All Right Jack ••• (59; a only)**, **The League of Gentlemen ••• (60; a only)**, **Only Two Can Play ••• (62; a only)**, **The Great Escape ••• (63; a only)**, Seance on a Wet Afternoon •• (64; a only), **The Flight of the Phoenix ••• (65; a only)**, The Sand Pebbles • (66; a only), Doctor Doolittle • (67; a only), **Oh! What a Lovely War •• (69)**, **10 Rillington Place •• (71; a only)**, Young Winston •• (72), The Chess Players •• (77; a only), A Bridge Too Far •• (77), Magic •• (78), **Gandhi ••• (82)**, A Chorus Line • (85), Cry Freedom •• (87), Chaplin •• (92), **Jurassic Park ••• (93; a only)**, **Shadowlands •••• (93)**, Miracle on 34th Street •• (94; a only)

Lauren Bacall (b. 1924)

Real name: Betty Joan Perske

The Miss Greenwich Village of 1942 was for a time a cinema usherette in Manhattan. She became a magazine cover model and was spotted by Howard Hawks's wife as a possible co-star for Humphrey Bogart in *To Have and Have Not*. Dubbed 'The Look' when the 19-year-old arrived in Hollywood, she claims that her sexy glance upwards through her eyelashes only came about because she was so scared that she had to keep her head down to stop it trembling. She and Bogart hit it off immediately off-screen as well as on and they were wed the following year. She was later married to Jason Robards for 12 years.

Quote: 'I'm not a member of the weaker sex.' • 'A woman isn't complete without a man. But where do you find a man – a real man – these days?' • 'Bogart fell in love with the character Bacall played in *To Have and Have Not*, so she had to keep playing it for the rest of her life.' [Howard Hawks]

Films: To Have and Have Not ••• **(44),** Confidential Agent •• (45), **The Big Sleep** •••• **(46),** Dark Passage ••• (47), **Key Largo** ••• **(48),** Young Man With a Horn ••• (50), How to Marry a Millionaire ••• (53), **Written on the Wind** •••• **(56),** Designing Woman •• (57), **Northwest Frontier** ••• **(59),** Harper ••• (66), **Murder on the Orient Express** • **(74),** The Shootist ••• (76), Health •• (79), Mr. North •• (88), Appointment with Death •• (88), Tree of Hands •• (89), **Misery** •••• **(90),** All I Want For Christmas • (91), Pret-a-Porter • (94)

Warren Beatty (b. 1937)

Real name: **Henry Warren Beaty**

The brother of Shirley MacLaine, he worked variously as rat-catcher, bricklayer, pianist and tunnel-builder to survive his early acting days. Stardom arrived with *Bonnie and Clyde*, which he also produced, a status he has retained ever since despite making relatively few successful films. For 25 years he vied with Jack Nicholson for the reputation of Hollywood's leading bachelor, dating some of the most famous actresses in the world. Ex-lover Carly Simon's song 'You're So Vain' is said to be about him. *Spy* magazine revealed that his chat-up line is 'Make a pass at me'. The film community was astounded when Beatty closed his black book and married Annette Bening, soon afterwards becoming a proud father. However, chat-show host David Letterman reckoned it was 'just so he can meet some babysitters'. He won an Oscar as Best Director for *Reds*.

Quote: 'If I come back in another life, I want to be Warren Beatty's fingertips.' [Woody Allen] • 'I'd like to do a love scene with him just to see what all the yelling is about.' [Shirley MacLaine, his sister] • 'It is a damn good thing he never co-starred with Lassie.' [Shirley MacLaine] • 'Think what Warren Beatty could have achieved if he'd been celibate.' [Shirley MacLaine]

Films: The Roman Spring of Mrs. Stone •• (61), **Bonnie and Clyde** •••• **(67),** **McCabe and Mrs. Miller** ••• **(71), The Parallax View** •• **(74),** The Fortune ••• (75), **Shampoo** • **(75; also s),** Heaven Can Wait ••• (78; also d&s), Reds ••• (81; also d&s), Ishtar • (87), Dick Tracy •• (90; also d), Bugsy •• (92), Love Affair •• (94; also s)

Robert Benchley (1889-45)

Urbane humourist Benchley enlivened a succession of films in the 40s by playing himself, an amiable but bumbling man with a martini-dry wit trying to make some sort of sense out of life and stealing the scene from whichever unfortunate 'star' happened to be on screen at the same time. An extremely witty man who was a pal of Dorothy Parker and a member of the famed Algonquin Round Table, Benchley also made a succession of droll short films, winning an Oscar for *How to Sleep*. They were gathered into a great collection, *Those Marvellous Benchley Shorts*. He was the grandfather of Robert Benchley, novelist and author of *Jaws*.

Quote: 'It took me 15 years to discover that I had no talent for writing. But by then I couldn't give it up because I was too famous.' • 'I'm glad this question came up, in a way, because there are so many different ways to answer it that one of them is bound to be right.' • 'A dog teaches a boy fidelity, perseverance, and to turn around three times before lying down.' • 'In Milwaukee last month a man died laughing at one of his own jokes. That's what makes it so tough for us outsiders. We have to fight home competition.' • 'The biggest obstacle to professional writing today is the necessity for changing the typewriter ribbon.' • 'I do most of my work sitting down. That's where I shine.' • 'I am the oldest living man, especially at seven in the morning.'

Films: Dancing Lady •• (33), **Foreign Correspondent** •• **(40; also s),** You'll Never Get Rich ••• (41), Bedtime Story •• (41), **I Married a Witch** •• **(42), The Major and the Minor** •• **(42),** The Sky's the Limit •• (43), Weekend at the Waldorf •• (45), Road to Utopia ••• (v)(45)

Ingrid Bergman (1915-82)

This beautiful Swedish actress starred in some of Hollywood's most fondly-remembered movies like *Casablanca*, *Gaslight* and *Notorious*. Her wholesome image was shattered when she abandoned her husband and daughter and took up with Italian director Roberto Rossellini, especially after she was seen in a state of pregnancy without the all-important ring on her finger. Bergman was attacked by religious groups, in the media and by politicians. In the Senate, she was called 'Hollywood's apostle of degradation'. As usual, financial expediency overcome moral scruples and, after a seven year ban, she worked in Hollywood again from the mid-50s. She is Isabella Rossellini's mother. Won Oscars for *Gaslight*, *Anastasia* and *Murder on the Orient Express*.

Quote: 'In America, people think if they buy their tickets they own you.' • 'I always wanted to do comedies but nobody discovered this until my old age. They think all Swedes are like Garbo.' • 'Happiness is good health – and a bad memory.' • 'I have no regrets. I wouldn't have lived my life the way I did if I was going to worry about what people were going to say.' • 'Sweden's greatest export since Garbo.' [Studio publicity] • 'If a face like Ingrid Bergman's looks at you as though you're adorable, everybody does. You don't have to act very much.' • 'When she walks on screen and says "Hello" people ask, "Who wrote that wonderful line of dialogue".' [Leo McCarey] • 'I reckon there wasn't a man who came within a mile of her who didn't fall in love with her.' [Anthony Quinn]

Films: Intermezzo ••• **(39)**, Dr. Jekyll and Mr. Hyde ••• (41), **Casablanca** •••• **(42)**, For Whom the Bell Tolls •• (43), Gaslight •• (44), **Spellbound** ••• **(45)**, Saratoga Trunk • (45), The Bells of St. Mary's •• (45), **Notorious** •••• **(46)**, Joan of Arc •• (48), Anastasia ••• (56), **Indiscreet** •• **(58)**, The Inn of the Sixth Happiness •• **(58)**, The Yellow Rolls-Royce •• (65), Cactus Flower •• (69), **Murder on the Orient Express** • **(74)**, Autumn Sonata ••• (78)

Eric Blore (1887-59)

A one-time insurance agent, Blore specialised in playing butlers and valets, though he varied between being subservient and rebellious depending on the movie. An outrageous over-actor, he was a wonderful comic addition to several of the Astaire-Rogers musicals and enlivened any film he was in.

Films Flying Down to Rio •• (33), The Gay Divorcee ••• (34), **Top Hat** •••• **(35)**, Diamond Jim ••• (35), **Swing Time** •••• **(36)**, Shall We Dance ••• (36), The Ex-Mrs. Bradford •• (36), Piccadilly Jim •• (36), Quality Street ••• (37), Swiss Miss •• (38), The Boys from Syracuse •• (40), **The Lady Eve** ••• **(41), Sullivan's Travels** •••• **(41)**, Road to Zanzibar • (41), **The Moon and Sixpence** ••• **(42)**, Love Happy •• (49), Fancy Pants •• (50)

Humphrey Bogart (1899-57)

Bogie must have given eternal thanks to George Raft, who got him more good movies than his agent. Raft turned down the leads in *Dead End*, *High Sierra* and *The Maltese Falcon* that turned Bogart from a contract player who specialised in wimps and cowards into Warner Bros. fastest-rising star. He didn't always have the tough-guy image he's known for. At just one year old, his picture was used on the labels of Mellin's baby food, so sweet was he. He came to movies from the stage, where he was the sort of young juvenile who bounded on in whites with a racket saying: 'Tennis, anyone?', those being, in fact, the first words he spoke as an actor. The famous scar on his lip probably didn't come, as Warners wanted people to believe, from a war wound but from an attempted escape by a prisoner he was escorting. Bogart was a hard drinker, whose friends tended to be those few who could keep up with him. After three troubled marriages, he struck lucky when he acted with Lauren Bacall in *To Have and Have Not*. They appear to have been one of Hollywood's happiest couples until his death from throat cancer. Unlike so many other male stars of the period, his anti-heroic image still strikes a potent chord with audiences today. He is said to be the seventh cousin twice removed of Princess Diana. He won his only Oscar for *The African Queen*.

Quote: 'I made more lousy pictures than any actor in history.' • 'Do I subscribe to the Olivier school of acting? Ah, nuts. I'm an actor. I just do what comes naturally.' • 'The only thing you owe the public is a good performance.' • 'The trouble with the world is that everybody in it is about three drinks behind.' • '"Bogart's a helluva nice guy till 11.30 p.m. After that, he thinks he's Bogart.' [Dave Chasen] • 'He was an extremely hard-working actor. He'd always pretend that he wasn't, that he didn't give a damn, but that wasn't true. One day I said to him, "Bogey, you're just a great big phoney." He put his finger to his lips and grinned at me. "Sure," he said, "But don't tell anyone".' [Howard Hawks] • 'He was playing Bogart all the time, but he was really just a big sloppy bowl of mush.' [Stanley Kramer] • 'I should never have switched from scotch to martinis.' [His supposed last words]

Films: The Petrified Forest •• **(36)**, Bullets or Ballots ••• (36), **Dead End** •• **(37)**, Marked Woman •• (37), Kid Galahad ••• (37), **The Amazing Dr. Clitterhouse**

•• (38), **Angels with Dirty Faces** ••• (38), **The Roaring Twenties** ••• **(39),** The Oklahoma Kid •• (39), Dark Victory ••• (39), They Drive By Night ••• (40), Brother Orchid •• (40), **The Maltese Falcon** •••• (41), **High Sierra** ••• (41), **Casablanca** •••• **(42),** Across the Pacific ••• **(42),** All Through the Night •• (42), Sahara •• (43), Thank Your Lucky Stars •• (43), **To Have and Have Not** ••• **(44),** Passage to Marseilles •• (44), **The Big Sleep** •••• **(46),** The Two Mrs. Carrolls • (47), Dark Passage ••• (47), **The Treasure of the Sierra Madre** ••• (48), Key Largo ••• (48), In a Lonely Place ••• (50), **The African Queen** •••• (51), **The Enforcer** ••• **(51), The Caine Mutiny** •••• **(54), Sabrina** ••• **(54),** Beat the Devil •• (54), The Barefoot Contessa •• (54), The Desperate Hours ••• (55), The Harder They Fall ••• (56)

Marlon Brando (b. 1924)

Real name: **Marlon Brando Jr.**

One of those actors who gives as much entertainment value off-screen as he does on. After his moody, disturbed youth roles, he has now graduated to the point where he can get millions for no more than a few screen minutes. While addicted to TV in his younger years, he binged on women the way Elvis binged on junk food. According to one TV mogul, 'He got TV stations to give him the phone numbers of any woman he found attractive on screen and half an hour later he was in bed with them.' His broken nose resulted from backstage playfulness with understudy Jack Palance during the Broadway run of *A Streetcar Named Desire*. A Method actor who seems to emphasise the madness in his method (see *Apocalypse Now*), Brando has never wanted to learn lines and in most of his movies, he reads them off idiot boards. Of late, though, he's adopted a new device that whispers the lines into his ear as he needs them. His passport lists as his occupation not 'Actor', but 'Shepherd'. He won Oscars for *On the Waterfront* and *The Godfather*.

Quote: 'I have the eyes of a dead pig.' • 'The only reason I'm in Hollywood is that I don't have the moral courage to refuse the money.' • 'An actor is a guy who, if you aren't talking about him, isn't listening.' • 'If you're successful, acting is about as soft a job as anybody could ever wish for. But if you're unsuccessful, it's

worse than having a skin disease.' • 'If you're rich and famous, getting laid a lot isn't difficult.' • 'Most of the time he sounds like he has a mouth full of wet toilet paper' [Critic Rex Reed] • 'An angel as a man, a monster as an actor.' [Director Bernardo Bertolucci] • 'Actors like him are good, but on the whole I do not enjoy actors who seek to commune with their armpits, so to speak.' [Greer Garson] • 'Brando is one of the finest actors we've had. I'm sorry he didn't have the benefit of older, more established friends – as I did – to help him choose the proper material in which to use his talent.' [John Wayne]

Films: **The Men** ••• **(50),** A Streetcar Named Desire ••• **(51),** Viva Zapata! ••• (52), **The Wild One** •• **(53),** Julius Caesar ••• (53), **On the Waterfront** ••• **(54),** Guys and Dolls ••• (55), The Teahouse of the August Moon ••• (56), The Young Lions ••• (58), One-Eyed Jacks • (61; also d), Mutiny on the Bounty •• (62), Bedtime Story •• (64), A Countess from Hong Kong • (67), Reflections in a Golden Eye •• (67), **The Godfather** •••• **(72), Last Tango in Paris** • **(73),** The Missouri Breaks •• (76), **Superman** ••• **(78), Apocalypse Now** ••• **(79),** A Dry White Season •• (89), The Freshman •••• (90), Christopher Columbus: The Discovery • (92), **Don Juan DeMarco** •••• **(95)**

Walter Brennan (1894-74)

Brennan got his break in the movies in 1923 when he stepped in to help out a director. The man was exasperated by a donkey that refused to bray on cue, so Brennan did it instead. The grouchy, toothless old man he played, often tinged with a spot of madness or booze – or both – were much in demand.

Films: **The Invisible Man** ••• **(b)(33), The Bride of Frankenstein** •••• **(b)(35),** Barbary Coast ••• (35), **Fury** ••• **(36),** The Moon's Our Home •• (36), The Story of Vernon & Irene Castle •• (39), Stanley and Livingstone ••• (39), The Westerner ••• (40), **Sergeant York** •• **(41),** Meet John Doe •• (41), The Pride of the Yankees ••• (42), **To Have and Have Not** ••• **(44),** The Princess and the Pirate •• (44), **My Darling Clementine** ••• **(46), Red River** ••• **(48),** The Far Country ••• (54), **Bad Day at Black Rock** •••• **(55),** Rio Bravo •• (59), **Support Your Local Sheriff** ••• **(68)**

Mel Brooks (b. 1926)

Real name: Melvin Kaminsky

WRITER-DIRECTOR. Like Woody Allen, Brooks began as a scriptwriter for TV comedian Sid Caesar, bursting into movies with a bang with his classic tasteless comedy *The Producers*. For a time, with movies like *Blazing Saddles* and *Young Frankenstein*, Brooks could do no wrong. But although still hysterically funny on chat shows, his later movies have singularly been lacking in laughs. His company Brooksfilms has backed some very original and interesting movies like *The Elephant Man* and *The Fly*. His sense of humour is presumably a family trait. When he told his mother that he was going to marry Anne Bancroft, Italian and non-Jewish, she said: 'Bring her over. I'll be in the kitchen...with my head in the oven.' He won an Oscar for the script of *The Producers*.

Quote: 'Bad taste is simply saying the truth before it should be said.' • 'My liveliness is based on an incredible fear of death. Most people are afraid of death, but I really *hate* it.' • 'We were so poor, my mother couldn't afford to have me. The lady next door gave birth to me.' • 'Critics can't even make music by rubbing their back legs together.'

Films: The Producers •••• (68; also s), The Twelve Chairs • (70; also a&s), **Blazing Saddles ••• (74; also a&s)**, **Young Frankenstein •••• (74; also s)**, Silent Movie •• (76; also a&s), High Anxiety • (77; also a&s), The Muppet Movie ••• (c)(79; a only), To Be or Not to Be •• (83; a only), Spaceballs •• (87; also a&s), Look Who's Talking Too • (v)(90; a only), Life Stinks •• (91; also a&s), Robin Hood: Men in Tights • (93; also a&s), The Little Rascals • (c)(94; a only)

Nigel Bruce (1895-53)

Real name: William Nigel Bruce

Mexican-born Bruce specialised in bluff, good-natured and invariably dim Englishmen. Though far from Conan Doyle's original vision of Dr. Watson, it is for that role in so many *Sherlock Holmes* films with Basil Rathbone that is best remembered.

Films: The Scarlet Pimpernel •••• (34), **The Charge of the Light Brigade ••• (36)**, The Trail of the Lonesome Pine ••• (36), The Last of Mrs. Cheyney •• (37), **The**

Adventures of Sherlock Holmes ••• (39), The Hound of the Baskervilles ••• (39), The Rains Came •• (39), **Rebecca •••• (40), Suspicion •• (41)**, Roxie Hart •• (42), Lassie Come Home ••• (43), Frenchman's Creek •• (44), The Pearl of Death ••• (44), The Scarlet Claw ••• (44), The Corn is Green ••• (45), The Two Mrs. Carrolls • (47), Limelight •• (52)

Sandra Bullock (b. 1966)

Although not yet strictly of 'classic' stature, surely nothing can stop the incredibly talented and beautiful Bullock from reaching the very top? I am far from being the only one to fall in love with her anew every time I see one of her movies yet, despite having star quality oozing out of every pore, she still comes across as the girl next door. As down to earth in real life as she is on screen, she still sticks to her pre-star hobbies of rock-climbing, DIY and Latin dancing. The daughter of an opera singer and a voice coach, she spoke her mother's native German as a girl and believes that Dr. Seuss is the greatest philosopher of our time.

Films: Demolition Man ••• (93), The Vanishing •• (93), Wrestling Ernest Hemingway •• (93), **Speed •••• (94)**, The Net •• (95), While You Were Sleeping ••• (95)

Richard Burton (1925-84)

Real name: Richard Jenkins

Thanks to the intervention of teacher Philip Burton, the mentor from whom he took his name, Richard Burton didn't become a coal miner like his father and most of those around him. He was the 12th of 13 children whose mother died when he was two. He was catapulted to stardom with his role on stage in *Camelot* but really hit the headlines performing with Liz Taylor on and off the set of *Cleopatra*. Their marriage was so exciting, they later did it all over again but it was even shorter the second time. An incredibly talented actor racked with unnecessary self-doubt, the years of hard living showed in his face and led to his early death. As with Peter O'Toole, Burton was nominated seven times for an Oscar, but never won one.

Quote: 'A spoiled genius from the Welsh gutter, a drinker, a womaniser. It's rather an attractive image.' • 'When I played drunks I had to remain sober because I didn't know how to play them when I was drunk.' • 'I've done the most awful rubbish in order to have somewhere to go in the morning.' • 'I've played the lot, a homosexual, a sadistic gangster, kings, princes, a saint, the lot. All that's left is a *Carry On* film. My last ambition.' • ''Richard is so discriminating he won't see a play with anybody in it but himself.' [Elizabeth Taylor] • Are we honestly supposed to believe that the Academy Awards are for acting ability when John Wayne has won the Oscar but Richard Burton, umpteen nominations and all, hasn't?' [Vic Morrow]

Films: My Cousin Rachel •• (52), The Desert Rats •• (53), The Robe •• (53), Alexander the Great •• (56), Look Back in Anger •• (59), The Longest Day ••• (62), **Cleopatra • (63),** The V.I.P.s •• (63), **Zulu •••• (v)(64),** The Night of the Iguana ••• (64), Beckett •• (64), **The Spy Who Came in from the Cold ••• (65), Who's Afraid of Virginia Woolf? ••• (66),** The Taming of the Shrew ••• (67), The Comedians •• (67), **Where Eagles Dare ••• (69),** Villain •• (71), Under Milk Wood •• (73), Equus •• (77), Wild Geese •• (78), 1984 •• (84)

James Cagney (1899-86)

Although known primarily for his gangster roles, Cagney was one of the greatest song and dance men in the movies, as can be seen in *Footlight Parade* and *Yankee Doodle Dandy*. His first performances on stage, however, were as a female impersonator. Warners took five years off his age in their publicity material to cash in on his baby-face appearance. He holds the record for the longest-surviving marriage in Hollywood, being wed to Frances 'Bill' Vernon for 63 years. He won an Oscar for *Yankee Doodle Dandy*.

Quote: 'With me, a career was the simple matter of putting groceries on the table.' • 'Once a song and dance man, always a song and dance man. Those few words tell as much about me professionally as there is to tell.' • 'When I drove through the studio gate, and the thrill was gone, I knew it was time to quit.' • 'Every time I see him work, it looks to me like a bunch of firecrackers going off all at once.' [Will Rogers] • 'I was never a fan of any actor outside of James Cagney...I always liked Cagney's style and energy. He was fearless.'

[Clint Eastwood] • 'Cagney's swift dialogue and swift movements had the glitter and precision of a meat-slicer.' [Louise Brooks]

Films: **The Public Enemy ••• (31),** Blonde Crazy •• (31), Winner Take All •• (32), **Footlight Parade •••• (33),** Hard to Handle •• (33), Lady Killer ••• (33), **A Midsummer Night's Dream •• (35),** G-Men ••• (35), Ceiling Zero •• (35), **Angels with Dirty Faces ••• (38),** Boy Meets Girl ••• (38), **The Roaring Twenties ••• (39),** The Oklahoma Kid •• (39), Each Dawn I Die ••• (39), **The Strawberry Blonde ••• (41),** The Bride Came C.O.D. •• (41), **Yankee Doodle Dandy •••• (42),** 13 Rue Madeleine •• (46), **White Heat •••• (49),** What Price Glory? •• (52), **Love Me or Leave Me ••• (55), Mister Roberts •• (55),** The Seven Little Foys •• (c)(55), Man of a Thousand Faces ••• (57), The Gallant Hours •• (60), One, Two, Three •• (61), Ragtime •• (81)

Michael Caine (b. 1933)

Real name: **Maurice Joseph Micklewhite Jr.**

Born in the Elephant and Castle, Caine is the son of a Billingsgate fish porter and a char-woman. He himself worked as a Smithfield meat porter while attending acting classes. He took his surname from the film *The Caine Mutiny* and made his mark with the films *Zulu*, *The Ipcress File* and *Alfie*. The most prolific of Hollywood stars, the many appaling films he's made don't stop him occasionally shining in the right movie. Once one of London's most swing-ing bachelors, he fell in love with Shakira Baksh when he saw her in a TV commercial and pulled weight to get her phone number. They have been married for over 20 years. He won an Oscar for *Hannah and Her Sisters*.

Quote: 'I'm a skilled, professional actor. Whether or not I've any talent is beside the point.' • 'I read books like mad, but I am careful not to let anything I read influence me.' • 'I'm not interested in directing. Now producing...! The director has to be there when it starts to rain. I notice on the set when it starts to rain, the only person who goes back to the hotel is the producer.' • 'I was rich from the day I was born, I just didn't have the money.' • 'He doesn't overact, he doesn't underact. With him, it's no sweat. His real energies go into reading too many scripts and saying 'Yes' too often.' [Ralph

Bellamy] • 'Wonderfully good company, ceaselessly funny and a brilliant actor.' [Laurence Olivier]

Films: **Zulu •••• (64), The Ipcress File ••• (65), Alfie ••** (66), Funeral in Berlin •• (67), Billion Dollar Brain •• (67), **The Italian Job ••• (69),** Battle of Britain •• (69), **Get Carter ••• (71), Sleuth ••• (72), The Man Who Would Be King ••• (75),** The Eagle Has Landed •• (76), A Bridge Too Far •• (77), California Suite ••• (78), The Swarm • (78), **Dressed to Kill ••• (80),** Escape to Victory • (81), The Hand • (81), Deathtrap •• (82), The Honorary Consul • (83), Educating Rita ••• (83), Blame it on Rio •• (84), The Holcroft Covenant • (85), Water • (85), **Hannah and Her Sisters ••• (86), Mona Lisa ••• (86),** Half Moon Street • (86), Sweet Liberty •• (86), Jaws the Revenge • (87), Surrender ••• (87), The Whistle Blower •• (87), The Fourth Protocol •• (87), **Dirty Rotten Scoundrels ••• (88),** Without a Clue • (88), Bullseye! • (90), A Shock to the System •• (90), Noises Off ••• (92), The Muppet Christmas Carol •• (92), Blue Ice • (92), On Deadly Ground • (94)

Frank Capra (1897-91)

DIRECTOR. Sicilian-born, this one-time gag writer for Mack Sennett found a home as a director at Poverty Row studio Columbia, where he was given unprecedented artistic freedom. Although he made a variety of movies in different genres, it was his sentimental comedies about the triumph of the individual against the system ('Capra-corn', they were dubbed) that hit the popular pulse in the Depression Era and transformed Columbia into one of the major players in Hollywood. However, in the postwar years, he seemed out of tune with the new mood. The political philosophy in many of his movies now seems naive and simplistic but some have stood the test of time, with *It's a Wonderful Life* now being a perennial favourite thanks to TV. He was given three Oscars, for *It Happened One Night*, *Mr. Deeds Goes To Town* and *You Can't Take It With You*.

Quote: 'I made some mistakes in drama. I thought drama was when the actors cried. But drama is when the audience cries.' • 'There are no rules in film-making, only sins. And the cardinal sin is dullness.' • 'I don't say, "Now I'm going to tell you a moral tale and you'd better like it." No, first I entertain them. I get them in a

spirit of laughter and then, perhaps, they might be softened up to accept some kind of moral precept.' • 'I'd rather be Capra than God, if there *is* a Capra.' [Grason Kanin]

Films: Miracle Woman •• (31), Platinum Blonde •• (31), The Bitter Tea of General Yen •• (33), Lady for a Day • (33), **It Happened One Night ••• (34), Mr. Deeds Goes to Town •••• (36), Lost Horizon •••• (37), You Can't Take It with You ••** (38), **Mr. Smith Goes to Washington •••• (39),** Meet John Doe •• (41), **Arsenic and Old Lace •••• (44), It's a Wonderful Life •••• (46; also s),** State of the Union • (48), Pocketful of Miracles • (61)

Charles Chaplin (1889-77)

Real name: Charles Spencer Chaplin

ACTOR-DIRECTOR. At one time, Chaplin was undoubtedly the most influential performer in the entire world, with his comedies popular in almost every single country. However, he behaved almost like the King Canute of legend when sound came, trying single-handedly to persuade everyone to go back to silent movies. He was born in London's East End and went to America with Fred Karno's troupe, Stan Laurel being another of the company. While some of his early shorts are still very funny, many now find his emphasis on sentimentality in his movies mawkish in the extreme. Richard Attenborough's film *Chaplin* did nothing to revive his reputation. He had something of an eye for young ladies, playing Svengali to a substantial number of budding actresses. He had four teenage brides, 16,16,19 and 18 respectively, and was done under the Mann Act for transporting a minor across state lines for immoral purposes, although he was found innocent. He became *persona non grata* in America during the McCarthy era, being refused entry to the country. Living out his declining years in Switzerland, he returned to America at the age of 72 to accept a special Academy Award. He once entered a Charlie Chaplin lookalike competition for a lark. He was placed third! Chaplin was knighted in 1975.

Quote: 'I am known in parts of the world by people who have never heard of Jesus Christ.' • 'All I need to make a comedy is a park, a policeman and a pretty girl.' • 'I don't think today's films stack up to mine. I'm very frank in saying that. They have no merit.' • 'I was loved by crowds, but I didn't have a single close

friend. I felt like the loneliest man alive.'
• 'Chaplin was a most terrible phoney. He
talked very pretentiously in this half-American,
half-Cockney accent. But, of course, he
couldn't escape from the unlikely fact that he
was a genius.' [Laurence Olivier] • 'When he
found a voice to say what was on his mind, he
was like a child of eight writing lyrics for
Beethoven's 9th.' [Billy Wilder] • 'If people don't
sit at Chaplin's feet, he goes out and stands
where they're sitting.' [Herman J. Mankiewicz]
• 'For me they are the most beautiful films in
the world. Chaplin means more to me than the
idea of God.' [François Truffaut] • 'The son of a
bitch is a ballet dancer! He's the best ballet
dancer that ever lived, and if I get a good
chance I'll strangle him with my bare hands.'
[W.C. Fields] • 'Chaplin is the one man in the
world I want to meet.' [Lenin]

Films: The Pawn Shop •• (16), The Rink ••
(16), The Cure ••• (17), Easy Street •• (17),
**The Gold Rush ••• (25), Show People •••
(c)(28), City Lights •• (31), Modern
Times •• (36),** The Great Dictator •• (40),
Monsieur Verdoux ••• (47), Limelight ••
(52), A Countess from Hong Kong • (c)(67)

Cyd Charisse (b. 1922)

Real name: Tula Ellice Finklea

As an actress, Charisse was little more than
competent. But as a dazzlingly slinky dancer,
partnering Astaire and Kelly, there were few to
outshine her in the musical heydays of the 40s
and 50s. Her memorably long legs are said to
have been insured for anything up to $5m.

Films: Ziegfeld Follies •• (46), The Harvey
Girls ••• (46), **Singin' in the Rain ••••
(52), The Band Wagon •••• (53),**
Brigadoon •• (54), It's Always Fair Weather
•• (55), **Silk Stockings ••• (57),** That's
Entertainment! III •••• (94)

Claudette Colbert (b. 1905)

Real name: Claudette Lily Chauchoin

French-born Colbert leapt to the public's attention when she bathed nude in milk in Cecil B.
DeMille's *Sign of the Cross*. But her career
seemed to be going nowhere until she made a
movie she thought was going to be a complete
turkey, *It Happened One Night*. In fact, it was
the first film to pick up all five major Oscars.
She was incredibly pernickety about how she

was lit on set. Crews hated her and called her
The Fretting Frog. She was once told by a
make-up specialist that her left side was her
best and from that moment on, she would not
let her right side be seen on film. Occasionally,
she insisted on whole sets being rebuilt so she
didn't have to expose it to the camera. Just to
make doubly sure it never appeared, she
daubed the right side of her face with green
greasepaint. Photographs of her looking
straight into the camera are extremely rare. Her
second husband won her hand after successfully treating her sinus problems. Her one
Academy Award was for *It Happened One
Night*.

Quote: 'Take Garbo. She was always sulking
on a sofa in her movies. Or Marlene Dietrich,
languishing in the shadows somewhere. I was
never idle. There always was a broom or a
vacuum cleaner in my fist, or I was at the sink
scrubbing away for dear life.' • 'I'd wring your
neck, if you had one.' [Noël Coward] • 'Pretty
rather than beautiful; she had some difficult
angles to her face. The right side of her face
was called "The other side of the moon"
because nobody ever saw it.' [Mary Astor]

Films: **It Happened One Night ••• (34),**
Cleopatra ••• (34), Bluebeard's Eighth Wife
• (38), **Midnight ••• (39),** Drums Along the
Mohawk ••• (39), **Boom Town ••• (40),**
Arise, My Love •• (40), **The Palm Beach
Story ••• (42), Since You Went Away ••
(44),** Without Reservations •• (46), The Egg
and I •• (47)

Ronald Colman (1891-58)

Invalided out of World War I, this British actor
moved to Hollywood in 1920 and soon cor-
nered the market in any role calling for a
distinguished gentleman. He was one of those
few actors who made the transition easily to
sound, when audiences discovered that the
voice was even smoother than his appearance.
He won an Oscar for *A Double Life*.

Quote: 'I wish I might find a Shangri-La.' • 'He
is an excellent director's dummy. He has no
personality of his own, only an appearance, and
for that reason he is an almost perfect actor for
the fictional screen.' [Graham Greene] • Mr.
Ronald Colman is, I understand, the greatest
male exponent of "sex-appeal" possessed by
the modern screen. He seems to me to be a
good-looking man who probably goes in first
wicket down, in scratch at golf, and would be

just about as interesting to talk to on any subject as a University Blue.' [James Agate]

Films: Bulldog Drummond •• (29), Raffles ••• (30), Bulldog Drummond Strikes Back ••• (34), **A Tale of Two Cities ••• (35)**, Clive of India •• (35), **The Prisoner of Zenda ••• (37)**, Lost Horizon •••• (37), The Light that Failed •• (39), **Random Harvest •••• (42)**, **The Talk of the Town ••• (42)**, A Double Life ••• (47), **Around the World in 80 Days •• (c)(56)**, The Story of Mankind • (57)

Sean Connery (b. 1930)

Real name: Thomas Connery

Dropping out of school at 13, Connery tried many different occupations – coffin polisher, bricklayer, milkman, lifeguard, cement mixer, steel worker, bodybuilder, even modelling swimming trunks – before joining the chorus of a West End production of *South Pacific*. It's said one of his main attractions as James Bond in *Dr. No* – for which he beat Richard Burton and Roger Moore – was the fact that he only cost £15,000 against the $1m a major star would have asked. Now, 40 films later and having at last escaped Bondage, he earns up to $10m a movie. He has an amazing array of accents, giving us over the years Russian-Scottish, Irish-Scottish, Spanish-Scottish, Arabian-Scottish, West Country Celtic-Scottish and English-Scottish. Won an Oscar for *The Untouchables*.

Quote: 'I never ask anybody what they earn and don't tell anybody what I earn. I want all I can get. I'm entitled to it. I don't believe all this stuff about starving in a garret or being satisfied with artistic appreciation only.' • 'I have always hated that damn James Bond. I'd like to kill him.' • 'I'm not mean, I'm Scottish.' • 'With the exception of Lassie, he's the only person I know who's never been spoiled by success.' [Terence Young, director] • 'May I say, as long as actors are going into politics, I wish for Christ's sake that Sean Connery would become King of Scotland.' [John Huston]

Films: Dr. No •••• (62), The Longest Day ••• (62), **From Russia With Love •••• (63)**, Marnie ••• (64), **Goldfinger •••• (64)**, **Thunderball •• (65)**, The Hill •• (65), **You Only Live Twice ••• (67)**, The Anderson Tapes •• (71), **Diamonds Are Forever •• (71)**, The Offence ••• (73), Zardoz • (74), **Murder on the Orient Express • (74)**, **The Man Who Would Be King ••• (75)**, Robin and Marian •• (76), A Bridge Too Far •• (77), The First Great Train Robbery ••• (79), Meteor • (79), Outland • (81), **Time Bandits ••• (81)**, The Man with the Deadly Lens ••• (82), **Never Say Never Again •• (83)**, Highlander •• (86), **The Name of the Rose •••• (86)**, **The Untouchables •••• (87)**, The Presidio •• (88), Family Business •• (89), **Indiana Jones and the Last Crusade •••• (89)**, Highlander II – the Quickening • (90), The Russia House •• (90), The Hunt for Red October ••• (90), **Robin Hood: Prince of Thieves ••• (c)(91)**, Medicine Man ••• (92), Rising Sun •• (93), A Good Man in Africa • (94), First Knight ••• (95), Just Cause •• (95)

Elisha Cook Jr. (1903-95)

Typecast from an early age in roles as a coward, a lightweight gangster and a turncoat, it's a rare movie that Cook survives until the closing credits. He was great at what he did though, never better than as Wilmer, Sydney Greenstreet's boy, in *The Maltese Falcon*. He lived a hillbilly existence in the High Sierra, catching trout with tied flies. When the studio needed him, they simply sent a messenger up into the hills to his mountain cabin, to tell him that he was wanted on set. He came, did the picture, and then disappeared again.

Films: Tin Pan Alley ••• (40), The Maltese Falcon •••• (41), **Hellzapoppin •••• (41)**, Ball of Fire •••• (41), Phantom Lady ••• (44), **The Big Sleep •••• (46)**, Don't Bother to Knock •• (52), **Shane •• (53)**, The Killing ••• (56), One-Eyed Jacks • (61), **Rosemary's Baby ••• (68)**, Hammett ••• (82)

Gary Cooper (1901-61)

Real name: Frank James Cooper

The leading screen example of the quiet man of integrity that Americans liked to believe were the backbone of their nation. He also shows a deft comic touch in movies like *Ball of Fire* and *Mr. Deeds Comes to Town*. Silent star Clara Bow's claim that 'he is hung like a horse and can go all night' did no harm to his reputation as one of the leading ladies' men in Hollywood. He won Oscars for *Sergeant York* and *High Noon*. Lee

Marvin was with him once when they stopped for petrol. When Cooper presented the attendant with a cheque for $10, the man was delighted, saying that he would frame it. Cooper admitted to Marvin that only about one in 10 of his cheques were ever cashed.

Quote: 'An oil man is allowed to deplete 27% annually as the oil is used up. An industrialist can depreciate his equipment as it ages. Now all I have to sell is me – this body of mine. If it's maimed or broken, I can't work. And it ages just as certainly as machine tools. But do they let me depreciate it? Heck no.' • 'That fellow is the world's greatest actor. He can do, with no effort, what the rest of us spend years trying to learn: to be perfectly natural.' [John Barrymore] • 'One of the most beloved illiterates this country has ever known.' [Carl Sandburg] • 'He got a reputation as a great actor just by thinking hard about the next line.' [King Vidor] • 'On the screen he's perfect, yet on the set you'd swear that it's the worst job of acting in the history of motion pictures.' [Sam Wood] • 'One of the nicest human beings I have ever met.' [Josef Von Sternberg]

Films: Wings •• (27), The Virginian •• (29), **Morocco ••• (30)**, A Farewell to Arms ••• (32), City Streets •• (32), If I Had a Million ••• (32), Design for Living •• (34), **The Lives of a Bengal Lancer ••• (35), Mr. Deeds Goes to Town •••• (36), Desire ••• (36)**, The General Died at Dawn •• (36), The Plainsman •• (36), The Adventures of Marco Polo •• (38), Bluebeard's Eighth Wife • (38), **Beau Geste ••• (39)**, The Westerner ••• (40), Northwest Mounted Police •• (40), **Ball of Fire •••• (41), Sergeant York •• (41)**, Meet John Doe •• (41), The Pride of the Yankees ••• (42), For Whom the Bell Tolls •• (43), Saratoga Trunk • (45), The Fountainhead •• (49), **High Noon •••• (52)**, Vera Cruz ••• (54), The Court-Martial of Billy Mitchell •• (55), **Friendly Persuasion ••• (56)**, Love in the Afternoon •• (57), Ten North Frederick •• (58), The Wreck of the Mary Deare •• (59)

Francis Ford Coppola (b. 1939)

DIRECTOR. Reputedly fired five times while making *The Godfather*, Coppola was the first of the movie-brat directors, himself Godfather to new talent like Scorsese, de Palma and Spielberg. He hates the studio system, but every time he sets up on his own he comes a

cropper financially and is forced to eat humble pie and make run-of-the-mill films, just so he can get enough money to set up on his own again and tell the studios to get lost once more. His first film, although he is slightly shy about it now, was *Tonight for Sure*, a mild porn pic. Nicolas Cage is his nephew and his sister is Talia Shire. He won screenwriting Oscars for *Patton*, *The Godfather* and *The Godfather, Part II* and Best Director Oscar for *The Godfather, Part II*.

Quote: 'The big studios make films like fast food.' • 'I probably have genius. But no talent.' • 'I'm very proud of my flops, as much as of my successes.'

Films: Dementia 13 •• (63; also s), Is Paris Burning? •• (66; s only), This Property is Condemned •• (66; s only), You're a Big Boy Now ••• (67; also s), Finian's Rainbow •• (68), The Rain People ••• (69; also s), **Patton •••• (70; s only), The Godfather •••• (72; also s), The Godfather, Part II ••• (74; also s), The Conversation •••• (74; also s)**, The Great Gatsby ••• (74; s only), **Apocalypse Now ••• (c)(79; also a&s)**, One from the Heart •• (82; also s), The Outsiders •• (83), Rumble Fish ••• (83; also s), The Cotton Club •• (84; also s), Peggy Sue Got Married ••• (86), Gardens of Stone ••• (87), Tucker: The Man and His Dream ••• (88), New York Stories •• (89; also s), **The Godfather, Part III ••• (90; also s)**, Bram Stoker's Dracula ••• (92)

Kevin Costner (b. 1955)

For some time, the most unseen actor ever. He left *Wargames* after shooting had begun, so that he could be in *The Big Chill*. However, his 10 minutes of screen time were cut. He later turned down leads in *Raising Arizona*, *Platoon* and *Jagged Edge*, until finally breaking through with *The Untouchables*, twelve years after his embarrassing tits'n'ass flick *Sizzle Beach USA*. During this fallow period, wife Cindy (his childhood sweetheart) brought home the bacon by working as Snow White at Disneyland. Costner has largely made his own career, shrewdly picking up films nobody else wanted to do like *No Way Out* and *Bull Durham* before astounding a sceptical Hollywood with *Dances with Wolves*. His supposed dalliance on *Waterworld*, where presumably he needed some distraction from the disaster around him, led to his wife suing for divorce.

Quote: 'They're going to have to stay up nights thinking how to cut me out of this one.' [On learning he was going to be in almost every scene in *Fandango*] • 'When I look at a film of Kevin Costner's I die of boredom.' [Mickey Rourke] • 'Kevin Costner is like Oakland: there is no there there.' [Marcello Mastroianni]

Films: Sizzle Beach, U.S.A. • (74), Night Shift •• (b)(82), Frances •• (b)(82), Testament ••• (83), Table for Five •• (b)(83), **The Big Chill** ••• **(b)(83)**, Silverado ••• (85), Fandango •• (85), **The Untouchables** •••• **(87), No Way Out** ••• **(87), Bull Durham** ••• **(88), Field of Dreams** •••• **(89), Dances With Wolves** •••• **(90; also d)**, Revenge •• (90), JFK •• **(91), Robin Hood: Prince of Thieves** •• **(91),** The Bodyguard •• (92), A Perfect World •• (93), Wyatt Earp •• (94), Waterworld ••• (95)

Joan Crawford (1904-77)

Real name: **Lucille Fay Le Sueur aka Billie Cassin**

Talk about from rags to riches. After a dirt-poor childhood, she passed through a period as a dancer, stripper and performer in explicit stag movies such as *Velvet Lips, The Casting Couch* and *Coming Home*, trying unsuccessfully in later years to buy up all the copies, an effort that is estimated to have cost over half a million dollars. One collector who kept discovering further last copies after having sword he had sold them lost his house in a mysterious fire. A champion Charleston dancer, Crawford managed to make it in silent movies in Hollywood and survived the transition to sound, establishing herself as the leading exponent of the art of suffering nobly on screen, although her image and personality now seem a lot stronger than the movies she starred in. She married the chairman of Pepsi-Cola and stayed on the board after he died. After her death, however, her adopted daughter Christina exploded the myth that she had been a good mother with the book that became the camp classic movie *Mommie Dearest*. Whenever she changed husbands, which happened on four occasions, she would cut their image out of every picture in the house, change all the toilet seats and then change the name of the house itself. Whenever she moved into a new house, she took the baths out, because she said it was totally unsanitary to sit in one's own dirty bathwater. Guests reported that she would follow them

around the house, wiping anything they touched. Dirty doorknobs were a particular phobia with her. When filming on the studio lot, her contracts insisted that the temperature had to be in the low 60s. Her face and body were covered with freckles, but she ordered them to be touched out of existence on every single publicity shot that was ever released of her. She had her back molars removed to give her the high cheekbones she is renowned for. She won an Oscar for *Mildred Pierce*.

Quote: 'I love playing bitches.' • 'I never go out unless I look like Joan Crawford the movie star. I you want to see the girl next door, go next door.' • 'She's like that joke about Philadelphia. First prize four years with Joan. Second, eight' [2nd husband Franchot Tone] • 'She is a 10-year-old girl who has put on her mother's dress – and has done it convincingly.' [Douglas Fairbanks Jr.] • 'Joan Crawford! I wouldn't sit on her toilet!' • 'Judy Holliday is the funniest comedic actress in pictures. And Joan Crawford is the funniest dramatic actress.' [Constance Bennett] • 'There is not enough money in Hollywood to lure me into making another picture with Joan Crawford. And I like money.' [Sterling Hayden]

Films: Our Dancing Daughters •• (28), **Grand Hotel** •• **(32),** Rain •• (32), Dancing Lady •• (33), Sadie McKee ••• (34), The Last of Mrs. Cheyney •• (37), **The Women** ••• **(39),** Strange Cargo •• (40), A Woman's Face ••• (41), Above Suspicion ••• (43), Hollywood Canteen •• (c)(44), **Mildred Pierce** •••• **(45),** Humoresque ••• (46), Possessed •• (47), Flamingo Road •• (49), Sudden Fear ••• (52), Female on the Beach •• (55), **Whatever Happened to Baby Jane?** •• **(62)**

Bing Crosby (1901-77)

Real name: **Harry Lillis Crosby**

Although he couldn't read a note of music, Bing became one of the most popular singers of all time. He also made many movies, most memorably as a priest or comic foil to Bob Hope. He picked his name from a comic strip, *The Bingville Bugle*, that he loved as a child. Nicknamed 'The Groaner' by the publicists, there was an early attempt to to pin back his prominent ears with gum. Unfortunately, when the lights of the studio had been on for a while, the gum softened and his ears would flap back into position with a loud noise. Eventually, he was accepted as he was. His reputation as a loving father of four boys was exploded after his death when one revealed that he was a domineering tyrant who beat his children so hard that he would sometimes draw blood. Like Bob Hope, he was a shrewd businessman and amassed a fortune of over $200m.

Quote: 'My favourite kind of picture would be one that opened with a shot of me sitting in a rocking chair on a front porch. The rest of the picture would be what I saw.' • 'Honestly, I think I've stretched a talent which is so thin it's almost transparent over a quite unbelievable term of years.' • 'He was an average guy who could carry a tune.' [His chosen epitaph] • 'Bing Crosby sings like all people think they sing in the shower.' [Dinah Shore] • 'The sticking-out ears of a pixie and the aloof demeanour of a camel.' [Ingrid Bergman]

Films: Mississippi ••• (35), Road to Singapore •• (40), **The Birth of the Blues ••• (41),** Road to Zanzibar • (41), **Road to Morocco ••• (42),** Holiday Inn •• (42), My Favorite Blonde •• (c)(42), Star Spangled Rhythm •• (42), **Going My Way ••• (44),** The Princess and the Pirate •• (c)(44), The Bells of St. Mary's •• (45), Road to Utopia ••• (45), Blue Skies • (46), Road to Rio ••• (47), My Favorite Brunette ••• (c)(47), The Emperor Waltz • (48), A Connecticut Yankee in King Arthur's Court • (49), Road to Bali •• (52), **White Christmas •• (54),** The Country Girl ••• (54), **High Society ••• (56),** Let's Make Love • (c)(60), The Road to Hong Kong •• (62), Robin and the Seven Hoods •• (64), Sing, You Sinners •• (68), **That's Entertainment! •••• (74)**

Tom Cruise (b. 1962)

Real name: Thomas Cruise Mapother IV

A one-time trainee monk who suffered from dyslexia as a child, Cruise took up acting out of boredom when he injured himself wrestling in high school. Initially little more than a smile on legs, he has proved himself capable of quality acting in a series of remarkably accomplished pictures. He was married for three years to Mimi Rogers, nine years his senior, and is now married to Nicole Kidman, who is two inches taller. They are both enthusiastic Scientologists.

Quote: 'He's a kid off a Wheaties box.' [Oliver Stone] • 'Tom Cruise is frighteningly polite. He's so nice, he's sick.' [Director Tony Scott]

Films: Endless Love • (81), Taps •• (81), **Risky Business •• (83),** Losin' It •• (83),

The Outsiders •• (83), Legend • (85), **Top Gun •• (86),** The Color of Money ••• (86), **Rain Man ••• (88),** Cocktail •• (88), Born on the Fourth of July •••• (89), Days of Thunder • (90), Far and Away •• (92), **A Few Good Men ••• (92),** The Firm ••• (93), Interview With the Vampire •• (94)

George Cukor (1899-83)

DIRECTOR. Cukor's reputation was as a woman's director. Gay himself, he was credited with drawing rounded, sensitive performances out of women like Katharine Hepburn and Joan Crawford. In fact, he was a good all-round craftsman with rather more taste and refinement than was often expected from the man with the megaphone. He brought his stylish touch to a range of genres, among them romantic comedies like *The Philadelphia Story*, costume dramas like *David Copperfield* and musicals like *My Fair Lady*. He was still directing until shortly before his death. He won an Oscar for *My Fair Lady*.

Quote: 'Give me a good script and I'll be a hundred times better as a director.'
• 'Personally, I adore clothes. I think they're one of the better inventions of mankind.' • 'Mr. Cukor is a hard task-master, a fine director and he took me over the coals giving me the roughest time I have ever had. And I am eternally grateful.' [Joan Crawford] • 'He has the ability to make me trust myself.' [Katharine Hepburn]

Films: The Royal Family of Broadway ••• (30), Bill of Divorcement •• (32), One Hour with You ••• (32), What Price Hollywood? •• (32), **Dinner at Eight ••• (33), Little Women •••• (33), David Copperfield •••• (35),** Sylvia Scarlett •• (35), **Camille ••• (37),** Holiday ••• **(38),** Gone with the Wind •••• (39), The Women ••• (39), **The Philadelphia Story ••• (40),** A Woman's Face ••• (41), Gaslight •• (44), **A Double Life ••• (47),** Adam's Rib •••• (49), **Born Yesterday ••• (50), Pat and Mike ••• (52), A Star Is Born •••• (54),** It Should Happen to You •• (54), Let's Make Love • (60), **My Fair Lady ••• (64)**

Tony Curtis (b. 1925)

Real name: Bernard Schwarz

One of Hollywood's great rags to riches success stories, Curtis was the son of a Hungarian immigrant who moved into acting after serving in the Navy in World War II. At his best in comedy, and never better than in *Some Like It Hot*, he proved he could cope with tougher roles in *Sweet Smell of Success*. He's almost better known, though, for his role with Roger Moore in TV's *The Persuaders* and for uttering one of cinema's most enduring lines in his best medieval Bronx accent: 'Yonda lies da castle of ma fadda'. His marriage to Janet Leigh, one of four, produced Jamie Lee Curtis and for that, if nothing else, he has made a major contribution to world cinema.

Quote: 'All you have to do is know your lines. What you have to avoid is acting.' • 'Finally now I am the man I want to be. I don't drink. I don't smoke. I make love. You want to know the secret of life? The saliva of young girls.' • 'Janet Leigh was years ago! Nowadays I wouldn't be caught dead married to a woman old enough to be my wife!' • 'I shared drugs with my dad many times when I was in my twenties. We had no relationship, really.' [Jamie Lee Curtis] • 'A perfect example of what ambition and bad career choices can do to fabulous good looks over the years.' [John Gielgud]

Films: Winchester '73 ••• (50), Trapeze •• (56), **Sweet Smell of Success ••• (57)**, The Vikings •• (58), The Defiant Ones •• (58), **Some Like It Hot •••• (59)**, **Operation Petticoat ••• (59), Spartacus •••• (60)**, The List of Adrian Messenger ••• (63), The Great Race •• (65), The Boston Strangler •• (68), Monte Carlo or Bust •• (69), The Last Tycoon ••• (76), Sextette • (78), Insignificance •• (85)

Michael Curtiz (1888-62)

Real name: **Mihaly Kertesz**

DIRECTOR. This Hungarian expatriate was Warner's most prolific director who turned his accomplished hand to whatever genre he was assigned. In the 30s, he was turning out four or five films a year for the penny-conscious studio and yet many of his movies achieved classic status. Renowned for his tyrannical behaviour on set, actors retaliated by ridiculing his loose grasp of the finer points of the English language. When making *Night and Day* for instance, he said: 'This man Cole Porter, he sticked to purpose of making good music, come hell or hayride.' A sign once went up at Warner Brothers saying: 'Curtiz spoken here'. He won an Oscar for *Casablanca*.

Quote: 'The next time I send a dumb sonafabitch to do something, I go myself.' • 'When I see the pictures you play in that theatre, it makes the hair stand on the edge of my seat.' • 'A savage, a real beast. A Hungarian Otto Preminger. He was a tyrant, he was abusive, he was cruel. Oh, he was just a villain, but I guess he was pretty good. We didn't believe it then.' [Olivia De Havilland]

Films: **The Mystery of the Wax Museum ••• (33)**, 20,000 Years in Sing Sing ••• (33), The Kennel Murder Case ••• (33), **Captain Blood ••• (35)**, Front Page Woman •• (35), **The Charge of the Light Brigade ••• (36)**, Kid Galahad ••• (37), **The Adventures of Robin Hood •••• (38)**, **Angels with Dirty Faces ••• (38)**, The Private Lives of Elizabeth and Essex ••• (39), Dodge City ••• (39), **The Sea Hawk ••• (40)**, Santa Fe Trail •• (40), **The Sea Wolf ••• (41), Casablanca •••• (42)**, **Yankee Doodle Dandy •••• (42)**, Passage to Marseilles •• (44), **Mildred Pierce •••• (45)**, Night and Day •• (46), **Life with Father ••• (47)**, Flamingo Road •• (49), Young Man With a Horn ••• (50), Trouble Along the Way •• (53), **White Christmas •• (54)**, King Creole •• (58)

Bette Davis (1908-89)

Real name: **Ruth Elizabeth Davis**

After her parents divorced when she was 10, Davis's mother began pushing her hard towards the limelight. Her unconventional looks made it a hard struggle. It's said nobody met her from the train when she arrived in Hollywood because the studio representative couldn't see anybody who looked like a film star. When she first saw herself on screen, she burst into tears. But within five years she was the Queen of Warners. Especially popular with women, she was not one to suffer fools gladly and fought a spectacular battle with the studio over the restrictions of her contract. Just when people wrote her off, she rescued her career time and again with movies like *All About Eve* and *Whatever Happened to Baby Jane?* So worried was she two months before *Baby Jane* came out that she took a full page ad in Variety: 'Mother of three, divorcee, American, 30 years' experience as an actress in motion pictures. Mobile still and more affable than rumour would have it. Wants steady employment in Hollywood (has had Broadway). Bette Davis. References upon request.' She is said by some to have given the name to the Oscar statuette because she said its backside resembled that of her first husband Oscar. She won her own Oscars for *Dangerous* and *Jezebel*.

Quote: 'I have eyes like a bullfrog, a neck like an ostrich and long, limp hair. You just *have* to be good to survive with that equipment.' • 'If Hollywood didn't work out I was all prepared to be the best secretary in the world.' • 'Would I consider remarriage? If I found a man who had $15m, would sign over half of it to me before the marriage, and guarantee he'd be dead within a year.' • 'I'm determined to die with my name above the titles.' • 'Why am I so good at playing bitches? I think it's because I'm not a bitch. Maybe that's why Miss Crawford always plays ladies.' • 'I don't hate Bette Davis even thought the press wants me to. I resent her – I don't see how she built a career out of a set of mannerisms instead of real acting ability. Take away the pop eyes, the cigarette an those funny clipped words and what have you got? She's phony, but I guess the public likes that.' [Joan Crawford] • 'The greatest actress of all time.' [James Mason] • 'I learnt more from watching Bette Davis than anyone else.' [George C. Scott] • 'I asked Bette Davis if she'd ever wanted to meet The Queen. She snapped at me. "What for? I am a queen." I wasn't going to argue with her!' [Natalie Wood] • 'I was never so scared in my life. And I was in the war!' [John Mills, on working with her] • 'Surely no one but a mother could have loved Bette Davis at the height of her career.'[Brian Aherne] • 'She did it the hard way.' [Her chosen epitaph]

Films: 20,000 Years in Sing Sing ••• (33), Of Human Bondage ••• (34), Front Page Woman •• (35), Dangerous •• (35), **The Petrified Forest** • **(36),** Marked Woman •• (37), Kid Galahad ••• (37), That Certain Woman •• (37), **Jezebel** ••• **(38),** Dark Victory ••• (39), Juarez •• (39), The Old Maid ••• (39), The Private Lives of Elizabeth and Essex ••• (39), **The Letter** ••• **(40), The Man Who Came to Dinner** ••• **(41), The Little Foxes** ••• **(41),** The Bride Came C.O.D. •• (41), The Great Lie •• (41), **Now, Voyager** ••• **(42),** Watch on the Rhine •• (43), Thank Your Lucky Stars •• (43), Old Acquaintance •• (43), Hollywood Canteen •• (44), Mr. Skeffington •• (44), The Corn is Green ••• (45), **All About Eve** •••• **(50),** Pocketful of Miracles • (61), **Whatever Happened to Baby Jane?** •• **(62),** Hush Hush Sweet Charlotte •• (65), The Nanny •• (65), Death on the Nile •• (78), The Whales of August ••• (87)

Olivia De Havilland (b. 1916)

This Tokyo-born British actress came to California when she was only three. The older sister of Joan Fontaine, with whom she feuded for many years, most of her roles exploited her demure, ladylike appearance. Bette Davis later said that of all the women in the world, she was the one that Errol Flynn truly loved. Despite their movies together, however, she was probably his only co-star not to succumb to his Tasmanian charm. She won Oscars for *To Each His Own* and *The Heiress*.

Quote: 'Life is a movie too.' • 'Joan deserved to win [an Oscar] and did. But Joan is 15 months younger than I, and I knew I would lose prestige with her if I lost – I had always been a heroine in her eyes – and I did! The goddess had feet of clay and she let me know it too!' • 'Olivia was up for the Oscar for *Hold Back the Dawn* and I was up for *Suspicion*. When my name was called, I thought she was going to pull out my hair.' [Joan Fontaine] • 'I wish I had a sister. I've always been the intruder in her life, the interloper. As my older sibling, Olivia could have looked after me. *Au contraire*, her desire my whole life has been to get me off-balance. We've not spoken since Mother's death in 1974, and that's it, kid. Never again.' [Joan Fontaine]

Films: Captain Blood ••• **(35), A Midsummer Night's Dream** •• **(35), The Charge of the Light Brigade** ••• **(36),** Anthony Adverse ••• (36), **The Adventures of Robin Hood** •••• **(38), Gone with the Wind** •••• **(39),** The Private Lives of Elizabeth and Essex ••• (39), Dodge City ••• (39), Raffles •• (40), Santa Fe Trail •• (40), **The Strawberry Blonde** ••• **(41),** They Died with Their Boots On ••• (41), Hold Back the Dawn ••• (41), Thank Your Lucky Stars •• (43), **The Dark Mirror** ••• **(46),** Devotion •• (46), To Each His Own •• (46), The Snake Pit ••• (48), **The Heiress** •••• **(49),** My Cousin Rachel •• (52), Hush Hush Sweet Charlotte (65), Airport '77 •• (77), The Swarm • (78)

Robert De Niro (b. 1943)

Almost more extraordinary than his electrifying acting is the length to which he goes to achieve his performance. He's encouraged scabs to grow on his face to play a junkie, learned to speak Sicilian for *The Godfather*, spent a month driving a taxi for *Taxi Driver*, lived for six weeks in a steel-mining town to understand his character in *The Deer Hunter*, gained 60 pounds on pasta to play *Raging Bull* and learned Latin to play a priest. He failed the test twice! He is said to have turned down the part of Jesus in *The Last Temptation of Christ* because there was no way he could research the role. His first acting role was as the Cowardly Lion in his school's production of *The Wizard of Oz*. De Niro's accomplished directorial debut, *A Bronx Tale*, showed considerable talent. He has won Oscars for *The Godfather, Part II* and for *Raging Bull*.

Quote: 'I only go to Los Angeles when I am paid for it.' • 'What I've always found remarkable about Bobby is his ability to not only become the person he is playing but to physically change the way he looks.' [Brian de Palma] • 'I can never recognise him from one movie to the next, so I never know who he is. To me he's just an invisible man. He doesn't exist.' [Truman Capote] • 'A Class A bastard.' [Liza Minnelli]

Films: Greetings •• (68), Bloody Mama •• (70), Hi, Mom! ••• (70), **Mean Streets ••• (73), The Godfather, Part II ••• (74),** The Last Tycoon ••• (76), **Taxi Driver ••• (76),** New York, New York •• (77), 1900 •• (77), **The Deer Hunter •• (78), Raging Bull ••• (80),** True Confessions •• (81), **The King of Comedy •••• (83),** Falling in Love •• (84), **Once Upon a Time in America •••• (84), Brazil •••• (85),** The Mission •• (86), **The Untouchables •••• (87),** Angel Heart •• (87), **Midnight Run •••• (88),** Jacknife •• (89), We're No Angels • (89), Awakenings ••• (90), **GoodFellas •••• (90),** Stanley & Iris •• (90), Cape Fear •• (91), Backdraft •• (91), Guilty by Suspicion •• (91), Mistress (92), Night and the City •• (92), This Boy's Life (93), Mad Dog and Glory ••• (93), **A Bronx Tale •••• (93; also d),** Mary Shelley's Frankenstein ••• (94)

James Dean (1931-55)

Real name: James Byron Dean

After his mother died when he was nine, Dean was sent to live on his aunt and uncle's farm. A keen debater at school, he drifted into dramatics. His first professional acting job was for a Pepsi ad and he made do between gigs as an usher at CBS and as a parking lot attendant. He was so badly off that he often slept in his car. Although he only has three notable films to his name, two of them came out after the speed-

obsessed Dean crashed his Porsche. Dean's post-death cult reputation equals Monroe's in its intensity and longevity, judging by the number of walls his poster still adorns. He was a bisexual around whom some very strange rumours have smouldered, not the least of which is the persistent story that he's really alive. Sure! No doubt he, Monroe and Elvis are running a diner together somewhere.

Quote: 'I hate all earthlings.' • 'James Dean was the strongest influence on any actor that ever stepped in front of the camera. Ever.' [Martin Sheen] • 'Intense, moody, incredible charisma. Short, myopic, not good-looking. You know who he was like? A young Woody Allen.' [Joan Collins] • 'If he'd have lived, they'd have discovered he wasn't a legend.' [Humphrey Bogart] • 'How could he *do* this to me after all my work to build him up into a big star? [Jack Warner, on learning of Dean's death]

Films: Sailor Beware •• (b)(51), Fixed Bayonets •• (b)(51), **Has Anybody Seen My Gal? ••• (b)(52),** Trouble Along the Way •• (b)(53), **Rebel Without a Cause •• (55), East of Eden ••• (55), Giant ••• (56)**

Marlene Dietrich (1901-92)

Real name: Maria Magdalene Dietrich

Already an established movie actor when she came to Hollywood in 1930 – although she denied ever making a film before *The Blue Angel* – Dietrich was taken under the wing of director Josef von Sternberg who established her elusive and ambiguous screen persona. She brought to Hollywood not only European style and sophistication, but also a cross-dressing decadence that shocked many even in Hollywood. The first female star to be seen wearing trousers, she also led the way with the first female-female kiss on screen. Never afraid to improve on what nature had given her she used make-up to change the apparent contours of her face, surgical tape to lift her breasts and had her top and bottom back molars taken out to give her high cheekbones. Just when her screen career seemed to fizzle out completely, she revived it with *Destry Rides Again*. She also proved a very successful cabaret performer. Her daughter Maria Riva lifted the lid on her extraordinary love and domestic life after her mother's death.

Quote: 'I was an actress. I made my films. Finish.' • 'When I die, I'd like to be buried in Paris. But I'd also like to leave my heart in

England. And in Germany – nothing.' • 'Age cannot with her, not custom stale her infinite sameness.' [David Shipman] • 'I know that every time I've seen Marlene Dietrich, it has done something to my heart…if she had nothing but her voice, she could break your heart with it. But she also had had that beautiful body and the timeless loveliness of her face.' [Ernest Hemingway] • 'You won't believe it, but the lady is extremely funny.' [Maximilian Schell]

Films: The Blue Angel ••• **(30)**, Morocco ••• **(30)**, Dishonoured •• (31), **Shanghai Express** ••• **(32)**, Blonde Venus •• (32), The Scarlet Empress •• (34), **Desire** ••• **(36)**, Knight Without Armour •• (37), **Destry Rides Again** •••• **(39)**, Foreign Affair ••• (48), No Highway ••• (51), **Rancho Notorious** ••• **(52)**, **Around the World in 80 Days** •• **(c)(56)**, **Witness for the Prosecution** ••• **(57)**, **Touch of Evil** ••• **(58)**, **Judgment at Nuremberg** •••• **(61)**

Robert Donat (1905-58)

British born Donat, of Polish descent, owed his mellifluous voice to training he underwent in childhood to overcome a stammer. Although a remarkably fine actor, his career was dogged by ill health from asthma which lost him several roles. He won an Oscar for *Goodbye, Mr. Chips.*

Quote: 'He is the only actor I have ever known who had a graph of his character development charted out on the wall of his dressing room.' [King Vidor] • 'One of the greatest actors of his generation, and probably the most unlucky. The gods gave him every grace and every gift but one – good health.' [Campbell Dixon]

Films The Private Life of Henry VIII ••• **(33)**, **The Count of Monte Cristo** ••• **(34)**, **The Ghost Goes West** •• **(35)**, **The 39 Steps** •••• **(35)**, Knight Without Armour •• (37), **The Citadel** ••• **(38)**, **Goodbye, Mr. Chips** ••• **(39)**, The Young Mr. Pitt •• (42), Perfect Strangers •• (45), **The Winslow Boy** ••• **(48)**, The Magic Box • (51), **The Inn of the Sixth Happiness** •• **(58)**

Kirk Douglas (b. 1916)

Real name: Iussur Danielovitch aka Isidore Demsky

Brought up in absolute poverty, the son of immigrants and the only boy in a family of seven, he saw acting as a better way out of the ghetto than his other talent, wrestling. In addition to possessing the most aggressive dimple known to mankind, Douglas was a formidable producer, who brought to the screen such movies as *Paths of Glory, Spartacus* and *Lonely are the Brave.* He only gave up on his long-cherished project, *One Flew Over the Cuckoo's Nest,* when he became too old to play the lead, but son Michael Douglas then took over.

Quote: 'I've made a career, in a sense, of playing sons of bitches.' • 'Virtue is not photogenic. What is it to be a nice guy? To be nothing, that's what. A big fat zero with a smile for everybody.' • 'My kids never had the advantage I had. I was born poor.' • 'If I knew he [Michael Douglas] was going to be that successful, I would have been nicer to him as a kid.' • 'Kirk would be the first to tell you he's a difficult man. I would be the second.' [Burt Lancaster] • 'I'm here to speak about his wit, his charm, his warmth, his talent…At last! A real acting job.' [Burt Lancaster] • 'We both came from, sort of, well, shall we say, humble beginnings. We were both young, brash, cocky, arrogant. We knew everything, were highly opinionated. We were invincible. Nobody liked us.' [Burt Lancaster] • 'Kirk never makes much of an effort toward anyone else. He's pretty wrapped up in himself. The film I made with Kirk, *Young Man With a Horn* was one of the few utterly joyless experiences I had in films.' [Doris Day]

Films: The Strange Love of Martha Ivers ••• (46), **Out of the Past** ••• **(47)**, **A Letter to Three Wives** ••• **(49)**, Young Man With a Horn ••• (50), **Ace in the Hole** •••• **(51)**, Detective Story ••• (51), **The Bad and the Beautiful** ••• **(52)**, **20,000 Leagues under the Sea** ••• **(54)**, The Man without a Star •• (55), Lust for Life ••• (56), **Paths of Glory** •••• **(57)**, **Gunfight at the OK Corral** •• **(57)**, The Vikings •• (58), **Spartacus** •••• **(60)**, **Lonely Are the Brave** ••• **(62)**, The List of Adrian Messenger ••• (63), **Seven Days in May** ••• **(64)**, The Villain •• (79), The Man from Snowy River ••• (83), Tough Guys •• (86), Oscar •• (c)(91), Greedy • (94)

Richard Dreyfuss (b. 1947)

From a bit part in *Valley of the Dolls* and *The Graduate,* Dreyfuss rose to become one of the biggest stars in Hollywood. But, as he admits, his drug habit did for him in the early 80s and although he's never really gone away, he has yet to claw his way back to the top. He became the youngest ever Best Actor Oscar winner for *The Goodbye Girl*.

Quote: 'The only difference between me and John Belushi is he's dead – and that's just the whim of the gods.'

Films: The Graduate ••• (b)(67), American Graffiti •••• (73), Jaws •••• (75), Close Encounters of the Third Kind •••• (77), The Goodbye Girl •••• (77), Stand by Me •• (86), Down and Out in Beverly Hills ••• (86), Tin Men ••• (87), Nuts •• (87), Stakeout ••• (87), Moon Over Parador •• (88), Always •• (89), **Postcards from the Edge •••• (90),** Rosencrantz and Guildenstern Are Dead •• (90), What About Bob? •• (91), Lost in Yonkers •• (93), Another Stakeout • (93), Silent Fall •• (95)

Margaret Dumont (1889-65)

Real name: **Margaret Baker**

Bewildered foil to the Marx Brothers in most of their films, Dumont also appeared with W.C. Fields and Laurel & Hardy. She is said to have understood little of the Marx Brothers' humour and was the butt of endless practical jokes from them. Nonetheless, without her statuesque and stoic dignity for them to play off, their movies wouldn't quite have been the same.

Quote: 'I was told that they needed an actress with dignity and poise, to lend legitimate balance to their comedy. After three weeks as Groucho's leading lady, I nearly had a nervous breakdown.' • 'Margaret Dumont had the regal bearing of a duchess. She really thought she was English. The only time I ever saw her lose her composure was when her wig slipped, fortunately not all the way off. I heard she was as bald as a cue ball underneath.' • 'She was a wonderful woman. She was the same off the stage as she was on it – always the stuffy, dignified matron. And the funny thing about her was she never understood the jokes." [Groucho Marx] • 'What are they laughing about?' [To Groucho, often] • 'Many people thought we were married.' [Groucho Marx]

Films: The Cocoanuts •• (29), **Animal Crackers ••• (30), Duck Soup •••• (33), A Night at the Opera •••• (35),** A Day at the Races ••• (37), **The Women ••• (39),** At the Circus •• (39), The Big Store •• (41), Never Give a Sucker an Even Break •• (41)

Clint Eastwood (b. 1930)

Real name: **Clinton Eastwood Jr.**

Fired from Universal – who originally spotted him when he was delivering dirt – for having an adam's apple that was too prominent, Eastwood was stuck in movies like *Revenge of the Creature* and *Tarantula* until he accepted $15,000 to be The Man With The No Name in *A Fistful of Dollars*, setting him on the trail to movie stardom. With his reputation now established, he is reckoned to be worth around $200m, although his fortune was dented by a $25m divorce settlement in 1980 and another $30m in palimony when he split from Sandra Locke in 1989. A fine director as well, he worked for $200 a month as the mayor of Carmel for two years in the mid-80s, enabling decent, honest folk to eat ice cream and wear high heels without being run out of town. He also owns a hamburger joint there, the Hog's Breath Bar. He and William Shatner once paid a group of mercenaries $50,000 to rescue American prisoners left in Cambodia after the Vietnam War, but Operation Lazarus was a flop. A stickler for work on the set, he once punched out a horse that he felt wasn't pulling its weight. Strangely enough, considering the time he has spent in the saddle, Eastwood is actually allergic to horses. If it wasn't for the tablets he takes, he'd be sneezing and wheezing through all his films. He is said to be a direct descendant of John Eastwood, the Mayor and Sheriff of Dublin in 1679. His coat of arms, centred around a wild boar, hangs in Clint's home. He won an Oscar for directing *Unforgiven*.

Quote: 'I squint because I can't take too much light.' • 'Movies are fun. But they're not a cure for cancer.' • 'Hardest thing in the world is to do nothing and he does it marvellously.' [Don Siegel] • 'Clint Eastwood is a man who walks softly and carries a big percentage of the gross.' [Bob Hope] • 'I think you'd have to be around for a year before you saw his ugly side, assuming he has one.' [Norman Mailer] • 'He isn't an actor, so one could hardly call him a bad actor. He'd have to do something before we could consider him bad at it.' [Pauline Kael]

Films: Revenge of the Creature •• (55), Tarantula • (55), **A Fistful of Dollars ••• (64),** For a Few Dollars More ••• (65), **The Good, The Bad and The Ugly ••• (67), Coogan's Bluff ••• (68),** Hang 'Em High •• (68), Paint Your Wagon •• (69), **Where Eagles Dare ••• (69),** Two Mules For Sister Sara •• (70), Kelly's Heroes •• (70), **Dirty**

Harry ••• (71), Play 'Misty' for Me ••• (71; also d), The Beguiled ••• (71), Joe Kidd •• (72), Magnum Force ••• (73), High Plains Drifter ••• (73; also d), Thunderbolt and Lightfoot •• (74), The Eiger Sanction •• (75; also d), The Enforcer •• (76), **The Outlaw Josey Wales ••• (76; also d),** The Gauntlet ••• (77; also d), **Every Which Way But Loose • (78), Escape from Alcatraz •• (79),** Any Which Way You Can •• (80), Bronco Billy ••• (80; also d), Honkytonk Man •• (82; also d), Firefox • (82; also d), Sudden Impact •• (83; also d), City Heat • (84), Tightrope •• (84), Pale Rider ••• (85; also d), Heartbreak Ridge •• (86; also d), The Dead Pool • (88), Bird ••• (88; d only), The Rookie • (90; also d), White Hunter, Black Heart •• (90; also d), **Unforgiven ••• (92; also d), In the Line of Fire ••• (93),** A Perfect World •• (93; also d), The Bridges of Madison County ••• (95; also d), Casper ••• (c)(95)

Denholm Elliott (1922-92)

Quote: 'I amended the actor's cliché to "Never work with children, animals or Denholm Elliott".' [Gabriel Byrne]

Films: **The Cruel Sea ••• (53),** The Heart of the Matter •• (53), **Alfie •• (66), Quest for Love ••• (71),** Robin and Marian • (76), Voyage of the Damned • (76), To the Devil a Daughter • (76), The Boys from Brazil •• (78), Zulu Dawn •• (79), **Bad Timing: A Sensual Obsession ••• (80), Raiders of the Lost Ark •••• (81),** The Missionary •••• (82), **Trading Places •••• (83),** The Wicked Lady • (83), **A Private Function ••• (85), A Room With a View •••• (86),** Defence of the Realm •••• (86), September • (87), Maurice • (87), Killing Dad • (89), **Indiana Jones and the Last Crusade ••• (89),** Stealing Heaven •• (89), Toy Soldiers •• (91), Noises Off ••• (92), Scorchers • (92)

W.C. Fields (1879-46)

Real name: **William Claude Dukenfield**

One-time vaudeville performer, all-time heavy drinker, Fields was by all accounts impossible to work with. However, he has a band of die-hard fans who adore his misanthropic, off-the-wall humour. A famous miser, he is said

to have left a fortune in up to 700 bank accounts around the world under bizarre names. He was so terrified of having his money stolen that he died (on Christmas Day) without ever having confided in anybody where the accounts were. Among the names for characters or pseudonyms for himself that he employed were Filthy McNasty, F. Snoopington Pinkerton, Elmer Prettywillie, Egbert Sousé, Mahatma Kane Jeeves, Otis Criblecoblis and Charles Bogle. There'll never be another quite like Fields.

Quote: 'Drat!' • 'Godfrey Daniels.' • 'I never drink anything stronger than gin before breakfast.' • 'If at first you don't succeed, try, try again. Then give up. No use being a damn fool about it.' • 'It was a woman who drove me to drink and I never had the decency to thank her.' • 'Somebody put too many olives in my martini last night.' • 'I never drink water. I'm afraid it will become habit forming.' • 'I make it a habit to keep a reasonable supply of medicinal stimulants on hand in case I encounter a venomous snake, which I also always keep on hand.' • 'I am free of all prejudices. I hate everybody equally.' • 'Somebody left the cork out of my lunch.' • 'There may be some things better than sex, and some things may be worse. But there is nothing exactly like it.' • 'Women are like elephants. I like to look at them but I wouldn't want to own one.' • 'If a thing's worth having, it's worth cheating for.' • 'Never give a sucker an even break.' • 'I'm looking for a loophole' [His explanation for reading the Bible on his deathbed] • 'Any man who hates small dogs and children can't be all bad.' [Leo Rosten] • 'A creative genius. I have only to see his face to laugh.' [John Betjeman] • 'I'd rather be in Philadelphia.' [Inscription he wanted for his tombstone]

Films: If I Had a Million ••• (32), International House • (33), **It's a Gift •••• (34; also s), You're Telling Me ••• (34),** The Old-Fashioned Way •• (34; also s), **David Copperfield •••• (35),** Mississippi ••• (35), My Little Chickadee •• (39; also s), **The Bank Dick •••• (40; also s),** Never Give a Sucker an Even Break •• (41), Mrs. Wiggs of the Cabbage Patch • (42)

Peter Finch (1916-77)

Real name: **William Mitchell**

Quote: 'I've grown accustomed to my face, as the song goes and, I gather, so have film producers. Others call it either aristocratic or baggy. You can call it sex appeal. I call it a character-filled face that has lived.' • 'Success is a very tough mistress. For years, while you're struggling, she wants nothing to do with you. Then, one day you find yourself in the room with her and even though the key is on the inside, you can't leave. "You've made your choice." she says. "I don't care how exhausted you are, you're going to stay here for the rest of your life making love to me".' • 'I never understood Finch. How could he do something as beautiful as *Sunday, Bloody Sunday*, but also make all that other shit? I mean, he could read, couldn't he?' [Alan Bates]

Films: The Miniver Story • (50), The Heart of the Matter •• (53), Father Brown •• (54), **The Nun's Story** ••• **(59),** The Trials of Oscar Wilde •• (60), The Pumpkin Eater •• (64), **The Flight of the Phoenix** ••• **(65), Far from the Madding Crowd** •• **(67), Sunday, Bloody Sunday** ••• **(71), Network** • **(76)**

Albert Finney (b. 1936)

Albert Finney burst onto British cinema screens carrying the kitchen sink with him and then proved there was more to him than just a northern accent in *Tom Jones*. Although one of the first Northern stars, he has an immensely impressive range that makes almost everything he does compelling viewing.

Quote: 'Now that I can afford all the shirts I want, I find people in shops insist I have them as a present.' • 'If we'd known he was going to be an actor, we'd have given him a fancier name.' [Mrs. Alice Finney, his mother]

Films: Saturday Night and Sunday Morning ••• **(60), The Entertainer** •• **(60), Tom Jones** •• **(63),** Two for the Road ••• (66), **Charlie Bubbles** •• **(68; also d),** Scrooge •• (70), Gumshoe •• (71), **Murder on the Orient Express** • **(74),** The Duellists ••• (77), Shoot the Moon •• (82), The Dresser ••• (83), Under the Volcano ••• (84), Orphans ••• (87), **Miller's Crossing** •••• **(90),** The Playboys •••• (92), Rich In Love •• (93), The Browning Version •• (94), A Man of No Importance ••• (94)

Errol Flynn (1909-59)

The Tasmanian Devil, Flynn was a whirlwind who

tore through most of the leading ladies in Hollywood. His on-screen image as a dashing swashbuckler was but a pale reflection of the high-living rake he was in his private life. He was a registered dope addict in England. He was very publicly accused of having sex with two teenage girls on his yacht, *Zaca*, on which he held his infamous parties. The case was thrown out but, unlike so many other Hollywood stars facing a scandal, the publicity only served to increase his reputation. He died young, though which of the diseases that then ravaged his body did for him was hard for the doctors to say.

Quote: 'My problem lies in reconciling my gross habits with my net income.' • 'If I have any genius, it is a genius for living.' • 'I felt like an impostor, taking all that money for reciting 10 or 12 lines of nonsense a day.' • 'The public always expected me to be a playboy and a decent chap never lets his public down.' • 'A star doesn't have to pursue or seduce any woman. What he needs, more likely, is a chastity belt for self-protection, as some of my movie pals will tell you.' • 'I've had a hell of a lot of fun and I've enjoyed every minute of it.' • 'He wasn't an admirable character, but he was a magnificent male animal and his sex appeal was obvious. It seemed not to matter whether he could act. He leapt from the screen into the projection room with the impact of a bullet.' [Hal Wallis] • 'You know Flynn. He's either got to be fighting or fucking.' [Jack L. Warner] • 'You knew where you were with Errol. He always let you down.' [David Niven]

Films: Captain Blood ••• **(35), The Charge of the Light Brigade** ••• **(36),** The Prince and the Pauper ••• (37), **The Adventures of Robin Hood** •••• **(38), Dawn Patrol** ••• **(38),** The Private Lives of Elizabeth and Essex ••• (39), Dodge City ••• (39), **The Sea Hawk** ••• **(40),** Santa Fe Trail •• (40), They Died with Their Boots On ••• (41), Gentleman Jim ••• (42), Thank Your Lucky Stars •• (43), Objective, Burma! ••• (45), Adventures of Don Juan ••• (48), That Forsyte Woman •• (49), The Master of Ballantrae •• (53), The Sun Also Rises •• (57)

Henry Fonda (1905-82)

At 10, Fonda had a story published in a local Omaha newspaper and decided he would be a journalist. He gave up after two years studying journalism at the University of Minnesota and was doing little when his mother's friend, Do

Brando, Marlon's mom, decided he would be just right for a play at the local theatre. Apparently too shy to say 'no', Fonda took to acting like the proverbial duck to water. He played so many American presidents that if he had run for office, he would have won on a landslide. He died five months after winning his one and only Oscar for *On Golden Pond*. He had been too ill to attend the ceremony.

Quote: 'I ain't really Henry Fonda. Nobody could have that much integrity.' • 'The best actors do not let the wheels show. This is the hardest kind of acting, and it works only if you look as if you are not acting at all.' • 'I have never known an actor with such craft, with such professional seriousness, such a pleasant man, full of humour, so reserved and so keenly quick-witted.' [Sergio Leone]

Films: The Trail of the Lonesome Pine ••• (36), The Moon's Our Home •• (36), **You Only Live Once ••• (37)**, That Certain Woman •• (37), **Jezebel ••• (38)**, The Mad Miss Manton •• (38), **Young Mr. Lincoln ••• (39)**, Jesse James ••• (39), The Story of Alexander Graham Bell ••• (39), Drums Along the Mohawk ••• (39), **The Grapes of Wrath •••• (40)**, The Return of Frank James •• (40), **The Lady Eve ••• (41)**, Tales of Manhattan •• (42), Rings on Her Fingers •• (42), **The Ox-Bow Incident ••• (43)**, **My Darling Clementine ••• (46)**, The Fugitive ••• (47), Fort Apache ••• (48), **Mister Roberts •• (55)**, War and Peace •• (56), **Twelve Angry Men •••• (57)**, The Wrong Man ••• (57), The Tin Star ••• (57), Stage Struck • (58), Advise and Consent ••• (61), How the West Was Won ••• (62), The Longest Day ••• (62), **Fail-Safe ••• (64)**, Battle of the Bulge •• (65), A Big Hand for the Little Lady • (66), Madigan •• (68), The Boston Strangler •• (68), **Once Upon a Time in the West •••• (69)**, The Cheyenne Social Club •• (70), The Great Smokey Roadblock •• (76), The Swarm • (78), Fedora •• (78), Meteor • (79), **On Golden Pond •• (81)**

Jane Fonda (b. 1937)

The son of Henry Fonda and brother of Peter, Jane Fonda seems to have spent her whole life trying to obliterate the sex bimbo image of *Barbarella*. For many years her political activities got more attention than her acting, although it was often hard to distinguish them

as she only seemed to go for films with liberal messages. She was reviled for a time in the US as 'Hanoi Jane' for her anti-Vietnam stance, particularly when she accused returning veterans of lying about their treatment at the hands of the North Vietnamese. She has now mellowed, established a multi-million dollar fitness empire and married TV mogul Ted Turner. She won Oscars for *Klute* and *Coming Home*.

Quote 'I found out that acting was hell. You spent all your time trying to do what they put people in asylums for.' • 'Life is not Hollywood.' • 'Working in Hollywood does give one a certain expertise in the field of prostitution.' • 'Jane has survived more bad movies than any actress should be able to in a lifetime.' [Henry Fonda] • 'From *Barbarella* to Stepford Wive.' [David Frost]

Films: Cat Ballou •• (65), **Barefoot in the Park •••• (67), Barbarella •• (68), They Shoot Horses, Don't They? ••• (69), Klute ••• (71), Steelyard Blues ••• (73)**, Julia ••• (77), California Suite •• (78), Coming Home •• (78), The Electric Horseman •• (79), **The China Syndrome ••• (79), 9 to 5 •• (80), On Golden Pond •• (81)**, Agnes of God ••• (85), The Morning After • (86), Old Gringo •• (89), Stanley & Iris •• (90)

Joan Fontaine (b. 1917)

Real name: Joan de Beauvoir De Havilland

British Fontaine was born in Tokyo but brought to Hollywood when she was two along with her elder sister Olivia De Havilland. Their respective careers advanced almost in parallel, but the two did not get on. The low point was the opening of the envelope that revealed Fontaine had won the Oscar for *Suspicion* while De Havilland went home from the evening empty-handed. Fontaine specialised in playing timid little mice, never better than in *Rebecca*.

Quote: 'Everyone wants to know about the feud between my sister and myself, and why shouldn't I admit that I haven't been able to forgive her for not inviting me to our mother's memorial service and for other cruelties. I married first, won the Oscar before Olivia did and if I die first, she'll undoubtedly be livid because I beat her to it.'

Films: Quality Street ••• (37), A Damsel in Distress •• (37), **Gunga Din •• (39), The Women ••• (39), Rebecca •••• (40), Suspicion •• (41), Jane Eyre •• (43)**, The

Constant Nymph ••• (43), Frenchman's Creek •• (44), **Letter from an Unknown Woman •••• (48)**, The Emperor Waltz • (48), Ivanhoe •• (52), Casanova's Big Night • (54), **South Pacific •• (c)(58)**, Voyage to the Bottom of the Sea •• (61)

Harrison Ford (b. 1942)

Ford was a favourite with the Hollywood community almost from the moment he arrived in LA – as a carpenter. Although he had short-term contracts as an actor with a couple of studios, it was carpentry that helped him survive. Sally Kellerman has a sign on her sundeck saying: 'This is the deck H.F. built.' He almost turned *American Graffiti* down because it paid less than carpentry. Despite the promise of *Star Wars*, it wasn't until *Raiders* that he became a star. His deal to be paid $50m for five Jack Ryan films was the biggest package Hollywood had ever seen. He is obsessed with tidiness. In his workshop, all the tools are arranged by size and category while in his wardrobe, the suits are hung in neat rows strictly according to colour. He hasn't bought any of them. He insists that on each film he makes, an extra suit is bought which he takes home with him when filming's finished.

Quote: 'The studio guys thought my name was too pretentious for a young man. As an alternative, I suggested the dumbest I could think of: Kurt Affair.' • 'He is a remarkable combination of Errol Flynn in *The Adventures of Don Juan* and Bogart as Fred C. Dobbs in *The Treasure of Sierra Madre*.' [Steven Spielberg] • 'You look at Harrison Ford and you *listen*. He looks like he's carrying a gun, even if he isn't.' [Carrie Fisher]

Films: **American Graffiti •••• (73)**, **The Conversation •••• (74)**, **Star Wars •••• (77)**, Force 10 From Navarone • (78), The Frisco Kid •• (79), Hanover Street • (79), **Apocalypse Now ••• (79)**, **The Empire Strikes Back •• (80)**, **Raiders of the Lost Ark •••• (81)**, **Blade Runner •••• (82)**, **Return of the Jedi ••• (83)**, **Indiana Jones and the Temple of Doom •• (84)**, **Witness •••• (85)**, The Mosquito Coast •• (86), **Working Girl •••• (88)**, Frantic •• (88), **Indiana Jones and the Last Crusade •••• (89)**, Presumed Innocent •• (90), Regarding Henry •• (91), Patriot Games •••• (92), **The Fugitive ••• (93)**, Clear and Present Danger •• (94)

John Ford (1895-73)

Real name: **Sean O'Fearna**

DIRECTOR. Although best known for his important contribution to the Western, Ford made many splendid films in other genres. In fact, bizarrely, he never received an Oscar for a Western, instead picking them up for *The Informer, Grapes of Wrath, How Green Was My Valley* and *The Quiet Man*. He had a wonderful eye for landscape and had such a firm idea of the way his films should look that he often needed no more than one take and rarely bothered visiting the editing room. He had no time for studio interference and, when a producer once visited the set and told him he was falling behind schedule, Ford ripped out 10 pages from the script and said: 'now we're three days ahead of schedule. Are you happy?'

Quote: 'My name's John Ford. I make Westerns.' • 'Westerns? I never look at them but I love to make them.' • 'I try to make people forget they're in a theatre. I don't want them to be conscious of a camera or a screen. I want them to feel that what they're seeing is real.' • 'Don't ever forget what I'm going to tell you. Actors are crap.' • 'A megaphone has been to John Ford what the chisel was to Michelangelo: his life, his passion, his cross.' [Frank Capra] • 'There's one general premise: almost anything that any of us has done you can find in a John Ford film.' [Sidney Lumet] • 'Jack Ford's idea of a love story is Ward Bond and John Wayne.' [Screenwriter Philip Dunne] • 'The set was anything but tranquil on a Ford picture. Ford believed that acting is a competitive thing. That it's good to be tense, good to be suspicious of other actors. His direction would be mostly asides, whispers. In a Ford film you were never exactly sure of what was going to happen next. And this is the way he wanted it.' [James Stewart] • 'He was so egomaniacal. He never would rehearse, didn't want to talk about a part…He loved getting his shot on the first take, which for him meant it was fresh. He would print the first take – even if it wasn't any good.' [Henry Fonda] • 'Actors were terrified of him because he liked to terrify them. He was a sadist.' [John Carradine]

Films: The Iron Horse •• (24), **The Lost Patrol ••• (34)**, **The Whole Town's Talking ••• (35)**, The Informer •• (35), **Stagecoach •••• (39)**, **Young Mr. Lincoln ••• (39)**, Drums Along the Mohawk ••• (39), **The Grapes of Wrath ••• (40)**, **How Green Was My Valley ••• (41)**, Tobacco

Road •• (41), They Were Expendable ••• (45), **My Darling Clementine ••• (46),** The Fugitive ••• (47), Fort Apache ••• (48), She Wore a Yellow Ribbon ••• (49), Rio Grande •• (50), **The Quiet Man ••• (52),** What Price Glory? •• (52), Mogambo •• (53), **Mister Roberts •• (55), The Searchers ••• (56),** The Last Hurrah ••• (58), The Man Who Shot Liberty Vallance •• (62), How the West Was Won ••• (62), Cheyenne Autumn •• (64)

Jodie Foster (b. 1962)

Real name: Alicia Christian Foster

It's hard to believe that Jodie Foster was once the Coppertone Girl, pictured on ads worldwide aged three with a puppy tugging at her knickers. Her breakthrough role as the 12-year-old hooker in *Taxi Driver* not only won her an Oscar nomination but also the unhealthy interest of would-be Reagan assassin John Hinckley Jr. Foster's parents divorced before her mother even knew that Jodie had been conceived. Although she studied literature and creative writing at Yale, she never took acting lessons. With her own company, Egg Productions, her abilities on both sides of the camera has made her one of the most powerful, as well as intelligent, powers in Hollywood. She has won Oscars for *The Accused* and *Silence of the Lambs.*

Films: Alice Doesn't Live Here Anymore ••• (74), Bugsy Malone •• (76), Taxi Driver ••• (76), Candleshoe •• (77), Foxes •• (80), Carny ••• (80), Hotel New Hampshire • (84), Siesta • (87), The Accused •• (88), Five Corners •• (88), Catchfire ••• (91), **The Silence of the Lambs ••• (91),** Little Man Tate ••• (92; also d), Shadows and Fog ••• (92), **Sommersby ••• (93),** Maverick ••• (94), Nell ••• (94)

Clark Gable (1901-60)

Real name: William Clark Gable

The King of Hollywood was mistakenly listed on his birth certificate as a girl. He worked in the oilfields like his father for a time. He was a telephone repair man when he met his first wife, a drama coach, whose phone he'd come to fix. She was 14 years older than him, while his second wife was 11 years his senior. His first

screen test, which he failed, forced him to wear a South Sea Islander costume with a flower stuck behind his ear. He was turned down at one point by producer Darryl F. Zanuck, who said: 'His ears are too big. He looks like an ape.' After an early experiment to tape back his ears was abandoned when they sprang back into place, he soon became one of Hollywood's major heart-throbs. He wore dentures and is reputed, at least by Vivien Leigh with whom he starred in *Gone With the Wind*, to have had appaling hygiene problems. Gable appeared to find happiness when he married Carole Lombard (his third of five marriages), but she died in a plane crash in 1942, leaving him distraught. He signed up for the Army. His discharge papers as a Major at the end of World War II were signed by Captain Ronald Reagan. After the war, he never seemed to reach the heights he commanded earlier. He won the Oscar for *It Happened One Night.*

Quote: 'When I did my first love scene, the director told me to use a longing expression, so I thought of a big, tender, rare steak.' • 'Hell, if I'd jumped on all the dames I'm supposed to have jumped on – I'd have had no time to go fishing.' • 'This 'King' stuff is pure bull. I eat and drink and go to the bathroom just like anybody else. I'm just a lucky slob from Ohio who happened to be in the right place at the right time.' • 'Clark Gable was highly professional. He was a bigger star than we could create today. I was just a mini-star when we did *Gone With the Wind*. I was afraid to talk to him. People can't understand it now, but we were in awe. Clark Gable didn't open supermarkets.' • 'Clark Gable was the only real he-man I've ever known, of all the actors I've met.' [John Huston] • 'His ears made him look like a taxicab with both doors open' [Howard Hughes] • 'You know how much I love Oappy, but to tell you the honest truth, he isn't such a hell of a good lay.' [Future wife Carole Lombard] • 'Listen, he's no Clark Gable at home' [Lombard] • 'If Clark had one inch less, he'd be the "Queen of Hollywood" instead of the King.' [Lombard] • 'Clark is the sort of guy, if you say "Hiya Clark, how are ya?", he's stuck for an answer.' [Ava Gardner] • 'Gable has enemies all right. But they all like him.' [David O. Selznick]

Films: Night Nurse ••• (31), Susan Lenox •• (31), **Red Dust •• (32),** No Man of Her Own •• (32), Strange Interlude •• (32), Dancing Lady •• (33), **It Happened One Night ••• (34),** Manhattan Melodrama ••• (34), **Mutiny on the Bounty ••• (35), San Francisco ••• (36),** Wife vs. Secretary ••

(36), Parnell • (37), Saratoga •• (37), Test Pilot •• (38), Too Hot to Handle ••• (38), **Gone with the Wind •••• (39),** Idiot's Delight •• (39), **Boom Town ••• (40),** Strange Cargo •• (40), The Hucksters •• (47), Mogambo •• (53), Run Silent, Run Deep ••• (58), Teacher's Pet ••• (58), **The Misfits •• (61)**

Greta Garbo (1905-90)

Real name: **Greta Louisa Gustafson**

Aloof, enigmatic, remote and fascinating. Nobody could ever figure out what Garbo was about either on or off screen. Born in poverty in Sweden, she was a barber's assistant at 13, lathering up the customers, then a salesgirl who got the chance to make some commercials. They led to movies and the introduction to a Hollywood which, at first, didn't know what to do with her. The public took to her on screen and MGM suddenly developed an enthusiasm for her that had earlier been lacking, with studio head Louis B. Mayer once saying: 'In America, men don't like fat women'. It was really the female cinemagoers who went for Garbo, although in those more censorious days, she usually had to die for her sins. However, one of her biggest fans appears to have been Adolf Hitler, who owned a copy of every movie she made. As far as Garbo was concerned, her private life was not for public consumption. Although she never married, she had many prominent love affairs, most spectacularly with silent star John Gilbert, whose cause she espoused when he failed to make the switch to talkies. After her ill-fated second comedy, *Two-Faced Woman* flopped in 1941, she retired from the screen and was wise enough never to make a comeback. Her most often quoted phrase, 'I vant to be alone', embodied her image both on and off screen.

Quote: 'My talent falls within definite limits. I'm not a versatile actress.' • 'Hollywood is my biggest regret. I let money, fame and greed ruin my life. Hollywood is where I wasted the best years of my life.' • 'A wonderful instrument.' [Director Rouben Mamoulian] • 'The most inhibited person I have ever worked with.' [Ernst Lubitsch] • 'What when drunk one sees in other women, one sees in Garbo sober.' [Kenneth Tynan] • 'Every man's harmless fantasy mistress. She gave you the impression that, if your imagination had to sin, it could at least congratulate itself on its impeccable taste.' [Alistair Cooke] • 'A deer in the body of a woman, living resentfully in the Hollywood zoo.' [Clare Boothe Luce] • 'I would rather spend an hour with Greta than a lifetime with any other woman.' [John Gilbert] • 'Like *Gone With the Wind*, Garbo is monumentally overrated. She's like a cardboard facade sprinkled with glitter, mysterious because you don't know what's behind it. Her voice is deep, she has no humour, her figure is flat, her carriage is not graceful, her feet are big, her private life is a fog. Only her face is perfect. But Garbo is smart; she quit when ageing began to betray her fabulous face.' [Alfred Hitchcock] • 'I got into an elevator at MGM once and there, in one of her famous men's hats, was Garbo. I said hello, and when there was no reply, I said, "Oh, sorry. I thought you were a fellow I knew".' [Groucho Marx] • 'Gary Cooper and Greta Garbo are the same person. After all, have you ever seen them in a movie together?' [Ernst Lubitsch]

Films: **Flesh and the Devil •• (27),** Anna Christie •• (30), Susan Lenox •• (31), **Grand Hotel •• (32),** Mata Hari •• (32), **Queen Christina •• (33),** Anna Karenina ••• (35), **Camille ••• (37), Ninotchka ••• (39),** Two-Faced Woman •• (41)

Ava Gardner (1922-90)

Ava Gardner may not have been the world's greatest actress, but she certainly had an impressive list of husbands, among them Mickey Rooney, bandleader Artie Shaw and Frank Sinatra. The green-eyed Gardner had originally gone to New York with the aim of becoming a secretary, only to be spotted by an MGM talent scout. She was perhaps the first actress whose tempestuous off-screen life was more dramatic than her performances. She lived her life the way she wanted to, right to the end. At her death, there were apparently five men who each believed that they were the most important man in her life.

Quote: 'I did it for the loot, honey, always the loot.' • 'Deep down, I'm pretty superficial.' • 'If people making a movie didn't keep kissing, they'd be at each other's throats.' • 'Although no-one believes me, I've always been a country girl, and still have country girl values.' • 'A lady of strong passions, one of them rage.' [Ex-husband Mickey Rooney]

Films: **The Killers •••• (46),** The Hucksters •• (47), Pandora and the Flying Dutchman •• (51), Showboat ••• (51), **The**

Band Wagon •••• (c)(53), Mogambo •• (53), The Barefoot Contessa •• (54), The Sun Also Rises •• (57), On the Beach ••• (59), 55 Days at Peking •• (63), **Seven Days in May ••• (64),** The Night of the Iguana •• (64), The Life and Times of Judge Roy Bean •• (72), Earthquake • (74), The Cassandra Crossing •• (77)

Judy Garland (1922-69)

Real name: **Frances Ethel Gumm**

The daughter of Vaudeville performers, Garland was on stage from the age of five. She later referred to her incredibly pushy mother as the 'Real Wicked Witch of the West'. When she arrived at MGM, it was a case of moving from the frying-pan to the fire. Studio boss Louis B. Mayer ought to have been done for accessory for murder. So convinced was he that she was fat, that this child star was forced onto a diet of chicken soup and appetite suppressant drugs. He also thought that she had a pug nose and had the make-up department run her up a false bridge she always had to wear. Mayer was over-heard to say: 'You see that girl? She used to be a hunchback. You see what I've made her into?' Winning the Special Oscar for *The Wizard of Oz* turned her into a star, but deprived her of a nor-mal childhood. The pressures of stardom swiftly took their toll, making her best movie, *A Star is Born*, all the more poignant. She was married to director Vincente Minnelli for five years, a marriage that produced Liza Minnelli.

Quote: 'I had the stage mother of all time. If I wasn't well, and didn't want to go on, she'd yell "Get out on that stage or I'll tie you to the bedpost".' • 'I was born at the age of 12 on the Metro-Goldwyn-Mayer lot.' • 'I've never looked through a keyhole without finding someone was looking back.' • 'If I'm such a legend, why am I so lonely?' • 'The only time I felt accepted or wanted was when I was on stage.' • 'Hollywood is a strange place when you're in trouble. Everyone is afraid it's contagious.' • 'The finest all-round performer we ever had in America...There was no limit to her talent. She was the quickest, brightest person i ever worked with.' [Gene Kelly] • 'Mayer treated Judy abominably. She was the lowest-paid star in *The Wizard of Oz*. Only Toto got paid less.' [James Mason] • 'There wasn't a thing that gal couldn't do – except look after herself.' [Bing Crosby] • 'Mother was the real-life Wicked Witch of the West.' [Liza Minnelli]

Films: Love Finds Andy Hardy •• (38), **The Wizard of Oz ••• (39),** Babes in Arms •• (39), Ziegfeld Girl •• (41), For Me and My Gal •• (42), Thousands Cheer •• (43), Girl Crazy ••• (43), **Meet Me in St. Louis •••• (44), The Clock •• (45),** Ziegfeld Follies •• (46), The Harvey Girls ••• (46), **Easter Parade ••• (48), The Pirate •• (48),** In the Good Old Summertime •• (49), Summer Stock •• (50), **A Star Is Born •••• (54),** Judgment at Nuremberg •••• (61)

Greer Garson (b. 1908)

This Anglo-Irish actress was Hollywood's idea of the ideal wife and mother, playing the role over and over again. On screen, she married Walter Pidgeon in nine of her movies. She won the Oscar for her best-known film *Mrs. Miniver*, although after the Academy members heard her speech – the longest ever given – they probably wished they'd voted for somebody else. Its inordinate length may well explain why, although nominated, she never won again.

Quote: 'If you're going to be typed, there are worse moulds in which you can be cast.' • 'Even when a petal falls from a rose, it keeps me awake.' • 'I gave up being serious about making pictures years ago, around the time I made a film with Greer Garson and she took 125 takes to say "No".' [Robert Mitchum]

Films: Goodbye, Mr. Chips ••• (39), **Pride and Prejudice •••• (40),** Blossoms in the Dust •• (41), **Random Harvest •••• (42), Mrs. Miniver •• (42),** Madame Curie •• (43), Mrs. Parkington •• (44), That Forsyte Woman •• (49), The Miniver Story • (50), Julius Caesar ••• (53)

Richard Gere (b. 1949)

Heart-throb whose career almost vanished with-out trace in the mid-80s, before being resurrected by the success of *Pretty Woman*. A musically-inclined Buddhist (he plays banjo, trumpet, guitar and piano), he's a personal mate of the Dalai Lama. Married supermodel Cindy Crawford in 1991, apparently on a whim. They split in 1995. She promptly decided to become a movie star herself.

Quote: 'My wife doesn't understand why I'm such a sex symbol. She came out of the screening of a film I did recently and said I didn't look any different from a guy you'd see on the street.' • 'Richard Gere and Cindy Crawford. Such a pair, and what a concept – his body's by Nautilus and her mind's by Mattel.' [Sam Kinison] • 'He's elastic and she's plastic.' [Sandra Bernhard]

Films: Looking for Mr. Goodbar •• (77), Bloodbrothers ••• (78), **Days of Heaven •••• (78),** Yanks •••• (79), **American Gigolo • (80), An Officer and a Gentleman •• (82),** Breathless • (83), The Honorary Consul • (83), The Cotton Club •• (84), King David •• (85), Power •• (86), No Mercy •• (86), Miles from Home •• (88), Internal Affairs •• (90), **Pretty Woman ••• (90),** Rhapsody in August • (91), Final Analysis •• (92), **Sommersby ••• (93),** Mr. Jones • (93), Intersection • (94), First Knight ••• (95)

Mel Gibson (b. 1956)

Gibson owes his career to being beaten up in a pub the night before the auditions for *Mad Max*. His battered look won him the title role in the low-budget pic that made $100m. The sixth of 11 children living in native New York, his railway-man father took the family to Australia when Mel was 12, partly to keep Mel's brothers out of the Vietnam draft. Bullied at school because of his accent, at one point he almost became a Catholic priest. Although frequently voted the sexiest man alive, he's a happily married and devoted father with six children.

Quote: 'If I've still got my pants on in the second scene of a film these days I think they've sent me the wrong script.' • 'I'm a guy that dances on tables, puts lampshades on his head, sticks his dick out in crowds. But I'm married now, got kids. I figure: Stay healthy, live longer.' • 'The most beautiful woman in the world can look like dog shit on camera. Fortunately for me, it also works the other way around.' • 'Mel Gibson is somewhere to the right of Attila the Hun. He's beautiful, but only on the outside.' [Susan Sarandon]

Films: **Mad Max •• (79), Mad Max 2 ••• (81),** Gallipoli ••• (81), The Year of Living Dangerously ••• (83), Mrs. Soffel •• (84), Bounty •• (84), The River •• (84), Mad Max Beyond Thunderdome ••• (85), **Lethal Weapon ••• (87),** Tequila Sunrise •• (88), Air America •• (89), **Lethal Weapon 2 •• (89),** Bird on a Wire •• (90), Hamlet •••

(90), **Lethal Weapon 3 •••• (92),** Forever Young ••• (92), The Man Without a Face ••• (93; also d), Maverick ••• (94), Braveheart •••• (95; also d), **Pocahontas ••• (v)(95),** Casper ••• (c)(95)

Gloria Grahame (1924-81)

Real name: **Gloria Grahame Hallward**

Gloria Grahame always played the girl you not only wouldn't take home to meet your mother but wouldn't even let your mother know existed. Nobody, but nobody, was better at playing girls who'd gone bad and who were enjoying life to the full. Grahame was known as The Girl with the Novocaine Lip, rumour having it that in the days before collagen she stuffed tissue paper under her top lip to give it an even more exaggerated and sensuous pout. After her career took a sharp nosedive, she ended up in Liverpool where she died of cancer. She won an Oscar for *The Bad and the Beautiful.*

Films: **It's a Wonderful Life •••• (46),** Song of the Thin Man •• (47), Crossfire •• (47), **In a Lonely Place ••• (50), The Bad and the Beautiful ••• (52),** The Greatest Show on Earth •• (52), Sudden Fear ••• (52), **The Big Heat ••• (53), Oklahoma! •• (55),** Melvin and Howard ••• (80)

Cary Grant (1904-86)

Real name: **Archibald Alexander Leach**

Born in Bristol, it is now hard to imagine that this debonair and suave leading man started off as a juggler, acrobat and song-and-dance man who decided to stay in America after a short tour. One of his early jobs there was as a stilt-walker at the Coney Island fairground. He is best-known for his part in many highly-regarded screwball comedies, although his habit of repeated double-takes now irritates rather than amuses. But his work for Hitchcock, which uncovered a darker side beneath the charm, still stands up well. His agent was once contacted by a journalist who sent a telegram saying: 'How old Cary Grant?' Grant sent the reply himself: 'Old Cary Grant fine. How you?' A notorious tightwad, as was Clark Gable, the two of them are rumoured to have got together after every Christmas to swap unwanted monogrammed gifts! Grant never, despite umpteen impressionists, uttered the words 'Judy, Judy, Judy' in a movie.

Quote: 'Everybody wants to be Cary Grant. *I* want to be Cary Grant.' • 'I improve on misquotation.' • 'I think making love is the best form of exercise.' • 'When I am married, I want to be single and when I am single, I want to be married.' • 'One doesn't direct Cary Grant; one simply puts him in front of a camera. And, you see, he enables the audience to identify with the main character. I meant by that, Cary Grant represents a man we know. He's not a stranger.' [Alfred Hitchcock] • 'Of all the people I performed with, I got to know Cary Grant least of all. He is a completely private person, totally reserved, and there is no way into him. Distant, very distant.' [Doris Day] • 'He was lucky – and he knew it.' [His own suggested epitaph]

Films: Blonde Venus •• (32), **I'm No Angel** ••• (33), **She Done Him Wrong** ••• (33), Sylvia Scarlett •• (35), **The Awful Truth** •• (37), **Topper** ••• (37), **Bringing Up Baby** ••• (38), **Holiday** ••• (38), Only Angels Have Wings •• (39), **Gunga Din** •• (39), In Name Only •• (39), **His Girl Friday** •••• (40), **The Philadelphia Story** ••• (40), **My Favorite Wife** ••• (40), Suspicion •• (41), Penny Serenade •• (41), **The Talk of the Town** ••• (42), Once Upon a Honeymoon •• (42), Destination Tokyo •• (43), **Arsenic and Old Lace** •••• (44), None But the Lonely Heart • (44), **Notorious** •••• (46), Night and Day •• (46), The Bachelor and the Bobby-Soxer •• (47), The Bishop's Wife •• (47), **Mr. Blandings Builds His Dream House** •• (48), I Was a Male War Bride ••• (49), People Will Talk • (51), Monkey Business •• (52), **To Catch a Thief** ••• (55), **An Affair to Remember** ••• (57), **Indiscreet** •• (58), Houseboat ••• (58), **North by Northwest** •••• (59), **Operation Petticoat** ••• (59), The Grass is Greener •• (60), That Touch of Mink •• (62), **Charade** •••• (63), Father Goose •• (64), Walk, Don't Run ••• (66)

Sydney Greenstreet (1879-54)

The English-born Sydney Greenstreet was once a tea planter and then spent 40 years as a stage actor. When he finally succumbed to the blandishments of Hollywood, he picked up an Oscar nomination for his first part on screen, as the electrifying Kasper Gutman in *The Maltese Falcon*. Although typecast as crooks, there were few quite as good at conveying the air of menace beneath a gentlemanly exterior. Twenty-stone Greenstreet was truly a heavyweight villain.

Films: **The Maltese Falcon** •••• (41), They Died with Their Boots On ••• (41), **Casablanca** •••• (42), **Across the Pacific** ••• (42), **The Mask of Dimitrios** ••• (44), Passage to Marseilles •• (44), Hollywood Canteen •• (c)(44), Between Two Worlds •• (44), **Christmas in Connecticut** •• (45), Three Strangers ••• (46), Devotion •• (46), The Hucksters •• (47), The Woman in White •• (48), Flamingo Road •• (49)

Alec Guinness (b. 1914)

Real name: **Alec Guinness de Cuffe**

There are few more natural screen actors than one-time advertising copywriter Sir Alec Guinness, whose long and varied career has spanned 50 years. Although he is best known to many as *Star War's* Obi-Wan Kenobi, a role that he apparently found completely bewildering, because he was on a percentage of profits it gave him a stellar return which has ensured he has financial independence for the rest of his life. He seems equally at home in comedy or drama and can be both gentle and menacing. One of cinema's greats, perhaps because he's kept pretty well clear of Hollywood whenever possible. He won an Oscar for *Bridge on the River Kwai*.

Quote: 'I don't really know who I am. Quite possibly, I do not exist at all.' • 'Until I decide how a character walks, nothing happens.' • 'I gave my best performances, perhaps, during the war, trying to be an officer and a gentleman.'

Films: **Great Expectations** •••• (46), **Oliver Twist** ••• (48), **Kind Hearts and Coronets** •••• (49), A Run for Your Money •• (49), **Last Holiday** ••• (50), The Mudlark •• (50), **The Lavender Hill Mob** •••• (51), **The Man in the White Suit** ••• (51), The Card •• (52), Father Brown •• (54), **The Ladykillers** •• (55), The Swan •• (56), **The Bridge on the River Kwai** ••• (57), The Horse's Mouth • (58), **Tunes of Glory** ••• (60), Our Man in Havana •• (60), **Lawrence of Arabia** •••• (62), **Doctor Zhivago** •• (65), The Comedians •• (67), Scrooge •• (70), Murder by Death • (76), **Star Wars** •••• (77), **The Empire Strikes Back** ••• (80), Raise the Titanic • (80), **Return of the Jedi** ••• (83), Lovesick •• (83), **A Passage to India** ••• (84), Little Dorrit ••• (87), A Handful of Dust •••• (88), Kafka ••• (91)

Edmund Gwenn (1875-59)

For most people, Welsh-born Gwenn is the image they have of Santa Claus, thanks to his cherubic portrayal of Kris Kringle in *Miracle on 34th Street*, for which he won an Oscar. Although acting on the stage and in films in Britain since as a youngster, he didn't pitch up in Hollywood until he was 60. But Gwenn proved an endearing character actor and was rarely out of work. He was responsible for the famous deathbed saying: 'It's tough – but not as tough as comedy!'

Films: **The Good Companions ••• (33),** Sylvia Scarlett •• (35), Anthony Adverse ••• (36), Parnell • (37), **Foreign Correspondent •• (40), Pride and Prejudice •••• (40), The Devil and Miss Jones •• (41),** Lassie Come Home ••• (43), Forever and a Day ••• (43), Between Two Worlds •• (44), **Miracle on 34th Street •••• (47), Life with Father •• (47), Them! ••• (54), The Trouble With Harry • (55),** A Yank at Oxford •• (68)

Gene Hackman (b. 1930)

Real name: **Eugene Alden Hackman**

There aren't many actors you can rely on to be good even in the most dreadful film, but Hackman is one. There are too many turkeys in Hackman's freezer but also some pretty choice prime cuts. He won Oscars for *The French Connection* and *Unforgiven*.

Quote: '75% of being successful as an actor is pure luck. The rest is just endurance.' • 'It really costs me a lot emotionally to watch myself on-screen. I think of myself and feel – like I'm quite young, and then I look at this old man with the baggy chins and the tired eyes and the ` receding hairline and all that.'

Films: **Bonnie and Clyde •••• (67),** Downhill Racer ••• (69), **The French Connection •••• (71), The Poseidon Adventure •• (72),** Scarecrow ••• (73), **Young Frankenstein •••• (c)(74), The Conversation •••• (74),** Night Moves ••• (75), French Connection II ••• (75), Lucky Lady •• (75), A Bridge Too Far •• (77), **Superman ••• (78), Superman II ••• (80),** Reds ••• (81), All Night Long ••• (81), Uncommon Valor •• (83), Under Fire •••• (83), **Eureka •••• (83),** Target •• (85), Twice in a Lifetime •• (85), Power •• (86),

No Way Out ••• **(87),** Superman IV: The Quest for Peace • (87), Best Shot ••• (87), Mississippi Burning •• (88), Another Woman • (88), Full Moon in Blue Water •• (88), BAT 21 ••• (88), The Package •• (89), Narrow Margin ••• (90), **Postcards from the Edge •••• (90),** Class Action ••• (91), **Unforgiven ••• (92),** The Firm ••• (93), Geronimo: An American Legend •• (93), Wyatt Earp •• (94), The Quick and the Dead • (95), Crimson Tide •••• (95)

Tom Hanks (b. 1956)

After his parents divorced when he was just five, he was raised by his father, a roving cook. Seemingly the all-round, affable, nice guy, Hanks became only the second actor ever to win two Best Actor Oscars in a row, with *Philadelphia* followed by *Forrest Gump*. If he has a fault, it's a tendency to become appallingly lachrymose and sentimental at awards ceremonies.

Quote: 'I had three mothers, five grammar schools and ten houses by the time I was ten.'

Films: He Knows You're Alone • (80), Bachelor Party • (84), **Splash •••• (84),** Volunteers • (85), Every Time We Say Goodbye • (86), Nothing in Common •• (86), The Money Pit • (86), Dragnet •• (87), **Big •••• (88),** Punchline ••• (88), The 'burbs ••• (89), Turner and Hooch •• (89), The Bonfire of the Vanities • (90), Joe Versus the Volcano • (90), A League of their Own •• (92), **Sleepless in Seattle •••• (93), Philadelphia •• (93), Forrest Gump ••• (94), Apollo 13 •••• (95)**

Cedric Hardwicke (1883-64)

Quote: 'Actors and burglars work better at night.' • 'I believe that god felt sorry for actors, so He created Hollywood to give them a place in the sun and a swimming pool. The price they had to pay was to surrender their talent.' • 'I suffer from what used to be called Sir tax. A knighthood inflates the cost of living beyond belief.' • 'Cedric Hardwicke is my fifth favourite actor, the first four being the Marx Brothers.' [George Bernard Shaw]

Films: **Les Miserables ••• (35), Things to Come •• (36), The Hunchback of Notre Dame ••• (39),** Stanley and Livingstone

••• (39), **Suspicion** •• **(41), The Picture of Dorian Gray** ••• (v)**(45), Rope** ••• **(48), The Winslow Boy** ••• **(48),** A Connecticut Yankee in King Arthur's Court • (49), The Desert Fox ••• (51), **The War of the Worlds** ••• (v)**(53),** Richard III ••• (55), **Around the World in 80 Days** •• (c)**(56),** The Ten Commandments •• (56), The Story of Mankind • (57), The Pumpkin Eater •• (64)

Jean Harlow (1911-37)

Real name: **Harlean Carpenter**

Jean Harlow's career was tragically short. In just a few movies, she proved that she could be not only one of the sexiest, most sultry temptresses, but also one of the sassiest comediennes. MGM producer Paul Bern married her and helped her career enormously but committed suicide under mysterious circumstances that still fascinate some. Although MGM put about the rumour that he was impotent, it is more likely that he was about to be exposed as a bigamist. A peroxide blonde, apparently not just up top, her off-screen life was pretty much as electric as the roles she played, with Margot Asquith being one of the few people to get the better of her. When asked by Harlow if the 't' in her name was pronounced out loud, she said: 'No, the 't' is silent, as in Harlow'. Her early death, at just 26, was a result, not as rumour sometimes has it, from peroxide poisoning but from a rare kidney disease. Had her mother not been a Christian Scientist and refused to allow her the necessary medical treatment, it is possible that Harlow might not have died.

Quote: 'I like to wake up feeling a new man' • 'Excuse me while I slip into something more comfortable.' [Line in *Hell's Angels*] • 'The men like me because I don't wear a brassiere. And the women like me because I don't look like a girl who would steal a husband. At least not for long.' • 'If audiences like you, you don't have to be an actress.' • 'She didn't want to be famous. She wanted to be happy.' [Clark Gable] • 'A square shooter if ever there was one.' [Spencer Tracy] • 'My God, she was beautiful. She had this low-cut dress on and I had to kiss her. Well…when it came to kissing, Harlow was the greatest. And Hollywood being what it was, we did the scene over and over again. They were happy days.' [James Stewart]

Films: Hell's Angels •• (30), **The Public Enemy** ••• **(31), City Lights** •• (b)**(31),**

Platinum Blonde •• (31), **Red Dust** •• **(32),** Red-Headed Woman •• (32), **Dinner at Eight** ••• **(33), Bombshell** ••• **(33), Libeled Lady** •• **(36),** Wife vs. Secretary •• (36), Saratoga •• (37)

Rex Harrison (1908-90)

Real name: **Reginald Carey Harrison**

The personification of the English gentleman who's got a spot of bad blood one generation back, Harrison was very much a ladies' man in real life as well. The old joke, 'I've had many wives, some of them my own', could have been invented with him in mind. There were six he got spliced to, including the wonderful but tragically short-lived Kay Kendall. Blind in one eye, he won an Oscar for *My Fair Lady*.

Quote: 'I'm now at the age where I've got to prove that I'm just as good as I never was.' •'If, next to him, Rex Harrison were not the funniest light comedy actor in the world, he'd be good for only one thing: selling cars in Great Portland Street.' [Noel Coward] • 'So pompous, he expects a lady to open the door for *him*!' [Ex-wife Rachel Roberts] • 'Rex is marvellous, but impossible…The only enduring relationship Rex had was with his basset hound Homer. Rex loved Homer.' [Elizabeth Harris Harrison]

Films: **The Citadel** ••• **(38), Night Train to Munich** •• **(40),** Major Barbara •• (40), **Blithe Spirit** •••• **(45),** The Rake's Progress •• (45), Anna and the King of Siam ••• (46), **The Ghost and Mrs. Muir** •••• **(47),** Unfaithfully Yours • (48), The Constant Husband •• (55), Midnight Lace •• (60), **Cleopatra** • **(63), My Fair Lady** ••• **(64),** The Yellow Rolls-Royce •• (65), The Agony and the Ecstasy • (65), Doctor Doolittle • (67)

Jack Hawkins (1910-73)

Quote: 'I would like some very bright spark to invent silent movies.' [After losing the use of his voice] • 'There is nobody else…really nobody who can with such a three-dimensional effect draw for us the reliable chap, conscientious but no tortoise, harassed but wryly surmounting frustration. Particularly the reliable policeman; Mr. Hawkins does a special line in policemen.' [Dilys Powell]

Films: **The Good Companions** ••• **(33), The Fallen Idol** •••• **(48), The Small**

Back Room ••• **(49)**, No Highway ••• (51), **The Cruel Sea** ••• **(53)**, **The Bridge on the River Kwai** ••• **(57)**, **Ben-Hur** ••• **(59)**, **The League of Gentlemen** ••• **(60)**, **Lawrence of Arabia** •••• **(62)**, **Zulu** •••• **(64)**, **Oh! What a Lovely War** •• **(69)**, Young Winston •• (72)

Howard Hawks (1896-77)

DIRECTOR. Hawks was at his happiest making action-based films about groups of men doing their job, usually under heavy pressure, such as *Only Angels Have Wings* and *To Have And Have Not*. In contrast to this are his comedies, which often subvert the professional ethos of his serious films, such as *His Girl Friday*, *Bringing Up Baby* and *I Was a Male War Bride*.

Quote: 'All I'm doing is telling a story.' • 'I learned right in the beginning from Jack (John) Ford, and I learned what not to do by watching Cecil De Mille.' • 'When you find out a thing goes pretty well, you might as well do it again.' • 'Howard Hawks called me up about *El Dorado*. "What about doing a Western with Duke Wayne?" Sounds good. Where? "Let's shoot it down in Old Tuscon, Arizona." Wonderful, great location, nice town. What's the story, Howard? "No story, Bob. Just characters. Stories bore people."'

Films: Dawn Patrol •• (30), **Scarface** ••• **(32)**, **Twentieth Century** •• **(34)**, Ceiling Zero •• (35), Barbary Coast ••• (35), **Bringing Up Baby** ••• **(38)**, **Only Angels Have Wings** •• **(39; also s)**, **His Girl Friday** •••• **(40)**, Ball of Fire •••• (41), Sergeant York •• (41), **To Have and Have Not** ••• **(44)**, **The Big Sleep** •••• **(46)**, **Red River** ••• **(48)**, **I Was a Male War Bride** ••• **(49)**, Monkey Business •• (52), **Gentlemen Prefer Blondes** ••• **(53)**, **Rio Bravo** •• **(59)**, Man's Favourite Sport •• (63)

Goldie Hawn (b. 1945)

Hawn was originally a caged go-go dancer, rising to become a Las Vegas show girl. She shot to stardom as the daffy blonde in the 60s TV show *Rowan and Martin's Laugh-In*. A shrewd businesswoman at odds with many of her screen roles, she has long been an item with Kurt Russell. She won the Best Supporting Actress Oscar for her first film, *Cactus Flower*, in 1969.

Quote: 'People have never wanted to see, still less to accept, the darker side of Goldie Hawn.' • 'Ditsy, my eye. She's the brightest dumb blonde since Queen Boadicea sliced Roman kneecaps.' [Victor Davis]

Films: Cactus Flower •• (69), There's a Girl in My Soup •• (70), **The Sugarland Express** •••• **(74)**, Shampoo • (75), Foul Play •• (78), Seems Like Old Times ••• (80), **Private Benjamin** •• **(80)**, Best Friends •• (82), Protocol •• (84), Overboard ••• (87), Bird on a Wire •• (90), Deceived •• (92), Housesitter •• (92), Death Becomes Her ••• (92)

Rita Hayworth (1918-87)

Real name: Margarita Carmen Cansino

The daughter of professional dancers and Ginger Rogers' cousin – their mothers were sisters – Hayworth was on the boards herself as a dancer from the age of 12, moving on to become a Hollywood nightclub singer, where she was spotted and snapped up for the movies. Originally dark-haired, her first husband gave up his business to look after her career, ordering her to change her hair to the distinctive auburn for which she is famous. She went through another four husbands, among them Orson Welles and Prince Aly Khan. She suffered at work from the over-attentive patronage of repulsive Columbia boss, Harry Cohn, whose major asset she was for many years. Her days ended unhappily, with Alzheimer's Disease taking its toll. Her quintessential role was as the vampish *Gilda*, although she later said it was a part that ruined her life: 'Every man I've known has fallen in love with Gilda and wakened with me'.

Quote: 'I never really thought of myself as a sex symbol, more as a comedienne who could dance.' • 'I haven't had everything from life. I've had too much.'

Films: **Only Angels Have Wings** •• **(39)**, **The Strawberry Blonde** ••• **(41)**, You'll Never Get Rich ••• (41), **You Were Never Lovelier** ••• **(42)**, Tales of Manhattan •• (42), Cover Girl •• (44), **Gilda** •••• **(46)**, **The Lady from Shanghai** ••• **(48)**, Miss Sadie Thompson •• (53), Fire Down Below •• (57), Pal Joey ••• (57), Separate Tables ••• (58)

Audrey Hepburn (1929-93)

Real name: Audrey Hepburn-Ruston

This Belgian-born actress was a top 50s star who bewitched audiences with her gamine, wide-eyed European charm. Hepburn was a natural at comedy and romance, although she occasionally shone in more serious dramatic roles. Her extraordinarily thin arms were the result of childhood deprivations hiding from the Nazis in occupied Europe. She wound down her screen career, to devote more time to her work for UNICEF, for which she was a special ambassador and a tireless worker. She won an Oscar for *Roman Holiday*.

Quote: 'I was asked to act when I couldn't act. I was asked to sing *Funny Face* when I couldn't sing and dance with Fred Astaire when I couldn't dance – and do all kinds of things I wasn't prepared for. Then, I tried like mad to cope with it.' • 'The kind of girl you know Mother would love, the kind they built musicals around.' [Frank Sinatra] • 'The patron saint of the anorexics.' [Orson Welles] • 'After so many drive-in waitresses in movies, here is class, someone who went to school, can spell and possibly play the piano…Titism has taken over the country. But Audrey Hepburn singlehanded may make bozooms a thing of the past. The director will not have to invent shots where the girl leans forward for a glass of scotch and soda.' [Billy Wilder]

Films: **The Lavender Hill Mob •••• (b)(51)**, Laughter in Paradise •• (b)(51), **Roman Holiday ••• (53), Sabrina ••• (54)**, War and Peace •• (56), **Funny Face ••• (57)**, Love in the Afternoon •• (57), **The Nun's Story ••• (59), Breakfast at Tiffany's •••• (61)**, The Children's Hour •• (62), **Charade •••• (63), My Fair Lady ••• (64)**, How to Steal a Million •• (66), Two for the Road ••• (66), **Wait until Dark ••• (67)**, Robin and Marian •• (76), Always •• (89)

Katharine Hepburn (b. 1907)

One of Hollywood's most intelligent, strong-willed and classy actresses, which at times made her unpopular not only with the studios but also with the public. She was once labelled 'box office poison' but fought back by bringing *The Philadelphia Story* to the screen. The upper-class Bryn Mawr-educated Hepburn married wealthy Ludlow Ogden Smith in 1928.

However, she insisted on him changing his name to Ogden Ludlow so that she wouldn't be known as 'Mrs. Smith'. The marriage lasted for three weeks and she refused to mention it again. Although the secret, incredibly, was kept by every gossip columnist in Hollywood, she and Spencer Tracy were lovers for a quarter of a century. Nominated a record 12 times, she won an unequalled four Oscars, for *Morning Glory*, *Guess Who's Coming to Dinner*, *The Lion in Winter* and *On Golden Pond*.

Quote: 'I have not lived my life as a woman. I have lived it as a man. I've done what I damn well wanted and I've made enough money to support myself.' • 'With all the opportunities I had, I could have done more. And if I'd done more, I could have been quite remarkable.' • 'When I started out, I didn't have any desire to be an actress or to learn how to act. I just wanted to be famous.' • 'I don't care what is written about me as long as it isn't true.' • 'Acting is the most minor of gifts and not a very high-class way to earn a living. After all, Shirley Temple could do it at the age of four.' • 'She has a face that belongs to the sea and the wind, with large rocking-horse nostrils and teeth that you just know bite an apple every day' [Cecil Beaton] • 'I always admired Katharine Hepburn's cheekbones. More than her films. She always wanted to be liked. Too much so. But I'd have killed for those cheekbones! [Bette Davis] • 'She makes dialogue sound better than it is by a matchless clarity and beauty of diction, and by a fineness of intelligence and sensibility that illuminates every shade of meaning in every line she speaks.' [Garson Kanin] • 'I *worship* that bloody woman. I've never enjoyed working with anyone so much in my whole life, not even Burton.' [Peter O'Toole] • 'She ran the gamut of the emotions from A to B.' [Dorothy Parker] • 'Katharine of Arrogance.' [Anon]

Films: Bill of Divorcement •• (32), **Little Women •••• (33)**, Morning Glory •• (33), **Alice Adams • (35)**, Sylvia Scarlett •• (35), **Stage Door ••• (37)**, Quality Street ••• (37), **Bringing Up Baby ••• (38), Holiday ••• (38), The Philadelphia Story ••• (40), Woman of the Year ••• (42)**, Stage Door Canteen •• (c)(43), State of the Union • (48), **Adam's Rib •••• (49), The African Queen •••• (51), Pat and Mike ••• (52)**, Summertime •• (55), Desk Set •• (57), Suddenly, Last Summer ••• (59), Long Day's Journey into Night ••• (62), **Guess Who's Coming to Dinner? •• (67), The Lion in Winter •• (68)**, The Madwoman of Chaillot •

(69), Rooster Cogburn •• (75), **On Golden Pond** •• **(81),** The Ultimate Solution of Grace Quigley •• (84), Love Affair •• (94)

Charlton Heston (b. 1924)

Real name: John Charlton Carter

A one-time nude model posing for New York art classes in the early 40s, if anyone was born to play God, it was Charlton Heston. He was the one actor anybody making an epic, ancient or modern, felt they *had* to have in the cast. Later on, he became typecast as the person it was handy to have around in a disaster. He won an Oscar for *Ben-Hur*.

Quote: 'I don't seem to have a Twentieth Century face.' • 'I haven't played a part with my pants on yet.' •'I have played three presidents, three saints and two geniuses. If that doesn't create an ego problem, nothing does.'
• 'Charlton Heston has a bad memory. He still thinks he's Moses parting the Red Sea.' [Barbara Stanwyck] • 'A graduate of the Mount Rushmore school of acting.' [Edward G. Robinson]

Films: The Greatest Show on Earth •• (52), Ruby Gentry •• (52), The Ten Commandments •• (56), **Touch of Evil** ••• **(58),** The Big Country •• (58), **Ben-Hur** ••• **(59),** The Wreck of the Mary Deare •• (59), El Cid •• (61), 55 Days at Peking •• (63), The Greatest Story Ever Told •• (65), Major Dundee ••• (65), The Agony and the Ecstasy • (65), Khartoum •• (66), **Planet of the Apes** ••• **(68), The Omega Man** ••• **(71), The Three Musketeers** •• **(73),** Soylent Green •• (73), Airport 1975 • (74), Earthquake • (74), Almost an Angel • (c)(90), Treasure Island ••• (90), Wayne's World 2 ••• (c)(93), Tombstone •• (c)(94), **True Lies** ••• **(c)(94),** In the Mouth of Madness •• (95)

Alfred Hitchcock (1899-80)

Real name: Alfred Joseph Hitchcock

DIRECTOR. No other director has been so strongly linked to a genre as Hitchcock has to the thriller. The London-born Hitch was already very successful on both sides of the Atlantic before he moved to Hollywood in 1939. He only returned twice to make further movies here, although he always insisted on tea being served on set at 4 o'clock every day. The universally acknowledged Master of Suspense, he specialised in witty, dark thrillers distinguished by technical innovation and a penchant for putting icy, blonde heroines through absolute hell. He made a habit of appearing somewhere in almost all of his movies, adding to the audience's enjoyment as they tried to spot him. Hitchcock's macabre sense of humour delighted audiences on screen, but his habit of playing rather savage and malicious practical jokes in real life didn't always endear him to his victims. Hitch once dared a technician to spend the night handcuffed to a particularly spooky set. He gave him a brandy nightcap to help him sleep, omitting to mention that it was laced with a laxative. Hitch liked train timetables to such an extent as a boy that he used to memorise them. His marriage to Alma Reville was the second longest in Hollywood history, lasting 54 years. Despite receiving five Oscar nominations, Hitchcock never won one. His legacy can be seen in umpteen, usually rather pale, imitations of his best work.

Quote: 'At a very early age I was frightened by a policeman. I'd been a bad boy. I can't remember what I'd done,but my father sent me to the police station with a note. The policeman read the note and locked me in a cell – for five minutes…I've been trying to escape from that cell ever since.' • 'I didn't say "actors are like cattle". I said "actors should be treated like cattle".' • 'The length of a film should be directly related to the endurance of the human bladder.' • 'A good film is when the price of the dinner, the theatre admission and the babysitter were worth it.' • 'Always make an audience suffer as much as possible.' • 'I am a typed director. If I made *Cinderella* the audience would be looking for a body in the coach.'
• 'There is no terror in a bang, only in the anticipation of it.' • 'Television has brought murder back into the home…where it belongs.'
• 'All love scenes shot on the set are continued in the dressing-room after the day's shooting is done. Without exception.' • 'Torture the heroine…that's always the best way.' 'Blondes are the best victims. They're like virgin snow which shows up the bloody footprints.' • 'I've never seen Hitchcock look through a camera. Some directors never stop.' [James Stewart]
• 'Any American director who says he hasn't been influenced by him is out of his mind.' [John Frankenheimer]

Films: Blackmail •• (29), The Man Who Knew Too Much ••• (34), **The 39 Steps** •••• **(35),** Secret Agent •• (36), **Young and Innocent** ••• **(37),** Sabotage ••• (37), **The**

Lady Vanishes ••• (38), Jamaica Inn • (39), **Foreign Correspondent •• (40)**, **Rebecca •••• (40)**, **Suspicion •• (41)**, Mr. and Mrs. Smith •• (41), Saboteur •• (42), **Shadow of a Doubt •••• (43)**, Lifeboat ••• (43), **Spellbound ••• (45)**, **Notorious •••• (46)**, The Paradine Case •• (47), **Rope ••• (48)**, **Strangers on a Train •••• (51)**, **Dial M For Murder •• (54)**, **Rear Window •••• (54)**, **To Catch a Thief ••• (55)**, **The Trouble With Harry • (55)**, The Man Who Knew Too Much •• (56), The Wrong Man ••• (57), **Vertigo •••• (58)**, **North by Northwest •••• (59)**, **Psycho •••• (60)**, **The Birds •• (63)**, Marnie ••• (64), Torn Curtain •• (66), Frenzy •• (72), Innocent Blood ••• (c)(92; a only)

Dustin Hoffman (b. 1937)

Real name: **Dustin Lee Hoffman**

Growing up with the worst acne in his neighbourhood, Hoffman originally wanted to be a concert pianist and studied music for a time. Switching to acting, he slept on Gene Hackman's floor, taking jobs washing dishes, checking coats and selling toys at Macy's. Paid only $17,000 for *The Graduate* he went back on the dole afterwards, as no-one was expecting it to be such an immense success. Reputed to be the biggest (though only 5 feet 6 inches) perfectionist in the business, his character in *Tootsie* is said to be very like the real him. He takes a back-stretching machine with him on set. Known by crews as 'The Humping Machine', he claims it's to keep him supple enough to live up to his younger wife's expectations in bed. He has won Oscars for *Kramer vs. Kramer* and *Rain Man*.

Quote: 'I decided to become an actor because I was failing in school and I needed the credits.' • 'I lived below the official American poverty line until I was 31.' • 'I do have this terrible suspicion that if I play myself I'm going to be bloody boring.' • 'I am obsessed with myself. I've always thought about myself. I get on the scale every day. I will look in the mirror. I've never been bored!' • 'Film is a personal effort and if you fail, you should fail for the right reasons – it's the only way of growing.' • 'You have to throw a little cold water on him every once in a while.' [Meryl Streep] • 'If you argue with him on something, he wants his point and he wants his way. Finally, if you say, "All right, we'll do it *your* way," he'll say, "No, I don't want to do it my way until you *like* doing it my way."

It's not enough to give in to him. You have to *like* what he wants, too!' [Teri Garr]

Films: The Graduate ••• (67), **Midnight Cowboy ••• (69)**, **Little Big Man ••• (70)**, **Straw Dogs • (71)**, Papillon ••• (73), Lennie ••• (74), **All the President's Men ••• (76)**, **Marathon Man ••• (76)**, Straight Time ••• (78), Agatha •• (79), **Kramer vs. Kramer ••• (79)**, **Tootsie •••• (82)**, Death of a Salesman ••• (85), Ishtar • (87), **Rain Man ••• (88)**, Family Business •• (89), Dick Tracy •• (90), Hook ••• (91), Billy Bathgate •• (92), **Accidental Hero •••• (92)**, Outbreak ••• (95)

William Holden (1918-81)

Real name: **William Franklin Beedle Jr.**

He won an Oscar for *Stalag 17*.

Quote: 'I like to think of emotions as being a series of cloaks hung on pegs. I take them down as I find I need them.' • 'Frankenstein and My Fair Lady are really the same story.' • 'I loved William Holden, but I could not have knowingly married an alcoholic.' [Audrey Hepburn]

Films: Sunset Boulevard •••• (50), **Born Yesterday ••• (50)**, **Stalag 17 •••• (53)**, The Moon is Blue • (53), **Sabrina ••• (54)**, Executive Suite ••• (54), The Bridges at Toko-Ri ••• (54), The Country Girl ••• (54), **The Bridge on the River Kwai ••• (57)**, **Casino Royale • (67)**, **The Wild Bunch •••• (69)**, **The Towering Inferno ••• (74)**, **Network • (76)**, Fedora •• (78), Escape to Athena •• (79)

Bob Hope (b. 1903)

Real name: **Leslie Townes Hope**

Although he hit his peak in the company of Bing Crosby in the *Road To* movies, British-born Hope's image of the cowardly, wisecracking common man stood him in good stead for umpteen solo vehicles during the 40s and 50s. In the light of his usual character, it seems hard to imagine him as a prizefighter, yet he had a small spell as one before moving into Vaudeville. An indefatigable performer on stage, whenever America has another 'foreign adventure', he's there entertaining the troops, a veteran of World War II who was still going in Desert Storm. Apparently a shrewd businessman with a substantial fortune, it was also recently revealed that despite the longevity of his marriage, he had rather more success with the ladies off-screen than he had in his films.

Quote: 'I do benefits for all religions. I'd hate to blow the hereafter on a technicality.' • 'They're doing things on the screen today that I wouldn't do in bed – if I could.' • 'They said I was worth $500m. If I was worth that much, I wouldn't have visited Vietnam, I'd have sent for it.' • 'There's nothing I wouldn't do for Bing, and there's nothing he wouldn't do for me. And that's the way we go through life – doing nothing for each other.' • 'Bob Hope would attend the opening of a supermarket.' [Marlon Brando] • 'There is a man.' [John Steinbeck] • 'Hope? Hope is not a comedian. He just translates what others write for him.' [Groucho Marx]

Films: **The Cat and the Canary ••• (39),** Road to Singapore •• (40), The Ghost Breakers •• (40), Road to Zanzibar • (41), **Road to Morocco ••• (42),** My Favorite Blonde •• (42), Star Spangled Rhythm •• (42), The Princess and the Pirate •• (44), Road to Utopia ••• (45), Road to Rio ••• (47), My Favorite Brunette ••• (47), **The Paleface ••• (48),** Fancy Pants •• (50), My Favorite Spy •• (51), The Lemon Drop Kid •• (51), Road to Bali •• (52), Son of Paleface ••• (52), Casanova's Big Night • (54), The Seven Little Foys •• (55), The Road to Hong Kong •• (62), The Muppet Movie ••• (c)(79)

Anthony Hopkins (b. 1937)

Although it took a chianti-swigging cannibal to *really* make Hopkins a household name, he is one of that rare breed of actors who combines stardom with a dazzling acting range. After a promising start in the late 60s, he had to overcome severe drink problems and a poor range of movies before developing a body of work in which he became spellbinding, almost regardless of the films' quality. There is scarcely a finer actor on screen today. He won an Oscar for *Silence of the Lambs*.

Quote: 'I was lousy in school. Real screwed-up. A moron. I was antisocial and didn't bother with the other kids. A really bad student. I didn't have any brains. I didn't know what I was doing there. That's why I became an actor.' • 'One of the better actors alive, in my estimation. Hopkins is the natural heir to Olivier.' [George C. Scott]

Films: The Lion in Winter •• (68), When Eight Bells Toll •• (71), Young Winston •• (72), A Bridge Too Far •• (77), Magic •• (78), **The Elephant Man •••• (80),** Bounty •• (84), The Good Father ••• (86), 84 Charing Cross Road ••• (87), The Dawning ••• (88), A Chorus of Disapproval •• (89), Desperate Hours •• (90), **The Silence of the Lambs ••• (91),** Freejack • (92), **Howard's End •••• (92),** Bram Stoker's Dracula ••• (92), Chaplin •• (92), Spotswood ••• (92), Remains of the Day ••• (93), **Shadowlands •••• (93),** The Innocent • (94), The Road to Wellville ••• (94), Legends of the Fall ••• (94)

Edward Everett Horton (1886-70)

This lanky supporting player is best known for being Fred Astaire's much put-upon comic side-kick in many of the musicals with Ginger Rogers. A superb comic performer, he kept working into his 80s, voicing the narration on the popular *Bullwinkle* cartoon TV series. Asked by the show's producer for the key to his long life, he said: 'Well, Bill, I'll tell you. Right now I'm on my way to my mother's birthday party'.

Films: The Front Page ••• (31), **Trouble in Paradise •••• (32),** The Gay Divorcee ••• (34), Design for Living •• (34), The Merry Widow •• (34), **Top Hat •••• (35),** Shall We Dance ••• (36), **Lost Horizon •••• (37), Holiday ••• (38),** Bluebeard's Eighth Wife • (38), **Here Comes Mr. Jordan •• (41),** Ziegfeld Girl •• (41), Forever and a Day ••• (43), **Arsenic and Old Lace •••• (44),** Summer Storm •• (44), The Story of Mankind • (57), Pocketful of Miracles • (61), **It's a Mad Mad Mad Mad World • (63)**

Leslie Howard (1893-43)

Real name: Leslie Howard Stainer

Although remembered as the perfect English gentleman, Howard was in fact the son of Hungarian parents and, although brought up in London, the language spoken at home was German. He only took up acting when he was invalided out of World War I suffering from shell shock. Educated at Dulwich College, where P.G. Wodehouse and Raymond Chandler had gone, he went to America and was successful both on stage and then in movies. When World War II broke out, he returned to Britain. The plane on which he was travelling back from Lisbon on in 1943 was shot down by the Germans, apparently under the misapprehension that Winston Churchill was on board. His daughter was named Leslie Ruth Howard and Bogart took a leaf out of his book, naming his daughter Leslie in gratitude for the help Howard had given him when he was still a struggling actor.

Quote: 'I wasn't cut out to be an actor. I haven't the energy for acting – it's too exhausting.' • 'I haven't the slightest intention of playing another weak, watery character such as Ashley Wilkes. I've played enough ineffectual characters already.' • 'My dear, he would have your hand while looking into your eyes and be rubbing his leg on somebody else's leg at the same time, while having the gate man phone him before his wife arrived…He was adorable. He was a little devil and just wanted his hands on every woman around…He just loved ladies.' [Joan Blondell]

Films: **The Scarlet Pimpernel** •••• **(34),** Of Human Bondage ••• (34), **The Petrified Forest** •• **(36), Pygmalion** •••• **(38; also d), Gone with the Wind** •••• **(39), Inter-mezzo** ••• **(39),** Forty-Ninth Parallel •• (41)

Trevor Howard (1916-88)

Quote: '*Faking* is the proper word for acting.' • 'One of the most remarkable actors of our century. His great films are classics. He was also one of the most popular actors in the business because he was so straight down the line. He always said what he felt.' [Peggy Ashcroft] • 'I believe Trevor Howard has quite a nice, gentle riposte to unwanted attention. Someone saw him in a bar once and said: "Are you Trevor Howard?" "Yes," he replied, "When I'm working I am".' [Charles Dance]

Films: **The Way Ahead** ••• **(44), Brief Encounter** •••• **(45), I See a Dark Stranger** ••• **(45), The Way to the Stars** ••• **(45), Green for Danger** ••• **(46), The Third Man** •••• **(49),** The Heart of the Matter •• (53), **Around the World in 80 Days** •• **(c)(56),** Sons and Lovers ••• (60), Mutiny on the Bounty •• (62), Father Goose •• (64), Von Ryan's Express ••• (65), The Charge of the Light Brigade •• (68), Battle of Britain •• (69), Ryan's Daughter •• (70), **Superman** ••• **(78),** Meteor •• (79), The Sea Wolves •• (80), **Gandhi** ••• **(82),** The Missionary •••• (82), Dust ••• (86), Foreign Body •• (86), The Dawning ••• (88), The Unholy •• (88), White Mischief •• (88)

Rock Hudson (1925-85)

Real name: **Roy Harold Scherer Jr.**

Hudson is now perhaps best known for being the first major public figure to acknowledge openly that he was suffering from AIDS. Six feet four inches tall, in his heyday he specialised in Douglas Sirk melodramas and fluffy comedies with Doris Day. His initial screen test for Fox was so lamentable, however, that it was kept and shown to other hopeful young movie actors as an example of how *not* to perform before the camera.

Quote: 'I need a script to order a sandwich.' • 'The only thing I can say in my defence is that I did the best I could. It was pretty rotten, I agree, but it was my best.'

Films: **Winchester '73** ••• **(50), Has Anybody Seen My Gal?** ••• **(52),** Bend of the River ••• (52), Magnificent Obsession •• (54), All That Heaven Allows ••• (55), **Written on the Wind** •••• **(56), Giant** ••• **(56),** Pillow Talk •• (59), **Lover Come Back** ••• **(61),** Man's Favourite Sport •• (63), Seconds ••• (66), Ice Station Zebra •• (68), The Ambassador ••• (85)

John Huston (1906-87)

WRITER-DIRECTOR. The crusty, unpredictable Huston had certainly seen plenty of life by the time he sat in the director's chair. He'd been a boxer, an officer in the Mexican Cavalry, a magazine editor and a bum in Europe, amongst other things. Then he turned his hand to scriptwriting movies like *High Sierra* and *Jezebel* before getting off to a running start as director with *The Maltese Falcon.* Although his output was variable, his films are distinguished by an ironic black humour and a strong literary sense. *The Dead* was his 41st film as director. He won an Oscar as director and screenwriter for *The Treasure of the Sierra Madre.*

Quote: 'I direct as little as possible. I relieve myself of the ardours of direction, simply by casting it right.' • 'Concentrate on the story, leave the details to others – and sit whenever you can.' • 'I don't try to guess what a million people will like. It's hard enough to know what I like.' • 'Tales of my toughness are exaggerated. I never killed an actor. Nearly lost a few.' • 'The man's as fascinating and as variable as his films. A Mephistopheles, an outrageously seductive, unfrocked cardinal, an amiable Count Dracula who drank only the best vintages of burgundy and never bared his teeth except to smile. He lives up to his living legend – and he lives it up.' [Orson Welles] • 'John, if you weren't the son of my beloved friend Walter, and if you weren't a brilliant writer and magnificent director, you'd be nothing but a common drunk.' [Gregory Ratoff] • 'A helmsman and a ham. Far too much of a ham to ever give up acting and hide his ego behind a camera.' [George Sanders] • 'John Huston couldn't care less about actresses. Men and horses, that is all! He gives better roles to the horses in his films than to the actresses.' [Delphine Seyrig]

Films: The Amazing Dr. Clitterhouse •• (38; s only), Jezebel ••• (38; s only), Dr. Ehrlich's Magic Bullet ••• (40; s only), The Maltese Falcon •••• (41; also s), Sergeant York •• (41; s only), High Sierra ••• (41; s only), Across the Pacific ••• (42), The Treasure of the Sierra Madre ••• (c)(48; also a&s), Key Largo ••• (48; also s), The Asphalt Jungle •••• (50; also s), The African Queen •••• (51), Beat the Devil •• (54), Moby Dick •• (56), The Misfits •• (61), The List of Adrian Messenger ••• (63; also a), The Night of the Iguana •• (64), Casino Royale • (67; also a), Reflections in a Golden Eye •• (67), Myra Breckinridge • (70; a only), The Life and Times of Judge Roy Bean •• (72; also a), Fat City ••• (72), Chinatown •••• (74; a only), The Man Who Would Be King ••• (75; also s), Winter Kills ••• (79; a only), Wise Blood ••• (79; also a), Lovesick • (c)(83; a only), Under the Volcano ••• (84), The Black Cauldron •• (v)(85; a only), Prizzi's Honor •• (85), The Dead ••• (87), Mr. North •• (88; s only)

Buster Keaton (1895-66)

Real name: Joseph Francis Keaton

Whereas Chaplin's comedy stemmed from its roots in theatre, Keaton's was far more purely cinematic and unsentimental. He got his nickname from family friend Harry Houdini who, after the six-year-old Keaton fell downstairs said: 'That was some buster he took'. After producing some of his greatest work himself, like *The General* and *Sherlock Junior*, he signed on with MGM and lost much of his independence. Combined with the arrival of sound, this signalled the end of Keaton's career. Reduced to

playing bit parts and providing gags for others' work, Keaton lost himself in the bottle. In the early 60s, the public seemed to rediscover him but, sadly, it was rather too late for Keaton. The best of his comedy seems as fresh and well-structured today as it ever did.

Quote: 'My ancestors didn't come on the *Mayflower*. But they met the boat.' • 'Chaplin clearly considered himself to be the clown for all ages – and that's why the stuff creaks a bit today. Buster Keaton holds up much better – and Keaton had no idea he was playing for posterity.' [John Crosby] • 'An altogether extraordinary emotional effect came from the dreamlike, obsessive, hallucinatory repetition of that strange frozen face. It was almost nightmarish – a phantasmagoria of masks. There is no question that Buster Keaton, among other things, was a surrealist even before surrealism.' [Albert Lewin]

Films Our Hospitality •• (23; also d), Sherlock Junior ••• (24; also d), The Navigator •• (24; also d), Seven Chances •• (25; also d), The General •••• (26; also d), Forever and a Day ••• (43), In the Good Old Summertime •• (49), Sunset Boulevard •••• (50), Limelight •• (52), Around the World in 80 Days •• (c)(56), It's a Mad Mad Mad Mad World • (63), A Funny Thing Happened on the Way to the Forum •• (66)

Gene Kelly (b. 1912)

Real name: Eugene Curran Kelly

The major performer in late 40s and 50s MGM musicals, Kelly brought much energy and originality to a genre that had been showing signs of over-familiarity. Some found his smile and insistence on putting extended ballet routines into every movie a trifle wearisome.

Quote: 'The joy of my kind of dancing is that you never forget it's an eternal fertility rite.' • 'I never wanted to be a dancer. It's true. I wanted to be a short-stop for the Pittsburgh Pirates.' • 'I got started dancing because I knew that was one way to meet girls.' • 'Fred Astaire represents the aristocracy when he dances. I represent the proletariat.' • 'You know, that Kelly, he's just terrific. That's all there is to it. He dances like crazy, he directs like crazy. I adore this guy. I really am crazy about his work.' [Fred Astaire]

Films: For Me and My Gal •• (42), Thousands Cheer •• (43), Cover Girl •• (44), Anchors

Aweigh •• (45), Ziegfeld Follies •• (46), **The Three Musketeers ••• (48), The Pirate •• (48), On The Town •• (49; also d),** Take Me Out to the Ball Game ••• (49), Summer Stock •• (50), **An American in Paris •••• (51), Singin' in the Rain •••• (52; also d),** Brigadoon •• (54), It's Always Fair Weather •• (55; also d), Invitation to the Dance •• (57; also d), Inherit the Wind ••• (60), Let's Make Love • (c)(60), The Guide for the Married Man • (67; d only), Hello Dolly! •• (69; d only), The Cheyenne Social Club •• (70; d only), **That's Entertainment! •••• (74),** That's Entertainment, Part 2 ••• (76; also d), That's Dancing •• (p)(85), That's Entertainment! III •••• (94)

Grace Kelly (1928-82)

This staggeringly beautiful ice-maiden comes across in many of her movies as being rather remote and wooden. It was really only Alfred Hitchcock who found the fire beneath that could melt the ice. After an extremely colourful private life that bore no resemblance to her aloof screen persona, she left Hollywood behind for an even more glamorous life when she married Prince Rainier of Monaco in 1956. She died in a car crash, around which much speculation has arisen, in 1982. She won an Oscar for *The Country Girl*.

Films: **High Noon •••• (52),** Mogambo •• (53), **Dial M For Murder •• (54), Rear Window •••• (54),** The Bridges at Toko-Ri ••• (54), The Country Girl ••• (54), **To Catch a Thief ••• (55),** High Society ••• **(56),** The Swan •• (56)

Deborah Kerr (b. 1921)

Real name: **Deborah Jane Kerr-Trimmer**

Quote: 'The camera always seems to find an innate gentility in me.' • 'I'm not very good at being me. That's why I love acting so much.' • 'She is the only star who genuinely treats each and everybody exactly alike.' [Julia Foster]

Films: Major Barbara ••• (40), Love on the Dole •• (41), **The Life and Death of Colonel Blimp •••• (43), I See a Dark Stranger ••• (45),** Perfect Strangers •• (45), **Black Narcissus ••• (46),** The Hucksters •• (47), King Solomon's Mines •• (50), Quo Vadis? •• (51), The Prisoner of Zenda •• (52), **From Here to Eternity ••**

(53), Julius Caesar ••• (53), **The King and I ••• (56),** Tea and Sympathy ••• (56), **An Affair to Remember •• (57),** Separate Tables ••• (58), **The Sundowners ••• (60),** The Grass is Greener •• (60), **The Innocents •••• (61),** The Night of the Iguana •• (64), **Casino Royale • (67),** The Assam Garden ••• (85)

Stanley Kubrick (b. 1928)

DIRECTOR. One of the most influential of postwar directors, the American Kubrick has achieved a remarkable degree of power independent of the big studios that is envied by his peers. He began making low-budget genre films like *The Killing* and *Paths of Glory*, discovered the welcome distance England gave him when he shot the controversial *Lolita* and has been here ever since. His increasingly rare work is marked by an obsessive perfectionism and considerable technical skill and innovation, although some find his work cold and remote. Though he holds a pilot's licence, he now refuses to fly anywhere in a commercial aircraft.

Quote: 'The great nations have always acted like gangsters, the small nations like prostitutes.' • 'He gives a whole new meaning to the word meticulous.' [Jack Nicholson] • 'An incredibly, depressingly serious man, with a wild sense of humour. But paranoid. He's a perfectionist.' [George C. Scott] • 'If Kubrick hadn't been a film director, he'd have been a General Chief of Staff of the US Forces. No matter what it is – even if it's a question of buying a shampoo – it goes through him. He just likes total control.' [Malcolm McDowell]

Films: The Killing ••• (56), **Paths of Glory •••• (57; also s), Spartacus •••• (60),** Lolita ••• (62), **Dr. Strangelove: Or How I Learned to Stop Worrying and Love the Bomb •••• (63; also s), 2001: A Space Odyssey •••• (68; also s), A Clockwork Orange •• (71; also s), Barry Lyndon •••• (75; also s), The Shining •••• (80; also s),** Full Metal Jacket ••• (87; also s)

Burt Lancaster (1913-94)

Real name: **Burton Stephen Lancaster**

Born in East Harlem, Lancaster escaped thanks to his athletic abilities, getting a scholarship to New York University. He dropped out and drifted around and was for a while a circus acrobat and a lingerie salesman – in the same store in Chicago where Dorothy Lamour was once a lift operator. He was discovered in a lift in New York by a producer. Although the system tried to typecast him in swashbuckling beefcake roles, Lancaster was always keen to stretch himself. He was one of the first actors to become a producer, setting up his own production company in the 50s to produce the sort of movies he *really* wanted to make like *Sweet Smell of Success*, although it also made movies he didn't star in like *Marty*. He continued to delight audiences into the 80s with *Atlantic City* and *Local Hero*. Despite his modest upbringing, he claimed to have been descended from the English House of Lancaster. He won an Oscar for *Elmer Gantry*.

Quote: 'I guess I'm the guy who always went to bed with the girl, even if it was only after the picture finished.' • 'Most people seem to think I'm the kind of guy who shaves with a blowtorch. Actually I'm bookish and worrisome.' • 'The living proof that you can be a sensitive actor and macho at the same time.' [Kirk Douglas] • 'Before he can pick up an ashtray he discusses his motivation for a couple of hours. You want to tell him to pick up the ashtray and shut up .' [Jeanne Moreau]

Films: **The Killers •••• (46)**, Brute Force ••• (47), **Sorry, Wrong Number ••• (48)**, Criss Cross •• (49), The Flame and the Arrow ••• (50), The Crimson Pirate ••• (52), Come Back, Little Sheba ••• (52), **From Here to Eternity •• (53)**, Vera Cruz •• (54), Apache •• (54), Trapeze •• (56), **Sweet Smell of Success ••• (57)**, **Gunfight at the OK Corral •• (57)**, Separate Tables ••• (58), Run Silent, Run Deep ••• (58), **Elmer Gantry ••• (60)**, **Judgment at Nuremberg •••• (61)**, Birdman of Alcatraz •• (62), **The Leopard ••• (63)**, The List of Adrian Messenger ••• (63), **Seven Days in May ••• (64)**, **The Train ••• (65)**, The Hallelujah Trail •• (65), The Professionals ••• (66), The Swimmer •• (68), **Airport ••• (70)**, 1900 •• (77), Executive Action • (77), The Cassandra Crossing •• (77), Zulu Dawn •• (79), **Atlantic City ••• (81)**, **Local Hero •••• (83)**, The Osterman Weekend •• (83), Tough Guys •• (86), **Field of Dreams •••• (89)**

Fritz Lang (1890-76)

DIRECTOR. Vienna-born Lang was a successful director in Germany with brilliantly-designed

movies like *Metropolis* but he fled the rising tide of Nazism to Hollywood. The success of *Fury* established him as a director with a strong expressionist vision and a pessimistic outlook of the human condition, as seen in *You Only Live Once* and *The Big Heat*. He was a ruthless tyrant and control freak on set and earned the enmity of most of the actors and crew he worked with. In 1956, fed up with continual rows over control with the studios, he left Hollywood for good. He claims to have invented the countdown procedure for rockets for *Woman in the Moon* in 1929 and was apparently furious that NASA later stole his idea without crediting him.

Quote: 'Directors are often blamed: "Why did you do this? And why did you do that?" But nobody ever says: "Even a director has to eat".'

Films: **Metropolis •• (26)**, **M •••• (31; also s)**, **Fury ••• (36; also s)**, **You Only Live Once ••• (37)**, The Return of Frank James •• (40), **Western Union ••• (41)**, Man Hunt ••• (41), **The Woman in the Window ••• (44)**, **Ministry of Fear ••• (44)**, Scarlet Street •• (45), **Rancho Notorious ••• (52)**, Clash by Night •• (52), **The Big Heat ••• (53)**

Jessica Lange (b. 1949)

She won Oscars for *Tootsie* and *Blue Sky*.

Quote: 'My teeth are crooked, my nose is broken. I've never thought of myself as beautiful.' • 'She is like a delicate fawn, but crossed with a Buick.' [Jack Nicholson]

Films: King Kong •• (76), **All That Jazz •• (79)**, The Postman Always Rings Twice •• (81), **Tootsie •••• (82)**, Frances •• (82), Country ••• (84), Sweet Dreams •• (85), Crimes of the Heart •• (86), Far North • (88), When I Fall in Love •• (88), Music Box ••• (89), Men Don't Leave •• (90), Cape Fear •• (91), Night and the City •• (92), Blue Sky ••• (94), Losing Isaiah •• (95), Rob Roy •• (95)

Charles Laughton (1899-62)

A great actor who was not above hamming it up outrageously if he felt the film was beneath him, Laughton's jowly features and distinctive voice have enlivened many colourful roles. His sole directorial venture, *Night of the Hunter*, was visually impressive but flopped badly. He won an Oscar for *The Private Life of Henry VIII*.

Quote: 'I am the incurable ham and Hollywood is a ham's paradise. I'm always acting even when I'm alone in a room. then I go prancing about.' • 'I have a face like the behind of an elephant.'• 'I have a face that would stop a sundial.' • 'They can't censor the gleam in my eye.' • 'Method actors give you a photograph. Real actors give you an oil painting.' • 'The only actor of genius I've ever met.' [Laurence Olivier] • 'The well from which a man draws his talents is deep, but Laughton's well had no bottom.' [Josef von Sternberg] • 'With him acting was an act of childbirth. What he needed was no so much a director as a midwife.' [Alexander Korda] • 'You can't direct a Laughton picture. The best you can hope for is to referee.' [Alfred Hitchcock] • 'The most vulgar actor of all. You always thought when you saw him, "What a great performance" or "What a ridiculous performance". It was brassy and extraordinary.' [Anthony Hopkins]

Films: **The Old Dark House** ••• (32), If I Had a Million ••• (32), **The Private Life of Henry VIII** ••• **(33)**, The Barretts of Wimpole Street •• (34), **Mutiny on the Bounty** ••• **(35)**, **Ruggles of Red Gap** •• **(35)**, **Les Miserables** ••• **(35)**, **Rembrandt** ••• **(36)**, **The Hunchback of Notre Dame** ••• **(39)**, Jamaica Inn • (39), They Knew What They Wanted •• (40), Tales of Manhattan •• (42), Forever and a Day ••• (43), The Paradine Case •• (47), **Hobson's Choice** ••• **(53)**, **The Night of the Hunter** •• **(55; d only)**, **Witness for the Prosecution** ••• **(57)**, **Spartacus** •••• **(60)**, Advise and Consent ••• (61)

Stan Laurel (1890-65) & Oliver Hardy (1892-57)

Real names: **Arthur Stanley Jefferson & Norvell Hardy**

After working separately making silent short comedies for Hal Roach, lanky British-born Laurel – who had come to America with Fred Karno's troupe as Charlie Chaplin's understudy – and stout Hardy became one of the best-loved comic duos in the entire world. They successfully made the transition to sound although Hollywood seemed to lose interest in them in the 40s after they left the guidance of Hal Roach. They didn't mix much socially off screen, but their bizarre on-screen friendship in

the face of frequently self-inflicted adversity and mayhem continues to delight audiences today. Laurel, intriguingly, was married eight times, but only to four wives. They won an Oscar for their 1932 short *The Music Box*.

Quote: 'Pardon me for a moment, my ear is full of milk.' • 'A lot of weather we've been having lately.' • 'Those two fellows we created, they were nice, very nice people. They never get anywhere because they are both so dumb, but they don't know they're dumb. One of the reasons why people like us, I guess, is because they feel superior to us.' [Ollie] • 'Babe would do anything Stan suggested. To him he was a god, and he had the greatest respect for Stan's genius for thinking up comic situations.' [Billy Gilbert] • 'All I know is just how to make people laugh.' [Stan] • 'He really is a funny, funny fellow, isn't he?' [Stan about Ollie] • 'Speaking for myself, I cannot like anyone who does not like Laurel and Hardy, nor love anyone who does not love them. In 104 films they never ran out of comic ideas, insane invention, charming conceits.' [Garson Kanin]

Films: Two Tars ••• (28), Big Business •••• (29), Hog Wild ••• (30), Laughing Gravy •••• (31), The Music Box •••• (32), Towed in a Hole •••• (32), Busy Bodies ••• (33), **Sons of the Desert** ••• **(34)**, Them Thar Hills ••• (34), Our Relations ••• (36), **Way Out West** •••• **(37)**, Swiss Miss •• (38), Blockheads ••• (38)

David Lean (1908-91)

DIRECTOR. Young David frequently ignored his Quaker parents' ban on seeing 'sinful' films. Consequently, he was filled with a burning desire to go into the film industry. He was the finest editor in 30s British films and began his directorial career in tandem with Noel Coward, first co-directing *In Which We Serve*, then other Cowards on his own before moving onto two highly regarded Dickens adaptations. In the late 50s, he began his love affair with the large-scale historical epic, the best known of which are his Oscar-winning *Bridge on the River Kwai* and *Lawrence of Arabia*. Others, like *Ryan's Daughter*, look rather overblown despite his considerable technical skills.

Quote: 'I hope the money men don't find out that I'd pay them to let me do this.' • 'There is a tendency to think that if a film is expensive, it's going to be an artistic failure.' • 'If he heard his best friend was dying while he was on the set, I doubt if he'd take it in. Once he's started a film, there's really nothing else in his life.' [Ronald Neame] • 'David Lean knows more about films than a banker knows about money.' [Katharine Hepburn]

Films: In Which We Serve ••• (42), This Happy Breed •• (44; also s), Blithe Spirit •••• (45; also s), Brief Encounter •••• (45; also s), Great Expectations •••• (46; also s), Oliver Twist ••• (48; also s), Hobson's Choice ••• (53; also s), Summertime ••• (55; also s), The Bridge on the River Kwai ••• (57), Lawrence of Arabia •••• (62), Doctor Zhivago •• (65), Ryan's Daughter •• (70), A Passage to India ••• (84; also s)

Christopher Lee (b. 1922)

Quote: 'Ours is a business both strange and unique, a business of starlight and glamour, one moment a place of dreams, the next of nightmares.' • 'There are many vampires in the world today. You only have to think of the film business.' • 'Lon Chaney and Boris Karloff didn't like the word "horror". they, like I, went for the French description: "The theatre of the *fantastique*".'

Films: Hamlet •• (b)(48), The Crimson Pirate ••• (52), The Curse of Frankenstein •• (56), **Dracula ••• (58),** The Hound of the Baskervilles •• (59), The Mummy •• (59), The Longest Day ••• (62), The Devil Rides Out • (68), **The Three Musketeers •• (73), The Wicker Man ••• (73), The Man with the Golden Gun • (74),** To the Devil a Daughter • (76), Airport '77 •• (77), 1941 •• (79), The Return of Captain Invincible •• (83), The Return of the Musketeers •• (89), Gremlins 2: The New Batch ••• (90), Treasure Island ••• (90), Police Academy: Mission to Moscow • (94), Funny Man • (94), A Feast at Midnight • (95)

Vivien Leigh (1913-67)

Real name: Vivien Mary Hartley

Born in Darjeeling to an Indian mother, this convent-educated actress had made several movies before her most famous role in *Gone With the Wind.* The married Leigh was already having her famous affair with Olivier when she became the Scarlett woman and the two married in 1940. Her lustrous beauty was matched by considerable talent but she was dogged by manic depression and tuberculosis. This kept her away from the screen for long periods, but she still managed to make such splendid films as *A Streetcar Named Desire.* She won Oscars for *Gone With the Wind* and *A Streetcar Named Desire.*

Quote: 'I never liked Scarlett. I knew it was a marvellous part, but I never cared for her.' • 'She wanted us to be like brother and sister. But, fortunately, occasional incest was allowed.' [Laurence Olivier] • 'A stunner whose ravishing beauty often tended to obscure her staggering achievements as an actress. Great beauties are infrequently great actresses, simply because they do not need to be. Vivien was different; ambitious, persevering, serious, often inspired.' [Garson Kanin]

Films: Dark Journey ••• (37), **Gone with the Wind •••• (39),** Waterloo Bridge ••• (40), Lady Hamilton ••• (41), Caesar and Cleopatra • (46), **A Streetcar Named Desire ••• (51),** The Roman Spring of Mrs. Stone •• (61), Ship of Fools ••• (65), Fire Over England •• (67), A Yank at Oxford •• (68)

Jack Lemmon (b. 1925)

Real name: John Uhler Lemmon III

Born in a lift, this son of the president of a doughnut company was educated at Harvard before moving into movies where he initially proved himself a fresh and versatile performer, equally at home in comedies and gritty dramas. He seems to opt only for earnest, down-trodden roles these days, but will long be remembered for his teaming with friend Walter Matthau in films like *The Odd Couple.* He has won Oscars for *Mister Roberts* and *Save the Tiger.*

Quote: 'The worst part about being me is when people want me to make them laugh.' • 'He has the greatest rapport with an audience since Chaplin. Just by looking at him people can tell what goes on in his heart.' [Billy Wilder] • 'I discovered Jack Lemmon, a fine actor. He's not one of those actors who'll bore you to death discussing acting. He'd rather bore you to death discussing golf.' [George Cukor]

Films: It Should Happen to You •• (54), **Mister Roberts •• (55),** My Sister Eileen ••• (55), Fire Down Below •• (57), Bell, Book and Candle •• (58), **Some Like It Hot •••• (59), The Apartment •••• (60),** Irma

469

la Douce •• (63), How to Murder Your Wife ••• (65), The Great Race •• (65), The Fortune Cookie ••• (66), **The Odd Couple ••• (68),** The Out-of-Towners • (70), Kotch •• (71; d only), Avanti! ••• (72), Save the Tiger • (73), **The Front Page •• (74),** The Prisoner of Second Avenue •• (75), Airport '77 •• (77), **The China Syndrome ••• (79),** Buddy Buddy • (81), Missing ••• (82), That's Life •• (86), Dad •• (89), **JFK •• (91), The Player ••• (c)(92),** Glengarry Glen Ross ••• (92), Short Cuts ••• (93), Grumpy Old Men •• (93)

Sergio Leone (1921-89)

DIRECTOR. This Italian director came to prominence in the early 60s by subverting and renewing the Western and making a star of Clint Eastwood. His 'Spaghetti Westerns' were marked by their cynical wit, extraordinary visual style and blood by the gallon. His last film, which flopped disastrously, was the ambitious gangster movie *Once Upon a Time in America* and he died before he could launch his $70m epic on the Siege of Leningrad.

Quote: 'They call me the father of the spaghetti western. In that case how many sons of bitches have I spawned?'

Films A Fistful of Dollars ••• (64; also s), *Films:* a Few Dollars More ••• (65), **The Good, The Bad and The Ugly ••• (67; also s), Once Upon a Time in the West •••• (69; also s), Once Upon a Time in America •••• (84; also s)**

Harold Lloyd (1893-71)

Lloyd was bumbling along in silent comedies when he put on a pair of glasses and discovered the character of the over-helpful and naive young man that made his considerable fortune. In the 20s, he was more successful than either Chaplin or Keaton. His distinctive combination of laughs with acrobatic thrills is seen to best effect in *Safety Last*. Although it has now been discovered that he didn't carry out all the stunts that he claimed, he was still responsible for many of them, despite having lost his right thumb and index finger when an explosive prop went wrong. He made quite a few talkies, but was never as popular again. He was a shrewd businessman, keeping the rights to all his movies which he profitably reissued. He was a

keen 3-D photographer and his extraordinary Hollywood photographs were recently collected into a book.

Quote: 'I was one of the first comics you could believe in.'

Films: **Safety Last ••• (23; also s),** The Freshman •• (25), The Kid Brother ••• (27), Feet First •• (30), **Movie Crazy ••• (32; also s),** The Cats's Paw •• (34; also s), Mad Wednesday • (47)

Carole Lombard (1908-42)

Real name: **Jane Alice Peters**

The greatest comedienne in the movies had everything; looks, class, brains, a glittering career and marriage to Clark Gable. Sadly, she was killed in a plane crash in the midst of raising money for the war effort. Her feisty, snappy wit enlivened many movies, most notably *To Be Or Not To Be* and *My Man Godfrey*. It was said there was no man in Hollywood who could outswear her. It was while she was working with Alfred Hitchcock on *Mr. and Mrs. Smith* that he came out with his famous taunt that actors were cattle. She responded by driving three heifers onto the set with the names of the main stars around their necks.

Quote: 'I live by a man's code designed to fit a man's world, yet at the same time I never forget that a woman's first job is to choose the right shade of lipstick.' • 'Hollywood is where they write the alibis before they write the story.' • 'A wonderful girl. Swore like a man. Other women try, but she really did. She was like one of the fellas, yet there she was, this beautiful girl.' [Fred MacMurray] • 'I found out Carole wasn't a natural blonde. We're in her dressing room, talking. She starts undressing. I didn't know what to do. She's talking away and mixing peroxide and some other liquid in a bowl. With a piece of cotton she begins to apply the liquid to dye the hair around her honeypot. She glanced up and saw my amazed look and smiled. "Relax, Georgie. I'm just making my collar and cuffs match".' [George Raft]

Films: No Man of Her Own •• (32), **Twentieth Century •• (34),** Bolero •• (34), Lady by Choice •• (34), **Hands across the Table ••• (35), My Man Godfrey ••• (36), Nothing Sacred •• (37),** In Name Only •• (39), Vigil in the Night •• (40), They Knew What They Wanted •• (40), Mr. and Mrs. Smith •• (41), **To Be or Not to Be •••• (42)**

Peter Lorre (1904-64)

Real name: Laszlo Loewenstein

Quote: 'All you need to imitate me is a pair of soft-boiled eggs and a bedroom voice.' • 'I can only dish it out. I can't take it. I don't go to see my movies. Once I had a terrible fight with Jack Warner, who asked me what I thought of a picture I had done with Humphrey Bogart. I told him I didn't go to see it. Mr. Warner was furious. I said that I only get paid for making pictures. If he wanted me to see them, he'd have to pay me extra.' • 'One of the finest and most subtle actors I have ever worked with. Beneath that air of innocence he used to such effect, one sensed a Faustian worldliness. I'd know he was giving a good performance as we put it on film, but I wouldn't know how good until I saw him in the rushes.' [John Huston]

Films: M •••• **(31),** The Man Who Knew Too Much ••• (34), Secret Agent •• (36), Strange Cargo •• (40), **The Maltese Falcon** •••• **(41),** The Face Behind the Mask •• (41), **Casablanca** •••• **(42),** All Through the Night •• (42), The Constant Nymph ••• (43), **Arsenic and Old Lace** •••• **(44), The Mask of Dimitrios** ••• **(44),** Passage to Marseilles •• (44), Hollywood Canteen •• (c)(44), Confidential Agent • (45), Three Strangers •• (46), The Beast with Five Fingers •• (46), My Favorite Brunette ••• (47), **20,000 Leagues under the Sea** ••• **(54),** Beat the Devil •• (54), **Around the World in 80 Days** •• (c)(56), **Silk Stockings** ••• **(57),** The Story of Mankind • (57), Voyage to the Bottom of the Sea •• (61), Tales of Terror •• (62), The Raven •• (63)

Myrna Loy (1905-93)

Real name: Myrna Adele Williams

Quote: 'They say the movies should be more like life. I think life should be more like the movies.'

Films: **The Jazz Singer** • (b)(27), **Love Me Tonight** ••• **(32),** The Mask of Fu Manchu •• (32), When Ladies Meet •• (33), **The Thin Man** •••• **(34),** Manhattan Melodrama ••• (34), **After the Thin Man** ••• **(36), Libeled Lady** •• **(36),** The Great Ziegfeld ••• (36), Wife vs. Secretary •• (36), Parnell • (37), Test Pilot •• (38), Too Hot to Handle ••• (38), The Rains Came •• (39), Another Thin Man •• (39), Love Crazy ••

(41), Shadow of the Thin Man •• (41), The Thin Man Goes Home •• (44), **The Best Years of Our Lives** •••• **(46),** Song of the Thin Man •• (47), The Bachelor and the Bobby-Soxer •• (47), The Senator Was Indiscreet •• (c)(47), **Mr. Blandings Builds His Dream House** •• **(48),** Cheaper by the Dozen •• (50), Belles on their Toes •• (52), Midnight Lace • (60), Airport 1975 • (74)

Ernst Lubitsch (1892-47)

DIRECTOR. At his funeral director Billy Wilder said, 'No more Lubitsch', to which William Wyler said, 'It's worse than that. No more Lubitsch pictures'. German-born Lubitsch brought to Hollywood a wit, style and sophistication all of his own, dubbed 'The Lubitsch Touch'. He conveyed a worldly sensuality to the romantic comedy and left a legacy of moving, charming and perceptive films about the joys and sorrows of love. His success in America was a spur for many other European directors to head across the Atlantic. As the publicity tag had it, "It's the Lubitsch touch that means so much." Lubitsch was a keen proponent of the casting couch. Billy Wilder arrived at his office one day and heard a starlet in the great man's office whose screams sound more like fear than joy. When Wilder dared enter, he found that Lubitsch had achieved the distinction of being the only major Hollywood executive to die on the casting couch.

Quote: 'I have directed 50 pictures and I'm still crapping in my pants on the first day.' • 'I let the audience use their imagination. Can I help it if they misconstrue my suggestions?' • 'All women are sirens at heart.' • 'I've been to Paris, France and I've been to Paris, Paramount. I think I prefer Paris, Paramount.' • 'The American public, with the mind of a 12-year-old child, you know. It must have life as it ain't.' • 'He was the only director in Hollywood who had his own signature.' [S.N. Behrman] • 'A great director, worthy of his enormous reputation, but I found working under him in *Design for Living* cramped my style a bit. He left one no leeway at all, telling you when to light a cigarette, when to put your hands in your pockets, regulating every movement and gesture, every expression. I felt like a robot after a few days.' [Fredric March] • 'We called him son-of-Lubitsch behind his back.' [Mae West]

Films: The Love Parade •• (29), If I Had a Million ••• (32; a only), **Trouble in Paradise** •••• **(32),** One Hour with You •••

(32), Design for Living •• (34), The Merry Widow •• (34), Bluebeard's Eighth Wife • (38), **Ninotchka ••• (39), The Shop around the Corner •••• (40), To Be or Not to Be •••• (42), Heaven Can Wait •••• (43)**

Sidney Lumet (b. 1924)

DIRECTOR. The archetypal postwar New York liberal director who brings good craftsmanship and concern for society to a varied range of pictures.

Films: **Twelve Angry Men •••• (57),** Stage Struck • (58), Long Day's Journey into Night ••• (62), **Fail-Safe ••• (64),** The Pawnbroker •• (65), The Hill •• (65), The Deadly Affair ••• (67), The Anderson Tapes •• (71), Serpico ••• (73), The Offence ••• (73), **Murder on the Orient Express • (74), Dog Day Afternoon ••• (75),** Network • (76), Equus •• (77), The Verdict •••• (82), Daniel •• (83), Power •• (86), The Morning After • (86), Running on Empty ••• (88), Family Business •• (89), Q & A •• (90), Close to Eden • (92), Guilty as Sin • (93)

Shirley MacLaine (b. 1934)

Real name: Shirley MacLean Beaty

After delighting us with a range of fresh and kooky performances in the 50s and 60s, MacLaine's more recent performances have had a tendency to be a little mannered and self-indulgent. A great believer in reincarnation, she apparently thinks that she was beheaded during a previous life in 18th-century France. Warren Beatty's sister, she won an Oscar for *Terms of Endearment*.

Quote: 'I'm certain I was a prostitute in some other life. I just have empathy for them.' • 'I've played so many hookers they don't pay me in the regular way any more. They leave it on the dresser.' • 'Her oars aren't touching the water these days.' [Dean Martin] • 'Shirley MacLaine's the sort of liberal that, if she found out who she was going to be in her next life, she'd make a will and leave all her money to herself.' • 'Who does she think she isn't?' [Yves Montand]

Films: **The Trouble With Harry • (55), Around the World in 80 Days •• (56), The Apartment •••• (60),** Can-Can •• (60), The Children's Hour •• (62), Irma la Douce

•• (63), The Yellow Rolls-Royce •• (65), Sweet Charity ••• (69), Two Mules For Sister Sara •• (70), The Turning Point •• (77), **Being There ••• (79),** Loving Couples •• (80), **Terms of Endearment ••• (83),** Cannonball Run II • (84), Madame Sousatzka ••• (88), Steel Magnolias ••• (89), **Postcards from the Edge •••• (90),** Waiting for the Light ••• (90), Defending Your Life •• (c)(91), Used People •• (92), Wrestling Ernest Hemingway •• (93), Guarding Tess • (94)

Fred MacMurray (1907-91)

A former saxophonist who moved from being a light comedian to playing paternal types in 60s Disney movies. He is most interested when cast against type in films like *Double Indemnity* and *The Apartment*, showing a dark and manipulative streak behind that easy grin.

Films: **Alice Adams • (35), Hands across the Table ••• (35),** The Trail of the Lonesome Pine ••• (36), Remember the Night •• (40), Too Many Husbands ••• (40), Above Suspicion ••• (43), **Double Indemnity •••• (44),** The Egg and I •• (47), **The Caine Mutiny •••• (54), The Apartment •••• (60),** The Absent Minded Professor •• (61), Sing, You Sinners •• (68), The Swarm • (78)

Fredric March (1897-75)

Real name: Frederick McIntrye Bickel

Quote: 'I never worried about typecasting. I always wanted to characterise. To me, it's the whole fun of acting. I like to imitate, maybe too much at times. These young actors, you don't find them fiddling around, putting on beards and so forth. Damn it, I think it takes a lot of the fun out of it. *Every* part is a character part.' • 'Keep interested in others, keep interested in the wide and wonderful world. Then, in a spiritual sense, you will always be young.' • 'He was able to do a very emotional scene with tears in his eyes and pinch my fanny at the same time.' [Shelley Winters]

Films: The Royal Family of Broadway ••• (30), **Dr. Jekyll and Mr. Hyde ••• (32),** Death Takes a Holiday •• (34), Design for Living •• (34), The Barretts of Wimpole Street •• (34), **Les Miserables ••• (35),**

Anna Karenina ••• (35), Anthony Adverse ••• (36), **Nothing Sacred** •• **(37), A Star Is Born** ••• **(37),** One Foot in Heaven ••• (41), Bedtime Story •• (41), **I Married a Witch** •• **(42),** Adventures of Mark Twain ••• (44), **The Best Years of Our Lives** •••• **(46),** Death of a Salesman ••• (51), Executive Suite ••• (54), The Bridges at Toko-Ri ••• (54), The Desperate Hours ••• (55), Alexander the Great •• (56), The Man in the Gray Flannel Suit ••• (56), Inherit the Wind ••• (60), **Seven Days in May** ••• **(64),** Hombre •• (67)

The Marx Brothers: Chico (1886-61), Harpo (1888-64), Groucho (1890-77) & Zeppo (1901-79)

***Real names:* Leonard (Chico), Adolph, called Arthur (Harpo), Julius Henry (Groucho) & Herbert (Zeppo)**

Named after characters in the comic strip Mager's Monks, the brothers worked themselves up from New York poverty to become one of the most successful Vaudeville acts in America. Their films reflected their manic, zany and anarchic humour, but weren't always appreciated by audiences in the midst of the Great Depression, When they switched to MGM, they became more popular, but some of the wit and mayhem was diluted by anodyne and unwatchable musical numbers. Harpo, who only spoke twice in his entire 47-year career. was a member of the group of American wits that comprised the Algonquin Round Table and an accomplished, self-taught harpist. Chico, the pianist with the fake Italian accent was a gambler and womaniser who once told his wife that he wasn't kissing the chorus girl she'd caught him with but whispering in her ear. The misanthropic wisecracking Groucho was the one with the loping walk, the tail coat, the cigar and the painted-on moustache. Gummo, the fifth brother, never appeared in their movies, leaving the act to become their agent and business manger. Straight-man Zeppo wisely opted out of their movies after a time and was later granted a US patent for a wristwatch that could check a person's heartbeat as well as tell the time.

Quote: 'There are three things that my brother Chico is always on: a phone, a horse, or a broad.' [Groucho] • 'A man's only as old as the woman he feels.' [Groucho] • 'I never forget a face, but in your case I'll make an exception.' [Groucho] • 'I am the most fortunate self-taught harpist and non-speaking actor who ever lived.' [Harpo] • 'Groucho, you're the greatest comedian of them all.' [Charlie Chaplin] • 'I never knew what bicarbonate of soda was until I wrote a Marx Brothers picture.' [Herman Mankiewcz] • 'Anybody who ever worked on any picture for the Marx Brothers said he would rather be chained to a galley and lashed at ten minute intervals until the blood spurted from his frame than ever work for these sons of bitches again.' [S.J. Perelman] • 'Je suis Marxiste, tendence Groucho.' [Grafitti in Paris, 1968]

Films: The Cocoanuts •• (29), **Animal Crackers** ••• **(30), Monkey Business** •••• **(31), Horse Feathers** ••• **(32), Duck Soup** •••• **(33), A Night at the Opera** •••• **(35), A Day at the Races** ••• **(37),** Room Service •• (38), At the Circus •• (39), The Big Store •• (41), Night in Casablanca ••• (46), Love Happy •• (49), The Story of Mankind • (57)

James Mason (1909-84)

Quote: 'Most of the motion pictures in Hollywood are made for half-wits and certainly not for intelligent people' • 'I think the question people should ask is: "Of all your films, which is the one you'd like most to have destroyed?"' • 'I'm tired of playing the lecherous, middle-aged chap who is forever vaulting the generation gap.' • 'He was a punctilious man, beautifully manners, quiet, generous and amusing. I never heard him say a vicious or bitter thing about anything or anyone.' [John Gielgud] • 'That Mason is the greatest actor.' [D.W. Griffith]

Films: The Man in Grey •• (43), Fanny by Gaslight • (44), **The Seventh Veil** ••• **(45), The Wicked Lady** • **(45), Odd Man Out** ••• **(47),** Madame Bovary ••• (49), Pandora and the Flying Dutchman •• (51), The Desert Fox ••• (51), **Five Fingers** ••• **(52),** The Prisoner of Zenda •• (52), Julius Caesar ••• (53), The Desert Rats •• (53), **A Star Is Born** •••• **(54), 20,000 Leagues under the Sea** ••• **(54), North by Northwest** •••• **(59), Journey to the Center of the Earth** ••• **(59),** The Trials of Oscar Wilde •• (60), **Lolita** ••• **(62),** The Pumpkin Eater •• (64), The Blue Max •• (66), Georgy Girl •• (66), Fire Over England •• (b)(67), The Deadly Affair ••• (67), Voyage of the Damned • (76), Heaven Can Wait ••• (78),

The Boys from Brazil •• (78), Murder by Decree •• (79), The Verdict •••• (82), Yellowbeard • (83), The Shooting Party ••• (85)

Walter Matthau (b. 1920)

Real name: Walter Matuschanskayasky

Matthau had an impoverished childhood in New York's Lower East side, sharing a bed with his brother while his mother slept in the bath. Among early jobs, he was a floor-scrubber, a boxing instructor and a cement-bag hauler. At 11, he was already 6 feet tall and claims that one of his neighbourhood friends was a young Rocky Graziano, whom he used to beat up from time to time. Some claim that his claimed real surname is a gag perpetrated on the compilers of film guides but it *is* certain that he played a character with that name in *Earthquake*. He won an Oscar for *The Fortune Cookie*.

Quote: 'A lot of parts I want they give to Robert Redford.' • 'He looks like a half-melted rubber bulldog' [John Simon]

Films: A Face in the Crowd ••• (57), King Creole •• (58), **Lonely Are the Brave ••• (62), Charade •••• (63), Fail-Safe ••• (64),** Ensign Pulver • (64), Mirage ••• (65), The Fortune Cookie ••• (66), The Guide for the Married Man • (67), **The Odd Couple ••• (68),** The Secret Life of an American Wife •• (68), Cactus Flower •• (69), Hello Dolly! •• (69), **A New Leaf ••• (70), Plaza Suite ••• (71),** Kotch •• (71), Pete'n'Tillie •• (72), **Charley Varrick •••• (73), The Front Page •• (74), The Taking of Pelham One Two Three ••• (74),** Earthquake • (74), **The Sunshine Boys ••• (75),** The Bad News Bears ••• (76), California Suite ••• (78), House Calls •• (78), **Hopscotch ••• (80),** Buddy Buddy • (81), Pirates •• (86), The Couch Trip • (88), **JFK •• (91),** Dennis •• (93), Grumpy Old Men •• (93), I.Q. ••• (94)

Steve McQueen (1930-80)

Real name: Terrence Steven McQueen

McQueen's mother was abandoned by her husband shortly after the baby was born. McQueen recalled that his stepfather was cruel and beat him frequently, but he doesn't seem to have been an angel himself. He was in reform school at 14 for stealing hubcaps and had a varied 'career' scrubbing the decks of an oil tanker, hawking gee-gaws at a travelling fair, selling ballpoint pens, making sandals, even as a towel boy in a brothel. He had joined the Marines at 17 and was a tank driver for three years. Forty-one days of that were spent in jail, part of the time on bread and water, for going Absent Without Leave. Aged 22, he got a two-line part, his first acting work, in a Yiddish play on Second Avenue and things changed for the better. His cool 60s image belied a fairly insecure and turbulent, almost brutal, domestic life. He was obsessed with motorbikes. Ali McGraw was the second of his three wives.

Quote: 'I am a limited actor. My range isn't that great and I don't have that much scope. I'm pretty much myself most of the time in my movies, and I have accepted that.' • 'In my own mind, I'm not sure that acting is something for a grown man to be doing.' • 'I took up acting because it let me burn off energy. Besides, I wanted to beat the 40 hour a week rap. But, man, I didn't escape. Now I'm working 72 hours a week! Acting's a hard scene for me. Every script I get is an enemy I have to conquer.' • 'One thing about Steve, he didn't like the women in his life to have balls' [Wife Ali McGraw] • 'A Steve McQueen performance just naturally lends itself to monotony. Steve doesn't bring much to the party.' [Robert Mitchum] • 'I can honestly say he's the most difficult actor I've ever worked with.' [Director Norman Jewison]

Films: Somebody Up There Likes Me ••• (56), The Blob •• (58), **The Magnificent Seven ••• (60), The Great Escape ••• (63),** The Cincinnati Kid •• (65), The Sand Pebbles • (66), **Bullitt ••• (68), The Thomas Crown Affair •• (68), The Getaway ••• (72),** Papillon ••• (73), **The Towering Inferno ••• (74)**

Liza Minnelli (b. 1946)

She first appeared in a movie, *Easter Parade*, aged just two, with mother Judy Garland and then the following year in *In the Good Old Summertime*, directed by father Vincente Minnelli. However her mother, knowing full well what it was like being a child star, refused to let her work on a movie again until she was over 16. Minnelli's second husband was Jack Haley Jr., son of the man who played The Tin Man in *The Wizard of Oz*. Her concert performances prove she is every bit as talented off screen as her mother was.

Quote: 'I look like a female Fred Astaire.'
• 'I think she decided to go into show business when she was an embryo, she kicked so much.' [Judy Garland]

Films: Easter Parade ••• (b)(48), In the Good Old Summertime •• (b)(49), **Charlie Bubbles** •• **(68),** The Sterile Cuckoo •• (69), **Cabaret •••• (72), That's Entertainment! •••• (74),** Lucky Lady •• (75), Silent Movie •• (c)(76), New York, New York •• (77), **Arthur ••• (81), The King of Comedy •••• (c)(83),** The Muppets Take Manhattan ••• (c)(84), That's Dancing • (p)(85), Arthur 2: On the Rocks •• (88), Stepping Out •• (91)

Vincente Minnelli (1910-86)

DIRECTOR. He was plucked from a highly successful Broadway musical career by MGM's Arthur Freed who trained him in direction. Together, the pair revolutionised the integrated musical in the 40s and 50s with enormous verve and fluid camera work, all rendered in the lush MGM house style. He was married to Judy Garland for six years, a marriage that produced Liza Minnelli. He won an Oscar for *Gigi*.

Quote: 'As you mull it over, you begin to see a form, a style…I think it is largely a matter of intuition. I think with my stomach more than with my head.' • 'He believes implicitly in the power of his camera to turn trash into art, and corn into caviar.' [Andrew Sarris] • 'Here lies Vincente Minnelli. He died of hard work.' [His chosen epitaph]

Films: Meet Me in St. Louis •••• (44), The Clock ••• (45), Ziegfeld Follies •• (46), **The Pirate** •• **(48),** Madame Bovary ••• (49), **Father of the Bride ••• (50), An American in Paris ••• (51),** Father's Little Dividend •• (51), **The Bad and the Beautiful ••• (52), The Band Wagon •••• (53),** Brigadoon •• (54), Kismet •• (55), Tea and Sympathy ••• (56), Lust for Life ••• (56), Designing Woman •• (57), **Gigi ••• (58),** On a Clear Day You Can See For Ever • (70)

Robert Mitchum (b. 1917)

His dad was killed in an accident when he was only one year old. Something of a troublemaker, he was thrown out of school and had to start work at 14. After a spell on a boat, he bummed around like many other Depression-era children, riding boxcars. He even did time on a chain gang for vagrancy, which he escaped after developing gangrene from the leg irons. Among jobs he held, he was a ditch digger, a coal miner, an nightclub bouncer, a promoter for a leading astrologer, a sheet-metal worker and a shoe salesman. Before he made it in the movies, one of his more extraordinary accomplishments was writing an oratorio about the plight of European Jewish refugees which Orson Welles put on at a Hollywood Bowl charity do. His early roles included eight Hopalong Cassidy movies. An insomniac (which gave him those sleepy eyes), he lived his bad-boy image as much off-screen as on. He was busted in 1949 and given 50 days in jail for possessing marijuana, but managed to persuade the judge to delay his sentence until he'd finished *The Big Steal*. He became the first star to refuse to shave his chest, even though he was frequently seen without his shirt on screen. It did nothing to harm his career. Ever the rebel, he avoided having to pose for studio beefcake shots by developing a pot belly. He married his childhood sweetheart, Dorothy, proposing to her with the words: 'Marry me and you'll be farting through silk.' His autobiography was called *It Sure Beats Working*.

Quote: 'I came back from the war and ugly heroes were in.' • 'Paint eyeballs on my eyelids and I'll sleepwalk through any picture.'
• 'Rumours? They're all true. Booze, broads. Make up some more if you want to.' • 'You know something? What I represent to the public is hope. They look at me and they think: If that big slob can get somewhere, there's a chance for us.' • 'Listen, I got three expression: looking left, looking right and looking straight ahead.'
• 'I've never been an actor – and I've got 70 movies to prove it.' • 'I kept the same suit for six years — and the same dialogue. We just changed the title of the picture and the leading lady.' • 'Every two or three years I knock off for a while. That way I'm constantly the new girl in the whorehouse. I'm a whore with a heart of gold. I just show up and do it.' • 'Movies bore me, especially my own.' • 'A sense of humour is a salvation. It's saved me so far. If you can't laugh, you're dead. I'm laughing all the time. You just never catch it.' • 'I've been smoking shit for about 40 years but it never got to be a habit with me.' • 'I started out to be a sex fiend but I couldn't pass the physical.' • 'People think I have an interesting walk. I'm just trying to hold my stomach in.' • 'The only difference between me and my fellow actors is that I've spent more

time in jail.' • 'Howard Hughes said one time: "My God, Mitch. You're just like a pay toilet. You don't give a shit for nothing".' • 'All his hip talk is a blind. He's a very fine man with wonderful manners and he speaks beautifully when he wants to. He won't thank you for destroying the tough image he's built up as a defence. In fact, he's a very tender man and very great gentleman…Bob would make the best Macbeth of any actor living.' [Charles Laughton] • 'Bob is one of the very great actors. His resources have never been fully tapped. He could play King Lear.' [John Huston] • 'You're the biggest fraud I ever met. You pretend you don't care a damn thing about a scene and you're the hardest working so-and-so I've ever known.' [Howard Hawks]

Films: Thirty Seconds Over Tokyo ••• (44), The Story of G.I. Joe ••• (45), **Out of the Past ••• (47)**, Crossfire •• (47), The Big Steal ••• (49), River of No Return •• (54), **The Night of the Hunter •• (55)**, Fire Down Below •• (57), **The Sundowners ••• (60)**, The Grass is Greener •• (60), **Cape Fear ••• (62)**, The Longest Day ••• (62), The List of Adrian Messenger ••• (63), Ryan's Daughter •• (70), **The Friends of Eddie Coyle ••• (73)**, Farewell, My Lovely ••• (75), The Yakuza •• (75), The Last Tycoon ••• (76), That Championship Season •• (83), Maria's Lovers ••• (84), The Ambassador ••• (85), Mr. North •• (88), Scrooged •• (88), Cape Fear •• (91), Tombstone •• (v)(94)

Marilyn Monroe (1926-62)

Real name: Norma Jean Mortenson/Baker

Over 30 years after her death, Monroe is still considered one of the greatest sex symbols, partly because of her early death and the conspiracy theories that still continue to swirl around its circumstances. Certainly, her image is better known these days than most of her films, many of which were pretty poor and only a few of which were outstanding. While people still debate her acting talent, her extraordinary beauty and skill as a comedienne cannot be doubted. After a difficult childhood and a tough struggle to become established as an actress, which involved a spell of prostitution and an overfamiliarity with the casting couch, she finally made it with *Niagara* and *Gentlemen Prefer Blondes*. She was, by all accounts, not the easiest of actresses to work with. She was unreliable in the extreme, bad at learning lines and

often rude to cast and crew, although her psychiatric condition and the anti-depressants she took probably exacerbated this. Her famous wiggle is said to have come about because she was slightly bow-legged. When she realised the effect that her gyrating hips had, she made it still more pronounced by sawing a quarter of an inch from the heel of her right shoe. Despite the legend, she was *not* the model used by Walt Disney for Tinkerbell in *Peter Pan*. Her second marriage was to baseball star Joe DiMaggio and her third to playwright Arthur Miller. Her grave is the most-visited in Hollywood. Joe DiMaggio had six red roses placed on it three times a week for 21 years until he died in 1982.

Quote: 'What do you wear when you go to bed?' – 'Chanel No. 5.' 'Didn't you have anything on?' – 'I had the radio on.' • 'The trouble with censors is they worry if a girl has cleavage. They ought to worry if she hasn't any.' • 'In Hollywood, a girl's virtue is much less important than her hairdo.' • 'Being a sex symbol is a heavy load to carry, especially when one is tired, hurt and bewildered.' • 'It's not really me that's late; it's the others who are always in a hurry.' • 'I can't memorise the words by themselves. I have to memorise the feelings.' • 'I don't mind living in a man's world as long as I can be a woman in it.' • 'I have too many fantasies to be a housewife.' • 'Yes, there was something special about me, and I knew what it was. I was the kind of girl they found dead in a hall bedroom with an empty bottle of sleeping pills in her hand.' • 'Marilyn Monroe was all woman. She had curves in places other women don't even have places' [Cybill Shepherd] • 'That broad's got a great future behind her.' [Constance Bennett] • 'Her body has gone to her head.' [Barbara Stanwyck] • 'Directing her was like directing Lassie. You needed 14 takes to get each one of them right.' [Director Otto Preminger] • 'Hollywood didn't kill Marilyn Monroe. But it's the Marilyn Monroes who are killing Hollywood.' [Billy Wilder] • 'It was like going to the dentist, making a picture with her. It was hell at the time, but after it was all over, it was wonderful.' [Billy Wilder] • 'I have a healthy aunt in Vienna who would come on set on time, know her lines, and always be ready. But no-one would pay to see her at the box office.' [Billy Wilder] • 'Slovenly, unappealing, unmanageable, unpleasant and dirty. No one wants to acknowledge that.' [Tony Curtis] • 'A vacuum with nipples.' [Director Otto Preminger] • 'Marilyn Monroe is a natural phenomenon like Niagara Falls or the Grand Canyon. You can't talk to it. It can't talk to you. All you can do is stand back and be awed by it.' [Nunnally Johnson] • 'A professional amateur.' [Laurence Olivier] • 'You are a very lovely lady.' [Nikita Kruschchev] • 'My God, I think there have been more books on Marilyn Monroe than on World War II and there's a great similarity.' [Billy Wilder]

Films: Love Happy •• (b)(49), **The Asphalt Jungle** •••• **(50)**, **All About Eve** •••• **(50)**, Clash by Night •• (52), Monkey Business •• (52), Don't Bother to Knock •• (52), **Gentlemen Prefer Blondes** ••• **(53)**, **Niagara** ••• **(53)**, How to Marry a Millionaire ••• (53), River of No Return •• (54), There's No Business Like Show Business •• (54), **The Seven Year Itch** •• **(55)**, **Bus Stop** •• **(56)**, The Prince and the Showgirl •• (57), **Some Like It Hot** •••• **(59)**, Let's Make Love • (60), **The Misfits** •• **(61)**

Demi Moore (b. 1962)

Real name: Demi Guynes

Beginning her career in the TV soap *General Hospital* Moore was getting nowhere slowly until she hit the big time with *Ghost*. Once engaged to Emilio Estevez, she has three daughters with husband Bruce Willis, called Rumer, Scout LaRue and Tallulah Belle. She posed naked when pregnant for Vanity Fair but stopped her 48-year-old mother taking her clothes off for *Playboy*. Just in case you happen to bump into her, she pronounces her name De-*MEE*, not *DE*-mee. Within the industry, she is nicknamed 'Gimmee' Moore because of her love for perks, apparently always insisting on the best trailer.

Quote: 'She's like a beautiful ballerina who can also kickbox and talk dirty.' [Alan Rudolph, director]

Films: Young Doctors in Love ••• (c)(82), Blame it on Rio •• (84), St. Elmo's Fire • (85), About Last Night... •• (86), The Seventh Sign • (88), We're No Angels • (89), **Ghost** •••• **(90)**, Mortal Thoughts •• (91), Nothing But Trouble • (91), The Butcher's Wife ••• (92), **A Few Good Men** ••• **(92)**, Indecent Proposal ••• (93), Disclosure •• (94)

Paul Newman (b. 1925)

Newman had a middle-class upbringing and for a time went into his late father's sporting goods business. He turned to acting when a knee injury stopped him playing American football. A famous graduate of Lee Strasberg's Actors Studio, he was pipped for the lead in *East of Eden* by James Dean. He was so appaled by his acting in his debut movie, *The Silver Chalice*, in 1954, that when it was shown on television he took out an ad in an LA paper to apologise for his performance. He claims to keep his youthful features by donning a snorkel and putting his head in a bucket of cold water for 20 minutes each morning. For years he was bedevilled by comparisons with Marlon Brando, before blazing a path of his own. During the making of the movie *Winning*, he became obsessed with motor racing and by the time he was 50 he was considered to be one of the top amateur drivers in America, coming second in the 24-hour Le Mans race. A leading Civil Rights campaigner and disarmer, Newman was number 19 on Richard Nixon's list of public enemies. He has been married to Joanne Woodward since 1958 and runs a very successful salad dressing, popcorn and spaghetti sauce business, the profits from which have ploughed over $40m into various charities. He won an Oscar for *The Color of Money*.

Quote: 'My own personality is so vapid and bland, I have to go steal the personalities of other people to be effective on the screen.' • 'I picture my epitaph: Here lies Paul Newman, who died a failure because his eyes turned brown.' • 'The embarrassing thing is that the salad dressing is out-grossing my films.' • 'There are three stages in an actor's career. The first is when he shows up on set and says: You should've seen the girl I was with last night. God! I didn't sleep. She was *amazing*! In the second stage, he's a leading man and says: You know, I found the most wonderful restaurant – you wouldn't believe the fish. By the third stage, he's a character actor. Now he says: Oh, I had the most lovely bowel movement last night.' • 'There's a stillness in his acting now that is quite magnetic. You can feel his intelligence, you can see him thinking. He has the depth of a clear pool of water.' [Sydney Pollack]

Films: Somebody Up There Likes Me ••• (56), **Cat on a Hot Tin Roof** ••• **(58)**, The Long, Hot Summer •• (58), Exodus •• (60), **The Hustler** ••• **(61)**, Sweet Bird of Youth ••• (62), **Hud** ••• **(63)**, The Prize •• (63), Torn Curtain •• (66), Harper ••• (66), **Cool Hand Luke** ••• **(67)**, Hombre •• (67), Rachel, Rachel (68; d only), **Butch Cassidy and The Sundance Kid** ••• **(69)**, Winning •• (69), The Life and Times of Judge

Roy Bean •• (72), **The Sting •••• (73), The Towering Inferno ••• (74),** The Drowning Pool •• (75), Silent Movie •• (c)(76), Slap Shot •• (77), Fort Apache – The Bronx (81), Absence of Malice ••• (81), The Verdict •••• (82), Harry and Son •• (84; also d&s), The Color of Money ••• (86), The Glass Menagerie ••• (87; d only), Blaze •• (89), Shadow Makers •• (89), Mr. and Mrs. Bridge ••• (90), The Hudsucker Proxy •• (93), **Nobody's Fool ••• (94)**

Jack Nicholson (b. 1937)

Nicholson's career took years to get anywhere. He worked as an office boy in the cartoon department of MGM, acted on TV, sold the rights to biker pics at Cannes, wrote and acted for schlockmeister Roger Corman and might never have been heard of had Rip Torn not dropped out of *Easy Rider*. Nicholson, the 32-year-old associate producer, stepped in and the rest, they say, is history. Although he lives modestly, he is one of the richest actors in the world, apparently earning over $50m from *Batman* and thus easily able to turn down an offer of $10m for half a day's work on a TV ad. He was for many years Anjelica Huston's partner. Only in the 70s did he learn that the woman he had thought was his mother was his grandmother and that his supposed sister was in fact his mother, a deception made to conceal his illegitimacy.

Quote: 'There are two ways up the ladder; hand over hand or scratching and clawing. It's sure been tough on my nails.' • 'My best feature's my smile. And smiles – praise heaven – don't get fat.' • 'I was always against authority, hated being told anything by my teachers, by parents, by anyone. At school I created a record by being in detention every day for a year. Today I suppose I'm still in love with what I think. I don't like listening to what other people think.' • 'I'm preoccupied with sex, an area of human behaviour that's underexplored, in general. And I like virgin territory.'

Films: The Raven •• (63), Ensign Pulver • (64), **Easy Rider •• (69), Five Easy Pieces ••• (70),** On a Clear Day You Can See For Ever • (70), **Carnal Knowledge •• (71),** Drive, He Said •• (71; d only), The King of Marvin Gardens ••• (72), **The Last Detail ••• (73), Chinatown •••• (74),** The Fortune ••• (75), The Passenger ••• (75),

Tommy ••• (75), **One Flew Over the Cuckoo's Nest •••• (75),** The Last Tycoon ••• (76), The Missouri Breaks •• (76), Goin' South ••• (78; also d), **The Shining •••• (80),** Reds ••• (81), The Postman Always Rings Twice •• (81), The Border •• (82), **Terms of Endearment ••• (83), Prizzi's Honor •• (85),** Heartburn • (86), **Broadcast News ••• (c)(87),** Ironweed •• (87), The Witches of Eastwick ••• (87), **Batman •• (89),** The Two Jakes •••• (91; also d), Man Trouble • (92), **A Few Good Men ••• (92),** Hoffa •• (92), Wolf ••• (94)

David Niven (1909-83)

***Real name:* James David Graham Niven**

Although considered the archetypal urbane Englishman, Niven was actually born in Scotland. In his two hilarious volumes of autobiography, *The Moon's a Balloon* and *Bring on the Empty Horses*, it is very hard to work out what is truth and what is a story told and embroidered so much over the years that Niven probably even believed it himself. Certainly he tried many different occupations before he arrived in Hollywood and was lucky enough to find friends among the stars there who helped him considerably. Sadly, while a handful of his films are excellent, many would need a great deal of work before you could even say they were 'dreadful'. Mercifully, he turned down the lead in the Hopalong Cassidy films or we'd probably never have heard of him. He was one of the first British artists in Hollywood to abandon their career and return to Blighty to pitch in with the war effort, serving with the Commandos, from which he emerged as a colonel. In most of his films, you should look out for a reference to somebody named Trubshawe. Michael Trubshawe was an old mate of his and even appeared in a few movies with Niven. He won an Oscar for *Separate Tables*.

Quote: 'I do only one movie a year and after each i am convinced nobody is going to ask me to do another.' • 'In 40 years, I've never been late. They pay me enough – so the least I can do is arrive sober, be on time and know all the jokes.' • 'I once described my face as a cross between two pounds of halibut and an explosion in an old clothes closet' • 'Print anything you like and I'll swear I said it.' • 'He was a model of how people who are famous and who enjoy the terrific privilege of stardom or public acclaim should behave.' [John Mortimer]

Films: Barbary Coast ••• (b)(35), **The Charge of the Light Brigade ••• (36), Dodsworth •••• (36),** The Prisoner of Zenda ••• (37), Dawn Patrol ••• (38), Bluebeard's Eighth Wife • (38), **Wuthering Heights ••• (39),** Bachelor Mother •• (39), Raffles •• (40), **The Way Ahead ••• (44), A Matter of Life and Death •••• (46),** The Bishop's Wife •• (47), The Moon is Blue • (53), Carrington, V.C. •• (55), **Around the World in 80 Days •• (56),** Separate Tables ••• (58), Please Don't Eat the Daisies •• (60), **The Guns of Navarone ••• (61), The Pink Panther ••• (63),** 55 Days at Peking •• (63), Bedtime Story •• (64), **Casino Royale • (67),** Candleshoe •• (77), Death on the Nile •• (78), Escape to Athena •• (79), The Sea Wolves •• (80), The Trail of the Pink Panther • (82), The Curse of the Pink Panther • (83)

Jack Norton (1889-58)

Real name: Mortimer J. Naughton

Almost nobody will have heard of Jack Norton, but we've all seen him. He propped up bars, or fell off them, in umpteen Hollywood films. Casting him against type would be having him drink beer instead of whisky although, bizarrely, off screen he never touched a drop. No film could be completely without merit if he appeared in it, even if he rarely got a mention on the credits.

Films: **Ruggles of Red Gap •• (35),** Marked Woman •• (37), **A Day at the Races ••• (37), Jezebel ••• (38),** The Roaring Twenties ••• (39), **The Bank Dick •••• (40),** The Ghost Breakers •• (40), **The Palm Beach Story ••• (42), Hail the Conquering Hero ••• (44)**

Maureen O'Hara (b. 1920)

Real name: Maureen Fitzsimmons

Quote 'She looked as if butter wouldn't melt in her mouth – or anywhere else.' [Elsa Lanchester]

Films: **The Hunchback of Notre Dame ••• (39),** Jamaica Inn • (39), **How Green Was My Valley ••• (41), Miracle on 34th Street •••• (47), Sitting Pretty ••• (48),** Rio Grande •• (50), **The Quiet Man ••• (52),** Our Man in Havana •• (60), Only the Lonely ••• (91)

Peter O'Toole (b. 1932)

Born in Ireland but raised in England, this talented star shot to fame with *Lawrence of Arabia* but frittered his career away on booze and bad movies. There were enough decent movies to win him seven Oscar nominations but, like Richard Burton who was also nominated for seven, he hasn't won one. Now sworn off the booze, even if his films aren't always wonderful his wit as a raconteur still makes him one of the best chat-show guests.

Quote: 'I was sort of the Vanessa Redgrave of the 50s.' • 'I'm not crazy, but I think everybody else is.' • 'I am deeply suspicious of people who do not go to pubs.' • 'For me, life has been either a wake or a wedding.' • 'I don't miss booze. I still cause mayhem. I'll always love to frolic, but now I can remember what I've done.' • 'Our old mistakes do come back to haunt us. Especially with video.' • 'Peter O'Toole looks like he's walking around just to save funeral expenses.' [John Huston]

Films: Lawrence of Arabia •••• (62), Beckett •• (64), What's New, Pussycat? •• (65), How to Steal a Million •• (66), **Casino Royale • (67), The Lion in Winter •• (68),** Goodbye, Mr. Chips •• (69), The Ruling Class ••• (72), Under Milk Wood •• (73), Zulu Dawn •• (79), The Stunt Man • (80), Caligula • (80), **My Favorite Year ••• (82),** Supergirl • (84), Creator •• (85), The Last Emperor ••• (87), High Spirits • (88), King Ralph ••• (91), Wings of Fame •• (91), Rebecca's Daughters ••• (92)

Laurence Olivier (1907-89)

Although regarded as one of the greatest actors of the century, his style now seems more appropriate to the Old Vic than the local multiplex. In many of his films, his performances can appear rather mannered on screen, particularly once he had donned the mantle of a 'Great Actor'. That said, occasionally he rose above this handicap and some of his performances are still strikingly brilliant. He did much to bring Shakespeare to the modern masses. When American TV showed his *Richard III*, more people saw that one transmission than had seen the play in its 350-year history. After a romantic, tempestuous affair and second marriage to Vivien Leigh, he then married actress Joan Plowright. He won a special Oscar for *Henry V* and was voted Best Actor for *Hamlet*.

Quote: 'Acting is a masochistic form of exhibitionism. It is not quite the occupation of an adult.' • 'Nothing is beneath me if it pays well. I've earned the right to damn well grab whatever I can in the time I've got left.' • 'You need to be a bit of a bastard to be a star.' • 'Larry Olivier is not an actor. He's a chameleon. He wears all that makeup and all those costumes and just disguises himself. Half the time you don't even know it's him.' • 'The most overrated actor on earth. Take away the wives and the looks and you have John Gielgud.' [Oscar Levant] • 'I see Sir Laurence as a rhinoceros.' [Salvador Dali]

Films: The Divorce of Lady X •• (38), **Wuthering Heights ••• (39), Q Planes ••• (39), Pride and Prejudice •••• (40), Rebecca •••• (40),** Lady Hamilton ••• (41), Forty-Ninth Parallel •• (41), **Henry V •••• (44; also d&s), This Happy Breed ••** (v)(44), **Hamlet •• (48; also d),** The Magic Box • (c)(51), Richard III ••• (55; also d&s), The Prince and the Showgirl •• (57), **Spartacus •••• (60), The Entertainer ••** (60), Othello •• (65), Khartoum •• (66), Fire Over England •• (67), Battle of Britain •• (69), **Oh! What a Lovely War •• (69), Sleuth ••• (72), Marathon Man ••• (76),** A Bridge Too Far •• (77), The Boys from Brazil •• (78), Bounty •• (84), Wild Geese II • (85)

Al Pacino (b. 1940)

Real name: Alfredo Pacino

The career of one of the greatest of all film actors was almost extinguished by the pitiable *Revolution,* a turkey so big it was several Christmases before Pacino was seen again. Raised by his mother and grandparents, they were so protective that, until he was seven, he was allowed out only to go to school and the cinema. A one-time dancer and stand-up comic, it was *The Godfather* that shot him to stardom. He is one of those actors who truly immerses himself in his roles. A brief affair several years ago resulted in a daughter, although he has never revealed who the mother is. He won an Oscar for *Scent of a Woman.*

Films: Me, Natalie ••• (69), The Panic in Needle Park ••• (71), **The Godfather •••• (72),** Serpico ••• (73), Scarecrow ••• (73), **The Godfather, Part II ••• (74), Dog Day Afternoon ••• (75),** Bobby Deerfield • (77), ...And Justice for All •• (79), Cruising • (80), Author! Author! •• (82), **Scarface •• (83),** Revolution • (85), **Sea of Love ••• (89),**

Dick Tracy •• (90), **The Godfather, Part III ••• (90),** Frankie & Johnny ••• (91), Glengarry Glen Ross ••• (92), Scent of a Woman ••• (92), Carlito's Way •• (93)

Eugene Pallette (1889-54)

This amply-covered supporting actor with the extraordinary rasping bullfrog voice was the icing on many already delicious comic confections. Although lucky enough to be in many great movies, being best known for his role as Friar Tuck in *The Adventures of Robin Hood,* this ex-streetcar conductor is one of those many lesser-known Hollywood actors whose mere presence on screen will raise a smile.

Films: **The Birth of a Nation •• (15), Intolerance •••• (16),** The Virginian •• (29), The Love Parade •• (29), **Shanghai Express ••• (32),** The Kennel Murder Case ••• (33), **The Ghost Goes West ••• (35), My Man Godfrey ••• (36), One Hundred Men and a Girl •••• (37), Topper ••• (37), The Adventures of Robin Hood •••• (38), Mr. Smith Goes to Washington •••• (39), The Mark of Zorro ••• (40), The Lady Eve ••• (41),** The Bride Came C.O.D. •• (41), **Heaven Can Wait ••• (43)**

Franklin Pangborn (1893-58)

Another of those supporting actors who enlivened many otherwise dull movies. Pangborn specialised in play fussy, interfering busybodies, often in the form of hotel managers.

Films: Design for Living •• (34), **My Man Godfrey ••• (36), Mr. Deeds Goes to Town •••• (36), Easy Living ••• (37), Stage Door ••• (37), A Star Is Born ••• (37),** Vivacious Lady ••• (38), Carefree ••• (38), Topper Takes a Trip •• (39), **The Bank Dick •••• (40), Christmas in July ••• (40), Sullivan's Travels •••• (41),** Never Give a Sucker an Even Break •• (41), **The Palm Beach Story ••• (42),** Now, Voyager ••• (42), **Hail the Conquering Hero ••• (44)**

Gregory Peck (b. 1916)

Real name: Eldred Gregory Peck

His father was a pharmacist and Peck studied to be a doctor but gave up to become a night watchman. He attended Berkeley but spent most of the time running and rowing, rather than studying. Then he had to give up sport because of a back injury which also kept him out of military service. He was a one-time tour guide at Radio City, where later 10 of his movies would be shown. He specialises in playing upright, honest citizens who are sometimes tormented by inner demons.

Quote: 'I'm glad I had a middle name to run to.'

Films: **Spellbound ••• (45), Duel in the Sun ••• (46),** The Yearling ••• (46), The Paradine Case •• (47), Gentleman's Agreement •• (47), Twelve O'Clock High ••• (49), **The Gunfighter ••• (50), Roman Holiday ••• (53),** The Man in the Gray Flannel Suit ••• (56), Moby Dick •• (56), Designing Woman •• (57), The Big Country •• (58), On the Beach ••• (59), **The Guns of Navarone ••• (61), Cape Fear ••• (62),** How the West Was Won ••• (62), **To Kill a Mockingbird** •• **(62),** Mirage •• (65), **The Omen** •• **(76),** The Boys from Brazil •• (78), The Sea Wolves •• (80), Silent Voice •• (87), Old Gringo •• (89), Other People's Money •• (91), Cape Fear •• (91)

Sam Peckinpah (1925-84)

Real name: **David Samuel Peckinpah**

DIRECTOR. Following military service in China and work on *Invasion of the Body Snatchers*, Peckinpah moved from TV Westerns to the big screen. His 60s Westerns are striking for their harsh beauty, nostalgia for the old West and, after *The Wild Bunch*, their frequent use of slow-motion violence.

Quote: 'Horses make some of the best actors. I'll take Trigger any day! They don't answer back – especially when they're stuffed.' • 'I'm a whore. I go where I'm kicked. But I'm a very good whore.'

Films: **Invasion of the Body Snatchers •••• (b)(56; a only),** Guns in the Afternoon •• (62), Major Dundee ••• (65), **The Wild Bunch •••• (69; also s), Straw Dogs • (71), The Getaway ••• (72), Bring Me the Head of Alfredo Garcia** •• **(74; also s),** The Osterman Weekend •• (83)

Michelle Pfeiffer (b. 1958)

Bizarre to think that if you were in the Seven-

Items-Or-Less queue in the Vons supermarket in El Toro, California in the late 70s, the blonde check-out girl in the red smock and black polyester trousers would have been Michelle Pfeiffer. Dissatisfied for some reason with retailing as a career, she took up modelling and commercials, winning the Miss Orange County competition but she was then pipped in the Miss LA contest. It took her over 10 years to become a star, probably because so many of her early films flopped.

Quote: 'I look like a duck. It's the way my mouth sort of curls up, or my nose tilts up. I should have played "Howard the Duck".' • 'Just standing around looking beautiful is so boring, really boring, so boring.' • 'Demi Moore was sold to Robert Redford for $1m. Uma Thurman went to Mr. De Niro for $40,000. And just three years ago Richard Gere bought Julia Roberts for $3,000. I'd say that was real progress.'

Films: Charlie Chan and the Curse of the Dragon Queen • (81), Grease 2 • (82), **Scarface** •• **(83),** Ladyhawke •• (85), Into the Night •• (85), Sweet Liberty •• (86), The Witches of Eastwick ••• (87), **Dangerous Liaisons ••• (88),** Married to the Mob •• (88), Tequila Sunrise •• (88), The Fabulous Baker Boys ••• (89), The Russia House •• (90), Frankie & Johnny ••• (91), **Batman Returns ••• (92),** The Age of Innocence •• (93), Wolf ••• (94)

Roman Polanski (b. 1933)

DIRECTOR. As a child, Paris-born Polanski fled the Crakow ghetto immortalised on film in *Schindler's List* and escaped from Nazi Germany. This traumatic childhood is reflected in the paranoia, violence and black humour of his best films made in Britain and America. His pregnant wife Sharon Tate was murdered by the Manson cult in 1969 and Polanski himself fled America in 1977 when he jumped bail after being charged with sex with an underage model. He has made his films in Europe ever since.

Quote: 'We are born; it means nothing; we die.' • 'Sometimes I am charmed by the fact that there are women with whom you can discuss the molecular theory of light all evening, and at the end they will ask you what is your birth sign.' • 'As a director, he was ten times more wonderful than as a lover.' [Nastassia Kinski]

Films: Knife in the Water •• (62; also s), **Repulsion ••• (c)(65; also a&s),** Cul de

Sac •• (66; also s), **Rosemary's Baby •••
(68; also s),** Macbeth ••• (72; also s),
Chinatown •••• (c)(74; also a), The
Tenant •• (76; also a&s), Tess •• (80; also
s), Pirates •• (86; also s), Frantic •• (88;
also s), Bitter Moon • (92; also s), Death and
the Maiden ••• (94)

Michael Powell (1905-90) &
Emeric Pressburger (1902-88)4)

Real name: Imre Pressburger

WRITER-DIRECTORS. Englishman Michael
Powell and Hungarian Emeric Pressburger were
introduced by Alexander Korda to make *The
Spy in Black.* Subsequently, they formed *The
Archers,* making the most exciting, original and
flamboyant British films for the ensuing 13
years. Some found their films gaudy, bizarre
and confusing, if not incomprehensible, but
they made a welcome change from the tradi-
tions of good taste and literary adaptation so
prevalent in the British film industry. Their reputation has soared in the past 20 years, helped
to a large extent by fan Martin Scorsese who
rescued Powell from career oblivion in the 80s.
Pressburger won an Oscar for the story of *The
49th Parallel.*

Quote: 'I got my first assignment as a director
in 1927. I was slim, arrogant, intelligent,
cocksure, dreamy and irritating. Today, I'm no
longer slim.' [Powell]

Films: The Spy in Black ••• (39), **The Thief
of Bagdad ••• (40),** Forty-Ninth Parallel ••
(41), **The Life and Death of Colonel
Blimp •••• (43; also s),** A Canterbury
Tale •• (44; also s), I Know Where I'm
Going! ••• **(45; also s), A Matter of Life
and Death •••• (46; also s),** Black
Narcissus ••• (46; also s), The Red
Shoes •• (48; also s), **The Small Back
Room ••• (49; also s),** Peeping Tom •••
(c)(59; also a)

William Powell (1892-84)

The personification of 30s and 40s sophistication. Suave, stylish and cynical, Powell is
forever remembered for his cocktail-sipping,
wisecrack-pulling teaming with Myrna Loy in the
Thin Man films. He also made a fine partner for
the likes of Carole Lombard and Lauren Bacall.

Films: One Way Passage ••• (32), The

Kennel Murder Case ••• (33), **The Thin
Man ••••** (34), **The Thin
Man ••••** (34), **My Man Godfrey ••• (36),** After the
Thin Man ••• (36), Libeled Lady •• (36),
The Great Ziegfeld ••• (36), The Ex-Mrs.
Bradford •• (36), The Last of Mrs. Cheyney
•• (37), Another Thin Man •• (39), Love
Crazy •• (41), Shadow of the Thin Man ••
(41), The Thin Man Goes Home •• (44),
Ziegfeld Follies •• (46), **Life with Father ••
(47),** The Senator Was Indiscreet •• (47),
Song of the Thin Man •• (47), How to Marry a
Millionaire ••• (53), **Mister Roberts •• (55)**

Claude Rains (1889-67)

Real name: William Claude Rains

Quote: 'I learn the lines and pray to God.'
• 'My favourite person to work with.' [Bette
Davis] • 'Film buffs "collect" Claude Rains
performances much as other people collect
fine porcelain, vintage port or antique silver,
relishing the delicate detail, the infinite variety
and the polished professionalism of his acting.
He was arguably Hollywood's greatest
character actor. But although he was
nominated for the Academy Award no less than
four times…it is an abiding scandal that he
never won his profession's greatest accolade.'
[Jeffrey Richards]

Films: **The Invisible Man ••• (33),**
Anthony Adverse ••• (36), The Prince and
the Pauper ••• (37), **The Adventures of
Robin Hood •••• (38), Mr. Smith Goes to
Washington •••• (39),** Juarez •• (39), **The
Sea Hawk ••• (40), Here Comes Mr.
Jordan •• (41), Casablanca •••• (42),**
Kings Row •••• (42), **Now, Voyager •••**
(42), Forever and a Day ••• (43), Passage
to Marseilles •• (44), Mr. Skeffington ••
(44), **Notorious •••• (46),** Caesar and
Cleopatra • (46), **Lawrence of Arabia ••••
(62),** The Greatest Story Ever Told •• (65)

Basil Rathbone (1892-67)

The South African-born Rathbone was one of
the most accomplished fencers in Hollywood, a
skill he demonstrated in umpteen villainous costume roles. Sadly, his career was overshadowed
by his success as *Sherlock Holmes,* a part he
seemed not to be able to break away from.

Quote: 'Two profiles pasted together.'
[Dorothy Parker]

Films: David Copperfield •••• (35), Captain Blood ••• (35), A Tale of Two Cities ••• (35), Anna Karenina ••• (35), **The Adventures of Robin Hood •••• (38), Dawn Patrol ••• (38),** The Adventures of Marco Polo •• (38), **The Adventures of Sherlock Holmes ••• (39), The Hound of the Baskervilles ••• (39), The Mark of Zorro ••• (40),** Above Suspicion ••• (43), Frenchman's Creek •• (44), The Pearl of Death ••• (44), The Scarlet Claw ••• (44), Casanova's Big Night • (54), **The Court Jester ••• (56),** The Last Hurrah ••• (58), Tales of Terror •• (62)

Robert Redford (b. 1937)

Real name: Charles Robert Redford Jr.

ACTOR-DIRECTOR. One of the biggest stars of the late 60s and 70s, Redford seems more interested now in his role behind the camera as a director. He is one of the few actors to give something back to the industry, having set up the annual Sundance Film Festival to encourage new cinematic talent. He won an Oscar for directing *Ordinary People.*

Quote: 'Critics are no longer able to judge my performances. My looks seem to get in the way.' • 'As a director, I wouldn't like me as an actor; as an actor, I wouldn't like me as a director.' • 'The centre of America, blond, blue-eyed, tall and thin.' [Barry Levinson] • 'Robert Redford's the very best kisser I ever met.' [Meryl Streep] • 'Bob Redford is a star in the shower. No water spray would dare him a hassle. The water would never be too hot or too cold and the eggs at breakfast would always come out of the pan perfect.' [Paul Newman]

Films: This Property is Condemned •• (66), **Barefoot in the Park •••• (67),** Downhill Racer ••• (69), **Butch Cassidy and The Sundance Kid ••• (69),** Jeremiah Johnson ••• (72), How To Steal a Diamond in Four Uneasy Lessons ••• (72), **The Candidate ••• (72), The Sting •••• (73), The Way We Were •• (73),** The Great Gatsby ••• (74), The Great Waldo Pepper ••• (75), **Three Days of the Condor •••• (75), All the President's Men ••• (76),** A Bridge Too Far •• (77), The Electric Horseman •• (79), **Ordinary People •• (80; d only),** The Natural •• (84), **Out of Africa ••• (85),** Legal Eagles ••• (86), The Milagro Beanfield War ••• (88; d only), Havana • (90),

Sneakers ••• (92), A River Runs Through It •• (92; d only), Indecent Proposal ••• (93), Quiz Show ••• (94; d only)

Burt Reynolds (b. 1936)

Quote: 'Nobody is worth what they pay me.' • 'I've become the No. 1 box office star in the world not because of my movies, but *in spite* of them.' • 'I think the most underrated thing in the world is a good hot bath. With bubbles.' • 'My movies were the kind they show in prisons and aeroplanes, because nobody can leave.' • 'We had such a good time, the public had a good time, too. That's the secret of *Cannonball* and *Smokey and the Bandit* – and films like *Police Academy.* They're laughing so much they didn't hear the words. If you listened to the words – you'd throw up!' • 'Clint Eastwood and I will never win an Oscar. We're too popular.' • 'Canada is where most of the crazy mail comes from; a lot of frustrated ladies in Canada, apparently. Girls sent me Polaroid pictures of themselves in the nude. One girl sent me pubic hair wrapped in wax paper. Their proposals weren't for marriage.' • 'What I look for mostly in a man is humour, honesty and a moustache. Burt has all three.' [Sally Field] • 'All Burt Reynolds has to do is wink at the camera and he's a star. I'm short and ugly and really have to act.' [Dustin Hoffman] • 'He is the one the ladies like to dance with and their husbands like to drink with. He is the larger-than-life actor of our times. He is gifted, talented, naughty – but nice.' [Frank Sinatra] • 'I thought Lyndon Johnson had an overgrown ego. Ol' Lyndon was a bashful country boy compared with this Reynolds asshole.' [Barry L. King, director of *The Best Little Whorehouse in Texas*]

Films: Everything You Always Wanted To Know About Sex (But Were Afraid To Ask) ••• (72), **Deliverance •••• (72),** The Man Who Loved Cat Dancing •• (73), The Longest Yard •• (74), Lucky Lady •• (75), At Long Last Love • (75), Silent Movie •• (c)(76), Nickelodeon ••• (76), Gator • (76; also d), Semi-Tough ••• (77), **Smokey and the Bandit • (77),** Hooper •• (78), Smokey and the Bandit II • (80), Best Friends •• (82), The Best Little Whorehouse in Texas •• (82), The Man Who Loved Women • (83), Cannonball Run II • (84), City Heat • (84), Switching Channels • (88), Breaking In •••• (89), All Dogs Go to Heaven •• (v)(89), Physical Evidence • (89), **The Player ••• (c)(92),** Cop and a Half • (93)

Edward G. Robinson (1893-73)

Real name: Emanuel Goldenberg

Although frequently typecast as a gangster, the Romanian-born Robinson was one of the more cultivated actors working in Hollywood. He spoke eight languages and put together a highly-regarded art collection. Films like *Double Indemnity* and *The Woman in the Window* showed that there was much more to him than just a hood with a gun.

Quote: 'Some people have youth, some have beauty. I have menace."Each part he plays, he enriches with deep and warm understanding of human frailties and compels us to pity rather than condemnation, always adding vivid colour to the intricate mosaic of motion picture reality.' [Fritz Lang]

Films: Little Caesar •• **(31), The Whole Town's Talking** ••• **(35),** Barbary Coast ••• (35), Bullets or Ballots ••• (36), Kid Galahad ••• (37), **The Amazing Dr. Clitterhouse** •• **(38),** A Slight Case of Murder ••• (38), Confessions of a Nazi Spy •• (39), **Dr. Ehrlich's Magic Bullet** ••• **(40),** Brother Orchid •• (40), **The Sea Wolf** ••• **(41),** Tales of Manhattan •• (42), **Double Indemnity** •••• **(44), The Woman in the Window** ••• **(44),** Scarlet Street •• (45), **The Stranger** ••• **(46), Key Largo** ••• **(48),** The Ten Commandments •• (56), The Prize •• (63), Cheyenne Autumn •• (64), Robin and the Seven Hoods •• (64), The Cincinnati Kid •• (65), Soylent Green •• (73)

Ginger Rogers (1912-95)

Real name: Virginia Katherine McMath

While Rogers remains best known for her 10 screen pairings with Fred Astaire, the Oscar on her mantelpiece for *Kitty Foyle* proved not only that she didn't need Astaire to shine, but that she could handle dramatic roles as well as the comedy that was her forte. She was Rita Hayworth's cousin, their mothers being sisters, and appears to have been one of the few Hollywood stars not to touch alcohol or, indeed, tobacco. She had a soda fountain in her house instead of a bar.

Quote: 'Cigarette me, big boy' [line in *Young Man of Manhattan*] • 'I wouldn't change places with Susie Glutz who works in an office for anything.' • 'A star is too tired to do anything but go home, and so to bed and to sleep.'

• 'She may have faked a little, but we knew we had a good thing going.' [Fred Astaire] • 'He gives her class and she gives him sex.' [Katharine Hepburn on teaming with Astaire] • 'Fellow actor made a picture with Ginger, came to me and said, "She's not very easy to know, is she?" I said, "Not if you're lucky, old man".' • 'She has a little love for a lot of people, but not a lot for anybody.' [George Gershwin] • One of the worst, red-baiting, terrifying reactionaries in Hollywood.' [Joseph Losey]

Films: **42nd Street** •••• **(33), Gold Diggers of 1933** •••• **(33),** Flying Down to Rio •• (33), Upperworld ••• (34), The Gay Divorcee ••• (34), **Top Hat** •••• **(35),** Roberta ••• (35), **Swing Time** •••• **(36),** Follow the Fleet ••• (36), Shall We Dance ••• (36), **Stage Door** ••• **(37),** Vivacious Lady ••• (38), Carefree ••• (38), The Story of Vernon & Irene Castle •• (39), Bachelor Mother •• (39), Kitty Foyle ••• (40), Tom, Dick and Harry •• (41), **The Major and the Minor** •• **(42),** Roxie Hart •• (42), Tales of Manhattan •• (42), Once Upon a Honeymoon •• (42), Lady in the Dark •• (44), Weekend at the Waldorf •• (45), The Barkleys of Broadway •• (49), Monkey Business •• (52)

Margaret Rutherford (1892-72)

Although she only began acting in her thirties, the multiple-chinned Rutherford quickly became an indispensable British comedy actress on stage and screen. Her pairing with Alastair Sim in *The Happiest Days of Your Life* seemed only proper, as there were times when one could imagine them as twins who had been separated early in life. She won an Oscar for *The VIPs*.

Films: Blithe Spirit •••• **(45),** Passport to Pimlico •••• **(49), The Happiest Days of Your Life** •••• **(50),** The Magic Box • (c)(51), **The Importance of Being Earnest** ••• **(52),** The Smallest Show on Earth •• (57), **I'm All Right Jack** ••• **(59),** Murder, She Said •• (62), The V.I.P.s •• (63), The Mouse on the Moon •• (63), A Countess from Hong Kong • (67), Chimes at Midnight ••• (67)

S.Z. "Cuddles" Sakall (1884-55)

Real name: B. Eugene Gero Szakall

Elderly, avuncular, with jowls you could have

hidden a string quartet in and mopping his forehead furiously, Sakall usually played 'Favourite Uncle' parts. He had fled Europe to escape the Nazis and when he first made movies in Hollywood, he had to learn his parts phonetically. To the delight of audiences and the benefit of his own pocket, he never completely mastered English, and is probably best known for offering language advice as the head waiter in *Casablanca*. His autobiography was called *The Story of Cuddles (My Life Under the Emperor Francis Joseph, Adolf Hitler and the Warner Brothers)*.

Quote: 'Alan Hale was such a good actor that if he was with you in a scene he could take it away, whether standing behind you, beside you or in front of you. He was full of tricks. I got him and S.Z. "Cuddles" Sakall together one night. Sakall was a funny old guy, but most actors hated him. He messed up the English language so much that they couldn't get their cues. Hale couldn't stand him. Naturally I brought them together as often as I could, and on this night Hale hollers, "For Chrissakes, Sakall, ain't it time you learned to speak English? You been here long enough!" Replied Sakall, "And for vy I should spik Englich better, ven mitt dis Englich I em makin' more vot iss you?"' [Errol Flynn]

Films: **Ball of Fire •••• (41)**, The Devil and Miss Jones •• (41), **Casablanca •••• (42)**, **Yankee Doodle Dandy •••• (42)**, Thank Your Lucky Stars •• (43), Hollywood Canteen •• (44), **Christmas in Connecticut •• (45)**, In the Good Old Summertime •• (49)

George Sanders (1906-72)

Quote: 'I was beastly but never coarse. A high-class sort of heel.' • 'An actor is not quite a human being. But then, who is?' • 'The important thing for a star is to have an interesting face. He doesn't have to move it very much. Editing and camerawork can always produce the desired illusion that a performance is being given.' • 'Acting is like roller-skating. Once you know how to do it, it is neither stimulating nor exciting.' • 'I am not one of those people who would rather act than eat. Quite the reverse. My own desire as a boy was to retire. That ambition has never changed.' • 'I never really thought I'd make the grade. And, let's face it, I haven't.' • 'I will have had enough of this earth by the time I am 65. After

that I shall be having my bottom wiped by nurses and being pushed around in a wheelchair. So I shall commit suicide.' • 'Dear World, I am leaving you because I am bored. I am leaving you with your worries in this sweet cesspool. Good luck.' [His suicide note] • 'The coldest man in movies was George Sanders. Oh, not on the screen. In real life. In real life, he made his movie characters seem sentimental.' [Anne Baxter]

Films: **The Man Who Could Work Miracles ••• (36)**, Confessions of a Nazi Spy •• (39), **Foreign Correspondent •• (40)**, **Rebecca •••• (40)**, Man Hunt ••• (41), **The Moon and Sixpence ••• (42)**, Tales of Manhattan •• (42), Summer Storm •• (44), **The Picture of Dorian Gray ••• (45)**, **The Ghost and Mrs. Muir •••• (47)**, **All About Eve •••• (50)**, Ivanhoe •• (52), **Village of the Damned ••• (60)**, **A Shot in the Dark ••• (64)**, **The Jungle Book •••• (v)(67)**

Susan Sarandon (b. 1946)

Real name: **Susan Abigail Tomaling**

The eldest of nine children in a Catholic family, she was more interested in ballet than acting and never went to drama class. But the agent of her ex-husband Chris Sarandon pushed her into signing up and she has since become one of the strongest and most sophisticated of Hollywood actresses. A political activist, together with partner Tim Robbins, she is also something of a keen amateur racing driver. And, just to set the record straight, her name is not pronounced the way most people do, but Sa-RAN-don.

Films: **The Front Page •• (74)**, The Great Waldo Pepper ••• (75), **The Rocky Horror Picture Show •• (75)**, The Great Smokey Roadblock •• (76), Dragonfly •• (76), The Other Side of Midnight •• (77), King of the Gypsies •• (78), **Pretty Baby •• (78)**, Loving Couples •• (80), **Atlantic City ••• (81)**, Tempest •• (82), The Hunger • (83), Compromising Positions •• (85), The Witches of Eastwick ••• (87), **Bull Durham ••• (88)**, Sweet Hearts Dance •• (88), A Dry White Season •• (89), The January Man • (89), **White Palace •• (90)**, **Thelma & Louise •••• (91)**, Light Sleeper • (92), **The Player ••• (c)(92)**, Bob Roberts ••• (c)(92), Lorenzo's Oil •• (92), The Client ••• (94), Little Women •• (94)

Arnold Schwarzenegger

(b. 1947)

The son of a Austrian policeman, he grew up in a house with no phone, fridge or toilet. By the age of 20 he was Mr. Europe, Mr. International and Mr. Universe. After studying business and economics part-time (as well as ballet), he had developed a shrewd business head on his enormous shoulders. While nobody took him seriously as *Hercules in New York*, a series of steadily more popular action pics has made him Hollywood's most bankable star. Apparently a neatness freak with an obsession for vanilla ice-cream, he's said to love cooking, cleaning and ironing and drives around in an armoured car. Despite being a leading Republican campaigner, he's succeeded in bringing together the Kennedys and the Republicans by marrying Maria Shriver, the niece of Teddy Kennedy. In partnership with Stallone and Willis, he owns the Planet Hollywood restaurant chain.

Quote: 'Money doesn't make you happy. I now have $50 million but I was just as happy when I had $48 million.' • 'I just use my muscles as a conversation piece, like someone walking a cheetah down 42nd Street.' • 'A condom stuffed with walnuts' [Clive James] • 'He has so many muscles that he has to make an appointment to move his fingers.' [Phyllis Diller] • 'Of course, if Arnold hadn't existed, we would have had to build him.' [John Milius]

Films: Hercules in New York • (70), **The Long Goodbye •••• (b)(73),** Stay Hungry ••• (76), Pumping Iron ••• (77), The Villain •• (79), Conan the Barbarian •• (82), **The Terminator •••• (84),** Conan the Destroyer •• (84), Commando •• (85), Red Sonja • (85), Raw Deal • (86), The Running Man •• (87), Predator •• (87), Twins •• (88), Red Heat •• (88), Kindergarten Cop •• (90), **Total Recall ••• (90), Terminator 2: Judgment Day ••• (91), Dave ••• (c)(93),** Last Action Hero •• (93), **True Lies ••• (94),** Junior •• (94)

Martin Scorsese (b. 1942)

DIRECTOR. An unhealthy child, plagued by asthma and other illnesses, Scorsese trained for the priesthood before being thrown out. He stopped attending Mass when a priest claimed that the Vietnam War was a holy cause and turned to film-making, startling the world with *Mean Streets* and *Taxi Driver* and courting controversy ever since. The majority of his films star either Harvey Keitel or Robert De Niro, while his mother is also usually in there somewhere. He was married, briefly, to Isabella Rossellini.

Quote: 'My friends used to say, "Jeez, Marty, do you really believe all that stuff the priests tell you?" Well I did believe it, every word of it. I wouldn't touch meat on Friday and I believed I would go to hell if I missed Mass on Sunday.'

Films: Who's That Knocking at My Door? ••• (68), Boxcar Bertha ••• (72), **Mean Streets ••• (c)(73; also a&s), Alice Doesn't Live Here Anymore ••• (74),** Cannonball •• (c)(76; a only), **Taxi Driver ••• (c)(76; also a),** New York, New York •• (77), The Last Waltz ••• (78), **Raging Bull ••• (80), The King of Comedy •••• (c)(83; also a),** After Hours •• (c)(85; also a), 'Round Midnight ••• (c)(86; a only), The Color of Money ••• (86), The Last Temptation of Christ •• (88), New York Stories •• (89), **GoodFellas •••• (90; also s),** Guilty by Suspicion •• (91; a only), Cape Fear •• (91), The Age of Innocence •• (93; also s), Quiz Show ••• (c)(94; a only)

George C. Scott (b. 1927)

Real name: **George Campbell Scott**

Quote: 'The essence of art should be life and change, and that can't be where films are concerned. The film freezes your art forever. No matter how much better you become, there is no way to improve the performance you've done for the camera. It's locked. And there's a certain, sad death in that.' • 'Don't you think it's a pretty spooky way to earn a living?' • 'It's a concentrated fury, a sense of inner rage, a kind of controlled madness.' [José Ferrer] • 'One of the best actors alive. But my opinion of him as an actor is much higher than my opinion of him as a man.' [John Huston]

Films: Anatomy of a Murder ••• (59), The Hustler ••• (61), Dr. Strangelove: Or How I Learned to Stop Worrying and Love the Bomb •••• (63), The List of Adrian Messenger ••• (63), The Yellow Rolls-Royce •• (65), **Patton •••• (70),** The Hospital •• (71), **Movie Movie •••• (78),** Taps •• (81), Firestarter • (84), The Exorcist III •• (90), The Rescuers Down Under ••• (v)(91), Malice (93)

Peter Sellers (1925-80)

Real name: Richard Henry Sellers

Sellers could have been the template for the tragic clown. His brilliant skills of mimicry and his ability to play several characters at once on screen concealed a tortured, eccentric personality racked with self-doubt. He came to attention with the zany, long-running radio series *The Goons* while starring in many pleasant British movies of the period. He became an international star with *Dr. Strangelove* and by stealing *The Pink Panther* from under David Niven's nose as Inspector Clouseau. Despite his amazing talents, his later career was a sad disappointment.

Quote 'There is no me. I do not exist. There used to be a me, but I had it surgically removed.' • 'I'm a classic example of all humorists – only funny when I'm working.' • 'People will swim through shit if you put a few bob in it.' • 'Sellers became a monsters. He just got bored with the part and became angry, sullen and unprofessional. He wouldn't show up for work and he began looking for anyone to blame but himself for his own madness, his own craziness.' [Blake Edwards, director of the *Pink Panther* films] • 'As a man he was abject, probably his own worst enemy, although there was plenty of competition.' [Roy Boulting] • 'Peter had an extraordinary sense of not being there. He genuinely felt that when he went into a room no-one could see him.' [Peter O'Toole]

Films: **The Ladykillers** •• **(55)**, The Smallest Show on Earth •• (57), **I'm All Right Jack** ••• **(59)**, **The Mouse that Roared** •• **(59)**, **Two Way Stretch** ••• **(60)**, The Millionairess • (60), **Only Two Can Play** ••• **(62)**, **Lolita** ••• **(62)**, The Road to Hong Kong •• (c)(62), The Wrong Arm of the Law •• (62), **Dr. Strangelove: Or How I Learned to Stop Worrying and Love the Bomb** •••• **(63)**, **The Pink Panther** ••• **(63)**, Heavens Above! •• (63), **A Shot in the Dark** ••• **(64)**, What's New, Pussycat? •• (65), **Casino Royale** • **(67)**, The Return of the Pink Panther •• (75), Murder by Death • (76), The Pink Panther Strikes Again •• (76), The Revenge of the Pink Panther • (78), **Being There** ••• **(79)**, The Trail of the Pink Panther • (82)

Don Siegel (1912-91)

DIRECTOR. Son of a mandolin soloist, after graduating from Cambridge graduate, Siegel started working for Warner Brothers. He directed the opening montage of *Casablanca* before moving onto low-budget, hard-hitting genre pieces like *Riot in Cell Block 11* and *Invasion of the Body Snatchers*. His lean, unpretentious style attracted him to Clint Eastwood and helped revive both their careers in the late 60s, starting with *Coogan's Bluff* and four subsequent collaborations.

Quote: 'Most of my pictures, I'm sorry to say, are about nothing. Because I'm a whore. I work for money. It's the American way.' • 'I once told Godard that he had something I wanted – freedom. He said: You have something I want – money.'

Films: The Big Steal ••• (49), **Riot in Cell Block 11** ••• **(54)**, **Invasion of the Body Snatchers** •••• **(56)**, **Coogan's Bluff** ••• **(c)(68; also a)**, Madigan •• (68), **Play 'Misty' for Me** ••• **(71; a only)**, **The Beguiled** ••• **(71)**, **Dirty Harry** ••• **(71)**, **Charley Varrick** •••• **(c)(73; also a)**, The Shootist ••• (76), **Escape from Alcatraz** •• **(79)**, Into the Night •• (c)(85; a only)

Alastair Sim (1900-76)

Quote: 'It was revealed to me many years ago with conclusive certainty that I was a fool and that I had always been a fool. Since then I have been as happy as any man has a right to be.' • 'There lives and breathes a comic genius of gargantuan proportions.' [Patricia Routledge]

Films: Gangway ••• (37), **This Man Is News** ••• **(38)**, Hue and Cry ••• (46), **Green for Danger** ••• **(46)**, **The Happiest Days of Your Life** •••• **(50)**, **Scrooge** •••• **(51)**, Laughter in Paradise •• (51), **The Belles of St. Trinians** •••• **(54)**, An Inspector Calls •• (54), **The Green Man** ••• **(56)**, Blue Murder at St. Trinian's •• (57), **School for Scoundrels** ••• **(60)**, The Millionairess • (60), The Ruling Class ••• (72)

Frank Sinatra (b. 1915)

Real name: Francis Albert Sinatra

Quote: 'I'm for anything that gets you through the night, be it prayer, tranquillizers or a bottle of Jack Daniels.' • 'If I had as many affairs as they say, I would now be speaking to you from a jar in the Harvard Medical School.' • 'He's the kind of guy that, when he dies, he's going up to heaven and give God a bad time for making him bald.'[Marlon Brando] • 'Terribly nice one minute, and…well…not so nice the next.' [Prince Charles] • 'When Frank Sinatra was down he was sweet but when he got back up he was hell.' [Ex-wife Ava Gardner] • 'I'm just one of those who thought they could *direct* Sinatra. It's like being one of the girls who thought they'd get Howard Hughes to marry them.' [Robert Aldrich] • 'I always knew Frank would end up in bed with a boy.' [Ex-wife Ava Gardner when Sinatra married Mia Farrow] • 'When Sinatra dies, they're giving his zipper to the Smithsonian.' [Dean Martin]

Films: Anchors Aweigh •• (45), **On The Town** ••• **(49),** Take Me Out to the Ball Game ••• (49), **From Here to Eternity** •• **(53),** Guys and Dolls ••• (55), **Around the World in 80 Days** •• (c)(56), **The Man with the Golden Arm** •• **(56), High Society** ••• **(56),** Pal Joey ••• (57), Can-Can •• (60), **The Manchurian Candidate** •••• **(62),** The List of Adrian Messenger ••• (63), Robin and the Seven Hoods •• (64), Von Ryan's Express ••• (65), **That's Entertainment!** •••• **(74),** Cannonball Run II • (c)(84), **Who Framed Roger Rabbit?** ••• **(v)(88)**

Steven Spielberg (b. 1947)

DIRECTOR. Though he's made some of the most phenomenally successful films ever, Spielberg appears to be a boy who's never grown up. A keen film-maker since childhood, his mother once cooked a cherries jubilee in a pressure cooker so that he could film the explosion for a home horror movie. He wasn't bright enough to get into film school but regularly bluffed his way onto the sets of directors like Hitchcock. He taps into the spirit of childhood magnificently well, but his films aimed at an adult audience were usually less commercially successful until *Schindler's List*. After the success of *ET*, Universal built a $3.5m complex for him on the lot. Querying the cost, Spielberg was told that the revenue from Bolivia alone would cover it! His divorce from actress Amy Irving cost a massive $59m and he is now married to actress Kate Capshaw, the heroine of *Indiana Jones and the Temple of Doom*. He finally received the Oscar he had been denied by the snobbishness of Academy voters for *Schindler's List*.

Quote: 'I've been really serious about this as a career since I was 12 years old.' • 'When I grow up I still want to be a director.' • 'The most expensive habit in the world is celluloid not heroin and I need a fix every two years.' • 'I've never been through psychoanalysis. I solve my problems with the pictures I make.' • 'I've discovered I've got this preoccupation with ordinary people pursued by large forces.' • 'The only person I've come across who fits my criteria of genius. And I don't throw that word around. Genius is imagination and attention to detail. The ability to achieve to the minutest detail what you perceive in your imagination…I don't think there's another person on earth who's as great a plot structurist or better storyteller.' [Richard Dreyfuss] • 'Spielberg isn't a filmmaker. He's a confectioner.' [Alex Cox]

Films: Duel •••• **(71), The Sugarland Express** •••• **(74), Jaws** •••• **(75), Close Encounters of the Third Kind** •••• **(77; also s),** 1941 •• (79), **The Blues Brothers** •••• **(c)(80; a only), Raiders of the Lost Ark** •••• **(81), E.T. The Extra-Terrestrial** •••• **(82), Poltergeist** •• **(82; s only),** Twilight Zone – The Movie •• (83), **Gremlins** ••• **(c)(84; a only), Indiana Jones and the Temple of Doom** •• **(84),** The Color Purple ••• (85), Empire of the Sun ••• (87), Always •• (89), **Indiana Jones and the Last Crusade** •••• **(89),** Hook ••• (91), **Jurassic Park** ••• **(93), Schindler's List** •••• **(93)**

Sylvester Stallone (b. 1946)

Real name: Michael Sylvester Stallone

Success was a long time coming. A failed trainee beautician, gym instructor at a Swiss girls' finishing school and lion-cage cleaner, his early acting career included a nudie revue and the now infamous semi-porn film *The Italian Stallion*. Offered $265,000 for his script of *Rocky* when he was down to his last $100 he refused, insisting that he star. The rest, as they say, is history. He was the first actor to earn $10m for a film and, in 1995, he became the first to be paid $20m upfront for a movie. Goodness knows what it will make him if it does well at the box office. Divorced noisily and expensively from Brigitte Nielsen, he has a son called Sage Moonblood and apparently believes that he was beheaded in a previous life in 18th-century France. He's a keen collector of art and even paints himself. Look out for his brief appearance as an uncredited mugger in Woody Allen's *Bananas*.

Quote: 'I see a body as a classy chassis to carry your mind around in. It will fade and you've got to have something left.' • 'I tried the kinder, gentler Stallone and it didn't work. Action is where I belong.' • 'You wouldn't believe some of the things they've said about me. Like Rex Reed saying my career is more mysterious than cot death!'

Films: Bananas •••• (b)(71), The Lords of Flatbush •• (74), Farewell, My Lovely ••• (75), Death Race 2000 ••• (75), Capone • (75), The Prisoner of Second Avenue •• (75), Cannonball •• (b)(76), **Rocky •••• (76; also s)**, F.I.S.T. ••• (78; also s), Paradise Alley • (78; also d&s), Rocky II •• (79; also d&s), Escape to Victory • (81), Nighthawks ••• (81), Rocky III ••• (82; also d&s), **First Blood •• (82; also s)**, Staying Alive •• (c)(83; also d&s), Rambo: First Blood Part II •• (85; also s), Rocky IV •• (85; also d&s), Cobra • (86; also s), Over the Top • (87; also s), Rambo III • (88; also s), Lock Up •• (89), Tango and Cash ••• (89), Rocky V •• (90; also s), Oscar •• (91), Stop! Or My Mom Will Shoot • (92), **Demolition Man ••• (93)**, Cliffhanger ••• (93), The Specialist • (94), Judge Dredd •• (95)

Barbara Stanwyck (1907-90)

Real name: Ruby Stevens

Stanwyck excelled as playing the tough, intelligent woman who had made it despite being born on the wrong side of the tracks. Although many of her roles had her as a hard woman who could give the men as good as they got, never better than in *Double Indemnity*, she was also capable of splendid comic performances, as in *The Lady Eve* and *Ball of Fire*.

Quote: 'Put me in the last 15 minutes of a picture and I don't care what happened before. I don't even care if I was in the rest of the damn thing, I'll take it all in those 15 minutes.' • 'I want to go on until they have to shoot me.' • 'Eyes are the greatest tool in film. Mr. Capra taught me that. Sure, it's nice to say very good dialogue, if you can get it. But great movie acting – watch the eyes.' • 'All I want, all any of the real pros want, is a decent script, a competent cast and a good director. The rest is a crock of shit.' • 'Here was an actress that never played just one side of a character. She always played the truth. I once asked Barbara Stanwyck the secret of acting, and she said, "Just be truthful. And if you can fake that, you've got it made".' [Walter Matthau]

Films: Miracle Woman •• (31), Night Nurse ••• (31), The Bitter Tea of General Yen •• (33), Baby Face ••• (33), Annie Oakley ••• (35), **Stella Dallas ••• (37)**, The Mad Miss Manton •• (38), Union Pacific ••• (39), Remember the Night •• (40), **Ball of Fire •••• (41), The Lady Eve ••• (41)**, Meet John Doe •• (41), **Double Indemnity •••• (44)**, Hollywood Canteen •• (c)(44), **Christmas in Connecticut •• (45)**, The Strange Love of Martha Ivers ••• (46), The Two Mrs. Carrolls • (47), **Sorry, Wrong Number ••• (48)**, The Furies •• (50), Clash by Night •• (52), Executive Suite ••• (54), Cattle Queen of Montana • (54)

James Stewart (b. 1908)

Real name: James Maitland Stewart

Stewart played the lanky, good-natured, slightly awkward, small-town American to perfection. But his often naive screen image belied a shrewd businessman. He was the first star to receive, not just a salary, but a percentage of the box office takings when he made *Broken Arrow* in 1950, opening the floodgates of a trend which helped bring about the collapse of the studio system. It was about that time that his screen image was toughened up with a brace of Westerns. Hitchcock, in four films, undermined the cuddly exterior, revealing aspects to his character that few had hitherto suspected. He had a distinguished war record, flying 20 combat missions as a bomber pilot and rising through the ranks from private to colonel. He won an Oscar for *The Philadelphia Story*.

Quote: 'I kept my own Western costume for most of my films. The hat, in particular. I wore it in every Western until one very sad day it completely disintegrated.' • 'James Stewart is the most nearly normal of all Hollywood stars.' [Louella Parsons] • 'Jimmy is everything the British audience wants an American to be but so rarely is.' [Anthony Quayle] • 'If Bess and I had a son, we'd want him to be just like Jimmy Stewart.' [President Harry S. Truman]

Films: After the Thin Man ••• (36), Rose Marie •• (36), Wife vs. Secretary •• (36), **You Can't Take It with You •• (38)**, Vivacious Lady ••• (38), Shopworn Angel •• (38), **Destry Rides Again •••• (39), Mr. Smith Goes to Washington •••• (39), The Philadelphia Story ••• (40), The Shop around the Corner •••• (40)**, The Mortal

Storm ••• (40), Ziegfeld Girl •• (41), **It's a Wonderful Life** •••• **(46), Rope** ••• **(48),** Call Northside 777 ••• (48), **Harvey** ••• **(50), Winchester '73** ••• **(50),** Broken Arrow ••• (50), No Highway ••• (51), The Greatest Show on Earth •• (52), Bend of the River ••• (52), The Naked Spur ••• (53), Thunder Bay ••• (53), **The Glenn Miller Story** ••• **(54), Rear Window** •••• **(54),** The Far Country ••• (54), The Man from Laramie ••• (55), The Man Who Knew Too Much •• (56), The Spirit of St. Louis •• (57), **Vertigo** •••• **(58),** Bell, Book and Candle •• (58), **Anatomy of a Murder** ••• **(59),** The Man Who Shot Liberty Vallance •• (62), How the West Was Won ••• (62), Cheyenne Autumn •• (64), **The Flight of the Phoenix** ••• **(65),** The Cheyenne Social Club •• (70), **That's Entertainment!** •••• **(74),** The Shootist ••• (76), Airport '77 •• (77), An American Tail: Fievel Goes West •• (v)(91)

Sharon Stone (b. 1958)

What fun it is looking at the embarrassing early films of future stars. There are so many dogs in Sharon Stone's kennel, you could start an American branch of the Battersea Dogs' Home. It would be nice to say one could see star quality shining through in her performance in *Allan Quatermain and the Lost City of Gold* or *Police Academy 4*. Nice, but totally untrue. However, one below-the-belt shot from a sneaky director in *Basic Instinct* and the world is hers, although a 1990 photo session in Playboy didn't hurt either. She is apparently one of the few beauty contestants to have combined cheesecake posing with a reading of the Gettysburg Address.

Quote: 'If you have a vagina *and* an attitude in this town, then that's a lethal combination.'
• 'It's a new low for actresses when you have to wonder what's between their ears instead of her legs.' [Katharine Hepburn]

Films: Diabolique (), Stardust Memories • (b)(80), Irreconcilable Differences • (84), King Solomon's Mines • (85), Allan Quatermain and the Lost City of Gold • (87), Police Academy 4: Citizens on Patrol • (87), Action Jackson •• (88), Nico •• (88), **Total Recall** ••• **(90),** Year of the Gun • (91), **Basic Instinct** •• **(92),** Sliver (93), Last Action Hero •• (c)(93), Intersection • (94), The Specialist • (94), The Quick and the Dead • (95)

Meryl Streep (b. 1949)

Real name: Mary Louise Streep

If producers need a leading actress to play a tortured martyr with an accent, there's only one place they need turn. Streep's already done Danish ('I haad a faaarm in Aaaafricaaa'), Polish, Italian, English, Australian ('A dingow stowl moy boyboi'). Some people love her performances, others find her mannered in the extreme.

Quote: 'You can't get spoiled if you do your own ironing.' • 'I could rip Madonna's throat out. I can sing better than she can.' • 'Meryl Streep is an acting machine in the same sense that a shark is a killing machine.' [Cher] • 'I am not a fan of Meryl Streep. Or as I call her, Meryl Creep. I think she's creepy. Anyway, life is difficult enough without Meryl Streep movies.' [Truman Capote]

Films: Julia ••• (b)(77), **The Deer Hunter** •• **(78),** The Seduction of Joe Tynan •• (79), **Manhattan** •••• **(79), Kramer vs. Kramer** ••• **(79), The French Lieutenant's Woman** •• **(81), Sophie's Choice** •• **(82),** Still of the Night •• (82), Silkwood ••• (83), Falling in Love •• (84), **Out of Africa** ••• **(85),** Plenty •• (85), Heartburn • (86), Ironweed •• (87), A Cry in the Dark •• (88), She-Devil • (89), **Postcards from the Edge** •••• **(90),** Defending Your Life •• (91), Death Becomes Her ••• (92), The House of the Spirits • (94), The River Wild •• (94), The Bridges of Madison County ••• (95)

Preston Sturges (1898-59)

Real name: Edmund P. Biden

WRITER-DIRECTOR. An occasional inventor whose proudest achievement was a waterproof lipstick, Sturges abandoned a playwriting career when he persuaded Paramount to let him direct his script for *The Great McGinty*. Its success led him briefly to become the king of 40s screwball comedy, with a string of films distinguished by madcap, irreverent humour put over by one of the greatest groups of repertory players ever assembled by a director. However, his star did not shine for very long and his later output was a pale shadow of his former achievement.

Quote: 'When the last dime is gone, I'll sit on the kerb outside with a pencil and a ten cent notebook, and start the whole thing over again.'

• 'One of the best, but crazy, a little nutty. He had a big desk and a horn on it that honked. Honk, honk. He thought it was goddamned funny.' [Screenwriter W.R. Burnett] • 'He was too large for this smelly resort and the big studios were scared to death of him. A man who was a triple threat, kept them awake nights and I'm positive they were waiting for him to fall on his face so they could pounce and devour this terrible threat to their stingy talents. They pounced and they got him good.' [Earl Felton]

Films: The Power and the Glory ••• (33; s only), **Easy Living** ••• **(37; s only)**, Ants In Your Pants of 1939 •• (38; s only), **Christmas in July** ••• **(c)(40; also a&s)**, The Great McGinty •• (40; also s), **The Lady Eve** ••• **(41; also s)**, **Sullivan's Travels** •••• **(41; also s)**, **The Palm Beach Story** ••• **(42; also s)**, **Hail the Conquering Hero** ••• **(44; also s)**, **The Miracle of Morgan's Creek** ••• **(44; also s)**, Mad Wednesday • (47; also s), Unfaithfully Yours • (48; also s)

Elizabeth Taylor (b. 1932)

Unquestionably a star, even from childhood, Taylor's much-married private life has provided more entertainment than most of her movies. Whether marrying or divorcing Richard Burton twice, befriending Michael Jackson or marrying a much younger construction worker she met in a detox clinic, she is rarely out of the news for long. She has given enough fine performances for us to regret that she sleep-walked her way through so many more. She won Oscars for *Butterfield 8* and *Who's Afraid of Virginia Woolf?*.

Quote: 'They have called me a scarlet woman for so long I'm almost purple.' • 'I don't pretend to be an ordinary housewife.' • 'If someone was stupid enough to offer me a million dollars to make a picture, I was certainly not dumb enough to turn it down.' • 'My toughest role was learning to grow up.' • 'Some of my best leading men have been horses and dogs.' • 'Beauty? Who wants it? I want a home in a quiet place, where no-one knows my name, except the grocer, the butcher and the milkman.' • 'I have a lust for diamonds, almost like a disease.' • 'She has a double chin and an overdeveloped chest and she's rather short in the leg. so I can hardly describe her as the most beautiful creature I've ever seen.' [Richard

Burton] • 'Liz is the only woman I have ever met who turns me on. She feels like the other half of me.' [Montgomery Clift] • 'There are three things I never saw Elizabeth Taylor do. Be on time. Tell a lie. Be unkind to anyone.' [Mike Nichols] • 'She should get a divorce and settle down.' [Jack Paar]

Films: Jane Eyre •• **(43)**, Lassie Come Home ••• (43), **National Velvet** ••• **(44)**, **Life with Father** •• **(47)**, Little Women •• (49), **Father of the Bride** ••• **(50)**, Father's Little Dividend •• (51), Quo Vadis? •• (c)(51), A Place in the Sun •• (51), Ivanhoe •• (52), Beau Brummel •• (54), **Giant** ••• **(56)**, Raintree County •• (57), **Cat on a Hot Tin Roof** ••• **(58)**, Suddenly, Last Summer ••• (59), Butterfield 8 •• (60), **Cleopatra** • **(63)**, The V.I.P.s •• (63), **Who's Afraid of Virginia Woolf?** ••• **(66)**, The Taming of the Shrew ••• (67), The Comedians •• (67), Reflections in a Golden Eye •• (67), Under Milk Wood •• (73), **That's Entertainment!** •••• **(74)**, **Winter Kills** ••• **(79)**, The Flintstones ••• (c)(94)

Terry-Thomas (1911-90)
Real name Thomas Terry Hoar-Stevens

There never was a better, more likeable bounder and cad than gap-toothed Terry-Thomas, a stand-up comic turned film actor. Forever associated with his repeated cry of 'absolute shower' in *Private's Progress*, he literally flew the flag for Britain when in Hollywood. He ran the Union Jack up his flagpole and drove round in a Rolls-Royce. His career was sadly curtailed by Parkinson's Disease, which left him unable to work for the last 13 years of his life.

Films: **The Green Man** ••• **(56)**, Private's Progress •• (56), Blue Murder at St. Trinian's •• (57), **I'm All Right Jack** ••• **(59)**, **School for Scoundrels** ••• **(60)**, **It's a Mad Mad Mad Mad World** • **(63)**, The Mouse on the Moon •• (63), How to Murder Your Wife ••• (65), Those Magnificent Men in their Flying Machines •• (65), The Guide for the Married Man • (c)(67), **Abominable Dr. Phibes** ••• **(71)**

Spencer Tracy (1900-67)

His pugnacious, no-nonsense, blue-collar image was best set off against the East Coast patrician Katharine Hepburn, with whom he starred in nine movies and had a long-standing secretive affair. He was a devout Catholic, however, and remained married to his long-suffering wife. His resolute determination to forge ahead where almost anybody else would have given up was seen to its best advantage in the superlative *Bad Day at Black Rock*. He won the Best Acting Oscar for *Captains Courageous* and *Boy's Town*, the first time anybody had won two years in a row, a record only equalled by Tom Hanks in 1994.

Quote: 'This mug of mine is as plain as a barn door. Why should people pay 35 cents to look at it?' • 'Acting is not an *important* job in the scheme of things. Plumbing is.' • 'Acting is not the noblest profession in the world. there are things lower than acting – not many, mind you – but politicians give you something to look down on from time to time.' • 'There were times my pants were so thin I could sit on a dime and tell if it was heads or tails.' • 'Anyone who stayed drunk for 25 years as I did would have to be in trouble. Hell, I used to take two-week lunch hours!' • 'Well, it's taken me 40 years of doing it for a living to learn the secret. I don't know that I want to give it away. Okay, I'll tell you. The secret of acting is – learn your line!.' • 'I've learned more about acting from watching Tracy than in any other way.' [Laurence Olivier] • 'Spence is the best we have, because you don't see the mechanism at work.' [Humphrey Bogart]

Films: 20,000 Years in Sing Sing ••• (33), The Power and the Glory ••• (33), Man's Castle ••• (33), **San Francisco •• (36), Libeled Lady •• (36), Fury ••• (36), Captains Courageous ••• (37),** Test Pilot •• (38), Boy's Town •• (38), Stanley and Livingstone ••• (39), **Boom Town ••• (40),** Edison, the Man ••• (40), Dr. Jekyll and Mr. Hyde ••• (41), **Woman of the Year ••• (42),** A Guy Named Joe •• (43), The Seventh Cross ••• (44), Thirty Seconds Over Tokyo ••• (44), State of the Union •• (48), **Adam's Rib •••• (49), Father of the Bride ••• (50),** Father's Little Dividend •• (51), **Pat and Mike ••• (52),** Broken Lance •• (54), **Bad Day at Black Rock •••• (55),** Desk Set •• (57), The Old Man and the Sea •• (58), The Last Hurrah ••• (58), Inherit the Wind ••• (60), **Judgment at Nuremberg •••• (61),** How the West Was Won ••• (v)(62), **It's a Mad Mad Mad Mad World • (63), Guess Who's Coming to Dinner? •• (67)**

John Travolta (b. 1954)

Travolta is surely the prime example of never writing an actor's career off. After languishing in the obscurity of video hell, he came back with *Look Who's Talking* and then vanished again, only to be rediscovered once more when fan Quentin Tarantino cast him in *Pulp Fiction*. Prior to this, few young filmgoers can have had any idea that he was once, thanks to *Saturday Night Fever* and *Grease*, one of the world's biggest heartthrobs. Although only receiving $150,000 for *Pulp Fiction*, he's now leapt so far back up the ladder that he can command $7m a movie.

Quote: 'Sex with love is about the most beautiful thing there is – but sex without love isn't so bad, either.' • 'If I'm androgynous, I'd say I lean towards macho-androgynous.' • 'He's not a dancer. What he did in those dance scenes was very attractive but he is basically not a dancer. I was dancing like that years ago, you know. Disco is just jitterbug.' [Fred Astaire]

Films: **Carrie ••• (76), Saturday Night Fever •• (77), Grease ••• (78),** Urban Cowboy ••• (80), Blow Out •• (81), Staying Alive •• (83), Two of a Kind • (83), Perfect • (85), Look Who's Talking ••• (89), Look Who's Talking Too • (90), Look Who's Talking Now • (93), **Pulp Fiction •••• (94)**

M. Emmet Walsh (b. 1935)

Real name: **Michael Emmet Walsh**

One of the greatest of current Hollywood character actors. You'll know his face, even if you can't put a name to it. No film is ever totally duff if M. Emmet Walsh is in it.

Films: **Midnight Cowboy ••• (69), Little Big Man ••• (70), What's Up, Doc? •••• (72),** Serpico ••• (73), The Prisoner of Second Avenue •• (75), Airport '77 •• (77), Slap Shot •• (77), Straight Time ••• (78), **Ordinary People •• (80),** Reds ••• (81), **Blade Runner •••• (82),** Silkwood ••• (83), Missing in Action • (84), The Pope of Greenwich Village •• (84), Scandalous • (84), Fletch • (85), **Blood Simple ••• (85),** Back to School • (86), Critters • (86), No Man's Land •• (87), Bigfoot and the Hendersons •• (87), Raising Arizona •••• (87), Clean and Sober ••• (88), Sunset • (88), War Party •• (89), The Mighty Quinn •• (89), Chattahoochee •• (90), Narrow Margin

•• (90), White Sands ••• (92), Wilder Napalm (93), Free Willy 2 ••• (95)

John Wayne (1907-79)

Real name: Marion Michael Morrison

A one-time props man who graduated to routine B-Westerns, John Wayne was catapulted to stardom when director John Ford decided that his old friend would be just right for the part of Ringo Kid in *Stagecoach*. He was to remain typecast as a cowboy for the rest of his life – with occasional soldiers and cops thrown in – but there was nobody better at the rugged, unswerving determination to do what a man's gotta do. Wayne was somewhat less accomplished as a director, though he remains the only film-maker to have made a pro-Vietnam War movie. He once won Lassie in a poker game, but gave her (in reality a 'him') back, saying he felt too guilty about it. His epitaph, written in Spanish, is: 'He was ugly, he was strong, and he had dignity'. He won an Oscar for *True Grit*.

Quote: 'At USC, I took Latin and romance Languages and mathematics through calculus. And when I started in movies, they had to teach me to say "Ain't".' • 'John Ford taught me what to do in front of the movie camera. He taught me not to *act* but to *react*.' • 'I play John Wayne in every picture regardless of the character, and I've been doing okay, haven't I?' • 'I never trust a man that doesn't drink.' • 'I've had three wives, six children, six grandchildren and I still don't understand women.' • 'Great legs and tight buttocks, a real great seat, and small, sensitive feet.' [Katharine Hepburn] • 'I certainly would have given anything to have worked with John Wayne. He's the most attractive man who ever walked the earth, I think.' [Bette Davis] • 'I did a movie with Duke Wayne and was very surprised to find out he had small feet, wore lifts and a corset. Hollywood is seldom what it seems.' [Rock Hudson] • 'John Wayne and his drinking buddy Ward Bond went around wrecking careers with their gung-ho willingness to blacklist anyone who politically disagreed with them during the 1950s.' [Melvyn Douglas]

Films: Baby Face ••• (b)(33), **Stagecoach •••• (39),** They Were Expendable ••• (45), Without Reservations •• (46), **Red River ••• (48),** Fort Apache ••• (48), She Wore a Yellow Ribbon ••• (49), Sands of Iwo Jima ••

(49), Rio Grande •• (50), **The Quiet Man ••• (52),** Trouble Along the Way •• (53), **The Searchers ••• (56), Rio Bravo •• (59),** The Alamo •• (60; also d), The Man Who Shot Liberty Vallance •• (62), How the West Was Won ••• (62), The Longest Day ••• (62), The Greatest Story Ever Told •• (65), The Green Berets • (68; also d), **True Grit ••• (69),** Rooster Cogburn •• (75), The Shootist ••• (76)

Orson Welles (1915-85)

WRITER-DIRECTOR. After he had co-founded the Mercury Theatre and terrified the American public with his radio broadcast of *The War of the Worlds*, RKO gave the *enfant terrible* carte blanche to save the struggling studio. His first movie, *Citizen Kane*, may now be thought of by many as the greatest film of all time, but that's not how RKO or William Randolph Hearst saw it then. He was never to have such freedom again, with the studios hampering and interfering with all his subsequent projects. He frequently acted in films he despised to raise cash for his own idiosyncratic projects. Sadly, towards the end of his life, he was better known by many people for his advertisements for sherry than for his contribution to world cinema. He won an Oscar for his work on the script of *Citizen Kane*.

Quote: 'I'm not bitter about Hollywood's treatment of me – but of its treatment of Griffith, von Sternberg, Buster Keaton and a hundred others.' • 'Every actor in his heart believes everything bad that's printed about him.' • 'I began at the top and I've been working my way down ever since.' • 'We should have the courage of our platitudes.' • 'I know little about Orson's childhood and seriously doubt if he ever was a child.' [Joseph Cotten] • 'A perpetual notion machine.' [Marlene Dietrich] • 'There, but for the grace of God, goes God.' [Herman Mankiewicz] • 'It's like meeting God without dying.' [Dorothy Parker] • 'Not true there was a cabal preventing Orson making more films. He simply never fulfilled himself after that magnificent start. His own fault – lack of self-discipline.' [Director Robert Wise, who edited *Citizen Kane*]

Films: Citizen Kane •• (41; also a&s), The Magnificent Ambersons •••• (v)(42; also a&s), Jane Eyre •• (43; a only), **The Stranger ••• (46; also a), The Lady from**

Shanghai ••• (48; also a&s), The Third Man •••• (49; a only), Moby Dick •• (56; a only), **Touch of Evil ••• (58; also a&s),** The Long, Hot Summer •• (58; a only), The Vikings •• (v)(58; a only), The V.I.P.s •• (63; a only), **A Man for All Seasons •••• (66; a only),** Casino Royale • (67; a only), Chimes at Midnight ••• (67; also a&s), Voyage of the Damned • (76; a only), Transformers – The Movie • (v)(86; a only)

Mae West (1892-80)

One of the most extraordinary stars ever to appear on a movie screen, the voluptuous Mae West managed to parody her image as a vamp hungry for men and money with her sly wit and endless double entendres. She first came to notoriety when her play *Sex* was raided by the police and, charged with obscenity, she was thrown in jail for 10 days. She only started making movies at the age of 40. Her early films like *I'm Not Angel* and *She Done Him Wrong* helped save Paramount from bankruptcy, but the advent of censorship and the Hays Office sanitised her brand of sexy humour. Operating her own form of casting coach, her leading men had to prove themselves worthy of the role before contracts were signed (although presumably not W.C. Fields). She was probably the only Hollywood star to be listed in the phone directory; she thought her fans ought to be able to get in touch with the people they paid good money to see in the cinema. There was a 35-year gap in her screen career, the longest ever retirement by a star before a comeback, although her final two movies were so bad many feel her return was one of the few professional mistakes she made.

Quote: 'I feel like a million tonight – but one at a time.' • 'A man in the house is worth two in the street.' • 'To err is human, but it feels divine.' • 'Let's forget the six feet and talk about the seven inches.' • 'It's better to be looked over than over-looked.' • 'I wouldn't let him touch me with a ten foot pole.' • 'I used to be Snow White, but I drifted.' • 'I'm the girl that works at Paramount all day and Fox all night.' • 'When I'm good I'm very good, but when I'm bad I'm better.' • 'Whenever I'm caught between two evils, I take the one I've never tried.' • 'Every man I meet wants to protect me. Can't figure out from whom.' • 'A hard man is good to find.' • 'An orgasm a day keeps the doctor away.' • 'You gotta get up early in the

morning to catch a fox and stay up late at night to get a mink.' • 'I'd be *insulted* if a picture I was in didn't get an X-rating. Don't forget, dear, I *invented* censorship.' • 'I come from a very good family, descendants from Alfred the Great.' • 'I never loved another person the way I loved myself.' • 'I enjoyed every inch of it.' • 'When they make a man better than George Raft, I'll make him too.' • 'She stole everything but the cameras.' [George Raft] • 'Mae West did have an hourglass figure. She had, besides, a minute attention span.' [Cary Grant] • 'She's a tremendous personality. I want to see whether there's anything I can learn from her. It may come in handy sometime.' [Ingrid Bergman] • 'A plumber's idea of Cleopatra.' [W.C. Fields]

Films: **I'm No Angel ••• (33; also s), She Done Him Wrong ••• (33; also s),** Belle of the Nineties •• (34; also s), Goin' to Town •• (35; also s), Klondike Annie •• (36; also s), My Little Chickadee •• (39; also s), Myra Breckinridge • (70), Sextette • (78)

Billy Wilder (b. 1906)

Real name: Samuel Wilder

WRITER-DIRECTOR. After a life as a journalist and a gigolo, the Viennese-born Wilder fled the Nazis and arrived in Hollywood speaking no English. He began writing scripts with Charles Brackett and really impressed the film colony with his third film as director, *Double Indemnity.* His films are marked by a black, corrosive wit, a delight in deception and disguise and a mordant view of the human race. He later collaborated with I.A.L. Diamond, their best work being *Some Like It Hot.* In his later years he has found it increasingly hard to get backing for his projects. He won Oscars for both Screenplay and Best Director for *The Lost Weekend* and *The Apartment* and for the Screenplay alone of *Sunset Boulevard.*

Quote: 'I have 10 commandments. The first 9 are, Thou Shalt Not Bore. The 10th is, Thou Shalt Have Right Of Final Cut.' • 'I do not believe in wasting money. On the other hand, nobody is going to go and see a picture simply because it came in under budget.' • 'My old films? I want to climb up there and change everything. It's like meeting a girl you slept with 15 years ago. You look at her and you think, "My God, did I go to bed with *that?*"' • 'What critics call dirty in our movies, they call lusty in foreign films.' • 'Of course there must be subtleties in filmmaking. Just make sure you make them obvious.' • 'It's not necessary for a director to know how to write, but it helps if he knows how to read.' • 'I'd worship the ground you walked on if only you lived in a better neighbourhood.' • 'France is a country where the money falls apart in your hands and you can't tear the toilet paper.' • 'I'd like to spend the rest of my life doing nothing but Billy Wilder films.' [Jack Lemmon] • 'Long before Billy Wilder was Billy Wilder, he thought he was Billy Wilder.' [Mrs. Wilder] • 'Let's face it, Billy Wilder at work is two people – Mr. Hyde and Mr. Hyde.' [Harry Kurnitz]

Films: Bluebeard's Eighth Wife • (38; s only), **Ninotchka ••• (39; s only), Midnight ••• (39; s only),** Arise, My Love •• (40; s only), **Ball of Fire •••• (41; s only), The Major and the Minor ••• (42; also s), Five Graves to Cairo •••• (43; also s), Double Indemnity •••• (44; also s), The Lost Weekend •••• (45; also s),** Foreign Affair ••• (48), The Emperor Waltz • (48), **Sunset Boulevard •••• (50; also s), Ace in the Hole •••• (51; also s), Stalag 17 •••• (53; also s), Sabrina ••• (54), The Seven Year Itch •• (55; also s), Witness for the Prosecution ••• (57; also s),** The Spirit of St. Louis •• (57), Love in the Afternoon •• (57), **Some Like It Hot •••• (59; also s), The Apartment •••• (60; also s),** One, Two, Three •• (61), The Fortune Cookie ••• (66), Avanti! ••• (72), **The Front Page •• (74; also s),** Fedora • (78), Buddy Buddy • (81)

Debra Winger (b. 1955)

Real name: **Mary Debra Winger**

Winger did three months basic training with the Israeli Army while living in Israel. Her first part in showbiz was as a furry troll at the Magic Mountain amusement park. In 1973, she had a serious accident which left her paralyzed and partially blinded. During her year-long recuperation she decided that she was going to be an actor. One of her early jobs was as Lynda Carter's younger sister Drusilla in 14 episodes of TV's *Wonder Woman*. Although she has a reputation for being difficult to work with, surely all anybody would have to do to quieten her would be to mention that her movie debut involved suggestively eating a banana and losing her virginity in *Slumber Party '57*.

Quote: 'I have to spend too much time extricating myself from a reputation I don't particularly want. As to how I got that reputation, all I can say is that a little spunk goes a long way in this business.'

Films: Urban Cowboy ••• (80), **An Officer and a Gentleman •• (82), E.T. The Extra-Terrestrial •••• (v)(82), Terms of Endearment ••• (83),** Legal Eagles ••• (86), Black Widow ••• (87), Made in Heaven •• (c)(87), Betrayed •• (88), Everybody Wins • (90), The Sheltering Sky • (90), Leap of Faith ••• (92), Wilder Napalm (93), A Dangerous Woman •• (93), **Shadowlands •••• (93)**

Roland Young (1887-53)

Born in London, Young took his moustache and thin thatch to America before World War I where he found ready employment on the stage. Often portraying those in the upper crust, his whimsical, puzzled air made him one of the most popular supporting actors in Hollywood, most notably in the *Topper* series, the first of which got him an Oscar nomination.

Films: One Hour with You ••• (32), **David Copperfield •••• (35), Ruggles of Red Gap •• (35), The Man Who Could Work Miracles ••• (36), Topper ••• (37), The Young in Heart ••• (38),** Topper Takes a Trip •• (39), **The Philadelphia Story ••• (40),** Two-Faced Woman •• (41), Topper Returns •• (41), Forever and a Day ••• (43), **And Then There Were None ••• (45)**